A DIRECTORY OF AMERICAN POETS AND FICTION WRITERS

2003–2004 Edition

A DIRECTORY OF AMERICAN POETS AND FICTION WRITERS

2003–2004 Edition

Names and addresses of over 7,300 contemporary poets,
fiction writers, and performance writers.

PUBLISHED BY POETS & WRITERS, INC.

Acknowledgements

In the two years between editions of *A Directory of American Poets and Fiction Writers*, we lose touch with some of the writers listed in it. We are very grateful to colleagues, agents, publishers, neighbors, and old beaus of these "lost" writers for helping us track them down. Special thanks to Talia Shalev, a summer intern at Poets & Writers, for finding hundreds of authors whose update forms were returned to us with no forwarding address.

Thanks also to the writers whose photographs appear on the cover, and to the photographers who granted us permission to use their photos. I appreciate the assistance I received from the publicity departments at New Directions, University of Pittsburgh Press, W.W. Norton & Co., and Coffee House Press in locating current, high-resolution photos of some of the authors.

I am grateful to Connie Lovatt, Amy Prins, and Talia Shalev for entering data from the 3,500 update forms returned to us and for deciphering the occasional, hard-to-read handwritten responses. I salute Joel Bernstein and Anna Cerami for the arduous task of proofreading.

A special thank-you goes to David Nielsen for his generous assistance in the production of this edition.

Amy Holman
Editor

Cover Photographs, clockwise, from upper right: Jack Grapes, David Bradley, Karen Tei Yamashita, Robert Creeley (Matt Valentine, photo), Tobias Wolff, Charles Baxter (Paul Thacker, photo), James Welch, Cathy Song, Nick Flynn, and Chocolate Waters.

Cover design of 2003–2004 edition by David Opie at H Plus, Inc., based on the redesign of the cover for the 1999–2000 edition by Lea Kalotay, also at H Plus. The *Directory* was originally designed by Stanley H. Barkan, Cross-Cultural Communications.

ISSN 0734-0605
ISBN 0-913734-63-2
Price: $29.95

Typeset by Westchester
Printed in Canada by Transcontinental

CONTENTS

Preface

A Directory of American Poets and Fiction Writers provides writers and publishing professionals an easy means by which to contact writers. Coordinators of reading series, conference directors in search of faculty, publicists at publishing houses, editors at magazines and presses, and old and new writing pals use the *Directory* to connect with writers, and offer them work, request blurbs, ask them to judge contests and rekindle old friendships. Peter Davison, a poet and the poetry editor at the *Atlantic Monthly*, says, " . . . It's an indispensable tool for any publishing person who needs a fingertips guide to the whereabouts of every substantial writer of verse or prose in the United States."

Every two years, Poets & Writers sends update forms to all of the writers listed in the *Directory* and asks them to verify their contact information and provide their most recent publication credits. We also ask writers whether they are interested in giving readings and whether they will travel to do so. Those who answered yes to these questions have icons of a microphone and an airplane after their names. (Please note that while the *Directory* lists this information, we leave the negotiation of fees and travel arrangements to the writers and groups that are hiring them.)

We also ask authors to list languages other than English in which they can give readings, one or two ways they would like to identify themselves (e.g., nationality, race, religion), and one or two community groups with which they like to work (e.g., seniors, prisoners). This edition of the *Directory* includes the information on Languages, Identity, and Community Groups in the indices.

Whether you are a poet, fiction writer, performance poet, editor, agent, or reading series coordinator, we hope the *Directory* will help you find the writers you are looking for.

Amy Holman
Editor

General Information About the *Directory*:

The 2003–2004 edition of the *Directory* contains information about 4,066 poets, 1,586 fiction writers, and 1,306 who are both poets and fiction writers. Some poets and fiction writers are also listed as performance poets. New York has the highest number of listed writers, in part because some fiction writers list themselves in care of their agents in New York City. California has the second highest number of writers listed.

The *Directory* does not list writers of journalism, translation, criticism, nonfiction, or dramatic writing. If the poets, fiction writers and performance poets listed in the *Directory* have published memoirs, translations, plays, screenplays, critical works, personal essays, book reviews, works for children under the age of 12, or articles, we do not include those credits in their listing.

A searchable online edition of the *Directory* may be found at www.pw.org. This edition lists over 4800 of the writers in the book, but does not list their phone numbers. The online edition lists only those authors who request being listed in it; every writer listed online is listed in the print edition.

A mailing list of writers listed in *A Directory of American Poets and Fiction Writers* is available for rental and can be segmented by state, zip code, or category of writing. The mailing list is available in many formats. For more information, please call Direct Communications at 802-747-3322.

How to Apply for Listing With Poets & Writers, Inc.

Poets & Writers uses a point system based on publication or performance credits in evaluating applications to be listed in the *Directory*. There is no fee to apply.

In general, if you have published a book or chapbook of poetry or fiction, or published three short stories or four poems in literary journals or anthologies, you will qualify for listing as a poet and/or fiction writer. If you have performed in six different venues work that has been created for performance or multimedia presentation, you will qualify for listing as a performance poet. We do not review work samples, but do require that the publications cited in your application follow standard publishing practices.

If you want to apply as a poet, fiction writer, or performance poet, you must request the appropriate application for each. Applications explain in detail eligibility and requirements for listing. You may call Poets & Writers at 212-226-0045, ext. 216, send an e-mail message with your name and postal address to aholman@pw.org, or download a PDF file from our Web site, www.pw.org.

How to Use *A Directory of American Poets and Fiction Writers*

The main body of *A Directory of American Poets and Fiction Writers* is organized by state. The District of Columbia, Guam, and Puerto Rico are included in this section. Within each state, writers are listed alphabetically. New York is divided into two sections: writers listed in the five boroughs of New York City and writers listed elsewhere in the state. Writers who live outside the United States are listed after the writers listed by state. The complete alphabetical listing of all writers follows the listing of writers who live abroad.

This edition has new indices following the general index:

Performance Index: performance poets, some of whom are listed also as poets or fiction writers

Index of Languages: languages other than English in which writers can read their work to audiences

Index of Identity: categories of identification (e.g., African American, Asian American, Woman)

Index of Community Groups: groups writers are interested in working with (e.g., children, seniors)

Index of Literary Agents: alphabetical listing of agents whom some writers list their addresses in care of

Each entry in the *Directory* includes the name of the writer, their category of listing, contact information, and publications. Some entries also include optional information—icons of a microphone and an airplane if the writer is willing to give readings and travel for them. Note: Information about identity, languages, and community groups that was included in each listing in the last edition of the *Directory* is now included in the indices only.

Below is a sample listing:

Jennifer Michael Hecht 🎤 ✈
144 First Ave, #2, New York, NY 10009, 212-674-7526
www.jennifermichaelhecht.com

The Next Ancient World (Tupelo Pr, 2001), *Poems to Live By In Uncertain Times:* Anth (Beacon Pr, 2001), *Best American Poetry 1999:* Anth (Scribner, 1999), *Denver Qtly, Antioch Rev, River City, Salmagundi, Prairie Schooner, Poetry*

Name: This is the name under which the writer writes, not necessarily the legal or full name.

Icons: 🎤 for willingness to read and ✈ for willingness to travel to read.

Category: Letter symbols to the right of entry indicate the type(s) of writer each is listed as.

P	=	poet
W	=	fiction writer
PP	=	performance poet
P&W	=	poet and fiction writer
PP&P	=	performance poet and poet
PP&W	=	performance poet and fiction writer
PP&P&W	=	performance poet, poet and fiction writer

Contact information: Every entry has a mailing address for the writer—home, business address, post office box, agent, or publisher. Telephone numbers, e-mail, and Web addresses are included only if the writers provide them. Please note that we do not list fax numbers.

Publications (Pubs): Every poet or fiction writer listed in the *Directory* has had work published. Books are listed first, then anthologies, and then magazines. Book and anthology titles are listed followed by publisher and date. When a writer has more than one book with a single publisher, the titles will be separated by commas, and the respective publication dates will also be separated by commas. Anthologies are designated as such by the abbreviation "Anth" following a colon if the word is not part of the book title (e.g., Pushcart Prize Anth; *Best American Poetry 1999:* Anth). Only magazine names are listed, not the titles of the works published in them. Performance poets may list performance pieces and venues where they've performed, as well as audio-tape/CD recordings.

All information is provided by the writers, who are mailed an update form every two years. Writers may also change their listings at any time by contacting Poets & Writers. If a writer does not provide new information, the entry from the last edition of the *Directory* is retained, unless we know that the address is incorrect. If the address is incorrect, the listing is not included in that edition. We try to list all of the information each writer provides, but due to space limitations, we are not always able to list all of the publication credits.

A list of Abbreviations Frequently Used precedes the listings in the *Directory*.

Please note that all writers in the *Directory* must meet Poets & Writers' publication requirements. We screen applications on a quarterly basis, and once a writer is accepted, his or her listing continues for life. Please see How to Apply for Listing.

Abbreviations Frequently Used

Space limitations have made it necessary to use abbreviations in listing author addresses, publication credits, and the indices. Some are standard mailing abbreviations, and others are used by the publications they represent. The following list has been created to serve as a general guide.

Acad	Academy	Knopf	Alfred A. Knopf
ACM	Another Chicago Magazine	Lang	Language
ALR	American Literary Rev	LIQ	Long Island Quarterly
Amer	American	Lit	Literary or Literature
Anth	Anthology	Little, Brown	Little, Brown & Company
APR	American Poetry Review	LSU	Louisiana State University
Assn	Association	Ltd	Limited
Assoc	Associates	Mag	Magazine
Ave	Avenue	Morrow	William Morrow & Company
Bk	Book	MPR	Manhattan Poetry Review
BkMk	BookMark	Mtn	Mountain
Bldg	Building	MWPA	Maine Writers & Publishers Alliance
BPJ	Beloit Poetry Journal	NAL	New American Library
c/o	care of	NAR	North American Review
CCC	Cross-Cultural Communications	NER	New England Review
Cir	Circle	Norton	W. W. Norton & Company
Ctr	Center	NW	Northwest
Cnty	County	NYQ	New York Quarterly
Co	Company	Pitt	Pittsburgh
CQ	California State Poetry Quarterly	Pl	Place
CSM	Christian Science Monitor	PO	Post Office
Ct	Court	Pr	Press
Dr	Drive	Pub	Publications
Edtn	Edition	Pubs	Publishers
Fdn	Foundation	QRL	Quarterly Review of Literature
FSG	Farrar, Straus and Giroux	Qtly	Quarterly
G/L/B/T	Gay/Lesbian/Bisexual/Transgender	Rev	Review
H Holt	Henry Holt	Rm	Room
H&R	Harper & Row	Rte	Route
HB	Harcourt Brace & Company	S&S	Simon & Schuster
HBJ	Harcourt, Brace, Jovanovich	SPR	Southern Poetry Review
HC	HarperCollins Publishers	St	Street
HM	Houghton Mifflin	Sta	Station
HR&W	Holt, Rinehart & Winston	Ste	Suite
Hse	House	SW	Southwest
Hwy	Highway	TLS	Times Literary Supplement
Inc	Incorporated	TriQtly	TriQuarterly
Inst	Institute	U/Univ	University
Intl	International	Unltd	Unlimited
Jrnl	Journal	VLS	Voice Literary Supplement

Poets & Writers: The Organization

Poets & Writers, Inc. is the primary source of information, support, and guidance for creative writers. Founded in 1970, it is the nation's largest nonprofit literary organization. Our national office is located in New York City. Our California office is based in Los Angeles.

Publications and Programs

Poets & Writers Magazine, the organization's flagship publication, is the leading journal of its kind for creative writers. Along with essays on the literary life and interviews with contemporary writers of poetry, fiction, and creative nonfiction, the magazine publishes articles with practical applications for both emerging and established writers. In addition, it provides the most comprehensive listing of literary grants and awards, deadlines, and prize winners available in print.

A Directory of American Poets and Fiction Writers lists names, addresses, and publication credits for 7,320 authors. The *Directory* encourages networking among writers and increases the accessibility of the authors listed in it. Published biennially, it is the only book of its kind that is national in its scope.

Poets & Writers Online includes a searchable database of over 4,800 listings from *A Directory of American Poets and Fiction Writers*; advice on topics such as copyright, publishing, and finding a writers conference; and links to over 1,000 Web sites of interest to writers. Another popular feature is the Speakeasy Message Forum, which serves as a central meeting place and community center of writers.

P&W's Publishing Seminars are offered via e-mail and on audiotape, and have been successful in teaching both emerging and published writer how to critically examine the potential market for their work, pitch their books to agents and publishers, and promote them once they have been published. Since 1995, when the seminars began, more than 800 writers from 40 states have participated.

Each year, through its Readings/Workshops Program, P&W sponsors more than 1,600 literary events—on average four events per day—throughout New York and California, as well as in Chicago and Detroit. P&W makes matching grants (restricted to the payment of writers' fees) to a variety of organizations—from grassroots to nationally acclaimed presenters—and distributes more than $170,000 annually to some 700 writers from 35 states.

In 1984, The Writers Exchange Contest was established to introduce writers to literary communities outside their home states. Each year, one poet and one fiction writer are selected from one state to participate in the program. Writers are selected based on manuscripts they submit to P&W and are flown to New York City for an all-expenses-paid, weeklong trip, at which time they meet with literary agents, editors, publishers, and writers. To date, 61 writers from 24 states have participated in this program.

As cofounder of the Literary Network, Poets & Writers continues to champion the cause of freedom of expression and advocates on behalf of writers for public funding of literature and the arts.

The Friends of Poets & Writers are a group of donors who provide financial support for P&W's programs. The Friends are writers, readers, and others who wish to support contemporary writers and literature. As thanks for their support, Friends receive special benefits.

NATIONAL OFFICE

Poets & Writers, Inc.
72 Spring St, Ste 301
New York, NY 10012
Phone (212) 226-3586
Fax (212) 226-3963

CALIFORNIA OFFICE

Poets & Writers, Inc.
2035 Westwood Blvd, Ste 211
Los Angeles, CA 90025
Phone (310) 481-7195
Fax (310) 481-7193

SUBSCRIPTION SERVICES

Poets & Writers Magazine
PO Box 543
Mount Morris, IL 61054
Phone (815) 734-1123

ALABAMA

Robin Behn 🎤 ✈   P
Univ of Alabama, English Department, Tuscaloosa, AL
35487-0244, 205-348-0766
Internet: rbehn@bama.ua.edu
    Pubs: *Horizon Note* (Wisconsin, 2001), *The Red Hour* (HC,
    1993), *Paper Bird* (Texas Tech U, 1988), *Iowa Rev, Field,
    Missouri Rev, Crazyhorse, Denver Qtly, Indiana Rev*

Richard G. Beyer   P
1131 Hermitage Dr
Florence, AL 35630, 205-764-6312
    Pubs: *Alabama Poets: Anth* (Livingston U Pr, 1990),
    Negative Capability, Panhandler, Potato Eyes

Margaret Key Biggs   P
Country Rd Box 852
Heflin, AL 36264, 205-748-3203
    Pubs: *Parnassus of India: Anth* (Parnassus of India, 1995),
    Pen Woman, Pelican Tracks, Earthwise, Negative Capability

Robert Boliek 🎤 ✈   P
1301 Panorama Dr
Birmingham, AL 35216
Internet: rboliek@home.com
    Pubs: *New Orleans Rev, The Formalist, MacGuffin, Hellas,
    RE:AL, Troubadour, Edge City Rev*

William Cobb   W
200 Shady Hill Dr
Montevallo, AL 35115, 205-665-7959
    Pubs: *A Walk Through Fire, A Spring of Souls* (Crane Hill,
    2000, 1999), *Somewhere in All This Green, Harry Reunited*
    (Black Belt Pr, 1998, 1995), *Amaryllis, Orpheus, Story,
    Southern Living, Arete, Shenandoah*

Robert Collins   P
205 Humanities Building, English Dept UAB, Birmingham, AL
35294, 205-934-4250
Internet: collinsr@uab.edu
    Pubs: *Lives We Have Chosen* (Middle Tennessee State U
    Pr, 1998), *The Glass Blower* (Pudding Hse, 1997), *The
    Inventor* (Glass Blower Pr, 1981), *Prairie Schooner, SPR,
    Portland Rev, Connecticut Rev*

Michael Driver   W
PO Box 6406
Montgomery, AL 36106-0406, 205-271-6384
    Pubs: *Infinity Ltd, Pearl, Road King Mag, Rockford Rev,
    Nihilistic Rev, NOMOS*

Robert Ely   P
659 South Hull St
Montgomery, AL 36104, 334-265-2002
Internet: relylaw@juno.com
    Pubs: *Encanchata* (New South, 2001), *Mose T's Slapout
    Family Album* (Black Belt Pr, 1996), *Standpoints: Anth*
    (Manchester CP, 1995), *Indiana Writes*

H. E. Francis 🎤 ✈   W
508 Clinton Ave E
Huntsville, AL 35801
    Pubs: *The Invisible Country, Goya, Are You With Me Now?,
    The Sudden Trees* (Beil, 2002, 1999, 1999), *Sudden
    Fictions* (Peregrine Smith, 1986), *A Disturbance of Gulls*
    (Braziller, 1983), *Naming Things* (U Illinois Pr, 1981),
    Itinerary of Beggars (Iowa, 1973)

C.S. Fuqua   P&W
15890 Estate Dr
Athens, AL 35613
http://csfuqua.freeyellow.com
    Pubs: *Butterflies Die: Audio, Deadlines: Audio, Death in
    Service: Audio* (Bks in Motion, 2001, 1998, 1997), *Year's
    Best Horror Stories: Anth* (DAW Bks, 1993, 1992, 1991),
    *Oasis, Pearl, Chiron Rev, Miller's Pond, Dark Regions,
    Space and Time, Grue*

Edward M. George   P
1548 Worthing Rd
Montgomery, AL 36117, 334-272-0738
    Pubs: *Espresso Evenings, Midnight Coffee* (New South,
    2002, 2001)

Charles Ghigna 🎤 ✈   P
204 W Linwood Dr,
Homewood, AL 35209-3926, 205-870-4261
Internet: pagoose@aol.com
    Pubs: *One Hundred Shoes, Mice Are Nice, See the Yak Yak*
    (Random Hse, 2002, 1999, 1999), *The Alphabet Parade*
    (River City Kids, 2002), *Haiku* (River City Pr, 2001), *Animal
    Trunk* (Abrams, 1999), *Plastic Soup: Dream Poems* (Black
    Belt Pr, 1998), *Harper's*

Virginia Gilbert   P
Alabama A&M Univ, Box 453, English Dept, Normal, AL
35762, 205-464-9130
    Pubs: *That Other Brightness* (Black Star Pub, 1996), *The
    Earth Above* (Catamount Pr, 1993), *Prairie Schooner, Mss.,
    PSA Poetry Rev, NAR*

Ralph Hammond   P
Box 486
Arab, AL 35016, 205-586-4151
    Pubs: *Vincent Van Gogh: A Narrative Journey* (Livingston Pr,
    1997), *Crossing Many Rivers: Poems Along the Way, Upper
    Alabama: Poems of Light* (Clemmons Creek Pr, 1995,
    1993), *Wolfe Rev, Amaryllis, Harp-String*

Peter Huggins 🎙 ✈   P
English Dept, Auburn Univ, 9030 Haley, Auburn Univ, AL
36849-5203, 334-844-3135
Internet: huggipm@auburn.edu
    Pubs: *In the Company of Owls* (New South Bks, 2003), *Blue
    Angels* (River City Pubs, 2001), *Hard Facts* (Livingston Pr,
    1998), *Natural Bridge, S Humanities Rev, Rhino, The
    Chattahoochee Rev, Calapooya, Mid-Amer Rev, Runes,
    Terrain, Slant, Amaryllis, Solo*

Sandy Huss 🎙 ✈   W
Univ Alabama, English Dept, Box 870244, Tuscaloosa, AL
35487, 205-348-5065
Internet: shuss@bama.ua.edu
    Pubs: *Labor for Love: Stories* (U Missouri Pr, 1992), *Georgia
    Rev, TriQtly, 2 Girls Rev, Chain, Prarie Schooner, Crazy-
    horse, River Styx, Spelunker Flophouse, Pearl*

Hank Lazer 🎙 ✈   P
1313 Newport Dr
Tuscaloosa, AL 35406-2611, 205-345-1543
Internet: hlazer@bama.ua.edu
    Pubs: *Days* (LavenderInk, 2002), *Simple Harmonic Motions*
    (INK-A! Pr, 2001), *As It Is* (Diaeresis, 1999), *3 of 10* (Chax
    Pr, 1996), *Doublespace* (Segue Bks, 1992), *Another South:
    Anth* (U Alabama Pr, 2002), *Callaloo, Chicago Rev, Salt,
    Virginia Qtly Rev*

Susan Militzer Luther 🎙 ✈   P
2115 Buckingham Dr SW
Huntsville, AL 35803-2017, 256-881-2245
Internet: smluther@hiwaay.net
    Pubs: *Greatest Hits: 1975-2000* (Pudding Hse, 2000),
    Breathing in the Dark (Banyon Swamp Creek Pr, 2000), *And
    What Rough Beast: Anth* (Ashland Poetry Pr, 1999),
    Ordinary & Sacred as Blood: Anth (River's Edge, 1999),
    Diner, The Lucid Stone

Fred A. Marchman 🎙 ✈   P
3006 Old Shell Rd
Mobile, AL 36607
    Pubs: *Dox Dixie Duograms* (Mail Pr, 1993), *Dr. Jo-Mo's
    Handy Holy Home Remedy Remedial Reader* (Nail Pr,
    1973), *Sparks of Fire: Anth* (North Atlantic Bks, 1982),
    Mobile Bay Monthly, For the Love of Life

Michael Martone 🎙 ✈   W
PO Box 21179
Tuscaloosa, AL 35402-0179, 205-344-5059
Internet: mmartone@english.as.ua.edu
    Pubs: *The Blue Guide to Indiana* (FC2, 2001), *Seeing Eye*
    (Zoland Bks, 1996), *Pensees* (Broadripple Pr, 1995), *Trying
    Fiction: Anth* (Colorado Rev, 2002), *The Scribner Anthology
    of Contemporary Short Fiction* (Scribner, 1999)

Charlotte Miller 🎙 ✈   W
c/o NewSouth Books, PO Box 1588, Montgomery, AL 36102
Internet: charlotte@prodigy.net
    Pubs: *Through A Glass Darkly, Behold This Dreamer*
    (NewSouth Bks, 2001, 2000), *Ordinary and Sacred As Blood:
    Alabama Women Speak: Anth* (Rivers Edge Pub, 1999)

Marianne Merrill Moates 🎙 ✈   W
640 Peckerwood Creek Trail
Sylacuaga, AL 35151, 256-249-4225
Internet: marimoates@aol.com
    Pubs: *Writer's Digest, Guideposts, Seventeen, Birmingham,
    Sewanee News*

Betty Oglesby Payne   W
c/o NewSouth Books, PO Box 1588, Montgomery, AL 36102
    Pubs: *Shine Annie* (New South, 2001), *Ebony Junior, True
    Love*

Georgette Perry 🎙 ✈   P
2519 Roland Rd SW
Huntsville, AL 35805-4147, 256-536-9801
    Pubs: *Uncommon Nature: Anth* (Wood Thrush Bks, 2002),
    2001: A Science Fiction Poetry Anthology (Anamnesis Pr,
    2001), *Bramblecrown* (Cedar Hill Pubs, 1999), *Ordinary &
    Sacred as Blood: Anth* (River's Edge Pub, 1999), *Edge City
    Rev, Hiram Poetry Rev, Amer Muse*

Carol J. Pierman 🎙 ✈   P
1508 13 St
Tuscaloosa, AL 35401
    Pubs: *The Age of Krypton* (Carnegie Mellon U Pr, 1989),
    Naturalized Citizen (New Rivers, 1981), *Iowa Rev, Carolina
    Qtly, Black Warrior Rev*

Thomas Rabbitt   P
Star Rte, Box 58
Elrod, AL 35458, 205-339-3548
    Pubs: *The Abandoned Country* (Carnegie Mellon, 1988),
    The Booth Interstate (Knopf, 1981), *Poetry*

Bonnie G. Roberts   P
1307 Wells Ave
Huntsville, AL 35801, 256-534-0823
Internet: bonnierpoet@yahoo.com
    Pubs: *Dances in Straw with a Two-Headed Calf, to Hide in
    the Light* (Elk River Rev Pr, 2002, 1998), *Greatest Hits*
    (Pudding Hse, 2002), *Ordinary and Sacred as Blood: Anth*
    (River's Edge Pr, 1999), *Croton Rev, American Muse,
    Kentucky Poetry Rev, Amelia, Bogg*

Charles Bernard Rodning 🎙 ✈   P
Univ South Alabama Med Center, 2451 Fillingim St, Mobile,
AL 36617-2293, 251-471-7034
Internet: crodning@usamail.usouthal.edu
    Pubs: *Tradition of Excellence, Love Knot* (American Literary
    Pr, 1994), *Swaying Grass, Papering Dreams* (Scots Plaid Pr,
    1998, 1994), *Negative Capability, Ko, Mayfly, Modern Haiku,
    New Cicada, Brussels Sprout*

Sue Scalf 🎤 ✈   P
152 Lawrence St
Prattville, AL 36067, 334-365-9661
members.aol.com/poetscalf
  Pubs: *South by Candlelight* (Elk River Pr, 1997), *Ceremony of Names* (Druid Pr, 1990), *Devil's Wine* (Troy State U Pr, 1978), *Southern Rev, America, Elk River Rev, Carolina Qtly, English Jrnl, Poem*

Carolynne Scott 🎤 ✈   W
5305 9th Ave S
Birmingham, AL 35212-4120, 205-595-3228
  Pubs: *The Green & the Burning Alike* (Portals Pr, 1994), *Belles' Letters: Anth* (Livingston Pr, 1999), *Outerbridge, Short Story Intl, Flannery O'Connor Bulletin, Aura, The Distillery, Noccalula*

Caroll Dale Short   W
PO Box 550057
Birmingham, AL 35233-0057
www.writerstoolkit.com
  Pubs: *The Shining Shining Path* (New South, 1995), *Contemporary Literature in Birmingham: Anth* (Thunder City Pr, 1983), *Redbook, Aspen Anth, Roanoke Rev, Southern Humanities Rev, Birmingham, Black Warrior Rev, Appalachian Jrnl, Southern Exposure*

Anne Nall Stallworth 🎤 ✈   P&W
4316 Wilderness Rd
Birmingham, AL 35213, 205-871-0140
Internet: www.coach1@mindspring.com
  Pubs: *Go, Go, Said the Bird, This Time Next Year* (Vanguard Pr, 1984, 1972), *McCall's, Birmingham Mag, This Week*

Lorraine Standish   P&W
10478 County Rd 99
Lillian, AL 36549-0657, 251-961-3259
  Pubs: *Life's Seasons: Anth* (Southern Poetry Association, 1994), *The Lillian News, Onlooker, The Legend, SPR, Best Poetry of 1997*

Joe Taylor 🎤 ✈   W
RR2, Box 90-D
Coatopa, AL 35470-9642, 205-652-3470
Internet: jwt@univ.westal.edu
  Pubs: *Oldcat & Ms. Puss* (Black Belt Pr, 1997), *TriQtly, Montana Rev, Cimarron Rev, Florida Rev, Virginia Qtly Rev*

Jeanie Thompson 🎤 ✈   P
Alabama State Council on the Arts, c/o Alabama Writers' Forum, 201 Monroe Street, Montgomery, AL 36130-1800, 334-242-4076x236
Internet: jeanie@arts.state.al.us
  Pubs: *White for Harvest, New and Selected Poems* (River City Pub, 2001), *Witness* (Black Belt Pr, 1995), *How to Enter the River* (Holy Cow! Pr, 1985), *Missouri Rev, Ploughshares, Black Warrior Rev, Southern Rev, Southern Humanities Rev*

Sandra S. Thompson   P
316 Woodland Dr
Birmingham, AL 35209, 205-879-3800

Sue Walker   P
Univ South Alabama, Humanities/English Dept, Mobile, AL 36688, 205-460-6146
  Pubs: *Baker's Dozen* (Druid Pr, 1988), *Traveling My Shadow* (Negative Capability Pr, 1982), *Kentucky Rev*

Wallace Whatley   P&W
7409 Lee Rd 54
Auburn, AL 36830-8550, 334-749-1966
  Pubs: *New Stories from the South: Best of 1986: Anth* (Algonquin Pr, 1986), *Minnesota Rev, Outerbridge, Virginia Qtly Rev, SPR, Kansas Qtly, Greensboro Rev*

James P. White 🎤 ✈   P&W
PO Box 428
Montrose, AL 36559-0428, 334-928-3711
Internet: james@americanartists.org
  Pubs: *Where Joy Resides* (FSG, 1993), *Clara's Call* (Texas Ctr for Writers Pr, 1991), *Birdsong, The Persian Oven & California Exit* (Methuen, 1990, 1989)

William J. Wilson   P&W
1239 Blevins Gap Rd SE
Huntsville, AL 35802, 205-881-8002
  Pubs: *Horror Story: Anth* (Underwood-Miller, 1990), *Poem, Haunts, Old Hickory Rev, The Scribbler, Black Lotus*

A. J. Wright 🎤 ✈   P
119 Pintail Dr
Pelham, AL 35124-2121, 205-663-3403
Internet: ajwright@uab.edu
  Pubs: *Right Now I Feel Like Robert Johnson* (Timberline Pr, 1981), *Alabama Poets: A Contemporary Anth* (Livingston U, 1990), *Aura, Morpo Rev, Semiotext* (e)

ALASKA

Jean Anderson 🎤 ✈   W
509 Aquila St
Fairbanks, AK 99712-1320, 907-457-7692
  Pubs: *In Extremis* (Plover Pr, 1989), *Inroads: Anth* (ASCA, 1988), *Prairie Schooner, Sugar Mule, Northern Rev, Polyarnya Izvezda, Alaska Qtly Rev, Chariton Rev, Stories, Connotations*

Ann Chandonnet 🎤 ✈   P
430 Hermit St
Juneau, AK 99801-1581
Internet: afchan@alaska.net
  Pubs: *Alaska's Arts, Crafts & Collectibles, Whispered Secrets* (Sedna Pr, 1998, 1991), *Last New Land* (Alaska Northwest Bks, 1996), *Canoeing in the Rain: Poems for my Aleut-Athabascan Son* (Mr. Cogito Pr, 1990), *Alaska, Lands' End Catalog*

Richard Dauenhauer P
3740 N Douglas Hwy
Juneau, AK 99801, 907-586-4708
    Pubs: *Phrenologies* (Thorp Springs Pr, 1988), *Frames of Reference* (Black Currant Pr, 1987), *Haa Tuwunaagu Yis, For Healing Our Spirit: Anth* (U Washington Pr, 1990)

Tim Jones 🎤 ✈ W
Box 1644
Valdez, AK 99686-1644, 907-835-4125
Internet: tjones@alaska.net
    Pubs: *Keep the Round Side Down* (McRoy & Blackburn, 1996), *Soundings*

Carolyn S. Kremers 🎤 ✈ P
PO Box 84223
Fairbanks, AK 99708, 907-458-8805
Internet: ckremers@mosquitonet.com
    Pubs: *A Whole Other Ballgame: Women's Literature on Women's Sport: Anth* (FSG, 1997), *Place of the Pretend People: Gifts from a Yup'ik Eskimo Village, Last New Land: Stories of Alaska Past & Present: Anth* (Alaska Northwest Bks, 1996), *Alaska Qtly Rev*

Nancy Lord W
PO Box 558
Homer, AK 99603
Internet: nlord@xyz.net
    Pubs: *The Man Who Swam with Beavers, Survival* (Coffee Hse Pr, 2001, 1991), *NAR, Ploughshares, High Plains Literary Rev, Passages North, Other Voices*

Donna Mack W
5000 Vi St
Anchorage, AK 99507, 907-349-2680
    Pubs: *The Whole Apple, Essence, Raven*

Linda McCarriston P
POB 111333
Anchorage, AK 99511, 907-345-0151
    Pubs: *Little River* (Nrthwstrn U Pr, 2002), *EVA-MARY* (TriQtly Bks, 1991), *Talking Soft Dutch* (Texas Tech U, 1984), *Atlantic, Sojourner, TriQtly, Poetry, Georgia Rev, Seneca U Rev*

John Morgan 🎤 ✈ P
3240 Rosie Creek Rd
Fairbanks, AK 99709-2818, 907-479-4936
Internet: ffjwm@aurora.alaska.edu
    Pubs: *Walking Past Midnight, The Arctic Herd* (U Alabama Pr, 1989, 1984), *New Yorker, APR, Poetry, Paris Rev, New Republic, Kenyon Rev*

James Ruppert P
3266 Bluebird Ave
Fairbanks, AK 99709, 907-479-3132
Internet: ffjkr@alaska.aurora.edu
    Pubs: *Natural Formations* (Blue Cloud Qtly Pr, 1981), *Contact II, New Mexico Humanities Rev, Blue Mesa*

Tom Sexton 🎤 ✈ P
1972 Wildwood Ln
Anchorage, AK 99517, 907-272-1060
Internet: sharyn@alaskalife.net
    Pubs: *Autumn in the Alaska Range* (Ireland Salmon Pub, 2000), *Leaving for a Year* (Adastra Pr, 1998), *The Bend Toward Asia* (Salmon Run, 1993), *Late August on the Kenai River* (Limner Pr, 1992), *Terra Incognita* (Solo Pr, 1974), *Hayden's Ferry Rev, Paris Rev*

Peggy Shumaker 🎤 ✈ P
100 Cushman St #210
Fairbanks, AK 99701-4674, 907-456-4098
Internet: peggyzoe@sprynet.com
    Pubs: *Underground Rivers* (Red Hen Pr, 2002), *Wings Moist from the Other World, The Circle of Totems* (U Pitt Pr, 1994, 1988), *Gettysburg Rev, Crazyhorse, Prarie Schooner, APR, NAR, Alaska Qtly Rev*

Ronald Spatz W
Dept of Creative Writing & Literary Arts, Univ Alaska
Anchorage, Anchorage, AK 99508, 907-786-4361
    Pubs: *Fiction, Transatlantic Rev, New Letters, Panache, Telescope, The Wayne Rev, Third Coast, In the Dreamlight, Inroads*

Ken Waldman 🎤 ✈ P&W
3705 Arctic, #1551
Anchorage, AK 99503
Internet: kenwaldman@hotmail.com
    Pubs: *To Live on This Earth, Nome Poems* (West End Pr, 2002, 2000), *Yankee, Exquisite Corpse, Manoa, BPJ, West End Pr*

Mark Arvid White P&W
PO Box 1771
Palmer, AK 99645, 907-746-2566
www.geocities.com/athens/acropolis/5766/erala.html
    Pubs: *Readers Break Vol III: Anth* (Pine Grove Pr, 1996), *Haiku Moment: Anth* (C. Tuttle Co., 1993), *Windows of the Soul: Anth* (Nat'l Arts Society, 1990), *Webster Rev, Modern Haiku, Candelabrum, riverrun, Woodnotes, Arnazella, Minas Tirith Evening-Star*

ARIZONA

C. S. Adler W
7041 N Cathedral Rock Pl
Tucson, AZ 85718
Internet: csawrite@mindspring.com
    Pubs: *No Place Cat, One Unhappy Horse* (Clarion/Houghton Mifflin, 2002, 2000)

Ai P
6125 E Indian School Rd, #108
Scottsdale, AZ 85251
    Pubs: *Vice, Greed* (Norton, 1999, 1993), *Fate, Sin, Killing Floor, Cruelty* (HM, 1991, 1986, 1979, 1973), *APR, Iowa Rev, Caprice, Poetry Intl, Agni, Onthebus*

Karl Arthur 🎤 ✈   W
Ravenhawk Books, 7739 E Broadway Blvd, #95, Tucson, AZ
85710, 520-886-9885
Internet: ravenhawk6dof@yahoo.com/www.ravenhawk.biz
    Pubs: *All . . . the Little . . ., Desert Dogs, Stalked to Death,
    Bank of Satan* (Ravenhawk Bks, 2002, 2001, 2000, 2000)

Dick Bakken 🎤 ✈   P
3 Old Douglas Rd
Bisbee, AZ 85603, 520-432-2771
Internet: dickbakken@yahoo.com
    Pubs: *Feet with the Jesus* (Lynx Hse, 1989), *The Other Side*
    (Brushfire, 1986), *Ironwood, Ploughshares, Yellow Silk,
    Poetry NW, Poetry Flash, Willow Springs*

Diane Beeson 🎤 ✈   P
685 S La Posada Cir, #1701
Green Valley, AZ 85614, 520-648-7949
Internet: dianekbeeson@hotmail.com
    Pubs: *Tiny Tales, Vols. 6, 4-5, 1-3* (Co-author; Mangold
    Santillana, 1991, 1990, 1989), *Parnassus of World Poets:
    Anth* (Venus Printers, 1994), *Poets & Peace International,
    Vol. 2: Anth* (Arc Pr, 1984)

Mark L. Berman   P
P.O. Box 44376
Phoenix, AZ 85064-4376
Internet: Mark53@home.com
    Pubs: *Meshi* (Aleph/beit Bks, 1982) *Eyes* (Brain Dream Pr,
    1975)

Jay Boyer   P&W
MFA Program, English Dept, Arizona State Univ, Tempe, AZ
85287-0302, 480-965-7644
Internet: jmboyer@asu.edu
    Pubs: *As Far Away As China* (Pratt, 1990), *Paris Rev,
    Nation*

Sandra Braman   P
1865 Gun Fury Rd
Sedona, AZ 86336
    Pubs: *A True Story* (Tansy/Zelot, 1985), *Spokeheards*
    (Longspoon, 1983), *Exquisite Corpse, Island*

Charles Brownson   W
Arizona State Univ Library, Tempe, AZ 85287
    Pubs: *In Uz* (Noumenon Pr, 1985), *Ancestors* (Jump River
    Pr, 1984)

Ron Carlson 🎤 ✈   W
Arizona State Univ, Eng Dept, Tempe, AZ 85287-0302,
480-965-7476
Internet: ron.carlson@asu.edu
    Pubs: *The Speed of Light* (HC, 2003), *At the Jim Bridger*
    (Picador, 2002), *The Hotel Eden, Plan B for the Middle
    Class, The News of the World, Betrayed by F. Scott
    Fitzgerald, Truants, Contemporary Fiction: Anth,* (Norton,
    1997, 1992, 1987, 1984, 1981, 1997)

Jefferson Carter   P
Pima Community College, 1255 N Stone, Box 5027, Tucson,
AZ 85709-3000, 520-884-6135
    Pubs: *Tough Love* (Riverstone Pr, 1993), *None of This Will
    Kill Me* (Moon Pony Pr, 1987), *Gentling the Horses* (Maguey,
    1979), *Metro, Carolina Qtly*

Emily Pritchard Cary 🎤 ✈   W
27653 N 72nd Way
Scottsdale, AZ 85255-1105, 480-502-0528
Internet: empcary@cs.com
    Pubs: *The Ghost of Whitaker Mountain* (Ogden Pr, 2002),
    My High Love Calling (Bouregy, 1977), *British Heritage, Phi
    Delta Kappan, Dog Fancy, Pittsburgh Pr Sunday Mag*

Virgil Chabre   P
7166 E Lindner Ave
Mesa, AZ 85208-4986
    Pubs: *San Fernando Poetry Jrnl, The Archer, Prophetic
    Voices, Deros, Poetica, Pub 9, Manna*

David Chorlton 🎤 ✈   P
118 W Palm Ln
Phoenix, AZ 85003, 602-253-5055
Internet: violon@mindspring.com
    Pubs: *Assimilation* (Main St Rag, 2000), *Outposts* (Taxus Pr,
    1994), *Forget the Country You Came From* (Singular Street,
    1992), *Fever Dreams: Anth* (U Arizona Pr, 1997), *Devil's
    Millhopper, Green Fuse, Heaven Bone, Poet Lore, Webster
    Rev, Lucid Stone*

Joel Climenhaga   P&W
115 San Jose Dr
Bisbee, AZ 85603-3009, 520-432-3410
Internet: joelrayc@hotmail.com
    Pubs: *Exploration of the Great Northwest While Traveling
    with the Fat Man* (Transient Pr, 1997), *Moan of Raping
    Bees, Bottom of the Spittoon, The Treachery of Innocence*
    (Shadow Pr, 1996, 1995, 1994), *Ascending Shadows,
    Mirage, Lucid Stone*

Jane Candia Coleman 🎤   P&W
1702 E Lind Rd
Tucson, AZ 85719, 520-795-5588
    Pubs: *Wives and Lovers, Country Music, The Italian Quartet,
    Desperate Acts, The O'Keefe Empire, Doc Holliday's Gone,
    I, Pearl Hart* (Thorndike 5-Star, 2002, 2002, 2001, 2001,
    1999, 1999, 1998), *Doc Holliday's Gone, Moving On*
    (Leisure Bks, 2001, 1999)

Paul Cook   P
1108 W Cornell
Tempe, AZ 85283, 602-831-7062
Internet: pcook@dancris.com
    Pubs: *The Engines of Dawn, Fortress on the Sun* (Penguin,
    1999, 1997), *On the Rim of the Mandala, Halo, Duende
    Meadow* (Bantam Bks, 1987, 1986, 1985), *Amazing Stories,
    Mag of Sci-Fi, New Letters*

David Coy P
The Writing School, Arizona Western College, PO Box 929,
Yuma, AZ 85364-0929, 602-344-7577
Internet: aw_coy@awc.cc.az.us
 Pubs: *Lean Creatures* (Church of the Head Pr, 1994), *Rural
Views* (Mother of Ashes Pr, 1991), *Antioch Rev, Widener
Rev, Colorado North Rev, Slant*

Barbara Cully 🎤 ✈ P
Univ Arizona, Dept of English, ML 445, Tucson, AZ 85721,
520-621-1836
Internet: cullyb@u.arizona.edu
 Pubs: *Desire Reclining* (Penguin, 2003), *The New Intimacy*
(Penguin 1997), *Shoreline Series* (Kore Pr, 1997)

Linda Lee Curtis P
1919 W Adams
Phoenix, AZ 85009-5240
 Pubs: *Head Shots* (Winter Wheat Pr, 1993), *Arizona
Journal: Anth* (High Desert Pub, 1995), *Lovestories, Loving
You, Dream Magic, Voices, True Liberty, Muse of Fire,
Quickenings, Roadrunner, Life Scribes*

Laura Deming 🎤 ✈ W
875 W Pecos Rd #3045
Chandler, AZ 85225, 480-720-4230
 Pubs: *Quadrant, The Prague Rev, Descant, Cimarron Rev*

Alison Hawthorne Deming 🎤 ✈ P
Univ of Arizona, Department of English, Tucson, AZ 85719,
520-621-3866
Internet: aldeming@aol.com
 Pubs: *Writing the Sacred Into the Real* (Milkweed, 2000),
The Edges of the Civilized World, Temporary Homelands
(Picador, 1998, 1996), *The Monarchs: A Poem Sequence,
Science & Other Poems* (Louisiana State U Pr, 1997, 1994)

Wally Depew P&W
PO Box 215
Patagonia, AZ 85624-0215, 520-394-2779
Internet: wdepew@dakotacom.net
 Pubs: *Girltalk, Pure Flip, Quatrains, Fortune, Book of the
Dead, Dead Birds, Toxic* (Bright Moments, 1996, 1996,
1991, 1991, 1991, 1991, 1991)

Norman Dubie P
700 W Brown #6
Tempe, AZ 85281, 603-965-3168
 Pubs: *Selected & New Poems* (Norton, 1983), *The City of
Olesha Fruit* (Doubleday, 1979)

Sally Ehrman P
PO Box 777
Bisbee, AZ 85603, 602-432-3995
 Pubs: *Fennel Stalk, Clarion, Z Misc, Piedmont Lit Rev, San
Fernando Poetry Jrnl, Archer*

Anne U. Forer W
4765 E Baker St
Tucson, AZ 85711-2116, 602-795-6245
 Pubs: *Hot Type: Anth* (Collier Bks, 1988), *Heresies, Green
Mountains Rev, Exquisite Corpse, Minotaur*

Rita Garitano P
3109 E Circulo Del Tenis
Tucson, AZ 85716-1074, 520-319-0877
 Pubs: *Rainy Day Man* (Norton, 1985), *Feeding the Hungry
Heart* (Bobbs-Merrill, 1982), *Walking the Twilight: Anth*
(Northland Pr, 1994), *Tucson Guide Qtly*

Michael Gessner 🎤 ✈ P&W
Central Arizona College, 8470 N Overfield Rd, Coolidge, AZ
85228, 520-297-6738
 Pubs: *Asphodel, Windhover, American Literary Rev,
Wallace Stevens Jrnl, Sycamore Rev, Pacific Rev, Poem,
Wisconsin Rev*

Beckian Fritz Goldberg 🎤 ✈ P
Arizona State Univ Dept of English, Box 870302, Tempe, AZ
85287, 480-965-3663
Internet: beckian@asu.edu
 Pubs: *Never Be the Horse* (U Akron Pr, 1999), *In the
Badlands of Desire, Body Betrayer* (Cleveland U Pr, 1993,
1991), *Pushcart Prize: Anth* (Pushcart Pr, 1998), *Best
American Poetry: Anth* (Scribner, 1995), *New Amer Poets of
the 90s Anth* (Godine, 1991)

Drummond Hadley P
Guadalupe Ranch, Box 1093
Douglas, AZ 85607
 Pubs: *Tierra: Contemporary Short Fiction of New Mexico:
Anth* (Cinco Puntos Pr, 1989)

Catherine Hammond P&W
1503 E Greentree Dr
Tempe, AZ 85284, 602-961-3337
Internet: cathmorrow@aol.com
 Pubs: *Contemporary Arizona Poets: Anth* (U Arizona, 1997),
*Chicago Rev, Mississippi Rev, NAR, Puerto del Sol, Laurel
Rev, Passages North*

Mark Harris W
2014 E Balboa Dr
Tempe, AZ 85282
 Pubs: *The Tale Maker, The Diamond: Baseball Writings,
Speed* (Donald I. Fine, 1994, 1994, 1990), *Arizona Qtly,
Denver Qtly, Virginia Qtly Rev, Sequoia, Esquire*

Dorothy L. Hatch P
2314 E Montecito Ave
Phoenix, AZ 85016-6218
 Pubs: *The Curious Act of Poetry, Waking to the Day* (Stone
Hse Pr, 1990, 1985)

Juanita Havill 🎤 ✈ P
PO Box 194
Sonoita, AZ 85637
Internet: lemotjuste@theriver.com
  Pubs: *Blossoms & Blizzards: Anth* (Pegasus Prose, 1986),
  The Inkling Selection: Anth (Inkling Pub, 1984), *Round Table*
  (1989), *Lucky Star* (1984)

Simon Hawke W
2080 W Speedway Blvd, Apt 2166
Tucson, AZ 85745-2171
  Pubs: *War, The Seeker* (TSR, Inc, 1996, 1994), *Whims of*
  Creation (Warner Bks, 1994)

Robert Haynes P
6117 E Nisbet Rd
Scottsdale, AZ 85254
Internet: bhaynes@inficad.com
  Pubs: *Poetry NW, Poet Lore, New Letters, Zone 3, Kentucky*
  Poetry Rev, Cape Rock, Cimarron Rev, Atom Mind

Laraine Herring W
4407 W Caron Dr
Glendale, AZ 85302-3817, 623-934-2001
Internet: raney@amug.org
  Pubs: *Monsoons* (Duality Pr, 1999), *Women Writers of the*
  Southwest: Walking the Twilight: Anth (Northland Pr, 1994)

Laurel Hogue P&W
PO Box 12220
Tucson, AZ 85732-2220, 520-747-2047
  Pubs: *Descant, Hollins Critic, Southern Humanities Rev,*
  Massachusetts Rev, Prairie Schooner, Santa Barbara Rev

Robert Houston W
Univ Arizona, English Dept, Tucson, AZ 85721
  Pubs: *The Fourth Codex* (HM, 1988), *The Line* (Ballantine,
  1986), *NER, BLQ*

Debra Hughes 🎤 ✈ W
2270 E Corte del Sabio
Tucson, AZ 85718
Internet: ddhughes@earthlink.net
  Pubs: *Walking the Twilight: Women Writers of the*
  Southwest: Anth (Northland, 1994), *Tierra: Contemporary*
  Short Fiction of New Mexico: Anth (Cinco Puntos Pr, 1989),
  New Letters, New Mexico Humanities Rev, Blue Mesa Rev

Will Inman P&W
2551 W Mossman Rd
Tucson, AZ 85746-5102, 520-883-3419
  Pubs: *Other Eye, Other Ear, End of the Ceaseless Road,*
  What Friend in the Labyrinth (Minotaur, 2000, 2000, 1999),
  you whose eyes enter me naked (Mille Grazie, 1999),
  Surfing the Dark Sound (Pudding Hse Pr, 1998), *Blackbird:*
  Anth (Phoenix Pr, 1998), *5 P.M.*

Nadine Kachur 🎤 ✈ P&W
PO Box 33511
Phoenix, AZ 85067
Internet: nkachur9@juno.com
  Pubs: *Sun Tennis, Art-Rag, Trails to Black Canyon,*
  exsanguinate, South Ash Pr, Ignis Fatuus Rev, Twisted
  Nipples, Damaged Wine, Mirage

Barbara Kingsolver P&W
PO Box 31870
Tucson, AZ 85751-1870
  Pubs: *The Poisonwood Bible, High Tide in Tucson, Pigs in*
  Heaven, Animal Dreams (HC, 1998, 1995, 1993, 1990),
  Another America (Seal Pr, 1992)

John Levy 🎤 ✈ P
8987 E Tanque Verde Rd, Box 111
Tucson, AZ 85749-9399, 520-740-5462
Internet: jdlevy@Azstarnet.com
  Pubs: *Scribble & Expanse* (Tel-Let, 1995), *We Don't Kill*
  Snakes Where We Come From (Querencia Pr, 1994),
  Origin, Shearsman, Longhouse

Robert Longoni 🎤 ✈ P
1872 E August Ave
Chandler, AZ 85249
  Pubs: *Woodpiles* (Moon Pony Pr, 1997), *Loft and Range:*
  Anth (Prima Pr, 2001), *Poetry of the Desert Southwest: Anth*
  (Baleen Pr, 1973)

Jonathan F. Lowe P&W
PO Box 26073
Tucson, AZ 85726, 520-326-3007
Internet: jonflowe@aol.com
  Pubs: *Dark Fire, Postmarked for Death* (E-pulp, 1998, 1998),
  Snapshots (Atlantic Disk Pub, 1996), *Ghost Rider*
  (Spectravision Electronic Pub, 1994), *Arizona Highways,*
  Rider, Porthole

Charlotte Ocean Lowe P&W
1530 N Blue Ridge Rd
Tucson, AZ 85745, 520-743-7596
Internet: Charlo@azstarnet.com
  Pubs: *APR, Tucson Poet, Changes Mag*

Delma Luben P
500 W Ocotillo Pl
Green Valley, AZ 85614-2051, 520-399-0893
Internet: dlubn3@yahoo.com
  Pubs: *The Universal Experience, The Writing World* (Hellyn
  Pr, 2002, 2001), *The Freedom Nation, Ghost Writers in the*
  Sky (Vision Pr, 1996, 1990), *Poems for Poets and Writers*
  (Mitchell Pubs, 1990), *Parnassus, Heartland Jrnl, New*
  Jersey Rev of Lit

Edward Lueders 🎤 ✈ P
715 W Camino del Poso
Green Valley, AZ 85614
   Pubs: *The Clam Lake Papers* (Wm. Caxton Ltd, 1996), *The Wake of the General Bliss* (U Utah Pr, 1989), *Poetry, Theology Today, Poetry Nippon, Terra Nova, Prairie Schooner, Weber Studies*

Nancy Mairs 🎤 ✈ P&W
1527 E Mabel St
Tucson, AZ 85719-4223, 602-623-2388
Internet: nmairs@earthlink.net
   Pubs: *Waist-High in the World, Voice Lessons, Ordinary Time* (Beacon, 1997, 1994, 1993), *American Voice, TriQtly, Mss*

Robert Matte, Jr. P
2190 N Calle El Trigo
Tucson, AZ 85749-8958, 520-721-4445
   Pubs: *Asylum Picnic* (Duck Down Pr, 1979), *Star Kissing* (Vagabond Pr, 1975), *Bellingham Rev*

Patricia McConnel W
Bldg 300-417, 2700 Woodlands Village Blvd
Dead Cat, AZ 86001
Internet: mcconnel@wordsculptors.com
   Pubs: *Eye of the Beholder* (Logoria, 1998), *Sing Soft, Sing Loud* (Atheneum, 1989), *Neon, Catalyst, Crosscurrents, Passages North, 13th Moon*

Judith McDaniel 🎤 ✈ P
1412 S Moonflower Ln
Tucson, AZ 85748-7431, 520-721-8915
Internet: jandj1412@aol.com
   Pubs: *Yes I Said Yes I Will* (Naiad Pr, 1996), *Just Say Yes, Metamorphosis, Sanctuary* (Firebrand, 1991, 1989, 1987)

Christopher McIlroy 🎤 ✈ W
2309 W Sumaya Pl
Tucson, AZ 85741-3708
Internet: mcilroyfamily@theriver.com
   Pubs: *All My Relations* (U Georgia Pr, 1994), *Best American Short Stories: Anth* (HM, 1986), *Colorado Rev, TriQtly, Missouri Rev, Fiction, Ploughshares, Puerto del Sol*

Gregory McNamee P&W
3380 E River Rd
Tucson, AZ 85718, 520-615-7955
   Pubs: *American Byzantium* (UNM Pr, 2001), *Blue Mountains Far Away* (Lyons Pr, 2000), *The Mountain World* (Random Hse, 2000)

Jane Miller 🎤 ✈ P
4990 N Acacia Ln
Tucson, AZ 85745-9262
   Pubs: *Wherever You Lay Your Head, Memory at These Speeds: Selected Poems, American Odalisque* (Copper Canyon Pr, 1999, 1996, 1987), *American Voice, Kenyon Rev, Ploughshares, APR*

Patricia Murphy 🎤 ✈ P
2333 E Geneva Dr
Tempe, AZ 85282-4146, 480-413-0371
Internet: pcm@asu.edu
   Pubs: *Seattle Rev, Qtly West, APR, Green Mountains Rev, Indiana Rev, Iowa Rev*

Sheila Ellen Murphy 🎤 ✈ P
3701 E Monterosa St, #3
Phoenix, AZ 85018-4848
Internet: shemurph@aol.com
   Pubs: *The Stuttering of Wings* (Stride Pr, 2002), *The Indelible Occasion, Falling in Love Falling in Love with You Syntax* (Potes & Poets Pr, 2000, 1998), *Arbitrariums* (Broken Boulder Pr, 2000), *The Immersion Tones* (Luna Bisonte Prods Pr, 2000),

Tenney Nathanson P
English Dept, Univ Arizona, 445 Modern Languages Bldg, Tucson, AZ 85721, 520-621-1836
Internet: nathanso@ccit.arizona.edu
   Pubs: *Rif/t, Social Text, Ironwood, Tamarisk, Caterpillar, Massachusetts Rev*

John L. Natkie P
Publisher-Editor, The Crazy Polack's Press, 5750 E Azalea Ave, Mesa, AZ 85206
   Pubs: *Screams! From an Unpadded Cell* (Cosmep Prison Project, 1979), *Greenfield Rev*

Steve Orlen 🎤 ✈ P
Univ Arizona, English Dept, Tucson, AZ 85721, 520-621-7405
Internet: sorlen@u.arizona.edu
   Pubs: *This Particular Eternity* (Ausable Pr, 2001), *Kisses, The Bridge of Sighs* (Miami U Pr, 1997, 1992), *New Bread Loaf Anth* (U Pr New England, 1999), *Best American Poetry: Anth* (Scribner, 1989), *A Place at the Table* (HR&W, 1982)

Nicolas Pastrone 🎤 ✈ P&W
17211 E Starflower ct
Queen Creek, AZ 85242, 480-988-4994
Internet: npastrone@disturbingtrend.com
   Pubs: *Happy, The Lucid Stone, Snake Nation Rev, Pinyon Poetry, Midwest Poetry Rev, Art:Mag, Burning Cloud Rev, Hodge Podge Poetry, Sierra Nevada College Rev, Small Pond Mag, NYQ, Poetry Motel Wallpaper Series*

Jonathan Penner 🎤 ✈ W
2232 E Seneca St
Tucson, AZ 85719-3834, 520-327-6961
Internet: exlibris@u.arizona.edu
   Pubs: *Natural Order* (Poseidon, 1990), *Private Parties* (U Pitt Pr, 1983), *Harper's, Commentary, Paris Rev, Antaeus, Grand Street, Ploughshares*

Melissa Pritchard 🎤 ✈   P&W
Arizona State Univ, English Dept, MFA Program, Tempe, AZ
85282, 480-965-7295
Internet: melissap@asu.edu
    Pubs: *Disappearing Ingenue: The Misadventures of Eleanor
Stoddard* (Doubleday, 2002), *Selene of the Spirits* (Ontario
Review Pr, 1998), *The Instinct for Bliss* (Zoland Bks, 1997),
Prize Stories 2000: The O. Henry Awards (Anchor, 2000)

Michael Rattee 🎤 ✈   P
33055 S Magda Ave
Tucson, AZ 85730-2721, 520-884-9392
Internet: mrattee@worldnet.att.net
    Pubs: *Calling Yourself Home* (Cleveland St U Pr, 1986), *Men
of Our Time: Anth* (U Georgia Pr, 1992), *Pivot, Laurel Rev,
Poet Lore, Santa Clara Rev, The Signal*

David Ray 🎤 ✈   P&W
2033 E 10 St
Tucson, AZ 85719-5925, 520-622-6332
Internet: djray@gci-net.com
    Pubs: *One Thousand Years* (Holy Cow! Pr, 2002), *Demons
in the Diner* (Ashland Poetry Pr, 1999), *Kangaroo Paws*
(Thomas Jefferson U Pr, 1995), *Wool Highways* (Helicon
Nine Edtns, 1993), *New Yorker, Paris Rev, Atlantic, Nation,
Grand Street*

Judy Ray 🎤 ✈   P&W
2033 E 10 St
Tucson, AZ 85719-5925, 520-622-6332
Internet: djray@gci-net.com
    Pubs: *Pigeons in the Chandeliers* (Timberline Pr, 1993), *The
Jaipur Sketchbook* (Chariton Rev Pr, 1991), *Fathers: Anth*
(St. Martin's Pr, 1997), *New Letters, Hampden Sydney
Poetry Rev, Paterson Lit Rev, Helicon Nine, New Millennium*

A. E. Reiff   P&W
2532 N Foote Dr
Phoenix, AZ 85008-1920
    Pubs: *Nineteen Women Without a Husband* (Papago Pr,
1997), *Living Jewels: A Treasury of Lyric Poetry* (Fine Arts
Pr, 1993), *Planet 3: Help Send This Book Into Space*
(Newfoundland Bks, 1986), *Broken Streets IV*

Del Reitz   P
c/o Newsletter Inago, PO Box 26244, Tucson, AZ 85726-6244,
520-294-7031
    Pubs: *Little Lieu & Other Waifs, Second Inago Anth of
Poetry, First Inago Anth of Poetry* (Inago Pr, 1996, 1995,
1985), *Various Artists, Mendocino Rev, South Ash Pr, Blue
Unicorn*

Jewell Parker Rhodes 🎤 ✈   W
Arizona State Univ, English Dept, Box 870302, Tempe, AZ
85287-0302, 602-965-6856
Internet: jprhodes9@aol.com
    Pubs: *Douglass' Women* (Atria, 2002), *Magic City* (HC,
1997), *Voodoo Dreams* (St. Martin's Pr, 1993), *Seattle Rev,
Callaloo, Feminist Studies, Calyx*

Alberto Alvaro Rios   P
English Dept, Arizona State Univ, Tempe, AZ 85287,
602-965-3168
    Pubs: *Teodoro Luna's Two Kisses* (Norton, 1990), *The Lime
Orchard Woman, Five Indiscretions* (Sheep Meadow Pr,
1988, 1985), *New Yorker, Story, APR, Paris Rev*

Lois Roma-Deeley 🎤 ✈   P
Paradise Valley Community College, 18401 N 32nd St,
Phoenix, AZ 85032, 602-787-6577
Internet: lois.roma-deeley@pvmail.maricopa.edu
    Pubs: *Looking for Home: Women Writing about Exile: Anth*
(Milkweed Edtns, 1990), *Classical Antiquity Street: Anth* (Pig
Iron Pr, 1994), *la bella figura: A Choice: Anth* (malafemmina
pr, 1993), *Iris, Midday Moon, Sow's Ear, Faultline, Pinyon
Rev, Confluence*

Yvette A. Schnoeker-Shorb   P
PO Box 12226
Prescott, AZ 86304-2226
    Pubs: *90 Poets of the Nineties: An Anthology of American
and Canadian Poets* (The Seminole Pr, 1998), *Weber
Studies, So to Speak, Clackamas Lit Rev, Midwest Qtly,
Green Hills Literary Lantern, Slant, Eureka Literary Mag,
Blueline, Puerto del Sol*

Susanne Shaphren   W
823 E Brook Hollow Dr
Phoenix, AZ 85022
    Pubs: *The Writer*

Richard Shelton 🎤 ✈   P
Univ Arizona, English Dept, Tucson, AZ 85721, 602-743-7864
    Pubs: *Going Back to Bisbee* (U Arizona Pr, 1992), *The
Other Side of the Story* (Confluence Pr, 1987), *Hohokam*
(Sun/Gemini Pr, 1986)

Shirley Sikes 🎤 ✈   W
PO Box 65496
Tucson, AZ 85728-5496, 520-299-5733
Internet: sikes7@juno.com
    Pubs: *Suns Go Down* (Sunflower U Pr, 2000), *A Line of
Cutting Women: Anth* (Calyx Pr, 1998), *O. Henry Prize
Stories: Anth* (Doubleday, 1973), *Potpourri, Sonora Rev,
Denver Qtly, Remark, Kansas Qtly, Calyx, Travelin' Woman*

Leslie Marmon Silko   P&W
8000 W Camino del Cerro
Tucson, AZ 85745
    Pubs: *Almanac of the Dead* (S&S, 1991), *Storyteller* (Seaver
Bks, 1981), *Ceremony* (Viking, 1977)

Beverly Silva   P&W
624 S Crows Nest Dr
Gilbert, AZ 85233-7129, 602-545-5842
Internet: silva_b@mc.maricopa.edu
    Pubs: *The Cat, The Second Street Poems* (Bilingual Pr,
1986, 1983), *Infinite Divisions: An Anth of Chicana
Literature* (U Arizona Pr, 1992)

Jim Simmerman 🎤 ✈   P
Northern Arizona Univ, Box 6032, English Dept, Flagstaff, AZ
86011, 520-523-6269
Internet: jim.simmerman@nau.edu
    Pubs: *Kingdom Come, Moon Go Away, I Don't Love You No
    More* (Miami U Pr, 1999, 1994), *Dog Music: Anth* (St.
    Martin's Pr, 1996), *Antaeus, Antioch Rev, Iowa Rev, Laurel
    Rev, New Letters, Poetry, Prairie Schooner*

Linda Smukler 🎤 ✈   P&W
POB 40442
Tucson, AZ 85717
Internet: junksa@earthlink.net
    Pubs: *Home in Three Days, Don't Wash* (Hard Pr, 1996),
    Normal Sex (Firebrand Bks, 1994), *Ploughshares, American
    Voice, Prose Poem: Intl Jrnl, Kenyon Rev*

John Spaulding 🎤 ✈   P
4140 W Lane Ave
Phoenix, AZ 85051-5759
    Pubs: *Walking in Stone* (Wesleyan, 1989), *Poet Lore, Poetry
    East, Yankee, APR, Poetry, Iowa Rev, Prairie Schooner*

Lawrence Sturhahn   W
PO Box 50704
Tucson, AZ 85703, 520-887-8878
    Pubs: *NAR*

Virginia Chase Sutton 🎤 ✈   P
1714 E Del Rio Dr
Tempe, AZ 85282, 480-839-5411
Internet: virginia.sutton@pcmail.maricopa.edu
    Pubs: *Fever Dreams: Contemporary Arizona Poetry Anth*
    (U Arizona Pr, 1997), *Paris Rev, Ploughshares, Witness,
    Antioch Rev, Boulevard, Poet Lore, Qtly West, Puerto del
    Sol, BPJ, Spoon River Poetry Rev*

Rhoda S. Tagliacozzo   W
4748 E Quail Creek Dr
Tuscon, AZ 85718
    Pubs: *Saving Graces* (St. Martin's, 1979), *New York Woman,
    Cosmopolitan*

Tobi Lopez Taylor 🎤 ✈   P&W
PO Box 66021
Tucson, AZ 85728, 602-526-8675
Internet: tobi.taylor@att.net
    Pubs: *Layers of History* (Northland Research, 1995), *An
    Apple a Day: Anth* (Half Halt Pr, 2001), *In My Life: Anth*
    (Fromm Intl, 1998), *Rockford Rev, Oregon Rev, South Ash
    Pr, Gryphon, Colorado North Rev, Ripples*

Anna Lee Walters   P&W
PO Box 276
Tsaile, AZ 86556, 602-724-3311
    Pubs: *Ghost Singer* (U New Mexico Pr, 1995), *Talking
    Indian* (Firebrand Bks, 1992), *The Spirit Seekers* (Chronicle
    Bks, 1989)

Peter Wild   P
Univ Arizona, English Dept, Modern Languages, Tucson, AZ
85721, 602-621-1836
    Pubs: *The Desert Reader* (U Utah Pr, 1991), *The Brides of
    Christ* (Mosaic, 1991), *APR, Iowa Rev*

Allen Woodman 🎤 ✈   W
PO Box 23310
Flagstaff, AZ 86002-2310
Internet: allen.woodman@nau.edu
    Pubs: *Saved by F. Scott Fitzgerald* (Livingston Pr, 1997), *All-
    You-Can-Eat, Alabama* (Apalachee Pr, 1994), *The Bear
    Who Came to Stay* (Bradbury Pr, 1994), *Cows Are Going to
    Paris* (Boyd Mills Pr, 1991), *Sudden Fiction* (Continued):
    Anth (Norton, 1996), *Story*

George T. Wright 🎤 ✈   P
2617 W Crown King Dr
Tucson, AZ 85741-2569, 520-575-1130
Internet: twrigh@earthlink.net
    Pubs: *Aimless Life* (North Stone Edtns, 1999), *New Yorker
    Book of Poetry: Anth* (Viking, 1969), *New Yorker, American
    Rev, Sewanee Rev, Esquire, Dacotah Territory*

Leilani Wright 🎤 ✈   P
247 W 9th St
Mesa, AZ 85201, 480-964-5211
Internet: laniw@aztec.asu.edu
    Pubs: *A Natural Good Shot* (White Eagle Coffee Store Pr,
    1994), *Contemporary Arizona Poets: Anth* (U Arizona Pr,
    1997), *Calyx, Talking River Rev, Atlanta Rev, Tampa Rev,
    Hawaii Rev, Hayden's Ferry Rev*

Ofelia Zepeda 🎤 ✈   P
Univ of Arizona, Dept of Linguistics, PO Box 210028, Tucson,
AZ 85721-0028
Internet: ofelia@u.arizona.edu
    Pubs: *Jewed I-hoi/Earth Movement* (Kore Pr, 1997), *Ocean
    Power, Home Places* (U Arizona Pr, 1995, 1995), *Poetry of
    the American Southwest: Anth* (Columbia U Pr, 1997),
    Reinventing the Enemy's Language: Anth (Norton Pr, 1997)

ARKANSAS

Mark Blaeuer 🎤 ✈   P
414 Veranda Trail
Pearcy, AR 71964-9318, 501-525-4798
    Pubs: *Avocet, Buzzwords, Cotyledon, Edge, City Rev,
    Parnassus Lit Jrnl, Piedmont Lit Rev, Potpourri, Pudding,
    Raintown Rev, Thorny Locust*

Andrea Hollander Budy 🎤 ✈   P&W
1433 Kahoka Rd
Mountain View, AR 72560-8980, 870-269-4586
Internet: ahbudy@mvtel.net
    Pubs: *The Other Life, House Without a Dreamer* (Story Line
    Pr, 2001, 1993), *What the Other Eye Sees* (Wayland Pr,
    1991), *NER, Poetry, Georgia Rev, Kenyon Rev, SPR, FIELD,
    DoubleTake*

Ralph Burns 🎤 ✈   P
Univ Arkansas, English Dept, Little Rock, AR 72204,
501-569-3160
Internet: rmburns@ualr.edu
　　Pubs: *Swamp Candles* (U Iowa Pr, 1996), *Mozart's Starling*
　　(Ohio Rev Bks, 1990), *Us* (Cleveland St U Pr, 1985), *Any*
　　Given Day (U Alabama Pr, 1985), *Poetry, Atlantic*

Crescent Dragonwagon   W
Rte 4, Box 7, 1 Frisco St
Eureka Springs, AR 72632-9401
Internet: 76500.3276@compuserve.com
　　Pubs: *Dairy Hollow House Soup & Bread* (Workman, 1992),
　　Home Place, The Year It Rained (Macmillan, 1991, 1984),
　　Lear's, Ms., Mode

Ellen Gilchrist   P&W
834 Easwood Dr
Fayetteville, AR 72701
　　Pubs: *Light Can Be Both Wave & Particle, The Anna Papers*
　　(Little, Brown, 1989, 1988)

Michael Heffernan   P
English Dept, Univ Arkansas, Fayetteville, AR 72701,
501-575-5990
　　Pubs: *The Man at Home* (U Arkansas Pr, 1988), *To the*
　　Wreakers of Havoc (U Georgia Pr, 1984), *Iowa Rev, The*
　　Qtly, Shenandoah

David Jauss 🎤 ✈   P&W
English Dept, Univ Arkansas, 2801 S University, Little Rock,
AR 72204, 501-569-8316
Internet: drjauss@ualr.edu
　　Pubs: *Black Maps* (U Massachusetts Pr, 1996), *Improvising*
　　Rivers (Cleveland State U Pr, 1995), *Ploughshares,*
　　Shenandoah, Nation, Iowa Rev, Paris Rev, Poetry, Georgia
　　Rev, NER

Paul Lake   P&W
2802 Honeysuckle Ln
Russellville, AR 72801, 501-967-2174
　　Pubs: *Among the Immortals* (Story Line Pr, 1994), *Another*
　　Kind of Travel (U Chicago Pr, 1988), *Paris Rev, Yale Rev,*
　　New Republic

Norman Lavers 🎤 ✈   W
3068 CR 901
Jonesboro, AR 72401-0754, 870-935-8543
　　Pubs: *Growing Up in Berkeley with the Bomb* (Summer Hse,
　　1998), *The Northwest Passage* (Fiction Collective, 1984),
　　APR, NAR, Short Story Intl, Missouri Rev

Jo McDougall 🎤 ✈   P
6 Perdido Cir
Little Rock, AR 72211-2142, 501-223-3540
Internet: jmcdougall@aristotle.net
　　Pubs: *Dirt* (Autumn Hse Pr, 2001), *From Darkening Porches,*
　　Towns Facing Railroads, The Made Thing: An Anth of
　　Contemporary Southern Poetry (U Arkansas Pr, 1996, 1991,
　　1999), *N Amer Rev, Hudson Rev, New Orleans Rev, New*
　　Letters, Kenyon Rev, Controlled Burn

Phillip H. McMath   W
711 W 3 St
Little Rock, AR 72201, 501-664-8990
　　Pubs: *Arrival Point* (M&M Pr, 1991), *Native Ground* (August
　　Hse, 1984)

Rebecca Newth 🎤 ✈   P&W
611 Oliver Ave
Fayetteville, AR 72701
Internet: rharriso@comp.uark.edu
　　Pubs: *19 Poems Plus Two, 19 Poems* (Picadilly Pr, 2002,
　　1993), *Great North Woods* (Will Hall Bks, 1994), *Sumac*
　　Reader: Anth (Michigan State U Pr, 1998), *The Whitest*
　　Wash: Anth (Lost Creek Pr, 1997), *Cries of the Spirit: Anth*
　　(Beacon Pr, 1991), *Iris*

Carter Patteson   W
2700 Harrisburg Rd
Jonesboro, AR 72401, 501-932-8453
　　Pubs: *Texas Qtly, Wind, Mississippi Valley Rev, Roanoke Rev*

James Whitehead   P&W
517 E Lafayette
Fayetteville, AR 72707, 501-575-4301

Miller Williams 🎤 ✈   P
1111 Valley View Dr
Fayetteville, AR 72701-1603, 479-521-2934
Internet: mwms1000@aol.com
　　Pubs: *The Lives of Kevin Fletcher: Stories Mostly Short*
　　(U Ga Pr, 2002), *Some Jazz a While* (U Illinois Pr, 1999),
　　Patterns of Poetry (LSU Pr, 1986)

Terry Wright 🎤 ✈   P
Univ Central Arkansas, Writing & Speech Dept, Conway, AR
72035, 501-450-5108
Internet: terryw@sbcglobal.net
　　Pubs: *Makeover, Safe House* (Wunder Kammer Pr, 2002,
　　2000), *No More Nature* (Kairos Edtns Pr, 1993), *Pig Iron,*
　　Rolling Stone, Urbanus, Puerto del Sol, Sequoia, Plastic
　　Tower

CALIFORNIA

William H. Abbott   W
5150 Babcock Ave
Valley Village, CA 91607
　　Pubs: *Cat's Eye, Seems, Trace, Sunset Palms Hotel, Citadel*

Steve Abee P&W
1614 Lucretia Ave
Los Angeles, CA 90026, 213-481-2677
Internet: abeecat@earthlink.net
    Pubs: *King Planet* (Bork Press/Incommunicado, 1997),
    Revival: Anth (Manic D Press, 1994), *Quarry West, Poet's
    Fest, Spillway*

Elmaz Abinader ♀ ✈ P
4096 Piedmont Ave 173
Oakland, CA 94611, 510-531-2513
Internet: elmaz@earthlink.net
    Pubs: *In the Country of My Dreams* (Sufi Warrior Pub,
    2000), *Children of the Roojne* (U Wisconsin Pr, 1997),
    Grape Leaves: A Century of Arab-American Poetry: Anth
    (U Utah Pr, 1988)

SDiane Adamz-Bogus P&W
1326 The Alameda, #368
San Jose, CA 95126
    Pubs: *Buddhism in the Classroom, The Chant of the
    Woman of Magdalena, Dykehands* (Woman in the Moon
    Pubs, 1996, 1994, 1994), *The New Age Reader: Anth* (S&S,
    1998), *MLA Newsletter, Connexions, Spirit, Sinister
    Wisdom, Common Lives, Black Scholar*

Kim Addonizio ♀ ✈ P&W
860 - 42nd St
Oakland, CA 94608
Internet: addonizio@mindspring.com
    Pubs: *Tell Me, Jimmy & Rita, The Philosopher's Club* (BOA
    Edtns, 2000, 1997, 1994), *In the Box Called Pleasure*
    (Fiction Collective 2, 1999), *The Best American Poetry
    2000: Anth* (Scribner, 2000), *The Beacon Best of 1999*
    (Beacon, 1999)

Opal Palmer Adisa ♀ ✈ P&W
PO Box 10625
Oakland, CA 94610-0625, 510-268-0704
Internet: opalpro@aol.com
    Pubs: *Leaf of Life, Traveling Woman* (Jukebox Pr, 2000,
    1979), *It Begins with Tears* (Heinemann, 1997), *Tamarind &
    Mango Women* (Sister Vision Pr, 1992), *Bake-Face & Other
    Guava Stories* (Kelsey Street Pr, 1986), *Zyzzyva, Obsidian
    II, Frontiers, Sage*

Frances Payne Adler ♀ ✈ P
California State Univ, Monterey Bay, 100 Campus Ctr,
Seaside, CA 93955-8001, 831-582-3982
Internet: frances_payne_adler@csumb.edu
    Pubs: *Raising the Tents* (Calyx, 1993), *When the Bough
    Breaks* (Newsage Pr, 1993), *Progressive, Women's Rev of
    Bks, Prism Intl, Ms., Exquisite Corpse*

Aelbert Clark Aehegma P
c/o Gail Walsh Agency, Oceanic Pub Co., 439 Mountain View,
Valley Cottage, CA 96772, 808-929-9101
    Pubs: *Turtle Dance: Poems of Hawaii* (Oceanic Pub, 1984)
    No Poems (Noh School of Poetry, 1972)

Mandy Aftel W
1518 Walnut
Berkeley, CA 94709, 510-841-2111
    Pubs: *Out of Step & Out of Detroit* (Inkblot, 1986)

Pancho Aguila P
c/o Esperanza Farr, 3341 18 St, San Francisco, CA 94110

Ellery Akers ♀ ✈ P&W
1592 Union, #211
San Francisco, CA 94123
    Pubs: *Knocking on the Earth* (Wesleyan, 1989), *Sierra,
    APR, Ploughshares, Intro 6*

Askia Akhnaton ♀ ✈ P
656 Lytton Ave #G123
Palo Alto, CA 94301, 650-326-3381
    Pubs: *Concurencie: This Season for Love, Sing When the
    Spirit Says Sing* (Vision Victory People, 2001, 2000), *The
    Last Black Man* (Soul Visions, 1994), *Indianapolis U Mag*

Mimi Albert ♀ ✈ W
English Dept, Napa Valley College, 2100 Napa Vallejo Hwy,
Napa, CA 94558, 510-918-5514
Internet: abriel@well.com
    Pubs: *Skirts* (Baskerville, 1994), *A Different Beat: Anth*
    (Serpent's Tail Pr, 1997), *The House on Via Gambito: Anth*
    (Two Rivers Pr, 1991), *Fiction Intl, Crazyquilt, SF Chronicle,
    Poetry Flash, Caprice, Southern Lights*

Adele Aldridge P
6363 Christie Ave, #2106
Emeryville, CA 94608-1945
    Pubs: *Once I Was a Square, Notpoems* (Magic Circle Pr,
    1974, 1972)

Jean Aldriedge P
1020 Bay St, Apt C
Santa Monica, CA 90405, 213-396-0825
    Pubs: *Circus Maximus, Interstate, Encore, Village Idiot,
    Dekalb Lit Arts Jrnl, Pig Iron*

Karl Alexander W
c/o Polly Fox, 1380 Manzanita Ave, Palm Springs, CA 92264,
760-327-2988
Internet: katkarl@pacbell.net
    Pubs: *Papa & Fidel* (Tor/St. Martin's Pr, 1989), *Curse of the
    Vampire* (Pinnacle, 1982), *Time After Time* (Delacorte/Dell,
    1979)

Blair H. Allen PP&P
PO Box 162
Colton, CA 92324-0162
    Pubs: *When the Ghost of Cassandra Whispers in My Ears*
    (Inevitable Pr, 1996), *Beyond the Realm: Anth, The
    Irreversible Man* (Pacificus Foundation, 1994, 1991), *Anti-
    War Poems Anth* (Vesta Pubs, 1984), *Northridge Rev,
    California Qtly, Space and Time*

T. Diener Allen　　　　　　　　　　　W
PO Box 2775
Carmel-By-The-Sea, CA 93921

Norma Almquist 🎤 ✈　　　　　　　P
415 W Ave 42
Los Angeles, CA 90065, 323-223-8257
　　Pubs: *Traveling Light* (Fithian Pr, 1997), *California Lyrics: Anth* (Live Poets Society at Huntington Library, 2000), *Where Icarus Falls: Anth* (Santa Barbara Rev, 1998), *Only Morning in Her Shoes: Anth* (Utah U Pr, 1990), Crosscurrents, New Orleans Rev

David Alpaugh 🎤　　　　　　　　　P
Small Poetry Press, PO Box 5342, Concord, CA 94524, 510-798-1411
Internet: davidalpaugh@attbi.com
　　Pubs: *Counterpoint* (Story Line Pr, 1994), *Outsiders: Anth* (Milkweed Edtns, 1999), *Asylum, BPR, Exquisite Corpse, The Formalist, Poetry, Wisconsin Rev*

Cathryn Alpert 🎤 ✈　　　　　　　W
Box 624
Aptos, CA 95001
Internet: cathryn@alpert.com
　　Pubs: *Rocket City* (Vintage, 1996), *Walking the Twilight I & II: Anth* (Northland Pub, 1996), *Sudden Fiction (Continued): Anth, Best of the West: Anth* (Norton, 1996, 1992), *Puerto del Sol, Zyzzyva*

Alta 🎤 ✈　　　　　　　　　　　P&W
PO Box 5540
Berkeley, CA 94705, 510-547-7545
　　Pubs: *Traveling Tales* (Acapella, 1990), *Deluged With Dudes* (Shameless Hussy Pr, 1989)

Alurista　　　　　　　　　　　　　P
California Polytechnic State, Foreign Languages Dept, San Luis Obispo, CA 93407, 805-546-2992
　　Pubs: *Z Eros, Et Tu, Raza?, Return* (Bilingual Pr, 1997, 1997, 1982), *Spik in glyph?* (Arte Publico Pr, 1981), *Calafia, Caracol*

Jorge Alvarez　　　　　　　　　　P
1004 S Ferris Ave
Los Angeles, CA 90022, 213-262-7120
　　Pubs: *Homenaje a la Ciudad de Los Angeles: Anth* (Xismearte Pr, 1982), *El Espejo: Selected Chicano Literature: Anth* (Quinto Sol Pubs, 1972)

Ameen Alwan　　　　　　　　　　P
992 N Madison Ave
Pasadena, CA 91104-3625, 213-684-4002
　　Pubs: *Nation, Kenyon Rev, New Republic, Michigan Qtly Rev, TriQtly, Chelsea, Epoch, Kayak*

Georgia Alwan　　　　　　　　　　P
992 N Madison Ave
Pasadena, CA 91104-3625
　　Pubs: *Paris Rev, Boundary 2, Canto*

Jan Lee Ande 🎤 ✈　　　　　　　P
8591C Via Mallorca
La Jolla, CA 92037-2549, 858-623-2748
Internet: ande@poetrywriter.com
　　Pubs: *Instructions for Walking on Water* (Ashland Pr, 2001), *In a Field of Words: Anth* (Prentice Hall, 2002), *Place of Passage: Anth* (Story Line Pr, 2000), *Clackamas, Poetry Intl, Mississippi Rev, New Letters, Image, Nimrod*

Karla M. Andersdatter 🎤 ✈　　　P
PO Box 790
Sausalito, CA 94966-0790, 415-383-8447
Internet: butterflytree@outrageous.net
　　Pubs: *Tambourine, White Moon Woman or the Education of Imogene Love* (In Between Bks, 2000, 1999), *Wild Onions, The Broken String* (Plain View Pr, 1994, 1990)

Douglas Anderson　　　　　　　　P
Pitzer College, 1050 N Mills Ave, Claremont, CA 91711-6110, 909-621-8000
　　Pubs: *The Moon Reflected Fire* (Alice James Bks, 1994), *The Four Way Reader: Anth* (Four Way Bks, 1996), *Virginia Qtly Rev, Ploughshares, Southern Rev, Massachusetts Rev*

Susan D. Noyes Anderson　　　　P
PO Box 2250
Saratoga, CA 95070-0250
　　Pubs: *At the End of Your Rope, There's Hope* (Deseret Bks, 1997), *Age Happens: Anth, For Better & for Worse: Anth, The Funny Side of Parenthood: Anth* (Meadowbrook Pr, 1996, 1995, 1994), *Lyric, Poetpourri*

Caron Andregg 🎤 ✈　　　　　　　P
1710 Panorama Rd
Vista, CA 92083, 760-643-0907
　　Pubs: *In the Language of Flesh, Of Chemistry & Voodoo* (Inevitable, 2001, 1997), *Line Dives: 100 Contemporary Baseball Poems: Anth* (Southern Illinois U Pr, 2002), *Spillway, Rattle, Sheila-Na-Gig, Talus & Scree, Poetry Intl, The Maverick Press*

Michael Andrews　　　　　　　　P&W
1092 Loma Dr
Hermosa Beach, CA 90254, 310-374-7672
　　Pubs: *In Country, The Poet From the City of the Angels* (Bombshelter Pr, 1994, 1991), *Arizona Qtly, Onthebus, Exquisite Corpse, Wormwood Rev*

Ralph Angel 🎤 ✈ P
838 Bank St
South Pasadena, CA 91030, 323-259-9049
Internet: ralph_angel@redlands.edu
Pubs: *Twice Removed* (Sarabande, 2001), *Neither World* (Miami U Pr, 1995), *Anxious Latitudes* (Wesleyan U Pr, 1986), *Poets of the New Century: Anth* (David R. Godine, 2001), *The Body Electric: Anth* (Norton, 2000) *APR, Antioch Rev, New Yorker, Poetry*

Roger R. Angle P&W
3837 Midway Ave Unit 2
Culver City, CA 90232, 310-287-1661
Internet: rogerangle@earthlink.net
Pubs: *BoldType, Caprice, California State Poetry Qtly, Kryptogame, StarWeb Paper, Italia America, Los Angeles Rev, Center, Fiction West, Coldspring Jrnl, El Corno Emplumado*

Eleanor Antin PP&P
Visual Arts Dept, B-027, Univ California/San Diego, La Jolla, CA 92093, 858-755-4619
Internet: eantin@ucsd.edu
Pubs: *100 Boots* (Running Pr, 1999), *Eleanora Antinova Plays* (Sun & Moon Pr, 1994), *Being Antinova* (Astro Artz Pr, 1984)

David Antin 🎤 ✈ P&W
PO Box 1147
Del Mar, CA 92014, 858-755-4619
Internet: dantin@ucsd.edu
Pubs: *What It Means to Be Avant Garde* (New Directions, 1993), *Selected Poems 1963-1973* (Sun & Moon Pr, 1991), *Conjunctions, Critical Inquiry, Genre*

Gloria E. Anzaldua 🎤 ✈ P&W
126 Centennial St
Santa Cruz, CA 95060-6502, 831-429-6041
Internet: anzaldua@pacbell.net
Pubs: *Prietita & the Ghost Woman/Prietita y la Llorona, Friends From the Other Side/Amigos del otro lado* (Children's Bk Pr, 1995, 1993), *Borderlands/La Frontera* (Spinsters/Aunt Lute, 1987), *Sinister Wisdom*

Roger Aplon P
16776 Bernardo Ctr Dr, Ste 110B
San Diego, CA 92128, 619-746-5250
Internet: 72172.1742@compuserve.com
Pubs: *It's Mother's Day* (Barracuda Pr, 1996), *By Dawn's Early Light at 120 MPH, Stiletto* (Dryad Pr, 1983, 1976)

Samuel Appelbaum 🎤 ✈ P
3929 Poppyseed Pl
Calabasas, CA 91302-2947, 818-880-0183
Internet: appelsam@pacbell.net
Pubs: *Chtcheglov, Judea Capta* (Asylum Arts, 1998, 1995), *Saturn* (Quixote Pr, 1978)

Jacki Apple PP
3532 Jasmine Ave #2
Los Angeles, CA 90034-4947
310-836-2771
Internet: jaworks@sprintmail.com or www.somewhere.org
Pubs: *A Stone's Throw* (Arcadia Club, Highways, 2000), *Noah's Folly* (Vocal Lounge, Salvation Theater, 2001), *Eco Geographies: CD, Ghost Dances/On the Event Horizon: CD* (Cactus, 1998, 1996), *Voice Tears: CD* (The Drama Rev, 1996), *Revista de arte sonora*

Helen Arana P
405 King Dr
South San Francisco, CA 94080, 415-877-8046

Ivan Arguelles 🎤 ✈ P
1740 Walnut St, #4
Berkeley, CA 94709, 510-848-6846
Internet: iarquell@hotmail.com
Pubs: *Tri Loka, Madonna Septet* (Potes & Poets, 2002, 2000), *Enigma & Variations* (Pantograph Pr, 1996), *Primary Trouble: Anth* (Talisman Hse Pubs, 1996), *Lost & Found Times*

Rae Armantrout 🎤 ✈ P
4774 E Mountain View Dr
San Diego, CA 92116, 619-563-3598
Internet: raea100900@aol.com
Pubs: *Veil: New and Selected Poems* (Wesleyan, 2001), *The Pretext* (Green InTeger, 2001), *Made to Seem, Necromance* (Sun & Moon, 1995, 1990), *Poems for the Millennium, Vol. 2: Anth* (U California, 1998), *Postmodern American Poetry: Anth* (Norton, 1994)

Mary Armstrong P
PO Box 571
Woodland Hills, CA 91365, 818-348-9668
Internet: mwarmstrong@socal.rr.com
Pubs: *Grand Passion: Anth* (Red Wind Bks, 1995), *Harbinger: Anth* (L.A. Festival, 1990), *Spoon River Poetry Rev, Kalliope, Zone 3, Birmingham Rev, Cream City Rev*

Alfred Arteaga 🎤 ✈ P
Chicano Studies, Univ of California, 506 Barrows, Berkeley, CA 94720-2570, 510-642-3563
Internet: bluebed@hotmail.com
Pubs: *Red* (Bilingual Rev Pr, 2000), *Love in the Time of Aftershocks, Cantos* (Chusma Hse, 1997, 1991), *House with the Blue Bed* (Mercury Hse, 1997), *Chicano Poetics* (Cambridge U Pr, 1997)

Kenneth John Atchity P
435 S Curson, #8E
Los Angeles, CA 90036
Internet: aeikja@lainet.com
Pubs: *A Writer's Time* (Norton, 1988), *Sleeping With an Elephant* (Valkyrie Pr, 1978), *Poetry/L.A., Southern Poetry, Huron Rev, Kansas Qtly, Ball State Forum*

Hope Athearn P
32 Bretano Way
Greenbrae, CA 94904, 415-461-0621
Pubs: *Asimov's, Amazing, Star*Line, Ploughshares, Blue Unicorn, Gaia*

Charles O. Atkinson P
4257 Fairway Dr
Soquel, CA 95073
Internet: atkinson@cats.ucsc.edu
Pubs: *Family* (Small Poetry Pr, 1994), *The Best of Us on Fire* (Wayland, 1992), *The Only Cure I Know* (San Diego Poets Pr, 1991), *Comstock Rev, Sow's Ear Pr, e, Pilgrim, The Ledge, Dogwood, Nimrod*

Sarai Austin 🎤 ✈ P
PO Box 460674
Escondido, CA 92046, 760-738-1769
Internet: sarai_austin@earthlink.net
Pubs: *The Flight of the Eagle: Poetry on the US-Mexico Border: Anth* (Binational Pr, 1994), *Tidepools, City Works, A Room of One's Own, Contact II, Pacific Poetry & Fiction Rev, Café Solo*

Mark Axelrod P&W
Dept of English & Comparative Literature, Chapman University, Orange, CA 92866, 714-997-6586
Internet: axelrod@chapman.edu
Pubs: *Cardboard Castles, Bombay California or Hollywood, Somewhere West of Vine* (Pacific Writers Pr, 1996, 1994), *Exquisite Corpse, Thanatos, Americas Rev, La Fusta, Iowa Rev, Splash, New Novel Rev, Pannus Index, Rev of Contemporary Fiction*

Hillary Ayer P
944 Fletcher Ln, #9
Hayward, CA 94544, 415-841-9032

Jane Bailey P
24 Kempton Ave
San Francisco, CA 94132
Pubs: *Tuning* (Slow Loris, 1978), *Pomegranate* (Black Stone, 1976), *Calyx, Columbia*

Eric Baizer P
PO Box 23042
Santa Barbara, CA 93121, 805-687-4067
Pubs: *Woodstock Poetry Rev, Coldspring Jrnl, Northern Pleasure, Cumberland Jrnl*

Laura Baker W
79 Roble Rd
Berkeley, CA 94705-2826
Pubs: *New Letters, San Francisco Focus, West Branch, Poetry East*

Charlene Baldridge 🎤 ✈ P
4435 Hamilton St, #5
San Diego, CA 92116-3079, 619-296-8044
Internet: charb81@home.com
Pubs: *Winter Roses* (Wordsperson Pr, 1990), *Poetry Conspiracy, Thirteen, Broomstick, Time of Singing, Sunrust, Song, Christianity Today*

Sheila Ballantyne W
Mills College, English Dept, 5000 MacArthur, Oakland, CA 94613, 510-430-2217
Pubs: *Life on Earth* (Linden Pr, 1988), *Imaginary Crimes, Norma Jean the Termite Queen* (Penguin, 1983, 1983)

Baloian P
PO Box 429
Half Moon Bay, CA 94019-0429
Pubs: *Eclipses* (Dark Sky Pr, 1995), *Ararat Papers* (Ararat Pr, 1979), *Anth of Mag Verse & Yearbook of Amer Poetry* (Monitor Bks, 1997), *Antioch Rev, Whole Notes, Poets On, Green Fuse, Ararat, Sensations, Midwest Qtly, Midwest Poetry Rev, Rain City Rev*

George Bamber W
2057 Willow Glen Rd
Fallbrook, CA 92028, 760-728-6786
Pubs: *The Sea Is Boiling Hot* (Ace Bks, 1971), *Rogue Mag*

Joan Baranow 🎤 ✈ P
73 Hillside Ave
Mill Valley, CA 94941-1180
Pubs: *Living Apart* (Plain View Pr, 1999), *Morning: Three Poems* (Radiolarian Pr, 1997), *Western Humanities Rev, Antioch Rev, Spoon River Poetry Rev, Cream City Rev, U.S. 1 Worksheets*

Ramon Sender Barayon W
3922 23rd St
San Francisco, CA 94114, 415-821-2090
Internet: rabar@well.com
Pubs: *A Death in Zamora* (U New Mexico Pr, 1989), *Zero Weather* (Family Pub Co., 1981)

John Barbato P
20391 New Rome Rd
Nevada City, CA 95959, 916-265-8757
Pubs: *Wild Duck Rev, Northern Contours, Tule Rev, Glyphs, Community Endeavor, Deepest Valley Rev, Zyzzyva*

Heather Doran Barbieri P&W
Cine/Lit Representation, PO Box 802918, Santa Clarita, CA 91380-2918
Pubs: *So to Speak: Anth* (George Mason Univ, 2001), *Explorations: Anth* (Univ of Alaska SE, 2000), *Pleasure Vessels: Anth* (Angela Royal, 1997), *Writing for Our Lives: Anth* (Running Deer Pr, 1996), *The Pursuit of Happiness: Anth* (Leftbank Bks, 1995), *Amelia*

George Barlow P
English Dept, DeAnza College, 21250 Stevens Creek Blvd,
Cupertino, CA 95014, 408-996-4547
 Pubs: *Gumbo* (Doubleday, 1981), *Gabriel* (Broadside Pr,
 1974), *Iowa Rev, River Styx, Antaeus, APR*

Dick Barnes P
English Dept, Pomona College, 140 W 6 St, Claremont, CA
91711-6335, 909-621-8873
Internet: rbarnes@pomona.edu
 Pubs: *Few & Far Between* (Ahsahta Pr, 1995), *A Lake on
 the Earth* (Momentum Pr, 1982), *Poetry, Paris Rev, Santa
 Monica Rev, Antioch, APR, Harvard*

Tony Barnstone P
English Dept, Whittier College Box 634, Whittier, CA 90608
Barnstone.com
 Pubs: *Impure* (U Pr Florida, 1999), *Seattle Rev, Lit Rev,
 Agni 38, Nimrod*

Dorothy Barresi ♥ ✈ P
English Dept, California State Univ, Northridge, CA
91330-8248, 818-677-3431
Internet: dorothy.barresi@csun.edu
 Pubs: *The Post-Rapture Diner* (U Pitt Pr, 1996), *All of the
 Above* (Beacon Pr, 1991), *Kenyon Rev, Antioch, Gettysburg
 Rev, Parnassus, Michigan Qtly Rev, Harvard Rev*

Anita Barrows P
546 The Alameda
Berkeley, CA 94707, 510-525-4899
 Pubs: *The Road Past the View* (QRL, 1992), *No More
 Masks* (Doubleday, 1973), *Nation, Revision, Bridges, Metis,
 Wild Duck Rev, Sonoma Mandala, Blind Donkey,
 Montemora, Aphra*

Ellen Bass ♥ ✈ P
PO Box 5296
Santa Cruz, CA 95063-5296, 831-426-8006
Internet: ebellenb@aol.com
 Pubs: *Mules of Love* (BOA, 2002), *No More Masks!: Anth*
 (HC, 1993), *DoubleTake, Field, Nimrod, Ms., Atlantic,
 Greensboro Rev, Calyx, Ploughshares*

Peter S. Beagle ♥ ✈ W
2135 Humboldt Ave
Davis, CA 95616-3084, 916-753-8538
Internet: psbeagle@juno.com
 Pubs: *A Dance for Emilia, Tamsin, Giant Bones*
 (Dutton/Signet, 2000, 1999, 1997), *The Rhinoceros Who
 Quoted Nietzsche* (Tachyon Pub, 1997), *The Unicorn
 Sonata* (Turner Pub, 1996), *In the Presence of Elephants*
 (Capra Pr, 1995), *Harper's, Saturday Evening Post*

Beau Beausoleil ♥ ✈ P
719 Lisbon St
San Francisco, CA 94112-3523
 Pubs: *Against the Brief Heavens* (Philos Pr, 2000), *Has That
 Carrying* (Jungle Garden Pr, 1985), *Aleppo* (Sombre
 Reptiles Pr, 1984)

Richard Beban ♥ ✈ P
6948 Vista del Mar Ln
Playa del Rey, CA 90293, 310-821-8455
Internet: beban@attbi.com
 Pubs: *Tree Stories: Anth* (Sun Shine, 2002), *Grrrrr: Anth*
 (Arctos, 2000), *What Have You Lost: Anth* (Greenwillow,
 1999), *Cider Pr Rev, Clay Palm Rev, Psychological
 Perspectives, Rivertalk, Solo*

Art Beck ♥ ✈ P
2528 25th Ave
San Francisco, CA 94116, 415-661-8502
Internet: artbeck@aol.com
 Pubs: *Simply to See* (Poltroon Pr, 1990), *Literature of Work:
 Anth* (U Phoenix Pr, 1992), *Once More with Feeling: Anth*
 (Vagabond, 1990), *Rilke* (Elysian Pr, 1983), *Translation Rev,
 Alaska Qtly, Artful Dodge, Painted Bride Qtly, Passages
 North, Invisible City*

Merle Ray Beckwith P
3732 Monterey Pine, #A109
Santa Barbara, CA 93105, 805-687-0310
 Pubs: *Abingdon Speeches & Recitations: Anth* (Abingdon,
 1994)

Robin Beeman ♥ ✈ W
PO Box 963
Occidental, CA 95465-0963, 707-874-2091
Internet: robinbee@monitor.net
 Pubs: *The Lost Art of Desire* (Texas Rev Pr, 2001), *A Minus
 Tide, A Parallel Life & Other Stories* (Chronicle Bks, 1995,
 1992), *Gettysburg Rev, Puerto del Sol, NAR, Crazyhorse,
 PEN Syndicated Fiction*

James Scott Bell P
22136 Clarendon St
Woodland Hills, CA 91367, 818-703-7875
 Pubs: *The Night Carl Sagan Stepped on My Cat*
 (Compendium Pr, 1988), *Broken Streets II*

Molly Bendall P
English Dept, Univ of Southern California, Los Angeles, CA
90089-0354, 213-740-3748
 Pubs: *Dark Summer* (Miami U Pr, 1999), *After
 Estrangement* (Peregrine Smith Bks, 1992), *Paris Rev,
 Poetry, Colorado Rev, APR*

Sheila Bender   P
3439 Keystone Ave #3, Los Angeles, CA 90034, 310-202-1225
Internet: sbender1@aol.com
   Pubs: *Sustenance: New and Selected, We Used to Be
   Wives: Anth* (Daniel & Daniel Pub, 1999, 2002), *Pockets Full
   of Garden Snails & Twigs* (Fithian Pr, 1999), *Boomer Girls:
   Anth* (U Iowa Pr, 1999), *Bellingham Rev, Poetry NW, Seattle
   Rev, Writers' Forum*

Karen Benke 🎤 ✈   P&W
92 La Verne Ave
Mill Valley, CA 94941, 415-380-9266
Internet: karenpoet@aol.com
   Pubs: *Gifts From Our Grandmothers: Anth* (Crown Pub,
   2000), *Beside the Sleeping Maiden: Anth* (Arctos Pr, 1997),
   An Intricate Weave: Anth (Iris Edtns, 1992), *Ploughshares,
   Santa Clara Rev, Clackamus Lit Rev, Convolvulus,
   California Qtly, Clark Street Rev*

Joyce Lorentzson Benson   P
1220 Hampel St
Oakland, CA 94602-1112
   Pubs: *Lift, Io, Caterpillar, Redhandbook II, Boundary II,
   Rolling Stock, Exquisite Corpse*

Rachelle Benveniste 🎤 ✈   P
5215 Sepulveda Blvd, #8-D
Culver City, CA 90230-5241, 310-398-9316
   Pubs: *Rapunzel, Rapunzel* (McBooks Pr, 1980), *Gridlock:
   An Anth About Southern California* (Applezaba Pr, 1990),
   13th Moon, Sing Heavenly Muse, Mindscapes, Playgirl

Sara Berkeley 🎤   P&W
PO Box 17
San Geronimo, CA 94963
   Pubs: *Shadowing Hannah, Playing the Field: Anth* (New
   Island Books, 2000, 1999), *The White Page: Anth* (Salmon
   Pub, 1999), *At the Year's Turning: Anth* (Dedalus, 1998)

Marsha Lee Berkman   W
1600 Hopkins Ave
Redwood City, CA 94062, 415-368-6516
   Pubs: *Mothers: Anth* (Northpoint Pr, 1996), *The Schocken
   Book of Contemporary Jewish Fiction: Anth* (Schocken Pr,
   1992), *Other Voices, Sifrut Rev*

Bill Berkson 🎤 ✈   P
25 Grand View Ave
San Francisco, CA 94114, 415-826-2947
Internet: berkson@pacbell.net
   Pubs: *25 Grand View* (Collorfleur, 2002), *Fugue State,
   Serenade* (Zoland, 2001, 2000), *Hymns of St. Bridget &
   Other Writings* (w/F. O'Hara; Owl Pr, 2001), *A Copy of the
   Catalogue* (Labyrinth, 1999), *Young Manhattan* (w/A.
   Waldman; Erudite Fangs, 1999), *Enough*

Mira-Lani Bernard 🎤 ✈   W
Art Options, PO Box 29476, Los Angeles, CA 90029-0476,
323-655-8433
Internet: artoptions@pacbell.net

Christopher Bernard 🎤 ✈   P&W
400 Hyde St, #606
San Francisco, CA 94109-7445
   Pubs: *The Dilettante of Cruelty: Deserts* (Meridien
   Pressworks, 1996), *Gilded Abattoir: Wreckage From a
   Journey* (Small Poetry Pr, 1986), *ACM, Caesura,
   Ampersand, Caveat Lector, The Drummer, Metier, Haight-
   Ashbury Jrnl*

Jeff Berner   P
PO Box 244
Dillon Beach, CA 94929-0244
Internet: jeffberner@jeffberner.com
   Pubs: *The Joy of Working From Home* (Berret-Koehler,
   1994), *The Photographic Experience* (Doubleday/Anchor,
   1975), *Kayak, Stolen Paper Rev, Antioch Rev, Liberation*

Alan Bernheimer   P
1613 Virginia St
Berkeley, CA 94703
   Pubs: *State Lounge* (Tuumba, 1981), *Up Late: Anth* (4 Walls
   8 Windows, 1987)

Elizabeth A. Bernstein 🎤   P
PO Box 94
Paradise, CA 95967-0094
   Pubs: *Many Moons Rising, Pull of the Tides* (Chiron Rev,
   2002, 1998), *Blue Collar Rev, Taj Mahal Rev, Visions Intl,
   Black Buzzard Rev, Piedmont, Taproot, Chiron Rev,
   Contemporary Rev*

Lisa (Lisa B) Bernstein 🎤 ✈   P
PO Box 20663
Oakland, CA 94620-0663, 510-336-3276
Internet: lisa@lisabmusic.com
   Pubs: *Free Me for the Joy* (Piece of Pie Records, 1999), *The
   Transparent Body* (Wesleyan, 1989), *Anorexia* (Five Fingers,
   1985), *Orpheus & Co: Anth* (Univ Pr of New England, 1999),
   *Lilith, Antaeus, Brilliant Corners, Poetry Intl, Zyzzyva, Calyx,
   Tikkun*

John Berry   P&W
579 Crane Blvd
Los Angeles, CA 90065
   Pubs: *Flight of White Crows, Krishna Fluting* (Macmillan,
   1960, 1959), *Chelsea, Manhattan Poetry Rev*

Jane Besen   P&W
1540 Arriba Dr
Monterey Park, CA 91754, 626-284-1161
   Pubs: *Happy Org*

Maur Bettman   W
Sonoma Mountain Rd
Petaluma, CA 94952, 707-763-3341
    Pubs: *Chicago Rev, Confrontation, Ascent, Virginia Qtly Rev,*
    Kansas Qtly, Apalachee Qtly

Michael F. Biehl 🎤 ✈   P
615 Central Ave, #301
Alameda, CA 94501-3875, 510-521-4063
    Pubs: *Slant, Owen Wister Rev, Graham House Rev, Concho*
    River Rev, Great River Rev, Creeping Bent, Interim, Image:
    A Jrnl of Arts & Religion, Callaloo

Duane Big Eagle   P&W
210 Cleveland Ave
Petaluma, CA 94952-1775, 707-778-3107
    Pubs: *America Street: Anth* (Persea Bks, 1993), *Zyzzyva,*
    Mattoid, Headlands Jrnl, Inside Osage

Judith Bishop 🎤 ✈   P
240 Fulton St
Palo Alto, CA 94301, 650-324-1379
Internet: jpishop1@earthlink.net
    Pubs: *Wheel of Breath* (Green Way Pr, 1994), *The Burning*
    Place (Fithian Pr, 1994), *The Longest Light* (Five Fingers
    Rev Pr, 1991), *The Muse Strikes Back: Anth* (Story Line Pr,
    1997), *Coastlight: Anth* (Coastlight Pr, 1981), *Americus Rev,*
    Kalliope

David Black   W
c/o David Wirtschafter, ICM, 8942 Wilshire Blvd, Beverly Hills,
CA 90211, 310-550-4000
    Pubs: *Peep Show* (Doubleday, 1986), *The Plague Years*
    (S&S, 1985), *Murder at the Met* (Dial, 1983), *Smart, Rolling*
    Stone, Harper's

Clark Blaise   W
130 Rivoli St
San Francisco, CA 94117
Internet: clarquito@aol.com
    Pubs: *If I Were Me, Man & His World, Lunar Attractions*
    (Porcupine's Quill, 1997, 1992, 1990), *I Had a Father*
    (Addison-Wesley, 1993), *Resident Alien* (Penguin, 1986),
    Mother Jones, Bomb, Descant

Ella Blanche   P
6817 Adolphia Dr
Carlsbad, CA 92009
    Pubs: *Whispering to God, Searching the Shadows* (Realities
    Library, 1986, 1984), *Maize, Poetry View, Impetus, Realities,*
    Poetic Justice

Douglas Blazek   P
2751 Castro Way
Sacramento, CA 95818-2709, 916-456-5734
    Pubs: *We Sleep As the Dream Weaves Outside Our Minds*
    (Alantansi Pr, 1994), *TriQtly, Seattle Rev, Prose Poem,*
    Zyzzyva, APR, Poetry, Nation

Lucy Jane Bledsoe   W
1226 Cedar St
Berkeley, CA 94702, 510-526-7771
Internet: lucyjane1@msn.com
    Pubs: *Working Parts, Sweat: Stories & a Novella* (Seal Pr,
    1997, 1995), *Newsday, Fiction Intl, Northwest Literary*
    Forum, Wig, Lambda Book Report, The Writer

Chana Bloch 🎤 ✈   P
12 Menlo Pl
Berkeley, CA 94707-1533, 510-524-8459
Internet: chana@mills.edu
    Pubs: *Mrs. Dumpty* (U Wisconsin Pr, 1998), *The Song of*
    Songs (U California, 1998), *The Past Keeps Changing*
    (Sheep Meadow, 1992), *Poetry, Field, Iowa Rev,*
    Ploughshares, Poetry NW, Atlantic, Nation, New Yorker,
    Marlboro Rev, Salmagundi

Layeh Bock Pallant   P
642 Alcatraz Ave #106
Oakland, CA 94609, 510-547-5360
    Pubs: *Through the Hill Anthology, Poetry Flash, Yellow Silk,*
    Haight-Ashbury Lit Jrnl, Beatitude

Maclin Bocock   W
635 Gerona Rd
Stanford, CA 94305, 415-327-6687
    Pubs: *New Directions 51 & 46: Anths* (New Directions, 1987,
    1983), *Southern Rev, Sequoia, Fiction*

Deborah Boe   P
PO Box 23851
Santa Barbara, CA 93121
    Pubs: *Mojave* (Hanging Loose Pr, 1987), *Poetry, Poetry NW,*
    Hanging Loose, Ohio Rev

Laurel Ann Bogen 🎤 ✈   P
2477 Silver Lake Blvd. #D
Los Angeles, CA 90039
Internet: labogen@mindspring.com
    Pubs: *Washing a Language* (Red Hen Pr, 2002), *Stand Up*
    Poetry: Anth (U Iowa Pr, 2002), *Outlaw Bible of Amer*
    Poetry: Anth (Thunder's Mouth Pr, 1999), *Rattapallax, Solo*

Abby Lynn Bogomolny 🎤 ✈   P&W
PO Box 9636
Oakland, CA 94613-0636
Internet: abbyb@earthlink.net
    Pubs: *People Who Do Not Exist* (Woman in the Moon,
    1997), *Black of Moonlit Sea, Nauseous in Paradise*
    (HerBooks, 1991, 1986), *Sexual Harrassment: Anth*
    (Crossing Pr, 1987) *Quarry West, Genre 10*

Lucile Bogue   W
2611 Brooks Ave
El Cerrito, CA 94530-1416, 510-232-0346
  Pubs: *One Woman, One Ranch, One Summer* (Strawberry
  Hill Pr, 1997), *I Dare You! How to Stay Young Forever* (Bristol
  Pub, 1990), *Pegasus Anth Series* (Kendall Hunt Pub, 1992),
  Pen Woman, Blue Unicorn, Galley Sail Rev

Margot Bollock   P
2015 Belle Monte Ave
Belmont, CA 94002, 415-593-7753

Maryetta Kelsick Boose   P
1537 W 20 St
San Bernardino, CA 92411, 714-887-6170
  Pubs: *Fragrant African Flowers* (Guild Pr, 1988), *Mosaic,
  Essence, Black American Lit Forum*

Millicent C. Borges ♣ ✈   P
16 Thorton Ave #105
Venice, CA 90291
Internet: MillB@aol.com
  Pubs: *Leading Me Towards Desperation* (Partisan Pr, 2000),
  Boomer Girls: Anth (U Iowa Pr, 1999), *Witness, Hubbub,
  Wallace Stevens Jrnl, Sycamore Rev, Tampa Rev, Seattle
  Rev, Laurel Rev, Madison Rev, Interim*

Terry Borst   P
PO Box 39804
Los Angeles, CA 90039-0804
Internet: tbor57@urfach.com
  Pubs: *Gargoyle, Asylum, American Classic Anth, Nebo,
  Blue Unicorn, Oyez Rev, Tequila Poetry Rev*

B.H. Boston   P
525 W. El Norte Pkwy, #242
Escondido, CA 92026
  Pubs: *How Much Earth: Anth* (The Round House Pr, 2001),
  The Geography of Home: Anth (Heyday Bks, 1999), *Crazy
  Horse, Black Warrior Rev, Ploughshares, Western
  Humanities Rev, Marlboro Rev, Blackbird, New Virginia Rev*

Greg Boyd ♣ ✈   P&W
c/o Asylum Arts Publishing, 5847 Sawmill Rd, Paradise, CA
95969, 530-876-1454
Internet: asyarts@sunset.net
  Pubs: *The Double* (Leaping Dog Pr, 2002), *Modern Love &
  Other Tall Tales* (Red Hen Pr, 2000), *Sacred Hearts* (Hi Jinx
  Pr, 1996), *Water & Power* (Asylum Arts, 1991), *Puppet
  Theatre, The Masked Ball* (Unicorn Pr, 1989, 1987), *Fiction
  Intl, Caliban, Bakunin*

Ray Bradbury   W
10265 Cheviot Dr
Los Angeles, CA 90064

Cecilia Manguerra Brainard ♣ ✈   W
PO Box 5099
Santa Monica, CA 90409, 310-452-1195
Internet: cbrainard@aol.com
  Pubs: *Magdalena* (Plain View Pr, 2002), *When the Rainbow
  Goddess Wept* (U Michigan Pr, 1999), *Acapulco at Sunset &
  Other Stories, Contemporary Fiction by Filipinos in America:
  Anth* (Anvil, 1995, 1998), *Filipinas Mag, Sunstar, Philippine
  Graphic*

Donn Brannon   P
Box 105
Castella, CA 96017, 916-235-2303
  Pubs: *Bread Jrnl*

Charles Brashear   W
5025 Old Cliffs Rd
San Diego, CA 92120, 619-287-0850
  Pubs: *Contemporary Insanities* (MacDonald & Reinecke,
  1990), *Aniyunwiya: Contemporary Cherokee Prose: Anth*
  (Greenfield Rev Pr, 1995), *Vignette, Callaloo*

Luke Breit ♣ ✈   P
2119 7th Ave
Sacramento, CA 95818-4312, 916-446-7638
Internet: luke@breitpoet.com
  Pubs: *Unintended Lessons, Messages: New & Selected
  Poems* (QED Pr, 1998, 1989), *Words the Air Speaks*
  (Wilderness Poetry Pr, 1978), *Editor's Choice II: Anth* (The
  Spirit That Moves Us Pr, 1987), *Bombay Gin, New Yorker,
  Haight-Ashbury Literary Rev, Poetry Now*

Summer Brenner ♣ ✈   W
1727 Addison St
Berkeley, CA 94703-1501, 510-644-3099
  Pubs: *Ivy: Tale of a Homeless Girl in San Francisco*
  (Creative Arts, 2000), *Presque nulle part* (France; Gallimard,
  1999), *One Minute Movies* (Thumbscrew Pr, 1996), *Dancers
  & the Dance* (Coffee Hse Pr, 1990)

David Breskin ♣ ✈   P&W
1061 Francisco St
San Francisco, CA 94109-1126, 415-921-3354
Internet: db233@msn.com
  Pubs: *Fresh Kills* (Cleveland State U Pr, 1997), *The Real
  Life Diary of a Boomtown Girl* (Viking Penguin, 1989),
  *Parnassus, New American Writing, Qtly West, American
  Letters & Commentary, New Yorker, TriQtly, Paris Rev,
  Boulevard, Nimrod, Salmagundi, NAW*

Peter Brett P
PO Box 1771
Ross, CA 94957-1771, 415-459-2566
   Pubs: *Borrowing the Sky* (Kastle, 1979), *California Qtly,
   Cotton Wood Qtly, Berkeley Poetry Rev, Generation,
   Seneca Rev, Kansas Qtly, Zyzzyva, Olympia Rev, Florida
   Rev, Wisconsin Poetry Rev, Rain City, Acorn, Red Owl,
   Silver Black Qtly, Lactuca*

Armand Brint P
215 Thompson St
Ukiah, CA 95482, 707-468-8906
   Pubs: *Plowman, Five Fingers Poetry, Lactuca, Pearl, Poetry
   Flash, North Atlantic Rev*

Mae Briskin 🎤 W
3604 Arbutus Dr
Palo Alto, CA 94303
   Pubs: *A Hole in the Water* (J. Daniel & Co, 2002), *The Tree
   Still Stands, A Boy Like Astrid's Mother* (Norton, 1991,
   1988), *Chicago Tribune Mag, San Francisco Chronicle Mag,
   St. Anthony Messenger, Western Humanities Rev*

Bill Broder W
68 Central Ave
Sausalito, CA 94965, 415-332-4364
   Pubs: *Remember This Time* (w/G.K. Broder; Newmarket
   Bks, 1983)

David Bromige P&W
461 High St
Sebastopol, CA 95472
   Pubs: *A Cast of Tens* (Avec Bks, 1994), *From the Other Side
   of the Century* (Sun & Moon Bks, 1994), *Avec, Object
   Permanence, River City, Sulfur, Fragmente*

Lynne Bronstein 🎤 ✈ P
215 Bay St, #1
Santa Monica, CA 90405-1003, 310-392-2728
   Pubs: *Thirsty in the Ocean* (Graceful Dancer Pr, 1980),
   Gridlock: Anth (Applezaba Pr, 1990), *Caffeine, California
   Poetry Calendar*

Brock Brower W
235 Denslow Ave
Los Angeles, CA 90049
Internet: brock.brower@valley.net
   Pubs: *Light, Smithsonian Mag*

Cecil Brown W
38 Panoramic Way
Berkeley, CA 94704

James Brown W
English Dept, California State Univ, 5500 University Pkwy, San
Bernardino, CA 92407, 909-880-5894
   Pubs: *Lucky Town* (HB, 1994), *Second Story Theatre & Two
   Encores* (Story Line Pr, 1993), *Final Performance* (Morrow,
   1988), *Chicago Tribune, L.A. Times Mag*

Stephanie Brown P
2818 Via Blanco
San Clemente, CA 92673
Internet: drbl@ix.netcom.com
   Pubs: *Allegory of the Supermarket* (U Georgia, 1998), *Best
   American Poetry: Anths* (Scribner, 1997, 1995, 1993), *APR*

Linda A. Brown P
1006 Hermes Ave
Leucadia, CA 92024
   Pubs: *Contemporary Women Poets* (Merlin, 1977), *Canta
   Una Mujer* (Athena, 1973), *Ms., Malahat Rev*

Beverly J. Brown W
121 Sierra St
Escondido, CA 92025
   Pubs: *True Story, True Love, True Confessions, True Life
   Secrets, Intimate Story*

Diana Brown W
PO Box 2846
Carmel, CA 93921-2846
   Pubs: *The Blue Dragon, The Hand of a Woman, The
   Sandalwood Fan* (St. Martin's, 1988, 1984, 1983)

Lennart Bruce P
31 Los Cerros Pl
Walnut Creek, CA 94598-3106, 925-932-8234
Internet: lensonb@aol.com
   Pubs: *The Coffee Break, The Ways of a Carpetbagger*
   (Symposion, 1995, 1993), *Speak to Me* (The Spirit That
   Moves Us Pr, 1990)

Bruce-Novoa P&W
Dept of Spanish & Portuguese, Univ California, Irvine, CA
92717, 714-856-7265
   Pubs: *RetroSpace* (Arte Publico, 1990), *Inocencia Perversa*
   (Baleen, 1976), *Periodico de Poesia, Confluencia, Plural,
   Quimera, Hispania*

John J. Brugaletta P
California State Univ, 800 N State College Blvd, Fullerton, CA
92634, 714-773-2723
   Pubs: *The Tongue Angles* (Negative Capability Pr, 1990),
   Random House Treasury of Light Verse: Anth (Random Hse,
   1995), *Formalist, Hellas Rev*

Christopher Buckley P
Univ California Riverside, Creative Writing Department,
Riverside, CA 92521-0118, 909-787-2414
Internet: cbuckley@mail.ucr.edu
  Pubs: *Fall from Grace* (BkMk Pr, 1998), *Camino Cielo*
  (Orchises Pr, 1997), *Dark Matter* (Copper Beech Pr, 1993),
  *APR, Poetry, Iowa Rev, Qtly West, Hudson Rev, Crazyhorse,
  Kenyon Rev*

Y. Stephan Bulbulian 🎤 ✈ P
113 Carter Way
Fowler, CA 93625-2000
  Pubs: *Saroyan's World* (William Saroyan Society, 1998),
  Poets of the Vineyard: Anths (Vintage, 1999, 1998, 1997,
  1996, 1995), *Ararat, Armenian Weekly, Hye Sharzoom,
  Asbarez, Poets of the Vineyard, Nor Hayastan*

Richard Alan Bunch P
248 Sandpiper Dr
Davis, CA 95616-7546
  Pubs: *Greatest Hits* (Pudding Hse, 2001), *Sacred Space*
  (Dry Bones Pr, 1998), *South by Southwest* (Cedar Bay Pr,
  1997), *Wading the Russian River* (Norton Coker Pr, 1993),
  Black Moon: Anth (Dream Tyger Prod, 1996), *Oregon Rev,
  Many Mountains Moving, Fugue*

Claire Burch P&W
Regent Press, 6020A Adeline, Oakland, CA 94608,
510-547-7602
  Pubs: *Homeless in the '90s, You Be the Mother Follies*
  (Regent Pr, 1994, 1994), *Life, McCall's, Redbook, SW Rev*

Jean Burden 🎤 P
1129 Beverly Way
Altadena, CA 91001
  Pubs: *Taking Light From Each Other* (U Pr Florida, 1992),
  Amer Scholar, Georgia Rev, Poetry

Herbert Burkholz W
Hamilburg Agency, 8671 Wilshire Blvd, Beverly Hills, CA
90211, 310-657-1501
  Pubs: *The FDA Follies* (Basic Bks, 1994), *Brain Damage*
  (Atheneum, 1992), *Writer-in-Residence* (Permanent Pr,
  1992), *New Republic, Longevity*

E.P. Burr W
1241 Irving Ave
Glendale, CA 91201
Internet: Epburr@aol.com
  Pubs: *The Light of the Morning* (Ensign Pub, 1988), *Utah
  Spring, Lightning in the Fog* (Herald Hse, 1979, 1977),
  Cimarron Rev, Forum, South, Writers' Jrnl

Robert A. Burton W
104 Caledonia St
Sausalito, CA 94965, 415-289-1316
Internet: raburton@pacbell.net
  Pubs: *Cellmates* (Russian Hill Pr, 1997), *Final Therapy*
  (Berkley, 1994), *Doc-in-a-Box* (Soho Pr, 1991)

Mary Bucci Bush W
English Dept, California State Univ/Los Angeles, 5151 State
University Drive, Los Angeles, CA 90032, 323-343-4140
Internet: mbush@calstatela.edu
  Pubs: *A Place of Light* (Morrow, 1990), *From the Margin:
  Anth* (Purdue U Pr, 2000), *Growing Up Ethnic In America:
  Anth* (Penguin, 1999), *The Voices We Carry: Anth*
  (Guernica Edtns, 1994), *Ploughshares, Missouri Rev, Black
  Warrior Rev*

Emilya Cachapero P
1101 Plymouth Ave
San Francisco, CA 94112

Michael Cadnum ✈ P
555 Pierce St #143
Albany, CA 94706
  Pubs: *Forbidden Forest, In a Dark Wood* (Orchard Bks,
  2002, 1998), *Redhanded, The Book of the Lion, Rundown,
  Heat, Taking It* (Viking, 2000, 2000, 1999, 1998, 1995), *The
  Judas Glass* (Carroll & Graf, 1996), *America*

Stratton F. Caldwell P
80 N Kanan Rd
Agoura, CA 91301-1105
  Pubs: *Somatics, Quest, Fat Tuesday, Parnassus Literary
  Jrnl, Yellow Butterfly, Pinchpenny, Arete, Mendocino Rev*

Pat Califia W
2215R Market St, #261
San Francisco, CA 94114
  Pubs: *Doc & Fluff* (Alyson, 1990), *Macho Sluts* (Alyson,
  1988), *The Advocate, On Our Backs*

Camincha P
723 Moana Way
Pacifica, CA 94044, 415-359-0890
  Pubs: *Hard Love: Anth* (Queen of Swords Pr, 1997),
  Apocalypse 4: Anth (Northeastern Illinois U Pr, 1997), *Four
  by Four: Anth* (Amaranth Edtns, 1993), *Cups, Passager*

Janine Canan 🎤 ✈ P
772 Ernest Dr
Sonoma, CA 95476-4614, 707-939-2771
Internet: jancanan@vom.com
  Pubs: *In the Palace of Creation: Selected Poems 1969
  1999, Journeys With Justine, Changing Woman* (Scars
  Pubs, 2002, 2002, 2000), *Her Magnificent Body* (Manroot,
  1986), *Exquisite Corpse*

Patricia E. Canterbury 🎤 ✈ P&W
PO Box 160127
Sacramento, CA 95816-0127, 916-483-1046
Internet: patmyst@aol.com, www.patmyst.com
  Pubs: *The Secret of Sugarman's Circus, Carlotta and the
  Locke Ghost Mystery, Carlotta and the Railfair Mystery, The
  Secret of Morton's End* (RBC Pub, 2004, 2004, 2003, 2002),
  Dreams of 21st Century: Rivers V (Sacramento Poetry Ctr,
  1993),

Jo-Anne Cappeluti 🎤 ✈   P&W
Brea, CA
Internet: jcappeluti@fullerton.edu
    Pubs: *Thorny Locust, Short Story, Lit Rev, Negative
    Capability, The Jrnl, Lyric, NYQ, South Coast Poetry Jrnl,
    Mosaic, Plains Poetry Rev, Bluegrass Literary Rev*

Eve La Salle Caram 🎤 ✈   P&W
The Writers' Program, UCLA Extension, Dept of Arts, 10995
Le Conte Ave, Los Angeles, CA 90024, 323-663-1095
    Pubs: *Rena: A Late Journey, Wintershine, Dear Corpus
    Christi* (Plain View Pr, 2000, 1994, 1991), *Avocet, Snowy
    Egret, Greenfield Rev, Sou'wester, Wisconsin Rev,
    Cottonwood*

Henry Carlisle   W
1100 Union St, #301
San Francisco, CA 94109-2019
Internet: hccarlisle@aol.com
    Pubs: *The Jonah Man, The Idealists* (w/O. Carlisle), (St.
    Martin's Pr, 2000, 1999)

R. S. Carlson 🎤 ✈   P
English Dept, Azusa Pacific Univ, 901 E Alosta Ave, Azusa,
CA 91702-4052, 818-815-6000
Internet: rcarlson@apu.edu
    Pubs: *Limestone Circle, Common Ground Rev, The Lucid
    Stone, The Kaleidoscope Rev, The Listening Eye, The
    Panhandler, Sunstone, Pacific Rev, Viet Nam War
    Generation Jrnl, Poet Lore, Hawaii Rev, Cape Rock, Hollins
    Critic*

Josephine Carson   W
PO Box 210240
San Francisco, CA 94121-0240
    Pubs: *Dog Star & Other Stories, Where Icarus Falls: Anth*
    (Santa Barbara Rev Pub, 1998), *Listening to Ourselves:
    Anth* (Anchor Bks, 1994), *American Short Fiction, Poetry
    USA, auto/bio*

Marie Cartier 🎤 ✈   P
974 Haverford Ave, #4
Pacific Palisades, CA 90272, 310-459-7601
Internet: ezmerelda@earthlink.net
    Pubs: *Freeze Count, Come Out, Come Out, Wherever You
    Are Stumbling Into Light* (Dialogos Pr, 1995 1995), *I Am
    Your Daughter, Not Your Lover* (Clothespin Fever Pr, 1995),
    Sinister Wisdom, Heresies, Colorado Rev

Peter Cashorali   P
857 1/2 N Hayworth
Los Angeles, CA 90046
    Pubs: *Bachy, Rara Avis, Poetry/L.A., Barney, Magazine,
    Beyond Baroque, Mouth of the Dragon*

Marsh G. Cassady 🎤 ✈   P&W
MCD R-03, PO Box 439016, San Diego, CA 92143
Internet: gary@telnov.com
    Pubs: *The Times of the Double Star, Perverted Proverbs &
    Sudden Drama* (Spectrum Pr, 1994, 1994), *Brussels Sprout,
    Chiron Rev*

Cyrus Cassells   P
c/o Mary Cassells, 2190 Belden Pl, Escondido, CA 92029,
619-745-9156
    Pubs: *The Mud Actor* (H Holt, 1982), *Under 35: The New
    Generation of American Poets: Anth* (Doubleday, 1989),
    Kenyon Rev, Ploughshares, Callaloo, Agni

Irene Chadwick 🎤 ✈   P
4336 Copper Cliff Ln
Modesto, CA 95355-8967, 209-524-3066
Internet: irenekooi@aol.com
    Pubs: *Dawn Pearl* (Ietje Kooi Pr, 1994), *Mindprint Rev, Napa
    Rev, INA Coolbrith Circle, Images of Oracle*

Pamela Herbert Chais   W
611 N Oakhurst Dr
Beverly Hills, CA 90210, 213-276-6215

Jeffrey Paul Chan   W
Asian American Studies Program, San Francisco State Univ,
1600 Holloway, San Francisco, CA 94132-1700, 415-338-1796
Internet: jefchan@sfsu.edu
    Pubs: *The Big Aiiieeeee!: Anth* (NAL, 1990)

Janet Carncross Chandler   P
c/o Dan Chandler, 436 Old Wagon Rd, Trinidad, CA 95570,
916-448-6248
    Pubs: *Why Flowers Bloom, Flight of the Wild Goose*
    (Papier-Mache Pr, 1994, 1989), *Significant Relationships*
    (Chandler, 1988)

Kosrof Chantikian 🎤 ✈   P
20 Millard Rd
Larkspur, CA 94939-1918
Internet: kosmos_books@att.net
    Pubs: *Prophecies & Transformations, Imaginations & Self-
    Discoveries* (KOSMOS, 1978, 1974)

Elizabeth Biller Chapman 🎤 ✈   P
121 Fulton St
Palo Alto, CA 94301-1320, 650-323-9331
Internet: thisbmagic@aol.com
    Pubs: *First Orchard* (Bellowing Ark Pr, 1999), *Creekwalker*
    (Mother Tongue Pr, 1995), *Best American Poetry 2002: Anth*
    (Scribner, 2002), *Poetry, American Tanka, GMR, Texas
    Observer, Prairie Schooner, Yankee*

Maxine Chernoff 🎤 ✈   P&W
369 Molino Ave
Mill Valley, CA 94941-2767, 415-389-1877
Internet: maxpaul@sfsu.edu
    Pubs: *Some of Her Friends That Year: New & Selected
    Stories, American Heaven* (Coffee Hse Pr, 2002, 1996),
    World:Poems 1991-2001 (Salt Pubs, 2001), *A Boy in Winter*
    (Crown, 1999), *Signs of Devotion, Plain Grief* (S&S, 1993,
    1991), *NAR, Sulfur, Chicago Rev*

Marilyn Chin 🎤 ✈   P
English Dept, San Diego State Univ, San Diego, CA
92182-8140, 619-697-1941
Internet: chin2@mail.sdsu.edu
    Pubs: *Rhapsody in Plain Yellow* (Norton, 2002), *The
    Phoenix Gone, The Terrace Empty* (Milkweed, 1994), *Dwarf
    Bamboo* (Greenfield Rev Pr, 1987), *Best American Poetry:
    Anth* (S&S, 1996), *Pushcart Prize XX: Anth* (Pushcart Pr,
    1996), *Paris Rev, Kenyon Rev*

Justin Chin 🎤 ✈   P&W
250-B Guerrero St
San Francisco, CA 94103-2313, 415-552-6542
Internet: jchin69@yahoo.com
    Pubs: *Burden of Ashes* (Alyson Pubs, 2002), *Harmless
    Medicine, Bite Hard* (Manic D Pr, 2001, 1997), *Word of
    Mouth: Anth* (Talisman House, 2000), *American Poetry:
    Anth* (Carnegie Mellon, 2000), *The World in Us: Anth* (St
    Martin's, 2000)

John Christgau   W
2704 Comstock
Belmont, CA 94002, 415-591-4045
    Pubs: *The Origins of the Jump Shot* (U Nebraska Pr, 1999),
    Mower County Poems, Sierra Sue II (Great Plains Pr, 1998,
    1994), *Spoon* (Viking, 1978), *Amelia, Window, Rainbow City
    Express, Camellia, Cream City Rev, Great River Rev*

Martha J. Cinader 🎤 ✈   PP&P&W
200 Brighton Dr
Vallejo, CA 94591-7035, 707-643-3597
Internet: mc@cinader.com
    Pubs: *When the Body Calls* (Harlem River Pr, 1999),
    Dreamscape (Tenth Avenue Edtns, 1995), *Dick for a Day:
    Anth,* (Villard Bks, 1997), *A Gathering of the Tribes,
    Nuyorican Poets Café, Knitting Factory, Royal Festival Hall,
    Hamburg Jazz Fest, Cody's Books*

Ralph Cissne 🎤 ✈   W
409 N Pacific Coast Hwy, #465
Redondo Beach, CA 90277-2870, 310-281-7341
Internet: cissne@earthlink.net
    Pubs: *American Way, Playboy, Writing on the Wall, Info*

Tom Clark   P&W
1740 Marin Ave
Berkeley, CA 94707
    Pubs: *Junkets on a Sad Planet: Scenes From the Life of
    John Keats* (Black Sparrow Pr, 1994), *The Exile of Celine*
    (Random Hse, 1987)

Kevin Clark 🎤 ✈   P
Dept of English, California Polytech State U, San Luis Obispo,
CA 93407, 805-756-2596
Internet: kclark@calpoly.edu
    Pubs: *In the Evening of No Warning* (New Issues Pr, 2002),
    One of Us (Millie Grazie Pr, 2001), *Window Under a New
    Moon* (Owl Creek Pr, 1990), *Granting the Wolf* (State St Pr,
    1984), *Georgia Rev, Denver Qtly, College English, Black
    Warrior Rev, Faultline*

Killarney Clary 🎤 ✈   P
2517 Kenilworth Ave
Los Angeles, CA 90039
    Pubs: *By Common Salt* (Oberlin College Pr, 1996), *Who
    Whispered Near Me* (FSG, 1989), *Ploughshares, APR, Yale
    Rev, Colorado Rev, Paris Rev, Partisan*

Karen Claussen 🎤 ✈   P
PO Box 188
Crescent City, CA 95531-0188, 707-465-3228
Internet: claussenkk@aol.com
    Pubs: *R. C. Lion, Primer, Poetry &, Altadena Rev,
    Janus/Seth*

Paul Clayton   W
800 Memorial Dr #2
San Francisco, CA 94080, 408-735-3438
    Pubs: *Calling Crow Nation* (Berkley 1997), *Flight of the Crow*
    (Berkley/Jove 1996), *Calling Crow* (Putnam/Berkley 1995)

Peter Clothier   P
2341 Ronda Vista Dr
Los Angeles, CA 90027, 213-661-6349
    Pubs: *Dirty-Down* (Atheneum, 1987), *Chiaroscuro* (St.
    Martin's Pr, 1985), *Art News, Artspace*

Jeanette Marie Clough 🎤 ✈   P
1330 Yale St #6
Santa Monica, CA 90404-2440
Internet: jclough@getty.edu
    Pubs: *Celestial Burn* (Sacred Beverage Pr, 1999), *Denver
    Qtly, Poetrybay, Nimrod, 13th Moon, Atlanta Rev, Ohio Rev,
    Paterson Lit Rev, Spillway, Wisconsin Rev*

David Cloutier   P
1023 Lincoln Way
San Francisco, CA 94122
Internet: ccmc@culturalmonterey.org
    Pubs: *Soft Lightnings, Tongue & Thunder* (Copper Beech,
    1982, 1980)

Cathy Cockrell W
3917 Elston Ave
Oakland, CA 94602-1620, 510-336-0484
Internet: cac@pa.urel.berkeley.edu
Pubs: *A Simple Fact, Undershirts & Other Stories* (Hanging Loose Pr, 1987, 1982), *Croton Rev, Hanging Loose Mag*

Judith Cody ♀ ✈ P
Box 1107
Los Altos, CA 94023-1107
Pubs: *Eight Frames Eight* (Xlibris Pub, 2002), *Woman Magic* (Kikimora Pub, 1977), *Atlantic Monthly Anth* (Atlantic Monthly Pr, 1973), *Cicada, Brussels Sprouts, Amelia, Haiku Headlines, Palo Alto Times, Lost & Found Times, Sequoia, Foreground, Stonecloud*

Tony Cohan ♀ W
Frederick Hill Assoc, c/o Bonnie Nadell, 1842 Union St, San Francisco, CA 94173, 415-921-2910
Internet: tobo101@cs.com
Pubs: *On Mexican Time* (Broadway Bks, 2000), *Mexicolor* (Chronicle Bks, 1998), *Opium* (S&S, 1984), *Canary* (Doubleday, 1981)

Wanda Coleman ♀ P
PO Box 11223
Marina Del Ray, CA 90295-7223, 310-641-6806
Internet: wcoleman44@hotmail.com
Pubs: *Mercurochrome, Mambo Hips & Make Believe, Bathwater Wine, Hand Dance, African Sleeping Sickness* (Black Sparrow, 2001, 1999, 1998, 1993, 1990), *Best American Poetry 1996: Anth* (Scribner, 1996), *Postmodern American Poetry: Anth* (Norton, 1994)

Michael R. Collings P&W
Humanities Division, Pepperdine Univ, Malibu, CA 90263, 805-469-3032
Pubs: *Matrix* (White Crow, 1995), *Dark Transformation* (Starmont, 1990), *In the Image of God* (Greenwood, 1990), *Georgetown Rev, Poet, Dialogue, Star*Line*

Julia Connor ♀ ✈ P
2265 2nd Ave
Sacramento, CA 95818-3116, 916-737-2736
Pubs: *X-ing the Acheron* (Poets Corner Pr, 2002), *A Canto for the Birds* (Tule Pr, 1995), *New Amer Writing, First Intensity, Tyuonyi*

Andree Connors W
PO Box 273
Mendocino, CA 95410
Pubs: *Amateur People* (Fiction Collective, 1977)

Geoffrey Cook ♀ ✈ P
PO Box 4233
Berkeley, CA 94704-0233, 510-654-9251
Internet: gcook69833@aol.com
Pubs: *The Heart of the Beast* (Hiram Poetry Rev, 1995), *Azrael* (Androgyne Pr, 1992), *Nation, Tropos, Poetpourri, Tight, Volume Number, Studia Mystica*

Carolyn Cooke W
25524 Ten Mile Cutoff, PO Box 462
Point Arena, CA 95468-0462, 707-882-2106
Internet: redtag@mcn.org
Pubs: *The Bostons, Best American Short Stories: Anth* (HM, 2001, 1997), *Prize Stories: The O. Henry Awards: Anth* (Anchor, 1998, 1997), *Breaking Up Is Hard to Do: Anth* (Crossing Pr, 1994), *Paris Rev, Ploughshares, NER*

Clark Coolidge P
108 Prospect St
Petaluma, CA 94952
Pubs: *Far Out West* (Adventures in Poetry, 2001), *On the Nameways: Vol 1 & 2* (The Figures, 2000, 2001), *Alien Tatters* (Atelos, 2000), *Bomb* (Granary Bks, 2000), *Research* (Tuumba, 1982), *Mine: The One That Enters the Stories* (The Figures, 1982)

M. Truman Cooper P
6575 Camino Caseta
Goleta, CA 93117-1533, 805-683-2340
Pubs: *Substantial Holdings* (Pudding Hse, 1987), *Poetry NW, New Letters, Prairie Schooner, South Dakota Rev, Tar River Poetry*

Lise King Couchot P&W
808 Mission St
San Luis Obispo, CA 93405-2343
Pubs: *Thin Scars/Purple Leaves* (Mudborn Pr, 1981), *Crosscurrents, Amelia, Connexions*

Gina Covina W
PO Box 145
Laytonville, CA 95454, 505-582-4226
Pubs: *The City of Hermits* (Barn Owl Bks, 1983), *Yellow Silk, Berkeley Works, New Age*

Michael Covino P&W
2525 Ashby Ave #4
Berkeley, CA 94705-2218
Pubs: *The Off-Season* (Persea Bks, 1985), *Unfree Associations* (Berkeley Poets Pr, 1982)

Lindsey Crittenden ♀ ✈ W
268 Frederick St.
San Francisco, CA 94117-4050
Internet: lindsc@pacbell.net
Pubs: *The View from Below* (Mid-List Pr,1999), *Santa Monica Rev, Faultline, River City, Qtly West*

Barney Currer   W
10280 Brooks Rd
Windsor, CA 95492-9464
Internet: barney45@aol.com
    Pubs: *Free Fire Zone Anth* (McGraw-Hill, 1973), *Hawaii Rev,
    Aboriginal Sci Fi, Antioch Rev, Thema*

Daniel Curzon 🎤 ✈   W
City College San Francisco, L 196, San Francisco, CA 94112,
415-585-3410
Internet: curzon@pacbell.net
    Pubs: *Not Necessarily Nice: Stories, Only the Good Parts*
    (Xlibris, 1999, 1998), *Superfag* (Igna Bks, 1996), *Queer
    View Mirror* (Arsenal Pump Pr, 1996), *Curzon in Love*
    (Knights Pr, 1988), *Kenyon Rev*

Bruce Cutler   P
260 High St #110
Santa Cruz, CA 95060, 408-420-1443
    Pubs: *Seeing the Darkness* (BkMk Pr, 1998), *Afterlife*
    (Juniper Pr, 1997), *The Massacre at Sand Creek* (U
    Oklahoma Pr, 1995), *Poetry, Shenandoah, New Letters*

Jane Cutler   W
352 27th St
San Francisco, CA 94131
    Pubs: *FM Five, Medical Heritage, Wind, Central Park West,
    Epoch, NAR, Ascent, Plainswoman*

Tony D'Arpino 🎤 ✈   P
1049 Market St #308
San Francisco, CA 94103, 415-255-9584
Internet: tonydarpino@netscape.net
    Pubs: *Seven Dials* (Kealakekua, 1997), *The Shape of the
    Stone* (Deep Forest, 1990), *Sierra Songs: Anth* (Hip Pocket,
    2002), *Runes, Terra Incognita, Pavement Saw, Carriage
    House Rev, Bloomsbury Rev*

Beverly Dahlen   P
15 1/2 Mirabel Ave
San Francisco, CA 94110-4614, 415-824-6649
    Pubs: *A Reading 8-10* (Chax Pr, 1992), *Moving Borders:
    Anth* (Talisman Hse, 1998), *The Art of Practice: Anth* (Potes
    & Poets, 1994), *River City, Bombay Gin, Iowa Rev, Temblor,
    Camerawork, Poetics Jrnl, Fourteen Hills, Mirage*

Ruth Daigon 🎤 ✈   P
86 Sandpiper Cir
Corte Madera, CA 94925-1057, 415-924-0568
Internet: ruthart@aol.com
    Pubs: *Greatest Hits of Ruth Daigon* (Pudding Hse, 2000),
    The Moon Inside (Newton's Baby Pr 2000), *Electronic
    Chapbook* (Alsop Rev, 1999), *ELF, Kansas Qtly, Atlanta Rev,
    Poet Lore, Tikkun, Mudlark, CrossConnect, Switched-On-
    Gutenberg, Recursive Angel*

Saralyn R. Daly   W
6211 Gyral Dr
Tujunga, CA 91042-2533
Internet: sharon.bassett@GTE.net
    Pubs: *Love's Joy, Love's Pain* (Fawcett, 1983), *Book of True
    Love* (Pennsylvania State U Pr, 1978), *A Shout in the Street,
    Western Humanities Rev, Beyond Baroque, Epos, Descant,
    Bywords*

Catherine Daly 🎤 ✈   P
533 S Alandele
Los Angeles, CA 90036-3250
323-933-3880
Internet: cadaly@pacbell.net
    Pubs: *Pubs: Locket* (Tupelo Pr, 2003), *The Last Canto*
    (Duration Pr, 1999), *Piers Plowman Marginalia* (Potes &
    Poets, Pr, 1999), *Mudlark, American Letters & Commentary,
    Combo, East Village, Hollins Critic*

John M. Daniel 🎤 ✈   W
PO Box 21922
Santa Barbara, CA 93121-1922, 805-962-1780
Internet: jmd@danielpublishing.com
    Pubs: *Generous Helpings* (Shoreline Pr, 2001), *The Woman
    by the Bridge* (Dolphin-Moon Pr, 1991), *Play Melancholy
    Baby* (Perseverance Pr, 1986), *Fish Stories, Qtly West,
    Zyzzyva, Amelia, Ambergris, Crosscurrents, Sequoia,
    Aberrations, Vignette*

Karen M. Daniels 🎤 ✈   P&W
46040 Paseo Gallante
Temecula, CA 92592
Internet: redwolfess@aol.com
    Pubs: *Dancing Suns, Mentor's Lair, Mindspark* (Vivisphere
    Pub, 2000, 2000, 2000), *Tenacity*

Keith Allen Daniels 🎤 ✈   P&W
PO Box 95
Ridgecrest, CA 93556, 760-375-8555
Internet: kdaniels@ix.netcom.com
    Pubs: *The Weird Sonneteers, I Think Therefore Iamb, Haiku
    by Unohu, Satan Is a Mathematician, What Rough Book*
    (Anamnesis Pr, 2000, 2000, 2000, 1998, 1992), *Loopy Is
    the Inner Ear* (Quick Glimpse Pr, 1993), *Analog, Asimov's
    SF, Recursive Angel, Weird Tales*

Jonathan Daunt   P
609 D St
Davis, CA 95616
    Pubs: *Stone Age Robin Hood* (Allegany Mtn Pr, 1979),
    Coyote's Jrnl: Anth (Wingbow Pr, 1982), *BPJ, Denver Qtly,
    Mississippi Rev, Prairie Schooner*

Michael Davidson 🎤 ✈   P
Dept of Literature, Univ California, San Diego, 9500 Gilman Dr,
Dept 0410, La Jolla, CA 92093-0410, 858-534-2101
Internet: mdavidson@uscd.edu
    Pubs: *The Arcades* (O Bks, 1999), *Post Hoc* (Avenue B Pr,
    1990), *Analogy of the Ion* (The Figures, 1988)

Angela J. Davis   P
505 S Beverly, #488
Beverly Hills, CA 90212, 310-277-3976
   Pubs: *Eureka Anth* (U Iowa Pr, 1995), *Art/Life, Onthebus, Permafrost, Yellow Silk, Sequoia, Cream City Rev*

Christopher Davis 🎤 ✈   W
2284 Norwic Pl
Altadena, CA 91001, 626-398-4109
   Pubs: *Dog Horse Rat* (Viking, 1990), *A Peep Into the 20th Century* (Arbor Hse, 1985), *Waiting for It* (H&R, 1980)

Richard Cortez Day   W
PO Box 947
Arcata, CA 95518-0947, 707-822-8877
Internet: rcday@humboldt1.com
   Pubs: *When in Florence* (Doubleday, 1986), *Imagining Worlds: Anth* (McGraw-Hill, 1995), *Kenyon Rev, Qtly West, Redbook, Carolina Qtly, NER, Witness*

Lucille Lang Day 🎤 ✈   P
1057 Walker Ave
Oakland, CA 94610-1511, 510-763-3874
Internet: lucyday@earthlink.net
   Pubs: *Infinities* (Cedar Hill Publications, 2002), *Wild One* (Scarlet Tanager Bks, 2000), *Fire in the Garden* (Mother's Hen, 1997), *Blue Unicorn, Hudson Rev, Threepenny Rev, Portland Rev, Chattahoochee Rev, Hawaii Pacific Rev, Poet Lore*

Jacqueline De Angelis   P&W
3244 Madera Ave
Los Angeles, CA 90039
Internet: jdeangelis@yahoo.com
   Pubs: *The Main Gate* (Paradise, 1984), *Hers: Anth* (Faber & Faber, 1996), *In a Different Light: Anth* (Clothespin Fever Pr, 1988), *Agni, Intl Qtly, Rara Avis, Momentum Mag*

Viviana Chamberlin De Aparicio   P&W
1769 Las Lunas St
Pasadena, CA 91106, 213-793-8379

Steve De France 🎤 ✈   P
5460 Las Lomas St
Lona Beach, CA 90815-4137, 562-494-4161
Internet: poet98@earthlink.net
   Pubs: *Mid Amer Poetry Rev, Rattle, Miller's Pond, ORBIS, Kit Kat, Lynx Eye, The Sun, Poetry Motel*

Marsha de la O 🎤 ✈   P
1296 Placid Ave
Ventura, CA 93004-2068, 805-671-5531
   Pubs: *Black Hope* (New Issues Pr, 1997), *Intimate Nature: Anth* (Ballantine, 1998), *Beyond the Valley: Anth* (Sacred Beverage Pr, 1998), *Barrow St, Passages North, Onset Rev, Black Warrior Rev, Solo, Third Coast, Art/Life*

Terri de la Peña 🎤 ✈   W
College of Letters & Science, Univ California, 405 Hilgard Ave, Los Angeles, CA 90095-1438, 310-206-1853
Internet: terrid@college.ucla.edu
   Pubs: *Faults* (Alyson Bks, 1999), *A Is for the Americas* (Orchard Bks, 1999), *Latin Satins, Margins* (Seal Pr, 1994, 1992), *Chicana Lesbians: Anth* (Third Woman Pr, 1992), *Lesbian Rev of Bks, Conmocion, Matrix*

Ruth de Menezes   P
2821 Arizona Ave
Santa Monica, CA 90404
e-mail 310-453-8448
   Pubs: *The Heart's Far Cry* (Small Poetry Pr, 1996), *Love Ascending* (Trinity Comm, 1987), *Woman Songs* (Claremont Pr, 1982), *Poetic Voices of America: Anth* (Sparrowgrass Poetic Forum, 1998), *America, Catholic World, Magnificat, St. Anthony Messenger, Visions*

Richard De Mille   W
960 Lilac Dr
Santa Barbara, CA 93108, 805-969-4887
   Pubs: *Two Qualms & A Quirk* (Capra Pr, 1973), *Antioch Rev*

John Deming   W
16634 McCormick
Encino, CA 91436, 818-501-5059
   Pubs: *Descant, Crosscurrents, Chariton Rev, Richmond Qtly, Uncommon Reader, Missouri Rev, Other Voices*

James DenBoer 🎤 ✈   P
1734 34th St
Sacramento, CA 95816, 916-731-4492
Internet: jamesdb@paperwrk.com
   Pubs: *Dreaming of the Chinese Army* (Blue Thunder Pr, 2000), *Lost in Blue Canyon* (Christopher's Bks, 1979), *Nine Poems* (Christopher's Bks, 1972)

Laura Denham 🎤 ✈   W
1590 Sacramento St #10
San Francisco, CA 94109
Internet: ldenham@aol.com
   Pubs: *Have You Seen Me* (Carroll & Graf, 2002), *S Dakota Rev, Fiction, Beloit Fiction Jrnl, 580 Split*

W.S. Di Piero 🎤 ✈   P
225 Downey St #5
San Francisco, CA 94117
   Pubs: *Skirts and Slacks* (Knopf, 2001), *Shooting the Works, Shadows Burning* (TriQtly Bks, 1996, 1995), *The Restorers* (U Chicago, 1992), *Out of Eden* (U California, 1991), *The Dog Star* (U Massachusetts Pr, 1989)

Diane di Prima 🎤 ✈   P&W
78 Niagara Ave
San Francisco, CA 94112-3335, 415-841-0717
  Pubs: *Recollections of My Life as a Woman* (Viking, 2001),
  Loba (Peguin, 1998), *Pieces of a Song* (City Lights, 1990),
  Unsettling America: Anth (Viking, 1994), *L.A. Times Book
  Rev, Disclosure, Paterson Lit Rev, Yoga Jrnl, Heaven Bone,
  First Intensity*

N. A. Diaman   W
2950 Van Ness Ave, #4
San Francisco, CA 94109-1036
Internet: personapro@aol.com
  Pubs: *Private Nation, Castro Street Memories, Reunion, Ed
  Dean Is Queer* (Persona Pr, 1997, 1988, 1983, 1978)

Ray Clark Dickson   P&W
Kerouac Connection/Beloit Poetry Jrnl, 1978 Oceanaire Dr,
San Luis Obispo, CA 93405-6829, 805-773-6530
  Pubs: *A Fine Excess: Fifty Years of Beloit Poetry Jrnl: Anth*
  (Beloit Poetry Jrnl, 2001), *Saturday Evening Post,
  Wormwood Rev, Haight-Ashbury Literary Jrnl, Coffeehouse
  Poets' Qtly, BPJ*

Millicent G. Dillon 🎤 ✈   W
83 6th Ave
San Francisco, CA 94118-1323
Internet: millicentd@mindspring.com
  Pubs: *A Version of Love* (Norton, 2003), *Harry Gold* (The
  Overlook Pr, 2000), *Dance of the Mothers,* (Dutton, 1991),
  The One in the Back Is Medea (Viking, 1973), *Michigan Qtly
  Rev, Ontario Rev, SW Rev*

Chitra Banerjee Divakaruni   P&W
Foothill College, English Dept, Los Altos, CA 94022,
415-949-7250
  Pubs: *Black Candle* (Calyx Bks, 1991), *The Reason for
  Nasturtiums* (Berkeley Poets Pr, 1990), *Ms., BPJ, Chicago
  Rev, Zyzzyva, Chelsea*

Mario Divok   P
5 Misty Meadow
Irvine, CA 92715, 714-854-1322
  Pubs: *Forbidden Island: Complete Works Two, The Birthday*
  (Triton, 1986, 1984), *Poetalk, California: A Qtly Mag, Amer
  Poetry*

Carl Djerassi 🎤 ✈   P&W
Dept of Chemistry, Stanford Univ, Stanford, CA 94305-5080,
650-723-2783
Internet: djerassi@stanford.edu
  Pubs: *No, Menachem's Seed, The Bourbaki Gambit*
  (Penguin, 2000, 1998, 1996), *Marx, Deceased* (U Georgia
  Pr, 1998, 1996), *The Clock Runs Backwards* (Story Line Pr,
  1991), *Hudson Rev, Southern Rev, New Letters, Grand
  Street, Kenyon Rev, Midwest Rev*

Harriet Doerr   W
494 Bradford St
Pasadena, CA 91105
  Pubs: *The Tiger in the Grass, Stones for Ibarra* (Viking,
  1995, 1984), *Consider This, Senora* (HB, 1993), *Under an
  Aztec Sun* (Yolla Bolly Pr, 1990)

Richard Dokey 🎤 ✈   W
4471 W Kingdon Rd
Lodi, CA 95242-9507, 209-463-8314
Internet: kingdon@inreach.com
  Pubs: *The Hollow Man* (Delta West, 1999), *Late Harvest*
  (Paragon Hse, 1992), *Intro to Literature: Anth, Intro to
  Fiction: Anth* (Norton, 1995, 1995), *TriQtly, Missouri Rev,
  SW Rev, New Letters*

Diane C. Donovan   P
12424 Mill St
Petaluma, CA 94952-9728
  Pubs: *General Store, Tightrope, Owlflight, Night Voyages,
  The Bookwatch, Kliatt Bk Guide*

Carol Dorf   P&W
1400 Delaware St
Berkeley, CA 94702, 510-848-4701
  Pubs: *A Breath Would Destroy That Symmetry* (E.G. San
  Francisco, 1989), *Feminist Studies, Five Fingers Rev,
  Liberty Hill, Heresies, Caprice, Metaphors*

Sharon Doubiago 🎤 ✈   P
2708 Stuart
Berkeley, CA 94705, 510-548-8368
  Pubs: *Body & Soul* (Cedar Hill Pubs, 2000), *Hard Country*
  (West End Pr, 1999), *The Husband Arcane, The Arcane of
  O* (Gorda Plate Pr, 1996), *South America Mi Hija* (U Pitt Pr,
  1992), *Psyche Drives the Coast* (Empty Bowl Pr, 1990), *El
  Nino* (Lost Roads Pr, 1989)

Philip Dow   P
2193 Ethel Porter Dr
Napa, CA 94558, 707-224-9463
  Pubs: *19 New American Poets of the Golden Gate: Anth*
  (HBJ, 1985), *Boundary 2*

Frank Dwyer   P
768 Canyon Wash Dr
Pasadena, CA 91107
Internet: dwyer@ctqla.org

Kathryn Eberly   P&W
301 Precita Ave, #2
San Francisco, CA 94110, 415-824-5809
Internet: keberly164@aol.com
  Pubs: *Women & Death* (Ground Torpedo Pr, 1996), *It's All
  the Rage: Anth* (Andrew Mountain Pr 1997), *If I Had a
  Hammer: Women's Work in Poetry & Fiction: Anth* (Papier-
  Mache Pr, 1990), *Rhino, Evergreen Chronicles, Ruah*

Bart Edelman ♪ ✈ P
394 Elmwood Dr
Pasadena, CA 91105, 213-340-8121
Internet: bedelman@glendale.cc.ca.us
 Pubs: *The Gentle Man, Alphabet of Love* (Red Hen Pr,
2001, 1999), *Under Damaris' Dress* (Lightning Pub, 1996),
Crossing the Hackensack (Prometheus Pr, 1993)

Nancy Edwards P
English Dept, Bakersfield College, 1801 Panorama Dr,
Bakersfield, CA 93305, 805-831-1067
 Pubs: *The Woman Within* (Bakersfield College, 1994),
*Network Africa, Orpheus, Amelia, Roadrunner, The Plastic
Tower, CQ, Little Balkans Rev, The Forum*

Susan Efros P
41 Pine Dr
Fairfax, CA 94930
 Pubs: *Two Way Streets* (Jungle Garden Pr, 1976), *This Is
Women's Work: Anth* (Panjandrum Pr, 1974), *Amelia,
Footwork, Lowell Pearl, Ascent, Paris Transcontinental,
Christopher Street*

Terry Ehret ♪ ✈ P
924 Sunnyslope Rd
Petaluma, CA 94952-4747, 707-762-2689
Internet: tehret99@attbi.com
 Pubs: *Translations from the Human Language* (Sixteen
Rivers Pr, 2001), *How We Go on Living* (Protean Pr, 1995),
Lost Body (Copper Canyon Pr, 1993)

Samuel A. Eisenstein ♪ ✈ P&W
1015 Prospect Blvd
Pasadena, CA 91103-2811
Internet: sameisenstein@hotmail.com
 Pubs: *Nudibranchia* (Red Hen Pr, 2000), *Rectification of
Eros, Price of Admission, The Inner Garden* (Sun & Moon
Pr, 2000, 1992, 1986)

Sergio D. Elizondo P
627 Lilac Ln
Imperial, CA 92251, 619-353-8233
 Pubs: *Suruma* (Dos Pasos, 1990), *Muerte en una Estrella*
(Sainz-Luiselli, 1984)

Ellen ♪ ✈ P
6353 Malibu Park Ln
Malibu, CA 90265, 310-457-3585
 Pubs: *4 Los Angeles Poets* (Bombshelter Pr, 2002), *Isis
Rising: Anth* (Temple of Isis, 2000), *In the Garden: Anth*
(International Forum, 1996), *ACM, Slant, COE Rev,
Coastal Forest Rev, Prime Time, Blue Unicorn, ArtLife,
Spillway*

Ella Thorp Ellis ♪ ✈ W
1438 Grizzly Peak
Berkeley, CA 94708, 510-549-9871
Internet: ehellis@ieee.org
 Pubs: *The Year of My Indian Prince* (Delacorte, 2001),
Swimming With the Whales (H Holt, 1995), *Hugo & the
Princess Nina, Sleepwalkers Moon* (Atheneum, 1983,
1980), *Mademoiselle*

Kenneth Ellsworth P&W
6055 Calmfield Ave
Agoura Hills, CA 91301, 818-991-4757
 Pubs: *Christian Blues: Anth* (Amador Pub, 1995), *Black
Buzzard Rev, Rivertalk, Toast, Illya's Honey, California Qtly,
Farmer's Market, Atom Mind, Sell Outs, Gargoyle,
Iconoclast, Bohemian Chronicle, Verve, Buffalo Bones,
Etcetera, Knocked*

Alan C. Engebretsen P
8220 Rayford Dr
Los Angeles, CA 90045, 310-649-1645
 Pubs: *A Rage of Blue* (Poetic Justice, 1985), *California
State Poetry Qtly, Wind, Pudding Mag, Prophetic Voices,
Orphic Lute, Proof Rock, Amelia*

Charles Entrekin P&W
10736 Indian Shack Rd
Nevada City, CA 95959
 Pubs: *In This Hour, Casting for the Cutthroat* (Berkeley
Poets, 1988, 1980), *Madison Rev, Passager, Xanadu,
Literature of Work, Birmingham Poetry Rev*

Catherine Henley Erickson ♪ ✈ P
764 Valparaiso
Claremont, CA 91711, 909-593-3511x4352
Internet: henleyer@ulv.edu
 Pubs: *Contemporary Women Poets: Anth* (Merlin Pr, 1977),
Rara Avis, Beyond Baroque, Poetry/L.A.

Maria Amparo Escandón ♪ ✈ W
2231 Overland Ave
Los Angeles, CA 90064
Internet: escandon@acento.com
 Pubs: *Esperanza's Box of Saints* (S&S, 1998), *Las Mamis*
(Knopf, 2000), *Palm Readings: Anth* (Plain View Pr, 1998),
*Onthebus, Manoa, Prairie Schooner, Herman Rev, West /
Word*

Rudy Espinosa W
250 Drake St
San Francisco, CA 94112, 415-585-0395

Maria Espinosa W
3396 Orchard Valley Ln
Lafayette, CA 94549, 510-283-4314
Internet: paulamar@aol.com
 Pubs: *Dark Plums, Longing, Three Day Flight: Anth* (Arte
Publico Pr, 1995, 1995, 1994)

Martha Evans 🎤 ✈   P
1022 57th St
Oakland, CA 94608-2706, 415-653-5566
    Pubs: *Landing Signals: Anth* (Sacramento Poetry Ctr, 1985),
    New Letters, Chelsea, NYQ, Chicago Rev, CutBank,
    Synapse, Ironwood

George Evans   P
1590 21st Ave
San Francisco, CA 94122
    Pubs: *Sudden Dreams: New & Selected Poems* (Coffee Hse
    Pr, 1991), *Conjunctions, New Directions, Sulfur*

Mary Fabilli   P
2445 Ashby Ave
Berkeley, CA 94705, 510-841-6300
    Pubs: *Winter Poems* (Inverno Pr, 1983), *Aurora Bligh &*
    Early Poems (Oyez, 1968), *Talisman, To, Sierra Jrnl*

B. H. Fairchild 🎤 ✈   P
706 W 11th St
Claremont, CA 91711
Internet: bhfairchil@aol.com
    Pubs: *Early Occult Memory Systems of the Lower Midwest*
    (Norton, 2002), *The Art of the Lathe* (Alice James Bks
    1998), *Local Knowledge* (QRL, 1991), *The Arrival of the*
    Future (Swallow's Tale Pr, 1986)

Marcia Falk 🎤 ✈   P
2905 Benvenue Ave
Berkeley, CA 94705, 510-548-8018
Internet: marciafalk@aol.com
    Pubs: *Book of Blessings, Song of Songs* (Harper, 1996,
    1990), *This Year in Jerusalem* (State Street, 1986), *Nice*
    Jewish Girls: Anth (Plume, 1996), *APR, Women's Rev of*
    Bks, Tikkun, PSA Bulletin, Anth of Mag Verse & Yearbook of
    American Poetry

Jennifer Crystal Fang-Chien 🎤 ✈   P
610 16 St Ste 506
Oakland, CA 94612
Internet: jennifer@art.net
    Pubs: *Louisville Rev, So to Speak, Pacific Rev, Haight-*
    Ashbury Lit Jrnl, Shades of December, Writing for Our Lives

Thomas Farber 🎤 ✈   W
Box 2, 1678 Shattuck Ave
Berkeley, CA 94709, 510-644-4193
    Pubs: *The Beholder* (Metropolitan, 2002), *Other Oceans*
    (U Hawaii Pr, 2001), *A Lover's Question: Selected Stories*
    (Creative Arts, 2000), *The Face of the Deep* (Mercury Hse,
    1998), *Through a Liquid Mirror* (Edtns Ltd, 1997), *On Water,*
    (Ecco Pr, 1994)

Dion N. Farquhar 🎤 ✈   P&W
249 Dickens Way
Santa Cruz, CA 95064-1064, 831-425-8680
Internet: dnfarquhar@aol.com
    Pubs: *The Other Machine* (Routledge, 1996), *Sulfur,*
    Crazyquilt, Poet Lore, Visions, Hawaii Rev, Red Bass,
    Painted Bride Qtly, Alea, Asylum, Boundary 2, Burning
    Cloud Rev, Juxta, New Novel Rev

Curtis Faville   P
34 Franciscan Way
Kensington, CA 94707, 415-526-3412

Raymond Federman 🎤 ✈   P&W
12428 Avenida Consentido
San Diego, CA 92128, 858-385-0849
Internet: moinous@aol.com
    Pubs: *Loose Shoes* (Weidler Verlag, 2002), *The Voice in the*
    Closet (Starcherone Books, 2002), *Aunt Rachel's Fur* (FC2,
    2001), *The Twofold Vibration, Smiles on Washington Square*
    (Sun & Moon, 1998, 1995), *To Whom It May Concern*
    (Fiction Collective 2, 1990)

Jean Femling   W
2384 Cornell Dr
Costa Mesa, CA 92626
Internet: jfemling@earthlink.com
    Pubs: *Getting Mine, Hush, Money* (St. Martin's, 1991, 1989),
    Interfaces: Anth (Ace, 1980), *Backyard* (H&R, 1975),
    Descant

Paul Fericano   P&W
Yossarian Universal News, PO Box 236, Millbrae, CA
94030-0236
    Pubs: *The One-Minute President* (w/Ligi), *Sinatra Sinatra*
    (Poor Souls Pr, 1987, 1982), *Stoogism: Anth* (Scarecrow
    Bks, 1977), *Wormwood Rev, Realist, Krokodil, Second*
    Coming, Free Lunch, Wine Rings

Lawrence Ferlinghetti   P&W
City Lights Books, 261 Columbus Ave, San Francisco, CA
94133, 415-362-1901
    Pubs: *These Are My Rivers: New & Selected Poems 1955-*
    1993 (New Directions, 1993), *Love in the Days of Rage*
    (Dutton/Penguin, 1989)

Anne Finger 🎤 ✈   W
5809 Fremont
Oakland, CA 94608, 510-594-6870
Internet: AnnieDigit@mindspring.com
    Pubs: *Bone Truth* (Coffee Hse Pr, 1994), *Past Due* (Seal Pr,
    1990), *Kenyon Rev, Southern Rev, Antioch Rev, 13th Moon,*
    Feminist Studies, Kaleidoscope

Molly Fisk 🎤 ✈　　　　　　　　　　　P
10068 Newtown Rd
Nevada City, CA 95959
Internet: molly@mollyfisk.com
　　Pubs: *Listening to Winter* (California Poetry Series, 2000),
　　Terrain (w/D. Bellm, et al; Hip Pocket Pr, 1998), *Salt Water
　　Poems* (Jungle Garden Pr, 1994)

Lawrence Fixel 🎤　　　　　　　　　　P&W
1496 Willard St
San Francisco, CA 94117-3721, 415-661-3870
　　Pubs: *Unlawful Assembly: Poems 1940-1992* (Cloud Forms,
　　1994), *Truth, War, & The Dream-Game: Selected Prose
　　Poems & Parables* (Coffee Hse Pr, 1992)

Ted Fleischman　　　　　　　　　　　P
293 Glorietta Blvd
Orinda, CA 94563, 510-376-3431
　　Pubs: *Half a Bottle of Catsup, Berkeley Poets Cooperative
　　Anth* (Berkeley Poets Pr, 1978, 1980), *Berkeley Poets Co-
　　op, Outerbridge, In a Nutshell*

Gerald Fleming 🎤 ✈　　　　　　　　P
PO Box 529
Lagunitas, CA 94938-0529, 415-488-4226
　　Internet: uncleennui@aol.com
　　Pubs: *Seeds Flying in a Fresh Light* (Allyn & Bacon, 1990),
　　*New Letters, Volt, Five Fingers Rev, Puerto del Sol,
　　Americas Rev, Pequod*

Stewart Florsheim 🎤 ✈　　　　　　P
170 Sandringham Rd
Piedmont, CA 94611
　　Internet: stewjay@pacbell.net
　　Pubs: *Bittersweet Legacy: Anth* (Univ Pr of Amer, 2001),
　　And What Rough Beast: Anth (Ashland Poetry Pr, 1999),
　　Unsettling America: Anth (Viking Penguin, 1994), *Ghosts of
　　the Holocaust: Anth* (Wayne State U Pr, 1989), *Rattle, 88,
　　DoubleTake, Karamu*

Jack Foley 🎤 ✈　　　　　　　　　　P&W
2569 Maxwell Ave
Oakland, CA 94601-5521, 510-532-3737
　　Internet: jasfoley@aol.com
　　Pubs: *Some Songs by Georges Brassens* (Goldfish Pr,
　　2001), *Advice to the Lovelorn* (Texture Pr, 1998), *New
　　Poetry from California: Dead/Requiem, Saint James ,
　　Exiles, Adrift* (Pantograph Pr, 1998 & 1998 w/Ivan
　　Arguelles), *1996, 1993)*

CB Follett 🎤 ✈　　　　　　　　　　P
PO Box 401
Sausalito, CA 94966-0401, 415-331-2503
　　Internet: runes@aol.com
　　Pubs: *At the Turning of the Light* (Salmon Run Pr, 2001),
　　Visible Bones (Plain View Pr, 1998), *Gathering the
　　Mountains,* (Hot Pepper Pr, 1995), *MacGuffin, Cumberland
　　Rev, The Bridge, Confluence, Calyx, Heaven Bone, New
　　Letters, Birmingham Poetry Rev*

Elizabeth Foote-Smith　　　　　　　P&W
2635 Regent St
Berkeley, CA 94704, 510-849-0800
　　Pubs: *Never Say Die, Gentle Albatross* (Putnam, 1980,
　　1978), *Michigan Qtly Rev*

Jeanne Foster　　　　　　　　　　　P
St. Mary's College, PO Box 4700, Moraga, CA 94575-4700,
925-631-4511
　　Internet: jfoster@stmarys-ca.edu
　　Pubs: *A Blessing of Safe Travel* (QRL, 1980), *Great Horned
　　Owl* (White Pine, 1980), *Ploughshares, Hudson Rev, TriQtly,
　　NAR, APR, Paris Rev*

William L. Fox 🎤 ✈　　　　　　　　P
503 S Fuller Ave
Los Angeles, CA 90036, 323-692-0889
　　Internet: wlfox@earthlink.net
　　Pubs: *One Wave Standing* (La Alameda Pr, 1998), *Silence &
　　License* (Light & Dust, 1994), *Geograph* (Black Rock Pr,
　　1994), *TumbleWords: Anth* (U Nevada Pr, 1995), *Caliban,
　　Chain*

Thaisa Frank　　　　　　　　　　　W
459 66thSt
Oakland, CA 94609, 510-658-1225
　　Pubs: *Enchanted Men, A Brief History of Camouflage* (Black
　　Sparrow Pr, 1994, 1991), *Whole Earth Rev, City Lights Rev,
　　Forehead*

Peter Frank　　　　　　　　　　　P
PO Box 24 A36
Los Angeles, CA 90024-1036, 310-271-9740
　　Internet: pfrank@scf.usc.edu
　　Pubs: *New, Used & Improved* (Abbeville Pr, 1987),
　　Travelogues (Sun & Moon Pr, 1982)

Kathleen Fraser　　　　　　　　　　P
1936 Leavenworth St
San Francisco, CA 94133, 415-474-8911
　　Internet: kfraser@sfsu.edu
　　Pubs: *il cuore: the heart, Selected Poems 1970-1997*
　　(Wesleyan U Pr, 1997), *When New Time Folds Up* (Chax,
　　1993), *Chicago Rev, Conjunctions, Talisman*

Devery Freeman　　　　　　　　　　W
320 N La Peer Dr, Apt 401
Beverly Hills, CA 90211
　　Pubs: *Father Sky* (Morrow, 1979), *American Mag, Liberty*

Mary Freericks 🎤 ✈　　　　　　　P
1074 Miramonte Dr, Unit #8
Santa Barbara, CA 93109, 805-899-4330
　　Pubs: *Poetry in the Garden: Anth* (Intl Forum, 1996), *For
　　She Is the Tree of Life: Grandmothers Through the Eyes of
　　Women Writers: Anth* (Conari Pr, 1995), *The Southern
　　California Anth* (USC, 1988), *Santa Barbara Commentary,
　　Ararat, CSM*

Melvyn Freilicher   PP&P
3945 Normal St, #5
San Diego, CA 92103, 619-299-4859
  Pubs: *120 Days in the FBI: My Untold Story by Jane Eyre*
  (Standing Stones Pr, 1998), *River Styx, New Novel Rev,*
  Fiction Intl, Frame-Work: Jrnl of Images & Culture, Central
  Park, Crawl out Your Window

Elliot Fried 🎤 ✈   P
Cal State Univ, Long Beach, English Dept, Long Beach, CA
90840
Internet: elliotfried@msn.com
  Pubs: *Marvel Mystery Oil* (Red Wind Pr, 1991), *New*
  Geography of Poets: Anth (U Arkansas Pr, 1993), *Movie*
  Poetry: Anth (Faber & Faber, 1993), *Green Mtns Rev*

Paula Naomi Friedman 🎤 ✈   P&W
5522 Tehama Ave
Richmond, CA 94804-5041, 510-527-3857
Internet: pnfpnf@aol.com
  Pubs: *Bittersweet Legacy: Anth* (U Pr of Amer, 2001),
  Touched by Adoption: Anth (Green River Pr, 1999),
  Gathered From the Center: Anth (Berkeley Women's Center,
  1995), *Out of Line, Earth's Daughters, Jewish Women's Lit*
  Annual, The Open Cell

S. L. Friedman   P
732 N June St
Los Angeles, CA 90038, 213-464-5802
Internet: carolineshona@sprynet.com
  Pubs: *Hanging by Our Teeth & Rising by Our Bootstraps,*
  Some Light Through the Blindfold (Friedman, 1991, 1988),
  Wordsworth's Socks, Plains Poetry Jrnl, California Poetry
  Jrnl, Quartet, Epos

Gloria Frym 🎤 ✈   P&W
2119 Eunice St
Berkeley, CA 94709-1416, 510-524-6069
Internet: gloriafrym@es.com
  Pubs: *Homeless at Home* (Creative Arts Bks, 2001),
  Distance No Object (City Lights Bks, 1999), *How I Learned*
  (Coffee Hse Pr, 1992), *By Ear* (Sun & Moon Pr, 1991)

Blair Fuller   W
565 Connecticut St
San Francisco, CA 94107, 415-824-8132
  Pubs: *A Butterfly Net & a Kingdom* (Creative Arts Bk Co.,
  1989), *Birth of a Fan: Anth* (Macmillan, 1993)

Len Fulton   W
Box 100
Paradise, CA 95967-0100, 530-877-6110
  Pubs: *Dark Other Adam Dreaming* (Dustbooks, 1976), *The*
  Grassman (Penguin, 1975)

Robert Funge 🎤 ✈   P
PO Box 1225
San Carlos, CA 94070-1225, 650-592-7720
  Pubs: *The Passage* (Ireland; Elo Pr, 2001), *What Have You*
  Lost?: Anth (Greenwillow Bks, 1999), *Witness, S Dakota*
  Rev, Lit Rev, Tampa Rev, Seattle Rev, Chariton Rev

Gary G. Gach 🎤 ✈   P
1243 Broadway, #4
San Francisco, CA 94109-2771, 415-771-7793
Internet: ggg@well.com
  Pubs: *Visions: Anth* (Nat'l Geographic, 2000), *The Book of*
  Luminous Things: Anth (Harcourt, 1998), *What Book!?: Anth*
  (Parallax, 1998), *Two Lines, APR, Zyzzyva*

Diane Gage   P
2541 Meddowlark Dr.
San Diego, CA 92123
Internet: dgage@san.rr.com
  Pubs: *Women Artists Datebook, Prayers to Protest: Anth,*
  The Unitarian Universalist Poets: Anth (Pudding Hse Pub,
  1998, 1996), *Pikeville Rev, Phoebe, Puerto del Sol*

Susan M. Gaines   W
1046 Elsbree Lane
Windsor, CA 95492
Internet: smgaines@movinet.com.uy
  Pubs: *Carbon Dreams* (Creative Arts, 2001), *Sacred*
  Ground: Writings About Home: Anth (Milkweed Edtns,
  1996), *Best of the West: Anth* (Norton, 1992), *Cream City*
  Rev, NAR, Missouri Rev

Kate Gale   P&W
Red Hen Press, PO Box 902582, Palmdale, CA 93590-2582,
818-831-0649
Internet: kgale@bigfoot.com
  Pubs: *Where Crows & Men Collide, Blue Air* (Red Hen Pr,
  1995, 1995), *Water Moccasins* (Tidal Wave Pr, 1994)

Robin Galguera 🎤   P
PO Box 9046
Oakland, CA 94613, 510-569-5766
Internet: quirkyangel@ earthlink.net
  Pubs: *I Feel A Little Jumpy Around You: Anth* (S&S, 1996),
  Mothering, Santa Barbara Rev, Qtly West, New Letters,
  WALRUS

Sally M. Gall   P
5820 Folsom Dr
La Jolla, CA 92037-7323
Internet: librettist@aol.com
  Pubs: *Eleanor Roosevelt* (Oxford U Pr, 1996), *Kill Bear*
  Comes Home (VM Music, 1994), *Southern Rev,*
  Ploughshares, Confrontation, Present Tense, Missouri Rev,
  The Humanist, Footwork

Dick Gallup P
1450 Castro St, #17
San Francisco, CA 94114, 415-550-0638
Internet: ice@tlcs.com
    Pubs: *Plumbing the Depths of Folly* (Smithereens Pr, 1983),
    Where I Hang My Hat (H&R, 1967)

Reymundo Gamboa P&W
408 Chaparral
Santa Maria, CA 93454, 805-922-1339
    Pubs: *Cenzotle: Chicano Literary Prize* (U California Irvine,
    1988), *The Baby Chook & Other Remnants* (Other Voices,
    1976), *Chicanos: Antologia Historica de Literatura* (Fondo
    de Cultura Economica, 1980), *Denver Qtly, Morning of '56,
    El Oficio, Script*

evvy garrett P
San Diego, CA
Internet: egarrett@peoplepc.com
    Pubs: *NYQ, AKA, Pearl, Capper's, Arizona Unconservative,
    Rant, Alura, December Rose, Copper Hill Qtly, Poetic
    Space, Radiant Woman*

Phyllis Gebauer ♀ ✈ W
515 W Scenic Dr
Monrovia, CA 91016-1511
Internet: pgebauer@earthlink.net
    Pubs: *The Pagan Blessing* (Viking, 1979), *Iowa English
    Bulletin, Modern Maturity, Sight Lines*

Dan Gerber ♀ ✈ P&W
PO Box 185
Santa Ynez, CA 93460
    Pubs: *Trying to Catch the Horses* (Michigan State U Pr,
    1999), *A Voice From the River, Grass Fires* (Clark City,
    1990, 1989), *Poetry, Best Amer Poetry, New Yorker, Nation,
    Georgia Rev*

Merrill Joan Gerber ♀ ✈ W
542 Santa Anita Ct
Sierra Madre, CA 91024-2623, 626-355-0384
www.cco.caltech.edu/~mjgerber
    Pubs: *Botticelli Blue Skies, Gut Feelings* (U Wisconsin Pr,
    2003, 2002), *Anna in the Afterlife, Anna in Chains* (Syracuse
    U Pr, 2002, 1998), *Old Mother, Little Cat, The Kingdom of
    Brooklyn* (Longstreet Pr, 1995, 1992), *American Scholar,
    New Yorker, Atlantic*

Amy Gerstler ♀ ✈ P&W
4430 Palo Verde Terr
San Diego, CA 92115
    Pubs: *Medicine* (Penguin Putnam, 2000), *Crown of Weeds,
    Nerve Storm* (Viking Penguin, 1997, 1993), *Bitter Angel*
    (North Point Pr, 1990)

Art Gibney W
PO Box 63
Tiburon, CA 94920
Internet: artgibney@earthlink.net
    Pubs: *Skin of the Earth* (U Nevada Pr, 2002), *Story Qtly,
    Zyzzyva, Estero, Clockwatch Rev, Tennessee Qtly, Intl Qtly,
    South Dakota Rev*

Barry Gifford ♀ ✈ P&W
833 Bancroft Way
Berkeley, CA 94710, 510-848-4956
    Pubs: *American Falls: The Collected Short Stories* (Seven
    Stories, 2002), *Wyoming* (Arcade, 2000), *My Last Martini*
    (Crane Hill, 2000), *Night People* (Grove Pr, 1993), *First
    Intensity, Esquire, Rolling Stone, Speak, Shenandoah,
    Projections, Exquisite Corpse*

Jack Gilbert P
136 Montana St
San Francisco, CA 94112, 415-585-6055
    Pubs: *Kochan* (Tamarack Pr, 1984), *Monolithos* (Knopf,
    1983), *Views of Jeopardy* (Yale U Pr, 1962)

Jeremiah Gilbert ♀ ✈ P&W
PO Box 753
Bryn Mawr, CA 92318
Internet: mersault@sprynet.com
    Pubs: *A Time of Trial: Anth* (Hidden Brook Pr, 2001), *Stirring,
    3rd Muse Poetry Jrnl, The Old Red Kimono, Clark St Rev*

Sandra M. Gilbert ♀ ✈ P&W
Univ California, English Dept, Davis, CA 95616, 916-752-2257
Internet: sgilbert@ucdavis.edu
    Pubs: *Kissing the Bread, Ghost Volcano* (Norton, 2000,
    1995), *Poetry, Ontario Rev, Kenyon Rev, Poetry NW, Field,
    APR*

D.H.L. Gilbert W
514 Lighthouse Ave
Santa Cruz, CA 95060
    Pubs: *Iowa Rev, NW Rev, NAR, Antioch Rev, Quarry West*

Molly Giles W
PO Box 137
Woodacre, CA 94973
    Pubs: *Rough Translations* (U Georgia Pr, 1985), *Caprice,
    San Jose Studies, Real Fiction, Manoa, Greensboro Rev,
    McCall's, Sundog, Shenandoah*

S. E. Gilman P&W
1725 Lehigh Dr
Davis, CA 95616, 916-757-1920
    Pubs: *Letters to Our Children* (Franklin Watts, 1997),
    Anyone Can Be a Target, Even Margaret (Consummated
    Productions, 1978), *Americas Rev, Modern Words*

Dana Gioia 🎤 ✈   P
7190 Faught Rd
Santa Rosa, CA 95403-7835
 Pubs: *The Gods of Winter, Daily Horoscope* (Graywolf Pr,
 1991, 1986), *Hudson Rev, Poetry, New Yorker*

Robert Franklin Gish   W
PO Box 947
San Luis Obispo, CA 93406, 805-756-2304
www.lavaland.com
 Pubs: *Dreams of Quivira* (Clear Light Pub, 1998), *Bad Boys
 & Black Sheep, First Horses* (U Nevada Pr, 1993), *North
 Dakota Qtly, New Mexico Mag, Mirage, Urbanus*

Maria Gitin   P
287 La Vida Rd
Aptos, CA 95003, 408-722-8535
Internet: msgitin@got.net
 Pubs: *Night Shift* (Blue Wind Pr, 1978), *The Melting Pot*
 (Crossing Pr, 1977), *Little Movies* (Ithaca Hse, 1976), *In
 Celebration of the Muse: Anth* (Quarry West/UC Santa Cruz,
 1997), *Poetry Flash, Alternative Press, Telephone, Sun &
 Moon, Hanging Loose*

David Gitin 🎤 ✈   P
PO Box 505
Monterey, CA 93942-0505, 831-646-9181
Internet: dgitin@mbay.net
 Pubs: *Fire Dance, This Once* (Blue Wind, 1989, 1979),
 Vacuum Tapestries (BB Bks, 1981), *Intent, Paideuma,
 Poetry Flash*

Jan Glading   P
1536 9th St #D
Alameda, CA 94501, 510-521-7366
 Pubs: *Gridlock: Anth* (Applezaba Pr, 1990), *Peace or Perish:
 Anth* (Poets for Peace, 1983), *Napa Rev, Kaleidoscope,
 Disability*

David Glotzer   P
1648 Waller
San Francisco, CA 94117, 415-752-1278
 Pubs: *Occasions of Grace* (Heron Pr, 1979), *Mulch, River
 Styx, Lillabulero, Works, B'way Boogie*

Robert Gluck 🎤 ✈   P&W
4303 20th St
San Francisco, CA 94114-2816, 415-821-3004
Internet: rgluck@sfsu.edu
 Pubs: *Jack the Modernist, Margery Kempe* (Serpent's
 Tail/High Risk, 1995, 1994), *Reader* (Lapis Pr, 1989)

Dale Going 🎤 ✈   P
541 Ethel Ave
Mill Valley, CA 94941-3327, 415-381-1243
Internet: dalegoing@aol.com
 Pubs: *Leaves From a Gradual* (Potes & Poets, 2000), *The
 View They Arrange* (Kelsey Street Pr, 1994), *She Pushes
 With Her Hands, Or Less* (Em Pr, 1992, 1991)

Herbert Gold 🎤 ✈   W
1051-A Broadway
San Francisco, CA 94133
 Pubs: *She Took My Arm As If She Loved Me, Daughter
 Mine* (St. Martin's Pr, 2000, 1997), *Bohemia: Digging the
 Roots of Cool, Best Nightmare on Earth: A Life in Haiti*
 (S&S, 1993, 1991)

Reuven Goldfarb   P
2020 Essex St
Berkeley, CA 94703, 510-848-0965
 Pubs: *To Be a Jew . . .* (Inter-oco Pr, 1977), *New Menorah,
 Exquisite Corpse, Oxygen, Voice of the Trees, Agada,
 Robert Frost Rev*

Juan Gomez-Quinones   P
507 Grande Vista Ave
Los Angeles, CA 90063
 Pubs: *5th & Grande Vista* (Editorial Mensaje, 1974), *Revista
 Chicano-Riquena*

Rafael Jesus Gonzalez 🎤   P&W
PO Box 5638
Berkeley, CA 94705, 510-841-5903
Internet: rjgonzal@sirius.com
 Pubs: *El Hacedor De Juegos/The Maker of Games* (Casa
 Editorial, 1978), *West Coast Rev, Contact II*

Cesar A. Gonzalez-T. 🎤 ✈   P&W
San Diego Mesa College, 7250 Mesa College Dr, San Diego,
CA 92111, 619-627-2751
 Pubs: *Unwinding the Silence* (Lalo-Bilingual Pr, 1987),
 Paper Dance: Anth (Persea Bks, 1995), *Ventana Abierto,
 RiverSedge, Prairie Schooner, Bilingual Rev*

Mary Lee Gowland   P
PO Box 958
Coarsegold, CA 93614, 559-683-6876
 Pubs: *Remembering August* (Mountain Arts Council, 1994),
 *Fresno Bee, Onthebus, Z Miscellaneous, Rag Mag,
 Poetry/L.A. Sculpture Gardens Rev, Fat Tuesday*

Taylor Graham 🎤 ✈   P
PO Box 39
Somerset, CA 95684-0039, 530-621-1833
Internet: piper@innercite.com
 Pubs: *An Hour in the Cougar's Grace* (Pudding Hse Pubs,
 2000), *Next Exit* (Cedar Hill Pub, 1999), *Casualties* (Coal
 City, 1995), *Poetry Intl, Santa Clara Rev, Willow Springs,
 America, Iowa Rev, Passages North, Southern Humanities
 Rev, 1997 Anth of Mag Verse*

Judy Grahn   P&W
4221 Terrace St
Oakland, CA 94611-5127
 Pubs: *Mundane's World* (Crossing Pr, 1988), *The Queen of
 Swords, Another Mother Tongue* (Beacon Pr, 1987, 1984)

Cynthia D. Grant 🎤 ✈ W
Box 95
Cloverdale, CA 95425-0095, 707-894-3420
Pubs: *The Cannibals, Starring Tiffany Spratt* (Roaring Brook Pr, 2002), *The White Horse, Mary Wolf, Uncle Vampire, Shadow Man, Keep Laughing* (Atheneum, 1998, 1995, 1993, 1993, 1991)

Jack Grapes 🎤 ✈ P
6684 Colgate Ave
Los Angeles, CA 90048, 323-651-5488
Pubs: *Lucky Finds, Breaking Down the Surface of the World, Trees, Coffee, & the Eyes of Deer* (Bombshelter Pr, 2000, 1998, 1987), *Men of Our Time: Anth* (U Georgia Pr, 1992), *The Maverick Poets: Anth* (Gorilla Pr, 1988), *Poetry East, Japanese American Mag*

Wallace Graves W
English Dept, California State Univ, Northridge, CA 91330, 818-885-3431

Alice Wirth Gray 🎤 P&W
1001 Merced St
Berkeley, CA 94707-2521, 510-524-8958
Internet: alicewirthgray@aol.com
Pubs: *What the Poor Eat* (Cleveland State U Poetry Ctr, 1993), *Amer Scholar, Atlantic, Poetry*

Benjamin Green 🎤 ✈ P&W
3415 Patricks Point Dr #3
Trinidad, CA 95570-9769, 707-677-3084
Internet: benjamingreen@earthlink.net
Pubs: *The Sound of Fish Dreaming* (Bellowing Ark, 1996), *Green Grace* (Punla Pub, 1993), *Monologs from the Realm of Silence* (Ransom Note Pub, 1990)

Geoffrey Green 🎤 ✈ W
English Dept, San Francisco State Univ, 1600 Holloway Ave, San Francisco, CA 94132-1700, 415-338-7414
Internet: ggreen@sfsu.edu
Pubs: *Fiction*

Suzanne Greenberg W
257 1/2 Park Ave
Long Beach, CA 90803
Pubs: *New Virginia Rev, Indiana Rev, Turnstile, Mississippi Rev, The Washington Rev, Florida Rev*

Linda Gregg P
PO Box 475
Forest Knolls, CA 94933-0475, 415-488-9587
Pubs: *Chosen by the Lion, The Sacraments of Desire* (Graywolf, 1994, 1991), *Paris Rev, Atlantic, The Qtly, TriQtly, Columbia Rev, Partisan Rev, Ploughshares*

Arpine Konyalian Grenier 🎤 ✈ P
990 S Marengo Ave
Pasadena, CA 91106-4255, 626-441-3249
Pubs: *Whores From Samarkand* (Florida Lit Fdtn Pr, 1993), *St. Gregory's Daughter* (U La Verne Pr, 1991), *Columbia Poetry Rev, Iowa Rev, Tinfish, Sulfur, CQ, Kiosk*

Susan Griffin 🎤 ✈ P&W
904 Keeler Ave
Berkeley, CA 94708-1420, 510-528-9296
Pubs: *What Her Body Thought* (HarperSF, 1999), *Bending Home Poems Selected & New, Unremembered Country* (Copper Canyon, 1998, 1988), *Women & Nature, The Poetry Inside Her: Anth* (Sierra Club Bks, 2000), *APR, Mother Jones, City Lights Rev, Utne Reader*

Morton Grinker P
1367 Noe St
San Francisco, CA 94131
Pubs: *The Gran Phoenician Rover: Book 5, Books 1-4, To the Straying Aramaean* (Thorp Springs, 1994, 1992, 1972)

Hugh Gross W
880 N Hilldale Ave #16
West Hollywood, CA 90069, 310-652-5844
Pubs: *16 Bananas, Same Bed, Different Dreams* (Mid-List Pr, 1995, 1991)

Richard Grossinger W
258 Yale Ave
Kensington, CA 94708
Internet: chard@lanminds.com
Pubs: *Out of Babylon, New Moon* (Frog Ltd, 1997, 1996), *The Night Sky* (J.P. Tarcher, 1988), *Embryogenesis* (North Atlantic Bks, 1986)

Richard Grossman 🎤 ✈ P
2000 DeMille Dr
Los Angeles, CA 90027, 323-665-2116
http://www.richardgrossman.com
Pubs: *The Book of Lazarus* (FC2, 1997), *The Alphabet Man* (Fiction Collective, 1993), *The Animals* (Graywolf, 1990), *Tycoon Boy* (Kayak, 1977)

Mark Grover P&W
3525 Del Mar Heights Rd Box 273
San Diego, CA 92130
Pubs: *What Touched His Life* (Noble Crown, 1995), *Words & Poets* (Revorg, 1994)

Albert J. Guerard W
English Dept, Stanford Univ, Stanford, CA 94305, 415-327-6687
Pubs: *The Hotel in the Jungle* (Baskerville Pub, 1996), *Gabrielle* (Donald I. Fine, 1992), *Christine/Annette* (Dutton, 1985), *Fiction*

Judith Guest   W
Patricia Karlan Agency, 3575 Cahuenga Blvd Suite 210, Los
Angeles, CA 90068
    Pubs: *Errands* (Ballantine Bks, 1997), *The Mythic Family*
    (Milkweed Edtns, 1988), *Ordinary People* (Viking Penguin
    Pr, 1976)

Thom Gunn ♪ ✈   P
1216 Cole St
San Francisco, CA 94117
    Pubs: *Boss Cupid, Collected Poems, The Man with Night
    Sweats* (FSG, 2000, 1994, 1992), *Threepenny Rev, TLS*

Carol L. Gunther   P
PO Box 876
Sutter Creek, CA 95685, 209-267-0332
    Pubs: *The Return of Mr. Trespass* (Black Tape Pr, 1990),
    Cincinnati Poetry Rev, Boston Lit Rev

Katharine Haake ♪ ✈   W
California State Univ/Northridge, English Dept, Northridge, CA
91330-8248, 818-677-3427
Internet: kate.haake@csun.edu
    Pubs: *That Water, Those Rocks: A Novel, The Height &
    Depth of Everything* (U Nevada Pr, 2003, 2001), *No Reason
    on Earth* (Dragon Gate, 1986), *Iowa Rev, Mississippi Rev,
    Minnesota Rev, Michigan Qtly Rev, Qtly West, Witness,
    NER/BLQ*

Philip Hackett ♪ ✈   P
PO Box 330168
San Francisco, CA 94133-0168
    Pubs: *Two American Poets* (Little City Pr, 1997), *Iraq,
    Jordan, & Egypt Poems, Poems to My Son Dylan* (Pegasus,
    1994, 1992), *SF Call, The Monthly, Beatitude, SF Bay
    Guardian, Boston Mag, Electrum, Stone Country, Deep
    Valley, A Publications, Haight-Ashbury*

Ray Hadley ♪ ✈   P
PO 16696
South Lake Tahoe, CA 96151, 800-541-6967
Internet: Rhadley@oakweb.com
    Pubs: *Smoking Mt. Shasta* (Blackberry, 1975), *Dacotah
    Territory, Kyoi, Kuksu, MidAtlantic, Sierra Nevada Rev,
    Scree 6, South & West, Yellow Brick Road*

Jane Hall   P&W
1516 Euclid Ave
Berkeley, CA 94708, 510-849-2540
    Pubs: *Anth of New England Writers* (New England Writers,
    1997), *Fourteen Hills, Berkeley Poetry Rev, Ruah, Sonoma
    Literary Rev, Americas Rev*

Judith Hall ♪ ✈   P
28239 Via Acero
Malibu, CA 90265
    Pubs: *The Promised Folly* (TriQtly Bks/NWstrn U Pr, 2002),
    Anatomy, Errata (Ohio State, 1998), *To Put the Mouth To*
    (Morrow, 1992)

Irving Halperin   W
San Francisco State Univ, 1600 Holloway Ave, San Francisco,
CA 94132, 415-338-2578
    Pubs: *Here I Am: A Jew in Today's Germany* (Westminster
    Pr, 1971), *Prairie Schooner, Massachusetts Rev, NER*

James A. Hamby   P
Drawer 1124
Arcata, CA 95518-1124, 707-826-0725
    Pubs: *New Mexico Mag, Idaho Heritage, Pandora, Western
    Rev, South Dakota Rev*

Forrest Hamer ♪ ✈   P
3 Commodore Dr
Emeryville, CA 94608, 510-654-4731
Internet: FHamer8580@aol.com
    Pubs: *Middle Ear* (Roundhouse, 2000), *Call & Response*
    (Alice James Bks, 1995), *Word of Mouth: Anth* (Talisman
    Hse, 2000), *Best American Poetry: Anth* (Scribner, 2000,
    1994), *Geography of Home: Anth* (Heyday Bks, 1999)

Rose Hamilton-Gottlieb ♪ ✈   W
2997 Lakeview Way
Fullerton, CA 92835, 714-526-6395
Internet: rjhg@aol.com
    Pubs: *Generation to Generation, At Our Core: Women
    Writing About Power: Anth, Grow Old Along With Me: Anth*
    (Papier-Mache Pr, 1998, 1998, 1997), *Farm Wives & Other
    Iowa Stories: Anth* (Mid-Prairie Bks, 1995), *The Ear, Room
    of One's Own*

Sam Hamod ♪ ✈   P
PO Box 1722
San Marcos, CA 92079, 760-583-5444
Internet: shamod@cox.net
    Pubs: *The Arab Poems, The Muslim Poems* (Cedar Creek
    Pr, 2001, 2000, 2000), *Unsettling America:American Ethnic
    Poetry: Anth* (Viking/Penguin, 1994), *Konch,
    todaysalternativenews.com*

Stephanie Han   P&W
55 Navy St #204
Venice, CA 90291, 310-396-3991
Internet: buddhafun@aol.com
    Pubs: *L.A (Lovers Anonymous)* (LaLa Pr, 1995), *Sheila Na
    Gig*

Joseph Hansen   P&W
2638 Cullen St
Los Angeles, CA 90034, 213-870-2604
    Pubs: *Living Upstairs* (Dutton, 1993), *Bohannon's Country*
    (Viking, 1993), *Ellery Queen's Mystery, Alfred Hitchcock's
    Mystery, South Dakota Rev*

C. G. Hanzlicek 🎤 ✈ P
738 E Lansing Way
Fresno, CA 93704-4223, 209-226-1528
Internet: chazh@cvip.net
  Pubs: *The Cave* (U Pitt Pr, 2001), *Against Dreaming* (U
  Missouri Pr, 1994), *When There Are No Secrets, Calling the
  Dead* (Carnegie Mellon U Pr, 1986, 1982)

Maria Harris 🎤 ✈ W
29377 Quail Run Dr
Agoura Hills, CA 91301, 818-889-8238
  Pubs: *Die, Die My Darling, Bullseye* (Books in Motion, 1999,
  1997), *Baroni, The Joseph File* (Putnam, 1975, 1974)

Mark Jonathan Harris 🎤 ✈ W
School of Cinema-TV, Univ Southern California, Los Angeles,
CA 90089, 213-740-3317
Internet: mjonharris@aol.com
  Pubs: *Into the Arms of Strangers* (Bloomsbury, 2000), *Solay,
  Come the Morning* (Bradbury Pr, 1993, 1989)

William Harrison W
William Morris Agency, 151 El Camino Dr, Beverly Hills, CA
90212, 310-274-7451
  Pubs: *Three Hunters* (Random Hse, 1989), *Burton & Speke*
  (St. Martin's Pr, 1982)

John Hart 🎤 ✈ P
PO Box 4262
San Rafael, CA 94913-4166, 415-507-9230
Internet: jh@johnhart.com
  Pubs: *The Climbers* (U Pitt Pr, 1978), *Ascent, Aethlon, Blue
  Unicorn, Interim, SPR*

William Hart 🎤 P&W
2721 Piedmont #3
Montrose, CA 91020
  Pubs: *Journeyman's Dues* (Musclehead Pr, 2002), *Never
  Fade Away* (Daniel & Daniel Pubs, 2002), *Wildcat Road*
  (Timberline Pr, 2000), *Hard Bucks* (Swan Duckling Pr, 2000)

Suzanne Hartman 🎤 ✈ W
17290 Redwood Springs Dr
Fort Bragg, CA 95437
Internet: sbyerley@mcn.org
  Pubs: *Kansas Qtly, Mississippi Valley Rev, Ladies Home
  Jrnl, Confrontation, Woman's Day, Gamut*

Gerald Haslam 🎤 ✈ W
PO Box 969
Penngrove, CA 94951-0969, 707-792-2944
Internet: ghaslam@sonic.net
  Pubs: *Manuel & the Madman, The Great Tejon Club Jubilee*
  (Devil Mountain Bks, 2000, 1996), *Straight White Male,
  Condor Dreams & Other Fictions* (U Nevada Pr, 2000,
  1994), *L.A. Times Mag, Nation, Sierra, This World, Sky*

Robert Hass 🎤 ✈ P
Box 807
Inverness, CA 94937
  Pubs: *Sun Under Wood* (Ecco, 1996), *Human Wishes,
  Twentieth Century Pleasures* (Ecco Pr, 1988, 1984)

Barbara Hauk 🎤 P
10181 Beverly Dr
Huntington Beach, CA 92646-5426, 714-968-7530
  Pubs: *Confetti* (Event Horizon Pr, 1993), *Pearl, Chiron Rev,
  Onthebus, Cape Rock, Genre, BPJ*

Marjorie Hawksworth P
2516 Selrose Ln
Santa Barbara, CA 93109
  Pubs: *Silent Voices* (Ally Pr, 1978), *Connecticut Poetry Rev,
  Centennial Rev, Pulpsmith, Spectrum, NYQ*

Gwen Head 🎤 ✈ P
72 Eucalyptus Rd
Berkeley, CA 94705-2802, 510-654-6525
Internet: Oaxaca508@earthlink.net
  Pubs: *Fire Shadows* (Louisiana State U Pr, 2001),
  Frequencies: A Gamut of Poems (U Utah Pr, 1992), *The Ten
  Thousandth Night* (U Pitt Pr, 1979), *Southern Rev, APR,
  Yale Rev*

Eloise Klein Healy 🎤 ✈ P
Antioch Univ Los Angeles, 13274 Fiji Way, Marina Del Rey, CA
90292, 310-578-1080
Internet: ekhpoet@hotmail.com
  Pubs: *Passing* (Red Hen Pr, 2002), *Another City: Writings
  from Los Angeles: Anth* (City Lights Bks, 2001), *The World
  in Us: Anth* (St Martin's Pr, 2000), *Geography of Home: Anth*
  (Heyday Bks, 1999), *Artemis in Echo Park* (Firebrand,
  1991), *Solo, Zyzzyva*

Kevin Hearle 🎤 ✈ P
137 14th Ave
San Mateo, CA 94402, 650-571-6390
Internet: kevinhearle@rcn.com
  Pubs: *Each Thing We Know Is Changed Because We Know
  It & Other Poems* (Ahsahta Pr, 1994), *Organization &
  Enviroment, Georgia Rev, Yale Rev, Qtly West, Windsor Rev,
  Poetry Flash*

Susan Hecht 🎤 ✈ P&W
19801 Meadow Ridge Dr #52
Trabuco Canyon, CA 92679, 949-858-2057
Internet: sahecht@cox.net
  Pubs: *Beware of Islands* (Inevitable Pr, 1998), *Devil's
  Millhopper, Calyx, Onionhead, Sou'wester, Hawaii Pacific
  Rev*

Mary Hedin P&W
182 Oak Ave
San Anselmo, CA 94960, 415-454-4422
  Pubs: *Direction* (West Country, 1982), *Fly Away Home*
  (U Iowa, 1980)

Anne Hedley   P
5870 Birch Ct
Oakland, CA 94618, 510-655-1430

Lyn Hejinian 🎤 ✈   P
2639 Russell St
Berkeley, CA 94705-2131, 510-548-1817
    Pubs: *The Language of Inquiry* (U California Pr, 2000),
Happily (Post-Apollo Pr, 2000), *Sight* (Edge Bks, 1999), *The
Cold of Poetry, My Life* (Sun & Moon Pr, 1994, 1987), *Oxota*
(The Figures, 1991)

Padma Hejmadi 🎤 ✈   W
2135 Humboldt Ave
Davis, CA 95616-3084, 530-753-8538
Internet: padma@den.davis.ca.us
    Pubs: *Birthday Deathday* (Penguin Bks India, 1992), *Dr.
Salaam & Other Stories* (Capra Pr, 1978), *Mirrorwork: Anth*
(Owl Pr, 1997), *New Yorker, Parabola, American Book Rev,
Southern Rev*

Carol Henrie 🎤 ✈   P
24929 Minnie Ct
Hayward, CA 94541-6910, 510-886-1018
Internet: reachus@pacbell.net
    Pubs: *Virginia Qtly Rev, Salt Hill Jrnl, New Zoo Poetry Rev,
Field, Nation, Poetry NW, New Republic, Prairie Schooner*

Barbara Hernandez   P
1432 Celis St
San Fernando, CA 91340

Juan Felipe Herrera 🎤 ✈   P
5340 N Campus Dr
Fresno, CA 93740-0097
Internet: juanlherrera@csufresno.edu
    Pubs: *Thunderweavers, Border-Crosser With Lamborghini
Dream, Night Train to Tuxtla* (U Arizona Pr, 2000, 1999,
1994), *Erashbloomlove* (U New Mexico Pr, 1999), *Love After
the Riots* (Curbstone Pr, 1997)

Elizabeth Carothers Herron 🎤   P&W
PO Box 41
Bodega, CA 94922
    Pubs: *Language for the Wild* (Hillside Pr, 2001), *The Stones
the Dark Earth* (Harlequin Ink, 1995), *While the Distance
Widens* (Floating Island, 1994), *Desire Being Full of
Distances* (Calliopea, 1983)

John Herschel   P
Univ California, Q-022, La Jolla, CA 92093, 619-534-3068
    Pubs: *The Floating World* (New Rivers Pr, 1979), *Minnesota
Rev, Invisible City, Seattle Rev, APR*

Jerry Hicks 🎤 ✈   P
2614 W 181 St
Torrance, CA 90504, 310-532-1200
Internet: beach.poet@worldnet.att.net
    Pubs: *California Poetry Calendar, Traffic Report Mag, Rattle
Mag, Spillway Mag, One (Dog) Press Mag, ZamBomba,
California Qtly*

Marvin R. Hiemstra 🎤 ✈   PP
166 Bonview St
San Francisco, CA 94110-5147, 415-826-4485
Internet: drollmarv@aol.com
    Pubs: *Two-Way Zipper Dream, A Turquoise Coyote Under
Your Pillow* (Zippy Digital Prdns, 2002, 1997), *I Mouse
Therefore I Am!* (Rhyme & Reason, 2000), *In Deepest USA*
(Prairie Lights Bks, 1996)

Donna Hilbert 🎤 ✈   P&W
5615 E Seaside Walk
Long Beach, CA 90803-4454, 562-434-4172
Internet: donnahilbert1@charter.net
    Pubs: *Traveler in Paradise: New and Selected Poems* (Pearl
Edtns, 2004), *Transforming Matter* (Pearl Edtns, 2000),
Deep Red (Event Horizon Pr, 1993)

Nellie Hill 🎤 ✈   P&W
16 The Crescent
Berkeley, CA 94708, 510-540-0886
    Pubs: *Having Come This Far* (Keeler, 1978), *Coast &
Ocean, Teacup, Sideshow, Aikido Today, Harvard Mag,
Studia Mystica, Margin, Amer Writing*

Brenda Hillman   P
St. Mary's College, Moraga, CA 94575, 925-631-4472
    Pubs: *Cascadia, Loose Sugar, Bright Existence, Death
Tractates, Fortress* (Wesleyan, 2001, 1997, 1993, 1992,
1989), *APR*

Mimi Walter Hinman   P
1085 Normington Way
San Jose, CA 95136, 408-723-0522
Internet: DeskAnt@aol.com
    Pubs: *Autumn Sun* (Zapizdat Pubs, 1995), *Wind Five-
Folded* (AHA Bks, 1994), *Marilyn, My Marilyn: Anth*
(Pennywhistle Pr, 1998), *Poetpourri, Japanophile, Poet,
Pearl, Cicada, Thema*

Jack Hirschman   P
1314 Kearny St
San Francisco, CA 94133, 415-398-1953
    Pubs: *The David Arcane, The Donmeh* (Amerus Pr, 1982,
1980)

Jane Hirshfield 🎤 ✈   P
Michael Katz, 367 Molino Ave, Mill Valley, CA 94941-2767,
415-381-2319
Internet: jh@well.com
  Pubs: *Given Sugar, Given Salt, The Lives of the Heart, The
  October Palace* (HC, 2001, 1997, 1994), *Of Gravity &
  Angels* (Wesleyan, 1988), *Atlantic, New Yorker*

Sandra Hoben   P
129 Sunnyside
Mill Valley, CA 94941, 415-388-7641
  Pubs: *Snow Flowers* (Westigan Rev Pr, 1979), *Partisan Rev,
  Ironwood, Qtly West, Mickle Street Rev*

Marilyn Hochheiser 🎤 ✈   P
5406 E Los Angeles Ave, #93
Simi Valley, CA 93063-4167, 805-527-5534
  Pubs: *Autumn Harvest* (Quill Bks, 2001), *Anthology Issue, A
  View Through the Thicket* (Outpost Pubs, 1990, 1977), *Last
  Words, California Confederation of the Arts, Art/Life,
  Crosscurrents, Poetry USA*

Cecelia Holland   W
520 Palmer Blvd
Fortuna, CA 95540

Scott C. Holstad   P
PO Box 10608
Glendale, CA 91209-3608
Internet: sch@well.com
  Pubs: *Places* (Sterling Hse, 1995), *Distant Visions, Again &
  Again* (Poet Tree, 1994), *Poetry Ireland Rev, Textual Studies
  in Canada, Arkansas Rev, Minnesota Rev, Wisconsin Rev,
  Southern Rev*

Paul Hoover   P&W
369 Molino Ave
Mill Valley, CA 94941-2767, 415-389-1877
Internet: viridian@hotmail.com
  Pubs: *Winter* (Mirror) (Flood Edtns, 2002), *Rehearsal in
  Black* (Salt Pubs, 2001), *Totem & Shadow* (Talisman Hse,
  1999), *Viridian* (U Georgia Pr, 1997), *Postmodern American
  Poetry: Anth* (Norton, 1994), *APR, Conjunctions, New
  Republic, Boston Rev, TriQtly*

Toke Hoppenbrouwers 🎤 ✈   W
Psychology Dept, California State Univ, 1811 Nordhoff St,
Northridge, CA 91330-8255, 818-667-2827
Internet: hcpsy009@csun.edu
  Pubs: *Autumn Sea* (Astarte Shell Pr, 1996)

Bill Hotchkiss   P&W
Sierra College, 5000 Rocklin Rd, Rocklin, CA 95677,
916-624-3333
Internet: 75213.20@compuserve.com
  Pubs: *Yosemite, Sierra Santa Cruz, To Fell the Giants*
  (Bantam, 1995, 1992, 1991)

Lindy Hough   P
258 Yale Ave
Kensington, CA 94708-1048
  Pubs: *Outlands & Inlands* (Truck Pr, 1984), *Nuclear Strategy
  & the Code of the Warrior: Anth* (North Atlantic Bks, 1984)

Sevrin Housen   P
3408 L St
Sacramento, CA 95816-5334, 916-451-7659
  Pubs: *Feathers & Bones* (Halcyon Pr, 1981), *Bellingham
  Rev, Quercus, Suttertown News*

James D. Houston 🎤 ✈   W
2-1130 E Cliff Dr
Santa Cruz, CA 95062-4836
  Pubs: *Snow Mountain Passage* (Knopf, 2001), *The Last
  Paradise* (U Oklahoma Pr, 1998), *In the Ring of Fire*
  (Mercury Hse, 1997), *Continental Drift* (U California Pr,
  1996), *Wild Duck Rev, Zyzzyva, Utne Reader, Manoa,
  Ploughshares*

Noni Howard   P
20 Driftwood Trl
Half Moon Bay, CA 94019-2349, 650-726-5939
  Pubs: *Tiger Balm, The Politics of Love* (New World Pr, 1997,
  1996), *Share My Fantasies* (Beatitude, 1996), *Bloodjet
  Literary Mag, Haight-Ashbury Literary Jrnl*

George F. Howell   P&W
3342 Hamilton Way
Los Angeles, CA 90026
  Pubs: *The Sartre Situation* (Howell, 1984), *Working Book*
  (Periplus Pr, 1978), *Angle of Repose*

Mary Hower   P
1831 Castro St
San Francisco, CA 94131
Internet: maryhower@aol.com
  Pubs: *The World Between Women: Anth* (Her Bks, 1987),
  *Virginia Qtly Rev, Threepenny Rev, Pacific Intl, California
  Qtly, Iowa Rev, Hubbub, Bellingham Rev*

Andrew Hoyem 🎤 ✈   P
The Presidio, 1802 Hays St, San Francisco, CA 94129,
415-561-2542
Internet: andrew.hoyem@arionpress.com
  Pubs: *What If: Poems 1969-87, Picture/Poems* (Arion Pr,
  1987, 1975)

Elias N. Hruska 🎤 ✈   P
PO Box 2157
Los Gatos, CA 95031-2157, 408-866-2229
  Pubs: *Perceptions Volume III: Anth* (The Wright Experience,
  1992), *Many Voices/Many Lands: Anth* (Poetry Ctr, 1989),
  Cafe Solo Anth (Solo Pr, 1974), *Poetry Mag*

Richard G. Hubler   W
PO Box 793
Ojai, CA 93023, 805-646-3200
    Pubs: *Inside Ojai, Wheeler* (Creek Hse, 1976, 1970), *Soldier & Sage* (Crown Pub, 1966)

Nan Hunt 🎤 ✈   P&W
23301 Clarendon St
Woodland Hills, CA 91367-4162, 818-887-0031
Internet: huntnanwritr@earthlink.net
    Pubs: *The Wrong Bride* (Plain View, 1999), *If I Had My Life to Live Over: Anth* (Papier-Mache Pr, 1992), *To Be a Woman: Anth* (J.P. Tarcher/St. Martin's Pr, 1991), *Slant, Daybreak, Rivertalk, Sheila Na Gig, BPJ, Borderlands, Crosscurrents*

Maureen Hurley   P
7491 Mirabel Rd, #5
Forestville, CA 95436, 707-887-2046
    Pubs: *Atomic Ghost: Poets Respond to the Nuclear Age: Anth* (Coffee Hse Pr, 1995), *Poems on the Korean War Conflict: Anth* (Ctr for Korean Studies, 1995), *House on Via Gambito: Women Writers Abroad: Anth* (New Rivers Pr, 1991)

Paula Huston 🎤 ✈   W
The Thomas Grady Agency, 209 Bassett Street, Petaluma, CA 94952-2668, 707-765-6229
    Pubs: *Daughters of Song* (Random Hse, 1995), *Image, Story, American Short Fiction, NAR, Missouri Rev, Mss., Massachusetts Rev*

Kathleen Iddings 🎤 ✈   P
PO Box 8638
La Jolla, CA 92038
Internet: kathleeniddings@aol.com
    Pubs: *Sticks, Friction & Fire* (West Anglia Pub, 2001), *Here's to Humanity: Anth* (People's Pr, 2000), *Streams: Anth* (Pudding Hse Pr, 2000), *The Muse Strikes Back: Anth* (Story Line Pr, 1997), *Poet's Market, L.A. Times, Writer's Digest, English Jrnl*

Momoko Iko   W
c/o J. McCloden, PO Box 172, Hollywood, CA 90028

Ruth G. Iodice   P
22 Avon Rd
Kensington, CA 94707, 510-526-8439
    Pubs: *And What Rough Beast: Poems at the End of the Century* (Ashland Poetry Pr 1999), *Out of Season: Anth* (Amagansett Pr, 1993), *South Coast Poetry Jrnl, Blue Unicorn, Poet Lore, Long Pond Rev, Negative Capability*

Susan K. Ito 🎤 ✈   P&W
6034 Valley View Rd
Oakland, CA 94611-2026, 510-339-0622
Internet: skito@sprintmail.com
    Pubs: *A Ghost at Heart's Edge: Anth* (North Atlantic Pr, 1999), *Making More Waves: Anth* (Beacon Pr, 1997), *Growing Up Asian American: Anth* (Morrow, 1993), *Two Worlds Walking: Anth* (New Rivers, 1992), *Side Show: Anth* (Somersault Pr, 1992), *Hip Mama*

Spoon Jackson   P
B-92377, #2184, CMC-East Box 8101, San Luis Obispo, CA 93409-8101
    Pubs: *African American Wisdom* (New World Library, 1994), *Rivers* (Sacramento Poetry Rev, 1992), *No Distance Between Two Points* (Month of Mondays Pr, 1987), *Brother's Keeper: Anth* (M. Datcher, 1992), *Exquisite Corpse, Community Endeavor*

Maggie Jaffe   P
3730 Arnold Ave
San Diego, CA 92104
Internet: mjaffe@mail.sdsu.edu
    Pubs: *The Prisons* (Cedar Hill Pub, 2001), *7th Circle* (Cedar Hill Pub, 1998), *How the West Was One, Continuous Performance* (Burning Cities Pr, 1996, 1992), *Getting By: Anth* (Bottom Dog Pr, 1996), *Cedar Hill Rev, Rattle, Pemmican Pr, Viet Nam Generation, Green Fuse, Intl Qtly*

Frances Jaffer   P
801 27th St
San Francisco, CA 94131
    Pubs: *Alternate Endings* (How/Ever, 1985), *She Talks to Herself in the Language of an Educated Woman* (Kelsey Street Pr, 1980)

T. R. Jahns   P
1220 E 13th St
Upland, CA 91786-3415
    Pubs: *Poetry NW*
    Denver Qtly, SWRev, Ohio Rev

Marnell Jameson   W
3957 Pacheco Dr
Sherman Oaks, CA 91403, 818-784-2204
    Pubs: *The Book of Blessings, The Song of Songs* (Harper, 1995, 1990), *California Palms* (Sunstone Pr, 1990), *L.A. Times, Valley Mag, Cimarron Rev, APR, Tikkun*

Jean Janzen 🎤 ✈   P
5508 East Ln
Fresno, CA 93727, 559-251-9006
Internet: jjanzen@qnis.net
    Pubs: *Tasting the Dust* (Good Bks, 2000), *How Much Earth: Anth* (Roundhouse Pr, 2001), *The Geography of Home: Anth, Highway 99: Anth* (Heyday Bks, 1999, 1996), *What Will Suffice: Anth* (Gibbs-Smith, 1995), *Piecework: Anth* (Silver Snakes Pr, 1987), *Poetry*

Estelle Jelinek P&W
1301 Bonita Ave #3
Berkeley, CA 94709-1983
Internet: ejel@uclink.berkeley.edu
  Pubs: *Berkeley Poets Collective, Berkeley Works, Dream Machinery, Razorslit*

Joyce Jenkins ♦ ✈ P
1450 4th St #4
Berkeley, CA 94710-1328, 510-525-5476
Internet: editor@poetryflash.org
  Pubs: *Portal* (Pennywhistle Pr, 1993), *Prayers at 3 AM: Anth* (HC, 1995), *Berkeley Poetry Rev, Zyzzyva*

Francisco Jimenez ♦ ✈ W
Santa Clara Univ, Modern Languages & Literatures, Santa Clara, CA 95053-0001, 408-554-5175
Internet: fjimenez@scu.edu
  Pubs: *Senderos Fronterizos, Breaking Through, Cajas de Carton, The Christmas Gift, La Mariposa* (HM, 2002, 2001, 2000, 2000, 1998), *The Circuit: Stories from the Life of a Migrant Child* (U New Mexico Pr, 1997), *Mosaico de la Vida* (HBJ, 1984), *Riversedge*

Donas John P&W
1629 Cimarron St
Los Angeles, CA 90019-6317, 323-732-3359
Internet: donaswest2@aol.com
  Pubs: *Peace Is Our Profession* (East River Pr, 1981), *Now Times, Rainbow City Pr, Gypsy, Connecticut Fireside, Poet Lore, Archer*

Robin Johnson P
Wide Awake Ranch, Rd 208
Madera, CA 93638, 209-822-2528
  Pubs: *Denver Qtly, Massachusetts Rev, Poetry NW, Antioch Rev, SW Rev, Outerbridge*

Diane Johnson W
24 Edith
San Francisco, CA 94133
  Pubs: *Le Divorce* (Dutton, 1997), *Natural Opium, Health & Happiness, Persian Nights* (Knopf, 1993, 1990, 1987)

Sheila Goldburgh Johnson ♦ ✈ P&W
1498 Tunnel Rd
Santa Barbara, CA 93105-2139, 805-682-4618
Internet: chtodel@gss.ucsb.edu
  Pubs: *After I Said No, Santa Barbara Stories: Anth, Shared Sightings: Anth* (John Daniel & Co, 2000, 1998, 1996), *Walking the Twilight II: Anth* (Northland Pub, 1996), *Atlanta Rev, Puerto del Sol, Negative Capability, Crosscurrents*

Alice Jones ♦ ✈ P
6239 College Ave, #304
Oakland, CA 94618-1384, 510-420-8803
Internet: ajones@idiom.com
  Pubs: *Extreme Directions* (Omnidown, 2002), *Isthmus, The Knot* (Alice James Bks, 2000, 1992), *Best American Poetry: Anth* (Scribner, 1994), *Volt, Colorado Rev, Poetry, Denver Qtly, Ploughshares*

Diem Jones ♦ ✈ P
4200 Park Blvd #138
Oakland, CA 94602, 510-482-4799
Internet: sufiwarrior@california.com
  Pubs: *Black Fish Jazz* (Sufi Warrior Pubs, 2002), *Sufi Warrior* (Juke Box Pr, 1998), *Walrus 2000: Anth* (Mills College Lit Rev, 2000), *Drumvoices Rev: Anth* (Southern Illinois U), *Zyzzyva*

Jorg P
125 Beach, #44
Santa Cruz, CA 95060
  Pubs: *Revolution Fruit Pie, Honking Geese* (Stone Pr, 1978, 1978), *Sitting Frog*

Andrew Joron ♦ ✈ P
2009 Cedar St
Berkeley, CA 94709, 510-843-7853
Internet: ajoron@earthlink.net
  Pubs: *The Removes* (Hard Pr, 1998), *Primary Trouble* (Talisman Hse, 1996), *Science Fiction* (Pantograph Pr, 1992), *Force Fields* (Starmont Hse, 1987), *Sulfur, New American Writing*

Natasha Josefowitz ♦ ✈ P
2235 Calle Guaymas
La Jolla, CA 92037-6915, 858-456-2366
  Pubs: *If I Eat I Feel Guilty, If I Don't I'm Deprived, Too Wise to Want to Be Young Again* (Blue Mountain Pr, 1999, 1995)

David Joseph P&W
298 9th Ave
San Francisco, CA 94118, 415-387-3412
  Pubs: *Homeless But Not Helpless: Anth* (Harvest, 1988), *Central Park, Rolling Stone*

Mifanwy Kaiser ♦ ✈ P
20592 Minerva Ln
Huntington Beach, CA 92646, 714-968-0905
Internet: mifanwy@earthlink.net
  Pubs: *News from Inside, Raising the Roof: Anth* (Bombshelter Pr, 1996, 1999), *Onthebus, Spillway*

Gerald Kaminski ♦ P&W
200 Davey Glen #413
Redding, CA 94002, 530-221-8979
Internet: geraldak@digital-star.com
  Pubs: *People Wanting Children, Circumstantial Evidence* (Cove View Pr, 1998, 1993), *Iconoclast, Main Street Rag, University Rev*

Howard Kaplan   W
2242 Guthrie Dr
Los Angeles, CA 90034-1030
 Pubs: *Passage to Baalbek* (Atheneum, 1979), *The
 Damascus Cover* (Dutton, 1977)

Pamala Karol   P
Loyola Marymount Univ, School of Film & Television, MS8230,
Los Angeles, CA 90045-2659, 310-338-3033
Internet: pamalakarol@mciworld.com
 Pubs: *Adventures on the Isle of Adolescence* (City Lights
 Bks, 1989), *Scars: Anth* (U Alabama Pr, 1996), *AMC,
 Threepenny Rev, City Lights Rev, Jacaranda Rev*

Pearl L. Karrer ♀   P
570 Kingsley Ave
Palo Alto, CA 94301-3224
 Pubs: *Knowing Stones: Poems of Exotic Places: Anth* (John
 Gordon Burke Pubs, 2000), *Weathering* (Slapering Hol Pr,
 1993), *Clackamas Lit Rev, Slant, Whetstone, Visions Intl,
 CQ, Berkeley Poetry Rev*

Hiroshi Kashiwagi   P&W
4314 Pacheco St
San Francisco, CA 94116-1056
 Pubs: *Only What We Could Carry: Anth* (Heyday Bks, 2000),
 The Big Aiiieeeee: Anth (Meridian-Penguin Bks, 1991), *On a
 Bed of Rice: Anth* (Anchor Bks, 1995)

Michael J. Katz   W
1631 Barry Ave #6
Los Angeles, CA 90025, 213-826-9475
 Pubs: *The Big Freeze, Last Dance in Redondo Beach*
 (Putnam, 1990, 1989)

Sam Keen   W
16321 Norrbom Rd
Sonoma, CA 95476
 Pubs: *Faces of the Enemy* (H&R, 1987)

George Keithley ♀ ✈   P&W
1302 Sunset Ave
Chico, CA 95926-2650, 530-345-0865
 Pubs: *Flesh and Dust* (Will Hall Bks, 2002), *The Midnight
 Train* (Small Poetry Pr, 2001), *Living Again* (Bear Star Pr,
 1997), *Earth's Eye* (Story Line Pr, 1994), *The Donner Party*
 (Braziller, 1989), *Harper's, Sewanee Rev, Agni, Kenyon Rev,
 TriQtly*

Robert Kelsey   W
650 N McPherson St
Fort Bragg, CA 95437, 707-964-7649
 Pubs: *Virginia Qtly Rev, Massachusetts Rev, The Sun, New
 Press, Snake Nation Rev*

Robert Kendall ♀ ✈   P
1800 White Oak Dr
Menlo Park, CA 94025-6129
www.wordcircuits.com/kendall
 Pubs: *A Life Set for Two* (Eastgate Systems, 1996), *A
 Wandering City* (Cleveland State U Poetry Ctr, 1992),
 WPWF Poetry: Anth (Bunny & Crocodile Pr, 1992), *Iowa
 Rev Web, Cortland Rev, Contact II, River Styx, NYQ,
 Indiana Rev*

Susan Kennedy ♀ ✈   P
PO Box 108
Duncans Mills, CA 95430, 707-865-9536
 Pubs: *Dancing With the Dog* (Philos Pr, 2002), *Cazadero
 Poems* (Floating Island Pr, 1994), *A New Geography of
 Poets: Anth* (U Arkansas Pr, 1992), *First Leaves,
 Explorations 2000, The Temple, White Heron Poetry Rev,
 The Tomcat, Haight-Ashbury Lit Jrnl, Zyzzyva*

Rolly Kent ♀ ✈   P
5501 Tuxedo Terrace
Los Angeles, CA 90068, 323-462-3332
Internet: rolly@inkcafe.com
 Pubs: *Queen of Dreams* (S&S, 1991), *Spirit, Hurry*
 (Confluence Pr, 1985), *The Wreck in the Post Office Canyon*
 (Maguey Pr, 1977)

Joseph Kent   P
1372 Pine St
San Francisco, CA 94109
 Pubs: *Streams, White Wind* (Sunlight Pub, 1996, 1989), *The
 Irreversible Man: Anth* (Ars Poetica Pr, 1991), *In the
 Company of Poets, CQ*

Roger Lee Kenvin ♀ ✈   W
575 Fairview Ave
Arcadia, CA 91007, 626-445-4420
Internet: jlybl@earthlink.net
 Pubs: *Trylons & Perispheres, The Cantabrigian Rowing
 Society's Saturday Night Bash, Harpo's Garden* (July Blue
 Pr, 1999, 1998, 1997), *South Carolina Rev, Garm Lu,
 Spindrift, Roanoke Rev, Oasis, The Distillery, ELF, Crescent
 Rev, Other Voices, New Letters*

Karen Kenyon ♀ ✈   P
PO Box 12604
La Jolla, CA 92039-2604, 858-587-9027
 Pubs: *Sunshower* (Putnam/Marek, 1981), *Redbook, Ladies
 Home Jrnl, CSM, British Heritage, Westways, Writer's
 Digest*

T. S. Kerrigan 🎤 ✈ P
14651 Morrison St
Sherman Oaks, CA 91403-1650, 818-905-8084
Internet: tkerrigan@hq.dir.ca.gov
Pubs: *Good Poetry* (Viking-Penguin, 2002), *Acumen,
Amer Reporter, Illuminations, Outposts, Poetry Greece,
Poetry, Poetry Monthly, Good Poetry, Another Bloomsday
at Molly Malone's Pub & Other Poems, Southern Rev, Intl
Poetry Rev*

Jascha Kessler 🎤 ✈ P&W
218 16th St
Santa Monica, CA 90402-2216
Internet: jkessler@ucla.edu
Pubs: *An Egyptian Bondage, Collected Poems, Rapid
Transit: 1948* (Xlibris, 2000, 2000, 2000), *Siren Songs: 50
Stories* (McPherson & Co., 1992), *Catullan Games: Poems*
(Marlboro Pr, 1989)

Christian Kiefer PP&P&W
P.O.Box 2553
Rocklin, CA 95677
www.christiankiefer.com
Pubs: *Feeding Into Winter* (March St Pr, 2000), *Antioch Rev,
Wild Duck Rev, Santa Monica Rev, Psychotrain, Think,
Recursive Angel, Tule Rev, Sublette's Barn, Poet's Corner,
Junkyard Dog*

Stanley Kiesel P&W
490 30th St
San Francisco, CA 94131-2307
Pubs: *The War Between the Pitiful Teachers & the Splendid
Kids, Skinny Malinky Leads the War for Kidness* (Avon,
1994, 1985)

Kathy Kieth 🎤 P
4708 Tree Shadow Pl
Fair Oaks, CA 95628, 916-966-8620
Internet: kathykieth@hotmail.com
Pubs: *The Acorn,The Iconoclast, Nostalgia, riverrun,
Midwest Poetry Rev, Poets Forum Mag, Limestone Circle,
Nanny Fanny, Northern Stars, PDQ, Northeastern States
Poetry Contest: Best Poems 1986*

Daphne Rose Kingma P
c/o Molly Stuart
1810 Markham Way
Sacramento, CA 95818, 916-498-1455
Internet: www.daphnekingma.com
Pubs: *The Book of Love* (Conari Pr, 2001), *Kansas Qtly,
Spectrum, Circus Maximus,*

Maxine Hong Kingston 🎤 ✈ W
Univ California, English Dept, Berkeley, CA 94720,
510-643-5127
Pubs: *The Fifth Book of Peace* (Knopf, 2003), *To Be the
Poet* (Harvard U Pr, 2002), *Hawaii One Summer* (Meadow
Pr, 1987; U of Hawaii Pr, 1998)

Diane Kirsten-Martin 🎤 ✈ P
68 Ashton Ave
San Francisco, CA 94112-2206, 415-337-7408
Internet: dianemartin@earthlink.net
Pubs: *NER, Third Coast, Five A.M., Crazyhorse, Santa
Clara Rev, Zyzzyva, Hayden's Ferry, Blue Mesa,
Bellingham Rev*

Ed Kissam P
Box 2041
Sebastopol, CA 95473, 707-829-5696
Pubs: *Poems of the Aztec Peoples* (Bilingual Rev Pr, 1983),
Jerusalem & the People (Anvil, 1975)

Pat Kite W
5318 Stirling Ct
Newark, CA 94560-1352
Pubs: *Highlights, Prime Monthly, Botanical Garden*

Carolyn Kizer 🎤 ✈ P
19772 8th St E
Sonoma, CA 95476-3849
Pubs: *Cool, Calm & Collected, Harping on Poems: 1985-
1995, The Nearness of You, Mermaids in the Basement*
(Copper Canyon Pr, 2000, 1996, 1986, 1984), *Pro Femina*
(BkMk Pr, 2000), *YIN* (BOA, 1984), *100 Great Poems By
Women: Anth* (Ecco Pr, 1995), *Paris Rev*

Edward Kleinschmidt Mayes 🎤 ✈ P
1700 Monterey Blvd
San Francisco, CA 94127-1928
Internet: girasole@pacbell.net
Pubs: *Works & Days* (U Pitt Pr, 1999), *Bodysong* (Heyeck
Pr, 1999), *Speed of Life* (Apogee Pr, 1999), *New Yorker,
APR, Poetry, NER, Massachusetts Rev, Volt*

August Kleinzahler P
325A Frederick St
San Francisco, CA 94117
Pubs: *Live From the Hong Kong Nile Club, Red Sauce,
Whiskey & Snow* (FSG, 2000, 1995), *New York Times,
London Rev of Bks, New Yorker, Harper's*

Mary Julia Klimenko 🎤 ✈ P
1392 West K St
Benicia, CA 94510-2445, 707-746-1645
Internet: mjklimenko@aol.com
Pubs: *Territory* (Brighton Pr, 1993), *Gargoyle, West Wind
Rev, Wisconsin Rev, Willow Rev, Sulphur River Rev, New
Letters, Berkeley Poetry Rev*

Arthur Winfield Knight 🎤 ✈ P&W
PO Box 544
Citrus Heights, CA 95611, 916-721-1827
Internet: robertcharlesmartel@msn.com
 Pubs: *Blue Skies Falling, Johnnie D.* (Forge Bks, 2001,
 2000), *Outlaw Voices* (CC Marimbo Comm, 2000), *The
 Darkness Starts Up Where You Stand* (Depth Charge,
 1996), *The Secret Life of Jesse James* (Burnhillwolf, 1996),
 NYQ, Poet Lore, Windsor Rev

Kit Knight 🎤 ✈ P
PO Box 2580
Citrus Heights, CA 95611, 916-721-1827
Internet: robertcharlesmartel@msn.com
 Pubs: *Women of Wanted Men* (Potpourri Pr, 1994), *Redneck
 Rev, Caprice, Pittsburgh Qtly, Waterways, Green's Mag*

Jeff Knorr P
2942 Highland Ave
Sacramento, CA 95818, 916-454-4323
www.scc.losrios.cc.ca.us/~knorrj
 Pubs: *Western Reach* (Red Hen Pr, 2002), *Standing Up to
 the Day* (Pecan Grove Pr, 1999), *Clockpunchers: Anth*
 (Partisan Pr, 2002), *American Diaspora: Anth* (U Iowa,
 2001), *Connecticut Rev, Clackamas Lit Rev, Chelsea,
 Oxford Mag, Fugue, Red Rock Rev, MacGuffin*

Chris Kobayashi P
298 Coleridge St
San Francisco, CA 94110, 415-821-3012
 Pubs: *Networks* (Vortex Edtns, 1979), *Azumi* (Japanese
 American Anth Committee, 1979)

Michael Koepf 🎤 ✈ W
PO Box 1055
Elk, CA 95432, 707-877-3518
Internet: bigfish1@saber.net
 Pubs: *The Fisherman's Son* (Broadway Bks, 1998), *Icarus*
 (w/M. Crawford; Atheneum, 1987), *Save the Whale*
 (McGraw-Hill, 1978)

Phyllis Koestenbaum 🎤 ✈ P
982-E La Mesa Terr
Sunnyvale, CA 94086-2402, 408-732-2756
 Pubs: *Doris Day and Kitschy Melodies* (La Questa, 2001),
 Criminal Sonnets (Writer's Ctr Edtns and Jacaranda, 1998),
 A Formal Feeling Comes: Anth (Story Line Pr, 1994), *Best
 American Poetry: Anth* (Macmillan, 1993, 1992), *Michigan
 Qtly Rev, Epoch*

Ken Kolb W
59280 Hwy 70
Cromberg, CA 96103, 530-836-2332
 Pubs: *Night Crossing, Aspects of Love: Anth* (Playboy, 1974,
 1972), *Couch Trip* (Random Hse, 1970), *Getting Straight*
 (Chilton, 1967), *Redbook, Esquire, Playboy*

Susan Kolodny 🎤 ✈ P
6239 College Ave Ste 304
Oakland, CA 94618, 510-339-2877
Internet: slk1012@aol.com
 Pubs: *Outsiders: Anth, Verse & Universe: Anth* (Milkweed
 Edtns, 1999, 1998), *Anthology of Magazine Verse: Anth*
 (Yrbk of American Poetry, 1997), *88, NER, Bellingham Rev,
 River Styx*

Lynda Koolish 🎤 ✈ P
1020 Grizzly Peak Blvd
Berkeley, CA 94708-1526, 510-524-4994
Internet: lkoolish@mail.sdsu.edu
 Pubs: *Journeys on the Living* (Ariel, 1973), *Mosaic,
 Networks, Yellow Silk, Berkeley Poets Co-op*

Stephen Kopel 🎤 ✈ P
187 Beaver St
San Francisco, CA 94114-1516, 415-626-1395
 Pubs: *Crux* (Calliope Pr, 2001), *Baby Blessings: Anth*
 (Harmony Bks, 2002), *Family Celebrations: Anth* (Andrews
 McMeel, 1999), *Antigonish Rev, Hampden-Sydney Poetry
 Rev, CQ, 580 Split, WordWrights!, Cape Rock, Ginger Hill,
 Sensations Mag, Onthebus, Oxford Mag*

Steve Koppman W
1960 Magellan Dr
Oakland, CA 94611, 510-339-6339
 Pubs: *The Literature of Work: Anth* (U Phoenix Pr, 1991),
 *Zyzzyva, Berkeley Monthly, Jewish Currents, Agada, Sifrut,
 Wind*

Dennis Koran P
6156 Wilkinson Ave
North Hollywood, CA 91606
 Pubs: *After All* (Norton Coker Pr, 1992), *Vacancies* (Mother
 Hen, 1975), *Poetry Now, Beatitudes, Abraxas, Panjandrum*

Steve Kowit P
PO Box 184
Potrero, CA 91963-0184, 619-478-2129
 Pubs: *Pranks* (Bloody Twin Pr, 1990), *Lurid Confessions*
 (Carpenter Pr, 1983), *The Maverick Poets: Anth* (Gorilla Pr,
 1988)

Michael H. Krekorian 🎤 ✈ W
San Diego State Univ, English Dept/Comparative Literature,
San Diego, CA 92182-8140, 619-594-6515
Internet: mkrekorian@juno.com
 Pubs: *Channel Zero* (Plover Pr, 1996), *Corridor* (Ashod Pr,
 1989), *New Novel Rev, Fiction Intl, AM Lit, Bateria, Central
 Park, Mississippi Mud*

Susan Allyx Kronenberg ♀ ✈ PP&P&W
502 Colorado Blvd, Ste 405
Santa Monica, CA 90401
Internet: jardine3@juno.com
  Pubs: *Confessions of a Travel Junkie* (Yardbird Pr, 2002), *Incantations of the Grinning Dream Woman* (Sagittarius Pr, 1990), *Always I Was Getting Ready to Go* (Black Heron Pr, 1989), *California Qtly, MPR, Dark Horse, Telephone, Slipstream*

Judy Kronenfeld ♀ ✈ P
3314 Celeste Dr
Riverside, CA 92507-4051, 909-682-5096
Internet: jkronen@citrus.ucr.edu
  Pubs: *Disappeared Down Dark Wells & Still Falling* (Inevitable Pr, 2000), *Shadow of Wings* (Bellflower Pr, 1991), *Proposing on the Brooklyn Bridge: Anth, Essential Love: Anth* (Grayson Bks, 2003, 2000), *Potpourri, MacGuffin, Poetry Intl, Free Lunch, Hubbub*

Lewis Kruglick P
118 Calera Canyon Rd
Salinas, CA 93908
  Pubs: *Spring Bandits* (Leviathan Pr, 1981), *The Unknown Angel* (Tree Bks, 1971)

James Krusoe P
504 Pier Ave
Santa Monica, CA 90405
  Pubs: *Hotel de Dream, ABCDEFGHIJKLMNOPQRSTUVWXYZ* (Illuminati, 1991, 1984), *Jungle Girl* (Little Caesar, 1982), *APR, Field, Denver Qtly*

Geraldine Kudaka P
4470-107 Sunset Blvd, Ste 331
Los Angeles, CA 90027
Internet: 103070.266@compuserve.com
  Pubs: *Persona* (Street Agency Pub, 1988), *Numerous Avalanches at the Point of Intersection* (Greenfield Rev Pr, 1979), *Y'Bird*

Joanne Kyger ♀ ✈ P
PO Box 688
Bolinas, CA 94924-0688, 415-868-0272
  Pubs: *As Ever: Selected Poems* (Penguin Putnam, 2002), *Again* (La Alameda Pr, 2001), *Some Life* (Post Apollo Pr, 2000), *Patzcuaro* (Blue Millennium Pr, 1999), *Just Space* (Black Sparrow Pr, 1991), *Phenomenological* (Further Studies, 1989)

John L'Heureux ♀ ✈ P&W
Stanford Univ, Dept of English, Stanford, CA 94305-2087, 650-725-1209
Internet: jex@leland.stanford.edu
  Pubs: *The Miracle, Having Everything* (Atlantic, 2002, 1999), *The Handmaid of Desire* (Soho Pr, 1996), *The Shrine at Altamira* (Penguin, 1995), *An Honorable Profession* (Viking, 1991), *Atlantic, New Yorker*

Joan La Bombard ♀ P
814 Teakwood Rd
Los Angeles, CA 90049-1330, 310-476-5437
  Pubs: *The Winter Watch of the Leaves, The Counting of Grains* (San Diego Poets Pr, 1993, 1990), *Glencoe Literature: Anth* (Glencoe/McGraw-Hill, 2000), *Wherever Home Begins: Anth* (Orchard Bks, 1995), *Cimarron Rev, Tar River Poetry, Colorado Rev, Nation*

Joyce La Mers ♀ ✈ P
2514 Greencastle Ct
Oxnard, CA 93035-2901, 805-985-6336
Internet: joylam@aol.com
  Pubs: *Grandma Rationalizes an Enthusiasm for Skydiving* (Mille Grazie Pr, 1996), *A Christmas Collection: Anth* (July Lit Pr, 2001), *The Muse Strikes Back: Anth* (Story Line Pr, 1997), *Light Qtly, Formalist, Solo, Sticks, Lyric, Potpourri*

Salvatore La Puma W
PO Box 20147
Santa Barbara, CA 93210-0147, 805-569-1633
  Pubs: *A Time for Wedding Cake* (Norton, 1991), *The Boys of Bensonhurst* (U Georgia, 1987)

A. LaFaye ♀ ✈ W
3416 Genevieve Street
San Bernardino, CA 92405, 909-475-9533
Internet: alafayebooks@aol.com
  Pubs: *Strength of Saints, Dad, in Spirit, Strawberry Hill, Nissa's Place, The Year of the Sawdust Man* (S&S, 2002, 2001, 1999, 1999, 1998), *Edith Shay* (Viking, 1998)

Jennifer Lagier ♀ ✈ P&W
165 Dolphin Cir
Marina, CA 93933-2220, 408-883-9587
Internet: pcmc@igc.org
  Pubs: *Second-Class Citizen* (Bordighera, 2000), *Where We Grew Up* (Small Poetry Pr, 1999), *Coyote Dream Cantos* (Iota Pr, 1992), *New to North America: Anth* (Burning Bush Pub, 1998), *At Our Core: Anth* (Papier-Mache Pr, 1998)

Philip Lamantia P
c/o City Lights Bookstore, 261 Columbus Ave, San Francisco, CA 94113, 415-362-1901
  Pubs: *Bed of Sphinxes, Meadowlark West, Becoming Visible* (City Lights Bks, 1997, 1986, 1981), *Sulfur, City Lights Rev, Arsenal, Exquisite Corpse, Caliban*

Jeanne Lance ♀ ✈ P
218 Appleton Dr
Aptos, CA 95003-5002, 831-685-9518
  Pubs: *Autumn Harvest, Student Guide, Red Wheelbarrow, 6ix, Switched-On Gutenberg, Santa Cruz County Sentinel*

Maxine Landis   P
553 N Pacific Coast Hwy #B130
Redondo Beach, CA 90277
Internet: hireapoet@aol.com
    Pubs: *News From Inside: Anth* (Hand Maid Bks 1994), *San
    Fernando Poetry Jrnl, Voices, Volno, Struggle, Onthebus,
    Earth Bound, Blood Pudding, Quill, Spillway*

Mervin Lane ♪   P
258 E Mountain Dr
Santa Barbara, CA 93108, 805-969-2990
    Pubs: *Going to Town* (Sadhe Pr, 1987), *Black Mountain
    College: Sprouted Seeds: Anth* (U Tennessee, 1990)

A. J. Langguth   W
Univ Southern California, ASC102, Los Angeles, CA
90089-0281, 213-740-3919
Internet: langguth@usc.edu

Daniel J. Langton ♪ ✈   P
1673 Oak St
San Francisco, CA 94117-2013
    Pubs: *Greatest Hits* (Pudding Hse, 2002), *Life Forms, The
    Inheritance* (Cheltenham, 1995, 1989)

Marina deBellagente LaPalma   PP&P
329 Pope St
Menlo Park, CA 94025, 650-326-4981
Internet: lapalma@well.com
    Pubs: *Half-Life* (The Present Pr, 1990), *Persistence: Anth*
    (Diderot Pr, 1994), *Rooms, Antigones, Afterimage,
    Resolutions*

John Laue ♪   P
8 Morehouse Dr
La Selva Beach, CA 95076-1629, 408-684-0854
    Pubs: *Paradises Lost* (North Star Pr, 1997), *Snapshots of
    Planet Earth: Anth* (Oxford U Pr, 1998), *Grow Old Along
    With Me: Anth* (Papier-Mache Pr, 1996), *English Jrnl, Chiron
    Rev, Santa Barbara Rev, New Press Qtly, Modern Poetry,
    Chaminade Rev*

J. T. Ledbetter   P
California Lutheran Univ, Thousand Oaks, CA 91360,
805-492-2411
Internet: ledbette@clunet.edu
    Pubs: *Sewanee Rev, Sou'wester, Laurel Rev, Nimrod,
    Atlanta Rev, Puerto del Sol, The Formalist, Kansas Qtly,
    Poetry, Others*

Stellasue Lee ♪ ✈   P
4169 Greenbush Ave
Sherman Oaks, CA 91423-4305, 818-986-3274
Internet: stellasue1@aol.com
    Pubs: *Crossing the Double Yellow Line, Over to You, After I
    Fall: Anth* (Bombshelter Pr, 2000, 1991, 1991), *Sheila-Na-
    Gig, Cedar Hill Rev, Raising the Roof, Onthebus, Herman
    Rev, On Target, Voices, Bloodpudding, Inky Blue, Rattle,
    Spillway*

Diane Lefer ♪ ✈   W
Los Angeles, CA
Internet: desilef@cs.com
    Pubs: *Radiant Hunger* (Authors Choice, 2001), *Very Much
    Like Desire* (Carnegie Mellon U Pr, 2000), *The Circles I
    Move in* (Zoland Bks, 1994), *LA Under the Influence: Anth*
    (Doublewide Pr, 2002), *Another City: Anth* (City Lights,
    2001), *Santa Monica Rev*

John Leggett   P&W
1781 Partrick Rd
Napa, CA 94558
    Pubs: *A Daring Young Man* (Knopf, 2002), *Making Believe,
    Gulliver House* (HM, 1986, 1979), *Ross & Tom* (S&S, 1974)

Carolyn Lei-lanilau ♪ ✈   P
6167 Harwood Ave
Oakland, CA 94618-1339
    Pubs: *Ono Ono Girl's Hula* (U Wisconsin, 1997), *Best
    American Poetry: Anth* (Scribner, 1996), *APR, Chicago Rev,
    Blue Mesa, Manoa, Raven Chronicles, Amer Voice,
    Occident, NAW*

Emily Wortis Leider   P
PO Box 210105
San Francisco, CA 94121
    Pubs: *WPFW 89.3 FM Anth, Rapid Eye Movement: Anth*
    (Bunny & Crocodile Pr, 1992, 1976), *Curious Rooms,
    Chicago Rev, Poets On, Mockingbird, Berkeley Poetry Rev*

Lucia Lemieux   P
Le Muse Productions, PO Box 2081, Thousand Oaks, CA
91359
www.lemuse.com
    Pubs: *Dancing Across County Lines, Moving Pictures: 9 LA
    Poets* (Best Pr, 2001, 1997), *Cadabra, Art Scene, Rattle,
    Imaginari, Spillway, Onthebus, Falling Star, ArtLite Lmtd
    Edtn Monthly*

Cornel Adam Lengyel ♪ ✈   P&W
El Dorado National Forest, 7700 Wentworth Springs Rd,
Georgetown, CA 95634-9534, 916-333-4224
    Pubs: *Late News From Adam's Acres* (Dragon's Teeth,
    1985), *Blood to Remember: Anth* (Texas Tech U Pr, 1991),
    *Old Crow, Confrontation, CQ, Dusty Dog, Mandrake,
    Poetry Rev*

Russell C. Leong ♪ ✈   P&W
3924 Tracy St
Los Angeles, CA 90027-3208, 310-825-2974
Internet: rleong@ucla.edu
    Pubs: *Phoenix Eyes & Other Stories* (U Washington Pr,
    2000), *Country of Dreams & Dust* (West End Pr, 1993),
    Strange Attraction: Anth (U Nevada, 1995), *The Open Boat:
    Anth* (Doubleday, 1993), *Charlie Chan Is Dead: Anth*
    (Penguin, 1993), *Tricycle Buddhist Rev*

George H. Leong P
1819 25th Ave
San Francisco, CA 94122, 415-441-2458
Pubs: *A Lone Bamboo Doesn't Come From Jackson Street* (Isthmus, 1977), *Califia, Time to Greez*

Arthur Lerner P
13511 Contour Dr
Sherman Oaks, CA 91423-4701, 213-936-4992
Pubs: *Words for All Seasons* (Being Bks, 1983), *Spring, Lit Rev, Poet & Critic, Poet, Orbis*

Eugene Lesser P
Box 656
Woodacre, CA 94973, 415-488-4760

Ken Letko 🎤 ✈ P
College of the Redwoods, 883 W Washington Blvd, Crescent City, CA 95531-8361, 707-465-2360
Internet: ken-letko@delnorte.redwoods.cc.ca.us
Pubs: *All This Tangling* (Mardi Gras Pr, 1995), *Shelter for Those Who Need It* (O2 Pr, 1985), *Greenfield Rev, Cottonwood, Permafrost, World Order*

Bob Levin 🎤 ✈ W
2039 Shattuck, #201
Berkeley, CA 94704, 510-848-3868
Pubs: *The Pirates and the Mouse* (Fantagraphics, 2003), *Fully Armed* (Baskerville, 1995), *The Best Ride to New York* (H&R, 1978), *Karamu, Comics Jrnl, Massachusetts Rev, Berkeley Insider, Cavalier, Carolina Qtly*

Philip Levine 🎤 ✈ P
4549 N Van Ness Blvd
Fresno, CA 93704, 209-226-3361
Pubs: *So Ask* (U of Michigan Pr, 2002), *The Mercy, The Simple Truth* (Knopf, 1994), *New Yorker, Atlantic, Poetry, Five Points, Paris Rev, Nation, Hudson Rev*

Aurora Levins-Morales W
1678 Shattuck Ave, Box 133
Berkeley, CA 94709, 510-524-0617
Pubs: *Getting Home Alive* (Co-author; Firebrand, 1986), *In Other Words: Anth* (Arte Publico, 1994), *Ms., American Voice, Bridges, Callaloo*

Frieda L. Levinsky 🎤 ✈ P&W
1697 Calle Leticia
La Jolla, CA 92037
Pubs: *Writers of the Desert Sage, La Jolla Village News, Heritage, San Diego Jewish Pr, Chiron Rev, Pegasus Rev, Poetic Liberty, Tucumcari Rev, San Fernando Poetry Jrnl, Dog River, Parnassus, Atticus, Hob-Nob, Omnific, Poetpourri*

James Heller Levinson P&W
21727 Tuba St
Chatsworth, CA 91311-2931, 818-882-9331
Pubs: *Bad Boy Poems* (Bombshelter Pr, 1993), *Pulled Apart* (Third Lung Pr, 1989), *Sulfur, Hawaii Rev, Dog River Rev, Spoon River Poetry Rev, Center, Bakunin, Nexus, Hunger, Small Pond*

Genny Lim P
New College of California, 766 Valencia St, San Francisco, CA 94110
Internet: meehdj516@aol.com
Pubs: *The Politics of Experience* (Temple U, 1993), *Winter Place* (Kearney Street Wkshp, 1991), *Wings for Lai Ho* (East/West, 1982), *Oxford Book of Women's Writing: Anth* (Oxford U Pr, 1995)

Jim Lindsey P
PO Box 1470
Ukiah, CA 95482
Pubs: *The Difficult Days* (Princeton U Pr, 1984), *In Lieu of Mecca* (U Pitt Pr, 1976)

Shelley List W
2919 Grand Canal
Venice, CA 90291

Leo Litwak W
246 Chattanooga St
San Francisco, CA 94114

D. H. Lloyd W
Applezaba Press, PO Box 4134, Long Beach, CA 90804
Pubs: *Bible Bob Responds to a Jesus Honker* (Applezaba Pr, 1986), *Wormwood Rev, AKA Mag, Pearl*

Mona Locke 🎤 ✈ P
PO Box 1800
Paradise, CA 95969-2926, 530-872-4934
Internet: mmlocke@netzero.net
Pubs: *Labyrinth: Anth* (PWJ Pub, 2001), *The Gathering 6: Anth* (Small Poetry Pr, 2001), *Coffeehouse Poetry: Anth* (Bottom Dog Pr, 1996), *Mid-America Poetry Rev, South Dakota Rev, Onthebus, Negative Capability, CQ, Poets On*

Gerald Locklin 🎤 ✈ P&W
English Dept, California State Univ, Long Beach, CA 90840, 310-985-5285
Internet: glocklin@csulb.edu
Pubs: *The Life Force Poems, Candy Bars, Go West, Young Toad, Charles Bukowski: A Sure Bet* (Water Row Pr, 2002, 2000, 1998, 1995), *The Firebird Poems* (Event Horizon Pr, 1992), *Chiron Rev*

Rachel Loden 🎤 ✈   P
3072 Stelling Dr
Palo Alto, CA 94303-3968, 650-493-4799
Internet: rloden@concentric.net
  Pubs: *Hotel Imperium* (U Georgia Pr, 1999), *The Last
  Campaign* (Slapering Hol Pr, 1998), *Like Thunder: Anth*
  (U Iowa Pr, 2002), *Pushcart Prize XXVI: Anth* (Pushcart Pr,
  2001), *NAR, Jacket, Amer Letters & Commentary, Paris
  Rev, NAW*

Ron Loewinsohn   P
University of California, Department of English, Berkeley, CA
94702
Internet: ronloewi@socrates.berkeley.edu
  Pubs: *Goat Dances* (Black Sparrow Pr, 1975), *Meat Air*
  (HBJ, 1970)

Jonathan London   P
PO Box 537
Graton, CA 95444, 707-823-4003
  Pubs: *The Candystore Man* (Morrow, 1998), *Hip Cat*
  (Chronicle Bks, 1993), *The Owl Who Became the Moon*
  (Dutton, 1993), *All My Roads* (Beehive Pr, 1981), Gargoyle

Cathleen Long 🎤 ✈   P
English Dept, Santa Monica College, 1900 Pico Blvd, Santa
Monica, CA 90405, 310-434-4242
  Pubs: *Truth & Lies That Press for Life: Anth* (Artifact Pr,
  1991), *The New Los Angeles Poets: Anth* (Bombshelter Pr,
  1989), *Sculpture Gardens Rev*

Perie J. Longo 🎤 ✈   P
987 Barcelona Dr
Santa Barbara, CA 93105-4501, 805-687-9535
  Pubs: *The Privacy of Wind, Milking the Earth* (John Daniel &
  Co, 1997, 1986), *Prairie Schooner, Lucid Stone, CQ,
  Pudding, Rattle, Embers*

David Wong Louie   W
806 Crestmore Pl
Venice, CA 90291
Internet: louie@humnet.ucla.edu
  Pubs: *The Barbarians Are Coming* (Berkeley, 2001, Putnam,
  2000), *Pangs of Love* (Knopf, 1991), *Best American Short
  Stories: Anth* (HM, 1989), *Chicago Rev, Ploughshares,
  Fiction Intl*

Iven Lourie   P
PO Box 2119
Nevada City, CA 95959, 530-272-0180
Internet: ilourie@oro.net
  Pubs: *Miro's Dream* (Gateways Bks, 1988), *Alternatives,
  Poetry, Hanging Loose, Midstream*

B. D. Love 🎤 ✈   P&W
3740 Valleybrink Rd
Los Angeles, CA 90039-1427, 323-669-1332
Internet: bdlove@earthlink.net
  Pubs: *Water at the Women's Edge* (Urthona Pr, 2001), *Meat
  Wisdom* (Pudding Hse Pr, 2000), *Cut Salt Fire Grace*
  (Rhythm Dog Edtns, 1995), *Sweet Nothings: Anth* (Indiana
  U Pr, 1994), *Nimrod, New Orleans Rev, Tennessee Qtly,
  Many Mountains Moving, Lit Rev*

Bia Lowe   P&W
2252 Bronson Hill Dr
Los Angeles, CA 90068
Internet: bialowe@aol.com
  Pubs: *Wild Ride* (HC, 1995), *Helter Skelter: Anth* (Los
  Angeles Museum of Contemporary Art, 1993), *Kenyon Rev,
  Witness, Harper's, Salmagundi*

Naomi Ruth Lowinsky 🎤   P
241 Courtney Ln
Orinda, CA 94563-3630
Internet: nlowsky@hotmail.com
  Pubs: *red clay is talking* (Scarlet Tanager Bks, 2000), *Rattle,
  Patterson Lit Rev, Many Mountains Moving*

Suzanne Lummis 🎤 ✈   P
PO Box 27924
Los Angeles, CA 90027, 323-255-5223
Internet: lapoetryfestival@earthlink.net
  Pubs: *In Danger* (Roundhouse Pr 1999), *Stand Up Poetry:
  Anth* (California State U Pr, 1994), *Ploughshares, Solo,
  SPR, Poetry Daily, Poetry Intl*

Kirk Lumpkin 🎤 ✈   P
5505 Macdonald Ave
El Cerrito, CA 94530-1639, 415-474-6159
  Pubs: *The Word-Music Continuum* (Detour Prdctns, 1998),
  Earth First! Campfire Poems (Feral Pr, 1998), *Co-Hearing*
  (Zyga Multimedia Research, 1983), *Peace Or Perish: Anth*
  (Poets for Peace, 1983), *Verve, Talking Leaves, Tenderloin
  Times, Terrain*

Rick Lupert 🎤 ✈   P
5336 Kester Ave #103
Sherman Oaks, CA 91411, 818-995-4457
Internet: rick@poetrysuperhighway.com
  Pubs: *Stolen Mummies, Feeding Holy Cats, Up Liberty's
  Skirt* (Cassowary Pr, 2002, 2001), *Brendan Constantine Is
  My Kind of Town* (Inevitable Pr, 2001), *Chiron Rev, Beyond
  the Valley of the Contemporary Poets, 51%, Blue Satellite,
  Caffeine*

Toby Lurie 🎤 ✈   P
2022 High St, #B
Alameda, CA 94501-1726, 510-523-8629
  Pubs: *Highway Erotica, Word-Scales, Hiroshima, Duets*
  (Mellen Poetry Pr, 2002, 2000, 1997, 1996)

Glenna Luschei P
5146 Foothill Rd
Carpinteria, CA 93013, 805-543-1058
Internet: berrypress@aol.com
 Pubs: *Shot With Eros* (John Daniel & Co, 2002), *The
 Geography of Home* (Heydey Bks, 2002), *Matriarch* (The
 Smith, 1992), *Bare Roots Seasons* (Oblong, 1990), *Farewell
 to Winter* (Daedalus, 1988), *Pembroke Mag, Artlife, Prairie
 Schooner, Blue Mesa Rev*

Celia S. Lustgarten 🎤 ✈ P&W
317 3rd Ave
San Francisco, CA 94118-2402, 415-386-3592
Internet: cswilldfi@pacbell.net
 Pubs: *Shock Treatment* (Peak Output Unlimited, 1988),
 Apocalypse 3: Anth (Apocalypse Literary Arts Coalition,
 1997), *For Poets Only, Perceptions, Chanticleer, New
 Canadian Rev, Z Misc, Grasslands Rev*

William Luvaas W
25593 1st St
Hemet, CA 92544, 619-739-1817
 Pubs: *Going Under* (Putnam, 1994), *The Seductions of
 Natalie Bach* (Little, Brown, 1986), *Glimmer Train, Village
 Voice, ALR, Confrontation*

Kathleen Lynch 🎤 ✈ P&W
4807 Miners Cove Circle
Loomis, CA 95650-7112, 916-652-7315
Internet: kalynch@aol.com
 Pubs: *How to Build an Owl, Times Ten: Anth* (Small Poetry
 Pr, 1995, 1997), *The Next River Over* (New Rivers Pr, 1993),
 *Poetry, Nimrod, Qtly West, Poetry East, Spoon River Poetry
 Rev, Sycamore Rev, Midwest Qtly, Poetry NW*

Annette Peters Lynch 🎤 P
833 Garfield Ave
South Pasadena, CA 91030-2819, 626-799-7836
 Pubs: *Christmas Blues: Anth* (Amador Pub, 1995),
 *Wisconson Rev, Spectrum, CQ, Blue Unicorn, Pointed
 Circle, Poem, Maryland Poetry Rev*

Susan Macdonald P
Printers Inc. Bookstore, 310 California Ave, Palo Alto, CA
94025, 415-323-7342
 Pubs: *A Smart Dithyramb* (Heyeck Pr, 1979), *Dangerous As
 Daughters* (Five Trees Pr, 1976)

Mary Mackey W
California State University, Sacramento, 6000 J Street,
Department of English, Sacramento, CA 95819, 916-457-3831
Internet: mm@well.com
 Pubs: *The Fires of Spring* (Penguin, 1998), *The Horses at
 the Gate, The Year the Horses Came* (HarperSF, 1996,
 1993), *The Dear Dance of Eros* (Fjord Pr, 1987), *A Grand
 Passion* (S&S, 1986), *The Feminist Pr, Book Passage Pr,
 Switched-on Gutenberg*

Amy MacLennan 🎤 ✈ P
2379 Lyall Way
Belmont, CA 94002
Internet: amaclennan@earthlink.net
 Pubs: *Wisconsin Rev, Slant, Confluence, Rattle, Lynx Eye,
 South Dakota Rev*

Samuel Maio P
Univ San Jose, One Washington Square, San Jose, CA
95192, 408-924-4483
 Pubs: *Antioch Rev, Bloomsbury Rev, Chariton Rev,
 Formalist, Southern California Anth*

Clarence Major 🎤 ✈ P&W
Univ California, English Dept, One Shields Ave, Davis, CA
95616-7532, 916-752-5677
Internet: clmajor@uc.davis.edu
 Pubs: *Come by Here* (Wiley, 2002), *Waiting for Sweet Betty,
 Configurations* (Copper Canyon Pr, 2002, 1998), *Dirty Bird
 Blues, Such Was the Season* (Mercury Hse, 1996, 1989),
 Painted Turtle: Woman with Guitar (Sun & Moon, 1988)

Devorah Major 🎤 ✈ P
PO Box 423634
San Francisco, CA 94142-4209, 415-621-1664
Internet: devmajor@pachell.net
 Pubs: *with more than tongue* (Creative Arts Book Co, Inc.,
 2002), *Brown Glass Windows, Street Smarts* (Curbstone,
 2002, 1996), *An Open Weave* (Seal Pr, 1995), *Obsidian III,
 New Progressive, Zyzzyva Black Scholar, Shooting Star,
 Caprice, Callaloo*

River Malcolm W
625 Serpentine Dr
Del Mar, CA 92014, 619-755-7845
 Pubs: *Womanspirit, Sinister Wisdom, Thursday's Child*

Lee Mallory 🎤 ✈ P
Santa Ana College, 17th at Bristol, Santa Ana, CA 92706,
714-564-6526
 Pubs: *Incidental Buildings and Accidental Beauty: Anth*
 (Tebot Bach Pr, 2001), *Two Sides Now* (w/M. Mallory;
 FarStarFire Pr, 1999), *Holiday Sheer* (Inevitable Pr, 1997),
 Full Moon, Empty Hands (Lightning Pubs, 1994), *Invisible
 City, Hyperion, The Smith, Forum*

Eileen Malone 🎤 P&W
1544 Sweetwood Dr
Colma, CA 94015-2029, 650-756-5279
Internet: wrigrps@aol.com
 Pubs: *Mudfish, Salt Hill, Madison Rev, Americas Rev, SPR,
 New Millennium, Half Tones to Jubilee, Louisville Rev, Briar
 Cliff Rev, Abiko Qtly, Icarus, Ariel, Lucid Stone, Fugue, Sun
 Dog, West Wind Rev, Disquieting Muses, Poetry Mag*

Oscar Mandel 🎤 ✈   P&W
California Inst Technology, Humanities & Social Sciences,
Pasadena, CA 91125, 626-395-4078
Internet: om@hss.caltech.edu
 Pubs: *Sigismund* (U Pr America, 1988), *Antioch Rev*,
 Kenyon Rev, Prairie Schooner

Angela Consolo Mankiewicz 🎤 ✈   P
752 N Mansfield Ave
Los Angeles, CA 90038-3406
Internet: acmank@earthlink.net
 Pubs: *Wired* (Aquarius West Pr, 2001), *Cancer Poems*
 (UBP-Los Angeles, 1995), *Montserrat, The Temple,
 Lummox Jrnl, Lynx Eye, Artword, Orange Willow, Yefief,
 Chiron Rev, Comstock Rev, Slipstream, Hawaii Rev, Amelia,
 Phase & Cycle, Karamu, The Lyric*

Victoria Lena Manyarrows   P
PO Box 411403
San Francisco, CA 94141-1403
Internet: earrows@itsa.ucsf.edu
 Pubs: *Songs From the Native Lands* (Nopal Pr, 1995), *Visit
 Teepee Town: Anth* (Coffee Hse Pr, 1999), *The Arc of Love:
 Anth* (Scribner, 1996), *Phati'tude, Indigenous Woman,
 Callaloo*

Morton Marcus 🎤 ✈   P
1325 Laurel St
Santa Cruz, CA 95060, 831-429-9085
Internet: dmekis@pacbell.net
 Pubs: *Shouting Down the Silence* (Creative Arts Bks, 2002),
 Moments Without Names (White Pine Pr, 2002), *When
 People Could Fly* (Hanging Loose Pr, 1997), *Geography of
 Home: Anth* (Heyday Bks, 1999), *TriQtly, Ploughshares, The
 Prose Poem, Denver Qtly*

Adrianne Marcus 🎤 ✈   P&W
79 Twin Oaks
San Rafael, CA 94901-1915, 415-454-6062
Internet: medea999@aol.com
 Pubs: *Carrion House World of Gifts* (St. Martin's Pr, 1993),
 *Potomac Rev, Poetry Ireland, Crescent Rev, Confrontation,
 Solo, Cosmopolitan*

William J. Margolis   P
1507 Cabrillo Ave
Venice, CA 90291-3709
 Pubs: *A Book of Touch & Other Poems* (Mendicant Edtns,
 1988), *Beat Voices: Anth* (H Holt, 1995), *Black Ace 5, Grist
 On-Line, Venice West Rev, Galley Sail*

Stefanie Marlis 🎤 ✈   P
36 Madrone Ave
San Anselmo, CA 94960, 415-459-2920
Internet: marlis@well.com
 Pubs: *Fine* (Apogee Pr, 2000), *Rife* (Sarabande Bks, 1998),
 Sheet of Glass (Floating Island Pr, 1994), *Slow Joy* (U
 Wisconsin Pr, 1989), *APR, Manoa, Plum Rev, Poetry,
 Poetry East, Zyzzyva, Arshile, Five Fingers Rev, Gettysburg
 Rev, Ploughshares, Volt*

Jack Marshall   P
845 Everett St
El Cerrito, CA 94530-2922
 Pubs: *New & Selected Poems:1960-2000, Millennium Fever,
 Sesame, Arabian Nights* (Coffee Hse Pr, 2002, 1997, 1993,
 1987), *APR, Zyzzyva, Exquisite Corpse*

Jim Martin   P
303 Estrella Dr
Scotts Valley, CA 95066
Internet: bjxmsc@tevm2.nsc.com
 Pubs: *Shadows of My World* (Rush-Franklin Pub, 1993)

Joan M. Martin   P
670 Walton Dr
Red Bluff, CA 96080
Internet: diakeuast@aol.com
 Pubs: *Z Miscellaneous, The Courier, Times-Argus,
 Prophetic Voices, Yellow Butterfly, Deros*

Eliud Martinez 🎤 ✈   W
137 Nisbet Way
Riverside, CA 92507-4627, 909-682-5396
Internet: eliud.martinez@ucr.edu
 Pubs: *Voice-Haunted Journey* (Bilingual Rev Pr, 1990),
 Grow Old Along with Me: Anth (Papier-Mache Pr, 1996)

Jack Matcha   W
7716 Teesdale Ave
North Hollywood, CA 91605
 Pubs: *No Trumpets, No Drums* (Powell, 1970), *Prowler in
 the Night* (Fawcett, 1959), *Gamma*

David Matlin   P&W
4635 56th St
San Diego, CA 92115, 619-583-7572
Internet: dmatlin@mail.sdsu.edu
 Pubs: *How the Night Is Divided* (McPherson & Co., 1993),
 Dressed in Protective Fashion (Other Wind, 1990), *Avant-
 Pop: Fiction Anth* (Black Ice Bks, 1993), *Apex of the M*

Clive Matson 🎤 ✈   P
472 44th St
Oakland, CA 94609-2136, 510-654-6495
Internet: clive@matson.ford.com
 Pubs: *Squish Boots* (Broken Shadow, 2000), *Hourglass*
 (Seagull Pr, 1988), *Equal in Desire* (Manroot, 1983),
 Exquisite Corpse, Nimrod, Visions Intl, Fine Madness

George Mattingly 🎤 ✈   P
820 Miramar Ave
Berkeley, CA 94707-1807, 510-525-2098
Internet: gmd@dnai.com
    Pubs: *Driven, Breathing Space* (Blue Wind Pr, 2000, 1975),
    Big Bridge, MSNBC Poetry Anthology

Sara McAulay   W
California State Univ, English Dept, Hayward, CA 94542
www.tinamou2.com
    Pubs: *Chance, Catch Rides* (Knopf, 1982, 1975), *Hot
    Flashes: Anth* (Faber & Faber, 1996), *Zyzzyva, Third Coast,
    Chili Verde Rev, Southern Ocean Rev, Black Warrior Rev,
    Real Fiction, California Qtly*

Kate McCarthy   W
14854 Sutton St
Sherman Oaks, CA 91403, 818-784-0711
    Pubs: *Calliope, Exquisite Corpse, Sewanee Rev*

Lee McCarthy   P&W
8200 Kroll Way, #174
Bakersfield, CA 93311
    Pubs: *Good Girl, Desire's Door* (Story Line Pr, 2002, 1991),
    Combing Hair With a Seashell (Ion Bks, 1992), *Solo, Third
    Coast, Great River Rev*

Michael McClintock 🎤 ✈   P
807 Prospect Ave, Suite 107
South Pasadena, CA 91030-2448, 626-441-1853
    Pubs: *Cockroach Feet* (Hermitage West, 2002), *Anthology
    of Days* (Backwoods Broadsides, 2002), *Summer Dreams:
    Anth, Up Against the Window: Anth* (Red Moon Pr, 2002,
    2000), *The Haiku Anthology* (Norton, 2000), *Modern Haiku,
    Blithe Spirit, Pemmican, Tundra*

Mark McCloskey 🎤 ✈   P&W
1724 N Edgemont St, #114, Los Angeles, CA 90027,
323-913-1840
    Pubs: *Sometime the Cow Kick Your Head: Anth, Light Year
    '87: Anth* (Bits Pr, 1988, 1987), *Mag of Fantasy & Sci-Fi,
    Many Mountains Moving, Rafters, Confrontation, Poetry NW,
    Zone 3, Poetry/L.A., American Literary Rev*

Frances Ruhlen McConnel   P
Mary Routt Hall, Scripps College, Claremont, CA 91711,
714-621-8000
    Pubs: *Gathering Light, One Step Closer* (Pygmalion Pr,
    1979, 1975), *Iowa Rev, Seattle Rev, The Nation*

Brian McCormick   P&W
c/o Martin Baum, Creative Artists Agency, 9830 Wilshire Blvd,
Beverly Hills, CA 90212
    Pubs: *The Immortality Project* (Word Made Flesh/Printed
    Matter Bks, 1991), *Atlantic, Permafrost, Blueline, Zyzzyva,
    Fine Madness, Harper's, Santa Monica Rev*

Jennifer McDowell   P
PO Box 5602
San Jose, CA 95150
    Pubs: *Ronnie Goose Rhymes for Grownups, Contemporary
    Women Poets: Anth* (Merlin Pr, 1984, 1977), *Chock, Snowy
    Egret, X, Tigris & Euphrates, Open Cell*

Whitman McGowan 🎤 ✈   P
PO Box 471493
San Francisco, CA 94147-1493, 415-441-0846
Internet: margwhit@ix.netcom.com
    Pubs: *Ghost Worker* (Deep Forest, 2001), *POFU, Contents
    May Have Shifted* (Viridiana, 2000, 1994), *No, I Am Not
    Walt Whitman's Great Grandson* (Mel Thompson Pub,
    1993), *Left Hand Maps: Anth* (Small Garlic Pr, 1998), *Kinky
    Verse: Anth* (Daedalus, 1996)

Thomas R. McKague 🎤 ✈   P&W
14094 Sosna Way
Guernewood Park, CA 95446, 707-869-3922
    Pubs: *Sea and Stones: Voices from Atlantia* (GLB Pubs,
    2001), *The Violet Hours, Stormlight* (Mellon Poetry Pr, 1996,
    1995), *Waterlight Dreams* (New Pr, 1995), *A Natural Beauty*
    (Florida Pr, 1991)

Michael McLaughlin 🎤 ✈   P&W
c/o Don't Trip Press, PO Box 14244, San Luis Obispo, CA
93401
Internet: mycalmac@thegrid.net
    Pubs: *Upholstery of Heaven* (Don't Trip Pr, 1996), *Chiron
    Rev, Art World, Crack, Convolvulus, Asylum Annual, Frank*

Thomas McNamee   P
2382 Bush St
San Francisco, CA 94115
    Pubs: *A Story of Deep Delight* (Viking, 1990), *The Grizzly
    Bear* (Penguin, 1990)

Elnora McNaughton 🎤 ✈   P
PO Box 7054
Oxnard, CA 93031, 805-485-5425
    Pubs: *Solo* (Solo Pr, 2001), *Hold the Moon Bursting* (Mille
    Grazie Pr, 1999), *Rivertalk: Anth* (Little Horse Pr, 1997-
    1994), *Verve, Embers, Art/Life, Wind, CQ, Daybreak*

Carol Alma McPhee 🎤 ✈   W
67 Benton Way
San Luis Obispo, CA 93405
    Pubs: *Staying Under* (Papier-Mache Pr, 1998)

Sandra McPherson   P
2052 Calaveras Ave
Davis, CA 95616-3021, 530-753-9672
Internet: sjmcpherson@ucdavis.edu
    Pubs: *The Spaces Between Birds, Edge Effect: Trails &
    Portrayals* (Wesleyan/UPNE, 1996, 1996), *The God of
    Indeterminacy* (U Illinois Pr, 1993), *New Yorker*

Kat Meads 🎤 ✈   P&W
8665 Hihn Rd
Ben Lomond, CA 95005
Internet: katmeads@aol.com
    Pubs: *Stress in America* (March St Pr, 2001), *Not Waving*
    (Livingston Pr/U W Alabama, 2001), *Night Bones, The*
    Queendom (Linear Arts Pr, 2000, 1998), *Born Southern &*
    Restless (Duquesne U Pr, 1996), *Wayward Women* (Illinois
    Writers Inc., 1995)

Maude Meehan   P
2150 Portola Dr
Santa Cruz, CA 95062, 408-476-6164
    Pubs: *Washing the Stones: A Collection 1975-1995* (Papier-
    Mache Pr, 1996), *Before the Snow* (Moving Parts, 1991),
    Chipping Bone (Embers Pr, 1988)

Ib J. Melchior   W
8228 Marmont Ln
Los Angeles, CA 90069, 213-654-6679
    Pubs: *Quest* (Presidio Pr, 1990), *Steps & Stairways* (Co-
    author; Rizzoli, 1989)

David Meltzer 🎤 ✈   P&W
PO Box 9005
Berkeley, CA 94709, 510-237-6919
Internet: dmelt@earthlink.net
    Pubs: *San Francisco Beat: Talking With the Poets* (City
    Lights, 2001), *No Eyes: Lester Young, Arrows* (Black
    Sparrow Pr, 2001, 1993), *Under* (Rhinoceros Bks, 1998),
    Writing Jazz: Anth, Reading Jazz: Anth (Mercury Hse, 1999,
    1994), *Washington Post, Davka*

Roger Ladd Memmott 🎤   P&W
512 S Crawford Ave
Willows, CA 95988-3313, 530-934-7062
Internet: rlmstory@aol.com
    Pubs: *Riding the Absolute* (Creative Edtns, 2002), *The*
    Gypsy Lover, Gardening Without Gloves (Gemstone Bks,
    2001, 2001), *Many Mountains Moving, New Millenium*
    Writings, ByLine, Colorado Qtly, Confrontation, Sou'wester,
    Cumberland Poetry Rev

Ann Menebroker   P
10 Azorean Court
Sacramento, CA 95833
    Pubs: *Mailbox Boogie* (w/Robertson; Zerx Pr, 1991), *Time*
    Capsule: Anth (Creative Time, 1995), *Caprice, Atom Mind,*
    Pearl, Painted Bride Qtly, Bogg, Smell Feast, Thunders
    Mouth Press

Sarah Menefee 🎤 ✈   P
1655 Sacramento #1
San Francisco, CA 94109
    Pubs: *Like the Diamond* (Calliope Pr, 2001), *Reamed Heart*
    (Deleriodendron Pr, 1997), *This Perishable Hand*
    (Multimedia Edizioni, 1995), *Please Keep My Word* (Worm
    in the Rain Pub, 1991), *The Blood About the Heart,*
    (Curbstone Press, 1992)

Douglas Messerli   P
Sun & Moon Press, 6026 Wilshire Blvd, Los Angeles, CA
90036, 213-857-1115
    Pubs: *The Walls Come True: An Opera for Spoken Voices,*
    Along Without: A Film for Fiction in Poetry (Littoral, 1994,
    1993)

Deena Metzger   P&W
PO Box 186
Topanga, CA 90290, 213-455-1089
    Pubs: *Tree: Essays & Pieces* (North Atlantic Bks, 1997), *A*
    Sabbath Among the Ruins (Parallax Pr, 1992), *What Dinah*
    Thought (Viking, 1989), *Intimate Nature: Anth* (Ballantine,
    1998), *Anima, Turning Wheel, Poetry Flash, Creation,*
    Jacaranda Rev, Lilith

Leonard Michaels   W
English Dept, Univ California, Berkeley, CA 94720,
415-642-2764
    Pubs: *I Would Have Saved Them If I Could* (FSG, 1975)

Rondo Mieczkowski 🎤 ✈   P&W
PO Box 29478
Los Angeles, CA 90029-0478, 323-661-0478
Internet: Rondowriter@aol.com
    Pubs: *Sundays at Seven: Anth* (Alamo Square Pr, 1996),
    Sonora Rev, James White Rev, Wisconsin Rev, Modern
    Words, Poetry/L.A.

Sara Miles   P
824 Shotwell St
San Francisco, CA 94110-3213
Internet: smiles@igc.org
    Pubs: *Native Dancer* (Curbstone Pr, 1986), *Ordinary*
    Women (Ow Bks, 1984), *Opposite Sex: Anth* (NYU Pr,
    1998), *Iowa Rev, Essence, Ms., XXXFruit, Nation, New*
    Yorker, Wired, Essence

Carolyn Miller 🎤 ✈   P&W
1195 Green St
San Francisco, CA 94109
Internet: cmiller355@aol.com
    Pubs: *After Cocteau* (Sixteen Rivers Pr, 2002), *Urban*
    Nature: Anth (Milkweed, 2000), *Wild Song: Poems of the*
    Natural World: Anth (Univ of Georgia Pr, 1998), *Southern*
    Rev, Gettysburg Rev, Shenandoah, Nimrod, Qtly West,
    Appalachia, Seattle Rev, Georgia Rev

Adam David Miller 🎤 ✈   P
PO Box 162
Berkeley, CA 94701-0162, 510-845-8098
Internet: eliseadm@sirius.com
    Pubs: *Land Between, New & Selected Poems, Apocalypse Is*
    My Garden (Eshu Hse Pub, 2000, 1997), *Forever Afternoon*
    (Michigan State U Pr, 1994), *Neighborhood & Other Poems*
    (Mina Pr, 1993), *Dices or Black Bones* (HM, 1973)

Brown Miller P
English Dept, City College of San Francisco, 50 Phelan Ave,
San Francisco, CA 94112, 415-239-4793
Pubs: *Hiroshima Flows Through Us* (Cherry Valley Edtns,
1977), *New Letters, Xanadu, Ohio Rev*

Lorraine Millings 🎤 ✈ P
PO Box 2291
Lancaster, CA 93539-2291, 805-949-8687
Internet: PoetRaini@aol.com
Pubs: *America at the Millennium, Verve, Plaza, Pirate
Writings, Poetic Eloquence, Friendship Rose*

Paul L. Mills PP
3426 Keystone Ave #4
Los Angeles, CA 90034-4731
Pubs: *The Co-op Songbook* (New York Musicians Co-op,
1983), *Think & Do* (Co-op Records, 1983), *Boston Phoenix,
Creem, Fusion, Outpost, Stroker*

Stephen Minkin W
320 Pitt Ave
Sebastopol, CA 95472
Internet: smink@sover.net
Pubs: *A No Doubt Mad Idea* (Ross/Back Roads Bks, 1979),
First Leaves, American Square Dancing

Stephen Minot 🎤 W
2225 Mt Vernon Ave
Riverside, CA 92507-2500, 909-369-3938
Internet: s.minot@juno.com
Pubs: *Bending Time* (Permanent Pr, 1997), *Surviving the
Flood* (Second Chance Pr, 1986), *Virginia Qtly Rev,
Sewanee Rev, Harper's, Agni, Paris Rev, Atlantic*

Janice Mirikitani P
Glide Foundation, 330 Ellis St, San Francisco, CA 94102,
415-771-6300
Pubs: *We the Dangerous, Shedding Silence: Anth* (Celestial
Arts Pub, 1995, 1990), *Awake in the River* (Isthmus Pr, 1982)

Hayley R. Mitchell 🎤 ✈ P
23106 Kent Ave
Torrance, CA 90505-3527
Internet: grimmgirl@aol.com
Pubs: *Bite to Eat: Anth* (Redwood Coast Pr, 1995), *Black
Buzzard Rev, Cimarron Rev, SPR, New Delta Rev, Poetry
NW, Wordwrights*

Mark J. Mitchell 🎤 ✈ P
2547 California St
San Francisco, CA 94115
Internet: Rfk40a@aol.com
Pubs: *Sir Gawain's Little Green Book* (Xlibris, 2000), *Line
Drives: Anth* (S Illinois Univ Pr, 2002), *Blue Unicorn,
Spelunker Flophouse, Verve, Tucumcari Lit Rev, Medicinal
Purposes, Kayak, Black Bough, Chachalaca Poetry Rev,
Blue Violin, Lynx*

Bill Mohr 🎤 ✈ PP&P
9130 Regents Rd, #C
La Jolla, CA 92037-1437, 858-587-4836
Internet: bmohr@ucsd.edu
Pubs: *Thoughtful Outlaw* (Inevitable Pr, 2000), *Vehemence*
(Cassette/CD; New Alliance, 1992), *hidden proofs*
(Bombshelter, 1982), *Zyzzyva, Wormwood Rev, Antioch
Rev, Blue Mesa Rev, Santa Monica Rev, Sonora Rev,
Onthebus*

Leslie Monsour 🎤 ✈ P
2062 Stanley Hills Dr
Los Angeles, CA 90046
Internet: metermade@hotmail.com
Pubs: *Earth's Beauty, Desire & Loss* (RLB Pr, 1998),
Indelibility (Aralia Pr, 1999), *Visiting Emily: Anth* (U Iowa Pr,
2000), *A Formal Feeling Comes: Anth* (Story Line Press,
1994), *The Formalist, Edge City Rev, Dark Horse, Hellas,
Lyric, Plum Rev, Poetry*

Rod Val Moore 🎤 ✈ W
5800 Fulton Ave
Van Nuys, CA 91401
Internet: Rod_V._Moore@antiochla.edu
Pubs: *Igloo Among Palms* (Hinterlands, 1997)

Raylyn Moore W
302 Park St
Pacific Grove, CA 93950, 408-372-0113
Pubs: *What Happened to Emily Goode After the Great
Exhibition* (Donning, 1978)

Rosalie Moore P
1130 7th St, #B-26
Novato, CA 94945, 415-892-3073
Pubs: *Learned & Leaved* (Marin Poetry Center, 1989), *Of
Singles & Doubles* (Woolmer/Brotherson, 1979)

Cherrie Moraga P&W
1042 Mississippi St
San Francisco, CA 94107
Pubs: *Loving in the War Years* (South End Pr, 1983)

Dorinda Moreno P
c/o Rose Gabaldon, 5505 Esplanada, Orcutt, CA 93455, 805-
937-3067

Richard W. Morris P
2421 Buchanan St
San Francisco, CA 94115-1927
Internet: rwmorris@ix.netcom.com
Pubs: *Adventures of God* (Ghost Dance Pr, 1994),
Assyrians (The Smith, 1991)

Henry J. Morro 🎤 ✈   P
2209A Dufour Ave
Redondo Beach, CA 90278-1414, 310-370-9659
Internet: henrymorro@adelphia.net
    Pubs: *Corpses of Angels* (Bombshelter Pr, 2000), *Outlaw Bible of Amer Poetry: Anth* (Thunder's Mouth Pr, 1999), *Invocation L.A.: Anth* (West End Pr, 1989), *Chiron Rev, New Letters, Seneca Rev, Black Warrior Rev, Pacific Rev*

Carlos Morton   P&W
San Francisco Mime Troupe, 855 Treat St, San Francisco, CA 94110
    Pubs: *White Heroin Winter* (One Eye Pr, 1971)

Lois Moyles   P
4243 Norton Ave
Oakland, CA 94602, 510-531-1375
    Pubs: *Alleluia Chorus* (Woolmer/Brotherson, 1979), *Partisan Rev, Shenandoah, Delos, Hawaii Pacific Rev, New Yorker, Manhattan Rev*

Frederick Mugler, Jr.   W
580 St Francis Pl
Menlo Park, CA 94025, 650-322-9650
Internet: fredmugler@aol.com
    Pubs: *Pavilion* (Putnam, 1982), *Emergency Room* (Delacorte 1975)

Harryette Mullen   P
UCLA English Dept, 405 Hilgard Ave, Los Angeles, CA 90095, 310-825-7553
    Pubs: *Muse & Drudge* (Singing Horse Pr, 1995), *Trimmings* (Tender Buttons Bks, 1991), *Callaloo, Agni, Chain, Antioch, World, Bombay Gin*

Alejandro Murguia   W
1799 Revere Ave
San Francisco, CA 94124-2345, 415-822-2543
    Pubs: *Southern Front* (Bilingual Rev Pr, 1988), *Farewell to the Coast* (Heirs Pr, 1980)

Pat Murphy   W
c/o Exploratorium, 3601 Lyon St, San Francisco, CA 94123, 415-561-0336
    Pubs: *Points of Departure, The Shadow Hunter, The City, Not Long After* (Bantam, 1990, 1990, 1989)

William K. Murphy   P
6635 Sepulveda Blvd
Van Nuys, CA 91411-1204, 818-787-2764
Internet: uxorcist@pacbell.net
    Pubs: *Nightland, Walk Along the Seashore* (Solo Pr, 1988, 1987), *Redstart, Cafe Solo, Kite*

Merilene M. Murphy 🎤 ✈   P
Telepoetics, Inc, 1939 1/4 W Washington Blvd, Los Angeles, CA 90018-1635, 323-419-0001
Internet: peazritr@mediaone.net
    Pubs: *darchitecture* (Love Is a House Lightshow, 1999), *under peace rising* (Woman in the Moon Pubs, 1994), *Trouble: Anth* (Kavayantra Pr, 1995), *Coffee House Poets Qtly, L.A. Mag*

Carol Muske-Dukes   P&W
English Dept, Univ Southern California, University Park Campus, Los Angeles, CA 90089-0354, 213-740-2808
Internet: carolmd@usc.edu
    Pubs: *Sparrow* (Random Hse, 2002), *An Octave Above Thunder: New & Selected* (Penguin, 1997), *Women & Poetry* (U Michigan Pr, 1997), *Red Trousseau, Saving St. Germ* (Viking, 1993, 1993), *Dear Digby* (Washington Square Pr, 1991), *Paris Rev, APR, New Yorker, Field*

Edward Mycue   P
PO Box 640543
San Francisco, CA 94164-0543, 415-922-0395
    Pubs: *Old Jack-A Napa Valley Story & Other Poems, Night Boats* (Norton Coker Pr, 2004, 1999), *Sunlight & Cobweb* (Minotaur Edtns, 2003), *The Poem of San Francisco, Because We Speak the Same Language* (Spectacular Diseases Pr 2002, 1994),

Majid Naficy   P
1144 12th St #103
Santa Monica, CA 90403, 310-395-6993
    Pubs: *In a Tiger's Skin* (Amir Kabir, 1969), *Literary Rev*

Peter Najarian 🎤 ✈   W
1521 Stuart St
Berkeley, CA 94703, 510-548-1407
    Pubs: *The Great American Loneliness* (Blue Crane Bks, 1999), *Daughters of Memory* (City Miner, 1986), *Voyages* (Ararat, 1980), *Wash Me on Home, Mama*

Martin Nakell   P&W
1201 Larrabee St, Apt 207
Los Angeles, CA 90069
Internet: mnakell@chapman.edu
    Pubs: *Goings* (Margin-to-Margin Bks, 2002), *Two Fields That Face & Mirror Each Other* (Green Integer Pr, 2001), *The Library of Thomas Rivka* (Sun & Moon Pr, 1996), *The Myth of Creation* (Parenthesis Writing Series, 1993), *Literal Latte, Hanging Loose*

Rochelle Nameroff 🎤 ✈   P
1102 Neilson St
Albany, CA 94706-2400, 510-524-2477
Internet: rnameroff@earthlink.net
    Pubs: *Body Prints* (Ithaca Hse, 1972), *Hard Choices: Anth* (U Iowa Pr, 1996), *Diamonds Are a Girl's Best Friend: Anth* (Faber & Faber, 1995), *Sweet Nothings: Anth* (Indiana U Pr, 1994), *Iowa Rev, Qtly West, Antioch Rev, Poetry NW, Michigan Qtly Rev*

Brenda Nasio P
216 Fair Oaks St
San Francisco, CA 94110
   Pubs: *Paris Rev, Open Places, Amelia, Negative Capability,
   CutBank, Crab Creek Rev, Pudding*

Jim Natal ♪ ✈ P
311 Bora Bora Way #205
Marina del Rey, CA 90292-8305, 310-821-3906
   Pubs: *Talking Back to the Rocks, In the Bee Trees* (Archer
   Bks, 2003, 2000), *Mischief, Oil on Paper, Explaining Water
   with Water* (Inevitable Pr, 2000, 1997), *Caprice and Other
   Poetic Strtgs: Anth* (Red Hen Pr, 2002), *Clay Palm Rev,
   Solo, Yalobusha Rev*

Leonard Nathan P
40 Beverly Rd
Kensington, CA 94707
   Pubs: *Tears of the Old Magician, The Potato Eaters*
   (Orchises Pr, 2003, 1997), *Diary of a Left-Handed
   Birdwatcher* (Graywolf Pr, 1996), *Carrying On: New &
   Selected Poems* (U Pitt Pr, 1985), *Manoa, Poet Lore,
   Salmagundi, Atlantic, Southwestern Rev, New Yorker*

Opal Louis Nations P
c/o KFPA, 1939 M L King Jr Way, Berkeley, CA 94704
   Pubs: *Neo-Absurdities* (Changed Species Pr, 1988), *Coach
   House Poets Collection: Anth* (Norton, 1988), *Rampike*

Louise Nayer ♪ ✈ P
1165 Bosworth St
San Francisco, CA 94131-2801, 415-587-4475
Internet: lnayer50@aol.com
   Pubs: *The Houses Are Covered in Sound* (Blue Light Pr,
   1990), *Keeping Watch* (Birthstone Pr, 1981)

Peter E. Nelson P
1303 Allesandro St
Los Angeles, CA 90026
   Pubs: *Spring Into Light* (Green Tree Pr, 1978), *Between
   Lives* (Ironwood Pr, 1974), *Choice, Poetry*

Mildred Nelson P&W
2000 S Melrose Dr #147
Vista, CA 92083
   Pubs: *The Island* (Pocket Bks, 1973), *Light Year: Anth* (Bits
   Pr, 1986), *Mediphors, Georgia Rev, McCall's, San Fernando
   Poetry Jrnl, Writers Jrnl, Crosscurrents*

Ray Faraday Nelson ♪ W
333 Ramona Ave
El Cerrito, CA 94530, 510-526-7378
   Pubs: *Virtual Zen* (Avon, 1996), *Dog Headed Death*
   (Strawberry Hill, 1988), *Timequest* (Tor, 1985)

Crawdad Nelson ♪ ✈ P&W
PO Box 219
Bayside, CA 95524-0219, 707-269-0611
Internet: mrsteelie@aol.com
   Pubs: *Road Kill & Other Stories, A Pocket Full of Revolution*
   (Bare Minimum Pr, 2002), *The Bull of the Woods, When the
   Eagle Shits* (Gorda Plate Pr, 1997, 1996), *Truth Rides to
   Work* (Poetic Space Bks, 1993), *Valley Advertiser, Arcata
   Free Pr, Arcata Eye*

David Nemec ♪ ✈ W
1517 Irving St
San Francisco, CA 94122-1908, 415-564-6506
   Pubs: *Stonesifer* (Robert D. Reed, 1999), *Early Dreams*
   (Baseballl Pr, 1999), *The Beer & Whisky League* (Lyons &
   Burford, 1994), *The Systems of M.R. Shurnas* (John Calder,
   1986), *Mad Blood* (Dial Pr, 1983), *Transatlantic Rev,
   Playgirl, Twilight Zone*

Peter Neumeyer P&W
45 Marguerita Rd
Kennsington, CA 94707-1019, 619-463-2229
   Pubs: *The Phantom of the Opera, Homage to John Clare*
   (Peregrine Smith, 1988, 1980), *Donald & The . . .* (Addison-
   Wesley, 1969), *New Mexico Qtly*

Felice Newman P
Cleis Press, PO Box 14684, San Francisco, CA 94114,
412-937-1555
Internet: fncleis@aol.com
   Pubs: *The Second Coming* (Alyson, 1996), *Herotica 5: Anth*
   (Down There Pr, 1997)

Rebecca Newman W
20 Bali Ln
Pacific Palisades, CA 90272, 310-573-2028
   Pubs: *Ely & the Komodo Dragon* (Ancient Mariners Pr,
   1991), *Adam the Detective* (Midwest Express, 1991), *The
   Divorce of Mrs. Dracula* (Redstart, 1988)

Jeanne M. Nichols ♪ ✈ P
4234 Camino Real
Los Angeles, CA 90065-3958, 323-222-0014
Internet: jeannenichols@mymailstation.com
   Pubs: *Leaning Over the Edge* (Fithian Pr, 1993), *California
   Lyrics: Anth* (Live Poets' Society, Huntington Lbry 2000),
   Where Icarus Falls: Anth (Santa Barbara Rev Pub, 1998),
   Only Morning in Her Shoes: Anth (Utah State U Pr, 1990),
   College English, Nimrod

Sheila Nickerson P&W
PO Box 637
Atwater, CA 95301, 209-358-3154
   Pubs: *In an August Garden* (Black Spruce Pr, 1997), *Feast
   of the Animals* (Old Harbor Pr, 1991), *In the Compass of
   Unrest* (Trout Creek Pr, 1988)

Ann Nietzke 🎤 ✈   W
466 N Hobart Blvd, #12
Los Angeles, CA 90004-1851, 323-660-5983
　Pubs: *Solo Spinout, Windowlight* (Soho Pr, 1996, 1996),
　Shenandoah, Other Voices, Massachusetts Rev

Nona Nimnicht   P
303 Adams, #210
Oakland, CA 94610
　Pubs: *In the Museum Naked* (Second Coming Pr, 1978),
　*Ploughshares, Poetry NW, Qtly West, Crosscurrents, Prairie
　Schooner, Nimrod*

Jim Nisbet 🎤 ✈   P&W
571 Ivy St
San Francisco, CA 94102, 415-701-7772
Internet: 76040.2210@Compuserve.com
　Pubs: *Prelude to a Scream* (Carroll & Graf, 1997), *Death
　Puppet, Lethal Injection, The Damned Don't Die* (Black
　Lizard Bks, 1989, 1987, 1986), *American Poets Say
　Goodbye to the 20th Century: Anth* (Four Walls Eight
　Windows, 1996), *City Lights Jrnl*

Larry Niven   W
11874 Macoda Ln
Chatsworth, CA 91311
Internet: organlegger@earthlink.net
　Pubs: *The Burning City* (w/J. Pournelle; Pocket Bks, 2001),
　Saturn's Race (w/S. Barnes; Tom Doherty Assoc, 2001)

Rick Noguchi 🎤 ✈   P
5315 Etheldo Ave
Culver City, CA 90230
　Pubs: *Flowers From Mariko* (Lee and Lou Bks, 2001), *The
　Ocean Inside Kenji Takezo* (U Pitt Pr 1996), *The Wave He
　Caught* (Pearl Edtns, 1995)

Harold Norse   P&W
157 Albion St
San Francisco, CA 94110-1103
　Pubs: *Memoirs of a Bastard Angel* (Morrow, 1989), *The
　Love Poems: 1940-85* (Crossing Pr, 1986)

John Norton 🎤 ✈   P&W
444A 14th St
San Francisco, CA 94103-2359, 415-558-9066
Internet: jnorton100@hotmail.com
　Pubs: *Re: Marriage, The Light at the End of the Bog* (Black
　Star Series, 2000, 1992), *Posthum(or)ous* (e.g. Pr, 1986),
　Before Columbus Fdn: Anth (Norton, 1991), *NAW, Oxygen,
　CrossConnect, Coracle*

John Noto 🎤 ✈   P&W
2470 Washington #101
San Francisco, CA 94115
　Pubs: *Simulcast Yearning* (Wordcraft of Oregon, 1999),
　Psycho-Motor Breathscapes (Vatic Hum Pr, 1997), *Volt,
　Talisman, Caliban, Central Park, Fiction Intl, NAW, Ctheory,
　American Letters & Commentary*

Joyce Nower 🎤 ✈   P
9333 Dillon Dr
La Mesa, CA 91941
Internet: jnower@mail.sdsu.edu
　Pubs: *Column of Silence* (Avranches Pr, 2001), *Year of the
　Fires* (CWSS Pub, 1983), *Common Ground Rev, Catbird
　Seat, GW Rev, Talus and Scree, Taproot Lit Rev,
　Grasslands Rev*

Susan Nunes 🎤 ✈   W
Berkeley, CA 94708-1925
Internet: suminu@aol.com
　Pubs: *The Last Dragon* (Clarion, 1995), *A Small Obligation
　& Other Stories of Hilo, Intersecting Circles: Anth* (Bamboo
　Ridge, 1982, 2000), *Graywolf Annual: Anth* (Graywolf, 1991),
　Home to Stay: Anth (Greenfield Rev, 1990)

Naomi Shihab Nye 🎤 ✈   W
Steven Barclay Agency, 12 Western Ave, Petaluma, CA 94952,
888-965-7323
Internet: nshihab@aol.com
　Pubs: *19 Varieties of Gazelle, Come with Me* (Greenwillow,
　2002, 2000), *Mint Snowball* (Anhinga, 2001), *Fuel, Red
　Suitcase* (BOA Edtns, 1998, 1994), *Words Under the Words*
　(Far Corner Bks, 1995), *Atlantic, Iowa Rev, Ploughshares,
　SW Rev, Wilderness,*

Heidi Nye   P
2213 Granade Ave
Long Beach, CA 90815
　Pubs: *Water From the Moon* (Forever a Foreigner Pr, 1992),
　*Australian Wellbeing, California Poetry Qtly, L.A. View, Pearl,
　Natural Health, Bad Haircut*

Philip F. O'Connor   W
821 Gonzalez Dr
San Francisco, CA 94123-2235
　Pubs: *Martin's World* (Bottom Dog Pr, 1993), *Finding
　Brendan* (S&S, 1991), *Defending Civilization* (Weidenfeld &
　Nicolson, 1988)

Jamie O'Halloran   P
8446 Fenwick St
Sunland, CA 91040, 818-353-7203
Internet: ohalloran@mindspring.com
　Pubs: *The Landscape From Behind* (V.C. Pr, 1997), *Grand
　Passion: Poets of Los Angeles: Anth* (Red Wind Bks, 1995),
　*Cream City Rev, Southern California Anth, Blue Satellite,
　Seattle Rev, Blue Moon Rev, 51%, Snakeskin*

Diana O'Hehir 🎤 ✈   P
2855 Jackson St, #301
San Francisco, CA 94115, 415-928-1261
　Pubs: *Spells for Not Dying Again* (Eastern Washington U Pr,
　1997), *Home Free, I Wish This War Were Over* (Atheneum,
　1988, 1984), *Mother Songs: Anth* (Norton, 1991), *Prarie
　Schooner, Poetry, Kenyon Rev, Poetry NW, Shenandoah*

Regina O'Melveny P
3071 Crest Rd
Rancho Palos Verde, CA 90275, 310-833-6580
    Pubs: *Blue Wolves* (Bright Hill Pr, 1997), *Cathedrals of the Spirit: Anth* (Harperperennial, 1996), *Spreading the Word/L.A. Poetry Contest Winners: Anth* (Red Wind Bks, 1993), *Yellow Silk Anth* (Crown Pubs, 1990), *The Sun, Jacaranda Rev, Poetry/L.A.*

Raymond Obstfeld W
2936 Ballesteros Ln
Tustin, CA 92680
    Pubs: *The Remington Contract* (Worldwide, 1988), *The Reincarnation of Reece Erikson* (Tor, 1988)

Joyce Odam P
2432 48th Ave
Sacramento, CA 95822
    Pubs: *Lemon Center for Hot Buttered Roll* (Hibiscus Pr, 1975), *Blue Unicorn, Impulse*

Jennifer Olds P
1403 W Locust St
Ontario, CA 91762-5327
    Pubs: *Rodeo & the Mimosa Tree* (Event Horizon Pr, 1991), *Gypsy, Tsunami, Pearl, Slipstream, Staple, Onthebus, Envoi, New Spokes*

Carole Simmons Oles ♀ ✈ P
California State Univ, English Dept, Chico, CA 95929-0001, 530-898-5240
    Internet: coles@csuchico.edu
    Pubs: *Sympathetic Systems* (Lynx Hse, 2000), *Stunts* (GreenTower, 1992), *The Deed* (LSU Pr, 1991), *Field, Kenyon Rev, Poetry, NER, Prairie Schooner, APR, Georgia Rev*

Beverly Olevin W
2252 Beverly Glen Pl
Los Angeles, CA 90077-2506, 310-474-0959
    Internet: 74634.1153@compuserve.com
    Pubs: *The Breath of Juno* (Elk Horn Pr, 1996), *Sweet Peas* (Juno Pr, 1991), *Ms., America West, Sun Dog: SE Rev, Oxford Mag, Portland Rev, MacGuffin*

Robert Oliphant W
English Dept, California State Univ, Northridge, CA 91330
    Pubs: *A Trumpet for Jackie, A Piano for Mrs. Cimino* (Prentice-Hall, 1983, 1980)

Daniel A. Olivas ♀ ✈ P&W
24638 Canyonwood Dr
West Hills, CA 91307, 213-897-2705
    Internet: olivasdan@aol.com
    Pubs: *Assumption and Other Stories, Fantasmas: Anth* (Bilingual Rev Pr, 2003, 2001), *The Courtship of Maria Rivera Pena* (Silver Lake Pub, 2000), *Love to Mama: Anth* (Lee & Low Bks, 2001), *MacGuffin, Pacific Rev, Exquisite Corpse, Paumanok Rev*

David Oliveira ♀ ✈ P
820A W Victoria St
Santa Barbara, CA 93101-4782, 805-963-8408
    Pubs: *In the Presence of Snakes* (Brandenburg Pr, 2000), *A Near Country* (Solo Pr, 1999), *Geography of Home: Anth* (Heyday Bks, 1999), *Poetry Intl, Third Coast, Cafe Solo, Americas Rev*

Tillie Olsen ♀ ✈ W
2333 Ward St
Berkeley, CA 94705, 510-649-7472
    Pubs: *Mother to Daughter, Daughter to Mother* (Feminist Pr, 1986), *Silences* (Delacorte, 1978), *Tell Me a Riddle* (Bantam/Doubleday/Dell, 1962), *Yonnondio: From the Thirties* (Bantam/Doubleday Dell, 1978), *First Words: Anth:* (Alqonquin, 1998), *Iowa Rev*

Sharon Olson P
Palo Alto Main Library, 1213 Newell Rd, Palo Alto, CA 94303, 650-329-2438
    Internet: slopoet@well.com
    Pubs: *Clouds Brushed in Later* (San Jose Poetry Ctr Pr, 1987), *Fire in the Hills: Anth* (Adler, 1992), *Convolvulus, Sand Hill Rev, Kalliope, Santa Clara Rev, Palo Alto Rev, Kansas Qtly, Seattle Rev, American Literary Rev, Worcester Rev*

Philip D. Ortego P&W
English Dept, San Jose State Univ, San Jose, CA 95912, 408-277-2242

Antonio G. Ortiz P
2006 S Genesee Ave
Los Angeles, CA 90016
    Pubs: *Flor y Canto II & I* (U Southern California Pr, 1978, 1976), *Urbis Mag, New Mexico Mag*

Mark Osaki ♀ ✈ P
6615 Fordham Way
Sacramento, CA 95831-2246, 916-421-4090
    Internet: m.osaki@worldnet.att.net
    Pubs: *Carrying the Darkness: Anth* (Texas Tech U Pr, 1989), *Hawaii Rev, Berkeley Poetry Rev, South Carolina Rev, Georgia Rev*

John Jay Osborn ♀ ✈ W
14 Fair Oaks St
San Francisco, CA 94110
    Internet: osborn67@post.harvard.edu
    Pubs: *The Paper Chase* (Whitson Pub, 2002), *The Associates, The Man Who Owned New York* (HM, 1982, 1981)

Ernest John Oswald P
Thumb Tree Poetry Service, 128 Laguna St, San Francisco, CA 94102, 415-431-8791
    Pubs: *Apricot Two Step* (E. Oswald, 1976), *NYQ, Small Pond, Cincinnati Rev, Offerta Speciale*

Louis Owens W
Univ of California, English Dept, Davis, CA 95616
Pubs: *I Hear the Train, Dark River, Mixedblood Messages, Bone Game, The Sharpest Sight, Other Destinies* (U Oklahoma Pr, 2001, 1999, 1998, 1994, 1992, 1992), *Nightland* (Dutton, 1996), *Wolfsong* (West End Pr, 1995)

Richard Oyama P&W
2809 B Cherry St
Berkeley, CA 94705, 510-653-8118
Internet: royama@ccac_art.edu
Pubs: *The NuyorAsian Anth* (Asian American Writers Workshop, 1999), *Image and Imagination: Anth* (Freedom Voices, 1997), *Premonitions: Anth* (Kaya Production, 1995), *Dissident Son: Anth* (Quarry W, 1991), *Breaking Silence* (Greenfield Rev Pr, 1983)

Rosella Pace P
2750 Hilltop Ct
Arcata, CA 95521-5221
Pubs: *Portugal: The Villages, Anth of Los Angeles Poets* (Red Hill Pr, 1977, 1972), *Cafe Solo, Bachy, Beyond Baroque, San Marcos Rev*

Javier Pacheco PP&P
5162 Berryman Ave
Culver City, CA 90230, 213-390-2579
Pubs: *Canciones De La Raza* (Fuego De Aztlan, 1978), *Chismearte, Rayas, Electrum, Maize*

Barbara Gordon Paine 🎤 P
Chaspaine, 803 15th Ave, Menlo Park, CA 94025-1947, 650-326-2212
Internet: chaspaine@aol.com
Pubs: *To Shout at the Fog* (Chaspaine, 1998), *Eidolon* (Ligda, 1962), *Reading & Interpreting: Anth* (Wadsworth, 1968), *Prairie Schooner, NYQ*

Charlotte Painter 🎤 ✈ W
6450 Mystic St
Oakland, CA 94618, 510-595-3901
Internet: holywrit@pacbell.net
Pubs: *Who Made the Lamb* (E-reads, 2002), *Conjuring Tibet* (Mercury Hse, 1997), *Gifts of Age* (Chronicle Bks, 1986)

Michael Palmer 🎤 ✈ P
265 Jersey St
San Francisco, CA 94114-3822, 415-282-8522
Pubs: *The Promises of Glass, The Lion Bridge, At Passages* (New Directions, 2000, 1998, 1995), *Grand Street, Sulfur, Chicago Rev, NAW, Chain, Avec, Common Knowledge*

Nicole Panter W
PO Box 862
Venice, CA 90294, 310-396-4391
Internet: nicolep7@aol.com
Pubs: *Mr. Right On & Other Stories, Unnatural Disasters: Recent Writings From the Golden State: Anth* (Incommunicado Pr, 1994, 1996)

Julia Park 🎤 ✈ P
229 Cypress St
Alameda, CA 94501
Internet: juliapark222@hotmail.com
Pubs: *Women's Uncommon Prayers* (Moorhouse 2000), *Two Worlds Walking* (New Rivers Pr, 1994), *Moxie, Caprice, Green Fuse Poetry, Poetry Nippon, Ruah, Spectrum*

Richard Parque P&W
PO Box 327
Verdugo City, CA 91046-0327
Pubs: *A Distant Thunder, Flight of the Phantom, Firefight, Hellbound, Sweet Vietnam* (Zebra Bks, 1988, 1987, 1986, 1985, 1984)

Alicia Partnoy W
8918 Earhart Ave
Los Angeles, CA 90045, 310-216-9188
Internet: apartnoy@lmu.edu
Pubs: *Revenge of the Apple: Poems, The Little School* (Cleis Pr, 1992, 1986)

John B. Passerello P
6825 Ashfield Way
Fair Oaks, CA 95628-4207
Internet: passerellojandb@worldnet.att.net
Pubs: *Homeless Not Helpless: Anth* (Fox Sparrow, 1989), *We Speak for Peace: Anth* (KIT, 1993), *Tapjoe, Peace & Freedom, Pudding, Feelings, Aristos, CQ*

Louis Patler P
36 Shell Rd
Mill Valley, CA 94941, 415-388-8344
Internet: bit@nbn.com
Pubs: *An American Ensemble* (Poltroon Pr, 1980), *Acts, Intent, Rootdrinker, Convivid, Mill Valley Mag, Pacific Poetry & Fiction Rev*

Jim Paul P&W
1170 Guerrero St, Loft
San Francisco, CA 94110,
415-641-5308
Internet: jimpaul@sirius.com
Pubs: *Medieval in L.A.* (Counterpoint, 1996), *Catapult: Harry & I Build a Siege Weapon* (Villard Bks, 1991), *Antioch Rev, Paris Rev, Mss.*

Paul J. J. Payack P&W
5046 Blackhawk Dr
Danville, CA 94506, 650-812-6229
Internet: payack@post.harvard.edu
Pubs: *New Letters, Paris Rev, Boulevard, Creative Computing, New Infinity Rev*

C. D. Payne 🎤 ✈ W
PO Box 1922
Sebastopol, CA 95473
www.nicktwisp.com
    Pubs: *Youth in Revolt: The Journal of Nick Twisp*
    (Doubleday, 1995)

Gerrye Payne P
10582 Barnett Valley Rd
Sebastopol, CA 95472
    Pubs: *The Year-God* (Ahsahta Pr, 1992), *An Amateur Plays
    Satie* (Loon Pr, 1984), *Dog River Rev, Kansas Qtly, Kalliope,
    Creeping Bent, Loon, Primavera, Fish Drum, Karamu,
    Hayden's Ferry Rev*

Sherman Pearl 🎤 ✈ P
941 26th St
Santa Monica, CA 90403, 310-453-0183
Internet: shrmprl@cs.com
    Pubs: *Working Papers* (Pacific Writers Pr, 1999), *Anth of
    New England Writers* (New England Writers, 1998), *Grand
    Passion: Anth* (Red Wind Bks, 1995), *Atlanta Rev, Buffalo
    Bones, CQ, Ledge, Passager, Peregrine, Slant, Verve*

Victor Pearn P
215 1/2 Hollister Ave
Santa Monica, CA 90405, 310-450-4156
    Pubs: *Pyromaniac* (The Plowman, 1995), *Swans Pausing*
    (Foothills Pub, 1994), *Negative Capability, Long Islander,
    Midwest Qtly, Mind Matters Rev, Sulphur River Literary Rev,
    Whole Notes*

Noel Peattie 🎤 ✈ P&W
23311 County Rd 88
Winters, CA 95694-9008, 530-662-3364
Internet: nrpeattie@earthlink.net
    Pubs: *King Humble's Grave, In the Dome of Saint Laurence
    Meteor, Amy Rose* (Regent Pr, 2001, 1999, 1995), *Cape
    Rock, Second Coming, Cayo, Tule Rev, Poetry Now, Poetry
    Motel Wallpaper, Hammers*

Oscar Penaranda P&W
Logan High School, 1800 H St, Union City, CA 94587,
510-471-2520
    Pubs: *Fiction by Filipinos in America: Anth* (New Day Pubs,
    1993), *Filipinas Mag, Bay-Loot*

James Pendergast P
685 Fano Ln
Sonoma, CA 95476, 707-996-7743
    Pubs: *Anth of Mag Verse* (Monitor Book Co, 1981), *The New
    Mag, Ruhtra, Hyperion*

Sam Pereira 🎤 ✈ P
1326 Canal Farm Ln
Los Banos, CA 93635-3808, 209-826-2072
Internet: litsam@inreach.net
    Pubs: *Brittle Water* (Penumbra Pr, 1987), *The Marriage of
    the Portuguese* (L'Epervier Pr, 1978), *How Much Earth: Anth*
    (Roundhouse Poets, 2001), *The Body Electric: Anth*
    (Norton, 2000), *Piecework: Anth* (Silver Skates Publishing,
    1987), *APR, Poetry, Antioch Rev*

Anne S. Perlman P
41 Fifth Ave
San Francisco, CA 94118, 415-752-2517
    Pubs: *Sorting It Out* (Carnegie Mellon, 1984), *Songs from
    Unsung Worlds: Anth* (Aviva, 1987)

Robert Peters 🎤 ✈ P
9431 Krepp Dr
Huntington Beach, CA 92646, 714-968-7546
Internet: ptrachrp@aol.com
    Pubs: *Familial Love and Other Misfortunes* (Red Hen Pr,
    2001), *Feather: A Child's Death & Life* (U Wisconsin Pr,
    1997), *Selected Poems 1967-1994* (Asylum Arts Pr, 1994),
    *Amer Bk Rev, James White Rev, Chiron Rev, Bakunin,
    Small Press Rev, Chicago Rev*

Geoff Peterson P
25 San Juan Ave
San Francisco, CA 94112, 415-585-4808
    Pubs: *The Owning Stone* (Red Hen Pr, 2000), *Jim
    Peterson's Greatest Hits* (Pudding Hse, 2000), *Medicine
    Dog* (St. Martin's Pr, 1989), *Letter From Wyoming: Anth*
    (Wyoming Council on the Arts, 1991), *Peregrine, Z
    Miscellaneous, Aileron, NYQ*

Frances Phillips P
194 Onondaga Ave
San Francisco, CA 94112, 415-626-2787
    Pubs: *Up at Two, For a Living* (Hanging Loose Pr, 1991,
    1981), *Hanging Loose, Five Fingers Rev, Volt, NYQ,
    Zyzzyva, Feminist Studies, Hungry Mind Rev*

Dennis Phillips 🎤 ✈ P
Sun & Moon Press, 6026 Wilshire Blvd, Los Angeles, CA
90036, 213-857-1115
    Pubs: *Study for the Ideal City* (Seeing Eye Bks, 1999), *20
    Questions* (Jahbone, 1992), *Credence, From the Other Side
    of the Century: Anth, Arena, A World* (Sun & Moon Pr, 1996,
    1995, 1992, 1989), *The Hero Is Nothing* (Kajun Pr, 1985),
    Ribot, Rhizome, Volt

Susan Lewis Policoff P&W
2807 Milvia St
Berkeley, CA 94703
    Pubs: *Love's Shadow* (Crossing Pr, 1993), *Life on the Line*
    (Negative Capability, 1993), *Folio, Reed, Sequoia, Oxygen,
    Other Voices, First/For Women*

James Polster   W
3311 Mandeville Canyon Rd
Los Angeles, CA 90049, 310-471-1805
    Pubs: *Brown* (Longstreet Pr, 1995), *A Guest in the Jungle*
    (Mercury Hse, 1987), *Smoke, New Orleans Rev*

Melinda Popham   W
12179 Greenock Ln
Los Angeles, CA 90049, 310-471-4336
    Pubs: *Skywater* (Graywolf, 1990), *A Blank Book* (Bobbs-
    Merrill, 1974)

Michael Porges   P
850 Tucson Ct
San Dimas, CA 91773-1852
    Pubs: *Songs, Portraits, Poems, Songs out of Season*
    (Landor Pr, 1981, 1979), *Verve*

Paul C. Portuges   P
3888 Fairfax Rd
Santa Barbara, CA 93110, 805-682-2060
    Pubs: *Paper Song* (Ross-Erikson, 1984), *The Turquoise
    Mockingbird of Light* (Mudborn, 1979), *Eye*

Evelyn Posamentier   P
210 Hoffman Ave
San Francisco, CA 94114-3128, 415-285-0477
Internet: eposamentier@yahoo.com
    Pubs: *Bittersweet Legacy: Anth* (U Pr America, 2001),
    Ghosts of the Holocaust: Anth (Wayne State U Pr, 1989),
    *Processed World, APR, Chrysalis, Mississippi Rev, NYC Big
    City Lit*

Jonathan V. Post   P&W
3225 N Marengo Ave
Altadena, CA 91001, 818-398-1673
    Pubs: *Project Solar Sail* (NAL, 1990), *Nebula Awards Anth
    23* (HBJ, 1989), *Amazing Stories, Analog, Fantasy Book,
    Omni, Quantum, Science*

Holly Prado 🎤 ✈   P&W
1256 N Mariposa Ave
Los Angeles, CA 90029-1416, 213-664-3640
    Pubs: *Esperanza, Specific Mysteries* (Cahuenga Pr, 1998,
    1990), *Gardens* (HBJ, 1985), *Grand Passion: Anth* (Red
    Wind Bks, 1995), *Exquisite Corpse, Denver Qtly, Kenyon
    Rev, Colorado Rev, Poetry Intl, Tule Rev*

Ralph E. Pray 🎤 ✈   W
805 South Shamrock
Monrovia, CA 91016, 626-357-6511
    Pubs: *Jingu-The Hidden Princess* (Shen's Bks, 2002),
    *Reflections Lit Jrnl, Philae, New Authors Jrnl, Writers of the
    Desert Sage, Evenki News, Vintage NW, Tucumcari Lit Rev,
    Acorn, Thalia, Ralph's Rev, Timber Creek Rev, Lynx Eye,
    Writer's Gazette*

Jean Pumphrey 🎤 ✈   P
650 Main St
Sausalito, CA 94965-2338, 415-332-5436
Internet: atp397@cs.com
    Pubs: *Sheltered at the Edge* (Solo Pr, 1982), *Beside the
    Sleeping Maiden: Anth* (Arctos Pr, 1997), *Stones & Amulets:
    Anth* (Wordsworth, 1996)

Barbara Quick   P&W
17 Edgecroft Rd
Kensington, CA 94707-1412
Internet: bqwriter@aol.com
    Pubs: *Northern Edge: A Novel of Survival in Alaska's Arctic*
    (HC West, 1994), *Ms.*

Leroy V. Quintana 🎤 ✈   P
9230-C Lake Murray
San Diego, CA 92119-1471, 619-589-1171
Internet: thequintanas@aol.com
    Pubs: *Great Whirl of Exile* (Curbstone Pr, 1999), *My Hair
    Turning Gray Among Strangers, History of Home* (Bilingual
    Pr, 1995, 1993), *Interrogations* (Viet Nam Generation,
    1992), *Ploughshares, Progressive, Prairie Schooner, Puerto
    del Sol*

Frederick A. Raborg, Jr.   P&W
329 E St
Bakersfield, CA 93304-2031, 661-323-4064
Internet: amelia@lightspeed.net
    Pubs: *Posing Nude, Hakata, Tule* (Amelia Pr, 1989, 1988,
    1986), *Westways, Cimarron Rev, Tendril, Crazyquilt, Prairie
    Schooner*

Charles Radke 🎤   W
9695 N 10th St
Fresno, CA 93720
Internet: chuckradke@hotmail.com
    Pubs: *Gulf Stream Mag, Hayden's Ferry Rev, South
    Dakota Rev*

Rebecca Radner 🎤 ✈   P
3025 Steiner, #12
San Francisco, CA 94123-3911, 415-563-8746
Internet: rebecca@differentpsychic.com
    Pubs: *What Book!?: Anth* (Parallax Pr, 1998), *Harvard Mag,
    NER/BLQ, Berkeley Poets' Co-op, Iowa Rev, Minnesota Rev,
    California Qtly, Central Park, Caliban*

Sheila Raeschild 🎤 ✈   P&W
17105 El Camino Real
Encinitas, CA 92024-4956, 760-632-1910
Internet: child@cybermesa.com
    Pubs: *Earth Songs* (NAL, 1984), *The Defiant* (Dell, 1982),
    Trolley Song (Zebra, 1981), *Spectral Line: Anth* (IAIA, 2000),
    Redbook

Louise Rafkin W
5846 Vallejo St
Oakland, CA 94608, 510-595-3393
www.louiserafkin.com
  Pubs: *Other People's Dirt* (Algonquin Bks, 1998), *Queer & Pleasant Danger: Writing Out My Life, Different Mothers: Anth* (Cleis Pr, 1992, 1991)

James Ragan 🎤 ✈ P
1516 Beverwil Dr
Los Angeles, CA 90035-2911, 310-277-1914
  Pubs: *Lusions, The Hunger Wall* (Grove Pr, 1996, 1995), *Womb Weary* (Carol Pub, 1990), *Ohio Rev, Antioch Rev, NAR, Poetry, Nation*

Carl Rakosi 🎤 ✈ P
1464 17th Ave
San Francisco, CA 94122-3403, 415-566-3425
  Pubs: *The Old Poet's Tale, The Earth Suite* (England: Etruscan Bks, 1999, 1997), *Poems 1923-1941* (Sun & Moon Pr, 1995), *Collected Poems, Collected Prose* (Nat Poetry Fdn, 1986, 1983), *American Poetry: Anth* (LOA, 2000)

Karen Randlev Smith 🎤 ✈ P
390 Carrera Drive
Mill Valley, CA 94941, 415-389-1534
  Internet: Rrs42@cornell.edu
  Pubs: *Light Runner* (Fireweed Pr, 1987), *The Last New Land: Anth* (Alaska Northwest Bks, 1996), *A New Geography of Poets: Anth* (U Arkansas Pr, 1992), *Exquisite Corpse, CSM*

Jack Random 🎤 ✈ W
541 Hunter Ave
Modesto, CA 95350, 209-524-8148
  Pubs: *The Ghost Dance Insurrection* (Dry Bones Pr, 2000), *Lynx Eye, Mobius, AIM*

Jerry Ratch 🎤 ✈ P&W
6065 Chavot Rd
Oakland, CA 94618, 510-428-2660
  Pubs: *Wild Dreams of Reality* (Creative Arts Bks, 2001), *Light* (O Bks, 1990), *How the Net Is Gripped: Anth* (Stride, 1992), *Avec, Tight, Sonoma Mandala, Carolina Qtly, Contact II, Seems*

Stephen Ratcliffe P
Mills College, 5000 MacArthur Blvd, Oakland, CA 94613, 510-430-2245
  Internet: sratcliff@mills.edu
  Pubs: *Sculpture* (Littoral Bks, 1996), *Present Tense* (The Figures, 1995), *Conjunctions, Talisman, Chain, New American Writing, o.blek, Avec*

Susan Rawlins P
1517 Ada St
Berkeley, CA 94703, 510-527-1244
  Pubs: *Grand Street, Shenandoah, Zyzzyva, Feminist Studies, The Qtly, Poet & Critic*

Gg Re P
PO Box 191261
San Francisco, CA 94119-1261, 415-626-6298
  Internet: gg.re@writeme.com
  Pubs: *Clerestory, 247, Fanorama, Entropy, Prosodia, Fag Rag*

Dennis J. Reader P
2045 Green Valley Rd
Watsonville, CA 95076, 408-728-1988
  Pubs: *Coming Back Alive* (Avon, 1983), *Virginia Qtly Rev*

Claudia M. Reder P
1488 Foothill Rd
Ojai, CA 93023-1731
  Internet: poart@erols.com
  Pubs: *Chester H. Jones Anth* (Chester H. Jones Fdn, 1985), *Pennsylvania Rev, Nimrod, Quarry West, Kansas Qtly, Poet Lore, NAR, Intl Qtly, Poetry NW, Lit Rev*

Ishmael Reed P&W
PO Box 3288
Berkeley, CA 94703
  Pubs: *The Terrible Threes, The Terrible Twos* (St. Martin's Pr, 1989, 1982), *God Made Alaska for the Indians* (Garland, 1982), *Yardbird Reader*

Diane Reichick P
2058 Ardenwood Ave
Simi Valley, CA 93063
  Pubs: *Color Wheel, Vol No, Verve, Orphic Lute, CQ, Red Dancefloor*

Gay Beste Reineck P
1425 Cole St
San Francisco, CA 94117

Armando B. Rendon P&W
272 Purdue Ave
Kensington, CA 510-524-9291
  Internet: arendon@flash.net
  Pubs: *We Mutually Pledge* (Dallas-Ft Worth SSP Cncl 1978), *Chicano Manifesto* (Macmillan, 1971)

Lois Larrance Requist 🎤 ✈ P&W
PO Box 349
Benecia, CA 94510, 707-746-5070
  Internet: Loqu@aol.com
  Pubs: *A Family: From Fence to Fax Through the Twentieth Century* (NTPWA, 1999), *Alaska Qtly Rev, Black Maria, Connecticut River Rev*

Ingrid Reti 🎤 P
1650 Descanso St
San Luis Obispo, CA 93405-6109, 805-544-3605
  Pubs: *Each in Her Own Way: Anth* (Queen of Swords Pr, 1994), *We Speak for Peace: Anth* (KIT, 1993), *Mindprints, Iowa Woman, Portlandia,*

Doug Rice   W
California State U English Dept., 6000 J St, Sacramento, CA
95819-6075, 916-278-5989
Internet: rice@salem.kent.edu
   Pubs: *Blood of Mugwump* (Black Ice Bks, 1996), *Avant-
   Pop: Anth* (Illinois State U, 1993), *collages & bricolages, 2
   Girls Rev, Black Ice Mag, Spitting Image, Fiction Intl, New
   Novel Rev*

Marilee Richards   P
1725 San Jose Ave
Alameda, CA 94501, 510-865-2533
   Pubs: *Poetry NW, National Forum, The Jrnl, Lit Rev,
   Sou'wester, Cimarron Rev, Poet Lore*

Cena Golder Richeson 🎤 ✈   W
PO Box 268
Knightsen, CA 94548
   Pubs: *Tombstone Epitaph, Horse Tales: Anth* (Wordware,
   1994), *The West That Was: Anth* (Random Hse, 1993),
   Daughters of Our Land: Anth (Maverick Pub, 1988)

Steve Richmond   P
137 Hollister Ave
Santa Monica, CA 90405, 213-396-1996

John M. Ridland 🎤 ✈   P
1725 Hillcrest Rd
Santa Barbara, CA 93103-1844, 805-965-9613
Internet: jridland@silcom.com
   Pubs: *John the Valiant* (Budapest; Corrina Pr, 1999), *Life
   with Unkie* (Mille Grazie Pr, 1999), *Palms* (Buckner Pr,
   1993), *Poems of the American West: Anth* (Everyman,
   2002), *Solo, The Formalist, Into the Teeth of the Wind,
   Hudson Rev, Sticks, Light, Overland*

Agnes Riedmann   W
233 W Morris Ave
Modesto, CA 95354
   Pubs: *The Story of Adamsville* (Wadsworth Publishing Co,
   1977), *Dismal River Rev, Intro*

Tom Riley   P
1441 Brown St
Napa, CA 94559
   Pubs: *Writing Poems: Anth* (Little, Brown, 1987), *Byline, Art
   Times, Dialogue, The Lyric, The Formalist, Blue Unicorn*

Stuart Robbins   P&W
660 Santa Ray Ave
Oakland, CA 94610
   Pubs: *Poetry Now, Berkeley Poet's Co-op, Paragraph,
   Amazing Stories, Berkeley Poetry Rev, Ararat*

Doren Robbins   P
4161 Alla Rd
Los Angeles, CA 90066
Internet: pantagruli@aol.com
   Pubs: *The Donkey's Tale* (Red Wind Pr, 1998), *Driving Face
   Down* (Eastern Washington Univ, 2001), *Under the Black
   Moth's Wings* (Ameroot Pr, 1988), *Sympathetic Manifesto*
   (Perivale Pr, 1987), *APR, Sulphur, 5am, Indiana Rev*

Gillian Roberts 🎤 ✈   W
PO Box 423
Tiburon, CA 94920
Internet: judygilly@aol.com
   Pubs: *Whatever Doesn't Kill You* (St. Martin's Pr, 2001), *Adam
   and Evil, Helen Hath No Fury* (Ballantine Bks, 2000, 1999)

Lillian S. Robinson   P
1520 O'Farrell St
San Francisco, CA 94115, 415-567-4195
   Pubs: *The Old Life* (SUNY Buffalo, 1977)

Shelba Cole Robison   W
PO Box 6359
Los Osos, CA 93412, 805-528-4182
Internet: dwcs90a@prodigy.com
   Pubs: *Appalachian Heritage, Pembroke Mag, Poughkeepsie*

Alfred A. Robles   P
520 6th Ave
San Francisco, CA 94118, 415-387-5783
   Pubs: *Rappin' With Ten Thousand Carabaos in the Dark*
   (U California Pr, 1996), *Looking for Ifugao Mountain*
   (Children's Pr, 1976), *Amerasia Jrnl, Bridge*

Aleida Rodriguez   P
1811 Baxter St
Los Angeles, CA 90026-1935, 323-953-6372
Internet: areditor@pacbell.net
   Pubs: *Garden of Exile* (Sarabande, 1999), *Not for the
   Academy: Anth* (Only Women Pr, 1999), *Sleeping With One
   Eye Open* (Georgia Pr, 1999), *In Short: Anth* (Norton, 1996),
   Grand Passion: Anth (Red Wind Bks, 1995), *Ploughshares,
   Prairie Schooner, Kenyon Rev*

Zack Rogow 🎤 ✈   P
541 Hill St #A
San Francisco, CA 94131
Internet: zrogow@uclink.berkeley.edu
   Pubs: *Greatest Hits: 1979-2002* (Pudding Hse Pubs, 2002),
   The Selfsame Planet (Mayapple Pr, 1999), *San Francisco
   Bay Area Poets: Anth* (A Small Garlic Pr, 1998), *Runes,
   Illya's Honey, APR, Left-Hand Maps*

Richard Ronan   P
4845 17 St
San Francisco, CA 94117
   Pubs: *A Radiance Like Wind or Water, Narratives From
   America* (Dragon Gate Bks, 1984, 1982), *APR*

Wendy Rose ♦ ✈   P
41070 Lilley Mountain Dr
Coarsegold, CA 93614-9622, 209-658-8018
Internet: lostcooper@yahoo.com
 Pubs: *Itch Like Crazy, Bone Dance: New & Selected Poems*
 (U Arizona Pr, 2002, 1994), *Now Poof She Is Gone*
 (Firebrand Pr, 1994), *Going to War With All My Relations*
 (Northland Pr, 1993)

Gerald Rosen ♦ ✈   W
320 Winfield St
San Francisco, CA 94110-5512, 415-648-2140
Internet: jerrydutch@aol.com
 Pubs: *Growing Up Bronx, Mahatma Gandhi in a Cadillac*
 (North Atlantic Bks, 2000, 1995), *Carmen Miranda
 Memorial Flagpole* (Avon, 1978)

Sylvia Rosen ♦ ✈   P
5445 Sawmill Rd, #A
Paradise, CA 95969-5926
Internet: Srosen@Saber.net
 Pubs: *Dreaming the Poem, A Dream Journal* (Red Wind
 Bks, 1994), *Stand-Up Poetry: Anth* (USCLB Pr, 1994),
 Butte Beast

Lee Rossi   P
1341 Centinela Ave, #103
Santa Monica, CA 90404, 213-453-6303
 Pubs: *Grand Passion: Anth* (Red Wind Bks, 1995), *Beyond
 Rescue* (Bombshelter Pr, 1991), *Apalachee Qtly, Chelsea,
 Bakunin, Faultline, Poetry East, L.A. Times*

Alexis Rotella   P
16651 Marchmont Dr
Los Gatos, CA 95032-5608
 Pubs: *Looking for a Prince* (Jade Mountain Pr, 1991), *Haiku
 Moment: Anth* (Tuttle, 1993), *Blue Mesa Rev, New Letters,
 Median Literary Rev*

Jerome Rothenberg ♦ ✈   PP&P
1026 San Abella
Encinitas, CA 92024-3948, 619-436-9923
Internet: jrothenb@ucsd.edu
 Pubs: *A Paradise of Poets, Seedings & Other Poems* (New
 Directions, 1999, 1996), *A Book of the Book: Anth* (Granary
 Bks, 2000), *Poems for the Millennium: Anth* (U California Pr,
 1998, 1995), *Samizdat, Jacket, Sulfur, Conjunctions, Poesie*

Eugene Ruggles   P
106 Washington St, #326
Petaluma, CA 94952-2308
 Pubs: *The Lifeguard in the Snow* (U Pitt Pr, 1977),
 Passages North: Anth (Milkweed Edtns, 1990), *Poetry Now,
 New Yorker, Poetry, Nation, Manoa, Poetry NW, Field*

Jean Ryan ♦   W
1000 Stonybrook Dr
Napa, CA 94558, 707-226-8603
 Pubs: *Massachusetts Rev, Potpourri, Artisan, Other Voices,
 Pleiades, Lynx Eye, Evergreen Chronicles*

Kay Ryan ♦ ✈   P
60 Taylor Dr
Fairfax, CA 94930-1237, 415-453-2059
 Pubs: *Say Uncle, Elephant Rocks* (Grove Pr, 2000, 1996),
 Flamingo Watching (Copper Beech Pr, 1994), *New Yorker,
 Atlantic, New Republic, Paris Rev, Georgia Rev, Yale Rev*

Michael Ryan ♦ ✈   P
Univ California, English Dept, Irvine, CA 92697-0001,
949-824-8773
Internet: mryan@uci.edu
 Pubs: *Secret Life* (Vintage, 1995), *God Hunger* (Viking,
 1989), *In Winter* (HRW, 1981), *Threats Instead of Trees*
 (Yale, 1974)

Floyd Salas ♦ ✈   P&W
1206 Delaware St
Berkeley, CA 94702-1407, 510-527-2594
www.floydsalas.com
 Pubs: *Color of My Living Heart, State of Emergency, What
 Now My Love, Buffalo Nickel* (Arte Publico Pr, 1996, 1996,
 1994, 1992), *Tattoo the Wicked Cross* (Second Chance Pr,
 1982)

Rachel Salazar ♦ ✈   W
PO Box 6173
Albany, CA 94706-6173
 Pubs: *Spectator: A Novel* (Fiction Collective, 1986), *Chick-
 Lit 2: Anth* (FC2, 1996), *Mondo Elvis: Anth* (St. Martin's Pr,
 1994), *American Letters & Commentary*

Dixie Salazar ♦ ✈   P&W
704 E Brown
Fresno, CA 93704-5509, 559-227-6914
 Pubs: *Reincarnation of the Commonplace* (Salmon Run Pr,
 1999), *Limbo* (White Pine Pr, 1995), *Hotel Fresno* (Blue
 Moon, 1988), *Unsettling America: Anth* (Viking, 1994)

Dennis Saleh ♦ ✈   P
1996 Grandview
Seaside, CA 93955-3203, 831-394-4288
 Pubs: *This Is Not Surrealism* (Willamette River Bks, 1993),
 First Z Poems (Bieler Pr, 1980), *Prarie Schooner, Pearl,
 Psychological Perspectives, Social Anarchism, Artlife,
 Ozone, Bitter Oleander, Nedge, Poetry, Paris Rev, Happy*

Mark Salerno   P
PO Box 3749
Los Angeles, CA 90078-3749
 Pubs: *Hate* (96 Tears Pr, 1995), *Exquisite Corpse, Ribot,
 Arshile, Oxygen, Galley Sail Rev, First Intensity, Apex of the
 M, Explosive, Membrane, Mike & Dale's Younger Poets*

Louis Omar Salinas   P
2009 9th St
Sanger, CA 93657, 209-875-4747
  Pubs: *Follower of Dusk* (Flume Pr, 1991), *Sadness of Days*
  (Arte Publico Pr, 1989)

Benjamin Saltman   P
English Dept, California State Univ, Northridge, CA 91330,
818-885-3431
  Pubs: *Deck* (Ithaca Hse, 1980), *The Leaves the People* (Red
  Hill Pr, 1974), *Event, Hudson Rev*

Steve Sanfield 🎤 ✈   P
22000 Lost River Rd
Nevada City, CA 95959-8559, 530-292-3353
Internet: sands@oro.net
  Pubs: *Bit by Bit* (Penguin Putnam, 1999), *In One Year & Out
  the Other, American Zen by a Guy Who Tried It* (Larkspur Pr,
  1999, 1994), *No Other Business Here* (La Alameda Pr,
  1999), *The Great Turtle Drive* (Knopf, 1996), *The Girl Who
  Wanted a Song* (HB, 1996)

R. A. Sasaki 🎤 ✈   W
5916 Santa Cruz Ave
Richmond, CA 94804
Internet: rasasaki@aol.com
  Pubs: *The Loom & Other Stories* (Graywolf Pr, 1991),
  Selected Shorts: Anth (Radio; NPR, 1994), *Pushcart Prize:
  Anth* (Pushcart Pr, 1992), *Story*

Shelley Savren 🎤 ✈   P
317 S Seaward Ave
Ventura, CA 93003
Internet: poets@jetlink.net
  Pubs: *Solo Pr, Poet Mag, Santa Clara Rev, Hawaii Pacific
  Rev, Lucid Stone, ArtLife, Illya's Honey, Buckle &, Blue
  Violin*

Minas Savvas   P
San Diego State Univ, English & Comparative Literature, San
Diego, CA 92182, 619-582-5873
  Pubs: *The House Vacated* (Parentheses Series, 1989),
  TriQtly, Seneca Rev, Antioch Rev, APR

Eliot Schain   P&W
1338 Santa Fe Ave
Berkeley, CA 94702, 510-527-2831
  Pubs: *American Romance* (Zeitgeist, 1989), *APR,
  Ploughshares, ACM, Mothering, Stone Country*

Gilbert Schedler   P
Univ of the Pacific, Stockton, CA 95211, 209-946-2161
  Pubs: *Starting Over* (Pisces Pr, 1992), *Waking Before Dawn*
  (Wampeter Pr, 1978), *CQ, Blue Unicorn, Christian Century,
  California English, Minotaur, The Windless Orchard*

Linda Scheller   P
3125 Freitas Rd
Newman, CA 95360
  Pubs: *Poem, Aethlon, Notre Dame Rev, Ledge, Seattle Rev,
  Wisconsin Rev, Poetry East*

James Schevill 🎤 ✈   P&W
1309-1311 Oxford St
Berkeley, CA 94709-1424, 510-845-2802
  Pubs: *New & Selected Poems, The Complete American
  Fantasies* (Swallow/Ohio U Pr, 2000, 1996)

Tom Schmidt   P
8036 California Ave
Fair Oaks, CA 95628
  Pubs: *Watching From the Sky: Anth* (Pinyon Pine Pr, 1989),
  The Salmon, Pinchpenny, Poet News

Dennis Schmitz 🎤 ✈   P
1348 57th St
Sacramento, CA 95819-4242, 916-456-6641
  Pubs: *The Truth Squad* (Copper Canyon, 2002), *About Night*
  (Field Edtns, 1993), *Eden* (U Illinois Pr, 1989), *Singing,
  String* (Ecco Pr, 1985, 1980)

Darrell g. h. Schramm   P&W
101 Benson Ave
Vallejo, CA 94590, 415-221-8779
Internet: schrammd@usfca.edu
  Pubs: *A Member of the Family: Anth* (Dutton, 1992),
  Silences, Bones & Angled Rain (Bogota, 1974), *Alaska Qtly
  Rev, Pittsburgh Qtly, Carolina Qtly, Illinois Rev, North
  Dakota Qtly*

Ruth Wildes Schuler   P&W
94 Santa Maria Dr
Novato, CA 94947-3737
  Pubs: *Mistress of the Darkened Rooms & Other Short
  Stories, Shades of Salem* (Heritage Trails, 1988, 1988),
  *Greens Mag, Kavita India, Potpourri, Tears in the Fence,
  Yomimono, Timber Creek Rev*

Carol Schwalberg 🎤 ✈   P&W
629 Palisades Ave
Santa Monica, CA 90402-2723, 310-451-0098
Internet: cschwalberg@aol.com
  Pubs: *Am I Teaching Yet: Anth* (Heinemann, 2002), *Sailing
  on Land: Anth* (New Voices, 1993), *If I Had My Life to Live
  Over I Would Pick More Daisies: Anth* (Papier-Mache Pr,
  1992), *Krax, Potpourri, The Sunday Suitor, West, Wordplay,
  Black River Rev*

Ruth L. Schwartz 🎙 ✈   P
6035 Majestic Ave
Oakland, CA 94605, 510-333-3572
Internet: ruthpoet@aol.com
  Pubs: *Edgewater* (HC, 2002), *Singular Bodies* (Anhinga Pr,
2001), *Accordion Breathing and Dancing* (U Pitt Pr, 1996),
*Prairie Schooner, Chelsea, The Sun, Marlboro Rev, Crab
Orchard Rev*

Leah Schweitzer 🎙 ✈   P&W
23565 Windrose Pl
Valencia, CA 91354, 661-263-6401
Internet: leyeleh@aol.com
  Pubs: *Without a Single Answer* (Judah L. Magnes Museum,
1990), *Only Morning in Her Shoes* (Utah State U Pr, 1990),
*Jewish Women's Literary Annual, Jrnl of the Skirball
Cultural Ctr, Lit Monitor, Apalachee Qtly, Shirim,
Confrontation, Slipstream, CQ*

Edward Scott 🎙 ✈   P
6020-A Adeline
Oakland, CA 94608, 510-594-2467
Internet: GHayes3327@aol.com
  Pubs: *The Metamorphi of the Phenomeni* (Regent Pr, 1998),
The Afterbirth, No Reasonable Explanation Required
(Ebony Juan Pr, 1995, 1991)

James Scully   P
39 Dashiell Hammet St
San Francisco, CA 94108
  Pubs: *Raging Beauty* (Azul Edtns, 1994)

Anna Sears 🎙   W
1440 Guerrero St
San Francisco, CA 94110-4325, 415-285-3136
  Pubs: *Leavenworth Poets Summit* (Hospitality Hse, 2002),
Exile (Goddesses We Ain't Pr, 1996), *Caveat Lector,
Alchemy, Other Voices, Volition One*

Carolyn See 🎙 ✈   W
17339 Tramonto #303
Pacific Palisades, CA 90272
  Pubs: *Making History* (HM, 1991), *Golden Days*

Alison Seevak 🎙 ✈   P
1079 Neilson St.
Albany, CA 94706, 510-528-8964
  Pubs: *What Have You Lost?: Anth* (Greenwillow Bks, 1999),
*The Party Train: A Collection of North American Prose
Poetry: Anth* (New Rivers Pr, 1996), *Atlanta Rev, Many
Mountains Moving, Lilith, Sun, 13th Moon*

Hubert Selby, Jr. 🎙 ✈   W
550 N Orlando, #102
West Hollywood, CA 90048-2547
  Pubs: *Waiting Period, The Willow Tree, Song of the Silent
Snow* (Marion Boyars, 2002, 1998, 1988), *Requiem for a
Dream, The Demon* (Playboy, 1979, 1976), *Last Exit to
Brooklyn* (Grove, 1964)

Bárbara Selfridge 🎙 ✈   W
476 43rd St
Oakland, CA 94609-2138, 510-658-8351
Internet: banterw8@aol.com
  Pubs: *Serious Kissing* (Glad Day Bks, 1999), *Pushcart Prize
XVIII: Anth* (Pushcart Pr, 1994), *Witness, American Voice,
Global City Rev, The Sun, Caribbean Writer, Other Voices*

Peter Serchuk 🎙 ✈   P
10366 Lorenzo Dr
Los Angeles, CA 90064, 310-836-6329
Internet: jjpete@aol.com
  Pubs: *Waiting for Poppa at the Smithtown Diner* (U Illinois
Pr, 1990), *Poetry, Mississippi Rev, NAR, Poem*

Judith Serin 🎙 ✈   P
259 Staples Ave
San Francisco, CA 94112-1836
  Pubs: *Hiding in the World* (Eidolon Edtns, 1998), *Breaking
Up Is Hard to Do: Anth, What's a Nice Girl Like You Doing in
a Relationship Like This?: Anth* (Crossing Pr, 1994, 1992),
Barnabe Mountain Rev

Nina Serrano 🎙 ✈   P
551 Radnor Rd
Oakland, CA 94606, 510-763-8204
Internet: ninaserrano@yahoo.com
  Pubs: *Under the Fifth Sun: Latina Literature from CA: Anth*
(Heyday Bks, 2002), *In Other Words: Lit by Latinas of the
US: Anth* (Arte Publico Pr, 1994), *Madison: The Adventure of
Exile* (Temple U Pr, 1989), *Heart Songs* (Poncho Che, 1980)

Bruce W. Severy   P
827 Oxford Ave
Marina Del Rey, CA 90292-5431, 213-820-4111
  Pubs: *The Woman's Lib* (Plirto Pr, 1979)

Patty Seyburn 🎙 ✈   P
2042-F Santa Ana Ave
Costa Mesa, CA 92627-2178, 949-646-5439
Internet: PSeyburn@aol.com
  Pubs: *Mechanical Cluster* (Ohio State U Pr, 2003),
Diasporadic (Helicon Nine Edtns, 1998), *American Poetry:
Anth* (Carnegie Mellon U Pr, 2000), *American Diaspora:
Anth* (U Iowa Pr, 2000), *Bellingham Rev, Crazyhorse, Gulf
Coast, NER, New Letters, Paris Rev*

Shaka Aku Shango   P&W
c/o Horace Coleman, 334 Gladys Ave, Apt 105, Long Beach,
CA 90814-2431, 714-841-1293
  Pubs: *Incoming* (Island Pubs, 1994), *Between a Rock & a
Hard Place* (BkMk Pr, 1978), *Catalyst, Sacrifice the
Common Sense, New Letters, Iowa Rev, Poets On*

Helen Shanley 🎙 ✈   P&W
6601 Eucalyptus Dr, #97
Bakersfield, CA 93306-6829, 661-366-8693
  Pubs: *Poetry, Cream City Rev, CQ, Ecphorizer, Bohemian
Chronicle', Reach, Arts Connection*

Deirdre Sharett   P
106 Candlewood Dr
Petaluma, CA 94954, 707-763-3850
   Pubs: *Language of a Small Space* (Hartmus Pr, 1980),
   Poetry Now, Footwork, Eleventh Muse, Telephone, Sheaf,
   Star Route Jrnl

Saundra S. Pearl Sharp   P
Poets Pay Rent, Too, PO Box 75796, Sanford Sta, Los
Angeles, CA 90075, 323-993-6006
   Pubs: *On the Sharp Side* (Poets Pay Rent, Too, 1993),
   Black Women for Beginners (Writers & Readers, 1993),
   tenderheaded: Anth (Pocket/ S&S, 2001), *I Hear a*
   Symphony: Anth (Anchor Bks, 1994), *Healthquest, Black*
   Film Rev, Essence, Crisis

Robin Shectman 🎤 ✈   P
3015 Maiden Ln
Altadena, CA 91001
Internet: rshectman@earthlink.net
   Pubs: *Diner, NER, Berkeley Rev, Santa Barbara Rev, Poetry,*
   Amer Scholar, Kenyon Rev, BPJ, Cumberland Poetry Rev,
   Literary Rev, Seneca Rev, Yankee

Marcy Sheiner 🎤 ✈   P&W
PO Box 136, 4096 Piedmont Ave
Oakland, CA 94612
Internet: marquest@earthlink.net
   Pubs: *Aqua Erotica: Anth* (Three Rivers Pr, 2000), *First*
   Light: Anth (Calypso Pub, 1997), *My Story's On: Ordinary*
   Women/Extraordinary Lives: Anth (Common Differences Pr,
   1985), *Five Fingers Rev, Slipstream*

Martha A. Shelley   P
705 Shrader St
San Francisco, CA 94117
   Pubs: *Haggadah: A Celebration of Freedom* (Aunt Lute Bks,
   1997), *Lovers & Mothers* (Sefir Pub, 1981), *Crossing the*
   DMZ (Women's Pr Collective, 1974), *On the Issues,*
   Common Lives/Lesbian Lives, Amazon Qtly

Jack Shields   PP
PO Box 36
Railroad Flat, CA 95248, 209-293-4437
Internet: shieldsmusic@depot.net
   Pubs: *Heritage Festival, Lord Buckley Festival of Poetry &*
   Music, KDVS Radio, Whole Earth Fair

Nancy Shiffrin 🎤 ✈   P
PO Box 1506
Santa Monica, CA 90406
http://home.earthlink.net/~nshiffrin
   Pubs: *What She Could Not Name* (La Jolla Poets Pr, 1987)

P. Shneidre 🎤 ✈   P
6317 Vedanta Terr
Hollywood, CA 90068, 323-463-5683
Internet: tadbooks@earthlink.net
   Pubs: *Thus Spake the Corpse: An Exquisite Corpse Reader*
   1988-1998, Vol I-Poetry & Essays (Black Sparrow Pr, 1999),
   God Stole My Brain, The Idea of Light (Tadbooks, 1995,
   2000), *Zyzzyva, Rolling Stone, Paris Rev, Exquisite Corpse,*
   Antioch Rev

Max Shulman   W
1100 Alta Loma Rd, #1505
Los Angeles, CA 90069

Al Shultz 🎤 ✈   P
1422 Selborn Pl
San Jose, CA 95126-2151, 408-289-9555
Internet: alshultz@earthlink.net
   Pubs: *Phantasm, New Laurel Rev, California Oranges,*
   Sheaf, Dacotah Territory, Mango, Transfer

Aaron Shurin   P
1661 Oak St
San Francisco, CA 94117, 415-552-0991
   Pubs: *Unbound: A Book of AIDS, Into Distances* (Sun &
   Moon Pr, 1997, 1993), *A's Dream* (O Bks, 1989), *Grand*
   Street, Sulfur, Talisman, Hambone

Noelle Sickels 🎤 ✈   P&W
3424 Larissa Dr
Los Angeles, CA 90026-6212
Internet: noelvic@earthlink.net
   Pubs: *The Shopkeeper's Wife, Walking West* (St. Martin's Pr,
   1998, 1995), *The New Menopause Medicine: Anth*
   (Kensington Pubs, 2002), *Autumn Harvest: Anth* (Quill Bks,
   2001), *Exquisite Reaction: Anth* (Andrew Mountain Pr,
   2000), *Switched-On Guttenberg*

Richard Silberg 🎤 ✈   P&W
2140 Haste St
Berkeley, CA 94704-2019, 510-848-5156
   Pubs: *Doubleness* (Roundhouse Pr, 2000), *Totem Pole*
   (3300 Rev Pr, 1996), *The Fields* (Pennywhistle Pr, 1989),
   APR, Denver Qtly, Zyzzyva

John Oliver Simon 🎤 ✈   P
2209 California
Berkeley, CA 94703-1607, 510-549-2456
Internet: josimon@lanminds.com
   Pubs: *Caminante* (Creative Arts Bk Co, 2002), *Velocities of*
   the Possible (Red Dragonfly, 2000), *Puerto del Sol, Runes,*
   Rhino, Turnrow, Zyzzyva, Elysian Fields Qtly, The Temple,
   Two Lines, Poetry Flash, APR

Maurya Simon 🎤 ✈   P
Creative Writing Dept, Univ California Riverside, Riverside, CA
92521-0318, 909-787-2006
Internet: maurya.simon@ucr.edu
    Pubs: *A Brief History of Punctuation* (Sutton Hoo Pr, 2002),
    The Golden Labyrinth (U Missouri Pr, 1995), *Days of Awe,*
    The Enchanted Room (Copper Canyon, 1989, 1986), *New*
    Yorker, Gettysburg Rev, Poetry

Willie Sims 🎤 ✈   PP
11369 Gladstone Ave
Lake View Terrace, CA 91342, 818-899-7209
Internet: slowpokerr@msn.com
    Pubs: *Beyond the Valley of Contemporary Poets: Anth*
    (Sacred Beverage Pr, 1996), *Grand Passion: Poets of Los*
    Angeles: Anth (Red Wind Bks, 1995), *World Stage, Malibu*
    Jewish Ctr, Beverly Hills Library, Beyond Baroque, UCLA
    Wight Art Gallery

Jean Sirius   P
PO Box 9665
Oakland, CA 94613
    Pubs: *And Every One of Us a Witch* (Sirius Bks, 1982),
    Poetry of Sex: Anth (Banned Bks, 1992), *Wanting Women:*
    Anth (Sidewalk Revolution Pr, 1992)

G. P. Skratz   P&W
5524 Vicente Way
Oakland, CA 94609, 510-428-2915
    Pubs: *Sundae Missile* (Generator Pr, 1992), *The Gates of*
    Disappearance (Konglomerati Pr, 1982), *Exquisite Corpse,*
    High Performance, Score, Paragraph

Richard Slota 🎤 ✈   P
1058 Century Dr
Napa, CA 94558-4227, 707-258-0108
Internet: rslota@earthlink
    Pubs: *Famous Michael* (Samisdat Pr, 1989), *Abraxas, Blue*
    Buildings, Plainswoman, Deros, Quercus, Yellow Silk

Edward Smallfield 🎤 ✈   P&W
2466 Hilgard Ave #205
Berkeley, CA 94709, 510-548-0526
Internet: esmallf@aol.com
    Pubs: *The Pleasures of C* (Apogee Pr, 2001), *Trio* (Specter
    Pr, 1995), *Seven Hundred Kisses: Anth* (HarperSF, 1997),
    The Battery Rev, Fourteen Hills, Santa Clara Rev, Zyzzyva,
    Barnabe Mountain Rev, Fiction, Ironwood, Margin, Five
    Fingers Rev, Caliban, Manoa

Rick Smith   P
8591 Hamilton St
Alta Loma, CA 91701
    Pubs: *Hand to Mouth* (Deep Dish, 1981), *Exhibition Game*
    (G Sack Pr, 1973), *Poetry/L.A.*

Steven Phillip Smith   W
1847 S Sherbourne Dr
Los Angeles, CA 90035, 213-559-9370
    Pubs: *American Flyers* (Bantam, 1985), *First Born* (Pocket
    Bks, 1984), *American Boys* (Avon, 1984)

D. James Smith 🎤 ✈   P
62 E Fedora
Fresno, CA 93704-4507
    Pubs: *Fast Company* (DK Ink, 1999), *Prayers for the Dead*
    Ventriloquist (Ahsahta Pr, 1995), *The Qtly, Qtly West, SPR,*
    Carolina Qtly, Green Mountains Rev, Laurel Rev, New
    Virginia Rev, Stand

Lawrence R. Smith 🎤 ✈   P&W
PO Box 561
Laguna Beach, CA 92652-0561
Internet: smithlr@earthlink.net
    Pubs: *Annie's Soup Kitchen, The Map of Who We Are* (U
    Oklahoma Pr, 2003, 1997), *The Plain Talk of the Dead*
    (Montparnasse Edtns, 1988), *River Styx, Paris Rev, Iowa*
    Rev, Pacific Rev

Clifton Snider 🎤 ✈   P
2719 Eucalyptus Ave
Long Beach, CA 90806-2515, 562-426-3669
    Pubs: *Bare Roots, Wrestling With Angels: A Tale of Two*
    Brothers, Loud Whisper, (Xlibris 2001, 2001, 2000), *The*
    Alchemy of Opposites (Chiron Rev, 2000), *The Age of the*
    Mother (Laughing Coyote, 1992), *Impervious to Piranhas*
    (Academic & Arts Pr, 1989)

Gary Snyder   P
English Dept, Univ California, Davis, CA 95616
    Pubs: *No Nature* (Pantheon, 1992), *The Practice of the Wild,*
    Left Out in the Rain (North Point Pr, 1990, 1986), *Yale Rev,*
    Grand Street

Margery Snyder 🎤 ✈   P
PO Box 471493
San Francisco, CA 94147-1493
    Pubs: *The Gods, Their Feathers* (Blue Beetle Pr, 1992),
    Loving Argument (Viridiana, 1991), *The Astrophysicist's*
    Tango Partner Speaks, Bee Hive, Perihelion, Wise Woman's
    Garden, Coracle, Lynx Eye

Mary Ellen Solt   P
25520 Wilde Ave
Stevenson Ranch, CA 91381, 805-287-0089
    Pubs: *The People Mover 1968: A Demonstration Poem*
    (West Coast Poetry Rev, 1978), *A Book of Women Poets*
    From Antiquity to Now: Anth (Schocken Bks, 1980), *Poor*
    Old Tired Horse, Poetry, 13th Moon, Redstart, BPJ

Scott A. Sonders 🎤 ✈   PP&P&W
PO Box 17897
Encino, CA 91416
Internet: media411@earthlink.net
  Pubs: *Boned* (Titan Pr, 2003), *Orange Messiahs* (Yale Pr,
  1999), *Prisoners Rules* (Mangrove, 1998), *Litany* (Caravan
  Pr, 1987), *Meet the People* (Perf; PBS Special, 1995), *Write
  On! Best Short Stories: Anth* (Center Pr, 1995), *Harper's,
  Concordia Rev, LA Times,*

R. Soos, Jr. 🎤 ✈   P
2745 Monterey Rd #76
San Jose, CA 95111-3130, 408-578-3546
Internet: soosict@yahoo.com
  Pubs: *Train of Love, Guitars, Moaning & Groaning,
  California Breeze* (Redwood Family, 2001, 2000, 1999,
  1998), *Garden Songs, The Son Is Breaking Through, His
  Power* (Carpenter's Creative Rev, 1995, 1992, 1988)

Gary Soto   P&W
43 The Crescent
Berkeley, CA 94708-1701, 510-845-4718
  Pubs: *Amnesia in a Republican County, Poetry Lover* (U
  New Mexico Pr, 2003, 2001), *Fearless Fernie* (G.P.
  Putnam's Sons, 2002), *A Natural Man, Junior College*
  (Chronicle Bks, 1999, 1997), *Buried Onions* (HB, 1997)

Lily Iona Soucie   P
619 39th St
Richmond, CA 94805
  Pubs: *Ink Mag, Berkeley Poetry Rev, Lip Service Mag,
  Green's Mag, Crazyquilt Qtly, Earth's Daughters, San
  Francisco Qtly*

Barry Spacks 🎤 ✈   P&W
1111 Bath St
Santa Barbara, CA 93101
Internet: barry.spacks@verizon.net
  Pubs: *Brief Sparrow* (Illuminati, 1988), *Spacks Street* (Johns
  Hopkins, 1982)

Roswell Spafford 🎤 ✈   P
Kresge College, Univ California, Santa Cruz, CA 95064
Internet: rozl@cats.ucsc.edu
  Pubs: *Nimrod, Bellingham Rev, Quarry W, Networks,
  Mississippi Rev, Room*

Rona Spalten   W
6815 Paso Robles
Oakland, CA 94611, 415-339-2978
  Pubs: *New Worlds* (Avon, 1975), *City Miner, Fiction*

Roberta L. Spear   P
3712 E Balch St
Fresno, CA 93702
  Pubs: *The Pilgrim Among Us* (Wesleyan, 1991), *Talking to
  Water* (HRW, 1985), *Ploughshares, Field*

James Spencer 🎤 ✈   P&W
785 Berkeley Ave
Menlo Park, CA 94025, 650-323-0633
Internet: spencerjj@aol.com
  Pubs: *Best Amer Short Stories* (HM, 1999), *The Girl in the
  Black Raincoat: Anth* (Duell, Sloan, Pearce, 1966), *Virginia
  Qtly Rev, Ontario Rev, Gettysburg Rev, ALR, Hawaii Rev,
  Greensboro Rev, BPJ*

Lawrence P. Spingarn   P&W
Perivale Press & Agency, 13830 Erwin St, Van Nuys, CA
91401-2914
  Pubs: *Elegy for Amelia* (Typographeum Bks, 1994), *Journey
  to the Interior, Going Like Seventy* (Perivale Pr, 1992, 1988),
  Sephardic American Voices: Anth (Brandeis U Pr, 1997),
  *Critical Qtly, Harper's, New Yorker, The European,
  Transatlantic Rev*

Leslie Lehr Spirson 🎤   W
22631 Hatteras St
Woodland Hills, CA 91367, 818-348-3084
Internet: toolights@aol.com
  Pubs: *66 Laps* (Villard Bks, 2000)

Susan St. Aubin 🎤 ✈   P&W
5 Pastori Ave
San Anselmo, CA 94960-1815, 415-459-2100
Internet: st_aubin@sfsu.edu
  Pubs: *Best American Erotica: Anth* (S&S, 2003, 2000,
  1995), *Best Women's Erotica: Anth, Ripe Fruit: Anth* (Cleis
  Pr, 2002, 2002), *Herotica 7: Anth* (Down There Pr, 2002),
  Going Down: Anth (Chronicle Bks, 1998)

David St. John 🎤 ✈   P
Univ Southern California, University Park, English Dept, Los
Angeles, CA 90089-0354, 213-740-3748
Internet: dstjohn@usc.edu
  Pubs: *In the Pines, Where the Angels Come Toward Us*
  (White Pine Pr, 1999, 1995), *The Red Leaves of Night,
  Study for the World's Body* (HC, 1999, 1994), *Terraces of
  Rain* (Recursos Bks, 1991)

Mia K. Stageberg 🎤 ✈   W
633 York St
San Francisco, CA 94110
Internet: MiaStageberg@aol.com
  Pubs: *Chameleon 7 1/2, Dream Machinery, Furious Fiction,
  Kameleon, New Directions, Oxygen*

Jayne Lyn Stahl 🎤 ✈   P
208 E. Aliso, #10
Ojai, CA 93023
Internet: jstahl33@aol.com
  Pubs: *The Stiffest of the Corpse: Anth* (City Lights Bks,
  1989), *NYQ, Big Bridge, Sic: Vice & Verse, L.A. Woman,
  Beatitude, Exquisite Corpse, Jacaranda Rev, City Lights
  Rev, Pulpsmith, Big Bridge, Jack Magazine*

Hans Jorg Stahlschmidt 🎤   P&W
1446 Scenic Ave
Berkeley, CA 94708-1834, 510-848-4040
Internet: stahlschmidt@attbi.com
    Pubs: *Wetlands* (Small Poetry Pr, 2002), *The Practice of
    Peace: Anth, XY Files: Anth* (Sherman Asher Publishing,
    1998, 1997), *Anthology of Mag Verse, Yearbook of American
    Verse: Anth* (Monitor Bk Co, 1997, 1997), *Atlanta Rev,
    Cumberland Poetry Rev, Nightsun*

Albert Stainton   P
478 Bartlett St
San Francisco, CA 94110
    Pubs: *The Crossing* (Puckerbrush Pr, 1974), *Paris Rev,
    Poetry, Chelsea, Poetry Now, Wormwood Rev*

Domenic Stansberry   W
4104 24th St, #355
San Francisco, CA 94114, 415-821-7879
    Pubs: *Exit Paradise* (Lynx Hse Pr, 1991), *The Spoiler*
    (Atlantic Monthly Pr, 1987), *Ploughshares, Colorado State
    Rev, Mississippi Mud*

Scott Starbuck 🎤 ✈   P
872 Agate St
San Diego, CA 92109
Internet: cwaterstone@hotmail.com
    Pubs: *The Eyes of Those Who Broke Free* (Pudding Hse
    Pub, 2000), *Storyboard, Black Bear Rev, High Country
    News, Kerf, Going Down Swinging, Wild Earth, The
    Climbing Art, Calapooya Collage, Green Fuse, Mandrake
    Poetry Rev*

Elaine Starkman   P&W
PO Box 4071
Walnut Creek, CA 94596, 925-932-1144
Internet: estarkma@duc.edu
    Pubs: *Learning to Sit in the Silence* (Papier-Mache Pr,
    1993), *Vital Lines* (St. Martin's Pr, 1990), *Shaking Eve's
    Tree: Anth* (Jewish Pub Soc, 1991)

Marian Steele 🎤   P
1371 Marinette Rd
Pacific Palisades, CA 90272-2627, 310-454-1887
Internet: cmszego@ucla.edu
    Pubs: *The American Dream: Anth* (Pig Iron Pr, 1999), *Life
    on the Line: Anth* (Negative Capability Pr, 1992), *Jama, The
    Lyric, Ellipsis, South Dakota Rev, Black Buzzard Rev, Press
    Ltd, New Renaissance, Connecticut River Rev, Poets On*

Timothy Steele 🎤 ✈   P
1801 Preuss Rd
Los Angeles, CA 90035-4313
    Pubs: *All the Fun's in How You Say a Thing* (Ohio U
    Pr/Swallow, 1999), *Sapphics & Uncertainties, Missing Mea-
    sures* (U Arkansas Pr, 1995, 1990), *The Color Wheel* (Johns
    Hopkins U Pr, 1994)

Hannah Stein 🎤 ✈   P
1118 Bucknell Dr
Davis, CA 95616, 530-753-5382
Internet: hannahdstein@aol.com
    Pubs: *Earthlight* (La Questa Pr, 2000), *GRRR: Anth* (Arctos
    Pr,1999), *Schools of Flying Fish* (State Street Pr, 1990),
    *ALR, Amer Voice, BPJ, Calyx, Kalliope, Kansas Qtly, Lit Rev,
    Poetry Flash, Prairie Schooner, Solo*

Julia Stein 🎤   P
5025 Maplewood #16
Los Angeles, CA 90004
Internet: galiastein@earthlink.net
    Pubs: *Shulamith, Walker Woman, Under the Ladder to
    Heaven* (West End, 2002, 2002, 1984), *Desert Soldiers*
    (California Classics, 1992), *Calling Home: Anth* (Rutgers,
    1990), *Ikon, Onthebus, Women's Studies Qtly, Pearl,
    American Book Rev*

Dona Luongo Stein   P
318 Cliff Dr
Aptos, CA 95003
    Pubs: *Heavenly Bodies* (Jacaranda Pr, 1995), *Women of the
    14th Moon* (Crossing Pr, 1994), *Children of the Mafiosi*
    (West End Pr, 1977), *Prairie Schooner*

Gary C. Sterling   P&W
Marshall Secondary School, 990 N Allen Ave, Pasadena, CA
91104, 818-798-0713
    Pubs: *Puerto del Sol, The Clearing House, Oyez Rev, Palo
    Alto Rev, Reading Improvement, Habersham Rev*

Janet Sternburg 🎤 ✈   P
16065 Royal Oak Rd
Encino, CA 91436-3913
Internet: janet.sternburg@calarts.edu
    Pubs: *Prairie Schooner, Cargo, Between Women, Tangled
    Vines*

Doreen Stock 🎤 ✈   P&W
POB 442
Stinson Beach, CA 94970, 415-460-9296
Internet: thesleepinglady@yahoo.com
    Pubs: *The Politics of Splendor* (Alcatraz Edtns, 1984),
    Poetry Greece, Kerem, Redwood Coast Rev, NASHIM

Ben Stoltzfus 🎤 ✈   W
Univ California, Comparative Literature Dept, Riverside, CA
92521, 909-787-5007
    Pubs: *La Belle Captive* (U California Pr, 1995), *Red White &
    Blue* (York Pr, 1989), *The Eye of the Needle* (Viking, 1967),
    *Fiction Intl, NAR, Nobodaddies, North Carolina Qtly,
    Collages & Bricolages, New Novel Rev, Alaluz, Chelsea,
    Mosaic*

Earle Joshua Stone   P
72-685 Haystack Rd
Palm Desert, CA 92260
   Pubs: *Song of the Toad* (Paige Pub, 1989), *Pub Mirrors,
Pine Needles, Arts of Asia Mag, Haiku Headlines, Poetry
Nippon, Intl Art Collectors Mag*

Phyllis Stowell, PhD ♀ ✈   P
1256 Queens Rd
Berkeley, CA 94708-2112
Internet: pstowell@stmarys-ca.edu
   Pubs: *Who Is Alice?* (Pennywhistle, 1989), *Runes,
Psychopoetico, Fourteen Hills, New Orleans Rev, The
Montserat Rev, Pleiades, Slant, APR, Virginia Qtly Rev,
Wallace Stevens Rev, Phoebe, Poet Lore, Volt, Columbia,
International Qtly*

Austin Straus   P
7937 McConnell Ave
Los Angeles, CA 90045
   Pubs: *Drunk With Light* (Red Hen Pr, 2002), *Laureate
Without a Country: Poems 1976-1989* (Ambrosia Pr, 1992),
Hollywood Rev, Slipstream

Jane Strong ♀ ✈   P&W
1720 Spruce St, Apt C
Berkeley, CA 94709-1784, 510-883-0872
   Pubs: *Blue Unicorn, Primavera, Crosscurrents*

Joseph Stroud ♀ ✈   P
144 Hunolt St
Santa Cruz, CA 95060
   Pubs: *Below Cold Mountain* (Copper Canyon Pr, 1998),
Pushcart Prize XXIV: Anth (Pushcart Pr, 2000), *The
Geography of Home: Anth* (Heyday Bks, 1999)

Dorothy Stroup ♀ ✈   W
10 Claremont Crescent
Berkeley, CA 94705-2324, 510-841-9758
Internet: dstroup@uclink4.berkeley.edu
   Pubs: *In the Autumn Wind* (Scribner, 1987)

Denver Stull   P&W
318 Cliff Dr
Aptos, CA 95003, 408-662-0197
   Pubs: *It Only Hurts When I Smile* (Modern Images, 1988),
Women of the 14th Moon: Anth (Crossing Pr, 1991),
Looking for Home: Anth (Milkweed Pr, 1990)

Evelin Sullivan ♀   W
4050 Farm Hill Blvd, #8
Redwood City, CA 94061-1023, 650-367-7770
Internet: evelinsull@aol.com
   Pubs: *Four of Fools, Games of the Blind* (Fromm Intl Pub
Corp, 1995, 1994), *The Dead Magician* (Dalkey Archive Pr,
1989)

Amber Coverdale Sumrall ♀ ✈   P&W
434 Pennsylvania Ave
Santa Cruz, CA 95062-2434, 408-459-9377
Internet: ambers@sasquatch.com
   Pubs: *Litany of Wings* (Many Names Pr, 1998), *Atomic
Ghost* (Coffee House Pr, 1995), *Storming Heaven's Gate:
Anth* (Plume, 1997), *Quarry West*

David Swanger ♀ ✈   P
Univ California—Santa Cruz, 301 Dickens Way, Santa Cruz,
CA 95064, 408-426-1292
Internet: dswanger@cats.ucsc.edu
   Pubs: *Style* (Pudding Hse, 2000), *This Waking Unafraid*
(U Missouri Pr, 1995), *Geography of Home: Anth* (Heyday
Bks, 1999), *Georgia Rev, Poetry NW, Chariton Rev, Kansas
Qtly, Poet & Critic*

Robert Sward ♀ ✈   P&W
435 Meder St
Santa Cruz, CA 95060-2307, 831-426-5247
Internet: sward@bigfoot.com
   Pubs: *Rosicrucian in the Basement, Heavenly Sex* (Black
Moss Pr, 2002, 2002), *A Much Married Man* (Ekstasis
Edtns, 1996), *Four Incarnations: New & Selected Poems*
(Coffee House Pr, 1991), *New Yorker, Paris Rev, Poetry
Chicago*

Robert Burdette Sweet   W
1761 Edgewood Rd
Redwood City, CA 94062

Ruth Swensen ♀   P&W
2587 Daisy Ln
Fallbrook, CA 92028-8479, 760-728-1203
Internet: rswensen3@excite.com
   Pubs: *Magee Park Poets Anth* (Carlsbad Library, 2000),
Tide Pools Anth (Mira Costa College, 1993)

Rob Swigart   P&W
1975 Oak Ave
Menlo Park, CA 92025, 650-323-6061
Internet: rswigart@iftf.org
   Pubs: *Venom, Toxin, Portal* (St. Martin's Pr, 1991, 1989,
1988), *NER, Poetry NW*

Michael Sykes   P
PO Box 276
Cedarville, CA 96104-0276, 530-279-2766
Internet: floatingisalndbooks@citilink.net
   Pubs: *From an Island in Time* (Jungle Garden Pr, 1984), *Lit
Arts Hawaii, Neon, Northern Contours, Barnabe Mountain
Rev, Floating Island, Fallow Deer, Estero*

Luis Salvador Syquia P
574 8th Ave
San Francisco, CA 94118

Barbara Alexandra Szerlip 🎤 ✈ P
532-B Lombard St
San Francisco, CA 94133, 415-398-3112
Pubs: *The Ugliest Woman in the World & Other Histories*
(Gallimaufry, 1978), *The Party Train: A Collection of North
American Prose Poetry: Anth* (New Rivers Pr, 1996),
National Geographic, Elle

Phil Taggart P
PO Box 559
Ventura, CA 93002, 805-672-1756
Internet: ptagga@aol.com
Pubs: *Opium Wars* (Mille Grazie Pr, 1997)

Mark Taksa 🎤 ✈ P
1138 Langlie Court
Rodeo, CA 94572, 510-799-1973
jantaksa2aol.com
Pubs: *Cradlesong* (Pudding Hse Pubs, 1994), *Truant Bather*
(Berkeley Poets Workshop & Pr), *Folio, Laurel Rev,
Greensboro Rev, Phoebe, Cimarron Rev*

William Talcott P
1331 26th Ave
San Francisco, CA 94122, 415-566-3367
Internet: 104174.426@compuserve.com
Pubs: *Benita's Book* (Thumbscrew Pr, 1997), *Kidstuff*
(Norton Coker Pr, 1992), *Calling in Sick* (End of the Century
Bks, 1989), *Exquisite Corpse, NAW, 33 Rev*

Elizabeth Tallent W
Univ California, English Dept, Davis, CA 95616, 916-752-6388
Pubs: *Time With Children, Museum Pieces, In Constant
Flight* (Knopf, 1987, 1985, 1983), *New Yorker*

Judith Tannenbaum 🎤 ✈ P
3120 Yosemite Ave
El Cerrito, CA 94530-3430
Pubs: *In the Crook of Grief's Arm, Songs in the Night*
(Nehama Pr, 1993, 1988), *Poetry Flash, Rattle, Coracle,
100 Words, Tule Rev, Convolvulus*

Carol Tarlen P&W
1001 Bridgeway #729
Sausalito, CA 94965, 415-332-0305
Pubs: *Homeless Not Helpless: Anth* (Canterbury Pr, 1991),
Calling Home: Anth (Rutgers U Pr, 1990), *Exquisite Corpse,
Rain City Rev, Hurricane Alice*

Roger Taus P
1418 Stanford St, #7
Santa Monica, CA 90404-3147
Pubs: *If You Ask Me Where I've Been* (Igneus Pr, 1998),
Poems From the Combat Zone (Tao Anarchy Bks, 1984),
Going for Coffee: Anth (Canada; Harbour Pub, 1981),
Neologisms, Left Curve, Third Rail

Judith Taylor 🎤 ✈ P
3252 Mandeville Canyon Rd
Los Angeles, CA 90049-1016
Internet: judithtay@aol.com
Pubs: *Curios* (Sarabande Bks, 2000), *Burning* (Portlandia
Group, 1999), *Stand Up: Anth* (Iowa, 2002), *Ravishing
DisUnities: Real Ghazals in English: Anth* (Wesleyan, 2000),
Fence, Boston Rev, Prairie Schooner, APR, Crazyhorse,
Antioch Rev, Poetry

Kent Taylor 🎤 ✈ P
1450 10th Ave
San Francisco, CA 94122-3603, 415-665-8073
Pubs: *Night Physics* (Kirpan Pr, 2002), *Rabbits Have Fled,
Late Show at the Starlight Laundry* (Black Rabbit, 1991,
1989), *Rattle, Rattapallax, The Qtly, Abraxas, Onthebus*

Eleanor Wong Telemaque 🎤 ✈ W
1531 12th St
Santa Monica, CA 90401, 310-581-3589
Pubs: *It's Crazy to Stay Chinese in Minnesota* (Thomas
Nelson, 1995), *Haiti Through Its Holidays* (Blyden Pr, 1990)
A, Mei-Li in Minnesota

Susan Terence P
65 Manchester St, #2
San Francisco, CA 94110-5214, 415-995-2659
Pubs: *Nebraska Rev, San Francisco Bay Guardian,
Halftones to Jubilee, SPR, Negative Capability, Lake Effect*

Susan Terris 🎤 ✈ P&W
11 Jordan Ave
San Francisco, CA 94118-2502, 415-386-7333
Internet: sdt11@aol.com
Pubs: *Angels of Bataan, Killing in the Comfort Zone*
(Pudding Hse Pubs, 1999, 1995), *Eye of the Holocaust*
(Arctos Pr, 1999), *Curved Space* (La Jolla Poets Pr, 1998),
Nell's Quilt, Author! Author! (FSG, 1996, 1990), Missouri
Rev, Nimrod, Antioch Rev

Roland Tharp P
307 Dickens Way
Santa Cruz, CA 95064
Pubs: *Highland Station* (Poetry Texas Pr, 1977), *Prairie
Schooner, Hawaii Rev, SW Rev*

Raul Thomas 🎤 ✈ W
116 San Jose St, #2
San Francisco, CA 94110, 415-641-8766
Internet: raulthomasq@aol.com
   Pubs: *Las Caras de la Luna, dicen que soy . . . , y aseguran que estoy* (Spain; Betania, 1996, 1993)

Robert Thomas P
3612 Gilbert Court
South San Francisco, CA 94080
Internet: rwt@kvn.com
   Pubs: *Door to Door* (Fordham U Pr, 2002), *Atlantic Monthly, FIELD, New England Rev, The Paris Rev, Southern Rev, Yale Rev, The Iowa Rev, Kenyon Rev, North Amer Rev, Sewanee Rev*

Joanna Thompson P
1515 Umeo Rd
Pacific Palisades, CA 90272
   Pubs: *Amer Scholar California Qtly, SWRev, New Orleans Rev, Phantasm, America*

Sabina Thorne W
PO Box 1413
Bethel Island, CA 94511-2413
   Pubs: *Of Gravity & Grace* (Janus Pr, 1982), *Reruns* (Viking Pr, 1981)

Sheila Thorne W
1326 Spruce St
Berkeley, CA 94709-1435, 510-848-3826
Internet: MSapir@compuserve.com
   Pubs: *Iris, Writer's Forum, Green Hills Lit Lantern, North Atlantic Review, Literal Latte, Nimrod, Primavera, Stand Mag*

Terry Tierney P
1185 Glencourt Dr
Oakland, CA 94611, 510-339-0704
Internet: ttierney@geoworks.com
   Pubs: *Abraxas, Blue Buildings, California Qtly, Centennial Rev, Chattahoochee Rev, Concerning Poetry, Contact II, Cottonwood Rev, Great River Rev, Kalliope, Kansas Qtly, Milkweed Chronicle, Poetry at 33, Poetry NW, Puerto del Sol, South Dakota Rev*

JoAnn Byrne Todd P
21627 Ocean Vista Dr
South Laguna, CA 92677, 714-499-2112
   Pubs: *Voices Intl, Wind Chimes, Modern Haiku, Pulp, Blue Grass, Literary Rev*

Sotere Torregian P
PO Box 163
San Carlos, CA 94070-3746, 415-592-6079
   Pubs: *The Young Englishwoman* (Printmasters, 1989), *The Age of Gold* (Kulchur Fnd, 1976), *Paris Rev*

Paul Trachtenberg P
9431 Krepp Dr
Huntington Beach, CA 92646, 714-968-7546
   Pubs: *Alphabet Soup: A Laconic Lexicon* (Wordworks, 1997), *Ben's Exit, Making Waves* (Cherry Valley Edtns, 1994, 1990)

Truong Tran P
337 10th Ave, #5
San Francisco, CA 94118
Internet: celan@primenet.com
   Pubs: *Zyzzyva, ACM, American Voice, Crazyhorse, Poetry East, Onthebus, Prairie Schooner, Berkeley Poetry Rev, Blue Mesa Rev, Fourteen Hills, North Dakota Qtly, Reed*

Elizabeth Treadwell 🎤 ✈ P&W
PO Box 9013
Berkeley, CA 94709
Internet: eliztj@hotmail.com
   Pubs: *Chantry* (Chax Pr, 2003), *Populace* (Avec Book, 1999), *Eleanor Ramsey: The Queen of Cups* (San Francisco State U Pr, 1997), *World*

Laurel Trivelpiece P&W
23 Rocklyn Ct
Corte Madera, CA 94925, 415-924-9130
   Pubs: *Just a Little Bit Lost* (Scholastic, 1988), *Blue Holes* (Alice James Bks, 1987), *Poetry*

Quincy Troupe 🎤 ✈ P
1655 Nautilus St
La Jolla, CA 92037-6412, 858-534-3210
   Pubs: *Choruses: New Poems, Avalanche: New Poems* (Coffee Hse Pr, 1999, 1996), *Weather Reports: New & Selected Poems* (Harlem River Pr, 1991) *Tin House, Review: Latin Amer Lit & Arts, Long Shot, Kenyon Rev, Ploughshares, Pequod*

George Tsongas P
57A Boardman Pl
San Francisco, CA 94103
Internet: mtsongas@pacbell.net

Kitty Tsui P
c/o Sheryl B. Fullerton, 1010 Church St, San Francisco, CA 94114, 415-824-8460
Internet: baisve888@aol.com
   Pubs: *Breathless* (Firebrand, 1996)

Mike Tuggle P
PO Box 421
Cazadero, CA 95421, 707-632-5818
   Pubs: *Cazadero Poems* (Floating Island Pub, 1994), *White Heron Rev, Temple, Poetry Flash, Zyzzyva, Manoa, Americas Rev, CPITS Anth, Psychological Perspectives, Floating Island, Slant*

David L. Ulin   P&W
8126 Blackburn Ave
Los Angeles, CA 90048
 Pubs: *Cape Cod Blues* (Red Dust, 1992), *Unbearables:
 Anth* (Autonomedia, 1995), *Exquisite Corpse, Rampike,
 Vignette, Brooklyn Rev, B City, Sensitive Skin*

Charles Upton   P
245 Nova Albion Way
San Rafael, CA 94903-3529, 415-454-2343
 Pubs: *Snake of Mute River* (Artaud's Elbow, 1979), *Panic
 Grass* (City Lights Bks, 1968), *Longhouse*

Amy Uyematsu 🎤 ✈   P
14339 Victory Blvd
Van Nuys, CA 91401
Internet: uyematsua@yahoo.com
 Pubs: *Nights of Fire, Nights of Rain; 30 Miles from J-Town*
 (Story Line Pr, 1998, 1992), *Another City: Anth* (City Lights,
 2001), *Geography of Home: Anth* (Heyday, 1999), *What
 Book?: Anth* (Parallax, 1998)

Lequita Vance-Watkins   P
PO Box 221847
Carmel, CA 93922, 408-624-5068
 Pubs: *White Flash/Black Rain* (Milkweed Edtns, 1995), *Dark
 With Stars* (High Coo Pr, 1984), *Out of the Dark: Anth*
 (Queen of Swords Pr, 1995)

Paul Vangelisti 🎤 ✈   P
1533 Cerro Gordo St
Los Angeles, CA 90026
 Pubs: *Embarrassment of Survival: Selected Poems 1970-
 2000* (Marsilio, 2001), *Nemo* (Sun & Moon Pr, 1995), *Villa*
 (Littoral Bks, 1991)

Jose L. Varela-Ibarra   P
5622 University Ave, #13
San Diego, CA 92105
Internet: j_ibarra@acad.fandm.edu
 Pubs: *Revista Chicano-Riquena, Citybender, Poema
 Convidado, Papeles De La Frontera*

Cherry Jean Vasconcellos 🎤 ✈   P
436 Elmwood Dr
Pasadena, CA 91105-1329, 323-255-1770
 Pubs: *Before Our Very Eyes* (Pearl Edtns, 1997), *L.A.
 Woman: Anth* (Ariel-Verlag, 2000), *Matchbook: Anth, Grand
 Passion: Anth* (Red Wind Bks, 1999, 1995), *Jitters: Anth*
 (Fossil Pr, 1996)

Richard Vasquez   W
3345 Marengo
Altadena, CA 91001, 213-794-9825

Katherine Vaz   W
522 D St
Davis, CA 95616, 530-758-1219
Internet: kavaz@ucdavis.edu
 Pubs: *Mariana* (HC/Flamingo, 1997), *Fado & Other Stories*
 (U Pitt Pr, 1997), *Saudade* (St. Martin's Pr 1994), *Nimrod,
 Gettysburg Rev, American Voice, Other Voices, TriQtly*

Bob Vickery   W
769 Cole St #2
San Francisco, CA 94117, 415-386-3088
Internet: cseiter@concentric.net
 Pubs: *Cock Tales* (Leyland Pub, 1997), *Up All Hours* (Alyson
 Bks, 1997), *Butch Boys, Skin Deep* (Masquerade Bks, 1997,
 1994), *Advocate Men*

Alma Luz Villanueva 🎤 ✈   P
4135 Gladys Ave
Santa Cruz, CA 95062-4507
Internet: almaluzia@cs.com
 Pubs: *Vida* (Wings Pr, 2001), *Luna's California Poppies,
 Desire, Weeping Woman, Naked Ladies, Planet* (Bilingual
 Pr, 2001, 1998, 1994, 1993, 1993), *The Ultraviolet Sky*
 (Doubleday, 1993)

Marianne Villanueva 🎤 ✈   W
2431 Hopkins Ave
Redwood City, CA 94032-2157
Internet: mvillanueva@witty.com
 Pubs: *Tilting the Continent: Anth* (New Rivers Pr, 2000),
 Ginseng & Other Tales From Manila (Calyx Bks, 1991), *The
 Nuyorasian Anth, Flippin: Filipinos in America: Anth* (AAWW,
 1998, 1996), *Charlie Chan Is Dead: Anth* (Viking, 1993)

Victor Edmundo Villasenor   W
Rancho Villasenor, 1302 Stewart St, Oceanside, CA 92054,
619-454-1550
 Pubs: *Walking Star* (Arte Publico Pr, 1994), *Rain of Gold*
 (Dell, 1992), *Jury* (Little, Brown, 1978), *Macho* (Bantam,
 1973)

Stephen Vincent   P
3514 21st St
San Francisco, CA 94114, 415-641-0739
Internet: steph484@aol.com
 Pubs: *Walking* (Junction Bks, 1993)

Gerald Robert Vizenor   P
American Studies, Univ California, 301 Campbell Hall,
Berkeley, CA 94720, 510-642-6593
Internet: vizenor@uclink4.berkeley.edu
 Pubs: *Chancers* (U Oklahoma Pr, 2001), *Fugitive Poses*
 (U Nebraska Pr, 1998), *Hotline Healers* (Wesleyan U Pr,
 1997)

Eric B. Vogel   P
29190 Verdi Rd
Hayward, CA 94544, 510-538-1638
Internet: erichv@tdl.com
    Pubs: *Antigonish Rev, Stand, Envoi, Poetry Motel,
    Encodings, Sublime Odyssey, Raindog Rev, Mobius,
    Parting Gifts*

Arthur Vogelsang 🎤 ✈   P
1730 N Vista St
Los Angeles, CA 90046-2235, 323-874-2220
    Pubs: *Left Wing of a Bird* (Sarabande, 2003), *Cities & Towns*
    (U Mass Pr, 1996), *Twentieth Century Women* (U Georgia
    Pr, 1988), *A Planet* (H Holt, 1983)

Christy Wagner 🎤 ✈   W
PO Box 1628
Mendocino, CA 95460-1628, 707-964-0350
Internet: cwagner@mcn.org
    Pubs: *Mustang Je T'aime* (Gorde Plata Pr, 1996)

Marilyn Schoefer Wagner 🎤 ✈   W
PO Box 860
Fort Bragg, CA 95437-0860, 707-964-5063
Internet: mwagner@mcn.com
    Pubs: *Cats & Other Tales:* (Genesis Pr, 1999), *Coast Mag,
    OutLook*

Jeanne Wagner   P
23 Edgecroft Rd
Kensington, CA 94707, 510-526-4190
    Pubs: *Denny Poems, Ekphrasis, Poet's Guild, Blue Unicorn,
    Lucid Stone, Silver Quill, Spoon River*

John Walke   W
5671 E Waverly Ln
Fresno, CA 93727-5437, 209-456-9255
    Pubs: *Nethula Jrnl, Pulp, Apalachee Qtly, Bachy, Bridge,
    Backwash, Second Coming, Tandava*

Mary Alexander Walker   W
PO Box 151615
San Rafael, CA 94915, 415-461-1025
    Pubs: *Scathach & Maeve's Daughters, Brad's Box, Maggot,
    To Catch a Zombie* (Atheneum, 1990, 1988, 1980, 1979)

David Foster Wallace   W
Frederick Hill Assoc, 1842 Union St, San Francisco, CA 94123
    Pubs: *Girl With Curious Hair* (Norton, 1989), *Broom of the
    System* (Viking, 1987), *Harper's*

William Wallis 🎤 ✈   P
English Dept, Los Angeles Valley College, 5800 Fulton Ave,
Van Nuys, CA 91401-4062, 818-781-1200
Internet: walliswg@laccd.cc.ca.us
    Pubs: *Selected Poems 1969-99, Dutton's Books, Eros*
    (Stone & Scott Pubs, 2000, 1995, 1994), *Biographer's Notes*
    (Yellow Barn Pr, 1984)

Diane Ward 🎤 ✈   P
1023 Centinela Ave
Santa Monica, CA 90403-2315, 310-828-1060
Internet: dianeward@yahoo.com
    Pubs: *Portrait As If Through My Own Voice* (Margin to
    Margin, 2001), *Portraits & Maps* (NLF editori, 2000), *Human
    Ceiling* (Roof Bks, 1996)

Paul Watsky   P
1966 Green St
San Francisco, CA 94123
www.paulwatskypoetry.com
    Pubs: *More Questions Than Answers* (tel-let, 2001),
    Countless Leaves: Anth (Inkling Pr, 2001), *A New
    Resonance: Anth, The Red Moon Anth* (Red Moon Pr, 2000,
    2000, 1998, 1997, 1996), *Poetry Flash, Cream City Rev,
    Modern Haiku, Frogpond, Convolvulus, Tundra*

Lynn Watson 🎤 ✈   P&W
PO Box 1253
Occidental, CA 95465-1253
Internet: isabell@sonic.net
    Pubs: *Catching the Devil* (Keegan Pr, 1994), *Amateur Blues*
    (Taurean Horn Pr, 1990), *Oxygen*

Charles Harper Webb 🎤 ✈   P&W
English Dept, California State Univ, 1250 Bellflower Blvd, Long
Beach, CA 90840, 562-985-4244
Internet: cwebb@csulb.edu
    Pubs: *Tulip Farms and Leper Colonies* (BOA Edtns, 2001),
    Liver (U Wisconsin Pr, 1999), *Reading the Water*
    (Northeastern U Pr, 1997), *Stand Up Poetry: An Expanded
    Anth* (U Iowa Pr, 2002), *Best Amer Poetry, Pushcart Prize,
    Paris Rev, APR, Ploughshares*

Brenda Webster   W
2671 Shasta Rd, Berkeley, CA 94708
Internet: brenda1@well.com
    Pubs: *Paradise Farm* (SUNY Pr, 1999), *Tattoo Bird* (Fiction
    Net, 1996), *Sins of the Mothers* (Baskerville Pr, 1993)

Richard J. Weekley 🎤 ✈   P
24721 Newhall Ave
Newhall, CA 91321-1729, 661-254-5215
    Pubs: *The Scrubwoman, Small Diligences* (L.A. Poets Pr,
    2001, 1988), *Mayan Night* (Domina Bks, 1981), *These
    Things Happen: Anth* (Inevitable Pr, 1997), *Blue Buildings,
    Crosscurrents, Gryphon, Kansas Qtly, Poetry/L.A., Literary
    Rev*

Florence Weinberger 🎤 ✈   P
29500 Heathercliff Rd #168
Malibu, CA 90265, 310-457-5511
Internet: flopetw@earthlink.net
    Pubs: *The Invisible Telling Its Shape* (Fithian Pr, 1997),
    Breathing Like a Jew (Chicory Blue Pr, 1997), *Grand
    Passion: Anth* (Red Wind Bks, 1995), *Truth & Lies That
    Press for Life: Anth* (Artifact Pr, 1991), *Solo, Lit Rev, Art/Life,
    Tikkun, ACM, Calyx*

Kenneth Weisner P
528 Windham St
Santa Cruz, CA 95062, 831-426-5172
Internet: weisnerken@fhda.edu
  Pubs: *The Sacred Geometry of Pedestrians* (Hummingbird
  Pr, 2002), *Porter Gulch Rev, Oyez, Berkeley Poetry Rev,
  Brooklyn Rev, Antioch Rev, Lighthouse Point, Eye Prayers,
  New Honolulu Rev*

ruth weiss 🎤 ✈ P
PO Box 509
Albion, CA 95410-0509, 707-937-5619
www.leftcoastart.com
  Pubs: *A New View of Matter* (Mata Pub, 1999), *For These
  Women of the Beat* (3300 Pr, 1997), *Ragged Lion: Anth*
  (Vagabond Pr, 1998), *Women of the Beat Generation: Anth*
  (Conari Pr, 1996), *Gargoyle*

Jason Lee Weiss P
1101 Spruce St
Berkeley, CA 94707, 415-655-9694

Mark Weiss 🎤 ✈ P
Box 40537
San Diego, CA 92164-0537, 619-282-0371
Internet: junction@earthlink.net
  Pubs: *Fieldnotes* (Junction Pr, 1995), *A Blockprint by
  Kuniyoshi* (Four Zoas/Night Hse, 1994)

David Weissmann P
Creative Writing Program, Stanford Univ, Stanford, CA 94305,
415-497-1700
  Pubs: *Poetry, Southern Rev, Poetry NW, Antioch Rev,
  Shenandoah, Epoch, Stand*

Michael Dylan Welch 🎤 ✈ P
PO Box 4014
Foster City, CA 94404-0014, 650-598-0461
Internet: welchm@aol.com
  Pubs: *Haiku Poetry Ancient and Modern: Anth* (MQ Pubs,
  2002), *The New Haiku: Anth* (Snapshots Pr, 2001), *Acorn
  Book of Contemporary Haiku: Anth* (Acorn Bk Co, 2000),
  Global Haiku: Anth (Iron/Mosaic Pr, 2000), *The Haiku Anth*
  (Norton, 1999), *Tundra, Woodnotes*

Marion deBooy Wentzien W
19801 Merribrook Ct
Saratoga, CA 95070, 408-867-0306
  Pubs: *Desert Shadows* (Avalon Bks, 1988), *Seventeen, New
  Letters, This World, Fact & Fiction*

Michael West P
323 Martin
Rio del Mar, CA 95003, 408-688-6253
  Pubs: *Odes & Other Modes, Eye Quilt* (Wire Wind Ink, 1984,
  1971), *Street, Lost & Found Times, Paper Radio, Swift Kick,
  Bird Effort, Abbey*

David Westheimer W
11722 Darlington Ave, #2
Los Angeles, CA 90049
  Pubs: *Delay En Route* (1st Bks, 2002), *The Great Wounded
  Bird* (Texas Rev Pr, 2000), *Death Is Lighter Than a Feather*
  (U North Texas Pr, 1995), *Sitting It Out* (Rice U Pr, 1992),
  My Sweet Charlie (Doubleday, 1965)

Philip Whalen P&W
Hartford Street Zen Center, 57 Hartford St, San Francisco,
CA 94114
  Pubs: *You Didn't Even Try & Imaginary Speeches for a
  Brazen Head* (Zephyr, 1985)

Jackson Wheeler 🎤 ✈ P
PO Box 954
Ventura, CA 93002-0954, 805-483-1905
Internet: jw@tri-counties.org
  Pubs: *Swimming Past Iceland* (Mille Grazie Pr, 1993), *A
  Near Country: Anth* (Solo Pr, 1999), *And What Rough
  Beast: Anth* (Ashland U Pr, 1999), *Beyond the Valley of the
  Contemporary Poets: Anth* (Sacred Beverage Pr, 1997),
  Chiron Rev, Cider Press Rev

Betty Coon Wheelwright P
PO Box 1359
Pt Reyes Station, CA 94956-1359
  Pubs: *Seaward* (Berkeley Poets Co-op, 1978), *Calyx, SPR,
  Psych Perspectives, Women's Qtly Rev, Wooster Rev*

Robin White W
English Dept, California State Polytechnic, 3801 W Temple
Ave, Pomona, CA 91768, 714-869-3940
  Pubs: *Moses the Man* (Monograph, 1981), *San Francisco,
  Focus, Spring Harvest, Pulpsmith, Hard Copies, Portfolio,
  Arizona Qtly*

Theresa Whitehill 🎤 ✈ P
1751 Cameron Rd
Elk, CA 95432-9204, 707-877-1816
Internet: writing@coloredhorse.com
  Pubs: *Napa Valley* (Stags Leap Winery, 1998), *A Natural
  History of Mill Towns* (Pygmy Forest Pr, 1993), *Wood, Water,
  Air & Fire: Anth* (Pot Shard Pr, 1998), *Montserrat Rev, Semi-
  Dwarf Rev, Art/Life, Yellow Silk, Oxygen*

William Wiegand W
Writing Dept, San Francisco State Univ, 1600 Holloway Ave,
San Francisco, CA 94132
  Pubs: *The Chester A. Arthur Conspiracy* (Dial Pr, 1983),
  School of Soft Knocks (Lippincott, 1968)

Rosemary C. Wilkinson 🎤 ✈ P
3146 Buckeye Ct
Placerville, CA 95667-8334, 530-626-4166
  Pubs: *Sing in the Wind With Love* (1stBooks Library, 2002),
  Calendar Poetry, Spiritual, Nature, Collected Poems (E.J.
  Co, 2000, 1997, 1996, 1994), *Cambrian Zephyr* (Amarin
  Printing Group, 1994)

Sylvia Wilkinson   W
514 Arena St
El Segundo, CA 90245-3016, 310-322-2814
    Pubs: *On the 7th Day God Created the Chevrolet, Cale*
    (Algonquin Bks, 1993, 1986)

Paul Osborne Williams 🎤 ✈   P
2718 Monserat Ave
Belmont, CA 94002-1448, 415-591-2733
Internet: powms@aol.com
    Pubs: *The Nick of Time* (Press Here, 2001), *Outside Robins
    Sing* (Brooks Bks, 1999), *Footsteps in the Fog, Fig
    Newtons: Anth* (Press Here, 1994, 1993), *Modern Haiku,
    Frogpond, Woodnotes*

Daniel Williams 🎤 ✈   P
General Delivery
Yosemite, CA 95389-9999, 209-375-6721
    Pubs: *Grrrr: Anth* (Arctos Pr, 2000), *XY Files: Anth*
    (Sherman Asher Pub, 1997), *Poets West, Terminus, North
    Dakota Qtly, Manzanita, Kerf*

Alan Williamson   P
826 Oak Ave
Davis, CA 95616
Internet: Aabwilliamson@aol.com
    Pubs: *Presence* (Knopf, 1983), *Poetry, New Yorker,
    Ploughshares*

Paul Willis 🎤 ✈   P&W
Westmont College, English Dept, Santa Barbara, CA
93108-1099, 805-565-7174
Internet: willis@westmont.edu
    Pubs: *Poison Oak* (Mille Grazie, 1999), *No Clock in the
    Forest* (Avon Bks, 1993), *Best Spiritual Writing: Anth*
    (Harper SF, 1999), *Best American Poetry: Anth* (Scribner,
    1996), *Solo, Christian Century, Image, Poetry*

Eric Wilson   W
1319 Pearl St
Santa Monica, CA 90405, 213-452-3452
    Pubs: *Prize Stories 1985: The O. Henry Awards: Anth*
    (Doubleday, 1985), *Witness, Massachusetts Rev, Epoch*

Dick Wimmer 🎤 ✈   W
c/o James Leonard, 4215 Glencoe Ave, 2nd Flr, Marina Del
Rey, CA 90292, 310-821-9000
    Pubs: *The Irish Wine Trilogy* (Penguin, 2001), *Boyne's
    Lassie* (Zoland, 1998), *Irish Wine* (Mercury Hse, 1989),
    Tales of the Heart, Nassau Rev, Flash-Bopp

A. D. Winans 🎤 ✈   P&W
PO Box 31249
San Francisco, CA 94131-0249, 415-826-1768
    Pubs: *The Holy Grail: The Charles Bukowski and Second
    Coming Rev* (Dust Bks 2002), *A Bastard Child With No
    Place to Go* (12 Gauge Pr, 2002), *North Beach Revisited*
    (Green Bean Pr, 2000), *Outlaw Bible of Amer Poetry: Anth*
    (Thunder's Mouth Pr, 1997), *APR, NYQ*

Mary Wings   W
1521 Treat Ave
San Francisco, CA 94110
Internet: shecame@earthlink.net
    Pubs: *She Came by the Book* (Berkley Prime Crime, 1996),
    Divine Victim, She Came in a Flash (NAL, 1993, 1989), *She
    Came Too Late* (Crossing Pr, 1987)

Bayla Winters 🎤   P
2700 Scott Rd
Burbank, CA 91504-2314, 818-846-1879
Internet: wb6osc@aol.com
    Pubs: *Seeing Eye Wife, Shooting From the Lip* (Gideon Pr,
    1997, 1995), *Sacred & Propane* (Croton Rev, 1989), *Life
    on the Line: Anth* (Negative Capability Pr, 1992), *Graffiti
    Rag, Convolvulus, Maverick Pr, El Locofoco, Iconoclast,
    Phoenix, Fuel*

Sandra Adelmund Witt   P&W
60 Roberts Rd, #12
Los Gatos, CA 95032-4429
    Pubs: *Aerial Studies* (New Rivers Pr, 1994), *40 Days & 40
    Nights* (Iowa Arts Council, 1994), *Chaminade Literary Rev,
    Colorado Qtly, Cream City Rev, Confluence, CutBank*

Anne F. Wittels   P
2116 Via Alamitos
Palos Verdes Estates, CA 90274, 213-378-5812
    Pubs: *Lost & Found* (Coco Palm Tree Pr, 1982), *Bitterroot,
    Palos Verdes Rev, Women*

Maia Wojciechowska   W
Pebble Beach Press, PO Box 1171, Pebble Beach, CA
93953-1171
    Pubs: *Dreams of World Cup, Dreams of Wimbledon,
    Dreams of Golf* (Pebble Beach Pr, 1994, 1994, 1993)

Tad Wojnicki   P&W
PO Box 3198
Carmel, CA 93921, 408-770-0107
Internet: wojnicki@aol.com
    Pubs: *Lie Under the Fig Trees* (Angels by the Sea Pr, 1998),
    Scrawls on a Crate of Oranges (Pomost Pubs, 1987),
    Mosaic, Leviathan, Coffeehouse, Poets' Paper, Lit Jrnl

Murray E. Wolfe 🎤 ✈   P
PO Box 280550
Northridge, CA 91328-0550, 818-885-0101
Internet: mw@america2000.com
    Pubs: *Blessed Be the Beast* (Ambrosia Pr, 1981)

Tobias Wolff   W
Creative Writing Program, Dept of English, Stanford University,
Stanford, CA 94305-2087, 650-723-2635
    Pubs: *In Pharaoh's Army* (Knopf, 1994), *This Boy's Life*
    (Atlantic Monthly Pr, 1989)

Geoffrey Wolff   W
202 S Orange Dr
Los Angeles, CA 90036, 949-824-3745
Internet: gwolff@uci.edu
   Pubs: *Providence, The Duke of Deception* (Vintage, 1991,
   1990), *Granta, Esquire, Paris Rev, TriQtly, Atlantic*

Jean Walton Wolff   P&W
PO Box 851
Capitola, CA 95010, 831-475-4221
   Pubs: *Storming Heaven's Gate: Anth* (Plume, 1997),
   Sleeping With Dionysis: Anth (Crossing Pr, 1992), *Porter
   Gulch Rev, Milvia Street, Bakunin*

Blema Wolin 🎤   P
1400 Geary Blvd #1803
San Francisco, CA 94109-9311, 415-673-6846
   Pubs: *With Half an Eye* (Small Poetry Pr, 2001), *Orange
   Willow Rev, CQ, The Squaw Rev, Hawai'i Rev, Virginia,
   Antioch Rev, Bellowing Ark*

Joel M. Y. Wolk   PP
1343 Oak St
San Francisco, CA 94117, 415-552-3883
Internet: globalpoet@aol.com
   Pubs: *The Jazz Poetry Anthology* (Indiana U Pr, 1991), *Tree
   3, Sou'wester, Monument, Poetry Bag, Off the Wall, Sala De
   Puerto Rico at MIT, Hayden Gallery at MIT, Writers' Forum,
   Old Red Kimono, Focus Midwest*

Cecilia Woloch   P
5921 Whitworth Dr #201
Los Angeles, CA 90019, 213-933-8718
Internet: ceciwo@aol.com
   Pubs: *Sacrifice* (Cahuenga Pr, 1997), *Grand Passion: Anth*
   (Red Wing Bks, 1995), *Breaking Up Is Hard to Do: Anth*
   (Crossing Pr, 1994), *Catholic Girls: Anth* (Penguin/Plume,
   1992), *Prose Poem, Antioch Rev, Zyzzyva, Literal Latte,
   Chelsea Hotel*

Ko Won   P
2535 Rockdell St
La Crescenta, CA 91214, 818-236-3020
Northridge, CA 91326, 818-363-5325
   Pubs: *Some Other Time* (Bombshelter Pr, 1990), *The Turn
   of Zero* (CCC, 1974), *Amerasia, Chicago Rev, The Lit
   Realm, Bitter Oleander*

Nellie Wong 🎤 ✈   P
549 Chenery St
San Francisco, CA 94131-3031, 415-584-7097
Internet: nelliewongpoet@yahoo.com
   Pubs: *Stolen Moments, Crimson Edge: Anth* (Chicory Blue
   Pr, 1997, 2000), *The Death of Long Steam Lady* (West End
   Pr, 1986), *Dreams in Harrison Railroad Park* (Kelsey Street
   Pr, 1977), *HEArt, Forkroads, Open Boat, Dissident Song,
   Long Shot*

Nanying Stella Wong   P
1537 Comstock Ct
Berkeley, CA 94703-1030, 510-524-2229
   Pubs: *Bearing Dreams, Shaping Visions: Anth* (Washington
   State U Pr, 1993), *Peace & Pieces: Contemporary Amer
   Poetry: Anth* (Peace & Pieces Pr, 1973), *Sunset Mag,
   California Living*

Alice F. Worsley   P
California State College, English/Foreign Languages Dept,
Turlock, CA 95380, 209-633-2361

Elizabeth Wray   P
834 Elizabeth St
San Francisco, CA 94114
   Pubs: *Partisan Rev, Kayak, Epoch, Denver Qtly, Pacific Sun
   Lit Qtly, Berkeley Poets Co-op*

Kirby Wright   P&W
3259 Alma St
Palo Alto, CA 94306
   Pubs: *Artful Dodge, Blue Mesa Rev, Santa Clara Rev,
   Hawaii Rev, Welter Mag, West Mag*

Mitsuye Yamada 🎤 ✈   P&W
6151 Sierra Bravo Rd
Irvine, CA 92715, 714-854-8699
   Pubs: *Camp Notes and Other Writings* (Rutgers Univ Pr,
   1998), *Camp Notes & Other Poems, Desert Run: Poems &
   Stories* (Kitchen Table Pr, 1992, 1988), *Sowing Ti Leaves:
   Anth* (Multicultural Women Writers, 1991)

Hisaye Yamamoto DeSoto   W
4558 Mont Eagle Pl
Los Angeles, CA 90041
   Pubs: *Seventeen Syllables & Other Stories* (Rutgers U Pr,
   1998), *Charlie Chan Is Dead: Anth* (Penguin, 1993), *The Big
   Aiiieeeee!: Anth* (Meridian, 1991), *Rafu*

Stephen Yenser 🎤 ✈   P
10322 Tennessee Ave
Los Angeles, CA 90064-2508, 310-203-9833
Internet: yenser@humnet.ucla.edu
   Pubs: *The Fire in All Things* (LSU Pr, 1993), *Best American
   Poetry: Anth* (Scribner, 1995, 1992), *Paris Rev*

Marly Youmans 🎤 ✈   P&W
c/o Thomas F. Epley, Potomac Literary Agency, 838 East
Dayton Avenue, Fresno, CA 93704-4815, 301-208-0674
Internet: smyoumans@excite.com
   Pubs: *The Wolf Pit, Catherwood* (FSG, 2001, 1996), *Little
   Jordan* (David R. Godine, 1995), *Carolina Qtly, South
   Carolina Rev, Southern Humanities*

Gary Young 🎤 ✈   P
3965 Bonny Doon Rd
Santa Cruz, CA 95060-9706, 831-426-4355
Internet: gyounggrp@aol.com
    Pubs: *No Other Life* (Creative Arts Books, 2002), *Braver
    Deeds* (Gibbs-Smith Pub, 1999), *Days* (Silverfish Rev Pr,
    1997), *The Dream of a Moral Life* (Copper Beech Pr, 1990),
    Antaeus, APR, Kenyon Rev

C. Dale Young 🎤 ✈   P
4210 Judah St #303
San Francisco, CA 94122-1016
Internet: cdaleyoung@rocketmail.com
    Pubs: *The Day Underneath the Day* (TriQtly
    Bks/Northwestern U Pr, 2001), *The Best American Poetry
    1996: Anth* (Scribner, 1996), *Paris Rev, Partisan Rev,
    Ploughshares, Poetry, Southern Rev, Yale Rev*

Joyce E. Young   P
PO Box 5381
Berkeley, CA 94705-0381, 510-496-6095
Internet: joypoet@mindspring.com
    Pubs: *Skin Deep: Women Writing on Color, Culture and
    Identity: Anth* (Crossing Pr, 1994), *The Word, Vol I* (CD;
    Akashic Records, 1999), *A Wise Woman's Garden, San
    Francisco Bay Guardian, Konceptonline, Writing for Our
    Lives, Squaw Rev*

Al Young   P&W
514 Bryant St
Palo Alto, CA 94301, 415-329-1189
    Pubs: *Heaven: Collected Poems, 1956-1990* (Creative Arts
    Bk Co., 1992), *Seduction by Light* (Delacorte, 1988)

John A. Youril   P
8420 Olivine Ave
Citrus Heights, CA 95610, 916-729-7072
    Pubs: *Realm of the Vampire, Mixed Bag, Haunted Jrnl,
    Bitterroot, Stone Country, Metrosphere, Poetry & Fiction,
    Lapis, Poetry Today, The Archer*

Rich Yurman 🎤 ✈   P
2514 24th Ave
San Francisco, CA 94116-3036, 415-665-8649
Internet: clomax@pacbell.net
    Pubs: *Giraffe* (March St Pr, 2002), *A Perfect Pair: he
    whispered/she shouted* (Secon Avenyuh Pr, 1989), *Parting
    Gifts, Slipstream, NYQ, Mudfish*

Jeffrey A. Z. Zable   P&W
50 Parnassus Ave
San Francisco, CA 94117, 415-731-5250
    Pubs: *Zable's Fables* (Androgyne Pr, 1990), *Wormwood
    Rev, Writ, Long Shot, Central Park, Caliban, NYQ*

Stella Zamvil   P&W
821 Thornwood Dr
Palo Alto, CA 94303-4437, 650-494-7791
    Pubs: *In the Time of the Russias* (John Daniel, 1985),
    *Harpoon, Greensboro Rev, Palo Alto Rev, Canadian Jewish
    Outlook, Louisville Rev*

Franklin Zawacki   W
915 Sanchez St
San Franciso, CA 94114-3322, 415-643-9336
    Pubs: *Hell Coal Annual, Cowhunting*

Andrena Zawinski 🎤 ✈   P
485 Wickson Ave #2
Oakland, CA 94610, 510-268-9796
Internet: andrenaz@earthlink.net
    Pubs: *Zawinski's Greatest Hits, 1991-2001* (Pudding Hse,
    2002), *Elegies for My Mother* (TPQ/Autumn Hse, 1999),
    Traveling in Reflected Light (Pig Iron Pr, 1996), *Rattle,
    Slipstream, Gulf Coast, Qtly West, Santa Clara Rev*

Merla Zellerbach   W
Fred Hill Literary Agency, 1842 Union St, San Francisco, CA
94123, 415-751-4535
    Pubs: *Rittenhouse Square* (Random Hse, 1991), *Sugar,
    Cavett Manor* (Ballantine, 1989, 1987), *Reader's Digest,
    Cosmopolitan*

Rafael Zepeda 🎤 ✈   P&W
English Dept, California State Univ, Long Beach, CA 90840,
562-985-4243
    Pubs: *The Witchita Poems* (Pearl Pr, 1997), *Horse Medicine*
    (Applezaba Pr, 1993), *The Yellow Ford of Texas* (Vergin Pr,
    1993), *Higher Elevations: Anth* (Swallow Pr, 1993), *A New
    Geography of Poets: Anth* (U Arkansas Pr, 1993),
    Wormwood Rev, Pearl Mag

Paul Edwin Zimmer   P&W
Greyhaven, 90 El Camino Real, Berkeley, CA 94705,
510-658-6033
    Pubs: *La Chramata Degli Eroi* (Casa Editrice Nord, 1993),
    Return to Avalon: Anth (Daw Bks, 1996), *Mythic Circle,
    Berserkrgangr*

Lloyd Zimpel   W
38 Liberty St
San Francisco, CA 94110-2319, 415-647-2868
    Pubs: *Literature, Class & Culture: Anth* (Addison-Wesley,
    2000), *A Good Deal: Anth* (U Mass Pr, 1988), *Threepenny
    Rev, Missouri Rev, Alaska Qtly Rev, ACM, Arkansas Rev,
    North Dakota Qtly, South Dakota Rev*

Harriet Ziskin   W
187 Ney St
San Francisco, CA 94112
    Pubs: *The Adventures of Mona Pinsky* (Calyx Bks, 1995),
    Broomstick, Jacob's Letter, Ceilidh, Outerbridge

Bonnie Zobell   W
English Dept, Mesa College, 7250 Mesa College Dr, San
Diego, CA 92111, 619-388-2321
Internet: bzobell@sdccd.net
   Pubs: *American Fiction: Anth* (New Rivers, 1997), *Arts &
   Understanding, PEN Syndicated Project, Cimarron Rev,
   Bellingham Rev, Gulf Stream Mag*

Al Zolynas   P
2380 Viewridge Pl
Escondido, CA 92026, 760-740-9098
Internet: azolynas@usiu.edu
   Pubs: *Under Ideal Conditions* (Laterthanever Pr, 1994), *A
   Book of Luminous Things: Anth* (HB, 1996), *A New
   Geography of Poets: Anth* (U Arkansas Pr, 1992)

COLORADO

Keith Abbott 🎤 ✈   P&W
Naropa Writing Dept, 2130 Arapahoe, Boulder, CO
80302-6602, 303-682-9664
   Pubs: *The French Girl* (Rodent Pr, 1996), *Skin and Bone*
   (Tangram, 1993), *Downstream From Trout Fishing in
   America* (Capra Pr, 1989), *The First Thing Coming* (Coffee
   Hse Pr, 1987)

Joe Amato 🎤 ✈   P
Univ of Colorado at Boulder, Hellems 101 Campus Box 226,
Boulder, CO 80309-0226, 303-492-3401
Internet: joe.amato@colorado.edu
   Pubs: *Bookend: Anatomies of a Virtual Self* (SUNY Pr,
   1997), *Symptoms of a Finer Age* (Viet Nam Generation &
   Burning Cities Pr, 1994), *Jacket, New Amer Writing, Crayon*

Mark Amerika   W
PO Box 241
Boulder, CO 80306, 303-499-9331
http://www.altx.com
   Pubs: *Sexual Blood, The Kafka Chronicles* (Fiction
   Collective Two, 1995, 1993), *Lettre Intl, Fiction Intl, Witness,
   Central Park, Amer Book Rev*

Donald Anderson 🎤 ✈   W
2500 Hill Circle
Colorado Springs, CO 80904
Internet: donald.anderson@usafa.af.mil
   Pubs: *Fire Road* (U Iowa Pr, 2001), *Michigan Qtly, CT Rev,
   NAR, Columbia, Fiction Intl, PRISM Intl, Epoch, Western
   Humanities Rev, Aethlon*

Nancy Andrews   P
1942 Mt Zion Dr
Golden, CO 80401, 303-279-1277
   Pubs: *Kansas Qtly*

Linda "Gene" Armstrong   P
401 Rana Ct
Grand Junction, CO 81503, 970-257-1626
   Pubs: *Early Tigers* (Bellowing Ark Pr, 1995), *Birmingham
   Poetry Rev, Rockford Rev, Bitterroot, Earth's Daughters,
   Slant, Spirit That Moves Us*

Dana W. Atchley   P
Box 183
Crested Butte, CO 81224, 303-349-6506

Beth Ann Bassein 🎤   P
24 Stovel Circle
Colorado Springs, CO 80916-4704, 719-591-8210
Internet: bsein@msn.com
   Pubs: *Prairie Smoke: Anth* (U South Colorado Pr, 1990),
   Turquoise Land: Anth (Nortex Pr, 1974), *Denver Qtly, South
   Dakota Rev, West Wind Rev, riverrun, Chachalaca Poetry
   Rev, Voices Intl, Twigs, Human Voice, The Amer Bard*

Esther G. Belin 🎤 ✈   P
3549 W 2nd Ave
Durango, CO 81301, 970-247-2966
Internet: bitterwater@hotmail.com
   Pubs: *From the Belly of My Beauty* (U Arizona Pr, 1999)

Don Bendell   P&W
PO Box 276
Canon City, CO 81215, 719-269-3929
Internet: bendell@webtv.net
   Pubs: *Blazing Colts, The Matched Colts Series* (Dutton-
   Signet, 1999, 1990-1999), *The B-52 Overture, Valley of
   Tears* (Dell, 1992, 1992), *Crossbow* (Berkley Pub Group,
   1990), *Pembroke Mag, Bowhunter*

Bruce Berger   P
Box 482
Aspen, CO 81612-0482, 970-925-1647
Internet: bberger@rof.net
   Pubs: *Almost an Island* (U Arizona Pr, 1998), *The Telling
   Distance* (Anchor/Doubleday, 1991), *Poetry, Negative
   Capability, Poetry NW, New Letters, Sierra, Orion*

Paul Bergner   P
PO Box 20512
Boulder, CO 80308
   Pubs: *Off the Beaten Track: Anth* (Quiet Lion Pr, 1992),
   Portlander, Plazm, Stanza, Rain City Rev, Spoon, Sufi

Rita Brady Kiefer 🎤 ✈   P
c/o Michelle McIrvin, Univ Pr of Colorado, 5589 Arapahoe Rd,
Boulder, CO 80303
Internet: rbkiefe@bentley.unco.edu
   Pubs: *Nesting Doll* (U Pr Colorado, 1999), *Trying on Faces*
   (Monkshood Pr, 1995), *Unveiling* (Chicory Blue Pr, 1993),
   Beyond Lament: Anth (Northwestern U Pr, 1998),
   Ploughshares, Kansas Qtly, SW Rev, Bloomsbury Rev

Edward Bryant W
PO Box 18349
Denver, CO 80218-0349, 303-480-5363
Internet: ebryant666@aol.com
  Pubs: *Flirting With Death* (Deadline Bks, 1996),
  Strangeness & Charm (Voyager Bks, 1996), *Evening's
  Empires* (Nemo Pr, 1989), *Omni, Penthouse*

Reed Bye P
2227 W Nicholl St
Boulder, CO 80304, 303-440-4091
  Pubs: *Nice to See You: Homage to Ted Berrigan* (Coffee Hse
  Pr, 1990), *Out of This World: Anth* (Crown, 1991), *Up Late:
  Anth* (4 Walls 8 Windows, 1989)

Lorna Dee Cervantes P
UCB 266, University of Colorado, Englsh Dept - Creative
Wrtng Prgrm, Boulder, CO 80309-0226, 303-492-4620
  Pubs: *From the Cables of Genocide: Poems on Love &
  Hunger* (Arte Publico Pr, 1990), *Red Dirt*

James Ciletti P
1215 North Union Blvd
Colorado Springs, CO 80909-3650, 719-634-2367
Internet: jimciletti@worldnet.att.net
  Pubs: *At the Crack of Dawn* (Impavide Pubs, 2002),
  Plainsongs, Midwest Poetry Rev

Jim Cohn P
2100 Baseline Rd
Boulder, CO 80302-7707
  Pubs: *Prairie Falcon* (North Atlantic Bks, 1989), *Nada
  Poems: Anth* (Nada Pr, 1988), *Big Scream, Hanging Loose,
  Heaven Bone, Brief, Colorado North Rev, Exquisite Corpse*

Jack Collom 🎤 ✈ P
1838 Pine St
Boulder, CO 80302, 303-444-1886
  Pubs: *Red Car Goes By* (Tuumba Pr, 2001), *Calluses of
  Poetry* (CD; Treehouse Pr, 1996), *Arguing With Something
  Plato Said* (Rocky Ledge, 1990), *The Fox* (United Artists,
  1981)

Robert Cooperman 🎤 ✈ P
2061 S Humboldt St
Denver, CO 80210, 303-722-2107
  Pubs: *In the Colorado Gold Fever Mountains* (Western
  Reflections, 1999), *A Tale of the Grateful Dead* (Artword,
  2000), *In the Household of Percy Bysshe Shelley* (U Pr
  Florida, 1993), *Centennial Rev, Lit Rev, Poetry East, Santa
  Clara Rev, Comstock Rev*

Mary Crow 🎤 ✈ P
1707 Homer Dr
Fort Collins, CO 80521-3805, 970-482-9923
Internet: mcrow@lamar.colostate.edu
  Pubs: *I Have Tasted the Apple, Borders* (BOA Edtns, 1996,
  1989), *Massachusetts Rev, APR, Ploughshares, NAR, New
  Letters, Graham House Rev, Prairie Schooner*

Robert Dassanowsky PP&P
Dept of Languages/Cultures, Univ Colorado, Colorado
Springs, CO 80933
Internet: belvederefilm@yahoo.com
  Pubs: *Telegrams From the Metropole: Selected Poems
  1980-1998* (U Salzburg Pr, 1999), *Verses of a Marriage*
  (Event Horizon, 1996), *Osiris, Poet's Voice, Rampike, Salz,
  Poetry Salzburg Rev, Adirondack Rev*

Judy Doenges W
Dept of English, Colorado State Univ, Fort Collins, CO
80523-1773
Internet: jdoenges@lamar.colostate.edu
  Pubs: *Our Mothers, Our Selves: Anth* (Bergin & Garvey,
  1996), *Ohio Short Fiction: Anth* (Northmont, 1995),
  *Permafrost, Green Mountains Rev, Phoebe, Nimrod,
  Georgia Rev, Evergreen Chronicles, Equinox*

Sharon Doyle 🎤 ✈ P
PO Box 271156
Ft Collins, CO 80527-1156
  Pubs: *The Corner Poetry Project: Anth* (Fairview Pr, 2001),
  *Midwest Qtly, Brooklyn Rev, Nimrod, Bayou, Baltimore Rev,
  Montserrat Rev, Chaminade, Cue Rev*

James Doyle 🎤 ✈ P
PO Box 271156
Fort Collins, CO 80527-1156
  Pubs: *The Silk at Her Throat* (Cedar Hill, 1999), *Literature:
  An Intro to Critical Reading: Anth* (Prentice-Hall, 1996), *Iowa
  Rev, Poetry, Cimarron Rev, Chelsea, Lit Rev, Green
  Mountains Rev, Midwest Qtly, Descant, Puerto del Sol,
  Laurel Rev, New Orleans Rev*

Jean Dubois P
PO Box 1430
Golden, CO 80402
  Pubs: *The Same Sweet Yellow, Silent Stones, Empty
  Passageways* (San Miguel Pr, 1994, 1992), *Wind Five-
  Folded: Anth* (AHA Bks, 1994), *Cicada, Mayfly, Modern
  Haiku, Passager, Poets On, Sijo West, Still, Frogpond, Lynx,
  Black Bough*

Mark DuCharme 🎤 ✈ P
2965 13th St
Boulder, CO 80304, 303-938-9346
Internet: markducharme@hotmail.com
  Pubs: *Cosmopolitan Tremble* (Pavement Saw Pr, 2002),
  Anon (w/A. Hollo, L. Wright & P. Pritchett; Potato Clock
  Edtns, 2001), *Near to* (Poetry NY, 1999), *Desire Series*
  (Dead Metaphor Pr, 1999), *Contracting Scale* (Standing
  Stones Pr, 1996), *Antennae, Conundrum*

Bruce Ducker 🎤 ✈ P&W
1560 Broadway
Denver, CO 80202
Internet: bducker@denverlaw.com
 Pubs: *Bloodlines, Lead Us Not Into Penn Station, Marital Assets* (Permanent Pr, 2000, 1994, 1993), *Yale Rev, The Qtly, Poetry, Commonweal, NYQ*

Rikki Ducornet W
Denver Univ, University Park, Denver, CO 80208-0001,
303-871-2890
Internet: rducorne@du.edu
 Pubs: *The Word "Desire"* (H Holt, 1997), *Phospor in Dreamland, The Stain, The Complete Butcher's Tales, The Jade Cabinet* (Dalkey Archive, 1995, 1995, 1994, 1993), *Conjunctions, Parnassus, Sulphur*

Lawrence Dunning W
1655 Leyden
Denver, CO 80220-1621, 303-321-2658
Internet: leehlarryd@aol.com
 Pubs: *Taking Liberty* (Avon, 1981), *Stories from Virginia Qtly Rev: Anth* (U Pr Virginia, 1990), *High Plains Lit Rev, Weber Studies, Margin, Virginia Qtly Rev, Colorado Qtly, Aspen Anth, Carolina Qtly, Descant, Rio Grande Rev*

Jacqueline Eis 🎤 ✈ W
1006 Hinsdale Dr
Fort Collins, CO 80526-3902, 970-229-9790
 Pubs: *Imaginary Lives: Anth* (Mica Pr, 1996), *The 13th Moon, Wisconsin Rev, CSM, MacGuffin, Prairie Schooner, Writers' Forum, Happy, Greensboro Rev*

Larry Fagin P
Naropa Institute, 2130 Arapahoe Ave, Boulder, CO 80302,
303-444-0202
 Pubs: *Complete Fragments* (Z Pr, 1983), *I'll Be Seeing You* (Fullcourt Pr, 1978)

Ida Fasel P
165 Ivy St
Denver, CO 80220-5846, 303-377-4498
www.thaddeusbooks.com
 Pubs: *Journey of a Hundred Years, The Difficult Inch, All Real Living Is Meeting, Where Is the Center of the World?* (Small Poetry Pr, 2002, 2000, 1999, 1998), *Air, Angels & Us* (Argonne Hse Pr, 2002), *Aureoles* (Juniper Pr, 2002), *Blue Unicorn, Lucid Stone*

Fred Ferraris 🎤 ✈ P
PO Box 65
Lyons, CO 80540-0065, 303-823-9362
Internet: ferr@oneimage.com
 Pubs: *Prayers for a Thousand Years: Anth* (Harper SF, 1999), *Older Than Rain* (Selva Edtns, 1997), *Marpa Point* (Blackberry Bks, 1976), *Heaven Bone, Measure, Kuksu, Glassworks, Phase & Cycle*

Merrill Gilfillan 🎤 ✈ P&W
PO Box 18194
Boulder, CO 80308
 Pubs: *Grasshopper Falls* (Hanging Loose, 2000), *Chokecherry Places* (Johnson Bks, 1998), *Satin Street: Poems* (Moyer Bell, 1997), *Sworn Before Cranes* (Orion Bks, 1994), *Magpie Rising: Sketches from the Great Plains* (Vintage, 1991)

Karen Glenn 🎤 ✈ W
PO Box 6069
Snowmass Village, CO 81615, 970-922-2348
Internet: prahu@aol.com
 Pubs: *Laurel Rev, Cricket, Seattle Rev, NAR, Poetry NW, Cream City Rev, Waterstone, Chattahoochie Rev, National Forum, Tar River Poetry, Portland Rev, Scholastic Scope, Denver Qtly*

Sidney Goldfarb P
English Dept, Univ Colorado, Boulder, CO 80302,
303-443-2211

Art Goodtimes 🎤 ✈ P
Cloud Acre, Box 160, Norwood, CO 81423, 970-327-4767
Internet: goodtimes@independence.net
 Pubs: *As If the World Really Mattered* (Conundrum Pr, 2000), *Mushroom Cloud Redeye* (Western Eye Pr, 1990), *Slow Rising Smoke* (Blackberry Bks, 1987), *Upriver Downriver, Word, The Sun, Petroglyph, Poiesis, Wild Earth*

Robert O. Greer, Jr. 🎤 ✈ W
180 Adams St, Ste 250
Denver, CO 80206-5215, 303-320-6827
 Pubs: *Limited Time, The Devil's Backbone, The Devil's Red Nickel, The Devil's Hatband* (Warner/Mysterious Pr, 2000, 1998, 1997, 1996)

Aimee Grunberger P
2100 Mesa Dr
Boulder, CO 80304
 Pubs: *Ten Degrees Cooler Inside* (Dead Metaphor Pr, 1992), *American Poets Say Goodbye to the 20th Century: Anth* (Four Walls Eight Windows, 1995)

Danielle D'Ottavio Harned W
27657 Timber Trail
Conifer, CO 80433
 Pubs: *The Perimeter of Light* (New Rivers Pr, 1992), *Sing Heavenly Muse, Kansas Qtly, Permafrost*

Kent Haruf W
8500 Chapin St
Salida, CO 81201
 Pubs: *Where You Once Belonged* (S&S, 1990), *Where Past Meets Present: Anth* (U Colorado Pr, 1994), *Best American Short Stories: Anth* (HM, 1987), *Grand Street*

Joan Harvey   W
1100 Stage Rd
Aspen, CO 81611
Internet: jmharvey@sopris.net
  Pubs: *Between C&D: Anth* (Penguin, 1988), *ACM, To: A Jrnl
  of Poetry, Prose & Visual Arts, Global City Rev, Mississippi
  Mud, Bomb, Osiris, Tampa Rev*

Bobbie Louise Hawkins   P&W
2515 Bluff St
Boulder, CO 80304
  Pubs: *My Own Alphabet, One Small Saga* (Coffee Hse Pr,
  1988, 1984)

Jana Hayes   P
c/o Janice Hays, 4835 Stanton Rd, Colorado Springs, CO
80918-3909, 719-599-9633
  Pubs: *New House, A Book of Women* (San Marcos Pr,
  1972), *Wingbone: Anth* (Sudden Jungle Pr, 1986), *BPJ,
  Writers' Forum, Ithaca Women's Anth, South Dakota Rev,
  Eleventh Muse, Hamline Jrnl, Frontiers, Ekphrasis*

Lois Beebe Hayna   P
403 Locust Dr
Colorado Springs, CO 80907, 719-599-0502
Internet: lhayna@kktv.com
  Pubs: *Northern Gothic* (Morgan Pr, 1992), *Never Trust a
  Crow* (James Andrews Pub, 1990), *The Bridge, Nimrod*

James B. Hemesath   W
8058 Vectra Dr
Colorado Springs, CO 80920
Internet: jimhemesath@msn.com
  Pubs: *Where Past Meets Present: Anth* (U Colorado Pr,
  1994), *Best of Wind: Anth* (Wind Pub, 1994), *Redneck Rev
  of Lit, New Mexico Humanities Rev, Wind*

Jane Hilberry 🎤 ✈   P
Colorado College, English Dept, 14 E Cache la Poudre,
Colorado Springs, CO 80903, 719-389-6501
Internet: jhilberry@coloradocollege.edu
  Pubs: *The Girl With the Pearl Earring* (Jones Alley Pr, 1995),
  *Denver Qtly Rev, Mid-American Rev, Virginia Qtly Rev,
  Michigan Qtly Rev*

Linda Hogan 🎤 ✈   W
PO Box 141
Idledale, CO 80453-0141, 303-697-9097
  Pubs: *Power* (Norton, 1998), *Solar Storms* (Scribner, 1996),
  Book of Medicines (Coffee Hse Pr, 1993), *Mean Spirit*
  (Atheneum, 1990), *Ms., Amer Voice, Denver Qtly*

Anselm Hollo 🎤 ✈   P
c/o Poetics, Naropa Univ, 2130 Arapahoe Ave, Boulder, CO
80302, 303-449-0691
Internet: jdhollo@aol.com
  Pubs: *Notes on the Possibilities and Attractions of Existence*
  (Coffee Hse Pr, 2001), *Rue Wilson Monday* (La Alameda Pr,
  2000), *Postmodern American Poetry: Anth* (Norton, 1994),
  *Exquisite Corpse, NAW, Talisman, Conjuctions, Sulfur,
  Arshile, Gas*

Margaret Honton   P
421 W 20th St, Pueblo, Co 81003-2509
  Pubs: *The Visionary Mirror, I Name Myself Daughter*
  (Sophia Bks, 1983, 1982), *Hyperion, Pudding*

Joseph Hutchison 🎤 ✈   P
PO Box 266
Indian Hills, CO 80454-0266, 303-697-3344
Internet: joe@jhwriter.com
  Pubs: *The Rain at Midnight* (Sherman Asher, 2000), *The
  Heart Inside the Heart* (Wayland Pr, 1999), *Bed of Coals* (U
  Colorado Pr, 1996), *House of Mirrors* (J. Andrews & Co.,
  1992), Prairie Schooner, Zone 3, Poetry, Northeast,
  Midwest Qtly*

Mark Irwin 🎤 ✈   P
3875 S Cherokee St
Englewood, CO 80110-3511, 303-762-6336
Internet: irwin@bel-rea.com
  Pubs: *White City, Quick, Now, Always* (BOA Edtns, 2000,
  1996), *Against the Meanwhile* (Wesleyan U Pr, 1988),
  Antaeus, Kenyon Rev, Atlantic, Nation, APR

Don Jones 🎤 ✈   P
3005 Bay State Ave, #212
Pueblo, CO 81005-2380, 719-561-0676
  Pubs: *Medical Aid* (Samisdat, 1978), *Miss Liberty, Meet
  Crazy Horse* (Swallow, 1972), *Massachusetts Rev, SPR,
  Prairie Schooner, Poet & Critic*

Suzanne Juhasz   P
English Dept, Univ Colorado, Boulder, CO 80309,
303-492-8948
  Pubs: *Benita to Reginald: A Romance* (Out of Sight Pr,
  1978), *Conditions, San Jose Studies*

Steve Katz 🎤 ✈   P
669 Washington St #602
Denver, CO 80203-3837, 303-832-2534
Internet: elbonoz@earthlink.net
  Pubs: *Swanny's Ways, 43 Fictions* (Sun & Moon Pr, 1995,
  1992)

Jessica Kawasuna Saiki 🎤   W
1901 E 13 Ave, #9-C
Denver, CO 80206-2041
  Pubs: *From the Lanai & Other Hawaii Stories, Once, A Lotus
  Garden, The Talking of Hands: Anth* (New Rivers Pr, 1991,
  1987, 1998)

Bruce F. Kawin P
English Dept, Univ Colorado, Boulder, CO 80309-0226,
303-449-4845
Internet: bkawin@aol.com

Baine Kerr ♀ ✈ W
411 Spruce
Boulder, CO 80302
Internet: kerr@hbcllc.com
   Pubs: *Harmful Intent* (Scribner, 1999), *Where Past Meets
   Present: Anth* (U Colorado, 1994), *Jumping-Off Place* (U
   Missouri Pr, 1981), *Best American Short Stories: Anth* (HM,
   1977), *Stanford Mag, Southwest Rev, Shenandoah, Denver
   Qtly, Many Mountains Moving*

Patricia Dubrava Keuning P
2732 Williams St
Denver, CO 80205
   Pubs: *Holding the Light* (James Andrews & Co, 1994),
   These Are Not Sweet Girls: Anth (White Pine Pr, 1994), *Intl
   Qtly, Sulphur River Literary Rev*

Robert W. King P
1309 40th Ave
Greeley, CO 80634, 970-392-1928
   Pubs: *Naming Names* (Palanquin Pr, 2001), *A Circle of
   Land* (Dacotah Territory Pr, 1990), *Standing Around Outside*
   (Bloodroot, 1979), *Ascent, NER, Midwest Qtly, Poetry,
   Massachusetts Rev*

Karl Kopp P
1517 S Dexter Way
Denver, CO 80222, 303-759-5985
   Pubs: *Crossing the River: Anth* (Permanent Pr, 1987), *City
   Kite on a Wire: Anth* (Mesilla, 1986), *Chiron Rev,
   Bloomsbury Rev, Chariton Rev*

Leota Korns P&W
PO Box 1617
Durango, CO 81302, 970-247-4468
   Pubs: *Kansas Mag, Women: A Jrnl of Liberation, San Juan
   Voices, Matrix, Raindrops of Spring*

Marilyn Krysl ♀ ✈ P&W
2003 Mesa Dr #4
Boulder, CO 80304, 303-444-6643
Internet: krysl@spot.colorado.edu
   Pubs: *How to Accommodate Men* (Coffee Hse Pr, 1998),
   Warscape With Lovers (Cleveland State Poetry Ctr, 1997),
   Soulskin (NLN Pr, 1996), *Mozart, Westmoreland & Me*
   (Thunder's Mouth Pr, 1985), *Honey, You've Been Dealt a
   Winning Hand* (Capra Pr, 1980)

R. D. Lakin P
405 Scott
Ft Collins, CO 80521
   Pubs: *American Passport, The MacDowell Poems*
   (Typographeum Pr, 1992, 1977), *Kansas Qtly, West Coast
   Rev, Antioch Rev, Nation, Cottonwood Rev, Michigan Qtly*

Marcela Lucero P
8614 Princeton St
Westminster, CO 80030
   Pubs: *The Third Woman* (HM, 1979)

Barb Lundy ♀ ✈ P
2512 S. University Blvd. #206
Denver, CO 80210, 303-777-5561
   Pubs: *Slant: a Journal of Poetry, Poetry Depth Qtly,
   Plainsongs, Cider Pr Rev, Mad Poets Rev, New Stone
   Circle, HazMat Rev*

Russell Martin W
15201 County Rd 25
Dolores, CO 81323, 970-882-4775
Internet: russellmartin@compuserve.com
   Pubs: *Beautiful Islands* (S&S, 1988), *New Writers of the
   Purple Sage: Anth* (Penguin, 1992)

David Mason ♀ ✈ P&W
English Dept, Colorado College, 14 E Cache La Poudre,
Colorado Springs, CO 80903-3298, 719-389-6502
Internet: dmason@coloradocollege.edu
   Pubs: *The Country I Remember, The Buried Houses* (Story
   Line Pr, 1996, 1991), *Irish Times, Hudson Rev, Georgia Rev,
   Poetry, New Criterion, Harvard Rev, Amer Scholar*

Katherine "Kaki" May P
111 Emerson St, #1423
Denver, CO 80218-3791
   Pubs: *Some Inhuman Familiars* (Cabbage Head Pr, 1983),
   Brandings (Cummington, 1968), *New York Times*

Mary McArthur ♀ ✈ P
622 W Pine St
Louisville, CO 80027-1083, 303-665-7605
Internet: mary.mcarthur@colorado.edu
   Pubs: *Midwest Qtly, Nation, Luminaria, Maryland Poetry
   Rev, Light Year, Portland, Feminist Renaissance*

Peter Michelson P
Univ Colorado, Box 226, English Dept, Boulder, CO 80309,
303-492-7381
   Pubs: *Speaking the Unspeakable* (SUNY Pr, 1993), *Pacific
   Plainsong* (Another Chicago Pr, 1987), *Rolling Stock,
   Boundary 2, ACM, Notre Dame Rev, Exquisite Corpse,
   Cincinnati Poetry Rev, Spoon River Rev, Many Mountains
   Moving*

Tony Moffeit P
1501 E 7th
Pueblo, CO 81001, 719-549-2751
Internet: moffeit@uscolo.edu
   Pubs: *Poetry Is Dangerous, The Poet Is an Outlaw* (Floating
   Island Pubs, 1995), *Neon Peppers* (Cherry Valley Edtns,
   1992), *Amelia, Taos Rev, Chiron Rev*

Laura Mullen 🎤 ✈   P
English Dept, Colorado State Univ, 359 Eddy Hall, Ft Collins,
CO 80523, 303-419-6845
Internet: lmullen@vines.colostate.edu
    Pubs: *The Tales of Horror* (Kelsey Street Pr, 1999), *After I
    Was Dead* (U Georgia Pr, 1999), *The Surface* (U Illinois Pr,
    1991), *Amer Letters & Commentary, Agni, Denver Qtly,
    Antaeus, Volt*

Kent Nelson 🎤 ✈   W
221 Wood Ave
Salida, CO 81201, 719-539-9706
    Pubs: *Land That Moves, Land That Stands Still* (Viking
    Penguin, 2003), *Toward the Sun* (Breakaway Bks, 1998),
    Language in the Blood (Gibbs Smith, 1992), *Virginia Qtly
    Rev, Sewanee Rev, Gettysburg Rev, Glimmer Train,
    Southern Rev, Shenandoah*

David J. Nelson   PP
PO Box 2993
Denver, CO 80201, 302-294-0653
    Pubs: *Cracking the Pavement* (Baculite Pub Co, 1990),
    Rocky Mountain Arsenal

Tom Parson   P
157 S Logan
Denver, CO 80209, 303-777-8951
    Pubs: *Some Trouble* (Now It's Up to You Pr, 1980), *City Kite
    on a Wire: Anth* (Mesilla Pr, 1986)

Veronica Patterson 🎤 ✈   P
11 Gregg Dr
Loveland, CO 80538-3850, 303-669-7010
Internet: rpatterson@duke.com
    Pubs: *Swan, What Shores?* (NYU Pr, 2000), *The Bones
    Remember* (Stone Graphics, 1992), *How to Make a
    Terrarium* (Cleveland State U Poetry Ctr, 1987), *Many
    Mountains Moving, Willow Springs, Georgia Rev, Louisville
    Rev, Caliban, Malahat Rev*

Naomi Rachel 🎤 ✈   P&W
954 Arroyo Chico
Boulder, CO 80302-9730, 303-449-4031
Internet: milopapers@juno.com
    Pubs: *The Temptation of Extinction* (Senex Pr, 1993), *Yale
    Rev, Nimrod, NAR, Hampden-Sydney Poetry Anth,
    Canadian Lit, Hawaii Rev*

Bin Ramke 🎤 ✈   P
Univ Denver, English Dept, Denver, CO 80208, 303-871-2889
Internet: bramke@du.edu
    Pubs: *Wake, Massacre of the Innocents* (U Iowa Pr, 1999,
    1995), *The Erotic Light of Gardens* (Wesleyan, 1989), *The
    Language Student* (LSU Pr, 1986)

Carson Reed   P&W
4470 W Vassar Ave
Denver, CO 80219, 303-477-7058
Internet: lodo1@aol.com
    Pubs: *Tie Up the Strong Man* (Bread & Butter Pr, 1989),
    Eros: Anth (Stewart, Tabori & Chang, 1996), *The Book of
    Eros* (Harmony Bks, 1995), *RealPoetik, Metrosphere, Neon
    Qtly, Artisan, Bizara, Western Pocket, Open Minds, Sun,
    Yellow Silk, Spilled Ink, Harp*

Deborah Robson 🎤 ✈   W
PO Box 484
Fort Collins, CO 80522-0484, 970-226-3590
Internet: debrobson@fortnet.org
    Pubs: *Nantucket Rev, Seattle Post-Intelligencer, Writers'
    Forum, Twigs, Dogsoldier, Port Townsend Jrnl*

Pattiann Rogers 🎤 ✈   P
7412 Berkeley Cir
Castle Rock, CO 80104-9278, 303-660-0851
Internet: pattiannrogers@mindspring.com
    Pubs: *Song of the World Becoming: New & Collected
    Poems, 1981-2001, The Dream of the Marsh Wren*
    (Milkweed Edtns, 2001, 1999), *Hudson Rev, Paris Rev,
    Poetry, Georgia Rev, Gettysburg Rev*

Reg Saner 🎤 ✈   P
Univ Colorado, English Dept, Box 226, Boulder, CO 80309,
303-494-8951
    Pubs: *Four-Cornered Falcon* (Johns Hopkins U Pr, 1993),
    Red Letters (QRL, 1989), *Essay on Air* (Ohio Rev Bks,
    1984), *Poetry Comes Up Where It Can: Anth* (U Utah Pr,
    2000), *Orpheus & Company: Anth* (U Pr New England,
    1999), *Generations: Anth* (Penguin, 1998)

Bienvenido N. Santos   W
2524 W 13 St
Greeley, CO 80631, 303-356-1121
    Pubs: *What the Hell for You Left Your Heart in San Francisco*
    (New Day, 1987)

Andrew Schelling 🎤 ✈   P
Naropa Univ, 2130 Arapahoe Ave, Boulder, CO 80302-6697,
303-554-5916
    Pubs: *Wild Form Savage Grammar* (La Alameda, 2003),
    Tea Shack Interior: New & Selected Poetry (Talisman
    House, 2002), *The Road to Ocosigno* (Smokeproof Pr,
    1998), *The Cane Groves of Narmada River* (City Lights,
    1998), *Old Growth* (Rodent Pr, 1995), *Sulfur, NAW*

Joel Scherzer   P
PO Box 222
Pueblo, CO 81002
    Pubs: *More Bronx Zen* (Baculite Pub, 1992), *Bronx Zen*
    (Academic & Arts Pr, 1989), *Rocky Mountain Arsenal of the
    Arts, Blue Light Rev, Apalachee Qtly*

Jay Schneiders   P
3955 E Exposition Ave #316
Denver, CO 80209-5032, 303-649-6651
Internet: jaysch@concentric.net
    Pubs: *Georgia Rev, Qtly West, Manoa, The Jrnl, Tampa Rev,
    Prism Intl*

Gary Schroeder 🎤 ✈   P
1429 N Castlewood Dr
Franktown, CO 80116-9015, 303-660-6029
    Pubs: *Cricket in the House: A Year's Haiku, Adjacent
    Solitudes* (Wayland Pr, 1999, 1991), *Only Morning in Her
    Shoes: Anth* (Utah State U Pr, 1990), *Frogpond, Eleventh
    Muse, Pig Iron, Environment & Essence Issue, JaMa*

Steven Schwartz 🎤 ✈   W
2943 Skimmerhorn St, Fort Collins, CO 80526-6288,
970-282-8755
Internet: sschwartz@vines.colostate.edu
    Pubs: *A Good Doctor's Son* (Morrow, 1998), *Therapy: A
    Novel* (Penguin/Plume, 1995), *Lives of the Fathers* (U Illinois
    Pr, 1991), *Ploughshares, Tikkun, Redbook, Virginia Qtly,
    Antioch Rev, Epoch, Missouri Rev*

Sandra Shwayder   P&W
1955 Holly
Denver, CO 80220, 303-399-5927
    Pubs: *The Nun* (Plainview Pr, 1992), *Connections, The Long
    Story, The Dream, COE Rev*

Charles Squier   P
English Dept, Univ Colorado, Campus Box 226, Boulder, CO
80309, 303-492-7381
    Pubs: *Mrs. Beaton's Tea Party* (Reading Dog Pr, 1996),
    *Sniper Logic, Ohio Rev, Open Places, Midwest Qtly,
    Midwest Rev, Rolling Stock, Light Year, Chinook*

Stephanie Stearns   P&W
3980 W Radcliff
Denver, CO 80236
    Pubs: *The Saga of the Sword That Sings & Other Realities*
    (Dubless Pr, 1981), *Eldritch Tales*

Roger Steigmeier   P
2770 Moorhead Ave, #204
Boulder, CO 80303
    Pubs: *Light Traveling Dark Traveling Light* (First East Coast
    Theater & Pub Co, 1984), *Poet*

Constance E. Studer 🎤 ✈   P&W
1617 Parkside Cir
Lafayette, CO 80026-1967, 303-665-3818
Internet: cstjal@prodigy.net
    Pubs: *Intensive Care: Anth* (U Iowa Pr, 2003), *The Age of
    Koestler: Anth* (Practices of the Wind, 1994), *Birmingham
    Poetry Rev, Earth's Daughters, Zone 3*

Ronald Sukenick   W
Univ Colorado, English Dept, Box 226, Boulder, CO 80309,
303-492-7381
Internet: sukenick@spot.colorado.edu
    Pubs: *Up, 98.6* (FC 2, 1998, 1994), *Doggy Bag* (FC 2/Black
    Ice Bks, 1994), *Blown Away* (Sun & Moon Pr, 1986)

Steve Rasnic Tem   P&W
2500 Irving St
Denver, CO 80211, 303-477-0235
    Pubs: *Excavation* (Avon, 1987), *The Umbral Anth of Science
    Fiction Poetry* (Umbral Pr, 1982)

James Tipton 🎤 ✈   P&W
1122 Aquarius Ave
Fruita, CO 81521, 970-858-5014
Internet: jtpoet@aol.com
    Pubs: *The Wizard of Is* (Bread & Butter Pr, 1995), *The Third
    Coast Anth, Cimarron Rev, Greensboro Rev, High Plains Lit
    Rev, ALR, Writers' Forum, Pinyon Poetry, Woodnotes, South
    Dakota Rev, Nation, Esquire, APR*

Rawdon Tomlinson   P
2020 S Grant
Denver, CO 80210
    Pubs: *Deep Red* (U Pr Florida, 1995), *Spreading the Word:
    Anth* (Bench Pr, 1990), *Sewanee Rev, Commonweal,
    Kansas Qtly, Poetry NW, SPR, Ohio Rev, Midwest Qtly*

Bill Tremblay 🎤 ✈   P&W
3412 Lancaster Dr
Fort Collins, CO 80525-2817, 970-226-0311
Internet: watremblay@aol.com
    Pubs: *The June Rise* (Utah State U Pr, 1994), *A Gathering
    of Poets: Anth* (Kent State U Pr, 1993), *Jazz Poetry Anth*
    (Indiana U Pr, 1993), *Bloomsbury Rev, Manoa, Spoon River
    Poetry Rev, Connecticut Poetry Rev, Luna, High Plains
    Literary Rev, Massachusetts Rev*

Anne Waldman   PP&P
375 S 45 St
Boulder, CO 80303, 303-444-0202
Internet: a.waldman@mindspring.com
    Pubs: *Fast Speaking Woman* (City Lights, 1997), *Iovis: All Is
    Full of Jove: Bks II & I, A Poem* (Coffee Hse Pr, 1997, 1993),
    Kill Or Cure (Penguin, 1996), *Conjunctions, Sulfur, City
    Lights Jrnl, Apex of the M, Poetry Project Newsletter, APR*

Gail Waldstein, MD ✈   P&W
108 Cook St, #308
Denver, CO 80206-5307, 303-321-1137
Internet: GWaldstein@aol.com
    Pubs: *Slipstream, Mutant Mule, Sheila-Na-Gig, Inklings,
    Explorations 1998, High Plains Lit Rev, Nimrod, Negative
    Capability, Women: A Jrnl of Liberation*

Marc Weber 🎤 ✈ P
2 N 24 St
Colorado Springs, CO 80904, 719-634-8010
Internet: sugarmale@hotmail.com
　Pubs: *Quest* (Lion's Roar, 1989), *Circle of Light* (San Marcos, 1976)

Robert Lewis Weeks P
6767 E Dartmouth Ave
Denver, CO 80224, 303-756-4274
　Pubs: *As a Master of Clouds* (Juniper Pr, 1971), *APR, Sewanee Rev, Prairie Schooner, West Branch, Georgia Rev, The Qtly, Shenandoah, BPJ*

Thomas A. West, Jr. P&W
6282 Chimney Rock Trail, Morrison, CO 80465-2151, 303-697-4772
　Writing Under Fire: Anth (Dell, 1978), *Chiron Rev, Open Bone Rev, Wisconsin Rev, Cimarron Rev, Four Quarters, Connecticut River Rev, Panhandler, New Mexico Qtly Rev, Touchstone, Oxford Mag, Short Story Intl, Shorelines, Nebraska Mag, New Renaissance*

Richard Wilmarth 🎤 ✈ P
PO Box 2076
Boulder, CO 80306-2076, 303-875-5288
　Pubs: *Trying to Make Sense out of the Absurd, Alphabetical Order, Voices in the Room* (Dead Metaphor Pr, 2001, 1998, 1993), *More! Henry Miller Acrostics: Anth* (Standish Bks, 1996), *Barrow St, California Qtly, Edgz, Big Scream, Zillah, Shiny, Nedge*

Renate Wood 🎤 ✈ P
1900 King Ave
Boulder, CO 80302-8038, 303-447-2796
Internet: rwood38@juno.com
　Pubs: *Patience of Ice* (TriQtly Bks/Northwestern U Pr, 2000), *Raised Underground, Carnegie Mellon Poetry: Anth* (Carnegie Mellon U Pr, 1991, 1993), *Hammer and Blaze: Anth* (U Georgia Pr, 2002), *Virginia Qtly Rev, APR, TriQtly, Ploughshares, NER*

James Yaffe W
1215 N Cascade
Colorado Springs, CO 80903
　Pubs: *Mom Among the Liars, Mom Doth Murder Sleep, Mom Meets Her Maker* (St. Martin's Pr, 1992, 1991, 1990)

William Zaranka P&W
Univ Denver, Denver, CO 80110, 303-871-2966
　Pubs: *Blessing* (Wayland Pr, 1988), *Brand-X Anth of Fiction, Brand-X Anth of Poetry* (Applewood Pr, 1984, 1983), *Poetry, TriQtly, Prairie Schooner*

CONNECTICUT

Dick Allen 🎤 ✈ P
74 Fern Cir
Trumbull, CT 06611-4910, 203-375-1927
Internet: rallen10@snet.net
　Pubs: *The Day Before: New Poems, Ode to the Cold War: New & Selected Poems* (Sarabande Bks, 2003, 1997), *The Best American Poetry: Anths* (Scribner, 1999, 1998), *New Republic, Massachusetts Rev, Yale Rev, New Criterion, Ontario Rev, Gettysburg Rev, Poetry*

Talvikki Ansel P
PO Box 4
Old Mystic, CT 06372
　Pubs: *My Shining Archipelago* (Yale U Pr 1997)

Dennis Barone 🎤 ✈ P&W
Saint Joseph College, 1678 Asylum Ave, West Hartford, CT 06117, 860-231-5379
Internet: dbarone@sjc.edu
　Pubs: *Temple of the Rat, Separate Objects: Selected Poems* (Left Hand Bks, 2000, 1998), *Echoes* (Potes & Poets Pr, 1997), *The Returns* (Sun & Moon Pr, 1996), *Waves of Ice, Waves of Rumor* (Zasterle Pr, 1993)

Lou Barrett 🎤 ✈ P
40 Meadow View Dr
Westport, CT 06880, 203-227-6384
Internet: loubarrett@aol.com
　Pubs: *Homefronts* (Quill Pr, 2002), *Connecticut River Rev, Midstream*

Wendy Battin P
15 Rogers Dr
Mystic, CT 06355, 860-572-9323
Internet: wjbat@conncoll.edu
　Pubs: *Little Apocalypse* (Ashland Poetry Pr, 1997), *In the Solar Wind* (Doubleday, 1984), *The Sacred Place: Anth* (U Utah Pr, 1996), *Yale Rev, The Nation, Gettysburg Rev, Threepenny Rev, Poetry, NER*

Paul Beckman 🎤 ✈ W
PO Box 609
Madison, CT 06443, 203-245-0835
Internet: PaulBeckman@rcn.com
　Pubs: *Come! Meet My Family & Other Stories* (Weighted Anchor Pr, 1995), *Playboy, The Writer's Voice, Onthebus, Strope, Other Voices, Connecticut Rev, Web del Sol, Parting Gifts, Sugar Mule, Northeast Mag*

Ted Bent W
60 Hinkle Rd
Washington, CT 06793-1001
Internet: tedbent@snet.net
　Pubs: *The Girl in the Black Raincoat* (Duell, Sloan & Pearce, 1966), *Massachusetts Rev*

April Bernard 🎤 ✈ P&W
96 Everit Str
New Haven, CT 06511-1321, 203-787-9012
    Pubs: *By Herself* (Graywolf, 2000), *Psalms, Pirate Jenny* (Norton, 1993, 1990), *Blackbird Bye Bye* (Random Hse, 1989), *Joyful Noise: Anth* (Little, Brown, 1998)

Raymond Biasotti P
16 Gerardo Dr
Monroe, CT 06468, 203-261-3830
Internet: nkunderscorebiasotti@commnet.edu
    Pubs: *Village Voice, Red Fox Rev, Phantasm, Folio, A Letter Among Friends*

Elaine Bissell W
10-B Heritage Village
Southbury, CT 06488
    Pubs: *Empire* (Worldwide Library, 1990), *Family Fortunes* (St. Martin's Pr, 1986), *Let's Keep in Touch* (Pocket Bks, 1983), *Women Who Wait* (Popular Library, 1979)

Blanche McCrary Boyd W
Connecticut College, Box 5421, 270 Mohegan Ave, New London, CT 06320
    Pubs: *The Revolution of Little Girls, The Redneck Way of Knowledge* (Knopf, 1991, 1981), *VLS, Esquire*

George Bradley P
82 W Main St
Chester, CT 06412, 203-526-3900
    Pubs: *The Fire Fetched Down, Of the Knowledge of Good & Evil* (Knopf, 1996, 1991), *Terms to Be Met* (Yale U Pr, 1986), *New Yorker, Paris Rev*

Brian Butterick P
31 Friendship St
Willimantic, CT 06226

Jamie Callan 🎤 ✈ W
438 Whitney Ave
New Haven, CT 06511-2349, 203-787-4558
Internet: jamiecatcallan@aol.com
    Pubs: *Story, Missouri Rev, Buzz, American Letters & Commentary, American Way, Baffler*

Michael Casey 🎤 ✈ P
Yale Univ Press, 92A Yale Sta, New Haven, CT 06520
    Pubs: *The Million Dollar Hole* (Carnegie Mellon, 2001), *Millrat* (Adastra, 1996), *Obscenities* (Yale U Pr, 1972), *College English, TriQtly, Michigan Qtly Rev, Rolling Stone, Panhandler, America, Salmagundi, Ohio Rev*

Ina B. Chadwick P
2 Redcoat Rd
Westport, CT 06880, 203-221-0655
Internet: ibcamuse@aol.com
    Pubs: *Considerate Gestures of Love* (Greens Farms Pr, 1979), *Jewish Forward, Namat Woman, New York Times, Antioch Rev*

Pamela Christman 🎤 ✈ W
26 Flicker Ln
Rowayton, CT 06853, 203-299-1370
    Pubs: *Jane, West, Arden, Bluff City, Amaranth Rev, Parting Gifts, Sassy, GW Rev*

David Chura P
477 Newtown Turnpike
Redding, CT 06896-2017
Internet: dchura@ntplx.net
    Pubs: *Essential Love: Anth* (Grayson Bks/Poetworks, 2000), *Queer Dharma: Anth* (Gay Sunshine Pr, 1998), *Many Mountains Moving, Contemporary Justice Rev, Adirondack, Turning Wheel, English Jrnl, Blueline, Connecticut River Rev, Embers, Earth's Daughters*

Gene Coggshall W
The Perkin-Elmer Corp M/S 887, 100 Wooster Heights Rd, Danbury, CT 06810, 203-744-4000

Stanley I. Cohen W
322 Pine Tree Dr
Orange, CT 06477, 203-795-4058
    Pubs: *Angel Face* (St. Martin's Pr, 1982), *330 Park* (Putnam, 1977), *Year's Best Mystery & Suspense Stories: Anth* (Walker, 1991), *Best Detective Stories of the Year: Anth* (Dutton, 1975), *Alfred Hitchcock's Mystery, Ellery Queen's Mystery*

James Coleman W
Three Rivers C-T College, 7 Mahan Dr, English Dept, Norwich, CT 06360, 860-823-2896
    Pubs: *South Dakota Rev, Elkhorn Rev, December, Centennial Rev, St. Andrews Rev, Red Fox Rev, Information*

Martha Collins 🎤 ✈ P&W
c/o Space, 59 Prospect St, Bloomfield, CT 06002
Internet: martha.collins@oberlin.edu
    Pubs: *Some Things Words Can Do* (Sheep Meadow, 1998), *A History of Small Life on a Windy Planet* (U Georgia Pr, 1993), *The Arrangement of Space* (Peregrine Smith, 1991)

Tony Connor W
44 Brainerd Ave
Middletown, CT 06457, 860-344-0815
Internet: jconnor@wesleyan.edu
    Pubs: *Metamorphic Adventures, Spirits of the Place* (Anvil Poetry Pr, 1996, 1986)

Robert Cording 🎤 ✈   P
100 Shields Rd
Woodstock, CT 06281-2820, 860-974-0874
Internet: robert.cording@snet.net
    Pubs: *Against Consolation* (Cavan Kerry, 2002), *Life-List*
    (Ohio State U Pr, 1988), *What Binds Us to This World*
    (Copper Beech, 1991), *Heavy Grace* (Alice James, 1996),
    Poetry, New Yorker, Paris Rev, NER, Southern Rev

Charlotte Garrett Currier 🎤 ✈   P
12 Long Hill Farm
Guilford, CT 06437, 203-453-5472
Internet: ccurrier@cshore.com
    Pubs: *Not to Look Back* (CD; w/D. Currier), *Poem Box*
    (Trefoil Arts, 1998, 1993), *Presences* (The Pr of Night Owl,
    1977), *Southern Rev, Southern Humanities Rev*

David Curtis   P
126 Ardmore Rd
Milford, CT 06460, 203-874-5102
Internet: dcurtis@sacredheart.edu
    Pubs: *Update From Pahrump* (Wyndam Hall, 1992), *Four
    Quarters, Dalhousie Rev, Descant, The Writer, Poem,
    Pegasus Rev, Potato Eyes, Inlet*

Emily Davidson   P
358 Orange St #407
New Haven, CT 06511
    Pubs: *Z Misc, River Rat Rev, Black Buzzard Rev, City, Truck,
    New Voices, Connecticut Fireside, Sister, Amaranth Rev*

Cortney Davis 🎤 ✈   P
PO Box 678
West Redding, CT 06896-0678
    Pubs: *Details of Flesh* (Calyx Bks, 1997), *The Body Flute*
    (Adastra Pr, 1994), *Between the Heartbeats: Anth* (U Iowa
    Pr, 1995), *Hudson Rev, Crazyhorse, Poetry East, Witness,
    Prairie Schooner, Hanging Loose, Poetry, Ontario Rev*

Ellen Kitzes Delfiner 🎤 ✈   P
1 Strawberry Hill Ct #6J
Stamford, CT 06902-2531
Internet: eskd@juno.com
    Pubs: *Response, Art Times, New Authors Jrnl, Jam Today,
    Treasure House, Aura, Slant*

G. Scott Deshefy 🎤 ✈   P
35 Walnut Dr
Uncasville, CT 06382, 860-424-3334
Internet: scott.deshefy@po.state.ct.us
    Pubs: *Shadow Stones: Selected Poems, Houyhnhnms All:
    Selected Poems* (Ahimsa Pr, 2002, 1998), *Survival in
    Writing and Art 2001: Anth* (CT Trauma Coalition, 2001), *In
    Other Words: An American Poetry Anth* (Western Reading
    Services, 1995), *Eye Prayers, Gone*

Concetta Ciccozzi Doucette   P&W
2799 Ellington Rd
South Windsor, CT 06074-1703, 860-644-2352
    Pubs: *Autumn Harvest: Anth* (Quill Bks, 2001), *Footwork:
    Anth* (Passaic County Community College, 1995), *AIM,
    Italian Americana, Beanfeast, Mediphors, Apostrophe,
    Women's Words*

Franz Douskey 🎤 ✈   P
50 Ives St
Mount Carmel, CT 06518-2202, 203-248-4615
Internet: inwalkedlike@yahoo.com
    Pubs: *Archaeological Nights* (Pharos Bks, 1982), *Yankee,
    The Nation, Die Hard, Colorado Qtly, Carolina Qtly, Cavalier,
    Yellow Silk, Colorado Qtly, NYQ, New Yorker, Georgia Rev,
    Minnesota Rev*

Russell Edson 🎤 ✈   P&W
29 Ridgeley St
Darien, CT 06820-4110, 203-655-1575
    Pubs: *The House of Sara Loo* (Rain Taxi, 2002), *The
    Tormented Mirror* (U Pitt Pr, 2001), *The Tunnel* (Oberlin
    College Pr, 1994), *The Song of Percival Peacock* (Coffee
    Hse Pr, 1992)

Resurreccion Espinosa 🎤 ✈   P&W
265 Gardner Ave
New London, CT 06320, 860-443-8703
    Pubs: *Waking Dream* (Xlibris, 1998), *Bilingual Rev, INTI,
    Teatra*

James Finnegan 🎤 ✈   P
18 Woodrow St
West Hartford, CT 06107, 860-521-0358
Internet: jforjames@aol.com
    Pubs: *Poetry NW, Shenandoah, Tar River Poetry, Southern
    Rev, Chelsea, Ploughshares, Poetry East, Virginia Qtly Rev,
    Willow Springs*

Henry George Fischer 🎤 ✈   P
29 Mauweehoo Hill
Sherman, CT 06784-2312, 860-354-2719
    Pubs: *Light & Night & the Half-Light* (Pocahontas Pr, 1999),
    *More Timely Rhymes, Timely Rhymes From the Sherman
    Sentinel* (Singular Speech Pr, 1996, 1993), *Treasury of
    Light Verse: Anth* (Random Hse, 1995), *Light, Pivot,
    Verbatim, Lyric, Sparrow, ELF*

Eleni Fourtouni   P
1218 Forest Rd
New Haven, CT 06515, 203-397-3902
    Pubs: *Greek Women in Resistance, Watch the Flame*
    (Thelphini Pr, 1985, 1983)

Vernon Frazer 🎤 ✈   PP&P&W
132 Woodycrest Dr
East Hartford, CT 06118, 860-569-3101
Internet: vfrazer@attbi.com
  Pubs: *Relic's Reunions, Improvisations, Stay Tuned to This
  Channel, Sing Me One Song of Evolution* (Beneath the
  Underground, 2000, 2000, 1999, 1998), *Demolition Fedora,
  Free Fall* (Potes & Poets, 1999, 1999), *Jack Mag, First
  Intensity*

William T. Freeman   P
205 Orange St
Waterbury, CT 06704, 203-753-7743
  Pubs: *Obsidian, Greenfield Rev, Pudding, Parnassus,
  Laurels*

Jim Furlong   W
57 Fishtown Ln
Mystic, CT 06355-2007, 860-572-4186
Internet: jcfurlong@att.net
  Pubs: *Local Action* (Cozy Detective Mystery Mag, 1999),
  Literature of Work: Anth (U Phoenix Pr, 1991), *Licking River
  Rev, Palo Alto Rev*

Margaret Gibson 🎤 ✈   P
152 Watson Rd
Preston, CT 06365-8837, 860-886-1777
Internet: margibson@juno.com
  Pubs: *Autumn Grasses, Icon and Evidence, Earth Elegy,
  The Vigil, Out in the Open, Memories of the Future, Long
  Walks in the Afternoon* (LSU Pr, 2003, 2001, 1997, 1993,
  1989, 1986, 1982), *Southern Rev, Georgia Rev,
  Shenandoah, Iowa Rev, Gettysburg Rev*

John Gilmore   P
c/o Walter Pitkin, 11 Oakwood Dr, Weston, CT 06883,
203-227-3684

Jody Gladding   P
Yale Univ Pr, PO Box 209040, New Haven, CT 06520-9040,
203-432-0960
  Pubs: *Stone Crop* (Yale U Pr, 1995), *Best American Poetry:
  Anth* (S&S, 1995), *Paris Rev, Wilderness, Agni, Poetry NW,
  Yale Rev*

Antoni Gronowicz   P&W
128 Brookmoor Rd
Avon, CT 06001
  Pubs: *God's Broker* (Richardson & Snyder, 1984), *An
  Orange Full of Dreams* (Dodd, Mead, 1973)

Jayseth Guberman 🎤 ✈   P
PO Box 270357
West Hartford, CT 06127-0357
  Pubs: *Voices Israel, Martyrdom & Resistance, European
  Judaism, Rashi, Prophetic Voices, Poet, Black Buzzard Rev,
  Jewish Spectator*

Joan Joffe Hall 🎤 ✈   P&W
64 Birchwood Heights
Storrs, CT 06268
  Pubs: *Summer Heat: Three Stories* (Kutenai Pr, 1991),
  Romance & Capitalism at the Movies (Alice James Bks,
  1985), *Kansas Qtly, Alaska Qtly, North Dakota Qtly, Fiction
  Intl*

Jay Halpern   W
58 Jackson Cove Rd
Oxford, CT 06478, 203-888-4976
Internet: alicorn@wtco.net
  Pubs: *The Jade Unicorn* (Macmillan, 1979), *Icarus, Hobo
  Jungle, Noiseless Spider, Tapestry, Enigma*

Richard F. Harteis   P&W
337 Kitemaug Rd
Uncasville, CT 06382, 860-848-8486
Internet: rfhar@conncoll.edu
  Pubs: *Keeping Heart* (Orpheus Hse, 1996), *Marathon*
  (Norton, 1989), *Internal Geography, Window on the Black
  Sea: Anth* (Carnegie Mellon U Pr, 1987, 1992), *Virginia Rev,
  Ploughshares, Seneca Rev, New Letters*

Dolores Hayden 🎤 ✈   P
125 Prospect Ave
Guilford, CT 06437-3114
Internet: dolores.hayden@yale.edu
  Pubs: *Line Dance, Playing House* (Robert Barth, 2001,
  1998), *SW Rev, Slate, Yale Rev, Michigan Qtly Rev*

Hank Heifetz 🎤 ✈   W
548 Orange St #406
New Haven, CT 06511-3866, 203-865-8801
  Pubs: *The Four Hundred Songs of War & Wisdom* (w/G.L.
  Hart; Columbia U Pr, 1999), *The Origin of the Young God,
  For the Lord of the Animals* (U California Pr, 1990, 1987),
  Where Are the Stars in New York? (Dutton, 1973),
  Evergreen Rev, VLS

Peggy Heinrich 🎤 ✈   P
625 Gilman St
Bridgeport, CT 06605-3608, 203-333-3938
Internet: heinrich@snet.net
  Pubs: *Sharing the Woods* (Old Sandal Pr, 1992), *A Patch of
  Grass* (High/Coo Pr, 1984), *the loose thread: Anth* (Red
  Moon Pr, 2001), *Literal Latte, Ct River Rev, American Tanka,
  Negative Capability, Texas Rev, Blue Unicorn, Rio Grande
  Rev, Passager*

E. Ward Herlands 🎤   P
179 Fox Ridge Rd
Stamford, CT 06903, 203-322-3811
  Pubs: *Literature: Introduction to Poetry: Anth, Reading
  Fiction, Poetry, Drama & the Essay: Anth,* (McGraw-Hill,
  2000, 1998), *Prairie Schooner, Prose Poem: An Intl Jrnl,
  New York Times, Pittsburgh Qtly*

Pati Hill   P&W
20 Grand St
Stonington, CT 06378, 203-535-1747

Barbara Holder   P
55 Gallow Hill Rd
Redding, CT 06896, 203-938-4043
    Pubs: *Literature 4th Ed.: Anth, Modern American Poets:
    Voices & Visions: Anth* (McGraw-Hill 1998, 1993), *Writing
    Through Literature: Anth* (Prentice Hall Bks, 1995), *Slow
    Dancer, Wind, Earth's Daughters, Footwork, Poetic Justice,
    Kentucky Poetry Rev*

David Holdt 🎤 ✈   P
Watkinson School, 180 Bloomfield Ave, Hartford, CT
06105-1096, 860-236-5618
Internet: dmholdt@mindspring.com
    Pubs: *Heartbeat of New England: Anth* (Tiger Moon Pr,
    2000), *In the Place of the Long River: Anth* (Blue Moon Pr,
    1996), *River of Dreams: Anth* (Glover, 1990), *Northeast,
    Spitball, Stone Country, Amelia*

John Hollander 🎤 ✈   P
Yale Univ, English Dept, PO Box 208302, New Haven, CT
06520-8302, 203-432-2231
Internet: john.hollander@yale.edu
    Pubs: *Figurehead, Selected Poetry, Tesserae, Harp Lake*
    (Knopf, 1999, 1993, 1993, 1988), *Melodious Guile* (Yale U
    Pr, 1988), *Blue Wine* (Hopkins, 1979)

Donald Honig   W
2322 Cromwell Gdns
Cromwell, CT 06416

Susan Howe   P
115 New Quarry Rd
Guilford, CT 06437
    Pubs: *The Nonconformist's Memorial* (New Directions,
    1993), *Singularities* (Wesleyan, 1990), *American Poetry
    Since 1950: Anth* (Marsilio, 1993)

Bob Jacob 🎤 ✈   P
PO Box 1133
Farmington, CT 06034-1133, 860-677-0606
Internet: versebks@tlac.net
    Pubs: *The Day Seamus Heaney Kissed My Cheek in Dublin*
    (The Spirit That Moves Us Pr, 2000), *Café Rev*

Gray Jacobik 🎤 ✈   P
Eastern Connecticut State Univ, English Dept, Willimantic, CT
06226, 860-963-0440
Internet: gray@grayjacobik.com
    Pubs: *Brave Disguises* (U Pitt Pr, 2002), *The Surface of Last
    Scattering* (Texas Rev Pr, 1999), *The Double Task* (U Mass
    Pr, 1998), *The Best American Poetry: Anths* (Scribner, 1999,
    1997), *Kenyon Rev, Poetry, Prairie Schooner, Ploughshares,
    Georgia Rev*

Sharon Ann Jaeger 🎤 ✈   P
PO Box 620
Stamford, CT 06904-0620
Internet: sajaeger@hotmail.com
    Pubs: *The Chain of Dead Desire, Filaments of Affinity* (Park
    Slope Edtns, 1990, 1989), *X-Connect*

Leland Jamieson, Jr. 🎤   P
24 Birchwood Rd
East Hampton, CT 06424, 860-267-6519
Internet: leejamieson@erols.com
    Pubs: *Artword Qtly, Midwest Poetry Rev, Rattle, Sidewalks,
    Spillway, Wise Woman's Garden, Aurorean, Avocet,
    California Qtly, Coffee & Chicory, Inlet, Kansas Qtly*

John Jurkowski   W
6 Walnut Ridge Rd
New Fairfield, CT 06812-0214, 203-746-7673
    Pubs: *New Yorker, Redbook, Shenandoah, QRL, NAR*

Susan A. Katz 🎤 ✈   P
121 Painter Ridge Rd
Washington Depot, CT 06793-1710, 203-241-1836
    Pubs: *Two Halves of the Same Silence* (Confluence Pr,
    1985), *Life on the Line: Anth* (Negative Capability Pr, 1992),
    When I Am an Old Woman I Shall Wear Purple: Anth
    (Papier-Mache Pr, 1991)

Susan Baumann Kinsolving 🎤 ✈   P
PO Box 175
Bridgewater, CT 06752-0175
    Pubs: *Dailies & Rushes* (Grove Pr, 1999), *Among Flowers*
    (Clarkson Potter/Random Hse, 1993), *Paris Rev, Grand
    Street, Kansas Qtly, Western Humanities Rev, New
    Republic, The Nation, Harvard Mag, BPJ, Antioch Rev*

Binnie Klein   P
225 Cooper Lane
Hamden, CT 06514, 203-785-0639
Internet: binnie.nai@rcn.com
    Pubs: *Twilight Zones* (Co-author; U California Pr, 1997),
    *Sequoia, Dreamworks, Stone Country, Panache, Minnesota
    Rev, Confrontation, Center, Etcetera*

Kenneth M. Koprowski   P
340 Bayberrie Dr
Stamford, CT 06902

Eileen Kostiner 🎤   P
19 Thompson Rd
Storrs, CT 06268, 860-429-6983
Internet: ekostiner@sprynet.com
    Pubs: *Love's Other Face, Poetry Like Bread: Anth*
    (Curbstone Pr, 1982, 1994), *MacGuffin, Nostalgia, SPR,
    Mediphors, Labyris, Creative Woman, Paintbrush, Embers*

Norman Kraeft P
86 Bellamy Ln
Bethlehem, CT 06751-1203, 203-266-5113
    Pubs: *The Lyric, Sparrow, Orbis, Prairie Schooner,
    Connecticut River Rev, Bogg: An Anglo-American Jrnl,
    Pivot, Blue Unicorn*

Janet Krauss 🎤 P
585 Gilman St
Bridgeport, CT 06605-3634, 203-333-7779
    Pubs: *A Pamphlet of Poems* (Palanquin Pr, 1995), *Painted
    Hills, Green Hills Lit Lantern, California State Poetry Society,
    Jabberwok, Rockhurst Rev, Dickinson Rev, Chaffin Jrnl,
    South Carolina Rev, Offerings, Sand Hill Rev, Parting Gifts*

Philip Watson Kuepper P&W
233 Bouton St W
Stamford, CT 06907-1322, 203-968-0165
    Pubs: *Promise*

Ken Kuhlken 🎤 ✈ W
Donald Gastwirth & Assoc, 265 College St, Suite 10-N,, New
Haven, CT 06510
Internet: kkuhlken@mail.sdsu.edu
    Pubs: *The Angel Gang, The Venus Deal, The Loud Adios*
    (St. Martin's, 1994, 1992, 1991), *Midheaven* (Viking, 1980),
    Crime Through Time: Anth (Berkeley, 1998), *Esquire, Puerto
    del Sol, Kansas Qtly, Colorado Rev, Mss.*

Helen Lawson P&W
80 Wethersfield Ave, Apt 3
Hartford, CT 06114
    Pubs: *Live Me a River, Women As I Know Them* (Blue
    Spruce Pr, 1981, 1978), *Bronte Street, Caprice*

Rena Lee P
179 Ledge Dr
Torrington, CT 06790
    Pubs: *Present Tense, Pulp, Bitterroot, Poet Lore, Shofar*

Ann Z. Leventhal 🎤 ✈ P&W
19 Woodside Cir
Hartford, CT 06105-1120
Internet: azlhdl@ct2.nai.net
    Pubs: *Life-Lines* (Magic Circle Pr, 1986), *Publishers Weekly,
    Passages North, Cottonwood, Remark, Pacific Rev, Lake
    Effect, Georgia Rev, Other Voices, South Dakota Rev,
    Mississippi Rev*

Pam Lewis W
128 Courtyard Ln
Storrs Mansfield, CT 06250
    Pubs: *Wee Girls* (Spinifex, 1997), *New Yorker, Puerto del
    Sol, Intro 14*

David Low W
276 Court St, #105
Middletown, CT 06457
    Pubs: *American Families: Anth* (NAL, 1989), *Ploughshares*

Rick Lyon P
65 Main St, #17
Ivoryton, CT 06442, 860-767-0628
    Pubs: *Bell 8* (BOA Edtns, 1994), *Missouri Rev, Partisan Rev,
    Kansas Qtly, Agni, Massachusetts Rev, Nation, Tar River
    Poetry, APR, Ironwood, Colorado Rev*

Chopeta C. Lyons 🎤 W
198 Jared Sparks Rd
West Willington, CT 06279-1406
    Pubs: *Northeast, Primavera, Negative Capability, Aura*

Kathleen A. Magill P
50 Bell St Apt 47
Stamford, CT 06901
    Pubs: *Just Buffalo Pr, Deros, Common Ground, Up Against
    the Wall Mother*

Robin Magowan 🎤 ✈ P
PO Box 511
Salisbury, CT 06068, 860-435-9586
    Pubs: *Imporbable Journeys* (Northwestern U Pr, 2002),
    Memoirs of a Minotour (Story Line Pr, 1999), *Lilac Cigarette
    in a Wish Cathedral* (U South Carolina Pr, 1998)

Alice Mattison 🎤 ✈ P&W
15 Anderson St
New Haven, CT 06511, 203-624-0332
Internet: alicemattison@snet.net
    Pubs: *The Book Borrower, Men Giving Money, Women
    Yelling, Hilda & Pearl, The Flight of Andy Burns* (Morrow,
    1999, 1997, 1995, 1993), *New Yorker, Shenandoah,
    Glimmer Train, Boulevard, Ploughshares, Michigan Qtly Rev*

Carole Spearin McCauley 🎤 ✈ P&W
23 Buena Vista Dr
Greenwich, CT 06831-4210, 203-531-6192
Internet: mccaulea@concentric.net
    Pubs: *Cold Steal, Happenthing in Travel On* (Women's Pr,
    1991, 1990), *Nightshade Reader: Anth* (Nightshade Pr,
    1995), *Baba Yaga: Anth* (Woman of Wands, 1995),
    *Whispering Willows, Timber Creek Rev, Heaven Bone,
    Murderous Intent, Vermont, Ink*

J. D. McClatchy P
The Yale Review, Box 208243, New Haven, CT 06520-8243,
203-432-0499
    Pubs: *Ten Commandments, The Rest of the Way* (Knopf,
    1998, 1990), *Stars Principal* (Macmillan, 1986), *Scenes
    From Another Life* (Braziller, 1981), *Vintage Book of
    Contemporary American Poetry: Anth* (Vintage, 1990)

Kaye McDonough P
236 Santa Fe Ave
Hamden, CT 06517
Internet: greenlightpress@aol.com
    Pubs: *The Stiffest of the Corpse: An Exquisite Corpse Reader: Anth, City Lights Anth* (City Lights Bks, 1989, 1974), *City Lights, Beatitude, Vagabond Press*

Rennie McQuilkin 🎤 ✈ P
21 Goodrich Rd
Simsbury, CT 06070-1804, 860-658-1728
Internet: RMcQuil@juno.com
    Pubs: *Gettysburg Rev, Crazyhorse, NAR, Poetry, Yale Rev, Southern Rev, Poetry NW, Hudson Rev, Atlantic*

Angela M. Mendez 🎤 ✈ P
PO Box 26401
West Haven, CT 06516, 203-937-7324
Internet: poetryang@hotmail.com
    Pubs: *Essential Love: Anth* (Poetworks/Grayson Bks, 2000), *The Connecticut River Rev, Afterthoughts, Devil Blossoms, Lunar Offensive Pr, Underwood Rev, Rockhurst Rev, Artful Mind, Contraband, New Digressions, eNteLechy, Wolfhead Qtly, Conscience*

David L. Meth 🎤 ✈ P
Writers' Productions, PO Box 630, Westport, CT 06881-0630, 203-227-8199
Internet: dlm67@worldnet.att.net
    Pubs: *Cambric Poetry Project One, Hoosier Challenger, New World, American Pen, Confrontation, Poet Lore, Valley Views, Lake Superior Rev, Jeopardy*

Barbara Milton W
32 Elm St
Milford, CT 06460
    Pubs: *A Small Cartoon* (Wordbeat Pr, 1983), *Paris Rev, NAR, Apalachee Qtly*

David Morse W
64 Birchwood Hts
Storrs, CT 06268, 860-429-6803
Internet: dmorse@david_morse.com
    Pubs: *The Iron Bridge* (Harcourt, 1998)

H. L. Mountzoures W
29 Old Black Point Rd
Niantic, CT 06357-2815
    Pubs: *The Bridge, The Empire of Things* (Scribner, 1972, 1968), *New Yorker, Yankee, Redbook, Atlantic*

Bryanne Nanfito P
428 Broad St #2-South
Meriden, CT 06450, 203-634-6675
    Pubs: *Greenfield Rev, NYQ, Kansas Qtly*

Gunilla B. Norris P
193 Ocean View Ave
Mystic, CT 06355337, 860-536-8792
    Pubs: *Journeying in Place, Sharing Silence, Becoming Bread, Being Home* (Bell Tower Bks, 1994, 1994, 1992, 1991), *Learning From the Angel* (Lotus, 1985)

Hugh Ogden 🎤 ✈ P
331 Chestnut Hill Rd
Glastonbury, CT 06033, 203-657-3293
Internet: hugh.ogden@mail.trincoll.edu
    Pubs: *Gift, Two Roads & This Spring* (CRS OutLoud Bks, 1998, 1993), *Natural Things, Windfalls* (Andrew Mountain Pr, 1998, 1996), *New Letters, Poetry NW, North Dakota Qtly, Malahat Rev*

Maureen A. Owen 🎤 ✈ P
109 Dunk Rock Rd
Guilford, CT 06437, 203-453-1921
Internet: pomowen@ix.netcom.com
    Pubs: *American Rush: Selected Poems, Moving Borders: Anth* (Talisman Hse Pub, 1998, 1998), *Untapped Maps* (Potes & Poets Pr, 1993), *Imaginary Income* (Hanging Loose Pr, 1992), *Five Fingers Rev, o.blek, Long News in the Short Century, NAW, 6ix, Hanging Loose*

Fred Pfeil P&W
Dept of English, Trinity College, Hartford, CT 06106, 860-297-2464
Internet: john.pfeil@trincoll.edu
    Pubs: *What They Tell You to Forget* (Pushcart Pr, 1996), *Goodman 2020* (Indiana U Pr, 1985), *DoubleTake, Minnesota Rev, Georgia Rev, Fiction Intl, Sewanee Rev*

Joan Pond W
277 Long Mtn
New Milford, CT 06776
    Pubs: *Reflections, Rose Garden* (Life-Link Bks, 1990, 1989)

Joseph Raffa P
Box 414
Glastonbury, CT 06033, 203-659-3424
    Pubs: *No Archaeologist, Death Depends on Our Dark Silence* (John Brown Pr, 1987, 1986), *NYQ, Crosscurrents, Samisdat, Wisconsin Rev, Windless Orchard*

Charles Rafferty 🎤 ✈ P
6 Longview Rd
Sandy Hook, CT 06482-1304, 203-270-3438
Internet: cmrafferty@usa.net
    Pubs: *The Man on the Tower* (U Arkansas Pr, 1995)

Kit Reed 🎤 ✈ W
45 Lawn Ave
Middletown, CT 06457, 212-265-7330
www.focus-consulting.co.uk/kreed/reed.html
 Internet: Pubs: *@expectations* (Forge, 2000), *Seven for the Apocalypse, Weird Women, Wired Women* (Wesleyan U Pr, 1999, 1998), *J. Eden* (U Pr New England, 1996), *Twice Burned, Gone* (Little, Brown, 1993, 1992), *Thief of Lives & Other Stories* (U Missouri Pr, 1992)

Dr. Nicholas M. Rinaldi 🎤 ✈ P&W
Fairfield Univ, English Dept, Fairfield, CT 06430, 203-254-4000
Internet: nrinaldi01@snet.net
 Pubs: *The Jukebox Queen of Malta* (S&S, 1999), *Bridge Fall Down* (St. Martin's, 1985)

Becky Rodia 🎤 ✈ P
75 Pinehurst Rd
Stratford, CT 06614, 203-378-4616
Internet: brodyjean@aol.com
 Pubs: *Another Fire* (Adastra Pr, 1997), *Indiana Rev, Weber Studies, Laurel Rev, Cream City Rev, Poet Lore, Georgetown Rev*

Lawrence Russ 🎤 ✈ P
33 Westford Dr
Southport, CT 06890-1444, 860-808-5090
Internet: lawrencer@snet.net
 Pubs: *Atlanta Rev, NYQ, Yankee, The Nation, Image, Virginia Qtly Rev, Iowa Rev, Parabola, Chelsea*

Mark Saba 🎤 ✈ P&W
144 Woodlawn St
Hamden, CT 06517, 203-230-8365
Internet: mark.saba@yale.edu
 Pubs: *Nantucket: Anth* (White Fish Pr, 2001), *Essential Love: Anth* (Poetworks, 2000), *Elvis in Oz: Anth* (U Pr Virginia, 1992), *VIA, Mars Hill Rev, Phantasmagoria, Connecticut River Rev, Confrontation, Kentucky Poetry Rev, The Ledge, MacGuffin, Permafrost*

Domenic Sammarco P
54 Toquam Rd
New Canaan, CT 06840-3926, 203-866-3372
Internet: ticovismar@aol.com
 Pubs: *Wings* (Scholastic Bks, 1984), *Poem, The End of the Journey, American Scholar*

Maria Sassi 🎤 ✈ P
11 Paxton Rd
West Hartford, CT 06107-3325, 860-521-2095
 Pubs: *Rooted in Stars* (Singular Speech Pr, 1998), *What I See* (Hanover Pr, 1997), *Connecticut River Rev, Italian-Americana, Blue Unicorn, Pivot*

Leslie Scalapino P
Wesleyan Univ Press, 110 Mt Vernon St, Middleton, CT 06459-0433
 Pubs: *The Return of Painting* (Talisman Hse Pub, 1997), *The Front Matter Dead Souls* (Wesleyan U Pr, 1996), *Crowd & Not Evening Or Light, What Is the Inside What Is Outside?: Anth* (O Bks, 1992, 1991), *How Phenomena Appear to Unfold* (Potes & Poets, 1990)

Jeffrey Schwartz P
50 Tahmore Pl
Fairfield, CT 06432-2520
 Pubs: *Contending With the Dark* (Alice James Bks, 1978), *Pennsylvania Rev, Yankee, Connecticut Poetry Rev*

James R. Scrimgeour P
36 Caldwell Dr
New Milford, CT 06776, 860-355-0154
 Pubs: *We Are What We Have Loved* (Hanover Pr, 2001), *James R. Scrimgeour Greatest Hits* (Pudding Hse Pubs, 2001), *The Route and Other Poems* (Pikostaff Pubs, 1996), *Dikel, Your Hands* (Spoon River, 1979), *Pembroke Mag, Connecticut Rev, Green Mountains Rev*

Thalia Selz W
52 Coolidge St
Hartford, CT 06106-3720, 860-527-4141
 Pubs: *American Fiction 3: Anth* (Birch Lane, 1992), *Oktoberfest V: Anth* (Druid Pr, 1990), *Antaeus, Partisan Rev, Missouri Rev, New Letters, Chicago, Kansas Qtly*

Joan Shapiro P
17 Fairview Dr/Box 752
South Windsor, CT 06074, 203-644-2311
 Pubs: *The Puppet Lady: Poems, Coloring Book: Poems* (Blue Spruce, 1982, 1978)

Vivian Shipley 🎤 ✈ P
Southern Connecticut Univ, 501 Crescent St, New Haven, CT 06515, 203-392-6737
 Pubs: *When There Is No Shore* (Word Pr, 2002), *Down of Hawk* (Sows Ear Pr, 2001), *Fair Haven* (Negative Capability, 2000), *Echo & Anger, Still* (Southeastern Louisiana U Pr, 2000), *Crazy Quilt* (Hanover Pr, 1999), *Prairie Schooner, Amer Scholar*

Joan Seliger Sidney 🎤 ✈ P
74 Lynwood Rd
Storrs, CT 06268-2012, 860-429-7271
Internet: jsidney@juno.com
 Pubs: *The Way the Past Comes Back* (Kutenai Pr, 1991), *Deep Between the Rocks* (Andrew Mountain Pr, 1985), *Beyond Lament: Anth* (Northwestern U Pr, 1998), *Her Face in the Mirror: Anth* (Beacon Pr, 1994), *The Louisville Rev, Kaleidoscope*

Sharyn Jeanne Skeeter 🎤 ✈   P&W
PO Box 16819
Stamford, CT 06905, 866-892-4216
Internet: sjskeeter@writernetwork.com
Pubs: *The Second Word Thursdays: Anth* (Bright Hill Pr,
1999), *In Search of Color Everywhere: Anth* (Stewart, Tabori
& Chang, 1994), *Pearl, Connecticut River Rev, Callaloo,*
Fiction

Rod Steier   P
39 Pheasant Hill Dr
West Hartford, CT 06107
Pubs: *28 Days to Satori, Kevin* (Bartholomew's Cobble,
1976, 1975)

Jonathan Stolzenberg 🎤   P
31 Woodland St #11R
Hartford, CT 06105, 860-246-8374
Internet: jstolzenberg@snet.net
Pubs: *Connecticut Rev, Notre Dame Rev, Half Tones to*
Jubilee, Eureka Lit Mag, Licking River Rev, Louisville Rev,
Gulf Stream, Mangrove, Texas Rev

William Styron   W
Rucum Rd
Roxbury, CT 06783
Pubs: *This Quiet Dust, Sophie's Choice* (Random Hse,
1982, 1979)

Wally Swist   P
300 Summit St
Hartford, CT 06106-3100, 860-688-0174
Pubs: *Veils of the Divine* (Hanover Pr, 2001), *The White*
Rose (Timberline Pr, 2000), *The New Life* (Plinth Bks,
1998), *Intimate Kisses: Anth* (New World Library, 2001),
Stories from Where We Live: Anth (Milkweed Edtns, 2000)

Lisa C. Taylor 🎤 ✈   P
PO Box 484
Mansfield Center, CT 06250
Internet: imagine22@earthlink.net
Pubs: *Falling Open* (Alpha Beat Pr, 1994), *Written With a*
Spoon: Anth (Sherman Asher Publishing, 1995), *Cape*
Rock, Connecticut River Rev, Midwest Rev, Xanadu

Randeane Tetu 🎤 ✈   W
41 Old Turnpike Rd
Haddam, CT 06438, 860-345-4226
Pubs: *Flying Horses, Secret Souls, Merle's & Marilyn's Mink*
Ranch, When I Am an Old Woman I Shall Wear Purple: Anth
(Papier-Mache Pr, 1997, 1991, 1987), *Massachusetts Rev,*
Minnesota Rev

Sue Ellen Thompson 🎤 ✈   P
PO Box 326
Mystic, CT 06355-0326, 860-536-0215
Internet: iambic@aol.com
Pubs: *The Leaving: New & Selected* (Autumn Hse Pr, 2001),
The Wedding Boat (Owl Creek Pr, 1995), *This Body of Silk*
(Northeastern U Pr, 1986)

Jessica Treat 🎤 ✈   W
PO Box 752
Lakeville, CT 06039, 860-435-1259
Internet: jttreat@earthlink.net
Pubs: *Not a Chance* (Fiction Collective 2, 2000), *A Robber*
in the House (Coffee Hse Pr, 1993), *Wildcards: Anth*
(Virago, 1999), *Under the Sun, Terra Incognita, 3rd Bed,*
webdelsol, Ms., Epoch, Black Warrior Rev, Qtly West,
Pennsylvania English

Edwina Trentham 🎤 ✈   P
Asnuntuck Community Colllege, 170 Elm St, Enfield, CT
06082, 860-253-3103
Internet: as_et@commnet.edu
Pubs: *Atomic Ghost: Anth* (Coffee Hse Pr, 1995), *Pivot,*
Yankee Mag, Massachusetts Rev, Sun, Embers, Dickinson
Rev, Harvard Mag, American Voice, New Virginia Rev

Peter J. Ulisse 🎤 ✈   P
65 Rivercliff Dr
Devon, CT 06460-5025, 203-874-0618
Internet: pulisse@hcc.commnet.edu
Pubs: *Wings & Roots* (Icarus Pr, 1985), *Poet, Poets On,*
Poetry South, Wayfarers, Connecticut River Rev

Katrina Van Tassel   P
6 Broad St
Guilford, CT 06437, 203-453-2328
Pubs: *Trundlewheel* (Andrew Mountain Pr, 1981), *Yankee,*
Embers, Red Fox Rev, Stone Country, Footworks

Theresa C. Vara 🎤 ✈   P
56 Shane Dr
Southbury, CT 06488
Pubs: *Poeti Italo-Americani/Italian-American Poets: Anth*
(Italbooks, 1992), *Earthwise, Beanfeast, A New Song*

Patricia Volk 🎤 ✈   W
Box 295
Sharon, CT 06069
Pubs: *Stuffed* (Knopf, 2001), *All It Takes, White Light*
(Atheneum, 1990, 1987), *The Yellow Banana* (Word Beat,
1984), *Redbook, Playboy, New Yorker, Atlantic*

Marilyn Nelson Waniek   P
English Dept, U-25, Univ Connecticut, Storrs, CT 06268,
203-486-2141
http://www.ucc.uconn.edu/~waniek/
Pubs: *In Search of Color Everywhere: Anth* (Stewart, Tabori
& Chang, 1994), *Every Shut Eye Ain't Asleep: Anth* (Little,
Brown, 1994), *Southern Rev, Kenyon, APR*

Katharine Weber 🎙 ✈   W
108 Beacon Rd
Bethany, CT 06524-3018, 203-393-1559
Internet: katweber@snet.net
   Pubs: *The Music Lesson* (Crown, 1999), *Objects in Mirror
   Are Closer Than They Appear* (Picador, 1996), *Southwest
   Rev, New Yorker, Story, Redbook*

Max Wilk   W
29 Surf Rd
Westport, CT 06880, 203-226-7669

David Wilk   P
Inland Book Company, PO Box 120261, East Haven, CT
06512, 800-243-0138
   Pubs: *Get Up off Your Ass & Sing* (Membrane, 1985), *Tree
   Taking Root* (Truck, 1977), *Sixpack*

Adrienne Wolfert 🎙 ✈   P&W
3200 Park Ave 11171
BPT, CT 06604, 203-372-3802
Internet: wolfrite@aol.com
   Pubs: *Making Tracks* (Silver Moon Pr, 2000), *Blue Unicorn,
   Great River Rev, Greenfield Rev, NAR, Poem, Poetry Rev,
   The Country and Abroad*

Ann Yarmal   P
27 Northil St
Stamford, CT 06907, 203-322-5638
   Pubs: *The North Star & the Southern Cross, On This Crust
   of Earth: Anth of Fairfield County Poets* (Yuganta Pr, 1989,
   1987), *Black Bear Rev*

Virginia Brady Young   P
The Bridges, 1450 Whitney Ave, Hamden, CT 06517-2451,
203-288-0185
   Pubs: *The Way a Live Thing Moves* (Croton Rev Pr, 1989),
   Wind in the Long Grass: Anth (S&S, 1993), *Frogpond, Haiku
   Intl, Modern Haiku, Woodnotes Haiku Mag*

Sondra Zeidenstein 🎙 ✈   P
795 E St N
Goshen, CT 06756-1130, 860-491-2271
Internet: sondrea.zeidenstein@snet.net
   Pubs: *A Detail in That Story, Late Afternoon Woman*
   (Chicory Blue Pr, 1998, 1992), *Passionate Lives: Anth*
   (Queen of Swords Pr, 1998), *The Taos Rev, The MacGuffin,
   Calliope, The Ledge, Mudfish, Lungfull, Lilith, Earth's
   Daughters, Black Buzzard Rev, Rhino*

Feenie Ziner 🎙 ✈   W
182 Shore Dr
Branford, CT 06405-4857, 203-481-9095
   Pubs: *Within This Wilderness* (Akadine, 1999), *Squanto*
   (Shoe String Pr, 1988), *A Lively Oracle: Anth* (Larson Pub,
   1999), *I Always Meant to Tell You: Anth* (Pocket Bks, 1997),
   Na'amat Woman, Northeast

DELAWARE

Fleda Brown   P
Dept of English, University of Delaware
Newark, DE 19711, 302-831-6749
Internet: fleda@udel.edu
   Pubs: *Breathing In, Breathing Out* (Anhinga, Pr, 2002), *The
   Devil's Child,* (Carnegie Mellon U Pr, 1999), *Do Not Feel the
   Birches, Fishing With Blood* (Purdue U Pr, 1993, 1988),
   *Poetry, Georgia Rev, Ariel, Midwest Qtly, Indiana Rev, Iowa
   Rev, SPR*

Bernard Kaplan   W
Univ Delaware, English Dept, Newark, DE 19711,
302-831-2361
   Pubs: *Obituaries, Prisoners of This World* (Grossman,
   1976, 1970)

Devon Miller-Duggan   P
213 Sypherd Dr
Newark, DE 19711-3626, 302-453-0564

Francis Poole 🎙 ✈   P
335 Paper Mill Rd
Newark, DE 19711-2254
   Pubs: *Gestures* (Anhinga, 1979), *Zero Zero* (Broken Arrow
   Pr, 1972), *NYQ, Five Points, Rolling Stone, Lost & Found
   Times, Poetry East, Pearl, Blades, Exquisite Corpse, Poem*

Cruce Stark   W
1316 N Clayton St
Wilmington, DE 19806, 302-658-9440
   Pubs: *Chasing Uncle Charley* (SMU Pr, 1992)

Z. Vance Wilson   W
8 Phelps Ln
Newark, DE 19711-3512, 302-738-8755
   Pubs: *The Quick & the Dead* (Arbor Hse, 1986), *Jrnl of the
   Short Story in English, Missouri Rev*

DISTRICT OF COLUMBIA

Jonetta Rose Barras   P
PO Box 21232
Washington, DC 20009, 202-882-2838
Internet: jrbarras@aol.com
   Pubs: *The Corner Is No Place for Hiding* (Bunny & The
   Crocodile Pr, 1996), *In Search of Color Everywhere* (Tabori
   & Chang, 1995), *New Republic*

Edward L. Beach   W
Washington, DC
    Pubs: *Cold Is the Sea, Dust on the Sea, Around the World
    Submerged* (HRW, 1978, 1972, 1962),
    Proceedings,American Heritage, Reader's Digest

Wayne Biddle   W
2032 Belmont Rd NW, #210, Washington, DC 20009,
202-234-2868
    Pubs: *Barons of the Sky* (S & S, 1991), *Coming to Terms*
    (Viking, 1980), *The Nation*

Kate Blackwell 🎤 ✈   W
3131 P St NW
Washington, DC 20007, 202-333-5121
Internet: blackwell36@msn.com
    Pubs: *So to Speak, Tameme, New Letters, Nebraska Rev,
    Lit Rev, Greensboro Rev, Cresent Rev, Prairie Schooner,
    Agni Rev, Sojourner*

Dale S. Brown   P
4570 MacArthur Blv NW, #104
Washington, DC 20007, 202-338-7111
Internet: dalebrown1@compuserve.com
    Pubs: *I Know I Can Climb the Mountain* (Mountain Bks,
    1995), *Challenging Voices: Anth* (Lowell Hse, 1995), *Speak
    Out, The Little Flower Mag, The Acher*

Rick Cannon   P
c/o Gonzaga, 19 Eye St NW, Washington, DC 20001,
202-336-7123x7408
Internet: wcannon@gonzaga.org
    Pubs: *Poet Lore, Free Lunch, Comstock Rev, Xanadu,
    Sidewalks, Cumberland Poetry Rev, Slant, America, Iowa
    Rev, Verve, Whetstone, Midwest Qtly, Antietam Rev,
    Cimarron Rev, Folio, Mudfish*

Alan Cheuse   W
3611 35 St NW
Washington, DC 20016, 202-363-7799
Internet: acheuse@gmu.edu
    Pubs: *Lost & Old Rivers, The Light Possessed, The
    Grandmother's Club, The Tennessee Waltz* (SMU Pr, 1998,
    1998, 1994, 1992)

Eric Cheyfitz   P
English Dept, Georgetown Univ, Washington, DC 20057,
202-625-4949
    Pubs: *Bones & Ash* (Cymric Press, 1977), *Esquire, The
    New Rev, TLS*

Maxine Clair   P&W
English Dept, George Washington Univ, Washington, DC
20052, 202-994-6180
    Pubs: *Rattlebone* (FSG, 1994), *October Brown* (Time
    Printers, 1992), *Coping With Gravity* (Washington Writers'
    Pub Hse, 1988)

William Claire   P
Washington Resources, Inc., 1250 24th St NW, Ste 300,
Washington, DC 20037, 202-463-0388
    Pubs: *Delos, Horizon, American Scholar, Carleton
    Miscellany, Chelsea, The Nation, Washingtonian*

Shirley Graves Cochrane   P&W
127 Seventh St SE
Washington, DC 20003, 202-546-1020
    Pubs: *Letters to the Quick/Letters to the Dead, Everything
    That's All* (Signal Bks, 1998, 1991), *The Fair-haired Boy*
    (Word Works/Mica Pr, 1997), *Truths & Half Truths*
    (Washington Expatriates Pr, 1996), *Family & Other
    Strangers* (Word Works, 1986)

Maxine Combs 🎤 ✈   P&W
2216 King Pl NW
Washington, DC 20007
Internet: maxcombs@aol.com
    Pubs: *The Inner Life of Objects* (Calyx, 2000), *Handbook of
    the Strange* (Signal Bks, 1996), *The Foam of Perilous Seas*
    (Slough Pr, 1990), *Swimming out of the Collective
    Unconscious* (The Wineberry Pr, 1989)

Noemi Escandell   P&W
1525 Q St NW, #11
Washington, DC 20009-7802, 202-328-7197
    Pubs: *Palabras/Words, Cuadros* (SLUSA, 1986, 1982), *CPU
    Rev, Third Woman, Letras Femeninas, Plaza, Stone
    Country, Peregrine*

Laura Fargas   P
621 Lexington Pl NE
Washington, DC 20002, 202-546-2347
    Pubs: *Strange Luck* (U California Pr, 1994), *Reflecting What
    Light We Can't Absorb* (Riverstone Pr, 1993), *Georgia Rev,
    Paris Rev, Atlantic, Poetry*

Julia Fields   P
3636 16 St NW, #B-647
Washington, DC 20010
    Pubs: *A Summoning, A Shining* (Red Clay Pr, 1976), *East
    of Moonlight* (Poets' Pr, 1973)

Candida Fraze   P&W
3601 Connecticut Ave NW, #822
Washington, DC 20008
    Pubs: *Renifleur's Daughter* (H Holt, 1987), *Poet Lore*

Edward Gold   P
3702 Jenifer St NW
Washington, DC 20015, 202-966-5724
    Pubs: *Owl* (Scop Pub, 1983), *NYQ, Crab Creek Rev, Red
    Cedar Rev, Gargoyle, Poet Lore, Kansas Qtly*

Patricia Gray P&W
Library of Congress, 101 Independence Ave SE, Washington,
DC 20541-4912, 202-707-1308
Internet: pgray@ loc.gov
  Pubs: *The Denny Poems* (Lincoln U Pr, 1996), *Old Wounds,
  New Words: Anth* (Jesse Stuart Foundation, 1994),
  *MacGuffin, Poetry East, Shenandoah, Poet Lore, Cider
  Press Rev*

Ron Green P
Literature Dept, American Univ, Washington, DC 20016, 202-
687-2450

Patricia Browning Griffith 🎤 ✈ W
1215 Geranium St NW
Washington, DC 20012
  Pubs: *Supporting the Sky, The World Around Midnight*
  (Putnam, 1996, 1991), *Tennessee Blue* (Clarkson Potter,
  1981), *Harper's*

Anthony Hecht P
4256 Nebraska Ave NW
Washington, DC 20016
  Pubs: *The Venetian Vespers, The Hard Hours* (Atheneum,
  1979, 1967)

Errol Hess 🎤 ✈ P
515 E Capitol St, SE
Washington, DC 20003, 202-543-5560
Internet: errol@kitnet.net
  Pubs: *Homeworks: Anth* (U Tennessee Pr, 1996), *A
  Gathering at the Forks: Anth* (Vision Bks, 1993), *Sow's Ear
  Rev, Friends Jrnl, Lactuca, Potato Eyes, Pegasus Rev*

Anne Sue Hirshorn PP
2039 37th St NW
Washington, DC 20007

David E. Hubler W
Jenny Bent, Graybill & English, 1920 N St NW, #660,
Washington, DC 20036, 202-861-0106
  Pubs: *You Gotta Believe* (NAL/Signet, 1983), *McCall's,
  Amer Way, Lifestyles*

Mark C. Huey P
1515 Caroline St NW
Washington, DC 20009
  Pubs: *The Persistence of Red Dreams* (Alderman Pr, 1980),
  Shenandoah, Virginia Lit Rev

Gretchen Johnsen P
3038 N St NW
Washington, DC 20007, 202-333-1544
  Pubs: *Journal: August 1978-August 1981* (Cumberland Jrnl,
  1981), *Paper Air, Aerial, Frank, Bogg*

Dan Johnson P
1328 E Capitol St NE
Washington, DC 20003, 202-546-9865
Internet: johnsond@wfs.org
  Pubs: *Come Looking* (Washington Writer's Pub Hse, 1995),
  Suggestions From the Border (State Street Pr, 1983),
  Lullwater Rev, Dickinson Rev, Lip Service, Virginia Mag

Beth Baruch Joselow P
2927 Tilden St NW
Washington, DC 20008, 202-966-5998
Internet: bjoselow@cais.com
  Pubs: *Excontemporary, Broad Daylight* (Story Line Pr, 1989,
  1989), *Mississippi Rev, APR*

Yala Korwin 🎤 ✈ P
c/o Holocaust Publications, U.S. Holocaust Memorial Museum,
Washington, DC 20024
Internet: yalkor@aol.com
  Pubs: *Voices of the Holocaust: Anth* (Perfection Learning,
  1999), *Beyond Lament: Anth* (Northwestern U Pr, 1998),
  Images From the Holocaust: Anth (National Textbook, 1996),
  To Tell the Story, Poems of the Holocaust (Holocaust Pubs,
  1987), *Poetry Digest*

David Kresh 🎤 ✈ P
601 N Carolina SE
Washington, DC 20003
Internet: dakr@loc.gov
  Pubs: *Sketches After "Pete's Beer"* (Stone Man, 1986),
  Bloody Joy: Love Poems (Slow Dancer, 1981)

Kwelismith PP
1820 Valley Terr SE
Washington, DC 20032
  Pubs: *Brown Girl in the Ring* (Washington Writer's
  Publishing Hse, 1992), *Slavesong: The Art of Singing*
  (Anacostia Repertory Co., 1989)

Kala Ladenheim P
1707 Columbia Rd NW, #419
Washington, DC 20009
Internet: kalae@gwis2.circ.gwu.edu
  Pubs: *Not Far From the Mountains of the Moon* (Dog Ear Pr,
  1982), *Kennebec, Maze, 4 Zoas, Glitch, Cafe Rev, Frontiers,
  Maine Times*

Mary Ann Larkin 🎤 ✈ P
221 Channing St NE
Washington, DC 20002, 202-832-3978
Internet: pepperlarkin@juno.com
  Pubs: *White Clapboard* (Carol Allen, 1988), *The Coil of the
  Skin* (WWPH, 1982), *The Celtic Quest: Anth* (Welcome,
  2000), *Ireland in Poetry: Anth, America in Poetry: Anth*
  (Abrams, 1990, 1988), *Poetry Greece, Poetry Ireland, New
  Letters*

Joanne Leedom-Ackerman ♪ ✈   P&W
3229 R St NW
Washington, DC 20007
  Pubs: *The Dark Path to the River, No Marble Angels*
  (Saybrook Pub, 1988, 1987)

Kate Lehrer   W
Ronald Goldfarb & Assoc., 918 16th St NW, Washington, DC
20006
  Pubs: *Out of Eden, When They Took Away the Man in the*
  Moon (Harmony Bks, 1996, 1993), *Best Intentions* (Little,
  Brown, 1987)

Sharon Lerch   W
1733 Riggs Pl NW
Washington, DC 20009-6114, 202-462-2511
  Pubs: *Virginia Qlty Rev, Kansas Qtly, Lit Rev, Black Warrior*
  Rev

Vladimir Levchev ♪ ✈   P
5410 Connecticut Ave NW, Apt 516
Washington, DC 20015, 202-363-2297
Internet: vlevchev@aol.com
  Pubs: *Black Book of the Endangered Species* (Word Works,
  1999), *Leaves From the Dry Tree* (CCC, 1996), *Anthology of*
  Magazine Verse, Yearbook of American Poetry: Anth
  (Monitor Bk Co, 1997)

C. M. Mayo ♪ ✈   W
PO Box 58063
Washington, DC 20037
Internet: cmayo@starpower.net
  Pubs: *Sky Over El Nido, Listening to the Voices: Anth* (U
  Georgia Pr, 1999, 1998), *American Poets Say Goodbye to*
  the 20th Cntry: Anth (Four Walls Eight Windows Pr, 1996),
  NW Rev, Rio Grande Rev, Natural Bridge, Witness, SW Rev,
  Paris Rev, The Qtly, Chelsea

Richard McCann ♪ ✈   P
1734 P St NW #32
Washington, DC 20036, 202-885-2978
Internet: rmccann@american.edu
  Pubs: *Best American Essays: Anth* (Houghten Mifflen,
  2000), *Things Shaped in Passing* (Persea Bks, 1997),
  Ghost Letters (Alice James Bks, 1994), *Men on Men: Anth*
  (Dutton, 2000), *Gay Short Stories: Anth* (Penguin, 1995),
  Nation, Atlantic, Esquire

Larry McMurtry   W
1209 31st St
Washington, DC 20007
  Pubs: *Buffalo Girls, All My Friends Are Going to Be*
  Strangers, Anything for Billy (Pocket Bks, 1995, 1992, 1989),
  Cadillac Jack (S&S, 1982)

Robert Mezey ♪ ✈   P
3821 Cathedral Ave NW
Washington, DC 20016, 202-237-7841
  Pubs: *Collected Poems* (U Arkansas Pr, 2000), *Evening*
  Wind (Wesleyan, 1987), *New Criterion, Raritan, Paris Rev,*
  New Yorker, Hudson Rev, NYRB

E. Ethelbert Miller ♪ ✈   P
Howard Univ, PO Box 441, Washington, DC 20059, 202-291-
1560
Internet: emiller698@aol.com
  Pubs: *Beyond the Frontier, Whispers, Secrets & Promises,*
  First Light: New & Selected Poems (Black Classic Pr, 2002,
  1998, 1994), *Fathering Words* (St. Martins Pr, 2000), *In*
  Search of Color Everywhere: Anth (Stewart, Tabori &
  Chang, 1994)

Faye Moskowitz ♪ ✈   P&W
3306 Highland Pl NW
Washington, DC 20008, 202-363-8628
Internet: faymos@gwu.edu
  Pubs: *And the Bridge Is Love, Her Face in the Mirror: Anth*
  (Beacon Pr, 1991, 1994), *Story Qtly, Prairie Schooner, 13th*
  Moon, Woman's Day, Victoria Mag, Feminist Studies

Jean Nordhaus ♪ ✈   P
623 E Capitol St SE
Washington, DC 20003-1234, 202-543-1905
Internet: jnordhaus@att.net
  Pubs: *The Porcelain Apes of Moses Mendelssohn*
  (Milkweed Edtns, 2002), *My Life in Hiding* (QRL, 1991), *A*
  Bracelet of Lies (WWPH, 1987), *Poetry, APR, Prairie*
  Schooner, Hudson Rev, West Branch, Washington Rev

Michael Novak   W
American Enterprise Institute, 1150 17th St NW, Rm 1200,
Washington, DC 20036
  Pubs: *Naked I Leave* (Macmillan, 1970), *The Tiber Was*
  Silver (Doubleday, 1961)

Andrew Oerke   P
2949 Macomb St NW
Washington, DC 20008, 202-966-8819

Fred Rachford   P
609 12th St NE
Washington, DC 20002

Dwaine Rieves ♪ ✈   P
1907 New Hampshire Ave NW
Washington, DC 20009-3309
Internet: dcrieves@aol.com
  Pubs: *Georgia Rev, DoubleTake, Chelsea, River Styx,*
  Sycamore Rev

Elisavietta Ritchie 🎤 ✈ P&W
3207 Macomb St NW
Washington, DC 20008-3327, 202-363-8036
Internet: chfarnsworth@compuserve.com
    Pubs: *In Haste I Write You This Note* (Washington Writers'
    Pub Hse, 2000), *Elegy for the Other Woman, The Arc of the*
    Storm, Flying Time (Signal Bks, 1995, 1995, 1992), *Poetry,*
    American Scholar, NYQ, Press, Confrontation

Robert Sargent 🎤 ✈ P
815 A St NE, #2
Washington, DC 20002-6033, 202-543-1868
    Pubs: *Stealthy Days* (Forest Woods Media Pr, 1998), *A*
    Woman From Memphis, Aspects of a Southern Story (Word
    Works, 1987, 1983), *Poetry, College English*

Jack Shoemaker P
Publisher, Counterpoint Press, 717 D St NW, Ste 203,
Washington, DC 20004, 202-393-8088

Mary McGowan Slappey P
National Writers Association, 4500 Chesapeake St NW,
Washington, DC 20016, 202-363-9082
    Pubs: *Swiss Songs & Other Selected Poetry, Lafayette &*
    Harriet, Glory of Wooden Walls (Interspace Bks, 1995,
    1989, 1986)

Laurie Stroblas 🎤 ✈ P
c/o District Lines/Metro Muse, 2500 Wisconsin Ave NW, #549,
Washington, DC 20007, 202-333-1026
    Pubs: *The First Yes: Poems About Communicating: Anth*
    (Dryad Pr, 1997), *Hungry As We Are: Anth* (Washington
    Writers Pub Hse, 1995), *George Washington Rev, Poet*
    Lore, Gargoyle, Calyx, Asha Jrnl, Outerbridge

Mary Swope P
3927 Idaho Ave NW
Washington, DC 20008, 212-363-1394
    Pubs: *The Book of Falmouth: Anth* (Falmouth Historical
    Commission, 1986), *Radcliffe Qtly*

Joseph Thackery P&W
4201 Harrison St NW
Washington, DC 20015, 202-363-7675
    Pubs: *The Dark Above Mad River* (Washington Writers' Pub
    Hse, 1992), *Evidence of Community* (Center for Washington
    Area Studies, 1984)

Roberto H. Vargas P
1627 New Hampshire NW
Washington, DC 20009, 202-387-4371
    Pubs: *Nicaragua, I Sing You Kisses, Bullets, Visions of*
    Liberty (Pocho Che, 1979)

David Veronese 🎤 ✈ W
4200 Cathedral Ave NW, #907
Washington, DC 20016-4922, 202-234-0047
Internet: dveronese@aol.com
    Pubs: *JANA* (Serpent's Tail, 1993), *Prism Intl, Club, Mystery*
    Scene, Blue Zebra

Hugh Walthall P
1603 Kearny St NE
Washington, DC 20018, 202-232-1876
    Pubs: *Ladidah* (Ithaca Hse, 1978)

Edward Weismiller 🎤 ✈ P&W
2400 Virginia Ave NW, #C1119
Washington, DC 20037-2664, 202-223-0333
    Pubs: *Walking Toward the Sun* (Yale U Pr, 2002), *The*
    Serpent Sleeping (Frank Cass Ltd, 1998), *The Faultless*
    Shore (HM, 1946), *The Deer Come Down* (Yale Series of
    Younger Poets, 1936)

Faith Williams P
3768 McKinley St NW
Washington, DC 20015, 202-362-0189
Internet: fmwill@aol.com
    Pubs: *Woman the Gatherer: Anth* (Yale U Pr, 1981), *Bogg,*
    Poet Lore, Earth's Daughters, The Bridge, Nimrod, Kansas
    Qtly, Kalliope, Boston Lit Rev

Joyce Winslow 🎤 ✈ W
2800 Wisconsin Ave NW, #403
Washington, DC 20007-4705, 202-686-1747
Internet: joyce@sak.org
    Pubs: *Best American Short Stories: Anth* (HM, 1969), *New*
    Virginia Rev, River City, Yankee, Washington Post, Redbook

Mary Kay Zuravleff 🎤 ✈ W
3730 Jocelyn St NW
Washington, DC 20015-1808, 202-966-9535
    Pubs: *The Frequency of Souls* (FSG, 1996), *Women's*
    Glibber: Anth (Crossing Pr, 1993), *Gila Rev, Gargoyle,*
    Appearances, New Mexico Humanities Rev

FLORIDA

Marnie K. Adler 🎤 P
266 W Casurina Pl
Beverly Hills, FL 34465, 352-746-0998
    Pubs: *Florida State Poetry Society: Anths* (Florida State
    Poetry Society, 1995, 1994), *American Anthology of*
    Southern Poetry (Great Lakes Poetry Pr, 1987), *Bitterroot,*
    Harpstrings, Voices Israel

Mari Alschuler 🎤 ✈   P
5370 NW 32 Ct
Margate, FL 33063, 954-979-0069
Internet: poetmari@aol.com
    Pubs: *The Nightmare of Falling Teeth* (Pudding Hse Pr,
    1998), *The Poet Within: Anth* (DeeMar Communications,
    1997), *Blood to Remember: Anth* (Texas Tech U Pr, 1991),
    *Pudding Mag, Backbone, No Apologies, Berkeley Poets
    Cooperative, Shenandoah*

Eileen Annie   P&W
PO Box 485
Eastpoint, FL 32328, 904-670-8518
    Pubs: *Half the Bran Muffin Is Gone, Life on a Beanstalk*
    (Bench Pr, 1991, 1986), *Long Island Qtly, Confrontation*

Mark Ari   P&W
56 Dolphin Blvd
Ponte Vedra Beach, FL 32092, 904-285-9477
Internet: markari@aol.com
    Pubs: *The Shoemaker's Tale* (Zephyr Pr, 1994), *The Stroker
    Anthology* (Stroker, Papandrea, Schumann, 1995), *Lost
    Creek Letters, Home Planet News*

Mary Baron 🎤 ✈   P
English and Foreign Languages, Univ North Florida,
Jacksonville, FL 32224-2645, 904-620-2273
Internet: mbaron@unf.edu
    Pubs: *Wheat Among Bones* (Sheep Meadow Pr, 1990),
    Letters for the New England Dead (Godine, 1974), *Southern
    Rev, Northward Jrnl, Kalliope, Hayden's Ferry, ALAN Rev*

Lynne Barrett 🎤 ✈   W
English Dept, Florida International Univ, 3000 NE 151st St,
North Miami, FL 33181, 305-919-5506
    Pubs: *The Secret Names of Women, The Land of Go*
    (Carnegie Mellon U Pr, 1999, 1988), *Mondo Barbie: Anth*
    (St. Martin's Pr, 1993), *Tampa Rev, Other Voices, Redbook,
    Ellery Queen's Mystery Mag*

Dina Ben-Lev 🎤 ✈   P
1232 Riverbreeze Blvd
Ormond Beach, FL 32176, 904-441-5636
Internet: dinabeach@cs.com
    Pubs: *Broken Helix* (Mid-List Pr, 1997), *Sober on a Small
    Plane* (Wind Pub, 1995), *American Poetry: Anth* (Carnegie
    Mellon U Pr, 2000)

Judith A. Berke   P
5600 Collins Ave #9S, Miami Beach, FL 33140-2411,
305-868-3302
    Pubs: *Acting Problems* (Silverfish Rev Pr, 1993), *White
    Morning* (Wesleyan U Pr, 1989), *Sonora Rev, Paris Rev,
    APR, Atlantic, Poetry, Field, Massachusetts Rev, Ohio Rev,
    Iowa Rev*

Wendy Bishop   P
Florida State Univ, English Dept, Tallahassee, FL 32306,
850-893-1381
Internet: wbishop@english.fsu.edu
    Pubs: *Working Words: The Process of Creative Writing*
    (Mayfield Pub, 1992), *Colors of a Different Horse: Anth* (Natl
    Council of Teachers of English, 1994)

Margaret Blaker   P
210 Lake Howard Dr NW
Winter Haven, FL 33880-2302, 863-294-2226
    Pubs: *Dan River: Anth* (Dan River Pr, 2000, 2002), *Knowing
    Stones: Anth* (J.G. Burke, 2000), *When a Lifemate Dies:
    Anth* (Fairview Pr, 1997), *Troubador, Medical Purposes,
    New England Writers, Pig Iron, Archaeology, Florida Rev*

Bocaccio   PP
c/o Dewey, 1700 Glenhouse Dr, #406, Sarasota, FL
34241-6766

Graal Braun 🎤 ✈   P
4232 Preserve Pl
Palm Harbor, FL 34685
Internet: gbraun@tampabay.rr.com
    Pubs: *Wormwood and Whines* (SuperiorBooks.com, Inc,
    2000), *Villains, Victims and Babes in the Woods* (Talent Hse
    Pr, 1999), *Envoi, Mind in Motion, Light, Aethlon, Lyric,
    Hellas, The Classical Outlook*

Harry Brody 🎤 ✈   P
3033 Pinecrest St
Sarasota, FL 34239-7037, 941-923-5098
    Pubs: *For We Are Constructing the Dwelling of Feeling*
    (Bluestone Pr, 1992), *Fields* (Ion Bks, 1987), *Chariton Rev,
    Carolina Qtly, Spirit That Moves Us*

P. R. Brostowin 🎤 ✈   P
961 Swallow Ave #205, Marco Island, FL 34145, 239-394-6780
    Pubs: *In Other Words* (Alfalfa, 1976), *Kansas Qtly, Smith,
    Blue Unicorn, Windless Orchard*

Janet Burroway 🎤 ✈   P&W
English Dept, Florida State Univ, Tallahassee, FL 32306,
850-222-8272
Internet: jburroway@english.fsu.edu
    Pubs: *Cutting Stone* (HM, 1992), *Opening Nights*
    (Atheneum, 1986), *Prairie Schooner, New Letters, New
    Virginia Rev*

Robert Olen Butler   W
Florida State Univ, English Dept, Tallahassee, FL 32306-1580
www.webdelsol.com/butler
    Pubs: *Fair Warning, Mr. Spaceman* (Grove/Atlantic, 2002,
    2000), *The Deep Green Sea, Tabloid Dreams, They
    Whisper, A Good Scent From a Strange Mountain* (H Holt,
    1998, 1996, 1994, 1992), *Esquire, New Yorker, GQ, Paris
    Rev, Harper's, Sewanee Rev, Hudson Rev*

Howard Camner 🎤 ✈ P
10440 SW 76 St
Miami, FL 33173-2903, 305-255-2911
Internet: hcamner@aol.com
  Pubs: *Hiss* (Tri-State Bks, 2000), *Brutal Delicacies, Bed of Nails, Jammed Zipper, Banned in Babylon, Stray Dog Wail* (Camelot Pub Co., 1996, 1995, 1994, 1993, 1992), *Florida in Poetry: Anth* (Pineapple Pr, 1995), *Steel Point Qtly, Fluid Ink Pr, Melic Rev*

Rick Campbell 🎤 ✈ P
444 Winding Creek Rd
Quincy, FL 32351, 850-442-4146
Internet: rc2121@earthlink.net
  Pubs: *Setting the World in Order* (Texas Tech U Pr, 2001), *The Breathers at St. Marks* (Wellberry Pr, 1994), *Prairie Schooner, SPR, Missouri Rev, Georgia Rev, Puerto del Sol*

Eli Cantor P&W
384 N Washington Dr
Sarasota, FL 34236
  Pubs: *Love Letters, Enemy in the Mirror* (Crown, 1979, 1977), *Esquire, Story, Accent, Poetry Mag, Coronet, Saturday Rev*

Nick Carbo 🎤 P
2201 South Ocean Dr, #203
Hollywood, FL 33019, 954-926-6188
Internet: ncarbo@aol.com
  Pubs: *Secret Asian Man, El Grupo McDonald's* (Tia Chucha Pr, 2000, 1995), *Poetry, TriQtly, Indiana Rev, Poet Lore*

Ella Cavis P
1408 56th St W
Bradenton, FL 34209
  Pubs: *Florida Qtly, Sarasota Qtly, Mobius, Voices Intl, Tucumcari, Prophetic Voices, MPR, Slant, Orphic Lute, Old Hickory Rev, Parnassus*

Polly Chase 🎤 P
300 S Sykes Creek Pkwy
Merritt Is., FL 32952
  Pubs: *Cancelled Reservations* (Poet Pr, 1986), *Poet Lore, Driftwood East, Jean's Jrnl*

Joanne Childers P
3504 NW 7th Pl
Gainesville, FL 32607, 904-376-9773
  Pubs: *Moving Mother Out* (Florida Literary Fdn, 1992), *Aisles of Flowers: Anth* (Anhinga Pr, 1995), *Massachusetts Rev, Poet & Critic, Chattahoochee Rev, Kalliope, Kentucky Rev*

Nancy J. Cohen 🎤 W
PO Box 17756
Plantation, FL 33318
www.nancyjcohen.com
  Pubs: *Highlights to Heaven, Body Wave, Murder by Manicure, Hair Raiser, Permed to Death* (Kensington Publishing Corp, 2003, 2002, 2001, 2000,1999)

Elsa Colligan P
214 Elizabeth St
Key West, FL 33040
  Pubs: *The Aerialist* (Barlenmir Hse, 1979), *Nantucket: A Collection: Anth, Key West: A Collection: Anth* (White Fish Pr, 2001), *Harper's, NYQ, Chicago Rev, Poets On, BPJ, Footwork, Comstock Rev, Whiskey Island Mag, The Lucid Stone*

Kirby Congdon P
715 Baker's Ln
Key West, FL 33040-6819, 305-294-6979
  Pubs: *Cat Poems, Novels, Poems From Fire Island Pines & Key West* (Cycle Pr, 2002, 2002, 1999), *Gay Roots: Anth* (Gay Sunshine Pr, 1991), *Small Press Rev, Cayo*

John Charles Cooper P&W
70 E Cahill Ct
Big Pine Key, FL 33043
Internet: v-cooper@juno.com
  Pubs: *Cast a Single Shadow* (Northwest Pub Co., 1996), *Vicki's Lake* (Harrodsburg Herald, 1989), *Christianity Today, Scripset, Time of Singing, Rant, Wind*

Patricia Corbus 🎤 ✈ P
PO Box 5601
Sarasota, FL 34277-5601, 941-349-0325
Internet: brcorbus@aol.com
  Pubs: *Witness, Notre Dame Rev, Natural Bridge, 88: A Jrnl of Cntmpry Amer Poetry, Natural Bridge,Green Mountains Rev, Folio, Antigonish Rev, Wallace Stevens Jrnl, Windsor Rev, Greensboro Rev, South Carolina Rev, Cream City Rev, Paris Rev, Antioch Rev*

Harry Crews W
English Dept, Univ Florida, Gainesville, FL 32601, 904-392-0777

Carole Crowe 🎤 ✈ W
9 Vista Palm Ln, #206
Vero Beach, FL 32962, 772-778-7128
Internet: waiting4dolphins@aol.com
  Pubs: *Groover's Heart, Waiting for Dolphins, Sharp Horns on the Moon* (Boyds Mills Pr, 2001, 2000, 1998)

Edwin Crusoe 🎤 P
2222 Middle Torch Rd
Summerland Key, FL 33042-5805, 305-872-9073
  Pubs: *Wanderings* (Rip Off Pr, 1971), *Key West Poetry Guild: Anth* (Key West Poetry Guild, 1999, 1989), *Paradise: Anth* (Florida Literary Fdn Pr, 1995), *Hidden Path, Florida Keys Maritime Historical Jrnl, Key West Rev*

Kay Day 🎤 ✈   P
3573 Equestrian Court
Jacksonville, FL 32223

Ron De Maris 🎤 ✈   P
9621 SW 103 Pl
Miami, FL 33176
    Pubs: *APR, The Nation, Sewanee Rev, Poetry NW, New
    Letters, New Orleans Rev, Carolina Qtly, Southern Rev,
    NER, Ploughshares, Gettysburg Rev, Atlanta Rev, New
    Republic, Lit Rev, Southern Poetry Rev, Priarie Schooner*

Donna Decker   P
74 Westview
Panacea, FL 32346, 850-984-0151
    Pubs: *Under the Influence of Paradise: Voices of Key West*
    (Head & a Half Pr, 1999), *Three Thirds* (Word Banks Pr,
    1984), *North of Wakulla: Anth* (Anhinga Pr, 1989), *Amer
    Voice, New Collage, Snake Nation Rev, Gulf Stream*

Leonardo DellaRocca 🎤 ✈   P
2800 Fiore Way #107
Delray Beach, FL 33445-4551, 561-278-4072
Internet: dellarocca@earthlink.net
    Pubs: *Having a Wonderful Time: Anth* (S&S, 1999),
    *Wisconsin Rev, Nimrod, Poet Lore, Apalachee Qtly, Sun
    Dog, Seattle Rev*

Matthew Diomede 🎤 ✈   P
125 Tenth St E
Tierra Verde, FL 33715-2206
    Pubs: *Apalachee Qtly, Riverside Qtly, Rolling Coulter,
    Wisconsin Rev, Centennial Rev, Oyez Rev, Christianity &
    Literature, The Viet Nam Generation, Big Book, Black
    Buzzard Rev, Western Ohio Jrnl*

Frances Driscoll   P
56 Seaplace, 901 Ocean Blvd
Atlantic Beach, FL 32233, 904-241-5075
Internet: pbstudio@pbstudio.com
    Pubs: *The Rape Poems* (Pleasure Boat Studio, 1997), *Talk
    to Me* (Black River, 1987), *Pushcart Prize Anth XIX*
    (Pushcart Pr, 1994), *Mudlark, Ploughshares*

John Dufresne 🎤 ✈   P&W
1065 SE 6 Ave
Dania Beach, FL 33004, 954-926-1181
Internet: John.Dufresne@fiv.edu
    Pubs: *Deep in the Shade of Paradise* (W. W. Norton, 2003),
    *Love Warps the Mind a Little, Louisiana Power & Light, The
    Way That Water Enters Stone* (Norton, 1997, 1994, 1991),
    Mississippi Rev, Missouri Rev, Greensboro Rev

Denise Duhamel   P
2201 South Ocean Dr #203
Hollywood, FL 33019, 954-926-6188
Internet: sedna61@aol.com
    Pubs: *Queen for a Day* (U Pitt Pr, 2001), *The Star-Spangled
    Banner* (Southern Illinois U Pr, 1999), *Kinky* (Orchises Pr,
    1997), *Girl Soldier* (Garden Street, 1996), *The Woman With
    Two Vaginas* (Salmon Run, 1994), *Global City Rev, Third
    Coast, Salt Hill Rev, APR*

Page Edwards, Jr.   W
PO Box 1117
St Augustine, FL 32085-1117, 904-829-9341
Internet: oldhouse@aug.com
    Pubs: *The Search for Kate DuVal, American Girl, The Lake*
    (Marion Boyars Pub, 1996, 1990, 1986)

Sheila Natasha Simro Friedman   PP
15451 SW 67 Ct
Miami, FL 33157, 305-233-4280

Sue Gambill   W
509 Curtis Rd
Tallahassee, FL 32311, 904-942-6597
    Pubs: *Heartscape* (Naiad Pr, 1989), *Word of Mouth: Anth*
    (Crossing Pr, 1990), *Moonseed*

Nola Garrett 🎤 ✈   P
2228 Orchard Park Dr
Spring Hill, FL 34608, 352-666-5867
Internet: ngarrett@atlantic.net
    Pubs: *The Pastor's Wife Considers Pinball* (Wordart, 1998),
    The Muse Strikes Back: Anth (Story Line, 1997), *Odd
    Angles of Heaven: Anth* (Harold Shaw, 1994), *Tampa Rev,
    Marlboro Rev, Formalist, Georgia Rev, Cimarron Rev, Poet
    Lore, Crab Orchard Rev*

Jim Gerard   P
1227 W Orange
Lake City, FL 32055, 904-752-6325

Stephen M. Gibson   P
119 Royal Pine Cir North
Royal Palm Beach, FL 33411, 407-793-6552
    Pubs: *Bodies in the Bog* (Texas Rev Pr, 1984), *Paris Rev,
    NER, Poetry, Chelsea, Texas Rev, Boulevard*

Andrew Glaze 🎤 ✈   P
825 NW 14 Ct
Miami, FL 33125-3621, 305-649-6944
Internet: andrewglaze@juno.com
    Pubs: *Remembering Thunder* (New South, 2002), *Someone
    Will Go on Owing* (Black Belt Pr, 1992), *I Am the Jefferson
    County Courthouse* (Thundering Pr, 1981), *Home Planet
    News, Light, Atlantic, Pivot, New Yorker*

Bonnie Gordon W
2464 SW 19 Terr
Miami, FL 33145, 305-856-2776
Pubs: *Childhood in Reno* (Street New York, 1982), *Songs
From Unsung Worlds: Anth* (Birkhauser, 1986)

Deborah Eve Grayson 🎤 ✈ P
6800 W Commercial Blvd Ste #4
Fort Lauderdale, FL 33319, 954-741-1160
Pubs: *The Healing Fountain: Poetry Therapy for Life's
Journey* (North Star Press of St. Cloud, 2003), *Breath Marks
in the Wind* (Breath Marks/IDF, 1988), *Journal of Poetry
Therapy, Pudding Mag*

Daniel Green P
1248 Belleflower St
Sarasota, FL 34232-1107, 941-366-6573
Internet: d9green@aol.com
Pubs: *All Told, Better Late, On Second Thought* (Fithian Pr,
1997, 1994, 1992)

Debora Greger 🎤 ✈ P
Univ Florida, English Dept, PO Box 117310, Gainesville, FL
32611-7310, 352-392-0777
Internet: dgreger@english.ufl.edu
Pubs: *God, Desert Fathers, Uranium Daughters* (Penguin,
2001, 1996), *Norton Anthology of Poetry* (Norton, 1996),
*New Yorker, New York Times, New Republic, The Nation,
Yale Rev*

Jack Gresham 🎤 ✈ P
5385 SW 83 Pl
Ocala, FL 34476-3799, 352-873-3976
Pubs: *The Red Candle Treasury: Anth* (Red Candle Pr,
1999), *Candelabrum Poetry Mag, Envoi, Tirra Lirra, Kit-Cat
Rev, Amer Poets & Poetry, Mobius, Neovictorian/Cochlea,
Satire, Tucumcari Lit Rev*

Kelle Groom 🎤 ✈ P&W
1726 Gurtler Court #4
Orlando, FL 32804
Internet: kellegroom@hotmail.com
Pubs: *The New Yorker, Florida Rev, The SE Rev, Chiron
Rev, Flyway, Slipstream*

Bob Grumman 🎤 ✈ P
1708 Hayworth Rd
Port Charlotte, FL 33952-4529, 813-629-8045
Internet: bobgrumman@nut-n-but.net
Pubs: *A Selection of Visual Poems* (Xexoxial Edtns, 2001),
Doing Long Division in Color (Runaway Spoon Pr, 2001),
Mathemaku 1-5 (Tel-Let, 1992), *The World of Zines: Anth*
(Penguin, 1992), Score, Lost & Found Times, Windless
Orchard, Kaldron, Experioddicist

Jim Hall P
English Dept, Florida International Univ, Miami, FL 33199
Pubs: *False Statements, The Mating Reflex* (Carnegie
Mellon, 1985, 1980)

Barbara Hamby 🎤 ✈ P
1168 Seminole Dr, Tallahassee, FL 32301-4656, 850-877-7411
Internet: bhamby@nettally.com
Pubs: *The Alphabet of Desire* (NYU Pr, 1999), *Delirium* (U
North Texas Pr, 1995), *Kenyon Rev, Harvard Rev, Five
Points, Southern Rev, Iowa Rev, Paris Rev*

Peter Hargitai 🎤 ✈ P&W
English Dept, Florida International Univ, Miami, FL 33199,
305-348-3405
Internet: Hargitai@fiu.edu
Pubs: *Mi Universo* (Framo Pr, 2002), *Having a Wonderful
Time: An Anth of S Florida Wrtrs* (S&S, 1998), *My
POEmpire* (Framo Pr, 1997), *Atilla: A Barbarian's Bedtime
Story* (Puski-Corvin Press, 1994), *Fodor's Budget Zion*
(Palmetto Pr, 1991)

Anne Haskins P
4714 NW 57 Dr
Gainesville, FL 32606-4369
Pubs: *The Earthquake on Ada Street: Anth* (Jupiter Pr,
1979), *Overtures, Mati, Ommation*

Lola Haskins 🎤 ✈ P
PO Box 18
LaCrosse, FL 32658-0018, 386-462-3117
Internet: lola@cise.ufl.edu
Pubs: *Desire Lines* (BOA Edtns, 2004), *The Rim Benders*
(Anhinga, 2001), *Extranjera* (Story Line Pr, 1998), *Hunger*
(U Iowa Pr/Story Line Pr, 1996), *Atlantic, Southern Rev,
Georgia Rev, CSM, BPJ*

Gerald Hausman 🎤 ✈ P&W
12699 Cristi Way
Bokeelia, FL 33922-3321
Internet: ghausman@compuserve.com
Pubs: *The Jacob Ladder* (Orchard Bks, 2001), *Cats of Myth,
Tom Cringle* (S&S, 2000, 2000)

Hunt Hawkins 🎤 ✈ P
Florida State Univ, English Dept, Tallahassee, FL 32306,
850-644-0240
Internet: hhawkins@english.fsu.edu
Pubs: *The Domestic Life* (U Pitt Pr, 1994), *A New
Geography of Poetry: Anth* (U Arkansas Pr, 1992), *TriQtly,
Southern Rev, Georgia Rev, Apalachee Qtly, Poetry,
Minnesota Rev*

Jonellen Heckler   W
5745 SW 75 St, PMB322
Gainesville, FL 32608, 352-332-1005
Internet: jonellenh@aol.com
    Pubs: *Final Tour, Circumstances Unknown* (Pocket Bks,
    1994, 1993), *White Lies, A Fragile Peace, Safekeeping*
    (Putnam, 1989, 1986, 1983)

Judith Hemschemeyer ♀ ✈   P&W
436 Knowles Ave #2
Winter Park, FL 32789-3232
    Pubs: *Certain Animals* (Snake Nation Pr, 1998), *The
    Harvest* (Pig Iron Pr, 1998), *The Ride Home* (Texas Tech U
    Pr, 1987), *Very Close & Very Slow* (Wesleyan U Pr, 1975),
    Hudson Rev, Colorado Rev, Tampa Rev, Dickinson Rev,
    Florida Rev

Michael Hettich ♀ ✈   P
561 NE 95 St
Miami Shores, FL 33138-2731, 305-237-3187
Internet: mhettich@mdcc.edu
    Pubs: *Singing With My Father, Many Simple Things,
    Immaculate Bright Rooms* (March Street Pr, 2002, 1997,
    1994), *Sleeping With the Lights On* (Pudding Hse, 2000),
    The Point of Touching (LeBow, 2000), *Having a Wonderful
    Time* (S&S, 1997), *TriQrtly, Rhino*

Patricia Higginbotham   P
3211 Swann Ave #310
Tampa, FL 33109-4685, 813-874-3498
Internet: higginp2@yahoo.com
    Pubs: *Conjure This* (WJM Pr, 1997), *Orbis, Tower Poetry,
    ELF, Poetpourri, Lyric, The Formalist, Staple*

Rochelle Lynn Holt ♀ ✈   P&W
15223 Coral Isle Ct
Ft Myers, FL 33919
    Pubs: *Whispering Secrets* (Lyra Pr, 2002), *Wound, To Life:
    Anth* (Kings Estate, 2001, 2002), *Chiron Rev, RiverKing,
    University of Missouri at St Louis Jrnl, Louisiana Rev, 360
    Degrees*

Susan Hubbard ♀ ✈   P&W
PO Box 4009
Winter Park, FL 32793-4009, 407-823-3543
Internet: shubbard@pegasus.cc.ucf.edu
    Pubs: *Blue Money, Walking on Ice & Other Stories* (U
    Missouri Pr, 1999, 1990), *Natural Bridge, Kalliope, NAR,
    Ploughshares, Passages North, Wooster Rev, Dickinson,
    Green Mountains Rev, TriQtly, Mississippi Rev*

Philip K. Jason   P
12823 Valewood Dr
Naples, FL 34119, 239-598-2880
Internet: pjason@aol.com
    Pubs: *Making Change* (Argonnettse Pr, 2001), *The
    Separation* (Viet Nam Generation, 1995), *Creative Writer's
    Handbook* (Prentice Hall, 1990), *Near the Fire* (Dryad, 1983)

John Kapsalis   P
5776 Deauville Lake Cir, #308
Naples, FL 34112
Internet: johnathy@aol.com
    Pubs: *The Saga of Chrysodontis Pappas, Tales of
    Pergamos* (Aegina Pr, 1994, 1988), *Bitterroot, Dark Horse,
    Indigo, Joycean Lively Arts Guild Rev, Northeastern Jrnl,
    Nebraska Rev*

David A. Kaufelt   W
PO Box 182
Key West, FL 33041, 305-292-1288
    Pubs: *The Winter Women Murders, The Fat Boy Murders*
    (Pocket Bks, 1994, 1993), *American Tropic* (Poseidon,
    1987), *Cosmopolitan*

Marcia Gale Kester-Doyle   P
516 NE 6 St
Pompano Beach, FL 33060
    Pubs: *Driving Through Nebraska* (Cooper Hse, 1991), *The
    Healing Stone: Anth* (Golden Apple Pr, 1998), *Baby's World,
    Green Hills Literary Lantern, SPR, Twinsworld,
    Bereavement, The Poet, Echoes*

Daniel Keyes   W
7491 N Federal Hwy, Ste C5-110
Boca Raton, FL 33487
Internet: dankeyes@usa.net
    Pubs: *Unveiling Claudia* (Bantam Bks, 1986), *The Minds of
    Billy Milligan* (Random Hse, 1981), *The Fifth Sally* (HM,
    1980), *Flowers for Algernon* (HB, 1966)

David Kirby ♀ ✈   P
1168 Seminole Dr
Tallahassee, FL 32301-4656, 850-877-7411
Internet: dkirby@english.fsu.edu
    Pubs: *Traveling Library* (Orchises, 2001), *House of Blue
    Light* (LSU Pr, 2000), *Five Points, Paris Rev, Parnassus,
    Kenyon Rev, Southern Rev, Ploughshares, NW Rev*

Smith Kirkpatrick   W
English Dept, Univ Florida, Gainesville, FL 32601,
904-392-0777
    Pubs: *The Sun's Gold* (HM, 1974)

Marjorie Klein ♀ ✈   W
11 Island Ave, #1710
Miami Beach, FL 33139, 305-538-3733
Internet: magicklein@aol.com
    Pubs: *Test Pattern* (William Morrow/HC, 2000)

Jeffrey Knapp   P
3457 Sheridan Ave
Miami Beach, FL 33140, 305-531-4309
    Pubs: *The Acupuncture of Heaven* (Do Something Pr,
    1989), *Palmetto Rev, Free Lunch, La Bete*

Nancy Roxbury Knutson   P
9791 NW 10 St
Plantation, FL 33322-4880
Internet: knutson27@aol.com
   Pubs: *Nothing Shall Fall to Waste* (Arts Wayland Fdn, 1983),
   If I Had a Hammer: Anth (Papier-Mache Pr, 1990), *APR,
   Calyx, Iowa Rev, Nimrod, New Virginia Rev*

Mary Sue Koeppel 🎤 ✈   P
3879 Oldfield Trail
Jacksonville, FL 32223, 904-646-2346
Internet: skoeppel@fccj.org
   Pubs: *In The Library of Silences, Poems of Loss* (Rhiannon
   Pr, 2001), *The Anth of New England Writers* (New England
   Writers, 1997), *Life on the Line, Selections on Words and
   Healing: Anth* (Negative Capability Pr, 1992), *CT Rev, Pike
   Creek Rev, Clockwatch Rev*

Alison W. Kolodinsky 🎤 ✈   P
1305 N Atlantic Ave
New Smyrna Beach, FL 32169-2205, 386-426-5864
Internet: AlisonKolodinsky@aol.com
   Pubs: *Isle of Flowers: Anth* (Anhinga Pr, 1995), *Florida in
   Poetry: Anth* (Pineapple Pr, 1995), *Poetry, Jama, Cream
   City Rev, Whetstone, Florida Rev, Kalliope*

Sam Koperwas   W
2701 NE 35 Dr
Ft Lauderdale, FL 33308
   Pubs: *Easy Money* (Morrow, 1983), *Hot Stuff* (Dutton, 1978)

Jose Kozer   P
500 Three Islands Blvd, Apt # 1209
Hallandale, FL 33009-2887
Internet: JoseKozer@aol.com
   Pubs: *Rosa Cubica* (Argentina: Tse Tse, 2002), *Bajo Este
   Cien y Otros Poemas* (Barcelona: El Bardo Editorial, 2002),
   No Buscan Reflejarse (Cuba: Letras Cubanas, 2001), *Al
   Traste* (Mexico: Trilce Ediciones, 1999), *Projimos/Intimates*
   (Spain; Carrer Ausias, 1991)

Ian Krieger 🎤 ✈   P
1415 Sturbridge Ct
Dunedin, FL 34698, 727-733-9575
   Pubs: *An Unnamed Aesthetic* (Stolen Images, 1987),
   Pavans (Ommation Pr, 1985)

Steve Kronen 🎤 ✈   P
2000 W Hampton Cir
Winter Park, FL 32792, 407-679-6973
Internet: skronen@mailcity.com
   Pubs: *Empirical Evidence* (U Georgia Pr, 1992), *Isle of
   Flowers: Anth* (Anhinga Pr, 1995), *Ploughshares, The
   Drunken Boat, Poetry, Paris Rev, Southern Rev, Georgia
   Rev, Agni, Virginia Qtly Rev, New Republic*

Elsie Bowman Kurz   P
Isle of Capri B50, Kings Point, Delray Beach, FL 33484,
407-498-2733
   Pubs: *Rhyming the Bible: Songs Your Mother Never Taught
   You, Endangered Species* (PPB Pr, 1996, 1996), *We
   Speak for Peace: Anth* (KIT, 1993), *Passager, Harp Strings,
   Poets Forum*

Zilia L. Laje   W
PO Box 45-1732 Shenandoah Station
Miami, FL 33245-1732, 305-856-9314
   Pubs: *Cartas Son Cartas, The Sugar Cane Curtain, La
   Contina de Bagazo* (Guarina Publishing, 2001, 2000, 1995)

P. V. LeForge   P&W
810 Annawood Dr, Tallahassee, FL 32305-5502, 850-878-1591
   Pubs: *The Secret Life of Moles* (Anhinga Pr, 1992), *The
   Principle of Interchange* (Paperback Rack Bks, 1990), *Q
   Mag, Nightstallion, Mid-Amer Rev*

Rose Lesniak   P
1000 West Ave #1410
Miami Beach, FL 33139, 305-534-8760
Internet: ralpi@aol.com
   Pubs: *Throwing Spitballs at the Nuns, Young Anger*
   (Toothpaste Pr, 1982, 1979), *Rolling Stone*

Edith Mize Lewis   P
8919 Old Pine Rd
Boca Raton, FL 33433-3152
   Pubs: *Haiku is . . . a Feeling* (Pippin Bks, 1990)

Duane Locke 🎤 ✈   P
2716 Jefferson St
Tampa, FL 33602-1620, 813-223-5174
Internet: duanelocke@netzero.net
   Pubs: *Watching Wisteria* (Vida Pr, 1995), *Ghost Dance:
   Anth* (Whitston, 1994), *Black Moon, Bitter Oleander, Glass
   Cherry, APR, ALR, Nation*

William Logan 🎤   P
Dept of English, University of Florida, Gainesville, FL 32611,
352-371-7780
Internet: wlogan@english.ufl.edu
   Pubs: *Macbeth in Venice, Night Battle, Vain Empires*
   (Penguin, 2003, 1999, 1998)

Carol Mahler 🎤 ✈   P
420 W Olympia Ave
Punta Gorda, FL 33950, 941-575-1976
Internet: CMahler4@cs.com
   Pubs: *The Hyer Family Odyssey: An American Pioneer
   History* (Punta Gorda, 2001), *When a Life Mate Dies:
   Stories of Love, Loss & Healing: Anth* (Fairview Pr, 1997),
   *Comstock Mag, Many Mountains Moving, Passages North,
   BPJ, Fan Mag, Poets On, Red Brick Rev*

Michael Margolin   P
1801 S Ocean Dr, #837
Hallandale, FL 33009-4947
   Pubs: *NAR, Shenandoah, Carleton Miscellany, SPR,
   Smith, Epoch*

Dionisio D. Martinez 🎤 ✈   P
4509 N Lincoln Ave
Tampa, FL 33614-6631, 813-874-6747
Internet: ddmartinez@aol.com
   Pubs: *Climbing Back, Bad Alchemy* (Norton, 2000, 1995),
   History as a Second Language (Ohio State U Pr, 1993),
   *New Republic, APR, Iowa Rev, Prairie Schooner, Virginia
   Qtly Rev, Georgia Rev, Denver Qtly, Kenyon Rev*

Richard Mathews 🎤 ✈   P
Univ of Tampa, PO Box 19-F, Tampa, FL 33606, 813-253-6266
Internet: rmathews@ut.edu
   Pubs: *Numbery* (Borgo Pr, 1995), *A Mummery*
   (Konglomerati, 1975), *SPR, Louisville Rev, Berkeley Rev*

Sharon Bell Mathis 🎤 ✈   P&W
PO Box 780714
Orlando, FL 32878-0714
   Pubs: *Running Girl: The Diary of Ebonee Rose*
   (HB/Browndeer Pr, 1997), *Red Dog, Blue Fly: Football
   Poems* (Viking Penguin, 1991)

Irma McClaurin 🎤 ✈   P
5128 NW 16 Pl
Gainesville, FL 32605-3302, 352-336-2154
Internet: l.mcclaurin@worldnet.att.net
   Pubs: *Pearl's Song* (Lotus Pr, 2000), *African-American
   Literature: Anth* (Glencoe/McGraw-Hill, 2000), *A Rock
   Against the Wind: Anth* (Perigee, 1996), *Essence, Drum
   Rev, Obsidian II*

Jane McClellan   P
2838 NE 14 Ave
Ocala, FL 34470-3700, 352-622-6145
Internet: doctorjmcc@aol.com
   Pubs: *Louisiana Lit, Eureka Lit Mag, Parting Gifts, Illya's
   Honey, Rattapallax, West Wind Rev, Poet Lore, Green Hills
   Lit Lantern, Cumberland Poetry Rev, MacGuffin, Skylark,
   Westview, Cape Rock, Blue Unicorn*

Tom McDaniel   P
249 Lake Ave E
Longwood, FL 32750-5442
   Pubs: *Pulpsmith, Wind, Plains Poetry Jrnl, Blue Unicorn,
   Florida Rev, Kansas Qtly*

Kevin McGowin   P&W
409 East Lane St. #1
Gainesville, FL 32604, 919367178
Internet: kmcgowin@mindspring.com
   Pubs: *The Benny Poda Years* (Levee67, 2001), *The Better
   Part of a Fortnight* (Funky Dog, 1999), *Love & Pity: CD* (A
   Priori, 2000), *Eclectica Mag, Rosebud, Whiskey Island,
   Yemassee, National Forum*

Campbell McGrath   P
Florida International Univ, N Miami Campus, North Miami, FL
33181, 305-919-5954
   Pubs: *Spring Comes to Chicago, American Noise* (Ecco Pr,
   1996, 1994), *New Yorker, Antaeus, Paris Rev, Ploughshares,
   TriQtly, Ohio Rev*

Peter Meinke 🎤 ✈   P&W
147 Wildwood Ln SE
St Petersburg, FL 33705-3222, 727-896-1862
Internet: meinkep@eckerd.edu
   Pubs: *Zinc Fingers, Scars, Liquid Paper* (U Pitt Pr, 2000,
   1996, 1991), *Atlantic, New Yorker, Georgia Rev, Poetry*

A. McA Miller 🎤 ✈   P
New Collage Magazine, 5700 N Tamiami Trail, Sarasota, FL
34243-2197, 813-359-4605
   Pubs: *BPJ, Epos, Gryphon, Negative Capability, Spirit That
   Moves Us, Tendril*

Karl F. Miller   P&W
1999 NW 83 Dr
Coral Springs, FL 33071-6274, 954-341-8672
   Pubs: *A Warning* (Merging Media, 1990), *Old Red Kimono,
   Comstock Rev, Cold Mountain Rev, Galley Sail Rev,
   Portland Rev, Mudfish, RE:AL, Glass Cherry*

Michael G. Minassian   P
1921 NW 93 Ave
Pembroke Pines, FL 33024, 305-431-2229
   Pubs: *Ararat, Wind, Western Poetry, Passaic Rev, Pegasus
   Rev, San Fernando Poetry Jrnl*

Susan Mitchell 🎤 ✈   P
9287-C Boca Gardens Circle S
Boca Raton, FL 33496-1797, 561-451-4326
Internet: sunmil@aol.com
   Pubs: *Erotikon, Rapture* (HC, 2000, 1992), *Atlantic, New
   Yorker, Yale Rev*

Harry Morris   P
3940 W Kelly Rd
Tallahassee, FL 32301, 904-877-4307

Bridget Balthrop Morton 🎤 ✈   P
736 Espanola Way
Melbourne, FL 32901-4140, 321-724-9636
Internet: bridgetbal@aol.com
    Pubs: *Florida in Poetry: Anth* (Pineapple Pr, 1995), *Song for
    Occupations: Anth* (Wayland Pr, 1991), *English Jrnl,
    Drought, America, Visions Intl, U.S. Air, Commonweal, Gulf
    Stream*

William Moseley 🎤 ✈   W
102 Highview Dr
Cocoa, FL 32922, 407-639-1538
    Pubs: *Earth Tones* (Vergin Pr, 1994), *People Around You:
    Anth* (Germany; Schoningh, 1997), *Polyphany: Anth of
    Florida Poets* (Panther Pr, 1989), *Kansas Rev, Scripsit,
    Virginia Qtly Rev*

Joseph M. Moxley   P&W
English Dept, Univ South Florida, Tampa, FL 33620,
813-974-2421
    Pubs: *Paragraph*

Patrick J. Murphy 🎤 ✈   W
3612 Monmouth Ct
Tallahassee, FL 32308, 850-386-8698
Internet: pjmurph@aol.com
    Pubs: *Way Below E* (White Pine Pr, 1994), *100% Pure
    Florida Fiction: Anth* (U Pr Florida, 2000), *Tampa Rev, New
    Orleans Rev, Cream City Rev, Buffalo Spree, Sequoia,
    Greensboro Rev, Confrontation, Fiction Mag, Other Voices*

George E. Murphy, Jr. 🎤 ✈   P
PO Box 2626
Key West, FL 33045-2626, 305-296-4244
Internet: gemurph@bellsouth.net
    Pubs: *The Key West Reader* (Tortugas, 1990), *Rounding
    Ballast Key* (Ampersand Pr, 1987)

Patricia Muse   W
2118 Cochise Trail
Casselberry, FL 32707
    Pubs: *Eight Candles Glowing* (Ballantine Bks, 1976), *The
    Belle Claudine* (Avalon Bks, 1971)

Norman Nathan   P&W
Stratford Ct #219, 6343 Via de Sonrisa del Sur
Boca Raton, FL 33433, 407-391-2716
    Pubs: *Prince William B* (Mouton, 1975), *Contemporary
    American Satire: Anth* (Exile Pr, 1988), *Poetry Event,
    Wisconsin Rev, Chaminade, Fiction, Z Miscellaneous, Poem*

Barbra Nightingale 🎤 ✈   P
2231 N 52 Ave
Hollywood, FL 33021-3310, 954-961-7126
Internet: bnighting@aol.com
    Pubs: *Greatest Hits* (Pudding Hse, 2000), *Singing in the Key
    of L* (NFSPS Pr, 1999), *Lunar Equations* (East Coast Edtns,
    1993), *Lovers Never Die* (Pteranodon Pr, 1981), *Having a
    Wonderful Time: Anth* (HB, 1997), *Barrow St, The Florida
    Rev, Appalachee Rev*

Sheila Ortiz-Taylor   P&W
Florida State Univ, English Dept, Tallahassee, FL 32306-1580,
850-644-5776
Internet: sotaylor@english.fsu.edu
    Pubs: *Imaginary Parents, Coachella* (U New Mexico Pr,
    1998, 1996), *Faultline* (Naiad Pr, 1982), *Americas Rev,
    Sinister Wisdom, Common Lives/Lesbian Lives, Innisfree,
    Apalachee*

Joseph Papaleo   W
150 Cypress Pl
Oldsmar, FL 34677, 813-781-4605
    Pubs: *Picasso at Ninety One* (Seaport Bks, 1988),
    Unsettling America: Anth (Viking Penguin, 1994), *Paterson
    Literary Rev, Paris Rev*

Ricardo Pau-Llosa   P
South Campus English Dept, Miami-Dade Community
College, 11011 SW 104 St, Miami, FL 33176, 305-237-2510
    Pubs: *Cuba* (Carnegie Mellon Pr, 1993), *Bread of the
    Imagined* (Bilingual Pr, 1992), *Kenyon Rev, TriQtly, APR,
    Denver Qtly, Missouri Rev, NER*

Nola Perez 🎤   P
4610 Village Dr
Fernandina Beach, FL 32034
Internet: nolaperez@yahoo.com
    Pubs: *The Continent of Dreams* (Sulphur River Lit Rev Pr,
    2000), *Bay Area Poets Coalition Anth* (BAPC, 1994),
    Bottomfish, Red Rock Rev, Outerbridge, U Windsor Rev

Diane Marie Perrine   P
11990 SW 141st Pl
Dunnellon, FL 34432-6627
    Pubs: *Nexus, Icon, Writers Haven Jrnl, Silver Wings,
    Prickly Pear*

Robin Perry   W
541 Nightingale Dr
Indialantic, FL 32903, 407-777-3310
    Pubs: *Videography, Shadows of the Mind* (Writer's Digest
    Bks, 1985, 1981)

Mario A. Petaccia 🎤 ✈   P&W
762 Sailfish Dr
Fort Walton Beach, FL 32548, 850-244-5001
Internet: mpetaccia1@cs.com
    Pubs: *Walking on Water* (CCC, 1986), *Florida in Poetry:
    Anth* (Pineapple Pr, 1995), *Yankee, Poet, SPR, NYQ, Poem
    Mag, Voices in Italian Americana, Philadelphia Daily News,
    Miami Herald*

Allan Peterson   P
5397 Soundside Dr
Gulf Breeze, FL 32561-9530, 850-932-3077
Internet: apeterson71@mchsi.com
    Pubs: *Anoymous Or* (Defined Providence Pr, 2002), *Small
    Charities* (Panhandler Pr, 1995), *Stars on a Wire* (Parallel
    Edtns, 1989), *Bellingham Rev, Pleiades, Agni, Gettysburg
    Rev, Willow Springs, River Styx, Epoch, Green Mountains
    Rev, Adirondack Rev*

Geoffrey Philp 🎤 ✈   P&W
1255 NE 200 Terr
North Miami Beach, FL 33179, 305-237-1699
Internet: d000094c@dcfreenet.seflin.lib.fl.us
    Pubs: *Xango Music, Hurricane Center, Wheel and Come
    Again* (Peepal Tree Pr, 2001, 1998, 1998), *Whispers From
    the Cotton Tree Root* (Invisible Cities, 2000), *Oxford Book of
    Caribbean Short Stories: Anth* (Oxford U Pr, 1999)

Padgett Powell   P&W
English 4008 TUR, Univ Florida, Gainesville, FL 32611,
904-392-0777
    Pubs: *A Woman Named Drown, Edisto* (FSG, 1987, 1984)

Ilmars Purens 🎤 ✈   P
1244 Bel Aire Dr
Daytona Beach, FL 32118-3639, 904-255-6644
    Pubs: *New Time, Kayak, Wisconsin Rev, Epoch, Poetry
    Now, Nation, The Little Rev*

Dawn E. Reno 🎤 ✈   W
RR22 Box 22636
Lake City, FL 32024
Internet: dawnreno@isgroup.net
    Pubs: *Somewhere Out There* (RFI Pr, 2001), *Foxglove*
    (Bookmice Pr, 2001), *Loving Marie* (Bookmice Pr, 2000),
    The Silver Dolphin (Zebra Bks, 1995), *All That Glitters*
    (Pinnacle Bks, 1993), *Vermont Voices: Anth* (League of
    Vermont Writers, 1991), *Green Mtns Rev*

Anne Giles Rimbey   P
14802 N Florida Ave, ApJ153
Tampa, FL 33613-1854,
813-989-1430
Internet: arimbey@ij.net
    Pubs: *Dusty Sandals* (Skin Drum Pr, 1992), *I Am Becoming
    the Woman I've Wanted: Anth* (Papier-Mache Pr, 1994),
    *Tampa Rev, Birmingham Poetry Rev, Kalliope, Press,
    Crosscurrents, The Alembic*

Andres Rivero 🎤 ✈   W
CSP Publications, PO Box 650909, Miami, FL 33265,
305-380-6833
Internet: andresrivero@msn.com
    Pubs: *Cuentos Torvos, Nina Melancolia, Somos Como
    Somos, Recuerdos* (CSP Pub, 1998, 1993, 1982, 1980),
    *SpanishUs.com, El Nuevo Herald, Diario Las Americas,
    Spanish Today Mag*

Dave Roberts 🎤 ✈   P&W
14310 SW 73 Ave
Archer, FL 32618, 352-495-3312
    Pubs: *Bellowing Ark, Frogpond, Aethlon, City Primeval,
    Black Dirt, Potpourri, Midwest Qtly, South Carolina Rev*

David B. Robinson   P
PO Box 1414
Miami Shores, FL 33153-1414
Internet: superbio@cheerful.com
    Pubs: *Simcoe Rev, The Writer's Lifeline, Black Creek Rev*

Marcia J. Roessler 🎤 ✈   P&W
377 Payne Hill Dr
Clayton, FL 30525
Internet: roess7170@aol.com
    Pubs: *Traveled Paths* (Haworth Society, 1998), *The Reach
    of Song: Anth* (Georgia Poetry Society, 2000),
    Wordspinners: Anth (Burlington County, 1994)

David Rosenberg   P
11121 SW 62 Ave
Miami, FL 33156-4003
Internet: fieldbridg@aol.com
    Pubs: *The Book of David* (Harmony Bks, 1997), *The Lost
    Book of Paradise, A Poet's Bible* (Hyperion, 1993, 1991),
    Five Fingers Rev, Harper's, APR, Nation

Sandra Russell   P&W
508 Simonton, #3
Key West, FL 33040
    Pubs: *Solares Hill, Ball State U Pr, Croton Rev, Forum,
    Aspen Anth, Amelia, Sunrust, Toad Highway*

Brian Salchert   P
1600 NE 12th Ave
Gainesville, FL 32601-4693
    Pubs: *Teasings, First Pick* (Thinking Lizard, 1986, 1982),
    Rooted Sky (Monday Morning Pr, 1972), *Wisconsin Rev,
    Sou'wester, Saltillo, Studia Mystica*

Nicholas Samaras 🎤 ✈   P
4028 Ligustrum Dr.
Palm Harbor, FL 34685-4116, 727-944-4455
Internet: saddlemaker@ij.net
    Pubs: *Survivors of the Moving Earth* (U Salzburg Pr, 1998),
    Hands of the Saddlemaker (Yale U Pr, 1992), *Paris Rev,
    Poetry, Amer Scholar, New Yorker, New Criterion, Poetry,
    Kenyon Rev*

Bonny Barry Sanders P
1411 E Blackhawk Trail
Jacksonville, FL 32225-2703, 904-744-3511
  Pubs: *New Voices: Anth* (Colorado State U, 1994), *Midwest Qtly, Avocet, CSM, Blueline, Skylark, Red Rock Rev, Hayden's Ferry Rev, Plainsongs, Puckerbrush Rev, CSM, George Washington Rev, South Dakota Rev, Kalliope, Negative Capability*

Christy Sheffield Sanford P&W
714 Northeast Blvd
Gainesville, FL 32601-4375, 352-375-7565
http://gnv.fdt.net/~christys/index.html
  Pubs: *Sur Les Pointes* (White Eagle Coffee Store, 1995), *The H's: The Spasms of a Requiem* (Bloody Twin, 1994), *Coffeehouse: Writings From the Web: Anth* (Manning, 1997), *American Poets Say Goodbye to the 20th Century: Anth* (4 Walls, 8 Windows, 1996)

Lin Schlossman P
4480 Deer Trail Blvd
Sarasota, FL 34238-5606
  Pubs: *Panhandler, Treasure House, Crazyquilt, Poem, Maryland Poetry Rev, Poetpourri, Birmingham Poetry Rev, Cincinnati Judaica Rev, Owen Wister Rev*

Peter Schmitt 🎤 ✈ P
Box 248145
Coral Gables, FL 33124, 305-284-4074
Internet: pschmittfl@aol.com
  Pubs: *Hazard Duty, Country Airport* (Copper Beech Pr, 1995, 1989), *The Nation, Paris Rev, Ploughshares, Poetry, Southern Rev, Hudson Rev*

Paul K. Shepherd P&W
1117 Lasswade Dr
Tallahassee, FL 32312
Internet: paulkeithshepherd@msn.com
  Pubs: *Other Testaments: Anth* (Other Testaments 1998), *Fiction, Beloit Fiction, Folio, Maryland Rev, Portland Rev, Prairie Schooner, William & Mary Rev*

Reginald Shepherd 🎤 ✈ P
741 Cornell Ave
Pensacola, FL 32514
Internet: rshepherd@worldnet.att.net
  Pubs: *Wrong, Angel, Interrupted, Some Are Drowning* (U Pitt Pr, 1999, 1996, 1994), *Best American Poetry: Anths,* (S&S, 2002, 2000, 1996, 1995),

Rose Sher P
7135 Collins Ave, Apt 1202
Miami Beach, FL 33141-3230
  Pubs: *Anthology Two* (Florida State Poets Assn, 1984), *Euterpe Housetops, Earthwise, Newscribes*

Edmund Skellings P
5835 SW 58th Ct
Davie, FL 33314-7303, 954-929-3595
Internet: poet1@laureate.cec.fau.edu
  Pubs: *Collected Poems 1958-1998, Selected Poems* (CD), *Living Proof, Showing My Age, Face Value* (U Pr Florida, 1998, 1997, 1987, 1978, 1977)

Elaine Campbell Smith W
5587 W Kelly Rd
Tallahassee, FL 32311
Internet: kamilane@yahoo.com
  Pubs: *A Wish Too Soon* (Silhouette, 1986), *Fantasy Lover* (Harlequin, 1984), *Southern Rev, Snap, Whispering Palms, Ellery Queen's Mystery Mag*

Patrick D. Smith W
1370 Island Dr
Merritt Island, FL 32952, 407-452-6590
  Pubs: *The Beginning, A Land Remembered, Allapattah* (Pineapple Pr, 1998, 1984, 1979), *Angel City* (Valkarie, 1978), *Forever Island* (Norton/Dell, 1973), *The River Is Home* (Little, Brown, 1953)

Jim Sorcic P
2348 NW 98 Way
Coral Springs, FL 33065, 305-345-3662
  Pubs: *This Could Lead to Dancing, The Cost of Living, The Secret Oral Teachings of Jim the House* (Morgan Pr, 1991, 1980, 1971)

Les Standiford 🎤 ✈ W
Creative Writing Program, Florida International Univ, Biscayne Bay Campus, North Miami, FL 33181, 305-253-7053
Internet: standifo@fiu.edu
  Pubs: *Havana Run, Bone Key, Deal With the Dead, Black Mountain* (Putnam, 2003, 2002, 2001, 1999), *Last Train to Paradise* (Crown, 2002), *Presidential Deal, Done Deal* (HC, 1998, 1993), *Spill* (Atlantic Monthly Pr, 1991), *Confrontation, Kansas Qtly, BPJ, Image*

Thomas Starling W
PO Box 2222
Cocoa, FL 32923-2222, 407-639-3162
Internet: dicki4@juno.com
  Pubs: *Peter Paladine of the Great Heart, Jethrow's Cabin* (Spindrift Pr, 1995, 1982)

Elisabeth Stevens 🎤 ✈ P&W
5353 Creekside Trail
Sarasota, FL 34243, 941-359-9712
  Pubs: *Cherry Pie & Other Stories, Lower Than the Angels: Anth* (Lite Circle, 2001, 1999), *Eranos* (Goss Pr, 2000), *Household Words* (Three Conditions Pr, 2000), *In a Certain Place: Anth* (SCOP, 1999), *In Foreign Parts, The Night Lover* (Birch Brook, 1997, 1995)

Virgil Suarez 🎤 ✈   P&W
F.S.U./ English Dept, Tallahassee, FL 32306-1580,
850-644-2521
Internet: vsuarez@english.fsu.edu
  Pubs: *In the Republic of Longing* (Bilingual Rev Pr, 1999),
  You Come Singing (Tia Chucha Pr, 1998), *Going Under*
  (Arte Publico Pr, 1996), *Havana Thursdays* (Arte Publico Pr,
  1995), *Latin Jazz* (William Morrow/Simon & Schuster, 1989)

Suzi 🎤   P
PO Box 831544
Ocala, FL 34483-1544, 352-687-1321
Internet: gnosticsuzi@aol.com
  Pubs: *Rogue Scolars, Conspire, Recursive Angel,
  Mesechabe, Long Shot, The New Laurel Rev, New
  American Writing, Exquisite Corpse*

Millie Taylor   P&W
PO Box 5001
Jacksonville, FL 32247-5001
  Pubs: *Thema, Kalliope, South Dakota Rev, Passager*

Sandra Thompson 🎤 ✈   W
4410 W Bay to Bay Blvd
Tampa, FL 33629, 813-831-3311
Internet: sandrachris@att.nt
  Pubs: *Wild Bananas* (Atlantic Monthly Pr, 1985), *Close-Ups*
  (U Georgia Pr, 1984)

Linda Trice 🎤 ✈   P&W
Box 17933
Sarasota, FL 34276
Internet: joyandhappiness@hotmail.com
  Pubs: *Pockets, Small Pond, Mini Romance, Sun & Shade,
  Papyrus, INK, Sarasvati, Show & Tell, Colorlines,
  Candlelight Poetry Jrnl, Idiolect, Short Stories, Writer's
  Gazette, Papyrus*

Dorothy Twiss   P
5125 Soundside Dr
Gulf Breeze, FL 32563-8923, 850-932-5619
Internet: dottwiss@aol.com
  Pubs: *Mississippi Writers: Reflections of Childhood & Youth:
  Anth* (U Pr Mississippi, 1988)

Kathryn Vanspanckeren 🎤 ✈   P
Univ Tampa, English Dept, Tampa, FL 33606, 813-251-1914
Internet: kvspanckeren@alpha.utampa.edu
  Pubs: *Salt & Sweet Water, Mountains Hidden in Mountains*
  (Empty Window, 1993, 1992), *APR, Ploughshares, 13th
  Moon, Carolina Qtly, Contact II, Boundary 2*

Mary Katherine Wainwright 🎤 ✈   P&W
111 3rd St S
Bradenton Beach, FL 34217
Internet: wainwrm@mccfl.us
  Pubs: *Sarasota Rev of Poetry: Anth* (Robert Abel Publishing,
  1999), *Harrington Lesbian Fiction Qtly, Kalliope, Rainbow
  Pages Mag*

Sterling Watson   W
Eckerd College, PO Box 12560/Letters Collegium, St
Petersburg, FL 33733, 813-864-8281
  Pubs: *Deadly Sweet* (S&S, 1994), *The Calling* (Dell, 1989),
  Blind Tongues (Delacorte, 1989)

Herbert J. Waxman   P
3502 Bimini Ln, #H4
Coconut Creek, FL 33066, 954-979-4593
  Pubs: *Where the Worm Grows Fat* (Full Court Pr, 1975),
  *Clarion, Voice of Wynmoor, NYQ, Speakeasy, Alive &
  Kicking*

Craig Weeden 🎤 ✈   P
151 Tall Trees Ct
Sarasota, FL 34232, 941-349-4702
Internet: muzzles@kudos.net
  Pubs: *American Sports Poems: Anth* (Orchard, 1988),
  *Poetry Now, New Orleans Rev, Chowder Rev, SPR,
  Cimarron Rev, Calliope*

Sarah Brown Weitzman 🎤 ✈   P
555 SE Sixth Ave, Apt 2B
Delray Beach, FL 33483-5252, 561-276-4464
  Pubs: *Nassau Rev, LIQ, Rattle, Poet Lore, CQ, Mid-Amer
  Rev, Kansas Qtly, Poet & Critic, Madison Rev, Croton Rev,
  Abraxas, New America*

Jean West   P
Box 2710, Rollins College
Winter Park, FL 32789-4499, 407-646-2666
  Pubs: *Holding the Chariot* (Open Hse, 1976), *Florida in
  Poetry: Anth* (Pineapple Pr, 1995), *Lullwater Rev, Kalliope,
  Confrontation, CSM*

William M. White 🎤 ✈   P&W
721 Navigator's Way
Edgewater, FL 32141, 904-423-8633
  Pubs: *Where I Stand* (Tudor Pubs, 1992)

Millie Mae Wicklund 🎤 ✈   P
3623 N Long Pine Point
Beverly Hills, FL 34465-3307
  Pubs: *Amer Writing: A Magazine, New Letters, Poets Forum*

Joy Williams   W
8128 Midnight Pass Rd
Siesta Key, FL 33581
  Pubs: *Escapes* (Atlantic Monthly Pr, 1990), *Breaking &
  Entering* (Random Hse, 1988), *Granta*

Robley Wilson 🎤 ✈ P&W
PO Box 4009
Winter Park, FL 32793-4009
Internet: robley.wilson@uni.edu
    Pubs: *Everything Paid For* (U Pr Florida, 1999), *The Victim's Daughter, Terrible Kisses* (S&S, 1991, 1989), *A Pleasure Tree* (U Pitt Pr, 1990), *Iowa Rev, Prairie Schooner, Epoch, Southern California Anth*

Nancy Leffel Wilson 🎤 ✈ P&W
4000 Old Settlement Road
Merritt Island, FL 32952-6210, 407-453-5224
Internet: Mtnannie@cfl.rr.com
    Pubs: *Pilgrimage, Onionhead, Saturday Evening Post, The Panhandler*

Norma Woodbridge P
2606 Zoysia Ln
North Fort Myers, FL 33917-2476
    Pubs: *Poetry Norma Woodbridge* (International Poets, 1995), *Graces* (Harper, 1994), *When God Speaks, Joy in the Morning, Resting Places* (Star Bks, 1991, 1990, 1988), *Christmas Blessings: Anth* (Time/Warner, 2002), *Get Well Wishes: Anth* (HarperSF, 2000)

Stephen Caldwell Wright P
Seminole Community College, 100 Weldon Blvd, Sanford, FL
32773-6199, 407-328-2063
    Pubs: *With Fortitude, The Chicago Collective, Circumference, Talking to the Mountains* (Christopher-Burghardt, 1991, 1990, 1989, 1988)

Fred W. Wright, Jr. P
PO Box 86158
St Petersburg, FL 33738, 813-595-5004
    Pubs: *Fiddler Crab, Pegasus, Reiki Jrnl, Gryphon, Chattahoochee Rev, Sharing, Pudding*

Wyatt Wyatt W
Univ Central Florida, English Dept, Orlando, FL 32816,
305-275-2212
    Pubs: *Deep in the Heart* (Atheneum, 1981), *Catching Fire* (Random Hse, 1977)

Jim Young P
4811 NW 17 Pl
Gainesville, FL 32605, 904-378-4208
    Pubs: *Plains Poetry Jrnl, Light Year, Lyric, Wind, Stone Country, Sunrust, Negative Capability*

Iris M. Zavala P
100 Kings Point Dr, #1707
Miami, FL 33160-4731
    Pubs: *Kiliagonia* (Mexico, 1980), *Que-Nadiemuera Sin Amar El Mar* (Spain, 1982), *Third Woman*

GEORGIA

Lynne Alvarez P
42 Vernon River Dr
Savannah, GA 31419
    Pubs: *On New Ground* (TCG, 1987), *Living With Numbers, The Dreaming Man* (Waterfront, 1987, 1984)

Ken Anderson P
Floyd College, 5198 Ross Rd, Acworth, GA 30102,
770-975-4150
Internet: kanderso@mail.FC.peachnet.edu
    Pubs: *Smooth 'N' Sassy, The Intense Lover: A Suite of Poems,* (Star Bks, 1998, 1995), *Chattahoochee Rev, Lullwater Rev, Connecticut Poetry Rev, James White Rev, Bay Windows, Beloit Poetry Rev*

Joan Anson-Weber P
Cherokee Publishing Co, 4331 Lake Chimney Ct, Roswell, GA
30075, 770-587-3077
    Pubs: *Snuffles* (Cherokee Pub Co, 1995), *The Gate of the Year* (Kingham Pr, 1993), *Before the Trees Turn Gray* (Wings Pr, 1981), *Poets at Work, Creative Arts & Science, Nashville Newsletter, Poets of Now, Ultimate Writer, Small Pond*

Rebecca Baggett 🎤 ✈ P
330 College Cir
Athens, GA 30605-3630, 706-548-0029
Internet: rbaggett@franklin.uga.edu
    Pubs: *Rebecca Baggett: Greatest Hits, Still Life With Children* (Pudding Hse Pub, 2001, 1996), *A More Perfect Union: Anth* (St. Martin's Pr, 1998), *Claiming the Spirit Within: Anth* (Beacon, 1996), *For She Is the Tree of Life: Anth* (Conari Pr, 1994)

Coleman Barks 🎤 ✈ P
196 Westview Dr
Athens, GA 30606, 706-543-2148
    Pubs: *The Book of Love, The Soul of Rumi, The Essential Rumi* (Harper SF, 2003, 2001, 1995), *Tentmaking, Club: Granddaughter Poems, Gourd Seed* (Maypop, 2002, 2001, 1992), *The Glance* (Viking, 1999)

Gloria G. Brame P&W
PO Box 18552
Atlanta, GA 31126
http://gloria-brame.com/
    Pubs: *Elf, Thermopylae*

Roy Bush   W
5450 Augusta Rd, #342
Garden City, GA 31408-1600

Lucas Carpenter 🎤 ✈   P
Oxford College of Emory Univ, English Dept, Oxford, GA
30267, 770-784-8301
Internet: lcarpen@emory.edu
    Pubs: *Perils of the Affect* (Mellen Pr, 2002), *Carolina Qtly,
    Minnesota Rev, Crescent Rev, Kansas Rev, College English,
    The Jrnl, Southern Humanities Rev, South Carolina Rev*

Turner Cassity 🎤 ✈   P
510 E Ponce De Leon Ave, Apt J
Decatur, GA 30030, 404-373-3514
    Pubs: *No Second Eden, The Destructive Element* (Ohio U
    Pr, 2002, 1998), *Between the Chains, Hurricane Lamp* (U
    Chicago Pr, 1991, 1986), *Poetry*

Peter Christopher 🎤 ✈   W
214 E Grady St Apt H
Statesboro, GA 30458
Internet: pchrstphr@gasou.edu
    Pubs: *Campfires of the Dead* (Knopf, 1989)

Mary Ann Coleman   P
205 Sherwood Dr
Athens, GA 30606
    Pubs: *Disappearances* (Anhinga Pr, 1978), *Kansas Qtly,
    National Forum, Negative Capability, Lit Rev*

Stephen Corey 🎤 ✈   P&W
357 Parkway Dr
Athens, GA 30606-4951, 706-542-3481
Internet: scorey@arches.uga.edu
    Pubs: *Greatest Hits: 1980-2000* (Pudding House, 2000),
    Mortal Fathers & Daughters (Palanquin Pr, 1999), *Hollins
    Critic, Runes, Shenandoah*

Gary Corseri   P&W
2455 Kingsland Dr
Atlanta, GA 30360, 404-396-8377
    Pubs: *Random Descent, North of Wakulla: Anth* (Anhinga
    Pr, 1989, 1989), *City Lights Rev, Redbook, Georgia Rev,
    Poetry NW, Florida Rev*

Doris Davenport   P&W
PO Box 135
Cornelia, GA 30531-0135, 704-535-3121
    Pubs: *Voodoo Chile/Slight Return* (Soque Street Pr, 1991),
    Eat Thunder & Drink Rain (Self, 1982), *Melus, Mid-Amer
    Rev, Women's Rev of Bks, Lesbian Studies*

Cynde Gregory De Acevedo Jerez   P
2615 Ridge Brook Trail
Duluth, GA 30096, 770-797-9099
Internet: nordgirl@earthlink.net
    Pubs: *Satori, Black Ice, Instructor Mag, BPJ, North Country
    Anth, Calyx*

Juni Dunklin   P&W
407 W Church St
Sandersville, GA 31082

John Ehrlichman   W
795 Hammond Dr #1607
Atlanta, GA 30328

Nadine Estroff   P
3134 Edinburgh Dr
Augusta, GA 30909-3316
    Pubs: *Hollins Critic, NYQ, Southern Rev, SW Rev, Carleton
    Miscellany, Texas Qtly, Kansas Qtly, Lyrical Voices*

Richard Flynn 🎤 ✈   P
310 Savannah Ave
Statesboro, GA 30458-5259, 912-489-1913
Internet: rflynn@gsvms2.cc.gasou.edu
    Pubs: *The Age of Reason* (Hawkhead Pr, 1993), *Reaper,
    Washington Rev, lower limit speech*

Starkey Flythe, Jr.   W
403 Telfair St
Augusta, GA 30901
    Pubs: *The American Story* (Curtis Pub, 1977), *Georgia Rev,
    Greensboro Rev, Ploughshares, Wind*

Walter Griffin 🎤 ✈   P
2518 Maple St
East Point, GA 30344-2432, 404-762-9196
Internet: sociolingo@aol.com
    Pubs: *Nights of Noise & Light* (Skidrow Penthouse, 1999),
    Western Flyers (U West Florida Pr, 1990), *Georgia Voices:
    Anth* (U Georgia Pr, 2000), *Atlantic, Evergreen, Paris Rev,
    Literary Rev, Southern Rev, New Criterion, Poetry, Harper's*

Gary D. Grossman 🎤   P
237 Highland Ave
Athens, GA 30606, 706-549-5897
Internet: grossman@uga.edu
    Pubs: *Mobius, Old Red Kimono, Brussels Sprout, In Your
    Face, Midwest Poetry Rev, Opus Lit Rev, Poetry Motel, Feh,
    The Acorn, Cotton Gin, Pearl, Lilliput Rev, Blood & Fire Rev*

Linda Lee Harper   P
3693 Inverness Way
Augusta, GA 30907
Internet: lleeharper@aol.com
  Pubs: *Blue Flute* (Adastra Pr, 1998), *Toward Desire* (Word
  Works, 1996), *A Failure of Loveliness* (Nightshade Pr,
  1994), *Anth of South Carolina Poets* (Ninety-Six Pr, 1994),
  *Georgia Rev, Massachusetts Rev, Illinois Rev, Kansas Qtly,
  Laurel Rev, Passages North*

Robert Hays   P
3360 Trickum Rd
Marietta, GA 30006-4683, 770-924-9228
Internet: haysr@aol.com
  Pubs: *Parnassus Lit Jrnl, Dekalb Lit Arts Jrnl, Reach of
  Song, Alura*

Katherine L. Hester   W
714 Woodland Ave SE
Atlanta, GA 30316
Internet: khandmc@bellsouth.net
  Pubs: *Eggs for Young America* (Penguin, 1998), *Ex-Files:
  New Stories About Old Flames: Anth* (Context Bks, 2000),
  Prize Stories 1994: The O. Henry Awards: Anth
  (Anchor/Doubleday, 1995), *Amer Short Fiction, Cimarron
  Rev, Five Points, Indiana Rev*

Robert W. Hill 🎤 ✈   P
Kennesaw State University, 1000 Chastain Rd, Kennesaw, GA
30144-5591, 770-423-6346
  Pubs: *Shenandoah, Southern Poetry Rev, Ascent, Billy Goat
  4, Southern Rev*

Robert Holland   P
140 Ridley Cir
Decatur, GA 30030, 404-378-2103
  Pubs: *Norton Introduction to Literature: Anth* (Norton, 1978),
  Georgia Rev, Midwest Qtly

T. R. Hummer   P
Univ of Georgia, c/o Georgia Review, Athens, GA 30602
  Pubs: *Useless Virtues, Walt Whitman in Hell* (LSU Pr, 2001,
  1996), *The 18,000-Ton Olympic Dream* (Morrow, 1991),
  Lower-Class Heresy, The Passion of the Right-Angled Man
  (U of Illinois Pr, 1987, 1984)

Emmett Jarrett   P
St. Michael and All Angels, Episcopal Church, 6740 Memorial
Dr, Stone Mountain, GA 30083-2235
  Pubs: *To Heal the Sin-Sick Soul* (Episcopal Urban Caucus,
  1996), *God's Body* (Hanging Loose Pr, 1975), *Hanging
  Loose, Fellowship Papers, Jubilee Pubs*

Greg Johnson 🎤 ✈   W
808 Amsterdam Ave
Atlanta, GA 30306, 770-423-6491
Internet: rjohn713@aol.com
  Pubs: *Sticky Kisses* (Alyson Bks, 2001), *Distant Friends* (U
  Georgia Pr, 1997), *I Am Dangerous & Other Stories, A
  Friendly Deceit* (Johns Hopkins Pr, 1996, 1992), *Pagan
  Babies* (Dutton, 1993), *Distant Friends* (Ontario Rev Pr,
  1990), *TriQtly, Georgia Rev*

Seaborn Jones 🎤 ✈   P
PO Box 469
Lizella, GA 31052-0469, 912-935-3659
  Pubs: *Lost Keys* (Snake Nation Pr, 1996), *X-Ray Movies*
  (Georgia Arts Council, 1988), *Drowning From the Inside Out*
  (Cherry Valley, 1983), *Georgia Voices: Anth* (U Georgia Pr,
  2000), *Atlanta Rev, Pearl, SPR, River Styx*

Anthony Kellman 🎤 ✈   P&W
796 Palatine Ave SE
Atlanta, GA 30316-2490
Internet: akellman@aol.com
  Pubs: *Wings of a Stranger, The Long Gap, The Coral
  Rooms, Watercourse* (Peepal Tree Pr, 2000, 1996, 1994,
  1990), *Chelsea, Callaloo*

Mary Torre Kelly 🎤 ✈   W
1176 St Louis Pl
Atlanta, GA 30306, 404-872-0934
Internet: noonie@mindspring.com
  Pubs: *Grasslands Rev, Poets, Artists 20, Madman,
  Manzanita, Touchstone, Pleiades, Black River Rev, Sun,
  Southern Humanities Rev, New South Rev*

Gary Kerley 🎤 ✈   P
4720 Creek Wood Dr
Gainesville, GA 30507-8870, 770-532-3430
  Pubs: *From the Green Horseshoe: Anth* (U South Carolina
  Pr, 1987), *SPR, Yankee*

Diane Kistner   P
738 Ormewood Ave SE
Atlanta, GA 30312
  Pubs: *Falling in Caves* (Bootlaig Pr, 1982), *Poem, Aura, Lit
  Arts Rev, North Carolina Sun*

Martin Lammon 🎤 ✈   P
Georgia College & State Univ, Arts & Letters, Campus Box 89,
Milledgeville, GA 31061, 478-445-1289
Internet: mlammon@gcsu.edu
  Pubs: *News From Where I Live* (U Arkansas Pr, 1998),
  *Chelsea, Connecticut Rev, Luna, Nimrod, Gettysburg Rev,
  Midwest Qtly Rev, Ploughshares*

M. Rosser Lunsford   P
456 Rockville Springs Dr
Eatonton, GA 31024, 404-485-3449
    Pubs: *Thoughts About Life* (Rainbow Bks, 1988),
    Sparrowgrass Anth (Washington U, 1998), *Reach of Song
    Anth* (Georgia Poetry Society, 1997), *Arizona Highways,
    Jean's Jrnl, Rhyme Time*

Marion Montgomery   P&W
Box 115
Crawford, GA 30630, 706-743-5359
    Pubs: *The Men I Have Chosen for Fathers* (U Missouri Pr,
    1990), *The Trouble With You Innerleckchuls* (Christendom
    College Pr, 1988)

Janice Townley Moore   P
Young Harris College, PO Box 144, Young Harris, GA 30582,
828-389-6394
    Pubs: *The Bedford Intro to Literature: Anth* (St. Martin's Pr,
    2002), *Prarie Schooner, JAMA, SPR, Georgia Rev, Atlanta
    Rev*

Cynthia A. Mortus   P
509 Cross Creek
Stone Mountain, GA 30087-5328
Internet: ca 425010@aol.com
    Pubs: *Connecticut River Rev, Black Bear Rev, Poem, Cotton
    Boll, Spoon River Qtly, Encore, Earth's Daughters, Virginia
    Country*

Chuck Oliveros   P
1206 Lyndale Dr SE
Atlanta, GA 30316, 404-624-1524
    Pubs: *Bleeding From the Mouth, The Pterodactyl in the
    Wilderness* (Dead Angel, 1992, 1982), *Caliban*

Robert Parham   P&W
Armstrong Atlantic State Univ, Dept of Languages, Lit, and
Philosophy, Savannah, GA 31419-1997, 912-927-5289
    Pubs: *The Low Fires of Keen Memory* (Colonial Pr, 1992),
    The Ninety-Six Sampler of South Carolina Poetry: Anth
    (Ninety-Six Pr, 1994), *SPR*

Lee Passarella 🎤 ✈   P
1384 Township Dr
Lawrenceville, GA 30043, 770-995-9475
    Pubs: *Swallowed Up in Victory* (White Mane, 2002), *Out of
    A/Maze: Anth* (Chiron Review Pr, 1996), *Poetry Bay,
    Antietam Rev, Wallace Stevens Jrnl, Mediphors, JAMA,
    Chelsea, Formalist,*

Phyllis E. Price   P
509 Cross Creek Pt
Stone Mountain, GA 30087, 404-841-5515
    Pubs: *Cotton Boll, Connecticut River Rev, Virginia Country
    Mag, Embers, Oxford, Appalachian Heritage, Poem*

Robert Earl Price   P&W
19 Ollie St NW
Atlanta, GA 30314, 404-753-3113
Internet: rep@rapid13.org
    Pubs: *Blues Blood* (CAC Pr, 1995), *Blood Elegy* (Poetry
    Atlanta Pr, 1987), *Blood Lines* (Togetherness Pr, 1984),
    Black Poetry of the '80s in the Deep South: Anth (Beans &
    Brown Rice Pub, 1990), *Snake Nation Rev, African
    American Rev, Atlanta Rev, Quest*

Rosetta Radtke   P&W
PO Box 2123
Savannah, GA 31402-2123
    Pubs: *Staten Island, Passages North, Blue Pitcher, Off Main
    Street, Wind, Pembroke, Poetry Now*

Barbara Ras   P
PO Box 82375
Athens, GA 30608, 706-552-3626
Internet: ras@ugapress.uga.edu
    Pubs: *Bite Every Sorrow* (Louisiana State U Pr, 1998), *The
    New American Poets: Anth* (U Pr New England, 2000),
    Georgia Rev, Massachusetts Rev

Paul Rice   P
Brunswick College, Altama at Fourth, Brunswick, GA 31523,
912-264-7357
    Pubs: *Georgia Rev, Chattahoochee Rev, Tar River Rev, Blue
    Unicorn, Barataria Rev, Mountain Rev*

William P. Robertson   P
PO Box 14532
Savannah, GA 31416
    Pubs: *Life After Sex Life* (Four Winds Pr, 1983)

Jalane Rogers   P
4461 Florence St
Tucker, GA 30084
    Pubs: *Broken Streets, Living Streams, Silver Wings,
    Parnassus, Red Pagoda, Archer Mag*

Larry Rubin 🎤 ✈   P
Box 15014, Druid Hills Branch, Atlanta, GA 30333
    Pubs: *Unanswered Calls* (Kendall/Hunt, 1997), *All My
    Mirrors Lie* (Godine, 1975), *Lanced in Light* (HBJ, 1967),
    The World's Old Way (U of Nebraska Pr,1963), *New Yorker,
    Harper's, Poetry, Yale Rev, Sewanee Rev, Kenyon Rev*

Esta Seaton 🎤   P
1200 Beech Valley Rd NE
Atlanta, GA 30306-3124, 404-874-0147

Bettie M. Sellers   P
PO Box 274
Young Harris, GA 30582
    Pubs: *Wild Ginger* (Imagery, 1988), *Liza's Monday & Other
    Poems* (Appalachian Consortium, 1986)

Ruth Knafo Setton 🎤 ⅄   P&W
Georgia College State Univ, Engl Dept, Milledgeville, GA 31061
   Pubs: *Nothing Makes You Free: Anth* (Norton, 2002), *The Road to Fez* (Counterpoint Pr, 2001), *With Signs & Wonders: Anth* (Invisible Cities Pr, 2001), *Lost on the Map of the World: Anth* (Peter Lang, 2001), *N Amer Rev, ACM, Nimrod, Tikkun*

L. S. Shevshenko   P&W
4008 Kemper Ave
Macon, GA 31206-1826, 912-784-8260
Internet: shevshenko@hotmail.com
   Pubs: *Rob Amsterdam, Ice House* (Moon Dog Pr, 1996, 1996), *The Paper Moon* (Moon Calf Pr, 1995), *In Our Own Words II & I: Anths* (MW Enterprises, 2000, 1999), *In the Wind, Expresso Poetry, Sounds of Poetry, Dream Intl Qtly, Deathrealm Mag, Poet's Rev*

Kristina Simms 🎤 ⅄   P
189 Harner Rd
Kathleen, GA 31047, 478-988-8560
Internet: ktina@alltel.net

Terrill Shepard Soules   P
2895 Mornington Dr Nw
Atlanta, GA 30327-1272, 404-352-9505
   Pubs: *Vacations, The Selectric Poems* (Pynyon Pr, 1986, 1983), *Esquire, Kayak, San Jose Studies*

Carol Speed   W
3016 Duke of Gloucester
East Point, GA 30346-5809
   Pubs: *Inside Black Hollywood* (Holloway Hse, 1980), *Buffalo Soldier Mag*

George E. Statham   P
699 McRidge Rd
Hiawassee, GA 30546, 706-896-5431
   Pubs: *Gunny's Rhymes, Poetic Injustice* (Fireside Pub, 1996, 1996), *Poetry Churg Mag, Writers Exchange, Parnassus Lit Jrnl, Laureate Letter Newsletter, Leatherneck Mag, Lines & Rhymes, Poetic Eloquence, Blind Man's Rainbow, Ultrafight Mag, Apostrophe*

Leon Stokesbury 🎤 ⅄   P
English Dept, Georgia State Univ, Atlanta, GA 30303, 404-651-2900
   Pubs: *Autumn Rhythm, The Made Thing, The Drifting Away* (U Arkansas Pr, 1996, 1987, 1986), *New Yorker, Georgia Rev, Kenyon Rev*

John Stone 🎤 ⅄   P
3983 Northlake Creek Ct
Tucker, GA 30084
Internet: jstone@medadm.emory.edu
   Pubs: *Where Water Begins, In the Country of Hearts, The Smell of Matches, Renaming the Streets, In All This Rain* (LSU, 1998, 1996, 1988, 1985, 1980)

Natasha Trethewey   P
Depart of English, Callaway Center, 537 Kilgo Circle, Emory Univ Atlanta, GA 30322, 404-727-6484
Internet: ntrenthe@emory.edu
   Pubs: Bellocg's Ophelia (Graywolf Pr, 2002) *Domestic Work* (Graywolf Pr, 2000), *The Best Amer Poetry: Anth* (Scribner, 2000), *The New Young Amer Poets: Anth* (Southern Illinois U Pr, 2000), *Boomer Girls: Anth* (U Iowa Pr, 1999), *Giant Steps: Anth* (HC, 2000), *NER, Southern Rev*

Memye Curtis Tucker 🎤 ⅄   P
184 Rhodes Dr
Marietta, GA 30068-3672, 770-971-1834
Internet: mc@tucker.net
   Pubs: *The Watchers* (Ohio U Pr, 1998), *Admit One* (State Street Pr, 1998), *Storm Line* (Palanquin Pr, 1998), *Holding Patterns* (Poetry Atlanta Pr, 1988), *Buck & Wing: Anth* (Shenandoah, 2000), *What Have You Lost?: Anth* (Greenwillow Bks, 1999), *Georgia Rev*

Dan Veach 🎤 ⅄   P
PO Box 8248
Atlanta, GA 31106, 404-636-0052
Internet: dan@atlantareview.com
   Pubs: *Annual Survey of American Poetry: Anth* (Roth, 1986), *Sotheby's Intl Poetry Competition: Anth* (Arvon 1982), *Irish Times, Sulphur Rev, CQ, Peabody Rev, Chattahoochie Rev, Pinchpenny*

Sharon Webb   W
2157 River Refuge Blvd
Blairsville, GA 30512, 706-745-4454
   Pubs: *Pestis 18* (Tor/St. Martin's Pr, 1987), *Ram Song* (Bantam, 1985)

GUAM

Richard E. Mezo 🎤 ⅄   P
PO Box 24814, GMF, APO, HQ
Useucom, AE, 09128, 07113057704
Internet: Richard_Mezo@eu.odedodea.edu
   Pubs: *Mainstreeter, Penny Dreadful, Colorado Qtly, Nantucket Rev, Christianity & the Arts, Poetry Motel, CQ, Buffalo Bones, Riverrun, SPR, Buffalo Spree, South Dakota Rev, HVE, Kaleido, Graffiti, George & Mertie's, Haight-Ashbury Literary Jrnl, Kimera*

HAWAII

Nell Altizer   P
English Dept, Univ Hawaii, 1733 Donaghho Rd, Honolulu, HI 96822
   Pubs: *The Man Who Died En Route* (U Massachusetts Pr, 1989), *Hawaii Rev, Ploughshares, Chaminade Rev, Massachusetts Rev*

Laureen Ching   P
2930 Varsity Cir, #4
Honolulu, HI 96826
 Pubs: *Rosalind, Thea* (Fawcett, 1985, 1985), *Hawaii Rev,*
 Mississippi Valley Rev, Dacotah Territory

Eric E. Chock   P
95-1053 Kopalani St
Mililani, HI 96789
 Pubs: *Last Days Here* (Bamboo Ridge Pr, 1990), *The Open*
 Boat, Poems of Asian America: Anth (Anchor, 1993), *Seattle*
 Rev, Zyzzyva, Jrnl of Ethnic Studies

Kermit Coad   P
1802 Mokehana Pl
Kihei, HI 96753-7920, 808-879-1782
 Pubs: *Poetry Hawaii: Anth* (U Hawaii Pr, 1979), *Stoogism*
 Anthology (Scarecrow Bks, 1977), *The Spirit That Moves*
 Us, Makali'i, Bamboo Ridge

Reuel Denney   P
2957 Kalakaua Ave, #315, Honolulu, HI 96815-4647,
808-923-9618
 Pubs: *Feast of Strangers* (Greenwood Pr, 1999), *The*
 Astonished Muse, In Praise of Adam (U Chicago Pr, 1989,
 1961), *The Lonely Crowd* (w/D. Reisman & N. Glazer; Yale U
 Pr, 1950), *New Directions, Kaimana, Poetry, Chelsea*

Ray Freed 🎤 ✈   P
PO Box 2883
Kailua-Kona, HI 96745-2883, 808-326-1138
www.tropweb.com/indigo/poems.htm
 Pubs: *All Horses Are Flowers, Much Cry Little Wool* (Street
 Pr, 1998, 1990), *The Juggler's Ball* (Hualalai Pr, 1996)

Norma W. Gorst   P&W
45-219 Kokokahi Pl
Kaneohe, HI 96744-2424, 808-235-2346
Internet: gorst@lava.net
 Pubs: *Bamboo Ridge, Kaimana, Sister Stew, Chelsea,*
 Cottonwood

Joy Harjo   P
1140-D Alewa Dr
Honolulu, HI 96817-1562, 808-595-8549
Internet: mekkopoet@earthlink.net
 Pubs: *How We Became Human, New and Selected Poems,*
 A Map to the Next World, Reinventing the Enemy's
 Language, The Woman Who Fell From the Sky (Norton,
 2002, 2000, 1997, 1994), *The Spiral of Memory* (U Michigan
 Pr, 1996), *In Mad Love & War* (Wesleyan, 1990)

Norman Hindley   P
46-049 Aliianela Pl, #1721
Kaneohe, HI 96744-3703, 808-236-2229
Internet: dlanska@lava.net
 Pubs: *A Good Man* (Fawcett, 1993), *Winter Eel* (Petronium
 Pr, 1984), *Chaminade Lit Rev, Hawaii Rev, Hawaii Lit Arts,*
 Poetry

Faye Kicknosway   P
English Dept, Univ Hawaii at Manoa, 412 Kuykendall,
Honolulu, HI 96822, 808-956-7619
 Pubs: *Listen to Me, The Violence of Potatoes* (Ridgeway Pr,
 1992, 1990), *All These Voices* (Coffee Hse Pr, 1986)

Irina Kirk   W
475 Front St, #323
Lahaina, HI 96761, 808-661-4835

Patrick Leahy   W
c/o NOAA, 3651 Ahukini Rd, Lihue, HI 96766-9713
 Pubs: *Bachy, Rocky Mountain Rev, Pulp*

Jo Ann Lordahl 🎤 ✈   P
70 Nahele Rd #A
Haiku, HI 96708, 808-575-9200
Internet: jlordahl@mindspring.com

Wing Tek Lum   P
80 N King St
Honolulu, HI 96817, 808-531-5200
 Pubs: *Expounding the Doubtful Points* (Bamboo Ridge, 1987)

Darrell H. Y. Lum 🎤 ✈   W
990 Hahaione St
Honolulu, HI 96825-1036, 808-626-1481
Internet: darrel@hawaii.edu
 Pubs: *Pass On, No Pass Back!, The Best of Bamboo*
 Ridge: Anth (Bamboo Ridge Pr, 1990, 1986), *Into the Fire:*
 Anth (Greenfield Rev Pr, 1996), *Seattle Rev, Manoa,*
 Chaminade Rev

Alan Decker McNarie   P&W
77 Mohouli St
Hilo, HI 96720, 808-935-7210
 Pubs: *Yeshua: The Gospel of St. Thomas* (Pushcart Pr,
 1993), *Chaminade Lit Mag, Hawaii Pacific Rev, Kaimana,*
 Bamboo Ridge, Cape Rock, Poultry, Wind

Adele Ne Jame 🎤 ✈   P
Hawaii Pacific Univ, 1188 Fort St, Honolulu, HI 96813
Internet: anejame@hpu.edu
 Pubs: *Field Work* (Petronium Pr, 1996), *Inheritance*
 (Ridgeway Pr, 1989), *The Poetry of Arab Women: Anth*
 (Interlink Pub Group, 2000), *Academy of American Poets*
 Anth (H.N. Abrams, 1996), *Denver Qtly, Hawaii Pacific Rev,*
 Blue Mesa Rev, Equinox, Ploughshares

William J. Puette   P
3363-A Keanu St
Honolulu, HI 96816
 Pubs: *The Hilo Massacre* (U Hawaii Pr, 1988), *Guide to the*
 Tale of Genji (Tuttle, 1983)

Tony Quagliano 🎤 ✈   P
509 University Ave #902
Honolulu, HI 96826-5002
    Pubs: *Snail Mail Poems* (Tin Fish Ntwrk, 1998), *Poetry of
    Solitude: Anth* (Rizzoli, 1995), *Rolling Stone, New
    Directions, NYQ, Harvard Rev, Exquisite Corpse, Yankee,
    JAMA, Kaimana*

Eric Paul Shaffer 🎤 ✈   P
101 Piliwale Rd
Kula, HI 96790-8875, 808-876-0149
Internet: eshaffer@hotmail.com
    Pubs: *Living at the Monastery, Working in the Kitchen,
    Portable Planet* (Leaping Dog Pr, 2001, 2000), *Threepenny
    Rev, Malahat Rev, Grain, Prose Ax, Poet Lore, ACM,
    Snowy Egret*

Robert Shapard   W
English Dept, Univ Hawaii-Manoa, 1733 Donaghho Rd,
Honolulu, HI 96822-2315, 808-956-3078
Internet: rshapard@hawaii.edu
    Pubs: *Stories in the Stepmother Tongue: Anth* (White Pine
    Pr, 2000), *Sudden Fiction Continued: Anth, Sudden Fiction
    Intl: Anths* (Norton, 1996, 1989), *Flaunt, NER, Kenyon Rev,
    Lit Rev, Prism Intl, Mid-Amer Rev, Cimarron Rev*

Stephen Shrader   P
41-945b Laumilo St
Waimanalo, HI 96795, 808-259-5692

Cathy Song 🎤 ✈   P
PO Box 27262
Honolulu, HI 96827, 808-735-3136
    Pubs: *The Land of Bliss, School Figures* (U Pitt Pr, 2001,
    1994), *Frameless Windows, Squares of Light* (Norton,
    1988), *Picture Bride* (Yale U Pr, 1983), *Poetry, Shenandoah,
    Southern Rev, Kenyon Rev, Michigan Qtly Rev, Carolina
    Qtly Rev, Poetry Ireland, NER*

Joseph Stanton 🎤 ✈   P
Dept. of Art, University of Hawaii at Manoa, Honolulu, HI
96822, 808-956-4050
Internet: jstanton@hawaii.edu
    Pubs: *Imaginary Museum* (Time Being Bks, 1999), *What the
    Kite Thinks* (U Hawaii Pr, 1994), *Cortland Rev, Ekphrasis,
    Poetry, Poetry East, Harvard Rev, NYQ, Image*

Frank Stewart   P
Univ Hawaii, English Dept, Honolulu, HI 96822, 808-956-3070
Internet: fstewart@hawaii.edu
    Pubs: *Flying the Red Eye, The Open Water* (Floating Island,
    1986, 1982), *Ploughshares, Zyzzyva, Ironwood, Orion*

Jean Yamasaki Toyama   P
European Languages/Literature, Univ Hawaii, 1890 East-West
Rd, Moore 485, Honolulu, HI 96822, 808-956-4185
Internet: toyama@hawaii.edu
    Pubs: *What the Kite Thinks: A Linked Poem* (U Hawaii Pr,
    1994), *The Forbidden Stitch: Anth* (Calyx, 1989),
    *Illuminations, Kaimana, Caprice, Redneck Rev, Michigan
    Qtly Rev*

Jeff Walt 🎤 ✈   P
2574 Pacific Heights Rd
Honolulu, HI 96813
www.JeffWalt.com
    Pubs: *The Danger in Everything* (Mad River Bks, 2001),
    Touched by Eros: Anth (The Live Poets Society, 2002),
    Intimate Kisses: The Poetry of Sexual Pleasure: Anth (New
    World Library, 2001), *Mourning Our Mothers: Poems About
    Loss: Anth* (Andrew Mtn Pr, 1998)

Dorothy Winslow Wright   P&W
2119 Ahapii Pl
Honolulu, HI 96821, 808-734-0846
    Pubs: *The Book Group Book: Anth* (Chicago Rev Pr, 1993),
    Poet, Mature Living, Blue Unicorn

IDAHO

Mark Geston   W
1829 Edgecliff Terr
Boise, ID 83702, 208-344-8535
    Pubs: *Mirror to the Sky* (Morrow, 1992), *The Siege of
    Wonder* (Doubleday, 1975), *The Day Star* (DAW, 1972), *Out
    of the Mouth of the Dragon* (Ace, 1969), *Lords of the
    Starship* (Ace, 1967), *Year's Best Short Fiction: Anth* (HC,
    1999), *Amazing Stories*

Gary Gildner 🎤 ✈   P&W
RR2, Box 219
Grangeville, ID 83530-9615, 208-983-1663
    Pubs: *My Grandfather's Book* (Michigan State U Pr, 2002),
    The Birthday Party (Limberlost Pr, 2000), *Blue Like the
    Heavens* (U Pitt Pr, 1984), *Bunker in the Parsley Fields, The
    Warsaw Sparks* (U Iowa Pr, 1997, 1990), *Georgia Rev, New
    Letters, Shenandoah, NAR*

Janet Campbell Hale   P&W
799 Wildshoe Dr
Desmet, ID 83824, 208-274-2034
    Pubs: *The Owl's Song & Other Stories* (HC, 1995),
    Bloodlines (Random Hse, 1993)

Janet Holmes 🎤 ✈   P
1304 N 26th St
Boise, ID 83702-2323
Internet: jholmes@boisestate.edu
    Pubs: *The Physicist at the Mall* (Anhinga Pr, 1994), *The
    Green Tuxedo* (U Notre Dame Pr, 1998), *Paperback
    Romance* (State Street Pr, 1984)

Denis Johnson   P&W
195 RR 34, Box 195A
Bonner's Ferry, ID 83805
    Pubs: *The Incognito Lounge* (Random Hse, 1982), *Inner
    Weather* (Graywolf, 1976)

Daryl Jones 🎤 ✈   P
Boise State Univ, 1910 University Dr, Boise, ID 83725,
208-385-1202
Internet: aprjones@bsu.idbsu.edu
    Pubs: *Someone Going Home Late* (Texas Tech U Pr, 1990),
    Sewanee Rev, TriQtly, New Orleans Rev

Ron McFarland 🎤 ✈   P&W
857 E 8 St
Moscow, ID 83843, 208-882-0849
Internet: ronmcf@uidaho.edu
    Pubs: *Catching First Light* (Idaho State Univ Pr, 2001),
    Stranger in Town (Confluence Pr, 2000), *Ballgloves* (Polo
    Grounds Pr, 2000), *The Hemingway Poems* (Pecan Grove
    Pr, 2000), *The Mad Waitress Poems* (Permafrost Pr, 2000)

James Masao Mitsui   P
229 Sandy Drive
Cocolalla, ID 83813
Internet: jim3wells@aol.com
    Pubs: *From a Three-Cornered World* (U Washington Pr,
    1997), *After the Long Train* (Bieler Pr, 1986), *Crossing the
    Phantom River* (Graywolf, 1978), *A Year in Poetry: Anth*
    (Crown Pub, 1995)

Helen Olsen   P&W
23289 Homedale Rd
Wilder, ID 83676
    Pubs: *The Lyric, Midwest Poetry Rev, Afterthoughts, Bogg,
    Maverick Pr, St. Anthony Messenger, St. Joseph's Mag,
    Time of Singing, Tree Spirit, Yankee Mag*

Susan Richardson 🎤 ✈   P&W
9533 Caraway Dr
Boise, ID 83704
Internet: tdmlundy@juno.com
    Pubs: *Rapunzel's Short Hair* (Embers, 1994), *Split Verse:
    Anth* (Midmarch, 2000), *What's Become of Eden: Anth*
    (Slapering Hol, 1994), *CQ, Faultline, Wisconsin Rev*

William Studebaker 🎤 ✈   P
2616 E 4000 N
Twin Falls, ID 83301, 208-733-8584
Internet: williamstudebaker@micron.net
    Pubs: *Short of a Good Promise* (Washington State U Pr,
    1999), *Travelers in an Antique Land* (U Idaho Pr, 1997),
    River Religion, The Rat Lady at the Company Dump
    (Limberlost, 1997, 1990), *Dickinson Rev, Ohio Rev, High
    Country News, George Washington Rev*

Eberle Umbach   W
Box 172
McCall, ID 83638
    Pubs: *NW Rev, Timbuktu, Oh Idaho Mag, Whole Earth Rev*

Norman Weinstein 🎤 ✈   P
1309 North 12th St
Boise, ID 83702, 208-433-1294
Internet: nweinste@mindspring.com
    Pubs: *Weaving Fire From Water* (Wolfpeach Pr, 2002), *A
    Night in Tunisia: Imaginings of Africa in Jazz* (Scarecrow Pr,
    1992), *Village Voice, Sulfur, Io, Tree*

Harald Wyndham 🎤 ✈   P
PO Box 595
Inkom, ID 83245-4966, 208-775-3216
    Pubs: *Tuscany* (Acid Pr, 2000), *The Christmas Sonnets,
    Heavenly Rhythm & Blues* (Blue Scarab Pr, 1996, 1993)

ILLINOIS

Carol M. Adorjan 🎤 ✈   W
1667 Winnetka Rd
Glenview, IL 60025, 847-657-8502
Internet: cmadorjan@aol.com
    Pubs: *I Can! Can You?* (Albert Whitman, 1990), *NAR,
    Redbook, Denver Qtly, Natl Radio Theatre*

Michael A. Anania 🎤 ✈   P&W
5755 Sunset Ave
La Grange, IL 60525
Internet: anania@uic.edu
    Pubs: *Once Again Flowered* (Haybarn, 2001), *In Natural
    Light*

Arnold Aprill   PP
2850 N Seminary
Chicago, IL 60657, 312-281-0927

Asa Baber   W
247 E Chestnut
Chicago, IL 60611

Mary Shen Barnidge 🎤   P
1030 W Dakin St
Chicago, IL 60613-2912
    Pubs: *Detours* (Lonesome Traveler Pub, 1997), *Piano Player
    at the Dionysia* (Thompson Hill, 1984), *Power Lines: Anth*
    (Tia Chucha Pr, 1999), *Whetstone, Overtures, Leatherneck,
    Howling Dog, Kaleidoscope, DEROS*

Jill Barrie   P
10S 272 Alma Ln
Naperville, IL 60564
Internet: jbarrie105@aol.com
    Pubs: *Calapooya Collage, Gulf Stream, ALR, Cimarron,
    New Virginia Rev, Calliope, Black River Rev, SPR*

Saul Bellow   W
1126 E 59 St
Chicago, IL 60637
  Pubs: *The Dean's December* (H&R, 1982), *Herzog* (Viking,
  1964)

Ronald Belluomini 🎤 ✈   P
2179 Spruce Pointe Court
Gurnee, IL 60031, 847-596-2179
  Pubs: *The Thirteenth Labor* (Dragon's Teeth Pr, 1985),
  Autumn Harvest: Anth (Quill Bks, 2001), *Rhino, FOC Rev,
  Menagerie*

Mary H. Ber 🎤 ✈   P
2015 Woodland Ln
Arlington Hts, IL 6004, 847-398-3594
Internet: maryhber@aol.com
  Pubs: *When a Lifemate Dies: Stories of Love, Loss, and
  Healing: Anth* (Fairview Pr, 1997), *Mutant Mule Review:
  Anth* (Finishing Line Pr, 1998), *13th Moon, Pudding Mag,
  100 Words*

Brooke Bergan   P
1150 N Lake Shore Dr #19F
Chicago, IL 60611-1025
  Pubs: *Storyville* (Moyer Bell, 1993), *Distant Topologies,
  Windowpane* (Wine Pr, 1976, 1974), *ACM, Oyez, Wire*

Susan Bergman 🎤 ✈   P&W
880 N Lake Shore Dr, #8AE
Chicago, IL 60611-1761, 888-408-7678
Internet: sbergman@previewport.com
  Pubs: *Anonymity* (FSG, 1994), *Martyrs: Anth* (HC, 1996),
  TriQtly, Ploughshares, Pequod

Leslie Bertagnolli   P
2800 Prudential Plaza
Chicago, IL 60601
  Pubs: *Family Photographs* (Red Herring Pr, 1979)

Leigh Buchanan Bienen   W
Northwestern School of Law, 357 E. Chicago Avenue,
Chicago, IL 60611-3067
Internet: lbbienen@nwu.edu
  Pubs: *The Left-Handed Marriage, The Ways We Live Now:
  Anth* (Ontario Rev Pr, 2001, 1986), *O. Henry Prize Stories
  1983: Anth* (Doubleday, 1983), *Descant, Ontario Rev*

James Bonk   P
400 N Main St
Mt Prospect, IL 60056, 312-253-7673
  Pubs: *Poetry Connection-Dial a Poem Chicago Anth* (City of
  Chicago, 1991), *America, Minnesota Rev, Commonweal*

Walter L. Bradford   P
932 E 50 St
Chicago, IL 60615, 312-373-2957

John M. Bradley 🎤 ✈   P
560 Normal Rd
DeKalb, IL 60115, 815-756-1533
  Pubs: *Best of the Prose Poem: Anth* (White Pine Pr, 2000),
  *Conduit, Luna, Rhino, Pavement Saw, Switched-on,
  Gutenberg, Arsenic Lobster*

Ardyth Bradley 🎤 ✈   P
514 Broadway
Libertyville, IL 60048, 708-362-4635
Internet: jbradley@enteract.com
  Pubs: *Light and Chance* (Mid-America Pr 2001), *Benchmark
  Anth of Contemporary Illinois Poetry* (Stormline Pr, 1988),
  Three Winter Poems: Anth (Penumbra Pr, 1986), *Inside the
  Bones Is Flesh* (Ithaca Hse, 1978), *Poetry, Parting Gifts,
  Shenandoah, Cutbank*

Becky Bradway 🎤 ✈   W
Millikin Univ, English Dept., Decatur, IL 62522, 217-362-6465
Internet: bbradway@mail.millikin.edu
  Pubs: *ACM, Amer Fiction, Ascent, Beloit Fiction Jrnl, Cream
  City Rev, Green Mountains Rev, Greensboro Rev, Laurel
  Rev, Lit Rev, NAR, Other Voices, River Styx, Third Coast,
  Troika, Writing on the Edge*

Alice G. Brand 🎤 ✈   P
1235 N. Astor St
Chicago, IL 60610, 312-664-4822
Internet: abrand@brockport.edu
  Pubs: *Court of Common Pleas* (Mellon Pr, 1994), *Studies
  on Zone* (BkMk Pr, 1989), *As It Happens* (Wampeter Pr,
  1983), *The New York Times, Thirteenth Moon, Kansas Qtly,
  Confrontation, River Styx, Nimrod, Paintbrush, New Letters,
  Minnesota Rev*

June Rachuy Brindel 🎤 ✈   P&W
2740 Lincoln Ln
Wilmette, IL 60091, 847-251-9228
  Pubs: *Phaedra* (St. Martin's Pr, 1985), *Nobody Is Ever
  Missing* (Story Pr, 1984), *Sound of Writing, Other Voices,
  Mss., Iowa Rev, Story Qtly, Cimarron Rev*

Rosellen Brown 🎤 ✈   P&W
5421 S Cornell, #16
Chicago, IL 60615, 773-288-3349
Internet: hoff@consortium-chicago.org
  Pubs: *Street Games* (Norton, 2001), *Half a Heart, Cora
  Fry's Pillow Book, Before & After* (FSG, 2000, 1994, 1992),
  Rosellen Brown Reader (U Pr New England, 1992)

Glen Brown 🎤 ✈   P
100 S Brainard Ave
La Grange, IL 60525-2100, 708-579-6300
Internet: ghbrown@enc.k12.il.us
    Pubs: *Yes, No, Maybe* (Lake Shore Pub, 1995), *Don't Ask
Why (Thorntree Pr, 1994), *Illinois Rev, Oyez Rev, Poetry,
Poet & Critic, Negative Capability, Spoon River Poetry Rev*

Michael H. Brownstein 🎤 ✈   P
PO Box 268805
Chicago, IL 60626-8805, 312-409-6762
Internet: garlic2222@aol.com
    Pubs: *The Principle of the Thing* (Tight Pr, 1994), *Poems
From the Body Bag* (Ommation Pr, 1989), *Always a
Beautiful Answer: Anth* (Kings Estate Pr, 1999), *Samisdat,
Cafe Rev, Rosewell Lit Rev, Artisan, Wordwrights, Potpourri,
Beyond Baroque*

Debra Bruce 🎤 ✈   P
English Dept, Northeastern Illinois Univ, 5500 N St Louis Ave,
Chicago, IL 60625
Internet: d-bruce-kinnebrew@neiu.edu
    Pubs: *What Wind Will Do* (Miami U Pr, 1997), *Sudden
Hunger, Pure Daughter* (U Arkansas Pr, 1987, 1984), *APR,
Kenyon Rev, Michigan Qtly Rev, Poetry, Virginia Qtly Rev,
Atlantic*

Nancy Burke   P
2206 Wesley Ave
Evanston, IL 60201
Internet: nbur@northwestern.edu
    Pubs: *The Neovictorian/Cochlea Pr, Mangrove, The Seattle
Rev, Seedhouse, Green Mountains Rev, Alligator Juniper*

Rex Burwell   P
1286 Robinwood Dr
Elgin, IL 60123
    Pubs: *Anti-History* (Smokeroot Pr, 1977), *Chicago Rev,
Shenandoah, Big Scream*

Anne Calcagno 🎤 ✈   W
English Dept, DePaul Univ, 802 W Belden, Chicago, IL
60614-3214, 773-325-1771
Internet: acalcagn@depaul.edu
    Pubs: *Pray for Yourself, Fiction of the Eighties: Anth* (TriQtly
Bks, 1993, 1990), *American Fiction: Anth* (Birch Lane Pr,
1991), *NAR, TriQtly, Epoch, Denver Qtly*

Paul Carroll   P
Univ Illinois, PO Box 4348, English Dept, Chicago, IL 60680,
312-996-3260
    Pubs: *Poems* (Spoon River Poetry, 1988), *The Garden of
Earthly Delights* (Chicago Public Library, 1986)

Ana Castillo   P&W
3036 N Sawyer
Chicago, IL 60618
    Pubs: *The Mixquiahuala Letters* (Bilingual Rev Pr, 1985),
Spoon River Qtly, River Styx, Maize

George Chambers   P&W
318 Sarah Barnewolt Dr
Peoria, IL 61604, 309-637-0454
    Pubs: *The Great Blue Sea* (Snowberries Pr, 1994), *The Last
Man Standing* (Fiction Collective Two, 1990), *Caprice,
Situation, Iowa Rev, Prose Poem*

Joan Colby 🎤 ✈   P
10N226 Muirhead Rd
Elgin, IL 60123, 847-464-5250
Internet: joanmc@aol.com
    Pubs: *The Atrocity Book* (Lynx Hse, 1987), *The Lonely
Hearts Killers* (Spoon River, 1986), *What Have You Lost:
Anth* (Greenwillow Bks, 1999), *Poetry, Illinois Rev, New Re-
naissance, Cream City Rev, Grand Street*

Judith Cooper   W
6620 N Glenwood
Chicago, IL 60626
Internet: dialexltd@aol.com
    Pubs: *Southern Rev, ACM, Whetstone, Black Warrior Rev,
Louisville Rev, Nebraska Rev, MacGuffin, Permafrost*

Mark Costello   W
English Dept, Univ Illinois, Urbana, IL 61801

Patricia Cronin 🎤 ✈   W
414 Audubon Rd
Riverside, IL 60546, 708-442-5098
Internet: patriciacronin@earthlink.net
    Pubs: *Jane's Stories II: Anth* (Wild Dove Studio & Press,
Inc., 2000), *Green Hills Lit Lantern, Actos de
Inconsciencias, Qtly West, Blue Skunk Companion,
Workshirts Writing Center, Inc., Alabama Lit Rev*

Carlos Cumpian   P
March, Inc., PO Box 2890, Chicago, IL 60690, 312-935-6188
    Pubs: *Coyote Sun, Emergency Tacos* (March/Abrazo Pr,
1990, 1989), *3rd World: Anth* (Pig Iron, 1989)

David Curry   P&W
2045 N Dayton
Chicago, IL 60614-4309
Internet: curryd@ada.org
    Pubs: *Contending to Be the Dream, Here* (New Rivers Pr,
1979, 1970), *Crab Orchard Rev, Fugue, Karamu*

Nat David   P
1718 Sherman Ave #203
Evanston, IL 60201
    Pubs: *Heartdance* (Doublestar Pr, 1989), *Primal Voices,
Strong Coffee, Hammers, Chaminade Lit Rev, Footwork:
The Paterson Lit Rev*

Marjorie Carlson Davis 🎤 ✈ W
292 W Hurst St
Bushnell, IL 61422
Internet: Mdavis@bushnell.net
    Pubs: *Stories From Where We Live: Great Lakes: Anth*
    (Milkweed Edtns, 2003), *Potpourri, Drexel Online Jrnl,*
    Baltimore Rev, Thema, Many Mountains Moving

Ronda Marie Davis P
10454 S Calumet
Chicago, IL 60628, 312-955-2971

Connie Deanovich P
c/o A. Denoyer, 5534 N Parkside, Chicago, IL 60630
    Pubs: *Watusi Titanic* (Timken, 1996), *Walk on the Wild Side:*
    Contemporary Urban Poetry Anth (Scribner, 1994),
    Parnassus, Sulfur, Gertrude Stein Awards, NAW, Grand
    Street, Bomb, See

Helen Degen Cohen P
1166 Osterman
Deerfield, IL 60015, 847-945-0487
    Pubs: *Sarajevo Anth, Blood to Remember: Poets on the*
    Holocaust: Anth (Texas Tech U Pr, 1993, 1991), *Partisan*
    Rev, ACM, Stand, Outerbridge

Mary Krane Derr 🎤 ✈ P
6105 S Woodlawn, #3S
Chicago, IL 60637, 773-288-2596
Internet: MaryKDerr@aol.com
    Pubs: *Conversing With Mystery: CD Anth* (The Hospice
    Poetry Recording Project, 2000), *Many Mountains Moving,*
    Seeding the Snow, Coyote, Switched-on Gutenberg,
    Pudding, Sacred Journey, Lilliput Rev, Poet Mag,
    Psychopoetica, Jrnl of Poetry Therapy, Mobius

John J. Desjarlais 🎤 ✈ W
934 Crest Ct
Byron, IL 61010
Internet: jdesjar@kougars.kish.cc.il.us
    Pubs: *Relics* (Thomas Nelson, 1993), *The Throne of Tara*
    (Crossway Bks, 1990), *The Karitos Rev, Apocalypse*

John Dickson P
2249 Sherman Ave
Evanston, IL 60201, 708-864-4793
    Pubs: *Waving at Trains* (Thorntree, 1986), *Victoria Hotel*
    (Chicago Rev Pr, 1979), *Poetry, TriQtly, Amer Scholar,*
    Willow Rev, Wire, Whetstone

John A. Domini W
1897 Sheridan Rd
Evanston, IL 60208
Internet: vojam@aol.com
    Pubs: *Bedlam* (Fiction Intl, 1982), *Pushcart Prize: Anth*
    (Pushcart, 1989), *Paris Rev, SW Rev, Ploughshares,*
    Threepenny Rev

George Drury 🎤 ✈ P
2674 N Burling St
Chicago, IL 60614-1514, 773-244-0095
    Pubs: *Massenmedien und Kommunikation, Pages, Strong*
    Coffee, Big Scream

Gerald Duff P&W
2 Foxmoor
Lebanon, IL 62254, 618-537-4029
Internet: gduff@mckendree.edu
    Pubs: *Coasters* (NewSouth Bks, 2001), *Snake Song,*
    Memphis Ribs (Salvo Pr, 2000, 1999), *That's All Right,*
    Mama (Bakersville Pubs, 1995), *The Kenyon Poets: Anth*
    (Kenyon College, 1990), *Ploughshares, Sewanee Rev,*
    Nation, Missouri Rev, Mississippi Rev, SPR

Elizabeth Eddy P
1050 W Jeffrey
Kankakee, IL 60901, 708-946-3167
    Pubs: *The Tie That Binds* (Papier-Mache Pr, 1988), *Spoon*
    River Qtly, Whetstone, Korone, New Poetry Jrnl

Cassie Edwards P&W
RR#3, Box 60
Mattoon, IL 61938
    Pubs: *Savage Thunder, Savage Sunrise, Savage Winds*
    (Leisure Bks, 1994, 1993, 1993), *Wild Splendor, Wild*
    Embrace, Wild Desire (NAL, 1994, 1993, 1993)

Charles Elwert 🎤 ✈ P
681-A Katherine Ln
Addison, IL 60101-6401, 630-916-4876
Internet: 85corvette@compuserve.com
    Pubs: *Poetry Connection 1981-1991* (Hydra, 1991), *Paris*
    Rev, Spoon River Qtly

Robert Klein Engler P
901 S Plymouth Apt 1801
Chicago, IL 60605
Internet: alphabpres@aol.com
    Pubs: *Medicine Signs, Shore Line* (Alphabeta Pr, 1997,
    1997), *Borderlands, Hyphen, Christopher Street, James*
    White Rev, Kansas Qtly, Fish Stories

Pamela Erbe W
3608 N Pine Grove Ave, #B7
Chicago, IL 60613-4556
    Pubs: *American Fiction: Anth* (New Rivers Pr, 1995), *New*
    Stories From the South: Anth (Algonquin Bks, 1994), *River*
    Oak Rev, Antioch Rev, Columbia, NAR, Ms.

Dave Etter 🎤 ✈ P
628 E Locust St
Lanark, IL 61046, 815-493-6778
    Pubs: *Greatest Hits* (Pudding Hse Pubs, 2002), *The*
    Essential Dave Etter, How High the Moon, Sunflower
    County (Spoon River, 2001, 1996, 1994)

H. R. Felgenhauer   P&W
PO Box 146486
Chicago, IL 60614, 312-772-8686
    Pubs: *IAPT3, Insects Are People Two* (Puffn' Stuff
    Productions, 1998, 1996), *Bouillabaisse, Gotta Write, Mind
    in Motion, Fantasy Commentator*

Peter Fellowes   P
3225 W Foster
Chicago, IL 60625
    Pubs: *Yale Rev, APR, Commonweal, Shenandoah, Ontario
    Rev, Epoch, Poetry Now, TriQtly*

Calvin Forbes   P
School of the Art Institute, 37 S Wabash Ave, Chicago, IL
60603, 312-899-5187
    Pubs: *From the Book of Shine* (Burning Deck, 1979), *Blue
    Monday* (Wesleyan U Pr, 1974)

Phyllis Ford-Choyke   P
23 Windsor Dr
Elmhurst, IL 60126-3971, 630-576-0777
    Pubs: *Apertures to Anywhere* (Harper Square Pr, 1979),
    Poetry NW, Voices Israel, Rhino

Rich Foss 🎤 ✈   P&W
19235 Plow Creek
Tiskilwa, IL 61368, 815-646-4264
Internet: richfoss@theramp.net
    Pubs: *Jonas & Sally* (Good Bks, 2000), *Poet's Page, North
    Country, Christian Poetry Jrnl, Christianity & Literature*

Alan Friedman   W
English Dept, Box 4348, Univ Illinois, Chicago, IL 60680,
312-413-2200
    Pubs: *Hermaphrodeity* (Knopf, 1972), *The Turn of the Novel*
    (Oxford U, 1966), *Raritan, Partisan Rev, Paris Rev*

Richard Friedman   P
5819 N Sacramento
Chicago, IL 60659, 312-275-7154
    Pubs: *Physical Culture* (Yellow Pr, 1979)

Paul Friedman   W
310 W Illinois St
Urbana, IL 61801, 217-328-3247
    Pubs: *Serious Trouble, And If Defeated Allege Fraud*
    (U Illinois Pr, 1986, 1971), *Mid-American Rev, Boulevard,
    Cimarron Rev*

Paul Friedrich   P
1130 E 59th St
Chicago, IL 60637-1539, 773-702-7004
    Pubs: *Speaking in Tongues: Anth* (Black Buzzard Pr, 1994),
    *Mutatis Mutandis, Mississippi Valley Rev, Blue Unicorn,
    Flutter By Pr, Kansas Qtly*

Robert Fromberg   W
734 N La Salle Dr, #1114
Chicago, IL 60610-3530, 312-440-9129
Internet: rmf880@nwu.edu
    Pubs: *Blue Skies* (Floating Island Pubs, 1992), *Indiana Rev,
    Bellingham Rev, Tennessee Qtly, Salmon, Colorado Rev,
    Northeast*

Al Gabor 🎤 ✈   P&W
1630 Mulford
Evanston, IL 60202, 847-475-2483
Internet: a-gabor@northwestern.edu
    Pubs: *XY Files: Anth* (Sherman Asher, 1997), *ACM, Cream
    City Rev, Ascent, Puerto del Sol, Great River Rev,
    Mississippi Valley Rev, Chattahoochee Rev, Plainsongs,
    Willow Rev*

Cynthia Gallaher 🎤 ✈   P
PO Box 2890
Chicago, IL 60690, 773-505-6508
Internet: swimmer53@yahoo.com
    Pubs: *Earth Elegance* (March Abrazo Pr, 2000), *Swimmer's
    Prayer* (Missing Spoke Pr, 1999), *Night Ribbons* (Polar Bear
    Pr, 1990), *Stand Up Poetry: Anth, Boomer Girls: Anth*
    (U Iowa Pr, 2002, 1999)

Bruce M. Gans 🎤 ✈   W
5324 Hyde Park Blvd #1
Chicago, IL 60615, 773-643-8888
Internet: bmg1030@earthlink.net
    Pubs: *Here's the Story: Fiction With Heart: Anth* (Spirit That
    Moves Us Pr, 1986), *Amer Scholar, Hawaii Rev, Playboy,
    Mademoiselle, Kansas Qtly, Memphis State Rev*

Bill Garson   P&W
PO Box 3126
Rockford, IL 61106-0126
    Pubs: *Where Are You Now, Boy Billie?* (Fithian Pr, 1992),
    Brother Earth (Imagination Plus), *Hardboiled Detective, Grit,
    Sunshine*

Lucia C. Getsi 🎤 ✈   P
English Dept, Illinois State Univ, Normal, IL 61790-4240,
309-438-7906
Internet: lcgetsi@ilstu.edu
    Pubs: *Intensive Care* (New Rivers, 1995), *No One Taught
    This Filly to Dance* (Pikestaff Pr, 1989), *Many Mountains
    Moving, Women's Rev of Bks, Willow Rev, Nimrod, Illinois
    Voices*

Reginald Gibbons 🎤 ✈   P&W
English Dept, Northwestern Univ, 215 University Hall,
Evanston, IL 60208-2240
Internet: rgibbons@northwestern.edu
    Pubs: *Antigone* (Oxford, 2003), *Homage to Longshot
    O'Leary* (Holy Cow! Pr, 1999), *Sweetbitter, Sparrow,* (LSU
    Pr, 2003, 1997), (Penguin, 1996), *Tikkun, APR, Harper's,
    Southern Rev, QRL, Atlantic*

Netta Gillespie   P
211 E Sherwin Dr
Urbana, IL 61802-7129, 217-328-7268
Internet: gillesp1@uiuc.edu
  Pubs: *Ophelia's Mother: Anth* (Perseus Pr, 2001), *A
  Christmas Collection: Anth* (July Lit Pr, 2001), *Knowing
  Stones: Anth* (John Gordon Burke, 2000), *Essential Love:
  Anth* (Grayson Bks/Poetworks, 2000), *Spoon River Poetry
  Rev, Snowbound, Wisconsin Rev, Karamu*

Philip Graham   P&W
605 W Vermont St
Urbana, IL 61801-4824, 217-337-6898
Internet: p-graham@uiuc.edu
  Pubs: *Interior Design, How to Read an Unwritten Language*
  (Scribner, 1996, 1995), *New Yorker, NAR, Paris Rev, Fiction,
  Missouri Rev, Washington Post*

Cindy Guentherman 🎤   P
7721 Venus St
Loves Park, IL 61111-3142, 815-654-8491
Internet: haikupup@aol.com
  Pubs: *Confluence: Anth* (Muhammad, Norwood, Swanberg,
  2000), *Frogpond, Korone, Acorn Whistle, Rockford Rev,
  Without Halos, Kumquat Meringue, Modern Haiku,
  Parnassus, Riverrun, Lynx, American Poets & Poetry*

Lee Gurga 🎤 ✈   P
514 Pekin St
Lincoln, IL 62656, 217-732-8731
Internet: gurga@ccaonline.com
  Pubs: *Haiku in My Pocket* (Laurel & Herbert, 2003), *Fresh
  Scent* (Brooks Bks, 1998), *In & Out of the Fog, The Mea-
  sure of Emptiness,* (Press Here, 1997, 1991), *Global Haiku:
  Anth* (Iron Pr, 2000), *The Haiku Anthology* (Norton, 1999)

Mary Hanford   P
c/o Jeanne McWherter, RR2, Box 78, Aledo, IL 61231
  Pubs: *Spoon River Qtly, Another Place to Publish, Brushfire,
  Spectrum, The Carillion*

Barbara Harr   P
c/o Juanita M. N. Harr, 20 S Fremont St, Naperville, IL
60540-4329, 708-778-9528
  Pubs: *The Mortgaged Wife* (Swallow, 1970), *The Nation,
  Rough Edges, Choice, Womanspirit, Shenandoah*

M. M. M. Hayes 🎤 ✈   W
431 Sheridan Rd
Kenilworth, IL 60043, 847-256-6998
Internet: hayesbox@interaccess.com
  Pubs: *New Stories From the South: Anth* (Algonquin Bks,
  1995), *Awards XVI: Katherine Anne Porter Award: Anth*
  (Nimrod, 1996), *NAR, Redbook, High Plains Lit Rev*

Robert R. Hellenga 🎤 ✈   W
Knox College, English Dept, Galesburg, IL 61401,
309-343-0112
Internet: rhelleng@knox.edu
  Pubs: *Blue Lessons, The Fall of a Sparrow* (Scribner, 2002,
  1996), *The Sixteen Pleasures* (Dell, 1995), *Chicago Tribune,
  New York Times, Mississippi Valley Rev, Chicago Rev, Iowa
  Rev, California Qtly, Columbia, Ascent, Crazyhorse, TriQtly*

Greg Herriges 🎤 ✈   W
c/o William Rainey, Harper College, 1200 Algonquin Rd,
Palatine, IL 60047
Internet: herriges3@aol.com
  Pubs: *The Winter Dance Party Murders* (Wordcraft, 1998),
  Secondary Attachment (Morrow, 1986), *Some Place Safe*
  (Avon, 1985), *Story Qtly*

Richard Holinger   P&W
335 Colonial Cir
Geneva, IL 60134-3640, 630-232-9996
www.rholinger.hotmail.com
  Pubs: *Iowa Rev, Witness, Boulevard, Southern Rev,
  Chelsea, Ohio Rev, ACM, Hampden-Sydney Poetry Rev,
  Cream City Rev, New Renaissance, Writers' Bar-B-Q, Zone
  3, Other Voices*

Barbara Savadge Horton   P
c/o V. Vedanta, 5423 S Hyde Park Blvd, Chicago, IL 60615,
773-667-8170
  Pubs: *The Verb to Love* (Silver Apples Pr, 1989), *Anth of
  Magazine Verse* (Monitor Bk Co, 1997), *Passages North,
  Poetry NW, Kansas Qtly, New Letters, SPR, ACM*

Dan Howell 🎤 ✈   P
738 W Aldine Ave, #1W
Chicago, IL 60657, 312-935-9244
  Pubs: *Lost Country* (U Massachusetts Pr, 1993)

Ivor S. Irwin 🎤 ✈   W
3012 South Farrell St
Chicago, IL 60608, 773-376-5748
Internet: iirwin@earthlink.net
  Pubs: *A Peacock or a Crow* (Willes e-Pr, 1998), *Cape
  Discoveries: Anth* (Sheep Meadow Pr, 1996), *Street Songs:
  Anth* (Longstreet Pr, 1990), *Actos de Inconsciencia, Oyez
  Rev, The Sun, Sycamore Rev, Sonora Rev, North Carolina
  Lit Rev, Emrys Jrnl, No Roses Rev*

John Jacob 🎤 ✈   P&W
417 S Taylor Apt 3B
Oak Park, IL 60302-4300, 708-383-3167
  Pubs: *Every Day I Got the Blues* (Small Poetry Pr, 1999),
  Hungers (Lake Shore Pub, 1995), *Long Ride Back*
  (Thunder's Mouth, 1988), *TriQtly, Partisan Rev, Poetry,
  Mississippi Rev, Chicago Mag*

Phyllis Janik   P
805 W Chicago Ave
Hinsdale, IL 60521, 708-887-1674
    Pubs: *Fuse* (ACP Bks, 1989), *No Dancing/No Acts of
Dancing* (BkMk Pr, 1982), *New Renaissance*

Honoree Fanonne Jeffers 🎙 ✈   P&W
982 N Prairie St Upper Floor
Galesburg, IL 61401
Internet: HoniJeff@aol.com
    Pubs: *Outlandish Blues* (Wesleyan U Pr, 2003), *The Gospel
of Barbeque* (Kent State U Pr, 2000), *Dark Matter: Anth*
(Warner/Aspect, 2000), *Callaloo, Brilliant Corners, Black
Warrior Rev, Ploughshares, Prairie Schooner, Indiana Rev,
Kenyon Rev*

Joyce Sandeen Johnson   P
6532 Spring Brook Rd #212
Rockford, IL 61114-8136
    Pubs: *Impressions Chapbook* (River City Pr, 1994), *Tanka
Splendor, American Tanka, Frogpond, Pegasus,
Midwestern Poetry Rev, Rockford Rev, Quarter Moon, Lynx*

Curt Johnson   W
PO Box 302
Highland Park, IL 60035, 847-940-4122
    Pubs: *Thanksgiving in Vegas* (Bottlehouse Pr, 1995), *The
Mafia Manager* (St. Martin's Pr, 1995), *Song for Three
Voices* (Carpenter Pr, 1984)

Allison Joseph 🎙 ✈   P
English Dept, Faner Hall, SIU-Carbondale, Carbondale, IL
62901-4503, 618-453-5321
Internet: aljoseph@aol.com
    Pubs: *Imitation of Life, Soul Train* (Carnegie Mellon U Pr,
2003, 1997), *In Every Seam* (U Pitt 1997), *What Keeps Us
Here* (Ampersand Pr 1992), *The New Young American
Poets: Anth* (SIU Pr, 2000), *Callaloo, Tamaqua*

Henry Kanabus   P
2925 N Kenneth Ave, Apt 1
Chicago, IL 60641, 312-725-3973
    Pubs: *Night Ministry & Other Stories* (Brigham Hse, 1990),
Capillary Sun (Lebensraum Pr, 1989)

David Michael Kaplan 🎙 ✈   P&W
4100 N Springfield
Chicago, IL 60618-1919, 773-509-0760
    Pubs: *Skating in the Dark* (Pantheon, 1991), *Comfort*
(Viking, 1987), *Mississippi Rev, Ohio Rev, Atlantic, Fiction,
Story, Playboy, Redbook, TriQtly, Mirabella*

John Keene 🎙 ✈   P&W
Northwestern University, University Hall 413, Evanston, IL
Internet: johnkeene@earthlink.net
    Pubs: *Annotations* (New Directions, 1995)

Brigit Pegeen Kelly   P
3402 Persimmon Circle
Urbana, IL 61802, 217-244-5873
Internet: b—kelly3@uiuc.edu
    Pubs: *Song* (BOA Limited Edtns, 1994), *In the Place of
Trumpets* (Yale U Pr, 1988), *NER, Antioch Rev, Southern
Rev, Yale Rev, Massachusetts Rev*

Kathryn Kerr   P
302 W. Graham St
Bloomington, IL 61701
Internet: kkerr@ilstu.edu
    Pubs: *I Feel a Little Jumpy Around You* (S&S, 1996), *First
Frost, Benchmark Anth* (Stormline Pr, 1985, 1987), *ACM,
Ascent, Thema, River Styx, Spoon River, Tamaqua, Karamu*

William Kir-Stimon   P
729 Emerson St
Evanston, IL 60201, 708-475-5548
    Pubs: *Inside the Open Cage* (Cooperfield, 1984), *Voices,
Pilgrimage, NU ILR Jrnl, Jrnl of Poetry Therapy, CPU Rev,
Midwest Rev*

Elizabeth Klein   P&W
610 S Chicago Ave
Champaign, IL 61821, 217-356-2683
Internet: EKleinS@aol.com
    Pubs: *Reconciliations* (Berkley Bks, 1984), *Approaches*
(Red Herring Pr, 1980), *ACM, Farmer's Market, Jewish
Spectator, Shofar, Prairie Schooner*

John Knoepfle 🎙 ✈   P
1008 W Adams
Auburn, IL 62615-1036, 217-438-6079
    Pubs: *The Chinkapin Oak* (Rosehill Pr, 1996), *Begging an
Amnesty* (Druid Pr, 1995), *Centennial Rev, Intl Qtly, Private
Arts, New Letters, Crosscurrents*

Art Lange 🎙 ✈   P
Chicago, IL
Internet: adlange@attbi.com
    Pubs: *Needles at Midnight* (Z Pr, 1986), *Evidence* (Yellow
Pr, 1981), *Postmodern American Poetry: Anth* (Norton,
1994), *New American Writing, Transfer, Partisan Rev,
Washington Rev*

William Leahy   W
4040 N Francisco Ave
Chicago, IL 60618-2662, 772-539-8445
    Pubs: *Verb, Cyphurs, Nit & Wit Mag, Northwest Challenge,
City, North Dakota Qtly*

Li-Young Lee   P
853 W Lawrence Ave
Chicago, IL 60640, 312-275-3054
    Pubs: *The City in Which I Love You, Rose* (BOA Edtns,
1990, 1986), *Grand Street, TriQtly*

Laurence Lieberman 🎤 ✈ P
Univ Illinois, 608 S Wright, 208 English Bldg, Urbana, IL
61801, 217-367-7186
    Pubs: *Flight From the Mother Stone, Compass of the Dying,
Dark Songs* (U Arkansas Pr, 2000, 1998, 1996), *The
Regatta in the Skies* (U Georgia Pr, 1998), *New & Selected
Poems: 1962-1992* (U Illinois Pr, 1993), *Body Electric: Anth*
(Norton, 2000), *Atlantic, APR*

Beth Lordan 🎤 ✈ W
Southern Illinois Univ, English Dept, Carbondale, IL 62901
Internet: crwr@siu.edu
    Pubs: *But Come Ye Back* (Morrow, 2003), *And Both Shall
Row* (Picador USA, 1998), *August Heat* (H&R, 1989), *O
Henry, Best Amer Short Stories, Atlantic, Gettysburg Rev*

William F. Love W
940 Cleveland Rd
Hinsdale, IL 60521, 708-325-9097
    Pubs: *Bloody Ten, The Fundamentals of Murder, The
Chartreuse Clue* (Donald I. Fine, 1992, 1991, 1990)

James M. Loverde P
3719 N Southport Ave #219
Chicago, IL 60613-3756
    Pubs: *Mutated Viruses, FEH!, Haunted Jrnl, 'scapes, Wolf's
Season, Silver Apple Branch, Art/Life*

Roslyn Rosen Lund 🎤 W
9220 E Prairie Rd, Apt #410
Evanston, IL 60203-1644
    Pubs: *Her Face in the Mirror: Anth* (Beacon Pr, 1995), *Loss
of the Ground-Note: Anth* (Clothespin Fever Pr, 1992),
Prism Intl, Crosscurrents, Ascent, Descant, Other Voices

Haki R. Madhubuti P
7822 S Dobson Ave
Chicago, IL 60619, 773-651-0700
Internet: twpress3@aol.com
    Pubs: *HeartLove, GroundWork, Black Men: Obsolete,
Single, Dangerous?, Earthquakes and Sunrise Missions,
Don't Cry, Scream* (Third World Pr, 1998, 1996, 1990, 1984,
1969), *Killing Memory, Seeking Ancestors* (Lotus Pr, 1987),
Book of Life (Broadside Pr, 1973)

Michael Patrick Malone 🎤 ✈ W
VP Development & University Relations, Northern Illinois Univ,
De Kalb, IL 60115, 815-753-6065
Internet: malone1916@aol.com
    Pubs: *PEN Short Story Collection: Anth* (Ballantine, 1986),
*Kansas Qtly, New Letters, Ascent, Chicago Reader, U.S.
Catholic, Mississippi Rev*

Norma Marder W
1009 W Church St
Champaign, IL 61821, 217-352-1824
Internet: marder@uiuc.edu
    Pubs: *An Eye for Dark Places* (Little, Brown, 1993), *Georgia
Rev, Gettysburg Rev*

Marion M. Markham 🎤 ✈ W
2415 Newport Rd
Northbrook, IL 60062
Internet: mmrbm@juno.com
    Pubs: *The St. Patrick's Day Shamrock Mystery, The April
Fool's Day Mystery* (HM, 1995, 1991), *McCall's, Alfred
Hitchcock's Mystery, London Mystery, Amer Way, Buffalo
Spree*

Cris Mazza 🎤 ✈ W
English Dept M/C162, Univ of Illinois at Chicago, Chicago, IL
60607, 312-413-2200
Internet: cmazza@uic.edu
    Pubs: *Girl Beside Him* (FC2, 2001), *Former Virgin,
Revelation Countdown* (FC2, 1997, 1993), *Dog People, Your
Name Here, Exposed, How to Leave a Country* (Coffee Hse
Pr, 1997, 1995, 1994, 1992), *Fiction Intl, High Plains Lit Rev*

James McGowan P
410 E Walnut St
Bloomington, IL 61701, 309-828-0807
Internet: jmcgowan@titan.iwu.edu

James McManus 🎤 ✈ P&W
School of the Art Institute, 37 S Wabash, Chicago, IL
60603-3017, 847-256-4109
    Pubs: *Positively Fifth Street* (FSG, 2003), *Going to the Sun,
Great America* (HC, 1996, 1993), *Out of the Blue, Ghost
Waves, Chin Music* (Grove Pr, 1989, 1988, 1987), *Best
American Poetry 1994: Anth* (S&S, 1994), *Harper's,
Atlantic, APR*

Erica Helm Meade 🎤 ✈ PP
Open Court Publishing Co., 332 S Michigan Ave, Ste #2000,
Chicago, IL 60604
Internet: meadwine@juno.com
    Pubs: *Tell It By Heart, Crossroads: Anth* (Open Court Pub,
1995, 1996), *Intimate Nature: Anth* (Ballantine, 1998),
Goddess: Anth (Stewart, Tabori & Chang, 1997), *The Sun*

Michael Mesic P
1725 Jenks St
Evanston, IL 60201, 847-328-7889

Robin Metz 🎤 ✈ P&W
695 N Broad St
Galesburg, IL 61401, 309-343-6746
    Pubs: *Unbidden Angel* (CCC, 1999), *National Poetry
Competition Anthology* (Chester H. Jones, 1996), *Abiko Qtly,
Paris Rev, Epoch, Other Voices, Writers' Forum, Visions Intl,
Intl Poetry Rev, Storytellers, December Mag, Medicinal
Purposes*

Effie Mihopoulos P
5548 N Sawyer
Chicago, IL 60625, 773-539-5745
    Pubs: *Languid Love Lyrics, The Moon Cycle* (Ommation Pr,
1993, 1991), *Tomorrow, Volume No, Lost & Found Times,
Hammers, Perceptions, Hob-Nob*

Jordan Miller 🎤 ✈   P
334 Hawthorn Ave
Glencoe, IL 60022, 847-835-2519
    Pubs: *Poets, Martyrs & Satyrs: New and Selected Poems,*
    1959-2001 (Lake View Pr 2002), *Gallery Poets, Choice,*
    Midwest

Pamela Miller 🎤 ✈   P
7538 N Bell, #3A
Chicago, IL 60645-1962, 773-973-6690
Internet: pmiller@enteract.com
    Pubs: *Recipe for Disaster* (Mayapple Pr, 2002), *Mysterious*
    Coleslaw (Ridgeway, 1993), *Fast Little Shoes* (Erie Street,
    1986), *Inhabiting the Body: Anth* (Moon Jrnl Pr, 2002), *A*
    Kiss Is Still a Kiss: Anth (Outrider Pr, 2001), *Pudding, Free*
    Lunch, Spout

Patricia Monaghan 🎤 ✈   P
De Paul Univ, 25 E Jackson, Chicago, IL 60604, 312-362-6773
Internet: pmonagha@depaul.edu
    Pubs: *Dancing With Chaos* (Salmon Poetry, 2002), *Irish*
    Spirit: Anth (Wolfhound Pr, 2001), *The Next Parish Over:*
    Anth (New Rivers Pr, 1994), *Creation Spirituality,*
    Sou'wester, River Oak Rev, NAR

Lisel Mueller 🎤 ✈   P
909 W Foster Ave #607
Chicago, IL 60640-2510
    Pubs: *Dependencies, Alive Together, Waving From Shore,*
    Second Language, The Need to Hold Still, The Private Life
    (LSU Pr, 1998, 1996, 1989, 1986, 1980, 1976), *Learning to*
    Play By Ear (Juniper Pr, 1990), *Paris Rev, Poetry*

G. E. Murray 🎤 ✈   P
1401 Jackson
River Forest, IL 60305, 312-366-4144
Internet: murrcorp@aol.com
    Pubs: *Arts of a Cold Sun* (U of Illinois Pr, 2003), *Oils of*
    Evening (Lake Shore Pr, 1996), *Walking the Blind Dog* (U
    Illinois Pr, 1992), *Repairs* (U Missouri Pr, 1979), *Poetry,*
    Hudson Rev

George Nelson   P
2304 Hastings Ave
Evanston, IL 60201, 847-475-7006
Internet: gnelson262@aol.com
    Pubs: *NAW, Wire, ACM, Private, The Critic*

Richard L. Newby   P
1007 Porter Ln
Normal, IL 61761, 309-452-1726
    Pubs: *Ball State University Forum, Mississippi Rev,*
    Gryphon, Descant, Small Pond

Dwight Okita   P
426 W Surf, #111
Chicago, IL 60657, 312-883-5219
    Pubs: *Crossing With the Light* (Tia Chucha Pr, 1992),
    Unsettling America: Anth (Penguin, 1994), *ACM, Hyphen*
    Mag, Asian Pacific American Jrnl, New City

Elaine Fowler Palencia   W
208 English Bldg, mc 718, University of Illinois-Urbana
Champaign, 600 S Wright, Urbana, IL 61801, 217-356-3893
Internet: epalenci@uiuc.edu
    Pubs: *Taking the Train* (Grex Pr, 1997), *Small Caucasian*
    Woman (U Missouri Pr, 1993), *Virginia Qtly Rev, Byline,*
    Pegasus, Other Voices, Sow's Ear Poetry Rev, Iowa Woman,
    Willow Rev, Chattahoochee Rev, Appalachian Heritage

Elise Paschen 🎤 ✈   P
1023 W. Oakdale Ave
Chicago, IL 60657, 773-871-6339
    Pubs: *Illinois Voices* (U Illinois Pr, 2001), *Ravishing*
    Disunities (Wesleyan U Pr, 2000), *Infidelities* (Story Line Pr,
    1996), *New Yorker, Poetry, New Republic, Nation*

Rob Patton   P
1142 S Euclid Ave
Oak Park, IL 60304
    Pubs: *Dare, Thirty-Seven Poems* (Ithaca Hse, 1977, 1971),
    Greenfield Rev

Mark Perlberg 🎤 ✈   P
612 Stratford Pl
Chicago, IL 60657-2632, 773-477-3287
Internet: perl@ripco.com
    Pubs: *The Impossible Toystore* (LSU Pr, 2000), *The Feel of*
    the Sun (Ohio U/Swallow, 1982), *The Burning Field*
    (Morrow, 1970), *New Yorker, Illinois Rev, Poetry East,*
    Poetry, Hudson Rev, Prairie Schooner

Bob Perlongo 🎤 ✈   P&W
820 Reba Pl
Evanston, IL 60202-2691, 847-475-6645
Internet: xyzzo@aol.com
    Pubs: *All Hours of the Night* (Writers Workshop Calcutta,
    1998), *Rolling Stone, New York Times, Boulevard, Reed,*
    The Little Mag, Massachusetts Rev, Playboy, Village Voice

Karen Peterson   P&W
633 S Lombard
Oak Park, IL 60304, 708-848-8498
    Pubs: *American Fiction 2: Anth* (Birch Lane Pr, 1991),
    Poetry, Qtly West, Other Voices, West Branch, Spoon River
    Qtly, Karamu

Deborah Rebollar Pintonelli   P&W
c/o Lee Webster, 77 W Wacker Dr, Chicago, IL 60601-1696,
312-326-8803
    Pubs: *Ego Monkey* (Another Chicago Pr, 1991),
    Unbearables: Anth (Autonomedia, 1995), *Jungles*
    D'Amerique: Anth (Arbres a Cames, 1993)

James Plath 🎤 ✈ P&W
Illinois Wesleyan Univ, English Dept, Bloomington, IL
61702-2900, 309-556-3352
Internet: jplath@titan.iwu.edu
Pubs: *Courbet, On the Rocks* (White Eagle Coffee Store Pr,
1994), *Men of Our Time: Anth* (U Georgia Pr, 1992), *The
Caribbean Writer, Amelia, Salt Hill Jrnl, Gulf Stream,
Apalachee Qtly, Mississippi Valley Rev, NAR, ACM*

Sterling Plumpp P
645 N Central Ave
Chicago, IL 60644, 312-996-4694
Pubs: *Blues Narratives* (Tia Chucha Pr, 1999), *Ornate With
Smoke, Hornman* (Third World Pr,1998, 1995),
*Johannesburg & Other Poems, Blues: The Story Always
Untold,* (Another Chicago Pr, 1993, 1989), *The Mojo Hands
Call, I Must Go* (Thunder's Mouth Pr, 1982)

Frederik Pohl W
855 S Harvard Dr
Palatine, IL 60067-7026, 847-991-6009
Pubs: *O Pioneer* (Tor, 1998), *Stopping at Slowyear* (Bantam
Bks, 1992), *Mining the Oort* (Ballantine/Del Rey, 1992), *The
World at the End of Time* (Ballantine, 1990)

Enid Levinger Powell 🎤 ✈ W
1300 Lake Shore Dr, #21B
Chicago, IL 60610, 312-787-7451
Internet: enidbert@prodigy.net
Pubs: *McCall's, Mississippi Valley Rev, Yankee*

Carmen M. Pursifull 🎤 ✈ P
809 West Maple St
Champaign, IL 61820-2810, 217-359-5056
Internet: llaque3605@aol.com
Pubs: *Brimmed Hat With Flowers, The Many Faces of
Passion, Elsewhere in a Parallel Universe* (Hawk
Productions, 2000, 1996, 1992), *Manhattan Memories*
(Esoterica Pr, 1989), *The Twenty-Four Hour Wake* (Red
Herring Pr, 1989), *Dan River Anth* (Dan River Pr, 2002)

David Radavich 🎤 ✈ P
1020 Williamsburg Dr
Charleston, IL 61920-4332, 217-345-9280
Internet: cfdar@eiu.edu
Pubs: *Greatest Hits* (Pudding House, 2000), *By the Way*
(Buttonwood, 1998), *Slain Species* (Court Poetry, 1980), *Die
Weiten Horizonte: Anth* (Pressler Verlag, 1985), *Orbis,
Connecticut River Rev, Intl Qtly, Kansas Qtly, Louisville Rev,
Northwoods Jrnl*

Eugene B. Redmond 🎤 ✈ P
English Dept, Southern Illinois Univ, Box 1431, Edwardsville,
IL 62026-1431, 618-650-3991
Pubs: *The Eye in the Ceiling* (Writers & Readers, 1991),
Furious Flowering: Anth (U Pr Virginia, 1999), *Drumvoices
Rev: Anth* (Southern Illinois U Pr, 1999), *Trouble the Water:
Anth* (Mentor, 1997), *Spirit & Flame: Anth* (Syracuse U Pr,
1997), New Rain

Rosemary Roberts P
RR1, Box 89
Broughton, IL 62817-9754
Pubs: *Let His Light Shine* (American Arts Assn, 1989),
Voices in Poetics: Anth (Yes Pr, 1986)

Carolyn M. Rodgers 🎤 ✈ P
PO Box 804271
Chicago, IL 60680-4104, 773-324-3003
Pubs: *The Salt of the Earth, A Train Called Judah, Chosen
to Believe* (Eden Pr, 1999, 1996, 1996), *Daughters of Africa*
(Pantheon, 1993), *Poetry, Essence, Nation, Black Scholar,
Caprice, Nommo*

Alane Rollings P
5455 S Ridgewood Ct
Chicago, IL 60615, 773-947-0759
Pubs: *The Logic of Opposites* (TriQtly Bks, 1998), *The
Struggle to Adore* (Story Line Pr, 1993), *In Your Own Sweet
Time* (Wesleyan, 1989), *Transparent Landscapes* (Raccoon
Bks, 1984)

Charles Rossiter 🎤 ✈ PP&P
705 S Gunderson Ave
Oak Park, IL 60304-1423, 708-660-9376
Internet: posey@juno.com
Pubs: *CR's Greatest Hits, What Men Talk About* (Pudding
Hse, 2002, 2000), *Back Beat* (Cross+Roads, 2001), *Cold Mt
2000* (Backroads, 2001), *Identity Lessons: Anth* (Penguin,
1999), *Passionate Hearts: Anth* (New World Lib, 1996),
Paterson Lit Rev, LIPS, NPR

Linda Roth 🎤 ✈ P
6207 Blomberg Rd
Cherry Valley, IL 61016-9760,815-874-7131
Internet: lroth65@aol.com
Pubs: *Grasslands Rev, Natural Bridge, Southern Rev,
Massachusetts Rev, Midwest Qtly, Rockford Rev*

Alice Ryerson Hayes 🎤 P
5550 S Shore Dr #615
Chicago, IL 60037-5032, 773-753-4395
Pubs: *Journal of the Lake* (Open Bks, 1997), *Water Sheba's
Story* (Bookwrights Pr, 1997), *New & Selected Poems*
(Spoon River, 1987), *Do Not Disturb: Anth* (Writer's Digest
Bks, 1989), *Spoon River Qtly, Prairie Schooner, Whetstone,
Women's Rev of Bks*

Thomas Sanfilip 🎤 ✈ P
526 Rose Ave.
Des Plains, IL 60016
Internet: thomassanfilip@hotmail.com
Pubs: *Myth/A Poem* (Iliad Pr, 2001), *By the Hours and the
Years* (Branden Pr, 1974), *Shore Poetry Anth* (Shore Pub,
1972), *Lyrics of Love: Anth* (Young Pub, 1972), *Letter Ex,
Towers, Thalassa, Nit & Wit, Ivory Tower, Tomorrow*

R. Craig Sautter 🎤 ✈   P
School for New Learning, DePaul Univ, 243 S Wabash Ave,
Chicago, IL 60604, 312-262-5806
    Pubs: *Wicked City Chicago* (w/C. Johnson), *Express Lane
    Through the Inevitable City* (December Pr, 1994, 1990),
    Central Park, Assembling

Whitney Scott 🎤 ✈   PP&P&W
Outrider Press, 937 Patricia Ln, Crete, IL 60417-1375,
708-672-6630
Internet: outriderpr@aol.com
    Pubs: *Dancing to the End of the Shining Bar, Earth Beneath
    Sky Above: Anth, Feathers Fins & Fur: Anth, Freedom's Just
    Another Word: Anth, Prairie Hearts: Anth* (Outrider Pr, 1995,
    2000, 1999, 1997, 1996), *After Hours, Amethyst, Pearl, CQ
    Rev, Arts Alive*

Maureen Seaton 🎤 ✈   P
Columbia College of Chicago, 33 E Congress, 3rd Floor,
Chicago, IL 60605, 312-344-8139
Internet: mseaton@popmail.edu
    Pubs: *Furious Cooking* (U Iowa Pr, 1996), *Fear of Subways*
    (Eighth Mountain, 1991), *Green Mountains Rev, Quarter
    After Eight, Paris Rev, Atlantic, Kenyon Rev*

Lynette Seator 🎤 ✈   P
1609 Mound Ave
Jacksonville, IL 62650-2257, 217-245-6427
Internet: lseator@csj.edu
    Pubs: *Mississippi Valley Rev, Praxis, Pulpsmith, Melus,
    Lodestar, Open Places, Kalliope*

Irene Sedeora   P&W
107 Cedar Ave
Morton, IL 61550-1007
Internet: itsedor@dpc.net
    Pubs: *Working Hard for the Money: Anth* (Bottom Dog Pr,
    2002), *Our Bundle of Joy: Anth* (Meadow Brook Pr, 2001),
    Love Poems for the Media Age: Anth (Ripple Effect Pr,
    2002), *The Mid-America Poetry Rev, Ariel, Good Foot, Blue
    Collar Rev, Crosscurrents*

John Sennett   P
237 Park Trail Ct
Schaumburg, IL 60173, 847-517-1690
Internet: TheSenate@attbi.com
    Pubs: *Magic Changes, Mississippi Valley Rev, Washout Rev,
    Derby City News, Bloodroot*

Gregg Shapiro   P&W
926 W Margate Terr
Chicago, IL 60640, 773-784-8258
Internet: gregg1959@aol.com
    Pubs: *Reclaiming the Heartland: Anth* (U Minnesota Pr,
    1996), *Unsettling America: Anth* (Viking, 1994), *Mondo
    Barbie: Anth* (St. Martin's Pr, 1993), *Blithe Hse Qtly, Velvet
    Mafia, Christopher St, Columbia Poetry Rev, Modern Words,
    Gargoyle, Illinois Rev*

Harry B. Sheftel   P
900 Coach Rd
Homewood, IL 60430-4143
    Pubs: *Quotations From My Questing, Of Truths &
    Wonderments, From Alpha to Omega* (Jesse Poet Pubs,
    1991, 1991, 1991), *CSM, Now Mag, Modern Maturity*

Barry Silesky   P&W
3709 N Kenmore
Chicago, IL 60613-2905, 773-248-7665
Internet: btsds@aol.com
    Pubs: *One Thing That Can Save Us* (Coffee Hse Pr, 1994),
    Greatest Hits (Pudding Hse Pr, 1999), *The New Tenants*
    (Eye of the Comet Pr, 1991), *Boulevard, Witness, NAW,
    Fiction, Poetry East, Poetry, The Prose Poem, Fiction Intl*

Brian Skinner   W
4044 N Avers
Chicago, IL 60618, 773-866-2610
Internet: gileac@earthling.net
    Pubs: *Liars, Tattlers & Weavers* (Monadnock Group Pubs,
    1992), *Christmas Blues: Anth* (Amador Pubs, 1995), *Other
    Voices, Magic Realism, Karamu, Atom Mind*

James Park Sloan   W
Univ Illinois, English Dept, Box 4348, Chicago, IL 60680,
312-996-3282
    Pubs: *The Last Cold-War Cowboy* (Morrow, 1987), *The
    Case History of Comrade U* (Avon, 1972)

Michael S. Smith 🎤 ✈   P
9428 Fond Du Lac Dr
Bloomington, IL 61704-5533, 309-828-0703
Internet: msslss@msn.com
    Pubs: *XY Files: Poems on the Male Experience: Anth*
    (Sherman Asher Pub, 1997), *Passionate Hearts: Anth* (New
    World Library, 1996), *Poet Lore, Plainsongs, Writers Forum,
    Spindrift, Spoon River Poetry Rev, Thema, Ledge, Cape
    Rock, Lynx Eye, Passager*

Jared Smith 🎤 ✈   P
2630 Longview Drive
Lisle, IL 60532, 630-357-2674
    Pubs: *Walking the Perimeters of the Plate Glass Window
    Factory* (Birch Brook Pr, 2000), *Keeping the Outlaw Alive*
    (Erie Street Pr, 1988), *NYQ, Rhino, After Hours, Letter-Ex*

Paul Andrew E. Smith   P&W
McHenry County Creative Comm, PO Box 354, Cary, IL
60013, 708-639-9200
    Pubs: *Scenes From the Postmodern Butler* (White Eagle
    Coffee Store Pr, 1992), *Postmodern Culture, Kalliope,
    Willow Rev, Hawaii Rev, Fly Rod & Reel, Whetstone, Alaska
    Qtly Rev, Carolina Qtly*

Sharon Solwitz   W
3709 N Kenmore
Chicago, IL 60613, 312-248-7665
   Pubs: *Blood & Milk* (Sarabande, 1997), *TriQtly, Ploughshares,
   American Short Fiction, Boulevard, Tikkun, Sassy*

Kevin Stein ♦ ✈   P
Bradley Univ, English Dept, Peoria, IL 61625, 309-677-2480
Internet: kstein@bradley.edu
   Pubs: *Chance Ransom, Bruised Paradise* (U Illinois Pr,
   2000, 1996), *A Circus of Want* (U Missouri Pr, 1992),
   Poetry, NAR

Richard Stern   W
Univ Chicago, English Dept, 1050 E 59 St, Chicago, IL 60637,
773-702-8536
Internet: rstern@midway.uchicago.edu
   Pubs: *What Is What Was* (U of Chicago, 2002), *Pacific
   Tremors* (Triuuaryly Bks, 2001), *A Sistermony* (Donald I.
   Fine, 1995), *One Person & Another* (Baskerville, 1993),
   Shares & Other Fictions (Delphinium, 1992), *Noble Rot:
   Stories* (ACP, 1991), *Paris Rev*

Anthony E. Stockanes   W
2201 E Vermont Ave
Urbana, IL 61801
   Pubs: *Ladies Who Knit for a Living* (U Illinois Pr, 1981),
   Sewanee Rev, Ascent, Chicago Magazine

Lucien Stryk ♦ ✈   P
342 Delcy Dr
Dekalb, IL 60115-1906, 815-756-8817
   Pubs: *And Still Birds Sing, Of Pen & Ink & Paper Scraps*
   (Swallow/Ohio U Pr, 1998, 1989), *Where We Are: Selected
   Poems & Zen Translations* (England; Skoob Bks Ltd, 1997)

Walter Sublette ♦ ✈   P&W
English Dept, Aurora Univ, 347 S Gladstone, Aurora, IL 60506,
708-844-5407
Internet: wsublette@aurora.edu
   Pubs: *Naked Exlie* (U Michigan Pr, 1991), *The Resurrection
   on Friday Night* (U Ohio Pr, 1981), *Go Now in Darkness*
   (Baker Pr, 1965)

Jean Thompson   W
Univ Illinois, 608 S Wright St, English Dept, Urbana, IL 61801
   Pubs: *The Woman Driver, Little Face, My Wisdom* (Watts,
   1985, 1984, 1982), *American Short Fiction, NER,
   Ploughshares, New Yorker*

Phyllis Alexander Tickle   P
c/o Joseph Durepos, 5114 1/2 Main St, Downers Grove, IL
60515, 630-852-5298
Internet: jdurepos@aol.com
   Pubs: *God-Talk in America, Re-Discovering the Sacred*
   (Crossroad Pub, 1997, 1996), *My Father's Prayer: A
   Remembrance* (Upper Room Bks, 1996)

Alpay K. Ulku ♦ ✈   P
5320 N Sheridan Rd #1302
Chicago, IL 60640, 773-334-1220
Internet: alpayulku@ziplip.com
   Pubs: *Meteorology* (Boa Edtns, 1999), *Ploughshares,
   Witness, Gettysburg Rev, Black Warrior Rev, Malahat Rev*

Martha M. Vertreace ♦ ✈   P
5232 South Greenwood Ave
Chicago, IL 60615-4316
   Pubs: *Dragon Lady* (Riverstone Pr, 1999), *Second
   Mourning, Light Caught Bending* (Diehard Pr, 1998, 1994),
   Smokeless Flame (Frith Pr, 1998), *Maafa: When Night
   Becomes a Lion* (Ion Bks, 1996), *Oracle Bones,* (White
   Eagle Coffee Store Pr, 1994)

Doris Vidaver   P&W
Professional Bldg 1106, Rush Univ, 600 S Paulina St,
Chicago, IL 60612, 312-942-2063
   Pubs: *Arch of a Circle* (Swallow, 1981), *Articulations: Anth*
   (U Iowa Pr, 1994), *Lit Rev, Illinois Rev, ACM, Prairie
   Schooner, Poetry, Amer Scholar, Chelsea*

Karen Volkman ♦ ✈   P
Department of English, U of Chicago, 1050 E. 59th St.,
Chicago, IL 60637, 773-684-1002
   Pubs: *Crash's Law* (Norton, 1996), *The Bread Loaf
   Anthology of New American Poets* (U Prs of New England,
   2000), *New American Poets: Anth* (S Illinois Pr, 2000), *Best
   American Poetry 1996: Anth* (Scribner, 1996), *Paris Rev,
   New Republic*

J. Weintraub ♦ ✈   P&W
UCP, 1427 E 60th St, Chicago, IL 60637
   Pubs: *Bite to Eat Place: Anth* (Redwood Coast Pr, 1995),
   Movieworks: Anth (Little Theatre Pr, 1990), *MacGuffin,
   Bellevue, Lit Rev, Karamu, Bryant Lit Rev, New Criterion,
   Formalist, Kansas Qtly, Chicago Reader*

Bill West ♦ ✈   P
666 W Irving Park Rd, I-2
Chicago, IL 60613-3125
   Pubs: *Aabye, Iota, Envoi, Mainichi, Asahi, Lynx, Tundra,
   Blue Collar Rev, Parnassus, Tanka Jrnl, Poetry Chain,
   Poetry Today, Lotus, Borderlines, Poet's Podium, T.O.P.S,
   Heron Qtly, Azami, Presence, Poetry Church Anth, Point
   Judith Light, American Tanka*

David Buffington Wham ♦ ✈   W
860 Hinman Ave, #724
Evanston, IL 60202-2341, 847-733-8015
   Pubs: *CPU Rev, Pilgrimage, Maelstrom, The Fair, Means,
   Charlatan, December, Woodwind*

Eugene Wildman   W
2705 N Mildred
Chicago, IL 60614, 312-281-7167

Anne Winters 🎤 ✈   P
English Dept (MC 162), Univ of Illinois at Chicago, 601 S
Morgan St, Chicago, IL 60607
    Pubs: *The Key to the City* (U Chicago Pr, 1986),
    Salamander (Princeton U Pr, 1979), *Paris Rev, Yale Rev,
    New Yorker*

S. L. Wisenberg   W
3752 N Sheffield Ave
Chicago, IL 60613-2904, 773-871-5361
Internet: slw644@nwu.edu
    Pubs: *Nice Jewish Girls: Anth* (Plume-Penguin, 1996),
    Feminism 3: Anth (Westview Pr, 1996), *Tikkun, New Yorker,
    NAR, Kenyon Rev, Wigwag, ACM, Calyx*

David Wojahn   P
1542 W Norwood
Chicago, IL 60660, 812-855-7967
Internet: wojahn@ucs.indiana.edu
    Pubs: *The Falling Hour, Late Empire, Mystery Train* (U Pitt
    Pr, 1997, 1994, 1990), *Poetry, New Yorker, APR, TriQtly,
    Ploughshares, Southern Rev*

Gene Wolfe   W
PO Box 69
Barrington, IL 60011
    Pubs: *Castleview, Soldier of Arete, There Are Doors* (Tor,
    1990, 1989, 1988)

Janet Wondra 🎤 ✈   P
School of Liberal Studies, Roosevelt Univ, 430 S Michigan
Ave, Chicago, IL 60605, 312-341-3710
Internet: jwondra@roosevelt.edu
    Pubs: *Long Division* (Holocene Pub, 1998), *The Wandering
    Mother, Emerging Island Cultures: Anth* (Emerging Island
    Cultures Pr, 1989, 1984), *Calyx, Connecticut Rev, Southern
    Rev, Michigan Qtly Rev, Denver Qtly, Witness, New Orleans
    Rev, Berkeley Poetry Rev*

G. K. Wuori   W
440 S California St
Sycamore, IL 60178
    Pubs: *An American Outrage, Nude in Tub* (Algonquin Books
    of Chapel Hill, 2000, 1999)

Joanne Zimmerman   W
18255 Perth Ave
Homewood, IL 60430-1615, 708-798-8136
    Pubs: *An Intricate Weave: Anth* (Iris Edtns, 1997),
    *Cottonwood Mag, Karamu, Out of Line, Arizona Qtly,
    Shenandoah, Antioch Rev, Descant*

Yvonne Zipter 🎤 ✈   P
4710 W Hutchinson
Chicago, IL 60641-1607
Internet: yz@press.uchicago.edu
    Pubs: *Contemporary Lesbian Love Poems: Anth* (Ballantine
    Bks, 1996), *Spoon River Poetry Rev, Modern Words,
    Columbia Poetry Rev, Primavera, The Bark*

INDIANA

Tony Ardizzone 🎤 ✈   P&W
Indiana Univ, Department of English, Bloomington, IN 47401
Internet: ardizzon@indiana.edu
    Pubs: *In the Garden of Papa Santuzzu* (Picador USA,
    2000), *Taking It Home* (U Illinois Pr, 1996), *Larabi's Ox:
    Stories of Morocco* (Milkweed Edtns, 1992), *Georgia Rev,
    Prairie Schooner, Gettysburg Rev, TriQtly, Witness*

William Baer   P&W
320 Hunter Dr
Evansville, IN 47711, 812-479-2975
    Pubs: *The Unfortunates* (New Odyssey Pr, 1997),
    Ploughshares, Hudson Rev, Iowa Rev, Poetry, Southern Rev

B. E. Balog   P
264 N Lake St
Gary, IN 46403
    Pubs: *Loaves & Fishes Anth* (Free Writer's Pr, 1982),
    Alternatives, Indiannual, Skylark

Willis Barnstone   P
Comparative Literature Dept, Indiana Univ, Bloomington, IN
47405, 812-855-9780
Internet: barnston@indiana.edu
    Pubs: *Selected Poems* (Sheep Meadow Pr, 1997), *The
    Secret Reader: 501 Sonnets* (U Pr New England, 1996),
    Partisan Rev, New Yorker

Marianne Boruch 🎤 ✈   P
415 Maple St
West Lafayette, IN 47906-3016, 765-743-1420
Internet: mboruch@purdue.edu
    Pubs: *A Stick That Breaks & Breaks, Moss Burning* (Oberlin
    College Pr, 1997, 1993), *Descendant* (Wesleyan U Pr,
    1989), *New Yorker, APR, Iowa Rev, Field, Georgia Rev,
    Denver Qtly*

James H. Bowden   P&W
2078 Ball Diamond Hill Rd
Lanesville, IN 47136
    Pubs: *Shenandoah, College English, Negative Capability*

Catherine Bowman   P
Indiana Univ, 442 Ballantine Hall English Dept, Bloomington,
IN 47401, 812-855-1834
Internet: cabowman@indiana.edu
  Pubs: *Rock Farm, 1-800-HOT-RIBS* (Gibbs Smith, 1997,
  1993), *Best American Poetry: Anths* (Scribner, 1995, 1994),
  TriQtly, River Styx, Paris Rev

Matthew Brennan ♦ ✈   P
Indiana State Univ, English Dept, Terre Haute, IN 47809,
812-237-3277
Internet: M-Brennan@Indstate.edu
  Pubs: *American Scenes* (Bliss Station, 2001), *The Music of
  Exile* (Cloverdale Bks, 1994), *Good Company: Anth* (Grinnell
  College, 2000), *Notre Dame Rev, South Dakota Rev, Blue
  Unicorn, Poem, Poetry Ireland Rev, Descant*

Edward Byrne   P
Valparaiso Univ, English Dept, Valparaiso, IN 46383,
219-464-5278
Internet: ebyrne@exodus.valpo.edu
  Pubs: *East of Omaha* (Pecan Grove Pr, 1996), *Words
  Spoken, Words Unspoken* (Chimney Hill Pr, 1995), *Along
  the Dark Shore* (BOA Edtns, 1977), *APR, Porch*

Jared Carter ♦ ✈   P
1220 N State Ave
Indianapolis, IN 46201-1162, 317-638-8136
  Pubs: *Les Barricades Mysterieuses, Work, For the Night Is
  Coming, After the Rain* (Cleveland State U Poetry Ctr, 1999,
  1995, 1993), *Poetry, New Yorker, Nation, Iowa Rev, TriQtly,
  Formalist, Kenyon Rev, New Letters*

Richard Cecil ♦ ✈   P
Indiana Univ, Ballantine Hall 442, English Dept, Bloomington,
IN 47405, 812-855-8224
Internet: cecilr@indiana.edu
  Pubs: *In Search of the Great Dead* (Southern Illinois U Pr,
  1999), *Alcatraz* (Purdue U Pr, 1992), *Einstein's Brain* (Utah
  U Pr, 1986), *APR, Poetry, Crazyhorse, NER, Ploughshares,
  Amer Scholar, Virginia Qtly, Georgia Rev*

Elizabeth Christman   W
American Studies Department, Univ Notre Dame, Notre
Dame, IN 46556, 219-239-7316
  Pubs: *Ruined for Life* (Paulist Pr, 1987), *A Broken Family*
  (Morrow, 1981), *The Critic*

Stephen R. Clark   P&W
36 Walnut St
Indianapolis, IN 46227-5187
  Pubs: *The Godtouch: Poems* (Northwoods Pr, 1985),
  *Christianity & Lit, Christian Herald, Encore, Face-to-Face,
  Alive Now!, Wellspring*

Ruth Allison Coates   P&W
8140 Township Line Rd
Indianapolis, IN 46260, 317-824-9548
  Pubs: *Waiting for the Westbound* (Ocean Tree Bks, 1992),
  Great American Naturalists (Lerner Pubs, 1974), *Minnesota
  Rev, Boys' Life, Byline*

Marilyn Durham   W
1508 Howard St
Evansville, IN 47713, 812-423-3342
  Pubs: *Flambard's Confession, Dutch Uncle, The Man Who
  Loved Cat Dancing* (HBJ, 1982, 1973, 1972)

Leslie Edgerton ♦ ✈   W
4941 Maple Ridge Dr
Fort Wayne, IN 46835-3930, 260-485-9207
Internet: edgertonL@cs.com
  Pubs: *Monday's Meal, The Death of Tarpons* (U North
  Texas Pr, 1997, 1996), *Best American Mystery Stories:
  Anth* (HM, 2001), *South Carolina Rev, Arkansas Qtly,
  Kansas Rev, Hopewell Rev, NAR, Breeze, Flyway Lit Rev,
  High Plains Lit Rev*

Douglas Eichhorn   P
208 W Main
Centerville, IN 47330, 317-855-3398
  Pubs: *Rituals: A Book of Poems* (Salt Mound Pr, 1968)

William C. Elkington   P
10433 Haverford Pl
Fort Wayne, IN 46845-6504
  Pubs: *Snowy Egret, Laurel Rev, Karamu, North Country,
  Denver Qtly, Aldebaran, Third Eye, Gravida*

Lenny Emmanuel   P
Indiana Univ Medical Center, 930 W Michigan St, Indianapolis,
IN 46223, 317-274-1744
  Pubs: *The Ice Cream Lady* (Ramparts, 1996), *The
  Cathartic, Descant, Poetry Rev, Outposts, Imago, Jrnl of
  Teaching Writing, Exquisite Corpse, Windless Orchard*

Mari Evans   P
PO Box 483
Indianapolis, IN 46206, 317-926-5229

Christine Farris   P
English Dept, Indiana Univ, Bloomington, IN 47405
  Pubs: *Mining the Beaches for Watches & Small Change*
  (Konglomerati Pr, 1981), *Some, Kairos*

Stephen Fredman   P
English Dept, Univ Notre Dame, Notre Dame, IN 46556,
219-631-7555
  Pubs: *Sagetrieb, Talisman, Boundary 2, o.ars, North Dakota
  Qtly, 20th Century Lit*

Alice Friman 🎤 ✈ P
6312 Central Ave
Indianapolis, IN 46220-1738, 317-257-2105
Internet: bgentry@uindy.edu
    Pubs: *Zoo* (U Arkansas Pr, 1999), *Inverted Fire* (BkMk Pr, 1997), *Driving for Jimmy Wonderland* (Barnwood Pr, 1992), *Insomniac Heart* (Years Pr, 1990), *Shenandoah, Poetry, Georgia Rev, Ohio Rev, Gettysburg Rev, Prairie Schooner, Poetry Rev* (U.K.), *Boulevard*

Helen Frost 🎤 ✈ P
6108 Old Brook Dr
Fort Wayne, IN 46835-2438, 260-485-1785
Internet: frost-thompson@worldnet.att.net
    Pubs: *Keesha's House* (FSG, 2003), *Skin of a Fish, Bones of a Bird* (Ampersand Pr, 1993), *The Sacred Place: Anth* (U Utah Pr, 1996), *Season of Dead Water: Anth* (Breitenbush, 1990), *River Styx, Ms., Chile Verde, Antioch Rev, Calyx, Calliope, Malahat Rev*

Sonia Gernes 🎤 ✈ P
Univ Notre Dame, 210 Decio Hall, Notre Dame, IN 46556, 219-631-5218
Internet: sonia.g.gernes.1@nd.edu
    Pubs: *A Breeze Called the Fremantle Doctor, Women at Forty* (U Notre Dame Pr, 1997, 1990), *Southern Rev, Poetry NW, Sewanee Rev, Amer Short Fiction, Georgia Rev, New Letters*

Paul E. Grabill W
905 S Spring St
Evansville, IN 47714, 812-477-2584
    Pubs: *Youth's a Stuff Will Not Endure* (Avon, 1977), *Bitterroot*

Matthew Graham 🎤 ✈ P
Univ Southern Indiana, 8600 University Blvd, Evansville, IN 47712, 812-464-1953
Internet: mgraham@usi.edu
    Pubs: *1946, New World Architecture* (Galileo, 1991, 1985), *Indiana Rev, Harvard Rev*

Nancy Hagen W
1133 Glenway St
West Lafayette, IN 47906, 765-497-1259
Internet: nancy@dcwi.com
    Pubs: *Alternatives: Roads Less Travelled: Anth, Prairie Hearts: Women View the Midwest: Anth* (Outrider Pr, 1997), *Mystery Time: Anth* (Hutton Pub, 1997)

Anne Haines 🎤 ✈ P
PO Box 2501
Bloomington, IN 47402-2501
Internet: ahaines@indiana.edu
    Pubs: *NW Rev, Kansas Qtly, Sojourner, Prairie Schooner, Sidewalks, Common Lives/Lesbian Lives, New Zoo Poetry Rev, Sinister Wisdom*

Patricia Henley P&W
PO Box 259
Battle Ground, IN 47920, 765-567-2058
Internet: phenley@omni.cc.purdue.edu
    Pubs: *The Secret of Cartwheels, Friday Night at Silver Star* (Graywolf, 1992, 1986), *Learning to Die* (Three Rivers, 1979), *Atlantic, Ploughshares*

Joe L. Hensley W
2315 Blackmore
Madison, IN 47250, 812-273-1683
    Pubs: *Grim City* (St. Martin's Pr, 1994)

Marc Hudson P
English Dept, Wabash College, Crawfordsville, IN 47933, 317-364-4232
    Pubs: *Journal for an Injured Son* (Lockhart Pr, 1991), *Kenyon Rev, Massachusetts Rev, Prairie Schooner, Poetry East, Fine Madness*

Karen I. Jaquish 🎤 ✈ P
4817 W Arlington Park Blvd
Fort Wayne, IN 46835-4311
Internet: jaquishka@yahoo.com
    Pubs: *Spoon River Poetry Rev, Prairie Schooner, Notre Dame Rev, SPR, Plainsongs, Connecticut Poetry Rev, 11th Muse, Poet Lore, South Carolina Rev, Nation, Denver Qtly*

Elisa Jenkins 🎤 ✈ W
3709 West Jackson St
Muncie, IN 47304-4202
    Pubs: *Fresh Ground, Emrys Journal, Oval, Side Show, Amer Fiction, Hopewell Rev, Literal Latte, Free Songs, Indiannual, Sun, Forum*

George Kalamaras 🎤 ✈ P
1202 Illsley Pl
Fort Wayne, IN 46807, 260-456-3151
Internet: kalamara@ipfw.edu
    Pubs: *Borders My Bent Toward* (Pavement Saw Pr, 2003), *The Theory and Function of Mangoes* (Four Way Bks, 2000), *Beneath the Breath* (Tilton Hse Pr, 1988), *Heart Without End* (Leaping Mountain Pr, 1986), *Best American Poetry: Anth* (S&S, 1997), *Sulfur, Epoch,*

Margaret Kingery 🎤 ✈ W
c/o Dimoplon, 4103 N Redding Rd, Muncie, IN 47304-1338, 317-289-5022
Internet: mdimoplo@bsuvc.bsu.edu
    Pubs: *Dark Horse* (Ball State U, 1997), *River Styx, Emrys Journal, Arts Indiana, Eureka Literacy Mag, Willow Rev, South Dakota Rev, Texas Rev, Confrontation, Prairie Schooner, Earth's Daughters, Thema*

Terry Alan Kirts 🎤 ✈   P
1620 Central Ave #102
Indianapolis, IN 46202, 317-921-9416
Internet: tkirts@iupui.edu
    Pubs: *ACM, Gastronomica, Third Coast, Green Mountains
    Rev, Sycamore Rev, Artful Dodge, The James White Rev*

Tom Koontz 🎤 ✈   P
Ball State Univ, Muncie, IN 47306, 765-288-0145
Internet: tkoontz@bsu.edu
    Pubs: *Rice Paper Sky* (Amelia, 2000), *In Such a Light*
    (Mississinewa Pr, 1996), *Black Fly Rev, Hopewell Rev,
    Birmingham Poetry Rev, Flying Island, PBQ*

Karen Kovacik 🎤 ✈   P
1325 N Central, #6
Indianapolis, IN 46202
Internet: kkovacik@inpui.edu
    Pubs: *Beyond the Velvet Curtain, Nixon & I, A Gathering of
    Poets: Anth* (Kent State U Pr, 1999, 1998, 1992), *Return of
    the Prodigal* (Poetry Atlanta Pr, 1991), *Salmagundi, BPJ,
    Confrontation*

Marcia H. Kruchten   W
442 S Maple St
Orleans, IN 47452, 812-865-2663
    Pubs: *Skyborn* (Schoastic, 1989), *I Don't Want to Be Like
    Her, Too Many Parents, The Ghost in the Mirror* (Willowisp
    Pr, 1996, 1996, 1986), *Indianapolis Woman, Writer's Digest,
    Prim-Aid, Black Box*

D. E. Laczi   P
805 S 9th St
Lafayette, IN 47905-1430, 317-742-2539
Internet: midwayog@mindspring.com
    Pubs: *Chicago Qtly Rev, Tears in the Fence, The Sow's Ear
    Poetry Rev, The Jrnl of Kentucky Studies, Limestone,
    Kentucky Writing*

John Matthias 🎤 ✈   P
Univ Notre Dame, English Dept, Notre Dame, IN 46556,
219-239-7226
Internet: john.e.matthias.1@nd.edu
    Pubs: *Pages: New Poems and Cuttings, Swimming at
    Midnight, Beltane at Aphelion* (Swallow Pr, 2000, 1995,
    1995), *TriQtly, Salmagundi, ACM, Southern Rev, Stand*

Kathy A. Mayer   P
PO Box 1135
Lafayette, IN 47902
    Pubs: *Haraka Pr, Story Circle Jrnl, Moon Jrnl, L'Ouverture,
    Outrider Pr, Flying Island, Earth's Daughters, Pike Creek Rev*

John A. McCluskey, Jr. 🎤 ✈   W
Afro-American Studies, Indiana Univ, Memorial Hall #28,
Bloomington, IN 47401
    Pubs: *Mr. America's Last Season Blues* (LSU Pr, 1983),
    *Ploughshares, Black Amer Lit Forum, Southern Rev,
    Callaloo*

Joan McIntosh 🎤 ✈   P
213 Wakewa Ave
South Bend, IN 46617, 574-232-4502
Internet: robert.p.mcintosh1@nd.edu
    Pubs: *Walking Amazed* (The Muse Rules, 2002), *Lake
    Michigan Shore, Branch & Shadow Branch* (Writer's Center
    of Indianapolis, 1997, 1982), *Flying Island, Cumberland
    Poetry Rev, Connecticut River Rev, Shenandoah*

Howard McMillen   W
5250 Cook Rd
West Terre Haute, IN 47885-9734, 812-237-3168
    Pubs: *The Many Mansions of Sam Peeples* (Viking, 1972),
    Lit Mag Rev, Gambling Times, Win Magazine

Margaret McMullan   W
Chair, English Dept, Univ of Evansville, 1800 Lincoln Ave,
Evansville, IN 47722
Internet: mm44@evansville.edu
    Pubs: *When Warhol Was Still Alive* (Crossing Pr, 1994),
    Catholic Girls & Boys: Anth (Penguin/NAL, 1994), *Chicago
    Tribune, Indianapolis Star, Boulevard, Brain, Child, Southern
    Accents, Greensboro Rev, New England Living*

Orlando Ricardo Menes 🎤 ✈   P
4364 Foxfire Drive
South Bend, IN 46628, 574-243-1125
Internet: orlando.menes.1@nd.edu
    Pubs: *Rumba Atop the Stones* (Peepal Tree Pr, 2001),
    Borderlands With Angels (Bacchae Pr, 1995), *New Letters,
    Green Mountains Rev, Ploughshares, Antioch Rev, Callaloo,
    Chelsea*

Roger Mitchell 🎤 ✈   P
1010 E 1st St
Bloomington, IN 47401, 812-332-1045
    Pubs: *Savage Baggage, Braid* (The Figures, 2001, 1997),
    The Word for Everything, Adirondack (BkMk Pr, 1996,
    1988), *Clearpond* (Syracuse U, 1991), *The Adirondack
    Reader: Anth* (Adirondack Mountain Club, 2002), *Tar River
    Rev, Pequod*

Neil Myers   P
901 N Chauncey
West Lafayette, IN 47906
    Pubs: *The Blade of Manjusri* (Sun Moon Bear, 1989), *All
    That, So Simple* (Purdue U Pr, 1980)

Susan Neville   W
Butler Univ, 4600 Sunset Ave, Box 135, Indianapolis, IN
46208, 317-940-9676
Internet: sneville@butler.edu
    Pubs: *Fabrication* (MacMurray & Beck, 2002), *Twilight in
    Arcadia, Indiana Winter* (Indiana U Pr, 2000, 1999), *In the
    House of Blue Lights* (Notre Dame U Pr, 1998), *Invention of
    Flight* (U Georgia Pr, 1984), *Missouri Rev, Gulf Stream,
    Nerve, NAR, Boulevard*

Tom Noyes ♫ ✈   W
English Department, Indiana State University, Terre Hante, IN
47809, 812-237-8552
Internet: noyestom@yahoo.com
    Pubs: *Behold Faith: Stories: Anth* (Dufour Edtns, 2002),
    *Ascent, High Plains Lit Rev, ALR, Pleiades, Third Coast,
    Image, Whetstone*

William O'Rourke ♫ ✈   W
Univ Notre Dame, English Dept, Notre Dame, IN 46556,
219-631-7377
Internet: william.a.o'rourke.1@nd.edu
    Pubs: *Campaign America 2000* (Preview Port Edtns, 2001),
    Campaign America '96 (Notre Dame U Pr, 2000), *Notts*
    (Marlowe & Co., 1996), *Signs of the Literary Times* (SUNY,
    1993), *Chicago Sun-Times, Commonweal*

Harry Mark Petrakis   W
80 E Rd, Dune Acres
Chesterton, IN 46304, 219-787-8283
    Pubs: *Collected Stories* (Ravenswood, 1990), *Days of
    Vengeance* (Doubleday, 1983), *Atlantic, Saturday Evening
    Post*

Roger Pfingston ♫ ✈   P
4020 Stoutes Creek Rd
Bloomington, IN 47404-1332, 812-339-2482
Internet: snapshot@bluemarble.net
    Pubs: *Singing to the Garden* (Parallel Pr, 2003), *Something
    Iridescent* (Barnwood Pr, 1987), *The Party Train: Anth* (New
    Rivers Pr, 1996), *Permafrost, Wind, Poet Lore*

Richard Pflum ♫ ✈   P
1473 Shannon Ave
Indianapolis, IN 46201-1758, 317-356-2048
Internet: drahcir@indy.net
    Pubs: *A Strange Juxtaposition of Parts* (Writers' Ctr Pr of
    Indiana, 1995), *A New Geography of Poets: Anth* (U
    Arkansas Pr, 1992), *Ploplop Mag, Poetry Tonight, Tears in
    the Fence, Flying Island, Hopewell Rev*

Michael Joseph Phillips ♫ ✈   P
238 N Smith Rd #25
Bloomington, IN 47408-3188, 812-336-2530
    Pubs: *Dreamgirls* (Cambric, 1989), *Selected Love Poems*
    (Wm. Hackett, 1980), *Massachusetts Rev, Nation*

Donald Platt ♫ ✈   P
Dept of English, Purdue Univ, 1356 Heavilon Hall, West
Lafayette, IN 47907-1356, 765-494-3740
    Pubs: *Cloud Atlas, Fresh Peaches, Fireworks, & Guns*
    (Purdue U Pr, 2002, 1994), *Leap Second at the Turn of the
    Millennium* (Ctr for Book Arts NY, 2000), *Best American
    Poetry: Anth* (Scribner, 2000), *Kenyon Rev, Nimrod, New
    Republic, Paris Rev, Qtly West*

Fran Quinn   P
599 W Westfield Blvd #38
Indianapolis, IN 46208, 317-259-9096
    Pubs: *The Goblet Crying for Wine* (Ally Pr, 1995), *At the
    Edge of the Worlds* (Presada Pr, 1994)

William Craig Rice   P
Liberty Fund, Inc, 8335 Allison Pointe Trail, Indianapolis, IN
46250-1684, 800-368-7897
Internet: wcrice@libertyfund.org
    Pubs: *Sewanee, New Criterion, Sparrow, Harvard Rev,
    Dog World*

Paulette Roeske ♫ ✈   P&W
7525 Syls Drive
Evansville, IN 47712, 812-985-5467
Internet: pauletteroeske@aol.com
    Pubs: *Bridge of Sighs: A Novella and Stories* (Story Line Pr,
    2002), *Anvil, Clock, & Last, Divine Attention* (LSU Pr, 2001,
    1995), *The Body Can Ascend No Higher* (Illinois Writers,
    1992), *Breathing Under Water* (Stormline, 1988),
    Threepenny Rev, Indiana Rev

Scott Russell Sanders   W
1113 E Wylie St
Bloomington, IN 47401
Internet: sanders1@indiana.edu
    Pubs: *Writing From the Center* (Indiana U Pr, 1995), *Staying
    Put, Secrets of the Universe* (Beacon Pr, 1993, 1991),
    Harper's, Omni, Georgia Rev, NAR

Valerie Sayers ♫ ✈   W
English Dept, Univ Notre Dame, Notre Dame, IN 46617,
219-631-7160
    Pubs: *Brain Fever, The Distance Between Us, Who Do You
    Love* (Doubleday, 1996, 1996, 1991), *Zeotrope, Image, Five
    Points*

John Sherman ♫ ✈   P
4175 Central Ave
Indianapolis, IN 46205-2604, 317-283-3330
Internet: shermco@earthlink.net
    Pubs: *Marjorie Main: Rural Documentary Poetry, America Is
    a Negro Child: Race Poems* (Mesa Verde Pr, 1999, 1981),
    Touched by Adoption: Anth (Green River Pr, 1999), *Dying: A
    Book of Comfort: Anth* (Doubleday, 1996), *Coe Rev, Amer
    Jones, Nebo, MM Rev*

R. E. Smith   W
520 Terry Ln
West Lafayette, IN 47906, 317-743-1074
    Pubs: *Unknown Texas: Anth* (Macmillan, 1988), *South By
    Southwest: Anth* (U Texas Pr, 1986), *Concho River Rev,
    Chariton Rev, Descant, Texas Rev*

Maura Stanton 🎤 ✈   P&W
Indiana Univ, Ballantine Hall 442, English Dept, Bloomington,
IN 47405, 812-855-1296
Internet: stanton@indiana.edu
    Pubs: *Do Not Forsake Me, Oh My Darling* (U Notre Dame
Pr, 2002), *Glacier Wine, Life Among the Trolls* (Carnegie
Mellon, 2001, 1998), *Tales of the Supernatural* (Godine,
1988), *The Country I Come From* (Milkweed Edtns, 1988),
Ploughshares, APR, Paris Rev

Felix Stefanile 🎤 ✈   P
103 Waldron St
West Lafayette, IN 47906-2836, 765-743-0530
    Pubs: *The Country of Absence* (Bordighera Pr, 2000), *The
Dance at St. Gabriel's* (Story Line Pr, 1995), *Unsettling
America: Anth* (Penguin, 1994), *Sewanee Rev, Hudson Rev,
Formalist, Poetry*

Leon Titche 🎤 ✈   P
510 Renard Rd
West Lafayette, IN 47906-9489, 765-743-1059
Internet: leontitche400@msn.com
    Pubs: *Reflections From a Desert Pond* (Century Pr, 1998)

Bronislava Volkova   P
926 Commons Dr
Bloomington, IN 47401, 812-339-3618
Internet: volkova@indiana.edu
    Pubs: *Shattered Worlds* (Votobia, 1995), *Courage of the
Rainbow* (Sheep Meadow, 1993), *The Deaf & Dumb Hand*
(Pm D, 1993), *Metamorphoses, Visions, Poetry East,
Nimrod, Midwest Poetry Rev, Witness*

Matt Wade   P
875 W 900 N
Fortville, IN 46040
    Pubs: *Black Dirt, Formalist, Mudfish, New Laurel Rev,
River Styx*

Elizabeth Weber   P
4771 Stansbury Ln
Indianapolis, IN 46254
    Pubs: *Small Mercies* (Owl Creek, 1984), *Puerto del Sol,
Florida Rev, 6ix*

Henry Weinfield 🎤 ✈   P
1113 N St Joseph
South Bend, IN 46617-1253, 219-288-7648
Internet: henry.m.weinfield.1@nd.edu
    Pubs: *The Sorrows of Eros & Other Poems* (U Notre Dame
Pr, 1999), *Sonnets Elegiac & Satirical, In the Sweetness of
New Time* (House of Keys, 1982, 1980), *Pequod, Denver
Qtly, Talisman*

Joanna H. Wos 🎤 ✈   W
8148 Lieber Rd
Indianapolis, IN 46260-2839, 317-255-6086
Internet: jhwriter@indy.net
    Pubs: *A House of Butter* (Writers Center Pr, 1998), *Loss of
the Groundnote: Anth* (Clothespin Fever Pr, 1992), *Flash
Fiction: Anth* (Norton, 1992), *Malahat Rev, Kalliope,
Permafrost, Webster Rev, MacGuffin, Qtly West*

Marguerite Young   P&W
2506 Knollwood Dr
Indianapolis, IN 46208-2188

IOWA

Nina Barragan 🎤 ✈   W
c/o Weinstein, 3880 Owl Song Ln SE, Iowa City, IA
52240-9044, 319-351-4700
Internet: ninaweinstein@aol.com
    Pubs: *Losers & Keepers in Argentina* (U New Mexico Pr,
2001), *No Peace at Versailles, The House on Via Gambito:
Anth* (New Rivers Pr, 1991, 1991), *B'nai B'rith Intl Jewish
Monthly*

Marvin Bell 🎤 ✈   P
1416 E College St
Iowa City, IA 52245, 319-337-5217
Internet: marvin-bell@uiowa.edu
    Pubs: *Nightworks: Poems 1962-2000, Ardor: The Book of
the Dead Man, Vol 2, The Book of the Dead Man* (Copper
Canyon, 2000, 1997, 1994), *Wednesday* (Ireland; Salmon
Pub, 1998)

Virginia Bensheimer   P
Route 1, Box 68
Macedonia, IA 51549
    Pubs: *Visions, Green's Mag, The Little Mag, Urthkin, Long
Pond Rev, Fine*

Frederick Bock   P
Embassy Manor Care Center, 200 S Eighth Ave E, Newton,
IA 50208
    Pubs: *The Fountains of Regardlessness* (Macmillan, 1961),
Ascent, Poetry, Antaeus, Iowa Rev

Michael Borich   P
1308 Vermont St
Waterloo, IA 50702, 319-232-0275
    Pubs: *Nana's Ark* (Thomas Nelson, 1984), *A Different Kind
of Love* (HR&W, 1984)

Jerry Bumpus   W
619 Church St, Suite 127
Ottumwa, IA 52501
    Pubs: *The Civilized Tribes* (U Akron Pr, 1995), *Dawn of the
Flying Pigs* (Carpenter Pr, 1992), *Esquire, Paris Rev,
Partisan Rev, Yellow Silk, December Mag*

Dan Campion 🎤 ✈   P
1700 E Rochester Ave
Iowa City, IA 52245
Internet: campion@act.org
    Pubs: *Calypso* (Syncline, 1981), *The North Amer Rev, Blue
    Unicorn, Poetry Daily, ACM, College English, English Jrnl,
    Midwest Qtly, Ascent, Light, Poetry, Poet Lore*

Rick Christman 🎤 ✈   W
6601 Lincoln Ave
Des Moines, IA 50322, 515-276-9317
    Pubs: *Falling in Love at the End of the World, The Party
    Train: Anth* (New Rivers Pr, 1998, 1996), *Clackamas Lit Rev,
    The Mochila Rev, Descant, River Oak Rev, Indiana Rev,
    River City, Red Rock Rev, Permafrost, Alembic*

Robert Dana   P
1466 Westview Dr
Coralville, IA 52241, 319-354-2171
Internet: robertdana@aol.com
    Pubs: *Hello Stranger: Beach Poems, Yes, Everything*
    (Another Chicago Pr, 1996, 1994), *Kenyon Rev, Manoa,
    Witness, Georgia Rev, High Plains Lit Rev*

Irma Dovey   P
1224 13th St NW, #321
Cedar Rapids, IA 52405-2404, 319-363-1966
    Pubs: *Long About Tuesday* (Dovey, 1989), *Lyrical Iowa:
    Anths* (Iowa Poetry Association, 1995, 1994, 1990),
    Midwest Chaparral, Thirteen, Quickenings, Story Friends

Jim Dunlap   P
2830 Brattleboro #2
Des Moines, IA 50311-4008, 515-279-3540
Internet: rhyme_master@yahoo.com
    Pubs: *Mobius, Dream Intl Qtly, Infinity Limited, Mind in
    Motion, Prophetic Voices, Candelabrum, Plainsongs, Stand
    Alone, Lyrical Iowa, Potpourri, Paris/Atlantic*

Gary Eller   W
1243 24th St
Ames, IA 50010, 515-232-4654
Internet: gbe4@aol.com
    Pubs: *Thin Ice & Other Risks* (New Rivers, 1994), *Flyway,
    Other Voices, Crescent Rev, River City, Sidewalks, New
    Press*

Jocelyn Emerson   P
English Dept, Univ of Iowa, 308 EPB, Iowa City, IA 52242
    Pubs: *Carolina Qtly, Colorado Rev, Common Lives/Lesbian
    Lives, Cosmos, Denver Qtly, The Jrnl, Seneca Rev,
    Sojourner, NAW*

William Ford 🎤 ✈   P
10 Forest Glen
Iowa City, IA 52245-1625, 319-354-1834
    Pubs: *The Graveyard Picnic* (Mid-America Pr, 2002), *Poetry,
    Iowa Rev, Southern Humanities Rev, The Pedestal,
    Pennsylvania Rev, Three Rivers Poetry Jrnl*

Harvey Hess   P
Professor of Enlgish Lang and Lit, University of Northern Iowa,
Cedar Falls, IA 50613
Internet: harvey.hess@uni.edu
    Pubs: *Skipped Stones: Faces in Time* (Eight Pound Tiger Pr,
    1994), *The Kona Coffee Cantata, Orchid Art & the Orchid
    Isle, The Singing Snails* (Malama Arts, 1985, 1982, 1980),
    Hawaii Lyrics (Finial, 1982)

Phillip H. Hey   P
2750 Malloy Rd
Sioux City, IA 51103, 712-277-2811
Internet: hey@briar-cliff.edu
    Pubs: *A Change of Clothes* (Celestial Light, 1989), *Voices
    on the Landscape: Anth* (Loess Hills Pr, 1996), *Zone 3,
    Art/Life, Briar Cliff Rev*

Jan D. Hodge 🎤 ✈   P
4920 Morningside Ave
Sioux City, IA 51106, 712-276-2999
Internet: jandhodge@aol.com
    Pubs: *Poems to Be Traded for Baklava* (Onionhead, 1997),
    Things Taking Shape (Harold's Pr, 1992), *Voices on the
    Landscape: Anth* (Loess Hills Pr, 1996), *NAR, Beloit Poetry
    Jrnl, South Coast Poetry Rev, ELF, Defined Providence*

Donald Justice   P
338 Rocky Shore Dr
Iowa City, IA 52246
    Pubs: *Orpheus Hesitated Beside the Black River* (Anvil Pr,
    1998), *New & Selected Poems* (Knopf, 1995)

Juliet Yli-Mattila Kaufmann   P
428 Clark St
Iowa City, IA 52240
    Pubs: *Cold Pastoral* (Virgil Burnett & Robert Williams, 1974),
    Lake Effect, Chicago Rev, Rochester Rev

Theodore Krieger ✈   P
PO Box 452
Charles City, IA 50616-0452, 641-228-2270
    Pubs: *Metal Monarch* (Plowman, 2000), *Bearing It Alone*
    (Ansuda, 1980), *Rattle, Comstock Rev, Maelstrom,
    Iconoclast, americas rev, Arachne, Sou'wester, Artword Qtly*

Rustin Larson   P
501 N C St
Fairfield, IA 52556, 515-472-1370
Internet: rlarson@lisco.com
    Pubs: *Voices on the Landscape: Anth* (Loess Hill Pr, 1996),
    *Iowa Rev, Cimarron Rev, William & Mary Rev, Passages
    North, New Yorker, Boundary 2, Poetry East, Indiana Rev,
    America*

Todd Lieber   W
789 Jesup St
Indianola, IA 50125, 515-961-7691
    Pubs: *Crazyhorse, Sycamore Rev, Nimrod, Mss., Missouri
    Rev, Yale Rev*

Lucille Gripp Maharry 🎤 ✈ P
300 N Sumner Ave
Creston, IA 50801-2041
    Pubs: *Pausing on the Attic Steps, Suddenly I Am Home*
    (Celestial Light, 2000, 1996), *Upper Case, Lyrical Iowa, The
    Pen Women, Bear Creek Haiku, Decision, Sunday Digest,
    Secret Place, Delta Kappa Gamma Bulletin, Bible Advocate*

Julie McDonald W
2802 E Locust St
Davenport, IA 52803-3430, 563-355-7246
Internet: jmcdonad@saunix.sau.edu
    Pubs: *The Watkins Man, North of the Heart* (1st Bks, 2001,
    2000)

James McKean 🎤 ✈ P
1164 E Court St
Iowa City, IA 52240-3232, 319-338-3976
    Pubs: *Tree of Heaven* (U Iowa Pr, 1995), *Headlong* (U Utah
    Pr, 1987), *Georgia Rev, Poetry, Southern Rev, Ironwood,
    Poetry NW, Seneca Rev, Iowa Rev*

James McPherson 🎤 ✈ W
711 Rundell St
Iowa City, IA 52240, 319-338-3136
    Pubs: *A Region Not Home, Crabcakes* (S&S, 2000, 1998),
    Fathering Daughters: Anth (Beacon Pr, 1998), *DoubleTake,
    Iowa Rev, Center Eight*

Gordon W. Mennenga W
1805 Windsor Ct
Iowa City, IA 52245, 319-338-7255
    Pubs: *Oxford Mag, Folio, NAR, Foothills Qtly, Seems, Seven*

Christopher Merrill 🎤 ✈ P&W
216 McLean St
Iowa City, IA 52246, 319-354-8197
Internet: christopher_merrill@uiowa.edu
    Pubs: *Watch Fire* (White Pine Pr, 1994), *The Grass of
    Another Country* (H Holt, 1993), *Paris Rev, Nation, Sierra,
    APR*

Chuck Miller P
PO Box 2814
Iowa City, IA 52244, 319-335-9223
    Pubs: *How in the Morning* (Spirit That Moves Us Pr, 1989),
    From Oslo (Friends Pr, 1988), *Harvesters* (Coffee Hse Pr,
    1984)

Eleanora Miller P
208 SW Church St
Leon, IA 50144-1349, 515-446-4401
    Pubs: *Interviewing the Ghosts* (Elm Grove Bks, 2001),
    Lyrical Iowa: Anth (Iowa Poetry Assn, 1999), *A Song of
    Myself: Anth* (CSS Pub, 1987), *Polestar, Sandcutters, Cats*

James Minor P
1450 Alta Vista St
Dubuque, IA 52001-4327
    Pubs: *Against the Night, A Measure of Light* (Juniper Pr,
    1986, 1984), *New Cicada, Northeast*

Nancy Price P&W
English Language & Literature Dept., Univ Northern Iowa,
Cedar Falls, IA 50614, 319-273-2821
    Pubs: *Two Liars and a Bride, Un Ecart de Jeunesse,
    L'Incendiaire* (Presses de la Cité, 2003, 2000, 1998), *Night
    Woman* (Pocket Bks, 1992), *Sleeping With the Enemy* (S&S,
    1987), *An Accomplished Woman* (Coward McCann
    Geoghegan, 1979)

Keith Ratzlaff 🎤 ✈ P
306 Liberty
Pella, IA 50219-1753, 515-628-8466
Internet: ratzlaffk@central.edu
    Pubs: *Man Under a Pear Tree* (Anhinga Pr, 1997), *Across
    the Known World* (Loess Hills Pr, 1997), *New Winter Light*
    (Nightshade Pr, 1994), *Out Here* (State Street Pr, 1984),
    Poets of the New Century: Anth (D. Godine, 2001), *NAR,
    Poetry NW, Jrnl, NER*

James Calvin Schaap 🎤 ✈ W
Dordt College, English Dept, Sioux Center, IA 51250,
712-722-6250
Internet: jschaap@dordt.edu
    Pubs: *Things Hoped For, Things Not Seen, Romey's Place,
    The Secrets of Barneveld Calvary, In the Silence There Are
    Ghosts* (Baker Bks, 2003, 1999, 1997, 1995), *Paternity:
    Stories* (Quiddity Pr, 2002), *Called to Die* (Eerdmans, 1994),
    Prairie Schooner

Sheryl St. Germain P
Dept of English, Iowa State Univ, Ross 203, Ames, IA
50011-1201, 515-294-8211
Internet: sgermain@iastate.edu
    Pubs: *The Journals of Scheherazade, How Heavy the
    Breath of God* (U North Texas Pr, 1996, 1994), *Making
    Bread at Midnight* (Slough Pr, 1992), *TriQtly, 5 A.M., Calyx*

Mary Helen Stefaniak 🎤 ✈ W
PO Box 2134
Iowa City, IA 52244-2134, 319-354-8515
Internet: mhs@creighton.edu
    Pubs: *Self Storage & Other Stories* (New Rivers Pr 1997), *A
    Sweet Secret: Anth* (Toronto; Second Story Pr, 1997),
    *Antioch Rev, Epoch, Iowa Rev, Nebraska Rev, NAR, Iowa
    Woman, Yale Rev, Calyx, Crescent Rev, Agni, Seattle Rev,
    Redbook*

Ann Struthers   🎤   ✈   P&W
503 Forest Dr SE
Cedar Rapids, IA 52403-4234, 319-362-3764
Internet: astruthe@coe.edu
    Pubs: *The Alcott Family Arrives* (Coe Rev Pr, 1993),
    Stoneboat & Other Poems (Pterodactyl Pr, 1988), *NAR,*
    Hampton-Sydney Rev, Calyx, The New Renaissance,
    Poetry, Hudson Rev, Amer Scholar, Iowa Woman

James Sutton   🎤   ✈   P
4324 Kingman Blvd
Des Moines, IA 50311-3418, 515-255-7031
Internet: jamessutton@juno.com
    Pubs: *Minnesota Rev, Phi Delta Kappan, College English,*
    Teacher, Stand Alone

Cole Swensen   P
Iowa Writers' Workshop
Dey House
507 N Clinton
Iowa City, Iowa 52242, 319-351-0891
Internet: xoxcole@cs.com
    Pubs: *Noon* (Sun & Moon Pr, 1996), *Numen* (Burning Deck,
    1995), *Conjunctions, Zyzzyva, Five Fingers Rev, Common*
    Knowledge, Avec, o.blek

Jody Swilky   P
Drake Univ, 2707 University Ave, Des Moines, IA 50312,
515-271-2853
    Pubs: *A City of Fences* (La Huerta Pr, 1977), *NAR, Mid-*
    Amer Rev, Chelsea, New Boston Rev, Yale Rev, Raccoon,
    Ohio Rev, Missouri Rev, Georgia Rev

Thomas Swiss   P
Drake Univ, English Dept, Des Moines, IA 50311,
515-271-3777
    Pubs: *Measure* (U Alabama, 1986), *Ploughshares, Amer*
    Scholar, Sewanee Rev

Fred Truck   P
4225 University
Des Moines, IA 50311, 515-255-3552
    Pubs: *Art Engine Texts* (Electric Bank, 1989), *Simulation*
    Stimulation (Art Com Electronic, 1986)

Melvin Wilk   P
3013 Terrace Dr
Des Moines, IA 50312, 515-255-3346
    Pubs: *In Exile* (BkMk Pr, 1979), *Mss, New Yorker, Poetry,*
    Massachusetts Rev

Frederic Will   P
617 7 St,N, Mt Vernon, IA 52314

Valorie Broadhurst Woerdehoff   🎤   ✈   P
3246 St Anne Dr
Dubuque, IA 52001-3951, 319-556-3534
Internet: vwoerde@loras.edu
    Pubs: How to Haiku: Anth, Haiku Moment: Anth (C.E. Tuttle
    Co, 2002, 1993),Haiku World: Anth (Kodansha America Inc,
    1996), Midwest Haiku: Anth (High/Coo Pr, 1992), *Modern*
    Haiku, Frogpond, Cottonwood Rev, Spoon River, Iowa
    Woman, 100 Words, Cicada

Ray A. Young Bear   P
751 Meskwaki Rd
Tama, IA 52339
Internet: blkeagle@pcpartner.net
    Pubs: *Black Eagle Child, Remnants of the First Earth*
    (Grove, 1997, 1996), *The Invisible Musician* (Holy Cow! Pr,
    1990), *Winter of the Salamander* (H&R, 1980), *Best*
    American Poetry: Anth (Scribner, 1996), *Ploughshares,*
    Akwekon

KANSAS

Marie A. Asner   🎤   ✈   P
PO Box 4343
Overland Park, KS 66204-0343
Internet: halmar9999@aol.com
    Pubs: *Tenebrae* (CSS Pubs, 2001), *3: An Interview of Poets,*
    Man of Miracles II: The Followers (New Spirit Pr, 1999,
    1994), *Angels* (Maka, 1998), *The Tree of Life* (Kindred Spirit
    Pr, 1996), *An Inquiring Mind* (Green Meadow Pr, 1993)

Thomas Fox Averill   🎤   ✈   W
Washburn Univ, 1700 College, Topeka, KS 66621,
913-231-1010
Internet: zzaver@washburn.edu
    Pubs: *Secrets of the Tsil CafÈ* (Blue Hen, 2001), *O. Henry*
    Award: Anth (Doubleday, 1991), *The Best of the West #4:*
    Anth (Norton, 1991), *NAR, Cimarron Rev, Cottonwood,*
    DoubleTake, Greensboro Rev

Gar Bethel   P
212 N Iowa
Winfield, KS 67156, 316-221-0939
    Pubs: *Small Wonder, Dust, Rivers & Stars* (Point Riders Pr,
    1996, 1992), *Fresh Eggs* (Wythe Hse Pr, 1992)

Donald Caswell   🎤   ✈   P
PO Box 171274
Kansas City, KS 66117, 913-321-7305
Internet: caswell@bigfoot.com
    Pubs: *Three-Legged Dog* (Anhinga Pr, 1999), *Fake*
    Picassos, The Boy That Was Made out of Wood (Wellberry
    Pr, 1994, 1991), *Poetry, New Letters, South Coast Poetry*
    Rev, Alaska Qtly Rev, Mid-Amer Rev, Apalachee Qtly

Victor Contoski P
4110 W 12 St
Lawrence, KS 66049, 913-842-5303
Pubs: *A Kansas Sequence* (Cottonwood-Tellus, 1983),
Names (New Rivers, 1979)

Marjorie Culver P
8027 W 113 St
Overland Park, KS 66210
Pubs: *Turn West at Jefferson* (Potpourri Pub Co, 1993), *A
Garden of Cucumbers* (Mid-America Pr, 1977), *Passager,
Missouri Poets, DeKalb Lit Arts*

Celia A. Daniels 🎙 ✈ P
1521 SW College Ave
Topeka, KS 66604-2759
Internet: cadaniel@ukans.edu
Pubs: *Fissures* (Singular Speech Pr, 1993), *Great Plains
Poets: Anth* (Midwest Qtly, 1995), *Common Journeys,
Sunflower Petals, Midwest Qtly, Cottonwood Rev, Nebraska
English Jrnl, Kansas Qtly, Spoon River Qtly, Inscape, Z-Misc*

A. A. Dewey P
PO Box 154
Eudora, KS 66025-0154, 913-842-1782
Pubs: *Heartland II: Poets of the Midwest: Anth* (Northern
Illinois U Pr, 1975), *Hanging Loose*

Bryan D. Dietrich 🎙 ✈ P
335 N Volutsia
Wichita, KS 67214
Internet: dietrichb@newmanu.edu
Pubs: *Paris Rev, Nimrod, Chelsea, Midwest Qtly, Prairie
Schooner, Western Humanities Rev, Bellingham Rev, NW
Rev, Qtly Rev*

Elizabeth Dodd 🎙 ✈ P
English Dept, Kansas State Univ, Manhattan, KS 66506,
785-532-0384
Internet: edodd@ksu.edu
Pubs: *Archetypal Light* (U Nevada Pr, 2001), *Like Memory,
Caverns* (NYU Pr, 1992), *Tar River Poetry, Seneca Rev,
Ascent, Crab Orchard Rev, Crazyhorse, High Plains
Literary Rev*

Carolyn Doty W
Univ Kansas, 1630 Barker, English Dept, Lawrence, KS
66044-3765, 785-843-6254
Internet: cdoty@kuhub.cc.ukans.edu
Pubs: *Whisper* (Scribner, 1992), *What She Told Him, Fly
Away Home, A Day Late* (Viking, 1985, 1982, 1980)

Harley Elliott P
328 E Beloit
Salina, KS 67401
Pubs: *The Monkey of Mulberry Pass* (Woodley Pr, 1991),
The Citizen Game (Basilisk Pr, 1988), *Darkness at Each
Elbow* (Hanging Loose Pr, 1981)

Albert Goldbarth P
English Dept, Wichita State Univ, Wichita, KS 67208,
316-683-6191
Pubs: *Marriage & Other Science Fiction* (Ohio State U Pr
1994), *Across the Layers: Poems Old & New* (U Georgia Pr,
1993), *New Yorker, Poetry, Paris Rev, Georgia Rev*

James Gunn 🎙 ✈ W
2215 Orchard Ln
Lawrence, KS 66049, 785-864-3380
Internet: jgunn@falcon.cc.ukans.edu
Pubs: *Human Voices* (Henan People's Pub Hse, 1999), *The
Joy Machine, The Mind Masters* (Pocket Bks, 1996, 1982),
Crisis! (Tor, 1986), *The Unpublished Gunn, Part Two, Tiger!
Tiger!* (Drumm, 1996, 1984), *Analog, Sci Fi Age*

Michael Hathaway 🎙 ✈ P
702 N Prairie
St John, KS 67576-1516, 620-786-4955
http://www.geocities.com/SoHo/Nook/1748
Pubs: *Cosmic Children* (Chiron Rev Pr, 2001), *Obsessed: A
Flesh & the Word Collection of Gay Erotica: Anth* (Penguin,
1999), *A Day for a Lay: A Century of Gay Poetry: Anth*
(Barricade, 1999), *Always the Beautiful Answer: Anth* (King's
Estate Pr, 1999)

Stephen Hathaway W
English Dept, Wichita State Univ, Wichita, KS 67208,
316-689-3130
Pubs: *A Kind of Redemption* (Louisiana State U Pr, 1990),
Accent on Fiction, Itinerary Four, Kansas Qtly

Jeanine Hathaway 🎙 ✈ P&W
Wichita State Univ, Box 14, Wichita, KS 67260-0014,
316-978-6696
Pubs: *The Self as Constellation* (U N Texas Pr, 2002),
Motherhouse (Hyperion, 1993), *Best Spiritual Writing: Anth*
(HarperSF, 2000), *DoubleTake, Image, Georgia Rev, Ohio
Rev, New Orleans Rev*

Steve F. Heller W
English Dept, Denison Hall, Kansas State Univ, Manhattan,
KS 66506, 913-532-6716
Pubs: *The Automotive History of Lucky Kellerman*
(Doubleday, 1989), *Chariton Rev*

Steven Hind P
Woodley Press, Washburn Univ, 1700 SW College, Topeka,
KS 66621
Pubs: *In a Place With No Map* (Woodley Pr, 1997), *That Trick
of Silence* (Ctr for Kansas Studies, 1990), *Anth of Magazine
Verse & Yearbook of American Poetry* (Monitor, 1997)

Jonathan Holden 🎤 ✈ P
Kansas State Univ, Denison Hall, English Dept, Manhattan,
KS 66506, 785-532-0388
Internet: jonhold@ksu.edu
    Pubs: *Knowing: New & Selected Poems* (U Arkansas Pr,
2000), *The Sublime* (U Texas Pr, 1996), *American Gothic* (U
Georgia Pr, 1992), *Against Paradise* (U Utah Pr, 1990), *The
Name of the Rapids* (U Massachusetts Pr, 1985)

Robert B. Hutchinson P&W
Regency Health Care Center, 915 McNair, Halstead, KS
67056, 316-835-2276
    Pubs: *Standing Still* (Eakins, 1971), *Poetry, Harper's,
Atlantic*

Kenneth Irby P
English Dept, Univ of Kansas, Lawrence, KS 66045,
913-864-3118
    Pubs: *Call Steps* (Station Hill/Tansy, 1992), *A Set, Catalpa*
(Tansy, 1983, 1977), *Orexis* (Station Hill, 1981)

Michael L. Johnson P
1621 N 1st St
Baldwin City, KS 66006-6901, 785-594-4823
    Pubs: *XY Files: Poems on the Male Experience: Anth*
(Sherman Asher, 1997), *Violence & Grace* (Cottonwood Pr,
1993), *Owen Wister Rev, Rhino, Oregon Rev, Chouteau
Rev, Midwest Qtly, Sequoia, Roanoke Rev, Lit Rev*

Ronald Johnson P
1422 Tyler
Topeka, KS 66612
    Pubs: *Ark* (drive he said pr, 1996), *Eyes & Objects* (Jargon
Pr, 1976), *Conjunctions, Sulfur, Chicago Rev, Sagetrieb,
Parnassus, Occident*

Denise Low 🎤 ✈ P
1916 Stratford Rd
Lawrence, KS 66044-4540
Internet: dlowweso@ross1.cc.haskell.edu
    Pubs: *New and Selected Poems, Touching the Sky: Essays,
Tulip Elegies* (Penthe, 1999, 1993, 1993), *Vanishing Point*
(Mulberry Pr, 1991), *Starwater* (Cottonwood Pr, 1988), *NAR,
Connecticut Rev, Flint Hills Rev, Cottonwood, Chariton Rev,
Faultline*

Stephen Meats 🎤 ✈ P&W
2310 E 8 St
Pittsburg, KS 66762, 316-231-2998
Internet: smeats@pittstate.edu
    Pubs: *Looking for the Pale Eagle: Poems, Kansas Stories:
Anth* (Woodley, 1994, 1989), *Hurakan, Leftbank Rev, The
Qtly, Blue Unicorn, Poetry East, Tampa Rev*

W. R. Moses 🎤 P
314 Denison Ave
Manhattan, KS 66502, 785-537-1954
    Pubs: *Tu Fu Poems, Edges, Memoir, Double View* (Juniper
Pr, 1996, 1994, 1992, 1984)

Michael Paul Novak 🎤 ✈ P
Saint Mary College, Leavenworth, KS 66048, 913-682-5151
Internet: novakm@hub.smcks.edu
    Pubs: *From the Tower* (Forest of Peace, 1996), *Whatever
Flames Upon the Night* (Potpourri, 1994), *A Story to Tell*
(BkMk Pr, 1990), *Kenyon Rev, Confrontation, Hudson Rev,
New Letters*

Emanuela O'Malley P
Box 279 Nazareth
Concordia, KS 66901, 913-243-2113
    Pubs: *Cloud of Darkness: The Pain of Apartheid* (Winston-
Derek, 1990)

Cynthia S. Pederson 🎤 ✈ P
1521 SW College Ave
Topeka, KS 66604, 785-232-0332
Internet: pederson@ccp.com
    Pubs: *Fissures* (Singular Speech Pr, 1993), *Of Frogs &
Toads: Anth* (Ione, 1998), *Climb Into My Lap: Anth, Call
Down the Moon: Anth* (S&S, 1998, 1995), *Roll Along: Anth*
(Macmillan, 1993), *Midwest Qtly, Poets On, Cottonwood,
Great River Rev, Kansas Qtly*

Antonia Quintana Pigno P
Modern Languages Dept, Kansas State Univ, Eisenhower
Hall, Manhattan, KS 66506, 785-532-1924
Internet: apigno@ksu.edu
    Pubs: *Old Town Bridge, La Jornada* (Zauberberg Pr, 1987,
1987), *Kenyon Rev, Kansas Qtly, Puerto del Sol, Cyphens,
Writers' Forum, Ploughshares*

Trish Reeves 🎤 ✈ P
5307 W 51 St
Roeland Park, KS 66205-1242
Internet: seachanger@aol.com
    Pubs: *In the Knees of the Gods* (U Missouri-Kansas Cty Pr,
2001), *Returning the Question* (Cleveland State U Pr, 1988),
New Letters, Ploughshares, Ironwood

R. Stephen Russell P
English Dept/Box 14, Wichita State Univ, Wichita, KS 67208,
316-689-3130
    Pubs: *Paris Rev, Carleton Miscellany, Denver Qtly, Kansas
Qtly, Midwest Qtly, Impact*

Mark Scheel 🎤 ✈ P&W
5738 Maple Dr
Shawnee Mission, KS 66202-2723, 913-262-4281
Internet: markscheel@hotmail.com
    Pubs: *A Backward View* (5th Street Irregulars Pr & Leathers
Pub, 1998), *Poet, Kansas Qtly, Cincinnati Poetry Rev, Facet,
Telescope*

Ann Slegman   P&W
6531 Overbrook, Shawnee Mission, KS 66208-1941,
913-362-7885
Internet: slegdog@aol.com
  Pubs: *Return to Sender, Spud Songs: Anth* (Helicon Nine
  Edtns, 1995, 1999), *The Same, Coal City Rev, New Letters,
  Helicon Nine, Kansas City Star*

Wyatt Townley ♀ ✈   P
PO Box 13302
Shawnee Mission, KS 66282-4307, 913-381-1984
  Pubs: *The Breathing Field* (Little, Brown, 2002), *Perfectly
  Normal* (The Smith, 1990), *Ravishing Disunities: Anth*
  (Wesleyan U Pr, 2000), *Prayers for a Thousand Years: Anth*
  (HC, 1999), *JM: A Remembrance: Anth* (Academy of
  American Poets, 1996)

Roderick Townley ♀ ✈   P&W
PO Box 13302
Shawnee Mission, KS 66282-4307, 913-381-1984
  Pubs: *Into the Labyrinth, The Great Good Thing* (Atheneum,
  2002, 2001), *Final Approach* (Countryman Pr, 1986), *Minor
  Gods* (St. Martin's Pr, 1977), *Paris Rev, NAR, Yale Rev, New
  Letters*

Donna Trussell ♀ ✈   P&W
7520 Briar
Prairie Village, KS 66208, 913-648-1632
Internet: mensawhitetrash@aol.com
  Pubs: *Texas Bound Book II: Anth* (Southern Methodist U Pr,
  1998), *Growing Up Female: Anth* (Mentor/Penguin, 1993),
  New Stories from the South: Anth (Algonquin Bks, 1990),
  NAR, TriQtly, Poetry, Chicago Rev, Poetry NW

KENTUCKY

Rebecca Bailey ♀ ✈   P&W
2465 Rock Fork Rd
Morehead, KY 40351, 606-783-1811
Internet: r.bailey@morehead-st.edu
  Pubs: *A Wild Kentucky Garden* (Jesse Stuart Fdn, 1998),
  Reign of the Girl-King (Esterling Pr, 1998), *Three Women
  Alone in the Woods* (Trillium, 1992), *Literal Latte, Jrnl of
  Kentucky Studies, Asheville Poetry Rev, Emrys Jrnl*

Garry Barker ♀ ✈   P&W
692 Orchard Rd
Bald Hill, KY 41041, 606-845-0707
Internet: garrybarker@netscape.net
  Pubs: *Notes From a Native Son, Appalachia Inside Out:
  Anth* (U Tennessee Pr, 1995, 1995), *Groundwater: Anth*
  (Lexington Pr, 1992), *Appalachian Heritage, M Mag, Arts
  Across Kentucky, Mountain Spirit.*

Joy Bale Boone   P
PO Box 188
Elkton, KY 42220-0188

Pat Carr   W
Western Kentucky Univ, English Dept, Bowling Green, KY
42101, 502-745-5998
  Pubs: *Sonahchi* (Cinco Puntos Pr, 1994), *Our Brother's War*
  (Sulgrave Pr, 1993), *Southern Rev, Southern Mag, Texas
  Monthly, Kansas Qtly, Arizona Qtly*

Rick Clewett   P
English Dept, Eastern Kentucky Univ, Lexington, KY 40475,
606-272-4247
  Pubs: *Salome, Encore, Bitterroot, Confrontation, Poetry
  Mag, Pudding, Samisdat, Microcosm*

Jenny Galloway Collins ♀ ✈   P&W
25 Wolfpen Dr
Thornton, KY 41855
  Pubs: *A Cave & A Cracker* (Elkhorn Pub, 1996), *Blackberry
  Tea* (Appalapple Productions, 1988), *Appalachian Heritage,
  Back Home in Kentucky*

Guy Davenport   P&W
621 Sayre Ave
Lexington, KY 40508, 606-257-6972
  Pubs: *Charles Burchfield's Seasons* (Pomegranate Bks,
  1994), *A Table of Green Fields* (New Directions, 1993),
  Antaeus, New Criterion, Yale Rev

Judith Degroote ♀ ✈   P
Box 72, 2nd St, Corydon, KY 42406, 502-533-6753
  Pubs: *Visions Intl, Blue Unicorn, Phoenix, Birmingham
  Poetry Rev, South Florida Poetry Rev, Thema, Another
  Small Mag*

Kim Edwards   W
2929 Montavesta
Lexington, KY 40502

Normandi Ellis   W
2369 Sullivan Ln
Frankfort, KY 40601
Internet: normandi@aol.com
  Pubs: *Voice Forms* (Watersign Pr, 1998), *Sorrowful
  Mysteries* (Arrowood Bks, 1991), *Agni Rev, Appalachian
  Heritage, Southern Humanities Rev, Between C & D, New
  Blood, Mediphors, Wind*

Jane Gentry   P
c/o Jane Gentry Vance, 340 Morgan St, Versailles, KY 40383,
606-873-5700
Internet: jgvanc00@ukcc.uky.edu
  Pubs: *A Garden in Kentucky* (LSU Pr, 1995), *Cries of the
  Spirit* (Beacon Pr, 1990), *Elvis in Oz: Hollins Writing
  Program Anth* (U Pr Virginia, 1992), *Amer Voice*

Sarah Gorham 🎤 ✈   P
Sarabande Books, 2234 Dundee Rd, Ste 200, Louisville, KY
40205, 502-458-4028
Internet: sarabandes@aol.com
    Pubs: *The Cure, The Tension Zone* (Four Way Bks, 2003,
1996), *Don't Go Back to Sleep* (Galileo Pr, 1989), *APR,
DoubleTake, Paris Rev, Poetry, Georgia Rev, Ohio Rev,
Grand Street*

Jonathan Greene 🎤 ✈   P
PO Box 475
Frankfort, KY 40602-0475, 502-223-1858
Internet: jgnomon@aol.com
    Pubs: *Fault Lines* (Larkspur Pr, 2002), *A Little Ink in the
Paper Sea* (Tangram, 2001), *Of Moment, Inventions of
Necessity* (Gnomon Pr, 1998, 1998)

Robert Gregory   P
706 Hambrick Ave
Lexington, KY 40508, 859-455-9114
Internet: rdgreg0@pop.uky.edu
    Pubs: *Change* (The Skinny Man) (Lynx Hse, 2003), *Clouds
& Green Police* (Mudlark, 2001), *Boy Picked Up the Wind*
(Bluestem Pr, 1992), *Good Foot, Willow Springs, Amherst
Rev, Hanging Loose, Diagram, Many Mountains Moving,
Grasslands, Berkeley Poetry Rev*

James Baker Hall   P&W
617 Dividing Ridge Rd S
Sadieville, KY 40370, 859-234-6481
    Pubs: *Yates Paul, His Grand Flights, His Tootings* (U
Kentucky Pr, 2002), *Praeder's Letters, The Mother on the
Other Side of the World* (Sarabande Bks, 2002, 2001), *Fast
Signing Mute* (Larkspur Pr, 1993), *New Yorker,
Ploughshares, Hudson Rev, Paris Rev*

Wade Hall   P
1568 Cherokee Rd
Louisville, KY 40205, 502-451-5516
Internet: adeway@aol.com
    Pubs: *Conecuh People* (Black Belt Pr, 1999), *Passing for
Black, Hell-Bent for Music: The Life of Pee Wee King, The
Rest of the Dream: Black Odyssey of Lyman Johnson* (U Pr
Kentucky, 1997, 1996, 1988), *Jefferson Rev*

Marcia L. Hurlow 🎤 ✈   P
Asbury College, Wilmore, KY 40390-1198, 859-223-1579
Internet: hurlow9@aol.com
    Pubs: *A Tree Ogham* (Nova Hse, 2002), *Dangers of Travel*
(Riverstone, 1994), *Aliens Are Intercepting My Brain Waves*
(State St Pr, 1991), *Karamu, Spoon River, Wind, Nimrod,
Poetry, Poetry NW, Poetry Wales, Chicago Rev, ACM,
Malahat Rev*

Ann Jonas 🎤 ✈   P
2425 Ashwood Dr
Louisville, KY 40205-2439, 502-459-0701
    Pubs: *Kentucky Authors-200 Yrs: Anth* (Kentucky U Pr,
2003), *So Small This Arc* (The Clandestine Pr, 2002),
Writing Who We Are: Anth (Western Kentucky U Pr, 1999),
Ipso Facto: Anth (Hub Pub, 1975), *Louisville Rev, Chaffin
Jrnl, Amer Voice, Poetry Rev, Orbis*

Gayl Jones   P
440 Locust Ave
Lexington, KY 40505
    Pubs: *Song for Anninho* (Lotus, 1981), *Callaloo,
Ploughshares, Obsidian*

Jane Wilson Joyce   P
Classics Dept, Centre College, Danville, KY 40422,
606-236-5211
    Pubs: *Appalachian Heritage, Sing Heavenly Muse!, Laurel
Rev, Appalachian Jrnl, Poet Lore*

Tamara Kennelly   W
Rt 3
Owenton, KY 40359
Internet: tjk@vt.edu

Kenneth King 🎤 ✈   P
POB 1015
Somerset, KY 42502, 606-423-3553
Internet: kenneth_e@eudoramail.com
    Pubs: *Poetry NW, College English, NW Rev, Kansas Qtly,
Appalachian Jrnl*

Wallace E. Knight   W
819 16th St
Ashland, KY 41101, 606-324-0867
    Pubs: *Lightstruck* (Little, Brown, 1979), *The Literature of the
South* (Scribner, 1979), *Atlantic*

Karen S. Lee   P
12892 Hwy 42
Walton, KY 41094
    Pubs: *SPA's Finest: Anth* (Southern Poetry Assoc, 1992),
Riding on Golden Wings: Anth (Geryon Pr, 1989), *Feelings,
Kentucky Explorer, The Jrnl, Tucumcari Lit Rev, Instructor
Mag, Southern Poetry Assoc, Rio Grande Pr, Poetry Only,
Poetry Pr*

George Ella Lyon 🎤 ✈   P&W
913 Maywick Dr
Lexington, KY 40504, 859-278-3956
Internet: ginalyon2001@yahoo.com
    Pubs: *Mother to Tigers, Gina.Jamie.Father.Bear.,*
(Atheneum, 2003, 2002), *Where I'm From, Where Poems
Come From* (Absey & Co, 1999), *Counting on the Woods,*
(DK Ink, 1998), *The United States of Poetry: Anth* (Harry N.
Abrams, 1996), *Mossy Creek Reader*

Leah Maines 🎤 ✈   P
PO Box 76181
Highland Heights, KY 41076-0181
    Pubs: *Beyond the River* (Kentucky Writers Coalition Pr,
    2002), *Looking to the East with Western Eyes* (Finishing
    Line Pr, 1998), *Flyway, Nebo, Licking River Rev, Owen
    Wister Rev*

Davis McCombs 🎤 ✈   P
PO Box 1045
Munfordville, KY 42765-1045, 270-524-3593
Internet: dmmc69@aol.com
    Pubs: *Ultima Thule* (Yale U Pr, 2000)

Kristina McGrath   P&W
1214 Cherokee Rd
Louisville, KY 40204
    Pubs: *House Work* (Bridge Works, 2001), *Pushcart Prize
    XIV: Anth* (Pushcart Pr, 1989), *Iowa Rev, Paris Rev, Kenyon
    Rev, Amer Voice, Yale Rev, Harper's*

Judith Moffett   W
2336 Glensboro Rd
Lawrenceburg, KY 40342-9508
Internet: eirving@compuserve.com
    Pubs: *Homestead Year* (Lyons & Burford, 1995), *Time, Like
    an Ever-Rolling Stream, The Ragged World* (St. Martin's Pr,
    1992, 1991), *Pennterra* (Congdon & Weed, 1987), *Kenyon
    Rev, New Yorker, Poetry, Asimov's Sci Fi, Georgia Rev*

R. Meir Morton   P
3923 Central Ave
Louisville, KY 40218, 502-458-7396
    Pubs: *Pegasus, Reaching, Brentwood Bee*

Joseph Napora   P
2205 Moore St
Ashland, KY 41101, 606-324-1953
Internet: napora@ramlink.net
    Pubs: *The Walam Olum* (Greenfield Rev Pr, 1990), *Bloom
    Blood* (Bottom Dogs Pr, 1988), *Texture, First Intensity,
    Asheville Poetry Rev, Small Press Rev*

Alan Naslund 🎤 ✈   P&W
2028 Emerson Ave
Louisville, KY 40205-2512
Internet: alanaslund@aol.com
    Pubs: *Silk Weather* (Fleur-de-lis Pr, 1999), *Pleiades,
    Louisville Rev, Amelia, Jefferson Rev, Pegasus, Calliope,
    River City Rev*

Sena Jeter Naslund   W
English Dept, Univ Louisville, Louisville, KY 40208
    Pubs: *Ice Skating at the North Pole* (Ampersand, 1989),
    Michigan Qtly Rev, Georgia Rev, Amer Voice

Gurney Norman   W
43 1/2 Richmond Ave
Lexington, KY 40502, 606-269-9594
    Pubs: *Divine Rights Trip, Kinfolks* (Gnomon Pr, 1990, 1990),
    Crazy Quilt (Larkspur, 1990).

Rose Orlich   P
1345 Knapp Ave
Morehead, KY 40351-1141, 606-784-6384
    Pubs: *The Rosewood Poems* (Small Poetry Pr, 1996), *Rose-
    Bloom at My Fingertips* (Adams Pr, 1981), *Autumn Harvest:
    Anth* (Quill Bks, 2001), *America at the Millenium: Anth* (Intl
    Library of Poetry, 2000), *Wind, Catholic School Jrnl, Poet*

Phil Paradis   P
Northern Kentucky Univ, Literature & Language Dept,
Highland Heights, KY 41076, 606-572-6636
    Pubs: *Along the Path* (White Fields, 1996), *Something of
    Ourselves* (Cedar Creek Pr, 1994), *Poetry, Cimarron Rev,
    Amer Scholar, Poet & Critic, Tar River Poetry*

Lee Pennington   P&W
Univ Kentucky, PO Box 1036, Louisville, KY 40202,
502-584-0181
    Pubs: *Appalachian Quartet, The Scotian Women* (Arion Pr,
    1984, 1984), *Writer's Digest, Wind*

Nolan Porterfield   W
564 Boyce Fairview Rd
Alvaton, KY 42122-9648
    Pubs: *Sewanee Rev, NAR, Harper's*

Bruce Rogers   P
5615 Ridgecrest Rd
Louisville, KY 40218
    Pubs: *Starships* (Whippoorwill Pr, 1973), *Minnesota Rev,
    New Salt Creek Reader, Handsel, Dust*

Daryl Rogers 🎤 ✈   P
PO Box 24198
Lexington, KY 40524
Internet: river25rat@aol.com
    Pubs: *June 10, Malibu Drive* (March St Pr, 2001), *Chaffin
    Journal, Black Bear Rev, Blue Beat Jacket, Chiron Rev,
    Parting Gifts, Clutch, Krax, Abbey, Atom Mind, Fuck!, Sepia,
    Dufus, Slipstream, Graffiti Rag, Main Street Rag*

Jeffrey Skinner 🎤 ✈   P&W
Director of Creative Writing, Univ Louisville, College of Arts &
Sciences, Louisville, KY 40292, 502-588-5920
Internet: jtskin01@aol.com
    Pubs: *Gender Studies* (Miami University Pr, 2002), *The
    Company of Heaven* (U Pitt Pr, 1992), *Real Toads in
    Imaginary Gardens* (Chicago Rev Pr, 1991), *Last Call: Anth*
    (Sarabande Bks, 1997), *Atlantic*

Frederick Smock   P&W
Bellarmine College, 2001 Newburg Rd, Louisville, KY 40205,
502-452-8000
　　Pubs: *Gardencourt: Poems* (Larkspur Pr, 1997), *Iowa Rev,*
　　Poetry, Intl Qtly, Poet & Critic

Philip St. Clair 🎤 ✈   P
Ashland Community College, 1400 College Dr, Ashland, KY
41101
Internet: philip.stclair@kctcs.edu
　　Pubs: *Acid Creek* (Bottom Dog Pr, 1997), *Little-Dog-of-Iron,*
　　At the Tent of Heaven (Ahsahta Pr, 1985, 1984), *Harper's,*
　　Cincinnati Poetry Rev, Gettysburg Rev, Greensboro Rev,
　　Minnesota Rev, Ploughshares, Black Warrior Rev,
　　Chattahoochee Rev, Shenandoah

Martha Bennett Stiles   W
861 Hume-Bedford Rd
Paris, KY 40361, 606-987-4158
　　Pubs: *Lonesome Road* (Gnomon Pr, 1998), *Kate of Still*
　　Waters, Sarah the Dragon Lady (Macmillan, 1990, 1986),
　　Esquire, TriQtly, Georgia Rev, Virginia Qtly Rev, Missouri
　　Rev, New Orleans Rev, Horsemen's Jrnl

James Still   P&W
Univ Press Kentucky, PO Box 865, Hindman, KY 41822
　　Pubs: *An Appalachian Mother Goose, Sporty Creek, Jack &*
　　the Wonder Beans, The Wolfpen Notebooks, The Wolfpen
　　Poems, Pattern of a Man, The Run for the Elbertas (U Pr
　　Kentucky Pr, 1998, 1998, 1996, 1991, 1986, 1976, 1953),
　　Amer Voice

George Strange   W
347 Wolf Gap Rd
Berea, KY 40403, 606-986-1257
　　Pubs: *Lullwater Rev, Descant, Appalachian Heritage,*
　　Habersham Rev

Jane Stuart   P&W
1000 W-Hollow Rd
Greenup, KY 41144
　　Pubs: *A Heart Shaped Moon, Candlelady* (Cameo, 2002,
　　2002), *Sestinas* (Cameo, 2000), *Journeys* (Summit Poetry
　　Pr, 1998), *Moon Over Miami* (Poetry Forum Pr, 1995),
　　Passage Into Time (Big Easy Pr, 1994), *Bloodroot: Anth* (U
　　Kentucky Pr, 1998), *Byron Poetry Works*

Joe Survant 🎤 ✈   P
English Dept, Western Kentucky Univ, Bowling Green, KY
42101, 270-745-5709
Internet: joesurvant@home.com
　　Pubs: *Rafting Rise* (Univ Pr of Florida, 2002), *The Presence*
　　of Snow in the Tropics (Singapore:Landmark Bks, 2001),
　　Anne & Alpheus, 1842-1882 (U Arkansas Pr, 1996), *We Will*
　　All Be Changed (State Street Pr, 1995), *Ring of Words: Anth*
　　(Sutton Pub Ltd, 1998)

Dorothy Sutton 🎤 ✈   P&W
Eastern Kentucky Univ, Dept of English, Richmond, KY 40475,
859-623-6071
Internet: dorothy.sutton@eku.edu
　　Pubs: *Startling Art* (Finishing Line Pr 1999), *Darwin: Anth*
　　(Norton, 2001), *Poetry, Hudson Rev, Poetry Ireland Rev,*
　　Southern Rev, Poetry Wales, Virginia Qtly Rev,
　　Shenandoah, Prairie Schooner, Antioch Rev, Carolina Qtly

Lynne Taetzsch   W
105 Country East
Morehead, KY 40351, 606-784-6905
Internet: l.taetzsch@morehead-st.edu
　　Pubs: *Hippo, Eotu, Pacific Rev, Asylum, Atticus Rev, Potato*
　　Eyes

Richard Taylor   P&W
335 Holt Ln
Frankfort, KY 40601, 502-223-5775
　　Pubs: *Earth Bones* (Gnomon Pr, 1979), *Girty* (Turtle Island
　　Foundation, 1977)

Jeff Worley   P
136 Shawnee Pl
Lexington, KY 40503, 606-277-0257
Internet: jworley@pop.uky.edu
　　Pubs: *A Simple Human Motion* (Larkspur Pr, 2000), *The*
　　Only Time There Is (Mid-List Pr, 1995), *Natural Selections*
　　(w/Lance Olsen; Still Waters Pr, 1993), *New Virginia Rev,*
　　Missouri Rev, Boulevard, Yankee College English,
　　Threepenny Rev, Poetry NW

LOUISIANA

Thomas Atkins   W
Univ New Orleans, Drama & Communications Dept, New
Orleans, LA 70148, 504-286-6345
　　Pubs: *The Blue Man, The Fire Came By* (Doubleday, 1978,
　　1976)

Fredrick Barton   W
63 Versailles Blvd
New Orleans, LA 70125, 504-861-1668
　　Pubs: *With Extreme Prejudice* (Villard/Random Hse, 1993),
　　The El Cholo Feeling Passes (Dell, 1988), *Xavier Rev,*
　　Louisiana Lit 99, Cresset

John Biguenet   P&W
Loyola Univ, Box 50, English Dept, New Orleans, LA 70118,
504-865-2474
Internet: biguenet@loyno.edu
　　Pubs: *Foreign Fictions* (Vintage, 1978), *NAR, Witness,*
　　Ploughshares, Boulevard, Threepenny Rev, Georgia Rev,
　　Granta, Story

Thomas Bonner, Jr. 🎙 ⊀   P&W
25 W Park Pl
New Orleans, LA 70124, 504-488-9014
    Pubs: *Louisiana Rev, War, Lit and the Arts, Xavier Rev,
    Potpourri, Maple Leaf Rag, New Laurel Rev, Negative
    Capability, Old Hickory Rev, Bluegrass Lit Rev*

Vance Bourjaily   W
c/o English Dept, Louisiana State Univ, Baton Rouge, LA
70803, 504-388-2862
    Pubs: *Old Soldier* (Donald I. Fine, 1990), *The Great Fake
    Book* (Weidenfeld & Nicolson, 1987), *A Game Men Play*
    (Dial, 1980)

Catharine Savage Brosman 🎙 ⊀   P
1550 2nd St #7-I
New Orleans, LA 70130, 504-899-6016
Internet: cbrosman@tulane.edu
    Pubs: *Places in Mind* (LSU Pr, 2000), *Passages, Journeying
    From Canyon de Chelly* (Louisiana State U Pr, 1996, 1990),
    The Swimmer and Other Poems, Abiding Winter (R. L.
    Barth, 2000, 1983), *South Carolina Rev, Snowy Egret,
    Southern Humanities Rev, Sewanee Rev*

Maxine Cassin 🎙 ⊀   P
2131 General Pershing St
New Orleans, LA 70115-5437,
504-891-3458
Internet: maxine_cassin@yahoo.com
    Pubs: *The Other Side of Sleep* (Portals Pr, 1995), *Turnip's
    Blood* (Sisters Grim Pr, 1985), *Uncommonplace: Anth* (LSU
    Pr, 1998), *Chicago Rev, New Republic, New York Times*

Christopher Chambers   P&W
934 St Roch Ave
New Orleans, LA 70117
Internet: chambers@loyno.edu
    Pubs: *This Is What I Hear* (Stillwater Pr, 1997), *Gettysburg
    Rev, Carolina Qtly, Epoch, Washington Square, Crazyhorse,
    3rd Bed, Bomb Mag, Exquisite Corpse, Florida Rev,
    Hayden's Ferry Rev, Mid-Amer Rev, Quarter After Eight,
    Qtly West*

Andrei Codrescu 🎙 ⊀   P&W
Louisiana State Univ, English Dept, Baton Rouge, LA
70803-0001
    Pubs: *Messiah* (S&S, 1999), *A Bar in Brooklyn, Alien
    Candor* (Black Sparrow, 1999, 1998), *License to Carry a
    Gun* (Carnegie Mellon U Pr, 1998)

Carlos Colon 🎙 ⊀   P
185 Lynn Ave
Shreveport, LA 71105-3523, 318-868-8932
Internet: ccolon@shreve.net
    Pubs: *In the Ship's Wake: Anth* (Iron Pr, 2001), *Thin Curve:
    Anth* (Red Moon Pr, 2000), *Haiku World: Anth* (Kodansha
    Intl, 1996), *Louisiana Lit, Louisiana English Jrnl, Modern
    Haiku, Writer's Digest, Frogpond, Piedmont Literary Rev*

Peter Cooley 🎙 ⊀   P
English Dept, Tulane Univ, New Orleans, LA 70118,
504-862-8174
Internet: pjcooley@msn.com
    Pubs: *A Place Made of Starlight, Sacred Conversations, The
    Astonished Hours, The Van Gogh Notebook* (Carnegie
    Mellon, 2003, 1998, 1992, 1987), *New Yorker, Atlantic,
    Poetry, Esquire, Nation, New Republic*

Pearl Garrett Crayton   P&W
1727 Harvard St
Alexandria, LA 71301, 318-449-1720
    Pubs: *Kente Cloth: Anth* (U of North Texas Pr, 1997), *Rites
    of Passage: Anth* (Hyperion Bks, 1994), *Trials, Tribulations,
    & Celebrations: Anth* (Intercultural Pr, 1992), *Out of Our
    Lives: Anth* (Howard U Pr, 1975), *Reed Mag, Pudding Mag*

Moira Crone 🎙 ⊀   W
English Dept/Allen Hall, Louisiana State Univ, Baton Rouge,
LA 70808, 504-864-9976
Internet: moiracrone@aol.com
    Pubs: *Dream State* (U Pr Mississippi, 1995), *Period of
    Confinement* (Harper Torch, 1988), *Winnebago Mysteries*
    (Fiction Collective, 1985), *New Stories by Southern Women:
    Anth* (U South Carolina Pr, 1989), *New Yorker, Louisiana Lit*

Joel Dailey   P
3003 Ponce De Leon St
New Orleans, LA 70119, 504-943-5198
    Pubs: *Release Window* (Semiquasi Pr, 1998), *Audience,
    Ambience, Ambulance* (Blank Gun Silencer Pr, 1993),
    Doppler Effects (Shockbox Pr, 1993), *American Poets Say
    Goodbye to 20th Century: Anth* (Four Walls Eight Windows,
    1996), *Exquisite Corpse*

Jim Donahoe   P
1380 Sigur Ave
Metairie, LA 70005, 504-833-3893

Charles East   W
1455 Knollwood Dr
Baton Rouge, LA 70808-8650, 225-926-3304
    Pubs: *Distant Friends & Intimate Strangers* (U Illinois Pr,
    1996), *Where the Music Was* (HBJ, 1965), *Sewanee Rev,
    Yale Rev, Southern Rev*

Maura Gage   P
Division of Liberal Arts, Lousiana State Univ at Eunice, PO
Box 1129, Eunice, LA 70535, 377-550-1328
Internet: mgage@lsue.edu
    Pubs: *Make Me Spring and Other Poems* (Mt Olive College
    Pr), *Quercus Rev, Southeastern Rev, Chiron Rev, Sundog,
    Big Scream, Louisiana Lit, Tar River Poetry, Poetry Depth
    Qtly*

Ernest J. Gaines   W
Univ Southwestern Louisiana, PO Box 44691, Lafayette, LA
70503
    Pubs: *A Lesson Before Dying, A Gathering of Old Men*
    (Knopf, 1993, 1984)

Timothy Martin Gautreaux   P&W
Southeastern Louisiana Univ, PO Box 889, Hammond, LA
70402, 504-549-5022
Internet: runner@i-ss.com
    Pubs: *The Next Step in the Dance, Same Place, Same
    Things* (Picador/St. Martin's, 1998, 1996), *New Stories From
    the South: Anth* (Algonquin Pr, 1996), *Harper's, Atlantic,
    GQ, Story, Massachusetts Rev, Virginia Qtly Rev*

Andrea Saunders Gereighty   P
257 Bonnabel Blvd
Metairie, LA 70005-3738, 504-835-8472
Internet: ager80@worldnet.att.net
    Pubs: *The Beat of the Forum* (Circasoft Pr, 2001), *Restless
    for Cool Weather, The Season of the Crane* (Gris Gris Pr,
    2000, 1998), *Illusions & Other Realities* (Medusa Pr, 1974),
    New Laurel Rev, Dalliance

Norman German   P&W
108 McVay St
Lake Charles, LA 70605, 318-478-1285
    Pubs: *No Other World* (Blue Heron Pr, 1992), *The Liberation
    of Bonner Child* (Aegina, 1992), *Hawaii Rev, BPJ, Worcester
    Rev, Wisconsin Rev*

John Gery 🎤 ✈   P
English Dept, Univ New Orleans, New Orleans, LA
70148-2315, 504-280-6133
Internet: jgery@uno.edu
    Pubs: *American Ghost* (CCC, 1999), *The Enemies of
    Leisure* (Story Line Pr, 1995), *Three Poems* (Lestat Pr,
    1989), *The Burning of New Orleans* (Amelia Pr, 1988), *Iowa
    Rev, Kenyon Rev, Louisiana Lit, Paris Rev, Sparrow, West
    Branch*

Hedwig Irene Gorski   PP
327 Clinton St
Lafayette, LA 70501-8101, 318-261-0239
Internet: hxg6638@usl.edu
    Pubs: *Slow Paradise, Polish Gypsy With Ghost* (Shinebone
    Pr, 1998, 1998)

Claudia K. Grinnell 🎤   P&W
4507 Churchill Circle
Monroe, LA 71203, 318-345-4263
Internet: grinnell@spock.ulm.edu
    Pubs: *Conditions Horizontal* (Missing Consonant Pr, 2001),
    *Exquisite Corpse, New Orleans Rev, CQ, Hayden's Ferry
    Rev, Phoebe, Bottomfish, Princeton Arts Rev*

Lee Meitzen Grue 🎤 ✈   P
New Laurel Review, 828 Lesseps St, New Orleans, LA 70117,
504-947-6001
    Pubs: *Three Poets in New Orleans* (Xavier Review Press,
    2000), *Good Bye Silver, Silver Cloud* (Plain View Pr, 1994),
    Live! On Frenchmen Street (CD; Cyberstudio, 2000)

Nancy C. Harris 🎤   P
8418 Freret St
New Orleans, LA 70118-1158, 504-861-7162
Internet: apewoman@poetic.com
    Pubs: *Mirror Wars, Maple Leaf Rag II: Anth* (Portals Pr,
    1999, 1994), *The Ape Woman Story* (Pirogue, 1989), *From
    a Bend in the River: Anth* (Runagate Pr, 1998), *Hawaii Rev,
    New Orleans Rev, Ellipsis, Negative Capability*

Ava Leavell Haymon 🎤 ✈   P
672 Nelson Dr
Baton Rouge, LA 70808-5066, 225-766-4739
Internet: avahaymon@aol.com
    Pubs: *Why the Groundhog Fears Her Shadow* (March Street
    Pr, 1995), *Staving Off Rapture* (Flume Pr, 1994), *Built in
    Fear of Heat* (Nightshade Pr, 1994)

Don A. Hoyt   P
RR2 Box 107
Downsville, LA 71234, 318-644-2012
    Pubs: *A New Kerygma* (Bootleg Pr, 1993), *Crossroads,
    Redneck Rev, Avra, Florida Rev, Whiskey Island, Oxford
    Mag, Pacific Rev, Pannus Index, MacGuffin*

Joe C. Ireland 🎤 ✈   P
410 Huntlee Dr
Algiers, LA 70131-3722, 504-394-8003
    Pubs: *Short Order* (New Orleans Poetry Forum, 1974), *The
    Smith, Dust, Bouillabaisse, Kumquat Meringue, Oxy*

Rodger Kamenetz   P
1209 Pine St
New Orleans, LA 70118-5218
    Pubs: *The Jew in the Lotus* (Harper SF, 1994), *The Missing
    Jew: New & Selected Poems* (Time Being Bks, 1992), *New
    Republic, Grand Street, Prairie Schooner, Ploughshares*

Julie Kane 🎤 ✈   P
Dept. of Language & Communication, Northwestern State
Univ, 316 Kyser Hall, Natchitoches, LA 71497, 318-352-8002
Internet: julkane@hotmail.com
    Pubs: *The Bartender Poems* (Greville Pr, 1991), *Body &
    Soul* (Pirogue Pub, 1987), *The Southern Rev, The Formalist,
    London Mag, Feminist Studies, Epoch*

Katherine Kane   P
955 Laurie La, #1
St Gabriel, LA 70776, 504-642-5743
Internet: jebkane@aol.com
    Pubs: *Ferry All the Way Up* (Porch, 1978), *Iowa Rev,
    Missouri Rev, Ontario Rev, Poetry Now, New Letters,
    Virginia Qtly Rev*

John Cantey Knight 🎙 ✈ P
4440 W Esplanade
Metairie, LA 70006
Internet: John_C_Knight@homail.com
   Pubs: *California Qtly, Borderlands, Big Muddy, Cotyledon, Jrnl of Kentucky Studies, Appalachian Heritage, Louisiana Lit*

Pinkie Gordon Lane 🎙 ✈ P
2738 77th Ave
Baton Rouge, LA 70807-5607, 225-356-3450
Internet: pinkieg@aol.com
   Pubs: *Elegy for Etheridge, Girl at the Window* (LSU Pr, 2000, 1991), *Double Stitch: Anth* (Beacon Pr, 1991)

David Madden 🎙 ✈ PP&P&W
614 Park
Baton Rouge, LA 70806, 225-344-3630
Internet: dmadden@lsu.edu
   Pubs: *Cassandra Singing, Sharpshooter* (U Tennessee Pr, 1998, 1996), *Southern Rev, New Letters, Gettysburg Rev, Kenyon Rev, Playboy*

Carolyn Maisel P
English Dept, Univ New Orleans/Lakefront, New Orleans, LA 70148
   Pubs: *Witnessing* (L'Epervier Pr, 1978), *NAR, New Yorker, Choice*

Leo Luke Marcello 🎙 ✈ P&W
PO Box 5508
Lake Charles, LA 70606
   Pubs: *Nothing Grows in One Place Forever* (Time Being Bks, 1998), *The Secret Proximity of Everywhere* (Blue Heron Pr, 1994), *Blackrobe's Love Letters* (Xavier Rev Pr, 1994), *Paterson Lit Rev, America, Italian Americana, Voices in Italian Americana*

Martha McFerren 🎙 ✈ P
2679 Verbena St
New Orleans, LA 70122-6037, 504-944-2707
   Pubs: *Women in Cars* (Helicon Nine Edtns, 1992), *Contours for Ritual* (LSU Pr, 1988), *Georgia Rev, Southern Rev, Shenandoah, New Laurel Rev, Louisiana Lit, Poetry NW*

Bryan T. McMahon P
PO Box 743
Ponchatoula, LA 70454, 504-386-2877
   Pubs: *Kree* (New Voices Pr, 1971), *The Ponchatoula Times*

Harold B. McSween P&W
PO Box 12907
Alexandria, LA 71315, 318-442-3215
   Pubs: *Hampden-Sydney Poetry Rev, South Carolina Rev, Virginia Qtly Rev, Poet & Critic, Sewanee Rev, Southern Rev*

Kay A. Murphy P&W
"F" St. John Ct
New Orleans, LA 70119
   Pubs: *The Autopsy* (Spoon River Poetry Pr, 1985), *Fiction Intl, St. Andrews Rev, Poetry*

James Nolan 🎙 ✈ P
925 Dauphine St
New Orleans, LA 70116-3036, 504-522-5934
   Pubs: *What Moves Is Not the Wind, Why I Live in the Forest* (Wesleyan U Pr, 1980, 1974), *Georgia Rev, City Lights Rev, Southern Rev, Exquisite Corpse, Poetry, New Letters*

Brenda Marie Osbey P
c/o LSU Press, The French House, Baton Rouge, LA 70122
Internet: osbey@bellsouth.net
   Pubs: *All Saints: New & Selected Poems* (LSU Pr, 1997), *Desperate Circumstance, Dangerous Woman* (Story Line Pr, 1990), *In These Houses* (Wesleyan U Pr, 1988), *APR, Callaloo, Amer Voice, Georgia Rev, Southern Rev*

Sue Owen P
7825 Rue Cache Ct
Baton Rouge, LA 70808, 225-769-3449
   Pubs: *My Doomsday Sampler* (Louisiana State U Pr, 1999), *The Book of Winter* (Ohio State U Pr, 1988), *Harvard Mag, Iowa Rev, Massachusetts Rev, Nation, Poetry, Southern Rev*

Burton Raffel 🎙 ✈ P&W
203 Mannering Ave S
Lafayette, LA 70508-4829, 337-232-4112
Internet: bnraffel@earthlink.net
   Pubs: *Beethoven in Denver & Other Poems* (Conundrum Pr, 1999), *Founders Fury* (Pocket Bks, 1988), *Paris Rev*

Stan Rice P
1239 1st St
New Orleans, LA 70130, 504-566-1544
Internet: stantravisrice@aol.com
   Pubs: *Red to the Rind, The Radiance of Pigs, Fear Itself, Singing Yet: New & Selected Poems* (Knopf, 2002, 1998, 1995, 1992), *Body of Work* (Lost Roads, 1983), *Some Lamb* (Figures, 1976), *Whiteboy* (Mudra, 1975)

Kenneth Robbins 🎙 ✈ W
Louisiana Tech Univ, School of the Performing Arts, Ruston, LA 71272-0001, 318-257-2711
   Pubs: *The Baptism of Howie Cobb* (U South Dakota Pr, 1995), *Buttermilk Bottoms* (U Iowa Pr, 1987)

Kalamu ya Salaam P&W
Box 52723
New Orleans, LA 70152, 504-523-4443
   Pubs: *What Is Life?* (Third World Pr, 1994), *Word Up: Black Poetry of the '80s From the Deep South: Anth* (Beans & Brown Rice, 1990), *African Amer Rev*

Dave Smith   P&W
1430 Knollwood Dr
Baton Rouge, LA 70808, 504-923-0388
    Pubs: *Fate's Kite* (Louisiana State U Pr, 1996), *Night
    Pleasures* (Bloodaxe Bks, 1992), *Cuba Night* (Morrow,
    1992), *New Yorker, Atlantic, Yale Rev, Poetry, Georgia Rev*

Garland Strother ⚇ ✈   P
516 Hester Ave
River Ridge, LA 70123-1405, 504-737-1278
Internet: glstroth@bellsouth.net
    Pubs: *Tucumcari Lit Rev, Sierra Nevada Rev, Sunstone,
    Arkansas Rev, Blue Cloud Qtly, North Dakota Qtly,
    Pontchartrain Rev, South Dakota, Southern Exposure*

Don Ray Thornton   P
Thornton Publishing, 1504 Howard St, New Iberia, LA 70560,
318-364-2752
    Pubs: *Ascending, Mentor* (Thornton Pub, 1993, 1993), *A
    Walk on Water* (Cajun Pub, 1985), *Catalyst, Slipstream,
    Muse*

Keith Veizer   W
825 Gallier St
New Orleans, LA 70117
    Pubs: *Intro, NAR, Sou'wester, Exquisite Corpse, Fell Swoop,
    Story Qtly, Pulpsmith*

Jan Villarrubia ⚇ ✈   P
38 Crane
New Orleans, LA 70124-4309, 504-288-0153
    Pubs: *Odd Fellows Rest* (Xavier Rev Pr, 1996), *Miz Lena's
    Backyard* (Dramatic Pub Co, 1994), *Mississippi Valley Rev,
    Third Wind, Lit Rev, Negative Capability*

Bernice Webb   W
159 Whittington Dr
Lafayette, LA 70503, 318-234-5397
    Pubs: *Mating Dance, Spider Web* (Spider Pr, 1996, 1993),
    Born to Be a Loser (w/Johnnie Allan; Jadfel Pub Co, 1993),
    Voices Intl

Leilah Wendell   P
5219 Magazine St
New Orleans, LA 70115-1858
    Pubs: *The Necromantic Ritual Book, The Complete Books
    of Azrael, Shadows in the Half-Light* (Westgate Pr, 1994,
    1992, 1989), *Carpe Noctem, Esoterra, Elegia*

Gail White ⚇ ✈   P
1017 Spanish Moss La
Breaux Bridge, LA 70517-6711
    Pubs: *The Price of Everything* (Mellen Pr, 2001), *Landscape
    With Women* (Singular Speech Pr, 1998), *The Muse Strikes
    Back: Anth, A Formal Feeling Comes: Anth* (Story Line Pr,
    1998, 1994), *The Formalist, Cape Rock, Cream City Rev,
    Hellas, Light, Midwest Qtly*

John Wood ⚇ ✈   P
McNeese State Univ, Lake Charles, LA 70609, 337-475-5326
    Pubs: *Selected Poems 1968-1998* (U Arkansas Pr, 1999),
    The Gates of the Elect Kingdom, In Primary Light (U Iowa
    Pr, 1997, 1994)

Angus Woodward ⚇ ✈   W
1045 E River Oaks
Baton Rouge, LA 70815
Internet: awoodw@mailcity.com
    Pubs: *Talking River Rev, Pennsylvania English, Dominion
    Rev, Laurel Rev, Habersham Rev, Gulf Stream, Louisiana
    Literature*

Yictove ⚇ ✈   P
2832 St Bernard Ave
New Orleans, LA 70119-2120
    Pubs: *Blue Print* (Portals Pr, 1997), *D. J. Soliloquy* (Thrown
    Stone Pr, 1988), *A Bend in the River: 100 New Orleans
    Poets: Anth* (Runagate Pr, 1998), *Identity Lessons: Anth*
    (Penguin, 1997), *Gathering of the Tribes*

Andy Young ⚇ ✈   P
935 Gov Nicholls, #4
New Orleans, LA 70116, 504-529-2634
Internet: Andimuse@aol.com
    Pubs: *Mine* (Lavender Ink, 2000), *What Have You Lost: Anth*
    (Greenwillow Pr, 1999), *Exquisite Corpse, Stinging Fly,
    Pierogi Pr, mind the gap, Snow Apple, New Laurel Rev,
    Appalachian Heritage, Florida Rev, New Orleans Rev, Texas
    Observer, Mesechabe*

Ahmos Zu-Bolton, II   P
1616 Marigny St
New Orleans, LA 70117
    Pubs: *The Widow Paris: A Folklore of Marie Laveau*
    (Copastetic, 1986), *Marquee, Black Voices*

MAINE

Jonathan Aldrich   P
41 Oakhurst Rd
Cape Elizabeth, ME 04107
    Pubs: *The Death of Michelangelo* (Puckerbrush Pr, 1985)

Kate Barnes   P
432 Appleton Ridge Rd
Appleton, ME 04862
    Pubs: *Where the Deer Were* (Godine, 1994), *Crossing the
    Field* (Blackberry Bks, 1992), *BPJ, Harper's, NER, Kenyon
    Rev, New Yorker*

Ingrid Bengis   W
Box 421
Stonington, ME 04681
    Pubs: *The Writer & Her Work* (Norton, 1980), *I Have Come
    Here to Be Alone* (S&S, 1977)

Steve Benson 🎙 ✈   P
33 Blackberry Lane
Surry, ME 04684
    Pubs: *Roaring Spring* (Zasterle Pr, 1998), *Reverse Order*
(Potes & Poets, 1991), *Blue Book* (The Figures, 1988),
*Poetics Jrnl, Language, Aerial, Zyzzyva, o.blek, Avec,
Crayon, This, Writing, Raddle Moon*

Jim Bishop   P
PO Box 1448
Bucksport, ME 04416-1448
    Pubs: *Mother Tongue* (Contraband Pr, 1976)

Alice Bolstridge 🎙 ✈   P&W
Maine School of Science & Mathematics, 77 High St,
Limestone, ME 04750, 207-325-3303
Internet: bolstridgea@mssm.org
    Pubs: *An Intricate Weave: Anth* (Iris Edtns, 1997), *Nimrod,
The Maine Scholar, Animus, Cimarron Rev, Mediphors,
Cincinnati Poetry Rev, Slant, Kalliope, Passager, Magic
Realism*

Philip Booth   P
95 Main St
Castine, ME 04421-0330, 207-326-4644
    Pubs: *Lifelines, Pairs, Selves, Relations: Poems 1950-1985*
(Penguin, 1999, 1994, 1990, 1986), *Trying to Say It* (U
Michigan Pr, 1996), *The Best American Poetry: Anth*
(Scribner, 1999), *Georgia Rev, APR, DoubleTake, Poetry,
Yale Rev, BPJ*

Myrna Bouchey   P
RR1, Box 2285
Jonesport, ME 04649-9717
    Pubs: *Malahat, Niagara, BPJ, Hard Pressed, Heirs, Maine
Times, Kennebec, Lakes & Prairies*

Henry Braun 🎙 ✈   P
Box 84
Weld, ME 04285, 207-585-2218
Internet: jhbraun@tds.net
    Pubs: *The Body Electric* (Norton, 2000), *The Vergil Woods*
(Atheneum, 1968), *Maine Speaks: Anth* (Maine Writers &
Publishers, 1989), *Painted Bride Qtly, APR, Poetry,
Massachusetts Rev*

William Carpenter 🎙 ✈   P&W
Box 1297
Stockton Springs, ME 04981, 207-567-4172
Internet: carpenter@acadia.net
    Pubs: *The Wooden Nickel* (Little, Brown, 2002), *A Keeper of
Sheep* (Milkweed Edtns, 1994), *Speaking Fire at Stones*
(Tilbury Hse, 1992), *Rain* (Northeastern U Pr, 1985)

Erleen J. Christensen   P&W
Rte 1, Box 2315
Unity, ME 04988
    Pubs: *Kennebec, Amelia, Wind, Prairie Schooner, Kansas
Qtly, Cottonwood, Memphis State Rev*

Robert M. Chute 🎙 ✈   P
85 Echo Cove Ln
Poland, ME 04274
    Pubs: *Thirteen Moons/Treize Lunes/'Sanko Kisuksok,
Sweeping the Sky* (Cider Pr, 2002, 2000), *Androscoggin
Too, Woodshed on the Moon* (Nightshade Pr, 1997, 1991),
Barely Time to Study Jesus (Cider Pr, 1996), *Samuel Sewall
Sails for Home* (Coyote Love Pr, 1986)

Roger L. Conover   P
55 Lambert Rd
Freeport, ME 04032
    Pubs: *The Last Lunar Baedeker* (Jargon Pr, 1982),
Shenandoah, Ironwood, Montemora, Epoch

Paul G. Corrigan, Jr. 🎙 ✈   P
PO Box 641
Greenville, ME 04441, 207-695-2100
Internet: corrigan@midmaine.com
    Pubs: *At the Grave of the Unknown Riverdriver* (North
Country Pr, 1992)

H. R. Coursen   P&W
Frog Prince Manor, 21 Toad's Landing, Brunswick, ME 04011,
207-725-2130
    Pubs: *History Lessons, The Green of Spring* (Mad River
1998, 1997), *The Search for Archerland, Graves of the
Poets* (EM Pr, 1994, 1993), *Tar River, Small Pond, Lit Rev,
Hollins Critic, South Carolina Rev, Iconoclast*

Alfred DePew   W
31 Pine St
Portland, ME 04102-3807
    Pubs: *The Melancholy of Departure* (U Georgia Pr, 1991)

Leigh Donaldson   P&W
790 Congress St
Portland, ME 04102
    Pubs: *City River of Voices, Cafe Rev, Shooting Star Rev,
Atelier, Art & Understanding, World Poetry 1998, Catalyst
Mag, Intl Poetry Rev, Potato Eyes, Manhattan Poetry Rev,
Portfolio Mag, Hawaii Rev, Obsidian II, AIM Qtly, Art Times,
Minnesota Ink*

Kathleen Lignell Ellis 🎙 ✈   P
9 Harris Rd
Orono, ME 04473-1522, 207-581-3858
Internet: kathleen.ellis@umit.maine.edu
    Pubs: *Entering Earthquake Country* (C.C. Marimbo, 2001),
Red Horses (Northern Lights, 1991), *The Eloquent Edge*
(Acadia, 1989), *NER, Columbia, Antioch, NAR, SW Rev,
New Letters, BPJ*

Theodore Enslin 🎤 ✈   P
RFD Box 289, Kansas Rd, Milbridge, ME 04658, 207-546-7636
  Pubs: *Then, & Now* (Natl Poetry Fdn, 1999), *Re-Soundings*
  (Talisman Hse, 1999), *Sequentiae* (London; Stop Pr, 1999),
  Skeins (Origin-Longhouse, 1998), *The House of the Golden
  Windows, Love & Science* (Light & Dust Bks, 1993, 1990),
  Conjunctions, Talisman

Christopher Fahy 🎤 ✈   P&W
15 Mechanic St
Thomaston, ME 04861, 207-354-8191
Internet: fahy@midcoast.com
  Pubs: *Fever 42* (Overlook Connection Pr, 2002), *Limerock:
  Maine Stories* (Coastwise Pr, 1999), *The Fly Must Die*
  (Washington Inst for Creative Activity, 1993)

Tom Fallon 🎤 ✈   P&W
239 Spruce St
Rumford, ME 04276, 207-364-7237
Internet: editor@aopoetry.com
  Pubs: *The Man on the Moon* (Small-Small Pr, 1988), *Maine
  Speaks: Anth* (MWPA, 1991), *Foliage, Panhandler, Black Fly
  Rev, Kennebec, Cafe Rev, Puckerbrush Rev, La Riviere,
  Animus*

Rod Farmer   P
10 Anson St
Farmington, ME 04938, 207-778-9298
Internet: farmer@maine.edu
  Pubs: *Universal Essence* (Brunswick Pub Co, 1986), *ELF,
  Phase & Cycle, Riverrun, Webster Rev, Thorny Locust,
  Without Halos*

Robert Farnsworth 🎤 ✈   P
19 Ware St
Lewiston, ME 04240, 207-784-0416
Internet: rfarnswo@bates.edu
  Pubs: *Honest Water, Three or Four Hills & a Cloud*
  (Wesleyan U Pr, 1989, 1982), *Michigan Qtly, Southern Rev,
  NER, BPJ, Hudson Rev*

Richard Flanagan 🎤 ✈   W
179 Covell Rd
Fairfield, ME 04937, 617-239-4256
Internet: flanagan@babson.edu
  Pubs: *Last of the Hippies* (Paycock, 1984), *San Jose
  Studies, Earth's Daughters*

Richard Foerster 🎤 ✈   P
PO Box 1040
York Beach, ME 03910-1040, 207-363-8220
Internet: rafoerster@aol.com
  Pubs: *Double Going, Trillium* (BOA Edtns, 2002, 1998),
  Patterns of Descent, Sudden Harbor (Orchises Pr, 1993,
  1992), *Paris Rev, Kenyon Rev, Southern Rev, Poetry,
  Gettysburg*

Elaine Ford   W
Univ Maine, 304 Neville, Orono, ME 04469, 207-581-3834
Internet: Elaine.Ford@umit.maine.edu
  Pubs: *Life Designs* (Zoland, 1997), *Monkey Bay, Ivory
  Bright* (Viking, 1989, 1986), *Missed Connections* (Random
  Hse, 1983)

M. Ekola Gerberick   P
999 High St
Bath, ME 04530
  Pubs: *Siirtolaisuus, Kansas Qtly, Passages North, Finnish
  Americana, BPJ, Gravida*

Paul Guernsey   W
1247 Middle Rd
Warren, ME 04864
  Pubs: *Angel Falls* (S&S, 1990), *Unhallowed Ground*
  (Morrow, 1986)

Gunnar Hansen   P
PO Box 268
Northeast Harbor, ME 04662
  Pubs: *True Coast* (Harpswell, 1991), *Mt. Desert: An Informal
  History* (Mt. Desert, 1989)

Anne Hazlewood-Brady   P
Box 534
Kennebunkport, ME 04046
  Pubs: *One to the Many* (Puckerbrush Pr, 1979), *The Cross,
  the Anchor & the Heart* (Victoria, 1976)

Nancy Heiser 🎤 ✈   W
25 Hemlock Rd
Brunswick, ME 04011, 207-725-4253
Internet: nheiser@blazenetme.net
  Pubs: *Nightshade Nightstand Reader: Anth* (Nightshade Pr,
  1995), *Seattle Rev, Potpourri, Footwork, Out of the Cradle,
  Thema, Paterson Lit Rev, Alkali Flats*

Lucille Iverson   P&W
133 N Main St
Morrill, ME 04952-9750, 207-342-5792
Internet: lucylake@hotmail.com
  Pubs: *We Become New* (Bantam, 1975), *Outrage* (Know
  Inc, 1974), *Soho Weekly News, Connections, Sunbury*

James Koller   P&W
PO Box 629
Brunswick, ME 04011
Internet: jindejinak@aol.com
  Pubs: *Et Nous Les Os* (La Main Courante, 1996), *Dans La
  Gueule Du Loup* (AIOU, 1995), *AIOU, Gate, Active in
  Airtime, Copice Biancaneve, Doc(k)s*

Sharon Kraus 🎤 ✈ P
c/o Alice James Books, 238 Main St, Farmington, ME 04938
Internet: Sharon5554@aol.com
    Pubs: *Strange Land* (U Pr Florida, 2002), *Generation* (Alice
James Bks, 1997), *Barrow Street, Georgia Rev,
Massachusetts Rev, Puerto del Sol, Qtly West, Agni,
TriQtly, Prairie Schooner, Mississippi Rev, Columbia: A
Jrnl of Lit & Art*

Diane Kruchkow 🎤 ✈ P
3 Saltmarsh Rd
New Sharon, ME 04955
Internet: kruch@exploremaine.com
    Pubs: *Green Isle in the Sea* (December, 1986), *Stony Hills,
Small Press News*

Daniela Kuper 🎤 ✈ W
836 Bargaduce Rd
Brooksville, ME 04617
Internet: daniela@acadia.net
    Pubs: *Cherries in the Snow* (Picador USA, 1999), *Storming
Heaven's Gate: Anth* (Penguin, 1996), *Many Mountains
Moving, The Sun, Cream City Rev, Coe Rev, Amaranth Rev,
Mobius, Lilith, Poetry Forum, Black Warrior Rev*

Kris Larson 🎤 ✈ P
PO Box 418
East Machias, ME 04630, 207-255-4924
    Pubs: *Second Thoughts, Groundwork* (Salt-Works Pr,
1976, 1974), *Maine Times, The Egg, Opinion, Downeast
Coastal Press*

Gary Lawless 🎤 ✈ P
617 E Neck Rd
Nobleboro, ME 04555, 207-729-5083
    Pubs: *In Ruins* (Blackberry Bks, 2002), *Caribudismo*
(Edizioni Arcobaleno Fiammeggiante, 2000), *BPJ, Wild
Earth, Animus, Raise the Stakes, Gate*

Denis Ledoux 🎤 ✈ W
Soleil Press, 95 Gould Rd, Lisbon Falls, ME 04252-9707,
207-353-5454
Internet: memoirs@ime.net
    Pubs: *What Became of Them & Other Stories From Franco-
America, Lives in Translation: Anth* (Soleil Pr, 1988, 1991),
Mountain Dance & Other Stories (Coastwise Pr, 1990)

James Lewisohn P
25 W St Ext Apt 2
Bar Harbor, ME 04609, 207-288-4078
    Pubs: *Finkel, New & Selected Poems* (Horizon Pr, 1990),
New Yorker, NYQ, Sojourner

Carl Little 🎤 ✈ P
PO Box 273
Mount Desert, ME 04660-0273, 207-288-5015
Internet: ckl@ecology.coa.edu
    Pubs: *3,000 Dreams Explained* (Nightshade Pr, 1992),
Maine Times, Puckerbrush Rev

Leni Mancuso 🎤 ✈ P
Box 303
Castine, ME 04421, 207-326-9381
    Pubs: *In Rothko's Cave* (Puckerbrush Rev Portfolio #6,
1998), *Off the Coast, Trenton Rev, BPJ, CSM, Potato Eyes,
Paideuma, Maine Times*

Katherine McAlpine 🎤 ✈ P
11 Mitchell St
Eastport, ME 04631
    Pubs: *Garlic & Sapphires: Selected Sonnets* (RL Barth,
1999), *The Muse Strikes Back: Anth* (Story Line Pr, 1997),
Literature: The Human Experience: Anth (St. Martin's Pr,
1997), *The Best Contemporary Women's Humor: Anth*
(Crossing Pr, 1994), *Formalist, Light*

James McKenna P
51 Central St
Hallowell, ME 04347-1204, 207-622-9104
    Pubs: *Zone 3, Potato Eyes, Negative Capability, Ledge,
Kennebec, Slant, WordWrights*

Wesley McNair 🎤 ✈ P
1 Chicken St
Mercer, ME 04957, 207-587-4681
    Pubs: *Fire, Mapping the Heart, Talking in the Dark, The
Town of No & My Brother Running* (Godine, 2001, 2000,
1998, 1997), *Atlantic, Poetry, Iowa Rev, Sewanee Rev,
Ploughshares, Gettysburg Rev*

Mark Melnicove P
132 Water St
Gardiner, ME 04345, 207-737-8116
Internet: thpub@aol.com
    Pubs: *Uncensored Guide to Maine* (Lance Tapley, 1984),
Advanced Memories (Bern Porter, 1983), *Kennebec, Cold-
Drill, Puckerbrush Rev*

Robin Morgan 🎤 ✈ P
c/o Edite Kroll, Edite Kroll Literary Agency, 12 Grayhurst Park,
Portland, ME 04102
    Pubs: *A Hot January: Poems 1996-1999, Upstairs in the
Garden: Selected Poems* (Norton, 1999, 1991), *The Mer-
Child: A New Legend* (CUNY Feminist Pr, 1991), *Dry Your
Smile* (Doubleday, 1989)

Mark Nakell W
11 Oceanwood Dr
Scarborough, ME 04074
Internet: mnakell@gui.net

Paul Nelson P
HC 70, Box 1085, Machiasport, ME 04655
    Pubs: *The Hard Shapes of Paradise* (U Alabama Pr, 1988),
Days Off (U Pr Virginia, 1982)

Edward Nobles 🎤 ✈ P
139 Kenduskeag Ave
Bangor, ME 04401, 207-973-3331
Internet: enobles@maine.edu
Pubs: *The Bluestone Walk, Through One Tear* (Persea, 2000, 1997), *Poetry 180, Tin House, Colorado Rev, Boulevard, Denver Qtly, Gettysburg Rev, Paris Rev, Volt, Witness, Kenyon Rev*

Patricia O'Donnell 🎤 ✈ W
Univ Maine, Roberts Learning Center, Farmington, ME 04938, 207-645-4872
Internet: podonnel@maine.edu
Pubs: *Woman Running Anth* (Her Books, 2001), *The Quotable Moose: Anth* (New England Pr, 1994), *Prairie Schooner, New Yorker, NAR, Agni, Short Story*

Carolyn Page P
Nightshade Pr, Ward Hill Rd, Troy, ME 04987, 207-948-5088
Pubs: *Barn Flight, Life on the Line: Anth* (Negative Capability, 1995, 1992), *Troy Corner Poems* (Nightshade Pr, 1994), *Parnassus, Comstock Rev, Now & Then, Pembroke, Fiddlehead, Zone 3*

Arnold Perrin P
PO Box 809
Union, ME 04862, 207-785-4355
Pubs: *Window* (Talent Hse Pr, 1998), *Noah* (East Coast Edtns, 1993), *View from Hill Cabin* (Northwoods Pr, 1979), *Puckerbrush Rev, Kennebec, Potato Eyes, Maine Life, CSM, The Sun*

Mary Peterson W
148 Pepperrell Rd
Kittery Point, ME 03905, 207-439-1640
Pubs: *Mercy Flights* (U Missouri Pr, 1985), *Story Qtly, South Dakota Rev, NAR, Ms.*

J. A. Pollard 🎤 ✈ P&W
RFD #2, Eames Rd, Box 5115
Winslow, ME 04901-9661, 207-873-6443
Pubs: *Sheltering Pines Fdn: Anth* (Sheltering Pines, 2002), *Currents II, The Spirit of the Woman in the Moon, The Lamp-Post, Space and Time, Weber Studies, Legions of Light, Penny-A-Liner, Bibliophiles, Pig Iron, Grace Notes*

Sylvester Pollet 🎤 ✈ P
963 Winkumpaugh Rd
Ellsworth, ME 04605-3030, 207-667-2255
Internet: pollet@maine.edu
Pubs: *The Dandelion Sutras* (Backwoods Broadsides Chaplets, 1994), *Maine Speaks: Anth* (MWPA, 1989), *Exquisite Corpse, Poetry NY, NYQ, Bullhead*

Bern Porter 🎤 ✈ P&W
50 Salmond St
Belfast, ME 04915
Pubs: *Symbols* (Spoon Pr, 1994), *Less Than Overweight* (Plaster Cramp, 1993), *Sounds That Arouse Me* (Tilbury, 1992), *Bern Porter's Pillow Book, The Best Period of My Life* (Roger Jackson, 1996, 1996), *Numbers, Neverends* (Runaway Spoon, 1989, 1988)

Patricia Smith Ranzoni 🎤 ✈ P
HCR 78, Box 173, Bucksport, ME 04416-9618
Internet: pranzoni@aol.com
Pubs: *Settling, Claiming* (Puckerbrush Pr, 2000, 1995), *Prayers to Protest: Anth* (Pudding Hse Pubs, 1998), *CSM, Animist, Shearsman, Spoon River Poetry Rev, Yankee, Cafe Rev, Blueline, Green Fuse*

Kenneth Rosen P
English Dept, Univ Southern Maine, Portland, ME 04103, 207-780-4296
Pubs: *Reptile Mind, Longfellow Square* (Ascenius Pr, 1993, 1993), *Paris Rev, Ploughshares, Western Humanities Rev, Massachusetts Rev, Poetry*

John Rosenwald 🎤 ✈ P
c/o Granite Rose Farm, Box 389, South Andover, ME 04216-0389, 207-392-1872
Internet: rosey@beloit.edu
Pubs: *Descant, Wisconsin Poets Calendar, BPJ, Kennebec, Kansas Qtly, Lit Rev*

Ira Sadoff 🎤 ✈ P&W
53 Middle St
Hallowell, ME 04347-1114
Internet: isadoff@colby.edu
Pubs: *Barter, Grazing* (U Illinois Pr, 2003, 1998), *An Ira Sadoff Reader* (U New England Pr, 1992), *Emotional Traffic* (Godine, 1990), *APR, New Yorker, Antaeus, Paris Rev*

Colin Sargent 🎤 ✈ P&W
114 Baxter Blvd
Portland, ME 04101, 207-775-4339
Internet: editor@portlandmonthly.com
Pubs: *Luftwaffe Snowshoes* (Portsmouth Fine Arts, 1984), *Poet Lore, Nexus, Panhandler, Gargoyle*

Lee Sharkey 🎤 ✈ P&W
RR1 Box 4122
Vienna, ME 04360-9500, 207-293-2390
Internet: sharkey@maine.edu
Pubs: *To a Vanished World* (Puckerbrush Pr, 1995), *Prairie Schooner, Marlboro Rev, Manhattan Rev, Green Mountains Rev, Cream City Rev*

Norma Voorhees Sheard P
551 Sunset Dr
Deer Isle, ME 04627
Internet: normasheard@hypernet.com
 Pubs: *NYQ, Maryland Rev, Black Fly Rev, Nimrod,
 Footworks, U.S. 1 Worksheets, Dragonfly, Jrnl of New
 Jersey Poets, Paterson Literary Rev, Cape Rock Rev*

Betsy Sholl P
24 Brentwood St
Portland, ME 04103, 207-774-9414
 Pubs: *The Red Line* (U Pitt Pr, 1992), *Pick a Card*
 (Coyote/Bark Pub, 1991), *Rooms Overhead* (Alice James
 Bks, 1986)

Alix Kates Shulman ♫ ✈ W
Long Island, ME 04050
 Pubs: *A Good Enough Daughter* (Schocken, 1999), *Drinking
 the Rain* (FSG, 1995), *In Every Woman's Life, On the Stroll,
 Burning Questions* (Knopf, 1987, 1981, 1978)

Mike Silverton P
86 Church St
Belfast, ME 04915, 207-338-5585
Internet: LaFoliaEd@aol.com
 Pubs: *Battery Park* (Thing Pr, 1966)

Jonathan Sisson P
7 Barron Road
Eastport, ME 04631-1601, 617-825-5430
 Pubs: *Where Silkwood Walks* (Lake Street Rev Pr, 1981),
 Poetry, Paris Rev, Antaeus

Michael Smetzer P&W
PO Box 3112
Portland, ME 04104-3112
Internet: m.smetzer@usa.net
 Pubs: *Teaching the Clergy to Dance* (Manic Monkey Bks,
 1996), *A Quiet Man* (Baggeboda Pr, 1988)

Karen South ♫ ✈ P
PO Box 235
Matinicus Island, ME 04851-0235, 207-366-3425
Internet: islandink@msn.com
 Pubs: *National Forum, Abraxas, Hampden-Sydney Poetry
 Rev, Ploughshares, MPR*

Debra Spark ♫ ✈ W
English Dept, Colby College, 5284 Mayflower Hill Dr,
Waterville, ME 04901-8852, 207-872-3257
Internet: daspark@colby.edu
 Pubs: *The Ghost of Bridgetown* (Graywolf, 2001), *Coconuts
 for the Saint* (Faber & Faber, 1996), *On the Tail of the Dog
 Star* (Avon, 1990), *Twenty Under Thirty: Anth* (Scribner,
 1986), *Passages North, Boston Globe Mag, Epoch, Agni,
 NAR, Ploughshares, Esquire*

Martin Steingesser ♫ ✈ PP&P
PO Box 7575
Portland, ME 04112-7575, 207-828-9937
Internet: msteings@maine.rr.com
 Pubs: *Brothers of Morning* (Deerbrook Edtns, 2002), *The
 Wildman, Speaking of New England* (North Country Pr,
 1998, 1993), *Motion: Anth* (U Iowa Pr, 2001), *Poetry Comes
 Up Where It Can: Anth* (U Utah Pr, 2000), *Nimrod, Rattle,
 Patterson Lit Rev, Progressive*

Linda Tatelbaum ♫ ✈ P&W
1050 Guinea Ridge Rd
Appleton, ME 04862, 207-785-4634
Internet: ltatelb@colby.edu
 Pubs: *Yes and No: Paris 1969/1137, Writer on the Rocks,
 Carrying Water As a Way of Life* (About Time Pr, 2004,
 2000, 1997), *Utne Reader, Maine Times*

Lewis Turco ♫ ✈ P&W
Mathom Bookshop, 40 Blinn Hill Rd, Dresden Mills, ME 04342,
207-737-4512
Internet: mathom@gwi.net
 Pubs: *The Green Maces of Autumn: Voices in an Old Maine
 House* (Mathom, 2002), *A Book of Fears* (Bordighera,
 1998), *An Exaltation of Forms: Anth* (Michigan, 2002)

Carol Wainright P
RR1, Box 449
Deer Isle, ME 04627
 Pubs: *Distant Mountain* (Wind Chimes Pr, 1985), *CSM*

David C. Walker ♫ ✈ P
Box 82
Freedom, ME 04941-0082, 207-382-6267
Internet: dwalker@maine.edu
 Pubs: *Voiceprints* (Romulus Edtns, 1989), *The Maine
 Reader: Anth* (HM, 1991), *Poetry, NW Rev, New Yorker,
 Georgia Rev, Antioch Rev*

Richard B. Weber P
142 Bay Point Rd
Georgetown, ME 04548, 207-729-5793
 Pubs: *Beard Poems* (Karma Dog Edtns, 1995), *The Fishing-
 Print Poems, Poems From the Xenia Hotel* (Street Pr, 1984,
 1980), *Oxalis*

Douglas "Woody" Woodsum P
90 Summer St Apt #3
Waterville, ME 04901, 207-872-0460
 Pubs: *Animus Rev, The Pucker Brush Rev, Antioch Rev,
 Southern Rev, Massachusetts Rev, Prairie Schooner,
 Denver Qtly, Yankee, Webster Rev, Exquisite Corpse, Sun
 Dog, Albany Rev*

Baron Wormser 🎤 ✈ P
19 1/2 Pleasant St Pl
Hallowell, ME 04347
Internet: baronw@gwi.net
    Pubs: *Mulroney and Others, When* (Sarabande Bks, 2000, 1997), *Atoms, Soul Music & Other Poems* (Paris Rev Edtns, 1989), *Harper's, New Republic, Paris Rev*

Leroy Zarucchi 🎤 ✈ P
Nightshade Press, Ward Hill Rd, Troy, ME 04987,
207-948-3427
Internet: potatoeyes@uninets.net
    Pubs: *Gunner's Moon* (Cider Pr, 1996), *Sparse Rain* (Pygmy Forest Pr, 1996), *Spirit That Moves Us: Anth* (Spirit That Moves Us, 1993), *Onthebus, Pembroke Mag, Fiddlehead*

MARYLAND

Karren LaLonde Alenier 🎤 ✈ P&W
4601 North Ave, #301
Chevy Chase, MD 20815, 301-652-7638
Internet: karren77@aol.com
    Pubs: *Looking for Divine Transportation* (Bunny & Crocodile Pr, 1999), *Winners: The Washington Prize: Anth* (Word Works, 1999), *MacGuffin, Crescent Rev, Jrnl of Poetry Therapy, Poet Lore, Negative Capability, Mississippi Rev, Jewish Currents*

Indran Amirthanayagam P
4810 Mercury Dr
Rockville, MD 20853, 301-946-8085
Internet: iamirthanayagam@hotmail.com
    Pubs: *The Elephants of Reckoning* (Hanging Loose Pr, 1993), *Four Way Reader: Anth* (Four Way Bks, 1996), *United States of Poetry: Anth* (Abrams, 1996)

Ellen Argo W
63 Conduit St
Annapolis, MD 21401, 301-268-3151
    Pubs: *Yankee Girl, Crystal Star, Jewel of the Seas* (Putnam, 1981, 1979, 1977)

Barri Armitage P
13904 N Gate Dr
Silver Spring, MD 20906-2217, 301-871-6656
    Pubs: *Double Helix* (Washington Writers Pub Hse, 1993), *Prairie Schooner, Poet Lore, Bridge, Poetry, Georgia Rev, Ohio Rev*

Ed Baker P
8215 Flower Ave
Takoma Park, MD 20912-6858, 301-587-1875
    Pubs: *Shrike* (tel-let, 2000), *Nine Perfect Ensos, Okeanos Rhos, The City, Hexapoem I, II, & III, This Wood* (Red Ochre Pr, 2000, 1995, 1994, 1982), *Amelia, Frogpond, Modern Haiku, Persimmon, Black Bough, Tundra, Bongos of the Lord, Hummingbird*

Diane DeMichele Barkett P
5394 Annapolis Dr
Mount Airy, MD 21771-5709
    Pubs: *Tempest, Archer, Up Against the Wall Mother, San Fernando Poetry Jrnl, Piedmont Literary Rev*

John Barth W
c/o The Writing Seminar, Johns Hopkins Univ, Baltimore, MD 21218, 410-516-7562
    Pubs: *On With the Story, The Last Voyage of Somebody the Sailor* (Little, Brown, 1996, 1991)

Robin Bayne P&W
215 Treherne Rd
Lutherville, MD 21093-1244
    Pubs: *The Will of Time, Shifters: Anth* (New Concepts Pub, 1999, 2002), *Charity's Prisoner* (Treble Heart Bks, 2001), *His Brother's Child* (Mountain View Pub, 1999)

Mary Beach W
Cherry Valley Editions, 3510 Olympic St, Silver Spring, MD 20906

David Beaudouin P
2840 St Paul St
Baltimore, MD 21218-4311, 410-467-6292
    Pubs: *The American Night* (Blue Nude, 1992), *Catenae— Set 1* (Apathy Pr, 1988), *Open 24 Hours, Stony Run*

Madison Smartt Bell W
Goucher College, English Dept, Towson, MD 21204, 410-337-6282
Internet: mbell@goucher.edu
    Pubs: *Ten Indians, All Soul's Rising* (Pantheon, 1996, 1995), *Doctor Sleep* (HBJ, 1991), *Barking Man* (Ticknor & Fields, 1990), *Harper's, Hudson Rev*

Donald Berger P
105 Hodges Ln
Takoma Park, MD 20912-4229
    Pubs: *Quality Hill* (Lost Roads, 1993)

David Bergman 🎤 ✈ P
3024 N Calvert St, #C5
Baltimore, MD 21218, 410-467-8070
Internet: dbergman@towson.edu
    Pubs: *Heroic Measures, Cracking the Code* (Ohio State, 1998, 1985), *Gaiety Transfigured* (U Wisconsin, 1991), *Poetry, New Republic, Raritan, Paris Rev, Kenyon Rev, New Criterion*

Cathy Drinkwater Better P
119 Caraway Rd Apt B1
Reisterstown, MD 21136, 410-833-1537
Internet: cbetter@juno.com
Pubs: *The Moon Tonight* (Los Hombres Pr, 1996), *Don't Hit Your Brother With Your Mouth Full* (Acme Pr, 1995), *Writer's Digest, St. Anthony Messenger, Modern Haiku, Amer Cowboy Poet Mag, Silver Web, Humpty Dumpty Mag, Psychopoetica, Raw Nervz*

Jody Bolz ♪ ✈ P
4004 Maryland Ave
Brookmont, MD 20816-2671, 301-229-6578
Pubs: *Her Face in the Mirror: Anth* (Beacon Pr, 1994), *The Amer Scholar, Gargoyle, Indiana Rev, SPR, River Styx, Women's Rev of Bks, Ascent, Ploughshares*

Betty Booker P
27826 Island Dr
Salisbury, MD 21801, 410-546-1712
Pubs: *Plainsong, Croton Rev, Stone Country, Artemis, Christian Century, America, Poetry Now*

Alan Britt ♪ ✈ P
233 Northway Rd
Reisterstown, MD 21136-2136, 410-833-9424
Pubs: *Bodies of Lightning* (Cypress Bks, 1995), *Fathers: A Collection of Poems: Anth* (St. Martin's Pr, 1997), *Rising Waters: Anth* (Pekitanoui Pub, 1995), *Black Moon, Bitter Oleander, Chariton Rev, Exquisite Corpse, Borderlands: Texas Rev, New Letters*

Melvin Edward Brown P
1311 Kitmore Rd
Baltimore, MD 21239, 410-323-3708

Barbara Browne P
6120 Edmondson Ave
Catonsville, MD 21228, 301-747-1090
Pubs: *Studia Mystica, Wind, Anima, Poet's Pride*

Marion Buchman ♪ P
11 Slade Ave, #315
Baltimore, MD 21208, 410-764-3327
Pubs: *In His Pavilion* (Haskell Hse Pub, 1986), *America* (Thornhill Pr, 1976), *Redbook, Stanza*

Lynn Buck P
13801 York Rd, Apt K-10
Cockeysville, MD 21030-1899, 410-771-0916
Pubs: *Two Minus One* (Birnham Wood, 1994), *Autumn Fires* (Red Creek Pr, 1989), *Blueline, The Body Politic, Crazyquilt, Live Poets, Long Pond Rev, LIQ, Heartland*

Roser Caminals-Heath W
Hood College, 401 Rosemont Ave, Frederick, MD 21701,
301-696-3474
Internet: rheath@nimue.hood.edu
Pubs: *Un Segle De Prodigis* (Spain; Columbia, 1995), *Once Remembered, Twice Lived* (Peter Lang Pub, 1993), *Georgia Rev, Amer Book Rev*

Kit Carlson ♪ P&W
1122 Cresthaven Dr
Silver Spring, MD 20903
Internet: kitcarlson@hotmail.com
Pubs: *New Collage Mag, Proofrock, Driftwood, The Roses, The Pub, Pudding, Discovery Channel Mag, Ambo*

Grant Carrington ♪ W
PO Box 1219
Laurel, MD 20725-1120, 301-490-6142
Internet: gcarrington@hotmail.com
Pubs: *Time's Fool* (Doubleday, 1981), *Amazing, Fantastic, Cavalier, Canadian Forum, Eternity, Isaac Asimov's SF Mag*

John Carter P
332 Lincoln Ave
Takoma Park, MD 20912
Pubs: *Impetus, Poetry USA, Poetry SF, The Pearl, Prisoners of the Night, Gargoyle, Lactuca*

Merritt Clifton P&W
The Animals' Agenda, PO Box 25881, Baltimore, MD
21224-0581
Pubs: *Samisdat*

Lucille Clifton ♪ ✈ P
St. Mary's College, St Mary's City, MD 20686
Pubs: *Blessing the Boats, Terrible Stories, Quilting* (BOA Edtns, 2000, 1996, 1991), *The Book of Light* (Copper Canyon Pr, 1994), *Ten Oxherding Poems* (Moving Parts Pr, 1988)

Michael Collier ♪ ✈ P
111 Smithwood Ave
Catonsville, MD 21228-4945, 410-719-7312
Internet: mc33@umail.umd.edu
Pubs: *The Ledge* (HM, 2000), *The Neighbor* (U Chicago Pr, 1995), *The Folded Heart* (Wesleyan U Pr, 1989), *Atlantic, New Yorker*

Sarah Cotterill P
9624 Evergreen St
Silver Spring, MD 20901, 301-588-8983
Pubs: *In the Nocturnal Animal House* (Purdue U Pr, 1991), *The Hive Burning* (Sleeping Bird Pr, 1983), *APR, Poetry NW, Ploughshares, Nimrod, Kansas Qtly*

Judith Speizer Crandell 🎤 ✈   W
12 Hilltop Rd
Silver Spring, MD 20910, 301-588-2538
Internet: crandellink@juno.com
> Pubs: *Hudson River Anthology, Cleveland Mag, Allied Pub,
> Laughing Bear, Whiskey Island*

James Cross   W
c/o Hugh J. Parry, 4814 Falstone Ave, Chevy Chase, MD
20815, 301-652-5665
> Pubs: *To Hell for Half a Crown* (Random Hse, 1968), *Mary-
> land Poetry Rev*

Bruce V. J. Curley 🎤 ✈   P&W
4210 Candice Drive
Mount Airy, MD 21771-7464, 301-829-3794
Internet: civilization@adelphi.net
> Pubs: *Electric Life, Red Booth Rev, Wired Heart, Under a
> Gull's Wing: Anth* (Down the Shore Pr, 1996), *Baltimore Rev,
> Pannus Index, Lynx Eye, Mad Poets Rev, Voices Israel,
> Potomac Rev, WordWrights*

Ann Darr   P
4902 Falstone Ave
Chevy Chase, MD 20815, 301-652-4292
Internet: anndarr@aol.com
> Pubs: *Flying the Zuni Mountains* (Forest Woods Media
> Productions, 1994), *Hungry As We Are: Anth* (Washington
> Writers Pub Hse, 1995)

Robert Day   W
The O'Neil Literary House, Washington College, 300
Washington Ave, Chestertown, MD 21620, 410-778-2800
> Pubs: *Speaking French in Kansas* (Cottonwood, 1989), *The
> Four Wheel Drive Quartet* (Galileo, 1986), *TriQtly*

Nan DeVincent-Hayes, Ph.D 🎤 ✈   W
5736 Royal Mile Boulevard
Salisbury, MD 21801
Internet: ndh02252@umes-bird.umes.edu
> Pubs: *Jacob's Trouble, Thy Brother's Reaper* (Renaissance
> Alliance Pub, 2001, 2000), *22 Friar Street* (Flower Valley Pr,
> 2000), *Grit, Mature Years, Redbook, Slipstream, Sojourner*

Enoch Dillon 🎤   P
6310 Hollins Dr
Bethesda, MD 20817-2351, 301-530-7795
Internet: enochdillon@msn.com
> Pubs: *Love, From the Ends of the Earth, The Bicentennial
> Blues* (Fithian Pr, 1990, 1988), *The Lyric, America, Poet
> Lore, Visions, Light, Friends Jrnl, Mediphors*

Stephen Dixon 🎤 ✈   W
Johns Hopkins Univ, Writing Seminars Gilman 135, Baltimore,
MD 21218, 410-825-8038
> Pubs: *I.* (McSweeney's Bks, 2002), *Tisch* (Red Hen Pr,
> 2000), *30* (H Holt, 1999), *Sleep* (Coffee Hse Pr, 1999),
> *Gould, Interstate* (Owl Bks, 1998, 1997), TriQtly, Boulevard,
> Harper's, Virginia Qtly Rev, Speak, Fence

Thomas A. Dorsett   P
4408 Wickford Rd
Baltimore, MD 21210, 410-467-4316
> Pubs: *Dance Fire Dance* (Icarus Pr, 1992), *Confrontation,
> Descant, Verse, Paintbrush, America, Slant, Intl Poetry Rev*

Maura Eichner   P
College of Notre Dame, Baltimore, MD 21210
> Pubs: *Hope Is a Blind Bard* (Harold Shaw Pub, 1989), *What
> We Women Know* (Sparrow, 1980)

Daniel Mark Epstein 🎤 ✈   P
843 W University Pkwy
Baltimore, MD 21210-2911
> Pubs: *The Traveler's Calendar* (The Overlook Pr, 2001), *The
> Boy in the Well, Spirits* (The Overlook Pr/Viking, 1995,
> 1987), *Sister Aimee* (HB, 1993), *Love's Compass* (Addison-
> Wesley, 1990), New Yorker, Atlantic, New Republic, Paris
> Rev, Nation

Michael Fallon   P
3041 St Paul St
Baltimore, MD 21218-3943, 410-366-6850
> Pubs: *A History of the Color Black* (Dolphin Moon Pr, 1989),
> *The Salmon, Puerto del Sol, Poets On, Maryland Poetry
> Rev, Potomac Rev*

Diana J. Felts   P
113 Byway Rd
Owings Mills, MD 21117, 301-356-6984
> Pubs: *Impetus, Up Against the Wall Mother, Piedmont
> Literary Mag, The Mountain Laurel, Proof Rock*

Elizabeth Follin-Jones   P&W
4896 Chevy Chase Blvd
Chevy Chase, MD 20815, 301-652-4346
> Pubs: *Bite to Eat Place* (Redwood Coast Pr, 1995), *One
> Flight From the Bottom* (Artscape, 1990), *Poet Lore, Mary-
> land Poetry Rev, Embers, Free State*

Martin Galvin 🎤 ✈   P
4100 Blackthorne Street
Chevy Chase, MD 20815
Internet: galvin1@starpower.net
> Pubs: *Appetites* (Bogg Pub, 2000), *Wild Card* (Washington
> Writer's Pub Hse, 1989), *Making Beds* (Sedwick Hse, 1989),
> *Best American Poetry: Anth* (Scribner, 1997), *Painted Bride
> Qrtly, Midwest Qtly, Poetry, Atlantic, New Republic*

CJeanean Gibbs   P
Palm Tree Enterprises, Inc., 1514 Roosevelt Ave, Landover,
MD 20785
> Pubs: *Spirits of the Ancestors, Gurus & Griots* (Palm Tree
> Enterprises, 1993, 1987)

Michael S. Glaser 🎤 ✈   P
PO Box 1
Saint Mary's City, MD 20686-0001, 301-862-9676
Internet: msglaser@osprey.smcm.edu
Pubs: *In the Men's Room & Other Poems* (Painted Bride
Qtly, 1996), *A Lover's Eye* (Bunny & Crocodile Pr, 1989),
Light-Gathering Poems: Anth (H Holt, 2000), *Outsiders:
Anth* (Milkweed Edtns, 1999), *Unsettling America: Anth*
(Penguin, 1994), *CSM, New Letters*

Barbara Goldberg   P
6623 Fairfax Rd
Chevy Chase, MD 20815, 301-907-7994
Internet: bgoldberg@asha.org
Pubs: *Marvelous Pursuits* (Snake Nation Pr, 1995),
Cautionary Tales (Dryad Pr, 1990), *Paris Rev, Poetry, NER,
American Scholar, Poet Lore*

Ivy Goodman 🎤 ✈   W
3911 Spring Meadow Dr
Ellicott City, MD 21042
Pubs: *A Chapter From Her Upbringing* (Carnegie Mellon U
Pr, 2001), *Heart Failure* (U Iowa Pr, 1983), *Gettysburg Rev,
Epoch, Witness, Michigan Qtly Rev, Ploughshares*

Beatrice Greene   W
6418 Bannockburn Dr
Bethesda, MD 20817
Pubs: *New Orleans Rev, Mississippi Rev, Panache, The
Fiddlehead, Style, Calvert Rev*

Allen R. Grossman   P
English Dept, Johns Hopkins Univ, Baltimore, MD 21218
Pubs: *The Ether Dome & Other Poems New & Selected
1979-1991, The Bright Nails Scattered on the Ground* (New
Directions, 1991, 1986)

Greg Hannan   P
207 Hodge St
Takoma Park, MD 20912
Pubs: *A Shout in the Street, The Poet Upstairs, Gargoyle,
Cycloflame*

Jean Harmon   P&W
12813 Falmouth Dr
Silver Spring, MD 20904, 301-622-0442
Pubs: *Ancient Paths, Constal Pubs, Legions of Light, Popu-
lar Reality, Robin's Nest, Thirteen, Z Misc, Popular Reality,
Renegade, Amer Organist, Anathema Rev, 'Scapes, New
Voices, Metropolitain, Opera Monthly, Neologisms, Verse
Unto Us*

Reginald Harris 🎤 ✈   P&W
PO Box 7184
Baltimore, MD 21218
Internet: rmharris2001@hotmail.com
Pubs: *Ten Tongues* (Three Conditons Pr, 2002), *Black Silk:
Anth* (Warner, 2002), *Role Call: Anth* (Third World, 2002),
Bum Rush the Page: Anth (Three Rivers, 2001), *Bayou,
5am, High Plains Lit Rev, Eye Ball, In Posse Rev, African-
American Rev*

Clarinda Harriss 🎤 ✈   P
English Dept, Chair, Towson Univ, Towson, MD 21252,
401-830-2869
Internet: charriss@towson.edu or www.towson.edu
Pubs: *License Renewal for the Blind* (Cooper Hse, 1994),
The Night Parrot (Salmon Pub, 1989), *Forms of Verse*
(Appleton-Century Croft, 1975), *The Bone Tree* (NPS,
1973), *Poetry, Southern Rev, Spoon River Anth*

John Hayes   P&W
1300K Scottsdale Rd
Bel Air, MD 21015, 410-420-7749
Internet: johnhayesaw@worldnet.att.net
Pubs: *Great Writers, Great Stories: Anth* (IM Pr, 1999), *Fire
on the Hills: Anth* (Highlights for Children, 1995), *Lynx Eye,
Bogg, Alabama Lit Rev, Thema, Rockford Rev, Onionhead,
Fresh Ground, Implosion, Baltimore Rev, MacGuffin,
Antipodean*

William Heath 🎤 ✈   P
Mount St. Mary's College, Emmitsburg, MD 21727,
301-694-5365
Internet: heath@msmary.edu
Pubs: *The Children Bob Moses Led* (Milkweed, 1997), *The
Walking Man* (Icarus, 1994), *Kenyon Rev, Southern Rev,
Massachusetts Rev, South Carolina Rev, Texas Rev,
Monocacy Valley Rev, Cortland Rev*

David Hilton   P
413 Grinstead Rd
Severna Park, MD 21146
Pubs: *No Relation to the Hotel* (Coffee Hse Pr, 1989),
Huladance (Crossing Pr, 1976), *Poetry NW, BPJ, Exquisite
Corpse, Poetry, Iowa Rev*

Geoffrey Himes 🎤 ✈   P
8 E 39 St
Baltimore, MD 21218-1801, 410-235-6627
Internet: geoffhimes@aol.com
Pubs: *City Paper, Salt Lick, Columbia Flier, Maryland En-
glish Jrnl, Baltimore Sun, December*

Carol F. Hoover 🎤 ✈   W
4817 Tallahassee Ave
Rockville, MD 20853, 301-949-2514
Pubs: *Story, Denver Qtly, Texas Qtly, Potomac Rev,
Crescent Rev*

Gary Hotham 🎤 ✈ P
10460 Stansfield Rd
Laurel, MD 20723
    Pubs: *Breath Marks* (Canon Pr, 1999), *Footprints &
    Fingerprints* (Lilliput Rev Pr, 1999), *Bare Feet* (Longhouse,
    1998), *Quadrant, Presence, The Heron's Nest, Snapshots,
    Modern Haiku, Northeast, Tundra, Puckerbrush Rev*

Josephine Jacobsen P&W
13801 York Rd #T-366
Cockeysville, MD 21030, 410-527-9472
    Pubs: *The Instant of Knowing* (U Michigan Pr, 1997), *What
    Goes Without Saying, In the Crevice of Time* (Johns Hopkins
    Pr, 1996, 1995), *Distances* (Bucknell U Fine Edtns, 1992),
    On the Island (Ontario Rev Pr, 1988), *Of Leaf & Flowers:
    Anth* (Perrea Books, 2001)

Rod Jellema P
1003 S. Robinson Rd
Baltimore, MD 21224, 410-276-2248
Internet: rjellema@wam.umd.edu
    Pubs: *The Sound That Remains* (Eerdmans, 1990), *The
    Eighth Day* (Dryad Pr, 1985), *Field, Plum Rev, Atlanta Rev,
    Nimrod, Many Mountains Moving, Nightsun, Image,
    Christian Century, Poet Lore*

Lane Jennings 🎤 ✈ P
6373 Barefoot Boy
Columbia, MD 21045, 301-596-2943
Internet: lanejen@aol.com
    Pubs: *Fabrications: New & Collected Poems, White Lies*
    (Black Buzzard Pr, 1998, 1984), *Virtual Futures* (Other
    Worlds Pr, 1996), *White Lies, Visions, Amelia, Catalyst,
    Gargoyle, Starline, Treasure House*

Lynn Kanter W
3312 Camalier
Chevy Chase, MD 20815
    Pubs: *The Mayor of Heaven, On Lill Street* (Third Side Pr,
    1997, 1992), *Breaking Up Is Hard to Do: Anth, The Time of
    Our Lives: Anth* (Crossing Pr, 1994, 1993)

Wayne Karlin 🎤 ✈ W
PO Box 239
St Mary's City, MD 20686-0239, 301-862-9871
Internet: waynek@csm.cc.md.us
    Pubs: *The Wished-for Country, Prisoners, Rumors &
    Stones* (Curbstone Pr, 2002, 1998, 1996), *Us, The Extras,
    Lost Armies* (H Holt, 1993, 1989, 1988), *Crossover*
    (Harcourt, 1989)

Terrance Keenan 🎤 ✈ P
1468 Blue Mount Road
Monkton, MD 21111, 410-357-9578
Internet: jikai@mac.com
    Pubs: *St. Nadie in Winter* (Charles Tuttle Pubs, 2001),
    Practicing Eternity (Basfal Bks, 1996), *Herbal* (Great Elm Pr,
    1988), *Georgia Rev, Poetry Now, Epoch, Ironwood*

Madeleine Keller P
4613 Wilmslow Rd
Baltimore, MD 21210
    Pubs: *Pearl, Stony Run, Tamarind, Telephone, Niagara, The
    Spirit That Moves Us, Knock-Knock*

Marta Knobloch 🎤 ✈ P
111 Hamlet Hill Road #908
Baltimore, MD 21210-1513, 410-464-1829
    Pubs: *The Room of Months/La Stanza dei Mesi* (Book
    Editore, 1995), *Sky Pond* (SCOP Pubs, 1992), *Beyond
    Lament: Anth* (Northwestern U Pr, 1998), *Leggere Donna,
    Maryland Poetry Rev, Lyric, Visions Intl, Delos, Poesie,
    Poetry Australia*

Ann B. Knox 🎤 ✈ P&W
PO Box 65
Hancock, MD 21750-0065, 717-294-3272
Internet: tinkerword@aol.com
    Pubs: *Staying Is Nowhere* (SCOP Pubs, 1996), *Late
    Summer Break* (Papier-Mache, 1995), *Flamecrop*
    (Washington Writers Publishing Hse, 1990), *Poetry, Atlanta
    Rev, Plum Rev, Poets On, MacGuffin, Cumberland Poetry
    Rev, Potomac Rev*

Susan Land W
7004 Exsair Rd
Bethesda, MD 20814, 301-652-4982
    Pubs: *Confrontation, Quarry West, West Branch, Other
    Voices, Wind, Kansas Qtly, Mississippi Rev, Alaska Qtly Rev*

Charles R. Larson W
3600 Underwood St
Chevy Chase, MD 20815, 301-656-9370
    Pubs: *Arthur Dimmesdale* (Avon, 1984), *The Insect Colony*
    (HRW, 1978)

Joyce E. Latham 🎤 ✈ P
10205 Green Holly Terr
Silver Spring, MD 20902, 202-966-2494
Internet: jlcomm@erols.com
    Pubs: *Circumference of Days: Anth* (Westmoreland PA Arts
    Center, 1999), *My Mama Always Said: Anth* (Faith Byrnie,
    1998), *Poetry Motel, Sliver Quill, Allusive Images, Art
    Inspires Writing, Poet Mag, Federal Poet, Jrnl of Graduate
    Liberal Studies, Poetry Today*

Kevin J. Lavey 🎤 ✈ W
20 North Montford Ave
Baltimore, MD 21224, 410-752-4708
Internet: kjlumb@earthlink.net
    Pubs: *Dan River Anth* (Dan River, 1995), *42opus,
    Slipstream, Z Miscellaneous, Licking River Rev*

Barbara F. Lefcowitz 🎤 ✈ P&W
4989 Battery Ln
Bethesda, MD 20814, 301-652-0835
Internet: blefcowitz@aol.com
Pubs: *The Politics of Snow, A Hand of Stars* (Dancing Moon Bks, 2001, 1999), *The Minarets of Vienna* (Chestnut Hills, 1996), *Shadows & Goatbones* (SCOP Pubs, 1992), *Other Voices, Prairie Schooner*

Harrison Edward Livingstone W
PO Box 7149
Baltimore, MD 21218
Pubs: *Baltimore, Harvard, John* (Conservatory Pr, 1988, 1987), *The Wild Rose: A Novel of the Sea* (Word of Mouth Pr, 1980), *David Johnson Passed Through Here* (Little, Brown, 1971)

Barbara Lockheart W
5602 Le Compte Rd
Rhodesdale, MD 21659
Internet: loc@dmv.com
Pubs: *Requiem for a Summer Cottage* (Southern Methodist U Pr, 2002), *Generation to Generation: Anth* (Papier Mache Pr, 1998), *Greensboro Rev, Women's Words, Pleiades*

Kathy Auchincloss Lorr P
302 Windsor St
Silver Spring, MD 20910, 301-585-7667
Pubs: *Science 82, Poet Lore, Poets On, Dark Horse, Vision, Womanspirit, Gargoyle*

Kathy Mangan P
3003 St Paul St
Baltimore, MD 21218, 410-243-0242
Internet: kmangan@wmdc.edu
Pubs: *Above the Tree Line* (Carnegie Mellon U Pr, 1995), *Pushcart Prize XV: Anth* (Pushcart Pr, 1991), *Georgia Rev, Gettysburg Rev, Shenandoah, Southern Rev*

Lena Dale Matthews P
4014 Roland Ave
Baltimore, MD 21211

John Mazur 🎤 ✈ P
247 S Ellwood Ave
Baltimore, MD 21224, 410-342-6843
Pubs: *Autumn Harvest: Anth* (Quill Bks, 2001), *Lover's Lane: Anth, Ever Green & Sunsets Red: Anth, Little Verse, Big Thought: Anth* (Golden Apple Pr, 1998, 1997, 1995), *Images of the Mind: Anth* (Modern Poetry Society, 1996)

Phillip McCaffrey 🎤 ✈ P
4121 Westview Rd
Baltimore, MD 21218
Pubs: *Freud & Dora* (Rutgers U Pr, 1984), *Teaching the Door to Close* (Lame Johnny, 1983), *Poetry*

Jean McGarry W
Johns Hopkins Univ, The Writing Seminars, Baltimore, MD 21218
Pubs: *Gallagher's Travels, Home at Last, The Very Rich Hours* (Johns Hopkins U Pr, 1997, 1994, 1987), *The Courage of Girls* (Rutgers U Pr, 1992), *New Yorker, SW Rev, Boulevard, Yale Rev*

Ann Landis McLaughlin W
6702 Maple Ave
Chevy Chase, MD 20815, 301-654-6877
Pubs: *The House on Q Street, Maiden Voyage, Sunset at Rosalie, The Balancing Pole, Lightning in July* (John Daniel & Co, 2002, 1999, 1996, 1991, 1989)

Terry McMillan 🎤 W
c/o Speakers Worldwide, PO Box 30195, Bethesda, MD 20814, 800-408-7757
Internet: spkrsww@aol.com
Pubs: *A Day Late and a Dollar Short, How Stella Got Her Groove Back, Waiting to Exhale, Disappearing Acts, Breaking Ice: Anth* (Viking, 2001, 1996, 1992, 1989, 1990), *Mama* (HM, 1987), *Essence, Esquire*

Margaret Meacham 🎤 ✈ W
Box 402, 10430 Falls Rd, Brooklandville, MD 21022
Internet: mmeac@aol.com
Pubs: *Standing Up to Hammerhead* (Holiday Hse, 2001), *Oyster Moon* (Tidewater, 1997), *Call Me Cathy* (Archway Pocket, 1995), *Vacation Blues, Love in Focus* (Berkley Pubs, 1985, 1983)

Elizabeth J. Morris W
8708 Ewing Dr
Bethesda, MD 20817, 301-530-3267
Pubs: *Metropolitan, The Writing on the Wall, Gyst 6, Short Story, Crazyquilt*

Phyllis Reynolds Naylor W
9910 Holmhurst Rd
Bethesda, MD 20817, 301-530-2340
Pubs: *Achingly Alice, Sang Spell, The Fear Place, All But Alice, Shiloh, Send No Blessings* (Atheneum, 1998, 1998, 1994, 1992, 1991, 1990)

Gloria Oden 🎤 ✈ P
Eng Dept, Univ Maryland, Baltimore County, 1000 Hilltop Circle, Baltimore, MD 21250, 410-242-0581
Pubs: *The Tie That Binds, Resurrections* (Olivant Pr, 1980, 1978), *Ms., Saturday Rev, Nimrod*

Linda Pastan 🎤 ✈ P
11710 Beall Mountain Rd
Potomac, MD 20854, 301-299-2362
Internet: lpastan@att.net
Pubs: *The Last Uncle, Carnival Evening: New & Selected Poems, An Early Afterlife, Heroes in Disguise* (Norton, 2002, 1998, 1995, 1991), *Paris Rev, Kenyon Rev, Ohio Rev, Poetry, Gettysburg Rev, Georgia Rev*

Kathy Pearce-Lewis   P
10501 Montrose Ave #102
Bethesda, MD 20814-4141, 301-530-4692
Internet: klew@erols.com
   Pubs: *Autumn Harvest: Anth* (Quill Bks, 2001), *Weavings
   2000: Anth* (Maryland Commission for Celebration 2000,
   2000), *Waiting for You to Speak: Anth* (Mekler & Deahl,
   1999), *Free State: Anth, The Cooke Book: A Seasoning of
   Poets: Anth* (SCOP Pub, 1989, 1987)

Lia Purpura 🎤 ✈   P
5116 Norwood Rd
Baltimore, MD 21212-4101
Internet: lpurpura@loyola.edu
   Pubs: *Increase* (U Georgia Pr, 2000), *Stone Sky Lifting* (Ohio
   State U Pr, 2000), *The Brighter the Veil* (Orchises Pr, 1996)

Marijane G. Ricketts 🎤   P
10203 Clearbrook Pl
Kensington, MD 20895-4121, 301-564-0852
Internet: marijan@ioip.com
   Pubs: *Autumn Harvest: Anth* (Quill Bks, 2001), *Maryland
   Millennial Anth* (St Mary's College, 2000), *The Child
   Without, The Child Within: Anth* (Earth's Daughters, 1994),
   Prose & Poetry: Anth (Writers League of Washington, 1992),
   Quirks, Washington Post

Phyllis Ringler   P&W
2306 Tucker Ln
Baltimore, MD 21207-6638, 410-448-2740
   Pubs: *Nerval's Magic Alphabet* (Peter Lang Pub, 1989),
   *Catonsville Times, Arbutus Times, Baltimore Sun, Sub-
   Stance, Modern Language Notes, Minnesota Rev*

Doris Rochlin   W
10100 Baldwin Ct
Bethesda, MD 20817, 301-581-0051
   Pubs: *In the Spanish Ballroom* (Doubleday, 1991),
   Frobisch's Angel (Taplinger Pub Co, 1987)

Peter Sacks   P
Writing Seminars, Johns Hopkins Univ, 34th & N Charles St,
Baltimore, MD 21218, 301-338-7564
   Pubs: *Promised Lands* (Viking, 1990), *In These Mountains*
   (Macmillan, 1986)

Karen Sagstetter 🎤 ✈   P&W
6004 Madawaska Rd
Bethesda, MD 20816-3105, 301-229-2370
   Pubs: *Ceremony* (State Street Pr, 1981), *New Stories From
   the South: Anth* (Algonquin Bks, 2000), *Antietam Rev,
   Glimmer Train, Poet Lore*

Diane Scharper   P
Towson Univ, 8000 York Rd-Linthicum 219K, Towson, MD
21204-0001, 410-830-2868
Internet: dscharpe@towson.edu
   Pubs: *Radiant* (Cathedral Fdn Pr, 1996), *The Laughing
   Ladies* (Dolphin Moon Pr, 1993), *Maryland Rev, City Paper,
   Saltimbanquers*

Steven Schutzman   P&W
2903 Ailsa Ave
Baltimore, MD 21214-2524, 410-254-7870
   Pubs: *Smoke the Burning Body Makes* (Panjandrum, 1978),
   The History of Sleep (Gallimaufry, 1976), *Sudden Fiction:
   Anth* (Gibbs Smith, 1986), *TriQtly*

Myra Sklarew   P&W
6521 Marywood Rd
Bethesda, MD 20817, 202-885-2811
Internet: msklarew@erols.com
   Pubs: *Over the Rooftops of Time* (SUNY Pr, 2002), *The
   Witness Trees* (Cornwall Pr, 2000), *Lithuania: New &
   Selected Poems* (Azul Edtns, 1997)

Susan Sonde 🎤 ✈   P
2011 St Stephens Woods Dr
Crownsville, MD 21032-2200, 301-858-1528
Internet: susansonde@msn.com
   Pubs: *In the Longboats With Others* (New Rivers, 1988),
   *Qtly West, Carolina Qtly, Cimarron, Conjunctions, NW Rev,
   Chelsea, Ohio Rev New and Selected*

Elizabeth Spires 🎤 ✈   P
6208 Pinehurst Rd
Baltimore, MD 21212-2532, 410-532-9752
   Pubs: *Now the Green Blade Rises* (Norton, 2002), *The
   Mouse of Amherst* (FSG, 1999), *Worldling* (Norton, 1995),
   Annonciade (Viking Penguin, 1989), *Swan's Island* (H Holt,
   1985)

Margaret Stavely   P
26096 Lambs Meadow Rd PO Box 8
Worton, MD
21678-0008, 410-348-2320
   Pubs: *Stopping the Sun* (Kent County Arts Council, 1982),
   *The Poets Domain: A Little Nonsense Vol 14: Anth, The
   Poets Domain: Straightaway Dangerous: Anth* (Road Pub,
   1997, 1996), *Sun Mag, Little Balkans Rev, Tapestry of the
   Mind, Maryland Poetry Rev*

Adele Steiner 🎤 ✈   P
6211 Wagner Ln
Bethesda, MD 20816-1028
Internet: beardog9@aol.com
   Pubs: *Freshwater Pearls* (Mellen Pr, 1997), *Refracted Love*
   (Bootleg Pr, 1993), *Promise Mag, Lucid Stone, Wordwrights,
   Black Buzzard Rev, M Mag, So to Speak, Maryland Rev*

Joseph McNair Stover   P&W
20854 Sandstone St
Lexington Park, MD 20653-2439
   Pubs: *Commander Coatrack Returns* (HM, 1989), *South
   Florida Poetry Rev, Florida Rev, The Cathartic, Potomac
   Rev, Connections*

Ron Tanner   W
Loyola College, Writing & Media Dept, 4501 N Charles St,
Baltimore, MD 21210-2699, 410-617-2434
   Pubs: *Best of the West: Anth* (Norton, 1991), *The Pushcart
   Prize XIV: Anth* (Pushcart Pr, 1990), *20 Under 30: Anth*
   (Scribner, 1986), *New Letters, Literary Rev, Iowa Rev,
   Michigan Qtly Rev*

James Taylor 🎤 ✈   P
Dolphin-Moon Press, PO Box 22262, Baltimore, MD 21203,
410-444-7758
   Pubs: *Shocked & Amazed! On & Off the Midway, Artifacture*
   (Dolphin-Moon Pr, 1995, 1989), *Puerto del Sol, Lips*

Henry Taylor 🎤 ✈   P
6930 Selkirk Dr
Bethesda, MD 20817, 301-320-5930
Internet: htaylor@american.edu
   Pubs: *Brief Candles: 101 Clerihews, Understanding Fiction:
   Poems 1986-1996, The Flying Change* (LSU Pr, 2000, 1996,
   1986), *Poetry, Sewanee Rev, New Republic, Shenandoah*

Chezia Thompson Cager 🎤 ✈   P&W
Spectrum of Poetic Fire: Reading Series, Maryland Institute of
College of Art, 1300 Mount Royal Ave, Baltimore, MD 21217,
410-947-8618
Internet: mstrand@bellatlantic.net
   Pubs: *The Presence of Things Unseen: Giant Talk*
   (Maisonneuve Pr, 1996), *Power Objects* (Baltimore Festival
   of the Arts, 1996), *When Divas Laugh: Anth* (Black Classic
   Pr, 2001), *Catch the Fire!!!: Anth* (Riverhead Bks, 1998),
   Poet Lore, Gargoyle, Potomac Rev

Michelle M. Tokarczyk 🎤 ✈   P
English Dept, Goucher College, 1021 Dulaney Valley Rd,
Baltimore, MD 21204-2794, 410-337-6165
Internet: mtokarcz@goucher.edu
   Pubs: *The House I'm Running From* (West End Pr, 1989),
   For a Living: Poetry of Work: Anth (U Illinois Pr, 1995),
   College English, Minnesota Rev, Pearl, Poetry NY

Margot Treitel   P
5508 Mystic Ct
Columbia, MD 21044-1856, 410-730-8575
   Pubs: *The Inside Story* (Tropos Pr, 1987), *Chicago Rev,
   Prairie Schooner, Lit Rev, NER, Carolina Qtly*

Mary M. Truitt   W
418 Duvall La
Annapolis, MD 21403, 410-268-8526
   Pubs: *1990 PEN Syndicated Fiction Project, Louisville Rev,
   Gargoyle, Mississippi Mud*

Stacy Tuthill 🎤 ✈   P&W
713 Maiden Choice La,   Apt 5303
Catonsville, MD 21228-3935, 410-536-1877
Internet: 102047.3727@compuserve.com
   Pubs: *House of Change* (Forest Woods Media, 1996), *Taste
   of Smoke* (East Coast Bks, 1995), *Wisconsin Rev, Hawaii
   Pacific Rev, Poet Lore, Emrys Jrnl, Poets On*

Anne Tyler   W
222 Tunbridge Rd
Baltimore, MD 21212-3422
   Pubs: *Back When We Were Grownups, A Patchwork Planet,
   Breathing Lessons, The Accidental Tourist* (Knopf, 2001,
   1998, 1988, 1985)

Kevin Urick   W
114 Hutchins Ct
Havre de Grace, MD 21078, 410-939-7062
   Pubs: *Snow World, The Death of Colonel Jones* (White Ewe,
   1983, 1980)

Patricia Valdata 🎤 ✈   P&W
36 Gina Ct
Elkton, MD 21921-2300
   Pubs: *Crosswind* (Wind Canyon Pub, 1996), *In Praise of
   Pedagogy: Anth* (Calendar Island, 2000), *Boomer Girls:
   Anth* (U Iowa, 1999), *Salt River Rev, Grasslands Rev, Icarus*

John Vieira 🎤 ✈   P
PO Box 59243
Potomac, MD 20859
Internet: john_vieira@adidam.org
   Pubs: *Points on a Hazard Map* (Runaway Spoon, 1999),
   Half-Life (Score, 1999), *Self-Portrait with Demons* (Runaway
   Spoon, 1997), *Reality Slices* (Runaway Spoon, 1996), *Many
   Mountains Moving, Rolling Stone, Typewriter, Assembling,
   Kaldron, Hummingbird, AGNI*

Davi Walders 🎤 ✈   P
4704 Essex Ave
Chevy Chase, MD 20815, 301-657-3282
Internet: dwalders@yahoo.com
   Pubs: *Gifts* (Orit Edtns, 2001), *Beyond Lament: Poets of the
   World Bearing Witness to the Holocaust: Anth*
   (Northwestern U Pr, 1998), *A More Perfect Union: Poems
   and Stories About the Modern Wedding: Anth* (St Martins Pr,
   1998), *JAMA, Ms., Amer Scholar*

Michael Waters 🎤 ✈   P
English Dept, Salisbury Univ, 1101 Camden Ave, Salisbury,
MD 21801-6860, 410-742-2559
Internet: mgwaters@salisbury.edu
   Pubs: *Parthenopi: New & Selected Poems, Green Ash, Red
   Maple, Black Gum* (BOA Edtns, 2001, 1997), *Bountiful, The
   Burden Lifters, Anniversary of the Air* (Carnegie Mellon U Pr,
   1992, 1989, 1985)

Riggin Waugh 🎤 ✈ P&W
PO Box 5243
Takoma Park, MD 20913-5243, 301-891-3953
Internet: rigginwaugh@aol.com
Pubs: *Life's a Stitch: The Best of Contemporary Women's Humor: Anth* (Random House, 2001), *Dykes with Baggage: Anth* (Alyson Pubs, 2000), *Ex-Lover Weird Shit: Anth* (TOOTS, 1994), *Women's Glib: Anth, Word of Mouth: Anth* (Crossing Pr, 1991, 1991)

Howard Weinstein W
7814 Edmunds Way
Elkridge, MD 21075
Pubs: *Power Hungry, Deep Domain, The Covenant of the Crown* (Pocket Bks, 1989, 1987, 1981)

Irving Weiss 🎤 ✈ P&W
319 Rosin Dr
Chestertown, MD 21620-2823, 410-778-2951
Internet: irving@dmv.com
Pubs: *Water Aphorisms in Writing on Water* (MIT Pr, 2001), *Number Poems, Visual Voices* (Runaway Spoon Pr, 1997, 1994), *Score, Caliban, Context, Wordimage, Lazy Bones Rev, Montserrat Rev, Synaesthetic, Ubu, Rio Mag, Spilled Ink Forum, Abraxas*

Julia Wendell 🎤 ✈ P
3637 Blackrock Rd
Upperco, MD 21155-9322, 410-239-4662
Internet: jawendell@aol.com
Pubs: *Wheeler Lane* (Igneous Pr, 1998), *An Otherwise Perfect History* (Ithaca Hse, 1988), *Missouri Rev, Prairie Schooner, Crazyhorse, The Jrnl*

John Milton Wesley P
c/o Jamal A. Rahman, 3942 Resierstown Rd, Baltimore, MD 21215, 410-578-8226
Pubs: *The Soybean Field* (Wesley, 1985), *Black Southern Voices: Anth* (NAL, 1985), *Metropolitan*

Philip Wexler P
9208 Chanute Dr
Bethesda, MD 20814, 301-897-8367
Internet: philip_wexler@nlm.nih.gov
Pubs: *Slow Dancer, Kansas Qtly, Z Miscellaneous, Painted Hills Rev, Mudfish, Jacaranda Rev, Monocacy Valley Rev*

Reed Whittemore P
4526 Albion Rd
College Park, MD 20740
Pubs: *Six Literary Lives* (U Missouri Pr, 1993), *The Past, the Future, the Present* (U Arkansas Pr, 1990)

Terence Winch 🎤 ✈ P
10113 Greeley Ave
Silver Spring, MD 20902, 301-681-8956
Internet: tpwinch@netkonnect.net
Pubs: *The Drift of Things* (The Figures, 2001), *The Great Indoors,* (Story Line Pr, 1995), *Best American Poetry 1997: Anth* (Scribner, 1998), *Paris Rev, NAW, APR, New Republic, Western Humanities Rev*

Michele Wolf 🎤 ✈ P
4615 N Park Ave, #810
Chevy Chase, MD 20815-4514, 301-718-9408
Internet: michelewolf@juno.com
Pubs: *Conversations During Sleep* (Anhinga Pr, 1998), *The Keeper of Light* (Painted Bride Qtly, 1995), *When I Am an Old Woman I Shall Wear Purple: Anth* (Papier-Mache Pr, 1987), *Rattapallax, Poetry, Hudson Rev, Boulevard, Antioch Rev, SPR, Poet Lore*

Winnie Zerne P
731 Old Herald Harbor Rd
Crownsville, MD 21032-1524
Pubs: *Maria, Daughter of Shadow* (Pacific Pr, 1976)

MASSACHUSETTS

Janet E. Aalfs 🎤 ✈ P&W
PO Box 1064
Easthampton, MA 01027, 413-586-6831
Pubs: *Reach* (Perugia Pr, 1999), *Full Open* (Orogeny Pr, 1996), *Sister/Stranger* (Sidewalk Revolution Pr, 1993), *And a Deer's Ear* (Cleis Pr, 1990), *Onion River Rev, California State Poetry Qtly, Peregrine, Evergreen Chronicles*

Jonathan Aaron P
100 Larch Rd
Cambridge, MA 02138
Pubs: *Corridor* (Wesleyan-New England, 1992), *Second Sight* (H&R, 1982), *The Best American Poetry: Anths* (Scribner, 1992, 1991), *Partisan Rev*

Robert H. Abel 🎤 ✈ W
27 Stockwell Rd
North Hadley, MA 01035-9644, 413-584-6257
Internet: robert.abel@the-spa.com
Pubs: *Riding a Tiger* (Asia, 2000, 1997), *Ghost Traps* (U Georgia Pr, 1991), *Glimmer Train, Manoa, Writer's Forum, Colorado Rev*

Kathleen Aguero 🎤 ✈ P
3 Gladstone St
Cambridge, MA 02140
Internet: agueroka@pmc.edu
Pubs: *The Real Weather* (Hanging Loose Pr, 1987), *Thirsty Day* (Alice James Bks, 1977), *Southwest Rev, Poetry, Sojourner*

Samuel Albert P
1550 Worcester Rd, #102W
Framingham, MA 01701, 508-879-5113
    Pubs: *As Is* (Wampeter, 1983), *Hozannah The Home Run*
    (Little, Brown, 1972), *This Sporting Life: Anth* (Milkweed,
    1987), *Atlantic, Hudson Rev, BPJ, Harvard Mag, Agni*

Alan Albert ♀ ⊀ P
27 Auburn St #5
Framingham, MA 01701, 508-393-9014
Internet: aa1000@aol.com
    Pubs: *Worcester Rev, California Qtly, Mississippi Rev,*
    Wisconsin Rev, APR, Madrona, SW Rev, Kansas Qtly,
    Obras Mag, New Infinity Rev

Francis Alix ♀ ⊀ P
226 The Jamaicaway
Boston, MA 02130, 617-522-9787
    Pubs: *Ordinary Time: Anth* (Daedalus Pr, 2000), *Black*
    Creek Rev, Pine Island Rev, Poet Lore, Sahara, Aurorean,
    Black Bear Rev

Samuel W. Allen P
145 Cliff Ave
Winthrop, MA 02152, 617-846-1996
    Pubs: *Every Round & Other Poems* (Lotus Pr, 1987), *Paul*
    Vesey's Ledger (Paul Breman Pr, 1975)

Keith Althaus ♀ ⊀ P
PO Box 163
North Truro, MA 02652-0163, 508-487-2557
    Pubs: *Tikkun, Rival Heavens* (Provincetown Arts Pr, 1993),
    APR, Agni, Virginia Qtly Rev, Seneca Rev, Provincetown
    Arts, Grand Street

Ray Amorosi P
Box 376
Marshfield Hills, MA 02051
    Pubs: *Flim Flam, A Generous Wall* (Lynx Hse Pr, 1980,
    1976), *Field, Iowa Rev*

Peter Anastas ♀ ⊀ W
PO Box 211
Gloucester, MA 01931-0211, 978-283-4582
Internet: panastas@shore.net
    Pubs: *Maximus to Gloucester* (Ten Pound Island Bk Co,
    1992), *Polis, Larcom Rev, Split Shift, Cafe Rev, Sulfur*

Frieda Arkin W
6 Manning St
Ipswich, MA 01938-1922, 978-356-2128
    Pubs: *The Essential Kitchen Gardener* (H Holt, 1990), *The*
    Dorp (Dial, 1969), *Beyond Lament: Anth* (Northwestern U
    Pr, 1998), *McCall's, Georgia Rev, Yale Rev, Transatlantic*
    Rev, California Qtly, Kenyon Rev

Jeannine Atkins W
PO Box 226
Whately, MA 01093
    Pubs: *Fiction Network, NAR, Pacific Rev, PEN Syndicated*
    Fiction, Jam To-Day

Robert Bagg ♀ ⊀ P
582 Pfersick Rd
Shelburne Falls, MA 01370-9590
    Pubs: *Body Blows: Poems New & Selected* (U
    Massachusetts, 1988), *The Scrawny Sonnets & Other*
    Narratives (Illinois U Pr, 1973), *Atlantic, Poetry, Boston Rev*

Donald W. Baker P&W
61 Seaway
East Brewster, MA 02631, 508-896-7963
    Pubs: *Search Patterns, The Readiness* (Sugar
    Creek/Steppingstone, 1996, 1995), *The Day Before,*
    Unposted Letters, Formal Application (Barnwood Pr, 1988,
    1985, 1982)

Carol Baker ♀ ⊀ P
2 Main St, PO Box 307
Montague, MA 01351-0307, 413-367-0367
    Pubs: *Sojourner, Ploughshares, NYQ, Mississippi Rev,*
    Stand, Women's Rev of Bks, Massachusetts Rev, Nation

Stanislaw Baranczak P
Harvard Univ, 313 Boylston Hall, Cambridge, MA 02138
    Pubs: *Breathing Under Water, A Fugitive From Utopia*
    (Harvard U Pr, 1991, 1987), *Selected Poems: The Weight of*
    the Body (Another Chicago Pr, 1989)

Rachel Barenblat ♀ ⊀ P
Box 669
Williamstown, MA 01267, 413-499-4565
www.rachelbarenblat.com
    Pubs: *What Stays* (Bennington Alum Chpbk Series, 2002),
    The Skies Here (Pecan Grove Pr, 1995), *Holding True: Anth*
    (Mad River Pr, 1999), *The Best of Pif Magazine Off-Line:*
    Anth (Fusion Pr, 1999), *Mangrove, Phoebe, Confrontation,*
    New Orleans Rev

R Bartkowech ♀ ⊀ W
54 Beach St
Woburn, MA 01801-3125, 781-937-0389
Internet: rayb@ziplink.net
    Pubs: *Fiction Intl, Mississippi Rev, SPR, ACM, Greenfield*
    Rev, APR

Edward Bartok-Baratta ♀ ⊀ P&W
PO Box 358
Northampton, MA 01061
    Pubs: *Like Thunder: Poets Respond to Violence in America*
    (U Iowa Pr, 2002), *Magazine Verse & Yearbook of American*
    Poetry: Anth (Monitor, 1998), *Ploughshares, Denver Qtly,*
    Manoa: A Pacific Jrnl of Intl Writing, African Amer Rev,
    Beloit Fiction Jrnl

Milton Bass   W
View Dr, Rte 49
Pittsfield, MA 01201, 413-698-2271
    Pubs: *The Broken-Hearted Detective, The Half-Hearted
    Detective* (Pocket Bks, 1994, 1993)

Guy R. Beining 🎤 ✈   P
156 West Park St., Unit 9
Lee, MA 01238
    Pubs: *Measurement of Night* (CC Marimbo, 2002), *Writing
    to be Seen: Anth* (Light & Dust, 2001), *Too Far to Hear,
    Chapters XIV-XXVI* (Standing Stones Pr, 1997), *Carved
    Erosion* (Elbow Pr, 1995), *The Capilano Rev, Borderlands,
    Black Warrior Rev, Kiosk*

June Beisch   P
19 Brown St
Cambridge, MA 02138, 617-497-2241
    Pubs: *A Fatherless Woman* (Cape Women's Pr, 2000), *Take
    Notes* (Epiphany Pubs, 1992), *Radcliffe Qtly, Epiphany,
    North Essex Rev, Dialogue, Northland Qtly, Lit Rev, Tendril,
    NE Corridor, Florida Rev, Cape Women Mag*

Richard N. Bentley 🎤 ✈   P&W
24 N. Prospect St
Amherst, MA 01002, 413-256-0240
Internet: rbentley@acad.umass.edu
    Pubs: *Postfreudian Dreaming* (AWA Pr, 2002), *Lumina,
    Westview, Pleiades, Paris Transcontinental, Southern
    Indiana Rev*

Suzanne E. Berger   P
23 Billingham St
Somerville, MA 02144, 617-625-3041
    Pubs: *Legacies* (Alice James Pr, 1984), *These Rooms*
    (Penmaen Pr, 1979), *Harvard Rev, New York Times, We
    Animals, Texas Qtly Anth, Ploughshares, Sojourner*

Denise Bergman   P
82 Elm St
Cambridge, MA 02139
    Pubs: *City River of Voices: Anth* (West End Pr, 1992),
    *Mudfish, Frontiers, Kalliope, Moving Out, 5 A.M., Sojourner,
    South Florida Poetry Rev, Sing Heavenly Muse, Pig Iron,
    Nimrod, Oxford Rev*

Anne Bernays   W
16 Francis Ave
Cambridge, MA 02138, 617-354-2577
    Pubs: *Professor Romeo* (Weidenfeld & Nicolson, 1989),
    Growing Up Rich (Little, Brown, 1975), *Sports Illustrated,
    New Woman, Amer Heritage, New Republic, Sophisticated
    Traveler, Nation*

MaryEllen Beveridge 🎤 ✈   W
40 Linnaean St, #11
Cambridge, MA 02138-1566
    Pubs: *Other Voices, Emrys Jrnl, Writers Mag, South
    Carolina Rev, New Orleans Rev, New Renaissance,
    Georgia Rev*

Frank Bidart 🎤 ✈   P
63 Sparks St #3
Cambridge, MA 02138, 617-497-1226
    Pubs: *Music Like Dirt* (Sarabande Books, 2002), *Desire, In
    the Western Night: Collected Poems 1965-90* (FSG, 1997,
    1990)

F. C. Blessington 🎤 ✈   P
English Dept, Northeastern Univ, Boston, MA 02115,
617-437-2512
    Pubs: *The Last Witch of Dogtown* (Curious Traveller Pr,
    2001), *Wolf Howl* (BkMk Pr, 2000), *Lorenzo de Medici* (U Pr
    America, 1992), *Lantskip* (Wm. L. Bauhan, 1987), *Wind,
    Southern Rev, Piedmont Lit Rev, Cumberland Poetry Rev,
    Harvard Mag, Arion*

W. F. Bolton 🎤 ✈   P
119 Beechwood Rd
Halifax, MA 02338, 781-293-2220
    Pubs: *An Introduction to Literature: Anth* (Addison Wesley
    Longman, 2001), *Explorations: Anth* (Univ of Alaska
    Southeast, 1994), *Poetry, Bridgeway Rev*

Harold Bond   P
11 Chestnut St
Melrose, MA 02176-5306, 781-662-7806
    Pubs: *Articulations: The Body in Poetry: Anth* (U Iowa Pr,
    1994), *The Magical Pine Ring: Anth* (Wayne State U Pr,
    1992), *Ararat, Kaleidoscope, Raft*

Mary Bonina 🎤 ✈   P
44 Thingvalla Ave
Cambridge, MA 02138, 617-491-6416
    Pubs: *City River of Voices: Anth* (West End Pr, 1992),
    Noctiluca, Red Brick Rev, Hanging Loose, English Jrnl

Paula Bonnell   P
44 Codman Hill Ave
Boston, MA 02124, 617-367-5990
    Pubs: *Poet Lore, Blue Buildings, SPR, Manhattan Poetry
    Rev, Blue Unicorn, Pulpsmith, Floating Island, Invisible City*

Lisa Borders 🎤 ✈   W
47 Avon St
Somerville, MA 02143-1601
Internet: lisaborders@aol.com
    Pubs: *Cloud Cuckoo Land* (River City Pub, 2002), *Crescent
    Rev, Washington Square, Painted Bride Qtly, Black Warrior
    Rev, Bananafish, NE Corridor, Iowa Woman, Agassiz Rev,
    Snake Nation Rev*

Daniel Bosch 🎤 ✈					P
Expository Writing, 8 Prescott St, Cambridge, MA 02138-3929
Internet: bosch@fas.harvard.edu
    Pubs: *Crucible* (Other Pr, 2002), *Agni, New Republic, Harvard Rev, Western Humanities Rev, Denver Qtly, BPJ*

Marguerite Guzman Bouvard 🎤 ✈			P
6 Brookfield Cir
Wellesley, MA 02181, 781-237-1340
Internet: marguerite.bouvard@worldnet.att.net
    Pubs: *Wind, Frost & Fire* (AB Collector Pubs, 2001), *The Body's Burning Fields* (Wind Pub, 1997), *Of Light & Silence* (Zoland Bks, 1990), *With the Mothers of the Plaza de Mayo* (Igneus Pr, 1993), *Journeys Over Water, 50th Anniversary Anth* (QRL, 1980, 1994)

William C. Bowie						P
30 Smith Rd
Ashfield, MA 01330
Internet: info@wcbowie.com
    Pubs: *The Conservator's Song* (U Arkansas Pr, 1993)

Sally Ryder Brady						W
Brady Literary Management, 267 Dudley Rd, Bedford, MA
01730, 617-275-1842
    Pubs: *Yankee Christmas* (Yankee Bks/Rodale Pr, 1993), *Instar* (Doubleday, 1976), *Catholic Digest*

Jeanne Braham						P&W
239 River Rd
Sunderland, MA 01375
    Pubs: *Starry, Starry Night* (Brookline Bks/Lumen Ed, 1998), *Crucial Conversations* (Teachers College Pr/Columbia, 1995), *A Sort of Columbus* (U Georgia Pr, 1984), *One Means of Telling Time* (Geryon Pr, 1981)

Melanie Braverman					P&W
PO Box 1404
Provincetown, MA 02657, 508-487-6576
Internet: mrb@mail1.wn.net
    Pubs: *East Justice* (Permanent Pr, 1996), *Welcome to Your Life: Anth* (Milkweed Edtns, 1998), *Amer Voice, Carolina Qtly, Provincetown Arts, APR*

Lucie Brock-Broido					P
Creative Writing Dept, Harvard Univ, 34 Kirkland St,
Cambridge, MA 02138
    Pubs: *A Hunger* (Knopf, 1988), *Amer Voice, Paris Rev, APR, New Republic, SW Rev, Ploughshares, Virginia Qtly, Mississippi Rev, Ironwood, Kenyon Rev*

Martin Broekhuysen 🎤 ✈				P
120 Pearl St
Cambridge, MA 02139, 617-492-4510
    Pubs: *Ararat, New Letters, Aspect, Nation, SPR, Nimrod,*

Ben Brooks 🎤 ✈						W
PO Box 440387
West Somerville, MA 02144-0387, 617-623-3719
Internet: bbrooks@mos.org
    Pubs: *The Icebox* (Amelia Pr, 1987), *Virginia Qtly Rev, Sewanee Rev, Mississippi Rev, O. Henry Prize Stories, Amer Short Fiction, Alaska Qtly Rev*

Olga Broumas 🎤 ✈					P
162 Mill Pond Dr
Brewster, MA 02631, 508-240-6452
Internet: broumas@brandeis.edu
    Pubs: *Rave: Poems 1975-1999, Sappho's Gymnasium, Perpetua* (Copper Canyon Pr, 1999, 1994, 1989), *APR, Amer Voice, Sonora Rev, Zyzzyva*

Robert Edward Brown					P
PO Box 442
Brimfield, MA 01010-0442
    Pubs: *Gathering Light* (Red Hill Pr, 1976), *Altadena Rev, Bachy, Coast, Sunset Palms Hotel*

Steven Ford Brown					P
22 Everett Ave
Sommerville, MA 02145
    Pubs: *Invited Guest: An Anth of 20th Century Southern Poetry* (U Virginia Pr, 2001), *Astonishing World* (Milkweed Edtns, 1993), *Considered Music* (Harrington-Black, 1989), *Harvard Rev, Seneca Rev*

Jane Brox							P
1334 Broadway
Dracut, MA 01826
    Pubs: *Here & Nowhere Else* (Beacon Pr, 1995), *In Short: Anth* (Norton, 1996), *Georgia Rev, Gettysburg Rev, Salamander, NER, Hudson Rev*

Roy Bryan							P
Cross Place Rd
Washington, MA 01235, 413-623-6446
    Pubs: *Winter Lightning* (Wild Thistle Pr, 1979), *Poetry East, Home Planet News*

Ruth Buchman 🎤 ✈					P
33 Endicott Ave
Somerville, MA 02144, 617-623-3874
    Pubs: *Sou'wester, Harvard Rev, Antioch Rev, Embers, Birmingham Poetry Rev, Cricket, Sojourner, Sing Heavenly Muse*

Claudia Buckholts 🎤 ✈				P&W
15 Clarendon Ave
Somerville, MA 02144-1704, 617-666-9040
Internet: lanbuck@ix.netcom.com
    Pubs: *Southern Poetry Rev, Prairie Schooner, Harvard Mag, Connecticut Poetry Rev, Minnesota Rev, Midwest Qtly, Kansas Qtly*

Julia Budenz 🎤 ✈   P
1616 Massachusetts Ave, Apt 5
Cambridge, MA 02138, 617-868-4769
    Pubs: *From the Gardens of Flora Baum* (Wesleyan U Pr, 1984), *North Stone Rev, CloeliaRhino, Notre Dame Rev*

George Buggs   P
333 VFW Pkwy
Chestnut Hill, MA 02167-3715
Internet: ogbuggs@msn.com

Michael Burkard   P
4 Brewster St #7
Provincetown, MA 02657
    Pubs: *Entire Dilemma* (Sarabande Bks, 1998), *My Secret Boat* (Norton, 1990), *The Fires They Kept* (Metro Bk Co., 1986), *Paris Rev, APR, Epoch, Denver Qtly, Exquisite Corpse, Central Park, Salt Hill Jrnl, Volt, Plum Rev, Zone 3*

Carol Burnes   P
Box 364
Weston, MA 02193, 781-899-7518
Internet: jburnes@earthwatch.org
    Pubs: *An Episode of Buttons* (Flarestack Pub U.K., 1998), *Fine Lines* (Headland Pubs, 1992), *Roots & Wings* (Emerald Pr, 1986), *13th Moon, Little Mag, Pipe Works UK, Rhino, Sail, CSM, Connections, Connecticut Mag*

Stanley Burnshaw   P&W
PO Box 1147
W Tisbury, MA 02575, 508-693-9389
    Pubs: *Complete Poetry and Selected Prose* (U Texas Pr, 2002), *The Seamless Web* (Braziller, 1991), *A Stanley Burnshaw Reader* (U Georgia Pr, 1990), *Atlantic, Sewanee Rev, Poetry, Saturday Rev, Nouvelle Rev*

Teresa Cader   P
20 Clarke St
Lexington, MA 02173, 617-863-0166
    Pubs: *Guests* (Ohio State U Pr, 1991), *Touchstones: Anth* (U Pr New England, 1996), *TriQtly, Harvard Mag, Ploughshares, Agni, Parnassus: Poetry in Rev*

Rafael Campo 🎤 ✈   P
330 Brookline Ave
Boston, MA 02215
Internet: rcampo@caregroup.harvard.edu
    Pubs: *Diva, What the Body Told* (Duke U Pr, 1999, 1996), *The Desire to Heal* (Norton, 1997), *The Other Man Was Me* (Arte Publico Pr, 1994), *Beacon Best American Poetry: Anth* (Scribner, 1995), *Best of 1999: Anth* (Beacon, 1999)

Jeffrey A. Carver 🎤 ✈   W
102 Melrose St
Arlington, MA 02474
Internet: jeff@starrigger.net
    Pubs: *Eternity's End, The Infinite Sea, Strange Attractors, Neptune Crossing, Dragon Rigger, Dragons in the Stars* (Tor, 2000, 1996, 1995, 1994, 1993, 1992), *From a Changeling Star* (Bantam, 1989), *The Infinity Link* (Bluejay, 1984), *Science Fiction Age*

John Case   P&W
37A Prentiss St
Cambridge, MA 02140

Helen Marie Casey 🎤 ✈   P
85 Pokonoket Ave
Sudbury, MA 01776, 978-443-4753
Internet: HMCasey@aol.com
    Pubs: *Mischief, Caprice, and Other Betic Stragegies: Anth* (Red Hen Pr, 2002), *Connecticut Rev, America, Larcom Rev, NE Corridor, Laurel Rev, Windhover, Worcester Rev, CSM, Passager*

Elena Castedo 🎤 ✈   P&W
Accent Media, 36 Lancaster St, Cambridge, MA 02140-2840, 617-492-6026
    Pubs: *Paradise* (Grove Pr, 1995), *El Paraiso* (Ediciones B, 1994), *Prairie Schooner, New Letters, Phoebe, Afro-Hispanic Rev, Listening to Ourselves, Iguana Dreams, Mirrored Garden*

Naomi Feigelson Chase   P
PO Box 1231, 66 Depot Rd
Truro, MA 02666-1231, 508-349-1991
    Pubs: *Stacked, Waiting for the Messiah in Somerville, Massachusetts* (Garden Street Pr, 1998, 1993), *Listening for Water* (Archival Pr, 1987), *Harvard Rev, South Coast Poetry Jrnl, Yankee, ALR, Prairie Schooner, Amaranth, ELF, Lowell Rev*

Karen Chase 🎤 ✈   P&W
PO Box 634
Lenox, MA 01240, 413-637-0505
    Pubs: *Kazimierz Square* (Cavan Kerry Pr, 2000), *Introduction to Literature: Anth, Introduction to Poetry: Anth* (Norton, 1998, 1998), *Yellow Silk: Anth* (Crown, 1990), *Southern Rev, New Republic, Yale Rev, New Yorker*

Helen Chasin   P
9 South St Ct
Rockport, MA 01966, 508-546-2937
    Pubs: *Casting Stones* (Little, Brown, 1975), *Coming Close* (Yale U Pr, 1968)

Laura Chester   P&W
25 Rose Hill
Alford, MA 01230, 413-528-0458
    Pubs: *The Story of the Lake* (Faber & Faber, 1995), *Bitches
    Ride Alone* (Black Sparrow, 1991), *The Unmade Bed: Anth*
    (HC, 1992)

James William Chichetto   P
PO Box 136
South Easton, MA 02375-0136
Internet: chichetto@stonehill.edu
    Pubs: *Homage to Father Sorin* (Connecticut Poetry Rev Pr,
    1993), *Blood to Remember: American Poets on the
    Holocaust: Anth* (Texas Tech U Pr, 1991), *Poem, Colorado
    Rev, Boston Globe*

M. Riesa Clark   P
14 Windsor Rd
Beverly, MA 01915-2626, 978-524-0157
    Pubs: *Laurels: Anth* (Laurel Pr, 1994), *Parnassus, Night
    Roses, Moonstone Blue, World Order, Poetry Peddler,
    Bitterroot*

John J. Clayton 🎤 ✈   W
English Dept, Univ Massachusetts, Amherst, MA 01003,
413-548-9645
Internet: jclayton@english.umass.edu
    Pubs: *Radiance* (OSU Pr, 1998), *Man I Never Wanted to
    Be* (Permanent Pr, 1998), *Bodies of the Rich* (U Illinois,
    1984), *What Are Friends For?* (Little, Brown, 1979), *Heath
    Intro to Fiction* (HM, 1999), *Esquire, Agni, Playboy, TriQtly,
    Georgia Rev*

Bradley Clompus 🎤 ✈   P
75 Brookings St
Medford, MA 02155
    Pubs: *The Journal, Tampa Rev, Tar River Poetry, Willow
    Springs, Passages North, West Branch, Poet Lore*

Dick Cluster   W
33 Jackson St
Cambridge, MA 02140-2424, 617-876-8464
Internet: dick.cluster@umb.edu
    Pubs: *Obligations of the Bone* (St. Martin's Pr, 1992),
    Repulse Monkey, Return to Sender (Dutton, 1989, 1988)

Andrew Coburn   W
3 Farrwood Dr
Andover, MA 01810, 508-475-8701
    Pubs: *Birthright* (S&S, 1997), *Voices in the Dark, No Way
    Home* (Dutton, 1994, 1992), *Goldilocks* (Scribner, 1989),
    Love Nest, Sweetheart (Macmillan, 1987, 1985), *A Woolf in
    Vita's Clothing, Lilacs, Charley Judd, Transatlantic Rev,
    Ellery Queen*

Judith Beth Cohen 🎤 ✈   W
Lesley College Graduate School, 29 Everett St, Cambridge,
MA 02138
    Pubs: *Seasons* (Permanent Pr, 1984), *High Plains Lit Rev,
    Rosebud, Rockford Rev, Amer Rev, New Letters*

Pat Lowery Collins   P&W
3 Wauketa Rd
Gloucester, MA 01930-1423, 978-283-2749
Internet: patlc19@idt.net
    Pubs: *The Fattening Hut, Just Imagine, Signs & Wonders*
    (HM, 2003, 2001, 1999), *Schooner* (Commonwealth Edtns,
    2002), *The Quiet Woman Wakes Up Shouting* (Folly Cove
    Bks, 1998), *I Am an Artist* (Millbrook Pr, 1992), *CQ, Wind,
    Small Pond, Yankee*

William Conelly 🎤 ✈   P&W
131 Montague Rd
Leverett, MA 01054, 413-548-9430
    Pubs: *Downward Towns: Anth, Touring* (Van Zora Press,
    1999, 1998), *A Green Sleep, Foothills, Nine Years After:
    Anth* (R. L. Barth, 1996, 1987, 1989), *Light, Tennessee Qtly,
    Dark Horse, Poets On, Pleiades, Epigrammatist, Sticks*

William Corbett   P
9 Columbus Sq
Boston, MA 02116, 617-266-5466
    Pubs: *City Nature III, On Blue Note* (Zoland Bks, 1991,
    1989), *o.blek, Lift, NAW, Talisman, Notus*

Bill Costley 🎤 ✈   P
One Sunset Rd
Wellesley, MA 02482, 781-431-1314
Internet: billcostley@yahoo.com
    Pubs: *Siciliconia* (Beehive Pr, 1995), *Terrazzo* (Malfunction
    Pr, 1993), *A(y)s(h)a, Rag(a)s* (Ghost Dance, 1988, 1978),
    Ploughshares

Steven Cramer 🎤 ✈   P
130 Bedford St
Lexington, MA 02420, 781-862-1704
    Pubs: *Dialogue for the Left & Right Hand* (Lumen Edtns,
    1997), *The World Book* (Copper Beech, 1992), *Atlantic,
    Nation, New Republic, Paris Rev, Poetry*

Dean Crawford   W
800 Northwest Hill Rd
Williamstown, MA 01267
    Pubs: *Lay of the Land* (Viking, 1987), *Epoch, NER*

D. L. Crockett-Smith 🎤 ✈   P
131 Old State Rd
Berkshire, MA 01224, 413-499-9877
    Pubs: *Civil Rites, Cowboy Amok* (Black Scholar Pr, 1996,
    1987), *Black Scholar, Open Places, Minnesota Rev, New
    Collage*

George Cuomo   P&W
121A Brattle St
Cambridge, MA 02138, 617-576-0972
Internet: jgcuomo@aol.com
  Pubs: *A Couple of Cops, Trial by Water* (Random Hse,
  1995, 1993)

Siouxie D   P
12 Wendell St #3
Cambridge, MA 02138, 617-491-8973
Internet: recept4@harvard.edu
  Pubs: *After Gary, It's Only Life* (Self/Aardvark Enterprises,
  1996, 1992), *Quest, Heartlight Jrnl, Poet's Pen Qtly, Pagan
  America, Vision Seeker*

Ellen Darion   W
335A Harvard St, Apt 12
Cambridge, MA 02139, 617-492-2793
  Pubs: *Gettysburg Rev, Special Report: Fiction, Epoch*

Helene Davis   P
19 Cherry St
Somerville, MA 02144

Hope Hale Davis   W
1600 Massachusetts Ave, #704
Cambridge, MA 02138, 617-497-5988
  Pubs: *Great Day Coming* (Steerforth Pr, 1994), *The Dark
  Way to the Plaza* (Doubleday, 1968), *New Leader, New
  Yorker, Radcliffe Qtly*

Peter Davison 🎤 ✈   P
70 River St
Boston, MA 02108-1125, 617-742-0342
Internet: davispoe@aol.com
  Pubs: *Breathing Room: New Poems, The Poems of Peter
  Davison 1957-1995* (Knopf, 2000, 1995), *The Fading Smile:
  Poets in Boston 1955-1960: Anth* (Norton, 1996), *Atlantic,
  Yale Rev, Frank, Nation, New Republic, Five Points,
  DoubleTake, Poetry, APR*

Corinne Demas 🎤 ✈   W
Mount Holyoke College, English Dept, South Hadley, MA
01075, 413-538-2801
Internet: cdemas@mtholyoke.edu
  Pubs: *If Ever I Return Again* (HC, 2000), *Eleven Stories High*
  (SUNY Pr, 2000), *What We Save for Last* (Milkweed, 1992)

Benjamin Demott   W
English Dept, Amherst College, Amherst, MA 01002

Diana Der-Hovanessian   P
2 Farrar St
Cambridge, MA 02138, 617-864-2224
  Pubs: *The Burning Glass, Any Day Now, Circle Dancers,
  Selected Poems* (Sheep Meadow Pr, 2002, 1999, 1997,
  1994), *Harvard Rev, Poetry, Partisan Rev, Amer Scholar,
  Agni, Graham Hse, Partisan Rev, CSM, Nation, Prairie
  Schooner, Yankee*

William Devoti   P
Foley Rd
Sheffield, MA 01257, 413-229-8461
Internet: dotbill@bcn.net
  Pubs: *October Mountain* (Mountain Pr, 1991), *Coming Out
  of It* (Hollow Springs, 1981), *Third Berkshire Anth* (Berkshire
  Writers, 1982)

Robb Forman Dew   W
218 Bulkley St
Williamstown, MA 01267, 413-458-3477
  Pubs: *The Evidence Against Her* (Little Brown, 2001), *A
  Southern Thanksgiving, The Family Heart* (Addison-Wesley,
  1995, 1994), *Fortunate Lives, The Time of Her Life* (Morrow,
  1992, 1984), *Dale Loves Sophie to Death* (FSG, 1982)

Richard Dey 🎤 ✈   P
178 Gardner St
Hingham, MA 02043, 617-740-2920
  Pubs: *New Bequia Poems* (Offshore Pr, 1996), *The Bequia
  Poems* (Caribbean; Macmillan, 1989), *Sail, Poetry, Harvard
  Mag, Light, Caribbean Writer, Caribbean Compass*

Gerard Dombrowski   P
PO Box C
Somerville, MA 02143, 617-623-8017

David F. Donavel   P
54 Pearl St
Amesbury, MA 01913, 508-388-2337
  Pubs: *Cape Rock, Windless Orchard, Tendril, Snowy Egret,
  Wind, Fireland Arts Rev, Kansas Qtly*

Susan Donnelly 🎤 ✈   P
32 Shepard St, #21
Cambridge, MA 02138, 617-491-4559
Internet: sedonne@aol.com
  Pubs: *Tenderly Pressed* (Every Other Thursday Pr, 1993),
  Eve Names the Animals (Northeastern U Pr, 1985), *Norton
  Introduction to Poetry: Anth* (Norton, 1995), *Ploughshares,
  SPR, Poetry, Atlantic*

Susan Donovan P
Box 2662
Amherst, MA 01004-2662, 413-545-3897
Pubs: *White Lobster* (Blue Willow Inn, 1980), *Georgia Rev, Massachusetts Rev, New Letters*

Mary Harris Driscoll P
206 W Main St
Milbury, MA 01527, 508-865-4242
Pubs: *Soundings East: Anth* (Salem State College, 1985), *Skylark, Pegasus, Night Sun, Sounds of Poetry, Manhattan Poetry Rev, Embers, Riverwind, Potpourri, Prairie Dog, Green Mountains Rev, Black Fly Rev*

Amy Dryansky 🎤 ✈ P
19 Hidden Ledge Dr
Conway, MA 01341
Internet: 70604.2363@compuserve.com
Pubs: *How I Got Lost So Close to Home* (Alice James Bks, 1999), *Luna, DoubleTake, Bloomsbury Rev, SPR, Mudfish, Harvard Rev, NER, Marlboro Rev*

Andre Dubus, III W
24 Allen St
Newburyport, MA 01950-3002, 978-462-1010
Pubs: *House of Sand and Fog* (Norton, 1999), *Bluesman* (Faber & Faber, 1993), *The Cage Keeper & Other Stories* (Dutton, 1989)

Ann duCille P
Bridgewater State College, English Dept, Bridgewater, MA 02324, 617-697-1258
Pubs: *For Neruda/For Chile: Anth* (Beacon Pr, 1975), *APR, Bridgewater Rev, Iowa Rev, New Letters*

Alan Dugan P
Box 97
Truro, MA 02666
Pubs: *New & Collected Poems: 1961-1983* (Ecco Pr, 1983)

Susan Eisenberg 🎤 ✈ P
9 Rockview St
Jamaica Plain, MA 02130
Internet: ssneisnbrg@aol.com
Pubs: *Literature, Class and Culture: Anth* (Addison Wesley Longman, 2001), *Pioneering* (Cornell U Pr, 1998), *It's a Good Thing I'm Not Macho* (Whetstone, 1984), *The Progressive, Alaska Qtly Rev, Orion, The Women's Rev of Bks, Prairie Schooner, Mothering*

Craig Ellis 🎤 ✈ P
159 Thoreau St, #1
Concord, MA 01742, 978-369-3450
Pubs: *Sparrow in the Supermarket* (Beehive Pr, 1997), *Aspect, Assembling, Gallimaufry, Intrepid, Nostoc, Wormwood Rev, Same As Day Pr*

David Ely W
PO Box 1387
East Dennis, MA 02641
Pubs: *A Journal of the Flood Year, Always Home & Other Stories* (Donald I. Fine, 1992, 1991), *Mr. Nicholas* (Putnam, 1974), *Walking Davis* (Charterhouse, 1972), *Poor Devils* (HM, 1970), *Time Out, The Tour* (Delacorte, 1968, 1967), *Trot, Seconds* (HM, 1963, 1963)

Leslie Epstein 🎤 ✈ W
23 Parkman St
Brookline, MA 02146, 617-734-3896
Internet: leslieep@bu.edu
Pubs: *Ice Fire Water: A Leib Goldkorn Cocktail, King of the Jews, Pinto & Sons* (Norton, 1999, 1992, 1992), *Goldkorn Tales* (SMU Pr, 1998), *Pandaemonium* (St. Martin's, 1998), *Playboy, Georgia Rev, Harper's, Atlantic, TriQtly, Yale Rev, Nation*

Martin Espada P
Univ Massachusetts, English Dept, Bartlett Hall, Amherst, MA 01003, 413-545-6594
Pubs: *Imagine the Angels of Bread, City of Coughing & Dead Radiators* (Norton, 1996, 1993), *Rebellion Is the Circle of a Lover's Hands* (Curbstone, 1990)

Rhina P. Espaillat 🎤 P
12 Charron Dr
Newburyport, MA 01950-3705
Internet: espmosk@juno.com
Pubs: *An Introduction to Poetry: 10th Ed.: Anth* (Longman Pubs, 2002), *Rehearsing Absence* (U Evansville Pr, 2001), *Mundo y Palabra/The World & the Word* (Oyster River Pr, 2001), *Landscapes With Women: Anth* (Singular Speech Pr, 2000), *The Dark Horse*

Nancy Esposito 🎤 ✈ P
34 Trowbridge St
Belmont, MA 02478-4002, 617-484-7479
Internet: nesposito@bentley.edu
Pubs: *Changing Hands, QRL 50th Anniverary: Anth* (QRL, 1984, 1993), *Stand, Eclipse, Prairie Schooner, SW Rev, Indiana Rev, Nation, APR, Seattle Rev*

Richard J. Fein 🎤 ✈ P
46 Irving St
Cambridge, MA 02138, 617-354-2785
Pubs: *I Think of Our Lives* (Creative Arts Books, 2002), *Ice Like Morsels, To Move Into the House, At the Turkish Bath* (Chestnut Hills Pr, 1999, 1996, 1994), *Kafka's Ear* (The New Poets Series, 1990)

Alan Feldman 🎤 ✈ P&W
399 Belknap Rd
Framingham, MA 01701-2807, 508-877-4370
Pubs: *Harvard Rev, Best American Poetry: Anth* (Collier Books, 2001), *Anniversary* (Chekhov & Co, 1992), *Poetry, Virginia Qtly Rev*

Jyl Lynn Felman 🎤 ✈   W
8 High Meadow Rd
Florence, MA 01062, 413-586-8080
    Pubs: *Cravings, Her Face in the Mirror: Anth, The Tribe of
    Dina: Anth* (Beacon, 1997, 1994, 1989) *Hot Chicken Wings*
    (Aunt Lute Bks, 1992)

William Ferguson   P&W
1 Tahanto Rd
Worcester, MA 01602, 508-757-1683
    Pubs: *Freedom & Other Fictions* (Knopf, 1984), *Mississippi
    Rev, Fiction, Harper's, Paris Rev*

Vincent Ferrini   P
126 E Main St
Gloucester, MA 01930, 978-283-5640
    Pubs: *Deluxe Daring* (Atelier, 1994), *Magdalene Silences, A
    Tale of Psyche* (Igneus, 1992, 1991), *Why, Atelier, First
    Intensity, House Organ, Left Curve*

David Ferry 🎤 ✈   P
8 Ellery St
Cambridge, MA 02138, 617-354-7327
Internet: dferry@wellesley.edu
    Pubs: *Raritan*

Andrew Fetler   W
125 Amity St
Amherst, MA 01002-2202
    Pubs: *Norton Anth of Short Fiction* (Norton, 1994), *Prize
    Stories: The O. Henry Awards Anth* (Doubleday, 1984),
    Guggenheim, Atlantic, TriQtly, NAR

Thomas Filbin   W
104 Clear Pond Dr
Walpole, MA 02801
    Pubs: *William & Mary Rev, Cache Rev, Proof Rock,
    Mississippi Valley Rev, Boston Rev, New Renaissance*

Peter Filkins 🎤 ✈   P
PO Box 34
Williamstown, MA 01267, 413-743-9103
Internet: pfilkins@simons-rock.edu
    Pubs: *After Homer* (George Braziller, 2002), *What She
    Knew* (Orchises Pr, 1998), *The New Republic, Partisan Rev,
    VERSE, Southwest Rev, The Amer Scholar, The Formalist,
    AGNI, The New Criterion*

Brent Filson   W
RFD White Oaks Rd
Williamstown, MA 01267, 413-458-5285
    Pubs: *Exploring With Lasers* (S&S, 1984), *The Puma*
    (Doubleday, 1984), *Yankee, Vermont Life*

Jack Flavin   P
634 Armory St
Springfield, MA 01104
    Pubs: *Atlantic, Massachusetts Rev, Epoch, Poetry NW,
    Plains Poetry Rev, Galley Sail Rev, Sonoma Mandala,
    Apalachee Qtly, Spoon River Poetry Rev, Midwest Qtly*

Marjorie Fletcher   P
36 Moon Hill Rd
Lexington, MA 02173, 617-861-9659
    Pubs: *33, Us: Women* (Alice James Bks, 1976, 1974)

Maria Flook   P&W
PO Box 2022
Truro, MA 02666, 508-487-7918
    Pubs: *You Have the Wrong Man, Open Water, Family Night*
    (Pantheon, 1996, 1995, 1993), *New Yorker, New Criterion,
    Ploughshares, Bomb*

Nick Flynn 🎤 ✈   P
Box 1341
Provincetown, MA 02657
    Pubs: *Blind Huber, Some Ether* (Graywolf Pr, 2002, 2000),
    New American Poets, A Bread Loaf Anth (U Pr New En-
    gland, 2000), *American Poetry: The Next Generation: Anth*
    (Carnegie Mellon U Pr, 2000), *Ploughshares, NER, BOMB,
    Kenyon Rev, Paris Rev*

Aaron Fogel 🎤 ✈   P
English Dept, Boston Univ, 236 Bay State Rd, Boston, MA
02215
Internet: amfogel@acs.bu.edu
    Pubs: *The Printer's Error* (Miami U Pr, 2001), *Best American
    Poetry: Anths* (Scribner, 1995, 1990), *The Stud Duck, Agni,
    Boulevard, Amer Poet*

Jan Frazier 🎤 ✈   P
75 Lyman Rd
Northfield, MA 01360, 413-498-5435
Internet: janf@javanet.com
    Pubs: *Our Mothers, Our Selves: Anth* (Bergin & Garvey,
    1996), *Yankee Mag, Passages North, Plum Rev, High Plains
    Lit Rev, Artful Dodge, Kalliope, Calyx*

K. C. Frederick   W
68 Chestnut St, #1
West Newton, MA 02165-2549
Internet: frederick@umbsky.cc.umb.edu
    Pubs: *Country of Memory* (Permanent Pr, 1998), *Sacred
    Ground* (Milkweed Edtns, 1996), *Epoch, Shenandoah,
    Kansas Qtly, Fiction Intl, Ascent, Qtly West, Beloit Fiction Jrnl*

Jan Freeman 🎤 ✈   P
PO Box 487
Ashfield, MA 01330
Internet: parispr@crocker.com
  Pubs: *Simon Says* (Paris Pr, 2000), *Hyena* (Cleveland State
  U Poetry Ctr, 1993), *Autumn Sequence* (Paris Pr, 1993),
  Oxford Book of Women's Writing in the U.S.: Anth (Oxford U
  Pr, 1995), *Chelsea, Massachusetts Rev, APR, Amer Voice*

Margaret Howe Freydberg   W
RR Box 21 Stonewall Pond
Chilmark, MA 02535
  Pubs: *Growing Up in Old Age* (Parnassus, 1998), *Winter
  Concert* (Countryman, 1985)

D. Dina Friedman 🎤 ✈   P
PO Box 1164
Northampton, MA 01061-1164, 413-586-2388
Internet: dina@frugal.fun.com
  Pubs: *Calyx, The Sun, Hurricane Alice, Paragraph, Black
  Bear Rev, Amelia, Oxalis, Worcester Rev, Permafrost,
  Pacific Poetry & Fiction Rev*

Barbara Friend 🎤 ✈   P
Atticus Books, 8 Main Street, Amherst, MA 01002,
413-542-2328
  Pubs: *Thirtieth Year to Heaven* (Jackpine Pr, 1980), *NEQ,
  Cumberland Rev, Commentary, Virginia Qtly Rev, Ms.,
  Yankee*

Kenny Fries 🎤 ✈   P
42 Day Ave
Northampton, MA 01060-2353
  Pubs: *Desert Walking, Anesthesia* (Advocado Pr, 2000,
  1996), *The Healing Notebooks* (Open Bks, 1990), *Kenyon
  Rev, American Voice, Ploughshares, Progressive*

Rocco Fumento   W
1100 Main St
Dalton, MA 01226-2202, 413-684-4006
Internet: rfumento@webtv.net
  Pubs: *A Decent Girl Always Goes to Mass on Sunday*
  (Exlibris Pr, 2002), *The Sea Wolf* (SIU Pr, 1998), *42nd
  Street* (U Wisconsin Pr, 1980), *Tree of Dark Reflection*
  (Knopf, 1963), *Penguin Book of Italian American Writing:
  Anth* (Penguin, 2002), *Chicago, Ramparts*

Erica Funkhouser 🎤 ✈   P
179 Southern Ave
Essex, MA 01929
  Pubs: *Pursuit, The Actual World, Sure Shot* (HM, 2002,
  1997, 1992), *Natural Affinities* (Alice James Bks, 1983)

Brendan Galvin 🎤 ✈   P
PO Box 383
Truro, MA 02666-0383
  Pubs: *Place Keepers, The Strength of a Named Thing, Sky
  & Island Light, Saints in their Ox-Hide Boat, Wampanoag
  Traveler* (LSU Pr, 2003, 1999, 1997, 1992, 1989), *Hotel
  Malabar* (U Iowa Pr, 1998), *Great Blue: New & Selected
  Poems* (U Illinois Pr, 1990)

Kinereth Gensler   P
221 Mt Auburn St, #404, Cambridge, MA 02138, 617-576-7243
Internet: kgens@worldnet.att.net
  Pubs: *Journey Fruit: Poems & a Memoir, Without Roof* (Alice
  James Bks, 1997, 1981), *Connection* (Teachers & Writers,
  1978), *Amer Voice, The Bridge, Poetry, Ploughshares,
  Sou'wester, Massachusetts Rev*

Faye George 🎤 ✈   P
21 Old Forge Rd
Bridgewater, MA 02324, 508-697-5577
  Pubs: *The Four Way Reader #2: Anth* (Four Way Bks, 2001),
  A Wound on Stone (Perugia Pr, 2001), *Poetry Comes Up
  Where It Can: Anth* (U Utah Pr, 2000), *Orpheus and
  Company: Contemporary Poems on Greek Mythology: Anth*
  (Univ of New England Pr, 1999)

David Giannini   P
PO Box 630
Otis, MA 01253-0630
  Pubs: *Rim* (Indian Mountain Pr, 1998), *Others' Line* (Cityful
  Pr, 1997), *The Unmade Bed: Anth* (HC, 1992), *Sonora Rev,
  Tel-Let, Talisman, Longhouse, Hummingbird*

Celia Gilbert 🎤 ✈   P
15 Gray Gardens W
Cambridge, MA 02138, 617-864-8778
Internet: cgilbert@nucleus.harvard.edu
  Pubs: *An Ark of Sorts, Bonfire* (Alice James Bks, 1998,
  1983), *Queen of Darkness* (Viking, 1977), *Tin House,
  Poetry, New Yorker*

Michael Gizzi   P
36 Cliffwood St
Lenox, MA 01240, 413-637-4215
  Pubs: *Continental Harmony* (Roof Bks, 1991), *Vers
  d'Aigrefin* (Les Cahiers de Royaumont, 1991), *TXT, Shiny,
  Talisman, Tyuonyi, Sulfur, Temblor*

Perry Glasser   W
Box 1913
Haverhill, MA 01831, 508-373-2687
  Pubs: *Singing on the Titanic* (U Illinois Pr, 1987), *Suspicious
  Origins* (New Rivers Pr, 1983), *Ms., NAW, TriQtly,
  Confrontation, Special Reports: Fiction*

James Glickman　　　　　　　　　　　W
51 McGilpin Rd
Sturbridge, MA 01566-1230
Internet: jaglickman@aol.com
 Pubs: *Sounding the Waters* (Crown, 1996), *Kansas Qtly, Redbook, Ladies' Home Jrnl*

Louise Gluck 🎤 ✈　　　　　　　　　　P
14 Ellsworth Park, #2
Cambridge, MA 02139-1011
 Pubs: *Vita Nova, Meadowlands, The Wild Iris, Ararat, The Triumph of Achilles* (Ecco, 1999, 1996, 1992, 1990, 1985), *New Yorker, APR, Threepenny Rev, Yale Rev, Tikkun*

Georgia Gojmerac-Leiner　　　　　　P
9 Union St
Natick, MA 01760-4709, 508-655-8073
Internet: gojmerac@bcvms.bc.edu
 Pubs: *Whose Woods These Are: Anth* (Word Works, 1983), *96 Inc, Vermont Times, Onion River Rev, Embers, Green Mountains Rev*

E. S. Goldman 🎤 ✈　　　　　　　P&W
PO Box 561
South Orleans, MA 02662-0561, 508-255-2312
 Pubs: *The Palmer Method, Big Chocolate Cookies* (John Daniel Co, 1995, 1988), *Earthly Justice* (TriQtly, 1990), *Atlantic, Missouri Rev, Cimarron*

Elizabeth Goldring　　　　　　　　P
383 Old Ayes Rd
Groton, MA 01450
Internet: goldring@mit.edu
 Pubs: *Laser Treatment* (Blue Giant Pr, 1983), *Without Warning* (Helicon Nine Edtns, 1995), *Asylum, Helicon Nine*

Deborah Gorlin 🎤 ✈　　　　　　　P
20 Maplewood Dr
Amherst, MA 01002-1843, 413-549-4146
Internet: dgorlin@hampshire.edu
 Pubs: *Bodily Course* (White Pine Pr, 1997), *Best Spiritual Writing: Anth* (HM, 2000), *Green Mountains Rev, Harvard Rev, Antioch Rev, Bomb, APR, Massachusetts Rev, Poetry, Prairie Schooner, NER*

Jennifer Gostin 🎤　　　　　　　　W
330 Salt Winds Dr
Eastham, MA 02642
Internet: ghostie@c4.net
 Pubs: *Peregrine's Rest* (Permanent Pr, 1996), *A Sense of Place: Anth* (G. Drake, 2002), *The Mage, North Shore Life, The Gamut, Whiskey Island, Byline, Monocacy Valley Rev*

Tzivia Gover 🎤 ✈　　　　　　　P&W
3 Vassar Circle
Holyoke, MA 01040
Internet: tz11@aol.com
 Pubs: *Love Shook My Heart, 2: Anth* (Alyson Pubs, 2001), *Grrr: A Collection of Poems About Bears: Anth* (Arctos Pr, 1999), *My Lover Is a Woman: Anth* (Ballantine Bks, 1996), *Berkshire Rev, Bark Mag, Peregrine, Malachite & Agate, Sinister Wisdom, Sojourner*

E. J. Graff 🎤 ✈　　　　　　　　W
c/o Beacon Press, 25 Beacon St, Boston, MA 02108
Internet: ejgraff@aol.com
 Pubs: *What Is Marriage For?* (Beacon Pr, 1999), *Tasting Life Twice: Anth* (Avon Morrow, 1995), *Voices of the X-iled: Anth* (Doubleday, 1994), *Iowa Rev, Kenyon Rev, Nation*

Jorie Graham　　　　　　　　　　P
Department of English, Harvard Univ, Barker Center, 12 Quincy St, Cambridge, MA 02138, 617-495-1189
 Pubs: *Swarm, The Errancy, The Dream of the Unified Field, Materialism, Region of Unlikeness, End of Beauty* (Ecco, 2000, 1997, 1996, 1990, 1987, 1983), *Erosion, Hybrids of Plants & of Ghosts* (Princeton, 1983, 1980)

Maria Grande-Conley 🎤　　　　　P
724 Plymouth St
Holbrook, MA 02343
 Pubs: *The Rolling Coulter* (Missouri Western State College, 1990), *Anth of Italian American Poets* (Malefemmina Pr, 1993), *Soundings East, Permafrost, Poem, The Laurel Rev, Haydn's Ferry Rev, Nimrod, Puerto del sol, la bella figura*

Christina J. Green　　　　　　　P
40 Ocean Ave
Salem, MA 01970-5406
Internet: c1phd@aol.com
 Pubs: *Up Against the Wall Mother, Poetalk, Wide Open Mag, Poetry Peddler, Free Focus, Jrnl of Poetry Therapy, The Pen, Poems of the World, Not Your Average Zine, Event*

Barbara L. Greenberg　　　　　P&W
770 Boylston St, Apt 6-1
Boston, MA 02199-7705
 Pubs: *What Nell Knows* (Summer Hse/Snowberries Pr, 1997), *The Never-Not Sonnets* (U Pr Florida, 1989), *Fire Drills* (U Missouri Pr, 1982)

Bette Greene　　　　　　　　　W
338 Clinton Rd
Brookline, MA 02146, 617-232-9855
 Pubs: *Them That Glitter* (Knopf, 1983), *Philip Hall Likes Me* (Dial, 1974)

Carole Gregory P
25 Custer St, Apt 5
Jamaica Plain, MA 02130-3130

Carolyn Gregory P
50 Green St, #106
Brookline, MA 02146
   Pubs: *Playing by Ear* (Green Street Pr, 1994), *Tour of Light: Anth* (Pressford, 1996), *Artword Qtly, Yankee, MacGuffin, Seattle Rev, Georgetown Rev*

Joe Haldeman ♀ ⊀ P&W
MIT, Writing Program, 14E-303, Cambridge, MA 02139
Internet: haldeman@mit.edu
   Pubs: *Forever Free, Forever Peace* (Berkley, 1999, 1997), *Saul's Death & Other Poems* (Anamnesis Pr, 1997), *None So Blind* (Avon, 1996), *1968, Worlds Enough & Time, Hemingway Hoax, Buying Time* (Morrow, 1995, 1992, 1990, 1989), *Worlds Apart* (Viking, 1983)

Anne Halley P&W
244 Amity St
Amherst, MA 01002, 413-549-5083
   Pubs: *Rumors of the Turning Wheel* (Aife Pr, 1986), *The Bearded Mother* (U Massachusetts Pr, 1979)

Paul Hannigan W
22 Fayette St, #2
Cambridge, MA 02139-1112
   Pubs: *Bringing Back Slavery* (Dolphin Edtns, 1976)

George Harrar ♀ ⊀ W
10 Oxbow Rd
Wayland, MA 01778
Internet: gharrar@mediaone.net
   Pubs: *First Tiger* (Permanent Pr, 1999), *Best American Short Stories: Anth* (HM, 1999), *Dickinson Rev, Quarter After Eight, Rockford Rev, SideShow, Story*

Jeffrey Harrison ♀ ⊀ P
77 Haven St
Dover, MA 02030
Internet: jwharrsion@mediaone.net
   Pubs: *Feeding the Fire* (Sarabande, 2001), *Signs of Arrival* (Copper Beech Pr, 1996), *The Singing Underneath* (Dutton, 1988), *Nation, Paris Rev, New Yorker, New Republic, Poetry*

Ken Harvey ♀ ⊀ W
55 Columbus Ave
Waltham, MA 02451
Internet: Bruceken24@aol.com
   Pubs: *If You Were With Me Everything Would be all Right* (Pleasure Boat Studio, 2001), *Baltimore Rev, Bananafish, Evergreen Chronicles, Green Mountains Rev, Gulf Stream, James White Rev, Laurel Rev, Massachusetts Rev, Nebraska Rev, Other Voices, River Styx, Worcester Rev*

James Haug ♀ ⊀ P
15 Washington Ave
Northampton, MA 01060-2861, 413-584-0169
Internet: alix1@attbi.com
   Pubs: *Walking Liberty* (Northeastern, 1999), *Fox Luck* (Center for Book Arts, 1998), *The Stolen Car* (U Massachusetts Pr, 1989), *APR, Brilliant Corners, DoubleTake, Gettysburg Rev, Ploughshares, Massachusetts Rev, Crazyhorse*

Stratis Haviaras P&W
Poetry Room, Harvard Univ, Cambridge, MA 02138, 617-495-2454
   Pubs: *The Heroic Age, When the Tree Sings* (S&S, 1984, 1979), *Crossing the River Twice* (Cleveland State U Pr, 1976), *Harvard Rev, Iowa Rev, Columbia Rev*

Mary Hazzard ♀ ⊀ W
452 Woodward St
Waban, MA 02468-1521, 617-332-6009
Internet: mdhazzard@juno.com
   Pubs: *Close His Eyes* (pseud. Olivia Dwight, revi, iUniverse, 2000), *Family Blood* (Ariadne Pr, 1999), *Sheltered Lives* (Pinnacle, 1981), *Idle & Disorderly Persons* (Madrona, 1981), *We Used to Be Wives: Anth* (Fithian Pr, 2002)

Judy Ann Heitzman P
20 Old Barn Pathe
Marshfield, MA 02050
   Pubs: *Maybe Grace* (Sandstone Pub, 1994), *Intro to Literature: Anth* (Bedford Bks, 1993), *Agni, New Yorker, Sojourner, Yankee*

Grey Held ♀ ⊀ P
658 Watertown St.
Newtonville, MA 02460, 617-630-1661
Internet: gheld@lyra.com
   Pubs: *My Heart's First Steps: Anth* (Adams Media Corp, 2003), *Poems For a Beach House: Anth* (Salt Marsh Poetry Pr, 2003), *The Antigonish Rev, Slipstream, Spoon River Poetry Rev, The MacGuffin, Concho River Rev, The Lucid Stone, Carriage Hse Rev, Puckerbrush*

DeWitt Henry W
33 Buick St
Watertown, MA 02172, 617-924-0012
Internet: bakofpak@aol.com
   Pubs: *Fathering Daughters: Anth* (Beacon, 1998), *The Pushcart Prize XIV: Anth* (Pushcart Pr, 1989), *Boulevard, Texas Rev, Agni, Antioch Rev, Missouri Rev, Iowa Rev, Nebraska Rev, Colorado Rev, Amer Voice, Nerve*

Marcie Hershman ♀ ⊀ W
46 Stanton Rd
Brookline, MA 02445-6839
Internet: marcie.hershman@tufts.edu
   Pubs: *Safe in America, Tales of the Master Race* (HC, 1996, 1992), *American Fiction: Anth* (Birch Lane Pr, 1990), *Tikkun, Ms., Ploughshares, Agni*

Emily Hiestand   P
Palmer & Dodge Agency, 1 Beacon St, Boston, MA 02108,
617-573-0468
Internet: collard@delphi.com
    Pubs: *Angela the Upside-Down Girl, The Very Rich Hours*
(Beacon Pr, 1998, 1992), *Green the Witch-Hazel Wood*
(Graywolf Pr, 1989), *New Yorker, Atlantic, Partisan Rev,
Georgia Rev, Michigan Qtly Rev, Nation, Orion, SE Rev*

John Hildebidle 🎤 ✈   P&W
MIT, 14N-434, Cambridge, MA 02139, 617-253-4452
Internet: jjhildeb@mit.edu
    Pubs: *Signs, Translations, Defining Absence* (Ireland;
Salmon Pub, 2004, 1999), *One Sleep, One Waking*
(Wyndham Hall Pr, 1994), *The Errand of Keeping Alive: Anth*
(Harvard U Pr, 1989), *Yankee, Ploughshares, Poetry, Thema*

Hollis Hodges   W
PO Box 436
Stockbridge, MA 01262, 413-298-4980
    Pubs: *Norman Rockwell's Greatest Painting* (Paul S.
Eriksson, 1988)

Richard Hoffman   P
3 Gladstone St
Cambridge, MA 02140, 617-661-8043
    Pubs: *Half the House* (HB, 1995), *An Ear to the Ground:
Anth* (U Georgia Pr, 1990), *Hudson Rev, Shenandoah, The
Sun, Amer Rev*

William Holinger 🎤 ✈   W
128 Academy Hill Rd
Boston, MA 02135-3906, 617-254-0185
    Pubs: *The Football Wars, 21st Century Fox* (Scholastic,
1992, 1989), *Fence-Walker* (SUNY Pr, 1985), *Iowa Rev,
Texas Rev, New Directions, Agni*

Lucy Honig 🎤 ✈   W
111 Dorchester St
Squantum, MA 02171
Internet: lhonig@bu.edu
    Pubs: *Open Season* (Scala Hse, 2002), *The Truly Needy &
Other Stories* (U Pitt Pr, 1999), *Prize Stories: O. Henry
Awards: Anths* (Doubleday, 1996, 1992), *Best American
Short Stories: Anth* (HM, 1988), *Gettysburg Rev, Witness,
Georgia Rev, Fiction*

Shel Horowitz 🎤 ✈   P
PO Box 1164
Northampton, MA 01061, 413-586-2388
Internet: www.frugalfun.com or shel@frugalfun.com
    Pubs: *XY Files: Anth* (Sherman-Asher, 1997), *Breathe!*
(Warthog Pr, 1980), *Against the Wall, Riverrun, Pudding,
Home Planet News, North Country, Anvil*

William Hunt   P
125 Christian Hill Rd
Great Barrington, MA 01230, 413-528-1639
    Pubs: *Oceans & Corridors of Orpheus* (Elpenor Pr, 1979),
Of the Map That Changes (Swallow Pr, 1974), *APR, Paris
Rev, TriQtly, Formations*

Lewis Hyde   P
PO Box 43
North Truro, MA 02652, 508-926-6047
Internet: HYDEL@Kenyon.edu
    Pubs: *APR, Massachusetts Rev, Southshore, Green House*

Barbara Helfgott Hyett 🎤 ✈   P
71 Mason Terr
Brookline, MA 02146-2602
Internet: bhelfgotthyett@attbi.com
    Pubs: *The Tracks We Leave, The Double Reckoning of
Christopher Columbus* (U Illinois Pr, 1996, 1992), *Hudson
Rev, New Republic, Partisan Rev, Nation, Prairie Schooner,
Agni*

Ruth Ice   W
204 Aspinwall Ave
Brookline, MA 02146
    Pubs: *Epoch, Lit Rev, Kansas Qtly, Catholic Worker*

Mildred M. Jeffrey 🎤 ✈   P&W
10 Longwood Dr #316
Westwood, MA 02090
    Pubs: *Detours & Intersections* (Pleasure Dome Pr, 1987),
Exquisite Reaction: Anth (Andrew Mtn Pr, 2000), *Heartbeat
of New England: Anth* (Tiger Moon, 2000), *Amer Land
Forum, NAR, Live Poets, Xanadu*

Paul Jenkins   P
POB 74
Conway, MA 01341
    Pubs: *Six Small Fires, Radio Tooth* (Four Way Bks, 2002,
1997), *Forget the Sky* (L'Epervier Pr, 1979), *Ploughshares,
Agni, New Yorker, Gettysburg Rev, Paris Rev, Kenyon,
Prairie Schooner, Chelsea, Poetry NW, Malahat Rev*

Donald Junkins   P
63 Hawks Rd
Deerfield, MA 01342, 413-774-3475
    Pubs: *Playing for Keeps* (Lynx Hse, 1991), *Crossing By
Ferry* (U Massachusetts Pr, 1978), *APR, New Yorker,
Atlantic, Sewanee Rev, Antioch Rev, Poetry*

Paul Kahn   P
24 Pitcher Ave
Medford, MA 02155, 617-488-4380
    Pubs: *Secret History of the Mongols* (North Point Pr, 1984),
January (Tuumba, 1978)

Roberta Kalechofsky 🎤 ✈   W
255 Humphrey St
Marblehead, MA 01945-1645, 781-631-7601
Internet: micah@micahbooks.com
    Pubs: *Justice, My Brother, My Sister, Bodmin, 1349* (Micah
    Pub, 1996, 1995, 1993, 1988), *Figlie di Sarah: Anth* (Passigli
    Editori, 1997), *The Woman Who Lost Her Names: Selected
    Writing by Amer Jewish Women: Anth* (H&R, 1980),
    Sou'Wester, Forum, Confrontation

Mark Karlins   P
88 Green St
Newburyport, MA 01951
    Pubs: *A Christmas Fable* (Atheneum, 1990), *Narrative of the
    Broken Winter* (North Atlantic Bks, 1988), *Origin, Sulfur*

Judy Katz-Levine 🎤   P
10 Hillshire Ln
Norwood, MA 02062-3009, 617-769-5931
    Pubs: *A Curious Architecture: Anth* (Stride Pr, 1996),
    Diamonds Are a Girl's Best Friend: Anth (Faber & Faber,
    1994), *Switched on Guttenberg, The Plaza, Haifa, Bitter
    Oleander, Fence, 96 Inc., Salamander, Hummingbird,*

William Kemmett   P
PO Box 777
Bryantville, MA 02327-0777, 617-293-9915
    Pubs: *The Bradford Poems, Flesh of a New Moon* (Igneus
    Pr, 1995, 1991), *Faith of Stone* (Wampeter Pr, 1983), *Poetry
    East, Seattle Rev, Atelier*

X. J. Kennedy 🎤 ✈   P
22 Revere St
Lexington, MA 02420-4424
    Pubs: *The Lords of Misrule: Poems, 1992-2001* (Johns
    Hopkins U Pr, 2002), *Exploding Gravy* (Little, Brown, 2002)

Rod Kessler 🎤 ✈   W
Salem State College, English Dept, Salem, MA 01970,
978-542-6247
Internet: rkessler@salem.mass.edu
    Pubs: *Off in Zimbabwe* (U Missouri Pr, 1985), *Outsiders:
    Anth* (Milkweed Edtns, 1999), *Flash Fiction: Anth* (Norton,
    1992), *Sextant, North Shore Mag, Dudley Rev, Chariton
    Rev, Calliope, Harvard Rev, Radcliffe Qtly*

Liza Ketchum 🎤 ✈   W
7 Arthur Terrace
Watertown, MA 02472
Internet: tortuga96@earthlink.net
    Pubs: *Orphan Journey Home* (Avon, 2000), *Blue Coyote*
    (S&S, 1997), *The Gold Rush* (Little, Brown, 1996), *Twelve
    Days in August* (Holiday Hse, 1993)

Claire Keyes 🎤 ✈   P
12 Higgins Rd
Marblehead, MA 01945-2122, 781-631-9454
Internet: ckeyes@erols.com
    Internet: Pubs: *Rising & Falling* (Foothills, 1999), *Sarasota
    Rev, Onset Rev, Larcom Rev, Talking River Rev, Blueline,
    Fresh Ground, Vermont Lit Rev, Spoon River Poetry Rev,
    Earth's Daughters, Zone 3, Crania@digitaldaze.com,
    Eleventh Muse, Sojourner*

Robert Lord Keyes   P
40 S Valley Rd
Amherst, MA 01002-9768, 413-253-2739
    Pubs: *Massachusetts Rev, Fresh Ground, Green Age,
    Spitball, Westwind Rev, Green Mountains Rev, Critical
    Times, Embers, The Fan, Wind, BPJ*

Rudy Kikel 🎤 ✈   P
154 W Newton St
Boston, MA 02118, 617-421-6987
Internet: rudyk@aol.com
    Pubs: *Gottscheers, Period Pieces* (Pride & Imprints, 1998,
    1997), *Long Division* (Writers Block Pub, 1993), *Lasting
    Relations* (Sea Horse, 1984), *Kenyon Rev, Massachusetts
    Rev, Shenandoah*

Richard E. Kim   W
59 Leverett Rd
Shutesbury, MA 01072
    Pubs: *In Search of Lost Years* (Korea; Sun Moon Pub, 1985)

Norman Andrew Kirk   P
14 Bayfield Rd
Wayland, MA 01778
    Pubs: *Panda Zoo* (West of Boston, 1983), *Some Poems My
    Friends* (Four Zoas/Night Hse, 1981), *Atlantic, Bitterroot,
    Poet Lore, Poem, Negative Capability*

Stanley Koehler   P
54 Hills Rd
Amherst, MA 01002, 413-549-1505
    Pubs: *The Perfect Destroyers: Poems of WWII* (Stinehour Pr,
    1995), *The Fact of Fall* (U Massachusetts Pr, 1969),
    Sewanee Rev, Poetry, Yale Rev, Massachusetts Rev

Zane Kotker 🎤 ✈   W
45 Lyman Road, Northampton, MA 01060-4248, 413-586-5207
Internet: zane@crocker.com
    Pubs: *Try to Remember* (Random Hse, 1997), *White Rising,
    A Certain Man, Bodies in Motion* (Knopf, 1981, 1976, 1972),
    Mademoiselle

Norman Kotker   W
45 Lyman Rd
Northampton, MA 01060-4248, 413-586-5207
    Pubs: *Billy in Love* (Zoland, 1996), *Learning About God* (H
    Holt, 1988), *Miss Rhode Island* (FSG, 1978)

Herbert Krohn   P
53 Centre St
Brookline, MA 02146, 617-232-6904
    Pubs: *Partisan Rev, Nation, New Yorker, Evergreen Rev,*
    Boston Phoenix, Chelsea, Village Voice

Susan N. Landon   🎤 ✈   P
Somerville, MA 02144-1203, 617-628-3944
Internet: landon_susan@hotmail.com
    Pubs: *Wedding Blessings: Anth* (Broadway Bks, 2003),
    Mothers and Daughters: Anth (Harmony Bks, 2001),
    Freedom's Just Another Word: Anth (Outrider Pr, 1998),
    Rising to the Dawn: Anth (Little Treasures Pub, 1998),
    Ibbetson St Pr

Joseph Langland   🎤 ✈   P
16 Morgan Cir
Amherst, MA 01002-1131, 413-549-6517
    Pubs: *Selected Poems* (APR, 1992), *Twelve Poems* (Adastra
    Pr, 2002), *A Dream of Love* (Pleiades Pr, 1986), *The Wheel
    of Summer* (Dial Pr, 1964), *New Yorker, Paris Rev,*
    Massachusetts Rev, Nation

Jacqueline Lapidus   P
PO Box 902
Provincetown, MA 02657
    Pubs: *Ultimate Conspiracy* (Lynx Pubs, 1987), *Starting Over*
    (Out & Out, 1977), *Conditions, Sinister Wisdom, Hanging*
    Loose, Women's Rev of Bks

Anne D. LeClaire   🎤 ✈   W
PO Box 656
South Chatham, MA 02659-1512, 508-432-6395
Internet: analee@capecod.net
    Pubs: *Leaving Eden, Entering Normal* (Ballantine, 2002,
    2001), *Sideshow* (Viking, 1994), *Grace Point* (Signet, 1993),
    Every Mother's Son, Land's End (Bantam, 1987, 1985), *I've*
    Always Meant to Tell You: Anth (Pocket Bks, 1997)

Jane Lecompte   W
PO Box 1393
Boston, MA 02117-1393
    Pubs: *Moon Passage* (H&R, 1989)

Jacob Leed   P
111 Gore St
Cambridge, MA 02141
    Pubs: *3x3* (Toucan Pr, 1986), *You Reading, Looking at*
    Chinese Pictures (Shelley's Pr, 1983, 1981)

Judith Leet   P
16 Gate House Rd
Chestnut Hill, MA 02167, 617-277-3857
    Pubs: *Flowering Trees & Shrubs: The Botanical Painting of*
    Esther Heins (H. Abrams, 1987), *Agni*

Brad Leithauser   🎤 ✈   P&W
Mount Holyoke College, English Dept, South Hadley, MA 01075
    Pubs: *Hence* (Knopf, 1989)

Ruth Lepson   🎤 ✈   P
49 Phillips St
Watertown, MA 02472-3917, 617-926-6990
Internet: rlepson@lynx.neu.edu
    Pubs: *Dreaming in Color* (Alice James Bks, 1980),
    POTEPOETZINE, Agni, Women's Rev of Bks,
    Ploughshares, Helicon Nine, Sojourner, Contact II, Harbor
    Rev, Poet Lore

Kathleen Leverich   W
40 Rogers Ave
Somerville, MA 02144
    Pubs: *The New You* (Scholastic Pr, 2000), *Best Enemies,*
    Hilary and the Troublemakers (Beechtree Bks, 1999, 1998),
    Best Enemies Forever (Greenwillow Bks, 1995), *Brigid the*
    Bad, Brigid the Bewitched (Random Hse, 1995, 1994),
    Ascent, Yankee, Mademoiselle

Ruth Levin   P
221 Mt Auburn St, #307
Cambridge, MA 02138-4847, 617-491-7229
    Pubs: *Birthmark* (CCC, 1992), *To Whom It May Concern*
    (William L. Bouhan, 1986), *Southern Rev, Sewanee Rev,*
    New Renaissance, Prairie Schooner, Nation

Miriam Levine   🎤 ✈   P
26-A Academy St
Arlington, MA 02174, 617-646-2618
Internet: miriamlevine39@aol.com
    Pubs: *In Paterson* (SMU Pr, 2002), *APR, Paris Rev, Kenyon*
    Rev, Ploughshares, Amer Voice

Sharon Libera   P
139 Taylor St
Granby, MA 01033-9588
    Pubs: *Cries of the Spirit: Anth* (Beacon Pr, 1991),
    Ploughshares Poetry Reader: Anth (Ploughshares Bks,
    1986), *I Hear My Sisters Saying: Anth* (Thomas Y. Crowell,
    1975), *Ploughshares, Poetry*

Karen Lindsey   P
33 Jefferson St
Cambridge, MA 02141
    Pubs: *A Company of Queens* (Bloody Mary Pr, 1977),
    Falling off the Roof (Alice James Bks, 1975)

Judith Liniado   🎤   P
305 Fuller St.
W. Newton, MA 02465
Internet: jalindo@earthlink.net
    Pubs: *Dream International Qtly, Ibbetson St Pr, Night*
    Roses, Psychopoetica, Frogpond, Point Judith Light,
    Tucumcari Lit Rev

Paul Lisicky W
19 Pearl St
Provincetown, MA 02657-2313
Internet: Badflorida@aol.com
    Pubs: *Lawnboy* (Turtle Point Pr, 1999), *Best American Gay Fiction 2: Anth* (Little, Brown, 1997), *Men on Men 6: Anth* (Dutton, 1996), *Flash Fiction: Anth* (Norton, 1992), *Boulevard, Qtly West, Gulf Coast, Provincetown Arts, Mississippi Rev*

Margaret Lloyd 🎤 ✈ P
17 Lilly St
Florence, MA 01062, 413-584-2752
Internet: mlloyd@spfldcol.edu
    Pubs: *This Particular Earthly Scene* (Alice James Bks, 1993), *Seneca Rev, Poetry East, NER, The Jrnl, Willow Springs, Gettysburg Rev, Planet*

Edward Locke 🎤 ✈ P
12 Flagstaff Hill Terr
Canton, MA 02021, 781-828-3978
Internet: jlocke6@aol.com
    Pubs: *What Time Is It?, Names for the Self, Green Bank, Advancing Back* (Harlequinade Pr, 1998, 1997, 1995, 1994), *Partisan Rev, Yale Rev, Poetry, Georgia Rev, Dalhousie Rev, BPJ, Nation*

Edward Lodi 🎤 ✈ W
41 Walnut St
Middleboro, MA 02346, 508-946-4738
    Pubs: *Northcote Anth of Short Stories* (Harold Shaw Pub, 1992), *Light, The Aurorean, Snowy Egret, Space & Time, Mediphors, New England Writers Network, Terminal Fright*

Gian S. Lombardo 🎤 ✈ P
781 E Guinea Rd
Williamsburg, MA 01096-9736, 413-268-7012
Internet: lombardo@quale.com
    Pubs: *Sky Open Again, Standing Room, Between Islands*, (Dolphin-Moon, 1997, 1989, 1984), *Puerto del Sol, Lift, Denver Qtly, Talisman, Prose Poem, Iowa Rev, Agni, Quarter After Eight, Third Coast, Qtly West*

Dick Lourie P
16 Alder-Sea, Prospect Hill
Somerville, MA 02143
    Pubs: *Anima* (Hanging Loose, 1977), *Stumbling* (Crossing, 1973), *Sun, Cottonwood Rev, Nation*

Steve Lowe W
2 Laurie La
Natick, MA 01760, 508-655-8701
    Pubs: *Aurora* (Dodd, Mead, 1985)

Michael Lowenthal 🎤 ✈ W
11 Seaverns Ave #3F
Jamaica Plain, MA 02130-2873
Internet: maxfranz@aol.com
    Pubs: *Avoidance* (Graywolf Pr, 2002), *The Same Embrace* (Dutton, 1998), *Neurotica: Anth* (Norton, 1999), *Best American Gay Fiction: Anth* (Litttle, Brown, 1996), *Men on Men 5: Anth* (Penguin/Plume, 1994), *Southern Rev, Tin House, Witness, Kenyon Rev*

Betty Lowry P
79 Moore Rd
Wayland, MA 01778
Internet: bettylowry@aol.com

Jean Lunn 🎤 ✈ P
25 Harvard St
Hyannis, MA 02601
    Pubs: *Yankee, Manhattan Poetry Rev, Sow's Ear, Hampden-Sydney Rev, Devil's Millhopper, Webster Rev*

Thomas Lux P
52 Chester Ave
Waltham, MA 02154
    Pubs: *The Drowned River, Half-Promised Land, Sunday* (HM, 1990, 1986, 1979), *Antaeus, Ploughshares*

David Lyon 🎤 ✈ P
6 Crawford St, #11
Cambridge, MA 02139, 617-864-0361
    Pubs: *The Sound of Horns* (L'Epervier Pr, 1984), *Massachusetts Rev, NAR, BPJ*

Daniel Lyons W
73 Pearl St
Charlestown, MA 02129-1918
    Pubs: *The Last Good Man* (U Massachusetts Pr, 1992)

Jeanette C. Maes 🎤 ✈ P
64 Harrison Ave
Lynn, MA 01905, 781-599-1349
    Pubs: *They Come No More, The Way of Ignorance, Fantastic Confusions* (Sunlit Waters Pr, 2002, 1994, 1990)

Carol Magun 🎤 ✈ W
90 Marion Rd
Watertown, MA 02172-4708, 617-924-8874
    Pubs: *Circling Eden* (Academy Chicago Pub, 1995), *Amer Fiction, Artful Dodge, Jewish Women's Literary Annual*

Elissa Malcohn P&W
PO Box 1764
Cambridge, MA 02238, 617-547-6533
    Pubs: *Full Spectrum: Anth* (Bantam, 1988), *Tales of the Unanticipated, Ice River, Diarist's Journal*

John Maloney 🎤 ✈ P
Allen Farm Rd
Chilmark, MA 02535, 508-645-9688
Internet: jmaloney@vineyard.net
  Pubs: *Proposal* (Zoland Bks, 1999), *The Boston Bk Rev,
  Poetry, Poetry NW, Ploughshares, SPR, New York Times,
  North Atlantic*

Marvin Mandell W
102 Anawan Ave
West Roxbury, MA 02132
  Pubs: *Best American Short Stories: Anth* (HM, 1972), *Cape
  Cod Compass, English Jrnl, Offshore*

Paul Mariani P
PO Box M
Montague, MA 01351, 413-367-2820
Internet: pmariani@english.umass.edu
  Pubs: *The Great Wheel, Salvage Operations: New &
  Selected Poems* (Norton, 1996, 1990), *Image, America,
  Poetry*

Paul Marion 🎤 ✈ P&W
Communications/Univ Massachusetts Lowell, 1 University Ave,
Lowell, MA 01854, 978-934-3107
Internet: MarionPF@aol.com
  Pubs: *Line Drives: Anth* (S Illinois U Pr, 2002), *French Class*
  (Loom Pr, 1999), *For a Living: Anth* (U Illinois Pr, 1995), *The
  Larcom Rev, Sport Literate, VYU, Jack Mag, Steak Hache,
  The Acre, CSM, Bridge Rev*

Ralph G. Martell P
Foreign Language & Literature Dept, Westfield State College,
Westfield, MA 01086
  Pubs: *Palabras/Words, Cuadros, Ciclos* (Slusa, 1986, 1982,
  1982), *Peregrine, Stone Country*

Richard J. Martin 🎤 ✈ P
40 Searle Rd
West Roxbury, MA 02132-3014, 617-323-2547
Internet: dckmrtn.@aol.com
  Pubs: *Modulations* (Asylum Arts, 1998), *Negation of
  Beautiful Words* (Igneus, 1996), *White Man Appears on
  Southern California Beach* (Bottom Fish Pr, 1991),
  American Poets Say Goodbye to the 20th Century: Anth
  (Four Walls Eight Windows, 1996), *Fell Swoop, ACM*

Valerie M. Martin W
Houghton Mifflin Co, 222 Berkeley St, Boston, MA
02116-3764, 617-725-5000
  Pubs: *Alexandra, Set in Motion* (FSG, 1979, 1978)

Tara L. Masih 🎤 ✈ P&W
18 Dufton Rd
Andover, MA 01810-2716
Internet: masiht@aol.com
  Pubs: *Essential Love: Anth* (Poetworks, 2000), *Two Worlds
  Walking: Anth* (New Rivers Pr, 1994), *Word of Mouth: Anth*
  (Crossing Pr, 1990), *Confrontation, Hayden's Ferry Rev, The
  Indian-American, Mind in Motion, New Millennium Writings,
  Ledge, Pangolin Papers*

Suzanne Matson 🎤 ✈ P&W
English Dept, Boston College, Chestnut Hill, MA 02467,
617-552-3716
Internet: suzanne.matson@bc.edu
  Pubs: *A Trick of Nature, The Hunger Moon* (Norton, 2000,
  1997), *Durable Goods, Sea Level* (Alice James Bks, 1993,
  1990), *Harvard Rev, APR, Poetry, Indiana Rev,
  Shenandoah, Poetry NW*

Mary Maxwell P
PO Box 1120
Truro, MA 02666
  Pubs: *New Republic, Nation, Western Humanities Rev, Paris
  Rev, Salmagundi, Southern Rev, Pequod*

Ben Mazer P
41 Tyler Rd
Belmont, MA 02478, 617-484-6808
Internet: benmazer@aol.com
  Pubs: *White Cities* (Barbara Matteau Edtns, 1995),
  *Agenda, Pequod, Fulcrum, Leviathan Qtly, Thumbscrew,
  Verse, Harvard Mag, Poetry East, Boston Phoenix, Stand,
  Jacket*

Grace Dane Mazur 🎤 ✈ W
35 Arlington St
Cambridge, MA 02140, 617-547-3895
Internet: gdm@math.harvard.edu
  Pubs: *Trespass* (Graywolf Pr, 2002), *Silk* (Brookline Bks,
  1996), *Southern Rev, Harvard Rev, NER/BLQ, Story*

Gail Mazur 🎤 ✈ P
5 Walnut Ave
Cambridge, MA 02140, 617-868-5753
  Pubs: *They Can't Take That Away From Me, The Common*
  (U Chicago Pr, 2001, 1995), *The Pose of Happiness* (David
  Godine, 1986), *Atlantic, New Republic, Partisan Rev,
  Boulevard, Agni, Slate, Ploughshares, Poetry*

David R. McCann P
Harvard Univ, EALC 2 Divinity Ave, Cambridge, MA 02138
Internet: dmccann@fas.harvard.edu
  Pubs: *Winter Sky* (QRL, 1981)

Elizabeth McKim   P
108 Winthrop Rd
Brookline, MA 02146
    Pubs: *Boat of the Dream* (Troubadour, 1988), *Burning Through, Family Salt* (Wampeter, 1987, 1981), *To Stay Alive* (Audiotape; Talking Stone Pr, 1992)

Reginald McKnight   W
Christina Ward, PO Box 515, N Scituate, MA 02060, 781-545-1375
    Pubs: *White Boys* (H Holt, 1998), *The Kind of Light That Shines on Texas* (SMU Pr, 1996), *O. Henry Awards 1990: Anth* (Doubleday, 1990), *New Stories From the South: Anth* (Algonquin, 1990), *Kenyon Rev, Callaloo, Black Amer Lit Forum*

Anthony McNeill   P
CCEMBS Program, Univ Massachusetts, Amherst, MA 01002, 413-545-0031

Michael McWey   W
34 Sparks St
Cambridge, MA 02138, 617-876-1784
    Pubs: *Redbook, Seventeen, Special Report, YM, 'Teen, Apalachee Qtly, Crescent Rev, Sou'wester, Woman, Faith 'N Stuff, Rosebud, Satire, Guideposts for Kids*

Mameve Medwed 🎤 ✈   W
58 Washington Ave
Cambridge, MA 02140, 617-868-8805
    Pubs: *The End of an Error, Host Family, Mail* (Warner Bks, 2003, 2000, 1997), *Ascent, Yankee, Redbook, Playgirl, Boston Globe, Missouri Rev*

Ed Meek 🎤 ✈   P&W
345 Cross St
Belmont, MA 02478
Internet: ecmeek@aol.com
    Pubs: *Walk Out* (Ibbetson St Pr, 2000), *The Larcom Rev, NAR, Confrontation, College English, North Dakota Rev*

Ifeanyi Menkiti   P
8 Malvern Ave
Somerville, MA 02144, 617-666-2855
    Pubs: *The Jubilation of Falling Bodies* (Pomegranate, 1978), *Affirmations* (Third World, 1971)

Gary Metras   P
16 Reservation Rd
Easthampton, MA 01027-1227, 413-527-3324
    Pubs: *Today's Lesson* (Bull Thistle Pr, 1997), *Seagull Beach* (Adastra Pr, 1995), *Atomic Ghost* (Coffee Hse, 1995), *Amer Voice, Poetry East, Potlatch, North Dakota Qtly*

Karen Michalson   W
PO Box 332
Southbridge, MA 01550, 508-248-1799
www.karenmichalson.com
    Pubs: *Enemy Glory* (Tor Bks, 2001)

Richard Michelson 🎤 ✈   P
PO Box 657
Amherst, MA 01004-0657, 413-586-3964
Internet: rm@rmichelson.com
    Pubs: *Too Young for Yiddish* (Charlesbridge, 2002), *Masks* (Gehenna Pr, 1999), *Intro to Poetry: Anth* (Norton, 1999), *Animals That Ought to Be* (S&S, 1996), *Tap Dancing for the Relatives* (U Central Florida Pr, 1985)

Paul Milenski   W
PO Box 592
Dalton, MA 01227-0592, 413-684-2066
    Pubs: *Power Play: Individuals in Conflict: Anth* (Prentice Hall Regents, 1996), *Sudden Fiction Intl: Anth* (Norton, 1989), *Witness, Wind Lit Jrnl, World of English, Berkshire Rev, Qtly West, Great River Rev*

Christopher Millis   P
290 Massachusetts Ave, Cambridge, MA 02139, 617-225-9608
Internet: ninadm@mit.edu
    Pubs: *Impossible Mirrors* (Singular Speech Pr, 1995), *On the Verge, Emerging Poets & Artists: Anth* (Agni Pr, 1993), *The Qtly, Intl Qtly, Harvard Rev, Seneca Rev*

Joan Millman   W
30 Ackers Ave, #1
Brookline, MA 02445-4160
Internet: joanmillmn@aol.com
    Pubs: *The Effigy & Other Stories* (U Missouri Pr, 1990), *Carolina Qtly, Virginia Qtly Rev, Ascent, Cimarron, Moment Mag*

Helena Minton   P
5 Random Ln
Andover, MA 01810, 508-475-6345
Internet: minton@noble.mass.edu
    Pubs: *The Canal Bed, Personal Effects* (Alice James Bks, 1985, 1976), *Poet & Critic, 5 A.M., Soundings East*

Wendy Mnookin 🎤 ✈   P
40 Woodchester Dr
Chestnut Hill, MA 02467-1033, 617-964-7759
Internet: wmnookin@post.harvard.edu
    Pubs: *What He Took, To Get Here* (BOA Edtns, 2002, 1999), *Guenever Speaks* (Round Table, 1991), *Urban Nature: Anth* (Milkwood, 2000), *Boomer Girls: Anth* (Iowa, 1999) *Arthurian Literature by Women: Anth* (Garland Pub, 1999)

Jean Monahan   P
55 Ord St
Salem, MA 01970-1152, 978-740-5008
Internet: jehane@world.std.com
　　Pubs: *Believe It Or Not* (Orchises Pr, 1999), *Hands*
　　(Anhinga, 1992), *Shenandoah, Seneca, New Republic,*
　　Graham Hse, Chelsea, Webster Rev, Columbia, Nimrod

Richard Moore ♀ ✈   P&W
81 Clark St
Belmont, MA 02478-2450, 617-489-0519
　　Pubs: *The Naked Scarecrow* (Truman State U Pr, 2000),
　　Pygmies & Pyramids, No More Bottom (Orchises Pr, 1998,
　　1991), *The Mouse Whole*

Richard Moore ♀ ✈   P&W
81 Clark St
Belmont, MA 02478-2450, 617-489-0519
　　Pubs: *The Naked Scarecrow* (Truman State U Pr, 2000),
　　Pygmies & Pyramids, No More Bottom (Orchises Pr, 1998,
　　1991), *The Mouse Whole* (Negative Capability, 1996), *The*
　　Investigator (Story Line Pr, 1991), *Poetry, Hudson Rev,*
　　APR, New Yorker, Harper's

Andrea Moorhead ♀ ✈   P
PO Box 297
Deerfield, MA 01342-0297
Internet: moorhead@deerfield.edu
　　Pubs: *From a Grove of Aspen* (U Salzburg Pr, 1997), *le vert*
　　est fragile, la blancheur absolue, le silence nous entoure
　　(Les Ecrits des Forges, 1999, 1995, 1992), *Winter Light*
　　(Oasis, 1994), *Abraxas, Estuaire, Midwest Qtly*

Emma Morgan ♀ ✈   P
491 Bridge Rd #724
Northampton, MA 01062
Internet: emmaloo@earthlink.net
　　Pubs: *Gooseflesh* (Clothespin Fever Pr, 1993), *Ma'Yan*
　　Journey, Lucid Stone

Geoffrey Movius   P&W
Harvard Univ, 124 Mount Auburn st, Cambridge, MA 02138
　　Pubs: *Agenda, Tufts Rev, Peace Feelers, Harvard Advocate,*
　　Boston Rev, Silo

Rich Murphy ♀   P
31 Eureka Ave
Swampscott, MA 01907
Internet: rmurphy277@aol.com
　　Pubs: *E: Anth* (Universities West Pr, 1999), *Poetry Mag,*
　　Borderlands: Texas Poetry Rev, Alligator Jumper, Natural
　　Bridge, Americas Rev, Icarus, Montserrat Rev, Spillway,
　　Connecticut Poetry Rev, Grand Street, Slant, Seattle Rev,
　　Blue Unicorn, Intl Poetry Rev

Dennis Must ♀ ✈   W
1 Valiant Way
Salem, MA 01970
Internet: must@attbi.com
　　Pubs: *Banjo Grease* (Creative Arts Bk Co, 2000), *Blue*
　　Cathedral: Anth (Red Hen Pr, 2000), *Exquisite Corpse, Big*
　　Bridge, Linnaean St, Elimae, Salt Hill Jrnl, Writers' Forum,
　　Crossconnect, Blue Moon Rev, Sou'wester, RE:AL,
　　Rosebud, SE Rev

Valery Nash   P
12 Linwood Ave
Rockport, MA 01966, 978-546-2900
　　Pubs: *October Swimmer* (Folly Cove Bks, 1996), *The*
　　Narrows (Cleveland State U Pr, 1980), *Field, Poetry NW,*
　　Yankee, SPR, New Virginia Rev, The Bridge

Mildred J. Nash   P
39 Sunset Dr
Burlington, MA 01803, 781-272-0206
　　Pubs: *Beyond Their Dreams* (Pocahontas Pr, 1989),
　　Troubadour, California Qtly, Formalist, Polyphon

Tema Nason ♀ ✈   W
93 Longwood Ave, #4
Brookline, MA 02146
　　Pubs: *Ethel: Fictional Autobiography of Ethel Rosenberg*
　　(Syracuse U Pr, 2002), *Crimson Tide: Anth, Full Moon*
　　(Chicory Blue Pr, 1996, 1993), *NAR, Puckerbrush Rev*

Judith Neeld ♀ ✈   P
PO Box 132
Menemsha, MA 02552
　　Pubs: *To Fit Your Heart Into the Body* (Bright Hill Pr, 1999),
　　Naming the Island (Thorntree Pr, 1988), *Sea Fire* (Adastra
　　Pr, 1987), *Tar River Poetry, Texas Rev, Yarrow, Rhino,*
　　Massachusetts Rev

Leslea Newman ♀ ✈   P&W
PO Box 815
Northampton, MA 01061-0815, 413-584-3865
Internet: lezel@aol.com
　　Pubs: *Best Short Stories of Leslea Newman, She Loves Me,*
　　She Loves Me Not, Heather Has Two Mommies, Girls Will
　　Be Girls (Alyson, 2003, 2002, 2000, 2000), *Runaway*
　　Dreidel (H Holt, 2002), *Cats, Cats, Cats!* (S&S, 2001)

James M. Neylon   P
215 Kings Hwy, #A6
West Springfield, MA 01089-2517, 413-731-9448
　　Pubs: *Kimera, Diner, Chachalaca, Barbaric Yawp, Brooklyn*
　　Rev, Blueline, California Qtly, Pegasus, Bitterroot, New York
　　Times, BPJ, Commonweal, Motive, Nightshade

Philip Nikolayev P
334 Harvard St Apt D-2
Cambridge, MA 02139, 617-864-7874
Internet: nikolay@fas.harvard.edu
    Pubs: *Artery Lumen* (Barbara Matteau Edtns, 1996), *Verse,
Grand Street, Culture Front, Exquisite Corpse

Joan Norris P
1126 Broadway
Hanover, MA 02339-2705, 781-826-8931
    Pubs: *Banquet* (Penmaen Pr, 1978), *Prairie Schooner,
Nation, Ploughshares*

Marian Novick W
313 Brookline St
Needham, MA 02192-3523
    Pubs: *At Her Age* (Scribner, 1985), *O. Henry Awards: Anth*
(Doubleday, 1981), *Massachusetts Rev*

Nina Nyhart 🎤 P
185 Warren St
Brookline, MA 02445, 617-734-2698
Internet: nnyhart@aol.com
    Pubs: *French for Soldiers, Openers* (Alice James Bks, 1987,
1979), *The Poetry Connection* (T&W, 1978), *Speaking for
Yourself: Poems in Different Voices* (HC, 2000), *The Party
Train: Anth* (New Rivers Pr, 1996)

Mary Oliver P
Molly Malone Cook Agency, Box 338, Provincetown, MA
02657, 508-487-1931
    Pubs: *New & Selected Poems, House of Light* (Beacon,
1992, 1990), *Dream Work* (Atlantic Monthly Pr, 1986), *Paris
Rev, Sierra, Southern Rev, Poetry*

David Olsen P
14 Vine Brook Rd
Westford, MA 01886-4212, 978-392-8617
Internet: davidolsen65@alum.calberkeley.org
    Pubs: *Greatest Hits* (Pudding Hse, 2001), *Literature of
Poverty: Anth* (World Bank, 1998), *The Gulf War: Many
Perspectives: Anth* (Vergin Pr, 1992), *Homeless Not
Helpless: Anth* (Canterbury Pr, 1991), *Larcom Rev, Poetry
SF, Black Bear, Amelia, Cicada, Bogg*

Rosalind Pace 🎤 ✈ P
Box 687
Truro, MA 02666-0687, 508-349-2487
Internet: rpace@massed.net
    Pubs: *Carnegie Mellon Anth of Poetry* (Carnegie Mellon U
Pr, 1993), *APR, Ploughshares, Ontario Rev, Denver Qtly*

Pamela Painter 🎤 ✈ W
65 Marlborough St
Boston, MA 02116, 617-267-6799
Internet: Pamela_Painter@emerson.edu
    Pubs: *The Long & Short of It* (Carnegie Mellon Pr, 1999),
Getting to Know the Weather (U Illinois Pr, 1985), *Atlantic,
Harper's, Story, Ploughshares, NAR, Harvard Rev*

Carol Ann Parikh 🎤 W
54 Babcock St
Brookline, MA 02446, 617-731-2175
    Pubs: *Side Show: Anths* (Somersault Pr, 1996, 1995),
*Queen St Qtly, Confrontation, Indiana Rev, Lit Rev, The
Jrnl, Canto*

Ruth M. Parks P
1550 Beacon St, #11A
Brookline, MA 02246
    Pubs: *Treacle on the Tongue* (Penrose Pub Co, 1994),
*SPSM&H, The Lyric, Byline, Time of Singing, Coastal Forest
Rev, Senior Times*

Marian Parry P
60 Martin St
Cambridge, MA 02138-1637, 617-876-0407
    Pubs: *Margin, Shenandoah, Grand Street, 2+2, Negative
Capability, Antioch Rev, Carleton Miscellany*

Mark Pawlak 🎤 ✈ P
44 Thingvalla Ave
Cambridge, MA 02138, 617-491-6416
Internet: mark.pawlak@umb.edu
    Pubs: *Special Handling: Newspaper Poems New &
Selected, All the News* (Hanging Loose, 1993, 1985),
*Lungfull, The World, Abraxas, Transfer, Exquisite Corpse,
Imagine, Bogg, Hanging Loose, Synaesthetic*

Peter Payack P
64 Highland Ave
Cambridge, MA 02139-1054, 617-492-2913
    Pubs: *The Zen of America* (The Idea Works, 1992), *No Free
Will in Tomatoes* (Zoland Bks, 1989), *Paris Review Anth*
(Norton, 1990), *Asimov's Sci-Fi Mag*

Edith Pearlman 🎤 ✈ W
21 Elba St
Brookline, MA 02146, 617-731-1387
Internet: chestersan@aol.com
    Pubs: *Love Among the Greats and Other Stories* (Eastern
Washington U Pr, 2002), *Vaquita and Other Stories* (U Pitt
Pr, 1996)

Roland F. Pease, Jr. P
Zoland Books, Inc, 384 Huron Ave, Cambridge, MA 02138,
617-864-6252
    Pubs: *Held Up for Answers* (Imaginary Pr, 1980),
Dreamworks, New York Times, Paris Rev

Jean Pedrick P
48 Mt Vernon St
Boston, MA 02108, 617-227-9731
    Pubs: *Mitteleuropa* (Small Poetry Pr, 1992), *An Ear to the
Ground: Anth* (U Georgia Pr, 1989), *Yankee, Granite Rev,
Compost, Antioch Rev, Southern Rev, Light, Press,
Passager*

Robin B. Pelzman   🎤 ✈   P
65 Babcock St, #5
Brookline, MA 02446, 617-513-6315
Internet: robinpelzman@mindspring.com
    Pubs: *The Antigonish Rev, The Lucid Stone, Carriage Hse
    Rev, The Comstock Rev, Salamander, The Senior Times*

Joyce Peseroff   🎤 ✈   P
24 Balfour St
Lexington, MA 02421, 781-862-9333
Internet: jpeseroff@aol.com
    Pubs: *Mortal Education, The Hardness Scale, A Dog in the
    Lifeboat* (Carnegie Mellon U, 2000, 2000, 1991),
    Ploughshares, Agni, Kenyon Rev, Massachusetts Rev

Stuart Peterfreund   P
250 Brattle St, #32
Cambridge, MA 02138-4855
Internet: speterfr@lynx.neu.edu
    Pubs: *Interstatements* (Curbstone, 1986), *Harder Than Rain*
    (Ithaca Hse, 1977), *Sow's Ear, New Rev, The Bridge,
    Wallace Stevens Jrnl, Abiko Qtly, Compost*

Joan K. Peters   W
c/o Lisa Warren, Assoc. Director of Pub, Perseus Books, One
Jacob Way, Reading, MA 01867, 212-929-1583
Internet: info@joankpeters.com
    Pubs: *Manny & Rose* (St. Martin's Pr, 1985), *Global City
    Rev, Family Life*

Michael Pettit   P
217 W Pelham Rd
Shutesbury, MA 01072, 413-259-1602
Internet: mpettit@alumni.princeton.edu
    Pubs: *Cardinal Points* (U Iowa Pr, 1988), *American Light* (U
    Georgia Pr, 1984), *Kenyon Rev, Gettysburg Rev, Southern
    Rev, Atlantic*

Steven J. Peyster   🎤 ✈   P
66 West St
New Salem, MA 01355-9721, 978-544-3887
Internet: speyster@mindspring.com
    Pubs: *Alphabet for Zina* (Window Edtns, 1981), *City Lights
    Jrnl, River Styx, Telephone, Poets On, Home Planet News,
    National Poetry Mag of the Lower East Side*

Stephen Philbrick   P
34 Shaw Rd
Windsor, MA 01270-9573
    Pubs: *The Smith, Poetry Now, Chouteau Rev, Anyart Jrnl,
    Grub Street, Greensboro Rev*

Marge Piercy   🎤 ✈   P&W
Box 1473
Wellfleet, MA 02667-1473, 508-349-3163
Internet: hagolem@c4.net
    Pubs: *Three Women* (Morrow, 1999), *Early Grrrl* (Leapfrog
    Pr, 1999), *The Art of Blessing the Day, What Are Big Girls
    Made Of* (Knopf, 1999, 1997), *Storm Tide* (w/Ira Wood), *City
    of Darkness, City of Light* (Fawcett, 1998, 1996)

Ronald William Pies, M.D.   P&W
PO Box 332
Bedford, MA 01730, 978-740-3230x111
Internet: ronpies@mass.med.org
    Pubs: *The Alzheimer Sonnets* (JAMA, 2001), *Ethics of the
    Sages* (Jason Aronson, 2000), *Riding Down Dark*
    (Nightshade Pr, 1992), *Blood to Remember: Anth* (Texas
    Tech U Pr, 1991), *Vital Signs: Anth* (UCLA Med School,
    1990), *Lit Rev, Oasis*

Helene Pilibosian   🎤 ✈   P
171 Maplewood St
Watertown, MA 02472-1324, 617-926-2602
Internet: hsarkiss@attbi.com
    Pubs: *At Quarter Past Reality, Carvings from an Heirloom*
    (Ohan Pr, 1998, 1983), *NAR, Lit Online, Half Tones to
    Jubilee, New Mexico Humanities Rev, Pacific Rev, Hawaii
    Rev, Cape Rock*

Robert Pinsky   🎤 ✈   P
Creative Writing Dept, Boston Univ, 236 Bay State Rd, Boston,
MA 02215, 617-353-2821
Internet: rpinsky@acs.bu.edu
    Pubs: *Jersey Rain, The Figured Wheel* (FSG, 2000, 1996),
    The Want Bone (Ecco Pr, 1990), *Agni, New Yorker,
    Threepenny Rev*

John Paul Pirolli   🎤 ✈   PP&P
The Buddah, PO Box 705, Watertown, MA 02471-0705
Internet: DaemonMag@aol.com
    Pubs: *Madman on the Merrimac* (Alpha Beat Pr, 1994),
    *Voices in Italian America, Poesy, Bouillabaisse, Amer
    Dissident Mag, Ibbetson Street Pr, Stone Soup Poets:
    Original Gallery, New Writers Poetry Guild: Community
    Church of Boston*

Susan Lyon Pope   W
PO Box 82
Monument Beach, MA 02553
    Pubs: *Catching the Light* (Viking, 1990), *Best of Wind: Anth*
    (Wind Pubs, 1994), *Northern New England Rev, Calliope,
    The Writing Self*

Linda Portnay   P
21 Robbins Rd
Lexington, MA 02173, 617-862-6004
    Pubs: *Wishing for the Worst* (Warthog Pr, 1993), *Radcliffe
    Qtly, Northern Rev, Gulfstream, Thema, Kalliope,
    Sandscript, Slant, Worcester Rev, Wisconsin Rev*

Carol Potter   P
27 Taylor Heights, PO Box 72
Montague, MA 01351
    Pubs: *Before We Were Born* (Alice James Bks, 1990),
    *Blueline, Massachusetts Rev, Sojourner, Iowa Rev,
    Out/Look, Field, APR, High Plains, Women's Rev of Bks,
    New Letters*

Patricia Powell ♀ ✈   W
1 Dana St #11
Cambridge, MA 02138-5404
Internet: pepowell@fas.harvard.edu
    Pubs: *The Pagoda* (Knopf, 1998), *A Small Gathering of
    Bones, Me Dying Trial* (Heinemann, 1994, 1993)

Stan Proper   P
Wentworth Institute, 550 Huntington Ave, #8-408, Boston, MA
02115, 617-442-9010
    Pubs: *Portraits: Kith, Kin & Neighbors, Love Lyrics* (Poets'
    Pr, 1998, 1996), *Laurels: Anth* (E. Blanche, 1994), *We
    Speak for Peace: Anth* (KIT, 1993)

Lawrence Raab ♀ ✈   P
139 Bulkley St
Williamstown, MA 01267-2020, 413-458-3870
Internet: lawrence.e.raab@williams.edu
    Pubs: *Visible Signs: New & Selected Poems, The Probable
    World, What We Don't Know About Each Other* (Penguin,
    2003, 2000, 1993), *Other Children* (Carnegie Mellon, 1987)

Pat Rabby ♀ ✈   P
23 Meriam St
Lexington, MA 02420, 781-861-0692
Internet: patrabby@hotmail.com
    Pubs: *Bellevue Lit Rev, Connecticut Poetry Rev, Lynx,
    Boston Today, Glassworks, The Bridge, Antigones*

Richard F. Radford ♀ ✈   W
8 Juniper St, #29
Brookline, MA 02445-7112, 617-734-9893
Internet: radfordrf@aol.com
    Pubs: *Drug Agent USA* (St. Martin's, 1991), *Trooper*
    (Quinlan, 1987), *New England Sampler, Alcoholism, Amer
    Man, Pegasus, New Earth Rev, The Word*

David Raffeld   P
1763 Commonwealth Ave
Auburndale, MA 02466-2727, 617-558-9539
    Pubs: *The Ballad of Harmonica George & Other Poems*
    (Adastra Pr, 1989), *Poetry East, Phoebe, October Mountain,
    Longhouse*

Peter Rand   W
35 Falmouth St
Belmont, MA 02478
    Pubs: *China Hands* (S&S, 1995), *Gold From Heaven, The
    Private Rich* (Crown, 1988, 1984), *Firestorm* (Doubleday,
    1969)

Edward Rayher   P
c/o Swamp Press, 15 Warwick Rd, Northfield, MA 01360-1105,
413-498-4343
    Pubs: *Buffalo Spree, Antigonish Rev, Washout Rev,
    Colorado Qtly*

Monica E. Raymond   P
57 Brookline
Cambridge, MA 02139
    Pubs: *Sinister Wisdom, Iowa Rev, Heresies, Sojourner,
    Village Voice, Light*

Jennifer Regan   P
992 Memorial Dr, #206
Cambridge, MA 02138-4872
    Pubs: *Cries of the Spirit: Anth* (Beacon Pr, 1991), *Black
    Mountain Rev, Prairie Schooner, The Reaper, Ohio Rev,
    Confrontation, Hudson Rev, Chelsea*

James S. Reinbold   W
44 School St
Rehoboth, MA 02769-2204

Steven Riel ♀ ✈   P
PO Box 679
Natick, MA 01760-0006
    Pubs: *How to Dream* (Amherst Writers & Artists, 1992),
    Badboy Book of Erotic Poetry: Anth (Masquerade Bks,
    1995), *The River Rev, The Gay and Lesbian Rev, Art &
    Understanding*

Eve Rifkah   P
11 Rosemont Rd
Worcester, MA 01605
Internet: seavoice@mac.com
    Pubs: *MacGuffin, Worcester Rev, California Qtly, Southern
    New Hampshire Lit Jrnl, Sahara, Jabberwock Rev*

David Rivard ♀ ✈   P
72 Inman St, Apt A
Cambridge, MA 02139-1213, 617-661-6388
Internet: drivard@channel1.com
    Pubs: *Bewitched Playground, Wise Poison* (Graywolf, 2000,
    1996), *Torque* (U Pitt Pr, 1988), *Poetry, Ploughshares,
    TriQtly, NAR, NER*

Laura Rodley ♀ ✈   P
PO Box 63
Shelburne Falls, MA 01370-0063
    Pubs: *Way Station Mag, Albatross, Blueline Anth, Tuesday's
    Storm, Greyhound Terminal, Massachusetts Rev, Prose
    Poem, Connecticut River Rev, Paragraph, Blueline, Earth's
    Daughters, Sanctuary, Zahara*

Tony Rogers 🎤 ✈   W
58 Larchmont Ave
Waban, MA 02468-2031, 617-965-5125
Internet: ttrogers@attbi.com
    Pubs: *North Dakota Qtly, Larcom Rev, Painted Hills Rev,
    Outerbridge, Half Tones to Jubilee, Wooster Rev, Four
    Quarters, Boston Monthly, Oak Square, Wind, Thema*

John J. Ronan 🎤 ✈   P
Box 5524
Gloucester, MA 01930-0007, 978-525-2022
Internet: jronan@nscc.mass.edu
    Pubs: *Sad Little Breathings: Anth* (PublishingOnline, 2001),
    *Recorder, Notre Dame Rev, The Curable Corpse, The
    Catching Self* (Folly Cove Bks, 1999, 1996), *Threepenny
    Rev, SPR, Folio, Greensboro Rev, NER*

Daniel Asa Rose 🎤 ✈   W
138 Bay State Rd
Rehoboth, MA 02769, 508-252-6315
Internet: rose@forward.com
    Pubs: *Small Family With Rooster, Flipping for It* (St. Martin's
    Pr, 1988, 1987), *Esquire, Playboy, New Yorker, Partisan Rev*

Jennifer Rose 🎤 ✈   P
94 Prospect St
Waltham, MA 02453-8501, 781-893-0361
Internet: jenr@tiac.net
    Pubs: *The Old Direction of Heaven* (Truman State U Pr, 2000)

George H. Rosen   W
2 Barberry Heights Rd
Gloucester, MA 01930-1202, 978-281-3561
Internet: georosen@tiac.net
    Pubs: *Black Money* (Scarborough Hse, 1990), *Descant,
    NAR, Yale Rev, Harper's, A Matter of Crime, Ascent*

Karen Rosenberg   W
c/o Society of Fellows, Harvard Univ, 78 Mount Auburn St,
Cambridge, MA 02138, 617-495-2485
    Pubs: *Water Baby: Anth* (John Murray, 1995), *The Year's
    Best: Anth* (Tickled by Thunder, 1996), *Orbis, Metropolitan,
    Vigil, Potato Eyes, Oasis, Swansea Rev, Response, Prop*

Sarah Rossiter   W
72 Church St
Weston, MA 02193, 617-894-6184
    Pubs: *Beyond This Bitter Air* (U Illinois Pr, 1987), *The
    Human Season* (Little, Brown, 1987)

Eleanor Roth   W
131 Clarendon St
North Dartmouth, MA 02747-3269, 508-993-3328
Internet: ebroth@gis.net
    Pubs: *Female, Living, Herworld, The Humanist, Asia Mag,
    Green's Fiction Mag*

Lee Rudolph   P
Math Dept, Clark Univ, 950 Main St, Worcester, MA 01610
    Pubs: *Contemporary New England Poetry: Anth* (Texas Rev
    Pr, 1987), *New Yorker, Clark Now*

Mary Ruefle 🎤 ✈   P
410 Old Montague Rd, #9
Amherst, MA 01002-2001
    Pubs: *Apparition Hill* (Cavan Kerry Pr, 2002), *Among the
    Musk Ox People, Post Meridian, Cold Pluto* (Carnegie
    Mellon U Pr, 2002, 2000, 1996), *The Adamant* (U Iowa Pr,
    1989), *Life Without Speaking* (U Alabama Pr, 1987)

Marieve Rugo   P
31 Fayerweather St
Cambridge, MA 02138-3329, 617-969-6667
    Pubs: *Fields of Vision* (U Alabama Pr, 1983), *Kenyon Rev,
    Chelsea, Black Warrior, New Letters, SPR, North Dakota Qtly*

Hilary Russell   P
PO Box 578
Sheffield, MA 01257, 413-229-2549
    Pubs: *BPJ, Ploughshares, Carolina Qtly, Country Jrnl,
    Boulevard*

Catherine Sasanov 🎤 ✈   P
50 Follen St, Apt 101
Cambridge, MA 02138-3506
    Pubs: *All the Blood Tethers* (Northeastern U Pr, 2002), *Las
    Horas de Belén: A Book of Hours* (Mabou Mines, 1999),
    Traditions of Bread & Violence (Four Way Bks, 1996)

Peter Saunders 🎤 ✈   P
Steppingstone, Box 327, Chatham, MA 02633, 508-945-5283
Internet: poetpeter@juno.com
    Pubs: *Heartbeat of New England: Anth* (Tiger Moon, 2000),
    Ask Any Frog (Steppingstone, 2000), *Pitkin Rev, Prime Time
    Mag, Provincetown Mag, CSM, Poetry In Your Face-P'town,
    WOMR-FM Poetry Corner, Longfellow, Aurorean, Cape
    Codder*

Cheryl Savageau   P&W
19 Walnut Hill Dr
Worcester, MA 01602, 508-752-3953
    Pubs: *Dirt Road Home, Poetry Like Bread: Anth* (Curbstone
    Pr, 1995, 1994), *Massachusetts Rev, Agni, River Styx,
    Indiana Rev, Nebraska English Jrnl, Boston Rev*

Randi Schalet 🎤 ✈   W
157 DeForest St
Boston, MA 02131-4907, 617-323-1942
Internet: rgschalet@cs.com
    Pubs: *Lunch* (Clothespin Fever Pr, 1994)

Jeanne Schinto   W
53 Poor St
Andover, MA 01810-2501, 978-475-5001
    Pubs: *Children of Men* (Persea Bks, 1991), *Shadow Bands*
    (Ontario Rev Pr, 1988), *The Literary Dog: Anth* (Atlantic
    Monthly Pr, 1990), *Virginia Qtly Rev, Yale Rev*

Ada Jill Schneider 🎤 ✈   P
120 Friends Cove
Somerset, MA 02726-5900, 508-672-5989
Internet: adajillschneider@yahoo.com
    Pubs: *The Museum of My Mother, Fine Lines & Other*
    Wrinkles (Gratlau Pr, 1996, 1993), *Her Face in the Mirror:*
    Anth (Beacon Pr, 1994), *Nedge, Synaesthetic, Newport*
    Rev, Crone's Nest, Mediphors, Midstream, The Sow's Ear
    Poetry Rev

Pat Schneider 🎤 ✈   P&W
PO Box 1076
Amherst, MA 01004, 413-253-3307
    Pubs: *A Continuing Passion: Writing Alone & With Others*
    (Oxford U Pr, 2003), *Ms., Sewanee Rev, Chrysalis*

Nina Schneider   W
Music St
West Tisbury, MA 02575, 508-693-5746
    Pubs: *The Woman Who Lived in a Prologue* (HM, 1980),
    Paris Rev

Jan Schreiber 🎤 ✈   P
210 Reservoir Rd
Brookline, MA 02467, 617-566-2516
Internet: jansch19@spire.com
    Pubs: *Sketch of a Serpent* (RL Barth, 1986), *Digressions*
    (Aliuando Pr, 1970), *Poemtree, TheHyperTexts*

Ron Schreiber 🎤 ✈   P
9 Reed St
Cambridge, MA 02140-2413
    Pubs: *John* (Hanging Loose Pr/Calamus Bks, 1988),
    Tomorrow Will Really Be Sunday (Calamus, 1985)

Lloyd Schwartz 🎤 ✈   P
27 Pennsylvania Ave
Somerville, MA 02145-2217, 617-666-3233
Internet: lloyd.schwartz@umb.edu
    Pubs: *Cairo Traffic, Goodnight, Gracie* (U Chicago Pr, 2000,
    1992), *Handbook of Heartbreak: Anth* (Morrow, 1998), *Best*
    American Poetry 1994: Anth (Scribner/Macmillan, 1994),
    New Yorker, Paris Rev

Elizabeth Searle 🎤 ✈   W
18 College Ave
Arlington, MA 02474-2253, 781-641-2906
Internet: esearle@attbi.com
    Pubs: *Celebrities in Disgrace, A Four-Sided Bed* (Graywolf
    Pr, 2001, 1998), *My Body to You* (U Iowa Pr, 1993), *Lovers:*
    Anth (Crossing Pr, 1992), *Ontario Rev, Michigan Qtly Rev,*
    Five Points, Ploughshares, Redbook, Kenyon Rev,
    Boulevard, Agni

Richard Seltzer 🎤 ✈   W
PO Box 161
West Roxbury, MA 02132
www.samizdat.com
    Pubs: *The Lizard of Oz* (B&R Samizdat Express, 1994), *The*
    Name of the Hero (J.P. Tarcher/HM, 1981), *Antic, Analog*

Richard C. Shaner 🎤 ✈   P
701 Nantascot Pl, 155 George Washington Blvd
Hull, MA 02045-3000, 617-925-2654
Internet: shaner@umbsky.cc.umb.edu
    Pubs: *A Nantucket Bestiary* (Poets Corner Pr, 1980),
    College English, American Land Forum, Passages North,
    Waves, Hanging Loose

Robert B. Shaw   P
English Dept, Mount Holyoke College, South Hadley, MA
01075, 413-538-2444
Internet: rshaw@mtholyoke.edu
    Pubs: *Below the Surface, The Post Office Murals Restored*
    (Copper Beech Pr, 1999, 1994), *The Wonder of Seeing*
    Double (U Massachusetts Pr, 1988), *Comforting the*
    Wilderness (Wesleyan U Pr, 1977)

Beverly Shaw-Johnson   P
217 Scudder Ave
Hyannis, MA 02601, 508-771-3471
    Pubs: *Massachusetts State Poetry Society Anth*
    (Massachusetts State Poetry Society, 1980), *Arizona*
    Highways, Back Bay View, Worcester Rev, Itsblotto Karmics,
    Jlag Rev, Gargoyle

Tom F. Sheehan 🎤 ✈   P
217 Central St
Saugus, MA 01906-2110, 617-233-5041
Internet: tomsheehan@mediaone.net
    Pubs: *A Gathering of Memories* (Millennium Assoc, 2000),
    Reflections From Vinegar Hill (Slagpile Pr, 1999), *Hummers,*
    Knucklers & Slow Curves (U Illinois Pr, 1991), *The Best of*
    Spitball: Anth (Pocket Bks, 1989), *MacGuffin, Aethlon,*
    Snowbound, Electric Acorn

Eve Shelnutt 🎤 ✈   P&W
College of Holy Cross, One College St, English Dept,
Worcester, MA 01610-2395, 508-752-8756
    Pubs: *First a Long Hesitation, Recital in a Private Room*
    (Carnegie Mellon, 1992, 1988), *The Writing Room*
    (Longstreet Pr, 1989)

Nancy Sherman   P
2 Brenda Ln
Belchertown, MA 01007-9758, 413-586-6151
Internet: nsherman@hampshire.edu
   Pubs: *Ploughshares, Grolier Annual, Massachusetts Rev,
   Seneca Rev, Cream City Rev, AWP Chronicle*

Lazare Seymour Simckes   W
Williams College, 301 Stetson, Williamstown, MA 01267
   Pubs: *The Comatose Kids* (Fiction Collective, 1976), *Seven
   Days of Morning* (Random Hse, 1963)

R. D. Skillings   W
730 Commercial St
Provincetown, MA 02657-1761, 508-487-3768
Internet: rdskillings@attbi.com
   Pubs: *Obsidian* (Arts End Bks, 2001), *How Many Die,
   Where the Time Goes* (U Pr New England, 2001, 1999)

John Skoyles 🎤 ✈   P
PO Box 2022
Truro, MA 02666-2022, 508-487-7918
Internet: john_skoyles@emerson.edu
   Pubs: *Definition of the Soul, Permanent Change, A Little
   Faith* (Carnegie Mellon, 1998, 1990, 1981), *The Smoky
   Mountain Cage Bird Society* (Kodansha America, 1997)

David R. Slavitt 🎤 ✈   P&W
35 W St #5
Cambridge, MA 02139, 617-497-1219
Internet: drslavitt@attbi.com
   Pubs: *Propertius in Love* (U California Pr, 2002), *Falling
   From Silence, Ps3569.L3, A Gift* (LSU Pr, 2001, 1998,
   1996), *A Crown for the King, Sixty-One Psalms of David*
   (Oxford U Pr, 1998, 1996), *Hudson Rev, Poetry, New
   Criterion, Pequod, Shenandoah*

Tom Sleigh 🎤 ✈   P
1 Stinson Ct #3
Cambridge, MA 02139, 617-876-9002
   Pubs: *The Far Side of the Earth* (HM, 2003), *The Dream-
   house, The Chain, Waking* (U Chicago Pr, 1999, 1996,
   1990), *After One* (HM, 1983), *New Yorker, Poetry,
   Threepenny Rev, Partisan Rev, New Republic, Grand Street,
   Slate, TriQtly, Paris Rev*

Joel Sloman 🎤 ✈   P
82 Harvard Ave
Medford, MA 02155, 781-488-3788
Internet: jmsloman1931@aol.com
   Pubs: *Cuban Journal, Stops* (Zoland Bks, 2000, 1997),
   Virgil's Machines (Norton, 1966)

William Jay Smith 🎤 ✈   P
63 Luther Shaw Rd
Cummington, MA 01026-9787, 413-634-5546
   Pubs: *The Girl in Glass: Love Poems* (Books & Co, 2002),
   The Cherokee Lottery (Curbstone Pr, 2000) *Around My
   Room, Laughing Time* (FSG, 2000, 1990), *The World Below
   the Window: Poems 1937-1997* (Johns Hopkins U Pr, 1998),
   New Criterion

Stephen Sossaman 🎤 ✈   P
Westfield State College, English Dept, Westfield, MA 01086,
413-572-5335
Internet: ssossaman@foma.wsc.ma.edu
   Pubs: *Bridge Traffic: Anth* (Tiny Poems Pr, 1999), *Viet Nam:
   Anth* (Bowling Green U Pr, 1987), *South Coast Poetry Rev,
   Southern Humanities Rev, Antigonish Rev, Ball State U
   Forum, Modern Haiku, Paris Rev, Formalist, Dalhousie Rev,
   Centennial Rev*

Kathleen (Drucker) Spivack 🎤 ✈   P&W
53 Spruce St
Watertown, MA 02472, 617-926-1637
Internet: kspivack@earthlink.net
   Pubs: *The Break-up Variations* (Zoland Bks, 2002), *The
   Honeymoon* (Graywolf Pr, 1986), *The Beds We Lie In*
   (Scarecrow Pr, 1986), *Kenyon Rev, New Letters, Harvard
   Rev, NAR, Poetry, Ploughshares, Agni, New Yorker*

Conrad Squires 🎤 ✈   P
17 Little Nahant Rd
Nahant, MA 01908, 781-599-8963
Internet: csquires@attbi.com
   Pubs: *Dancing With the Switchman* (Pudding Hse Pubs,
   2001)

Sue Standing 🎤 ✈   P
Wheaton College, English Dept, Norton, MA 02766
Internet: sstandin@wheatonma.edu
   Pubs: *Gravida* (Four Way Bks, 1995), *Deception Pass* (Alice
   James Bks, 1984), *APR, Iowa Rev, Nation, Partisan Rev,
   Poetry NW, SW Rev*

Judith W. Steinbergh 🎤 ✈   P
99 Evans Rd
Brookline, MA 02445-2117, 617-734-1416
Internet: judithst@aol.com
   Pubs: *Writing My Will, A Living Anytime* (Talking Stone Pr,
   2001, 1988), *Winners: Washington Prize: Anth* (Word Works
   Pr, 1999), *Sojourner, Calyx*

Robert Steinem   P
40 Stranahan
Colrain, MA 01340, 413-624-3709
Internet: robstei@aol.com
   Pubs: *This Wood Sang Out: Anth* (Literacy Project, 1995),
   *Optimist, Poetry Motel, Sanctuary, ELF, Poems for a Livable
   Planet, Written Arts, Peregrine, Folio*

Harry Stessel P
Westfield State College, Westfield, MA 01086, 413-568-3311
    Pubs: *American Studies* (Raindust Pr, 1975), *Connecticut
    River Rev, SPR, Xanadu, Mss., Cottonwood Rev,
    Commonwealth Rev, Kansas Qtly*

Jadene Felina Stevens P
Salt Wind Poets, 12 Olde Homestead Way, East Harwich, MA
02645, 508-432-6661
    Pubs: *The Original Trinity* (Stepping Stone Pr, 1994), *Salt
    Wind Poets Anth* (Blue Moon Pr, 1991), *Quilt, Proof Rock,
    Transnational Perspectives, Sunrust*

Susan Stinson 🎤 ✈ P&W
PO Box 1272
Northampton, MA 01061
Internet: sestinson@aol.com
    Pubs: *Martha Moody, Fat Girl Dances With Rocks* (Spinsters
    Ink, 1995, 1994), *Mammoth Book of Lesbian Erotica: Anth*
    (Robinson, 2000), *Diva, Curve, Kenyon Rev, Sinister
    Wisdom, Heresies, Yellow Silk, Bay Windows*

Jane Strete P
106 Pleasant St, #2
Cambridge, MA 02139, 617-354-9487
    Pubs: *City River Voices* (West End Pr, 1992), *Ourselves,
    Growing Older: Anth* (S&S, 1987), *South Coast Poetry Intl,
    Timbrel, Maine Times*

Jonathan Strong 🎤 ✈ W
English Dept, Tufts Univ, Medford, MA 02155
    Pubs: *A Circle Around Her, The Old World, Offspring, An
    Untold Tale, Companion Pieces, Secret Words* (Zoland,
    2000, 1997, 1995, 1993, 1993, 1992), *Elsewhere*
    (Ballantine, 1985)

Jack Sughrue P
52 Heritage Dr
Whittinsville, MA 01588-2358
    Pubs: *The Book of Books, The Link* (Pakka Pr, 1993, 1978),
    Jlag Rev, Poets, Little Apple, The Lobe, Gargoyle

James Sullivan 🎤 ✈ P
590A Sunrise Ave, PO Box 451
Barre, MA 01005-0451, 978-355-4389
    Pubs: *In Order of Appearance: 400 Poems* (Adams Printing
    Co, 1988), *America, Commonweal, Worcester Rev*

Stanley Sultan 🎤 ✈ W
1 Prospect Ave
Boston, MA 02131-3727, 617-325-1482
Internet: ssultan@clarku.edu

Harris Sussman 🎤 ✈ P
51 Craigie St
Somerville, MA 02143, 617-629-0048
Internet: harris@sussman.org
    Pubs: *So Far, Two Step* (Lizard Head Pr, 1979, 1978), *The
    Sun, Wall Paper*

John T. P
7 Silverwood Terr
South Hadley, MA 01075

Cecilia M. Tan 🎤 ✈ W
Circlet Press Inc, 1770 Massachusetts Ave, #278, Cambridge,
MA 02140, 617-864-0492
Internet: ctan@circlet.com
    Pubs: *THE VELDERET* (Circlet Pr, 2001), *Black Feathers*
    (HC, 1998), *Isaac Asimov's Sci Fi Mag, Blithe House Qtly,
    Herotica, Penthouse, Paramour, Looking for Mr. Preston, On
    a Bed of Rice* (Anchor Bks, 1995), *Best Amer Erotica, By
    Her Subdued, No Other Tribute*

Stephen J. Tapscott P
66 Martin St, #2
Cambridge, MA 02138, 617-876-6121
    Pubs: *From the Book of Changes* (Carcanet, 1996), *Another
    Body* (Cleveland State U Poetry Ctr, 1989), *Mesopotamia*
    (Wesleyan U Pr, 1975)

James Tate 🎤 ✈ P
16 Jones Rd
Amherst, MA 01002-9715
    Pubs: *Dreams of a Robot Dancing Bee* (Verse Pr, 2002),
    *Memoir of the Hawk, Shroud of the Gnome, Worshipful
    Company of Fletchers* (Ecco Pr, 2001, 1997, 1994),
    Distance From Loved Ones, Reckoner (Wesleyan U Pr,
    1990, 1986), *APR, Poetry, Massachusetts Rev*

Janice Thaddeus P
58 Garfield St
Cambridge, MA 02138, 617-547-7806
    Pubs: *Lot's Wife* (Saturday Pr, 1986), *Mountain Rev,
    Louisville Rev, Shenandoah, Cold*

Alexander Louis Theroux   W
Willow St
West Barnstable, MA 02668

Daniel Tobin 🎤 ✈   P
Emerson College, 120 Boylston St, Boston, MA 02116
    Pubs: *Double Life* (LSU Pr, 2003), *Where the World Is
    Made, New American Poets: Anth* (Middlebury/U Pr of New
    England, 1999, 2000), *Norton Introduction to Poetry: Anth*
    (Norton, 2002), *Southern Rev, Prairie Schooner, Boulevard,
    Poetry, Ploughshares, Paris Rev*

Jessica Treadway   W
17 Old Colony Ln
Arlington, MA 02174-3205, 781-646-2748
    Pubs: *And Give You Peace* (Graywolf Pr, 2001), *Absent
    Without Leave & Other Stories* (Delphinium Bks, 1993),
    Ploughshares, Agni, Atlantic, Hudson Rev

Florence Trefethen   P
1010 Waltham St
Lexington, MA 02421-8044, 781-862-0644
    Pubs: *The Little Brown Reader: Anth* (HC, 1993), *Fairbank
    Remembered: Anth* (Harvard U Pr, 1992), *Bellingham Rev,
    Connecticut Rev, Negative Capability*

Jean Tupper 🎤 ✈   P
165 Tilting Rock Rd
Wrentham, MA 02093-1360
    Pubs: *Castings: Anth* (Aubade Pr, 1991), *Madison Rev,
    MacGuffin, Nebraska Rev, Paterson Lit Rev, Sanskrit Rev,
    SPR, Worcester Rev*

Gregoire Turgeon   P
5 Sherlock La
Westford, MA 01886
    Pubs: *Painted Bride Qtly, Poetry, Poetry NW, SPR,
    Louisville Rev*

Sondra Upham   P
37 Manters Pt
Plymouth, MA 02360
    Pubs: *Freight* (Slapering Hol Pr, 2000), *Times of Sorrow,
    Times of Grace: Anth* (Backwater Pr, 2002), *We Speak for
    Peace: Anth* (KIT, 1993), *Prairie Schooner, Phoebe, New
    Virginia Rev, FIELD, Sojourner, Eclectic Lit Forum*

Cornelia Veenendaal   P
14 Wellesley Pk
Dorchester, MA 02124, 617-825-7262
    Pubs: *What Seas What Shores* (Rowan Tree Pr, 1984),
    *Arvon Fdn, Prairie Schooner, Sojourner, Soundings East,
    Ploughshares, Hanging Loose, Commonweal*

Peter Viereck   P
12 Silver St
South Hadley, MA 01075-1616, 413-534-5504
    Pubs: *Tide & Continuities* (U Arkansas Pr, 1995), *The
    Unadjusted Man* (Greenwood Pr, 1973), *New Yorker, Paris
    Rev, Parnassus, APR, New Republic*

Tino Villanueva 🎤 ✈   P
1112 Boylston St, Ste 270
Boston, MA 02215, 617-267-2592
    Pubs: *Chronicle of My Worst Years* (Northwestern U Pr,
    1994), *Scene From the Movie Giant* (Curbstone Pr, 1993),
    Bloomsbury Rev, Agni

Arturo Vivante 🎤 ✈   W
Box 3005
Wellfleet, MA 02667-3005, 508-349-6619
    Pubs: *The Tales of Arturo Vivante* (Sheep Meadow Pr,
    1990), *TriQrtly, Formations, Notre Dame Rev, New Yorker,
    Yankee*

Dan Wakefield   W
Po Box 1190
Burlington, MA 01803-6190
Internet: wakespace@aol.com
    Pubs: *Home Free* (Delacorte, 1977)

Diane Wald   P
52 Paine St
Boston, MA 02131, 617-524-0072
    Pubs: *Double Mirror* (Runaway Spoon Pr, 1996), *My Hat
    That Was Dreaming* (Literary Renaissance, 1994), *Boston
    Lit Rev, APR, New Rev, Kayak, Missouri Rev*

Victor Walter 🎤 ✈   W
204 Aspinwall Ave
Brookline, MA 02446-6960, 617-566-0233
Internet: manush@bu.edu
    Pubs: *The Craftsmen* (Lyric Pr, 2001), *The Voice of Manush*
    (White Pine Pr, 1996), *A Ghost at Heart's Edge: Anth* (North
    Atlantic Bks, 1999), *Boston Globe Mag, Ellipsis, Short Story,
    Cimarron Rev, NER, Chaminade Rev, Magic Realism*

Richard Waring 🎤 ✈   P
33 Chandler St
Belmont, MA 02478-5026, 617-489-1630
Internet: rwaring@nejm.org
    Pubs: *Listening to Stones, The Unitarian Universalist Poets:
    Anth* (Pudding Hse Pr, 1999, 1996), *Mothering, Pine River
    Papers, Noctiluca, Dark Horse, Dragonfly, Contact II, Zone*

Rosanna Warren   P
28 Tappan Street
Roslindale, MA 02131
    Pubs: *Stained Glass, Each Leaf Shines Separate* (Norton,
    1993, 1984)

Ellen Doré Watson 🎤 ✈ P
40 Manning Rd
Conway, MA 01341, 413-585-3368
Internet: ewatson@smith.edu
  Pubs: *Ladder Music* (Alice James Bks, 2001), *We Live in Bodies* (Alice James Bks, 1997), *Broken Railings* (Owl Creek Pr, 1997), *Night Out: Anth* (Milkweed Edtns, 1997), *New Yorker, Boulevard, APR, Ploughshares, Prairie Schooner*

Nancy Dingman Watson 🎤 ✈ W
Box 32
Truro, MA 02666-0032, 508-349-2324
  Pubs: *Tommy's Mommy's Fish* (Viking, 1996), *Blueberries Lavender* (Addison Wesley, 1977)

Anne Sweeter Watson 🎤 P
105 Allen's Point
Marion, MA 02738-2301, 508-748-0674
Internet: oldsalt@compuserve.com
  Pubs: *Prisms of the Soul: Anth* (Morehouse Pub, 1996), *The Living Church, Noetic Sciences Rev, Starting Point, Time of Singing, Jrnl of Poetry Therapy, Human Quest, Journeys, New England Writers Network*

Suellen Wedmore P
155 South St
Rockport, MA 01966, 978-546-3754
Internet: swedmore@massed.net
  Pubs: *Anthology of American Poetry* (Monitor Bks, 1997), *I Am Becoming the Woman I Wanted to Be: Anth* (Papier-Mache Pr, 1994), *College English, Boston Poet, Green Mountains Rev, Byline Mag, Teaching Voices, Phoebe, Writer's Ink, The Artful Mind, Stuff Mag*

Hannah Weiner PP&P
64 Hillside Ave
West Newton, MA 02165
  Pubs: *Silent Teachers Remembered* (Tender Buttons Pr, 1993), *The Fast* (United Artists, 1992), *Raddle Moon, Motel, Paper Air, Object, Grist, Writing*

Howard L. Weiner W
114 Somerset Rd
Brookline, MA 02146, 617-738-5343
  Pubs: *The Children's Ward* (Putnam, 1980)

Ron Welburn 🎤 ✈ P&W
PO Box 420
Hadley, MA 01035-0420, 413-584-0419
Internet: rwelburn@english.umass.edu
  Pubs: *Coming Through Smoke & the Dreaming* (Greenfield Rev Pr, 2000), *Council Decisions* (American Native Pr Archives, 1991), *Returning the Gift: Anth* (U Arizona Pr, 1995), *Durable Breath: Anth* (Salmon Run, 1994), *Red Owl, Cimarron Rev, Callaloo*

Susan B. Weston P&W
80 Park St #55
Brookline, MA 02146, 617-566-8672
  Pubs: *Children of the Light* (St. Martin's Pr, 1985), *Other Voices, Kansas Qtly, Fiction Rev, Croton Rev, Literal Latte, Press, Potpourri, Changes*

Dara Wier 🎤 ✈ P
504 Montague Rd
Amherst, MA 01002-1008
Internet: daraw@hfa.umass.edu
  Pubs: *Hat on a Pond* (Verse Pr, 2002), *Voyages in English, Our Master Plan, Blue for the Plough, The Book of Knowledge* (Carnegie Mellon U Pr, 2001, 1999, 1992, 1988), *Fence, Washington Square, APR, Gettysburg Rev, Seattle Rev, Hollins Critic, Conduit*

Elie Wiesel W
Boston University, 745 Commonwealth Avenue, Boston, MA 02215-1401, 617-353-4566
  Pubs: *The Forgotten* (Schocken Bks, 1992), *The Fifth Son, The Testament* (Summit Bks, 1985, 1981), *A Beggar in Jerusalem* (RH, 1970), *The Gates of the Forest, The Town Beyond the Wall* (HR & W, 1966, 1964), *Dawn* (Hill and Wang, 1961)

Richard Wilbur 🎤 ✈ P&W
87 Dodwells Rd
Cummington, MA 01026-9705
  Pubs: *Mayflies* (Harcourt, 2000), *More Opposites, New & Collected Poems* (HBJ, 1991, 1988)

Bosley Wilder 🎤 ✈ P
121 Cold Hill
Granby, MA 01033, 413-467-3191
Internet: bosleywilder@attbi.com
  Pubs: *Portraits & Landscapes* (The Asia Connection, 2002), *Dragons and Pomegranates* (South Pr, 1996), *You Once Had Wings* (China; Heilongjiang People's Pub Hse, 1991), *The Wind Is Mine* (Academic Bks, 1985), *Medusa* (Janus Pr, 1962), *Zuzu's Petals Qtly*

Emmett Williams P
Carpenter Visual Arts Center, Harvard Univ, Cambridge, MA 02138
Internet: Emmett@virtualitas.com

Jane Williams W
19 Cottage St
Cambridge, MA 02139
  Pubs: *Family Affairs* (H&R, 1977), *Harvard Mag, Boston Globe*

Irene Willis 🎤 ✈ P
2 Cornwall Dr
Great Barrington, MA 01230-1592, 413-528-1924
  Pubs: *They Tell Me You Danced* (U Pr Florida, 1995), *For a Living: The Poetry of Work: Anth* (U Illinois Pr, 1995), *Crazyhorse, Laurel Rev, NYQ, Kansas Qtly, Yankee, Florida Rev*

Joseph Wilson   P
RFD #1, Irish La
Rutland, MA 01543, 617-886-6786

Joyce Wilson 🎤 ✈   P
158 Hollett St
Scituate, MA 02066-2037, 781-545-0731
Internet: jpwilson@world.std.com
    Pubs: *Spruce Etymology* (Rhino, 2000), *Allium, The
    Formalist, Harvard Rev, Atigonish Rev*

Irene K. Wilson   P
1010 Waltham St A208
Lexington, MA 02421
    Pubs: *The Cat's Meow!: Anth* (Maine Rhode Pubs, 1996),
    *Rosebud, Tucumcari Lit Rev, Redbook, Piedmont Lit Rev,
    Calapooya Collage, Poetry Nippon, Pegasus*

Ellen Wittlinger 🎤 ✈   P
47 Beach Ave
Swampscott, MA 01907-1765, 781-599-6951
Internet: pritchwitt@aol.com
    Pubs: *The Long Night of Leo & Bree, Razzle, Gracie's Girl,
    What's in a Name, Hard Love* (S&S, 2002, 2001, 2000,
    1999), *Noticing Paradise, Lombardo's Law* (HM, 1995,
    1993), *Breakers* (Sheep Meadow Pr, 1979), *Iowa Rev, Amer
    Voice, Midwest Qtly, Ploughshares*

Margot Wizansky   P
12 Lincoln Rd
Brookline, MA 02445, 617-566-7726
Internet: margot.wiz@verizon.net
    Pubs: *Proposing on the Brooklyn Bridge: Anth* (Grayson
    Bks, 2003), *Heartbeat of New England: Anth* (Tiger Moon,
    2000), *Concrete Wolf, Poetry Motel, Antigonish Rev,
    Kalliope*

J. Barrett Wolf   P
118 Captain Lijahs Rd
Centerville, MA 02632-1600
    Pubs: *Old North Field & Other Poems* (Bear Pause Pubs,
    1993), *Enchante Mag, Black Bear Rev, Fireheart*

Ira Wood   W
Box 1473
Wellfleet, MA 02667, 508-349-1925
Internet: leapfrog@c4.net
    Pubs: *Storm Tide* (Fawcett-Columbine, 1998), *Going Public,
    The Kitchen Man* (Ballantine, 1992, 1987)

Douglas Worth 🎤 ✈   P
31 Maple Ave, #1
Cambridge, MA 02139-1115, 617-441-3983
    Pubs: *Some Sense of Transcendence, Once Around
    Bullough's Pond* (William L. Bauhan, 1999, 1987), *From
    Dream, From Circumstance: New & Selected Poems 1963-
    1983* (Apple-Wood Bks, 1984)

Rosalind Wright   W
12 Gardner St
Chelsea, MA 02150

Mark Wunderlich 🎤 ✈   P
4 Brewster St #1
Provincetown, MA 02657, 508-487-1690
Internet: MarkCWunderlich@aol.com
    Pubs: *The Anchorage* (U Mass Pr, 1999), *New American
    Poets: Anth* (U Pr New England, 2000), *American Poetry:
    Anth* (Carnegie Mellon U Pr, 2000), *The World in Us: Anth*
    (St. Martin's Pr, 2000), *Paris Rev, Boston Rev, Poetry,
    Fence, SW Rev,*

Xiaodo Xiao   W
135 Belchertown Rd
Amherst, MA 01002
Internet: xiado@javanet.com
    Pubs: *DoubleTake, North Dakota Qtly, Confrontation,
    Antaeus, Atlantic*

Gene Zeiger 🎤 ✈   P
RFD 1, #274 Patten Hill Rd
Shelburne, MA 01370, 413-625-6113
    Pubs: *Leaving Egypt* (White Pine Pr, 1994), *Sudden
    Dancing* (Amherst Writers & Artists Pr, 1988), *Georgia Rev,
    Tar River Poetry, Prose Poem, The Sun*

Tony Zizza   P
13 Butterworth Rd
Beverly, MA 01915, 508-922-5704
    Pubs: *The Magic of an Open Mind* (Readable Heart Pub,
    1987)

Marilyn Zuckerman 🎤   P
153 Medford St
Arlington, MA 02174-3118, 617-643-8483
Internet: marizuck@aol.com
    Pubs: *Amerika/America* (Cedar Hill Pubs, 2002), *Marilyn
    Zuckerman-Greatest Hits, 1970-2000* (Pudding Hse Pubs,
    2001), *Poems of the Sixth Decade* (Garden Street Pr, 1993),
    Claiming the Spirit Within: Anth (Beacon Pr, 1996), *Mystic
    River Rev*

MICHIGAN

Betsy Adams   P
Chelsea Cats, Inc., PO Box 296, Dexter, MI 48130
    Pubs: *The Dead Birth, Itself* (Paul Green/Spectacular
    Diseases, 1990)

Debra Allbery 🎤   P
8267 Mast Rd
Dexter, MI 48130, 734-477-1560
    Pubs: *Walking Distance, The Pittsburgh Book of
    Contemporary American Poetry: Anth* (U Pitt Pr, 1991,
    1993), *Hammer & Blaze: Anth* (U Georgia Pr, 2002), *Poetry,
    Iowa Rev, TriQtly*

Alvin Aubert 🎤 ✈   P
18234 Parkside Ave
Detroit, MI 48221, 313-345-4790
Internet: ad8722@wayne.edu
   Pubs: *Harlem Wrestler* (Michigan State U Pr, 1995), *If Winter Come* (Carnegie Mellon U Pr, 1994), *African Amer Rev, Callaloo, Drumvoices*

Carolyn Balducci   W
Univ Michigan, Residential College, Ann Arbor, MI
48109-1245, 734-647-4388
   Pubs: *Earwax* (HM, 1972), *Alternative Rev, Sipario Intl, Antologia Nuova*

Michael J. Barney 🎤 ✈   P
27030 Havelock, Dearborn Heights,, MI 48127
Internet: mikeb@dhol.org
   Pubs: *The Perils of Warm Flesh* (Gravity Pr, 2001), *True Life Adventures* (Budget Pr, 1998), *Silhouettes in the Electric Sky: Anth* (Newton's Baby, 1998), *Midwest Poetry Rev, Wordwrights*

Jackie Bartley   P
646 Pinecrest Dr
Holland, MI 49424, 616-392-6556
Internet: bartley@hope.edu
   Pubs: *The Terrible Boundaries of the Body* (White Eagle Coffee Store Pr, 1997), *When Prayer Is Far From Our Lips* (Franciscan U Pr, 1994), *For a Living: Anth* (U Illinois Pr, 1995), *West Branch, Calliope, Cincinnati Poetry Rev, Aileron, Blue Mesa Rev*

Therese Becker 🎤 ✈   P&W
2401 Eaton Gate Rd
Lake Orion, MI 48360, 248-391-1093
Internet: rbecker115@aol.com
   Pubs: *The Fear of Cameras* (Ridgeway Pr, 2000), *Contemporary Michigan Poetry: Anth* (Wayne State U Pr, 1988), *Woman Poet, The Midwest: Anth* (Women in Literature, 1985), *Double Take, Puerto del Sol, The Beloit Poetry Jrnl, Poetry East, Witness, NYQ*

Elinor Benedict 🎤 ✈   P&W
8627 S Lakeside Dr
Rapid River, MI 49878, 906-474-9273
Internet: elifax@aol.com
   Pubs: *All That Divides Us* (Utah State U Pr, 2000), *The Tree Between Us, Chinavision* (March Street Pr, 1997, 1995), *The Green Heart* (Illinois State U Pr, 1994)

Terry Blackhawk 🎤 ✈   P
16215 Warwick Rd
Detroit, MI 48219, 313-532-5763
Internet: terry260@earthlink.net
   Pubs: *I Have My Own Story for It:Modern Poems of Ohio: Anth* (U Akron Pr, 2002), *Body & Field* (Michigan State U Pr, 1999), *Trio: Voices From the Myths* (Ridgeway Press, 1998), *Michigan Qtly Rev, Controlled Burn, CALYX, Spoon River Rev, Ekphrasis*

Norma Blair   P
2025 McCann Rd
Hastings, MI 49058
   Pubs: *What's a Nice Girl Like You Doing in a Relationship Like This?: Anth* (Crossing Pr, 1992), *CityBook V: Sideshow Anth* (Flying Buffalo, 1991)

Shanda Hansma Blue 🎤 ✈   P
29509 Fawn River Rd
Sturgis, MI 49091, 616-651-3050
   Pubs: *Southern Indiana Rev, Louisville Rev*

Beth Brant   P&W
18890 Reed
Melvindale, MI 48122, 313-381-3550
   Pubs: *Food & Spirits* (Firebrand Bks, 1991), *Kenyon Rev, Amer Voice, Turtle Qtly, Forum, Tiger Lily, Woman of Power*

Alfred J. Bruey 🎤 ✈   P
201 S Grinnell St
Jackson, MI 49203, 517-784-1411
Internet: ajbruey@aol.com
   Pubs: *Greatest Hits, Practising Insanity* (Pudding Hse Pub, 2001, 1987), *Wherever You Go, There You Are* (Suburban Wilderness Pr, 1985), *Pudding, Poetry Motel, Amelia, Attention Please*

Gary Bundy   P
172 Jacaranda
Battle Creek, MI 49015
Internet: gbundy2034@aol.com
   Pubs: *CQ, Poetry Motel, Sell Outs Lit Mag, Without Halos, Chiron Rev, Spitball, Blue Light Rev, Birmingham Poetry Rev, Westering, Boar's Tusk*

Elizabeth Kane Buzzelli   W
60185 Lamplight Ct
Washington, MI 48094
   Pubs: *Gift of Evil* (Bantam, 1983)

Gladys H. Cardiff 🎤 ✈   P
980 Ironwood Dr, #357
Rochester, MI 48307-1316, 248-650-4771
   Pubs: *A Bare Unpainted Table* (New Issues Pr, 1999), *Contemporary Native American Poets of the Twentieth Century* (H&R, 1988), *Seattle Rev*

John Carpenter   P
1606 Granger Ave
Ann Arbor, MI 48104-4429, 734-996-4351
   Pubs: *Paris Rev, Chicago Rev, Manhattan Rev, Slant, Embers, New Yorker, NYRB, Kenyon Rev, Grand Street, Michigan Qtly, Crosscurrents*

Carol Carpenter 🎤 P&W
10005 Berwick
Livonia, MI 48150, 734-525-6586
Internet: CarolCarpenter@mindspring.com
  Pubs: *Resourceful Woman* (Visible Ink Pr, 1994),
  Generation to Generation: Anth (Papier-Mache Pr, 1998),
  Yankee, Louisiana Lit, Weber Studies, Hawaii Rev,
  Wisconsin Rev, Qtly West, Indiana Rev, Confrontation, Iowa
  Woman, America, Carolina Qtly, CSM

Andrew G. Carrigan P
212 W Henry St
Saline, MI 48176, 313-429-5868
  Pubs: *To Read, To Read, The King, You Poems* (Crowfoot Pr,
  1981, 1981, 1979)

Patricia Clark P
Grand Valley State Univ, English Dept, Allendale, MI 49401,
616-895-3199
Internet: clarkp@gvsu.edu
  Pubs: *North of Wondering* (Women-In-Literature, 1998),
  Worlds in Our Words: Anth (Blair/Prentice Hall, 1997),
  Seattle Rev, Mississippi Rev, New Criterion, CutBank, NER,
  NAR, Nebraska Rev, Poetry

Charles Cline P
9866 S Westnedge
Portage, MI 49024, 616-327-7135
  Pubs: *Ultima Thule* (Tagore Inst of Creative Writing, 1984),
  Riverrun, Poet, Auraq, Sou'wester

Lyn Coffin P&W
2034 Norfolk
Ann Arbor, MI 48103, 734-663-1589
Internet: Lyn_Coffin@msn.com
  Pubs: *Crystals of the Unforeseen* (Plain View Pr, 1998),
  Poetry of Wickedness (Ithaca Hse, 1980), *Human Trappings*
  (Abbattoir Edtns, 1980), *Wind Eyes: Anth* (Plain View Pr,
  1996), *Best American Short Stories: Anth* (HM, 1969)

Margaret Jean Condon 🎤 P
c/o Margaret Condon Taylor, 400 Maynard St, Ste 506, Ann
Arbor, MI 48104, 734-995-8627
  Pubs: *Topographics* (Lame Johnny Pr, 1977)

Peter Ho Davies W
English Language and Literature, Univ of Michigan, 4200
Angel Hall, Ann Arbor, MI 48109286, 734-764-6330
Internet: phdavies@umich.edu
  Pubs: *The Ugliest House in the World, Best American Short*
  Stories: Anths (HM, 1997, 1996, 1995), *Paris Rev, Story,*
  Agni, Harvard Rev, Gettysburg Rev, Antioch Rev

Nicholas Delbanco 🎤 ✈ W
Univ Michigan, Hopwood Room, 1006 Angell Hall, Ann Arbor,
MI 48109
  Pubs: *The Lost Suitcase* (Columbia U Pr, 2000), *What*
  Remains, Old Scores, In the Name of Mercy (Warner Bks,
  2000, 1997, 1995), *Running in Place* (Atlantic Monthly Pr,
  1989)

Michael Delp 🎤 ✈ P
Interlochen Arts Academy, PO Box 199, Interlochen, MI
49643, 616-276-9747
  Pubs: *The Coast of Nowhere, Under the Influence of Water,*
  Over the Graves of Horses (Wayne State U Pr, 1998, 1992,
  1988), *Playboy, Poetry NW, Memphis State Rev*

Patricia Demetri P
11313 Rockland Ave
Redford, MI 48239
  Pubs: *Manna, Alura, Iadr, Buselinesii, Jean's Journal,*
  Canadian Contingent Pr, Still Night Writings

Pamela Ditchoff P&W
605 Butterfield
East Lansing, MI 48823
Internet: pamela@voyager.net
  Pubs: *The Mirror of the Monsters & Prodigies* (Coffee Hse
  Pr, 1995), *Lexigram Learns* (Interact Pr, 1994), *Home for the*
  Holidays: Anth (Papier-Mache Pr, 1997), *Whose Woods*
  These Are: Anth (Ecco Pr, 1993), *West*

Stephen Dunning 🎤 ✈ P&W
517 Oswego St
Ann Arbor, MI 48104, 734-668-7723
Internet: dunnings@umich.edu
  Pubs: *Hunter's Park: 13 Stories, To the Beautiful Women:*
  Stories (S. Russell, 1996, 1990), *Good Words* (March Street
  Pr, 1991), *New Letters, Crescent Rev, Synaesthesia,*
  Fourth Genre

Stuart Dybek 🎤 ✈ P&W
320 Monroe
Kalamazoo, MI 49006, 616-344-5590
  Pubs: *The Coast of Chicago* (Knopf, 1990), *Childhood &*
  Other Neighborhoods (Ecco, 1987), *Harper's, New Yorker,*
  Atlantic, DoubleTake, Poetry, Paris Rev

Ed Engle, Jr. P
1 Birnwick
Adrian, MI 49221, 517-265-2035
  Pubs: *Baking Catholic* (Summer Stream Pr, 1985), *Blue*
  Horse, Crab Creek Rev, New Collage Mag

Gary James Erwin 🎤 ✈ W
2460 Somerville Dr
Oxford, MI 48371
Internet: gerwin@kettering.edu
  Pubs: *PrePress Awards Vol II: Anth* (PrePress Pub 1995),
  Driftwood Rev, Meat Whistle Qtly, Santa Fe Lit Rev, Sun,
  MacGuffin, Red Cedar Rev

Clayton Eshleman 🎤 ✈   P
210 Washtenaw Ave
Ypsilanti, MI 48197, 313-483-9787
  Pubs: *From Scratch, Under World Arrest* (Black Sparrow Pr,
  1998, 1994), *Antiphonal Swing: Selected Prose 1962-87*
  (McPherson, 1988), *Terra Nova, Lusitania, Poesie* (Paris),
  Hambone, Grand Street, Paris Rev

Leslie D. Foster   P
1901 Division St. Apt. 41
Marquette, MI 49855, 906-228-5131
Internet: lfoster@nmu.edo
  Pubs: *Myths for Dorothy* (Foster, 1992), *Northeast, Georgia
  Rev, Christian Century, Sisters Today, Interim, Anglican
  Theological Rev, Ariel*

Linda Nemec Foster 🎤 ✈   P
2024 Wilshire Dr SE
Grand Rapids, MI 49506-4014, 616-452-7204
Internet: mfapwgrr9@aol.com
  Pubs: *Amber Necklace From Gdansk* (LSU Pr, 2001), *Living
  in the Fire Nest* (Ridgeway Pr, 1996), *New Poems From the
  Third Coast: Anth* (Wayne State U Pr, 1999), *Poet Lore,
  Atlanta Rev, Mid-Amer Rev, Georgia Rev, Indiana Rev, Qtly
  West, River Styx, Nimrod*

Lucia Fox   P&W
Michigan State Univ, 546 Wells Hall, East Lansing, MI 48823
  Pubs: *Tales of an Indian Princess, Un Cierto Lugar*
  (Shambhala, 1979, 1978)

Randall R. Freisinger   P
Michigan Technological Univ, Humanities Dept, Houghton, MI
49931, 906-487-3229
Internet: rfreisi@mtu.edu
  Pubs: *Plato's Breath* (Utah State U Pr, 1997), *Hand
  Shadows* (Green Tower, 1988), *Running Patterns* (Flume,
  1985), *Tar River Poetry, Cream City Rev, Zone 3, New
  Letters, Tendril, Centennial Rev, Atlanta Rev*

Sonya Friedman   W
111 S Woodward, Ste 212B
Birmingham, MI 48009, 313-644-4794
  Pubs: *A Hero Is More Than Just a Sandwich* (Putnam, 1986)

Alice Fulton   P&W
2370 LeForge Rd,, Ypsilanti, MI 48198-9638, 313-482-7197
Internet: slippage@umich.edu
  Pubs: *Felt* (Norton, 2001), *Feeling as a Foreign Language:
  The Strangeness of Poetry* (Graywolf, 1999), *Sensual Math*
  (Norton, 1995), *Powers of Congress* (Godine, 1990),
  Palladium (U Illinois Pr, 1986), *Best Amer Poetry, New
  Yorker, Atlantic, Nation, Conduit*

Ken Gaertner   P&W
11447 Weiman Dr
Pinckney, MI 48169, 313-878-3711
  Pubs: *Koan Bread* (Survivor's Manual, 1977), *Christian
  Century, New Oxford Rev, America, Poem*

Laurence Goldstein 🎤 ✈   P
408 2nd St
Ann Arbor, MI 48103, 734-769-9899
  Pubs: *Cold Reading, The Three Gardens* (Copper Beech,
  1995, 1987), *The Faber Book of Movie Verse: Anth* (F&F,
  1994), *Iowa Rev, Ontario Rev, Poetry, Salmagundi, TriQtly*

Jaimy Gordon 🎤 ✈   P&W
Western Michigan Univ, English Dept, Kalamazoo, MI 49008,
616-381-6606
Internet: gordonj@wmich.edu
  Pubs: *Bogeywoman* (Sun & Moon Pr, 1999), *She Drove
  Without Stopping* (Algonquin, 1990), *Best American Short
  Stories: Anth* (HM, 1995), *Colorado Rev, Witness, Michigan
  Qtly Rev, Ploughshares, Missouri Rev, Shankpainter*

Judith Goren 🎤   P
21525 W 13 Mile Rd
Beverly Hills, MI 48025
Internet: judithg@comcast.net
  Pubs: *The Tao of Awakening* (Sunrise Pr, 1998), *Traveling
  Toward the Heart* (Ridgeway Pr, 1994), *Contemporary
  Michigan Poetry: Anth* (Wayne State U Pr, 1988), *Driftwood
  Rev, Centennial Rev, Green River Rev, The Bridge*

Delcie Southall Gourdine 🎤 ✈   W
325 Yellow Creek Dr
St Joseph, MI 49085-9326, 616-429-8393
  Pubs: *Redbook, Obsidian, Green's Mag*

Linda Gregerson 🎤 ✈   P
4881 Hidden Brook Ln
Ann Arbor, MI 48105, 734-996-2702
Internet: gregerso@umich.edu
  Pubs: *Waterborne, The Woman Who Died in Her Sleep* (HM,
  2002, 1996), *Fire in the Conservatory* (Dragon Gate, 1982),
  Atlantic, Poetry, TriQtly, Yale Rev

Jim Gustafson   P
411 Pleasant
Birmingham, MI 48009, 313-642-1542
  Pubs: *Aloha Street* (Avatar Edtns, 1989), *Virtue &
  Annihilation* (The Alternative Pr, 1988)

Robert Haight 🎤 ✈   P
PO Box 744
Marcellus, MI 49067-0744, 616-372-5452
Internet: robthaight@aol.com
  Pubs: *Emergences and Spinner Falls* (New Issues, 2002),
  Water Music (Ridgeway Pr, 1993), *New Poems From the
  Third Coast: Anth* (Wayne State U Pr, 2000), *Passages
  North: Anth* (Milkweed Edtns, 1990), *Contemporary
  Michigan Poetry: Anth* (Wayne State U Pr, 1989)

Charles Hanson   P
449 Moran Rd
Grosse Pointe Farm, MI 48236, 313-882-3627
   Pubs: *Poetry Ohio, Ego Flights, Anth of Mag Verse, White
Rock Rev, Yellow Butterfly, BPJ, Stone Country, Crab
Creek Rev*

Bill Harris   P
Univ Wayne State, 51 W Warren, Detroit, MI 48202
   Pubs: *The Ringmaster's Array* (Past Tents Pr, 1997),
Yardbird Suite: Side One (Michigan State U Pr, 1997),
Dispatch Detroit

Jim Harrison   P&W
PO Box 135
Lake Leelanau, MI 49653-0135
   Pubs: *Sundog* (Dutton, 1984), *Warlock, Legends* (Delacorte,
1981, 1979), *Farmer* (Viking, 1976)

Chris Haven   W
Grand Valley State Univ, 102 Lake Superior Hall, Allendale, MI
49401, 281-591-0524
Internet: chaven@bayou.uh.edu
   Pubs: *Threepenny Rev, RE:AL, Massachusetts Rev, Hawaii
Rev, Press*

Shayla Hawkins 🎤 ✈   P
20236 Redfern
Detroit, MI 48219-1269, 313-255-2698
Internet: imagoodpoet@yahoo.com
   Pubs: *Role Call: Anth* (Third World Pr, 2002), *Calabash,
Drumvoices Revue, Graffiti Rag, Maxis Rev, Paris/Atlantic*

Janet Ruth Heller 🎤 ✈   P
611 E. Porter St, Albion College-English Dept
Albion, MI 49224, 616-387-2572
Internet: jheller@albion.edu
   Pubs: *Modern Poems on the Bible: Anth* (Jewish Pub
Society, 1994), *Women's Glib: A Collection of Women's
Humor: Anth* (Crossing Pr, 1991), *The Minnesota Rev,
Midstream, Anima*

Conrad Hilberry 🎤 ✈   P
1601 Grand Ave
Kalamazoo, MI 49006, 616-345-5951
Internet: hilberry@kzoo.edu
   Pubs: *Player Piano* (LSU Pr, 1999), *Taking Notes* (Snowy
Egret, 1999), *Sorting the Smoke* (U Iowa Pr, 1990), *Luke
Karamazov* (Wayne State U Pr, 1987), Tamaqua, Gettysburg
Rev, Shenandoah, Virginia Qtly, Poetry

Sheryl Morang Holmberg 🎤   P&W
45077 Custer
Utica, MI 48317-5701, 810-726-6615
Internet: sholmberg99@hotmail.com
   Pubs: *Driftwood Rev, Pike Creek Rev, Heron Qtly, Los,
Indefinite Space, Ship of Fools, Eratica, Iconoclast,
Cumberland Poetry Rev, SLUGfest, Ltd, Piedmont Lit Rev,
Ever Dancing Muse, Cicada, black bough, Quantum Tao*

Patricia Hooper 🎤 ✈   P
616 Yarmouth Rd
Bloomfield Township, MI 48301
   Pubs: *At the Corner of the Eye* (Michigan State U Pr, 1997),
The Flowering Trees (State Street Pr, 1995), *Other Lives*
(Elizabeth Street Pr, 1984), *Ploughshares, Atlantic, New
Criterion, Poetry, Hudson Rev, American Scholar*

Daniel Hughes   P
17524 3rd Ave, #104
Detroit, MI 48203
   Pubs: *You Are Not Stendhal* (Wayne State U Pr, 1992),
Spirit Traps, Falling (Copper Beech Pr, 1988, 1979)

Christine Hume 🎤 ✈   P
641 N 5th Ave
Ann Arbor, MI 48104, 734-327-3667
Internet: chume@online.emich.edu
   Pubs: *Musca Domestica* (Beacon Pr, 2000), *American
Poetry: The Next Generation: Anth* (Carnegie Mellon, 2000),
Best American Poetry 1997: Anth (Scribner, 1997), *Boston
Rev, The New Rep, Fence, Rhizome, New American Writing*

David James 🎤 ✈   P
PO Box 721
Linden, MI 48451, 248-522-3685
Internet: dljames@occ.cc.mi.us
   Pubs: *Do Not Give Dogs What is Holy* (March Street Pr,
1994), *A Heart Out of This World* (Carnegie Mellon, 1984),
*Qtly West, Rattle, Lit Rev, Bryant Lit Rev, California Qtly,
Iowa Rev, Poem, Caliban, Kansas Qtly*

Arnold Johnston 🎤 ✈   P&W
471 W South St #102
Kalamazoo, MI 49008, 616-381-6316
Internet: arnie.johnston@wmich.edu
   Pubs: *What the Earth Taught Us* (March Street Pr, 1996),
Third Coast: Anth (Wayne State U Pr, 2000), *Embers,
Rockford Rev, ELF, Malahat Rev, Colorado Qtly, Alabama
Literary Rev, Indiana Rev, Cumberland Poetry Rev,
Passages North, Hiram Poetry Rev*

Laura Kasischke   P
2997 S Fletcher Rd
Chelsea, MI 48118, 313-475-7485
   Pubs: *Suspicious River* (HM, 1996), *Housekeeping in a
Dream* (Carnegie Mellon, 1995), *Wild Brides* (NYU Pr,
1991), *Poetry*

Janet Kauffman   P&W
14671 W Cadmus Rd, Rte 1
Hudson, MI 49247, 517-448-4973
   Pubs: *Rot* (New Issues Pr, 2001), *Characters on the Loose,
The Body in Four Parts* (Graywolf, 1997, 1993)

Josie Kearns 🎤 ✈   P
120 Litchfield
Clinton, MI 49236, 517-456-4970
Internet: jakearns@umich.edu
　Pubs: *Boomer Girls* (Iowa U Pr, 2001), *Contemporary Michigan Poetry* (Wayne State U Pr, 2000), *New Numbers* (March Street Pr, 2000, 1998), *Iowa Rev, Georgia Rev, Poetry NW*

Elizabeth Kerlikowske 🎤 ✈   P
2423 Russet Dr
Kalamazoo, MI 49008-4316, 616-343-4003
Internet: mme642@aol.com
　Pubs: *The Seven, Her Bodies, Postcard* (March Street Pr, 1997, 1995, 1990), *Stand-Up Poetry: Anth* (U California Pr, 1993), *Sow's Ear, Natural Bridge, Graffiti Rag, Louisiana Rev, Driftwood, Encore, The Comstock Rev, Mid Amer Poetry Rev, Garfield Rev*

Judith Kerman   P
Dept of English, Saginaw Valley State Univ, 7400 Bay Rd, University Center, MI 48708, 989-964-4063
Internet: kerman@tardis.svsu.edu
　Pubs: *Plane Surfaces/Plano de Incidencia* (Mayapple Pr, 2002), *Three Marbles* (Cranberry Tree Pr, 1999), *Mothering & Dream of Rain* (Ridgeway, 1997), *Driving for Yellow Cab* (Tout Pr, 1985), *Mothering* (Uroboros/Allegheny Mtn Pr, 1978), *Salt Hill, Calyx*

Lionel Bruce Kingery   P
947 Francis
Rochester Hills, MI 48307
　Pubs: *The Popular Songs of Bruce Kingery* (North American Mentor, 1980), *Arcadia Poetry Anth* (Arcadia Poetry Pr, 1992), *Verses, Voices Intl, Second Coming*

Margo LaGattuta   P
2134 W Gunn Rd
Rochester, MI 48306, 810-693-7227
Internet: lagapvp@aol.com
　Pubs: *Embracing the Fall* (Plain View Pr, 1994), *The Dream Givers* (Lake Shore Pub, 1990), *Sun, Yankee, The Bridge, Passages North, Calliope, Woman Poet*

Christine Lahey   P
1540 Boulan Rd
Troy, MI 48084, 810-643-6525
　Pubs: *Blood to Remember: American Poets on the Holocaust: Anth* (Texas Tech U Pr, 1991), *All's Normal Here: Anth* (Ruddy Duck Pr, 1985), *Planet Detroit, Michigan Qtly Rev*

Betty Rita Gomez Lance   P&W
1562 Spruce Dr
Kalamazoo, MI 49008-2227, 616-345-0649
　Pubs: *Siete Cuerdas* (Ediciones Cardenoso, 1996), *Alas en el Alba* (Compotex, 1987), *Hoy Hacen Corro las Ardillas* (Editorial Papiro, 1985)

Douglas W. Lawder   P
Michigan State Univ, Morrill Hall, East Lansing, MI 48824
　Pubs: *Trolling* (Little, Brown, 1977), *Nation, Poetry, Virginia Qtly Rev, The Seventies*

Joseph Lease   P
Central Michigan Univ, Dept of English, Mt. Pleasant, MI 48859, 989-773-3187
Internet: joseph.lease@cmich.edu
　Pubs: *Human Rights* (Zoland Bks, 1998), *Best American Poetry: Anth* (Scribner, 2002), *Grand Street, Talisman, Paris Rev, Lingo, Colorado Rev, Denver Qtly, Pequod, Agni, NAW, Boston Rev*

David Dodd Lee 🎤 ✈   P
2627 Lorraine Ave
Kalamazoo, MI 49008
　Pubs: *Arrow Pointing North* (Four Way Bks, 2002), *Downsides of Fish Culture* (New Issues Pr, 1997), *Green Mountains Rev, Quarterly, Worcester Rev, Willow Springs*

Stephen Leggett 🎤 ✈   P
PO Box 4551
Ann Arbor, MI 48106, 734-461-1574
　Pubs: *The Form It Takes* (Ridgeway Pr, 1988), *The All-Forest* (Waves, 1980)

Christopher Towne Leland 🎤 ✈   W
English Dept, Wayne State Univ, 51 W Warren, Detroit, MI 48202, 313-577-2450
Internet: ctllnd@aol.com
　Pubs: *Letting Loose, The Professor of Aesthetics* (Zoland, 1996, 1994), *The Book of Marvels* (Scribner, 1990), *Mrs. Randall* (HM, 1987), *Mean Time* (Random Hse, 1982)

Kathleen Ripley Leo 🎤 ✈   P
42185 Baintree Cir
Northville, MI 48167-3447, 248-349-4827
http://northville.lib.mi.us/NAC/krleo.htm
　Pubs: *Familiar Ground* (Gravity Press, 2002), *The Circle Is Assembled: Glass Poems, The Old Ways* (Sun Dog Pr, 1994, 1991), *Town One South, Northville Poems* (Northville Arts, 1988)

M. L. Liebler 🎤 ✈   P&W
PO Box 120
Roseville, MI 48066, 313-577-7713
Internet: mlliebler@aol.com
　Pubs: *Breaking the Voodoo* (Adastra Pr, 2001), *Written in Rain* (Tebot Bach Bks, 2000), *Stripping the Adult Century Bare* (Viet Nam Generation Pr, 1994), *Identity Lessons: Anth* (Viking, 1999), *Paterson Literary Rev, Hong Kong U Jrnl, Long Shot*

Judith Wood Lindenau   P
7707 Fouch Rd
Traverse City, MI 49684-9513, 616-947-9803

Thomas Lynch ♦ ✈   P&W
328 E Liberty
Milford, MI 48381, 810-684-6645
Internet: thoslynch@aol.com
    Pubs: *Bodies in Motion & at Rest, Still Life in Milford, The
    Undertaking* (Norton 2000, 1998, 1997), *Grimalkin & Other
    Poems* (Cape/Random Hse, 1994), *New Yorker, Harper's,
    Poetry, London Rev of Bks, Paris Rev*

Naomi Long Madgett ♦ ✈   P
18080 Santa Barbara Dr
Detroit, MI 48221-2531, 313-342-9174
Internet: nlmadgett@aol.com
    Pubs: *Octavia Long: Guthrie and Beyond* (Lotus Pr, 2002),
    Remembrances of Spring (Michigan State U Pr, 1993),
    *Great Lakes Rev, Witness, Essence, Obsidian, Michigan
    Qtly Rev, Sage, Black Scholar*

Denise Martinson   P&W
Poetic Page, PO Box 71192, Madison Heights, MI 48071-0192
    Pubs: *Pieces of Eight: Anth* (Wordsmith Pub, 1992), *Canto,
    Elk River Rev, Mobius, Metro Singles Lifestyle*

Beverly Matherne ♦ ✈   P
English Dept, Northern Michigan Univ, 1401 Presque Isle,
Marquette, MI 49855-1556, 906-227-1386
Internet: bmathern@nmu.edu
    Pubs: *Le Blues Braillant, La Grande Pointe* (CCC, 1999,
    1995), *Uncommonplace: Anth* (LSU Pr, 1998), *Two Worlds
    Walking: Anth* (New Rivers Pr, 1994), *Paterson Lit Rev,
    Runes, Verse, Great River Rev, Kansas Qtly,
    Metamorphoses*

Kathleen McGookey ♦ ✈   P
135 Lakeview Dr
Wayland, MI 49348, 616-792-6011
Internet: kathleen.mcgookey@wmich.edu
    Pubs: *Whatever Shines* (White Pines Pr, 2001), *The Party
    Train: Anth* (New Rivers Pr, 1996), *Verse, Plougshares,
    Boston Rev, Epoch, Field*

Richard E. McMullen ♦   P
128 Marvin St
Milan, MI 48160-1356, 313-439-7112
    Pubs: *Like Heaven* (Limited Mailing Pr, 1993), *Trying to Get
    Out* (Crowfoot Pr, 1981), *I Feel a Little Jumpy Around You:
    Anth* (S&S, 1996), *CSM, Commonweal, Epoch, Hanging
    Loose, Massachusetts Rev, New York Times, SPR,
    Wisconsin Rev*

Ken Mikolowski   P
1207 Henry St
Ann Arbor, MI 48104-4340, 313-662-1286
    Pubs: *Big Enigmas* (Past Tents Pr, 1991), *Little Mysteries*
    (Toothpaste Pr, 1979), *Re:view, Rolling Stock, Exquisite
    Corpse, Notus*

Sam Mills   P
116 W Maple St
Lansing, MI 48906, 517-482-4037
    Pubs: *Burning the Stratocaster* (Sleeping Buddha Pr, 1992),
    A Long Drink (Poetry Centre, 1975), *In This Corner, Red
    Cedar Rev, Triage*

Ronald Milner   P
15865 Montevista
Detroit, MI 48238

Judith Minty ♦ ✈   P
7113 S Scenic Dr
New Era, MI 49446-8005, 231-894-2121
Internet: judminty@aol.com
    Pubs: *Walking With the Bear* (MSU Pr, 2000), *Mad Painter
    Poems* (March Street Pr, 1996), *Yellow Dog Journal*
    (Parallax Pr, 1991), *Bloomsbury Rev, Poetry, Iowa Rev,
    Hawaii Rev, Prairie Schooner, Luna, Poetry Flash, Passages
    North, Controlled Burn*

Edward Morin ♦ ✈   P
2112 Brockman Rd
Ann Arbor, MI 48104-4530, 734-668-7523
Internet: eacmorso@core.com
    Pubs: *Labor Day at Walden Pond* (Ridgeway Pr, 1997), *The
    Dust of Our City* (Clover Pr, 1978), *Michigan Qtly Rev, New
    Letters, Windsor Rev, Hudson Rev, Ploughshares, TriQtly,
    Iowa Rev, River Styx*

Carol Morris   P
912 Rose Ave
Ann Arbor, MI 48104-4349, 313-761-5616
Internet: silkrhino@aol.com
    Pubs: *Atomic Picnic* (Stellar Productions, 1995), *Sweet
    Uprisings* (Years Pr, 1990), *Slipstream, MacGuffin,
    Psychopoetica*

Julie Moulds ♦ ✈   P
7546 S Crooked Lake Dr
Delton, MI 49046-8427, 616-623-3099
    Pubs: *Woman With a Cubed Head* (New Issues Pr, 1998),
    American Poetry: The Next Generation: Anth (Carnegie
    Mellon U Pr, 2000), *Cream City Rev, Gulf Coast, Marlboro
    Rev, NYQ*

William P. Osborn ♦ ✈   W
145 Crestwood NW
Grand Rapids, MI 49504, 616-791-0049
    Pubs: *Passages North, Cream City Rev, Quarter After Eight,
    Gettysburg Rev, Carolina Qtly, Mississippi Rev, Faultline,
    Louisville Rev*

David Palmer 🎤 ✈ P
2310 Calumet St
Flint, MI 48503-2811, 810-238-5919
  Pubs: *Quickly, Over the Wall* (Wake-Brook, 1966), *Songs From Unsung Worlds: Anth* (AAAS, 1985), *Peace or Perish: Anth* (Poets for Peace, 1983), *Beloit, Kayak, Passages North, Poets On, Immobius, Slipstream*

Charlene Noel Palmer P
2310 Calumet St
Flint, MI 48503-2811
  Pubs: *Anti-War Poem, Vol. II: Anth* (Stephen Gill, 1986), *Voices for Peace: Anth* (Disarmament & Peace Task Force, 1983), *Peace or Perish: A Crisis Anth* (Poets for Peace, 1983), *Odyssey, Axios, Christian Century, Mediphors, December, Handmaiden*

Miriam Pederson 🎤 P
Aquinas College, English Dept, 1607 Robinson Rd SE, Grand Rapids, MI 49506-1705, 616-459-8281
Internet: pedermir@aquinas.edu
  Pubs: *Essential Love: Anth* (Poetworks, 2000), *New Poems From the Third Coast: Anth, The Third Coast: Anth* (Wayne State U Pr, 2000, 1990), *The Book of Birth Poetry: Anth* (Bantam Bks, 1995), *Passages North, MacGuffin, Sing Heavenly Muse*

William S. Penn 🎤 ✈ W
963 Lantern Hill Dr
East Lansing, MI 48823, 517-337-7313
Internet: penn@msu.edu
  Pubs: *Feathering Custer, All My Sins Are Relative* (U Nebraska Pr, 2002, 1994), *Killing Time with Strangers* (U Arizona Pr, 2000), *This Is the World* (Michigan State U Pr, 2000), *The Absence of Angels* (Permanent Pr, 1994), *Antaeus, Stand, Grain, Qtly West*

Rosalie Sanara Petrouske P
324 East Jefferson St
Grand Ledge, MI 48837, 517-627-4207
Internet: Prosaliepoet@aol.com
  Pubs: *The Geisha Box* (March Street Pr, 1996), *New Poems From the Third Coast: Anth* (Wayne State U Pr, 2000), *It's All the Rage: Anth* (Andrew Mountain Pr, 1997), *Eclectic Woman, Parting Gifts, Plainsongs, Poets On, Paintbrush, MacGuffin, Passages North, SPR*

Patricia Rachal P
2133 Ridge Rd
Kalamazoo, MI 49008, 616-345-3682

Rebecca B. Rank 🎤 ✈ P
1888 Oak
Birmingham, MI 48009, 248-642-6243
Internet: seasonone@aol.com
  Pubs: *Feminist Studies, MacGuffin, Phoebe: An Interdisciplinary Jrnl of Feminist Scholarship, River City, Iris, Smartish Pace, Sow's Ear Rev, Antigonish Rev, So to Speak, Rockford Rev, CQ, Aurorean*

Greg Rappleye P
Box 441
Grand Haven, MI 49417, 616-844-3335
  Pubs: *The PrePress Awards, 1992-1993: A Sampler of Emerging Michigan Writers: Anth* (PrePress Publishing of Michigan, 1993), *Mississippi Rev, Southern Rev, Prairie Schooner, Qtly West, Sky Books*

John R. Reed 🎤 ✈ P
English Dept, Wayne State Univ, 51 W Warren, Detroit, MI 48202, 313-861-4298
Internet: john.reed@wayne.edu
  Pubs: *Dear Ruth, Great Lake* (Ridgeway Pr, 2002, 1995), *Life Sentences* (Wayne State U Pr, 1996), *Poetry, Amer Scholar, Michigan Qtly Rev, Ontario Rev, SW Rev, Partisan Rev*

Danny Rendleman 🎤 ✈ P
Univ Michigan, 326 French Hall, Flint, MI 48502, 810-762-3388
Internet: dannyr@flint.umich.edu
  Pubs: *The Middle West, Victrola* (Ridgeway Pr, 1995, 1994), *APR, Field, o.blek, Epoch, Passages North, Antigonish Rev*

Jack Ridl P
6625 147th Ave
Holland, MI 49423, 616-335-7435
Internet: ridl@hope.edu
  Pubs: *Against Elegies* (Ridgeway Pr, 2002), *Approaching Poetry* (St. Martin's Pr, 1997), *Poems From the Same Ghost & Between* (Dawn Valley Pr, 1993), *For a Living: Poems of Work: Anth* (U Illinois Pr, 1995), *Georgia Rev, Artful Dodge, Poetry East, Ploughshares*

Daniel Rosochacki P
2223 Fremont
Grand Rapids, MI 49504

Gil Saenz 🎤 ✈ P
19211 Wall St
Melvindale, MI 48122-1876
Internet: GilSaenz@msn.com
  Pubs: *Poems of Life/Poemas de la vida* (Laredo Pub Co, 2001), *Dreaming of Love* (Pentland Pr, 1999)

William Schoenl 🎤 ✈ P
2643 Roseland
East Lansing, MI 48823-3870, 517-351-0456
  Pubs: *Big Two-Hearted, Alura Qtly, Riverrun, Parnassus*

Herbert Scott P
2328 Oakland Dr
Kalamazoo, MI 49003-2254, 616-342-5715
Internet: herbert.scott@wmich.edu
  Pubs: *The Wishing Heart* (Sutton Hoo Pr, 1999), *Durations* (LSU Pr, 1984), *Groceries* (U Pitt Pr, 1976), *Poetry NW, Michigan Qtly Rev, Black Warrior Rev, Shenandoah, Kenyon Rev*

Heather Laurie Sellers 🎤 ✈   P&W
Hope College, 126 E 10 St, Holland, MI 49423-9000, 616-
395-7116
Internet: sellers@hope.edu
    Pubs: *Georgia Underwater* (Sarabande, 2001), *Your Whole
Life* (Panhandler, 1994), *William & Mary Rev, Sonora Rev,
The Sun, Five Points, New Virginia Rev, Indiana Rev, Alaska
Qtly Rev*

Diane Seuss 🎤 ✈   P
144 Monroe St
Kalamazoo, MI 49006-4475, 616-337-7038
Internet: dseussb@kzoo.edu
    Pubs: *It Blows You Hollow* (New Issues Pr, 1998), *Boomer
Girls: Anth* (U Iowa Pr, 1999), *Poetry NW, Alaska Qtly, Third
Coast, Primavera, Indiana Rev, Tamaqua, NW Rev,
Cumberland Poetry Rev*

Maryl Shackett 🎤   P
323 Jefferson
Marine City, MI 48039-1620, 810-765-4383
    Pubs: *That Other Woman, Lucidity* (Bear House Pub, 2000,
2000), *This Is My Beloved* (Anderie Poetry Pr, 1997),
Changes in the Heart (Lyre Loon, 1996)

Marc Sheehan   P
21518 Brady Lake Blvd
Morley, MI 49336, 231-856-4202
Internet: sheehanm@ferris.edu
    Pubs: *Greatest Hits* (New Issues Pr, 1999), *Third Coast,
Sky, Controlled Burn, Burning World, Pannus Index,
Gulfstream, Parting Gifts*

Linda K. Nerva Sienkiewicz 🎤   P
520 W Third St
Rochester, MI 48307-1914, 248-652-3235
Internet: Fade2Blue@aol.com
    Pubs: *Edge City Rev, Wayne Lit Rev, Heartlands Today,
Spoon River Poetry Rev, Maverick Pr, Thema, Muddy River
Poetry Rev, Touchstone Rev, Poetry Motel*

Anita Skeen 🎤 ✈   P
Michigan State Univ, 201 Morrill Hall, English Dept, East
Lansing, MI 48824, 517-355-7570
Internet: skeen@msu.edu
    Pubs: *The Resurrection of the Animals, Outside the Fold,
Outside the Frame* (MSU Pr, 2002, 1999), *Portraits* (Kida Pr,
1993), *Each Hand a Map* (Naiad Pr, 1986), *Ploughshares,
New Letters, Prairie Schooner, Ms., Nimrod, 13th Moon,
The Atlantic Rev*

Julie L. Stone   P
1890 Carriage Rd #215
Muskegon, MI 49442, 616-773-0885
    Pubs: *Playgirl, Berkeley Monthly, The Poet, The Hunter,
Scene, Vega, Hoosier Challenger*

Keith Taylor 🎤 ✈   P&W
1715 Dexter Ave
Ann Arbor, MI 48103-4007, 734-665-5341
Internet: keitay@umich.edu
    Pubs: *Everything I Need* (March Street Pr, 1996), *Life
Science & Other Stories* (Hanging Loose Pr, 1995), *Detail
From the Garden of Delights* (Limited Mailing Pr, 1993),
*Witness, Hanging Loose, Story, Pivot, Caliban, Michigan
Qtly Rev*

Robert Tell   P
29401 Windmill Ct
Farmington Hill, MI 48334
    Pubs: *Dialogue Through Poetry: Anth* (Fictionopolis, 2001),
Arts Borealis, Peninsula Poets, Mediphors, PKA's Advocate

Vonnie Thomas   P
8757 Berridge Rd
Greenville, MI 48838, 616-754-8698
    Pubs: *Gift of Time, Changing View* (Belding, 1992, 1990),
The View Beyond the Tree (Greenville, 1981)

F. Richard Thomas 🎤 ✈   P
Dept of American Thought/Language, Michigan State Univ,
East Lansing, MI 48824-1033, 517-355-2400
Internet: thomasff@msu.edu
    Pubs: *Death at Camp Pahoka, New Poems From the Third
Coast: Anth* (Michigan State U Pr, 2000, 2000), *Miracles*
(Canoe Pr, 1996), *Frog Praises Night* (Southern Illinois U
Pr, 1980)

Ben Tibbs   P
c/o R. Tibbs, 2127 Audley Dr NE, Grand Rapids, MI 49505,
616-349-2763
    Pubs: *Graffiti Book, Italics Mine, Approaches* (Stovepipe Pr,
1984, 1983, 1982), *Celery*

Richard Tillinghast 🎤 ✈   P&W
1317 Granger Ave
Ann Arbor, MI 48104-4480, 734-930-0532
Internet: rwtill@umich.edu
    Pubs: *Six Mile Mountain* (Story Line Pr, 2000), *Today in the
Cafe Trieste* (Salmon/Dufour, 1997), *The Stonecutter's Hand*
(David R. Godine, 1995), *Our Flag Was Still There*
(Wesleyan U Pr, 1984), *Paris Rev, New Yorker, Nation,
Atlantic, New Criterion*

Eric Torgersen 🎤 ✈   P&W
8475 Chippewa Trail
Mount Pleasant, MI 48858-9488, 517-773-4559
Internet: eric.torgersen@cmich.edu
    Pubs: *Inside Unity House, The Door to the Moon,* (March
Street Pr, 1999, 1993), *Dear Friend* (Northwestern U Pr,
1998), *Good True Stories* (Lynx Hse, 1994), *Hudson Rev,
APR, Lit Rev, Gettysburg Rev, River Styx*

Stephen H. Tudor P
14447 Harbor Island
Detroit, MI 48215, 313-822-4895
www.quicklink.com/~monella/haul.html
 Pubs: *Haul-Out: New & Selected Poems, Hangdog Reef: Poems Sailing the Great Lakes* (Wayne State U Pr, 1996, 1989), *Michigan Qtly Rev, Bridge*

Christina-Marie Umscheid 🎤 P
149 Washington St
Petoskey, MI 49770-2948, 231-347-1775
Internet: christinu@voyager.net
 Pubs: *Images & Language* (Writers North, 1987), *Voices of Michigan: Anth* (Mackinac Jane Pub Co, 1999), *At the Edge of Mirror Lake: Anth* (Plainview Pr, 1999), *Poetry Tonight, Napalm Health Spa, Hiram Poetry Rev, MacGuffin, Caliban, Chicago Rev*

Robert Vandermolen 🎤 ✈ P
2771 Glencairin Dr NW
Grand Rapids, MI 49504-2388, 616-453-7056
 Pubs: *Breath* (New Issues Pr, 2000), *Peaches* (Sky Pr, 1998), *Night Weather* (Northern Lights Pr, 1991), *London Rev of Bks, Mudfish, NAW, Artful Dodge, Sulfur, Grand Street, House Organ, Epoch*

Diane Wakoski 🎤 ✈ P
607 Division St
East Lansing, MI 48823-3428, 517-332-3385
Internet: dwakoski@aol.com
 Pubs: *The Butcher's Apron, Argonaut Rose, The Emerald City of Las Vegas, Jason the Sailor, Medea the Sorceress* (Black Sparrow Pr, 2000, 1998, 1995, 1993, 1990)

Morrie Warshawski P
1408 W Washington St
Ann Arbor, MI 48103-4285, 734-332-9768
http://www.warshawski.com
 Pubs: *Out of Nowhere* (Press-22, 1985), *Indiana Rev, Apalachee Qtly, Hayden's Ferry Rev, Exquisite Corpse, Modern Poetry Studies, NYQ*

Sylvia Watanabe W
145 Crestwood NW
Grand Rapids, MI 49504
 Pubs: *Talking to the Dead & Other Stories* (Doubleday, 1992)

Barrett Watten 🎤 ✈ P
English Dept, Wayne State University, Detroit, MI 48202, 313-577-3067
Internet: b.watten@wayne.edu
 Pubs: *Bad History* (Atelos Pr, 1998), *Frame,* (Sun & Moon Pr, 1997), *Under Erasure* (Zasterle Pr, 1991), *Leningrad: American Writers in the Soviet Union* (w/M. Davidson, et al; Mercury Hse, 1991), *Conduit* (Gaz, 1986), *The World, Common Knowledge, Poetics Jrnl*

Ron Weber P
2160 N County Line Rd
Watervliet, MI 49098-9535, 616-463-4049
 Pubs: *Bluff View From the Twin Cities: Poems From the West Bank* (Harbor Hse 1993), *Voices Intl, Tempo, Catalyst, Peninsula Poets, Poet, Analecta*

Robert E. Wegner W
Alma College, Alma, MI 48801
 Pubs: *The Third Coast: Anth* (Wayne State, 1982), *Short Story Intl, Karamu, SW Rev*

Mary Ann Wehler 🎤 ✈ P
The Writer's Voice, YMCA Metro Detroit, 6361 Emerald Lake, Troy, MI 48085, 248-879-3013
Internet: mawehler@wideopenwest.net
 Pubs: *Throat, Variations On the Ordinary: Anth* (Bottom Dog Pr, 2002, 1995), *Walking Through Deep Snow* (Plain View Pr, 1997), *What Have You Lost: Anth* (Green Willow Bks, 1999), *Rattle, Graffiti Rag, The Heartlands Today, MacGuffin*

Patricia Jabbeh Wesley 🎤 ✈ P&W
English Department, Western Michigan Univ, Spau Tower, Kalamazoo, MI 49008-5092, 616-387-2572
Internet: pjabbah@juno.com
 Pubs: *Becoming Ebony* (SIU Pr, 2003), *Before the Palm Could Bloom* (New Issues Pr, 1998), *Crab Orchard Rev, New Orleans Rev, East, Midday Moon, English Acad Rev, Inst for Liberian Studies Jrnl*

Gloria Whelan 🎤 ✈ W
Oxbow, 9797 N Twin Lake Rd NE, Mancelona, MI 49659, 231-587-9501
 Pubs: *Homeless Bird, Return to the Island, Farewell to the Island* (HC, 2000, 2000, 1998), *Forgive the River, Forgive the Sky* (Eerdmans, 1998)

Carolyn White 🎤 ✈ P&W
1661 Mt Vernon Ave
East Lansing, MI 48823-3740, 517-351-5866
 Pubs: *The Adventure of Louey & Frank* (Greenwillow, 2001), *Whuppity Stoorie* (Putnam, 1997), *The Tree House Children* (S&S, 1994), *Parabola, Magical Blend, Book of Contemporary Myth, Michigan Qtly Rev, Studia Mystica*

Laurie Anne Whitt P
PO Box 195
Chassell, MI 49916, 906-523-4566
Internet: lawhitt@mtu.edu
 Pubs: *Words for Relocation* (Will Hall Bks, 2001), *A Long Dream of Difference* (Frith Pr, 2001), *Spoon River Poetry Rev, Puerto del Sol, Wisconsin Rev, Cottonwood, Hawaii Rev, Malahat Rev, Prism Intl*

Margaret Willey   P&W
431 Grant St
Grand Haven, MI 49417-1834, 616-846-1759
Internet: joannisr@river.it.gvsu.edu
    Pubs: *Facing the Music, The Melinda Zone, Saving Lenny*
    (Bantam, 1996, 1993, 1990), *If Not for You, Finding David
    Dolores* (H&R, 1988, 1986), *Hungry Mind Rev, New Moon
    Network, Calyx, Passages North, Redbook, Qtly West*

Willie Williams   P
3836 Courville
Detroit, MI 48224, 313-824-4086
    Pubs: *Spillway, Way Station Mag, Red Cedar Rev, Howling
    Dog, Graffiti Rag, Triage*

Thomas Wiloch ♪ ✈   P&W
PMB #226, 42015 Ford Rd, Canton, MI 48187
Internet: mssunltd@postmark.net
    Pubs: *Neon Trance, Decoded Factories of the Heart*
    (Runaway Spoon Pr, 1997, 1994), *Mr. Templeton's Toyshop*
    (Wordcraft, 1995), *Back Brain Recluse, Exquisite Corpse,
    Recursive Angel, Graffiti Rag, Bitter Oleander, Winedark
    Sea, Carpe Noctem*

Terry Wooten ♪ ✈   PP
12754 Stone Circle Dr
Kewadin, MI 49648, 231-264-9467
www.go.to/terrywooten
    Pubs: *Michigan Association of Media Educators Conference,
    Camp Michigania, North Central Michigan College Poetry
    Series, Michigan's Great Outdoors Culture Tour*

Janice Zerfas ♪ ✈   P
English Dept, Lake Michigan College, 2755 E Napier Ave,
Benton Harbor, MI 49022-1899, 616-927-3571
Internet: zerfas@lmc.cc.mi.es
    Pubs: *Parting Gifts, The Way In, MacGuffin, Indiana Rev,
    Sky, Paterson Lit Rev, Graffiti Rag*

Jack Zucker   P
14050 Vernon St
Oak Park, MI 48237
    Pubs: *From Manhattan* (Pointe Pr, 1989), *Beginnings*
    (Katydid Pr, 1982), *The Bridge, Poetry NW, Esquire,
    Literary Rev*

MINNESOTA

Cezarija Abartis ♪ ✈   W
English Dept, St. Cloud State Univ, St Cloud, MN 56301, 612-
255-3061
    Pubs: *Nice Girls and Other Stories* (2002), *Manoa, Twilight
    Zone Mag, Lady's Circle, The Qtly*

Harold Adams ♪   W
12916 Greenwood Rd
Minnetonka, MN 55343, 612-938-6426
    Pubs: *Lead So I Can Follow, No Badge No Gun, The Icepick
    Artist, The Hatchet Job, The Ditched Blonde, A Way With
    Widows, A Prfctly Prpr Mrdr, The Mn Who Was Tllr Thn God*
    (Walker, 1999, 1998, 1997, 1996, 1995, 1994, 1993, 1992)

Paulette Bates Alden   W
4900 Washburn Ave S
Minneapolis, MN 55410, 612-920-1896
    Pubs: *Crossing the Moon* (Hungry Mind Pr, 1996), *Feeding
    the Eagles* (Graywolf Pr, 1988), *Ploughshares, Mississippi
    Rev, Antioch Rev, First*

Floyce Alexander ♪ ✈   P&W
1211 Beltrami Ave NW
Bemidji, MN 56601-2826
Internet: fmklalex@paulbunyan.net
    Pubs: *Succor, Memory of the Future* (Red Dragonfly Pr,
    2002, 1998), *Red Deer* (L'Epervier, 1982), *Bottom Falling
    Out of the Dream* (Lynx Hse Pr, 1976), *Nation, TriQtly,
    Greenfield Rev, Contact II, Colorado Rev*

Daniel Bachhuber ♪ ✈   P
1288 Osceola Ave
St Paul, MN 55105, 612-699-1560
    Pubs: *Mozart's Carriage, Party Train: Anth* (New Rivers Pr,
    2001, 1996), *Atlanta Rev, Visions Intl, SPR, Green Hills Lit
    Lantern, Iowa Rev*

Patricia Barone ♪ ✈   P
686 Kimball St NE
Fridley, MN 55432-1643, 612-784-3386
Internet: baronel@juno.com
    Pubs: *Handmade Paper, The Wind, The Talking of Hands:
    Anth, One Parrish Over: Anth* (New Rivers Pr, 1994, 1987,
    1998, 1995), *American Voices: Anth* (Merrill, 1998), *Bless
    Me Father: Anth* (Penguin, 1994), *Visions Intl, And Rev,
    Pleiades*

Charles Baxter   P
134 Groveland Terrace
Minneapolis, MN 55403, 612-377-6234
    Pubs: *The Feast of Love, Believers* (Pantheon, 2000, 1997),
    Burning Down the House (Graywolf, 1997), *Shadow Play, A
    Relative Stranger* (Norton, 1993, 1990)

David Bengtson ♪ ✈   P
626 Oak Ct S
Long Prairie, MN 56347-1629, 320-732-6297
Internet: david_bengtson@mail.lpge.k12.mn.us
    Pubs: *blink: Anth* (Spout Pr, 2001), *Open Windows* (Juniper
    Pr, 1990), *26 Minnesota Writers: Anth* (Nodin Pr, 1995),
    Biggy's Candy Store: Anth (The Loft, 1992), *Ascent, New
    Letters, NER, Northeast, Sidewalks, Lake County Jrnl*

Sigrid Bergie P
1000 W Franklin Ave, Apt 120
Minneapolis, MN 55405
 Pubs: *Turning Out the Lights* (New Rivers Pr, 1988)

Candace Black 🎤 ✈ P
824 Baker Ave
Mankato, MN 56001, 507-625-6104
 Pubs: *The Volunteer* (New Rivers Press, 2003), *Key West: A Collection: Anth* (White Fish Pr, 2001) *Willow Springs, The Pharos, White Pelican Rev, The Decade Dance: Anth* (Sandhills Pr, 1991), *Sport Literate, Passages North, Folio, Conscience*

Carol Blair P
208 2 St NW Apt 405
East Grand Forks, MN 56721-1876
 Pubs: *Nobody Gets off the Bus* (Viet Nam Generation, 1994), *The Color of Grief & Morning Glories* (Wolfe D. T. Pub, 1991), *The American Poetry Anthology* (Amer Poetry Assoc, 1983), *New Press Lit Qtly*

Carol Bly W
1668 Juno Ave
St Paul, MN 55116-1415
Internet: carolmbly@aol.com
 Pubs: *My Lord Bag of Rice: New and Selected Stories* (Milkweed Edtns, 2000), *Changing the Bully Who Rules the World: Anth* (Milkweed Edtns, 1996), *New Yorker, TriQtly, Laurel Rev, Iowa Rev*

Robert Bly 🎤 ✈ P
1904 Girard Ave S
Minneapolis, MN 55403-2945, 612-377-9817
 Pubs: *Eating the Honey of Words: New & Selected Poems, Morning Poems, Meditations on the Insatiable Soul, What Have I Ever Lost by Dying?* (HC, 1999, 1997, 1994, 1993), *Nation, The Sun, Kenyon Rev, Common Boundary*

William Borden 🎤 ✈ P&W
10514 Turtle River Lake Rd NE
Bemidji, MN 56601-8635, 218-586-2765
Internet: wborden@paulbunyan.net
 Pubs: *Eurydice's Song* (St. Andrews, 1999), *Superstore* (Orloff, 1996), *Slow Step & Dance* (Loonfeather Pr, 1991), *Minnesota Poetry Calendar: Anth* (Black Hat, 2001), *Fresh Water: Anth* (Pudding Hse, 2000), *Flyaway, Rag Mag, Midwest Qtly, Poets On, Quantum Tao*

Jonathan Brannen 🎤 ✈ P&W
817 Portland Ave
St. Paul, MN 55104
Internet: jhbrannen@earthlink.net
 Pubs: *Deaccessioned Landscapes* (Chax Pr, 2002), *No Place to Fall* (Sink Press, 1999), *Thing Is the Anagram of Night, The Glass Left Waltzing* (Meow Pr, 1996), *Nothing Doing Never Again* (Score Pr, 1995)

Jill Breckenridge P
708 N 1st St, #534
Minneapolis, MN 55401-1152
 Pubs: *How to Be Lucky* (Blue Stem Pr, 1990), *Civil Blood* (Milkweed Edtns, 1986), *Noeva: 3 Women Poets: Anth* (Dakota Pr, 1975)

Kerri R. Brostrom P
2512 E 125 St
Burnsville, MN 55337-3139, 612-728-0053
 Pubs: *Oregon East, Pointed Circle, Ellipsis, Pearl, Old Red Kimono, Alura, Cape Rock, Maryland Poetry Rev, Black River Rev, Rattle, Madison Rev*

Michael Dennis Browne 🎤 ✈ P
English Dept, Univ Minnesota, Lind Hall, 207 Church St, Minneapolis, MN 55455, 612-626-9555
Internet: mdb@umn.edu
 Pubs: *Selected Poems 1965-1995, You Won't Remember This, Smoke From the Fires, The Sun Fetcher* (Carnegie Mellon, 1997, 1992, 1985, 1978), *APR, TriQtly*

Emilie Buchwald P&W
6808 Margaret's Lane
Edina, MN 55439, 612-332-3192
 Pubs: *The Most Wonderful Books, The Sporting Life: Anth, The Poet Dreaming in the Artist's House: Anth, Transforming a Rape Culture: Anth* (Milkweed Edtns, 1996, 1987, 1984, 1993)

Alan Burns W
English Dept, 207 Lind Hall, Univ Minnesota, 207 Church St SE, Minneapolis, MN 55455, 612-625-3363
 Pubs: *Revolutions of the Night* (Schocken, 1987), *The Day Daddy Died* (Allison & Busby, 1981)

John Caddy P
8870 202nd St N
Forest Lake, MN 55025
 Pubs: *The Color of Mesabi Bones, Eating the Sting* (Milkweed Edtns, 1989, 1986), *Dacotah Territory*

Kathy Callaway 🎤 ✈ P&W
c/o S. Callaway, 802 SW 3rd Ave, Grand Rapids, MN 55744
Internet: kathyjcallaway@hotmail.com
 Pubs: *Lithuanian Letters,* (Archipelago, 2001), *Estonian Letters* (Archipelago, 2001), *Heart of the Garfish* (U Pitt Pr, 1982), *The Bloodroot Flower* (Knopf, 1982)

Katherine Carlson W
2912 34th Ave S, #2
Minneapolis, MN 55406, 612-296-6605
 Pubs: *Casualties* (New Rivers, 1982), *Minneapolis/St. Paul Mag, New Directions for Women, In These Times, VIA, Minnesota Women's Pr, Spirit*

Barry Casselman 🎤 ✈   P
1414 S 3rd St, #102
Minneapolis, MN 55454-1172, 612-321-9044
Internet: barcass@mr.net
    Pubs: *The Boat of the Blue Rose, Among Dreams* (Kraken
Pr, 2002, 1985), *Language Is Not Words* (Lingua Pr, 1980),
APR, ACM, Calcutta 2000, Kansas Qtly, North Stone Rev

Nadia Christensen   P
1545 Fulham St
St Paul, MN 55108
    Pubs: *Turkestan* (w/Kling; France; Chene, 1991), *Action,
Reflection, Celebration* (ARC, 1988)

Kathleen Coskran 🎤 ✈   W
152 Bank St SE
Minneapolis, MN 55414-1033
Internet: kac1122@aol.com
    Pubs: *The High Price of Everything, Tanzania on Tuesday:
Anth* (New Rivers Pr, 1988, 1997), *Living on the Edge:
Anth* (Curbstone Pr, 1999), *Going Up Country: Anth*
(Scribner, 1994)

Jeanette M. Cox 🎤 ✈   P&W
28 Davis Dr
Silver Bay, MN 55614, 218-226-0057
    Pubs: *War and Peace* (Zigzag Press, 1996), *Dust & Fire: An
Anth of Women's Writing* (Bemidji State U, 1994), *North
Coast Rev*

Florence Chard Dacey   P
Box 31
Cottonwood, MN 56229, 507-423-6652
    Pubs: *The Necklace* (Midwest Villages & Voices, 1988), *The
Swoon* (Minnesota Writers Pub Hse, 1979)

Philip Dacey 🎤 ✈   P
English Dept, Southwest State Univ, Marshall, MN 56258, 507-
537-7155
Internet: dacey@ssu.southwest.msus.edu
    Pubs: *The Deathbed Playboy* (Eastern Washington U Pr,
1999), *Night Shift at the Crucifix Factory* (U Iowa Pr, 1991),
*Qtly Rev of Lit, Nation, Hudson Rev, Poetry, Georgia Rev,
Paris Rev, Partisan Rev*

Alan Davis 🎤 ✈   P&W
Minnesota State Univ, PO Box 38, Moorhead, MN 56563, 218-
236-4681
Internet: davisa@mnstate.edu
    Pubs: *Alone With the Owl, Rumors From the Lost World* (New
Rivers, 2000, 1996, 1995), *The Qtly, Hudson Rev, North
Dakota Qtly, South Dakota Rev, Chattahoochee Rev, Image*

Emilio DeGrazia 🎤 ✈   W
211 W 7 St
Winona, MN 55987, 507-454-6564
Internet: edegrazia@vax2.winona.msus.edu
    Pubs: *A Canticle for Bread & Stones, Seventeen Grams
Worth of Soul* (Lone Oak Pr, 1997, 1994), *Billy Brazil* (New
Rivers Pr, 1992)

Scott Edelstein   W
4445 Vincent Ave S, #2
Minneapolis, MN 55410-1527, 612-823-5838
Internet: comconse@aol.com
    Pubs: *Ellery Queen's Mystery Mag, Artist's Mag, Writer's
Yearbook, Artlines, New Worlds, City Miner*

Michael Finley   P
1814 Dayton Ave
St Paul, MN 55104, 651-644-4540
    Pubs: *Looking for China* (Kraken Pr, 1994), *Pushcart Prize
XI: Anth* (Pushcart Pr, 1986), *Paris Rev, New American &
Canadian Poetry, Great River Rev*

Kevin FitzPatrick   P
PO Box 40214
St. Paul, MN 55104
    Pubs: *Kevin Fitzpatrick-Greatest Hits: 1975-2000* (Pudding
Hse Pubs, 2001), *Rush Hour, Down on the Corner* (Midwest
Villages & Voices, 1997, 1987)

David J. Fraher   P
c/o Arts Midwest, Hennepin Center for the Arts, 528 Hennepin
Ave, Ste 310, Minneapolis, MN 55403
    Pubs: *Western Humanities Rev, APR, New Letters,
Slackwater Rev*

Mary Gardner 🎤 ✈   W
235 Arundel St, #5
St Paul, MN 55102, 651-291-8722
    Pubs: *Boat People* (Norton, 1995), *Milkweed* (Papier-Mache,
1994), *Keeping Warm* (Atheneum, 1987)

Terry A. Garey 🎤 ✈   P
3149 Park Ave S
Minneapolis, MN 55407, 612-824-5157
    Pubs: *Time Frames: Anth of Speculative Poetry* (Rune Pr,
1991), *Raw Sacks: Anth* (Bag Person Pr, 1991), *Hurricane
Alice, Weird Tales, Star*Line, Asimovs, Tales of the
Unanticipated*

Diane Glancy 🎤 ✈   P
Macalester College, 1600 Grand, St Paul, MN 55105,
651-696-6516
Internet: glancy@macalester.edu
    Pubs: *The Relief of America* (Tia Chucha Pr, 2000), *The
Voice That Was in Travel* (U Oklahoma Pr, 1999), *Fuller
Man, Flutie* (Moyer Bell, 1999, 1998), *The West Pole* (U
Minnesota Pr, 1997), *Pushing the Bear* (HB, 1996)

Kate Green P&W
c/o Lazear Agency, 430 1st Ave N, Ste 416, Minneapolis, MN
55401, 612-332-8640
Pubs: *Shooting Star* (HC, 1992), *The Fossil Family Tales*
(Creative Education, 1992), *Night Angel* (Delacorte, 1989),
APR, Hungry Mind Rev

Alvin Greenberg P&W
1113 Lincoln Ave
St Paul, MN 55105, 612-290-9732
Internet: greenberg@macalester.edu
Pubs: *How the Dead Live* (Graywolf Pr, 1998), *Why We Live
With Animals, The Man in the Cardboard Mask* (Coffee Hse
Pr, 1990, 1985), *Heavy Wings* (Ohio Rev Pr, 1988), *NAR,
Gettysburg Rev, Georgia Rev, Chelsea, ALR*

Keith Gunderson P
1212 Lakeview Ave S
Minneapolis, MN 55416, 612-374-4339
Pubs: *A Continual Interest in the Sun & Sea & Inland
Missing the Sea* (Nodin, 1977), *Milkweed, North Stone Rev,
Baja Jrnl*

Patricia Hampl 🎤 ✈ P
286 Laurel Ave
St Paul, MN 55102-2190
Internet: hampl@umn.edu
Pubs: *I Could Tell You Stories, A Romantic Education*
(Norton, 1999, 1999), *Virgin Time* (FSG, 1992), *Spillville*
(Milkweed Edtns, 1987), *New Yorker, Antaeus, Paris Rev*

Joanne Hart P
Box 356
Grand Portage, MN 55605
Pubs: *Minnesota Poetry Calendar: Anth* (Black Hat Pr,
1998), *The Women's Great Lakes Reader: Anth* (Holy Cow!
Pr, 1998), *Inheriting the Land: Anth* (U Minnesota Pr,
1993), *Mixed Voices: Anth* (Milkweed Edtns, 1991), *North
Coast Rev*

Margaret M. Hasse P
1698 Lincoln Ave
St Paul, MN 55105, 612-699-9138
Pubs: *In a Sheep's Eye, Darling* (Milkweed Edtns, 1988),
Sisters of the Earth: Anth (Vintage, 1991), *Tendril,
Primavera, Milkweed Chronicle*

Susan Carol Hauser 🎤 ✈ P
21963 Erica Ln NW
Puposky, MN 56667, 218-243-2402
Internet: schauser@paulbunyan.net
Pubs: *Outside After Dark: New & Selected Poems* (Loon
Feather Pr, 2002), *Poetry Motel, North Coast Rev*

Ellen Hawley 🎤 ✈ W
3223 36th Ave S
Minneapolis, MN 55406-2128, 612-729-8813
Internet: ellenhawley@yahoo.com
Pubs: *Trip Sheets* (Milkweed Edtns, 1998), *Hers 3: Anth*
(Faber & Faber, 1999)

Allison Adelle Hedge Coke P&W
C/O Coffee House Press, 27 N 4th St Ste 400, Minneapolis,
MN 55401, 612-338-0125
Internet: aahedgecoke@aol.com
Pubs: *Dog Road Woman* (Coffee Hse Pr, 1997), *The Year of
the Rat* (Grimes Pr, 1995), *Santa Barbara Rev, Little Mag,
Caliban, 13th Moon, Cross Culture Poetics, Gatherings*

Robert Hedin P
PO Box 59
Frontenac, MN 55026, 612-388-6103
Pubs: *Tornadoes* (Ion Bks, 1990), *Alaska: Reflections on
Land & Spirit* (U Arizona Pr, 1989)

Donal Heffernan 🎤 ✈ P
8570 Jewel Ave North
Stillwater, MN 55082
Internet: donal@zelium.net
Pubs: *Duets of Motion, Orion* (Lone Oak Pr, 2001, 1994),
Hillsides (Anvil, 1990), *Artword, CPU Rev, Crisp Pine, Fan,
Minnesota Poetry Calendar, Paintbrush*

Scott Helmes 🎤 ✈ P
862 Tuscarora
St Paul, MN 55102-3706, 612-339-9260
Internet: skaadenhelmes@compuserve.com
Pubs: *Non Additive Postulations* (Runaway Spoon Pr, 2000),
Poems 1972-1997 (Helmes, 1997), *Writing to Be Seen:
Anth* (Light & Dust Bks, 2001), *Dictionary of the Avant-
Gardes: Anth* (Schirmer, 2000), *Art Postale: Anth* (AAA
Edizioni, 1999)

Mary Ann Henn P
104 Chapel Ln
St Joseph, MN 56374-0220
Pubs: *Nu-N-Human, Nun-Plus* (Fig Pr, 1993, 1990), *Time of
Singing, Upsouth, Poets at Work, Parnassus, Explorer,
Smiles, Silver Wings, Simply Words, San Fernando Poetry
Jrnl, Waterways, Reflect*

Stephen Hesla W
c/o Alma Hesla, #8 Lincoln Ln, Northfield, MN 55057
Pubs: *The Hawthorn Conspiracy* (Dembner Bks, 1984)

Jim Heynen 🎤 ✈   P&W
960 Portland Ave
St. Paul, MN 55104, 651-228-7017
Internet: jheynen60@yahoo.com
   Pubs: *Standing Naked* (Confluence 2001), *The Boys' House*
   (MN Hist Scty Pr, 2001), *Cosmos Coyote and Wiliam the*
   Nice, Being Youngest (Holt 2000, 1997), *The One-Room*
   Schoolhouse (Knopf, 1993), *You Know What Is Right* (North
   Point Pr, 1985), *Harpers*

Rolando Hinojosa   W
Univ Minnesota, 224 Church St SE/493 Ford Hall,
Minneapolis, MN 55455, 612-373-9707

H. Edgar Hix   P
5144 45th Ave South
Minneapolis, MN 55417-1625, 612-724-4362
   Pubs: *God's Special Book* (Concordia Pub, 1980), *Impetus,*
   Waterways, Time of Singing, Midland Rev, Lilliput Rev,
   South Coast Poetry Jrnl, Burning Light, Untitled

Richard D. Houff 🎤 ✈   P
604 Hawthorne Ave East
St Paul, MN 55101, 651-793-4369
   Pubs: *News from the Border* (Limited Edtn Pr, 2000),
   Endless tongue: 22 Semi-Automatics For Andre Breton,
   (Benway Inst, 1999) *Cardboard Pastries* (Scrooge's Ledger
   Pr, 1999), *Earthquake School: Anth* (Many Beaches Pr,
   1998), *Gryphon, Brooklyn Rev*

Alyce Ingram   W
Mears Park Place, 401 Sibley St #622
St Paul, MN 55101
   Pubs: *Best of Wind: Anth* (Wind Pub, 1994), *Sexual*
   Harassment (Crossing Pr, 1992), *Nightshade Short Story*
   Reader: Anth (Nightshade Pr, 1991), *Small Pond, Slate,*
   Happy, Peep, Knocked, Potato Eyes, Pittsburgh Qtly, ELF,
   Briar Cliff Rev, Potpourri, Q Rev

Louis Jenkins 🎤 ✈   P
101 Clover St
Duluth, MN 55812-1103, 218-724-6382
Internet: louis@skypoint.com
   Pubs: *Just Above Water, Nice Fish* (Holy Cow! Pr, 1997,
   1995), *All Tangled Up With the Living* (Nineties Pr, 1991)

Jim Johnson   P
New Rivers Press, 420 N 5 St, Ste 910, Minneapolis, MN
55401, 612-339-7114
   Pubs: *Wolves* (New Rivers Pr, 1993), *A Field Guide to*
   Blueberries, Finns in Minnesota Midwinter (North Star Pr,
   1992, 1986)

Deborah Keenan 🎤 ✈   P
1168 Laurel Ave
St Paul, MN 55104, 612-647-0276
   Pubs: *Happiness* (Coffee Hse Pr, 1995), *Looking for Home:*
   Anth (Milkweed Edtns, 1990), *Santa Monica Rev,*
   Shenandoah

Garrison Keillor   W
Minnesota Public Radio, 45 E 7th St, St Paul, MN 55101

N. M. Kelby 🎤 ✈   W
553 Selby Ave
St. Paul, MN 55102-1728, 651-298-8544
Internet: nkelby@yahoo.com
   Pubs: *In the Company of Angels* (Hyperion Pr, 2001),
   Mississippi Rev

Patricia Kirkpatrick 🎤 ✈   P
1256 Osceola
St Paul, MN 55105, 612-690-0089
   Pubs: *What Have You Lost?: Anth* (S&S, 2000), *The Writing*
   Path: Anth (U Iowa Pr, 1995), *The Threepenny Rev,*
   Bloomsbury Rev, Luna, Antioch Rev, Hungry Mind Rev

Allan Kornblum   P
Coffee House Press, 27 N 4 St, Ste 400, Minneapolis, MN
55401, 612-338-0125
   Pubs: *Awkward Song* (Toothpaste Pr, 1980), *The Salad*
   Bushes (Seamark Pr, 1975)

Cinda Kornblum   P
Coffee House Press, 27 N 4 St, Ste 400, Minneapolis, MN
55401
   Pubs: *Bandwagon* (Toothpaste Pr, 1976), *The Actualist Anth*
   (The Spirit That Moves Us, 1977)

Jack Kreitzer   P
1031 Prior Ave S
Saint Paul, MN 55116
   Pubs: *Dark Moon* (Bald Mountain Pr, 1979), *Through Fire &*
   Deep Water (RVK Publishing, 1976)

J. L. Kubicek   P
16757-512 Lane, Rt 1, Box 167
Lake Crystal, MN 56055-9757, 507-546-3775
   Pubs: *Blood to Remember: Anth* (Texas Tech U Pr, 1990),
   Czech-American Writing: Anth (New Rivers, 1990), *Intl*
   Poetry Rev, New Laurel Rev, Midstream, New Hope Intl,
   Queen's Qtly, Prism Intl, Voices Israel, Greensboro Rev,
   Mobius

Brett Laidlaw   W
2087 Princeton Ave
St Paul, MN 51105, 612-646-2472
   Pubs: *Blue Bel Air* (Norton, 1993), *Three Nights in the Heart*
   of the Earth (NAL, 1989), *Elvis in Oz: Anth* (U Virginia, 1992)

Joseph Maiolo   W
English Dept, Univ Minnesota, Duluth, MN 55812,
218-726-8226
   Pubs: *Ploughshares, Sewanee, Shenandoah, Texas Rev,*
   New Virginia Rev

Freya Manfred 🎤 ✈ P
33487 Winnamakee Shores Rd
Pequot Lakes, MN 56472, 218-543-5052
Internet: thompope@uslink.net
  Pubs: *Flesh and Blood* (Red Dragonfly Pr, 2001), *American Roads* (Viking, 1985), *APR, New Letters, Antioch Rev*

Galen Martini P
104 Chapel La
St. Joseph, MN 56374
  Pubs: *The Heart's Slow Race* (North Star, 1976), *Northwoods Jrnl, New Amer and Canadian Poetry, Great River Rev, Christian Poetry Jrnl, America, Sing Heavenly Muse*

Ken McCullough 🎤 ✈ P&W
2490 Garvin Heights Rd
Winona, MN 55987, 507-454-5079
Internet: kmccullough@VAX2.winona.msus.edu
  Pubs: *Obsidian Point* (Lone Oak Pr, 2002), *Sycamore Oriole* (Ahsahta Pr, 1991), *Travelling Light* (Thunder's Mouth Pr, 1987)

Bill Meissner 🎤 ✈ P&W
618 6th Ave N
St Cloud, MN 56303
  Pubs: *The Sleepwalker's Son* (Ohio U Pr, 1989), *Hitting Into the Wind* (SMU Pr, 1997), *Twin Sons of Different Mirrors* (w/Jack Driscoll; Milkweed Edtns, 1989)

Leslie Adrienne Miller 🎤 ✈ P
English Dept, Mail 30F, Univ St. Thomas, 2115 Summit Ave, St Paul, MN 55105-1096, 651-962-5604
Internet: lmille8@attglobal.net
  Pubs: *Yesterday Had a Man in It, Ungodliness, Staying Up for Love* (Carnegie Mellon U Pr, 1998, 1994, 1990), *APR, Kenyon Rev, NER, Georgia Rev, Ploughshares, Nimrod*

John Minczeski 🎤 ✈ P
1300 Dayton
St Paul, MN 55104, 651-646-9434
  Pubs: *Circle Routes* (U Akron Pr, 2001), *Gravity* (Texas Tech U Pr, 1991), *The Reconstruction of Light* (New Rivers Pr, 1981), *Qtly W, Mid-Amer Rev, Notre Dame Rev, Agni, Meridian, Marlboro Rev, Pleiades, Free Lunch, Cape Rock, Cream City Rev*

Valerie Miner 🎤 ✈ W
English Dept, Univ Minnesota, Minneapolis, MN 55455, 612-625-3363
Internet: miner002@umn.edu
  Pubs: *The Low Road* (Michigan State U Pr, 2001), *Ranging Light* (Zoland, 1998), *A Walking Fire* (SUNY Pr, 1994), *Rumors From the Cauldron* (U Michigan Pr, 1992), *VLS, New Letters, Salmagundi, Michigan Qtly Rev, Ploughshares, Nation, Virginia Qtly Rev*

David R. Moffatt P
Rte 3, Box 228
Pine City, MN 55063, 612-629-2816
  Pubs: *The Folded Paper Dream* (Tiger Moon Pr, 1992), *Riverrun, Verve, Poetic Knight, Star Triad, Shawnee Silhouette, The Archer*

James Moore 🎤 ✈ P
438 Laurel Ave, #5
St Paul, MN 55102-2049, 651-227-0047
Internet: laurel438@aol.com
  Pubs: *The Long Experience of Love, The Freedom of History* (Milkweed Edtns, 1995, 1988), *Pushcart Prize Anth* (Pushcart Pr, 2002), *Luna, Bloomsbury Rev, APR, Paris Rev, Nation, Kenyon Rev, Antioch Rev, Threepenny Rev*

Michael Moos P
2223 Dayton Ave
St Paul, MN 55104, 612-642-0181
  Pubs: *Great River Review Anth* (Great River Rev, 1989), *Minnesota Writers: Anth* (Milkweed, 1987)

David Mura 🎤 ✈ P
1920 E River Terr
Minneapolis, MN 55414-3672
Internet: davsus@aol.com
  Pubs: *The Colors of Desire* (Anchor, 1995), *After We Lost Our Way* (Carnegie Mellon U Pr, 1989), *APR, NER, New Republic, Conjunctions, Mother Jones, New York Times*

James Naiden 🎤 ✈ P
The North Stone Review, Box 14098, Minneapolis, MN 55414-0098, 612-781-7594
Internet: jack123904@aol.com
  Pubs: *Summer Poems* (Tendon Pr, 2002), *Asphyxiations #1-40* (Metron Pr, 2001), *The Orange Notebook* (Metron Pr, 1973), *ShortStory.org, Poetry, Eire-Ireland, Nantucket Rev, New Hibernia Rev, Willow Avenue Rev, Wolf Head Qtly*

Josip Novakovich W
Graywolf Press, 2402 University Ave, Ste 203, St. Paul, MN 55114, 612-641-0007
  Pubs: *Salvation & Other Disasters* (Graywolf, 1995), *Antaeus, Paris Rev, Ploughshares*

W. Scott Olsen 🎤 ✈ W
443 42nd Ave
Moorhead, MN 56560-6719, 218-236-7037
Internet: olsen@cord.edu
  Pubs: *The Sacred Place* (U Utah Pr, 1996), *Acts of Illumination* (St. Mary's U Pr, 1996), *Meeting the Neighbors* (North Star Pr, 1993), *Just This Side of Fargo* (Ironwood Pr, 1992), *Ascent, Kenyon Rev, Willow Springs, North Dakota Qtly, Weber Studies*

Lon Otto P&W
270 MacKubin St
St Paul, MN 55102, 612-227-7883
Pubs: *Cover Me, Water Bodies* (Coffee Hse, 1988, 1986), *A Nest of Hooks* (U Iowa Pr, 1978)

Tom Peacock P
1507 Lockling Rd
Cloquet, MN 55720, 218-879-7326

Mary Ellis Peterson P
13887 85th Pl N
Maple Grove, MN 55369-9237, 763-420-2901
Internet: maryellisp@yahoo.com
Pubs: *Journey Into Motherhood* (Riverhead Bks, 1996), *Motherpoet* (Mothering Pub, 1984), *And I Shall Be Your Ancestor* (Guild Pr, 1980)

Joan Wolf Prefontaine P
18562 Nokay Lake Rd
Deerwood, MN 56444
Internet: prewolf@emily.net
Pubs: *Thirty-three Minnesota Poets: Anth* (Nodin Pr, 2000), *The Divided Sphere* (Floating Island Pr, 1985)

Sister Bernetta Quinn P
Sisters of St. Francis, Box #4900, Rochester, MN 55903, 507-282-7441
Pubs: *Dancing in Stillness* (St. Andrews, 1983), *Sewanee Rev, Yale Rev, America, English Jrnl, Sign*

Thomas Dillon Redshaw P
1944 Carroll Ave
St Paul, MN 55104, 612-645-7669
Pubs: *The Floating World* (Truck Pr, 1979), *Sewanee Rev, Antioch Rev, Carleton Miscellany*

John Calvin Rezmerski 🎤 ✈ P
Box 202
Eagle Lake, MN 56024-0202, 507-257-3491
Internet: rez@gac.edu
Pubs: *What Do I Know?* (Holy Cow! Pr, 2000), *One & Twenty Poems by Grace Lord Stoke* (Bootless Pub, 1999), *Growing Down* (Minnesota Writers Pub Hse, 1982)

Melanie Richards P
16570 22nd St S
St Mary's Point, MN 55043, 612-436-1666
Pubs: *26 Minnesota Writers: Anth* (Nodin, 1996), *Harvard Rev, Yankee, Kalliope, Shenandoah, Negative Capability, Passages North*

Richard Robbins 🎤 ✈ P
Minnesota State Univ, 230 Armstrong Hall, Mankato, MN 56001, 507-389-1354
Internet: richard.robbins@mnsu.edu
Pubs: *Famous Persons We Have Known* (Eastern Washington U Pr, 2000), *The Invisible Wedding* (U Missouri Pr, 1984), *NAR, Nation, Poetry NW*

George Roberts P
1022 Sheridan Ave N
Minneapolis, MN 55411, 612-588-3723
Pubs: *Scrut* (Holy Cow! Pr, 1983), *Night Visits to a Wolf's Howl* (Oyster Pr, 1979)

Mordecai M. Roshwald W
Univ Minnesota, 314 Ford Hall, Minneapolis, MN 55455, 612-521-7955
Pubs: *A Small Armageddon, Level 7* (NAL, 1976, 1961), *Judaism, Nation*

Ruth Roston P
Parkshore Pl, 3663 Park Center Blvd, #501, Minneapolis, MN 55416, 612-926-7132
Pubs: *The Poet Dreaming in the Artist's House* (Milkweed Edtns, 1984)

CarolAnn Russell P
English Dept, Bemidji State Univ, 1530 Birchmont Dr NE, Bemidji, MN 56601, 218-755-2880
Pubs: *Silver Dollar* (West End Pr, 1995), *Feast* (Loonfeather Pr, 1993), *Verse, Pemmican, Midwest Qtly, Hurakan, Puerto del Sol, Great River Rev*

Mark Ryan 🎤 ✈ W
5604 Upton Ave S
Minneapolis, MN 55410-2623, 612-926-6095
Internet: markdryan@aol.com
Pubs: *Things That Fall From the Sky: Anth* (The Loft, 1994), *Pinehurst Jrnl, Alabama Lit Rev*

Sally Jo Sorensen P
PO Box 611
Dassel, MN 55325
Internet: mznpho@cmgate.com
Pubs: *A Turban Lily* (State Street Pr, 1990), *Zone 3, Laurel Rev, Sycamore Rev, Painted Bride Qtly, Poet & Critic, Yarrow, West Branch, Amaranth, Nebraska Qtly, Poem, Poet Lore*

Robert T. Sorrells 🎤 W
529 5th St SW
Rochester, MN 55902-3280, 507-289-0997
Internet: sorrelli@aol.com
Pubs: *The Blacktop Champion of Ickey Honey & Other Stories* (U Arkansas Pr, 1988), *Full Court: Anth, Tennis & the Meaning of Life: Anth* (Breakaway Pr, 1996, 1995), *Pudding Mag*

Madelon Sprengnether 🎤 ✈   P
Univ Minnesota, 207 Church St, English Dept, Minneapolis,
MN 55455
Internet: spren001@umn.edu
   Pubs: *Crying at the Movies* (Gray Wolf Pr, 2002), *La Belle et
la Bîte* (Sarasota Poetry Theater Pr, 1999), *Rivers, Stories,
Houses, Dreams, The Normal Heart, The House on Via
Gombito: Anth* (New Rivers Pr, 1983, 1981, 1990)

Francine Sterle 🎤 ✈   P
4023 River Rd
Iron, MN 55751-8044, 218-262-2503
Internet: fmsterle@uslink.net
   Pubs: *Every Bird Is One Bird* (Tupelo Pr, 2001), *The White
Bridge* (Poetry Harbor, 1999), *Great River Rev, Midwest
Qtly, NAR, Nimrod, BPJ, CutBank, Zone 3, Birmingham
Poetry Rev, Atlanta Rev*

Barton Sutter 🎤 ✈   P&W
1321 E 8th St
Duluth, MN 218-724-2736
   Pubs: *My Father's War* (U Minnesota Pr, 2000), *Book of
Names* (BOA Edtns, 1993), *Pine Creek Parish Hall & Other
Poems* (Sandhills, 1985), *Sequoyah* (Ox Head, 1983),
Poetry

Susan Marie Swanson 🎤 ✈   P
818 Seal St
St Paul, MN 55114
   Pubs: *Letter to the Lake, Getting Used to the Dark* (DK Ink,
1998, 1997), *Primavera, How(ever), Ironwood, Hungry Mind
Rev, APR, Minnesota Writes, Cricket*

Steve Swanson   P
910 St Olaf Ave
Northfield, MN 55057, 507-645-6017
   Pubs: *The First Fall: Ytterboe Hall, 1946* (Nine Ten Pr, 1997),
Moving Out on Your Own, Is There Life After High School?
(Augsburg, 1994, 1991)

Marcella B. Taylor   P
English Dept, St. Olaf College, Northfield, MN 55057,
507-646-2222
   Pubs: *The Lost Daughter* (Renaissance Pr, 1985), *The
Butterfly Tree: Anth* (New Rivers Pr, 1991), *Poetry, Tampa
Bay Rev*

Richard Terrill 🎤 ✈   P
English Dept, Minnesota State Univ, Mankato, MN 56001,
507-389-5500
Internet: richard.terrill@mankato.mnsu.edu
   Pubs: *Fakebook* (Limelight Edtns, 2000), *The Cross & the
Red Star* (Asian Pacific Fdn, 1994), *New Letters, NAR, Mid-
Amer Rev, Iowa Rev, Michigan Qtly, Trafika*

Susan Allen Toth   W
4820 Penn Ave S
Minneapolis, MN 55409, 612-927-0594
   Pubs: *A House of One's Own* (Potter, 1991), *Blooming*
(Little, Brown, 1981)

Mark Vinz 🎤 ✈   P&W
510 5th Ave S
Moorhead, MN 56560-2723, 218-236-5226
Internet: fac026@binghamton.edu
   Pubs: *Affinities* (Dacotah Territory, 1998), *Late Night Calls*
(New Rivers Pr, 1992), *Minnesota Gothic* (Milkweed Edtns,
1992), *Mixed Blessings* (Spoon River Poetry Pr, 1989)

Ping Wang   P&W
2118 Hendon Av
St. Paul, MN 55108, 612-332-3344
Internet: ping@macalester.edu
   Pubs: *Of Flesh & Spirit, Foreign Devil, American Visa*
(Coffee Hse Pr, 1999, 1996, 1994), *New Generation: Poetry
From China Today* (Hanging Loose Pr, 1999), *Sulfur, The
World, Talisman, Manoa, Chicago Rev, River City, Asylum,
Literary Rev, Westcoast Line*

Susan Steger Welsh   P
181 Vernon St
St. Paul, MN 55105-1921, 651-699-2318
Internet: sswwriter@aol.com
   Pubs: *Rafting on the Water Table* (New Rivers Pr, 2000),
Essential Love: Anth (Grayson Bks, 2000), *A Definitive
Guide to the Twin Cities: Anth* (Spout Pr, 1997), *Black Hat
Pr, Wolf Head Qtly*

Jay P. White 🎤 ✈   P
4616 W 56 St
Minneapolis, MN 55424-1557, 612-925-0616
Internet: jaywhite1@sprintmail.com
   Pubs: *The Sleeper at the Party* (Defined Providence Pr,
2001), *The Salt Hour* (U Illinois Pr, 2001), *The
Pomegranate Tree Speaks From the Dictator's Garden* (Holy
Cow Pr, 1988)

Warren Woessner 🎤 ✈   P
34 W Minnehaha Pkwy
Minneapolis, MN 55419-1365, 612-822-7848
Internet: wwoessner@slwk.com
   Pubs: *Iris Rising* (BkMk Pr of UMKC, 1998), *Clear to
Chukchi* (Poetry Harbor Pr, 1995), *Storm Lines* (New Rivers
Pr, 1987)

Karen Tei Yamashita 🎤 ✈   W
Coffee House Press, 27 N 4th St, Ste 400, Minneapolis, MN
55401, 612-338-0125
Internet: ktyamash@cats.ucsc.edu
   Pubs: *Circle K Cycles, Tropic of Orange, Brazil-Maru,
Through the Arc of the Rain Forest* (Coffee Hse Pr, 2001,
1997, 1992, 1990), *Los Angeles Times, Amerasia Jrnl*

MISSISSIPPI

Angela Ball 🎤 ✈   P
Box 5037, Southern Sta
Hattiesburg, MS 39406-5037, 601-266-4321
   Pubs: *The Museum of the Revolution, Quartet* (Carnegie
   Mellon, 1999, 1995), *Possession* (Valentine Pub Group,
   1996), *NAR, Field, Southern Rev, Denver Qtly, New Yorker,
   Ploughshares*

D. C. Berry 🎤 ✈   P
306 Washington Ave
Ocean Springs, MS 39564-4628, 601-872-1927
Internet: david3berry@aol.com
   Pubs: *Divorce Boxing* (Eastern Washington Pr, 1998),
   Jawbone (Thunder City Pr, 1978), *Saigon Cemetery* (U
   Georgia Pr, 1972), *Poetry, Chicago Rev*

Carol Cox   P
PO Box 188
Tougaloo, MS 39174-0188, 601-956-2610
   Pubs: *The Water in the Pearl* (Hanging Loose Pr, 1982),
   Mississippi Writers: Anth (U Pr Mississippi, 1988)

David Galef 🎤 ✈   W
Univ Mississippi, English Dept, University, MS 38677-1848,
662-915-7439
Internet: dgalef@olemiss.edu
   Pubs: *Laugh Track* (U Pr Miss, 2002), *Even a Stone
   Buddha Can Talk* (Tuttle, 2000), *Turning Japanese, Flesh*
   (Permanent Pr, 1998, 1995), *Tracks* (Morrow, 1996), *The
   Supporting Cast* (Penn State U Pr, 1993), *North Dakota
   Qtly, Gettysburg Rev, Crossroads*

Patricia Minter Grierson 🎤 ✈   P
PO Box 55808
Jackson, MS 39296, 601-982-3674
Internet: patg5000@cs.com
   Pubs: *Boston U Jrnl, Kansas Qtly, Mississippi Rev, Poem,
   Florida Qtly, Researcher*

Barry Hannah   W
211 Eagle Springs Rd
Oxford, MS 38655, 601-234-2453
   Pubs: *Never Die, Boomerang* (Seymour Lawrence/HM,
   1991, 1989), *Esquire, The Qtly, Southern Rev, Chicago Rev,
   Harper's, Georgia Rev*

Charles Henley   W
426 11th Ave NW, #5
Magee, MS 39111-3365, 601-371-7827
   Pubs: *The Smith, The Phoenix, Intro, Mississippi Rev,
   Carolina Qtly*

John Horvath, Jr. 🎤 ✈   P
222 Melrose Dr
Jackson, MS 39211
Internet: PRSeditor@aol.com
   Pubs: *Greatest Hits* (Pudding Hse, 2003), *Reverend
   Terrebonne Walker: CD* (Artvilla, 2002), *Illiana Region
   Poems* (Zebooks, 2001), *CONUS* (Ebookstand, 2000),
   *Dalhousie Rev, Nimrod, Seeker, Facets, Audax, Of(f)
   Course, Red Coral, Ascent, Ygdrasil, Swagazine*

Gary Myers   P
English Dept, Mississippi State Univ, Drawer E, Mississippi
State, MS 39762, 601-325-3644
   Pubs: *Lifetime Possessions* (Riverstone Pr, 1997), *World
   Effects* (Nevertheless Pr, 1990), *New Yorker, Poetry, Indiana
   Rev, Kansas Qtly, Louisville Rev, Bitterroot*

Helon Howell Raines 🎤 ✈   W
2330 Kelly Ave
Gulfport, MS 39501, 228-822-2961
Internet: hraines2502@cs.com
   Pubs: *Denver Qtly, Mississippi Rev, Outerbridge, Earth's
   Daughters, Worksheet, Wind Singers*

William Russell   W
PO Box 35
Tunica, MS 38676, 601-363-2196
   Pubs: *Berlin Embassy* (Macfadden Bks, 1962), *A Wind Is
   Rising* (Scribner, 1950)

Larry Marshall Sams   W
339 W Monroe Ave
Greenwood, MS 38930
   Pubs: *Words of Wisdom, Ancient Paths, Mississippi Rev,
   Seedhouse, Aura, Cotton Patch*

Glenn Robert Swetman   P
PO Box 146
Biloxi, MS 39533-0146
   Pubs: *Concerning Carpenters* (Pterodactyl Pr, 1979), *Deka
   #2* (Paon Pr, 1979), *Texas Qtly*

Margaret Walker   W
2205 Guynes Ave
Jackson, MS 39213

Jerry W. Ward, Jr.   P
1872 Lincolnshire Blvd
Ridgeland, MS 39157-1213, 601-957-5062
Internet: jerryward31@hotmail.com
   Pubs: *Trouble the Water: 250 Years of African-American
   Poetry: Anth* (Mentor, 1997), *Black Southern Voices: Anth*
   (NAL, 1992), *Callaloo, ADE Bulletin, Obsidian II, Open
   Places, Mississippi Qtly, Southern Qtly, Callaloo, Black
   American Lit Forum*

Claude Wilkinson 🎤 ✈   P
2895 Lester Rd
Nesbit, MS 38651-9190, 662-429-4935
    Pubs: *Reading the Earth* (Michigan State U Pr, 1998), *The Chattahoochee Rev, The Oxford American, Atlanta Rev, Blue Mesa Rev, CQ, A New Song, Poem, Southern Rev, Xavier Rev*

Joan Williams   W
908 Old Taylor Rd
Oxford, MS 38655-4619
    Pubs: *Pay the Piper* (Dutton, 1988), *Pariah & Other Stories* (Atlantic Monthly Pr, 1983), *Esquire, Southern Accents*

Benjamin J. Williams   P
3004 29th St
Gulfport, MS 39501, 601-864-6911
    Pubs: *Obsidian, Negro History Bulletin, Phylon, Black Scholar, Callaloo, Kitabu Cha Jua, Jrnl of Black Poetry, Afro Amer Qtly, Sphinx*

Austin Wilson   P&W
English Dept, Millsaps College, Jackson, MS 39210,
601-974-1305
Internet: wilsola@millsaps.edu
    Pubs: *From the Green Horseshoe: Anth* (U South Carolina Pr, 1987), *Mississippi Writers: Reflections: Anth* (U Pr Mississippi, 1985), *New Orleans Rev, Hiram Poetry Rev, Southern Humanities Rev, Descant, Mississippi Rev, Roanoke Rev*

Steve Yates   W
875 William Blvd, #412
Ridgeland, MS 39157-1519
    Pubs: *Arkansas Rev/Kansas Qtly, Ontario Rev, Missouri Rev, Nebraska Rev, Turnstile, Western Humanities Rev, Chariton Rev, Red Cedar Rev, Texas Rev, Laurel Rev, South Carolina Rev*

MISSOURI

Rosa M. Arenas   P
7731 Gannon, #1 E
St Louis, MO 63130, 314-726-1145
    Pubs: *She Said Yes* (Fallen Angel Pr, 1981), *Kenyon Rev, Calyx, River Styx, Blue Mesa Rev, Americas Rev, Sycamore Rev*

Mary Jo Bang 🎤 ✈   P
Department of English, c/o Washington Univ, Box 1122, One Brookings Dr, St. Louis, MO 63130-4899, 314-935-5190
Internet: maryjobang@aol.com
    Pubs: *The Downstream Extremity of the Isle of Swans* (U Georgia Pr, 2001), *Louise in Love* (Grove Pr, 2001), *Apology for Want, The New American Poets: A Bread Loaf Anthology* (U Pr New England, 1997, 2000), *Best American Poetry 2001: Anth* (Scribner, 2001)

Stanley E. Banks 🎤 ✈   P
7120 Indiana
Kansas City, MO 64132, 816-333-8705
Internet: banksSE@mail.avila.edu
    Pubs: *Blue Beat Syncopation* (BkMk Pr, 2002), *Rhythm and Guts, Coming From a Funky Time & Place* (Georgia AB Pr, 1992, 1988)

Walter Bargen 🎤 ✈   P
PO Box 19
Ashland, MO 65010, 573-657-2636
Internet: bargenw@missouri.edu
    Pubs: *Harmonic Balance, Water Breathing Air, The Vertical River* (Timberline Pr, 2001, 1999, 1995), *Mysteries in the Public Domain* (BkMk Pr, 1990), *Georgia Rev, New Letters, Iowa Rev, Boulevard*

Jim Barnes 🎤 ✈   P
The Chariton Review, Truman State Univ, Kirksville, MO 63501, 660-785-4499
Internet: jbarnes@truman.edu
    Pubs: *On a Wing of the Sun, Paris, Sawdust War* (U Illinois Pr, 2001, 1997, 1992), *La Plata Cantata* (Purdue U Pr, 1989), *Numbered Days* (New Odyssey, 1999), *Poetry, Qtly West, Nation, Sewanee Rev, Kenyon Rev, NAR, SW Rev, TriQtly*

Ben Bennani 🎤 ✈   P
1103 Cherry Ln
Kirksville, MO 63501-2097, 660-665-1103
Internet: bbennani@truman.edu
    Pubs: *Psalms for Palestine* (Three Continents Pr, 1993), *Bread, Hashish & Moon* (Unicorn Pr, 1982), *A Bowl of Sorrow* (Greenfield Rev Pr, 1977)

Edward Boccia   P
600 Harper Ave
Webster Groves, MO 63119, 314-962-5081
    Pubs: *A Light in the Grapes* (Frank Cat Pr, 2000), *No Matter How Good the Light Is* (Time Being Bks, 1998), *Edward Boccia: Twelve Greatest Hits, Moving the Still Life* (Pudding Hse, 2000, 1993), *Against the Grain: Anth* (CSS Pubs, 1988), *Flash Point*

James J. Bogan 🎤 ✈   P
Univ Missouri, Philosophy & Liberal Arts Dept, Rolla, MO 65409-0670, 573-341-4755
Internet: jbogan@umr.edu
    Pubs: *Trance Arrows, Ozark Meandering* (Timberline Pr, 2002, 1999), *Sparks of Fire* (North Atlantic Pr, 1982), *Exquisite Corpse, River Styx, Latin American Lit Rev*

Michelle Boisseau 🎤 ✈   P
English Dept, Univ of Missouri—KC, 5100 Rockhill Rd, Kansas
City, MO 64110-2499, 816-235-2561
Internet: boisseaum@umkc.edu
    Pubs: *Understory* (Northeastern U Pr, 1996), *No Private Life*
    (Vanderbilt U Pr, 1990), *Three Penny Rev, Yale Rev,*
    Shenandoah, Poetry, Agni, Ploughshares, Ohio Rev, Crazy-
    horse, Southern Rev, Georgia Rev, Gettysburg Rev

Louis Daniel Brodsky   P
10411 Clayton Rd, Ste 201-203
St Louis, MO 63131, 314-432-1771
    Pubs: *Shadow War, Paper-Whites for Lady-Jane,*
    Disappearing in Mississippi Latitudes, The Capital Cafe,
    Gestapo Crows (Time Being Bks, 2002, 1995, 1994, 1993,
    1992)

Catherine Browder 🎤 ✈   W
3611 Gladstone Blvd
Kansas City, MO 64123-1145, 816-483-8949
Internet: catherine_browder@yahoo.com
    Pubs: *The Heart: A Story* (Helicon Nine Edtns, 1995), *The*
    Clay That Breathes: Stories (Milkweed Edtns, 1991), *The*
    Broken Bridge: Anth (Stone Bridge Pr, 1997), *Kansas City*
    Star, Shenandoah, New Letters, Prairie Schooner, Kansas
    Qtly

Richard Burgin 🎤 ✈   P&W
7545 Cromwell Dr, #2N
St Louis, MO 63105, 314-862-2643
    Pubs: *The Spirit Returns, Fear of Blue Skies* (Johns Hopkins
    U Pr, 2001, 1997), *Pushcart Prize Anth* (Pushcart Pr, 2001,
    1998, 1987, 1982), *Ghost Quartet* (Northwestern U Pr,
    1999), *Private Fame, Man Without Memory* (U Illinois Pr,
    1991, 1989)

R. A. Burns 🎤 ✈   P
English Dept, Southeast Missouri State Univ, Cape Girardeau,
MO 63701
Internet: raburns@semovm.semo.edu
    Pubs: *Black Dirt, Potpourri, River King Poetry Supplement,*
    American Poets & Poetry, Satire, Poetry Now, College
    Composition & Communication

Marcus Cafagña 🎤 ✈   P
English Dept, 209C Pummill Hall, 901 S National Ave,
Springfield, MO 65804
Internet: msc607f@mail.smsu.edu
    Pubs: *Roman Fever* (Invisible Cities Pr, 2001), *The Broken*
    World (U Illinois Pr, 1996), *The Beacon Best of 1999: Anth*
    (Beacon Pr, 1999), *American Poetry Rev, Boulevard,*
    DoubleTake, Field, Poetry, Southern Rev, Threepenny Rev,
    TriQtly

Scott Cairns 🎤 ✈   P&W
University of Missouri, English Dept Tate Hall #107, Colombia,
MO 65211, 573-882-0669
Internet: CairnsS@missouri.edu
    Pubs: *Philokalia: New and Selected Poems* (Zoo Pr, 2002),
    Recovered Body (Braziller, 1998), *Figures for the Ghost* (U
    Georgia Pr, 1994), *Paris Rev, New Republic, Atlantic,*
    Image, Prairie Schooner, Colorado Rev

David Carkeet   W
9307 Old Bonhomme Rd
St Louis, MO 63132, 314-994-7532
Internet: engdcark@jinx.umsl.edu
    Pubs: *The Error of Our Ways* (H Holt, 1997), *The Full*
    Catastrophe (S&S, 1990), *Carolina Qtly, Kansas Qtly, NAR,*
    Village Voice, Oxford American

Michael Castro 🎤 ✈   P
8368 Richard Ave
St Louis, MO 63132, 314-432-0236
Internet: michael.castro@usa.net
    Pubs: *Human Rites* (Neshui Pub, 2002), *The Man Who*
    Looked Into Coltrane's Horn (Caliban Pr, 1998), *(US)*
    (Ridgeway Pr, 1991), Interpreting the Indian (U Oklahoma
    Pr, 1991), *Drum Voices Rev, Mississippi Valley Rev, Tampa*
    Rev, Edge, Printed Matter, Long Shot

Jan Garden Castro 🎤 ✈   P
7420 Cornell
St Louis, MO 63130, 314-725-0602
Internet: jcastro@prodigy.net
    Pubs: *The Last Frontier* (Eclectic Pr, 2001), *New Letters,*
    Eclectic Press, Missouri Rev, River Styx, Wind, Southwinds,
    Greenfield Rev, Exquisite Corpse, Abraxas, Focus Midwest

David Clewell 🎤 ✈   P
Webster Univ, English Dept, 470 E Lockwood, St Louis, MO
63119, 314-968-7170
    Pubs: *Jack Ruby's America, The Conspiracy Quartet* (Garlic
    Pr, 2000, 1997), *Now We're Getting Somewhere* (U
    Wisconsin Pr, 1994), *Blessings in Disguise* (Viking, 1991),
    Poetry, Georgia Rev, Kenyon Rev, Harper's, Ontario Rev,
    NER

Carole Knipp Cohen 🎤   P
8030 Delmar
St. Louis, MO 63130, 314-862-2503
Internet: carcoh7@aol.com
    Pubs: *And What Rough Beast* (Ashland Poetry Pr, 1999),
    Midwest Qtly, Sou'wester, Cape Rock, Madison Rev, Prism,
    Ascent, Spoon River

Gene Doty 🎤 ✈   P
Univ Missouri, English Dept, Rolla, MO 65401, 573-364-5322
Internet: gino@rollqnet.org
     Pubs: *Nose to Nose* (Brooks Bks, 1998), *Zero: 30 Ghazals*
(AHA Bks Online, 1998), *Wind Five-Folded* (AHA Bks,
1994), *Uncommon Places: Anth* (Mayapple Pr, 2000),
Midwest Haiku Anth (High/Coo Pr, 1992), *Rolling Coulter,
Lynx, Phase & Cycle, Woodnotes*

Jon Dressel   P
376 Walton Row
St Louis, MO 63108, 314-361-3478
     Pubs: *Face to Face, The Road to Shiloh* (Gomer Pr, 1997,
1994), *Out of Wales* (Alun Bks, 1985), *Prairie Schooner,
Epoch, Poetry Wales, Counter-Measures, New Welsh Rev,
Planet*

Debra L. Edwards 🎤 ✈   P
3406 Arlington Ave
St. Louis, MO 63120
     Pubs: *Black Rose* (Upstream Productions, 1977), *Home
Planet News, Natl Poetry Mag of the Lower East Side,
Poetry NY, Limelight, Gulf Times, Cover, Barefoot Grass
Jrnl, Quarter Horse*

Donald Finkel 🎤 ✈   P
2051 Park Ave #D
St Louis, MO 63104, 314-241-4426
Internet: dfinkel@artsci.wustl.edu
     Pubs: *The Road Back: Poems, Selected and New* (Midlist
Pr, 2002), *The Question of Seeing* (U Arkansas Pr, 1998),
The Wake of the Electron, Selected Shorter Poems
(Atheneum, 1987, 1987), *Yale Rev, SW Rev, Paris Rev,
Kenyon Rev, Denver Qtly*

Robert A. Frauenglas   P&W
2624 Roseland Terr, #19
St. Louis, MO 63143-2328, 314-647-9002
     Pubs: *The Eclectic Musings of a Brooklyn Bum* (Somrie Pr,
1980), *Blood to Remember: Anth* (Texas Tech U Pr, 1991),
Scottish Book Collector, Cups, Waterways

William H. Gass   W
6304 Westminster Pl
St Louis, MO 63130, 314-725-0317
Internet: iwc@artsci.wustl.edu
     Pubs: *Cartesian Sonata, Finding a Form, The Tunnel* (Knopf,
1998, 1996, 1995), *On Being Blue* (Godine, 1975), *New
Republic, Harper's, Conjunction, Salmagundi*

Paul Gianoli   P
2600 S 14 Ave
Ozark, MO 65721, 417-581-0895
Internet: gianoli@cofo.edu
     Pubs: *Blueprint, Focus: Midwest, Wisconsin Rev,
Mississippi Rev*

John F. Gilgun 🎤 ✈   W
PO Box 7152
St Joseph, MO 64507-7152, 816-233-8374
Internet: gilgun@griffon.mwsc.edu
     Pubs: *The Dooley Poems* (Robin Price, 1991), *From the
Inside Out* (3-Phase, 1991), *Music I Never Dreamed Of*
(Amethyst, 1989)

Galen Green   P&W
201 Westport Rd
Kansas City, MO 64111-2239
     Pubs: *World-Weary Polka* (Fireweed Pr, 1977), *NYQ, Poetry
Now, West Coast Rev*

Charles Guenther 🎤 ✈   P
9877 Allendale Dr
St Louis, MO 63123-6450, 314-544-0563
     Pubs: *Moving the Seasons* (BkMk Pr, 1994), *Phrase-
Paraphrase* (Prairie Pr, 1970), *Poetry, APR, Kenyon Rev, Lit
Rev, Formalist, Black Mountain Rev, Critic*

Frank Higgins   P
12500 E 53 Terr
Kansas City, MO 64133, 816-353-4529
     Pubs: *Eating Blowfish* (Raindust Pr, 1996), *Starting From
Ellis Island* (BkMk Pr, 1981), *New Letters, Dacotah Territory,
Kansas Qtly, Chariton Rev, Poetry Now*

Peter Daniel Hilty   P
632 Bellevue
Cape Girardeau, MO 63701, 314-335-8332
     Pubs: *Thomas Crook's Shoebox, How Far Is Far?*
(Southeast Missouri State U Pr, 1996, 1990)

Jane Hoogestraat   P
English Dept, Southwest Missouri State Univ, 901 S National,
Springfield, MO 65802, 417-836-6613
Internet: jah905f@vma.smsu.edu
     Pubs: *Poetry, Southern Rev, Iowa Woman, High Plains Lit
Rev, Poem, SPR*

Jane Ellen Ibur   P
3536 Victor St
St Louis, MO 63104, 314-771-7661
     Pubs: *If I Had a Hammer: Women & Work Anth* (Papier-
Mache Pr, 1990), *Webster Rev, Slipstream, Crazyquilt,
Literati Internationale, Spitball, Pastiche*

Donn Irving 🎤 ✈   W
Thornhill Fold, 707 NW 100 Rd, Centerview, MO 64019,
660-656-3832
     Pubs: *III Novellas* (Woodley Pr, 1993), *Jazz, Theatre & a
Prayer* (Potpourri Pubs, 1993), *These & Other Lands*
(Westphalia Pr, 1986), *ALR, New Letters, Crescent Rev,
Habersham Rev*

Jeanne Lebow   P
Northeast Missouri State Univ, Division of Language &
Literature, Kirksville, MO 63501, 816-785-5677
    Pubs: *The Outlaw James Copeland & the Champion-Belted
    Empress* (U Georgia Pr, 1991), *Nimrod, Sun Dog*

Thomas John Lochhaas   W
2349 S 11 St
St Louis, MO 63104, 314-771-7923
    Pubs: *Chicago Rev, Writers' Forum, Subject to Change,
    Sawtooth, Slackwater Rev*

Barbara Loots 🎤 ✈   P
7943 Charlotte
Kansas City, MO 64131, 816-361-3844
Internet: bkloots@earthlink.net
    Pubs: *Sibyl & Sphinx* (Rockhill Pr, 1988), *Landscapes With
    Women: Anth* (Singular Speech Pr, 1999), *The Muse Strikes
    Back: Anth* (Story Line Pr, 1997), *Random House Treasury
    of Light Verse: Anth* (Random Hse, 1995), *Lyric, Christian
    Century, Sparrow*

Kathleen M. McCann 🎤 ✈   P
103 N. Sixth St.
Elsberry, MO 63343, 573-898-5080
Internet: katemccann@juno.com
    Pubs: *Worcester Rev, Red Rock Rev, Writer's Forum,
    Descant, Sonoma Mandala Lit Rev, Midwest Qtly,*

James McKinley   W
Professional Writing Program, Univ Missouri, 5100 Rockhill
Rd, Kansas City, MO 64110, 816-235-1120
    Pubs: *The Fickleman Suite & Other Stories* (U Arkansas Pr,
    1993), *Acts of Love* (Breitenbush Bks, 1987)

Ronald W. McReynolds   P
High Field, RR#5, Warrensburg, MO 64093, 816-747-8810
    Pubs: *The Blooding & Other Missouri Poems* (Mid-America
    Pr, 1979), *Chariton Rev*

Jerred Metz   P
2318 Albion Pl
St Louis, MO 63104
    Pubs: *Halley's Comet, 1910: Fire in the Sky* (Singing Bone,
    1985)

Philip Miller   P
1841 Pendleton
Kansas City, MO 64124, 816-842-5872
    Pubs: *Dork* (Mulberry Pr, 1991), *Boulevard, College English,
    Lit Rev, Confrontation, Mudfish, New Letters, Kansas Qtly,
    Puerto del Sol*

Michael Murphy   W
4304 McCausland
St Louis, MO 63109, 314-647-4363
    Pubs: *AKA Ormand Sacker* (Norfolk-Hall, 1984),
    Hemingsteen (Autolycus Pr, 1978), *Esquire, Life*

Martin Musick   P
1661 Vassier Ave
St Louis, MO 63133, 314-389-2354
    Pubs: *Para*phrase, Midwest Poetry Rev*

Bob Myers   W
16503 3rd St N
Independence, MO 64056
    Pubs: *Kill the Fine Young Dreamers* (Abiding Mystery Pr,
    1998), *Good Old Hillmont High* (Crescent, 1979), *Mystery
    Forum Mag*

Robert Nazarene   P
PO Box 250
Chesterfield, MO 63006-0250
Internet: margiereview@aol.com
    Pubs: *5 AM, Callaloo, Green Mountains Rev, Indiana Rev,
    National Forum, Ploughshares, Fourteen Hills, Boulevard,
    BPJ*

Christina V. Pacosz 🎤 ✈   P&W
2003 NE Russell Rd #102
Kansas City, MO 64116-2473
Internet: pacosz@earthlink.net
    Pubs: *Christina V. Pacosz-Greatest Hits, One River* (Pudding
    Hse Pr, 2002, 2000), *This Is Not a Place to Sing* (West End,
    1987), *Some Winded, Wild Beast* (Black & Red, 1985),
    *Midwest Qtly, Calyx, Sing Heavenly Muse, Pig Iron,
    Exquisite Corpse*

Tom Padgett 🎤 ✈   P
523 N Park Pl
Bolivar, MO 65613-1576, 417-326-5406
Internet: tpadgett@microcore.net
    Pubs: *What Got Me, Barking Barkwards, The Magpie, The
    Weasel, Prodigal Poet, Pets, Second Tuesday: Anth*
    (Barnowl, 2001, 1998, 1997, 1997, 1995, 1990, 1999),
    Grist: Anth (MSPS, 2002, 2001, 2000), *Encore: Anths*
    (NFSPS, 2001, 2000, 1999, 1998)

Michelle Paulsen 🎤 ✈   P
HC83, Box 64
Salem, MO 65560-8404, 573-743-6848
Internet: paulsens@yahoo.com
    Pubs: *Dirt* (Hope & Allen, 2001), *What Wells Up* (Mellen
    Poetry Pr, 1997), *Sixteen Voices: Anth* (Mariposa, 1994),
    *Weber Studies, Midland Rev, Howling Dog, Recursive
    Angel, Fox Cry*

William Peden   W
603 Rollins CT
Columbia, MO 65205
    Pubs: *Twilight at Monticello* (HM, 1975)

David Perkins   P
Box 10016
Kansas City, MO 64111, 816-756-1744
    Pubs: *Wrapped Mind & Other Essays* (Woods Colt Pr,
    1988), *License to Kill* (BkMk Pr, 1974)

Carl Phillips P
English Dept, Box 1122, One Brookings Dr, St. Louis, MO
63130, 314-935-7133
Internet: phillips@artsci.wustl.edu
   Pubs: *Rock Harbor, The Tether* (FSG 2002, 2001), *Pastoral,
   From the Devotions, Cortege* (Graywolf, 2000, 1998, 1995),
   In the Blood (Northeastern U Pr, 1992)

Carol Poster P&W
Univ Missouri, 107 Tate Hall, English Dept, Columbia, MO
65211, 314-449-0765
   Pubs: *Surrounded by Dangerous Things* (Singular Speech
   Pr, 1994), *Deceiving the Worms* (Sleeping Lizard Pr, 1984),
   Poetry East, Formalist, Ploughshares

Cathleen Quirk P
c/o Dr. Thomas Quirk, 418-A N Clay St, Kirkwood, MO 63122,
314-909-1562
   Pubs: *Rue & Grace* (Crossing Pr, 1987), *Burden & Other
   Poems* (Orpheum Pr, 1980), *Ploughshares Poetry Reader:
   Anth* (Ploughshares Bks, 1994)

Carter Revard P
6638 Pershing Ave
St Louis, MO 63130, 314-727-9358
Internet: ccrevard@artsci.wustl.edu
   Pubs: *An Eagle Nation* (U AZ Pr, 1993), *Cowboys and
   Indians Christmas* (Point Riders Pr, 1992), *Urban Nature:
   Anth, Outsiders: Anth, Verse & Universe: Anth* (Milkweed
   Edtns, 2000, 1999, 1998), *Prairie Schooner, Caiban,
   American Indian Culture & Research Jrnl*

Suzanne Rhodenbaugh ♦ ✦ P
3734 Arsenal St
St. Louis, MO 63116-4802, 314-772-6587
Internet: srhodenb@aol.com
   Pubs: *Lick of Sense* (Helicon Nine Edtns, 2001), *Greatest
   Hits* (Pudding Hse Pr, 2001), *The Shine on Loss* (Painted
   Bride Qtly Pr, 1998), *Hudson Rev, NER, Amer Scholar,
   Cimarron Rev, Salmagundi, Michigan Qtly Rev*

Carol Lee Sanchez ♦ ✦ P
13918 Longwood Rd
Hughesville, MO 65334-2217, 660-827-5261
Internet: carolee@sockets.net
   Pubs: *Rainbow Visions & Earth Ways* (U Osnabrueck,
   1998), *From Spirit to Matter* (Taurean Horn Pr, 1997), *She
   Poems, Crimson Edge: Anth* (Chicory Blue Pr, 1995, 2000),
   Reinventing the Enemy: Anth (Norton, 1997)

Jo Sapp ♦ ✦ W
1025 Hickory Hill Dr
Columbia, MO 65203-2322, 573-443-8964
Internet: disapp@attglobal.net
   Pubs: *Fiction 100: Anth* (Prentice Hall, 2000), *Norton Anth of
   Short Fiction, Flash Fiction: Anth* (Norton, 1995, 1992), *NAR,
   Intro, Epoch, Washington Rev, Kansas Qtly, Long Pond*

Howard Schwartz ♦ ✦ P&W
14 Hill N Dale Lane
St Louis, MO 63132, 314-997-4553
Internet: hschwartz@umsl.edu
   Pubs: *The Four Who Entered Paradise* (Jason Aronson Inc,
   1995), *Gabriel's Palace* (Oxford U Pr, 1993), *Sleepwalking
   Beneath the Stars* (BkMk Pr, 1992)

Jory Sherman P
3044 Shepherd Hill Expy, #642
Branson, MO 65616-8168
   Pubs: *Grass Kingdom, Trapper's Moon* (Tor/Forge, 1994,
   1994), *The Medicine Horn* (Tor Bks, 1991)

Peter L. Simpson P
5261 Westminster Pl
St Louis, MO 63108, 314-361-5342
   Pubs: *Press Box & City Room, Stealing Home* (BkMk Pr,
   1988, 1985), *Choice, New Letters*

Roland E. Sodowsky W
Southwest Missouri State Univ, English Dept, Springfield, MO
65804, 417-882-5791
   Pubs: *Interim in the Desert* (TCU Pr, 1990), *Un-Due West*
   (Corona, 1990), *Things We Lose* (U Missouri Pr, 1989),
   Concho River Rev, Atlantic

Evelyn Somers W
1136 7 St
Boonville, MO 65233
Internet: rogerses@missouri.edu
   Pubs: *Descant, Crazyhorse, Many Mountains Moving*

Arnold Stead P&W
Univ Missouri, Tate Hall, Rm 1, Columbia, MO 65202, 314-
882-0681
   Pubs: *The Blood of This Need* (Kawabata Pr, 1987),
   Woodrose, Sepia, Loonfeather, Lake Street Rev

Marjorie Stelmach P
708 Carman Oaks Ct
Ballwin, MO 63021
   Pubs: *Night Drawings* (Helicon Nine Pr, 1995), *Kenyon Rev,
   Tampa Rev, The Jrnl, Chelsea, Ascent, River Styx, New
   Letters*

Robert Stewart ♦ ✦ P
7714 Summit St
Kansas City, MO 64114-1742, 816-444-6870
   Pubs: *Letter From the Living* (Borderline Pubs, 1992),
   Plumbers (BkMk Pr, 1988), *Prairie Schooner, Notre Dame
   Rev, Stand*

Anthony J. Summers W
1825 Bender Ln
Arnold, MO 63010, 314-752-3703
   Pubs: *Moving* (The Smith, 1981), *Metamorphosis*
   (Cornerstone Pr, 1979)

William L. Sutherland   W
654 W Bethel Dr
Columbia, MO 65203, 314-442-7241
    Pubs: *News From Fort God* (Midlist Pr, 1992)

Gladys Swan   W
2601 Lynnwood Dr
Columbia, MO 65203-2936, 573-442-9129
Internet: swangl@missouri.edu
    Pubs: *News From the Volcano, A Visit to Strangers, Do You
    Believe in Cabeza de Vaca?* (U Missouri Pr, 2000, 1996,
    1991), *Ghost Dance: A Play of Voices, Of Memory & Desire*
    (LSU Pr, 1992, 1989)

Marilyn R. Tatlow   W
1507 Keegan Ct
Columbia, MO 65203-6251
Internet: marilynt@gte.net
    Pubs: *Paradise* (Florida Literary Fdn, 1994), *Missouri
    Women Writers: Anth* (Sheba Rev, 1987), *Prism Intl,
    Slugfest, Pleiades, Poets' Edge, Palo Alto Rev*

Brian Taylor   P
4376 Maryland Ave, #A-4
St Louis, MO 63108-4101, 314-531-1437
    Pubs: *Transit* (London Mag Edtns, 1986), *River Styx,
    Antioch Rev, Missouri Rev, London Mag, The Listener,
    NER/BLQ, Sewanee Rev, Paris Rev, Stand*

Julius Eric Thompson   P
Black Studies Program, Univ Missouri, 313 Gentry Hall,
Columbia, MO 65211, 573-814-1592
    Pubs: *Blues Said: Walk On* (Energy, Earth Comm, 1977),
    Hopes Tied Up in Promises (Dorrance & Co, 1970), *Trouble
    With the Water: 250 Years of African American Poetry: Anth*
    (Penguin, 1997), *Freedomways, Phylon, Black Creation,
    Callaloo*

William Trowbridge   P
907 S Dunn St
Maryville, MO 64468, 660-582-3961
    Pubs: *Flickers, O Paradise, Enter Dark Stranger* (U
    Arkansas Pr, 2000, 1995, 1989), *Prairie Schooner, Epoch,
    Georgia Rev, Gettysburg Rev, Poetry*

Mary Troy   W
Univ of Missouri/English Dept, 8001 Natural Bridge, St Louis,
MO 63121-4401, 314-516-6845
Internet: marytroy@umsl.edu
    Pubs: *Alibi Café and Other Stories* (Bkmk Pr, 2002), *Joe
    Baker Is Dead* (U Missouri Pr, 1998), *Greensboro Rev,
    Chicago Tribune, Amer Fiction, Boulevard, River Styx,
    Ascent, ALR*

Mona Van Duyn   P
7505 Teasdale Ave
St Louis, MO 63130, 314-863-1943
    Pubs: *Firefall, If It Be Not I, Near Changes* (Knopf, 1993,
    1993, 1990), *Merciful Disguises* (Atheneum, 1982)

Gloria Vando   P
Helicon Nine Editions, The Writers Place, 3607 Pennsylvania,
Kansas City, MO 64111, 816-753-1095
Internet: vandog@aol.com
    Pubs: *Promesas* (Arte Publico Pr, 1993), *American
    Diaspora: Anth, 9MM: Anth* (U Iowa Pr, 2000, 2000), *Verse
    & Universe: Anth* (Milkweed, 1998), *Touching the Fire: Anth*
    (Anchor Bks, 1998), *River Styx, Western Humanities Rev,
    Kenyon Rev, New Letters*

Maryfrances Wagner   P
5021 Tierney Dr
Independence, MO 64055-6930
Internet: zinnia@planetkc.com
    Pubs: *Red Silk, Tonight Cicadas Sing* (Mid-America Pr,
    1999, 1984), *Salvatore's Daughter* (BkMk Pr, 1995),
    Unsettling America: Anth (Penguin, 1994), *Coal City Rev,
    Birmingham Poetry Rev, Laurel Rev, New Letters, Nebraska
    Rev, Midwest Qtly*

Richard Watson   W
756 Harvard Ave
St Louis, MO 63130, 314-862-7646
Internet: rawatson@artsci.wustl.edu
    Pubs: *The Philosopher's Diet* (Godine, 1998), *The
    Philosopher's Demise* (U Missouri Pr, 1995), *Niagara*
    (Coffee Hse Pr, 1993)

Jane O. Wayne   P
6376 Washington Ave
St Louis, MO 63130-4705, 314-725-6291
Internet: jowayne@inlink.com
    Pubs: *A Strange Heart* (Helicon Nine Edtns, 1996),
    Looking Both Ways (U Missouri Pr, 1985), *Poetry, Iowa
    Rev, Ploughshares, Amer Scholar, Massachusetts Rev,
    Michigan Qtly*

Susan Whitmore   P
5148 Baltimore Ave
Kansas City, MO 64112, 816-561-4226
Internet: susanwhitmore@aol.com
    Pubs: *The Invisible Women* (Singular Speech Pr, 1991)

Rebecca M. Wright   P
2011 Rutger St #A
St Louis, MO 63104, 314-231-0441
    Pubs: *Ciao Manhattan* (Telephone Bks, 1976), *Brief Lives*
    (Ant's Forefoot, 1974)

Joan Yeagley   P
Rte 1, Box 1306
Stella, MO 64867-9623, 417-435-2341
Internet: hayeagley@juno.com
    Pubs: *The Studs of McDonald County, In the Middle:
    Midwestern Women Poets: Anth* (BkMk Pr, 1987, 1985)

MONTANA

Sandra Alcosser 🎤 ✈ P
5791 W County Line Rd
Florence, MT 59833-6056, 406-273-0560
Internet: alcosser@mail.sdsu.edu
  Pubs: *A Woman Hit by a Meteor, Glyphs, Sleeping Inside
  the Glacier* (Brighton, 2001, 2001, 1997), *Except By Nature*
  (Graywolf, 1998), *A Fish to Feed All Hunger* (U Pr Virginia,
  1986, Ahsata, 1992), *APR, New Yorker, Paris Rev,
  Ploughshares, Poetry*

Minerva Allen P
Box 5270 HC63
Dodson, MT 59524, 406-673-3596
  Pubs: *Winter Smoke, Thematic Approach Curriculum: Anth*
  (Flores Hill County Printing Havremt, 1996, 1996), *The Last
  Place: A Centennial Anth* (Montana Historical Society,
  1988), *Montana Mag of Western History*

Margaret Bridwell-Jones W
135 Village Ln
Bigfork, MT 59911, 406-837-0248
  Pubs: *Northwood Jrnl, Calliope, Green's Mag, Colorado-
  North Rev, Hob-Nob*

Ed Chaberek 🎤 ✈ P
PO Box 424
Superior, MT 59872-0424, 406-822-4848
Internet: gchaberek@hotmail.com
  Pubs: *Voices From German Graveyards, Types, Vol. I*
  (Superior Poetry Pr, 2003, 1998), *The Berkshire Polish Bar*
  (Ibbetson Street Pr, 1999), *Spare Change, Midwest Qtly,
  Blue Collar Rev, Plainsongs, Superior Poetry News*

Karyn Follis Cheatham 🎤 ✈ W
PO Box 442
Helena, MT 59624
  Pubs: *Kansas Dreamer: Fury in Sumner County, Spotted
  Flower and the Ponokomita* (KAIOS Bks, 2002, 2001), *The
  Adventures of Elizabeth Fortune* (Blue Heron Publishing,
  2000), *Writers of the Gulch: Anth* (The Artist Group, 2002)

Geraldine Connolly 🎤 ✈ P
86 Romain Dr
Big Fork, MT 59911
  Pubs: *Province of Fire* (Iris Press, 1998), *Food for the
  Winter* (Purdue U Pr, 1990), *Boomer Girls: Anth* (U Iowa Pr,
  1999), *Gettysburg Rev, Prairie Schooner, Poetry, Georgia
  Review, Connecticut Rev, West Branch, Shenandoah*

Michele Corriel 🎤 ✈ P
23 Snowcrest Dr
Belgrade, MT 59714
  Pubs: *ABC No Rio: Anth* (1986), *Natl Poetry Mag of the
  Lower East Side, Manzanita Qtly, Montana Mag, Big Sky Jrnl*

James Crumley W
PO Box 9278
Missoula, MT 59807, 406-728-8602
  Pubs: *Dancing Bear, The Last Good Kiss, The Wrong Case*
  (Random Hse, 1983, 1978, 1975)

Art Cuelho, Jr. P&W
PO Box 249
Big Timber, MT 59011
  Pubs: *Fiction 100* (Macmillan, 1994), *As Far As I Can See*
  (Windflower Pr, 1989), *California Childhood* (Creative Arts
  Bks, 1989)

David Dale 🎤 ✈ P
PO Box 257
Big Arm, MT 59910, 406-849-5702
  Pubs: *Stumbling Over Stones, What We Call Our Own*
  (Wright Impressions, 2002, 1991), *Skating Backwards,
  Montana Primer, The Way a Bear Is* (Big Mountain Pub,
  1999, 1996, 1994), *Frog Pond, Portland Rev, Talking River
  Rev, Bellowing Ark, Camphorweed*

Martha Elizabeth P&W
Once Only Productions, Box 9444, Missoula, MT 59807,
406-728-8602
Internet: crumdog@aol.com
  Pubs: *The Return of Pleasure* (Confluence Pr, 1996), *Basics
  of the Dance, Inheritance of Light: Anth* (U North Texas Pr,
  1990, 1996), *Grow Old Along With Me: Anth* (Papier-Mache
  Pr, 1996), *Georgia Rev, NER, New Virginia Rev*

Pete Fromm 🎤 ✈ W
2908 3rd Ave N
Great Falls, MT 59401
  Pubs: *How All This Started, Night Swimming* (Picador 2000,
  1999), *Blood Knot, Dry Rain, Indian Creek Chronicles* (Lyons
  Pr, 1998, 1997, 1993), *Monkey Tag* (Scholastic, 1994), *The
  Tall Uncut* (John Daniel & Co, 1992), *Glimmer Train*

Marilyn Kay Giuliani P
716 S 6th W
Missoula, MT 59801
  Pubs: *Poetic Eloquence, Dreambuilding Crusade Idea
  Company, Capper's*

Patricia Goedicke 🎤 ✈ P
Univ of Montana, Creative Writing Prgrm, Missoula, MT 59812,
406-549-0343
Internet: goedicke@selway.umt.edu
  Pubs: *As Earth Begins to End* (Copper Canyon, 2000),
  Invisible Horses, Paul Bunyan's Bearskin (Milkweed, 1996,
  1992), *Denver Qtly, Yale Rev, Seneca Rev, Alaska Qtly,
  Green Mountains Rev, Hudson Rev, BPJ, Manhattan Rev,
  Gettysburg Rev*

Valerie Harms   W
PO Box 1123
Bozeman, MT 59771-1123, 406-587-3356
Internet: valerie@valerieharms.com
    Pubs: *The Inner Lover* (Aslan, 1999), *The Ecology of
Everyday Life* (Putnam, 1994)

John Holbrook 🎤 ✈   P
328 S 5th W
Missoula, MT 59801, 406-728-6223
Internet: jholbrok@mssl.uswest.net
    Pubs: *Loose Wool, River Tackle, Pencil Drafts* (Pudding
House Pubs, 2002), *Clear Water on the Swan* (Falcon Pr,
1992), *Big Sky Jrnl, Pinyon Rev, The Iconoclast, Comstock
Rev, Montana Crossroads, Kumquat Meringue, Hubbub,
SPR, Poetry NW, Kinesis, Rain City*

Lowell Jaeger   P
E Lake Shore
Bigfork, MT 59911, 406-982-3269
Internet: ljaeger@spot1.fvcc.cc.mt.us
    Pubs: *Hope Against Hope, War on War* (Utah State U Pr,
1990, 1988), *CutBank, High Plains Lit Rev, Poetry NW*

William Kittredge   W
143 S 5th E
Missoula, MT 59801, 406-549-6605
    Pubs: *Who Owns the West* (Mercury Hse, 1996), *Hole in the
Sky* (Vintage, 1993), *The Last Best Place: Anth* (Montana
Historical Society Pr, 1988), *Paris Rev*

King D. Kuka   P
907 Ave C NW
Great Falls, MT 59404, 406-452-4449

David Long   W
820 3rd Ave E
Kalispell, MT 59901, 406-755-8490
Internet: long@digisys.net
    Pubs: *The Falling Boy, Blue Spruce* (Scribner, 1997, 1995),
The Flood of '64 (Ecco, 1987), *New Yorker, GQ, Story,
Sewanee Rev, Antaeus*

Maria R. Maris   P
2332 Ash
Billings, MT 59101, 406-259-1977
    Pubs: *Plains Poetry Jrnl, The Lyric, Poet Lore, Piedmont Lit
Rev, Wind, Kansas Qtly, Z Miscellaneous*

Ruth McLaughlin   W
2506 1st Ave N
Great Falls, MT 59401
    Pubs: *Best American Short Stories: Anth* (HM, 1979),
California State Poetry Qtly

Elsie Pankowski 🎤   P
1404 11 Ave S
Great Falls, MT 59405-4632, 406-452-0127
    Pubs: *Leaning Into the Wind* (HM, 1997), *Bellowing Ark,
Midwest Qtly, Thema, Midland Rev, Birdwatcher's Digest,
Manhattan Poetry Rev, Yankee*

Greg Pape 🎤 ✈   P
English Dept, Univ Montana, Missoula, MT 59812,
406-243-5231
Internet: pape@selway.umt.edu
    Pubs: *Sunflower Facing the Sun* (U Iowa Pr, 1992), *Storm
Pattern, Black Branches, Border Crossings* (U Pitt Pr, 1992,
1984, 1978), *Atlantic, DoubleTake, Poetry*

Marnie Prange   P&W
231 Eagle's Pt
Stevensville, MT 59870, 406-777-5689
    Pubs: *Dangerous Neighborhoods* (Cleveland State Poetry
Ctr, 1994)

Lloyd Van Brunt 🎤 ✈   P&W
31 Hillside, PO Box 161
Basin, MT 59631-0161, 406-225-3577
Internet: lloyd@onewest.net
    Pubs: *Poems New & Selected 1962-1992, Working
Firewood for the Night* (The Smith, 1993, 1990), *Exquisite
Corpse, The Generalist Papers, Re-Publish, APR*

James Welch   PW
2321 Wylie St
Missoula, MT 59802, 406-549-6713
    Pubs: *The Heart Song of Charging Elk* (Doubleday, 2000),
Fools Crow (Viking, 1986)

Ivon W. White, Jr. 🎤 ✈   P
PO Box 637
Billings, MT 59103-0637, 406-245-6875
    Pubs: *Gates Left Open: Anth* (Montana Inst of the Arts,
1989), *Portable Wall, Alkali Flats, Thomas Wolfe Rev, The
Villager, Art Times*

Paul Zarzyski   P
PO Box 1315
Augusta, MT 59410, 406-453-1856
    Pubs: *Words Growing Wild* (CD; Jim Rooney Productions,
1998), *All This Way for the Short Ride* (Museum of New
Mexico Pr, 1996), *Poetry of The American West: Anth, The
Last Best Place* (U Columbia Pr, 1996, 1988), *Poetry,
Chariton Rev, Prairie Schooner*

NEBRASKA

Jonis Agee   P&W
8005 W Pioneers Blvd
Denton, NE 68339-3059
    Pubs: *South of Resurrection* (Viking, 1997), *Strange Angels, Sweet Eyes* (HC, 1994, 1992), *.38 Special & a Broken Heart, Bend This Heart* (Coffee Hse Pr, 1995, 1989)

Susan Aizenberg ♀ ✈   P
Creighton Univ - Eng Dept, 2500 California Plz, Omaha, NE 68178, 402-280-2823
    Pubs: *Muse* (Crab Orchard Series, S Illinois U Pr, 2002), *Peru* (Graywolf Pr, 1997)

Grace Bauer ♀ ✈   P
Univ of Nebraska English Dept, 202 Andrews, PO Box 880333, Lincoln, NE 68588-0333, 402-472-0993
Internet: gbauer@unlserve.unl.edu
    Pubs: *Field Guide to the Ineffable* (Snail's Pace Pr, 2000), *Women at the Well* (Portals Pr, 1998), *Where You've Seen Her* (Pennywhistle Pr, 1993), *House Where I've Never Lived* (Anabiosis Pr, 1993), *Colorado Rev, Natural Bridge, DoubleTake, ALR*

Stephen Behndart ♀ ✈   P
English Dept, Univ of Nebraska, Lincoln, NE 68588-0333, 402-472-1806
Internet: sbehrendt1@unl.edu
    Pubs: *A Step in the Dark, Instruments of the Bones* (Mid-List Pr, 1996, 1992), *Sewanee Rev, Hudson Rev, Texas Rev, Midwest Qtly*

Miriam Ben-Yaacov   P&W
1870 Mayfair Dr
Omaha, NE 68144, 402-333-1115
    Pubs: *Nexus, Short Story Intl, Nebraska English Jrnl, The Long Story, Smackwarm, Trans-Missouri Art View, Metropolitan*

Robert Beum   P
PO Box 29303
Lincoln, NE 68529, 402-466-7814
    Pubs: *A House In Milo, Inscriptions* (Dolphin Press, 2000, 2000), *Celebrations* (Armstrong State U Pr, 1987), *Poems and Epigrams* (Regnery, 1964)

J. V. Brummels ♀ ✈   P
Two Cow
Winside, NE 68790, 402-286-4891
Internet: twocow@nntc.net
    Pubs: *Cheyenne Line* (Backwaters Pr, 2000), *Clay Hills* (Nosila Pr, 1996), *Sunday's Child* (Basfal Bks, 1994), *Deus Ex Machina* (Bantam Bks, 1989), *614 Pearl* (Abattoir Edtns, 1986), *Ellipsis, Chariton Rev, Puerto del Sol, Prairie Schooner*

Roger Burkholder ♀ ✈   W
PO Box 4406
Omaha, NE 68104, 402-551-7863
www.rogerburkholder.com
    Pubs: *How Did That Sun Get Out* (Writer's Showcase, 2000)

Marilyn Dorf ♀   P
4149 "E" St
Lincoln, NE 68510, 402-489-3104
    Pubs: *This Red Hill* (Juniper Pr, 2003), *Bison Poems* (U Nebraska, 2002), *Of Hoopoes and Hummingbirds, Windmills Walk the Night* (Cricket-Ink Pr, 1998, 1992), *Willow Rev, Christian Science Monitor, Northeast, Midwest Poetry Rev, Whole Notes*

Richard Duggin   W
Writer's Workshop, Univ Nebraska, Fine Arts 223, Omaha, NE 68182, 402-554-4801
Internet: rduggin@cwis.unomaha.edu
    Pubs: *The Music Box Treaty* (Abbatoir Edtns, 1982), *Kansas Qtly, Laurel Rev, Playboy, Pulpsmith, NAR, Fiction Jrnl, ALR, Beloit, The Sun*

Lorraine Duggin ♀ ✈   P&W
932 N 74 Ave
Omaha, NE 68114-3114, 402-397-6153
    Pubs: *Nebraska Poets Calendar* (Black Star Pr, 2001, 2000), *The Heartlands Today* (Firelands Writing Ctr, 1995), *In a New Land* (Natl Textbook Co, 1992), *Boundaries of Twilight: Anth* (New Rivers Pr, 1991)

Charles Fort ♀ ✈   P
Univ of Nebraska, English Dept, Kearney, NE 68849-1320, 308-865-8164
Internet: fortc@unk.edu
    Pubs: *Darvil* (St. Andrews, 1993), *The Town Clock Burning, Carnegie Mellon Anth of Poetry* (Carnegie Mellon U Pr, 1991, 1993), *The Best of the Prose Poem: Anth* (White Pine Pr, 2000), *Best American Poetry: Anth* (Scribner, 2000)

Mark Edwin Fuehrer   P
Imperial, NE 69033, 308-882-4219

Patrick Worth Gray   P
1109 Kingston Ave
Bellevue, NE 68005, 402-292-1908
    Pubs: *Spring Comes Again to Arnett* (Mr. Cogito Pr, 1987), *Disappearances* (U Nebraska Pr, 1978)

Twyla Hansen ♀ ✈   P
4140 N 42 St Cir
Lincoln, NE 68504-1210, 402-466-5839
Internet: twylahansen@alltel.net
    Pubs: *Potato Soup* (Backwaters Pr, 2003), *Sanctuary Near Salt Creek* (Lone Willow Pr, 2001), *In Our Very Bones* (A Slow Tempo Pr, 1997), *How to Live in the Heartland* (Flatwater Edtns, 1992), *Woven on the Wind: Anth* (HM, 2000), *Prairie Schooner, Laurel Rev*

Arthur Homer ♪ ✦   P&W
Dogrose Farm, RR1, Box 76, Peru, NE 68421, 402-556-4691
Internet: ahomer@unomaha.edu
    Pubs: *The Drownt Boy* (U Missouri Pr, 1994), *Skies of Such
    Valuable Glass* (Owl Creek Pr, 1990), *Poetry, Prairie
    Schooner, Brevity, Southern Rev, Georgia Rev, NAR, The
    Sun, Green Mountains Rev*

William Kloefkorn   P
2502 N 63
Lincoln, NE 68507, 402-466-1032

Ted Kooser ♪ ✦   P
1820 Branched Oak Rd
Garland, NE 68360-9303, 402-588-2272
Internet: kr 84428@navix.net
    Pubs: *Local Wonders* (U Nebraska Pr, 2002), *Winter
    Morning Walks; 100 Postcards to Jim Harrison* (Carnegie
    Mellon Pr, 2000), *Weather Central* (U Pitt Pr, 1994),
    Atlantic, Kenyon Rev, Hudson Rev, Poetry

Greg Kosmicki ♪ ✦   P
Backwaters Press, 3502 N 52nd St, Omaha, NE
68104-3506, 402-451-4052
Internet: Gkosm62735@aol.com
    Pubs: *Greg Kosmicki: Greatest Hits 1975-2000* (Pudding
    Hse Pubs, 2001), *tables, chairs, wall, window, For My Son in
    a Motel Room* (Sandhills Pr, 2000, 1999), *nobody lives here
    who saw this sky* (Missing Spoke Pr, 1998), *How Things
    Happen* (bradypress, 1997)

Greg Kuzma   P
English Dept, Univ Nebraska, Lincoln, NE 68588
    Pubs: *Good News* (Carnegie Mellon, 1994), *Wind Rain &
    Stars & the Grass Growing* (Orchises, 1993), *TriQtly, Crazy-
    horse, Harvard Rev, Virginia Qtly, Massachusetts Rev*

Wopashitwe Mondo Eye Langa   P
PO Box 2500
Lincoln, NE 68542-2500
    Pubs: *Morning of the Bright Bird* (Third World Pr, 1992),
    *Shooting Star Qtly Rev, Nebraska Humanities, Obsidian,
    Black Scholar, Nantucket Rev, Pacifica Rev, Argo*

James Magorian   P
1225 N 46 St
Lincoln, NE 68503
    Pubs: *Hearts of Gold* (Acme Pr, 1996), *The Hideout of the
    Sigmund Freud Gang* (Black Oak Pr, 1987), *Plainsongs,
    Nebraska Rev, River Styx, Sewanee Rev, Atlanta Rev, SPR*

Mordecai Marcus   P
7920 Lillibridge St
Lincoln, NE 68506-3137, 402-488-7831
Internet: mmarcus@unlinfo.unl.edu
    Pubs: *Pursuing the Lost* (Whole Notes Pr, 1993), *Poet Lore,
    Tar River Poetry, Poet & Critic, Cats Mag, South Dakota Rev,
    Santa Barbara Rev*

Nancy McCleery ♪ ✦   P
3025 P St
Lincoln, NE 68503-3434, 402-477-8363
    Pubs: *Girl Talk* (Backwaters Pr, 2002), *Blown Roses*
    (bradypress, 2001), *Polar Lights* (Transient Pr, 1994),
    Staying the Winter (Cummington Pr, 1987), *Many Mountains
    Moving, Cafe Solo, Calyx*

Hilda Raz ♪ ✦   P
Univ of Nebraska, 201 Andrews Hall, Lincoln, NE 68588-0334,
402-472-1812
Internet: hraz1@unl.edu
    Pubs: *Trans, Divine Honors* (Wesleyan U Pr, 2001, 1997),
    The Bone Dish (State Street Pr, 1989), *Cancer in the Voices
    of Ten Women: Anth* (Pandora/HC, 1997), *Southern Rev,
    Women's Rev of Bks, Ploughshares*

James Reed ♪ ✦   W
1009 Hickory St
Omaha, NE 68108-3617, 402-345-3711
Internet: jpreed@radiks.net
    Pubs: *West Branch, Whetstone, Talking River Rev,
    Flash!Point, Apalachee Qtly, Tennessee Qtly, Aura Lit/Arts
    Rev, Carolina Qtly, Buffalo Spree, William & Mary Rev, River
    Styx, Brilliant Corners*

Roy Scheele ♪ ✦   P
2020 S 25th St
Lincoln, NE 68502-3017, 402-477-1102
Internet: rscheele@doane.edu
    Pubs: *From the Ground Up: Thirty Sonnests by Roy Scheele*
    (Lone Willow Pr, 2000), *Keeping the Horses* (Windflower Pr,
    1998), *Short Suite* (Main-Traveled Roads, 1997), *To the
    Clear Fountains: Anth* (Dolphin Pr, 2002), *The Formalist,
    Amer Scholar, Poetry*

Michael Skau ♪ ✦   P
Univ Nebraska, 60th & Dodge, English Dept, Omaha, NE
68182, 402-554-3314
Internet: mskau@mail.unomaha.edu
    Pubs: *Me & God Poems* (Bradypress, 1990), *Paintbrush,
    Kansas Qtly, Passaic Rev, Sequoia, Carolina Qtly, NW Rev,
    Cumberland Poetry Rev, Midland Rev*

James Solheim ♪ ✦   P&W
3707 S 97th St
Omaha, NE 68124-3740, 402-393-6108
jamessolheim.com
    Pubs: *It's Disgusting . . . and We Ate It* (Scholastic, 1999),
    Pushcart Prize XV: Anth (Pushcart Pr, 1991), *ACM, Poetry,
    Kenyon Rev, Iowa Rev, NW Rev, Chicago Rev, Missouri Rev,
    Cimarron Rev*

Brent Spencer ♪ ✦   P&W
Creighton Univ, English Dept, Omaha, NE 68178,
402-280-2192
Internet: spencr@creighton.edu
    Pubs: *Are We Not Men?, Lost Son* (Arcade, 1996, 1995),
    GQ, Glimmer Train, Antioch Rev, Missouri Rev, Atlantic

Don Welch 🎙 ✈   P
611 W 27 St
Kearney, NE 68847, 308-237-3861
Internet: pigeondw@aol.com
    Pubs: *Inklings* (Sandhills Pr, 2001), *A Brief History of Feathers* (Slow Tempo Pr, 1996), *Carved by Obadiah Verity* (Colorado College Pr, 1993), *Prairie Schooner, Georgia Rev, Laurel Rev*

Nancy G. Westerfield   P
505 W 22 St, #2
Kearney, NE 68847, 308-237-7107
    Pubs: *Welded Women* (Kearney State College Pr, 1983), *Prairie Schooner, Poem, Trains, Grain*

Hargis Westerfield   W
505 W 22nd St
Kearney, NE 68845-5245, 308-237-7107
    Pubs: *The Forty-First Division* (Turner Pub Co, 1993), *SW Rev, Christian Century, Saturday Rev, Trains*

Fredrick Zydek 🎙 ✈   P&W
5002 Decatur St
Omaha, NE 68104-5023, 402-551-0343
Internet: zydek007@aol.com
    Pubs: *Dreaming on the Other Side of Time* (Holmes Hse Pubs, 2002), *The Abbey Poems* (Lone Willow Pr, 1998), *Ending the Fast* (Yellow Barn Pr, 1984), *Poetry, Antioch, NER, Nimrod, Poetry NW, Prairie Schooner, SW Rev*

NEVADA

Aliki Barnstone 🎙 ✈   P
University of Nevada, Las Vegas, Department of English, Las Vegas, NV 89154-5011, 702-895-4341
Internet: aliki@nevada.edu
    Pubs: *Wild with It* (Sheep Meadow Pr, 2001), *Voices of Light: Anth* (Shambhala, 2000), *Madly in Love, Bright Snow* (Carnegie Mellon U Pr, 1997, 1997), *A Book of Women Poets from Antiquity to Now: Anth* (Random Hse, 1992), *Agni, Antioch Rev, Poetry*

J.T. Cavender 🎙 ✈   P
1950 Wren St.
Reno, NV 89509
Internet: j.t.cavender@worldnet.att.net
    Pubs: *Permafrost, Borderlands, Talking River Rev, Nassau Rev, Chaffin Jrnl, Carolina Qtly, Black Fly Rev, Panhandler, Descant*

Charles H. Crump   P
11 Condor Cir
Carson City, NV 89701, 702-883-6380
    Pubs: *Desert Wood* (U Nevada Pr, 1991), *Piedmont Literary Rev, Redneck Rev, Poultry, Manna, Silver State Quill, Bellowing Ark*

Elaine Dallman   P
PO Box 60550
Reno, NV 89506, 702-972-1671
Internet: edall@ios.com
    Pubs: *A Parallel Cut of Air* (Medallion Guild, 1996), *Woman Poet: The West* (Women in Literature, 1994), *Black Buzzard Rev, Flat Tired, Northern Contours*

John H. Irsfeld   W
Professor of English, Univ Nevada, 4505 Maryland Pkwy, Las Vegas, NV 89154, 702-895-4877
Internet: irsfeldj@nevada.edu
    Pubs: *Little Kingdom* (SMU, 1989), *Rats Alley* (U Nevada, 1987), *New Texas '91: Anth* (U North Texas Pr, 1991), *American Literary Rev, Kansas Qtly, The Writer*

Stephen Shu Ning Liu 🎙 ✈   P
4024 Deerfield Ave
Las Vegas, NV 89117-4542, 702-871-5987
    Pubs: *My Father's Martial Art* (U Nevada Pr, 1999), *Dream Journeys to China* (New World Pr, 1982)

Melanie Perish 🎙 ✈   P
Univ Nevada, College of Engineering, MS256, Reno, NV 89557, 775-784-6433
Internet: mperish@equinox.unr.edu
    Pubs: *Traveling the Distance* (Rising Tide, 1981), *Notes of a Daughter from the Old Country* (Motherroot, 1978), *Calyx, Sinister Wisdom, Desert Wood, eNVee*

George Perreault   P
3553 Arches Ct
Reno, NV 89509, 775-827-2728
Internet: gmp@unr.edu
    Pubs: *All the Verbs for Knowing* (Black Rock Pr, 2002), *Trying to Be Round* (Singular Speech Pr, 1994), *Curved Like an Eye* (Ahsahta Pr, 1994), *Jrnl of American Culture, Shenandoah, High Plains Literary Rev, NW Rev, The Lyric, Blue Mesa Rev*

Elizabeth Perry   P
PO Box 61324
Boulder City, NV 89006, 702-294-0021
Internet: peg_pub@ix.netcom.com
    Pubs: *Desert Wood* (U Nevada Pr, 1991), *Gathered Echoes* (Pegasus Pr, 1991), *Interim, Midwest Poetry Rev*

Kirk Robertson   P
PO Box 1047
Fallon, NV 89407, 775-423-1440
    Pubs: *Just Past Labor Day: New & Selected Poems* (U Nevada Pr, 1996), *Music: A Suite & 13 Songs* (Floating Island Pr, 1995), *Driving to Vegas: Poems 1969-1987* (Sun/Gemini Pr, 1989), *New Directions*

G. J. Scrimgeour   W
PO Box 2809
Reno, NV 89505, 702-786-1442
  Pubs: *A Woman of Her Times* (Putnam, 1982)

NEW HAMPSHIRE

Allan Block   P
944 Bible Hill Road
Francestown, NH 03043, 603-547-2934
  Pubs: *Unopened Mail* (Flatiron Pr, 2002), *In Noah's Wake*
  (William L. Bauhan, 1972), *Nation, Massachusetts Rev,*
  Prairie Schooner

Christopher Brookhouse   P&W
PO Box 2567
New London, NH 03257
  Pubs: *A Selfish Woman, Dear Otto* (Permanent Pr, 2001,
  1995), *Passing Game* (Safe Harbor Bks, 2000), *The Light*
  Between the Fields (Signal Pr, 1998), *Wintermute* (Dutton,
  1978)

W. E. Butts 🎤 ✈   P
827 State St #5
Portsmouth, NH 03801-4330, 603-427-6963
  Pubs: *The Required Dance* (Igneus Pr, 1990), *Magazine*
  Verse: Anth (Monitor Bks, 1997), *Atlanta Rev, Contemporary*
  Rev, Spillway, Mid-American Rev, Poet Lore, Calliope,
  Cimarron Rev, Defined Providence

Martha Carlson-Bradley 🎤 ✈   P
18 Summer St
Hillsborough, NH 03244, 603-464-4033
Internet: mcarlson@conknet.com
  Pubs: *Each Nest Full of Cries* (Adastra, 2000), *Anth of Mag*
  Verse & Yearbook of American Poetry (Monitor Bk Co,
  1997), *BPJ, Poetry East, Carolina Qtly, Calliope,*
  Chattahoochee Rev, Poets On, NER, Marlboro Rev

Dan Carr   P
PO Box 111/30 Main St
Ashuelot Village, NH 03441, 603-239-6830
  Pubs: *Intersection* (Golgonooza Letter Foundry & Pr, 1990),
  Mysteries of the Palaces of Water (Four Zoas Night Hse,
  1985), *Connecticut Poetry Rev*

Carolyn C. Carrara 🎤 ✈   P
HCR 58, Box 254
East Hebron, NH 03232, 603-744-5101
  Pubs: *California State Poetry Qtly, Underwood Rev, Blue*
  Violin, Halftones to Jubilee, Sojourner, Phoebe, Onion River
  Rev, Lucid Stone, Live Poets Society, Pebbles

Mark DeCarteret 🎤 ✈   P
106 Glengarry Dr
Stratham, NH 03885, 603-778-9960
Internet: MARKDCART@AOL.COM
  Pubs: *The Great Apology* (Oyster River Pr, 2001), *American*
  Poetry: The Next Generation: Anth (Carnegie Mellon Pr,
  2000), *Atlanta Rev, Chicago Rev, Salt Hill*

Jeannine Dobbs   P
PO Box 1076
Merrimack, NH 03054
  Pubs: *Threesome Poems* (Alice James Bks, 1976), *Ohio*
  Rev, Midwest Qtly, Shenandoah, Amicus Jrnl, Merrimack

William Doreski 🎤 ✈   P
79 Murphy Rd
Peterborough, NH 03458, 603-924-7987
Internet: wdoreski@keene.edu
  Pubs: *Suburban Light* (Cedar Hill, 1999), *Sublime of the*
  North (Frith Pr, 1998), *Pianos in the Woods* (Pygmy Forest
  Pr, 1998), *Ghost Train* (Nightshade Pr, 1991), *Cimarron Rev,*
  Swamproot, Colorado Rev, Harvard Rev, Atlanta Rev

Christopher Dornin   P
1 Appleton St
Concord, NH 03301-5942
  Pubs: *Contemporary Religious Poetry: Anth* (Paulist Pr,
  1987), *Nimrod, Plains Poetry Rev, Gamut, Mudfish, Amelia,*
  Blue Unicorn, Soundings East, Lucky Star

Merle Drown 🎤 ✈   W
60 W Parish Rd
Concord, NH 03301, 603-224-7985
Internet: drown@mediaone.net
  Pubs: *The Suburbs of Heaven* (Berkley Bks, 2001), *Plowing*
  Up a Snake (The Dial Pr, 1982), *New Hampshire College*
  Jrnl, Other Voices

Robert Dunn 🎤 ✈   P
53 Whidden St
Portsmouth, NH 03801
  Pubs: *I Hear America Singing: Sometimes It Troubles Me,*
  Under the Legislature of Stars: Anth (Oyster River Pr, 2001,
  1999) *Quo, Musa, Tendis* (Peter Randall, 1983), *Larcom*
  Rev, Black & White, Trayfull of Lab Mice, Aspect, Bellowing
  Ark, CSM

Patricia Fargnoli 🎤 ✈   P
PO Box 132
Walpole, NH 03608
Internet: arielpf123@aol.com
  Pubs: *Lives of Others* (Oyster River Pr, 2001), *Necessary*
  Light (Utah State U Pr, 1999), *SPR, Crab Orchard Rev,*
  Malahat Rev, Atlanta Rev, Laurel Rev, Indiana Rev, Poetry
  NW, Poet Lore, Spoon River Rev, Poetry, Green Mountains
  Rev, Ploughshares, Cimarron

Alice B. Fogel 🎤 ✈ P
PO Box 25
Acworth, NH 03601, 603-835-6783
Internet: fogeledson@mindspring.com
  Pubs: *I Love this Dark World, Elemental* (Zoland Bks, 1996, 1993)

Richard Frede 🎤 ✈ W
58 Concord St
Peterborough, NH 03458-1511, 603-924-6609
Internet: rfrede@frede.mv.com
  Pubs: *The Boy, Devil, And Divorce* (Pocket Bks, 1993), *The Nurses* (NAL, 1986), *Harper's, McCall's, Short Story Intl, Poetry, Fantasy & Sci Fi*

Jeff Friedman 🎤 ✈ P
PO Box 187
Hanover, NH 03755-0187, 603-643-8255
Internet: jhfriedman@hotmail.com
  Pubs: *Taking Down the Angel, Scattering the Ashes* (Carnegie Mellon Pr, 2002, 1998), *The Record-Breaking Heat Wave* (BkMk Pr, 1986), *APR, Missouri Rev, NER, Poetry, Press, Manoa, Boulevard, Antioch Rev, 5 A.M.*

Barbara Gibbs P
c/o Barbara Gibbs Golffing, 272 Middle Hancock Rd,
Peterborough, NH 03458, 603-924-3487
  Pubs: *Possibility* (w/Francis Golffing; Peter Lang, 1991), *The Meeting Place of the Colors* (Cummington Pr, 1972), *New Yorker, Yankee, Helicon 9*

Donald Hall 🎤 ✈ P&W
24 US Route 4, Eagle Pond Farm
Wilmot, NH 03287
  Pubs: *The Painted Bed, Without, Old & New Poems* (HM, 2002, 1998, 1990), *New Yorker, Atlantic, Nation, New Republic, Gettysburg Rev, Iowa Rev*

Marie Harris 🎤 ✈ P
PO Box 203
Barrington, NH 03825, 603-664-7654
Internet: isinglas@metrocast.net
  Pubs: *G is for Granite: A New Hampshire Alaphabet* (Sleeping Bear Pr, 2003), *Your Sun, Manny* (New Rivers, 1999), *Weasel in the Turkey Pen* (Hanging Loose Pr, 1992), *The Party Train, A Collection of North American Prose Poetry: Anth* (New Rivers, 1996)

Hugh Hennedy P
456 Lincoln Ave
Portsmouth, NH 03801, 603-431-2829
  Pubs: *Under the Legislature of Stars: Anth, Halcyon Time* (Oyster River Pr, 1999, 1993), *Tar River Poetry, Hawaii Rev, James Joyce Qtly, Brownstone Rev*

Elizabeth Hodges P
30 Graham Rd
Concord, NH 03301-6900
  Pubs: *A Green Place: Anth* (Delacorte Pr, 1982), *NAR, Connecticut River Rev, Greenfield Rev*

Cynthia Huntington 🎤 ✈ P
60 Lyme Rd
Hanover, NH 03755, 603-643-6232
Internet: Cynthia.Huntington@Dartmouth.edu
  Pubs: *The Radiant* (Four Way Bks, 2003), *We Have Gone to the Beach* (Alice James Bks, 1996), *The Fish-Wife* (U Hawaii Pr, 1986)

J. Kates 🎤 ✈ P
PO Box 221
Fitzwilliam, NH 03447
Internet: jkates@monad.net
  Pubs: *Under the Legislature of Stars* (Oyster River, 1999), *XY Files: Anth* (Sherman Asher, 1997), *The Gospels in Our Image: Anth* (HB, 1995), *Larcom Rev, Cream City Rev, Cyphers, Florida Rev, Mississippi Rev, Denver Qtly*

Dolores Kendrick P
Phillips Exeter Academy, Exeter, NH 03833
  Pubs: *The Women of Plums* (PEA Pr, 1991), *Columbia, Ms.*

Lawrence Kinsman 🎤 ✈ P&W
PO Box 305
Manchester, NH 03105-0305
Internet: lkinsman@minerva.nhc.edu
  Pubs: *Water from the Moon, A Well-Ordered Life* (Abelard, 1998, 1995), *Kentucky Poetry Rev, MacGuffin, Pacific Rev, New Laurel Rev*

Maxine Kumin 🎤 ✈ P&W
40 Harriman Ln
Warner, NH 03278-4300, 603-456-3709
  Pubs: *Quit Monks or Die!* (Story Line Pr, 1999), *The Long Marriage, Selected Poems 1960-1990, Connecting the Dots* (Norton, 2001, 1997, 1996)

Ron Kurz W
PO Box 164
Antrim, NH 03440, 603-588-3323
  Pubs: *Black Rococo, Lethal Gas* (M. Evans, 1976, 1974)

Nancy Lagomarsino 🎤 ✈ P
6 Brook Rd
Hanover, NH 03755, 603-643-3959
  Pubs: *The Secretary Parables, Sleep Handbook* (Alice James Bks, 1991, 1987)

Esther M. Leiper   P
Box 87
Jefferson, NH 03583, 603-586-4505
   Pubs: *The Wars of Faery* (Amelia, 1994), *Stone Country*
   (Caro-Lynn Pub, 1993), *Writer's Jrnl, North Country Weekly,*
   The Answer

P. H. Liotta   P&W
2 Coach Rd
Exeter, NH 03833
   Pubs: *Rules of Engagement* (Cleveland State U Poetry Ctr,
   1991)

Ruth Doan MacDougall 🎤   W
285 Range Rd
Center Sandwich, NH 03227, 603-284-6451
www.ruthdoanmacdougall.com
   Pubs: *Snowy, The Cheerleader* (Frigate Bks, 2002, 1998),
   Snowy (St. Martin's Pr, 1993), *A Lovely Time Was Had By*
   All (Atheneum, 1982)

Rodger Martin   P&W
Goosebrook, 54 Sargeant Camp Rd, Harrisville, NH 03450,
603-924-7342
Internet: rodgerwriter@prodigy.net
   Pubs: *Gettysburg* (Lewis, 2000), *The Nemo Poems*
   (Goosebrook, 1992), *Selected Poems of Contemporary Eu-*
   ropean & American Poets: Anth (Spring Breeze Pub, 1989),
   Granite Rev, Appalachia

Cleopatra Mathis 🎤 ✈   P
39 Carriage Lane
Hanover, NH 03755, 603-643-8381
Internet: cleopatra.mathis@dartmouth.edu
   Pubs: *What To Tip the Boatman?* (Sheep Meadow Pr, 2001),
   Guardian, The Center for Cold Weather, The Bottom Land,
   Aerial View of Louisiana (Sheep Meadow Pr, 1995, 1990,
   1983, 1980)

Bridget Mazur   W
Lebanon College, 1 Court St, Lebanon, NH 03766
   Pubs: *Iowa Rev, Shenandoah, Beloit Fiction Jrnl, Buffalo*
   Spree, Apalachee Qtly, Cimarron, Buffalo Magazine

Mekeel McBride   P
Univ New Hampshire, English Dept, Hamilton Smith, Durham,
NH 03824, 603-862-4216
   Pubs: *Red Letter Days, The Going Under of the Evening*
   Land (Carnegie Mellon U Pr, 1988, 1983)

Rollande Merz   P
Province Rd, Box 70A
Strafford, NH 03884
   Pubs: *Pictures: Life & Still Life* (Andrew Mountain Pr, 1984),
   Calliope, Bitterroot

Edith Milton   W
PO Box 237
Francestown, NH 03043-0237
   Pubs: *Best American Short Stories: Anth* (HM, 1988),
   Ploughshares, Tikkun, Witness, Yale Rev, Prairie Schooner

John Morressy 🎤 ✈   W
PO Box 33
Sullivan, NH 03445
   Pubs: *English Lite* (#31 Pr, 2002), *The Domesticated Wizard*
   (Meisha Merlin, 2002), *The Juggler* (H Holt, 1996),
   Mammoth Book of Science Fiction: Anth, Mammoth Book of
   Comic Fantasy II: Anth (Carroll & Graf, 2002, 1999)

Deborah Navas 🎤   W
1-H Bass St
Newmarket, NH 03857-1151
   Pubs: *Murdered By His Wife* (U Mass Pr, 2000), *Things We*
   Lost, Gave Away, Bought High & Sold Low (SMU Pr, 1992),
   New Fiction from New England: Anth (Yankee Bks, 1986),
   PEN Syndicated Fiction

Julia Older 🎤 ✈   P&W
PO Box 174
Hancock, NH 03449-0174
   Pubs: *The Ossabaw Book of Hours, City in the Sky* (Oyster
   River Pr, 2001, 2001), *Hermaphroditus in America, The*
   Island Queen: Celia Thaxter of the Isles of Shoals, Higher
   Latitudes (Appledore Bks, 2000, 1998, 1995), *New Yorker,*
   Nimrod

Norval Rindfleisch   W
6 Village at Maplewood
Bethlehem, NH 03574, 603-869-5737
   Pubs: *The Season of Letting Go* (Claritas Imprints, 1995), *In*
   Loveless Clarity (Ithaca Hse, 1970), *Epoch, Literary Rev,*
   Yale Literary Mag, Northern New England Rev

Rebecca Rule   W
178 Mountain Ave
Northwood, NH 03261, 603-942-8174
Internet: beckyrule@earthlink.net
   Pubs: *True Stories, Creating The Story* (w/Susan Wheeler;
   Heinemann, 2000, 1993), *The Best Revenge* (U Pr New En-
   gland, 1995), *Yankee, Echoes, Whetstone, Northern Rev*

Steve Sherman   W
PO Box 174
Hancock, NH 03449-0174, 603-525-3581
   Pubs: *Highboy, Primary Crime, The Maple Sugar Murders*
   (Appledore, 2001, 2000, 1999), *The Hangtree* (Major Bks,
   1977), *Ellery Queen*

Charles Simic   P&W
PO Box 192
Strafford, NH 03884-0192
   Pubs: *Orphan Factory* (Michigan U, 1997), *Walking the*
   Black Cat, A Wedding in Hell, The Book of Gods & Devils
   (HB, 1996, 1994, 1990), *Selected Poems* (Braziller, 1990)

Mark Smith   W
English Dept, Univ New Hampshire, Hamilton-Smith, Durham,
NH 03824, 603-862-1313
   Pubs: *Smoke Street, Doctor Blues* (Morrow, 1984, 1983),
   The Delphinium Girl (H&R, 1980)

Sidney L. Surface   P&W
17 Old Milford Rd
Brookline, NH 03033, 603-673-4943
Internet: shall@jlc.net
   Pubs: *Small Town Tales, What We Will Give Each Other*
   (Hobblebush Bks, 1997, 1993), *Dog Music: Anth* (St.
   Martin's, 1996), *L.A. Times Book Rev, Graham House Rev,
   Chattahoochee Rev, California Qtly, Hollins Critic, Midwest
   Qtly*

Parker Towle 🎤 ✈   P
836 Easton Valley Rd
Franconia, NH 03580-5407, 603-823-8157
Internet: parker.a.towle@hitchcock.org
   Pubs: *Our Places* (Andrew Mountain Pr, 1998), *Handwork*
   (Nightshade Pr, 1991), *Search for Doubloons* (Wings Pr,
   1984), *Appalachia, Blueline, Cape Rock, Calliope, Great
   River Rev, Galley Sail Rev*

Dianalee Velie 🎤 ✈   P&W
PO Box 290
Newbury, NH 03255, 603-763-8863
Internet: leeopal@aol.com
   Pubs: *Grandmother Earth VII 2001: Anth* (Grandmother
   Earth Creations, 2001), *Earth Beneath, Sky Beyond: Anth*
   (Outrider Pr, 2000), *Neovictorian/Cochlea, Half Tones to
   Jubilee, Kit-Cat Rev, A Summer's Reading, New Millennium
   Writings, Pikeville Rev*

Donald Wellman 🎤 ✈   P
21 Rockland Rd
Weare, NH 03281-4725, 603-529-1060
Internet: wellman@dwc.edu
   Pubs: *Fields* (Light & Dust, 1995), *Frames, Fields, Meanings*
   (O.ars, 1993), *Generator, Tyuonyi, Room, Puckerbrush Rev,
   O.ars, Boundary 2*

W. D. Wetherell 🎤 ✈   W
PO Box 84
Lyme, NH 03768-0084
   Pubs: *Morning* (Pantheon, 2001), *Chekhov's Sister* (Little,
   Brown, 1990)

Marc Widershien   P
Dawn Christensen, Managing Editor, Four Arts, Main St, PO
Box 641, Wilton, NH 03086
   Pubs: *Essays #0-11* (Four Arts, 1994), *Middle Journeys*
   (Northwoods Pr, 1994), *Atelier, Small Press Rev, Library
   Jrnl, New Directions, Small Mag Rev*

NEW JERSEY

Marion Arenas 🎤 ✈   P
694 Birchwood Dr
Wyckoff, NJ 07481-1007, 201-891-1051
   Pubs: *The U-U Poets: Anth* (Pudding Hse, 1996), *Life on the
   Line: Anth* (Negative Capability Pr, 1992), *Jrnl of New
   Jersey Poets, Lyric*

Sylvia Argow   P
33 Osborne ST
Bloomfield, NJ 07003-2714
   Pubs: *Poet, Bitterroot*

Renee Ashley 🎤 ✈   P&W
210 Skylands Rd
Ringwood, NJ 07456, 973-962-1142
Internet: reneea@bellatlantic.net
   Pubs: *Someplace Like This: A Novel* (The Permanent Pr,
   2003), *The Revisionist's Dream, The Various Reasons of
   Light* (Avocet Pr, 2001, 1998), *Salt* (U Wisconsin Pr, 1991),
   Writing Poems: Anth (HC, 1996), *Poetry, Bellevue Rev,
   Harvard Rev, Amer Voice*

Jay S. Auslander 🎤 ✈   P
1492 River Rd
Teaneck, NJ 07666, 201-836-1174
   Pubs: *A New Majority* (Broncho Pr, 1987), *Uncharted Lines:
   Anth* (Boaz Pub, 1999), *MacGuffin, Orphic Lute, Lucky Star,
   Blow, Connecticut River Rev, Jrnl of American Medical
   Assoc, Sonoma Mandala*

Beth Bahler   P&W
201 S Livingston, #2F
Livingston, NJ 07039
   Pubs: *Parting Gifts, Footwork, New York Times, Pinehurst
   Jrnl, Lilliput, Highlights for Children*

Neil Baldwin   P
340 Washington St
Glen Ridge, NJ 07028, 212-685-0261

Jan Barry 🎤 ✈   P
109 N Mountain Ave
Montclair, NJ 07042-2339, 973-746-5941
Internet: janbarry61@hotmail.com
   Pubs: *Times of Change: Vietnam and the 60's: Anth*
   (Perfection Learning, 2001), *From Both Sides Now: Anth*
   (Scribner, 1998), *The Vietnam War in America: Anth* (St
   Martin's, 1996), *Paterson Lit Rev, Jrnl of Amer Culture*

Lee Barwood   P&W
65 Main St
Oceanport, NJ 07757, 732-544-8547
Internet: msatter@erols.com
    Pubs: *Catfantastic V: Anth, Catfantastic III: Anth, Horse-*
    fantastic: Anth (DAW Bks, 1999, 1994, 1991), *Sisters in*
    Fantasy II: Anth (NAL, 1992), *Weirdbook, Fantasy, Ellery*
    Queen's Mag, Paradox, Haunts

Ronald D. Bascombe   P
77 Orange Road
Montclair, NJ 07042, 973-655-1809
Internet: rbascombe@usa.net
    Pubs: *Black Creation, 360 Degrees of Blackness Comin' at*
    You, The Universal Black Writer

Emily Trafford Berges 🎤   W
English Dept, New Jersey City Univ, 2039 Kennedy Blvd,
Jersey City, NJ 07305, 201-200-3100
Internet: bflorimel@aol.com
    Pubs: *The Flying Circus* (Morrow, 1985)

Laura Boss 🎤 ✈   P
Lips, PO Box 1345, Montclair, NJ 07042, 201-662-1303
Internet: LBOSS79270@aol.com
    Pubs: *Arms: New & Selected Poems* (Guernica, 1999),
    Reports from the Front (CCC, 1995), *Outsiders: Anth*
    (Milkweed, 1999), *Identity Lessons: Anth* (Penguin, 1999),
    Unsettling America: Anth (Viking/Penguin, 1995), *Abraxas,*
    Greenfield Rev, New York Times

Claude Brown   W
381 Broad St, #1605
Newark, NJ 07104

Sarah Browning 🎤 ✈   P
48 Birch Ave, #2
Princeton, NJ 08542, 609-430-9351
Internet: browning@womenarts.org
    Pubs: *Elixir, Confrontation, Midnight Mind, Apostrophe, Out*
    of Line, Flint Hills Rev, Permafrost, Borderlands, Flyway,
    Hubbub, Larcom Rev, Literary Rev, Many Mountains
    Moving, Midwest Qtly, Mudfish, Natural Bridge, NYQ,
    Peregrine, Poet Lore, Sycamore Rev

Michael E. Burczynski   P&W
909 Reed Court
Flemington, NJ 08822, 908-704-5669
Internet: mburczyn@prius.jnj.com
    Pubs: *The Kerf, Lucid Stone, Poet's Attic, Coastal Forest Rev*

Salvatore Amico M. Buttaci 🎤   P
124 Garfield Ave
Lodi, NJ 07644-1510
Internet: sambpoet@yahoo.com
    Pubs: *Labyrinth* (PWJ Pub, 2002), *Uno* (Comrade Pr, 2002),
    A Time of Trial (Hidden Brook Pr, 2002), *Greatest Hits:*
    1970-2000 (Pudding Hse Pub, 2000), *Friction Mag, Steel*
    Point Qtly, The Writer, PoetryMagazine, Bereavement Mag,
    Anemone, Black Mountain

Kevin O. Byrne 🎤 ✈   P
24 Dogwood La
New Providence, NJ 07974-1402, 908-464-2711
    Pubs: *The Panhandler, Poet & Critic, Bitterroot, CQ,*
    Cottonwood, Concerning Poetry, Wisconsin Rev

Richard Carboni   P
38 Marion Rd
Montclair, NJ 07043, 973-783-0598

Rafael Catala   P&W
Ometeca Institute, PO Box 38, New Brunswick, NJ
08903-0038, 908-435-0152
Internet: catala@mariner.rutgers.edu
    Pubs: *Escobas De Milo* (Ometeca Institute & Ventura One,
    1998), *Cuban Poets in New York: Anth* (Betania Madrid,
    1988), *Ometeca, Trasimagen, Paterson Literary Rev,*
    Realidad Aparte, Poesia De Venezuela

Roberta Chester   P
234 Passaic Ave
Passaic, NJ 07055-3603
    Pubs: *The Eloquent Edge: Anth of Maine Women Writers*
    (Acadia Pr, 1989), *Tar River Poetry*

Donna L. Clovis 🎤 ✈   P&W
PO Box 0741
Princeton Junction, NJ 08550-0741
Internet: dclovis@home.com
    Pubs: *Locket of Dreams* (Books for Black Children, 2000),
    Sound (Addison-Wesley, 1998), *Native American Storybook*
    (Cherubic Pr, 1998), *Struggles for Freedom* (Dillon Pub,
    1994), *Survival Through These Hard Times, Metamorphosis*
    (Northwoods Pr, 1991, 1988)

Robert J. Conley 🎤 ✈   P
Cherry Weiner Literary Agency, 28 Kipling Way, Manalapan,
NJ 07726, 732-446-2096
Internet: rjconley@fullnet.net
    Pubs: *Cherokee Dragon, War Woman* (St. Martin's Pr,
    2000, 1997), *Barjack, Brass* (Dorchester Pub, 2000, 1999),
    The Meade Solution (U Pr Colorado, 1998), *Mountain*
    Windsong (U Oklahoma Pr, 1992), *Nickajack* (Doubleday,
    1992), *True West*

Edmund Conti 🎤 ✈   P
79 Tulip St
Summit, NJ 07901, 908-273-7632
Internet: edmundpoet@aol.com
  Pubs: *Greatest Hits: 1980-2000* (Pudding Hse, 2000), *The Ed C. Scrolls, Eddies* (Runaway Spoon Pr, 1996, 1994), *Light, Light Year, Abbey, Lyric, Studies in Contemporary Satire, Bogg, S.L.U.G.fest*

David Cope 🎤 ✈   P
c/o Humana Press, 999 Riverview Dr, Ste #2, Totowa, NJ 07512
Internet: dcope@yahoo.com
  Pubs: *Silences for Love, Coming Home, Fragments from the Stars, On the Bridge, Quiet Lives* (Humana Pr, 1997, 1993, 1990, 1986, 1983), *Sierra, Lame Duck, Napalm Health Spa, Heaven Bone*

Steven Corbin   W
168 3rd St
Jersey City, NJ 07302-2514
  Pubs: *Fragments That Remain* (GMP Ltd, 1992), *No Easy Place to Be* (S&S, 1989), *Breaking Ice, More Like Minds, Passport 3*

Louie Crew 🎤 ✈   P
377 S Harrison St, 12D
East Orange, NJ 07018-1225, 973-395-1068
Internet: lcrew@andromeda.rutgers.edu,
http://newark.rutgers.edu/~lcrew
  Pubs: *Book of Revelations* (Integrity, 1991), *From Queen Lutibelle's Pew* (Dragon Disks, 1990), *Midnight Lessons* (Samisdat, 1987)

Paula Bramsen Cullen 🎤 ✈   P
980 Stuart Rd
Princeton, NJ 08540, 609-924-9128
Internet: cullen@eticomm.net
  Pubs: *Journey of Storms* (Millstone River Pr, 1994), *Anthology of Magazine Verse and Yearbook of American Poetry* (Monitor Bk Co, 1981), *Cimarron Rev, Kansas Qtly, Connecticut Fireside & Book Rev, Poem*

Walter Cummins   W
English Dept, Fairleigh Dickinson Univ, 285 Madison Ave,
Madison, NJ 07940, 973-443-8564
Internet: wcummins@worldnet.att.net
  Pubs: *Where We Live* (Lynx Hse Pr, 1983), *Witness* (Samisdat, 1975), *Virginia Qtly Rev, Other Voices, Laurel Rev, Confrontation, North Atlantic Rev, Connecticut Rev*

Anne E. Cusack   P
975 Garrison Ave
Teaneck, NJ 07666, 201-836-4790
  Pubs: *Chelsea, Northeast Jrnl, 13th Moon, Open Places*

Mona Da Vinci   P&W
65 Spruce St
Bloomfield, NJ 07003, 201-748-6275
  Pubs: *Out of This World, Unnatural Acts, The Herald*

Melody Davis   P&W
24 Childsworth Ave
Bernardsville, NJ 07924, 908-630-0572
Internet: melodydavis@juno.com
  Pubs: *The Center of Distance* (Nightshade Pr, 1992), *Chelsea, Brooklyn Rev, Poetry, BPJ, West Branch, Poetry NW, Verse, Sing Heavenly Muse!*

Elaine Denholtz   W
13 Birchwood Dr
Livingston, NJ 07039, 973-992-5480
  Pubs: *Playing for High Stakes* (Freundlich, 1986), *Having It Both Ways* (Stein & Day, 1981), *New Jersey, Woman, New Woman, Daily Record*

Emanuel Di Pasquale   P
392 Ocean Ave, #1G
Long Branch, NJ 07740, 908-222-6313
  Pubs: *Genesis* (Jostro, 1997), *Literature* (HC, 1993), *Men of Our Time* (Georgia U Pr, 1991), *APR, Sewanee Rev, Nation, NYQ, New York Times*

Concetta Mary Diana 🎤 ✈   P
1405 Cypress Ln
East Brunswick, NJ 08816
Internet: poetess27@aol.com
  Pubs: *Is That You My God?* (Zinnia Bks, 1997)

George-Therese Dickenson   P
125 Rock Lodge Rd
Stockholm, NJ 07460-1148
  Pubs: *Candles Burn in Memory Town* (Segue, 1988), *Transducing* (Roof, 1985), *Tricycle, Big Allis, Assassin, Amsterdam News, The World, Annoi*

Juditha Dowd   P
440 Rosemont Ringoes Rd
Stockton, NJ 08559, 908-439-2144
  Pubs: *Earth's Daughters, Black Fly Rev, California Qtly, Jrnl of New Jersey Poets, U.S. 1 Worksheets, Footwork, Kelsey Rev, Exit 13*

John Drexel 🎤 ✈   P
42 Edgewood Rd
Glen Ridge, NJ 07028, 973-680-8834
Internet: castlepoet@yahoo.com
  Pubs: *A Fine Excess: Anth* (Sarabande Bks, 2001), *U.S. 1 Worksheets, Paris Rev, Acumen, Verse, Seneca Rev, Illuminations, Oxford Poetry, Southern Rev, Hudson Rev, Outposts, Image, Salmagundi, First Things*

Rosalyn Drexler 🎤 ✈   P&W
60 Union St #1S
Newark, NJ 07105-1430
Internet: watch2@earthlink.net
    Pubs: *Art Does "Not!" Exist* (Fiction Collective 2, 1996)

Sandra R. Duguid 🎤 ✈   P
114 Forest Ave
West Caldwell, NJ 07006, 973-226-1096
    Pubs: *America, Jrnl of New Jersey Poets, Anglican
    Theological Rev, Earth's Daughters, Modern Poetry Studies,
    West Branch*

Lora Dunetz 🎤   P
PO Box 113
Whiting, NJ 08759, 732-350-9236
    Pubs: *To Guard Your Sleep & Other Poems* (Icarus, 1987),
    *Anth of American Mag Verse 1997, Hellas, Without Halos,
    Blue Unicorn, Ararat, Amelia, Baltimore Rev, New Renais-
    sance, Arkansas Rev*

Stephen Dunn 🎤 ✈   P
Richard Stockton College
Pomona, NJ 08240, 609-652-4354
Internet: sdunn55643@aol.com
    Pubs: *Different Hours, Riffs & Reciprocities, Loosestrife,
    New & Selected Poems: 1974-1994, Landscape at the End
    of the Century, Between Angels* (Norton, 2000, 1998, 1996,
    1994, 1991, 1989)

Valerie L. Egar 🎤 ✈   P
40 Fern Ridge Ln
Titusville, NJ 08560, 609-737-0682
    Pubs: *River Styx, Lullwater Review, Poetry Northwest,
    Kalliope, Flyway*

Wendy Einhorn   P
234 Passaic Ave
Passaic, NJ 07055
    Pubs: *Do Not Say That She Is Happy Being Crazy* (Einhorn,
    1975), *New Maine Writing, Kennebec*

Pamela Brett Erens 🎤 ✈   P&W
44 Curtiss Pl
Maplewood, NJ 07040, 973-762-6476
Internet: erens1@aol.com
    Pubs: *Chicago Rev, Lit Rev, Boston Rev, Bellingham Rev,
    ACM, No Roses Rev*

K. S. Ernst   P
13 Yard Ave
Farmingdale, NJ 07727, 908-938-4297
    Pubs: *Sequencing* (Xerox Sutra Edtns, 1984), *Interstate,
    Earth's Daughters, Lost & Found Times*

Karen Ethelsdattar 🎤 ✈   P
229 Ogden Ave
Jersey City, NJ 07307, 201-653-3523
Internet: ethelsdatr@aol.com
    Pubs: *The Cat Poems* (Linden Pr, 2002), *Earthwalking &
    Other Poems* (Xlibris, 2001), *Proposing on the Brooklyn
    Bridge: Anth, To Love One Another: Anth* (Poetworks, 2003,
    2002), *We Used to Be Wives: Anth* (Fithian Pr, 2002), *Inside
    Grief: Anth* (Wise Pr, 2001)

Prescott Evarts, Jr.   P
19 Linden Ave
West Long Branch, NJ 07764, 201-222-4205
    Pubs: *Harvard Mag, Hudson Rev, Cimarron Rev, Nebraska
    Rev, BPJ, Kansas Qtly*

Firth Haring Fabend   W
54 Elston Rd
Upper Montclair, NJ 07043, 201-746-5336
    Pubs: *A Dutch Family in the Middle Colonies, 1660-1800*
    (Rutgers U, 1991)

John L. Falk 🎤 ✈   P
8 Fieldston Rd
Princeton, NJ 08540-6416, 609-452-1977
Internet: johnlfalk@comcast.net
    Pubs: *Snow & Other Guises* (Guernica Edtns, 2000),
    Antigonish Rev, Osiris, Prism Intl, Visions Intl

Sean-Thomas Farragher   P
160 Bergen Ave
Ridgefield Park, NJ 07660, 201-248-2688
Internet: www.seanfarragher.com
    Pubs: *Modern Rivers, Taxi Murders Sextet Vol. V Christina*
    (Hudson River Pr, 1998, 1997), *Bluestones & Salthay: Anth*
    (Rutgers U Pr, 1990), *Home Planet News, Dublin Mag, Jrnl
    of New Jersey Poets, Hipnosis, BPJ*

Patricia Fillingham   P
29 S Valley Rd
West Orange, NJ 07052, 973-731-9269
    Pubs: *Report to the Interim Shareholders, John Calvin*
    (Warthog Pr, 1991, 1988)

Bernadine Fillmore   PP
8 Vincent Court #1A
Newark, NJ 07105
    Pubs: *Safe Haven Community Center, House of Bishops,
    Mental Health Assoc, Here Come the Poets*

Frank Finale 🎤 ✈   P
19 Quail Run
Bayville, NJ 08721-1376, 732-237-0776
Internet: ffinale@aol.com
    Pubs: *To the Shore Once More* (Jersey Shore Pubs, 2002,
    2000, 1999), *Tree Stories: Anth* (SunShine Pr Pubs, 2002),
    Identity Lessons: Anth (Penguin, 1999), *Shore Stories: Anth,
    Under a Gull's Wing: Anth* (Down the Shore Pub, 1998,
    1996), *the new renaissance*

Patricia Ellen Flinn W
PO Box 2
Gillette, NJ 07933
    Pubs: *Loss of the Ground-Note: Anth* (Clothespin Fever Pr,
    1992), *Lynx Eye, Lullwater Rev, Alabama Literary Rev, Mind
    in Motion, Portable Wall, Portland Rev*

Nancy Flynn P&W
c/o Paul Reese, 115 Mine Hill Rd, Hackettstown, NJ 07840,
201-852-5912
    Pubs: *Room, Because You Talk, Gallery Works, Minotaur,
    Anthropology of Work Rev, Center*

Edward Foster P
Talisman House Publishers, PO Box 3157, Jersey City, NJ
07303-3157, 201-938-0698
    Pubs: *The Boy in the Key of E* (Goats & Compasses, 1998),
    All Acts Are Simply Acts (Rodent Pr, 1995), *The
    Understanding* (Texture Pr, 1994), *Boston Book Rev, River
    City, Bombay Gin, Five Fingers Rev, Boxkite, Amer Letters &
    Commentary*

Hanna Fox W
Fox Associates, 175 Hamilton Ave, Princeton, NJ 08540-3857,
609-924-2990
Internet: foxly@aol.com
    Pubs: *Transatlantic Rev, Jewish Frontier, Jewish Roots,
    Kelsey Rev*

Sheldon Frank W
221 Jackson St, #9J
Hoboken, NJ 07030, 201-653-7534

Thomas Friedmann 🎤 ✈ W
The Writer's Workbench, PO Box 117, Marlboro, NJ 07746
    Pubs: *Skills in Sequence* (St. Martin's Pr, 1988), *Damaged
    Goods* (Permanent Pr, 1984), *Footworks*

Sondra Gash 🎤 P
82 Martins La
Berkeley Heights, NJ 07922, 908-464-6780
Internet: sondraregine@comcast.net
    Pubs: *Silk Elegy* (Cavankerry Pr, 2002), *Calyx, U.S. 1
    Worksheets, Paterson Lit Rev*

Dan Georgakas P&W
Smyra Press, PO Box 1151, Union City, NJ 07087-1151
    Pubs: *New to North America* (Burning Bush, 1997),
    Solidarity Forever (Lake View Pr, 1985), *Greece in Print,
    Greek American, Greek Star, Mr. Cogito, Odyssey Mag*

Emery George 🎤 ✈ P
16 Buckingham Ave
Trenton, NJ 08618-3312, 609-984-8375
    Pubs: *A Year in Poetry: Anth* (Crown Pubs, 1995),
    Contemporary East European Poetry: Anth (Oxford U Pr,
    1993), *Blue Unicorn, Denver Qtly, Partisan Rev, Jrnl of New
    Jersey Poets*

Richard Gessner P&W
PO Box 661
Montclair, NJ 07042-0661, 201-744-1744
    Pubs: *Excerpts from the Diary of a Neanderthal Dilettante &
    the Man in the Couch* (Bombshelter, 1991), *Air Fish: Anth*
    (Cat's Eye Bks, 1993), *Happy, The Pannus Index, Java
    Snob, Devil Blossoms, Raw Vision*

Janet Frances Gibbs 🎤 ✈ P&W
39 Tiffany Dr
East Hanover, NJ 07936-2517, 973-386-8987
Internet: coner5039@aol.com
    Pubs: *Past & Promise: Women of New Jersey: Anth*
    (Scarecrow Pr, 1990), *Bitterroot, Sandsounds, Footworks*

Maria Mazziotti Gillan 🎤 ✈ P
40 Post Ave
Hawthorne, NJ 07506, 201-423-2921
www.pccc.cc.nj.us/Poetry
    Pubs: *Things My Mother Told Me, Where I Come From*
    (Guernica Edtns, 1999, 1995), *Identity Lessons: Anth,
    Growing Up Ethnic in America: Anth* (Penguin/Putnam,
    1999, 1999), *Unsettling America: Anth* (Viking, 1994), *New
    Myths, Borderlands*

Martin Golan 🎤 ✈ P&W
196 Inwood Ave
Upper Montclair, NJ 07043-1947
Internet: mgolan@softhome.net
    Pubs: *My Wife's Last Lover* (Creative Arts, 2000), *Bitterroot,
    Poet Lore, Lit Rev*

Edward M. Goldman 🎤 P
43 W 32 St
Bayonne, NJ 07002, 201-436-4796
    Pubs: *Emes Mit Poemes* (Chortelach Pr, 1992), *Frost in
    Spring: Anth, Celebrating T.S. Eliot: Anth* (Wyndham Hall Pr,
    1989, 1988)

Marion Goldstein P
84 Highland Ave
Montclair, NJ 07042-1910, 973-746-0726
Internet: miggold@aol.com
    Pubs: *The Tie That Binds: Anth* (Papier-Mache Pr, 1988),
    CSM, Pivot, Croton Rev

Roger Granet 🎤 ✈ P
261 James St, Ste 2E
Morristown, NJ 07960-6348, 973-540-9490
Internet: RBG@aol.com
    Pubs: *Museum of Dreams* (Ross-Hunt Pub, 1999), *The
    World's a Small Town* (Negative Capability Pr, 1993)

Max Greenberg P
127 Aycrigg Ave
Passaic, NJ 07055, 201-778-0937
    Pubs: *Country of the Old* (Chrysalis Pr, 1982), *Present Tense*

Patricia Celley Groth 🎤 ✈   P
Tree House Press, Inc., PO Box 268, Ringoes, NJ 08551,
908-806-3446
Internet: 102741.11611@compuserve.com
    Pubs: *The Gods' Eyes, Different Latitude: Anth* (DVP, 1998,
    1998), *Before the Beginning* (Belle Pr, 1987), *U.S. 1*
    Worksheets, Jrnl of New Jersey Poets, Paterson Lit Rev,
    Encore, Stone Country

James Haba 🎤 ✈   P
436 E Mountain Rd
Hillsborough, NJ 08844, 908-874-6209
Internet: jehaba@earthlink.net
    Pubs: *Ten Love Poems* (Ally Pr, 1981), *Jrnl of New Jersey*
    Poets, Paterson Lit Rev, U.S. 1 Worksheets, Sunrust,
    George Washington Rev

Daniel Halpern   P
100 W Broad St
Hopewell, NJ 08525
    Pubs: *Selected Poems, Foreign Neon* (Knopf, 1994, 1991),
    Tango, Seasonal Rights, The Art of the Tale: Anth (Viking,
    1987, 1982, 1986)

Therese Halscheid 🎤 ✈   P
1143 Mt Vernon Ave
Haddonfield, NJ 08033, 856-428-0232
Internet: thalscheid@hotmail.com
    Pubs: *Without Home* (Kells Media Group, 2001), *White*
    Pelican Rev, New Millennium Writings, Midwest Qtly,
    Paterson Lit Rev, Spindrift, Lullwater Rev, Grasslands Rev

Patrick Hammer, Jr.   P
400 Fairview Ave, #3E
Fort Lee, NJ 07024, 201-585-0435
    Pubs: *Elements* (North River Pr, 1993), *The Yank: Irish*
    Poems, Coming to Light (Sub Rosa Pr, 1989, 1987), *Poet,*
    North River Rev

Joan Cusack Handler 🎤 ✈   P
6 Horizon Rd
Fort Lee, NJ 07024-6652, 201-224-9653
Internet: cavankerry@mindspring.com
    Pubs: *Westview, Southern Humanities Rev, Poetry East,*
    Agni, Painted Bride Qtly, Feminist Studies, Confrontation,
    Kalliope, Madison Rev, Negative Capability, Jrnl of New
    Jersey Poets

Terri Hardin   P
19 Morford Pl, Apt 3B
Red Bank, NJ 07701-1042, 908-530-6490
Internet: terrih1742@aol.com
    Pubs: *Nimue* (Guignol Bks, 1984), *Cuz I & II, Dyslexia*

Y. L. Harris   W
23 Topeka Pass
Willingboro, NJ 08046, 609-871-5168
    Pubs: *Hindu-Kush* (Ashley Bks, 1990)

Lois Marie Harrod 🎤 ✈   P
111 Taylor Terr
Hopewell, NJ 08525, 609-466-1945
Internet: lmharrod@worldnet.att.net
    Pubs: *Spelling the World Backwards, This Is a Story You*
    Already Know, Part of the Deeper Sea (Palanquin U Pr of
    South Carolina, 2000, 1999, 1997), *Cool Women Vol II & I:*
    Anths (Cool Women Pr, 2002, 2001), *Crazy Alice*

Penny Harter 🎤 ✈   P&W
From Here Press, P.O. Box 1402, Summit, NJ 07902
Internet: handh@att.net
    Pubs: *Buried in the Sky* (La Alameda Pr, 2001), *Lizard*
    Light: Poems from the Earth (Sherman Asher Pub, 1998),
    Turtle Blessing (La Alameda Pr, 1996), *Stages & Views*
    (Katydid Books, 1994), *American Nature Writing 2002: Anth*
    (Fulcrum, 2001)

Elizabeth Hartman   P
127 Westmont Ave
Haddonfield, NJ 08033-2318, 856-354-9061
Internet: r.b.hartman@worldnet.att.net
    Pubs: *Iconoclast, Nomad's Choir, Muse of Fire, Jersey*
    Woman, Poetry Scope, Midwest Poetry Rev, Encore, Day
    Tonight/Night Today, Bitterroot

Sheila Hellman   P
100 High St
Leonia, NJ 07605, 201-947-5534
    Pubs: *In the Outbook: A Dreaming* (March Street Pr, 1999)

David Sten Herrstrom 🎤 ✈   P
P.O. Box 219, 15 Farm La, Roosevelt, NJ 08555
    Pubs: *Appearing by Daylight* (Aegina Pr, 1993), *The*
    Disappearance of Jonah (Ambrosia Pr, 1989), *Footwork,*
    Nimrod, U.S. 1 Worksheets, Stone Country, Columbia, New
    River

William J. Higginson 🎤 ✈   P&W
From Here Press, PO Box 1402, Summit, NJ 07902
Internet: handh@att.net
    Pubs: *Red Fuji* (From Here Pr, 1997), *Met on the Road*
    (Press Here, 1993), *Wind in the Long Grass* (S&S, 1991),
    Haiku World: Anth (Kodansha Intl, 1996), *Center, Edge,*
    Frogpond, Modern Haiku, Still, Albatross

Mark Hillringhouse 🎤 ✈   P
428 Mountain View Rd
Englewood, NJ 07631, 201-816-1588
Internet: m.hillringhouse@worldnet.att.net
    Pubs: *Chester H. Jones Natl Poetry Winners: Anth* (Chester
    H. Jones Fdn, 1996), *Bluestones & Salthay: Anth* (Rutgers U
    Pr, 1991), *Hanging Loose, New Jersey Monthly, Literary*
    Rev, Blade, APR, Kshanti Literary Rev, Paterson Lit Rev,
    Fitzroy Dearborn

Madeline Hoffer 🎤 P&W
5 Woodview Dr
Cranbury, NJ 08512, 609-655-2774
Internet: ProfrHofr@aol.com
  Pubs: *Classical Outlook, Thema, Kelsey Rev, Conservative Rev, Exit 13, Encodings, California Qtly, This Broken Shore, Everdancing Muse, Hammers*

Jean Hollander 🎤 ✈ P
592 Provinceline Rd
Hopewell, NJ 08525
  Pubs: *Moondog* (QRL, 1996), *Crushed Into Honey* (Saturday Pr, 1986), *Sewanee Rev, American Scholar, Poem, Southern Humanities Rev*

Lew Holzman P
95 Hillside Ave
Tenafly, NJ 07670
  Pubs: *Men's Bodies, Men's Selves* (Deta, 1979), *Neo Neo Dodo, Riverrun, Film Library Qtly*

Deborah L. Humphreys 🎤 ✈ P
55 Barbara St
Newark, NJ 07105
Internet: deborahsc@aol.com
  Pubs: *Conventional Wisdom* (Salmon Poetry, 2000), *Affilia, Christianity & the Arts, U.S. 1 Worksheets*

Susan G. Jackson 🎤 ✈ P
66 Holland Rd
Far Hills, NJ 07931
Internet: sgj7@yahoo.com
  Pubs: *South Mountain: Anth* (Millburn Free Public Library, 1993), *Between Two Rivers: Anth* (From Here Pr, 1980), *Nimrod, Paterson Lit Rev*

Judah Jacobowitz 🎤 ✈ P
206 Cleveland La
Princeton, NJ 08540-9513, 732-329-6306
Internet: Bianca1@erols.com
  Pubs: *A Taste of Bonaparte* (Golden Quill Pr, 1990), *Massachusetts Rev, River City, Small Pond, Green Mountains Rev, Touchstone, Crab Creek Rev*

Dana Andrew Jennings W
34 Godfrey Rd
Montclair, NJ 07043-1330
  Pubs: *Woman of Granite* (HBJ, 1992), *Mosquito Games* (Ticknor & Fields, 1989)

Maynard Johnson P
1907 Sunset Ave
Surf City, NJ 08008, 609-361-9630
Internet: wgcl09a@prodigy.com
  Pubs: *National Poetry Jrnl, Black Bear Rev, Lehigh Valley Anth, Chester Country Anth*

Morris A. Kalmus P
c/o Yares, 227 Sandringham Rd, Cherry Hill, NJ 08003
  Pubs: *Prophetic Voices, Heartland Jrnl, Reflect, Common Ground, Poets Corner*

Edward Kaplan 🎤 ✈ P
213 Deland Ave
Cherry Hill, NJ 08034, 609-429-1836
Internet: edpicasso@aol.com
  Pubs: *Mechos* (Scotland; Glennifer Pr, 1983), *Pancratium* (Swamp Pr, 1978), *Adz, Sapiens, Sulfur, Menu, Black Box, Red Handbook II*

Jaleelah Karriem P
6907 Sussex Ave, #6907
East Orange, NJ 07018, 201-672-5205
  Pubs: *a gathering of hands . . . tryin' to keep time & tryin' to make a difference* (Ngoma's Gourd, 1991), *blackbooksbulletin* (Third World, 1991), *Essence*

Adele Kenny 🎤 ✈ P
207 Coriell Ave
Fanwood, NJ 07023-1613, 908-889-7223
Internet: amkenny@worldnet.att.net
  Pubs: *Chosen Ghosts* (Muse-Pie Pr, 2001), *Photographic Cases* (Schiffer, 2001), *At the Edge of the Woods, Castles & Dragons* (Yorkshire Hse Bks/Muse-Pie Pr, 1997, 1990), *Road to the Interior: Anth* (Charles E. Tuttle, 1997), *Paterson Lit Rev*

M. Deiter Keyishian 🎤 ✈ P&W
English Dept, Fairleigh Dickinson Univ, 285 Madison Ave, Madison, NJ 07940, 973-267-7901
Internet: keyishianm@hotmail.com
  Pubs: *Lit Rev, Ararat, Laurel Rev, Arts Mag, Fiction, Massachusetts Rev*

Kathryn Kilgore P
20 Nassau St, Ste 226
Princeton, NJ 08542, 212-865-5657
Internet: kilgorekey@aol.com
  Pubs: *Something for Nothing* (Seaview Bks, 1982)

Burt Kimmelman 🎤 ✈ P
9 Lancaster Ave
Maplewood, NJ 07040, 973-763-8761
Internet: kimmelman@njit.edu
  Pubs: *The Pond at Cape May Point* (Marsh Hawk Pr, 2002), *First Life* (Jensen/Daniels, 2000), *Musaics* (Spuyten Duyvil Pr, 1992), *Mudfish, First Intensity, Pequod, Poetry NY, Sagetrieb, Talisman, House Organ*

Kinni Kinnict P
113 Clover St
Mt Holly, NJ 08060
  Pubs: *Crosscurrents, Archer, The Poet, Touchstone, San Fernando Poetry Jrnl, Undinal Songs*

Nicholas Kolumban 🎤 ✈   P
150 W Summit St
Somerville, NJ 08876, 201-526-0682
     Pubs: *Flares at Dusk* (Szephalom Pr, 2001), *The Science of
     In-Between, Surgery on My Soul* (Box Turtle Pr, 1999,
     1996), *Antioch Rev, Artful Dodge, Chariton Rev, Mudfish,
     Onthebus, Poetry East, North Dakota Qtly*

Yusef Komunyakaa   P
185 Nassau St
Princeton, NJ 08544
     Pubs: *Thieves of Paradise, Magic City, Dien Cai Dau*
     (Wesleyan, 1998, 1992, 1988), *Kenyon Rev, Vox,
     Ploughshares, Threepenny Rev, Callaloo, Colorado Rev,
     Iowa Rev*

Donna Walters Kozberg 🎤 ✈   W
45 Dug Way
Watchung, NJ 07069-6011, 908-226-1178
Internet: dmrkozberg@aol.com
     Pubs: *Forms, Cream City Rev, Junction, Wind Literary Jrnl,
     Parachute, For Art's Sake*

Erlinda V. Kravetz 🎤 ✈   W
403 Hill Ln
Leonardo, NJ 07737-1802, 732-872-1749
Internet: ekravetz@earthlink.net
     Pubs: *Philippine American Short Stories: Anth* (Giraffe Bks,
     1997), *Americas Rev, Chiricu, Maryland Rev, Rosebud,
     Taproot Literary Rev*

T. R. LaGreca   P
788 Winding Way
River Vale, NJ 07675
     Pubs: *Cover/Arts New York, Ellipsis, Albany Rev, Wisconsin
     Rev, Parting Gifts, Jrnl of New Jersey Poets*

Shirley Warren Lake   P
459 S Willow Ave
Galloway, NJ 08201-4633
     Pubs: *The Bottomfeeders, Somewhere Between, Oyster
     Creek Icebreak* (Still Waters Pr, 1995, 1991, 1989), *Jrnl of
     New Jersey Poets, Georgia Rev, Amer Writing, Cream City
     Rev*

Bulusu Lakshman 🎤 ✈   P
19 J Reading Rd
Edison, NJ 08817
Internet: balakshman@hotmail.com
     Pubs: *The Villager, The Poet's Touchstone*

Michael Lally 🎤 ✈   P&W
40 Kensington Terr
Maplewood, NJ 07040
Internet: lallyjmf@earthlink.net
     Pubs: *It Takes One to Know One, It's Not Nostalgia* (Black
     Sparrow Pr, 2001, 1999), *Of* (Quiet Liou Pr, 1999), *Can't Be
     Wrong* (Coffee Hse Pr, 1996), *Catch My Breath* (Salt Lick Pr,
     1995), *Identity Lessons: Anth* (Penguin Pr, 1999)

Donald Lawder   P
Route 4, Box 4105
Hammonton, NJ 08037
     Pubs: *Amer Scholar, The Nation, Kansas Qtly, New Yorker,
     Crazyhorse, BPJ*

Caroline Leavitt 🎤   W
PO Box 497
Hoboken, NJ 07030
Internet: theleav@aol.com
     Pubs: *Coming Back to Me* (St Martin's Pr, 2001), *Living
     Other Lives, Into Thin Air* (Warner Bks, 1995, 1993), *Family*
     (Arbor Hse, 1984), *Lifelines* (Seaview Bks, 1980), *Father:
     Anth, Forever Sisters: Anth* (Pocket Bks, 2000, 1999)

Curt Leviant 🎤 ✈   W
PO Box 1266
Edison, NJ 08818
     Pubs: *Partita in Venice* (Livingston Pr, 1999), *The Man Who
     Thought He Was Messiah* (Jewish Publishing Society,
     1990), *Zoetrope, Chariton Rev, Writers' Forum*

Joel Lewis 🎤 ✈   P
PMB 260, 409 Washington St, Hoboken, NJ 07030
Internet: penwaves@mindspring.com
     Pubs: *Vertical's Currency: New & Selected Poems* (Talisman
     House, 1999), *House Rent Boogie* (Yellow Pr, 1992)

Antoinette Libro 🎤 ✈   P
College of Communication, Rowan Univ, Mullica Hill Rd,
Glassboro, NJ 08028, 609-256-4290
Internet: libro@rowan.edu
     Pubs: *The House at the Shore* (Lincoln Springs Pr, 1997),
     Women Without Wings (Blackbird Pr, 1993), *Wedge of Light:
     Anth* (Press Here, 1999), *Identity Lessons: Anth* (Penguin
     Putnam, 1999), *Modern Haiku, Jrnl of New Jersey Poets,
     Paterson Lit Rev*

Deena Linett 🎤 ✈   P&W
English Dept, Montclair State Univ, Upper Montclair, NJ
07043, 973-655-7320
     Pubs: *Rare Earths: Poems* (BOA Edtns, 2001), *The
     Translator's Wife* (Humanities & Arts Pr, 1986), *On Common
     Ground* (SUNY Pr, 1983), *The Texas Rev, Poetry Intl,
     Comstock Rev, Two Rivers Rev, Runes, Big Muddy*

Timothy Liu 🎤 ✈   P
William Paterson Univ, 300 Pompton Rd, Wayne, NJ 07470,
973-720-3567
Internet: liut@wpunj.edu
     Pubs: *Hard Evidence, Word of Mouth: Anth* (Talisman Hse,
     2001, 2000), *Say Goodnight, Burnt Offerings* (Copper
     Canyon Pr, 1998, 1995), *Vox Angelica* (Alice James Bks,
     1992), *Grand Street, Nation, Sulfur, Volt, Ploughshares,
     TriQtly, Paris Rev, Poetry*

Diane Lockward 🎤 ✈ P
4 Midvale Ave
West Caldwell, NJ 07006-8006, 973-226-0807
Internet: dslockward@aol.com
 Pubs: *Mischief, Caprice & Other Poetic Strategies: Anth*
 (Red Hen Pr, 2002), *Against Perfection* (Poets Forum,
 1998), *North American Rev, Poetry Intl, S. Dakota Rev,
 Rattapallax, BPJ, Cumberland Poetry Rev, Free Lunch,
 Kalliope, Lit Rev, Poet Lore*

Doughtry "Doc" Long 🎤 ✈ P
67 Garfield Ave
Trenton, NJ 08609, 609-695-8462
 Pubs: *Timbuktu Blues* (Palanquin Pr, 2001), *Rules For Cool*
 (Xlibris, 2001), *A Rock Against the Wind: Anth* (Perigee Bks,
 1996), *Painted Bride Qtly, Obsidian*

Joyce Greenberg Lott 🎤 ✈ P
5 Toth La
Rocky Hill, NJ 08553, 609-921-2492
Internet: lottofjoy@aol.com
 Pubs: *A Teacher's Stories* (Boynton/Cook/Heinemann,
 1994), *The Writer's Chronicle, Cool Women: Vol 1 & 2,
 Kalliope, Writing for Our Lives, Ms., U.S. 1 Worksheets,
 English Jrnl, Jrnl of New Jersey Poets, Footwork: Paterson
 Lit Rev*

Valerie Loveland 🎤 ✈ P
98 Oak St #1414
Lindenwold, NJ 08021-2423
Internet: corvash@home.com
 Pubs: *Mad Poet's Rev, Maelstrom, Pegasus, RE:AL, Thema,
 Third Coast, Thorny Locust*

Radomir Luza, Jr. P
36 Liberty Ave #2
Jersey City, NJ 07306, 201-798-8963
Internet: radluza@aol.com
 Pubs: *Shoes in a Magazine, Broken Headlights, Airports
 and Railroads* (Pigling Bland Pr, 2000, 1997,1997), *Porch
 Light Blues* (B.T. Pubs, 1995), *This N' That, Handwriting
 from a Wounded Heart* (Dinstuhl, 1994), *Poet, New Laurel
 Rev, Anterior Bitewing, Papyrus*

Julia Macdonnell 🎤 ✈ W
211Bunce Hall, Rowan University, Mullica Hill Rd, Glassboro,
NJ 08028, 856-256-4500
Internet: CHANG@ROWAN.EDU
 Pubs: *A Year of Favor* (Morrow, 1994), *ALR, Heart Qtly,
 Larcom Rev*

Pamela Malone 🎤 ✈ P&W
169 Prospect St
Leonia, NJ 07605, 201-944-7104
Internet: pamwings@juno.com
 Pubs: *That Heaven Once Was My Hell* (Linear Arts, 2000),
 Anth of Contemporary American Poetry (Finishing Line Pr,
 1999), *Hungry Poets Cookbook: Anth* (Applezaba Pr, 1987),
 *The Sun, Chelsea, Belletrist Rev, Bellowing Ark, West
 Branch, Blue Unicorn*

Joe L. Malone 🎤 ✈ P&W
169 Prospect St
Leonia, NJ 07605, 201-944-7104
Internet: pamwings@juno.com
 Pubs: *Carmina Gaiana, Above the Salty Bay* (Linear Arts,
 2000, 1998), *Wings, Iconoclast, Brooklyn Literary Rev, Jrnl
 of New Jersey Poets, Hellas, New Press*

Charlotte Mandel 🎤 ✈ P&W
60 Pine Dr
Cedar Grove, NJ 07009, 973-256-5053
Internet: charmandel@aol.com
 Pubs: *Sight Lines* (Midmarch Arts Pr, 1998), *The Marriages
 of Jacob* (Micah Pubs, 1991), *The Life of Mary* (Saturday Pr,
 1988), *River City, Indiana Rev, Mississippi Valley Rev,
 Nimrod, Seneca Rev, New Millennium Writings*

Stanley Marcus 🎤 P
658 Valley Rd I-3
Upper Montclair, NJ 07043-1434, 973-783-7353
 Pubs: *For a Living: The Poetry of Work: Anth* (U Illinois Pr,
 1995), *Stand, Permafrost, Gun Rev, College English, Poetry
 East, Virginia Qtly Rev, Literary Rev, Denver Qtly, Prairie
 Schooner, Minnesota Rev, North Dakota Qtly*

David Matthew 🎤 ✈ P&W
East Rutherford, NJ 201-438-1658
Internet: daopen@yahoo.com
 Pubs: *New Press, Rag Shock, Up Front News, Pagan Place,
 Open Moments, Pinched Nerves, The Rift*

Cathy Mayo P
33 W Paul Ave
Trenton, NJ 08638-4513
 Pubs: *Her Soul Beneath the Bone: Anth* (U Illinois Pr, 1988),
 *Up Against the Wall Mother, Plainsongs, Tsunami, Bogg,
 Connecticut River Rev*

James T. McCartin W
Lincoln Springs Press, PO Box 269, Franklin Lakes, NJ 07417,
718-833-2036
 Pubs: *The Crazy Aunt & Other Stories* (Lincoln Springs Pr,
 1988), *Arizona Qtly, Footwork, Descant*

Florence McGinn 🎤 ✈ P
46 Featherbed La
Flemington, NJ 08822-5638, 908-782-0894
Internet: fmcginn@hcrhs.k12.nj.us
  Pubs: *Blood Trail* (Pennywhistle Pr, 2000), *Midwest Poetry Rev, Parnassus, Poetry Flash, Modern Haiku, Cicada, Eclectic Lit Forum*

Rochelle Hope Mehr P
5 Silver Spring Rd
West Orange, NJ 07052-4317, 973-731-0433
Internet: rochellemehr@hotmail.com
  Pubs: *World Healing Book: Anth, Book of Hope: Anth* (Beyond Borders, 2002, 2002), *Offerings, Concrete Wolf, Verbicide, Anthology, CER*BER*US*

Yvette Mintzer P
159 Cedar La
Princeton, NJ 08540, 609-430-9245
  Pubs: *Dreamline Express* (Inwood Pr, 1975)

Marilyn Mohr 🎤 ✈ P
109 Rynda Rd
South Orange, NJ 07079, 201-762-5403
Internet: Mmohr@klezpoets.com
  Pubs: *Satchel* (CCC, 1992), *Blood to Remember: Anth* (Texas Tech U, 1991), *Sarah's Daughters Sing: Anth* (KTAV Pub, 1990), *Medicinal Purposes, Jewish Women's Lit Annual, Lips, Noctiluca, Home Planet News*

Rory Morse P
53 Parlin Ln
Watchung, NJ 07060, 908-769-0780
  Pubs: *Golden Retriever World, Arulo, Vega, CSP World News, Hob-Nob, Wings, Night Writers, True Romance, Robin's Nest, Retriever's Qtly, Dog Song, Red Owl*

Peter E. Murphy 🎤 ✈ P
18 N Richards Ave
Ventnor, NJ 08406-2136, 609-823-5076
Internet: pembroke9@earthlink.net
  Pubs: *Yellow Silk: Anth* (Harmony Bks, 1990), *Laurel Rev, Natural Bridge, Cortland Rev, Atlanta Rev, Commonweal, Many Mountains Moving, Witness, BPJ, NYQ*

Walter Dean Myers W
2543 Kennedy Blvd
Jersey City, NJ 07304
  Pubs: *Me, Mop, & the Moondance Kid* (Delacorte Pr, 1988), *Black World, Essence, Espionage*

Murat Nemet-Nejat 🎤 ✈ P
1122 Bloomfield St
Hoboken, NJ 07030-5304, 201-420-7790
Internet: muratnn@aol.com
  Pubs: *A Blind Cat Black & Orthodoxies* (Sun & Moon Pr, 1997), *I, Orhan Veli* (Hanging Loose, 1989), *The Bridge* (Martin Brian & O'Keeffe, 1978), *Thus Spake the Corpse: Anth* (Black Sparrow Pr, 1999), *Talisman, World, Little Mag, Transfer*

Dawn O'Leary P
47 Oakwood Ave
Upper Montclair, NJ 07043, 201-783-6729
  Pubs: *Antioch Rev, Poetry NW, New Letters, Commonweal, NW Rev*

Joyce Carol Oates P&W
9 Honeybrook Dr
Princeton, NJ 08540
  Pubs: *My Heart Laid Bare, Man Crazy, We Were the Mulvaneys, A Bloodsmoor Romance* (Dutton, 1998, 1998, 1997, 1982), *Invisible Woman* (Ontario Rev Pr, 1982)

Vanessa L. Ochs W
57 Fairmount Ave
Morristown, NJ 07960, 201-984-3913
  Pubs: *Words on Fire: One Woman's Journey Into the Sacred* (HBJ, 1990)

Alicia Ostriker 🎤 ✈ P
33 Philip Dr
Princeton, NJ 08540, 609-924-5737
Internet: ostriker@rci.rutgers.edu
  Pubs: *The Volcano Sequence, The Little Space: New & Selected Poems, The Crack in Everything* (U Pitt Pr, 2002, 1998, 1996), *The Nakedness of the Fathers* (Rutgers U Pr, 1994), *Paris Rev, APR, Kenyon Rev, New Yorker, TriQtly*

Christopher Parker 🎤 ✈ P
PO Box 43206
Upper Montclair, NJ 07043, 973-509-0523
Internet: parkerc@mail.montclair.edu
  Pubs: *Newshole, Poetry NW, Jrnl of New Jersey Poets, New Jersey Poetry, Waterways, Spirit, Calliope, Footwork, Phoenix, Crazyquilt*

Angela Peluso P
180 Eagle Rock Ave #2
Roseland, NJ 07068, 973-364-9855
Internet: mrsangelkiss@hotmail.com
  Pubs: *Womansong: Anth, The Seasons of Childeren:Anth, Mind Matters Rev, Wide Open Mag*

George Pereny P
134 Van Ave
Pompton Lakes, NJ 07442, 201-831-7411
  Pubs: *New Worlds Unlimited: Anth* (Sal Buttaci, 1985), *English Jrnl, Slant, Footwork, Black Belt*

Alfred "Sonny" Piccoli PP
41 James St
Bloomfield, NJ 07003, 973-748-9856
  Pubs: *Phenomenal Lives* (1st Bks, 1997), *Municipal Access TV, NewArk Writers Collective, Franklin School, Christian Faith Center, First Congregational Church, Nuyorican Poets Cafe, Barnes & Noble*

Minnie Bruce Pratt 🎤 ✈ P
PO Box 8212
Jersey City, NJ 07308, 201-659-2326
Internet: mbpratt@earthlink.net
  Pubs: *The Dirt She Ate: Selected and New Poems, Walking Back Up Depot Street* (U Pitt Pr, 2003, 1999), *S/HE, Crime Against Nature* (Firebrand Bks, 1995, 1990), *Ploughshares, NER, Progressive, Amer Voice, Village Voice, Out/Look, TriQtly, Hungry Mind Rev*

Norman Henry Pritchard, II P
45-A Phelps Ave
New Brunswick, NJ 08901-3712
  Pubs: *Eecchhooeess* (NYU Pr, 1971), *The Matrix: Poems 1960-1970* (Doubleday, 1970), *The Chronicle of the Horse*

Rich Quatrone P
c/o Millennium Editions, PO Box 732, Spring Lake, NJ 07762
  Pubs: *Lucia's Rain* (Passaic Rev Pr, 1989), *Beehive, Aquarian, Lips, Footwork, Jrnl of New Jersey Poets, Long Shot, Steppingstones, Passaic Review, New Leaves, Phatitude, Lucid Moon, Alphabeat Soup*

Jan Emily Ramjerdi P&W
c/o Boonstra, 56 Oakwood Dr, Wayne, NJ 07470, 973-694-8197
  Pubs: *RE.LA.VIR, Degenerative Prose: Anth* (Black Ice/FC2, 1999, 1995), *Tasting Life Twice: Anth* (Avon, 1995), *Qtly West, Fiction Intl, Black Ice, The Little Mag, 13th Moon, Mid-Amer Rev, Denver Qtly*

Thomas Reiter 🎤 ✈ P
105 Sycamore St
Neptune, NJ 07753-3933, 732-922-3437
  Pubs: *Powers and Boundaries, Pearly Everlasting* (LSU Pr, 2004, 2000), *Poetry, Georgia Rev, Gettysburg Rev, NER, Ohio Rev*

Robert R. Reldan P
ACSU 62212/557463, Bag "R", Rahway, NJ 07065, 201-894-1927
members.tripod.com/~r_r_r/index.html
  Pubs: *96 Inc, Lummox Jrnl, Paterson Lit Rev, Climbing the Walls, U.S. 1 Worksheets, Kelsey Rev*

James Richardson 🎤 ✈ P
Creative Writing Program, Princeton Univ, 185 Nassau St, Princeton, NJ 08544-2095, 609-258-4712
Internet: jrich@princeton.edu
  Pubs: *Vectors: Aphorisms and Ten-Second Essays* (Ausable, 2001), *How Things Are* (Carnegie Mellon, 2000), *As If* (National Poetry Series, 1992), *Best American Poetry 2001: Anth* (Scribner, 2001)

Ruby Riemer P
Box 210, Village Rd, Green Village, NJ 07935
  Pubs: *Jrnl of New Jersey Poets, Multicultural Rev, Exquisite Corpse, Belles Lettres, SPR, Nation, Amer Book Rev, APR, Poet Lore, Anth of Mag Verse*

Ed Roberson 🎤 ✈ P
9 Edgeworth Pl
New Brunswick, NJ 08901-3021, 732-220-2920
Internet: roberson@aesop.rutgers.edu
  Pubs: *Atmosphere Conditions* (Sun & Moon Pr, 1999), *Just In/Word of Navigational Challenges* (Talisman Hse, 1998), *Voices Cast Out to Talk Us In* (U Iowa Pr, 1996)

Sarah Rodgers P
44 Wiggins St
Princeton, NJ 08540, 609-924-9448
  Pubs: *Croton Rev, Day Tonight/Night Today, Impact, Dark Horse, Chelsea, Second Coming, Urthkin*

Wilhelm Hermann Röhrs 🎤 P
Dunhill & Clark of New York, 82 Jacoby St, Maplewood, NJ 07040-3052
  Pubs: *Tears of Time, The Zeneida Cycle, Against the Tide* (Small Poetry Pr, 1998, 1996, 1994), *Mortal Truth* (Dunhill & Clark, 1987), *New Yorker, Staatszeltung, Maplewood-S Orange News Record, NAR, Cambridge Collection, Independent Rev, New Jersey Free Pr*

Martin C. Rosner 🎤 ✈ P
234 Vivien Ct
Paramus, NJ 07652-4615, 201-262-7749
Internet: roscape@aol.com
  Pubs: *The Doctor in the Night* (ABC Pub Co, 2002), *Pilgrim at Sunset* (Research Triangle Pub, 1994), *Hormones & Hyacinths* (Libra Pub, 1981), *Cape Codder, Voices Intl, New Jersey Poetry Monthly, Essence, New York Times*

Diana Kwiatkowski Rubin 🎤 ✈ P
The Cognitive Overload Press, PO Box 398, Piscataway, NJ 08855-0398
  Pubs: *A Gathered Meadow* (Prospect Pr, 2000), *Visions of Enchantment* (JVC Bks, 1991), *Poet, Touchstone, Fox Cry, Minetta Rev, Antigonish Rev, Amelia*

Frank Rubino P&W
76 High St
Bloomfield, NJ 07003, 201-667-9162
  Pubs: *Toy of the Evil Genie* (New Observations Pr, 1983), *The World*

Dorothy Rudy 🎤 ✈   P
161 W Clinton Ave
Tenafly, NJ 07670-1916, 201-569-7771
  Pubs: *Voices Through Time & Distant Places* (Willdor Pr,
  1993), *Knightscapes, Poem, Laurel Rev, Write Connection,
  Bergen Poets, Footnotes, Lips, Connection Collection*

James Ruffini   P
20 E Elro Dr
Oak Ridge, NJ 07438, 973-208-7250
  Pubs: *Against Suburbia* (Ocean Size Pr, 1991), *Busy
  Signals from the Holy City* (Sub Rosa, 1988), *Earth Bound,
  Poetry Motel, Cicada, Blank Gun Silencer*

Dorothy Ryan 🎤   P
3 N Bridge Dr
Long Valley, NJ 07853-3205, 973-584-7028
Internet: rothrite7@aol.com
  Pubs: *Animal Weaver* (Carpenter Pr, 2002), *To Love One
  Another: Anth* (Grayson Bks, 2002), *Rambunctious Rev,
  Many Mountains Moving, Parting Gifts, The Pedestal,
  America, Off the Coast, Paterson Literary Rev, CSM*

Mark SaFranko 🎤 ✈   W
5 Amherst Pl
Montclair, NJ 07043, 973-655-1645
Internet: marksafranco@yahoo.com
  Pubs: *Nerve Cowboy, Nebo, First Class, Hawaii Rev, Green
  Hills Lit Lantern, Wind, Sulphur River Lit Rev, MacGuffin,
  Footwork, NAR, New Orleans Rev, Soundings East, Art
  Times, Cimarron Rev, Pig Iron, The Panhandler, South
  Carolina Rev*

Brandi Scollins-Mantha 🎤 ✈   W
21 Prospect Ave
Plainsboro, NJ 08536
Internet: brandi.scollins@comcast.net
  Pubs: *My Intended* (Morrow, 2000), *Kelsey Rev, Pleiades,
  Folio, City Primeval*

Sylvia Semel   P
109 Oakland Ave
Somerset, NJ 08873
  Pubs: *Possession* (For Poets Only, 1988), *Innisfree,
  Modern Haiku*

Robbie Clipper Sethi 🎤 ✈   P&W
English Dept, Rider Univ, 2083 Lawrenceville Rd,
Lawrenceville, NJ 08648-3099, 609-895-5578
Internet: sethi@rider.edu
  Pubs: *The Bride Wore Red* (Picador, 1997), *Other Voices,
  Atlantic, Philadelphia Inquirer Mag, Massachusetts Rev,
  California Qtly, Wind, Ascent, Alaska Qtly Rev, Crescent
  Rev, Mademoiselle, Boulevard, Lit Rev*

Fatima Shaik 🎤 ✈   W
English Dept, St. Peter's College, 121 Glenwood Ave, Jersey
City, NJ 07306, 201-915-9325
Internet: fshaik@aol.com
  Pubs: *Melitte* (Puffin, 2000), *On Mardi Gras Day, Jazz of
  Our Street,* (Dial Bks, 1999, 1998), *Breaking Ice: Anth*
  (Viking Penguin, 1990), *Southern Rev, Tribes, Rev of
  Contemporary Fiction, Double Dealer Redux, Xavier Rev,
  Callaloo*

Harry S. Shapiro   PP
530 Upper Mountain Ave
Upper Montclair, NJ 07043
  Pubs: *Journey to Harmony* (Rachel Pub, 1984), *Spaceships
  Are Too Slow, Seeds of the Universe* (Intl Printing, 1973,
  1971), *Dream Shop*

Barry Sheinkopf 🎤 ✈   W
601 Palisade Ave
Englewood Cliffs, NJ 07632-1802, 201-567-4017
Internet: 102100.1065@compuserve.com
  Pubs: *Live from the Limelight: Selected Poems, 1973-1993*
  (Full Court Pr, 2002), *The Ivory Kitten, The Longest Odds*
  (Lynx Bks, 1990, 1989)

William Sherman 🎤 ✈   P
9300 Atlantic Ave, #218
Margate, NJ 08402-2340, 609-822-7050
  Pubs: *From the South Seas* (Roman F. Garbacik, 1997), *A
  Tale for Tusitala* (Branch Redd, 1993), *Tahitian Journals*
  (Hearing Eye, 1990), *Spanner, Fire*

Herschel Silverman 🎤 ✈   PP&P
47 E 33 St, #1
Bayonne, NJ 07002, 201-339-3880
  Pubs: *Tokyo Stroll* (Sisyphis Pr, 2002), *Bookshelf Cowboy*
  (Beehive/Arts End, 2001), *Lift Off: New and Selected Poems
  1961-2001* (Water-Row/Longshot 2002), *Outlaw Bible of
  Amer Poetry: Anth* (Thunder's Mouth Pr, 2000), *Long Shot,
  Talisman, Blue Beat Jacket*

Diane Simmons   W
9 Lancaster Ave
Maplewood, NJ 07040, 201-763-8761
Internet: simmons@admin.njit.edu
  Pubs: *Dreams Like Thunder* (Story Line Pr, 1992), *Let the
  Bastards Freeze in the Dark* (S&S, 1980), *Green Mountains
  Rev, NW Rev, Whetstone*

Ed Smith 🎤 ✈   P
1413 Winesap Dr
Manasquan, NJ 08736-4020
Internet: edsmith@lmxac.org
  Pubs: *Under a Gull's Wing: Anth* (Down the Shore, 1996),
  Bluestones & Salthay: Anth (Rutgers U Pr, 1990), *Boog City,
  Talisman, Footwork, The World*

Carol Sturm Smith 🎤 ✈ W
41 Aunt Molly Rd
Hopewell, NJ 08525, 609-466-8229
  Pubs: *Cosmic Clowns* (Subscription Edtns, 1999), *Only a
  Dream, Partners, Renewal* (Ballantine, 1984, 1982, 1982)

Elizabeth Anne Socolow P
64 Pine St
Princeton, NJ 08542-3810, 609-921-0834
Internet: elizacup@earthlink.net
  Pubs: *Laughing at Gravity, Conversations with Isaac Newton*
  (Beacon, 1988), *Bluestones & Salthay: Anth* (Rutgers U Pr,
  1990), *Michigan Qtly Rev*

Mark Sonnenfeld 🎤 ✈ P
45-08 Old Millstone Dr
East Windsor, NJ 08520-4674, 609-443-0646
www.experimentalpoet.com
  Pubs: *Independent Small Pub, Dash* (Marymark Pr, 2002,
  2001), *Sky, Washington Rev, Bathtub Gin, De'Pressed Intl,
  Lost Continent Rev, Neologisms, Suffusion, Quicksilver*

Donna Baier Stein 🎤 ✈ P&W
15 Main St, PO Box 659
Peapack, NJ 07977-0659, 908-781-7849
Internet: dbstein@aol.com
  Pubs: *I Always Meant to Tell You: Letters from Women
  Writers to Their Mothers: Anth* (S&S, 1997), *Virginia Qtly
  Rev, New York Stories, Kansas Qtly, BPJ, The Lit Rev,
  Florida Rev, Poet Lore*

Toby Stein W
45 Church St
Montclair, NJ 07042
  Pubs: *Only the Best* (Arbor Hse, 1984), *Getting Together*
  (Atheneum, 1980), *Moment, Reconstructionist*

Gerald Stern 🎤 ✈ P
89 Clinton St
Lambertville, NJ 08530-1912, 609-397-2562
  Pubs: *American Sonnets, Last Blue, This Time, Odd Mercy,
  Bread Without Sugar* (Norton, 2002, 2000, 1998, 1995, 1992)

Shane Stevens W
PO Box 1927
Hoboken, NJ 07030
  Pubs: *Hot Tickets, Jersey Tomatoes* (Arbor Hse, 1987,
  1986), *The Anvil Chorus* (Delacorte, 1985)

D. E. Steward 🎤 ✈ P&W
PO Box 1239
Princeton, NJ 08542-1239
  Pubs: *A Letter to a Writer Down the Line* (Oasis, 1987),
  Contact Inhibition (Avant, 1985), *NAR, Hawaii Rev, Chicago
  Rev, Epoch, Sulfur, Conjunctions, Temblor, Chelsea, SW
  Rev, Denver Qtly, Fiction Intl, NW Rev*

Carole Stone 🎤 ✈ P
16 Howard St
Verona, NJ 07044-1412, 973-655-7312
  Pubs: *Lime & Salt* (Carriage Hse Pr, 1997), *Orphan in the
  Movie House* (Andrew Mtn Pr, 1997), *Ravishing Disunities:
  Anth* (Wesleyan U Pr, 2000), *Anthology of Father Poems* (St.
  Martin's Pr, 1997), *BPJ, Orbis, The North, Devil's Millhopper*

Adam Szyper P
220 W Jersey St
Elizabeth, NJ 07202-1354, 908-659-0652
  Pubs: *And Suddenly Spring* (CCC, 1992), *The Current, New
  Hope Intl Writing*

Marcia Tager W
193 Elm St
Tenafly, NJ 07670
  Pubs: *Shaking Eve's Tree: Anth* (Jewish Pub, 1990), *The
  Literary Rev, North Dakota Qtly, Confrontation, Wind,
  Ascent*

Madeline Tiger 🎤 ✈ P
126 Beverly Rd
Bloomfield, NJ 07003
  Pubs: *Cutting the Pines: Selected & New Poems* (Marsh
  Hawk Pr, 2003), *White Owl* (Spuyten Duyvil, 2000), *Water
  Has No Color* (New Spirit Pr, 1992), *Mary of Migdal* (Still
  Waters Pr, 1991), *My Father's Harmonica* (Nightshade Pr,
  1991), *Sow's Ear, One Trick Pony*

Inge Trachtenberg W
288 Oakwood Rd
Englewood, NJ 07631
  Pubs: *An Arranged Marriage, So Slow the Dawning* (Norton,
  1977, 1973)

Steve Troyanovich 🎤 ✈ P
1 Pelle Ct
Florence, NJ 08518-1615, 609-499-3878
Internet: stephen.troyanovich@worldnet.att.net
  Pubs: *Dream Dealers & Other Shadows* (Triton, 1978),
  *Quarry, Argonaut, Yellow Butterfly, Abraxas, Moody Street
  Irregulars, Eric Burdon Connection*

Robert Blake Truscott P
88 Guilden St
New Brunswick, NJ 08901, 201-846-3767
  Pubs: *Cumberland Poetry Rev, Literary Rev, Virginia Qtly
  Rev, Stone Country*

Rod Tulloss P
PO Box 57
Roosevelt, NJ 08555-0057, 609-448-5096
Internet: ret@njcc.com
  Pubs: *The Machine Shuts Down* (Berkeley Poets Pr, 1982),
  Bluestones & Salthay: Anth (Rutgers U Pr, 1990), *Archae,
  U.S. 1 Worksheets, Exquisite Corpse, Nimrod*

Lois Van Houten   P
16 Harlow Cres
Fairlawn, NJ 07410
    Pubs: *Korone Women's Voices: Anth* (Womanspace Inc,
    1996), *Women & Death: Anth* (Ground Torpedo Pr, 1994),
    Footwork, Stone Country, Jrnl of New Jersey Poets

Lourdes Vázquez 🎤 ✈   P&W
Alexander Library, Rutgers Univ, 169 College Ave, New
Brunswick, NJ 08901-1063
    Pubs: *Historias de Pulgarcito* (Cultural, 1999), *La Rosa*
    Mec·nica (Huracan, 1991), *Sortilegio de Tifinagh: Anth*
    (Alcance, 1998), *Tertuliando/Hanging Out: Anth* (Santo
    Domingo; Comision Permanente de la Feria del Libro,
    1997), *Revista Casa de las Americas*

Patrick Walsh 🎤 ✈   P
321 Witherspoon St
Princeton, NJ 08540
Internet: pdwalsh67@hotmail.com
    Pubs: *Cimarron Rev, College Green, Hudson Rev, Press,*
    The Recorder, The Shop, U.S. 1

William John Watkins   P&W
The Sand Agency, 1406 Garven Ave, Ocean, NJ 07712,
201-988-2287
Internet: wwatkins@brookdale.cc.nj.us
    Pubs: *Cosmic Thunder* (Avon Bks, 1996), *Tracker: The Story*
    of Tom Brown, Jr. (Prentice-Hall, 1978), *Commonweal,*
    Asimov's, Rhino, Hellas, MacGuffin, Satire

Daniel Weeks 🎤 ✈   P
15 Sandspring Dr
Eatontown, NJ 07724, 732-389-4484
Internet: jazzlamic@aol.com
    Pubs: *Ancestral Songs* (Libra Pubs, 1992), *X Poems* (Blast
    Pr, 1991), *Blue Unicorn, Fox Cry, Cimarron Rev, Mudfish,*
    Slant, Fennel Stalk

Richard K. Weems 🎤 ✈   W
101 E Gibbsboro Rd #511
Clementon, NJ 08021-1912
Internet: richardweems@hotmail.com
    Pubs: *Best of Pif Mag Off-Line: Anth* (Fusion Pr, 1999),
    Story Bytes, Eratica, Sparks, Papyrus, New Works Rev,
    Wired Hearts, Southern Ocean Rev, Barcelona Rev, La
    Petite Zine, Oval, Beloit Fiction Jrnl, Bluff City, Mississippi
    Rev, Eclectica, Crescent Rev

Theodore Weiss 🎤 ✈   P
26 Haslet Ave
Princeton, NJ 08540, 609-921-6976
    Pubs: *Selected Poems* (TriQtly Bks, 1995), *A Sum of*
    Destructions (LSU Pr, 1994), *Collected Poems* (Macmillan,
    1990), *New Republic, Poetry, APR, Paris Rev, New*
    Criterion, Partisan Rev

Alix Weisz   P
PO Box 720
Gladstone, NJ 07934-0720, 908-879-8775
Internet: cetaitmoi@aol.com
    Pubs: *Lobotomy, Alix Poems Weisz* (New Broom Pr, 1993,
    1992), *Do You Sense an Angel: Anth* (Ashby Lane Pr, 1993),
    Fenice, Phoenix Sheets, Pegasus Rev, Iota, Whisper

Debbie Lee Wesselmann 🎤 ✈   W
19 Elm St
Hopewell, NJ 08525, 609-466-8868
Internet: dlw@trutor.net
    Pubs: *The Earth & the Sky* (SMU Pr, 1998), *Trutor & the*
    Balloonist (MacMurray & Beck, 1997), *Lit Rev, Ascent, Folio,*
    Gulf Stream Mag, Beloit Fiction Jrnl, Pennsylvania English,
    NAR, Florida Rev, Fiction, Philadelphia Inquirer

John A. Williams 🎤 ✈   P&W
693 Forest Ave
Teaneck, NJ 07666
    Pubs: *Captain Blackman, Clifford's Blues* (Coffee Hse Pr,
    2000, 1999), *Safari West* (Hochelaga Pr, 1998), *Sons of*
    Darkness, Sons of Light, (Northeastern U Pr, 1999), *Click*
    Song, The Man Who Cried I Am (Thunder's Mouth Pr,
    1987, 1985)

Meredith Sue Willis 🎤 ✈   W
311 Prospect St
South Orange, NJ 07079-1806, 973-378-8361
Internet: msuewillis@aol.com
    Pubs: *Oradell at Sea* (WVU, 2002), *Trespassers* (Hamilton
    Stone Edtns, 1997), *Marco's Monster* (HC, 1996), *In the*
    Mountains of America (Mercury Hse, 1994)

Ted Wilson   P
342 Warwick Ave
South Orange, NJ 07079, 973-763-9550
Internet: theodorel@worldnet.att.net
    Pubs: *In Defense of Mumia: Anth* (Writers & Readers, 1996),
    Amiri Baraka: The Kaleidoscope Torch: Anth (Steppingstone
    Pr, 1985), *Nobo, Drumvoices, Essence, Callaloo, Black*
    Nation

Barbara Wind 🎤 ✈   P
10 Londonderry Way
Summit, NJ 07901, 908-608-1748
Internet: barbmwind@aol.com
    Pubs: *Jacob's Angels* (Emmet Pr, 1998), *South Mountain:*
    Anth (Milburn Public Library, 1993), *Poetry Works: Anth*
    (NewArk Writers Collective, 1993), *JAMA, Footwork,*
    Whiskey Island, Negative Capability, Pleiades, Philae,
    Paterson Lit Rev

Holly Woodward 🎤 ✈   W
76 Jackson St, Apt #3
Hoboken, NJ 07030-6054
Internet: artictfox@aol.com
    Pubs: *Drunken Boat, Archipelago, Story, New Letters,*
    Chicago Rev

Michael T. Young P
219 Liberty Ave Apt 2
Jersey City, NJ 07306-4936
Internet: michaeltyoung@go.com
  Pubs: *Transcriptions of Daylight* (Rattapallax Pr, 2000),
  Because the Wind Has Questions (Somers Rocks Pr, 1997),
  *Pivot, Red Jacket, The Lyric, Hiram Poetry Rev, Birmingham
  Rev, Inkshed*

Ruth Zimmerman P
7 Marianna Pl
Morristown, NJ 07960-2708
Internet: rewritez@aol.com
  Pubs: *Winter Sun* (Carpenter Pr, 1999), *Kalliope, Verve,
  Poets Online, Thema, Dream Intl Qtly, Passages North, Jrnl
  of New Jersey Poets, Embers, Mary Jane, Yet Another
  Small Mag, The Ledge, Mediphors, Buffalo Bones,
  Sensations, Nostalgia*

Sander Zulauf ♦ ✈ P
County College of Morris, 214 Center Grove Rd, Randolph, NJ
07869, 973-328-5471
Internet: szulauf@ccm.edu
  Pubs: *Succasunna New Jersey* (Breaking Point Inc, 1987),
  The Art & Craft of Poetry: Anth (Writer's Digest, 1994),
  Editor's Choice III: Anth (Spirit That Moves Us Pr, 1991),
  *Sewanee Rev, Lips, CSM, Journal of NJ Poets, Paterson
  Lit Rev*

NEW MEXICO

Ward Abbott P
632 Adams NE
Albuquerque, NM 87110
Internet: wabbott@unm.edu

Anya Achtenberg ♦ ✈ P&W
1313 La Poblana NW
Albuquerque, NM 87107
Internet: aachtenberg@earthlink.net
  Pubs: *A Pocketful of Prose: Anth* (HRW, 1991), *Harvard Rev,
  ACM, Paterson Literary Rev, Blue Mesa Rev, New Letters*

Rudolfo Anaya ♦ ✈ W
5324 Canada Vista NW
Albuquerque, NM 87120-2412
  Pubs: *Elegy on the Death of Cesar Chavez* (Cinco Puntos
  Pr, 2000), *Farolitos for Abuelo, The Farolitos of Christmas*
  (Hyperion, 2000, 1995), *My Land Sings* (HC, 1999),
  *Shaman Winter, Rio Grande Fall, Zia Summer, Bless Me
  Ultima* (Warner)

Rudy S. Apodaca W
829 Canterbury Arc
Las Cruces, NM 88005-3715, 505-525-8421
Internet: xqx@prodigy.net
  Pubs: *The Waxen Image* (Titan Publishing Co, 1977)

Elizabeth Ayres ♦ ✈ P
PO Box 933
Abiquiu, NM 87510, 505-685-0524
Internet: eayres@creativewritingcenter.com
  Pubs: *Writing the Wave* (Putnam, 1999), *Fresh Paint: Anth*
  (Ailanthus Pr, 1978), *Malahat Rev, Aspect, Hanging Loose,
  Encore, Bitterroot*

Aztatl ♦ ✈ P&W
PO Box 8251
Albuquerque, NM 87198
Internet: aztatlxikano@hotmail.com
  Pubs: *Chicharones, Next Exit* (Chichimecatl Pr, 2002, 1999),
  Todo Nada (Red Age Unlimited Pr, 1998), *Masks, Folk
  Dances & a Whole Bunch More* (Ridgeway Pr, 1989),
  *Callaloo, California Qtly, Black Bear Rev, Poetry East,
  Gatherings*

Lee Bartlett P
Box 250, Star Rte, Placitas, NM 87043, 505-867-4891
  Pubs: *The Greenhouse Effect* (Lords of Language, 1994),
  Sagetrieb

Laura Beheler P&W
3 Placita Rafaela
Santa Fe, NM 87501-2845, 505-983-9166
  Pubs: *Clay's Tablet* (1st Bks Library, 2001), *The Snow
  Moon* (Pentland, Ltd, 1986), *Phone Calls Late at Night to
  God* (Four Winds, 1983), *The Dragon Thread* (Hystry-
  Mystry Hse Ltd, 1981), *Admit One* (Harlow, 1978),
  Alegorias (Dorrance, 1969)

Charles Greenleaf Bell P&W
1260 Canyon Rd
Santa Fe, NM 87501-6128, 505-983-6035
  Pubs: *Five Chambered Heart* (Persea, 1985), *New Yorker,
  Atlantic, Harper's*

Carol Berge P&W
2070 Calle Contento
Santa Fe, NM 87505-5406, 505-438-3979
  Pubs: *Zebras* (Tribal Center Pr, 1991), *Thus Spake the
  Corpse: Anth* (Black Sparrow Pr, 1999), *A Secret Location
  on the Lower East Side: Anth* (NYPL, 1998), *Literature: Anth*
  (St. Martin's Pr, 1998), Art & Antiques, Fiction Intl, TriQtly,
  ACM, Caprice

Stanley Berne ♦ ✈ P&W
American-Canadian Pub, Inc, PO Box 4595, Santa Fe, NM
87502-4595, 505-983-8484
  Pubs: *Legal Tender, Swimming to Significance, Gravity Drag,
  To Hell with Optimism, Every Person's Little Book of P-L-U-
  T-O-N-I-U-M* (w/Zekowski; Rising Tide, 2003, 2000, 1999,
  1996, 1992), *Living Underground: Anth* (Whitston Pr, 1999)

Mei-mei Berssenbrugge P
PO Box 831
Abiquiu, NM 87510-0831
    Pubs: *Four Year Old Girl, Sphericity* (Kelsey Street Pr, 1998,
    1993), *Empathy* (Station Hill Pr, 1988)

Sallie Bingham 🎤 ✈ W
369 Montezuma, #316
Santa Fe, NM 87501-2626, 505-989-1205
Internet: sabingham@aol.com
    Pubs: *Straight Man, Matron of Honor, Small Victories*
    (Zoland Bks, 1996, 1994, 1992), *Upstate* (Permanent Pr,
    1993), *Passion & Prejudice* (Knopf, 1989), *SW Rev, New
    Woman/New Fiction, Amicus Jrnl*

Imogene L. Bolls 🎤 ✈ P
1466 Monterey Dr.
Taos, NM 87571, 505-751-9414
Internet: ibolls@wittenberg.edu
    Pubs: *Advice for the Climb, Earthbound* (Bottom Dog, 1999,
    1989), *Glass Walker* (Cleveland State U, 1983), *Antioch Rev,
    Georgia Rev, Ohio Rev, SPR, South Dakota Rev, Texas Rev*

Robert Boswell W
New Mexico State Univ, English Dept, Box 3E, Las Cruces,
NM 88003, 505-527-2335
    Pubs: *Living to Be a Hundred, Mystery Ride, The
    Geography of Desire* (Knopf, 1994, 1993, 1989), *Iowa Rev,
    New Yorker*

John Brandi 🎤 ✈ P&W
56 Priestly Pl
Corrales, NM 87048
    Pubs: *Reflections in the Lizard's Eye* (Western Edge, 2000),
    Visits to the City of Light (Milk Pr, 2000), *Stone Garland*
    (Tooth of Time, 2000), *Weeding the Cosmos* (La Alameda,
    1998), *Heartbeat Geography* (White Pine, 1995)

Paul Bufis 🎤 ✈ P
123 1/2 Martinez St
Santa Fe, NM 87501-2219, 505-983-1951
Internet: zeebufi@interserv.com
    Pubs: *XY Files: Anth* (Sherman Asher Pub, 1997), *Saludos
    Poemas De Nuevo Mexico/Poems of New Mexico: Anth*
    (Pennywhistle Pr, 1995), *SPR, River Styx, Visions, Blue
    Unicorn, Permafrost, Rhino, Wind, Phantasm*

Barney Bush 🎤 ✈ PP&P
Box 22779
Santa Fe, NM 87502-2779, 508-289-2003
Internet: barneybush@redwinds.org
    Pubs: *By Due Process* (Selene Edizioni Pr, 2004),
    Redemption of the Serpent (Paris; Albin Michelle Pr, 2000),
    *A Sense of Journey, Left for Dead, Remake of the
    American Dream, Oyate* (CD; Paris; Nato Records, 1996,
    1995, 1994, 1989)

Laura Calvert P
1029 Guadalupe del Predo NW
Albuquerque, NM 87107, 505-345-7064
    Pubs: *Discurso Literario, Studia Mystica, The
    Backwoodsman, Southern Rev, North Dakota Rev*

Nash Candelaria W
111 E San Mateo Rd
Santa Fe, NM 87505-4721, 505-983-0795
Internet: nashcan@aol.com
    Pubs: *Uncivil Rights & Other Stories, Leonor Park* (Bilingual
    Pr, 1998, 1991), *Growing Up Latino: Anth* (Houghton Mifflin,
    1993), *Growing Up Ethnic in America: Anth* (Penguin, 1999),
    Americas Rev, Puerto del Sol, Bilingual Rev

Alvaro Cardona-Hine 🎤 ✈ P
PO Box 326
Truchas, NM 87578-0326
    Pubs: *Thirteen Tangos for Stravinsky, A History of Light*
    (Sherman Asher Pub, 1999, 1997), *A Garden of Sound*
    (Pemmican Pr, 1996), *When I Was a Father* (New Rivers Pr,
    1982), *The Half-Eaten Angel* (Nodin Pr, 1981), *American
    Writing, Chelsea*

Ioanna Carlsen 🎤 ✈ P&W
PO Box 307
Tesuque, NM 87574, 505-983-6910
    Pubs: *Saludos Poemas De Nuevo Mexico/Poems of New
    Mexico: Anth* (Pennywhistle Pr, 1995), *Beloit Poetry Jrnl,
    Glimmertrain, Poetry 180, Poetry Daily, Ploughshares, Field,
    Marlboro Rev, The Qtly, Poetry, Cafe Solo, Nimrod, Chelsea,
    Blue Mesa Rev*

Christine Cassidy P
369 Montezuma, Ste 158
Santa Fe, NM 87501, 505-986-1953
Internet: cccassidy@aol.com
    Pubs: *First Time Ever: Anth* (Naiad Pr, 1995), *Persistent
    Desire: Anth* (Alyson, 1992), *Lambda Book Report, Mudfish,
    BPJ, Chalk Circle*

Susan Chapman P
5801 Lowell St NE, #5A
Albuquerque, NM 87111
    Pubs: *Conversations with Dracaena* (Word Merchant Pr,
    1982), *The Spirit That Wants Me: Anth* (Duff, 1991), *Haiku
    Qtly, Pudding Mag, Frogpond*

James Colbert W
Dept of English Language and Literature, Univ New Mexico,
Humanities Bldg 217, Albuquerque, NM 87131-1106,
505-277-6347
Internet: colbert@unm.edu
    Pubs: *God Bless the Child, All I Have Is Blue, Skinny Man*
    (MacMillan, 1993, 1992, 1990), *No Special Hurry, Profit &
    Sheen* (HM, 1988, 1986)

Joseph L. Concha P
c/o Mr. & Mrs. Alex Concha, Box 1184, Taos, NM 87571

Michele Connelly P
PO Box 28
Coyote, NM 87012
    Pubs: *Rebirth of Power: Anth* (Mother Courage, 1987),
*Hudson Valley Writers' Ctr River Anth, Reed Mag, High
Country News, Sinister Wisdom, Swamproot*

Sheila Cowing 🎤 ✈ P
5 Bonito Rd
Santa Fe, NM 87505-8793, 505-466-4163
    Pubs: *Stronger in the Broken Places* (Sherman Asher,
1999), *Living in Storms: Anth* (Purdue U Pr, 2000),
Saludasi: Anth (Pennywhistle, 1996), *Chattahoochee Rev,
Warren Wilson Rev, Georgia Rev, Dalhousie Rev, Mid-
American Rev, New Laurel Rev, MacGuffin*

Stanley Crawford 🎤 ✈ W
PO Box 56
Dixon, NM 87527-0056, 505-579-4288
Internet: scrawford@newmexico.com
    Pubs: *The River in Winter: New & Selected Essays* (Univ of
New Mexico Pr, 2003), *A Garlic Testament* (HC, 1992),
Mayordomo (U New Mexico Pr, 1988), *Some Instructions*
(Knopf, 1978)

Judson Crews W
2323 Kathryn SE, #531
Albuquerque, NM 87106-3456, 505-266-2938
    Pubs: *The Brave Wild Coast* (Dumont Pr, 1997), *The Clock
of Moss* (Ahsahta Pr, 1983), *Wormwood Rev, New York Rev,
Xib, Burning World, Zen Tattoo, Atom Mind*

Richard Currey W
160 Washington SE, #185
Albuquerque, NM 87108, 505-255-9801
    Pubs: *Lost Highway, Fatal Light* (HM, 1997, 1997), *The Wars
of Heaven* (Vintage, 1991), *Witness, NAR, Utne Reader*

R. P. Dickey 🎤 ✈ P&W
PO Box 87
Ranchos de Taos, NM 87557-0087
    Pubs: *Collected Poems, The Way of Eternal Recurrence*
(21st Century Pr, 1999, 1994), *The Little Book on Racism &
Politics* (Mohualu Pr, 1990), *New Yorker, Atlantic, Poetry*

John Duncklee 🎤 ✈ P&W
1201 2nd St.
Las Cruces, NM 88005
Internet: jpduncklee@earthlink.net
    Pubs: *Manchado and His Friends, Peach Trees* (Barbed
Wire Pub, 2002, 2001), *Double Vengeance, Graciela of the
Border, Genevieve of Tombstone,* (Dorchester Pub, 2001),
Quest for the Eagle Feather (Northland Pub, 1997)

Howard Faerstein 🎤 ✈ P
PO Box 748
Arroyo Seco, NM 87514
Internet: hfaerstein@aol.com
    Pubs: *Diner, Chiron Rev, Larcom Rev, Downtown Brooklyn,
Pegasus, Pine Island Jrnl, West Wind Rev, Confrontation,
Painted Bride Qtly, Berkshire Rev*

Thomas Fitzsimmons 🎤 ✈ P
1 Balsa Rd
Santa Fe, NM 87508, 505-466-9909
    Pubs: *Iron Harp* (La Alameda Pr, 1999), *The Dream Machine*
(Pennywhistle Pr, 1996), *Water Ground Stone, The New
Poetry of Japan: Anth* (Katydid Bks/U Hawaii Pr, 1992, 1993)

Phillip Foss P
PO Box 1322
San Juan Pueblo, NM 87566-1322
    Pubs: *Venaculture* (Jensen/Daniels, 1999), *Chromatic
Defacement* (Chax Pr, 1998), *Courtesan of Seizure, The
Excesses, The Caprices* (Light & Dust Bks, 1993, 1990),
Tyuonyi, Conjunctions, Avec, Sulfur, Hambone

Gene Frumkin 🎤 ✈ P&W
3721 Mesa Verde NE
Albuquerque, NM 87110-7723, 505-266-1319
    Pubs: *The Old Man Who Swam Away & Left Only His Wet
Feet* (La Alameda Pr, 1998) *Saturn Is Mostly Weather*
(Cinco Puntos Pr, 1992), *Comma in the Ear* (Living Batch,
1990), *Paris Rev, Manoa, Prairie Schooner*

Carl Ginsburg P
3212 Monte Vista NE
Albuquerque, NM 87106, 505-266-6699
    Pubs: *Medicine Journeys: Ten Stories* (Center Pr, 1991),
The Spirit That Wants Me: A New Mexico Anth (Duff, 1991),
Southwest Discovery

Larry Goodell 🎤 ✈ PP&P
PO Box 571
Placitas, NM 87043, 505-867-5877
Internet: larryg@nmia.com
    Pubs: *Samurai Dog Biscuits* (Duende Pr, 2002), *The Bonk
of Phooey* (Dirge Pr, 2001), *From Here on Earth: A Book
of Sonnets* (Alameda Pr, 1996), *Out of Secrecy* (YooHoo
Pr, 1992), *New Mexico Poetry Renaissance: Anth* (Red
Crane, 1994)

MacDonnell Gordon P
1026 Governor Dempsey
Santa Fe, NM 87501
    Pubs: *Loon, Road Apple Rev, Greenfield Rev, Alembic,
Hard Pressed, Cedar Rock, Blue Buildings*

Becky Hagenston   W
2510 S Espina St #4B
Las Cruces, NM 88001, 505-541-9313
    Pubs: *A Gram of Mars* (Sarabande Bks, 1999), *Prize
    Stories: Anth* (Doubleday, 1996), *Shenandoah, Crescent
    Rev, Press, Antietam Rev, Carolina Qtly, Folio, TriQtly,
    Witness, Southern Rev*

Nancy Harrison ♪ ✈   P&W
PO Box 227
Ocate, NM 87734, 505-666-2519
    Internet: naranhill@nmt.net
    Pubs: *Powers of Desire: Anth* (Monthly Rev Pr, 1983),
    Fiction & Poetry by Texas Women: Anth (Texas Center for
    Writers Pr, 1975), *Feminary, Sinister Wisdom, Kalliope*

Nancy Peters Hastings   P
PO Box 1374
Las Cruces, NM 88004, 505-382-7446
    Pubs: *A Quiet I Carry with Me* (A Slow Tempo Pr, 1994),
    The Spirit That Wants Me: Anth (Duff, 1988), *Kansas Qtly,
    Poetry, Prairie Schooner, Connecticut River Rev*

Mary Rising Higgins ♪ ✈   P
801 Malachite Dr SW
Albuquerque, NM 87121
    Internet: mrhigns@tvi.cc.nm.us
    Pubs: *locus TIDES, OCLOCK* (Potes & Poets Pr, 2002,
    2000), *red tables* (La Alameda Pr, 1999), *Kenning, No
    Roses Rev, O.ars, Tyuoni, Denver Qtly, Big Allis, Hambone,
    Central Park*

Judyth Hill ♪ ✈   P
HC 69 Box 20-H
Sapello, NM 87745-9602, 505-454-9628
    Internet: rockmirth@cybermesa.com
    Pubs: *Black Hollyhock, First Light* (La Alameda Pr, 2000),
    Men Need Space, A Presence of Angels (Sherman Asher
    Pubs, 1996, 1995), *Altar of the Ordinary* (Ya-Hoo Pr, 1993),
    Goddess Cafe (Fish Drum, 1990)

Suzanne Marie Hobbs   P
4805 Downey St NE
Albuquerque, NM 87109, 505-296-4662

J. R. Humphreys   W
Box 5461
Santa Fe, NM 87502, 505-983-5685
    Pubs: *Maya Red* (Cane Hill, 1989), *Timeless Towns &
    Haunted Places* (St. Martin's, 1989), *Chelsea*

Kelley Reynolds Jacquez ♪ ✈   W
841 Camino Vistas Encantada
Sante Fe, NM 87507, 505-424-6020
    Pubs: *Fantasmas: Anth* (Bilingual Pr, 2000), *Walking the
    Twilight II: Anth* (Northland Pub, 1996), *Eratica, Writing for
    Our Lives*

David Johnson   P
1025 Summit NE
Albuquerque, NM 87106, 505-266-9960
    Pubs: *Fire in the Fields* (Writers on the Plains, 1996),
    Western Literature in a World Context: Anth (St. Martin's Pr,
    1995), *Puerto del Sol, Cafe Solo*

Don Kurtz   W
PO Box 4182
Las Cruces, NM 88003, 505-521-4832
    Internet: donkurtz@nmsu.edu
    Pubs: *South of the Big Four* (Avon, 1996), *O. Henry Festival
    Stories: Anth* (Trans-Verse Pr, 1987), *Iowa Rev, Puerto del
    Sol, Epoch*

Elizabeth Searle Lamb   P
970 Acequia Madre
Santa Fe, NM 87501-2819, 505-982-8890
    Pubs: *Across the Windharp* (La Alameda Pr, 1999), *Casting
    Into a Cloud* (From Here Pr, 1985), *Zen Poems: Anth* (MQ
    Pub Ltd, 2002), *How to Haiku: Anth* (Tuttle, 2002), *Haiku
    Tanka Senryu: Anth* (Chugainippohsha, 2002), *Countless
    Leaves: Anth* (Inkling Pr, 2001)

Dana Levin   P
Creative Writing Program, College of Santa Fe, 1600 St
Michael's Dr, Santa Fe, NM 87505
    Internet: Dlevin@csf.edu
    Pubs: *In the Surgical Theatre* (APR, 1999), *Influence &
    Mastery: Anth* (Paul Dry Bks, 2001), *American Poetry: Next
    Generation: Anth* (Carnegie Mellon U Pr, 2000), *Pushcart
    Prize XXII: Anth* (Pushcart Pr, 1998), *Volt, Third Coast,
    Marlboro Rev, Ploughshares*

Robert Lloyd   P
English Dept, Univ New Mexico, 217 Humanities Bldg, Box
132, Albuquerque, NM 87131

Joan Logghe ♪ ✈   P&W
12C Eckards Way
Espanola, NM 87532, 505-753-3174
    Internet: jlogghe@espanola.com
    Pubs: *Sofia, Twenty Years in Bed with the Same Man* (La
    Alameda Pr, 1999, 1995), *Blessed Resistance* (Mariposa,
    1999), *Another Desert: Anth* (Sherman Asher, 1998), *Catch
    Our Breath: Anth* (Mariposa, 1996), *Frank, Women's Review
    of Books, Puerto del Sol*

Sandra Lynn   P
1814 Hermosa Dr NE
Albuquerque, NM 87110-4924, 505-255-0410
    Pubs: *Where Rainbows Wait for Rain* (Tangram, 1989),
    Inheritance of Light: Anth (U North Texas Pr, 1996), *Three
    Texas Poets: Anth* (Prickly Pear, 1986)

Hank Malone 🎤 ✈   P
1220-J Nakomis NE
Albuquerque, NM 87112
Internet: hanksharon@aol.com
  Pubs: *Urban Millennium Haiku, James Dickey On the Eve of
  the Millennium, Experiencing New Mexico: Lyrical & Critical
  Essays, New Mexico Haiku* (Poetic License Pr, 2000, 1999,
  1998, 1996), *Footstrikes & Spondees* (Parkville Pr, 1993)

E. A. Mares 🎤 ✈   P
202 Edith NE
Albuquerque, NM 87102-3526, 505-248-0946
Internet: tmares@swcp.com
  Pubs: *The Unicorn Poem & Flowers & Songs of Sorrow* (U
  New Mexico Pr, 1992), *Paper Dance: Anth* (Persea Bks,
  1995), *Frank, Santa Fe Poetry Broadside, Prairie Schooner,
  Blue Mesa Rev, Blanco Movil, Century Mag, Cafe Solo*

Barbara McCauley   P
PO Box 326
Truchas, NM 87578
  Pubs: *Small Mercies, Written with a Spoon* (Sherman Asher
  Pub, 1998, 1996), *Drug-Related Diseases* (Franklin Watts,
  1986), *Finding the Balance* (Red Hill, 1977), *Nation*

Karen Quelle McKinnon 🎤 ✈   P
PO Box 508
Sandia Park, NM 87047-0508, 505-281-9856
Internet: karennrich@aol.com
  Pubs: *Coming True* (Watermelon Mtn Pr, 2000), *Saludos
  Poemas De Nuevo Mexico/Poems of New Mexico: Anth*
  (Pennywhistle Pr, 1995), *Queen Anne's Lace: Anth*
  (Wildflowers Pr, 1994), *Blue Mesa Rev, Puerto del Sol*

Emerson Blackhorse Mitchell   P
Box #204
Shiprock, NM 87420

Carol Moldaw 🎤 ✈   P
RR5, Box 231
Santa Fe, NM 87506, 505-455-3074
Internet: cmoldaw@nets.com
  Pubs: *Through the Window, Chalkmarks on Stone* (La
  Alameda Pr, 2001, 1998), *Taken from the River* (Alef Bks,
  1993), *Another Desert: Anth* (Sherman Asher Pub, 1998),
  *Field, Denver Qtly, Parnassus, Chicago Rev, Volt, Manoa,
  Threepenny Rev*

N. Scott Momaday   P&W
PO Box 6
Jemez Springs, NM 87025-0006

Linda Monacelli-Johnson 🎤 ✈   P
308 W Houghton
Santa Fe, NM 87505-8849, 505-988-4569
  Pubs: *Campanile* (Drummer Pr, 1999), *Weathered*
  (Sunstone Pr, 1986), *Lacing the Moon* (Cleveland State U
  Poetry Ctr, 1978), *Zeta, CSM, Rio Grande Writers Qtly,
  South Florida Poetry Rev, Pembroke Mag, Tributaries*

Frank D. Moore 🎤 ✈   P
4 Glorieta Rd
Santa Fe, NM 87508-2257, 505-466-8450
  Pubs: *One Trick Pony, Literary Rev, Painted Bride Qtly,
  Passages North, Sou'wester, Four Quarters, Piedmont
  Literary Rev*

Todd Moore 🎤 ✈   P
3216 San Pedro Dr NE
Albuquerque, NM 87110-2634, 505-837-1167
Internet: moorebt@aol.com
  Pubs: *The Corpse Is Dreaming* (Lummox Pr, 2000), *Working
  on My Duende* (Kings Estate Pr, 1998), *Dillinger: Book II*
  (Primal Pub, 1992), *Outlaw Bible: Anth* (Thunder's Mouth Pr,
  1999), *Chiron Rev, Nerve Cowboy, Sin Fronteras, NYQ*

Barbara Beasley Murphy   W
Casa Esteban, 486 Circle Dr, Santa Fe, NM 87501,
505-983-9607
  Pubs: *Fly Like an Eagle, Join In* (Delacorte, 1994, 1993),
  Ace Hits It Big (Bantam, 1992)

Antonya Nelson   W
English Dept, Box 3E, New Mexico State Univ, Las Cruces,
NM 88003, 505-646-3536
  Pubs: *Nobody's Girl, Talking in Bed* (Scribner, 1998, 1997),
  Family Terrorists (HM, 1994), *In the Land of Men* (Avon,
  1993), *New Yorker, Story, Redbook, TriQtly, Esquire,
  Antioch Rev*

Dr. Tessa Nelson-Humphries 🎤 ✈   P&W
3228 Jupiter Rd, 4 Hills
Las Cruces, NM 88012-7742
Internet: gaucho@zianet.com
  Pubs: *Envoi: Summer Anth* (Poets Pubs, 1990), *Northwoods
  Jrnl, Array, New Frontiers New Mexico, Negative Capability,
  Alaskan Poetry Jrnl, Confrontations, Animal Cavalcade,
  Appalachian Heritage, Blue Unicorn, Cobblestones*

Kathleen Neuer   P
PO Box 2409
Taos, NM 87571-2409, 505-758-2994
  Pubs: *Prairie Schooner, Texas Rev, Pennsylvania Rev,
  Malahat, Black Warrior, Threepenny Rev*

Stanley Noyes   P&W
634 E Garcia
Santa Fe, NM 87501-2858, 505-982-4067
  Pubs: *Commander of Dead Leaves* (Tooth of Time, 1984),
  *Saludos Poemas De Nuevo Mexico/Poems of New Mexico:
  Anth* (Pennywhistle Pr, 1995), *Sin Fronteras, High Plains,
  Blue Unicorn*

Antony Oldknow   P
PO Box 1091
Portales, NM 88130, 505-359-0901
Internet: Antony.Oldknow@enmu.edu
  Pubs: *Ten Small Songs* (Paraiso Pr, 1985), *Consolation for
  Beggars* (Song Pr, 1978), *Antaeus*

Bill Pearlman 🎤 ✈   P
Box 613
Placitas, NM 87043-0613
Internet: b2pearl@juno.com
    Pubs: *Flareup of Twosomes* (La Alameda Pr, 1996)

V. B. Price 🎤 ✈   P
PO Box 6175
Albuquerque, NM 87197-6175
Internet: vbp@swcp.com
    Pubs: *Chaco Trilogy* (La Alameda Pr, 1998), *Saludos
    Poemas De Nuevo Mexico/Poems of New Mexico: Anth*
    (Pennywhistle Pr, 1995), *New Mexico Poetry Renaissance:
    Anth* (Red Crane Bks, 1994)

Margaret Randall   P
50 Cedar Hill Rd NE
Albuquerque, NM 87122-1928, 505-856-6543
Internet: mrandmeg@aol.com
    Pubs: *Hunger's Table* (Papier-Mache Pr, 1997), *Sandino's
    Daughters Revisited* (Rutgers U Pr, 1994), *Gathering Rage*
    (Monthly Review Pr, 1992), *American Voice, Ms., Ikon,
    Calyx, Berkeley Poetry Rev, Blue Mesa Rev*

Harvena Richter   P&W
1932 Candelaria Rd NW
Albuquerque, NM 87107-2855, 505-344-6766
    Pubs: *Frozen Light: The Crystal Poems* (Wildflower Pr,
    2002), *Innocent Island* (Puckerbrush Pr, 1999), *Green Girls,
    The Yaddo Elegies* (North Valley Pr, 1996, 1995), *The
    Human Shore* (Little, Brown, 1959), *South Dakota Rev, Blue
    Mesa Rev*

Janet Rodney   P
PO Box 8187
Santa Fe, NM 87504
    Pubs: *Orphydice* (Salt Works Pr, 1986), *Crystals* (North
    Atlantic Bks, 1979), *Conjunctions, Sulfur*

Del Marie Rogers 🎤 ✈   P
HCR 74 Box 24516
El Prado, NM 87529, 505-776-3266
    Pubs: *She'll Never Want More Than This* (Firewheel Pr,
    2002), *Close to Ground* (Corona, 1990), *Texas in Poetry:
    Anth* (TCU Pr, 2002), *Puerto del Sol, Texas Observer,
    Colorado Rev*

Leo Romero 🎤 ✈   P&W
34 Calle de Gancho
Santa Fe, NM 87507
    Pubs: *Seeing the Big Picture* (Intercultural Pr, 2001), *Real
    Things* (Indiana U Pr, 1999), *The Floating Borderlands* (U
    Washington Pr, 1998), *Rita & Los Angeles* (Bilingual Review
    Pr, 1994), *Going Home Away Indian* (Ahsahta Pr, 1990)

Sharman Apt Russell 🎤 ✈   W
1113 West St
Silver City, NM 88061-4633, 505-538-6345
Internet: sharman@zianet.com
    Pubs: *Last Matriarch* (U New Mexico Pr, 2000), *When the
    Land Was Young, Kill the Cowboy, Songs of the Fluteplayer*
    (Addison-Wesley, 1996, 1993, 1991), *The Humpbacked
    Fluteplayer* (Knopf, 1994)

Miriam Sagan 🎤 ✈   P
626 Kathryn Ave
Santa Fe, NM 87505
    Pubs: *New Jersey Book of the Dead* (Santa Fe Poetry
    Broadside, 2002), *The Widow's Coat* (Ahsahta, 2002),
    Archeology of Desire (Red Hen, 2001)

Scott Patrick Sanders   P
English Dept, Univ New Mexico, Albuquerque, NM 87131
Internet: ssanders@unm.edu
    Pubs: *Mr. Cogito, Rocky Mountain Rev of Language &
    Literature, Chiaroscuro, Spoon River Qtly, Weber Studies*

Roberto Sandoval   P
137 Romero St
Santa Fe, NM 87501, 505-982-9605

Lorna D. Saunders 🎤 ✈   P
Kralor Press, PO Box 1867, Magdalena, NM 87825
    Pubs: *The Elsewhere* (Kralor Pr, 2000), *Wild Outdoor World,
    Poet Lore, Bitterroot, Apprentice, Bloodroot, Planet X*

Ken Saville   P
Box 4662
Albuquerque, NM 87196, 505-268-0265
    Pubs: *20 Postcards* (Transient Pr, 1979)

Rebecca Seiferle 🎤 ✈   P
5602 Tarry Terr
Farmington, NM 87402-8261, 505-325-6145
Internet: seiferle@yahoo.com
    Pubs: *Bitters, The Poet's Child: Anth, Reversible
    Monuments: Anth* (Copper Canyon, 2001, 2002, 2002), *The
    Music We Dance To, The Ripped-Out Seam, Trilce* (Sheep
    Meadow Pr, 1999, 1993, 1992), *Best American Poetry: Anth*
    (Scribner, 2000)

Jeanne Shannon 🎤   P&W
The Wildflower Press, PO Box 4757, Albuquerque, NM
87196-4757, 505-296-0691
Internet: jspoetry@aol.com
    Pubs: *Sometimes the Light* (Wildflower Pr, 2000), *The
    House on Afternoon Street* (Penhaligon Page, 2000),
    Learning By Heart: Anth (U Iowa Pr, 1999), *In Good
    Company: Anth* (Live Wire Pr, 1999), *Hunger, Grasslimb,
    Quarter After Eight*

Sherri Silverman   P
PO Box 66
Santa Fe, NM 87504-0066, 505-984-0327
Internet: shrisilver@aol.com
    Pubs: *Crosswinds, Santa Fe Spirit Mag, Studia Mystica, Cicada, Sackbut Rev, Manna, Reconstructionist, Salome*

Katie Singer ♪ ✈   W
PO Box 6574
Santa Fe, NM 87502-6574, 505-820-0773
www.KatieSinger.com
    Pubs: *The Wholeness of a Broken Heart* (Riverhead Bks, 1999), *Heresies, Sojourner, Lilith*

Florentin Smarandache ♪ ✈   P&W
Univ New Mexico, 200 College Rd, Gallup, NM 87301-5603
Internet: smarand@unm.edu
    Pubs: *Leitmotives, Destiny, In Seven Languages, Defective Writings, I Exist Against Myself, Non Novel* (Aius, 2000, 2000, 2000, 1997, 1997, 1993), *Paradoxist Distichs* (Dorul, 1998), *Emigrant to Infinity* (Macarie, 1995), *Non Poems* (Xiquan Pub Hse, 1990)

Linda Wasmer Smith   P
12017 Kashmir St NE
Albuquerque, NM 87111, 505-296-3095
    Pubs: *Second Aid* (Fish Down Pr, 1993), *If I Had My Life to Live Over I Would Pick More Daisies: Anth* (Papier-Mache Pr, 1992), *Defined Providence*

Maryhelen Snyder   P
422 Camino Del Bosque NW
Albuquerque, NM 87114, 505-898-7047
Internet: mel@abq.com
    Pubs: *The Effect of Lilacs on Distance* (Potes & Poets, 2002), *No Hole in the Flame* (Wildflower Pr, 2002), *Undressing for Rodin, Because I Praise* (Watermelon Mtn Pr, 2002, 1998), *Enough* (Solo Pr, 1979), *The Practice of Peace: Anth* (Sherman Asher Pr, 1998)

Anthony Sobin   P
22 Alcalde Rd
Santa Fe, NM 87505
    Pubs: *The Sunday Naturalist* (Ohio U Pr, 1982), *Poetry, Poetry NW, BPJ*

Jane Somerville   P
2442 Cerillos Rd, Ste 455
Sante Fe, NM 87505-3262
    Pubs: *The Only Blessing* (Greenhouse Review Pr, 1992), *Making the Light Come* (Wayne State U Pr, 1990), *APR, Gettysburg Rev, Kansas Qtly, Ohio Rev*

Joseph Somoza ♪ ✈   P
1725 Hamiel Dr
Las Cruces, NM 88001-5222, 505-522-1119
Internet: josomoza@nmsu.edu
    Pubs: *Cityzen, Sojourner So to Speak* (La Alameda Pr, 2002, 1997), *Out of This World* (Cinco Puntos Pr, 1990), *New Mexico Poetry Renaissance: Anth* (Red Crane Bks, 1994)

Marcia Southwick   P
1001 Camino Pinones
Santa Fe, NM 87505, 505-989-8781
Internet: smouthwick@aol.com
    Pubs: *A Saturday Night at the Flying Dog* (Field Pr, 1998), *Why the River Disappears* (Carnegie Mellon U, 1990), *The Night Won't Save Anyone* (U Georgia, 1980), *APR, Harvard Rev, Field, Prairie Schooner, Antaeus, Poetry, Iowa Rev*

Arlene Stone   P&W
PO Box 2880
Sante Fe, NM 87504-2880
    Pubs: *Son Sonnets* (Emmanuel Pr, 1994), *The Double Pipes of Pan* (North Atlantic Bks, 1983), *Harper's, Yellow Silk, Contact II*

Mary Swander   P
Univ New Mexico, English Dept, Humanities Bldg 217, Albuquerque, NM 87131-1106
    Pubs: *Out of This World* (Viking, 1995), *Heaven-and-Earth House, Driving the Body Back* (Knopf, 1994, 1986), *New Republic, CSM, Nation, New Yorker, Poetry*

George Swaney   P
1825 Meadow Ln
Las Cruces, NM 88005
    Pubs: *Iowa Rev, Poetry East, Georgetown Rev, Gulf Stream, Mudfish, Rastown Rev, Antietam Rev, Haight Ashbury Jrnl, Jacaranda Rev, Sou'wester, Pittsburgh Qtly*

Arthur Sze ♪ ✈   P
PO Box 457
Santa Fe, NM 87504-0457, 505-455-3074
    Pubs: *The Silk Dragon, The Redshifting Web, Archipelago* (Copper Canyon Pr, 2001, 1998, 1995), *APR, Paris Rev, Manoa, Conjunctions, Kenyon Rev, Orion*

Nathaniel Tarn ♪ ✈   P
PO Box 871
Tesuque, NM 87574-0871, 505-982-3990
    Pubs: *Selected Poems: 1950-2000* (Wesleyan U Pr, 2002), *The Architextures* (Chax Pr, 2000), *Seeing America First* (Coffee Hse Pr, 1989), *Jacket, Sulfur, Conjunctions, First Intensity*

Phyllis Hoge Thompson 🎤 ✈   P
213 Dartmouth SE
Albuquerque, NM 87106-2219, 505-265-4214
    Pubs: *Letters from Jian Hui and other Poems* (The
    Wildflower Pr, 2001), *The Ghosts of Who We Were* (U Illinois
    Pr, 1986), *I Gotta Crow: Women, Voice and Writing: Anth*
    (Writer Bks, 2002), *Hudson Rev, Manoa*

John Tritica 🎤 ✈   P
3516 Haines NE
Albuquerque, NM 87106
    Pubs: *How Rain Records Its Alphabet* (La Alameda Pr,
    1998), *Central Park, Talisman*

Paul Edward Trujillo   P
Box 396
Peralta, NM 87042, 505-864-0307
    Pubs: *Bilingual Rev, Ceremony of Brotherhood, Poetry Now,
    Writers' Forum*

Sharon Oard Warner 🎤 ✈   W
English Language & Literature, Univ New Mexico, Humanities
Bldg 217, Albuquerque, NM 87131-1106, 505-277-6248
Internet: swarner@unm.edu
    Pubs: *Deep in the Heart* (Dial Pr, 2000), *Learning to Dance
    & Other Stories* (New Rivers Pr, 1992), *The Way We Write
    Now: Short Stories From the AIDS Crisis: Anth* (Citadel Pr,
    1995), *Prairie Schooner, Green Mountains Rev, Sonora Rev,
    AWP Chronicle*

Mark Weber   P
725 Van Buren Pl SE
Albuquerque, NM 87108, 505-255-3012
    Pubs: *Existential Hum* (Pearl Special Edtns, 1996),
    Swindler's Harmonica Siesta, Drunk City (Zerx Pr, 1994,
    1991), *Pearl, Wormwood Rev, Caprice, Chiron*

Joel Weishaus   P
401 14th St SW #11
Albuquerque, NM 87102-2871
    Pubs: *Woods, Shore, Desert: 1968 Notebook of Thomas
    Merton* (Museum of New Mexico Pr, 1983), *Artspace*

Kathleene West 🎤 ✈   P
New Mexico State Univ, PO Box 30001, English Dept, Las
Cruces, NM 88003-8001
Internet: kwest@nmsu.edu
    Pubs: *The Farmer's Daughter* (Sandhills, 1990), *Water
    Witching, Gift of Tongues: Anth* (Copper Canyon, 1984,
    1996), *TriQtly, Kenyon Rev, Prairie Schooner*

Keith Wilson 🎤 ✈   P
1500 S Locust #C-21
Las Cruces, NM 88001-5356, 505-522-8389
Internet: kewilson@nmsu.edu
    Pubs: *The Priesthood Quartette* (Whole Note Pr, 2002),
    Bosque Redondo (Penny Whistle Pr, 2000), *Graves
    Registry* (Clark City Pr, 1992)

Herta Wittgenstein   W
c/o B. J. Harris, PO Box 9848, Santa Fe, NM 87504,
505-984-1154
    Pubs: *Watching a Field of Zebras* (Demarais Studio Pr, 1992)

Ann E. Weisman   PP
New Mexico Arts Division
PO Box 1450
Santa Fe, NM 87504-1450, 505-827-6490
Internet: aweisman@cityof.lawton.ok.us
    Pubs: *Playing the message twice* (Rose Rock Pr, 2001), *Eye
    Imagine: Performances on Paper* (Point Riders Pr, 1991),
    Moonrise, The Eloquent Object (Philbrook Museum, 1989,
    1987)

Susan Yuzna 🎤 ✈   P
516 Austin, Apt 1
Truth or Consequences, NM 87901, 786-552-6957
Internet: yuzna@aol.com
    Pubs: *Pale Bird, Spouting Fire, Her Slender Dress* (U Akron
    Pr, 2000, 1996)

Arlene Zekowski 🎤 ✈   P&W
Pamela Tree, PO Box 6136, Santa Fe, NM 87502,
505-983-8484
    Pubs: *Against the Disappearance of Literature, The Living
    Underground: Anth* (Whitston Pr, 1998, 1999), *Every
    Person's Little Book of P-L-U-T-O-N-I-U-M* (w/Berne; Rising
    Tide Pr, 1992), *Dictionary of the Avant-Gardes: Anth* (A
    Cappella Pr, 1994), *Tyuonyi*

NEW YORK

Sam Abrams 🎤 ✈   P
Rochester Inst Technology, College of Liberal Arts, Rochester,
NY 14623, 716-475-2444
Internet: sxagsl@rit.edu
    Pubs: *The Old Pothead Poems* (Backwoods Broadsides,
    1999), *Jazz Poetry: Anth* (Indiana U Pr, 1991), *Out of this
    World: Anth* (Crown, 1991), *Up Late: Anth* (4 Walls 8
    Windows, 1987), *Talisman, Mesechabe, Exquisite Corpse,
    Napalm Health Spa Report, Alcatraz*

Ally Acker 🎤 ✈   P
8 Hayloft Ln
Roslyn Heights, NY 11577
Internet: ally@allyacker.com
    Pubs: *Waiting for the Beloved* (Red Hen Pr, 1999), *Surviving
    Desire* (Garden Street Pr, 1994), *American Voice, Poetry
    Kanto, Ploughshares*

Barbara Adams 🎤 ✈   P&W
59 Coach Ln
Newburgh, NY 12550-3818, 845-564-3499
Internet: bblockadams@aol.com
    Pubs: *Personal Narratives: Anth* (Haworth Pr, 2002), *The Muse
    Strikes Back: Anth* (Story Line Pr, 1997), *When a Lifemate
    Dies: Anth* (Fairview Pr, 1997), *Awakenings Rev, Texas Rev,
    Free Associations, Humanist, Breakfast All Day, Belles Lettres*

Elizabeth Adams W
Philip Spitzer Literary Agency, 750 Talmage Farm Lane, East
Hampton, NY 11937-4300
Pubs: *Phoebe, Caprice, Chicago Rev, Alaska Qtly Rev, NAR,
Groundswell, Intro 10, Raddle Moon, Massachusetts Rev*

Jeanette Adams ♦ ⊀ P
208 Old Country Rd
Elmsford, NY 10523
Pubs: *Poetry in Performance 19* (CUNY, 1991), *Parallels
Artists Poets: Anth* (Midmarch Arts, 1993), *Drumvoices
Revue: Anth* (U Southern Illinois, 1992)

Joan Albarella ♦ ⊀ P&W
3574 Clinton St
Buffalo, NY 14224-1401
Internet: jkea@juno.com
Pubs: *Called to Kill, Agenda for Murder* (Rising Tide Pr,
2000, 1999), *Spirit & Joy* (Alpha Pr, 1993), *Women, Flowers,
Fantasy* (Textile Bridge Pr, 1987)

Joan Alden ♦ ⊀ W
257 Warren St
Hudson, NY 12534, 518-822-1089
Pubs: *Before Our Eyes, Letting in the Night* (Firebrand Bks,
1993, 1989), *A Boy's Best Friend* (Alyson Pubs, 1992), *Mrs.
Cooper's Boarding House* (McGraw-Hill, 1980)

Linda Allardt ♦ ⊀ P
2 Ann Lynn Rd
Pittsford, NY 14534-3910, 585-248-5223
Pubs: *River Effect, Seeing for You* (State Street Pr, 1998,
1981), *The Names of the Survivors* (Ithaca Hse, 1979), *The
Bridge, BPJ, West Branch*

John Allman ♦ ⊀ P&W
28 Frances Dr
Katonah, NY 10536-3212, 914-232-3835
Internet: allmanej@cs.com
Pubs: *Inhabited World* (Wallace Stevens Society Pr, 1995),
Descending Fire & Other Stories (New Directions, 1994),
Poetry, Pivot, The Qtly, Beloit, Poetry NW

Karen Alpha ♦ ⊀ W
106 Welch Rd
Corning, NY 14830, 607-936-6576
Pubs: *Redbook, NAR, Blueline, North Dakota Qtly*

Kath M. Anderson ♦ ⊀ P
28 Arlington St
Rochester, NY 14607
Internet: dempander@earthlink.net
Pubs: *An Abbreviated History of Water* (State Street Pr,
1996), *Hauling Water* (Jumping Cholla Pr), *Poetry, Qtly West,
Georgia Rev, Carolina Qtly, Ploughshares, Sonora Rev, Orion*

Marjorie Appleman ♦ ⊀ P&W
PO Box 39
Sagaponack, NY 11962-0039, 631-537-1741
Internet: applemanmh@yahoo.com
Pubs: *Against Time* (Birnham Wood, 1994), *Confrontation,
Long Island Qtly, Poetry Pilot, Poetry Rev, Wind, Kentucky
Poetry Rev, Sojourner*

Philip Appleman ♦ ⊀ P&W
PO Box 39
Sagaponack, NY 11962-0039, 631-537-1741
Internet: appleman@yahoo.com
Pubs: *New & Selected Poems* (U Arkansas Pr, 1996), *Let
There Be Light* (HC, 1991), *Darwin's Ark* (Indiana U Pr,
1984), *Poetry, Partisan Rev, Yale Rev, Nation, Paris Rev*

Sondra Audin Armer ♦ ⊀ P
221 Cleveland Dr
Croton-on-Hudson, NY 10520, 914-271-6801
Internet: ssaphd@aol.com
Pubs: *Dog Music: Anth* (St. Martin's Pr, 1996), *Ravishing
DisUnities: Anth* (Wesleyan Poetry, 2000), *South Carolina
Rev, Blue Unicorn, Cumberland Poetry Rev, Edge City Rev,
Western Humanities Rev, Apalachee Qtly*

Deborah Artman ♦ ⊀ P&W
25 Hill 99
Woodstock, NY 12498-1424
Pubs: *Bite to Eat Place: Anth* (Redwood Coast Pr, 1995),
*Puerto del Sol, Fish Stories, American Short Fiction,
Carolina Qtly, Cottonwood, Seattle Rev, Ironwood,
Appearances*

Linda Ashear P
92 Paulding Ave
Tarrytown, NY 10591-5708
Internet: lingolite@aol.com
Pubs: *The Rowers, the Swimmers & the Drowned* (Morris
Pr, 1996), *Toward the Light* (Croton Rev Pr, 1989),
MacGuffin, Santa Barbara Rev, Without Halos

Rilla Askew ♦ ⊀ W
PO Box 324
Kauneonga Lake, NY 12749
Internet: raskew@bestweb.net
Pubs: *Fire in Beulah, Strange Business* (Viking Penguin,
2001, 1992), *The Mercy Seat* (Viking, 1997), *Prize Stories
1993: O. Henry Awards Anth* (Doubleday, 1993), *Nimrod,
Puerto del Sol, Carolina Qtly*

Katharine Assante P
22 Armand's Way
Highland Mills, NY 10930-9801, 914-534-8522
Pubs: *A Delicate Blue Veil, October's Child* (Assante, 1994,
1990), *Algonquin Qtly, On Course, Critical Mass*

Susan Astor ♦ ⊀ P
32 Jefferson Ave
Mineola, NY 11501-2928, 516-873-2547
Pubs: *Dame* (U Georgia Pr, 1980), *Paris Rev, Partisan Rev,
Poet Lore, Kansas Qtly, Confrontation, Croton Rev*

Brett Axel 🎤 ✈   P
726 Chestnut St.
Utica, NY 13502, 315-797-1195
Internet: axels@adelphia.net
  Pubs: *Disaster Relief* (Minimal Pr, 2002), *First on the Fire*
  (Genesis/Fly by Night Pr, 1999), *Princeton Arts Rev,*
  Unknown Writer, Algonquin Qtly, Heaven Bone, Longshot

David B. Axelrod 🎤 ✈   P
233 Mooney Pond Rd, PO Box 2344
Selden, NY 11784, 631-451-0478
poetrydoctor.org
  Pubs: *Random Beauty* (Amereon Hse, 2001), *Intro to*
  Literature: Anth (HC, 1998), *Long Island Qtly, Shi Kahn,*
  Kansas Qtly, Nasa Kniga, North Carolina Qtly

Donald Everett Axinn 🎤   P&W
131 Jericho Turnpike
Jericho, NY 11753-1024, 516-333-8500
  Pubs: *The Ego Makers* (Arcade, 1998), *The Latest Illusion,*
  Spin (Arcade, 1995, 1994), *Dawn Patrol* (CCC, 1992), *The*
  Colors of Infinity (Blue Moon Bks, 1990), *Antaeus, NER,*
  New York Qtly, Confrontation

George Bailin 🎤   P
Sacred Orchard, PO Box 298, Harriman, NY 10926-0298,
845-782-3849
Internet: sacredor@warwick.net
  Pubs: *Sage of Ananda, First Strike* (Seaport Poets & Writers
  Pr, 1993, 1988), *Dead Reckoning* (Dragonsbreath Pr, 1984),
  Evening News Report (Court Poetry Pr, 1984), *Meditators*
  Newsletter

Gay Baines 🎤   P&W
274 North St
East Aurora, NY 14052, 716-652-5037
Internet: gayb@buffnet.net
  Pubs: *Lighter Than Air: Anth* (Lighter Than Air, 1998),
  Clutter: Anth (Andrew Mtn Pr, 1998), *RE Arts & Letters,*
  Lullwater Rev, Licking River Rev, Oregon East, Hampden-
  Sydney Poetry Rev, Rio Grande Rev, Wellspring, Whiskey
  Island Mag, Lumina, Soundings East

Ansie Baird   P
17 Tudor Pl
Buffalo, NY 14222
  Pubs: *Paris Rev, Poetry NW, Denver Qtly, Poetry Now,*
  Vassar Qtly, The Qtly, Earth's Daughters, Southern Rev,
  South Dakota Rev, Green River Rev

Peter Balakian 🎤 ✈   P
Colgate Univ, English Dept, Hamilton, NY 13346
Internet: pbalakian@mail.colgate.edu
  Pubs: *June-Tree* (HC, 2001), *Reply from Wilderness Island,*
  Sad Days of Light (Sheep Meadow Pr, 1988, 1983), *Poetry*

Harry Barba   W
Harian Creative Books, 47 Hyde Blvd, Ballston Spa, NY
12020-1607, 518-885-7397
  Pubs: *Mona Lisa Smiles, The Day the World Went Sane,*
  Round Trip to Byzantium, Gospel According to Everyman
  (Harian Creative Bks, 1993, 1987, 1985, 1981)

Stanley H. Barkan 🎤 ✈   P
239 Wynsum Ave
Merrick, NY 11566-4725, 516-868-5635
Internet: cccmia@juno.com
  Pubs: *Naming the Birds* (Bulgaria; ALEKO, 2002),
  Bubbemeises & Babbaluci (Coop Ed Sicilian Antigruppo,
  2001), *Under the Apple Tree* (Poland; Oficyna Konfraterni
  Poetow, 1998), *Confrontation, Visions, Forward, Lips,*
  Shabdaguchha

Mildred Barker   W
229 Main St
Kingston, NY 12401
  Pubs: *Hot Stitches* (Crazy Ladies Pr, 2001), *Speaking the*
  Words: Anth (Word Thursdays/Bright Hill Pr, 1994), *If I Had*
  a Hammer: Women's Work: Anth (Papier-Mache Pr, 1990),
  Oxalis Literary Qtly, Nimrod

Nancy Barnes   P
Erie Community College, 121 Ellicott St, Buffalo, NY 14203,
716-851-1018
  Pubs: *Fine China: Twenty Years of Earth's Daughters: Anth*
  (Springhouse Edtns, 1993), *Pure Light, Earth's Daughters,*
  Black Mountain Rev, Centrum Jrnl

Linda Michelle Baron   PP
Panache Inc, PO Box 4051, Hempstead, NY 11551-4051
  Pubs: *The Sun Is On, Rhythm & Dues* (Harlin Jacque,
  1981, 1981)

Marylin Lytle Barr 🎤 ✈   P
PO Box 75
Grahamsville, NY 12740, 914-985-7337
  Pubs: *Unexpected Light, Food and Other Enemies: Anth*
  (Essex Pr, 1999, 2000), *Concrete Considerations*
  (Sweetwater Pub, 1993), *Drawn from the Shadows* (Egret
  Pr, 1991), *Alchemist 8: Anth* (Alchemy Club, 1995), *Poetry*
  Page, Oxalis, Zephyr, Outloud, The Rostrum

Jack Barry 🎤 ✈   P
121 North Way
Camillus, NY 13031-1254, 315-488-3566
  Pubs: *Hints & Hunches* (Garlic Pr, 1974), *New Letters, APR,*
  Notre Dame Rev, Poetpourri, Syracuse Rev

Michael Basinski 🎤 ✈   PP&P
Poetry/Rare Books Collection, SUNY Buffalo, 420 Capen Hall,
Buffalo, NY 14260-2200, 716-645-2917
Internet: basinski@acsu.buffalo.edu
  Pubs: *By* (Hse Pr, 1999), *Heebee-Jeebees, Cnyttan* (Meow
  Pr, 1996, 1993), *SleVep* (Tailspin Pr, 1995), *Abacus, Lung,*
  Boxkite

John Batki   P&W
211 Lockwood Rd
Syracuse, NY 13214

M. Garrett Bauman 🎤 ✈   W
Monroe Community College, English Dept, Rochester, NY
14623, 716-292-2000
Internet: garrettbauman@cs.com
    Pubs: *Ideas & Details* (HB, 2001), *New Letters, Story,
    Yankee, Greensboro Rev, Chrysalis*

E. R. Baxter, III   P
2709 Braley Rd
Ransomville, NY 14131, 716-791-4611
    Pubs: *Looking for Niagara, What I Want* (Slipstream Pub,
    1993, 1993), *Albany Rev, Black Mountain Rev, Earth's
    Daughters, Pig Iron*

Michael Benedikt   P&W
315 W 98 St, #6-A
New York, NY 212-865-4538
    Pubs: *The Badminton at Great Barrington* (U Pitt Pr, 1980),
    Night Cries (Wesleyan U Pr, 1976)

Bruce Bennett 🎤 ✈   P
PO Box 145
Aurora, NY 13026, 315-364-3228
Internet: brbennett@wells.edu
    Pubs: *Hey, Diddle Diddle* (FootHills Pub, 2001), *Navigating
    the Distances: Poems New & Selected* (Orchises, 1999), *It's
    Hard to Get the Angle Right* (Greentower Press, 1997),
    *Atlanta Rev, Green Mountains Rev, Harvard Rev, Laurel
    Rev, Tar River Poetry*

Saul Bennett 🎤 ✈   P
167 Broadview
Woodstock, NY 12498
Internet: saulben@aol.com
    Pubs: *Harpo Marx at Prayer, New Fields & Other Stones/On
    a Child's Death* (Archer Bks, 2000, 1998), *Jesus Matinees &
    Other Poems* (Pudding Hse, 1998), *Rattle, New York Times,
    Amelia, Christian Century, ELF, First Things, Peregrine,
    Pudding Mag*

Sally Bennett 🎤   P&W
846 Ostrom Ave
Syracuse, NY 13210-2902, 315-478-7129
Internet: sally@a-znet.com
    Pubs: *American Fiction: Anth* (Birch Lane Pr, 1990), *Anth of
    Magazine Verse & Yearbook of American Poetry* (Monitor
    Bks, 1987), *Pangolin Papers, Distillery, Poetry, Seneca Rev,
    Gulf Stream, Syracuse Scholar, Sycamore Rev*

Robert Bensen 🎤 ✈   P
14 Harrison Ave
Oneonta, NY 13820-1107, 607-431-4902
Internet: bensenr@hartwick.edu
    Pubs: *Scriptures of Venus* (Swamp Pr, 2000), *Agni, River
    Styx, Caribbean Writer, Paris Rev, Partisan Rev, Antioch
    Rev, Akwe:kon Jrnl, Cumberland Poetry Rev, Poetry Wales,
    Ploughshares, Cimarron Rev, Yankee*

Kimberly Berg 🎤 ✈   P
489 East Rd
Cadyville, NY 12918-2037
    Pubs: *Uncommon Nature* (Wood Thrush Bks, 2002),
    *Amerikua!, Phoebus, Hummingbird, Minkhill Jrnl, Colorwheel,
    Visions, High Rock Rev, Negative Capability, CSM*

Frank Bergon 🎤 ✈   W
Vassar College, Box 94, Poughkeepsie, NY 12604-0094,
845-437-5663
Internet: bergon@vassar.edu
    Pubs: *Wild Game, The Temptations of St. Ed & Brother S*
    (U Nevada Pr, 1995, 1993), *Shoshone Mike* (Viking
    Penguin, 1987)

Bruce Berlind 🎤 ✈   P
PO Box 237
Hamilton, NY 13346, 315-893-7078
    Pubs: *Charon's Ferry* (Northwestern U Pr, 2000), *Otto
    Orban's The Journey of Barbarus* (Passegiatta Pr, 1997),
    When You Became She (Xenos Bks, 1994), *Birds & Other
    Relations* (Princeton U Pr, 1987), *Partisan Rev, Kenyon Rev,
    Grand Street, Poetry, APR*

Cassia Berman 🎤 ✈   P
11 1/2 Tannery Brook Rd
Woodstock, NY 12498, 914-679-9457
Internet: cassia@netstep.net
    Pubs: *Divine Mother Within Me, Divine Mother Poems*
    (Divine Mother Communications, 1995, 1993), *Her Words:
    An Anth of Poetry About the Great Goddess* (Shambhala,
    1999), *APR, Chelsea, Northeast Jrnl, The Falcon, Poetry
    Studies, Collaboration*

Charles Bernstein 🎤 ✈   P
Poetics Program, SUNY, English Dept, 438 Clemens Hall,
Buffalo, NY 14260, 716-645-3810
Internet: bernstei@bway.net
    Pubs: With Strings, My Way: Speeches & Poems (U Chicago
    Pr, 2001, 1998), Republics of Reality: Poems 1975-1995
    (Sun & Moon Pr, 1999), A Poetics (Harvard U Pr, 1992),

Holly Beye   P&W
PO Box 1043
Woodstock, NY 12498, 914-679-2820
    Pubs: *Out of the Catskills & Beyond: Anth* (Bertha Rogers,
    1997), *In the City of Sorrowing Clouds* (Print Workshop,
    1953), *Oxalis, New Directions Annual*

Celia Bland 🎤 ✈ P
6 Friendship St
Tivoli, NY 12583
    Pubs: *Too Darn Hot: Anth* (Global City Rev/Persea Bks,
    1998), *Alembic, Mudfish, 13th Moon, Snake Nation Rev,
    Chain, Poet Lore, Pequod, Columbia Mag, Verse, Pavement,
    New Poetry from Oxford, Washington Rev, Madison Rev,
    Apalachee Qtly*

Pamela Wharton Blanpied W
19 Pinnard St
Rochester, NY 14610, 716-473-5483
    Pubs: *Dragons: An Introduction to the Modern Infestation*
    (Warner Bks, 1981)

J. J. Blickstein 🎤 ✈ P
PO Box 505
Rosendale, NY 12472, 854-658-9273
www.hungermagazine.com
    Pubs: *Vespers: Anth* (U Syracuse Pr, 2002), *American
    Diaspora: Poetry in Exile: Anth* (U of Iowa Pr, 2000), *Poets
    Gallery Press: The Subterraneans: Anth* (Poets Gallery Pr,
    1997), *Long Shot, Rattle, Louisiana Rev*

Sarah W. Bliumis P
8 Pheasant Dr
Armonk, NY 10504, 914-273-8324
    Pubs: *Spoon River Qtly, Ceilioh, Whetstone*

Etta Blum P
c/o Shrier, 397 Spruce Ln, East Meadow, NY 11554
    Pubs: *Poems* (Golden Eagle Pr, 1937), *Poetry, Paris Rev,
    Nation, New Republic, Open Places*

Barbara Boncek 🎤 ✈ P
39 Denman Mt Rd
Grahamsville, NY 12740, 845-985-2847
    Pubs: *Wide Open Mag, Stone Ridge Poetry, Oxalis,
    OutLoud, Echoes, Almanac*

(Bonnie Hoag) Bonnielizabethoag 🎤 ✈ PP
Dionondehowa Wildlife Sanctuary/School, 148 Stanton Rd,
Shushan, NY 12873-3215, 518-854-7764
    Pubs: *Interview with a Young Crone* (Orion Pr, 1996), *Sand
    Paintings* (Muse Room, 1995)

Audrey Borenstein 🎤 W
4 Henry Ct
New Paltz, NY 12561-3000
    Pubs: *One Journal's Life* (Impassio Pr, 2002), *Paradise:
    Anth* (Florida Lit Fdn, 1994), *Messages from the Heart,
    Medicinal Purposes Literary Rev, Oxalis, Albany Rev,
    MacGuffin, North Dakota Qtly, Kansas Qtly/Arkansas Rev,
    Albany Rev*

Emily Borenstein 🎤 ✈ P
189 Highland Ave
Middletown, NY 10940, 914-343-3796
Internet: eboren@warwick.net
    Pubs: *Night of the Broken Glass* (Time Being Bks, 2002),
    From a Collector's Garden (Timberline Pr, 2001), *Cancer
    Queen* (Barlenmir Hse, 1979), *Aura Literary/Arts Rev, Home
    Planet News, Pivot, Poet Lore, Response, Webster Rev*

Martin Boris W
Ghame Writing Corp, 1019 Northfield Ave, Woodmere, NY
11598, 516-374-2058
    Pubs: *Brief Candle* (Crown, 1990), *Woodridge, 1946* (Ace,
    1981), *Two & Two* (Ballantine, 1980)

Megan Boyd P
PO Box 27
Sag Harbor, NY 11963, 516-725-9220
    Pubs: *Gathering to Deep Water* (Quay Bks, 1988), *New
    Voices: Anth* (Acad of American Poets, 1984)

Maureen Brady 🎤 ✈ W
135 Winnie Rd
Mt Tremper, NY 12457
Internet: meb4444@prodigy.net
    Pubs: *Ginger's Fire* (Haworth Pr, 2003), *Mom* (Alyson,
    1998), *The Question She Put to Herself, Folly* (Crossing Pr,
    1987, 1982), *Intersections: Anth* (Banff Centre Pr, 2000),
    Pillow Talk 2: Anth (Alyson, 2000), *Cabbage & Bones: Anth*
    (H Holt, 1997)

Maura Alia Bramkamp 🎤 ✈ P
266 Elmwood Ave, #307
Buffalo, NY 14222
Internet: maura.bramkamp@verizon.net
    Pubs: *Resculpting* (Paper Boat Pr, 1995), *This Far Together:
    Anth* (Haight Ashbury Literary, 1995), *Haight Ashbury Jrnl,
    Exhibition, Synapse, Coffee Hse, Switched-on Gutenberg,
    Convolvulus, Half Tones to Jubilee*

Anthony Brandt P&W
54 High St
Sag Harbor, NY 11963, 516-725-1937
Internet: asbrandt@aol.com
    Pubs: *The People Along the Sand: Three Stories, Six Poems
    & a Memoir* (Canio's Edtns, 1992), *Prairie Schooner, NYQ,
    Boulevard, TLS*

Kate Braverman 🎤 ✈ P&W
PO Box 794
Alfred, NY 14802
    Pubs: *The Incantation of Frieda K., Lithium for Medea*
    (Seven Stories Pr, 2002, 2002), *Small Craft Warnings* (U
    Nevada Pr, 1998), *Wonders of the West, Squandering the
    Blue* (Ballantine, 1993, 1990), *Postcard from August*
    (Illuminati, 1990)

Susan Breen W
1 Riverview Ct
Irvington, NY 10533, 914-591-7841
Internet: szb4@yahoo.com
    Pubs: *Kinesis, Kansas Qtly/Arkansas Rev, American Literary Rev, North Dakota Qtly, Chattahoochee, New Delta*

Wendy Brenner W
150 Capen Rd
Brockport, NY 14420, 716-395-9159
    Pubs: *Large Animals in Everyday Life* (U Georgia Pr, 1996), *New Stories from the South: Anth* (Algonquin, 1995), *Ploughshares, Southern Exposure, Puerto del Sol*

Joseph E. Bruchac, III 🎤 ✈ P&W
PO Box 308
Greenfield Center, NY 12833-0308, 518-584-1728
Internet: nudatlog@earthlink.net
    Pubs: *Sacajawea, Between Earth & Sky* (HB, 2000, 1996), *No Borders* (Holy Cow Pr, 1999), *Dawn Land* (Fulcrum Pub, 1993), *Green Mountains Rev, Kestrel, Parabola, Gatherings, Puerto del Sol, Bullhead*

Judith Bruder W
132 Wagon Rd
Roslyn Heights, NY 11577
Internet: judithb@idt.net
    Pubs: *Convergence* (Doubleday, 1993), *Going to Jerusalem* (S&S, 1979)

Felice Buckvar W
43 Juneau Blvd
Woodbury, NY 11797, 516-692-5485
    Pubs: *Dangerous Dream* (Royal Fireworks Pr, 1998), *Ten Miles High* (Morrow, 1981), *Happily Ever After* (Zebra Bks, 1980), *Family Circle, Woman's Day, Reader's Digest, Real People*

Frederick Henderson Buell 🎤 ✈ P
72 Amity Rd
Warwick, NY 10990, 914-258-6076
Internet: buell@warwick.net
    Pubs: *Full Summer* (Wesleyan, 1979), *Theseus & Other Poems* (Ithaca Hse, 1971), *Poetry, Hudson Rev, NER, Little Mag, Kansas Qtly, Pembroke Mag, Southern Rev, SW Rev*

Brio Burgess 🎤 ✈ PP&P
c/o Gail Tolley, 5 Cuyler St, Albany, NY 12202, 518-447-7448
Internet: streetkids2@aol.com
    Pubs: *WAIL!* (Jacobs Ladder Pr, 2002), *The Butcher's Block Volume 1: Anth* (Butchershop Pr, 2000), *Street Kids & Other Plays: Anth* (Angel Enterprises, 1995), *Outlaw Blues: Anth* (Tawanna L. Brace Knowles, 1992), *Bay Area Poets Anth, Poetalk, Open Mic*

Gabrielle Burton 🎤 ✈ P&W
211 Le Brun Rd
Eggertsville, NY 14226, 716-835-5062
    Pubs: *Heartbreak Hotel* (Dalkey Archive Pr, 1999)

Frederick Busch 🎤 ✈ W
839 Turnpike Rd
Sherburne, NY 13460, 607-847-8646
Internet: fbusch@mail.colgate.edu
    Pubs: *A Memory of War* (Norton, 2003), *The Night Inspector* (Ballantine, 2000), *Don't Tell Anyone* (Norton, 2000), *Girls* (Fawcett, 1998), *A Dangerous Profession* (St. Martin's, 1998)

Rebecca Busselle W
RR2, PO Box 270, Millerton, NY 12546, 518-789-3413
Internet: rebline@pipeline.com
    Pubs: *An Exposure of the Heart* (Norton, 1999), *A Frog's-Eye View, Bathing Ugly* (Orchard Bks, 1990, 1989)

Don Byrd P
English Dept, SUNY Albany, 1400 Washington, Albany, NY 12222, 518-442-4055
    Pubs: *The Great Dimestore* (Station Hill Pr, 1986), *Technics of Travel* (Tansy-Zelot, 1984)

Charles Calitri W
30 Gristmill Ln
Halesite, NY 11743
    Pubs: *The Goliath Head, Father, Strike Heaven on the Face* (Crown, 1974, 1962, 1958)

Jimmie Gilliam Canfield P&W
Erie Community College/City Campus, 121 Ellicott St, Buffalo, NY 14203, 716-842-8676
    Pubs: *Pieces of Bread* (White Pine Pr, 1986), *Black Mountain 2 Rev, Earth's Daughters*

Joe Cardillo 🎤 ✈ P
Hudson Valley Comm College, MRV 214, Troy, NY 12180, 518-629-7577
Internet: cardijos@hvcc.edu
    Pubs: *Be Like Water* (Warner, 2003), *Pulse* (Dutton/Penguin, 1996), *The Rock N' Roll Journals, No Surrender* (Stone Buzzard Pr, 1996, 1993)

Michael Carrino 🎤 ✈ P
32 Edgewater Ests.
Plattsburgh, NY 12901, 518-564-2134
    Pubs: *Some Rescues* (New Poets Series, 1994), *Dalhousie Rev, Pottersfield Portfolio, Green Mountains Rev, Hudson Rev, Poetry East, Slant, Calliope, Hayden's Ferry Rev*

Hayden Carruth   P
RD 1, PO Box 128, Munnsville, NY 13409, 315-495-6665
    Pubs: *Collected Shorter Poems, 1946-1991* (Copper
    Canyon, 1992), *Tell Me Again How the White Heron Rises &
    Flies Across the Nacreous River at Twilight Toward the
    Distant Islands* (New Directions, 1991)

Shari Elaine Carter 🎤 ✈   PP
4677 North St Rd
Marcellus, NY 13108-9724, 315-673-1789

Fran Castan 🎤 ✈   P
PO Box 1923
Amagansett, NY 11930, 631-267-8646
Internet: waters.edge@hamptons.com
    Pubs: *Our Bundle of Joy: Anth* (Meadow Brook, 2001), *The
    Widow's Quilt: Poems* (Canio's Edtns, 1996), *From Both
    Sides Now: Poetry of Vietnam: Anth* (Scribner, 1998), *The
    Seasons of Women: Anth* (Norton, 1995), *The Doll House
    Anth* (Pushcart, 1995), *Poetry Mag*

Alan Catlin 🎤 ✈   P
143 Furman St
Schenectady, NY 12304-1113, 518-372-5016
Internet: catlinv@crisny.org
    Pubs: *Greatest Hits* (Pudding Hse Pub, 2002), *Ghost Road*
    (Main Street Rag, 2001), *Hair of the Dog That Bit Me* (Four
    Sep Pub, 2000), *Stop Making Sense* (March Street Pr,
    2000), *Celtic Twilight* (JVC Bks, 1999), *Pleiades*

Siv Cedering 🎤 ✈   P&W
PO Box 89, 93 Merchants Path
Sagaponack, NY 11962, 631-537-7525
Internet: siv@hamptons.com
    Pubs: *Seeing the Blue In Between: Anth* (Candlewick Pr,
    2002), *Heart to Heart: Anth* (Harry N. Abrams, 2001),
    Letters from an Observatory (Karma Dog Edtns, 1998),
    Letters from the Floating World (U Pitt Pr, 1984), *The Blue
    Horse* (Clarion Bks, 1979)

Lena London Charney 🎤 ✈   P
PO Box 145
Mohegan Lake, NY 10547-0145, 914-528-5162
    Pubs: *Beyond Lament: Anth* (Northwestern U Pr, 1998), *A
    Celebration of Poets: Anth* (Poetry Guild, 1998), *Lover's
    Lane: Anth, The Color of Gold: Anth* (Golden Apple Pr, 1998,
    1995), *We Speak for Peace: Anth* (KIT Pub, 1993),
    Wordplay, Raconteur, Robin's Nest

Robert Chatain   P&W
PO Box 1770
Amagansett, NY 11930
    Pubs: *Touring Nam: The Viet Nam War Reader: Anth*
    (Morrow, 1985), *Best of TriQtly: Anth* (Washington Sq Pr,
    1982)

L. John Cieslinski 🎤 ✈   P
8 Close Hollow Dr
Hamlin, NY 14464-9302, 716-964-2868
Internet: johnmore@concentric.net
    Pubs: *Amelia, Pearl, Stone Country, Karamu, Negative
    Capability, Magical Blend, Black Bear Rev, Voices Intl, Sore
    Dove, Piedmont Lit Rev*

Josephine Clare   P
435 Exchange St
Geneva, NY 14456, 315-789-9517
    Pubs: *Mammatocumulus* (Ocotillo Pr, 1977), *Deutschland &
    Other Poems* (North Atlantic Bks, 1974)

Barbara Moore Clarkson   P
26 N Helderberg Pkwy
Slingerlands, NY 12159-9260, 315-474-3533
    Pubs: *The Flame Tree* (Basfal Bks, 1996), *Farewell to the
    Body* (The Word Works, 1991), *APR, Georgia Rev,
    Massachusetts Rev, Poetry, Salmagundi, NER*

Suzanne Cleary 🎤 ✈   P
1315 Elm St
Peekskill, NY 10566
Internet: scleary@sunyrockland.edu
    Pubs: *Keeping Time* (Carnegie Mellon Univ Pr, 2002),
    *Georgia Rev, Poetry Northwest, Third Coast, Atlanta Rev,
    Massachusettes Rev, Ohio Rev, New Letters*

Mickey Clement   W
14 Bay Crest
Huntington Bay, NY 11743, 516-427-8316
    Pubs: *The Irish Princess* (Putnam, 1994)

Vince Clemente 🎤 ✈   P
25 Cornell Rd
Sag Harbor, NY 11963, 516-725-8905
Internet: clemente.ppc@yahoo.com
    Pubs: *Sweeter than Vivaldi* (CCC Pr, 2002), *Watergate
    Along the Thames, The Shining Place* (Birnham Wood, 1999,
    1992), *Place for Lost Children, Girl in the Yellow Caboose*
    (Karma Dog, 1996, 1992), *Confrontations, The Ledge*

Arthur L. Clements   P
English Dept, SUNY Binghamton, Binghamton, NY
13902-6000, 607-777-2168
    Pubs: *The Book of Madness and Love* (Bordighera, 2000),
    Dream of Flying (Endless Mountains, 1994), *Poetry of
    Contemplation* (SUNY Pr, 1990), *Common Blessings*
    (Lincoln Springs, 1987), *Bellingham Rev, LIPS, Paterson
    Literary Rev, Poet, Poet Lore, Ruah*

Stephen Clorfeine 🎤 ✈   PP
63 Cooper St
Accord, NY 12404-6200, 845-626-3096
Internet: goldsun@ulster.net
    Pubs: *Beginning Again* (The Advocate Pr, 1994), *Out of
    the Catskills: Anth* (Bright Hill Pr, 1999), *Parabola,
    Shambhala Sun*

Steven Coffman 🎤 ✈ W
1874 Dombroski Rd
Dundee, NY 14837, 607-243-7561

Joan Cofrancesco 🎤 ✈ P
1025 James St, #39
Syracuse, NY 13203, 315-423-8404
    Pubs: *Riding on Dragons, Cat Bones in the Tree* (Hale Mary
Pr, 2000, 1996), *Walpurgis Night* (San Diego Poets Pr,
1993), *Silverman Rev, Potato Eyes, 13th Moon,
Rejectioncollection.com, Sinister Wisdom, Kalliope,
Common Lives/Lesbian Lives, Aurora*

Jonathan Cohen 🎤 ✈ P
101-75 Sylvan Ave
Miller Place, NY 11764-2425, 631-331-9178
    Pubs: *Countersong to Walt Whitman* (Azul, 1993), *With
Walker in Nicaragua* (Wesleyan U, 1984), *American Voice,
Agni, City Lights Rev*

Arlene Greenwald Cohen 🎤 ✈ P
36 Colonial Ln
Bellport, NY 11713-2906
Internet: agc55@aol.com
    Pubs: *PPA Lit Rev, Pen Woman, Electric Umbrella, Island
Poets, Long Island Qtly, Taproot Jrnl, Oxalis, Wordworks,
Live Poets Society, Pegasus*

Arthur Coleman W
C. W. Post College, Greenvale, NY 11548
    Pubs: *A Case in Point, Petals on a Wet Black Bough*
(Watermill, 1979, 1973)

Zena Collier 🎤 ✈ W
83 Berkeley St
Rochester, NY 14607-2207, 585-442-6941
Internet: zenacollier@juno.com
    Pubs: *Ghost Note* (Grove Weidenfeld, 1992), *A Cooler
Climate* (British American, 1990), *New Letters, SW Rev,
Southern Humanities Rev*

Billy Collins P
RD #2, Route 202
Somers, NY 10589-9802
    Pubs: *Nine Horses, Sailing Alone Around the Room*
(Random Hse, 2002, 2001), *Picnic, Lightning, The Art of
Drowning* (U Pittsburgh Pr, 1998, 1995), *Questions About
Angels* (Morrow, 1991), *New Yorker, Paris Rev, Poetry*

Kathleen Collins 🎤 ✈ W
19 Victory Knoll Path
Miller Place, NY 11764-1748, 631-331-8876
Internet: andercoll@aol.com
    Pubs: *The Romantic Naiad, Lovers in the Present Afternoon*
(Naiad Pr, 1993, 1984), *The Mountain, The Stone*
(Puckerbrush Pr, 1978)

Judith W. Colombo 🎤 ✈ W
1354 NY Rt 41
Deposit, NY 13754
Internet: judithcolombo@hotmail.com
    Pubs: *The Fablesinger* (Writers Club Pr, 2001), *Night
Crimes* (America Hse, 2001)

Brenda Connor-Bey PP
501 Old Kensico Rd, #2R
White Plains, NY 10603-3118, 914-686-8187
Internet: jimm3@aol.com
    Pubs: *Thoughts of an Everyday Woman: An Unfinished
Urban Folktale, New Rain 6 & 7* (Blind Beggar Pr, 1995,
1991), *Phatitude: Asian African Diaspora: Anth* (Phatitude
Literary Mag, 1998), *Essence*

Helen Cooper P
English Dept, SUNY, Stony Brook, NY 11794, 516-632-7400
    Pubs: *13th Moon, City, Xanadu, Jrnl of New Jersey Poets,
U.S. 1, Gravida, 19th Century Fiction*

Teresa Marta Costa P&PP
PO Box 391
West Hurley, NY 12491, 845-331-6713
Internet: manxcat12491@yahoo.com
    Pubs: *Blessed Madonna, Frankenstein* (The Poets Gallery,
1993, 1993), *Poetry Motel, Chronogram, Art Times,*

James Finn Cotter 🎤 ✈ P
Mount Saint Mary College, Newburgh, NY 12550-3612,
845-569-3162
Internet: cotter@msmc.edu
    Pubs: *The Nation, Hudson Rev, America, Commonweal,
Thought*

Jack Coulehan 🎤 ✈ P
4 Townsend Ct
Setauket, NY 11733, 631-689-6958
Internet: jcoul44567@aol.com
    Pubs: *Medicine Stone* (Fithian Pr, 2002), *The Heavenly
Ladder* (Ginninderra Pr, 2001), *First Photographs of
Heaven, The Knitted Glove* (Nightshade Pr, 1994, 1991),
JAMA, Kansas Qrtly

Nancy Vieira Couto 🎤 ✈ P
508 Turner Pl
Ithaca, NY 14850-5630, 607-273-8559
Internet: nvcouto@juno.com
    Pubs: *The Face in the Water, Pittsburgh Bk of Contemporary
Poetry: Anth* (U Pittsburgh Pr, 1990, 1993), *Second Word
Thursdays: Anth* (Bright Hill Pr, 1999), *Iowa Rev, Kalliope,
Shenandoah, American Voice, Black Warrior Rev*

Joseph Cowley 🎤 ✈   W
69430 Main Rd
Greenport, NY 11944-2801, 631-477-8719
Internet: JoeCowley@cs.com
    Pubs: *The Night Billy Was Born and Other Love Stories,
    Home by Seven, The House on Huntington Hill* (Xlibris,
    2002, 2000, 2000), *Landscape with Figures* (Writers Club
    Pr, 2001), *Dust Be My Destiny* (Denlinger's, 2000), *The
    Chrysanthemum Garden* (S&S, 1981)

Timothy Craig   P
RR Box 150, Tug Hollow Farm
Shushan, NY 12873, 518-854-7601
    Pubs: *Advice to the Rain* (Grey Walls Pr, 1990), *Knots &
    Fans* (Tamara, 1985), *London Mag, Pale Fire, Xanadu*

Jack Crawford, Jr.   P
54 Joy Rd
Woodstock, NY 12498
    Pubs: *Poetry, Poetry NW, Virginia Qtly Rev, Massachusetts
    Rev, Prairie Schooner, Chelsea*

Robert Creeley 🎤 ✈   P&W
64 Amherst St
Buffalo, NY 14207, 7166452575 1018
Internet: creeley@acsu.buffalo.edu
    Pubs: *So There: Poems 1976-83, Life & Death* (New
    Directions, 1998, 1998), *Selected Poems* (U California Pr,
    1991)

James Crenner   P
English Dept, Hobart & Wm. Smith Colleges, Geneva, NY
14456, 315-781-3361
    Pubs: *My Hat Flies on Again* (L'Epervier Pr, 1979), *The
    Airplane Burial Ground* (Hoffstadt, 1976)

Mary Crescenzo   P&W
12 Campwoods Grounds
Ossining, NY 10562, 914-923-1703
    Pubs: *Italian-Americana, Trapani Nova, Le Bella Figura*

Ida Maria Cruzkatz   P
24 Fairlawn Ave
Dobbs Ferry, NY 10522, 914-693-4473
    Pubs: *Bitterroot, New Collage, Tempest, MPR, Windless
    Orchard, Samisdat*

Jack Curtis 🎤   P&W
Mildred Marmur Assoc LTC, 2005 Palmer Ave, Ste 127,
Larchmont, NY 10538, 408-667-2440
    Pubs: *Dawn Waters* (Spring Creek Pr, 1998), *Christmas in
    Calico* (Daybreak Pr, 1998), *Mercy Shot, Pepper Tree
    Rider* (Walker & Co., 1995, 1994), *The Fight for San
    Bernardo, Jury on Smoky Hill, Sheriff Kill* (Pocket Bks,
    1993, 1992, 1991)

Michele Cusumano   P
Box 117
New Suffolk, NY 11956, 516-734-6090
    Pubs: *Just as the Boy Dreams of White Thighs Under
    Flowered Skirts* (Street Pr, 1981), *Zephyr*

Vincent T. Dacquino 🎤 ✈   W
38 Curry Rd
Mahopac, NY 10541, 914-628-9092
    Pubs: *Max's Glasses* (Benchmark Education Co, 2002),
    Sybil Ludington: The Call to Arms (Purple Mountain Pr,
    2000), *Kiss the Candy Days Good-Bye* (Dell, 1983)

Kate Dahlstedt   P
10 Winthrop Ave
Albany, NY 12203, 518-438-1062
    Pubs: *Outpost, Brussels Sprout, Groundswell, Mildred,
    Voices*

Enid Dame 🎤 ✈   P&W
PO Box 455
High Falls, NY 12440, 845-687-4084
Internet: dame@admin.njit.edu
    Pubs: *Stone Shekhina* (Three Mile Harbor, 2002), *Anything
    You Don't See* (West End, 1992), *Lilith & Her Demons*
    (CCC, 1989), *The Poets Grimm: Anth* (Storyline Pr, 2003),
    *Runes, Heliotrope, Rattapallax, Many Mountains Moving,
    NYQ, Tikkun, American Voice, Phoebe*

George Davis   W
327 Claremont Ave
Mount Vernon, NY 10552
    Pubs: *Love, Black Love* (Doubleday, 1978), *Coming Home*
    (Random Hse, 1972), *Essence, Black World*

Marjorie De Fazio 🎤 ✈   P
254 Burrows Rd
Unadilla, NY 13849, 607-988-6358
Internet: jorie@dmcom.net
    Pubs: *A Quiet Noise* (The Poet's Pr, 1972), *Out of the
    Catskills & Just Beyond: Anth* (Bright Hill Pr, 1997), *Omen,
    Aphra, Michael's*

tatiana de la tierra 🎤 ✈   P&W
PMB 104, 266 Elmwood Ave, Buffalo, NY 14222
Internet: td6@acsu.buffalo.edu
    Pubs: *Gynomite: Fearless Feminist Porn: Anth* (New Mouth
    from the Dirty South, 2000), *Pillow Talk 2: Anth* (Alyson,
    2000), *Latino Heretics: Anth* (Black Ice/FC 2, 1999), *El
    Andar, Flyway Lit Rev, La Revista Calaca, Mid-American
    Rev, Cimarron Rev*

Beltran De Quiros 🎤 ✈   W
PO Box 6134
Syracuse, NY 13217, 315-476-8994
Internet: jromeu@ecs.syr.edu
    Pubs: *Narrativa y Libertad: Anth, La Otra Cara De La
    Moneda* (Ediciones Universal, 1996, 1984), *Los Unos, Los
    Otros y El Seibo '71*

Edward De Roo W
7 Bacon St
St. James, NY 11780, 516-862-9397
  Pubs: *Rumble in the Housing Project* (Ace Bks, 1944),
  Nassau Qtly Rev, New Mexico Qtly

Regina deCormier P&W
34 Sparkling Ridge
New Paltz, NY 12561
  Pubs: *Claiming the Spirits Within* (Beacon Pr, 1996), *Two
  Worlds Walking* (New Rivers Pr, 1994), *Hoofbeats on the
  Door* (Helicon Nine Edtns, 1993), *APR, Nation, Salmagundi,
  Poetry East, Nimrod*

Constance Dejong W
131 S Broadway, #3
Nyack, NY 10960
  Pubs: *I.T.I.L.O.E.* (Top Stories, 1984), *Satyagraha* (Tianam
  Pr, 1983)

Samuel R. Delany W
c/o Henry Morrison Inc, PO Box 235, Bedford Hills, NY 10507,
914-666-3500

Louise Budde DeLaurentis 🎤 P&W
983 Cayuga Heights Rd
Ithaca, NY 14850
  Pubs: *Outerbridge, Kalliope, Farm Jrnl, Plainswoman,
  Frontiers*

Bruce D. Delmont W
443 Wendel Ave
Buffalo, NY 14223-2211
  Pubs: *Art Voice, MDA Chronicle, The Villager, Buffalo Mag,
  Poetry Forum Short Stories*

Robert DeMaria W
106 Vineyard Pl
Port Jefferson, NY 11777, 631-928-3460
Internet: rdemaria@portjeff.net
  Pubs: *The White Road* (Permanent Pr, 2000), *That Kennedy
  Girl* (Vineyard Pr, 1999), *Stone of Destiny* (Ballantine, 1985),
  New Letters, Antaeus, Florida Rev

Mary Russo Demetrick 🎤 P&W
423 E Ellis St
East Syracuse, NY 13057-2413, 315-437-3474
Internet: mmdemetr@syr.edu
  Pubs: *Italian Notebook, First Pressing* (Hale Mary Pr, 1995,
  1994), *Hey!: Anth* (Durland Alternative Pr, 1998), *Malachite
  & Agate: Anth* (Grove Pr, 1997), *Word of Mouth: Anth*
  (Crossing Pr, 1990), *Asheville Poetry Rev, Footwork*

Carl Dennis P
49 Ashland Ave
Buffalo, NY 14222, 716-886-1331
Internet: cedennis@acsu.buffalo.edu
  Pubs: *Ranking the Wishes, Meetings with Time* (Penguin,
  1997, 1992), *The Outskirts of Troy, The Near World* (Morrow,
  1988, 1985)

Mark Dery P&W
19 White Ave
Nyack, NY 10960
Internet: markdery@aol.com
  Pubs: *Two Men Meet on a Beach* (Broadside; Atticus Pr,
  1982), *EFQ, Frank, Red Light Blue Light*

Rachel Guido deVries 🎤 ✈ P
PO Box 228
Cazenovia, NY 13035-0228, 315-655-8020
Internet: guidogirl@aol.com
  Pubs: *Gambler's Daughter, How to Sing to a Dago, The
  Voices We Carry: Anth* (Guernica Edtns, 2001, 1996, 1994),
  The Milk of Almonds: Anth (Feminist Pr, 2002), *Tender
  Warriors* (Firebrand Bks, 1986), *Paterson Lit Rev, Voices in
  Italian Americana*

Katherine Dewart P
333 Ellis Hollow Creek Rd
Ithaca, NY 14850, 607-272-8548

Bob Dial P
6 Willowbrook Rd
Glenville, NY 12302
Internet: JohnRDial@aol.com
  Pubs: *Gulf Coast, Ledge, MacGuffin, Chiron Rev, Writer,
  Plastic Tower*

Anthony DiFranco W
Suffolk Community College, 533 College Rd, English Dept,
Selden, NY 11784, 516-451-4159
Internet: difranco@sunysuffolk.edu
  Pubs: *Ardent Spring* (Bantam, 1986), *Prize Stories: O.
  Henry Awards: Anth* (Doubleday, 1986), *Four Quarters, NAR*

Arthur Dobrin P
613 Dartmouth St
Westbury, NY 11590, 516-997-8545
  Pubs: *Angles & Chambers* (CCC, 1990), *Out of Place*
  (Backstreet, 1982)

Anthony J. Dolan P&W
69 Sheryl Cres
Smithtown, NY 11787, 516-724-1859

Lynn Domina   🎤 ✈   P
472 Sherwood Rd
Delhi, NY 13753, 607-746-7847
Internet: dominalm@dehli.edu
    Pubs: *Corporal Works* (Four Way Bks, 1995), *Marlboro
Rev, Carolina Qtly, Indiana Rev, Poetry NW, Prairie
Schooner, SPR*

George Drew   🎤 ✈   P
PO Box 298
Poestenkill, NY 12140, 518-283-1339
Internet: drewgeo@hvcc.edu
    Pubs: *So Many Bones* (Rarus Pr, 1997), *Toads in a
Poisoned Tank* (Tamarack, 1986), *Southern Poetry Rev,
Maine Times, Vermont Lit Rev, Qtly West, Salmagundi*

Joseph Duemer   P
School of Liberal Arts, Clarkson Univ, Potsdam, NY 13699,
315-262-2466
Internet: duemer@polaris.clarkson.edu
    Pubs: *Static* (Owl Creek Pr, 1996), *Customs* (U Georgia Pr,
1987), *APR, Iowa Rev, NER, Boulevard, Mss., Tampa Rev,
Tar River Poetry*

Peter Kane Dufault   🎤 ✈   P
56 Hickory Hill Rd
Hillsdale, NY 12529, 518-672-4897
Internet: pkdufault@hotmail.com
    Pubs: *Looking in All Directions* (Worple Pr, 2000),
*Memorandum to the Age of Reason, New Things Come Into
the World* (Lindisfarne, 1993, 1989), *Norton Anth of Poetry*
(Norton, 1996), *New Yorker, New Republic, Atlantic,
Spectator*

Erika Duncan   🎤 ✈   W
105 Hampton St
Sag Harbor, NY 11963, 631-725-3177
Internet: kerika@earthlink.net
    Pubs: *Those Giants: Let Them Rise, Unless Soul Clap Its
Hands* (Schocken, 1985, 1985)

Mary Durham   🎤   P
PO Box 2856
Poughkeepsie, NY 12603-8856, 914-473-0405
Internet: mmd373@aol.com
    Pubs: *Crazy Ladies, Wise Women: Anth* (Crazy Ladies Pr,
1999), *Almanac, Outloud, Poetry Peddler, Home Planet
News, Kaatskill Life*

Arlene Eager   P
85 Edgewood Ave
Smithtown, NY 11787, 631-366-3437
    Pubs: *Essential Love: Anth* (Grayson Bks, 2000), *Atlanta
Rev, Five Points, Eureka Lit Mag, Hampden-Sydney Poetry
Rev, Hudson Rev*

M. D. Elevitch   🎤 ✈   W
Box 604
Palisades, NY 10964, 845-365-3772
    Pubs: *Dog Tags Yapping* (S Illinois U Pr, 2003), *Grips*
(Grossman, 1972), *Green Eternal Go* (Foolscap Pr, 1991),
Americans at Home (First Person, 1976), *New Directions
33: Anth* (New Directions, 1976), *Chelsea, TriQtly, Chicago
Rev, Pacific Coast Jrnl*

Virginia Elson   P
Smith Pond Rd, RD 2, Avoca, NY 14809, 607-566-8355
    Pubs: *And Echoes for Direction, Where in the Sun to Stand*
(State Street Pr, 1987, 1982), *Atlantic, Literary Rev, Prairie
Schooner, Poetry NW, Yankee*

Judith Sue Epstein   P
1859 Slaterville Rd
Ithaca, NY 14850, 607-277-4205
    Pubs: *Keeping Score* (Ithaca Hse, 1975), *Epoch, Hanging
Loose, The Trojan Horse, The Grapevine*

Amelia Etlinger   PP
44 Barney Rd
Clifton Park, NY 12065
    Pubs:

Graham Everett   🎤 ✈   P
PO Box 772
Sound Beach, NY 11789-0772
Internet: grahamever@aol.com
    Pubs: *Corps Calleux* (Street, 2000), *The Doc Fayth Poems*
(Mongrel, 1998), *Minus Green Plus* (Breeze/Street, 1995),
Minus Green (Yank This Pr, 1992), *Caprice, Long Island
Qtly, 4x4, Exquisite Corpse*

Frank C. Falcetta   🎤   P&W
10 Larry Dr
Commack, NY 11725-3306, 631-499-6530
    Pubs: *Lit Rev 2001, Emotions, Reader's Break, Orange
Willow Rev, Blind Man's Rainbow, Grit, Nomad's Choir,
Taproot*

Pat Falk   🎤 ✈   P
190-15 Merrick Rd.
Amityville, NY 11701, 631-598-4635
Internet: falkp@ncc.edu
    Pubs: *In the Shape of a Woman* (Canios Edtns, 1995), *And
What Rough Beast: Anth* (Ashland Poetry, Pr, 1999), *The
Muse Strikes Back: Anth* (Story Line Pr, 1997), *The Nassau
Rev, Xanadu, Petroglyph, 13th Moon, Poets On, Long
Island Qtly, Thema, Wordsmith*

Livio Farallo   🎤 ✈   P
4020 McKoon Ave.
Niagara Falls, NY 14305
    Pubs: *Spelunker Flophouse, Spillway Pubs, Rattle, Black
Bear Rev, Pavement Saw, Asheville Poetry Rev, Sheila-Na-
Gig, Acid Angel*

Patricia Farewell 🎤 ✈ P
PO Box 198
Pleasantville, NY 10570-0198, 914-769-7228
    Pubs: *Waltzing on Water: Anth* (Dell, 1989), *Desire: Anth* (St.
Martin's Pr, 1980), *Chelsea, Green Mountains Rev,
Formalist*

Irving Feldman 🎤 ✈ P
SUNY Buffalo, English Dept, Buffalo, NY 14260, 716-885-4122
Internet: feldman@acsu.buffalo.edu
    Pubs: *Beautiful False Things* (Grove, 2000), *The Life &
Letters* (U Chicago, 1994), *All of Us Here, Teach Me Dear
Sister, New & Selected Poems* (Viking Penguin, 1986,
1983, 1979)

Mary Ferrari 🎤 P
288 Weaver St
Larchmont, NY 10538, 914-834-2132
    Pubs: *Why the Sun Cannot Set: New and Selected Poems*
(Hanging Loose, 1994), *The Isle of the Little God* (Kulchur,
1981), *The Angel Hair Anthology* (Granary Bks, 2001), *The
13th Moon: Anth* (13th Moon Pr, 1996), *Curious Rooms, Sal
Mimeo, Hanging Loose*

Anne Lathrop Fessenden 🎤 ✈ P
PO Box 35
Willow, NY 12495-0035
    Pubs: *Newark Rev, Woodstock Times*

Sally A. Fiedler P
154 Morris Ave
Buffalo, NY 14214-1610
    Pubs: *Eleanor Mooseheart* (Weird Sisters Pr, 1992), *To
Illinois, With Love* (Tyler School of Art, 1975), *APR*

Jeanne Finley 🎤 ✈ P&W
125 Manning Blvd.
Albany, NY 12203, 518-438-8728
    Pubs: *Anth of Mag Verse & Yearbook of American Poetry*
(Monitor, 1988), *North Country: Anth* (Greenfield Rev Pr,
1986), *New Myths, Little Mag, Visions Intl*

Mike Finn P
930 Comfort Rd
Spencer, NY 14883, 607-277-2345
    Pubs: *And Death Is Watching, A Man Mistaking His Mother
for His Ego* (Poortree Bks, 1996, 1992), *Mothering,
Audit/Poetry, Choice, Second Growth, Not Man Apart*

Adam D. Fisher 🎤 ✈ P
11 Media Ln
Stony Brook, NY 11790-2811, 631-751-6606
Internet: adfisher@erols.com
    Pubs: *God's Garden, An Everlasting Name* (Behrman Hse,
1999, 1992), *Dancing Alone* (Birnham Wood, 1993), *Long
Island Qtly, West Hills Rev, MPR, NAR, CCAR Jrnl*

Lou Fisher 🎤 W
12 Julie Dr
Hopewell Junction, NY 12533
Internet: loufisher8@aol.com
    Pubs: *The Blue Ice Pilot* (Warner Bks, 1986), *Sunstop 8*
(Dell, 1978), *New Letters, Mississippi Rev, Other Voices,
Crescent Rev*

Harrison Fisher 🎤 ✈ P
50 N Allen St
Albany, NY 12203, 518-482-2402
    Pubs: *Poematics of the Hyperbloody Real: Poems 1980-
2001* (Xlibris, 2000), *House Organ*

Charles Fishman 🎤 ✈ P
56 Wood Acres Rd
East Patchogue, NY 11772, 631-776-2752
Internet: cfishman@notes.cc.sunysb.edu
    Pubs: *Chopin's Piano* (CCC, 2003), *Time Travel Reports*
(Timberline Pr, 2002), *The Firewalkers* (Avisson Pr, 1996),
The Death Mazurka, Blood to Remember: Anth (Texas Tech
U Pr, 1989, 1991), *Georgia Rev, Southern California Anth,
New Letters, NER*

Gregory Fitz Gerald P&W
32 Cherry Dr
Brockport, NY 14420, 716-637-9372
    Pubs: *October Blood & Other Stories* (Spectrum Pr, 1993),
The Hidden Quantum (Hobaugh Pubs, 1993), *The Druze
Document* (Cliffhanger Pr, 1987), *Galaxy, Aberrations, Red
Herring, Fantastic Worlds, Show & Tell*

Peggy Flanders 🎤 ✈ P
4956 St John Dr
Syracuse, NY 13215-1245, 315-488-8077
    Pubs: *An Array of Textures* (Threshold Pr, 2002), *Comstock
Rev, Queen's Qtly, Radiology, Voices Intl, South Florida Rev*

Lisa Fleck P
18 Glendale Rd
Ossining, NY 10562
    Pubs: *Musical Chairs in the Garden* (1st East Coast Theatre
& Publishing Co, 1987)

Sheldon Flory 🎤 ✈ P
6981 Rte 21
Naples, NY 14512
    Pubs: *A Winter's Journey* (Copper Beech, 1979), *Arvon Intl
Poetry Competition Anth* (Arvon, 1990), *Puckerbrush,
Graffiti Rag, Ekphrasis, Natl Prison Reform Association
News, New Yorker, Poetry, Iowa Rev, Seneca Rev,
Mangrove, Zone 3, Gulf Coast*

Jim Flosdorf 🎤 ✈ P
18 Lillian Ln
Troy, NY 12180-4700, 518-272-6210
Internet: jfpan@nycap.rr.com
    Pubs: *My Father Was Shiva* (Ablex, 1994), *North Country:
Anth* (Greenfield Rev Pr, 1986), *Groundswell, Voices*

Joan Elizabeth Ford   P
151 Woodward Ave
Buffalo, NY 14214, 716-886-7136
    Pubs: *Intrepid, Moody Street Irregulars, Swift Kick, Earth's
    Daughters*

Gertrude Ford   W
3 Midwood Cross
Roslyn, NY 11576-2414
    Pubs: *81 Sheriff Street* (Frederick Fell, 1981)

Peter Fortunato ♪ ✈   P
172 Pearsall Pl
Ithaca, NY 14850
www.lightlink.com/fortuna
    Pubs: *Letters to Tiohero* (Grapevine Pr, 1979), *A Bell or a
    Hook* (Ithaca Hse, 1977), *Nimrod, Seneca Rev, Yellow Silk,
    Voices in Italian Americana*

Walt Franklin   P
1205 County, Rte 60
Rexville, NY 14877, 607-225-4592
    Pubs: *The Singing Groves* (Timberline Pr, 1996), *Uplands
    Haunted by the Sea* (Great Elm Pr, 1992), *The Wild Trout*
    (Nightshade Pr, 1991), *Poem, Grain, Pig*

Darren Franz   P&W
733 Stowe Ave
Baldwin, NY 11510
    Pubs: *Jack Frost* (iuniverse, 2000), *Torniquet Heart: Anth*
    (Prime Bks, 2002), *Objet D'Evil: Anth* (Underside, 2001),
    *Martian Wave, Feline, Peridot Bks, Futures, Short Scary
    Tales, Alternate Realities, Mysterical-e, Story House,
    Nightmares, Outer Darkness*

Mary Lamb Freeman   P
182 Oxford Ave
Amherst, NY 14226
    Pubs: *Ripples, Crowdancing, Midwest Poetry Rev, Room of
    Our Own, Green Feather, Dream Intl Qtly*

Emanuel Fried   W
1064 Amherst St
Buffalo, NY 14216-3606, 716-873-4131
Internet: friedej@bscmail.buffalostate.edu
    Pubs: *The Un-American* (Springhouse Edtns, 1992), *Big
    Ben Hood, Elegy for Stanley Gorski* (Labor Arts Bks, 1988,
    1986), *Dramatists Qtly*

Lee Frisbee   P
91 Bev Ln
Brockport, NY 14420-1236, 716-637-5672
    Pubs: *Driftwood East, Encore, English Jrnl, Fiesta, New
    Infinity Rev, Rufus*

Richard Frost ♪ ✈   P
959 Co Hwy 7
Otego, NY 13825, 607-988-7170
Internet: frostrg@oneonta.edu
    Pubs: *Neighbor Blood* (Sarabande Bks, 1996), *The Family
    Way* (Devil's Millhopper Pr, 1994), *Jazz for Kirby* (State
    Street Pr, 1990), *Paris Rev, Poetry, Georgia Rev*

Carol Frost ♪ ✈   P
959 County Hwy 7
Otego, NY 13825, 607-988-7170
Internet: frostc@hartwick.edu
    Pubs: *Love & Scorn, Venus & Don Juan, Pure* (TriQtly Bks,
    2000, 1996, 1994), *Chimera* (Peregrine Smith, 1990), *Day
    of the Body* (Ion Bks, 1986), *APR, Atlantic, NER, TriQtly,
    Partisan Rev, Ploughshares, Kenyon Rev, Shenandoah,
    Southern Rev, Volt*

Gerard Furey   W
HGHS 70 Roaring Brook Rd
Chappaqua, NY 10514, 914-238-3911
    Pubs: *Pittsburgh Mag, St. Anthony Messenger, Ambit*

Enid Futterman ♪ ✈   W
661 Rte 23
Craryville, NY 12521, 518-851-6340
Internet: EnidF@aol.com
    Pubs: *Bittersweet Journey* (Viking, 1998)

Judith Gaberman   W
PO Box 135
South Salem, NY 10590
    Pubs: *In Summertime It's Tuffy* (Bradbury Pr, 1977)

Elizabeth Gaffney   P
English Dept, Westchester Community College, 75 Grasslands
Rd, Valhalla, NY 10595, 914-785-6194
    Pubs: *SPR, College English, Wordsmith, Descant, Wind,
    New Voices, The Smith, Dark Horse*

Diane Gallo ♪ ✈   P&W
9 Nilton St, POB 106
Gilbertsville, NY 13776, 607-783-2386
Internet: gallod@norwich.net
    Pubs: *Signs of Departure* (Pudding Hse Pr, 2000), *The
    Neighbor's Dog Howls* (Madwoman's Daughter Pr, 1996),
    Creating the Literature Portfolio: Anth (NTC Pub Group,
    1996), *Asheville Poetry Rev, Phoebe*

Beatrice Ganley ♪ ✈   P
4095 East Ave
Rochester, NY 14618-3732, 716-586-1000
Internet: bganley@ssjrochester.org
    Pubs: *The Sea of Connection* (Heirloom Pub, 1996), *Sisters
    Today, Broomstick, Lake Effect, Wyoming, Verity, Muse
    Reader*

Eric Gansworth   P&W
Niagara County Community College, 3111 Saunders
Settlement Rd, Sanborn, NY 14132, 716-614-6715
Internet: onondaga@localnet.com
Pubs: *Children of the Dragonfly* (U Arizona Pr, 2000), *Nickel Eclipse: Iroquois Moon, Indian Summers* (Michigan State U Pr, 2000, 1998), *Nothing But the Truth: Anth* (Prentice Hall, 2000), *Word Thursdays II: Anth* (Bright Hill, 1999)

Eugene K. Garber   W
13 Empire Circle
Rensselaer, NY 12144-9319, 518-434-3294
Internet: egarber1@nycap.rr.com
Pubs: *The Historian* (Milkweed Edtns, 1994), *Norton Anths of Contemporary Fiction* (Norton, 1989, 1988), *Paris Rev*

Lewis Gardner   P
16 Cedar Way
Woodstock, NY 12498, 914-679-4090
Pubs: *Columbia, Firewood, U.S. 1 Worksheets, Ethical Society*

Sandra Gardner   P
16 Cedar Way
Woodstock, NY 12498
Pubs: *We Used to be Wives: Anth* (Fithian Press, 2002), *Dyed-in-the-Wool: Anth* (Vivisphere Pubs, 2002), *Mutant Mule Rev: Anth* (Finishing Line Pr, 1999), *Freedom's Just Another Word: Anth* (Outrider Pr, 1998)

Thomas Gavin   W
Univ Rochester, English Dept, Rochester, NY 14627, 716-244-8052
Pubs: *Breathing Water* (Arcade, 1994), *The Last Film of Emile Vico* (Viking, 1986), *Kingkill* (Random Hse, 1977), *Icarus, Prairie Schooner, Georgia Rev, TriQtly*

Joan Austin Geier   P
39-91 48 St
Sunnyside Garden, NY 11104-1021, 718-899-5919
Internet: jag3634@aol.com
Pubs: *A Formal Feeling Comes* (Story Line Pr, 1994), *Mother of Tribes* (Four Circles Pr, 1987), *The Lyric, Potomac Rev, New Rev, U Portland Rev, Northern Spirit, Amelia, Negative Capability, Visions, Poets On*

Ruth Geller   W
270 Potomac Ave
Buffalo, NY 14213, 716-881-5391
Pubs: *Triangles, Nice Jewish Girls: Anth* (Crossing Pr, 1984, 1984), *Ms., Sojourner*

Willard Gellis   P&W
57 Seafield Ln
Bay Shore, NY 11706
Pubs: *Under Algol, Tramping Dirtyside* (Crippled Planet Pr, 2001, 1999), *No Grease on the Gump, Slaves of Algol* (CD's; Orpheophrenia, 2002, 2002), *Die Metal* (Big Easy Pr, 1996), *Bronco Junky* (Wild Strawberry Pr, 1994), *Penny Dreadful Rev, Beast Qtly*

Kathleen Gemmell   P
209 1/2 Pleasant St
Ithaca, NY 14850-5603, 607-273-6511
Internet: ksg3@cornell.edu
Pubs: *A Common Bond* (Allegheny Pr, 1976), *Bookpress, Bitterroot, Blackbird Circle, Pembroke Mag, Poet Lore, South Carolina Rev, Voices Intl*

Paul Genega   P
PO Box 1
Stuyvesant, NY 12173
Pubs: *Striking Water* (Ireland; Salmon, 1989), *Seagirt* (A Musty Bone, 1988), *Nation, Epoch*

William Gifford   W
English Dept, Vassar College, Box 344, Poughkeepsie, NY 12604-0344, 845-471-5132
Pubs: *Colorado Qtly, QRL, Apalachee Qtly, Peregrine, Open City*

Mary Gilliland   P
Writing Program, Cornell Univ, 172 Pearsall Pl, Ithaca, NY 14850, 607-273-6637
Pubs: *Gathering Fire* (Ithaca Hse, 1982), *LIT, Smartish Pace, Poetry, Southern California Anthology, Nimrod, Seneca Rev, Spoon River Qtly, Yellow Silk, Seattle Rev*

Gail Godwin   W
7 Laura Ln
Woodstock, NY 12498
Pubs:

Gail Kadison Golden   P
18 Zabella Dr
New City, NY 10956
Internet: peacepoet@aol.com
Pubs: *Awaiting Creation* (Xlibris, 2002), *The Evansville Rev, Thirteenth Moon, Pikesville Rev, Apalachee Rev, Visions, Korone, Embers, Footwork, Karamu, Outerbridge, Milieu*

Barry Goldensohn   P
11 Seward St
Saratoga Springs, NY 12866, 518-584-7962
Internet: bgoldens@skidmore.edu
Pubs: *Dance Music* (Cummington Pr, 1992), *The Marrano* (Natl Poetry Fdn, 1988), *Poets of the New Century: Anth* (Godine, 2001), *Poetry, Yale Rev, Agenda, Salmagundi, Agni*

Lorrie Goldensohn 🎤 ✈   P
11 Seward St
Saratoga Springs, NY 12866
    Pubs: *East Long Pond* (Cummington Pr, 1997), *The Tether*
    (L'Epervier, 1982), *Dreamwork* (Porch, 1980), *Salmagundi,*
    Ploughshares, Poetry

Cynthia R. Golderman   P
5 Edison Ave
Albany, NY 12208, 518-438-7360
    Pubs: *Oh, That We Would, At This Last Breach . . . The*
    Facility (Cerulean Pr, 1986, 1986)

Barbara Goldowsky 🎤   P&W
PO Box 705, East Hampton, NY 11937, 631-329-3816
Internet: Goldowsky@aol.com
    Pubs: *Restless Spirits, Ferry to Nirvana & New Poems*
    (Amereon Ltd, 1992, 1991), *Whelks Walk Rev,*
    Confrontation, The Round Table, Brookspring '92, Caprice

Ann Goldsmith 🎤 ✈   P
45 N Pearl St
Buffalo, NY 14202, 716-833-1879
Internet: anngold2@juno.com
    Pubs: *No One is the Same Again* (QRL, 1999), *Poets at*
    Work: Anth (Just Buffalo Literary Center, 1995), *The Qtly,*
    Helicon Nine

Catherine Gonick   P
48 Fair St #C4
Cold Spring, NY 10516-3009, 845-265-2775
Internet: gm@highlands.com
    Pubs: *Pivot, Plain Dealer Mag, New Boston Rev, Zone, City,*
    Mothering

Stephen Goodwin   W
PO Box 47
Bedford, NY 10506-0047
    Pubs: *The Blood of Paradise* (Dutton, 1979), *Kin* (H&R,
    1975), *Country Jrnl, Yankee*

Marea Gordett   P
1 Hunter's Run Blvd
Cohoes, NY 12047
    Pubs: *Freeze Tag* (Wesleyan U Pr 1984), *The Pushcart*
    Prize V: Anth (Pushcart Pr, 1980), *Georgia Rev,*
    Ploughshares, Antioch Rev

Kirpal Gordon   P
c/o Steven Hirsch, Heaven Bone Pr, PO Box 486, Chester, NY
10918, 718-797-3321
    Pubs: *Dear Empire State Building, This Ain't No Ballgame*
    (Heaven Bone Pr, 1990, 1988)

Shotsie Gorman   P
44 Hickory Hill Dr
Warwick, NY 10990
www.shotsiestattoo.com
    Pubs: *The Black Marks He Made* (Proteus Pr, 1999), *Will*
    Work For Peace: New Political Poems Anth (Zeropanik,
    1999), *Fertile Ground, Paterson Lit Rev, LIPS, Heaven*
    Bone, At Your Leisure Mag, Black Swan Rev

Marcia Grant   P
15 Miller Hill Dr
La Grangeville, NY 12540
    Pubs: *Connecticut River Rev, Oxalis, Z Misc, Bitterroot,*
    Alura Poetry Qtly, Midwest Poetry Rev, Archer

C. D. Grant 🎤 ✈   P
24 Bowbell Rd
White Plains, NY 10607-1106, 914-683-6792
Internet: consultingplus@compuserve.com
    Pubs: *Images in a Shaded Light, Keeping Time, New Rain*
    Vol. 9: Anth (Blind Beggar Pr, 1986, 1981, 1999), *Bum Rush*
    the Page: Anth (Three Rivers Pr, 2001), *Black Masks Mag,*
    Suburban Styles, Essence

Jerome Greenfield   W
English Dept, SUNY New Paltz, New Paltz, NY 12561,
914-257-2720
    Pubs: *Wilhelm Reich vs. the USA* (Norton, 1974), *The Chalk*
    Line (Chilton Bks, 1963), *Midstream*

Linda Greenwald 🎤 ✈   P&W
162 Elm St
Cobleskill, NY 12043-1021, 518-234-7162
Internet: greenwl@cobleskill.edu
    Pubs: *Word Thursdays II: Anth* (Bright Hill Pr, 1999), *Heart*
    Music: Anth (the unmade bed, 1988), *The Stories We Hold*
    Secret: Anth (Greenfield Rev Pr, 1986), *Comstock Rev*

Eamon Grennan 🎤 ✈   P
Vassar College, Box 352, Poughkeepsie, NY 12604-0352,
914-437-5655
    Pubs: *Still Life with Waterfall* (Gallery Pr, 2001), *Relations:*
    New & Selected Poems, So It Goes, As If It Matters
    (Graywolf, 1998, 1995, 1992), *What Light There Is & Other*
    Poems (North Point Pr, 1989), *New Yorker, Kenyon Rev,*
    Poetry

Susan Anne Gubernat 🎤 ✈   P
English Dept Dr, Nassau Community College, One Education,
Garden City, NY 11530, 516-572-7185
Internet: sgubernat@aol.com
    Pubs: *Flesh* (Helicon Nine Ednts, 1999)

Jorge Guitart 🎤 ✈ P
Univ Buffalo, 910 Clemens Hall, Buffalo, NY 14260-4620,
7166456000x1194
Internet: guitart@acsu.buffalo.edu
Pubs: *Film Blanc* (Meow Pr, 1996), *Foreigner's Notebook*
(Shuffaloff Bks, 1993), *Chain, Carolina Qtly, Exquisite
Corpse, First Intensity, Tin Fish, Kiosk*

Robert Guzikowski P
900 Pratt Dr
Vestal, NY 13850-3843
Pubs: *Letters, Grub Street, Tightrope*

Janet Hamill 🎤 ✈ P
24 Chaucer Ct
Middletown, NY 10941, 914-692-7263
Internet: nightsky@warwick.net
Pubs: *Flying Nowhere* (Not Records, 2001), *Lost Ceilings*
(Telephone Bks, 1999), *Nostalgia of the Infinite* (Ocean View
Bks, 1992), *Will Work for Peace: Anth* (zeropanik pr, 1999),
Living with the Animals: Anth (Faber & Faber, 1994), *For
Immediate Release*

Louis Hammer 🎤 ✈ P&W
PO Box 9
Old Chatham, NY 12136-0009, 518-794-8327
Pubs: *Poetry at the End of the Mind & Postmodern Poems*
(Sachem Pr, 1992), *The Mirror Dances* (Intertext, 1986)

J. C. Hand (Axelrod) 🎤 ✈ P&W
25C Nymph Rd
Rocky Point, NY 11778, 631-744-7058
Internet: swimmer@aol.com
Pubs: *Facts of Life, Entrances to Nowhere* (CCC, 1987,
1976), *Your Witch* (DESPA Pr, 1972), *West Hills Rev, New
Letters, Greenfield Rev*

Jim Handlin P
Rockland Country Day School, 34 Kings Hwy, Congers, NY
10920, 845-268-6802
Internet: jimhandlin@aol.com
Pubs: *Tea With the Lord of Death* (Tupelo Pr, 2003), *Editors'
Choice III: Anth* (The Spirit That Moves Us Pr, 1992),
Bluestones & Salthay: Anth (Rutgers, 1990), *The Haiku
Anth* (S&S, 1986), *Virginia Qtly, Rockland Cnty Jazz and
Blues Society Poetry Jazz Fest*

Gail Hanlon 🎤 ✈ P
100 Edge of Woods
Southampton, NY 11968
Internet: gailhanlon@aol.com
Pubs: *Best American Poetry: Anth* (Scribner, 1996), *Iowa
Rev, Poetry Flash, Calyx, Poet Lore*

Emily Hanlon W
RD 1, Chapman Rd, Yorktown, NY 10598
Pubs: *Petersburg* (Putnam, 1988), *Love Is No Excuse*
(Bradbury Pr, 1981)

Tom Hanna P
210 Eddy St
Ithaca, NY 14850, 607-255-3001
Pubs: *New Letters Reader 2: Anth* (U Missouri, 1984), *From
A to Z: Anth* (Swallow, 1981), *Epoch, New Letters, West
Coast Rev, The Stone, Latitudes*

Lisa A. Harris P&W
5111 Perry City Rd
Trumansburg, NY 14886, 607-387-6977
Internet: lizruth96@aol.com
Pubs: *Low Country Stories* (Bright Hill Pr, 1997), *Flight*
(Words & Spaces Pr, 1995), *Feminism 3: Anth* (HC, 1996),
Karamu, Fennel Stalk

Muriel Harris Weinstein 🎤 P&W
644 Pauley Dr
West Hempstead, NY 11552-2225
Pubs: *Sidewalks: Anth* (Sidewalks, 1996), *Listening Eye,
Nassau Rev, Outerbridge, Voices Intl, Ethereal Dances,
Nexus, Cape Rock*

Gayle Elen Harvey 🎤 ✈ P
11 Shaw St
Utica, NY 13502, 315-735-4194
Internet: gaylelen1@juno.com
Pubs: *White Light of Trees* (Permafrost, 1995), *Flower-of-
Turning-Away* (Geryon Pr, 1992), *Working the Air* (Winter
Creek Pr, 1991), *Montserrat Rev, Ledge, Yankee, Louisiana
Rev, Gulf Coast, Bitter Oleander, Yellow Silk, Poetry NW,
Zone 3, Atlanta Rev*

William Hathaway P
243 Maple Ave
Saratoga Springs, NY 12866
Pubs: *Churlsgrace, Look Into the Heart* (U Central Florida,
1992, 1988), *Gettysburg Rev, Southern Rev, NAR*

Barry T. Hawkins 🎤 ✈ W
PO Box 236
Middletown, NY 10940
Pubs: *Dark Medicine, Puppet Master* (Kensington Publishing
Corp, 1996, 1993)

Brooks Haxton P
835 Maryland Ave
Syracuse, NY 13210, 315-475-1570
Internet: bhaxton@syr.edu
Pubs: *Nakedness, Death, and the Number Zero, The Sun at
Night, Traveling Company* (Knopf, 2001, 1995, 1989), *Dead
Reckoning* (Story Line Pr, 1989), *APR, NER, Paris Rev*

Deborah C. Hecht 🎤 ✈   W
114 Burr's Ln
Dix Hills, NY 11746-6030, 631-491-1841
Internet: hecht@tourolaw.edu
Pubs: *A More Perfect Union: Anth* (St. Martin's Pr, 1998),
*Jabberwock Rev, in*tense, Fine Print, American Scholar,
Good Housekeeping, Women's World, Colorado North,
Nantucket Rev, The Writer*

Leslie Woolf Hedley 🎤   P&W
Susan Kelly, William Pell Agency, PO Box 912, Water Mill, NY
11976-0912
Internet: lwhedley@gte.net
Pubs: *The Holocaust Memorial Cantata* (CD; Polygram,
1996), *& Other Stories* (Exile Pr, 1992), *Blood to
Remember: Poems* (U Texas Tech Pr, 1991), *Baseball: The
Game of Life* (Birchbook Pr, 1990)

William C. Henderson 🎤 ✈   W
PO Box 380
Wainscott, NY 11975-0380, 631-324-9300
Pubs: *Tower* (FSG, 2000), *Her Father* (Faber & Faber,
1995), *The Kid That Could* (Chipps & Co, 1990), *His Son*
(Norton, 1981)

Safiya Henderson-Holmes   P&W
438 Columbus Ave, #1
Syracuse, NY 13210
Pubs: *Madness & a Bit of Hope* (Harlem River Pr, 1990),
Confirmation (Quill Pr, 1985), *Ikon*

Rick Henry   W
Dept of English, SUNY Potsdam, Potsdam, NY 13676,
315-267-2043
Internet: henryrm@potsdam.edu
Pubs: *Airfish: Anth* (Catseye Bks, 1993), *Between C&D:
Anth* (Penguin Bks, 1998), *Short Story, Acorn, Raconteur,
Salthouse*

Lance Henson   P
c/o Joseph Bruchac, 2 Middle Grove Rd, Greenfield Center,
NY 12833
Pubs: *A Motion of Sudden Aloneness* (American Native Pr
Archives, 1991), *Another Distance* (Point Rider's Pr, 1991),
Poetry East, Pig Iron, Tamaqua

William Heyen 🎤 ✈   P
142 Frazier St
Brockport, NY 14420, 716-637-3867
Internet: wheyen1@aol.com
Pubs: *Crazy Horse in Stillness* (BOA Edtns, 1996), *The
Host: Selected Poems 1965-1990* (Time Being Bks, 1990),
Contemporary American Poets (HM, 2000), *TriQtly, Ontario
Rev, Southern Rev*

Catherine Hiller   W
528 Munro Ave
Mamaroneck, NY 10543, 914-698-5328
Pubs: *Skin: Sensual Tales* (Carroll & Graf, 1997), *California
Time, 17 Morton Street* (St. Martin's Pr, 1993, 1990),
Redbook, Penthouse, State Mag

Edward D. Hoch   W
2941 Lake Ave
Rochester, NY 14612, 716-865-1179
Internet: ehoch@mcls.rochester.lib.ny.us
Pubs: *The Night People* (Five Star, 2001), *The Old Spies
Club, The Velvet Touch, The Ripper of Storyville,
Diagnosis: Impossible* (Crippen & Landru, 2001, 2000,
1997, 1996), *Year's Best Mystery & Suspense Stories:
Anth* (Walker, 1995)

Barbara Hoffman 🎤 ✈   P&W
1330 1st St
West Babylon, NY 11704
Pubs: *Each in Her Own Way: Anth* (Queen of Swords Pr,
1994), *Catholic Girls: Anth* (Penguin, 1992), *Poets On, BPJ,
Gryphon, Aura, Minnesota Rev*

Roald Hoffmann 🎤 ✈   P
Chemistry Dept, Cornell Univ, Baker Laboratory, Ithaca, NY
14853-1301, 607-255-3419
Internet: rh34@cornell.edu
Pubs: *Soliton* (Truman State Univ Pr, 2002), *Memory Effects*
(Calhoun Pr, 1999), *Gaps & Verges, The Metamict State* (U
Central Florida Pr, 1990, 1987), *Paris Rev, Prairie Schooner,
Yale Rev, Chelsea, Grand Street, Raritan*

Kay Hogan 🎤 ✈   W
154 East Ave
Saratoga Springs, NY 12866-2636
Internet: Khogan4866@aol.com
Pubs: *North Country* (Greenfield Pr, 1986), *Library Bound:
Anth* (Saratoga Springs Library, 1996), *Bless Me, Father:
Anth, Catholic Girls: Anth* (Penguin, 1995, 1993),
*Kaleidoscope, Spiritual Life, Descant, Jrnl of Irish Lit, Long
Pond Rev*

Susan Holahan   P&W
370 Mulberry St
Rochester, NY 14620-2514, 716-244-8052
Pubs: *Sister Betty Reads the Whole You* (Gibbs Smith,
1998), *Bitches & Sad Ladies: Anth* (Harper's, 1975), *Crazyhorse, Seneca Rev, American Letters, Spoon River Rev,
Women's Rev of Bks, Central Park*

Barbara D. Holender   P
263 Brantwood Rd
Snyder, NY 14226
Pubs: *Lifecycles II, I: Anth* (Jewish Lights, 1997, 1994), *Is
This the Way to Athens?* (Qtly Rev of Literature, 1996),
Ladies of Genesis (Jewish Women's Resource Ctr, 1991),
*Kerem, Jewish Women's Lit Annual, Helicon 9, Prairie
Schooner, Literary Rev*

Dennis Tilden Holzman P
13 Cherry Ave
Delmar, NY 12054, 518-463-8173
　Pubs: *Greenfield Rev, Berkeley Poets Cooperative,
　Washout Rev*

George J. Honecker P
453 Mineola Blvd
Williston Park, NY 11596, 516-746-3120
　Pubs: *Glass Bottom Boat* (John Street Pr, 1987), *Rampike,
　Fiction Intl, Sun & Moon, Little Mag*

Akua Lezli Hope 🎙 ✈ P
PO Box 33
Corning, NY 14830, 607-962-0935
Internet: akura@artfarm.com
　Pubs: *Embouchure Poems on Jazz & Other Musics* (Artfarm
　Pr, 1995), *Dark Matter: Anth* (Warner Bks, 2000), *Bluelight
　Corner: Anth* (Three Rivers Pr, 1998), *Sisterfire: Anth* (HC,
　1994), *Obsidian, Eyeball, Bluecage, Hambone, African
　American Rev*

Michael F. Hopkins P
18 Stanislaus St
Buffalo, NY 14212, 716-895-9749
　Pubs: *A Kind of Twilight* (Smiling Cat Pub, 1995), *The Fourth
　Man* (Textile Bridge Pr, 1981)

Mikhail Horowitz 🎙 ✈ P
302 High Falls Rd
Saugerties, NY 12477, 845-246-7441
Internet: horowitz@bard.edu
　Pubs: *The Opus of Everything in Nothing Flat* (Outloud/Red
　Hill, 1993), *Big League Poets* (City Lights, 1978), *Outlaw
　Bible of American Poetry: Anth* (Thunder's Mouth Pr, 1999),
　Long Shot

Nat Hough P&W
306 Lake Ave
Ithaca, NY 14850
　Pubs: *Ithaca Women's Anthology* (NYSCA, 1992), *About
　Chickadees: Anth* (Raspberry Pr, 1982), *Willow Springs,
　High Rock Rev*

Tom House 🎙 ✈ W
PO Box 856
Wainscott, NY 11975-0856, 631-907-0071
Internet: tomhouse1@aol.com
　Pubs: *The Beginning of Calamities* (Bridge Works, 2003),
　Men on Men: Anth (Plume, 2000), *Best American Gay
　Fiction: Anths* (Little, Brown, 1998, 1997), *Chicago Rev,
　Antioch Rev, SW Rev, Witness, NAR, Harper's, Gettysburg
　Rev, Other Voices*

Ben Howard P
English Division, Alfred Univ, Alfred, NY 14802, 607-871-2256
Internet: fhoward@bigvax.alfred.edu
　Pubs: *Midcentury* (Ireland; Salmon Pub, 1997), *The
　Pressed Melodeon* (Story Line Pr, 1996), *The Other Shore*
　(Passim Edtns, 1991), *Lenten Anniversaries: Poems 1982-
　89* (Cummington Pr, 1990), *Poetry, Sewanee Rev, Iowa Rev,
　Chelsea, New Hibernia Rev, Seneca Rev*

Eric Machan Howd P
106 Fayette St
Ithaca, NY 14850-5261
　Pubs: *Origami* (Sometimes Y Pubs, 1993), *Blaming Icarus*
　(Crane Pr, 1992), *Yankee, Calapooya Collage, Sun Dog,
　Chaminade Lit Rev, Round Table*

Edward Hower 🎙 ✈ W
1409 Hanshaw Rd
Ithaca, NY 14850
Internet: edwardhower@hotmail.com
　Pubs: *A Garden of Demons* (Ontario Rev Pr, 2003),
　Shadows and Elephants (Leapfrog Pr, 2002), *Queen of the
　Silver Dollar, Night Train Blues* (Permanent Pr, 1997, 1996),
　The Pomegranate Princess (Wayne State U Pr, 1991),
　Epoch, Atlantic Monthly

Joan Howlett P
14 High St
Norwood, NY 13668, 315-353-2713
　Pubs: *Variations of White, Against the Grain: Anth, A Song
　of Myself: Anth* (CSS, 1986, 1988, 1987)

William Humphrey W
RD #1, Box 139
Hudson, NY 12534
　Pubs:

Paul Humphrey 🎙 ✈ P
2329 S Union St
Spencerport, NY 14559-2229, 716-352-4421
www.lway.com/towpath
　Pubs: *Bedford Intro to Lit: Anth* (St. Martin's Pr, 1998),
　Ladies First: Anth (Tow Path Bks, 1996), *Saturday Evening
　Post, Cosmopolitan, Good Housekeeping, Ladies' Home
　Jrnl, True Love*

Rose Graubart Ignatow W
PO Box 1458
East Hampton, NY 11937-0995
　Pubs: *Surplus Love & Other Stories, Down the American
　River* (Copper Beech Pr, 1985, 1979)

Charles F. Itzin 🎙 ✈ P
PO Box 159
Fairhaven, NY 13064-0159, 315-947-5522
Internet: itzinhouse@redcreek.net
　Pubs: *New Letters, Visions, Greenfield Rev, NW Rev, Little
　Mag, Nimrod, Phoenix*

M.J. Iuppa 🎤 ✈ P
Writer-in-Residence, St. John Fisher College, 3690 East
Avenue, Rochester, NY 14618, 585-385-8150
Internet: mjiuppa@worldnet.att.net
    Pubs: *Greatest Hits 1986-2001, Freshwater: Anth* (Pudding
    Hse Pr, 2002, 2002), *Temptations* (Foothills Publishing,
    2001), *Voices in the Gallery* (U Rochester Pr, 2001), *Poetry,
    Tar River Poetry, Blueline, Clackamus Lit Rev, Eclipse, Many
    Mtns Moving*

Anita Jacobs W
3641 Regent Ln
Wantagh, NY 11793, 516-731-8188
Internet: caasi3641@aol.com
    Pubs: *Where Has Deedie Wooster Been All These Years*
    (Delacorte Pr, 1981)

Karoniaktatie Alex Jacobs P
RFD 1, Box 116
Bombay, NY 12914-9718, 518-358-4460
Internet: dogrezz@aol.com
    Pubs: *New Voices from the Longhouse: Anth* (Greenfield
    Rev, 1988), *Returning the Gift: Anth* (Sun Tracks, 1995),
    Akwesasne Notes, Semiotexte, Tribes

Susan Jacobson 🎤 ✈ P&W
2284 Cty Rt 8
Elizaville, NY 12523, 518-537-3762
    Pubs: *Shift-Change* (Main Street Rag, 2000), *Other
    Testaments* (Incarnate Muse Pub, 1997), *Life on the Line:
    Anth* (Negative Capability, 1992), *Pittsburgh Qtly, Heart Qtly,
    5AM, Pittsburgh Post-Gazette, Negative Capability*

Bev Jafek W
24-08 24 Ave
Astoria, NY 11102-2832
Internet: maqroll@ix.netcom.com
    Pubs: *The Man Who Took a Bite Out of His Wife* (Overlook
    Pr, 1995), *Best American Short Stories: Anth* (HM, 1985),
    Columbia, Yellow Silk, Missouri Rev

Robert Jagoda W
547 Lucas Ave Ext
Kingston, NY 12401-8215, 914-331-5473
    Pubs: *Nobody Wants My Resume: Anth* (McGraw-Hill,
    1979), *A Friend in Deed: Anth* (Norton, 1976)

Phyllis Janowitz 🎤 ✈ P
English Dept, Cornell Univ, Goldwin Smith Hall, Ithaca, NY
14853, 607-257-3279
    Pubs: *Temporary Dwellings* (U Pitt Pr, 1988), *Visiting Rites*
    (Princeton, 1982), *Epoch, Free Lunch, Verve, River Styx,
    The Qtly, The Bridge, Ithaca Women's Anth*

Joachim W
c/o Costas Parpas, 23 Cullen Dr, East Northport, NY 11731,
516-758-7647
    Pubs:

Polly Joan P
604 Taylor Pl
Ithaca, NY 14850, 607-277-3738
    Pubs: *The Living Alternative* (Human Sciences Pr, 1985),
    No Apologies (Women Writing Pr, 1975)

Bobby Johnson P
110 Normandy Ave
Rochester, NY 14619, 716-436-5929
    Pubs: *Mr. Parker Songbook, Clarissa Street Project*
    (Johnson, 1991, 1985)

Bonnie L. Johnson P
2316 Shadagee Rd
Eden, NY 14057
Internet: alice1933@aol.com
    Pubs: *The Jungle Book* (Textile Bridge Pr, 1983), *Fine
    China, Twenty Years of Earth's Daughters: Anth* (Spring-
    house Edtns, 1993), *Room of Our Own, Serendipity Pr*

Carlos Johnson W
30-98 Crescent St, #2B
Astoria, NY 11102, 718-956-3240
    Pubs: *Entre Nosotros, Centerpoint, Revista Chicano-
    Riquena, Chasqui, Linden Lane Mag, Inti*

Darren Johnson 🎤 ✈ P&W
PO Box 672
Water Mill, NY 11976-0672, 631-369-0518
Internet: rocketusa@delphi.com
    Pubs: *Jazz Poems* (So It Goes/U Pitt, 1996), *I Do Not Prefer
    to Have Sex* (NPI, 1994), *Hampton Shorts, Long Island Qtly,
    U-Direct, Plastic Tower, Impetus*

Ina Jones P&W
121 Cleveland Ave
Cobleskill, NY 12043
    Pubs: *Womenstory: Memoir: Anth* (Sing Heavenly Muse!,
    1997), *Out of the Catskills & Just Beyond: Anth, Word
    Thursdays: Anth* (Bright Hill Pr, 1997, 1995), *West Branch,
    Cape Rock*

Susan Jordan P
39 Beaufort St
Rochester, NY 14620, 716-271-1589
    Pubs: *Crystal Spirit* (Snakesisters Pr, 1988), *Benzene* (Truck
    Pr, 1977), *Ikon, And*

Barbara Jordan 🎤 ✈ P
5149 Old West Lake Rd
Honeoye, NY 14471, 716-229-4365
Internet: micaamber@aol.com
    Pubs: *Trace Elements* (Penguin, 1998), *Channel* (Beacon
    Pr, 1990), *Atlantic, Sulfur, Agni, New Yorker, Paris Rev*

Pierre Joris 🎤 ✈ P
English Dept, SUNY Albany, Albany, NY 12202, 518-442-4085
Internet: joris@cnsunix.albany.edu
    Pubs: *Poasis* (Wesleyan U Pr, 2001), *Breccia* (Edtns
    Phi/Station Hill, 1987)

Laurence Josephs P
c/o Wilolea Farm, 992 Locust Grove Rd, Greenfield Center,
NY 12833
    Pubs: *New & Selected Poems* (Copley Pub Group, 1988),
    Salmagundi, St. Johns Rev, Southern Rev

Frank Judge P
Syndicated News Service, 232 Post Ave, Rochester, NY
14619-1398, 716-328-2144
Internet: sns3@aol.com or fjudge1@aol.com
    Pubs: *The Flickering Dark* (Exit Pr, 1994), *24 Exposures*
    (Writers & Bks, 1988), *The Spy's Handbook, Two Voices*
    (Center Pr, 1987, 1985)

Franz Kamin W
c/o Station Hill Press, Station Hill Rd, Barrytown, NY 12507,
612-227-0225
    Pubs: *Scribble Death* (Station Hill Pr, 1986), *Hotel* (Prospect
    Bks, 1986)

Paul Kane 🎤 ✈ P
8 Big Island
Warwick, NY 10990-2408, 914-986-8522
Internet: kane@vassar.edu
    Pubs: *Drowned Lands* (U South Carolina Pr, 2000), *The
    Farther Shore* (George Braziller, 1989), *Paris Rev, New
    Republic, Grand Street, Sewanee Rev, Western Humanities
    Rev, Shenandoah, Poetry*

Ro'ee Bob Kaplan 🎤 ✈ P
774 Greenbelt Pkwy W
Holbrook, NY 11741-4213, 631-472-3416
    Pubs: *Poetry Today, New Thought Jrnl, Rosemaryes, All
    Pocket Poetry, Creations*

Mary Karr 🎤 ✈ P&W
English Dept, Syracuse Univ, Syracuse, NY 13244,
315-443-2173
    Pubs: *Viper Rum, The Devil's Tour* (New Directions, 1998,
    1993), *Abacus* (Wesleyan U Pr, 1987), *Seneca Rev, Poetry,
    Parnassus, Willow Springs, Ploughshares, Columbia*

Peter Katopes P&W
c/o Univ College, Adelphi Univ, Garden City, NY 11530
    Pubs: *The Vietnam Reader: Anth, The Human Condition in
    the Modern Age: Anth* (Kendall/Hunt, 1991, 1991)

Miriam Polli Katsikis 🎤 ✈ P&W
200 E Bayberry Rd
Islip, NY 11751
    Pubs: *PEN Fiction Award, St. Anthony Messenger,
    Primavera, Buffalo Spree, Playgirl, Plainswoman, Echoes,
    Earthwise Poetry Jrnl, Anemone, Cimarron, Ripples*

Rita Katz P
8 Greentree Rd
Mineola, NY 11501
    Pubs: *A Writing Woman, Outside My Window, Surviving the
    Distance* (Small Poetry Pr, 2002, 2000, 1999), *The Alembic,
    Piedmont Lit Rev, Long Island Qtly, Midwest Poetry Rev*

Stuart Kaufman P
English Dept, Nassau Community College, 1 Education Dr,
Garden City, NY 11530, 516-572-7185
Internet: bigcigarz@aol.com
    Pubs: *Fast Friends* (Minerva Pr, 1996), *The Ultimate Cigar &
    Other Poems* (First East Coast Pubs, 1984), *Verse, Mudfish,
    Poetry, Privates, Kingfisher*

Merilee Kaufman P
3256 Elliott Blvd
Oceanside, NY 11572
    Pubs: *Sarah's Daughters Sing: Anth* (K'Tav Pub Hse, 1990),
    *Confrontation, Nassau Rev, Slugfest, Live Poets, Messages
    from the Heart*

Bill Keith P
Howland Public Library, 313 Main St, Beacon, NY 12508,
914-831-1134
    Pubs: *Pictographs* (Left Hand Pr, 1996), *Wingdom*
    (Runaway Spoon Pr, 1992), *Writers Forum, African
    American Rev, Poems*

Emily Keller P
9354 Rivershore Dr
Niagara Falls, NY 14304-4449, 716-283-0606
http://www.bluemoon.net/~mbwbio
    Pubs: *Anth of Mag Verse & Yearbook of American Poetry*
    (Monitor Bks, 1984), *Kansas Qtly, Hollins Critic,
    Confrontation, Piedmont Lit Rev, McCall's, San Jose
    Studies, Poetry Now, Images*

Dave Kelly P
PO Box 53
Geneseo, NY 14454, 716-243-0987
    Pubs: *The Sumal Reader* (MSU Pr, 1996), *Talking to Myself*
    (State Street Pr, 1994), *Northern Letter* (Nebraska Rev Pr,
    1980), *The Paris Rev Anth* (Norton, 1990)

Robert Kelly P&W
Bard College, Annandale-on-Hudson, NY 12504,
914-758-6549
Internet: kelly@bard.edu
    Pubs: *Red Actions: Selected Poems 1960-93* (Black
    Sparrow Pr, 1995), *Queen of Terrors* (McPherson & Co,
    1994), *Conjunctions, Notus, Ashen Meal, Grand Street*

Sylvia Kelly   W
PO Box 53
Geneseo, NY 14454, 716-243-0987
    Pubs: *Conjunctions: 14* (Collier-Macmillan, 1989),
MacGuffin, Redstart Plus, Transpacific

Maurice Kenny 🎤 ✈   P
PO Box 1029, 55 Riverside Dr, Saranac Lake, NY 12983,
518-891-5865
    Pubs: *Carving Hawk: Poems Old & New, Backward to
Forward, Tekonwatonti* (White Pine Pr, 2002, 1997, 1992),
Tortured Skins & Other Fictions (MSU Pr, 2000), *Wooster
Rev, House Organ, River Styx, Cimarron, Adirondack Life,
Amicus*

Milton Kessler   P
25 Lincoln Ave
Binghamton, NY 13905, 607-772-1217
    Pubs: *The Grand Concourse* (Mss., 1993), *Riding First Car*
(Sulfur 31, 1993), *On Prejudice: Anth* (Doubleday, 1993),
Poems on the Underground, Walt Whitman Qtly

Siri Narayan Kaur Khalsa 🎤 ✈   P&W
460 Ashland Ave
Buffalo, NY 14222-1502, 716-881-5504
Internet: siri_naray@aol.com
    Pubs: *Dancing with the Guru* (White Lion Pr, 1996),
Unconditional Love, Life Junkies: Anth (Textile Bridge,
1992, 1991)

Robert Kimm 🎤 ✈   P
RR #2
Marcellus, NY 13108-9623
    Pubs: *Goin' Nowhere Sunday* (Bull Thistle Pr, 1996), *River
King Poetry Supplement, Edgz, Concrete Wolf, Nerve
Cowboy, Rhino, Apocalypse, Camellia, Fat Tuesday, Plastic
Tower, Hiram Poetry Rev, Connecticut Poetry Rev, Prairie
Schooner*

Joan Payne Kincaid   P
132 Du Bois Ave
Sea Cliff, NY 11579-1826, 516-671-2375
Internet: jpaynekincaid@juno.com
    Pubs: *Skinny Dipping* (Bogg Pubs, 1998), *Understanding
the Water* (Kings Estate Pr, 1997), *Art of Haiku: Anth* (New
Hope Intl, 2000), *Confrontation: Anth* (Long Island U Pr,
2000), *The Quarterly: Anth* (Random Hse, 1990),
Crosscurrents, Oyez, Black River Qtly

Janice King   PP&P
36 Post St
Kingston, NY 12401, 845-339-4939
www.goldennotebook.com
    Pubs: *Taking Wing* (Golden Note Pr, 2002), *Wildflowers:
Anth* (Shivastan Woodstock, 2001), *Out of the Catskills:
Anth* (Bright Hill Pr, 1997), *Woodstock Originals: Anth*
(Byrdcliff Writers, 1997), *Long Shot, Woodstock Times Lit
Supplement, Ulster*

Judith Kitchen 🎤 ✈   W
35 College St
Brockport, NY 14420, 716-637-0023
Internet: jkitchen@brockport.edu
    Pubs: *The House on Eccles Road* (Graywolf Pr, 2002),
Georgia Rev, Water-Stone

Jon Klimo   P
82 Main Ave
Sea Cliff, NY 11579, 516-671-5480

Ron Kolm 🎤 ✈   P&W
30-73 47 St, #3F
Long Island City, NY 11103, 718-721-0946
    Pubs: *Help Yourself!: Anth, Crimes of the Beats: Anth,
Unbearables: Anth* (Autonomedia, 2002, 1998, 1995),
Outlaw Bible of American Poetry: Anth (Thunder's Mouth Pr,
1999), *New Observations, Redtape, Pink Pages, Public
Illumination Mag*

Henry Korn   W
Guild Hall of East Hampton, 158 Main St, East Hampton, NY
11937
    Pubs: *Marc Chagall* (Artists Ltd Edtns, 1985), *Brooklyn
College Rev, Unmuzzled Ox, Congress Monthly, Staten
Island Advance, Connoisseur*

Nina Kossman 🎤 ✈   P&W
19-22A 22nd Rd
Long Island City, NY 11105
Internet: nkossman@columbia.edu
    Pubs: *Behind the Border* (Morrow, 1994), *Gods and Mortals:
Anth* (Oxford, 2001), *The Gospels in Our Image: Anth* (HB,
1995), *Confrontation, Michigan Qtly, Southern Humanities
Rev, Qtly West, Connecticut Poetry Rev, Prairie Schooner,
Columbia, Threepenny Rev*

Allen Kovler   P
90 Grandview Ave Ext
Catskill, NY 12414, 518-943-9479
    Pubs: *Prairie Smoke: Anth* (Pueblo Poetry Project, 1990),
Groundswell, Look Quick

Lynn Kozma   P
165 W Islip Rd
West Islip, NY 11795, 516-587-6479
    Pubs: *Catching the Light* (Pocahontas Pr, 1989), *Phases of
the Moon, If I Had My Life to Live Over: Anth, When I Am an
Old Woman: Anth* (Papier-Mache, 1994, 1992, 1991), *Dumb
Beautiful Ministers: Anth* (Birnham Wood, 1997), *Color
Wheel, Xanadu*

Thomas Krampf 🎤 ✈   P
4611 Gile Hollow Rd
Hinsdale, NY 14743, 716-557-2518
Internet: TOMFRAN@LOCALNET.COM
    Pubs: *Shadow Poems, Satori West* (Ischua Bks, 1997, 1987),
Subway Prayer & Other Poems (Morning Star Pr, 1976)

Norbert Krapf 🎤 ✈ P
134 Willow St
Roslyn Heights, NY 11577-1216, 516-299-2391
Internet: nkrapf@liu.edu
  Pubs: *The Country I Come From* (Archer Bks, 2002),
Bittersweet Along the Expressway (Waterline Bks, 2000),
Somewhere in Southern Indiana, Blue-Eyed Grass (Time
Being Bks, 1997, 1993), *Poetry, American Scholar, Ontario
Rev*

Nancy Kress W
50 Sweden Hill Rd
Brockport, NY 14420, 716-637-2339
Internet: n.kress1@genie.com
  Pubs: *Oaths & Miracles* (St. Martin's Pr, 1996), *Beggars &
Choosers* (TOR, 1994), *Omni, Asimov's Sci Fi, Analog,
Writer's Digest*

Gary Krist W
166 Colabaugh Pond Rd
Croton-on-Hudson, NY 10520
  Pubs: *Bone by Bone* (Harcourt Brace, 1994), *The Garden
State* (Vintage, 1989), *Boulevard, Tikkun, The Qtly, Hudson
Rev, Ladies' Home Jrnl*

Mindy Kronenberg P
PO Box 516
Miller Place, NY 11764, 631-331-4118
Internet: cyberpoet@msn.com
  Pubs: *Dismantling the Playground* (Birnham Wood, 1994), *I
Am Becoming the Woman I've Wanted: Anth* (Papier-Mache
Pr, 1994), *MPR, Hawaii Rev, Long Island Qtly, North Atlantic
Rev, Confrontation, Whelks Walk Rev*

Lawrence Kucharz P
International Audiochrome, PO Box 1068, Rye, NY 10580
Internet: intaudiocr@aol.com
  Pubs: *Poesie Sonore Internationale* (Edtns Jean-Michel
Place, 1979), *Dramatika, Assemblings, Against Infinity*

Lesley Kuhn P
58 18th Ave
Sea Cliff, NY 11579
  Pubs: *West Wind Rev, Innisfree, Footwork, Waterways,
Black Buzzard Rev, Poets On, Metis, North Shore, Women's
Newspaper*

Carol Scarvalone Kushner 🎤 ✈ W
4 Lore Ln
Red Hook, NY 12571-2310, 914-758-2014
  Pubs: *Crazyquilt Qtly, Passages North, Esprit, Italian-
Americana*

Billy Lamont PP&P
Other Perspective Management, PO Box 284, Northport, NY
11702
www.eskimo.com/~strobelt
  Pubs: *Into the 21st Century* (CD), *The Gallery of Light*
(National Post Modern Pubs, 1998, 1994)

Pedro M. Lastra P
Dept of Hispanic Languages, SUNY Stony Brook, Stony
Brook, NY 11794-3371
  Pubs: *Noticias Del Extranjero* (Chile; Editorial Univ, 1992),
Travel Notes/Notas de Viaje (La Yapa Editores, 1991)

Ann Lauterbach P
Ruth & David Schwab, Prof of Literature, Bard College,
Annandale-on-Hudson, NY 12504
  Pubs: *Clamor* (Viking/Penguin, 1991), *How Things Bear
Their Telling* (France; Collective Generation, 1990),
Conjunctions, o.blek, Ploughshares

Denize Lauture 🎤 ✈ P
St. Thomas Aquinas College, Rte 340, Sparkill, NY 10976,
914-398-4132
  Pubs: *Running the Road to ABC* (S&S, 1996), *Father & Son*
(Putnam/Grosset Group, 1993), *Caribbean Connections:
Anth* (Networks of Educators, 1998), *LittÈ RÈalitÈ Etudes
Francaises, Callaloo, Litoral, Presence Africaine, Black
American Literary Forum*

Dorianne Laux 🎤 ✈ P
BOA Editions, 260 East Ave, Rochester, NY 14604
Internet: dlaux@darkwing.uoregon.edu
  Pubs: *The Poet's Companion* (Norton, 1997), *Smoke, What
We Carry* (BOA Edtns, 2000, 1994), *Kenyon Rev, Southern
Rev, DoubleTake, Zyzzyva, APR, American Voice*

Patrick Lawler P&W
College of Environmental Science, Writing Project, Moon
LLRC, Syracuse, NY 13210, 315-451-3161
  Pubs: *A Drowning Man Is Never Tall Enough* (U Georgia,
1990), *Passages North, Southern Humanities Rev, Central
Park, APR, Iowa Rev, Ironwood, Nimrod*

Beverly Lawn P
Adelphi Univ, Garden City, NY 11530, 516-877-4020
  Pubs: *Throat of Feathers* (Pleasure Dome Pr, 1979), *New
Letters, Xanadu, Poetry Rev, Live Poets #4*

Naomi Lazard P
61 Pantigo Rd
East Hampton, NY 11937, 516-324-6104
Internet: naomilazard@worldnet.att.net
  Pubs: *Lives Through Literature* (Macmillan, 1990), *The True
Subject* (Princeton U Pr, 1987), *Ordinances* (Owl Creek Pr,
1984), *A Book of Luminous Things: Anth* (HB, 1996), *New
Yorker, Harper's, Frank, Solo*

John Leax 🎤 ✈ P
Houghton College, Houghton, NY 14744, 585-567-8412
  Pubs: *On Walking* (Baker Bks, 2000), *Country Labors,
Nightwatch* (Zondervan, 1991, 1989), *Image, Isle, Nimrod*

Julia Lebentritt   P
27 2nd St
Troy, NY 12180-3925, 518-274-6713
    Pubs: *The Kooken* (H Holt, 1992), *Universal Lullabies* (Song
    Bank, 1990), *Cultural Connections, New York Folklore*

Adam LeFevre ♦ ✈   P
2 Hummel Rd
New Paltz, NY 12561, 914-255-9275
    Pubs: *Everything All at Once* (Wesleyan, 1978), *Vital Signs:
    Anth* (U Wisconsin Pr, 1989), *APR, Ploughshares, Paris
    Rev, Nation, Grand Street*

Barbara Lekatsas   P
Comparative Literature Dept, Hofstra Univ, Hempstead, NY
11550, 516-463-6553
    Pubs: *Demeter in the Deep North, Persephone* (CCC, 1994,
    1986), *Artists & Influence*

Rhoda Lerman   W
135 Potter Hill Rd
Port Crane, NY 13833, 212-903-1163
Internet: bobrhoda@aol.com
    Pubs: *In the Company of Newfies, Animal Acts, God's Ear,
    Book of the Night, Eleanor* (H Holt, 1997, 1994, 1989,
    1984, 1979)

Naton Leslie   P&W
36 White St
Saratoga Springs, NY 12866-4342, 518-581-0214
    Pubs: *75 Readings: Anth* (McGraw-Hill, 1998), *Best
    American Essays: 1997: Anth* (HM, 1997), *Agincourt
    Irregular, Riverwind, Massachusetts Rev, Chariton Rev,
    Prairie Schooner, Yarrow, Puerto del Sol, Pikeville Rev, West
    Branch, Intl Poetry Rev*

Donald Lev ♦ ✈   P
PO Box 455
High Falls, NY 12440, 845-687-4084
    Pubs: *Enemies of Time* (Warthog Pr, 2000), *Twilight* (CRS
    Outloud Bks, 1995), *A New Geography of Poets: Anth* (U
    Arkansas Pr, 1992), *Rattapallax, House Organ, Caprice,
    Jews, And Then, Long Shot, Ikon, Home Planet News*

Marvin Levine   P
Dept of Psychology, SUNY Stonybrook, Stonybrook, NY
11794, 516-632-7804
    Pubs: *Look Down from Clouds* (Writers Ink Pr, 1997)

Stephen Lewandowski ♦ ✈   P
PO Box 943
Canandaigua, NY 14424-9502, 716-374-5473
    Pubs: *One Life* (Wood Thrush Bks, 2001), *Artesia* (FootHills
    Pub, 1989), *Wild Earth, Country Jrnl*

F. R. Lewis ♦ ✈   W
PO Box 12093
Albany, NY 12212-2093
Internet: frollop_frl@yahoo.com
    Pubs: *Each in Her Own Way* (Queen of Swords, 1994),
    Mother of the Groom: Anth (Distinctive Pr, 1996), *West
    Branch, Ascent, 13th Moon, Alaska Qtly Rev, Tampa Rev,
    Kinesis, William & Mary Rev*

George Liaskos ♦ ✈   P
PO Box 11-481
Loudonville, NY 12211-1481
    Pubs: *Library Bound: Anth* (Saratoga Springs Public Library,
    1996), *Saratogian, Mill Hunk Herald, MacGuffin, Poetalk,
    Ormfaer*

Lyn Lifshin ♦ ✈   P&W
2142 Appletree Ln
Niskayuna, NY 12309, 703-242-3829
Internet: onyxvelvet@aol.com
    Pubs: *Another Woman Who Looks Like Me, Before It's Light,
    Cold Comfort* (Black Sparrow Pr, 2002, 1999, 1997), *Blue
    Tattoo* (Event Horizon, 1995), *Marilyn Monroe Poems* (Quiet
    Lion, 1994), *Reading Lips* (Morgan Pr, 1992), *The Doctor
    Poems* (Applezaba Pr, 1991)

Leatrice Lifshitz ♦ ✈   P
PO Box 615
Pomona, NY 10970-0615, 914-354-2507
Internet: leatty@aol.com
    Pubs: *Only Morning in Her Shoes: Anth* (Utah State U Pr,
    1990), *Kalliope, Modern Haiku, Slant, Poets On, Sing
    Heavenly Muse!, Stone Country*

Ray Lindquist   P
Craig Rd
Pavilion, NY 14525, 716-584-3307
    Pubs: *By-Products* (Crossing Pr, 1972), *Mother Jones,
    West End*

Romulus Linney   W
289 Dales Bridge Rd
Germantown, NY 12526
    Pubs: *Sand Mountain, A Woman Without a Name*
    (Dramatists Play Service, 1986, 1985)

Geri Lipschultz ♦ ✈   PP
487 Old Country Rd
Huntington Station, NY 11746
Internet: glipschultz@juno.com
    Pubs: *Black Warrior Rev, Kalliope, NAR, New Federal
    Theater, The Bottom Line*

Mike Lipstock   W
132 Hazelwood Dr
Jericho, NY 11753, 516-681-0171
   Pubs: *Chicken Soup for the Soul: Anths* (Health
Communications Inc, 1998, 1997), *Gifts of Our Fathers:
Anth* (Crossing Pr, 1994), *A Loving Voice: Anth* (Charles Pr,
1994), *European Judaism, Ambassador, Aethlon, Rosebud,
Evansville Rev, Nassau Rev, Mediphors*

Robert Long 🎤 ✈   P&W
313A Three Mile Harbor, Hog Creek Rd
East Hampton, NY 11937-2014
Internet: rtlong@mindspring.com
   Pubs: *Gone to the Country* (Farrar, Straus & Giroux, 2004),
Blue (Canios Edtns, 2000), *What Happens* (Galileo Pr,
1988), *New Yorker, Partisan Rev, Poetry, New American
Poets of the '90s*

James Longstaff 🎤 ✈   P&W
8944 Syracuse Rd
Cazenovia, NY 13035, 315-655-1090
Internet: jflongst@aol.com
   Pubs: *River Poems: Anth* (Slapering Hol Pr, 1992), *South
Dakota Rev, Green Hills Lit Lantern, Chaminade Lit Rev,
Pike Creek Rev, North Stone Rev*

Michael Lopes   P
260 Jay St
Katonah, NY 10536, 914-232-4584
   Pubs: *Mr. & Mrs. Mephistopheles & Son* (Dustbooks, 1975),
Poets West, Hanging Loose, Kansas Qtly

Dennis Lucas   P&W
PO Box 263
Hunter, NY 12442, 518-263-4865
   Pubs: *Thirteen Ways of Looking at Crows, Poetic License:
Anth* (Left Hand Bks, 1992, 1997), *Amelia, Zone 3, Black
River Rev, Outloud, Satori, Flipside, Ploplop, Shockbox,
Creatum Sinistra*

Barbara Lucas   P
6 Briarcliff Ln
Glen Cove, NY 11542, 516-676-7686
   Pubs: *Confrontation, Xanadu, Nassau Rev, Dodeca,
Sharing, BPJ, Hiram Poetry Rev*

Sister Mary Lucina   P
Mount Mercy Convent, 625 Abbott Rd, Buffalo, NY 14220,
716-826-6192
   Pubs: *Webster Rev, Zone 3, Nimrod, Florida Rev, River City,
Greensboro Rev, Mid-American Rev, Sun Dog, Nebraska
Rev, Slant, National Forum*

Jack Ludwig   W
PO Box A-2028
Setauket, NY 11733
Internet: jludwig@ccmail.sunysb.edu
   Pubs: *The Great American Spectaculars* (Doubleday, 1976),
A Woman of Her Age (McClelland & Stewart, 1973), *Above
Ground* (Little, Brown, 1968), *Atlantic, Partisan Rev, London
Mag, Qtly Rev*

Susan Lukas   W
85 Rockland Rd
Sparkill, NY 10976
   Pubs: *Morgana's Fault* (Putnam, 1980), *Stereopticon, Fat
Emily* (Stein & Day, 1975, 1974)

Alan Lupack 🎤 ✈   P&W
375 Oakdale Dr
Rochester, NY 14618
Internet: alpk@db1.cc.rochester.edu
   Pubs: *The Dream of Camelot* (Green Chapel, 1990), *Pig
Iron, Aileron*

Alison Lurie   W
English Dept, Cornell Univ, Ithaca, NY 14853
Internet: al28@cornell.edu
   Pubs: *Women & Ghosts* (Doubleday, 1994), *Don't Tell the
Grownups, The Truth About Lorin Jones* (Little, Brown,
1990, 1988)

Dennis Lynds   W
c/o Henry Morrison, PO Box 235, Bedford Hills, NY 10507
www.dennislynds.com
   Pubs: *Fortune's World* (Crippen & Landru, 2000), *The
Cadillac Cowboy* (DIF-Penguin, 1995), *Talking to the World*
(John Daniel & Co., 1995), *Ellery Queen's Mystery Mag,
South Carolina Rev, Cimarron Rev*

Ali MacDonald 🎤 ✈   P&W
PO Box 33
St. Johnsville, NY 13452-0033, 518-568-7447
Internet: alijohn@klink.net
   Pubs: *Phoebe, LIQ*

Katharyn Howd Machan 🎤 ✈   P&W
PO Box 456
Ithaca, NY 14851-0456, 607-273-3744
Internet: machan@ithaca.edu
   Pubs: *Delilah's Veils* (Sometimes Y Pubs, 1999), *Bedford
Intro to Lit: Anth, Literature: Anth* (St. Martin's Pr, 2001,
2000), *Beloit, Seneca Rev, Louisiana Lit, Yankee, Nimrod*

Jennifer MacPherson 🎤 ✈ P
907 Comstock Ave
Syracuse, NY 13210-2813, 315-475-0339
Internet: jennymac@dreamscape.com
 Pubs: *Greatest Hits* (Pudding House, 2001), *As They Burn the Theater Down* (Hale Mary Pr, 1998), *Another Use for Husbands* (Saltfire Pr, 1990), *Lousiana Lit, Red Wheel Barrow, Poet Lore, The Distillery, CafÈ Rev, Poetry Intl, Clackamas Lit Rev, MPR*

Mary Makofske P&W
76 Drew Rd
Warwick, NY 10990, 845-986-9477
 Pubs: *The Disappearance of Gargoyles* (Thorntree, 1988), *Tangled Vines: Anth* (HBJ, 1992), *Poetry, Mississippi Rev, N Amer Rev, Natural Bridge, Lullwater Rev, Cream City Rev, Calyx, Cumberland Poetry Rev, Iris*

Dennis Maloney P
PO Box 236
Buffalo, NY 14201, 716-627-4665
Internet: dennismaloney@yahoo.com
 Pubs: *Between This Floating Mist* (Spring Hse Edtns, 1992), *The Map Is Not the Territory: Poems & Translations* (Unicorn Pr, 1990)

Bridget Manney P
165 E Dover St
Valley Stream, NY 11580
 Pubs: *Twigs, Unicorn, Hyacinths & Biscuits*

Paul Martin W
135 Parkwood Dr
Snyder, NY 14226
 Pubs: *The Floating World Cycle Poems* (Great Raven Pr, 1979), *Greenfield Rev, Contact II*

Grace B. Martin P&W
898 Richmond Ave
Buffalo, NY 14222-1118, 716-884-6942
 Pubs: *Grannies: 101* (Slipstream, 1992), *Buffalo News, Today, Forward*

Patricia Martin P&W
PO Box 773
New Paltz, NY 12561, 914-255-1664
 Pubs: *The Bombay Tree* (Phantom Pr, 1991), *Bitterroot, Wide Open Mag, Oxalis, Parnassus, Amelia, Maryland Poetry Rev, George Washington Rev, Art Times*

Janette Martin P
The Writer's Center at Chautauqua, 953 Forest Ave Ext, Jamestown, NY 14701, 716-483-0381
Internet: blsaid@madbbs.com
 Pubs: *Connecticut River Rev, Pudding, Bitterroot, Crazyquilt, Anemone, Harbinger*

Anne Marx P
315 Tallwood Dr
Hartsdale, NY 10530
 Pubs: *Love in Late Season* (Wm H Bauhan, 1992), *The Courage to Grow Old: Anth* (Ballantine Bks, 1989), *CSM, Amelia, Lyric, Good Housekeeping, Modern Maturity, South Florida Poetry Rev*

Dan Masterson 🎤 ✈ P
41 Fisher Ave
Pearl River, NY 10965, 845-735-5815
Internet: prdan@optionline.net
 Pubs: *All Things, Seen & Unseen, World Without End, Those Who Trespass* (U Arkansas Pr, 1997, 1991, 1985), *Southern Rev, Prairie Schooner, NYQ, Ontario Rev, Gettysburg Rev, Poetry NW, Georgia Rev, Sewanee Rev, Paris Rev*

Debby Mayer 🎤 ✈ W
PO Box C-25
Hollowville, NY 12530
Internet: dmayer@bard.edu
 Pubs: *Sisters* (Berkley, 1985), *New Yorker, Redbook, Fiction Intl, Plainswoman*

Harry Mazer W
7626 Brown Gulf Rd
Jamesville, NY 13078, 315-682-6799
Internet: hmazer @aol.com

Gerald McCarthy P
St. Thomas Aquinas College, Rt 340, Sparkill, NY 10976, 845-398-4134
Internet: gmccarth@stac.edu
 Pubs: *Home* (Crossing Pr, 2003), *Rattle, Nimrod, BPJ, Asheville Poetry Rev, Tri Qtly, Ohio Rev, Shoetown* (Cloverdale Library, 1992), *War Story* (Crossing Pr, 1977), *Mid-American Rev, New Letters, And Rev, America, Cloverdale Rev, Poet Lore*

Kenneth Anderson McClane 🎤 ✈ P
English Dept, Cornell Univ, 278 Goldwin Smith Hall, Ithaca, NY 14853, 607-255-9314
 Pubs: *Take Five: Collected Poems* (Greenwood, 1988), *A Tree Beyond Telling* (Black Scholar, 1983)

James McConkey 🎤 ✈ W
402 Aiken Rd
Trumansburg, NY 14886, 607-387-9830
Internet: jrm9@cornell.edu
 Pubs: *Stories from My Life with the Other Animals, Court of Memory* (Godine, 1993, 1993), *Anatomy of Memory: Anth* (Oxford U Pr, 1996), *American Scholor*

James McCorkle 🎤 ✈   P
790 S Main St
Geneva, NY 14456-3235, 315-789-2139
Internet: mccorkle@epix.net
  Pubs: *Best American Poetry: Anth* (Collier Bks, 1992),
*Kenyon Rev, Partisan Rev, Colorado Rev, Bomb, NER,
Poetry, SW Rev, Verse, Green Mountains Rev, Manoa,
Pequod, Turnstile, Boulevard, Plum Rev, Ontario Rev*

Maureen McCoy   W
Cornell Univ, Goldwin Smith 250, Ithaca, NY 14850
  Pubs: *Divining Blood, Summertime, Walking After Midnight*
(Poseidon, 1992, 1987, 1985)

Sandy McIntosh 🎤 ✈   P
2823 Rockaway Ave
Oceanside, NY 11572-1018, 516-766-1891
Internet: amcintos@optoline.net
  Pubs: *Between Earth and Sky* (Marsh Hawk Pr, 2002),
Endless Staircase (Street Pr, 1991), *Sleepers Awake,
Monsters of the Antipodes* (Survival Manual Bks, 1989, 1989)

Robert T. McLaughlin   W
24 Goodrich St
Williston Park, NY 11596
  Pubs:

Gary McLouth 🎤 ✈   P&W
490 Waterbury Rd
Nassau, NY 12123-9412, 518-766-4385
  Pubs: *North Country: Anth* (Greenfield Rev Pr, 1986),
*Baltimore Rev, Nassau Rev, 360 Degrees, Riversedge,
Sanskrit, ELM, RE:AL*

Susan Merrill   P
340 Grand St
Croton-on-Hudson, NY 10520, 914-271-3893
  Pubs: *Croton Rev, Kansas Qtly, Footwork, Pudding, NYQ,
Purchase Poetry Rev, Pomegranate Series*

Bart Midwood 🎤 ✈   W
64 Meadow St
Garden City, NY 11530, 516-747-6239
Internet: midwood2001@yahoo.com
  Pubs: *The World in Pieces* (Permanent Pr, 1999), *Bennett's
Angel* (British-American Paris Rev Edtns, 1989), *The
Nativity* (Bel Esprit, 1981), *Phantoms* (Dutton, 1970), *Bodkin*
(Random Hse, 1967)

Deborah Miller   W
31 Milo St
Hudson, NY 12534, 518-828-3493
  Pubs: *Alaska Qtly Rev, Antioch Rev, Cottonwood, Ascent,
PEN Fiction Project '87*

Carol Miller 🎤   P
30 Grace St
Oyster Bay, NY 11771, 516-922-0067
Internet: amelialives@att.net
  Pubs: *Life on the Line* (Negative Capability Pr, 1992), *The
Mennonite, Cape Rock, Wisconsin Rev, Oregon East,
Buffalo Spree, New Infinity Rev, Calapooya Collage,
Albatross, Confrontation*

Edmund Miller 🎤 ✈   P
English Dept, Long Island Univ, C W Post Campus, Brookville,
NY 11548-1300, 516-299-2391
Internet: edmund.miller@liu.edu
  Pubs: *Night Times* (Prowler, 2000), *Leavings* (Birnham
Wood, 1995), *Fucking Animals* (Florida Lit Fdn, 1994),
Pleasures of the Flesh: Anth (Starbooks, 1999), *Flashpoint:
Gay Male Sexual Writing: Anth* (Richard Kasak, 1996), *Vice,
Long Island Qtly*

Marianne Milton   P
6558 4 Section Rd, #149
Brockport, NY 14420-2472
Internet: miltonmc@earthlink.net
  Pubs: *Coal-Slit Dawn* (Bone & Flesh, 1997), *Practice of
Peace: Anth* (Sherman Asher, 1998), *Spoon River Poetry
Rev, Apalachee Qtly*

Phil Mintz   P
c/o Newsday
Melville, NY 11747, 516-843-2754
Internet: mintz@newsday.com
  Pubs: *Nation, Village Voice, Xanadu, The Smith*

Eugene Mirabelli   W
29 Bennett Terr
Delmar, NY 12054
Internet: mirabelli@global2000.net
  Pubs: *The Language Nobody Speaks* (Spring Harbor Pr,
1999), *The World at Noon* (Guernica Edtns, 1994), *No
Resting Place* (Viking, 1972), *Exquisite Corpse, Third Coast,
Via, Michigan Qtly, APR, Grand Street*

Jo Mish 🎤 ✈   P
10 Main St
Laurens, NY 13796, 607-432-2990
  Pubs: *The Alchemy Poems* (Serpent & Eagle Pr, 2002)

Eileen Moeller 🎤 ✈   P
20 Marvin St
Clinton, NY 13323, 315-853-4295
Internet: edmoelle@mailbox.syr.edu
  Pubs: *Cries of the Spirit: Anth, Claiming the Spirit Within:
Anth* (Beacon Pr, 2000, 1995), *The Nerve: Writing Women
1998: Anth* (Virago Pr, 1998), *Fine China: Twenty Years of
Earth's Daughters: Anth* (Springhouse Edtns, 1993), *Icarus
Rising, Kalliope*

Ann Mohin 🎤 ✈   P&W
338 Pike Rd
McDonough, NY 13801-0083
Internet: anchor@clarityconnect.com
    Pubs: *The Farm She Was: A Novel* (Bridge Works Pub,
    2000), *The Apple Orchard: Anth* (Syracuse U Pr, 2003), *An
    Encounter of the Senses, Vestal Rev, Milestones, Blueline*

Daniel Thomas Moran 🎤 ✈   P
PO Box 2008
Shelter Island, NY 11964, 631-749-2595
    Pubs: *From Hilo to Willow Pond* (Street Pr, 2002), *In Praise
    of August* (Canio's Edtns, 1999), *Commonweal, National
    Forum, Hawaii Pacific Rev, Oxford, Confrontation, Nassau
    Rev, Sulfur River*

Robert Morgan 🎤 ✈   P&W
427 Ferguson Rd
Freeville, NY 13068, 607-844-4538
    Pubs: *New and Selected Poems, Topsoil Road: Poems* (LSU
    Pr, 2003, 2001), *This Rock, Gap Creek, The Truest Plea-
    sure, The Hinterlands* (Algonquin Bks, 2001, 1999, 1995,
    1994), *The Balm of Gilead Tree: Stories* (Gnomou Pr, 1999)

Carole Morgan   W
45 Old Roaring Brook Rd
Mt Kisco, NY 10549, 914-241-0936
    Pubs: *Heirlooms* (Macmillan, 1981)

Mark Morganstern   P&W
PO Box 279
Rosendale, NY 12472, 914-658-3511
    Pubs: *Crescent Rev, New Southern Lit Messenger,
    Espresso, Tilt, Piedmont Lit Rev, Tempest*

David Morrell   W
Henry Morrison, Inc, PO Box 235, Bedford Hills, NY 10507,
914-666-3500
    Pubs: *Double Image, Desperate Measures, Assumed
    Identity, Covenant of the Flame, Fifth Profession* (Warner
    Bks, 1998, 1994, 1993, 1991, 1990)

Sylvia Moss 🎤 ✈   P
462 Weaver St
Larchmont, NY 10538-1307, 914-834-2724
Internet: sylviasmoss@aol.com
    Pubs: *Cities in Motion* (U Illinois, 1987), *Six Poets: Anth*
    (Russia; Abel, 1999), *Foreign Lit, New Letters, New Laurel
    Rev, Helicon Nine*

Elaine Mott   P
269 Steam Hollow Rd
Ellenville, NY 12428, 845-436-6812
    Pubs: *Blood to Remember: American Poets on the
    Holocaust: Anth* (Texas Tech U Pr, 1991), *Anth of Magazine
    Verse & Yearbook of American Poetry* (Monitor Bk Co, 1989)

William Mulvihill   W
PO Box 204
Sag Harbor, NY 11963
    Pubs: *Serengeti, God Is Blind* (Brickiln Pr, 1996, 1996),
    Night of the Axe (HM, 1972)

Christopher Munford   P
PO Box 255
Grahamsville, NY 12740
    Pubs: *Sermons in Stone* (Birch Brook Pr, 1993), *River Night*
    (Sub Rosa Pr, 1989), *Make Room for Dada, Home Planet
    News, Outerbridge, Sub Rosa*

Fred Muratori 🎤 ✈   P
John M Olin Library, Cornell Univ, Ithaca, NY 14853,
607-255-6662
Internet: fmm1@cornell.edu
    Pubs: *Despite Repeated Warnings* (Basfal Bks, 1994), *The
    Possible* (State Street Pr, 1988), *Best American Poetry:
    Anth* (Scribner, 1994), *Denver Qtly, Talisman, ACM*

Joan Murray 🎤 ✈   P
PO Box 214/Albany Turnpike
Old Chatham, NY 12136, 518-794-9722
    Pubs: *Dancing on the Edge, Queen of the Mist* (Beacon,
    2002, 1999), *Looking for the Parade* (Norton, 1999), *The
    Same Water* (Wesleyan, 1990), *Hudson Rev, Paris Rev,
    Ontario Rev, Nation, Atlantic, APR*

Mark Neider   P&W
4 Chestnut Ridge Way
Dobbs Ferry, NY 10522, 914-693-1237
    Pubs: *Mudfish, Cumberland Poetry Rev, Judaism, Cross
    Roads, Everyman, Medicinal Purposes, Lilliput Rev,
    Mediphors, Iconoclast, Hollins Critic, Magic Realism, De-
    cade, Pacific, New Mexico Qtly*

Howard Nelson 🎤 ✈   P
3617 Keesee Rd
Moravia, NY 13118, 315-364-8536
Internet: nelsonH33@hotmail.com
    Pubs: *Touched by Eros: Anth* (Live Poets Society, 2002),
    Roots & Flowers: Anth (H Holt, 2001), *Prayers for a
    Thousand Years* (Harper SF, 1999), *Bone Music*
    (Nightshade Pr, 1997), *Gorilla Blessing* (Falling Tree Pr,
    1993), *Blueline, Poetry East, West Branch*

Shirley Nelson   W
122 Lancaster St
Albany, NY 12210, 518-432-5163
    Pubs: *Fair, Clear, & Terrible* (British American, 1989), *The
    Last Year of the War* (Harold Shaw, 1989), *Image: A Jrnl of
    the Arts*

Mark Nepo P
136 Clermont St
Albany, NY 12203-2430
   Pubs: *Acre of Light* (Ithaca Hse, 1994), *Fire Without Witness*
   (British American, 1988), *Antaeus, Kenyon Rev, Chelsea,
   Sewanee Rev, Voices, Pilgrimage*

Lucia Nevai 🎤 W
PO Box 27
Malden Bridge, NY 12115
   Pubs: *Normal, Best American Short Stories of South: Anth*
   (Algonquin, 1997, 2002), *Star Game* (U Iowa Pr, 1987),
   Zoetrope: All Story: Anth (HB, 2000), *American Fiction: Anth*
   (Birch Lane Pr, 1993), *NAR, North Dakota Qtly, Iowa Rev,
   NER, New Yorker, ACM*

Tam Lin Neville P
PO Box 673
Keene Valley, NY 12943-0673
   Pubs: *Journey Cake* (BkMk Pr/U Kansas City, 1998), *Indiana
   Rev, APR, Ironwood, Crazyhorse, Massachusetts Rev*

Ben Nightingale 🎤 ✈ W
14 Soundview Ave, #C5-28
White Plains, NY 10606-3327, 914-428-5991
Internet: bnight@att.net
   Pubs: *Mendocino Rev, Network Africa, Obsidian*

David Michael Nixon 🎤 ✈ P
140-1 Lake Vista Court
Rochester, NY 14612-5332, 585-865-0965
   Pubs: *Season of the Totem* (Linear Arts, 1999), *Hunting the
   World* (FootHills Pub, 1989), *Blue Water Line Blues* (Mott
   Calligraphy, 1988), *Yankee, Miller's Pond, Blueline,
   Waterways, Gypsy, Home Planet News, Hazmat Rev, Potato
   Eyes, Comstock Rev*

Sharyn November P
81 Salem Rd
East Hills, NY 11577
   Pubs: *Poetry, NAR, Poetry Miscellany, Small Pond, New
   Infinity Rev*

Beatrice O'Brien 🎤 ✈ P
30 East Lake Rd
Cohocton, NY 14826
Internet: bobrien4@juno.com
   Pubs: *Echoes* (Poetry Forum Pr, 2001), *Loon Lake Jrnl,
   Words of Wisdom: Anth,* (H&H Pr, 2000, 2000), *Time of
   Singing*

Mary Beth O'Connor 🎤 ✈ P&W
Ithaca College, The Writing Dept, Ithaca, NY, 14850,
607-274-1576
   Pubs: *Life on the Line: Reflections on Words & Healing*
   (Negative Capability Pr, 1992), *Massachusetts Rev, Blithe
   Hse Qtly, Concourse 7, Nimrod*

Irene O'Garden P
39 Fox Glove Ln
Garrison, NY 10524
www.ireneogarden.com
   Pubs: *The Scrubbly Bubbly Car Wash, Maybe My Baby* (HC,
   2003, 1995), *Fat Girl* (HarperSF, 1993), *The Greatness of
   Girl: Anth* (Andrews McNeel, 2001), *Writer's Forum, Calyx,
   Chachalacas Poetry Rev, College English, Whiskey Island
   Mag, Skylark*

Sharon Olinka 🎤 ✈ P
23-38 28 St
Astoria, NY 11105, 718-267-1792
Internet: sazibree@aol.com
   Pubs: *A Face Not My Own* (West End Pr, 1995), *Bum Rush
   the Page: A Def Poetry Jam: Anth* (Random Hse, 2001),
   *Long Shot, Onthebus, Luna, Poetry Wales, Chaminade Lit
   Rev, Lungfull!, Brilliant Corners*

Lawrence Osgood W
PO Box 575
Germantown, NY 12526-0575, 212-673-5232
   Pubs: *Canadian Fiction Mag, Carleton Miscellany, London
   Mag*

Ron Overton 🎤 ✈ P
16 Renown St
Lake Grove, NY 11755-2014, 631-585-8032
Internet: ronoverton@hotmail.com
   Pubs: *Psychic Killed by Train, Hotel Me* (Hanging Loose Pr,
   2002, 1994), *Poetry, Hanging Loose, Downbeat,
   Commonweal, Salmagundi*

William B. Patrick 🎤 ✈ P
2 The Crossways
Troy, NY 12180-7263, 518-272-1446
Internet: caltap@worldnet.att.net
   Pubs: *We Didn't Come Here for This, These Upraised
   Hands, Roxa: Voices of the Culver Family* (BOA Edtns,
   1999, 1995, 1989), *Southern Rev, North Dakota Rev,
   Kansas Qtly, Carolina Qtly, Epoch*

Raymond R. Patterson 🎤 ✈ P
2 Lee Ct
Merrick, NY 11566, 516-868-3874
   Pubs: *Elemental Blues* (CCC, 1982), *Best American Poetry:
   Anth* (Scribner, 1996), *Every Shut Eye Ain't Asleep: Anth*
   (Little, Brown, 1994), *Drumvoices*

Elizabeth Patton   P
5273 Kingston Rd, PO Box 427
Elbridge, NY 13060

Basil Payne   P
c/o Keating, 43-30 46 St, #4B, Sunnyside, NY 11104,
718-388-2184

Theodore Pelton 🎤 ✈   W
340 Maryland St
Buffalo, NY 14201
Internet: tpelton@medaille.edu
 Pubs: *Endorsed by Jack Chapeau* (Starcherone Bks, 2000),
 *Paragraph, La Petite Zine, Fiction Intl, Gulf Coast, I.E. Mag,
 Southern Plains Rev, Half Tones to Jubilee, New Delta Rev,
 Fantasy Macabre*

Nita Penfold 🎤 ✈   P&W
c/o Penfold, 11385 Big Tree Rd, East Aurora, NY 14052,
617-846-5445
Internet: penfold5@juno.com
 Pubs: *Mile-High Blue Sky Pie, Woman with the Wild-Grown
 Hair* (Pudding Hse Pub, 2002, 1998), *Sacred Voices: Anth*
 (Harper San Francisco, 2002), *Family Celebrations: Anth*
 (Andrews McMeel Pubs, 1999), *Claiming the Spirit Within:
 Anth* (Beacon Pr, 1996)

Simon Perchik 🎤 ✈   P
10 Whitby Ln
East Hampton, NY 11937, 631-324-2834
Internet: simon@hamptons.com
 Pubs: *The Autochthon Poems* (Split/Shift Pr, 2002), *Hands
 Collected* (Pavement Saw Pr, 2001), *Partisan Rev, New
 Yorker, New Letters*

Michael Perkins 🎤 ✈   P&W
750 Ohayo Mountain Rd
Glenford, NY 12433, 845-657-6439
 Pubs: *Dark Star* (Avalon, 2002), *Night Moves* (Robinson,
 2000), *Dark Matter* (Titan Bks, 1996), *The Good Parts*
 (Kasak Bks, 1994), *Out of the Catskills: Anth* (Bright Hill,
 1997), *The Stiffest of the Corpse: Anth* (City Lights, 1988),
 Notre Dame Rev

John Niels Perlman 🎤 ✈   P
38 Ferris Pl
Ossining, NY 10562, 914-762-1978
Internet: johnperl@aol.com
 Pubs: *Legion Their Numbers* (Xtant, 2004), *The Natural
 History of Trees* (Potes & Poets Pr, 2004), *Edward John* (Tel-
 Let Pr, 1998), *Natural History of Trees* (Texture Pr, 1995),
 Anacoustic (Standing Stone Pr, 1993), *Talisman, O.ars,
 Shearsman, Juxta, Texture*

Ellen Perreault   P
34 Danker Ave
Albany, NY 12206, 518-459-2795
 Pubs: *Greenfield Rev, Hollow Springs Rev, Washout Rev,
 Laurel Rev, Three Sisters*

Marion Perry   P
Word Worth, PO Box 221, East Aurora, NY 14052,
716-851-1712
Internet: wordworth@wordworth.com
 Pubs: *Word Worth Volume 1* (Word Worth, 2001), *Dishes,
 Establishing Intimacy* (Textile Bridge, 1989, 1982), *Hiram
 Poetry Rev, Footwork, Esprit, Black Mountain Rev, Buckle,
 Earth's Daughters, Intrepid*

Bette Pesetsky 🎤 ✈   W
Hilltop Park
Dobbs Ferry, NY 10522
Internet: true132@aol.com
 Pubs: *Cast a Spell* (HB, 1993), *The Late Night Muse* (HC,
 1991), *Confessions of a Bad Girl, Midnight Sweets*
 (Atheneum, 1989, 1988), *Digs, Author from a Savage
 People, Stories Up to a Point* (Knopf, 1984, 1983, 1982)

Joan Peternel   P&W
138 Pelletreau St
Southampton, NY 11968, 516-723-0425
Internet: pesnik@aol.com
 Pubs: *Howl & Hosanna* (Whelks Walk Pr, 1997), *Anth of
 Magazine Verse* (Monitor Bk Co, 1997), *James Joyce Qtly,
 Small Press Rev, Mandrake Poetry Rev, Long Island Qtly*

Donald Petersen   P
12 Grand St
Oneonta, NY 13820, 607-432-8308
 Pubs: *The Spectral Boy* (Wesleyan U Pr, 1964), *New
 Criterion*

Tom Phelan 🎤 ✈   W
Glanvil Enterprises, Ltd, 237 Church St, Freeport, NY 11520
http://members.aol.com/glanvil2
 Pubs: *Derrycloney, Iscariot* (Brandon, 1999, 1995), *In the
 Season of the Daisies* (Four Walls, Eight Windows, 1996)

Anthony Piccione   P
Crow Hill Farm, Box 295, Prattsburgh, NY 14873,
607-522-3289
 Pubs: *For the Kingdom, Seeing It Was So* (BOA Edtns Ltd,
 1995, 1987), *APR, Choice, Iowa Rev, Chicago Rev, Literary
 Rev, Painted Bride Qtly*

Sonia Pilcer 🎤 ✈   W
63 Cherokee Dr
Hillsdale, NY 12529, 518-325-4170
Internet: pilmak@taconic.net
 Pubs: *The Holocaust Kid* (Bantam/Dell, 2002), *I-Land, Little
 Darlings* (Ballantine, 1987, 1983), *Maiden Rites* (Viking,
 1982), *Visions of America: Anth* (Persea Bks, 1993), *L.A.
 Times, The Forward*

Paul Pines   🎤   ✈   P&W
55 Garfield St
Glens Falls, NY 12801-2660, 518-798-2858
Internet: nazul@aol.com
    Pubs: *Adrift on Blinding Light: Selected Poems, Breath,*
    Pines Songs (Ikon Pr, 2003, 1996, 1992), *Hotel Madden*
    Poems (Contact II, 1991), *The Tin Angel* (Morrow, 1983),
    New Directions, Global City Rev, First Intensity

Joseph Pintauro   P&W
PO Box 531
Sag Harbor, NY 11963, 516-725-4141
    Pubs: *State of Grace* (Times Bks, 1983), *Cold Hands*
    (Signet, 1980)

Allen Planz   P
PO Box 1866
Sag Harbor, NY 11963, 631-725-1667
Internet: aplanz@earthlink.net
    Pubs: *Dune Heath* (Canio's Edtns, 1999), *Long Island*
    Poets: Anth (Permanent Pr, 1993), *Long Pond Rev, Wild*
    Dog, Massachusetts Rev

Allen Planz   P
PO Box 212
East Hampton, NY 11937, 516-725-1667
    Pubs: *A Night for Rioting* (Swallow, 1990), *Wild Craft* (Living
    Ports Pr, 1976), *Chonderhara Street Pr*

Mariquita Platov   P
Rte 1, Box 4
Tannersville, NY 12485, 518-589-0135
    Pubs: *Banana Girl* (Peace Creativity, 1988), *One Moment*
    (Plowshare Pr, 1961), *Groundswell, Fellowship, Concern,*
    Imprints Qtly, Inward Light, The Word

Charles Plymell   🎤   ✈   P&W
PO Box 303
Cherry Valley, NY 13320-0303, 607-264-3707
Internet: cveds@capital.net
    Pubs: *Hand on the Doorknob* (Water Row Bks, 2000),
    Forever Wider (Scarecrow Pr, 1985), *Trashing of America*
    (Kulchur Fdn, 1975), *Outlaw Bible of American Poetry: Anth*
    (Thunder's Mouth Pr, 1999)

Kathryn Poppino   P
1027 Hickory Rd
Schenectady, NY 12309
    Pubs: *The Smith, Tightrope, Yellow Brick Road, Chicago*
    Rev, Hanging Loose

Richard Posner   🎤   ✈   W
Henry Morrison, Inc., PO Box 235, Bedford Hills, NY 10507
    Pubs: *Terror Runs Deep, Sweet Sixteen & Never Been*
    Killed, Can You Hear Me Scream? (Pocket Bks, 1995,
    1994, 1994)

Shirley Powell   P&W
229 Main St
Kingston, NY 12401, 845-340-1567
    Pubs: *The Adventures of Margaret* (Crazy Ladies Pr, 2001),
    Other Rooms, Villages & Towns, Alternate Lives (Poets' Pr,
    1997, 1993, 1990), *Home Planet News, True West, Oxalis,*
    Art Times

Prem Nagpal Prasad   P&W
7 Roberta Ave
Farmingville, NY 11738, 516-698-0512
    Pubs: *Padmavati* (Birnham Wood, 1994), *We Speak for*
    Peace: Anth (Knowledge, Ideas & Trends Inc, 1993), *Long*
    Island Qtly, Bharti, Willow, Massachusetts Rev

Elaine Preston   🎤   ✈   P
Suffolk Community College-West, Sagtikos Bldg, Rm 202,
Brentwood, NY 11717, 631-851-6788
Internet: epwingz@aol.com
    Pubs: *Fishing Underground* (H&H Pr, 1997), *Look for a Field*
    to Land (Bridge Works Pub, 1994), *Always the Beautiful*
    Answer: Anth (Kings Estate Pr, 1999), *Confrontation, Jrnl of*
    Poetry Therapy, Poet Lore, Comstock Rev, Passager,
    Peregrine, NYQ

Dan Propper   🎤   ✈   P
PO Box 346
Bearsville, NY 12409-0346
    Pubs: *For Kerouac in Heaven, Fable of the Final Hour*
    (Energy Pr, 1980, 1958), *Tale of the Amazing Tramp* (Cherry
    Valley Edtns, 1976), *Maverick Poets: Anth* (Gorilla Pr, 1988),
    The Beats: Anth (Gold Medal, 1960), *Hunger, Woodstock*
    Seasoner, Love Lights

William Pruitt   🎤   ✈   P
294 Sagamore Dr
Rochester, NY 14617-2406, 585-467-9510
Internet: c21pruitt@earthlink.net
    Pubs: *Bold Cities and Golden Plains* (FootHills Pub, 2002),
    Editor's Choice: Anth (The Spirit That Moves Us Pr, 1980),
    Potato Eyes, Blueline, Ploughshares, Poetry Now

George Quasha   P
Station Hill Rd
Barrytown, NY 12507, 914-758-5291
    Pubs: *In No Time, Giving the Lily Back Her Hands* (Station
    Hill, 1988, 1979)

Stuart P. Radowitz   P
2484 Kayron Ln
North Bellmore, NY 11710, 516-826-3278
    Pubs: *Steppenwolf, Fragments, Crazyhorse, Aspen Leaves,*
    Process, Syracuse Poems, Star Web Rev

Diana Ramirez-De-Arellano   P
23 Harbor Cir
Centerport, NY 11721, 516-757-3498
    Pubs: *Adelfazar, Tree at Vespers/Arbol en Visperas* (Spain;
    Editorial Torremozas, 1995, 1987)

Larry Rapant 🎤 ✈   P
35 School Rd
Voorheesville, NY 12186-9615, 518-765-3471
Internet: lrapant@sescva.esc.edu
    Pubs: *Say* (CannedPhlegm Pr, 2002), *Kumquat Meringue,
Switched-On Gutenberg, Mobius, Nanny Fanny, Cranial
Tempest, The Silt Reader, RAW NerVZ, Alpha Beat Soup,
Modern Haiku, Cotyledon, Passages North, Slugfest,
Mildred, Mati, Knocked, Lynx Eye, Potpourri*

Nefretete S. Rasheed 🎤 ✈   P
65 McKinley Ave, Ste C3-4
White Plains, NY 10606
Internet: rasheedn@prodigy.net
    Pubs: *Child's Play* (Limelight, 1996), *Manhattan on the
Neva: Anth* (Perestroyka Pr, 1991), *Theatre: Anth*
(NTC/Contemporary Pub Grp, 1999), *Three Thirds: Anth*
(Wordbanks Pr, 1984), *Phoebe, Plum Rev, Salome*

Robert L. Reiff 🎤 ✈   P&W
8 Dover Dr
Latham, NY 12110, 518-783-8271
Internet: rlr47@aol.com
    Pubs: *MacGuffin, Proof Rock, Gargoyle, Antigonish Rev,
Schenectady Rev, Deros, Skylark, Alura, Augusta Spectator*

Samuel Reifler 🎤 ✈   W
PO Box 299
Clinton Corners, NY 12514-0299, 914-266-5186
Internet: rhinebeckrecords@compuserve.com
    Pubs: *Esquire, New Directions, TriQtly, Denver Qtly, Mid-
Atlantic Rev*

Donna Reis 🎤   P
201 Jessup Rd
Warwick, NY 10990-2543, 914-987-8179
Internet: dreis@warwick.net
    Pubs: *Dog Shows & Church, Incantations* (Eurydice Pr,
2000, 1995), *Beyond Lament: Anth* (Northwestern U Pr,
1998), *Women & Death: Anth* (Ground Torpedo Pr, 1994),
*Promethean, Lullwater Rev, Zone 3, Cumberland Poetry
Rev, A Gathering of the Tribes*

Elliot Richman 🎤 ✈   P
159 Oak St
Plattsburgh, NY 12901-1624, 518-562-1838
Internet: comrado@together.net
    Pubs: *Franz Kafka's Daughter Meets the Evil Nazi
Empire!!!, Honorable Manhood, The World Dancer* (Asylum
Arts, 1999, 1994, 1993), *Walk on Trooper* (Viet Nam
Generation Pr, 1994)

Frances Bragan Richman   P
237 Circle Ln
Webster, NY 14580, 716-671-6165
    Pubs: *Yellow Butterfly, Saturday Evening Post, Ladies'
Home Jrnl*

Jean Rikhoff   W
42 Sherman Ave
Glens Falls, NY 12801
    Pubs: *David Smith, I Remember* (The Loft Pr, 1985), *Where
Were You in '76?, The Sweetwater, One of the Raymonds*
(Dial Pr, 1978, 1976, 1974)

Mary Ann Malinchak Rishel   W
Ithaca College, Writing Dept, 204 Williams Hall, Ithaca, NY
14850, 607-274-3324
Internet: rishel@ithaca.edu
    Pubs: *Shankpainter, Scrivener, Red Cedar Rev, Hudson
Rev, Cornell Rev*

Helen Morrissey Rizzuto   P&W
548 E Bay Dr
Long Beach, NY 11561, 516-431-5263
    Pubs: *A Bird in Flight, Evening Sky on a Japanese Screen*
(Lintel, 1986, 1978), *Birmingham Poetry Rev, America,
Crazyquilt*

Sheryl Robbins   P
369 Maryland St
Buffalo, NY 14201, 716-885-0804
Internet: weirdsls@aol.com
    Pubs: *Or, The Whale* (Shuffaloff Bks, 1993), *Snapshots of
Paradise* (Just Buffalo Pr, 1981), *Denver Qtly, Works &
Days, Inc #2, Earth's Daughters*

Mary Elsie Robertson   W
3238 Brick Schoolhouse Rd
Hamlin, NY 14464, 716-964-8683
Internet: maryerobertson@earthlink.net
    Pubs: *Family Life* (Atheneum, 1987), *What I Have to Tell You*
(Doubleday, 1989), *Literary Outtakes: Anth* (Ballantine,
1990), *Ascent, Mississippi Rev, Nebraska Rev, NER, New
Virginia Rev, Outerbridge, Phoebe, Seattle Rev, Stand,
Virginia Qtly*

Bruce Robinson 🎤 ✈   P
PO Box 26
Albany, NY 12201-8026
Internet: wrobinso@mail.nysed.gov
    Pubs: *Weber Studies, Xavier Rev, Sow's Ear, Spoon River,
Greenfield Rev, Opera Jrnl, Paragraph, Fiction*

Anthony Robinson 🎤 ✈   W
153 Huguenot St
New Paltz, NY 12561, 914-255-8040
    Pubs: *The Member-Guest, The Whole Truth* (Donald I. Fine,
1991, 1990), *The Easy Way* (S&S, 1963), *A Departure From
the Rules* (Putnam, 1960)

Bertha Rogers 🎤 ✈ P
Bright Hill Farm, 6430 Co Hwy 16, Delhi, NY 13753-3123,
607-746-7306
Internet: bkrogers@catskill.net
  Pubs: *Beowulf* (Birch Brook Pr, 2000), *A House of Corners*
(Three Conditions Pr, 2000), *The Blueline Anthology*
(Syracuse U Pr, 2002), *Rain of the Ocean Anthology*
(Headwaters Pr, 2002), *Laurel Rev, Onthebus, Rattapallax,
AbleMuse, Many Mountains Moving*

Jay Rogoff 🎤 ✈ P
35 Pinewood Ave
Saratoga Springs, NY 12866-2622, 518-584-0912
Internet: jrogoff@skidmore.edu
  Pubs: *How We Came to Stand on That Shore* (River City,
2003), *The Cutoff* (Word Works, 1995), *The Progressive,
Southern Rev, Georgia Rev, DoubleTake, Kenyon Rev, Paris
Rev, Partisan Rev, Prairie Schooner, Shenandoah*

Ginny Rorby W
c/o Barbara Kouts, Barbara Kouts Agency, Box 560, Bellport,
NY 11715
Internet: grorby@mcn.org
  Pubs: *Dolphin Sky* (Putnam, 1996)

Liz Rosenberg P&W
English Dept, SUNY Binghamton, Binghamton, NY 13901,
607-777-2168
  Pubs: *The Fire Music* (U Pitt Pr, 1985), *The Angel Poems*
(State Street Pr, 1984), *Harper's*

William Rosenfeld W
Hamilton College, Clinton, NY 13323, 315-859-4462

Ira Rosenstein 🎤 ✈ P
PO Box 3102
Long Island City, NY 11103
  Pubs: *Twenty-two Sonnets, Left on the Field to Die* (Starlight
Pr, 1986, 1984)

Geri Rosenzweig 🎤 ✈ P
63 Mystic Dr
Ossining, NY 10562-1965, 914-762-7025
Internet: nidapa@aol.com
  Pubs: *Half the Story* (March Street Pr, 1997), *Under a
Jasmine Moon* (HMS Pr, 1993), *Lullwater Rev, Poet & Critic,
River City, Greensboro Rev, Verse*

Gary Earl Ross 🎤 ✈ P&W
228 Highgate Ave
Buffalo, NY 14215, 716-838-9786
Internet: geross@buffalo.edu
  Pubs: *Shimmerville, The Wheel of Desire and Other Intimate
Hauntings* (Writers Club Pr, 2002, 2000), *Sideshow 1995:
Anth* (Somersault Pr, 1994), *Artisans Anth of Fiction*
(Marienhelz Artisans, 1994), *Artvoice, Buffalo Mag, Buffalo
Spree, ELF, Pure Light*

Henry H. Roth W
288 Piermont Ave
South Nyack, NY 10960, 914-358-2399
  Pubs: *In Empty Rooms* (December Pr, 1980), *Kansas Qtly,
South Carolina Rev, Confrontation*

Paul B. Roth 🎤 ✈ P
4983 Tall Oaks Dr
Fayetteville, NY 13066-9776, 315-637-3047
Internet: bones44@ix.netcom.com
  Pubs: *Fields Below Zero* (Cypress Bks, 2002), *Nothing Out
There* (Vida Pr, 1996), *Half-Said* (Bitter Oleander Pr, 1977),
Immanentist: Anth (The Smith, 1973), *Puerto del Sol,
Louisiana Rev, Potpourri, Bitter Oleander, Borderlands*

Chuck Rothman 🎤 ✈ W
2012 Pyle Rd
Schenectady, NY 12303-3071, 518-356-4205
Internet: sf_writer@yahoo.com
  Pubs: *Staroamer's Fate* (Warner/Questar Bks, 1986), *Blood
Muse: Anth* (Donald I Fine, 1995), *Fantasy & Sci Fi Mag,
Aboriginal Sci Fi, Galaxy, Strange Horizons, Realms of
Fantasy, Tomorrow Sci Fi*

Berton Roueche W
PO Box 693
Amagansett, NY 11930, 516-267-3822

Carol Rubenstein 🎤 ✈ P
209 Giles St, #1
Ithaca, NY 14850-5911
  Pubs: *The Honey Tree Song: Poems & Chants of Sarawak
Dayaks* (Ohio U Pr, 1985), *Ms., The Bookpress*

Stan Sanvel Rubin 🎤 ✈ P
The Writers Forum, SUNY Brockport, Brockport, NY 14420,
716-395-5713
Internet: srubin@brockport.edu
  Pubs: *Midnight* (State Street Pr, 1985), *Chelsea, Virginia
Qtly Rev, Georgia Rev, Poetry NW, Tar River Poetry, Laurel
Rev, Ohio Rev, Kenyon Rev*

Helen Ruggieri 🎤 ✈ P
111 N 10 St
Olean, NY 14760-2101, 716-372-0935
Internet: hruggieri@localnet.com
  Pubs: *Glimmer Girls* (Mayapple Pr, 1999), *The Poetess*
(Allegheny Mountain Pr, 1981), *Poems of Passage: Anth*
(Story Line, 2000), *Under A Gull's Wing: Anth* (Down the
Shore, 1996), *Flutes of Power: Anth* (Great Elm Pr, 1995),
House Organ, Sport Literate

Michael Rumaker P&W
194 N Franklin St
Nyack, NY 10960-1937
Internet: mrb213@mail.tco.com
  Pubs: *To Kill a Cardinal* (Arthur Mann Kaye Pub, 1992),
Gringos & Other Stories (North Carolina Wesleyan College
Pr, 1991)

Paul Russell 🎤 ✈ W
Vassar College, English Dept, Poughkeepsie, NY 12604,
845-437-5645
Internet: russell@vassar.edu
    Pubs: *The Coming Storm* (St. Martin's Pr, 1999), *Sea of
    Tranquility, Boys of Life* (Dutton, 1994, 1991)

Michael Rutherford P
Alternative Literary Programs, RD 1, Box 147, Indian Ledge
Rd, Voorheesville, NY 12186, 518-765-2613

Sarah Ryder P
1588 Hereford Rd
Hewlett, NY 11557

Natalie Safir P
154 Martling Ave
Tarrytown, NY 10591, 914-332-8846
Internet: safarian@juno.com
    Pubs: *Made Visible* (Singular Speech Pr, 1998), *To Face the
    Inscription* (La Jolla Poets, 1987), *McGraw-Hill Book of
    Poetry: Anth* (McGraw-Hill, 1993), *Reading Poetry: Anth*
    (Random Hse, 1989), *Slant, Pivot, Roh Wedder, Poets On,
    MacGuffin, West Hills Rev*

Kenneth Salzmann 🎤 ✈ P
160 Second St
Troy, NY 12180, 518-272-6562
Internet: ksalzmann@theartscenter.cc
    Pubs: *Wired Art Peninsula Rev, Spillway, Piedmont Lit Rev,
    CQ, Medicinal Purposes, Rattle, Afterthoughts, Sheila-na-
    gig, Talus & Scree*

Edward Sanders 🎤 ✈ P&W
PO Box 729
Woodstock, NY 12498-0729, 914-679-6556
    Pubs: *America, A History in Verse: Vols 2 & 1, 1968: A
    History in Verse, Chekhov: A Biography in Verse, Hymn to
    the Rebel Cafe: Poems 1987-1991* (Black Sparrow, 2000,
    2000, 1997, 1995, 1992)

Pamela Sargent W
15 Crannell Ave
Delmar, NY 12054-1535
Internet: psargent@sff.net
    Pubs: *The Mountain Cage and Other Short Stories*
    (Meisha Merlin, 2002), *Behind the Eyes of Dreamers and
    Other Short Novels* (Thorndike Pr/Five Star, 2002), *Child
    of Venus* (Avon/HarperCollins, 2001), *Climb the Wind*
    (Harper Prism, 1999)

Judith Saunders 🎤 P
Marist College, Humanities Division, Poughkeepsie, NY
12601, 914-575-3000
    Pubs: *Check-Out Counter Suite* (Panhandler/U West Florida
    Pr, 1992), *Poetry USA, Potpourri, NAR, CSM, Aura, Art
    Times, Folio, Concho River Rev, Bay Windows, CQ*

Joan Sauro 🎤 P&W
315 Herkimer St
Syracuse, NY 13204-1609
    Pubs: *Weavings, U.S. Catholic, Critic, America,
    Commonweal, New Catholic World*

Robert J. Savino 🎤 ✈ P
363 Oak Neck Rd
West Islip, NY 11795-3616, 631-422-6934
Internet: dynsus@aol.com
    Pubs: *Sports Literate, Long Island Qtly, Urban Beat, In My
    Shoes, Angel Flesh, Wooden Head Rev, Surreal
    Underground, Conflict of Interest, Incoming, Tantra Pr, The
    Equinox, Avenging Spirit, Ellipsis, Axe Factory, Babylon Rev*

Lynne Savitt P
2646A Riverside Dr
Wantagh, NY 11793, 516-221-7182
    Pubs: *The Transport of Grandma's Yearning Vibrator* (Myskin
    Pr, 2002), *The Burial of Longing Beneath the Blue Neon
    Moon* (Ye Olde Fonte Shoppe, 1999), *Sleeping Retrospect
    of Desire* (Konocti Bks, 1993), *A New Geography of Poets:
    Anth* (Arkansas, 1992), *NYQ*

Boria Sax 🎤 ✈ P
25 Franklin Ave, #2F
White Plains, NY 10601-3819, 914-946-6735
Internet: vogelgreif@aol.com
    Pubs: *I Am That Snow Flake* (The Poet's Pr, 1990),
    Rhineland Market (Textile Bridge Pr, 1985), *Storytelling,
    Poesie Europe, Poet & Critic, Greenprints, Gegengift,
    Parabola*

Susan Schefflein 🎤 P&W
16 Partridge Ln
Putnam Valley, NY 10579-2800, 845-528-6338
    Pubs: *Each in Her Own Way* (Queen of Swords Pr, 1994),
    *Birmingham Rev of Poetry, Forum, Touchstone, Live
    Writers!, Prophetic Voices, Wind, Pandora*

Lorraine Schein 🎤 P&W
41-30 46 St, #5A
Sunnyside, NY 11104-1829
    Pubs: *The Raw Brunettes: Anth* (Wordcraft of Oregon,
    1995), *Wild Women: Anth* (Overlook Pr, 1994), *Gargoyle,
    Exquisite Corpse, Semiotext(e), Poetry NY*

Budd Schulberg W
c/o Miriam Altshuler Agency, RR 1, Box 5, Old Post Rd, Red
Hook, NY 12571
    Pubs: *Love, Action, Laughter & Other Sad Tales, What
    Makes Sammy Run?* (Random Hse, 1990, 1990)

Beatrice Schuman W
3604 Skillman Ave
Long Island City, NY 11101
    Pubs: *It's Not Easy to Marry an Elephant, Am I Greedy If I
    Want More* (Fred Fell, 1982, 1979)

Doris E. Schuyler 🎤 ✈ W
Canal Side Publishers, PO Box 137, RFD 3, Frankfort, NY
13340, 315-895-7535
    Pubs: *Adirondack Princess 2* (Canal Side Pubs, 1990),
Butlersbury (LED Pr, 1985), *Aunt Cad, Adirondack Princess*
(Worden Pr, 1984, 1982)

Patricia Roth Schwartz 🎤 ✈ P&W
PO Box 636, Weeping Willow Farm, 1212 Birdsey Rd,
Waterloo, NY 13165-9422, 315-539-0948
Internet: prschwartz@flare.net
    Pubs: *The Names of the Moons of Mars* (New Victoria,
1989), *The Laurel Rev, The Distillery, Blueline,
Phantasmagoria, Beloit Fiction Jrnl*

Joanna Scott 🎤 ✈ W
Univ Rochester, English Dept, Rochester, NY 14616,
716-275-4092
    Pubs: *Make Believe* (Little, Brown, 2000), *The Manikin,
Various Antidotes* (H Holt, 1997, 1994), *Arrogance* (S&S,
1990), *The Closest Possible Union* (Ticknor & Fields, 1988)

Dee Rossi Script 🎤 ✈ P&W
887 W Ferry St
Buffalo, NY 14209
Internet: dscript221@aol.com
    Pubs: *Textile, Buffalo Jrnl, ELF, Baker Street Jrnl, Moody
Street Irregulars, Lilith, Italian American Jrnl*

Hollis Rowan Seamon 🎤 ✈ W
College of Saint Rose, English Dept, Albany, NY 12203,
518-454-5207
Internet: seamonh@mail.strose.edu
    Pubs: *Body Work* (Spring Harbor Pr, 2000), *A Line of
Cutting Women: Anth* (Calyx Pr, 1998), *Sacred Ground:
Anth* (Milkweed Edtns, 1996), *Fiction Intl, Nebraska Rev,
Hudson Rev, McCall's, Crosscurrents, American Voice,
Creative Woman, Chicago Rev, 13th Moon*

G. J. Searles 🎤 ✈ P
Humanities Dept, Mohawk Valley Community College, 1101
Sherman Dr, Utica, NY 13501, 315-792-5439
Internet: gsearles@mvcc.edu
    Pubs: *Mudville Diaries: Anth* (Avon Bks, 1996), *Iodine,
Melting Trees, Oberon, Taproot, Rockhurst Rev, Greenfield
Rev, The Bridge, Light, Footwork, Lynx Eye, Main Street
Rag, Wings, Artword Qtly*

Barry Seiler 🎤 ✈ P
PO Box 82
Roxbury, NY 12474-0082, 607-326-7363
Internet: barryseiler@hotmail.com
    Pubs: *Frozen Falls, Black Leaf, The Waters of Forgetting* (U
Akron Pr, 2001, 1997, 1994), *Retaining Wall* (L'Epervier Pr,
1979)

Joanne Seltzer 🎤 ✈ P&W
2481 McGovern Dr
Schenectady, NY 12309-2433, 518-377-9049
Internet: sseltzer1@juno.com
    Pubs: *Uncommon Nature* (Wood Thrush Bks, 2002), *Inside
Invisible Walls* (Bard Pr, 1989), *Suburban Landscape* (MAF
Pr, 1988), *The Muse Strikes Back: Anth* (Story Line Pr,
1997), *Thema, Jewish Women's Lit Annual, Waterways,
Footsteps*

Wilfrid Sheed W
Stock Farm Ln/New Haven
Sag Harbor, NY 11963

Marilyn Pocius Shelton 🎤 ✈ P
13 Sunset Terr
Baldwinsville, NY 13027-1111, 315-638-4068
Internet: marp123@aol.com
    Pubs: *Bedside Prayers: Anth* (Harper SF, 1997), *Mudfish,
Bitter Oleander, Poetry Motel*

Alana Sherman P
183 Clark A Rd
Woodbourne, NY 12788
    Pubs: *Home Ground* (Alms Hse Pr, 1994), *Everything Is
Gates* (Willamette River Bks, 1991)

Beth Sherman W
4 Ellen Pl
Huntington Station, NY 11746

Carol Sherman 🎤 ✈ P
PO Box 2083
Bridgehampton, NY 11932-2083, 631-537-7006
    Pubs: *Swimming in Lavender* (Fieldside Pr, 1998), *Women
Under Assault, In Autumn: Anth* (Birnham Wood, 1995,
1994), *Celebrating Gaia: Anth, Olden Times: Anth* (Sweet
Annie & Sweet Pea Rev, 2000, 1999)

Edith Shiffert P
c/o Dennis Maloney, White Pine Press, 76 Center St, Fredonia,
NY 14063, 310-540-1880
    Pubs: *The Light Comes Slowly* (Katsura Pr, 1997), *When on
the Edge, Touching the Point, New & Selected Poems*
(White Pine Pr, 1991, 1990, 1979), *Forest House with Cat*
(Japan; Unio Corp, 1991), *New Yorker, CSM, Kyoto Jrnl*

Dan Sicoli 🎤 ✈ P
Slipstream, PO Box 2071, New Market Sta, Niagara Falls, NY
14301, 716-282-2616
Internet: slipdan@aol.com
    Pubs: *All Shook Up: Collected Poems about Elvis: Anth, A
New Geography of Poets: Anth* (U Arkansas Pr, 2001,
1992), *Louisiana Rev, Butcher's Block, Monkey's First, Main
Street Rag, Nerve Cowboy, Slipstream*

Peter Siedlecki 🎤 ✈   P
249 Winspear Ave
Buffalo, NY 14215-1035, 716-837-2863
Internet: psiedlec@daemen.edu
    Pubs: *Waterbirds* (Uprising Pr, 1994), *2 River View, Terra Poetica, Escarpment, New Kent Qtly, Stone Country, Slant, Nantucket Rev, Red Cedar, Buffalo Jrnl*

Joan I. Siegel 🎤 ✈   P&W
PO Box 99
Blooming Grove, NY 10914-0099, 845-496-9784
    Pubs: *Peach Girl* (Grayson Bks, 2002), *Beyond Lament: Anth* (Northwestern U Pr, 1998), *American Visions: Anth* (Mayfield Pub, 1994), *Atlantic Monthly, NAR, Gettysburg Rev, Prairie Schooner, Alaska Qtly Rev, Literary Rev, Yankee, Amicus Jrnl, Free Lunch*

Roberta Silman 🎤 ✈   W
18 Larchmont St
Ardsley, NY 10502-2327, 914-693-2816
    Pubs: *Beginning the World Again* (Viking, 1990), *The Dream Dredger* (Persea, 1986), *New England Stories: Anth* (Globe-Pequot Pr, 1992), *Voices Louder Than Words: Anth* (Vintage, 1991), *Virginia Qtly Rev, McCall's*

Nina Silver   P&W
190 Kripplebush Rd
Stone Ridge, NY 12484-5806, 845-687-0963
www.healingheart_harmonics.com
    Pubs: *Birthing* (Woman in the Moon Pubs, 1996), *Women's Glib: Anth* (Crossing Pr, 1991), *Off Our Backs, New Internationalist, New Press, Jewish Currents*

Maxine Silverman   P
224 Foss Dr
Upper Nyack, NY 10960, 914-353-4106
    Pubs: *Saturday's Women* (Saturday Pr, 1982), *Pushcart Prize III, Greenfield Rev*

Linda Simone 🎤 ✈   P
88 Dunwoodie St
Scarsdale, NY 10583
Internet: LindSim1@aol.com
    Pubs: *Moon* (Richard C. Owen Pubs, 2002), *Let the Poets Speak: Anth* (Arts & Culture Committee, Town of Greenburgh, 2001), *Essential Love, Poems about Mothers & Fathers, Daughters & Sons: Anth* (Poetworks/Grayson Bks, 2000), *Westview*

Louis Simpson 🎤 ✈   P&W
PO Box 119
Setauket, NY 11733, 631-689-0498
    Pubs: *There You Are* (Story Line Pr, 1995), *Jamaica Rooms* (Pr of Appletree Allet, 1993), *Hudson Rev, Southern Rev, APR, Five Points*

Susan Sindall 🎤 ✈   P&W
PO Box 527
Shady, NY 12409, 914-679-7490
    Pubs: *Confluence, Passager, Kenyon Rev, Prairie Schooner, Pivot, 13th Moon, Salamander, Fiddlehead*

Marcia Slatkin 🎤   P&W
PO Box 663
Shoreham, NY 11786-0663, 516-744-5023
Internet: mslatkin@juno.com
    Pubs: *Poems 1974-81* (Backstreet Pr, 1982), *Midstream, Portland Mag, NAR, Paris Rev, San Francisco Chronicle, Earth's Daughters, Xanadu, Bellingham Rev, Sycamore Rev*

Jordan Smith 🎤 ✈   P
English Dept, Union College, Schenectady, NY 12308,
518-383-0775
Internet: smithj@union.edu
    Pubs: *Three Grange Halls* (Swan Scythe Pr, 2002), *For Appearances* (U Tampa Pr, 2002), *The Household of Continuance* (Copper Beech, 1992), *Lucky Seven* (Wesleyan, 1988), *Agni, American Short Fiction, Antaeus, NER, Yale Rev*

Bill Smith   P&W
RFD 1, Box 280
Colton, NY 13625, 315-262-2436
    Pubs: *Adirondack Memories* (Tape; Northern Roads Productions, 1992), *I Always Tell the Truth: Anth* (Greenfield Rev Pr, 1990)

Barbara Leavell Smith   P
359 56 Rd, RD 1
Petersburg, NY 12138
    Pubs: *Appalachia, Waterways, Pegasus Rev, Footwork, Black Willow*

Mason Smith   P
N Point Rd
Long Lake, NY 12847, 518-624-6398
    Pubs: *Everybody Knows & Nobody Cares* (Knopf, 1971), *Blueline*

W. D. Snodgrass 🎤 ✈   P
3061 Hughes Rd
Erieville, NY 13061-9801, 315-684-3752
    Pubs: *Selected Translations, The Fuehrer Bunker, Each in His Season* (BOA Edtns, 1999, 1995, 1993), *Selected Poems 1957-1987* (Soho Pr, 1991, 1987)

Bonnie Snow   PP
41 Ft Putnam St
Highland Falls, NY 10928
    Pubs: *Milkweed Chronicle, Playing for Free* (Wartsenall Records, 1988)

Miriam Solan   P
1 Dolma Rd
Scarsdale, NY 10583, 914-725-1041
    Pubs: *Woman Combing* (Hard Pr, 1997), *For a Living: Anth*
    (U Illinois Pr, 1996), *Lingo, The World, Poetry NY*

J. R. Solonche 🎤   P
English Dept, Orange County Community College, 115 South
St, Middletown, NY 10940-6404, 914-341-4021
    Pubs: *Anth of Mag Verse* (Monitor, 1997), *Blood to
    Remember: Anth* (Texas Tech U Pr, 1991), *Mixed Voices:
    Anth* (Milkweed Edtns, 1991), *Poet & Critic, New Criterion,
    Poetry NW, American Scholar, Literary Rev, Cumberland
    Poetry Rev, Yankee*

Ted Solotaroff 🎤 ✈   W
19 Beachland Ave
East Quogue, NY 11942-4940
Internet: solotaroff@aol.com
    Pubs: *The Truth Comes in Blows: A Memoir* (Norton, 1998),
    A Few Good Voices in My Head (H&R, 1988), *The Red Hot
    Vacuum* (Godine, 1980)

Donna Spector 🎤 ✈   P&W
115 Blooms Corners Rd
Warwick, NY 10990-2305, 914-986-7718
Internet: dspector@warwick.net
    Pubs: *At Our Core: Anth* (Papier-Mache Pr, 1998), *XY Files:
    Anth* (Sherman Asher Pub, 1997), *Sycamore Rev,
    Greensboro Rev, Poet & Critic, Poet Lore, Paterson Literary
    Rev, Bellingham Rev, Hiram Poetry Rev*

Susan Fantl Spivack 🎤 ✈   P
250 Quarry St
Cobleskill, NY 12043, 518-234-3840
Internet: spivack@telenet.net
    Pubs: *Times River 2: Anth* (Singing Frog Pr, 2000), *Word
    Thursdays 2: Anth, Out of the Catskills & Just Beyond: Anth*
    (Bright Hill Pr, 1999, 1997), *Jewish Women's Lit Annual,
    Calyx, Kalliope, Earth's Daughters*

Michele Spring-Moore 🎤 ✈   P
21 Burkhard Pl
Rochester, NY 14620
Internet: springbyker@yahoo.com
    Pubs: *Boomer Girls: Poems by Women from the Baby Boom
    Generation: Anth* (U of Iowa Pr, 1999), *The Practise of
    Peace: Anth* (Sherman Asher Pub, 1998), *Onthebus, Many
    Mountains Moving, Hanging Loose, Sun Dog, Fireweed*

B. A. St. Andrews 🎤 ✈   P
Upstate Medical Univ - SUNY, Bioethics & Medical
Humanities, Syracuse, NY 13210, 315-464-6920
Internet: standreb@upstate.edu
    Pubs: *The Healing Muse* (Silverman Pr, 1999), *Stealing the
    Light* (Sous Pr, 1992), *Forbidden Fruit* (Whitston Pub, 1986),
    *JAMA, Critical Care Nursing, General Internal Medicine,
    Paris Rev, New Yorker, Commonweal, Gettysburg Rev,
    CSM, Carolina Qtly*

Marilyn Stablein 🎤 ✈   PP&P&W
122 St. James Street
Kingston, NY 12401, 845-331-4706
Internet: alterna@ulster.net
    Pubs: *Night Travels to Tibet* (Shivastan Pr, 2001), *Climate of
    Extremes: Landscape & Imagination, The Census Taker*
    (Black Heron Pr, 1995, 1992), *Vermin: A Bestiary* (Reservoir
    Pr, 1997), *Intrusions in Ice* (Wash'n Pr, 1988)

Megan Staffel 🎤 ✈   W
4635 East Valley
Andover, NY 14806, 607-478-8178
Internet: mstaffel@eznet.net
    Pubs: *The Notebook of Lost Things* (Soho Pr, 1999), *She
    Wanted Something Else* (North Point Pr, 1987), *A Length of
    Wire & Other Stories* (Pym Randall Pr, 1983),
    Ploughshares, Kansas State Qtly

Alice P. Stein   P
166 Kingsbury Ln
Tonawanda, NY 14150
    Pubs: *Lyric, California State Poetry Qtly, Erewhon, Pastiche,
    Snippets, Light Year '87, Light, Pearl*

Charles Stein   P
Station Hill Rd
Barrytown, NY 12507-5005, 914-758-3214
    Pubs: *The Hat Rack Tree, Selected Poems from
    Theforestforthetrees* (Station Hill Pr, 1994), *A Night of
    Thought* (St. Lazaire, 1987), *Little Mag*

Alan L. Steinberg   P
English Dept, Potsdam College, Potsdam, NY 13676,
315-267-2008
Internet: steinbal@potsdam.edu
    Pubs: *Cry of the Leopard* (St. Martin's Pr, 1997), *Divided*
    (Aegina Pr, 1996), *The Road to Corinth* (Players Pr, 1984),
    *Carolina Qtly, William & Mary Rev, New Rev, Louisville Rev,
    Poem, Wisconsin Rev, Blueline*

Russell Steinke   P
109 Matthews Rd
Oakdale, NY 11769, 516-589-4164
    Pubs: *Confrontation, Poetry Miscellany, Pembroke Mag,
    Charleton Rev, John O'Hara Jrnl*

Eugene L. Stelzig   P
6892 Bailey Rd
Groveland, NY 14462, 716-245-5273
Internet: stelzig@uno.ccgeneseo.edu
    Pubs: *Poetpourri, A Shout in the Street, Crab Creek Rev,
    Greenfield Rev, Literary Rev, Sou'wester, Desperate Act*

Jody T. Sterling   P
76 Esopus Ave
Ulster Park, NY 12487
    Pubs: *Bitterroot, Sunrust, Echoes, Art Times, Esprit*

Steve Stern   W
42 Bryan St
Saratoga Springs, NY 12866
    Pubs: *The Wedding Jester* (Graywolf, 1999), *A Plague of
Dreamers* (Scribner, 1993), *Harry Kaplan's Adventures
Underground* (Ticknor & Fields, 1990), *Lazer Malkin Enters
Heaven* (Viking, 1986), *The Moon & Ruben Shein* (August
Hse, 1984)

Lou Stevens   PP
PO Box 2524
East Hampton, NY 11937-0246
www.loustevens.com
    Pubs: *Fine Art Photography, The Personal Peace Program*
(Perf; PPP Prod, 1998, 1993), *Anamiles* (Perf; Clone Pub,
1992)

Margo Stever 🎤 ✈   P
157 Millard Ave
Sleepy Hollow, NY 10591, 914-332-4469
    Pubs: *Frozen Spring* (Mid-List Pr, 2002), *Reading the Night
Sky* (Riverstone Pr, 1996), *Imperiled Landscapes
Endangered Legends: Anth* (Rizzoli Intl Pub, 1997),
*Minnesota Rev, Ironwood, Chelsea, NER, West Branch,
Webster Rev, Seattle Rev*

Edward William Stever   P&W
Writers Edge, Box 284, Ridge, NY 11961, 516-924-7463
Internet: edactwrit@aol.com
    Pubs: *Propulsion, Transparency* (Writers Ink Pr, 1992,
1990), *Long Island Qtly, Chiron Rev, Poets On, Pearl, Live
Poets, Long Islander*

Ellen Greene Stewart   P
4 Roosevelt Ave
Roxbury, NY 12474-9778, 607-326-4340
    Pubs: *Prose & Poet Tastery: Anth* (Integrity Pr, 1999),
*Catskill Mountains News, Ailanthus, Up Against the Wall
Mother, Archer, Encore, Pudding*

Tom Stock 🎤   P
376 Mill Road
Manorville, NY 11949, 631-727-5250
Internet: tstock@suffolk.lib.ny.us
    Pubs: *The Ecozoic Reader Qtly, Long Island Qtly, San
Fernando Poetry Jrnl, Beginings Mag, Zephyr Mag*

Ken Stone   P
PO Box 392
Portlandville, NY 13834, 607-286-7500
    Pubs: *A Lust in My Bones* (MAF Pr, 1990), *A Man Holds a
Tree* (Pygmy Forest Pr, 1989), *Jrnl of Poetry Therapy,
Piedmont Lit Rev, Lilliput, Innisfree*

Marc J. Straus   P
707 Westchester Ave
White Plains, NY 10604, 914-328-9696
Internet: mjstraus@ibm.net
    Pubs: *Scarlet Crown* (Aureole Pr, 1994), *One Word* (TriQtly
Bks, 1994), *Field, Ploughshares, Kenyon Rev, Passages
North, Exquisite Corpse, Poetry East, TriQtly, Virginia Qtly
Rev*

David Levi Strauss   P
244 Rock Hill Rd
High Falls, NY 12440-5412, 914-687-7914
    Pubs: *Manoeuvres* (Aleph Pr/Eidolon Edtns, 1980), *49+1:
Nouveaux Poetes Americains* (Edtns Royaumont, 1991),
Apex of the M, Intent, Five Fingers Rev, Hambone

Kiel Stuart 🎤   P&W
12 Skylark Lane
Stony Brook, NY 11790
Internet: poetrybone@yahoo.com
    Pubs: *Mr. Darkmore's Neighborhood* (Weird Tales, 2000),
Disaster Quarterback (Columbia, 1999), *Dreams of
Darkness: Anth* (Tor Bks, 1997), *Dreams of Decadence,
Worlds of Fantasy and Horror, Columbia, Potomac Rev*

Julia P. Suarez 🎤 ✈   P
19 Tilton Ave
Oneonta, NY 13820-2619
Internet: suarezj@hartwick.edu
    Pubs: *The Lesser Light* (Swamp Pr, 1979), *Second Word
Thursdays: Anth, Word Thursdays: Anth* (Bright Hill Pr, 1999,
1997), *Phoebe, Wordsmith, Salmagundi, Tightrope*

Robyn Supraner 🎤 ✈   P&W
420 Bryant Ave
Roslyn Harbor, NY 11576-1125, 516-621-1779
Internet: rsupraner@aol.com
    Pubs: *Sam Sunday & the Mystery at the Ocean Beach
Hotel* (Viking, 1996), *Under Open Sky: Poets on Wm. Cullen
Bryant: Anth* (Fordham U Pr, 1986), *Berkeley Poetry Rev,
Massachusetts Rev, BPJ, Prairie Schooner, Ploughshares,
Confrontation*

Shulamith Surnamer 🎤 ✈   P&W
27 W Penn St
Long Beach, NY 11561-4003, 516-889-7163
Internet: judith27@aol.com
    Pubs: *From Adam to Zipporah* (Judi-isms, 1991), *Filtered
Images: Women Remembering Their Grandmothers: Anth*
(Vintage '45 Pr, 1992), *Caprice, Vulcan's Lyre, Midnight
Zines Café, LitvakSIG Poetry Page*

Hariette Surovell   W
c/o Henry Morrison, Henry Morrison Inc, PO Box 235, Bedford
Hills, NY 10507, 914-666-3500
    Pubs: *The Stiffest of the Corpse: Anth* (City Lights Pub,
1989), *New York Woman, Seven Days, Playgirl*

Harriet Susskind 🎤 ✈   P
670 Pittsford-Mendon Rd
Pittsford, NY 14534, 585-381-3436
    Pubs: *To See the Speech of Trees* (Amygdala Pr, 1995),
    Denver Qtly, Prairie Schooner, Seneca Rev, Nimrod,
    Georgia Rev, Ohio Rev

Phillip P. Sweeney   PP
137 Shamrock Pl, #2
Harpursville, NY 13787, 607-693-4138
    Pubs: *Wail* (Beverly Arts Council, 1991), *Fell Swoop: Big*
    Horror Reader: Anth (J Daily, 1989)

Bruce Sweet 🎤 ✈   P&W
34 Hannahs Terr
Rochester, NY 14612-4909
    Pubs: *Mixed Voices* (Milkweed Edtns, 1991), *Yankee,*
    Minnesota Monthly, Blueline, Commonweal

David Swickard   P
PO Box 800
Amagansett, NY 11930
    Pubs: *Confrontation, Nimrod, Bluefish, Poet Lore, Mid-*
    American Rev, CutBank, Panhandler

William Sylvester 🎤 ✈   P&W
411 Parkside Ave
Buffalo, NY 14216-3404, 716-838-6780
Internet: sylvester@acsu.buffalo.edu
    Pubs: *War & Lechery, Fever Spreading Into Light, Heavy*
    Metal from Pliny, Scarecrow Poetry: Anth (Ashland Poetry
    Pr, 1995, 1992, 1992, 1994), *Acre, No Exit, House Organ,*
    Exquisite Corpse, Chelsea, Poetry

Mary Vigliante Szydlowski 🎤 ✈   W
37 Normanside Dr
Albany, NY 12208-1018, 518-453-3613
Internet: maszyd@aol.com
    Pubs: *Worship the Night, Silent Song* (Back In Print, 2000), *I*
    Can't Talk, I've Got Farbles in My Mouth (Greene Bark Pr,
    1995), *Show & Tell, ESC! Mag, Surprises Mag*

Deborah Tall 🎤 ✈   P
Hobart & Wm Smith Colleges, Geneva, NY 14456,
315-781-3364
Internet: tall@hws.edu
    Pubs: *Summons* (Sarabande Bks, 2000), *The Poet's*
    Notebook (Norton, 1995), *From Where We Stand* (Knopf,
    1993)

Patti Tana 🎤 ✈   P&W
61 Kaintuck Ln
Locust Valley, NY 11560, 516-656-9070
    Pubs: *Make Your Way Across This Bridge: New and*
    Selected (Whittier Pubs, 2003), *When the Light Falls Short*
    of the Dream (Eighth Moon Pr, 1998), *Wetlands* (Papier-
    Mache Pr, 1993), *Hiram Poetry Rev, Anth of Magazine*
    Verse, Nassau Rev

Barry Targan 🎤 ✈   P&W
259 Mahaffey Rd
Greenwich, NY 12834, 518-692-9409
    Pubs: *Ark of the Marindor* (MacMurray & Beck, 1998),
    Tangerine Tango Equation (Thunder's Mouth, 1991), *Falling*
    Free, Surviving Adverse Seasons (U Illinois Pr, 1989, 1986),
    Kingdoms (SUNY Pr, 1981), *NAR, Yankee, Sewanee Rev,*
    Confrontations

Ronald Tavel   P
454 Linda Dr
East Meadow, NY 11554
    Pubs: *Street of Stairs* (Olympia Pr, 1968), *Night Mag,*
    Unmuzzled Ox, Brooklyn Literary Rev

Ted Taylor   P
1-1 Brook Club Dr
Ossining, NY 10562, 914-944-4935
Internet: tedtaylor@aol.com
    Pubs: *Whetstone, Atlanta Rev, The Bridge, Slugfest, No*
    Exit, Pebbles, Amaranth, Wolf Head Qtly, Kit-Cat Rev

Ann R. Taylor   P
91 Acacia Ave
Hempstead, NY 11550, 516-485-9206
    Pubs: *Feel 'N' Good* (Delar Pub Co., 1986), *Hopes &*
    Dreams (Panache Enterprises, 1986)

Gayl Teller 🎤 ✈   P
1 Florence Ln
Plainview, NY 11803-3903, 516-822-2760
    Pubs: *Moving Day* (Premier Poets Srs, 2001), *At the*
    Intersection of Everything You Have Ever Loved (San Diego
    Poets Pr, 1989), *Bronx Accent: Anth* (Rutgers Univ Pr,
    2000), *Sow's Ear Poetry Rev, Crone's Nest, Phoebe,*
    Halftones to Jubilee

Silvia Tennenbaum   W
763 Fireplace Rd
East Hampton, NY 11937, 516-324-9618
    Pubs: *Yesterday's Streets* (Random Hse, 1981), *Best*
    American Short Stories 1978, American Rev

Kathleen M. Tenpas 🎤   P
7549 Rte 474 N Clymer
Panama, NY 14767, 716-355-4176
Internet: hillfarm@cecomet.net
    Pubs: *Hill Farm* (Arachne, 1985), *Seedbed to Harvest: Anth*
    (Seven Buffalos, 1985), *Earth's Daughters, Artifacts*

Virginia R. Terris 🎤 ✈   P
84 N Bayview Ave
Freeport, NY 11520-1938, 516-378-3481
    Pubs: *PUR-R-R* (Channel Pr, 2001), *The Metaphysical*
    Raisin, Folding/Unfolding (Birnham Wood, 1996, 1992),
    Barkeater, Hanging Loose, Long Island Qtly, Confrontation,
    SPR, Hampden-Sydney Rev

Ed Tick P
18 Van Schoick Ave
Albany, NY 12208-2306, 518-438-1062
    Pubs: *Healing a Generation* (Guilford, 1991), *Sacred Mountain: Encounters with the Viet Nam Beast* (Moon Bear, 1989), *Voices, Key West Rev*

Ellen Tifft 🎤 ✈ P&W
45 Crane Rd
Elmira, NY 14901-9240, 607-732-4756
www.xenosbooks.com
    Pubs: *Moon, Moon, Tell Me True* (Xenos Bks, 1996), *Yale Rev, New Yorker, Poetry, New Letters, Laurel Rev, Transatlantic Rev*

Meredith Trede P
259 Hunter Ave
Sleepy Hollow, NY 10591
Internet: mtrede@kenyontrede.com
    Pubs: *Paris Rev, Blue Mesa Rev, Nebraska Rev, The Ledge, Western Humanities Rev, MacGuffin, West Branch, RE:AL, Babybury Rev*

Martin Tucker 🎤 ✈ P&W
161 Daniel Rd
North Massapequa, NY 11758-1919, 516-796-2562
    Pubs: *Attention Spans* (Potpourri Pub, 1997), *Homes of Locks & Mysteries* (Dovetail Pr, 1982), *Fathers: Anth* (St. Martin's Pr, 1999), *Confrontation, Boulevard, Sarasota Poetry Rev, Northern Centinel, Choice, Literary Rev, Collages & Bricolages*

Chase Twichell 🎤 ✈ P
Ausable Press, 46 East Hill Rd, Keene, NY 12942,
518-576-9273
Internet: chasetwichell@mindspring.com
    Pubs: *The Snow Watcher, The Ghost of Eden* (Ontario Rev Pr, 1998, 1995), *Perdido* (FSG, 1991), *The Odds, Northern Spy* (U Pitt Pr, 1986, 1981)

Jim Tyack 🎤 ✈ P
326 Echo Lake Rd
New Hampton, NY 10958-3522, 845-374-6042
Internet: moho@citlink.net
    Pubs: *Tundra, A Limousine to Nowhere* (Street Pr, 1997, 1994), *Thus Spake the Corpse: Anth* (Black Sparrow Pr, 1999), *McGraw-Hill Book of Poetry: Anth* (McGraw-Hill, 1994), *Exquisite Corpse, Rain City Rev, Prairie Schooner*

Barbara Unger 🎤 ✈ P&W
101 Parkside Dr
Suffern, NY 10901, 845-357-1683
    Pubs: *Bronx Accent: A Literary & Pictorial History of the Borough: Anth* (Rutgers U Pr, 2000), *Southern Humanities Rev, Confrontation, The Literary Rev, Amer Fiction, Beloit Poetry Journal, Beloit Fiction Jrnl, Massachusetts Rev, Nation, NYQ, Denver Qtly*

Sonia Usatch 🎤 ✈ PP
371 S Ocean Ave #2
Patchogue, NY 11772-3729, 631-289-9631
Internet: susatch@suffolk.lib.ny.us
    Pubs: *Noodle Kugel & Life's Other Meichels* (Writers Ink Pr, 1989), *Journal of Poetry Therapy*

Desire Vail 🎤 P
6136 Unionville Rd
Bath, NY 14810-8164, 607-776-9157
    Pubs: *In the Fold of a Hill, First Shine of Dawn, See How Wet the Street Sounds* (FootHills Pub, 2000, 1996, 1992)

Frank Van Zant 🎤 ✈ P
11 Metcale Ln
East Northport, NY 11731-4419, 516-368-6306
Internet: veezee@staffordnet.com
    Pubs: *The Lives of the Two-Headed Baseball Siren* (Kings Estate Pr, 2000), *Climbing Daddy Mountain* (Pudding Hse, 2000), *What's Become of Eden?* (Slapering Hol Pr, 1994), *Our Mothers, Our Selves: Anth* (Greenwood, 1996), *Yankee, Context South*

Janine Pommy Vega 🎤 ✈ P
PO Box 162
Bearsville, NY 12409-0162, 845-688-7068
    Pubs: *Mad Dogs of Trieste* (Black Sparrow Pr, 2000), *Tracking the Serpent* (City Lights Bks, 1997), *Women of the Beat Generation: Anth* (Conari Pr, 1996), *What We Know So Far: Anth* (St. Martin's Pr, 1995), *Long Shot, Nexus, Luna*

John Vernon 🎤 ✈ P&W
English Dept, Binghamton Univ, Box 6000, Binghamton, NY 13902-6000
Internet: fac026@binghamton.edu
    Pubs: *The Last Canyon, A Book of Reasons* (HM, 2001, 1999), *All for Love* (S&S, 1995), *Peter Doyle* (Random Hse, 1991), *Lindbergh's Son* (Viking, 1987), *The Book of Love: Anth* (Norton, 1998), *APR, Paris Rev, Poetry, Harper's*

Janine M. Veto 🎤 ✈ P&W
92 Crescent St
Sag Harbor, NY 11963
Internet: jmveto@optonline.net
    Pubs: *The Dream Book* (Syracuse Univ, 2000), *Iris* (Alyson, 1983), *Confrontation, la bella figura*

Paul Violi 🎤 ✈ P
23 Cedar Ledges
Putnam Valley, NY 10579-2133, 914-526-3392
    Pubs: *Breakers* (Coffee Hse Pr, 2000), *Fracas, The Curious Builder, Likewise* (Hanging Loose Pr, 1998, 1992, 1988), *Splurge* (Sun Pr, 1982), *Kenyon Rev, Partisan Rev, Harper's, NAW*

Helena Maria Viramontes   W
Cornell Univ, Dept of English, Ithaca, NY 14853,
607-255-6800
Internet: hmvz@ornell.edu
　　Pubs: *Under the Feet of Jesus* (Dutton/Penguin 1995), *The
　　Moths & Other Stories* (Arte Publico Pr 1985)

Les Von Losberg 🎤 ✈   P
10 Evergreen Way
Sleepy Hollow, NY 10591, 914-332-4961
　　Pubs: *Making Sense of Foreign Currency* (Poets Union Pr,
　　1983), *Riverrun, Pudding, Gryphon*

Anneliese Wagner 🎤 ✈   P
36 Shaw Pl
Hartsdale, NY 10530-1015, 914-761-5874
　　Pubs: *Murderous Music* (Chicory Blue Pr, 1995), *Fish Magic*
　　(Black Swan Pr, 1989), *NW Rev, West Branch, Paris Rev,
　　Prairie Schooner, Chelsea, Kenyon Rev, Ploughshares,
　　Threepenny Rev*

Phil Wagner 🎤 ✈   W
1675 Amazon Rd
Mohegan Lake, NY 10547-1804
　　Pubs: *Marlowe in the South Seas* (Cove View, 2001),
　　*Iconoclast, Libido, Reality & Meaning, Mediphors,
　　Objectivity, Common Journeys, Samisdat*

Eliot Wagner   W
651 Sheffield Rd
Ithaca, NY 14850-9253, 212-362-0609
　　Pubs: *My America!* (Kenan, 1980), *Better Occasions*
　　(Crowell, 1974), *Grand Concourse* (Bobbs Merrill, 1964),
　　Antioch Rev

Kathleen Wakefield   P
1840 Baird Rd
Penfield, NY 14526-1046, 716-586-1368
　　Pubs: *Notations on the Visible World* (Anhinga Pr, 2000),
　　There & Back (State Street Pr, 1993), *Georgia Rev, Kenyon
　　Rev, Image, The Jrnl, Poetry*

Lois V. Walker 🎤 ✈   P
149 Harbor S
Amityville, NY 11701-3820, 631-691-2376
Internet: lvwalkerappts@earthlink.net
　　Pubs: *You & You & Me* (Studio, 1993), *Saturday's Women:
　　Anth* (Saturday Pr, 1982), *Xanadu, Helicon 9, New Letters,
　　Sojourner, Poets On*

Charlotte Zoe Walker 🎤 ✈   W
Hummingbird House, PO Box 14, Gilbertsville, NY
13776-0014, 607-783-2278
Internet: walkercz@oneonta.edu
　　Pubs: *Condor & Hummingbird* (Women's Pr, 1987), *Intimate
　　Nature: Anth* (Ballantine, 1998), *Storming Heaven's Gate:
　　Anth* (Penguin, 1997), *O. Henry Awards: Anth* (Doubleday,
　　1991), *Ms., Georgia Rev*

George Wallace   P
Long Islander, 313 Main St, Huntington, NY 11743,
516-427-7000
　　Pubs: *Tales of a Yuppie Dropout* (Writers Ink, 1992), *The
　　Milking Jug* (Cross-Cultural Communications, 1989), *Lips,
　　Rialto, South Florida Poetry Rev*

Thom Ward 🎤 ✈   P
1054 Stafford Rd
Palmyra, NY 14522-9561, 315-597-1155
Internet: boaedit@frontiernet.net
　　Pubs: Small Boat with Oars of Different Size (Carnegie
　　Mellon, 1999), Tumblekid (Devil's Millhopper Pr, 1999) Anth
　　of Magazine Verse (Anth of Mag Verse, 1997), Atlantic,
　　Poetry NW, Tar River Poetry

David S. Warren   W
514 Edgewood Pl
Ithaca, NY 14850, 607-273-1283
　　Pubs: *Natural Bone, The World According to Two-Feathers*
　　(Ithaca Hse, 1979, 1973)

Rosanne Wasserman 🎤 ✈   P
PO Box 704
Hudson, NY 12534, 516-767-8503
Internet: zannie@aol.com
　　Pubs: *Other Selves* (Painted Leaf Pr, 1999), *Place du
　　Carousel* (w/ Eugene Richie; Zilvinas & Daiva Pubs, 2001),
　　No Archive on Earth, The Lacemakers (Gnosis Pr, 1995,
　　1992), *Best American Poetry: Anths* (MacMillan, 1998,
　　1994), *Sulfur, Boulevard, Broadway*

Angus M. Watkins   P
106 Pullman Ave
Kenmore, NY 14217-1516, 716-877-0963
　　Pubs: *Gathered at the River* (White Wolf Edtns, 1993), *River
　　Poems: Anth* (Hudson Valley Writers Ctr, 1992), *Poetic
　　Space, Blue Unicorn, Rolling Coulter*

Angela M. Weiler   W
SUNY Morrisville-Library, PO Box 902, Rt. 20, Morrisville, NY
13408, 315-684-6060
home.tweny.rr.com/aweiler/publications.htm
　　Pubs: *Concho River Rev, The Advocate, The Armchair
　　Aesthete, The Funny Paper*

Gregg Thomas Weinlein   P&W
35 Albany Pl
East Greenbush, NY 12061, 518-479-7221
　　Pubs: *In the Mirror of Departures* (Claddagh Pr, 1992), *The
　　Avenue of Tears* (Kelly Colm Pr, 1986), *Albany Rev,
　　American Family*

Paul Weinman   P
79 Cottage Ave
Albany, NY 12203, 518-482-3003
　　Pubs: *Tongue-Dancing* (Concrete Block Pr, 1993), *Suck My
　　Cock, White Boy* (Drew Blood Pr, 1992), *Shattered Wig,
　　Lost & Found Times, Pink Pages, NYQ*

Sigmund Weiss   P
7 Neil Dr
Lake Grove, NY 11755-2608, 516-751-3309
    Pubs: *Survivor in Limbo* (JVC Bks, 1990), *Impetus, Thirteen,
    San Fernando Poetry Jrnl, Orphic Lute, Omnific, Cerberus*

Beverley Wiggins Wells   P
Black Belles-Lettres, PO Box 2019, Sag Harbor, NY
11963-0058, 516-725-9128
    Pubs: *Simply Black* (Canio's Edtns, 1993), *A Rock Against
    the Wind: Anth* (Putnam Berkley Group, 1996), *Essence,
    Dickinson Rev, Texas Jrnl of Women & Law*

Bill Wertheim   P
100 Sycamore Ave
Mount Vernon, NY 10553, 914-664-5452
    Pubs: *Building a New Home* (First Issue Pr, 1977)

Paul West 🎤 ✈   W
126 Texas Ln
Ithaca, NY 14850-1755
    Pubs: *Cheops: A Cupboard for the Sun, A Fifth of
    November, The Dry Danube* (New Directions, 2002, 2001,
    2000), *O.K.* (Scribner, 2000), *First Intensity, Bomb,
    Conjunctions, Yale Rev, Parnassus, Witness*

William Wetmore   W
Cascade Mountain Vineyards, Flint Hill Rd, Amenia, NY
12501, 914-373-9021
    Pubs: *Here Comes Jamie* (Little, Brown, 1972), *All the Right
    People* (Doubleday, 1964)

Maxwell Corydon Wheat, Jr. 🎤 ✈   P
333 Bedell St
Freeport, NY 11520-5131, 516-623-5530
    Pubs: *Christian Century, Friends Jrnl, Bird Watcher's Digest,
    Appalachia, Confrontation, Nassau Rev*

Clark Whelton   W
15 Hudson St, PO Box422
Kinderhook, NY 12106-0422
    Pubs:

Steven F. White 🎤 ✈   P
St Lawrence Univ, Modern Languages Dept, Canton, NY
13617, 315-229-5160
Internet: swhite@stlawu.edu
    Pubs: *Transversions* (Colibri, 2001), *Fire that Engenders
    Fire* (Verbum, 2000), *From the Country of Thunder, For the
    Unborn, Burning the Old Year* (Unicorn, 1990, 1986, 1984),
    Ayahuasca Reader: Anth (Synergetic, 2000)

Claire Nicolas White 🎤 ✈   P&W
574 Moriches Rd
St James, NY 11780, 631-584-5736
    Pubs: *News from Home* (Birnham Wood Graphics, 1998),
    Riding at Anchor (Waterline Bks, 1994), *Fragments of
    Stained Glass* (Mercury Hse, 1981), *Best American Poetry:
    Anth* (Scribner, 2002), *World Poetry: Anth* (Norton, 1998),
    Witness, Partisan Rev, New Yorker

Marsha White   P
Mohawk Valley Community College, Floyd Ave, Rome, NY
13440
    Pubs: *The Mother Tongue* (Outland Pr, 1975), *Ironwood,
    New American Rev, New Jersey Poetry Jrnl*

Sea-Flower White Cloud Dawson 🎤 ✈   P
203 Concord Ln
Middletown, NY 10940, 914-342-6982
    Pubs: *Planetary Action* (CT Robinson, 1971), *Akwesasne
    Notes*

Gary J. Whitehead   P
34-A Wawayanda Rd
Warwick, NY 10990, 914-986-8089
Internet: defprov@aol.com
    Pubs: *Walking Back to Providence* (Sow's Ear Pr 1997),
    Voices on the Landscape: Contemporary Iowa Poets: Anth
    (Loess Hills Pr, 1996), *What's Become of Eden: Poems of
    Family at Century's End: Anth* (Slapering Hol Pr, 1994),
    DoubleTake, BPJ, Poet Lore

Max Wickert   P&W
Dept of English, 306 Clemens, Univ of Buffalo, Amherst, NY
14260, 7136452575x1032
Internet: wickert@acsu.buffalo.edu
    Pubs: *Pat Sonnets* (Street Pr, 2000), *All the Weight of the
    Still Midnight* (Outriders, 1972), *Poetry, Shenandoah,
    Sewanee Rev, APR, Chicago Rev, Choice, The Lyric,
    Xanadu, Pequod*

Laurance Wieder   W
114 Oak Street
Patchogue, NY 11772, 631-475-1142
Internet: mosesmuses@redsea.com
    Pubs: *Man's Best Friend* (Abrams, 1982), *Garden
    Intelligence* (Nobodaddt Pr, 1976), *New Yorker*

Patricia Wilcox   P&W
27 Chestnut St
Binghamton, NY 13905, 607-772-8750
    Pubs: *Shaped Notes* (Pageant Pr, 2001), *An Exile from
    Silence* (Alembic Pr, 1981), *A Public & Private Hearth*
    (Bellevue, 1978), *A House by the Side of the Road* (as E.V.
    Austin; Iris Pr, 1975), *The Muse Strikes Back: Anth* (Story
    Line Pr, 1997), *Colorado Rev*

Nancy Willard 🎤 ✈ P
Vassar College, Poughkeepsie, NY 12604
  Pubs: *Swimming Lessons, Sister Water* (Knopf, 1998, 1994),
  Telling Time: Angels, Ancestors, & Stories (HB, 1993)

Russ Williams 🎤 ✈ P
Greemantle, 12 S Helderberg Pkwy, Slingerlands, NY
12159-9262, 518-439-3260
Internet: students@senate.state.ny.us
  Pubs: *Gates to the City* (Albany Tricentennial, 1986), *North
  Country: Anth* (Greenfield Rev Pr, 1986), *The Hole in
  Jocelyn's Head & Other Poems* (SUNY Albany Pr, 1979),
  Blueline, Bullet, Glens Falls Rev

Gil Williams P
60 Schubert St
Binghamton, NY 13905, 607-771-6800
  Pubs: *Moving On* (Bellevue Pr, 1969), *Dear Winter: Anth*
  (Northwoods Pr, 1984), *Aspect, Shocks*

Robin Kay Willoughby P
1711 Amherst St
Buffalo, NY 14214, 716-837-7778
  Pubs: *Not a Poem* (Press Me Close, 1983), *Earth's
  Daughters, Contact II, Place Stamp Here*

Pearl Mary Wilshaw P
59 S Ocean Ave
Center Moriches, NY 11934-3332
  Pubs: *Mind Matters, Clark St Rev, Caveat Lector, Potpourri,
  Penny Dreadful, Plainsongs, Midwest Poetry Rev, Ginger
  Hill, Twilight Ending, Poetry Depth Qtly, Tucumacari Lit Rev,
  Mobius, Nomad's Choir*

Howard Winn 🎤 ✈ P
6 Arthur Lane
Poughkeepsie, NY 12603-4864, 845-462-1604
Internet: hwinn@alum.vassar.edu
  Pubs: *Bridges* (Springtown Pr, 1988), *Four Picture
  Sequence* (Front Street Pubs, 1978), *Southern Humanties
  Rev, Raven Chronicles, Caffin Jrnl, Rumble*

Janet Winn W
6 Arthur Lane
Poughkeepsie, NY 12603-4864, 845-462-1604
Internet: jwinn@alum.vassar.edu
  Pubs: *The Open Mind* (Peter Lang, 1989), *Connecticut Low*
  (HM, 1980), *Sucarnochee Rev, MacGuffin*

Daniel Wolff 🎤 ✈ P
12 Castle Heights
Upper Nyack, NY 10960
  Pubs: *The Memphis Blues Again* (Viking, 2001), *Work
  Sonnets* (Talisman, 2001), *You Send Me* (Morrow, 1995),
  *Partisan Rev, Musician, Paris Rev, Threepenny Rev, Sulfur,
  DoubleTake*

Amy An Mei Wong P&W
2089 Kodma Pl
East Meadow, NY 11554-2519, 516-794-9587
  Pubs: *55 to the Nth Possibilities* (Turn of River Pr, 1991),
  Long Island Chinese Center Jrnl

Bettie Wysor W
70 Cove Hollow Rd
East Hampton, NY 11937, 516-324-8664
  Pubs: *Echos, A Stranger's Eyes* (Jove, 1983, 1981), *To
  Remember Tina* (Stein & Day, 1975)

Carolyn Yalkut P&W
Director, Journalism Program, SUNY Albany, English Dept,
Albany, NY 12222, 518-442-4065
  Pubs: *Northeast Jrnl, West Hills Rev, Webster Rev, Poet &
  Critic, Tales*

R. H. Yodice P&W
PO Box 534
Hurley, NY 12443-0534
  Pubs: *Voices in the Wind* (DocWat, 1999), *Simply Words,
  Poets Podium, Free Xpression, Writer's World, Byline*

Christoper A. Zackey P&W
19 Chenango Ave S, #3
Clinton, NY 13323-1661, 315-853-3112
  Pubs: *My Legacy, New Hope Intl, Piedmont Lit Rev, Slant,
  Minas Tirith Evening-Star, Lost Worlds, Mythic Circle*

Leah Zazulyer 🎤 ✈ P
450 Rugby Ave
Rochester, NY 14619, 585-436-5035
Internet: fam_wats@uno.cc.geneseo.edu
  Pubs: *The Word Is a Wedding* (FootHills Pub, 1993), *Round
  Trip Year: A Book of Days* (Vick-Witte, 1992), *Literal Latte,
  Bridges, Ontario Rev, Georgia Rev, South Coast Poetry Jrnl,
  Negative Capability*

James A. Zoller 🎤 ✈ P&W
9800 Seymour St
Houghton, NY 14744-8703, 716-567-9465
Internet: jzoller@houghton.edu
  Pubs: *Literature: Anth* (McGraw-Hill, 1994), *Christian
  Century, Prose Poem, Laurel Rev, Red Dancefloor*

Carol Zuravleff P
RD 2, Box 73
Otego, NY 13825, 607-988-7170
  Pubs: *Venus & Don Juan, Pure* (TriQtly Bks, 1996, 1994),
  Chimera (Peregrine Smith Bks, 1990), *Day of the Body* (Ion
  Bks, 1986), *APR, Atlantic, NER, TriQtly, Partisan Rev,
  Ploughshares, Kenyon Rev, Shenandoah, Southern Rev, Volt*

NEW YORK CITY

Stephen Abbott   P
164 E 81 St
New York, NY 10028-1804
    Pubs: *Holy Terror* (Crossing Pr, 1989), *Skinny Trip to a Far Place* (e.g. Pr, 1988)

Walter Abish   P&W
PO Box 485 Cooper Sta
New York, NY 10276, 212-982-3074
    Pubs: *Eclipse Fever* (Knopf, 1993), *99: The New Meaning* (Burning Deck, 1990), *How German Is It* (New Directions, 1980)

Linsey Abrams   W
c/o Laurie E. Liss, Harvey Klinger Inc., 301 W 53 St, Ste 13B, New York, NY 10019, 212-581-7068
Internet: Globalcityreview@aol.com
    Pubs: *Our History in New York* (Great Marsh Pr/Umbrella Pubs, 1998), *The Reading Room: Writing of the Moment: Anth* (Great Marsh Pr, 2000), *Glimmer Train, Central Park, Colorado Rev, Seattle Rev, New Directions Annual, 13th Moon*

Richard S. Abrons   W
812 Park Ave, #4E
New York, NY 10021, 212-517-4230
    Pubs: *Nebraska Rev, MacGuffin, Sou'wester, Columbia, NAR, Cosmopolitan, Fiction Network, Other Voices*

Diane Ackerman   P
Random House, 201 E 50 St, New York, NY 10022
    Pubs: *I Praise My Destroyer, The Rarest of the Rare, Jaguar of Sweet Laughter: New & Selected Poems* (Random Hse, 1998, 1995, 1991)

Glenda Adams   W
Goodman Assoc, 500 W End Ave, New York, NY 10024
    Pubs: *The Tempest of Clemenza* (Faber & Faber, 1996), *Longleg* (Cane Hill, 1992), *TriQtly, Village Voice, Hanging Loose, Seattle Rev*

Lloyd E. Addison 🎤   P
1704 St Johns Pl, #7F
Brooklyn, NY 11233, 718-771-2778
    Pubs: *Mystery of The Invention of Doublecross Baseball* (Private Pubs, 1981), *Drum Voices Revue*

Joel Agee   W
Donadio & Olson, Inc, 121 W 27 St, Ste 704, New York, NY 10001, 212-691-8077
    Pubs: *Twelve Years: An American Boyhood in East Germany* (FSG, 1981), *New Yorker, Harper's*

Jack Agueros   P&W
212 W 14 St
New York, NY 10011, 212-243-2270
    Pubs: *Dominoes & Other Stories* (Curbstone Pr, 1993), *Sonnets from the Puerto Rican* (Hanging Loose Pr, 1996), *Parnassus, Callaloo, Agni*

Ellen Akins   W
c/o Marian Young, 156 Fifth Ave, Ste 617, New York, NY 10010, 212-229-2612
Internet: emakins@cheqnet.net
    Pubs: *Hometown Brew* (Knopf, 1998), *Public Life, Little Woman* (HC, 1993, 1990), *World Like a Knife* (Johns Hopkins U Pr, 1991), *Home Movie* (S&S, 1987), *Georgia Rev, Southern Rev, SW Rev, Missouri Rev*

Viki Akiwumi 🎤 ✈   PP&P
61 E 8th St, #180
New York, NY 10003-6450, 212-459-4540
    Pubs: *Sister Fire* (HC, 1994), *In the Tradition* (Harlem River Pr, 1993), *Ancient Youth & Elders Reborn* (Universal Black Writers Pr, 1985), *Essence, Testimony, Presstime*

Meena Alexander 🎤 ✈   P&W
English Dept, Hunter College, CUNY, 695 Park Ave, New York, NY 10021, 212-772-5200
Internet: MAlexander@gc.cuny.edu
    Pubs: *Illiterate Heart* (TriQtly Bks/Northwestern Univ Pr, 2002), *Manhattan Music* (Mercury Hse, 1997), *River & Bridge* (Toronto Rev Pr, 1996), *Shock of Arrival* (Southend Pr, 1996), *Grand Street, Poetry Rev*

Elena Alexander 🎤 ✈   P&W
103 Bowery
New York, NY 10002, 212-431-6496
    Pubs: *101 Stories: Anth* (New York Univ Pr, 2002), *Second Word Thursdays: Anth* (Bright Hill Pr, 1999), *Aloud: Voices from the Nuyorican Poets Cafe: Anth* (H Holt, 1994), *American Letters & Commentary, Hanging Loose, LUNGFULL!, Minnesota Rev, Bomb*

Charlotte Alexander   P
112 E 10 St, #2
New York, NY 10003
    Pubs: *Outerbridge, Mid-American Rev, Earth's Daughters, Three Gray Geese Anth, Tide Turning Anth, The Dolphin's Arc Anth*

Austin M. Alexis 🎤 ✈   P&W
58 E 4 St, #9
New York, NY 10003-8914, 212-260-7525
Internet: amalexisjj@yahoo.com
    Pubs: *Phatitude, Candelabrum Poetry Mag, Pieran Springs, Dana Lit Society On-line Jrnl, Pedestal Mag, The Jrnl, Obsidian II, Barrow Street, Connecticut River Rev, James White Rev*

Donna Allegra 🎤 ✈					P&W
60 E 4 St, #3
New York, NY 10003-8916, 212-477-1109
   Pubs: *Black Like Us-A Century of Lesbian, Gay and
   Bisexual African-Amer Fiction: Anth* (Cleis Pr, 2002),
   *Witness to the Leasure of Blond Hip Hop Dancers, Mom:
   Anth* (Alyson Pubs, 2001, 1998)

Deborah Allen 🎤					P
PO Box 1452, Stuyvesant Sta, New York, NY 10009
   Pubs: *Yellow Leaves* (A Musty Bone, 1990), *Three Mile
   Harbor, Salmon, Painted Bride Qtly, South Dakota Rev, BPJ,
   Blue Unicorn, Ledge*

Paula Gunn Allen					P
Sanford Greenburger Assoc, 55 Fifth Ave, New York, NY
10003-4301, 212-206-5600
   Pubs: *The Sacred Hoop* (Beacon Pr, 1992), *The Voice of the
   Turtle: Anth* (Ballantine Pr, 1994), *Chicago, Yefief, Global
   Rev, Transpersonal Rev*

Roberta Allen 🎤 ✈					W
c/o DeAnna Heindel, Georges Borchardt Inc, 136 E 57 St,
New York, NY 10022
Internet: roall@aol.com
   Pubs: *The Dreaming Girl* (Painted Leaf, 2000), *Certain
   People* (Coffee Hse Pr, 1997), *Amazon Dream* (City Lights,
   1993), *The Daughter* (Autonomedia, 1992), *The Travelling
   Woman* (Vehicle Eds, 1986), *Fast Fiction: Anth* (Norton,
   1997), *Open City, Epoch, Bomb*

Dorothy Allison 🎤 ✈					P&W
Frances Goldin Agency, 57 East 11th Street, #5B, New York,
NY 10003
Internet: rydab@aol.com
   Pubs: *Trash* (Plume, 2002), *Cavedweller, Two or Three
   Things I Know for Sure, Bastard Out of Carolina* (Dutton,
   1998, 1995, 1992)

Mindy Aloff					P
708 Eighth Ave, #4L
Brooklyn, NY 11215
   Pubs: *Night Lights* (Prescott Street Pr, 1979), *APR, Choice,
   St. Andrews Rev*

Harold Alvarado-Tenorio
1591 Third Ave, Box 6694
New York, NY 10128
Internet: alvaradotenorio@telesat.com.co
   Pubs: *Libro del extranado* (Colcultura, 1985), *Kavafis* (U del
   Valle, 1984), *Inti, Chasqui, Logos*

Julia Alvarez 🎤 ✈					P&W
Susan Bergholz Literary Services, 17 W 10 St, #5, New York,
NY 10011, 212-387-0545
   Pubs: *In the Name of Salome, Something to Declare, The
   Other Side, Yo!, Seven Trees, Homecoming, In the Time of
   the Butterflies, How the Garcia Girls Lost Their Accents*
   (Algonquin Bks, 2000, 1998, 1998, 1997, 1996, 1995, 1994,
   1991), *New Yorker*

Mark Ameen 🎤 ✈					P&W
235 E 4 St #5A
New York, NY 10009-7231
Internet: markjameen@aol.com
   Pubs: *The Buried Body* (Amethyst, 1990), *A Circle of Sirens*
   (Seahorse Pr, 1985), *James White Rev, Between C&D*

Jack Anderson 🎤 ✈					P
40 E 10 St, #1H
New York, NY 10003-6221, 212-677-7698
   Pubs: *Traffic* (New Rivers Pr, 1998), *Field Trips on the Rapid
   Transit* (Hanging Loose Pr, 1990), *Selected Poems* (Release
   Pr, 1983), *Poetry, Paris Rev, Caliban, Hanging Loose,
   Chelsea*

Poul Anderson					W
Scovil-Chichak-Galen Literary Agency, 381 Park Ave S, #1112,
New York, NY 10016, 212-679-8686
   Pubs: *The Stars Are Also Fire, Harvest of Stars* (Tor, 1994,
   1993), *Orion Shall Rise* (Timescape, 1983)

Beth Anderson 🎤 ✈					PP&P
135 Eastern Pkwy Apt 4D
Brooklyn, NY 11238, 718-636-6010
Internet: beand@interport.net
   Pubs: *St. Mark's Poetry Project, Merkin Hall, Whitney
   Museum, Text-Sound Texts, Dramatika Mag, Poetry Mailing
   List, Assemblings, Flash Art, Ear Mag*

Michael Andre 🎤 ✈					P
Unmuzzled Ox, 105 Hudson St, #311, New York, NY 10013,
212-226-7170
Internet: MAndreOX@aol.com
   Pubs: *Experiments in Banal Living* (Empyreal Pr, 1998), *It as
   It* (Money for Food Pr, 1990), *Letters Home* (Vehicle, 1981),
   Mudfish, O.ars, Exquisite Corpse, Coves, Small Pr Rev

Bruce Andrews 🎤 ✈					P
41 W 96 St, #10D
New York, NY 10025
   Pubs: *Lip Service* (Coach Hse, 2001), *I Don't Have Any
   Paper So Shut Up, Give Em Enough Rope* (Sun & Moon Pr,
   1990, 1987)

Lucy Angeleri					PP
71-34 Harrow St
Forest Hills, NY 11375, 718-544-2877
   Pubs: *Tidings #2* (Four Facet Pr, 1992), *Tidings* (Print
   Center, 1974), *Lake Effect, Oread, Z Misc, Nomad,
   Slipstream, American Lit Rev, Slant, Croton Rev*

Roger Angell   P&W
The New Yorker, 4 Times Square, New York, NY 10036
  Pubs: *Once More Around the Park* (Ballantine, 1991),
  Season Ticket (HM, 1988), *New Yorker*

Jacob M. Appel   W
140 Claremont Ave, Apt 30
New York, NY 10027, 212-663-3643
Internet: jma38@columbia.edu
  Pubs: *Cimarron Rev, South Dakota Rev, Real, Writers'
  Forum, Green Mountains Rev, Boston Rev, Fugue, Buffalo
  Spree*

Allan Appel 🎤 ✈   P&W
332 E 84 St, #5A
New York, NY 10028, 212-737-1946
  Pubs: *Club Revelation, High Holiday Sutra* (Coffee Hse Pr,
  2001, 1997), *The Rabbi of Casino Boulevard* (St. Martin's
  Pr, 1986), *A Pocket Apocalypse: Anth* (Riverhead Bks,
  1997), *Nation, National Lampoon*

Linda Arking   W
110 Thompson St
New York, NY 10012

Richard R. Armijo   P
PO Box 477, 128 E Broadway, New York, NY 10002,
212-228-3033
  Pubs: *Wishing on a Star* (American Idealism Rag, 1990),
  Suburban Ambush (Johns Hopkins U Pr, 1989), *A
  Gathering of the Tribes, New Leaves Rev, Zien, Blast*

Emily Arnold   W
3 Washington Sq Village, #16-I
New York, NY 10012-1809, 212-260-2246
  Pubs: *Life Drawing* (Delacorte, 1986), *A Craving* (Dell, 1986)

Katherine Arnoldi   W
77 Park Terrace East D19
New York, NY 10034, 212-569-1232
Internet: karnoldi2100@yahoo.com
  Pubs: *The Amazing True Story of a Teenage Single Mom*
  (Hyperion, 1998), *The Qtly: Anths* (Vintage, 1991, 1990,
  1989), *Blue Collar Rev, Room of One's Own, Fiction, World,
  The Qtly, Onthebus, Red Tape, A Gathering of the Tribes,
  New Observations*

Maria Arrillaga 🎤 ✈   P&W
140 Charles St., Apt 8E
New York, NY 10014, 212-929-4046
Internet: mariajoe@banet.net
  Pubs: *Manana Valentina* (Room of One's Own, 1995),
  These Are Not Sweet Girls (White Pine Pr, 1994), *Cascada
  de Sol* (Inst of Puerto Rican Culture, 1977), *Yo Soy Fili
  Mele: Anth* (U PR Pr, 1999), *Festa Da Palabra, Cupey,
  Tercer Milenio, Confrontation, PEN Intl*

Sarah Arvio   P
314 E 9 St, #1
New York, NY 10003
Internet: arvio@earthlink.net
  Pubs: *Visits From The Seventh* (Knopf, 2002), *KGB Bar Book
  of Poems: Anth* (Scribner, 2000), *Best American Poetry
  1998: Anth* (Scribner, 1998), *New Yorker, Yale Rev, Paris Rev,
  Raritan, Poetry, Literary Imagination, Southwest Rev*

Carol Ascher   W
158 W 23 St #5
New York, NY 10011
Internet: carol.ascher@nyu.edu
  Pubs: *The Flood* (Curbstone Pr, 1996), *Between Women*
  (Routledge, 1993), *Kenyon Rev, Shenandoah, Virginia Qtly
  Rev, Boulevard, Literary Rev, Ms., Witness, ACM*

Sheila Ascher   PP&P&W
PO Box 176
Rockaway Park, NY 11694-0176, 718-474-6547
www.ascher/straus.com
  Pubs: *ABC Street* (Green Interger, 2001), *The Menaced
  Assassin, The Other Planet, Red Moon/Red Lake*
  (McPherson, 1989, 1988, 1988), *Central Park,
  Confrontation, NAW*

Baron James Ashanti 🎤 ✈   PP&P
274 West 140 St #45
New York, NY 10030
Internet: brilancefactory@aol.com
  Pubs: *Nova* (Harlem River Pr, 1990), *Nubiana II* (Shamal Pr,
  1979), *Essence, Eye Ball Mag, Greenfield Rev, Race Today,
  Pan African Jrnl, Telephone Bar, Southern University,
  Howard University*

John Ashbery 🎤 ✈   P
Georges Borchardt Inc, 136 E 57 St, New York, NY 10022,
212-753-5785
  Pubs: *Chinese Whispers, Your Name Here, Girls on the Run,
  Wakefulness, And the Stars Were Shining* (FSG, 2002,
  2000, 1999, 1998, 1994), *As Umbrellas Follow Rain* (Qua,
  2001), *Hotel Lautreamont* (Knopf, 1992)

Gary Aspenberg 🎤 ✈   P
323-A E 89 St, #1W
New York, NY 10128
  Pubs: *Bus Poems* (Broken Moon Pr, 1993)

James Atlas   P
The New York Times, 229 W 43 St, New York, NY 10036
  Pubs: *The Great Pretender* (Atheneum, 1986), *New
  Republic, Atlantic*

Louis Auchincloss   W
1111 Park Ave
New York, NY 10028, 212-348-3723

Jean M. Auel   W
Jean V. Naggar Literary Agency, 216 E 75 St, Ste 1E, New
York, NY 10021, 212-794-1082
  Pubs: *The Plains of Passage, The Mammoth Hunters, The
  Valley of Horses, The Clan of the Cave Bear* (Crown, 1990,
  1985, 1982, 1980)

Jane Augustine ♦ ✈   P
PO Box 1289, Stuyvesant Sta, New York, NY 10009,
212-533-1928
Internet: AugustineJane@cs.com
  Pubs: *Arbor Vitae* (Marsh Hawk Pr, 2002), *Transitory*
  (Spuyten Duyvil, 2002), *French Windows* (Poetry NY, 1998),
  Journeys (Pig Pr, 1985), *Beneath a Single Moon: Anth*
  (Shambhala, 1991)

Paul Auster   P
c/o Carol Mann, Carol Mann Agency, 55 Fifth Ave, New York,
NY 10003
  Pubs: *Mr. Vertigo, Leviathan* (Viking, 1994, 1992)

Kofi Awoonor   W
Harold Ober Assoc, 425 Madison Ave, New York, NY 10017,
212-759-8600
  Pubs: *Until the Morning After* (Greenfield Rev Pr, 1987)

Jody Azzouni ♦ ✈   P&W
301 Hicks St
Brooklyn, NY 11201, 718-852-6282
Internet: jodyazzouni@mindspring.com
  Pubs: *The Lust for Blueprints* (Poet's Pr, 1999), *Quarter
  After Eight, Wisconsin Rev, Willow Springs, Hanging Loose,
  Artful Dodge, Bitter Oleander*

Virginia Bagliore   P
PO Box 244, Ryder St Sta, Brooklyn, NY 11234
  Pubs: *Oracles of Light* (Pella Pub, 1986), *The Inkling, Z
  Misc, Bitterroot, Eve's Legacy*

Alison Baker ♦ ✈   W
Gail Hochman, Brandt & Brandt Literary Agents, Inc, 1501
Broadway, New York, NY 10036
Internet: abaker@jeffnet.org
  Pubs: *Thousands Live!* (Helianthus Pr, 1996), *Loving
  Wander Beaver: Novella & Stories, How I Came West, &
  Why I Stayed: Stories* (Chronicle Bks, 1995, 1993), *Story,
  Zyzzyva*

Julius Balbin ♦ ✈   P
945 W End Ave, #9A
New York, NY 10025, 212-666-6526
  Pubs: *Inter Vivo Kaj Morto, Damnejoj* (Edistudio, 1996, 1992),
  Imperio De L'Koroj: Esperanto Poetry (Italy; Estudio, 1989)

Jean Balderston ♦   P
1225 Park Ave, #8C
New York, NY 10128-1758, 212-876-4111
  Pubs: *Visiting Emily: Anth* (U Iowa Pr, 2001), *A Poke in the I:
  Anth* (Candlewick Pr, 2001), *A More Perfect Union: Anth* (St.
  Martin's Pr, 1998), *Poetry from A to Z: Anth* (Bradbury Pr,
  1994), *NYQ, Wormwood Rev, Light, Poets On, Mudfish,
  Sing Heavenly Muse!*

J. G. Ballard   W
Robin Straus Agency, 229 E 79 St, New York, NY 10021

Robert Joseph Banfelder   W
53-38 195 St
Fresh Meadows, NY 11365, 718-357-7330
  Pubs: *No Stranger Than I* (Hudson View Pr, 1991)

Russell Banks ♦ ✈   P&W
Ellen Levine Literary Agency, 15 E 26 St, Ste 1801, New York,
NY 10010, 212-889-0620
Internet: rebstudio@aol.com
  Pubs: *Angel on the Roof, Cloudsplitter, Rule of the Bone,
  Sweet Hereafter* (HC, 2000, 1998, 1995, 1991)

William Henry Banks, Jr.   W
PO Box 2268
New York, NY 10163-2268, 203-562-7940
  Pubs: *A Love So Fine* (Pyramid Bks, 1974)

Barbara Baracks   P
427 15 St, #4B
Brooklyn, NY 11215, 718-783-2881
  Pubs: *Poems Out of Place* (Language, 1978), *No Sleep*
  (Tuumba Pr, 1977), *Village Voice, Ms.*

Amiri Baraka ♦ ✈   P
Sterling Lord Literistic, 65 Bleecker St, New York, NY 10012,
212-780-6050
Internet: ab11@erols.com
  Pubs: *The Fiction of LeRoi Jones/Amiri Baraka* (Lawrence
  Hill Bks, 1999), *Eulogies, Transbluesency* (Marsilio, 1997,
  1995), *Funklore* (Litoral, 1996), *Y's/Why's/Wise: The Griot's
  Song* (Third World Pr, 1995)

Benjamin R. Barber   W
370 Riverside Dr
New York, NY 10025
  Pubs: *Marriage Voices* (S&S, 1981), *Harper's, Salmagundi*

Barbara Barg   P&W
520 E 14 St, #26
New York, NY 10009, 212-529-8751
Internet: bestpoet@aol.com
  Pubs: *Origin of the Species* (Semiotext(e), *1994), Obeying
  the Chemicals* (Hard Pr, 1984), *Playboy, High Times, Short
  Qtly, Language Anth*

Helen Barolini 🎤   P&W
86 Maple Ave
Hastings-on-Hudson, NY 10706, 914-478-5774
Internet: helenbarolini@juno.com
    Pubs: *Festa* (Univ of Wisconsin Pr, 2002), *More Italian
    Hours & Other Stories* (Bordighera, 2001), *Love in the
    Middle Ages* (Morrow, iUniverse, 2000), *The Dream Book:
    Anth* (Syracuse U Pr, 2000), *Umbertina* (Feminist Pr, 1999),
    Antioch Rev, New Letters

Suze Baron 🎤   PP&P
549 E 34 St
Brooklyn, NY 11203, 718-282-7159
    Pubs: *When Black People Pray* (Self, 1990), *The P.S. 269
    Fivers* (P.S. 269, 1988), *Raven Chronicles, Z Misc, NYQ,
    Calapooya Collage, New Pr, Pegasus Rev, Word Thursdays*

Marvin Barrett   W
115 E 67 St, #3B
New York, NY 10021-5901

Fran Barst 🎤 ✈   P&W
115 E 9 St #11B
New York, NY 10003-5419, 212-677-8934
Internet: rblake@nyc.rr.com
    Pubs: *The Death Gods* (Intl Poetry & Fiction Pr, 1991), *Bitter
    Oleander, Negative Capability, Korone, Carolina Qtly, Indian
    American, Denver Qtly*

Tricia Bauer 🎤 ✈   P&W
Susan Gleason, Literary Agent, 325 Riverside Dr, New York,
NY 10025, 212-662-3876
Internet: hardwood@altavista.net
    Pubs: *Shelterbelt* (St. Martin's Pr, 2000), *Hollywood &
    Hardwood, Boondocking, Working Women & Other Stories*
    (Bridge Works Pub, 1999, 1997, 1995)

Jonathan Baumbach 🎤 ✈   W
English Dept, Brooklyn College, Brooklyn, NY 11210, 718-
856-6501
    Pubs: *D-Tours, Seven Wives* (FC2/Black Ice Bks, 1998, 1992)

Judith Baumel   P
3530 Henry Hudson Pkwy, #12M
Bronx, NY 10463, 718-548-3053
Internet: baumel@adlibv.adelphi.edu
    Pubs: *Now* (Miami U Pr, 1996), *The Weight of Numbers*
    (Wesleyan, 1988)

Ann Beattie   W
c/o Lynn Nesbit, Janklow & Nesbit Associates, 445 Park Ave,
New York, NY 10022, 212-421-1700
    Pubs: *What Was Mine, Picturing Will* (Random Hse, 1991,
    1990)

Jeanne Marie Beaumont 🎤 ✈   P
120 W 70 St, #2D
New York, NY 10023-4444
Internet: jeannebeaumont@att.net
    Pubs: *Curious Conduct* (BOA, 2004), *Placebo Effects*
    (Norton, 1997), *DoubleTake, Manhattan Rev, Conduit,
    Pleiades, Boston Rev, Verse, Nation, NAW, Denver Qtly*

Mary Ann Beban   P
22 Jones St, #3F
New York, NY 10014, 212-929-2511
    Pubs: *Lips Unsealed: Anth* (Capra Pr, 1990), *Slipstream,
    Connecticut River Rev, Blueline, The Writer's Eye*

Madeleine D. Beckman 🎤 ✈   P&W
131 Thompson St, #3A
New York, NY 10012, 212-533-2033
Internet: madi@echonyc.com
    Pubs: *Dead Boyfriends* (Linear Arts Bks, 1998), *Contact II,
    Fetishes, Skidrow Penthouse, Salonika Qtly, Happy,
    Confrontations, NYQ, Barrow Street, Tempus*

Joshua Saul Beckman   P
182 Franklin St, Apt E16
Brooklyn, NY 11222, 718-383-0042
    Pubs: *Things Are Happening* (APR/Copper Canyon Pr,
    1998), *There Is an Ocean* (WSW, 1997), *Blue Paradise, At
    the News of Your Death* (Permeable Pr, 1997, 1995), *ACM,
    APR, Gulf Coast, Response*

Louis Begley   W
Georges Borchardt Inc, 136 E 57 St, New York, NY 10022,
212-753-5785
    Pubs: *Das Gelobte Land* (Suhrkamp, 2001), *Schmidt
    Delivered, Mistler's Exit, About Schmidt, As Max Saw It, The
    Man Who Was Late, Wartime Lies* (Knopf, 2000, 1998,
    1996, 1994, 1993, 1991)

Judith Bell 🎤 ✈   W
Witherspoon Assoc Inc, 235 E 31 St, New York, NY 10016,
212-889-8626
Internet: belljort@aol.com
    Pubs: *Generation to Generation: Anth, Grow Old Along With
    Me: Anth* (Papier-Mache Pr, 1998, 1996), *Farm Wives &
    Other Iowa Stories: Anth* (Mid-Prairie Bks, 1995),
    *Washington Rev, First, Short Fiction by Women, Snake
    Nation Rev, Parting Gifts, ALR*

Bruce Benderson 🎤 ✈   W
257 E 7 St, #7
New York, NY 10009, 212-228-3114
Internet: bruxe@aol.com
    Pubs: *User* (Dutton/Plume, 1996), *Pretending to Say No,
    Flesh & the Word: Anth, Men on Men 6: Anth* (Plume, 1990,
    1997, 1996), *American Letters and Commentary, Between
    C & D, Purple, Central Park, Lit Rev, Outweek, NYQ,
    Advocate*

Frances Bendix PP
2676 Grand Concourse, #3H
Bronx, NY 10458-4939, 718-295-2697
    Pubs: *Resonance, Modern Images, Ararat, NY Poets Qtly,
    Poetry Jrnl, Bronx Arts, Words & Image, SlugFest, Visions*

Helen Benedict 🎤 ✈ W
Richard Parks Literary Agency, 138 E 16 St #5D, New York,
NY 10003
    Pubs: *The Sailor's Wife* (Zoland, 2000), *Bad Angel, A World
    Like This* (Dutton, 1996, 1990), *Ontario Rev, Antioch Rev*

Ruth Benjamin P&W
1158 Fifth Ave, #5D
New York, NY 10029, 212-348-6624
    Pubs: *Naked at Forty* (Horizon Pr, 1984), *Albany Rev*

Nathan Bergenfeld P
2632 W 2 St
Brooklyn, NY 11223, 718-769-6773
    Pubs: *Life Spirals, Garden Gleanings* (NYC Dept of Parks,
    1987, 1986)

Rachel Berghash 🎤 P
7 E 20 St
New York, NY 10003-1106, 212-533-1541
Internet: rberghash@earthlink.net
    Pubs: *Chicago Rev, Anima, Waterways, Pulp, Jewish
    Frontier, Bitterroot, Blue Unicorn, Israel Horizons, West
    Wind Rev, Poetpourri*

Eleanor Bergstein W
210 Central Park S, Ste 14C
New York, NY 10019, 212-245-4313
    Pubs: *Ex-Lover* (Random Hse, 1989), *Advancing Paul
    Newman* (Viking Pr, 1973)

Nancy Berke P
164 Sterling Pl, #3D
Brooklyn, NY 11217
    Pubs: *Alternative Poetry & Fiction, Footwork, Pig Iron,
    Slipstream, Central Park, New Voices*

Constance E. Berkley P
Fordham Univ, Lincoln Center, Rm 414, New York, NY 10023

Howard Berland PP
3044 Kingsbridge Ave, #26
Bronx, NY 10463, 212-593-7552

Carol W. Berman 🎤 ✈ W
866 UN Plaza, #473
New York, NY 10017-1822, 212-758-2901
    Pubs: *Aphrodite Gone Berserk, Caprice, Challenging
    Destiny, Fetishes*

Kenneth Bernard P&W
800 Riverside Dr, #8H
New York, NY 10032, 212-927-8851
Internet: k.bernard@verizon.net
    Pubs: *The Qui Parle Play & Poems, The Baboon in the
    Night Club* (Asylum Arts Pub, 1999, 1994), *Clown at Wall*
    (Confrontation Pr, 1996), *From the District File* (Fiction
    Collective 2, 1992), *Chelsea, Fiction Intl, Salmagundi,
    Contre-Vox, Collages & Bricolages*

Louise Bernikow 🎤 ✈ P
318 W 105 St, #4A
New York, NY 10025, 212-662-6307
Internet: weezieman@aol.com
    Pubs: *Alone in America, Among Women* (H&R, 1985, 1982)

Burton Bernstein P&W
Donadio & Olson, Inc, 121 W 27 St, Ste 704, New York, NY
10001, 212-691-8077
    Pubs: *Plane Crazy* (Ticknor & Fields, 1985), *Family Matters*
    (Summit, 1982), *New Yorker, Esquire*

Daniel Berrigan P
220 W 98 St, #11-L
New York, NY 10025, 212-662-6358
    Pubs: *Whereon to Stand, Sorrow Built a Bridge: Friendship
    & AIDS* (Fortcamp Pr, 1991, 1990)

Eliot Berry W
c/o Carl Brandt, Brandt & Brandt Literary Agents, 1501
Broadway, New York, NY 10036
    Pubs: *Tough Draw* (H Holt/John MacRae Bks, 1992), *Four
    Quarters Make a Season* (Berkley Pr, 1973)

Lebert Bethune P&W
110 W 96 St, #16C
New York, NY 10025, 212-866-8059

Sarah Bird W
c/o Kristine Dahl, ICM, 40 W 57 St, New York, NY 10019,
212-556-5600
Internet: sbirdgirl@aol.com
    Pubs: *Virgin of the Rodeo, The Mommy Club* (Doubleday,
    1993, 1991), *Mademoiselle, Texas Observer, Cosmopolitan*

Ann Birstein 🎤 ✈ W
1623 3rd Ave, #27-J W
New York, NY 10128-3642, 212-289-0346
Internet: abirstein@aol.com
    Pubs: *The Last of the True Believers* (Norton, 1988), *The
    Rabbi on 47th Street* (Dial Pr, 1982), *McCall's, New Yorker,
    Confrontation*

Ellen Marie Bissert P
735 Kappock St, #9A/F
Riverdale, NY 10463
    Pubs: *The Immaculate Conception of the Blessed Virgin
    Dyke* (13th Moon, 1977), *Beyond Baroque, 13th Moon*

Star Black   P
111 E 36 St
New York, NY 10016, 212-683-6127
    Pubs: *October for Idas* (Painted Leaf Pr, 1997), *Waterworn*
    (Tribes Bks, 1995), *Doubletime* (Groundwater Pr, 1995)

Sophie Cabot Black 🎤 ✈   P
PO Box 528
New York, NY 10024
Internet: SCB49@aol.com
    Pubs: *The Misunderstanding of Nature* (Graywolf Pr, 1994),
    Atlantic, Antaeus, Partisan Rev, APR, Paris Rev

Isaac J. Black   P
119-10 225 St
Cambria Heights, NY 11411, 718-723-5148
    Pubs: *Obsidian, Callaloo, Hoodoo, First World, BPJ, Black
    World*

Nicole Blackman 🎤 ✈   PP&P
PO Box 534
New York, NY 10156
Internet: blackmanpr@aol.com
    Pubs: *Blood Sugar* (Incommunicado Bks, 2000), *Poetry
    Nation: Anth* (Vehicule Pr, 1999), *Will Work for Peace: Anth*
    (zeropanik pr, 1999), *Revival: Anth* (Manic D Pr, 1995),
    Aloud: Anth (Holt, 1994), *Oculus, Flexible Head, Gargoyle,
    Barrow Street*

George Blagowidow   W
Hippocrene Books, 171 Madison Ave, New York, NY 10016,
212-685-4371
    Pubs: *In Search of the Lady Lion Tamer* (HBJ, 1987)

Barbara A. Blatner 🎤 ✈   P
c/o Frankel, 900 West End Ave, #10A, New York, NY 10025,
212-866-4130
    Pubs: *No Star Shines Sharper* (Baker's Plays, 1990), *The
    Pope in Space* (Intertext Pr, 1986), *Apalachee Qtly, Poetry
    NW, Compost, 13th Moon, Lift, Fireheart, NYQ, Mildred,
    Groundswell*

Lucienne S. Bloch   W
1111 Park Ave
New York, NY 10128
    Pubs: *Finders Keepers* (HM, 1982), *On the Great-Circle
    Route* (S&S, 1979)

Lawrence Block   W
Knox Burger, 39 1/2 Washington Sq S, New York, NY 10012
    Pubs: *A Walk Among the Tombstones, A Dance at the
    Slaughterhouse* (Morrow, 1992, 1991), *Playboy, American
    Heritage*

Amy Bloom   W
c/o Phyllis Wender, Rosenstone/Wender, 3 E 48 St, New York,
NY 10077, 212-832-8330
Internet: amybloom@aol.com
    Pubs: *Come to Me* (HC, 1993), *Best American Short
    Stories: Anths* (HM, 1992, 1991), *New Yorker*

Laurel Blossom 🎤 ✈   P
920 Park Ave, #2B
New York, NY 10028-0208, 212-628-0239
Internet: lbaines920@aol.com
    Pubs: *The Papers Said* (Greenhouse Rev Pr, 1993), *Lights,
    Camera, Poetry: Anth* (HB, 1996), *Paris Rev, Poetry,
    Pequod, Confrontation, APR, Lips, Many Mountains Moving*

Bonnie Bluh 🎤 ✈   W
55 Bethune St, #1007A
New York, NY 10014, 212-255-3322
Internet: bbluh@aol.com
    Pubs: *The Eleanor Roosevelt Girls* (LyreBird Bks, 1999),
    The Old Speak Out (Horizon, 1979), *Banana* (Macmillan,
    1976), *Woman to Woman* (Starogubski, 1974)

Victor Bockris   P
106 Perry St
New York, NY 10014

Richard Bodtke   P
175 W 93 St, #5A
New York, NY 10025
    Pubs: *Tragedy & the Jacobean Temper* (U Salzburg, 1972),
    World of Undisguise (Nauset, 1968)

Karen Iris Bogen   P
c/o Letitia Lee, Ann Elmo Literary Agency, 60 E 42 St, New
York, NY 10165, 212-661-2883
    Pubs: *Will the Circle Be Unbroken: Anth* (Spinsters/Aunt
    Lute Pr, 1986), *SPR*

Nancy Bogen 🎤 ✈   W
31 Jane St, #17B
New York, NY 10014-1982, 212-741-2417
Internet: nancybogen@hotmail.com
    Pubs: *Klytaimnestra Who Stayed at Home, Bagatelle
    Guinevere, Bobe Mayse: A Tale of Washington Square*
    (Twinkenham Pr, 1998, 1995, 1993)

Magda Bogin   P&W
425 Riverside Dr
New York, NY 10025, 212-662-9434
    Pubs: *Natalya, God's Messenger* (Scribner, 1994)

Portia Bohn 🎤 ✈   W
49 W 12 St, Apt 5G
New York, NY 10011-8531, 646-486-6736
    Pubs: *Confrontation, Carolina Qtly, Short Story Intl,
    Massachusetts Rev, Other Voices, Kalliope*

Thomas Bolt P
110 Suffolk St, #6B
New York, NY 10002
    Pubs: *Out of the Woods* (Yale U Pr, 1989)

Roger Bonair-Agard 🎤 ✈ PP&P
748 Madison St, #2
Brooklyn, NY 11221
Internet: bonairpoet@aol.com
    Pubs: *and chaos congealed* (Fly by Night Pr, 2000), *Burning Down the House: Anth* (Soft Skull Pr, 2000), *360: A Revolution of Black Poets: Anth* (Black Words Pr, 1998), *Phati'tude, 13 Bar/Lounge, Nuyorican Poets Cafe, Spy, Antioch College*

Gina Angeline Bonati P
607 E 11 St, #10
New York, NY 10009, 212-473-1950
    Pubs: *Resurrection* (Venom Pr, 1993), *The Weight of a Place* (Enemy Loose Pub, 1990), *Curare, Village Voice, Resister*

Rafael Bordao P
Arcas, PO Box 023617, Brooklyn, NY 11202-3617
    Pubs: *Libro De Las Interferencias, Escurridduras De La Soledad* (Editorial Palmar, 1995, 1995), *Diario Las Americas, Cuzcatlan, Latino Stuff Rev, El Diario*

Laure-Anne Bosselaar 🎤 ✈ P
122 Washington Pl
New York, NY 10014, 212-462-4281
    Pubs: *Small Gods of Grief, The Hour Between Dog & Wolf* (BOA Edtns, 2001, 1997), *Urban Nature: Anth, Outsiders: Anth, Night Out: Anth, Drive They Said: Anth* (Milkweed Edtns, 2000, 1999, 1997, 1995)

David Bottoms P&W
Maria Carvainis Literary Agency, 235 W End Ave, New York, NY 10023, 212-580-1559
Internet: engdhb@panther.gsu.edu
    Pubs: *Vagrant Grace, Armored Hearts: New & Selected Poems* (Copper Canyon Pr, 1999, 1995), *Easter Weekend* (HM, 1990), *Under the Vulture-Tree, In a U-Haul North of Damascus* (Morrow, 1987, 1983), *Atlantic, New Yorker, Paris Rev, Harper's, Poetry, APR*

Matthew S. Boyd W
Little, Brown & Company, 1271 Ave of the Americas, New York, NY 10020, 212-522-8000
Internet: petithall@dcdu.com
    Pubs: *The Art of Breaking Glass* (Little, Brown, 1997), *Nightmare Logic* (Bantam, 1989)

T. Coraghessan Boyle 🎤 ✈ W
Georges Borchardt Inc, 136 E 57 St, New York, NY 10022, 212-753-5785
www.tcboyle.com
    Pubs: *Drop City, After the Plague, A Friend of the Earth, Riven Rock, T.C. Boyle Stories, The Tortilla Curtain, The Road to Wellville, East Is East, If the River Was Whiskey, World's End* (Viking, 2003, 2001, 2000, 1998, 1998, 1995, 1993, 1990, 1989, 1987)

David Bradley W
Wendy Weil Agency Inc, 232 Madison Ave, Ste 1300, New York, NY 10016, 212-685-0030
    Pubs: *The Chaneysville Incident* (H&R, 1990), *South Street* (Scribner, 1986), *Esquire, New Yorker, Philadelphia, Harper's*

Kathleen Brady W
305 E 72 St
New York, NY 10021
    Pubs: *Ida Tarbell: Portrait of a Muckraker* (U Pittsburgh, 1989), *Inside Out* (Norton, 1979)

Perry Brass 🎤 ✈ P&W
2501 Palisade Ave, #A1
Bronx, NY 10463-6104, 718-884-6606
Internet: belhuepress@earthlink.net
    Pubs: *The Substance of God, Warlock: A Novel of Possession, The Lover of My Soul, The Harvest, Sex-Charge* (Belhue Pr, 2003, 2001, 1998, 1997, 1991), *Columbia Anth of Gay Literature* (Columbia U Pr, 1998), *James White Rev, Christopher Street*

Kamau Brathwaite P
37 Washington Sq W, #4B
New York, NY 10011
    Pubs: *Sunpoem, The Arrivants* (Oup, 1982, 1973), *Savacou: Jrnl of the Caribbean Artists*

Brian Breger P
179 E 3 St, #33
New York, NY 10009
    Pubs: *Journeys to the Center of the Earth* (Piecework Pr, 1986), *Mojave* (# Pr, 1980), *Mulch*

Betty Bressi P
74 Claradon Ln
Staten Island, NY 10305, 718-273-1793
    Pubs: *Letternet II: Letters from Italy, Letternet I* (Glassworks Pr, 1998, 1990), *Poeti Italo Americani: Anth* (Alfonsi, 1985), *Small Pond, Box 749, Contact II, Jam Today*

Peter Bricklebank W
1803 Riverside Dr, #2J
New York, NY 10034, 212-567-3686
    Pubs: *American Voice, Crescent Rev, Mid-American Rev, Kansas Qtly, Carolina Qtly, Confrontation*

Richard P. Brickner   W
Lantz-Harris Literary Agency, 156 Fifth Ave, Ste 617, New
York, NY 10010, 212-924-6269
    Pubs: *After She Left* (H Holt, 1988), *Tickets* (S&S, 1981)

Les Bridges   P
313 E 10 St, #4
New York, NY 10009, 212-677-2799
    Pubs: *Read 'em & Weep, Fractured Snapshots* (LynDawn,
1993, 1992), *The Literature of Work* (U Phoenix Pr, 1991)

Stewart Brisby   P
463 West St, #G113
New York, NY 10014-2010, 212-633-1642
Internet: spb3@columbia.edu
    Pubs: *A Death in America* (Wolverine Pr, 1986), *Caprice,
Greenfield Rev, Berkeley Barb, Margins*

Jean Brody   W
Jean V Naggar Literary Agency, 216 E 75 St, Ste 1E, New
York, NY 10021, 212-794-1082
    Pubs: *Cleo* (St. Martins Pr, 1987), *A Coven of Women*
(Atheneum, 1987), *Gideon's House* (Putnam, 1984),
Special Report, Lear's

Janet Brof 🎤 ✈   P&W
380 Riverside Dr, #2F
New York, NY 10025-1801, 212-663-6254
    Pubs: *Through a Half-Open Door* (Catkin Pr, 1988), *Kansas
Qtly, Poets On, Negative Capability, Stone Country, Mid-
Stream, Mss.*

E. M. Broner   W
Charlotte Sheedy Literary Agency, 65 Bleecker St, New York,
NY 10012, 212-780-9800
    Pubs: *Mornings & Mournings, The Telling* (HC, 1994, 1993),
A Weave of Women, Her Mothers (HR&W, 1978, 1975)

Donna Brook 🎤 ✈   P
231 Wyckoff St
Brooklyn, NY 11217-2208, 718-643-9559
    Pubs: *A More Human Face, What Being Responsible Means
to Me, Notes on Space/Time* (Hanging Loose Pr, 1998,
1988, 1977), *Without Child: Anth* (Feminist Pr, 1999), *Verse,
Hanging Loose, Telephone, Alternative Pr, B'way II, River
Styx, The World*

Terry Brooks   W
Ballantine Books/Del Rey Fantasy, 201 E 50 St, New York,
NY 10022
    Pubs: *The Wishsong of Shannara, The Elfstones of
Shannara* (Del Rey/Ballantine Bks, 1985, 1982)

Millicent Brower 🎤 ✈   P&W
484 W 43 St, #10-F
New York, NY 10036, 212-239-1881
    Pubs: *Young Performers* (Julian Messner, 1985), *I Am Going
Nowhere* (Putnam, 1972), *Ingenue* (Ballantine, 1959),
Language Arts, Cricket

Kurt Brown 🎤 ✈   P
122 Washington Place
New York, NY 10014, 212-462-4281
Internet: kn.brown@verizon.net
    Pubs: *More Things in Heaven and Earth* (FourWay Books,
2002), *Return of the Prodigals* (Four Way Bks, 1999), *Verse
& Universe: Anth* (Milkweed Edtns, 1999), *Harvard Rev,
Crazyhorse, Indiana Rev, Ploughshares, SPR,
Massachusetts Rev, Agni*

Rita Mae Brown   P&W
Wendy Weil Agency Inc, 232 Madison Ave, Ste 1300, New
York, NY 10016
    Pubs: *Rest in Pieces, Wish You Were Here* (w/S.P. Brown),
Bingo (Bantam, 1992, 1990, 1988), *Southern Discomfort*
(H&R, 1982)

Andrea Carter Brown 🎤 ✈   P
355 S End Ave Apt 5A1
New York, NY 10280-1060, 212-321-2928
Internet: waterrail@aol.com
    Pubs: *Brook & Rainbow* (Sow's Ear Pr, 2001), *Poetry After
9-11: An Anth of NY Poets* (Melville House Pubs, 2002),
Girls: An Anthology (Global City Pr, 1997), *Ploughshares,
Many Mountains Moving, Phoebe, Mississippi Rev,
Gettysburg Rev, Marlboro Rev*

Kenneth H. Brown 🎤 ✈   P&W
150 74th St #3K
Brooklyn, NY 11209, 718-836-1116
    Pubs: *Hitler's Analyst* (Xlibris, 2000), *You'd Never Know It
from the Way I Talk* (Ashland Poetry Pr, 1990), *The Narrows*
(Dial Pr, 1971), *The Brig* (Hill & Wang, 1965), *Gallery Mag,
City Lights*

Michael Brownstein 🎤 ✈   P&W
21 E 2 St, #3
New York, NY 10003
    Pubs: *Self-Reliance* (Coffee Hse Pr, 1994), *The Touch*
(Autonomedia, 1993), *New Yorker, Open City*

Anne-Marie Brumm 🎤 ✈   P&W
175 W 13 St #8A
New York, NY 10011-7869, 212-255-5030
    Pubs: *Last Exit to Peace, Come Drink Coffee with Me*
(Widener & Lewis, 2000, 1994), *Confrontation, SW Rev,
Response, Abiko Qtly, Prospice, Paterson Lit Rev, Nexus,
Global City Rev, Urban Affairs, Intl Poetry Rev, Queen's
Qtly, Karam*

C. D. B. Bryan W
c/o Lynn Nesbit, Janklow & Nesbit Associates, 598 Madison Ave, New York, NY 10022-1614, 212-421-1700
 Pubs: *Beautiful Women, Ugly Scenes* (Doubleday, 1983), *Friendly Fire* (Putnam, 1976)

Frederick Buechner W
Harriet Wasserman Agency, 137 E 36 St, New York, NY 10016, 212-689-3257
 Pubs: *Godric, Whistling in the Dark* (Harper, 1988, 1980)

Melvin Jules Bukiet 🎤 ✈ W
c/o Jennifer Lyons, 21 W 26 St, New York, NY 10010, 212-685-2663
 Pubs: *Strange Fire* (Norton, 2001), *Signs & Wonders* (Picador, 1999), *After* (St. Martin's Pr, 1996), *While the Messiah Tarries* (HB, 1995), *Stories of an Imaginary Childhood* (Northwestern U Pr, 1992), *Antaeus, Paris Rev*

Aaron E. Bulman P
15 Magaw Pl, #1B
New York, NY 10033, 212-781-5498
 Pubs: *Plum Rev, Jewish Currents, Partisan Rev, Home Planet News, Small Pond Rev, Images, Paris Rev, Jewish Spectator*

France Burke P&W
170 Ave C, #21D
New York, NY 10009
 Pubs: *Women in Search of Utopia: Anth* (Schocken Bks, 1984), *Paris Rev, Confrontation, Panache, Dramatist Guild Qtly*

Kathe Burkhart 🎤 ✈ PP&P&W
47 S 5 St, 3rd Fl
Brooklyn, NY 11211-5106, 718-486-7383
Internet: domfemart@aol.com
 Pubs: *Deux Poids, Deux Mesures* (Hachette Litteratures, 2002), *The Double Standard* (Participant, 2002), *Velvet Revolution* (Italy; Galleria in Arco, 1993), *Red Tape: Anth* (M. Carter, 1993), *From Under the 8-Ball* (Line, 1985), *Williamsburg Observer*

Brian Burland P&W
W W Norton, 500 5 Ave, New York, NY 10110
 Pubs: *A Few Flowers for St. George, Love Is a Durable Fire, Fall from Aloft* (Grafton/Collins, 1987, 1987, 1987), *New Letters*

Diane Burnspesetsky P
46 E 1st St, #4B
New York, NY 10003, 212-475-5680
Internet: tribes@pop.interport.net
 Pubs: *Riding the One-Eyed Ford* (Contact/II Pr, 1981), *Aloud: Voices from the Nuyorican Poets Cafe: Anth* (New Worlds of Literature, 1994), *Greenfield Rev, A Gathering of the Tribes, Akwesasne Notes, Anishinabe Aki, LAC Court Oreilles Jrnl*

Anne Kelleher Bush W
Donald Maass Literary Agency, 157 W 57 St, Ste 1003, New York, NY 10019
Internet: ahay72a@prodigy.com
 Pubs: *The Misbegotten King, Children of Enchantment* (Warner Bks, 1997, 1996)

Naomi Bushman P
716 Broadway
New York, NY 10013, 212-421-1637
 Pubs: *West End, Trellis Two, Hanging Loose*

Peter Bushyeager 🎤 ✈ P
9 Stuyvesant Oval, #5F
New York, NY 10009
 Pubs: *Citadel Luncheonette* (Ten Dell Bks, 2002), *Help Yourself: Anth* (Autonomedia, 2002), *Vital Wires* (Unimproved Edtns Pr, 1986), *Synergism Anth* (Boshi Pr, 1995), *Talisman, The World, Pagan Place*

Edward Butscher P&W
84-01 Main St
Briarwood, NY 11435, 718-441-9766
 Pubs: *Child in the House: Poems* (Canio's Bks, 1995), *Eros Descending: A Selection* (Dusty Dog Pr, 1992)

Christopher Butters 🎤 ✈ P
488 12th St
Brooklyn, NY 11215-5205, 718-768-1724
 Pubs: *Americas* (Viet Nam Generation, 1996), *The Propaganda of a Seed* (Cardinal Pr, 1990), *Split Shift, Blue Collar Rev*

Cheryl Byron PP&P
Something Positive, 225 E 89 St, Box 20, New York, NY 10128, 212-289-3785
 Pubs: *Womantalk* (Heartbeat Records, 1986), *Womanrise* (Shamal Bks, 1978)

Luis Cabalquinto 🎤 ✈ P&W
PO Box 618, Stuyvesant Sta, New York, NY 10009-0618, 212-254-4514
 Pubs: *Bridgeable Shores* (Kaya Pr, 2001), *The Dog-Eater & Other Poems* (Kalikasan Pr, 1989), *APR, Prairie Schooner, Manoa, Trafika, Poetry Australia, River Styx*

Regie Cabico PP
Emerald Garden #136, 577 2nd Ave, New York, NY 10016
Internet: missbamboo@aol.com
 Pubs: *The Trick, I Saw Your Ex-Lover Behind the Starbucks Counter* (Bigfat Pr, 2000, 1997), *The Outlaw Bible of American Poetry: Anth* (Thunder's Mouth, 1999), *Onomatopoeia & a 1/4 Life Crisis* (Here Theater, 1999), *The Gene Pool* (Dixon Place, 1999)

Rosalie Calabrese 🎤 ✈   P
700 Columbus Ave, #16D
New York, NY 10025-6680, 212-663-6620
Internet: rcmgt@yahoo.com
   Pubs: *Wedding Blessings: Anth* (Broadway Bks, 2003),
   Mothers and Daughters: Anth (Harmony Bks, 2001), *Full
   Circle: Anth* (Pittenbrauch Pr, 1997), *Caprice, Byline,
   Thirteen, New Laurel Rev, Up Front Muse Intl Rev, And
   Then, Jewish Currents*

Justin Caldwell   P
410 W 24 St, #2A
New York, NY 10011, 212-675-3931
   Pubs: *The Sleeping Porch* (Lost Roads Pr, 1979), *Southern
   Rev, Poetry Now, Ironwood*

Hortense Calisher   W
Donadio & Olson, Inc, 121 W 27 St, Ste 704, New York, NY
10001, 212-691-8077
   Pubs: *Sunday Jews* (Harcourt, 2002), *In the Slammer with
   Carol Smith* (Marion Boyars, 1997), *The Novellas of
   Hortense Calisher, In the Palace of the Movie King* (Random
   Hse, 1997, 1993), *Kissing Cousins* (Weidenfeld, 1988)

Paulette Callen 🎤   W
215 W 83 St #1F
New York, NY 10024
Internet: paulettecallen@msn.com
   Pubs: *Beyond Lament: Poets of the World Bearing Witness
   to the Holocaust: Anth* (Northwestern U Pr, 1998), *Charity*
   (S&S, 1997), *Negative Capability*

James Camp   P
365 W End Ave, #7C
New York, NY 10024
   Pubs: *Paris Rev Anth* (Norton, 1990), *Light Year: Anth* (Bits
   Pr, 1989), *Cincinnati Rev, Poetry NY, Sagetrieb*

Tina Cane 🎤 ✈   P
178 Frost St
Brooklyn, NY 11211, 718-383-1629
   Pubs: *Girls: An Anthology* (Global City Pr, 1998), *Laisse de
   Mer: Anth* (Francoforum, 1999), *La Petite Zine, Barrow
   Street, Spinning Jenny, New Press Lit Qtly, Hanging Loose,
   Salt Hill Jrnl*

Ethan Canin   W
Maxine Groffsky Literary Agency, 853 Broadway, Ste 708, New
York, NY 10003, 212-979-1500
Internet: ecanin@aol.com
   Pubs: *Carry Me Across the Water, For Kings & Planets, The
   Palace Thief* (Random Hse, 2001, 1998, 1994), *Blue River,
   Emperor of the Air* (HM, 1991, 1988)

Steve Cannon   W
285 E 3 St, 3rd Fl
New York, NY 10009, 212-674-8262
   Pubs: *Groove, Bang & Jive Around* (Olympia Pr, 1968),
   American Rag, Sunbury, Pulp

Robert Canzoneri   P&W
c/o Roberta Pryor, 24 W 55 St, New York, NY 10019,
212-245-0420
   Pubs: *Potboiler: An Amateur's Affair with La Cuisine* (North
   Point, 1989), *Story, Chariton Rev, Modern Maturity*

Phyllis Capello   P&W
495 16th St
Brooklyn, NY 11215-5913
Internet: mjcpc9999@aol.com
   Pubs: *Journey into Motherhood* (Riverhead Putnam, 1996),
   Voices in Italian Americana: Anth (Purdue U Pr, 1997), *The
   Voices We Carry: Anth* (Guernica Edtns, 1993), *Footwork,
   Literary Mag, NYQ, Downtown Mag*

Alberto O. Cappas 🎤 ✈   P
85 Fourth Ave, Apt 3JJ
New York, NY 10003-5206, 212-353-9114
Internet: cappas@aol.com
   Pubs: *Dona Julia & Other Selected Poems* (1st Bks Library,
   2002), *The Pledge, Roots to Reality, Disintegration of the
   Puerto Ricans* (Don Pedro Enterprises, 1998, 1998, 1997),
   Echolalia: Verse & Vibration of Alberto O. Cappas (Carlton
   Pr, 1988)

Peter Carey 🎤 ✈   W
c/o Amanda Urban, ICM, 40 W 57 St, New York, NY 10019,
212-556-5600
Internet: caresummmer@aol.com
   Pubs: *True History of the Kelly Gang, Jack Maggs, The
   Unusual Life of Tristan Smith, The Tax Inspector* (Knopf,
   2001, 1997, 1995, 1992), *Oscar & Lucinda, Illywhacker,
   Bliss* (H&R, 1988, 1986, 1982), *The Fat Man in History*
   (Random Hse, 1980)

Don Carpenter   W
E P Dutton & Co., 375 Hudson St, New York, NY 10014,
212-366-2000

Julie A. Carr 🎤 ✈   P
11 Schermerhorn St #5FE
Brooklyn, NY 11201, 718-935-0935
Internet: george_lewes@msn.com
   Pubs: *Epoch, Greensboro Rev, NER, Pequod, Poet Lore,
   Salamander, TriQtly*

Mary Anne Cartelli   P
122 Spring St, #4S
New York, NY 10012, 212-334-5229
   Pubs: *The Little Mag, Bomb, Joe Soap's Canoe, World,
   Field, Luna Tack, Berkeley Poetry Rev*

Charlotte Carter   W
c/o Faith Childs, Charlotte Sheedy Literary Agency, 65
Bleecker St, New York, NY 10012, 212-780-9800
   Pubs: *Personal Effects* (United Artists, 1990), *Transfer*

Mary Casanova   W
Hyperion, 114 5th Ave, New York, NY 10011
www.marycasanova.com
  Pubs: *Stealing Thunder, Wolf Shadows, Riot, Moose Tracks*
  (Hyperion Bks, 1997, 1997, 1996, 1995), *Cricket, Once
  Upon a Time, Highlights, Loonfeather*

John Casey 🎤 ✈   W
Michael Carlisle & Co., 24 E 64 St, New York, NY 10026,
212-813-1881
Internet: anitraps@aol.com
  Pubs: *The Halflife of Happiness* (Knopf, 1998), *Spartina*
  (Vintage, 1998), *Testimony & Demeanor, An American
  Romance* (Avon, 1991, 1991), *New Yorker, L.A. Times*

Maud Casey 🎤 ✈   W
c/o Alice Tasman, Jean Naggar Agency, 216 E 75 St, #1E,
New York, NY 10021, 212-794-1082
Internet: mcasey@inch.com
  Pubs: *Drastic, The Shape of Things to Come* (Morrow,
  2002, 2001), *Gettysburg Rev, Prairie Schooner,
  Shenandoah, Confrontation, Georgia Rev, Beloit Fiction
  Jrnl, Threepenny Rev*

Kay Cassill   W
c/o Elise Goodman, Goodman Assoc, 500 W End Ave, New
York, NY 10024, 212-873-4806
  Pubs: *Twins: Nature's Amazing Mystery* (Atheneum, 1982),
  The Twins Letter

Joan Castagnone   P&W
484 W 43 St, #28C
New York, NY 10036, 212-592-1834
Internet: jcastagnone@cpg.org
  Pubs: *Kansas Qtly, North Dakota Qtly, Plainswoman,
  Louisville Rev, Random Hse Audio Bks*

J. N. Catanach   W
560 Riverside Dr, #20-F
New York, NY 10027
  Pubs: *The Last Rite of Hugo T.* (St. Martin's Pr, 1992),
  Brideprice, White Is the Color of Death (The Countryman Pr,
  1989, 1988)

Thomas M. Catterson 🎤 ✈   P
86-37, 120th St
Richmond Hill, NY 11418
  Pubs: *My Father's Paradox* (Founder's Hill Pr, 2002), *This
  Pot Has Pepper* (Cross-Cultural Lit Edtn, 1998)

Anita Mirenberg Caylor 🎤 ✈   PP&P
437 E 118 St
New York, NY 10035, 212-534-2764
  Pubs: *BPJ, East Coast Writers Anth, Bronx Roots*

Marisha Chamberlain   P
Bill Craver/Writers & Artists, 19 W 44 St, Ste #1000, New York,
NY 10036
Internet: marisha5t@aol.com
  Pubs: *A Line of Cutting Women* (Calyx Jrnl, 1998),
  Scheherazade (Dramatists Play Service, 1985), *Powers*
  (New Rivers Pr, 1983), *Minneapolis Rev of Baseball, City
  Pages, Hungry Mind Rev*

Clovr Chango   PP
631 E 11 St #24
New York, NY 10009

Laura Chapman   W
c/o Hruska, 1148 Fifth Ave, New York, NY 10128
  Pubs: *Multiple Choice* (Doubleday, 1978), *Legal Relations*
  (Dutton, 1977)

Steve Chapple   W
Ellen Levine Literary Agency, 15 E 26 St, Ste 1801, New York,
NY 10010
  Pubs: *Outlaws in Babylon* (S&S, 1984), *Don't Mind Dying*
  (Doubleday, 1980), *Los Angeles Times*

Suzy McKee Charnas 🎤 ✈   W
c/o Jennifer Lyons, The Writers House, 21 W 26 St, New York,
NY 10010, 212-685-2663
  Pubs: *The Slave & the Free, Conqueror's Child, Ruby Tear,
  Furies* (Tor Bks, 1999, 1999, 1997, 1995), *Vampire Tapestry*
  (U New Mexico Pr, 1993), *Kingdom of Kevin Malone* (HB,
  1993), *Golden Thread, Silver Glove* (Bantam, 1989, 1988)

Jerome Charyn   W
302 W 12 St, #10C
New York, NY 10014, 212-691-2879
  Pubs: *Elsinore, The Good Policeman* (Mysterious Pr, 1991,
  1990), *Movieland, Metropolis* (Putnam, 1989, 1986)

Peter Cherches   W
195 Garfield Pl, #3E
Brooklyn, NY 11215
  Pubs: *Between a Dream & a Cup of Coffee* (Red Dust,
  1987), *Condensed Book* (Benzene Edtns, 1986)

Kelly Cherry 🎤 ✈   P&W
c/o Elizabeth Sheinkman, Elaine Markson Agency, 44
Greenwich Ave, New York, NY 10011, 212-243-8480
Internet: kcherry@facstaff.wisc.edu
  Pubs: *The Society of Friends: Stories, Writing the World* (U
  Missouri Pr, 1999, 1995), *Augusta Played, Death &
  Transfiguration, God's Loud Hand* (LSU Pr, 1998, 1997,
  1993), *Lovers & Agnostics* (Carnegie Mellon U Pr, 1995),
  Atlantic, Commentary, Ms., Poetry

Edith Chevat 🎤 ✈   W
395 S End Ave, #19J
New York, NY 10280, 212-321-2524
Internet: echevat@aol.com
    Pubs: *Writers As World Witnesses* (Pen & Brush, 2000),
    Love Lesson (Valon Bks, 1998), *Girls: An Anth* (Global City
    Pr, 1997), *The One You Call Sister: Anth* (Cleis Pr, 1989),
    *Bridges, Global City Rev, Sojourner, Other Voices, Home
    Planet News*

Fay Chiang   P
60 E 4 St, #20
New York, NY 10003
    Pubs: *Voci Dal Silenzio* (I Canguri/Feltrinelli, 1996), *Miwa's
    Song, In the City of Contradictions* (Sunbury Pr, 1982,
    1979), *Girls: An Anth* (Global City Pr, 1997)

Evans Chigounis   P
224 E 18 St, #3A
New York, NY 10003
    Pubs: *Secret Lives* (Wesleyan U Pr, 1972)

China   P&W
44 Hamilton Terr #4FL
New York, NY 10031-6403
    Pubs: *Voices of Color* (Applause, 1993), *Feelings of Love
    Not Yet Expressed* (Folkways, 1978), *Essence, Yardbird
    Reader, Bergen Sun, Velvet Glove*

Sri Chinmoy 🎤 ✈   P
c/o Dr V Bennett, 85-38 151st St, Jamaica, NY 11432,
718-523-3826
    Pubs: *77,000 Service-Trees* (Agni Pr, 2002), *The Wisdom
    of Sri Chinmoy* (Blue Dove Pr, 2000), *The Wings of Joy*
    (S&S, 1997)

Kathleen Chodor   P
148 W 23 St
New York, NY 10011

Sonja Christina 🎤 ✈   P
PO Box 142 Lenox Hill
New York, NY 10021, 212-737-7691
    Pubs: *The Great Adventure* (ART Pr, 1997)

Nicholas Christopher 🎤 ✈   P&W
Janklow & Nesbit Associates, 445 Park Ave, New York, NY
10022-2606, 212-421-1700
    Pubs: *Franklin Flyer, A Trip to the Stars, Veronica* (Dial,
    2002, 2000, 1996), *Atomic Field: Two Poems, The Creation
    of the Night Sky* (HB, 2000, 1998), *5 Degrees & Other
    Poems, In the Year of the Comet* (Viking, 1995, 1992)

Jane Ciabattari 🎤 ✈   W
36 W 75 St #5A
New York, NY 10023
Internet: janeciab@aol.com
    Pubs: *Stealing the Fire: Stories* (Canio's Edtns, 2002),
    Winning Moves (Penguin, 1990), *Redbook, NAR, Denver
    Qtly, Blueline, Caprice, Hampton Shorts*

Jill Ciment 🎤 ✈   W
254 E 7 St, #15-16
New York, NY 10009
Internet: jillci@aol.com
    Pubs: *Teeth of the Dog, Half a Life* (Crown, 1999, 1996),
    The Law of Falling Bodies (Poseidon Pr, 1993), *Small
    Claims* (Weidenfeld & Nicholson, 1986), *Michigan Rev, CQ,
    South Carolina Rev*

Vivina Ciolli 🎤   P
PO Box 620797
Little Neck, NY 11362-0797, 718-279-4988
    Pubs: *Bitter Larder* (New Spirit Pr, 1994), *Negative
    Capability, Maryland Poetry Rev, Poets On, Long Island Qtly,
    Sistersong, Earth's Daughters*

Sandra Cisneros   P&W
Susan Bergholz Literary Services, 17 W 10 St, #5, New York,
NY 10011, 212-387-0545
    Pubs: *Loose Women* (Knopf, 1994), *Hairs-Pelitos, Loose
    Women, Woman Hollering Creek* (Random Hse/Vintage,
    1994, 1991), *The House on Mango Street* (Vintage, 1991),
    My Wicked, Wicked Ways (Third Woman Pr, 1987)

Jean Clark   W
Harold Ober Assoc, 425 Madison Ave, New York, NY 10017,
212-759-8600
    Pubs: *The Marriage Bed* (Putnam, 1983), *Untie the Winds*
    (Macmillan, 1976)

Jan Clausen 🎤 ✈   P&W
132 Maple St
Brooklyn, NY 11225
Internet: clausenj@newschool.edu
    Pubs: *Apples & Oranges* (HM, 1999), *Books & Life* (Ohio
    State U, 1989), *The Prosperine Papers, Sinking/Stealing*
    (Crossing Pr, 1988, 1985), *Kenyon Rev, 13th Moon, ACM,
    Out/Look, Feminist Studies, Women's Review of Books,
    Luna, The Progressive*

Russell Clay   P
585 W End Ave, #7E
New York, NY 10024, 212-877-4808
    Pubs: *Father Poems, From Ghost Through Bone to Man,
    Half-Life Poems* (West End Poetry Pr, 1998, 1997, 1997),
    *Georgia Jrnl, Poetry Jrnl, Share, Sow's Ear, Poetry Motel,
    Talking River Rev, Lucid Stone, Mediphors Jrnl*

Carol Clemeau W
Bobbe Siegel, Literary Agent, 41 W 83 St, New York, NY
10024, 212-877-4985
   Pubs: *The Ariadne Clue* (Scribner, 1982), *Ellery Queen's
   Mag*

Francois Clemmons 🎤 ✈ P
4 W 101 St, #35
New York, NY 10025
Internet: clemmons@middlebury.edu

Michelle Cliff W
c/o Faith Childs, Faith Childs Literary Agency, 915 Broadway,
Ste 1009, New York, NY 10010, 212-995-9600
   Pubs: *The Store of a Million Items: Short Stories, Best
   American Short Stories: Anth* (HM, 1998, 1997), *Free
   Enterprise, No Telephone to Heaven* (Dutton, 1993, 1987),
   *VLS, Parnassus, American Voice, Ms., Kenyon Rev, Nation,
   Agni, TriQtly*

William Leo Coakley 🎤 ✈ P
120 W 71 St
New York, NY 10023, 212-873-6884
   Pubs: *Humor in America: Anth* (Open Places, 1984),
   Sotheby's Poetry Competition Anth (Arvon Fdn, 1984),
   *NYQ, Harvard Gay & Lesbian Rev, Paris Rev, Nation,
   Christopher Street, Aquarius*

Judith Ortiz Cofer 🎤 ✈ P&W
c/o Jane Pasanen, Chelsea Forum, 377 Rector Pl, New York,
NY 10280, 212-945-3100
Internet: jocofer@aol.com
   Pubs: *An Island Like You* (Penguin, 1997), *The Latin Deli*
   (Norton, 1995), *Silent Dancing* (Arte Publico Pr, 1990), *The
   Line of the Sun* (U Georgia Pr, 1989), *Georgia Rev, Kenyon
   Rev, Southern Rev, Prairie Schooner, Parnassus*

Marc Cohen 🎤 ✈ P
1 University Pl, #3E
New York, NY 10003-4514, 212-228-6781
Internet: marc_cohen@schindler.com
   Pubs: *Mecox Road, On Maplewood Time* (Groundwater Pr,
   1996, 1989), *Blood and Tears: Anth* (Painted Leaf Pr, 2000),
   KGB Bar Book of Poems: Anth (Perennial, 2000), *Best
   American Poetry: Anths* (Scribner, 1993, 1991), *Grand
   Street, NAW, Paris Rev, Columbia, APR*

Gerald Cohen P&W
English Dept, BMCC, CUNY, 199 Chambers St, New York, NY
10007, 717-646-2858
Internet: wankele@msn.com
   Pubs: *Fire Readings/Tumbleweed: Anth* (Paris; Shakespeare
   & Co, 1996), *Chicago Rev, Lit Rev, NER, Confrontation,
   Poetry NW, Kansas Qtly*

Ira Cohen P
c/o Faye Cohen, 225 W 106 St, New York, NY 10025,
212-222-4068
   Pubs: *The Majoon Traveller* (CD; Sub Rosa, 1994), *Ratio:*
   (Media Shamans, 1991), *First Intensity, Third Rail, Exquisite
   Corpse*

Esther Cohen P&W
66 W 77 St
New York, NY 10024, 212-595-0122
   Pubs: *No Charge for Looking* (Schocken Bks, 1985)

Marvin Cohen 🎤 ✈ P&W
PO Box 460, Stuyvesant Sta, New York, NY 10009, 212-677-
2040
   Pubs: *Aesthetics in Art & Life* (Gull Bks, 1982), *The Inconve-
   nience of Living* (Urizen Bks, 1977), *Nation, Antaeus,
   Hudson Rev, Sun & Moon, Chelsea*

Alice Eve Cohen PP
250 W 77 St, #103
New York, NY 10024
   Pubs: *Book of Truth, Book of Lies* (Baltimore Museum of Art,
   1989), *Goliath on 74th Street vs. The Woman Who Loved
   Vegetables* (Manhattan Punchline, 1989)

Michael Cohen 🎤 ✈ P
59 Livingston St #3D
Brooklyn, NY 11201-4834, 718-797-9649
Internet: mcohen@arcllc.com
   Pubs: *In This Sea* (New School Pets Series, 1997)

Marty Cohen 🎤 ✈ P
600 W 246 St, #810
Bronx, NY 10471
Internet: mcohen@workinamerica.org
   Pubs: *A Traveler's Alphabet* (Prescott Street Pr, 1979),
   Parnassus, Northern Rev, Abraxas

Tram Combs P
5 Spring St #14
New York, NY 10012
   Pubs: *Art in America, Arts Mag, Noticias de Arte*

Elizabeth Cook-Lynn P&W
c/o Regula Noetzli, Charlotte Sheedy Literary Agency, 65
Bleecker St, New York, NY 10012, 212-780-9800
   Pubs: *I Remember the Fallen Trees* (Eastern Washington U
   Pr, 1998), *Woyake Kinikiya Vol II, Vol I: Anths* (Oak Lake
   Writers Pr, 1995, 1994), *Talking Up a Storm: Anth* (U
   Nebraska Pr, 1994), *The Writer's Perspective: Anth* (Prentice
   Hall, 1994), *Indian Artist*

Jane Cooper 🎤   P
545 W 111 St, #8K
New York, NY 10025, 212-663-3934
    Pubs: *The Flashboat: Poems Collected & Reclaimed*
    (Norton, 1999), *Green Notebook, Winter Road, Scaffolding:*
    Selected Poems (Tilbury Hse, 1994, 1993), *APR, Field,*
    New Yorker, Paris Rev, Kenyon Rev, Iowa Rev

Bernard Cooper 🎤 ✈   P&W
c/o Sloan Harris, ICM, 40 W 57 St, New York, NY 10019,
212-556-5600
Internet: bcooper635@aol.com
    Pubs: *Guess Again* (S&S, 2000), *Truth Serum* (HM, 1996), *A*
    Year of Rhymes (Viking Penguin, 1993), *Harper's, Paris Rev*

David Cooper 🎤 ✈   P
1149 Prospect Ave, #1R
Brooklyn, NY 11218, 718-965-9337
Internet: shoshndavid@yahoo.com
    Pubs: *XY Files: Poems on the Male Experience: Anth*
    (Sherman Asher Pub, 1997), *Green Mountains Rev,*
    Archipelago, New Works Rev, Synaesthetic, Kinesis,
    Response, Pudding, Davka, Literary Rev, Massachusetts
    Rev, Passages North, Painted Bride Qtly

Robert Coover   W
Georges Borchardt Inc, 136 E 57 St, New York, NY 10022,
212-753-5785
    Pubs: *John's Wife, Pinocchio in Venice, A Night at the*
    Movies, Whatever Happened to Gloomy Gus of the Chicago
    Bears? (S&S, 1996, 1991, 1987, 1987)

John Corrigan 🎤 ✈   W
Giles Anderson, The Anderson Literary Agency, 395 Riverside
Dr., New York, NY 10025, 212-280-1206
Internet: corriganj@mssm.org
    Pubs: *River Rev, Echoes, Red Owl, Rio Grande Rev,*
    Reader's Break, Author's, AIM, Advocate

Jayne Cortez 🎤 ✈   P
PO Box 96, Village Sta
New York, NY 10014, 212-431-5067
    Pubs: *Jazz Fan Looks Back* (Hanging Loose Pr, 2002),
    Taking the Blues Back Home (CD; Harmolodic/Verve, 1998),
    Somewhere in Advance of Nowhere (Serpent's Tail/High
    Risk Bks, 1996)

Angela Costa 🎤 ✈   PP
PO Box 1356, Canal St Station
New York, NY 10013-0877
http://www.angelacosta.com
    Pubs: *Howling Dog, Femme Mystique, Nuyorican Poets*
    Cafe, Knitting Factory, Living Theater, Mona's, St. Mark's
    Poetry Project

Jonathan Cott   P
247 E 33 St, #6A
New York, NY 10016
    Pubs: *Back to a Shadow in the Night* (Hal Leonard Pub,
    2002), *Homelands* (Cahuenga Pr, 2000), *Wandering Ghost:*
    The Odyssey of Lafcadio Hearn (Knopf, 1991), *The Search*
    for Omm Sety (Warner Bks, 1989)

Cynthia Cotts   W
59 E 7 St, #2
New York, NY 10003
    Pubs: *Art & Artists, Columbus Dispatch, Appearances,*
    Gargoyle, Telescope

Linda Cousins   P
The Universal Black Writer Pr, PO Box 5, Radio City Sta, New
York, NY 10101, 718-398-8941
    Pubs: *The Mystical Experiences of Harriet Tubman, Black &*
    in Brooklyn (Universal Black Writer Pr, 1992, 1983),
    Cottonwood (U Kansas Pr, 1986)

Stephanie Amy Cowell 🎤 ✈   W
585 W End Ave
New York, NY 10024, 212-877-4808
Internet: stephanie@cowell-clay.com
    Pubs: *The Players, The Physician of London, Nicholas*
    Cooke (Norton, 1997, 1995, 1993)

Douglas Crase   P
470 W 24 St
New York, NY 10011
    Pubs: *The Revisionist* (Little, Brown, 1981)

Gwyneth Cravens   W
c/o Amanda Urban, ICM, 40 W 57 St, New York, NY 10019
    Pubs: *The Gates of Paradise* (Ticknor & Fields, 1991),
    Heart's Desire, Love & Work (Knopf, 1986, 1982), *New*
    Yorker, Nation, Harper's

Marc Crawford   W
360 W 21 St, #4-M
New York, NY 10011, 212-675-7197
    Pubs: *The Lincoln Brigade* (Atheneum, 1989), *Emerge,*
    Freedomways, Time Capsule

Tad Crawford 🎤 ✈   W
10 E 23 St, Ste 400
New York, NY 10010
    Pubs: *Confrontation, Central Park, Phantasm*

Jennifer Crewe   P
285 Riverside Dr #3B
New York, NY 10025-5226, 212-865-6254
    Pubs: *Pequod, Tar River Poetry, American Muse, Poet &*
    Critic, Ploughshares, Piedmont Lit Rev

Angie Cruz 🎤 ✈   W
Ellen Levine Literary Agency,
15 E 26 St, Ste 801, New York, NY 10010
Internet: www.angiecruz.com
   Pubs: *Soledad* (S&S, 2001)

William Cullen, Jr.   P
910 Albemarle Rd
Brooklyn, NY 11218, 718-287-7507
Internet: bill_cullen_99@yahoo.com
   Pubs: *Heron's Nest, Mayfly, Snapshots, bottle rockets,
   International Herald, Tribune, Asahi Shimbun, Frogpond,
   Modern Haiku*

Elizabeth Cullinan   W
463 West St, Apt 817-D
New York, NY 10014
   Pubs: *A Change of Scene* (Norton, 1982), *House of Gold*
   (HM, 1969), *Shenandoah, Colorado Rev, Irish Lit
   Supplement, Threshold, New Yorker*

Lorraine Rainie Currelley   P
PO Box 562, College Sta
New York, NY 10030-0562
   Pubs: *Gaptooth Girlfriends The Third Act* (Gaptooth
   Girlfriends The Third Act, 1994)

David Curzon 🎤 ✈   P
254 W 82 St, #2B
New York, NY 10024-5450, 212-874-3989
   Pubs: *Dovichik* (Penguin Bks, 1996), *The View from Jacob's
   Ladder, Modern Poems on the Bible: Anth* (Jewish Pub Soc,
   1996, 1994), *The Gospels in Our Image: Anth* (HB, 1995),
   Midrashim (CCC, 1991), *Poetry, Antaeus, New Republic,
   Sewanee Rev, Formalist, Tikkun*

D.C. Cymbalista 🎤 ✈   W
63 Downing Street
New York, NY 10014
   Pubs: *Danger* (Dutton, 1990)

John D'Agata 🎤 ✈   P
c/o Matt McGowan, Francis Goldin Literary Agency, 57 E 11
St, New York, NY 10003, 212-777-0477
www.graywolfpress.org
   Pubs: *The Next American Essay, Halls of Fame* (Graywolf
   Pr, 2003, 2001), *Gettysburg Rev, North Amer Rev, Paris
   Rev, Ploughshares*

Vinni Marie D'Ambrosio 🎤   P
11 5 Ave, #3N
New York, NY 10003, 212-673-5875
   Pubs: *Mexican Gothic: A Frieda Kahlo Narrative* (Blue Heron
   Pr, 1996), *Life of Touching Mouths* (NYU Pr, 1971),
   McGraw-Hill Book of Poetry: Anth (McGraw-Hill, 1993), *Italo
   American Poets: Anth* (A Carello, 1985)

Susan Daitch   W
c/o Miriam Altshuler, 50 W 29 St, New York, NY 10001,
212-684-6050
   Pubs: *Storytown* (Dalkey Archive Pr, 1996), *Avant Pop
   Anthology* (Viking Penguin, 1995), *Top Stories, Rev of
   Contemporary Fiction, Bomb, Fiction Intl, VLS*

Rosemary Daniell 🎤 ✈   P&W
Wendy Weil Agency Inc, 232 Madison Ave, Ste 1300, New
York, NY 10016, 212-685-0030
   Pubs: *The Woman Who Spilled Words All Over Herself*
   (Faber & Faber, 1997), *The Hurricane Season* (Morrow,
   1992), *Fort Bragg & Other Points South, Sleeping with
   Soldiers* (H Holt, 1988, 1984), *American Voice,
   Chattahoochee Rev, Kalliope, Arts & Letters*

Kathryn Daniels   P&W
35-45 78 St, Apt #2
Jackson Heights, NY 11372
   Pubs: *If I Had a Hammer: Anth* (Papier-Mache Pr, 1990),
   Chrysanthemum, Earth's Daughters, Korone

Jack Dann   W
c/o Merrilee Heifetz, Writers House, 21 W 26 St, New York, NY
10010, 212-691-4575
Internet: jackmdann@aol.com
   Pubs: *Jubilee, The Man Who Melted* (HC Australia, 2001,
   1998), *The Silent, The Memory Cathedral* (Bantam Bks,
   1998, 1995), *The Counting Coup, High Steel* (w/J.C.
   Haldema) (Tor, 2001, 1993), *Nebula Awards 32: Anth* (HB,
   1998), *Playboy, Twilight Zone Mag*

Ruth Danon   P
NYU/ADSD, 225 Shimkin Hall, 50 W 4 St, New York, NY 10003
Internet: danon@is3.nyu.edu
   Pubs: *Triangulation from a Known Point* (North Star
   Line/Blue Moon Bks, 1990), *Bomb, Paris Rev*

Ann Darby 🎤 ✈   W
245 W 104 St, #2D
New York, NY 10025-4279
Internet: darbann@aol.com
   Pubs: *The Orphan Game* (Morrow, 1999), *The American
   Story: The Best of Story Qtly: Anth* (Cane Hill Pr, 1990),
   *NW Rev, Blue Light/Red Light, Story Qtly, Organica,
   Malahat Rev*

Alice Elliott Dark 🎤   W
Dunow & Carlson Agency, 27 W 20 St, New York, NY 10010
Internet: aedark@aol.com
   Pubs: *Think of England, In the Gloaming* (S&S, 2000),
   *Naked to the Waist, Best American Short Stories of the
   Century: Anth* (HM, 1991, 1999), *New Yorker, Harper's,
   DoubleTake, Redbook*

Eric Darton 🎤 ✈   P&W
315 8th Ave, #20F
New York, NY 10001, 212-242-0579
  Pubs: *Free City* (Norton, 1996), *Radio Tirane* (Conjunctions,
  1991), *After the World Trade Center: Anth* (Routledge,
  2002), *110 Stories: Anth* (NYU Pr, 2002), *Conjunctions 17
  Anth* (Bard, 1991), *NER, Confrontation, American Letters &
  Commentary, Central Park*

Kiana Davenport 🎤 ✈   W
Dunow & Carlson Agency, 27 W 20 St #1003, New York,
NY 10011, 212-645-7606
  Pubs: *Song of the Exile* (Ballantine, 2000), *Shark Dialogues*
  (Plume, 1995), *Charlie Chan Is Dead: Anth* (Penguin, 1993)

Richard Davidson   P
200 W 94 St, #3E
New York, NY 10025, 212-749-0870
  Pubs: *Tower Nine* (Ann Salazar, 1986), *The Gentleman from
  Hyde Park* (Bard, 1982), *Jewish Affairs, Home Planet News,
  People's Weekly World, Arts Muse*

Thulani Davis   P
Grove Weidenfeld Press, 841 Broadway, New York, NY 10003
  Pubs: *Playing the Changes* (Wesleyan U Pr, 1985), *All the
  Renegade Ghosts Rise* (Anemone, 1978)

Christina Davis   P
60 W 13 St
New York, NY 10011
Internet: cdavis@twc.org
  Pubs: *Boston Rev, Paris Rev, New Republic, Gettysburg
  Rev, Colorado Rev, NER*

Lydia Davis 🎤 ✈   W
c/o Denise Shannon, ICM, 40 W 57 St, New York, NY 10019,
212-556-6727
  Pubs: *Almost No Memory, The End of the Story, Break it
  Down* (FSG, 1997, 1995, 1986), *Best American Poetry:
  Anth* (Scribner, 1999), *KGB Bar Reader: Anth* (Morrow,
  1998), *Granta, Harper's, Grand Street, Paris Rev,
  Conjunctions*

Beatrice G. Davis 🎤 ✈   P
270-26V Grand Central Parkway
Floral Park, NY 11005, 718-352-6995
Internet: beegeedee@aol.com
  Pubs: *Looking Out with an Inner Eye* (Small Poetry Pr,
  2000), *Reflections of Life* (EPS Pub, 1996), *Mother of the
  Groom: Anth* (Distinctive Pub, 1996), *Whispers from
  Heaven, Rock River News, Steck-Vaughn Test Practice
  Series, Apple Blossom, Writer's Haven*

Bradley B. Davis   P
8383 118 St
Jamaica, NY 11452442, 718-847-5609

L. J. Davis 🎤 ✈   W
138A Dean St
Brooklyn, NY 11217, 718-625-3365
  Pubs: *Billionaire Shell Game* (Doubleday, 1998)

Cecil Dawkins   W
Charlotte Sheedy Literary Agency, 65 Bleecker St, New York,
NY 10012, 212-780-9800
  Pubs: *The Quiet Enemy, Charleyhorse* (Viking Penguin,
  1986, 1985), *The Live Goat* (H&R, 1971), *Paris Rev, SW
  Rev, Sewanee Rev, McCall's, Redbook*

Storm De Hirsch   P
1760 3rd Ave, #721B
New York, NY 10029

James De Jongh   W
6 Fordham Hill Oval, #9D
Bronx, NY 10468, 718-933-6131
Internet: jimdejongh@aol.com
  Pubs: *Vicious Modernism: Black Harlem & the Literary
  Imagination* (Cambridge U Pr, 1990), *City Cool: A Ritual of
  Belonging* (Random Hse, 1978)

John Del Peschio   P
35 Orange St, #6F
Brooklyn, NY 11201, 718-488-8979
Internet: JohnDelPeschio@aol.com
  Pubs: *Queer Dog: Anth* (Cleis Pr, 1997), *Planet Authority,
  Time To Consider,*

John Del Peschio 🎤 ✈   P
35 Orange St, #6F
Brooklyn, NY 11201
  Pubs: *Queer Dog: Anth* (Cleis Pr, 1997), *Planet Authority,
  Time to Consider*

Irma Del Valle 🎤   P
96-07 42nd Ave
Corona, NY 11368-2146
  Pubs: *Polvo Poetico, Senderos Contigo, Ilusiones* (Archer
  Bks, 1990, 1974, 1966)

Don DeLillo   W
Wallace Literary Agency, 177 E 70 St, New York, NY 10021
  Pubs: *Underworld* (Scribner, 1997), *Mao II, Libra, White
  Noise* (Viking, 1991, 1988, 1985), *The Names* (Knopf, 1982)

Jane DeLynn 🎤 ✈   W
Promethean Artists Management, 1133 Broadway, New York,
NY 10010, 212-219-9038
Internet: janed@prodigy.net
  Pubs: *Don Juan in the Village* (Pantheon, 1990), *Real
  Estate* (Poseidon/S&S, 1988), *Bad Sex Is Good: Anth, New
  York Sex: Stories: Anth* (Painted Leaf Pr, 1998, 1998), *Paris
  Rev, Harper's*

Arto DeMirjian, Jr. W
311 W 24 St, Apt 20-G
New York, NY 10011, 212-989-4967
   Pubs: *Not a Clue* (Popular Pr, 1974), *Ararat Qtly*

Alice Denham ♦ ✈ W
Claudia Menza Literary Agency, 1170 Broadway, Ste 807, New
York, NY 10001
   Pubs: *Amo* (Putnam, 1975), *Coming Together* (Lancer,
   1970), *My Darling from the Lions* (Bobbs-Merrill, 1967),
   Great Tales of City Dwellers (Pyramid & Lion, 1965), *Best of
   the Missouri Rev: Anth* (U Missouri Pr, 1991), *Confrontation,
   Playboy, Discovery, Nation*

Alma Denny P
353 W 56 St, #3B
New York, NY 10019, 212-757-4648
   Pubs: *Blinkies: Funny Poems to Read in a Blink* (Spectacle
   Lane Pr, 1992), *Lyric, Cosmopolitan, Ladies' Home Jrnl,
   Good Housekeeping, Light Qtly*

Shira Dentz ♦ ✈ P
71 Ocean Pkwy Apt 5B
Brooklyn, NY 11218, 718-854-5050
   Pubs: *Escaping the Yellow Wallpaper: Anth* (Haworth Pr,
   2002), *Facture, Web del Sol, Natural Bridge, The Jrnl, Salt
   Hill Jrnl, Phoebe, Cimarron Rev, Illuminations, Barrow
   Street, No Exit, WV, 6ix, 13th Moon, So to Speak,
   Salamander, Paragraph, Modern Words*

Ed Depasquale P
59 Christopher St
New York, NY 10014, 212-675-0833
   Pubs: *Ally, Poems in Captivity, Velvet Wings, Helen Rev,
   Mati, Contact II, Poetry*

Graham Diamond W
2320 Parsons Blvd
Whitestone, NY 11357-3442
   Pubs: *Forest Wars* (Lion Pr, 1994), *Black Midnight* (Zeba
   Bks, 1989)

George Dickerson ♦ ✈ P&W
172 Bleecker St., #5
New York, NY 10012, 212-228-3745
Internet: ggdickerson44@hotmail.com
   Pubs: *The Cause* (Headwaters Pr, 2001), *George Dickerson
   Selected Poems 1959-1999* (Rattapallax Pr, 2000), *The
   Best Amer Short Stories of 1966: Anth* (HM Co, 1966),
   *Penthouse Mag, Mademoiselle Mag, The New Yorker, Poetz,
   Pivot, Medicinal Purposes Lit Rev*

Jeanne Dickey P&W
880 W 181 St, 5l
New York, NY 10033, 212-740-0081
Internet: jeannedickey@hotmail.com
   Pubs: *Amherst Rev, Parting Gifts, Long Shot, Poet Lore,
   Visions Intl, A Summers Reading, Rogue Scholars*

Joan Didion W
Janklow & Nesbit Associates, 445 Park Ave, New York, NY
10022, 212-421-1700

May Dikeman ♦ ✈ W
70 Irving Pl
New York, NY 10003, 212-475-4533
   Pubs: *The Devil We Know, The Angelica* (Atlantic/Little,
   Brown, 1973, 1971), *Atlantic, Harper's*

Annie Dillard P&W
c/o Tim Seldes, Russell & Volkening Inc, 50 W 29 St, 7E, New
York, NY 10001
   Pubs: *For the Time Being* (Knopf, 1999), *The Living* (HC,
   1992), *An American Childhood, Pilgrim at Tinker Creek*
   (H&R, 1987, 1974)

Carol Dine ♦ ✈ P
c/o Peter Rubie, Rubie & Assoc, 240 W 35 St, Ste 500, New
York, NY 10001
Internet: cdine@suffolk.edu
   Pubs: *Trying to Understand the Lunar Eclipse* (Erie Street
   Pr, 1992), *Naming the Sky* (Golden Quill, 1989), *Living on
   the Margins: Anth* (Persea Bks, 1999), *A Map of Hope: Anth*
   (Rutgers U Pr, 1999), *Women's Rev of Books, Prairie
   Schooner*

Susan Grathwohl Dingle ♦ ✈ P
166 E 96 St
New York, NY 10128
Internet: dingle0925@aol.com
   Pubs: *For Neruda, For Chile: Anth* (Beacon, 1975), *U.S.
   Submarine Veterans Reporter, Island Submariner, Mock
   Turtle, Parents Mag, APR, Partisan Rev, Ohio Rev*

Ray DiPalma ♦ ✈ P
301 W 108 St #6B
New York, NY 10025
   Pubs: *Letters* (Littoral Pr, 1998), *Motion of the Cypher* (Roof
   Bks, 1995), *Provocations* (Potes & Poets Pr, 1994), *Harvard
   Rev, Il Particolare, Le Nouveau Recueil, APR, First Intensity,
   Quaderno, Fence, La Polygraphe, Chicago Rev, Revue
   Pretexte, Iowa Rev*

Thomas M. Disch P&W
Karpfinger Agency, 357 W 20 St, New York, NY 10011-3379,
212-691-2690
   Pubs: *Dark Verses & Light, Yes, Let's: New & Selected
   Poems* (Johns Hopkins U Pr, 1991, 1989), *The M.D.: A
   Horror Story* (Knopf, 1991), *Poetry*

Stephen Dobyns P&W
Henry Holt & Co, 115 W 18 St, New York, NY 10011
   Pubs: *Cemetery Nights, A Boat Off the Coast* (Viking,
   1987, 1987)

E. L. Doctorow   W
c/o Amanda Urban, ICM, 40 W 57 St, New York, NY 10019

J. D. Dolan   W
c/o Amanda Urban, ICM, 40 W 57 St, New York, NY 10019,
212-556-5764
Internet: jd.dolan@wmich.edu
    Pubs: *New Stories from the South: Anth* (Algonquin, 1996),
    Esquire, Antioch Rev, Mississippi Rev, Shenandoah, Nation

Sharon Dolin 🎤 ✈   P
600 W 111 St, #11D
New York, NY 10025
Internet: sdolin@earthlink.net
    Pubs: *Realm of the Possible* (Four Way Bks, 2004), *Serious
    Pink* (Marsh Hawk Pr, 2003), *Mistakes* (Poetry New York,
    1999), *Climbing Mount Sinai* (Dim Gray Bar Pr, 1996), *Heart
    Work* (Sheep Meadow Pr, 1995), *Barrow Street, NAW,
    Jacket, Kenyon Rev, Ploughshares*

Bob Dombrowski 🎤 ✈   PP
805 Sixth Ave
New York, NY 10001, 212-741-2525
    Pubs: *A Song to Ecstasy, A Delicate Membrane* (DP
    Productions, 2002, 2001), *Help Yourself: Anth* (The
    Unbearables Productions, 2001), *The Spirit in the Words:
    Anth* (Daimler/Chrysler Pubs, 2000)

Jack Donahue 🎤 ✈   P
50-19 Bell Blvd
Bayside, NY 11364, 718-225-7992
Internet: jrdonahue@yahoo.com
    Pubs: *Folio, Poetry Motel, Dream Intl Qtly, Mediterranean
    Rev*

Stephen R. Donaldson 🎤 ✈   W
Howard Morhaim Agency, 175 Fifth Ave, #709, New York, NY
10010, 212-529-4433
Internet: steverd@umcphq.com
    Pubs: *Reave the Just and Other Tales, This Day All Gods
    Die, Forbidden Knowledge, The Real Story*
    (Bantam/Spectra, 1999, 1996, 1991, 1991), *Lord Foul's
    Bane* (Del Rey/Ballantine, 1977)

J. P. Donleavy   W
Seymour Lawrence Inc., 2 Park Ave, 17 Fl, New York, NY
10016, 212-725-1818

Alfred Dorn 🎤 ✈   P
PO Box 580174, Station A
Flushing, NY 11358-0174
    Pubs: *Voices from Rooms, From Cells to Mindspace*
    (Somers Rocks Pr, 1997, 1997), *Dark Horse, Edge City Rev,
    Hudson Rev, New Criterion, Formalist, Orbis, The Lyric,
    Pivot, Sparrow, Light*

Mark Doty 🎤 ✈   P&W
c/o Burnes and Clegg, 1133 Broadway, Ste 1020, New York,
NY 10010, 212-331-9880
    Pubs: *Source, Sweet Machine, Atlantis* (HC, 2001, 1998,
    1995), *My Alexandria* (U Illinois Pr, 1993), *New Yorker, Paris
    Rev, Boulevard, DoubleTake*

Ellen Douglas   W
RLR Assoc, 7 W 51 St, New York, NY 10017
    Pubs: *Can't Quit You, Baby* (Viking Penguin, 1989), *Black
    Cloud, White Cloud* (U Pr Mississippi, 1989)

Michael Drinkard   W
c/o Cynthia Cannell, Janklow & Nesbit Associates,
598 Madison Ave, New York, NY 10022-1614, 212-421-1700
    Pubs: *Disobedience* (Norton, 1993), *Green Bananas*
    (Knopf, 1989)

Sally Ann Drucker 🎤 ✈   P
PO Box 7888
New York, NY 10116-7888
    Pubs: *Walking the Desert Lion* (Ena, 1984), *Words on the
    Page, The World in Your Hands: Anth* (H&R, 1990),
    Bitterroot, Buckle, Epos, Pig Iron, Womanspirit

Nancy du Plessis 🎤 ✈   PP&P
150 W 80 St
New York, NY 10024
Internet: neduple@attglobal.net
    Pubs: *Notes des Cahiers Marocaine/Notes from the
    Moroccan Journals, Art New York* (Paris; L'Harmattan,
    1995), *Home Planet News*

Helen Duberstein 🎤 ✈   P&W
463 West St, #904D
New York, NY 10014
Internet: ghohel3@aol.com
    Pubs: *A Thousand Wives Dancing* (Xlibris, 2002), *Roma*
    (Metropolis Ink, 2002), *Shadow Self & Other Tales, The
    Shameless Old Lady* (Ghost Dance Pr, 1996, 1995), *The
    Radical Theatre Notebook* (Applause, 1994), *Signal
    Network Intl*

Maggie Dubris 🎤 ✈   P&W
27 1st Ave, #14
New York, NY 10003, 212-673-1583
Internet: dubris@aol.com
    Pubs: *Weep Not, My Wanton* (Black Sparrow Pr, 2002),
    Willieworld (Cuz Bks, 1998), *Ladies, Start Your Engines:
    Anth* (Faber & Faber, 1996), *Out of This World: Anth* (Crown,
    1991), *Cybercorpse, Big Bridge, Cuz, Tribes, Exquisite
    Corpse*

Margaret Mitchell Dukore   W
Bobbe Siegel Literary Agency, 41 W 83 St, New York, NY 10024
    Pubs: *Bloom, Survival of the Fittest* (Franklin Watts, 1985,
    1985), *Rev of Contemporary Fiction*

Harris Dulany W
273 Warren St
Brooklyn, NY 11201
Internet: hdulany@aol.com
    Pubs: *One Kiss Led to Another* (HC, 1994), *Falling*
(Saturday Rev Pr, 1971)

Gerald Dumas P
King Features Syndicate, 235 E 45 St, New York, NY 10017
    Pubs: *An Afternoon in Waterloo Park* (Wayne State U Pr,
1988), *Rabbits Rafferty* (Avon Camelot, 1985), *Atlantic,
Smithsonian*

Pearl Duncan 🎤 ✈ W
c/o Laurie Liss, Sterling Lord Literistic, 65 Bleecker St, New
York, NY 10012, 212-962-3944
Internet: pearl@pearlduncan.com
    Pubs: *A Rock Against the Wind: African-American Poems*
(Berkley/Perigee, 1996), *Water Dancing* (Aegina Pr,
1991), *Los Angeles Times, Essence, Black Enterprise,
Sailing, Sail*

Robert Dunn 🎤 ✈ P&W
c/o Coral Press, 252 W 81st St #15, New York, NY 10024,
718-776-8853
Internet: rddunn@aol.com
    Pubs: *Pink Cadillac* (Coral Pr, 2001), *The Sting Rays*
(Electron Pr, 2000), *Guilty as Charged, Zen Yentas in
Bondage* (Cross-Cultural Lit Edtns, 1999, 1997), *New
Yorker, Fiction Network, Atlantic, Sewanee Rev, Mother
Jones*

Martin S. Dworkin P&W
c/o Brian Cave, 245 Park Ave, New York, NY 10167-0002,
212-254-2960
    Pubs: *Northern Perspective, The World & I, Zymergy,
Contemporary Rev, Transnational Perspectives, ACM,
Poetry Ireland Rev, Takahe, Laurel Rev, Nutshell*

Miriam Dyak P
82 Garfield Pl
Brooklyn, NY 11215
    Pubs: *Dying, Fire Under Water* (New Victoria Pubs, 1979,
1978)

Cornelius Robert Eady 🎤 ✈ P
39 Jane St #GB
New York, NY 10014, 212-242-8646
    Pubs: *Brutal Imagination* (Putnam, 2001), *Victims of the
Latest Dance Craze, The Autobiography of a Jukebox, The
Gathering of My Name* (Carnegie Mellon, 1997, 1997,
1997), *You Donít Miss Your Water* (HH, 1995), *Seneca Rev,
Ploughshares*

Patricia Eakins 🎤 ✈ P&W
1200 Broadway, #4C
New York, NY 10001, 212-679-7413
www.fabulara.com/
    Pubs: *The Marvelous Adventures of Pierre Baptiste: Father
& Mother, First & Last* (NYU Pr, 1999), *The Hungry Girls*
(Cadmus, 1988), *Third Bed, American Letters &
Commentary, Sources, Parnassus, Iowa Rev, Conjunctions,
Storia, Paris Rev*

Elaine Edelman 🎤 ✈ P
444 E 86 St #27B
New York, NY 10028-6464, 212-535-7066
    Pubs: *Boom-de-Boom* (Pantheon, 1980), *Noeva: Three
Women Poets: Anth* (U South Dakota Pr, 1990), *Gettysburg
Rev, Out of Line, Mudfish, APR, Frontiers, Prairie Schooner,
Malahat Rev, Cape Rock*

John Ehle W
Donadio & Olson Inc, 121 W 27 St, Ste 704, New York, NY
10001, 212-691-8077
    Pubs: *The Widow's Trial, The Winter People* (H&R, 1989,
1984), *Trail of Tears* (Anchor, 1988)

Gretel Ehrlich P
Darhansoff & Verrill, 179 Franklin St, 4th Fl, New York, NY
10013
    Pubs: *Drinking Dry Clouds, Wyoming Stories* (Capra Pr,
1991, 1986), *Islands, The Universe, Home, Heart Mountain*
(Viking, 1991, 1988)

Janice Eidus 🎤 ✈ W
77 Seventh Ave, #14G
New York, NY 10011-6632, 212-924-3018
Internet: janiceeidus@mindspring.com
    Pubs: *Urban Bliss, The Celibacy Club, Vito Loves Geraldine*
(City Lights, 1998, 1996, 1990), *Neurotica: Jewish Writers
On Sex: Anth* (Norton, 1999), *The Oxford Book of Jewish
Stories: Anth* (Oxford Univ Pr, 1998), *SW Rev, Village Voice,
Witness, Asylum Arts*

J. Eigo 🎤 ✈ W
182 Ave A, #1B
New York, NY 10009, 212-533-2769
Internet: JIMEIGO@aol.com
    Pubs: *Quickies 2: Anth* (Arsenal Pulp Pr, 1999), *Best
American Gay Fiction 3: Anth* (Little, Brown, 1998), *Best
Gay Erotica 1997: Anth* (Cleis Pr, 1997), *Butch Boys: Anth*
(Bad Boy/Kasak Bks, 1997), *Boilermakers: Harrington Gay
Men's Fiction Qtly*

Bernard Lionel Einbond P
PO Box 307, Ft George Sta
New York, NY 10040, 718-960-8361
    Pubs: *The Tree As It Is* (Brander O'Neill Pr, 1996), *The
Coming Indoors* (Charles E. Tuttle, 1979), *Bogg, Wordsmith,
Modern Haiku, Frogpond*

Barbara Einzig 🎤 ✈   P
375 S End Ave, #27-N
New York, NY 10280, 212-912-1303
Internet: BEinzig@aol.com
    Pubs: *Distance Without Distance* (Kelsey Street Pr, 1994),
Life Moves Outside (Burning Deck Pr, 1987), *Five Fingers
Rev, Chelsea, Conjunctions, VLS, Fence, APR*

Deborah Eisenberg   W
c/o Lynn Nesbit, Janklow & Nesbit Associates, 598 Madison
Ave, New York, NY 10022-1614
    Pubs: *The Stories (So Far)* (Noonday, 1997), *All Around
Atlantis, Under the 82nd Airborne* (FSG, 1997, 1992),
Transactions in a Foreign Currency (Knopf, 1987)

Kim Elizabeth   P&W
c/o John Habermas, PO Box 120036, Staten Island, NY
10312-0036, 718-317-6110
    Pubs: *Netherworld* (Ghost Girl Graphix, 1995), *Darkworld
Vampires* (Millennium Pubs, 1995), *Dead of Night, The
Tome, Haunted Sun, Ghastly, Scream in the Dark*

Jim Elledge 🎤 ✈   P&W
English & Humanities, Pratt Inst, 200 Willoughby Ave,
Brooklyn, NY 11205, 718-636-3790
    Pubs: *The Chapters of Coming Forth by Day, Into the Arms
of the Universe* (Stonewall, 2000, 1995), *Indiana Rev,
Fiction Intl, Paris Rev*

Kate Ferguson Ellis   P
240 W 102 St
New York, NY 10025
    Pubs: *The Contested Castle* (U Illinois Pr, 1989), *Ms.,
Feminist Studies, Chrysalis, Salamander, Telephone,
Marxist Perspectives*

Harlan Ellison   W
Richard Curtis Assoc Inc, 171 E 74 St, New York, NY 10021
    Pubs: *Troublemakers* (ibooks & Edgeworks Abbey, 2001),
The Essential Ellison, Mind Fields (Morpheus, 2001, 1994),
Angry Candy, Slippage (HM, 1998, 1997), *Edgeworks 4,
Edgeworks 1* (White Wolf, 1997, 1996)

Patricia Elmore   W
c/o Marcia Amsterdam, 41 W 82 St, New York, NY 10024
    Pubs: *Susannah & the Purple Mongoose Mystery* (Dutton,
1992), *Susannah & the Blue House Mystery* (Scholastic
Apple, 1990)

Barbara Elovic 🎤 ✈   P
96 Schermerhorn St #6A
Brooklyn, NY 11201, 718-834-0291
    Pubs: *Time Out* (Amity Street Pr, 1996), *Second Word
Thursdays: Anth* (Bright Hill Pr, 1999), *Walk on the Wild
Side: Anth* (Scribner, 1994), *Marlboro Rev, Passages North,
New Laurel Rev, Poetry, Exquisite Corpse, Mss., Sonora
Rev, Onthebus*

Carol Emshwiller 🎤 ✈   W
210 E 15 St, #12E
New York, NY 10003-3938, 212-982-5779
Internet: cemsh@aol.com
    Pubs: *Report to the Men's Club, The Mount* (Small Beer Pr,
2002, 2002), *Leaping Man Hill, Ledoyt* (Mercury Hse,
1998, 1995), *Love Stories for the Rest of Us: Anth,
Pushcart Prize XXII: Anth* (Pushcart Pr, 1995, 1989),
Omni, TriQtly, Wild Women

Helen Engelhardt   P
805 E 21 St
Brooklyn, NY 11210, 718-859-5440
    Pubs: *Latitude 30'18', Intl Poetry Rev, Bitterroot, Dark
Horse, Mixed Voices*

Russell Epprecht   W
PO Box 734, Stuyvesant Sta
New York, NY 10009, 212-254-1004
    Pubs: *Yardstick, Further* (Domesday Bks, 1984, 1983),
Redtape, Homeless Catalogue

Elaine Equi   P
298 Mulberry St, #3L
New York, NY 10012, 212-941-8724
    Pubs: *Decoy, Surface Tension* (Coffee Hse Pr, 1994, 1989),
*Conjunctions, APR, Sulfur, Chelsea, NAW, Caliban, Paris
Rev*

Nancy Watson Erikson   P&W
c/o Writers Group, West Side Arts Coalition, PO Box 527,
Cathedral Sta, New York, NY 10025
    Pubs: *Splinters of Fear* (Avon, 1960), *This Singing Earth:
Anth* (Round Table, 1959), *Stories*

John Eskow   P
247 W 87 St, #23-F
New York, NY 10024, 212-662-5766

Sandra Maria Esteves   PP&P
3750 Broadway, #31
New York, NY 10032-1527, 212-926-0284
    Pubs: *Bluestown Mockingbird Mambo* (Arte Publico Pr,
1990), *Hanging Loose, Hispanic Women Write*

Eurydice   P&W
c/o Gear, 450 W 15 St, 5th Fl, New York, NY 10011,
212-771-7000
    Pubs: *F/32: The Second Coming* (Virago Pr, 1993), *F/32*
(Kasak Bks, 1993), *Barebreasted* (Greece; Fosti Edtns,
1980), *Iowa Rev, Black Ice, Cups, Texture, Open End, Spin,
Gear, Harper's, George*

David Evanier   P
184 Amity St
Brooklyn, NY 16201 718-522-4534

Bill Evans 🎙 ✈   P
99 E 4 St #3F
New York, NY 10003-9074, 212-982-5462
Internet: warwtithfun@msn.com
   Pubs: *Monologues from the Road: Anth, Elvis Monologues:
   Anth* (Heinemann Bks, 1999, 1998), *Engine Studios, Puerto
   del Sol, Quarry West, Antioch Rev, Mudfish, Exquisite
   Corpse*

RobertOh Faber 🎙   P
160 Claremont Ave
New York, NY 10027-4635, 212-864-6151
   Pubs: *NYQ, Light, Clown War, Poets, Kauri, Wormwood Rev,
   Daily World*

Andrea Falcetta   W
Wendy Weil Agency, Inc., 232 Madison Ave, Ste 1300, New
York, NY 10016, 212-685-0030
   Pubs: *Ship Fever & Other Stories* (Norton, 1996), *The
   Forms of Water* (Pocket Bks, 1993), *Story, Missouri Rev,
   Southern Rev, NER*

Arnold E. Falleder 🎙 ✈   P
160 W 87 St, #7B
New York, NY 10024-2951, 212-724-4712
   Pubs: *Midrash for Macbeth, The God-Shed* (Runaway
   Spoon Pr, 2000, 1992), *William Said, Generator 9: Anth*
   (Generator Pr, 1996, 1999), *Cover, The Poet, Christian
   Century, Onthebus, Stone Country, Purple, Rattle,
   Fiddlehead*

Louis Falstein   W
2571 Hubbard St
Brooklyn, NY 11235
   Pubs: *Sole Survivor* (Dell, 1954), *Chicago Jewish Forum*

John Fandel   P
609 Palmer Rd, Apt 2-L
Yonkers, NY 10701
   Pubs: *Ranging & Arranging* (Roth, 1990), *A Morning Answer*
   (Forward Movement Pub, 1988)

Philip Jose Farmer   W
c/o Ralph M. Vicinanza, Ltd, 111 Eighth Ave, New York, NY
10011, 212-924-7090
   Pubs: *Dayworld* (Putnam, 1985), *The Grand Adventure*
   (Byron Preiss Visual Pub, 1984)

Margot Farrington 🎙 ✈   PP&P
118 N 9 St
Brooklyn, NY 11211-1915, 718-388-2184
   Pubs: *Rising & Falling* (Warthog Pr, 1985), *Out of the
   Catskills & Just Beyond: Anth, Word Thursday Anth of Poetry
   & Fiction, Speaking the Words: Anth* (Bright Hill Pr, 1997,
   1995, 1994), *Poetry Wales, California Qtly, Phoebe, ALR*

Irvin Faust 🎙   W
417 Riverside Dr
New York, NY 10025-7928
   Pubs: *Jim Dandy* (Carroll & Graf, 1994), *Year of the Hot
   Jock* (Dutton, 1984), *Newsreel* (HBJ, 1980), *Contemporary
   Atlantic: Anth* (Atlantic Monthly, 1988), *O. Henry Prize
   Stories 1986: Anth, Michigan Qtly Rev, Esquire,
   Confrontation, Lit Rev, Paris Rev*

Naomi F. Faust 🎙 ✈   P
112-01 175 St
Jamaica, NY 11433-4135, 718-291-5338
   Pubs: *And I Travel by Rhythms & Words, All Beautiful Things*
   (Lotus Pr, 1990, 1983)

Susan C. Fawcett   P
67 Riverside Dr, #9B
New York, NY 10024
   Pubs: *Abandoned House* (Silver Apples Pr, 1988), *Michigan
   Qtly Rev, Nation, Montana Rev, Nimrod*

Cheri Fein 🎙 ✈   P&W
8 Stuyvesant Oval, #8F
New York, NY 10009, 212-995-5486
   Pubs: *Home Before Light* (Ridgeway Pr, 1991), *Pequod,
   Bomb, Ploughshares, Partisan Rev, Nimrod, Between C&D*

Frederick Feirstein   P
c/o Egon Dumler, 575 Madison Ave, New York, NY 10028
   Pubs: *New & Selected Poems, City Life* (Story Line Pr,
   1998, 1991), *Ending the 20th Century, Family History* (QRL,
   1994, 1991)

Eric Felderman   P&W
PO Box 194
Pelham, NY 10803
   Pubs: *Two Men and a Kangaroo Go Into a Bar* (Portmanteau
   Edtns, 1990)

Annette B. Feldmann   P
Shelley Society of New York, 77-07 138 St, #2F, Flushing, NY
11367, 718-969-7010
   Pubs: *The Carousel* (Diamond Hitch Pr, 1992), *The Scarab
   Beetle Speaks* (Iota Pr, 1993), *New Rev, Hellas, Mew Pr,
   Poetry Digest*

Jim Feraca   W
1428 Midland Ave
Bronxville, NY 10708
   Pubs: *Light Year Anth* (Bits Pr, 1985), *Green Hse, Rapport,
   Transatlantic Rev*

Daniel Fernandez   P
119 Payson Ave #3E
New York, NY 10034
   Pubs: *Apples from Hesperides* (Pegasus Pubs, 1971), *Intl
   Poetry Rev, The Lyric, Plains Poetry Jrnl, Christian Century,
   New Laurel Rev*

Jean Fiedler   W
69-23 Bell Blvd
Bayside, NY 11364-2532
    Pubs: *When a Sparrow Falls, Sisters in Crime: Anth*
    (Berkley, 1992, 1991), *The Year the World Was Out of Step
    with Jancy Fried* (HBJ, 1981)

Edward Field 🎤 ✈   P
463 West St, #A-323
New York, NY 10014
Internet: fieldinski@yahoo.com
    Pubs: *A Frieze for a Temple of Love, Counting Myself Lucky,
    Selected Poems 1963-1992* (Black Sparrow Pr, 1998, 1992),
    APR, Exquisite Corpse

Jennie Fields 🎤 ✈   W
452 8th St
Brooklyn, NY 11215-3616, 718-965-9335
    Pubs: *Crossing Brooklyn Ferry* (HarperPerennial, 2002),
    The Middle Ages (Morrow, 2002), *Lily Beach* (Warner, 1994)

Elliot Figman 🎤 ✈   P
15 W 11 St #5E
New York, NY 10011, 212-229-2398
Internet: elliotf@mindspring.com
    Pubs: *Big Spring* (Four Way Bks, 2003), *TriQtly, Poetry,
    Pequod*

Marlene Rosen Fine 🎤 ✈   P
490 W End Ave, #7E
New York, NY 10024-4331, 212-874-6671
    Pubs: *Clouds Fire the Smell of Wood* (Author, 1981),
    Ordinary Women: Anth (Common Differences Pr, 1985),
    Green Mountains Rev, Helen Rev, Atlantic, Connections

Miriam Finkelstein   W
680 W End Ave
New York, NY 10025
    Pubs: *Domestic Affairs* (HM, 1982), *Ascent, Arizona Qtly,
    Commonweal, Hanging Loose, Kalliope, Atlanta Rev, Kayak,
    Letters*

Cheryl Fish   P&W
40 Harrison St #23D
New York, NY 10013-2726
Internet: cfj@pipeline.com
    Pubs: *My City Flies By* (e.g. Pr, 1986), *African-American
    Travel Writing: Anth* (Beacon Pr, 1998), *Ladies, Start Your
    Engines: Anth* (Faber & Faber, 1998), *NAW, Long News,
    Response, Poetry NY, Talisman, Santa Monica Rev,
    Between C&D, B City*

Sally Fisher 🎤 ✈   P
98 Riverside Dr, #16C
New York, NY 10024
Internet: sallyxfish@aol.com
    Pubs: *Heliotrope, Turning Wheel, Field, Chelsea, Poetry
    East, New Directions, Tar River Poetry, The Sun*

Robert Fitterman   P
1 Washington Sq, Village #16-0
New York, NY 10012, 212-533-8030
Internet: rmf@is.nyu.edu
    Pubs: *Metropolis 1-15, Gertrude Stein Awards: Anth* (Sun
    & Moon Pr, 2000, 1996), *Metropolis 16-20* (Edge Bks,
    1998), *Ameresque* (Buck Downs Bks, 1996), *Leases*
    (Periphery Pr, 1989)

Jack Flam   W
Georges Borchardt Inc, 136 E 57 St, New York, NY 10022,
212-753-5785
    Pubs: *Bread & Butter* (Viking, 1977), *Zoltan Gorency*
    (Hodder & Stoughton, 1974)

Jane Flanders   P
1 Hazen St
Pelham, NY 10803-2408, 914-738-3776
Internet: stflanders@aol.com
    Pubs: *Timepiece* (U Pitt, 1988), *The Students of Snow* (U
    Massachusetts Pr, 1982), *Prairie Schooner, New Yorker,
    Paris Rev, Nation, New Republic, Poetry*

Bernice Fleisher 🎤   P
350 1st Ave, #4C
New York, NY 10010
    Pubs: *Poet Dreaming in Artist's House: Anth* (Milkweed
    Edtns, 1988), *East West: A Poetry Annual, Nostalgia,
    Leading Edge, Nimrod, Jam Today, Love Lyrics, Voices for
    Peace*

Eugene C. Flinn   W
Stewart H Benedict Literary Agency, 27 Washington Sq N,
New York, NY 10011-9165, 212-228-1440
    Pubs: *Strictly Fiction II: Anth* (Potpourri Pubs, 1995), *Best
    of Spitball: Anth* (Pocket Bks, 1988), *Thalia, Lynx Eye,
    Eclectic Literary Forum, Monocacy Valley Rev, Thin Ice,
    Small Pond Mag*

George Flynn   P
303 W 66 St, Apt 8CE
New York, NY 10023, 212-496-7658
    Pubs: *Zingers* (Letter Pr, 1978), *Kansas Qtly, Wisconsin
    Rev, Folio, Florida Qtly*

Helen Fogarassy 🎤 ✈   W
44 E 74th St, #3D
New York, NY 10021, 212-717-9859
    Pubs: *Mix Bender* (Quality Pubs, 1987), *Queen's Qtly, Our
    Town, Greenfeather, Gypsy, Sidewinder, Mildred, Home
    Planet News, Innisfree, Echoes, Nostalgia*

Dorothy Swartz Foley   P
81-48 169 St
Jamaica, NY 11432, 718-380-4134
    Pubs: *Bitterroot, Orphic Lute, Artist's Mag, Saturday
    Evening Post*

Montserrat Fontes W
W W Norton, 500 5th Ave, New York, NY 10110, 800-223-2584
Pubs: *Dreams of the Centaur, First Confession* (Norton,
1996, 1991), *High Contrast* (Naiad Pr, 1987), *Westways*

Richard Ford W
c/o Amanda Urban, ICM, 40 W 57 St, New York, NY 10019
Pubs: *Women with Men: Stories, Independence Day* (Knopf,
1997, 1995), *New Yorker, Esquire, Harper's, Granta*

Charles Henri Ford P
1 W 72 St, #103
New York, NY 10023
Pubs: *Water from a Bucket, I Will Be What I Am* (U Southern
Illinois Pr, 1993, 1992), *Out of the Labyrinth: Selected
Poems* (City Lights, 1986), *Arshile*

Vic Fortezza 🎤 W
2546 E 13th St, #B-12
Brooklyn, NY 11235
Internet: chinagame@flash.net
Pubs: *Black Petals, Cabal Asylum, Elements, The Black
Abyss, HELLP!, Neologisms, L'Ouverture, Forbidden Lines,
Blue Lady*

Geoffrey Edmund Fox 🎤 ✈ W
14 E 4 St, #812
New York, NY 10012, 212-505-2615
Internet: gefox@post.harvard.edu
Pubs: *Welcome to My Contri* (Lintel, 1988), *Yellow Silk
Erotic Arts & Letters: Anth* (Harmony Bks, 1990),
*Threepenny Rev, Fiction Intl, Yellow Silk, Central Park,
Exquisite Corpse, Copperfield Rev, In Posse, Linnaean
Street*

Paula Fox W
c/o Robert Lesher, 47 E 19 St, New York, NY 10003,
212-529-1790
Pubs: *The Eagle Kite, Western Wind, Monkey Island, The
Village by the Sea* (Orchard Bks, 1995, 1993, 1991, 1988),
The God of Nightmares (North Point Pr, 1990)

Elizabeth Fox 🎤 ✈ P&W
61 Eastern Pkwy #3-C
Brooklyn, NY 11238, 718-789-3640
Pubs: *Limousine Kids on the Ground* (Rocky Ledge Cottage
Edtns, 1983), *Asylum Annual 1994: Anth* (Asylum Arts Pubs,
1994), *The World, Transfer, Bombay Gin, Sugar Mule*

Patricia Weaver Francisco 🎤 ✈ W
Ellen Levine Literary Agency, 15 E 26 St, Ste 1801, New York,
NY 10010
Internet: pwf@bitstream.net
Pubs: *Village Without Mirrors* (Milkweed Edtns, 1989), *Cold
Feet* (S&S, 1988)

Don Frankel 🎤 ✈ W
2728 Henry Hudson Pkwy, Apt 35C
Riverdale, NY 10463, 718-581-0805
Internet: dfabmd@aol.com
Pubs: *Newscribes, Fan Mag, Steppingstones*

J. E. Franklin P
PO Box 517
New York, NY 10031-0517, 212-926-5974
Internet: je413@aol.com
Pubs: *Black Girl from Genesis: Revelations* (Howard U,
1977), *Voices of Color: Anth* (Applause Bks, 1992), *Black
Short Story Anth* (NAL, 1972), *Black Scholar*

Jonathan Franzen W
c/o Susan Golomb, 35 E 9 St, #90, New York, NY 10003,
212-505-7330
Pubs: *Strong Motion, The Twenty-Seventh City* (FSG, 1992,
1988), *Fiction Intl, Grand Street, Icarus*

Lynn Freed 🎤 ✈ W
William Morris, 1325 Ave of the Americas, 15th Floor, New
York, NY 10019, 212-903-1120
www.lynnfreed.com
Pubs: *House of Women* (Little, Brown & Co, 2002), *Friends
of the Family, The Bungalow, Home Ground* (Story Line Pr,
2000, 1999, 1998), *The Mirror* (Ballantine, 1999), *Tin House,
New Yorker, Atlantic, SW Rev, Harper's, Threepenny Rev*

Mathias B. Freese 🎤 ✈ W
9050 Union Turnpike, #1M
Glendale, NY 11385, 718-805-2420
www.vkinetic.com/freese
Pubs: *i* (Freese Pubs, 1997), *Confessions of Two Twigs*
(Brett Jordan Pubs, 1996), *Pilgrimage, Skywriters, Voices,
Global Stamp News*

Joan French P
427 E 73 St
New York, NY 10021, 212-840-1234
Pubs: *Voices Intl, Green's Mag, Intrepid, Modularist Rev,
Lake Superior Rev*

Mike Frenkel P
71-57 162 St
Fresh Meadows, NY 11365, 718-380-7599
Internet: Mfwriter@aol.com
Pubs: *Beyond Lament: Poets of the World Bearing Witness
on the Holocaust: Anth* (Northwestern U Pr, 1998), *Blood to
Remember: American Poets on the Holocaust: Anth* (Texas
Tech U Pr, 1991), *Bone & Flesh, Fan Mag*

Philip Fried 🎤 ✈   P
440 Riverside Dr, #45
New York, NY 10027
Internet: phfried@aol.com
    Pubs: *Quantum Genesis* (Zohar Pr, 1997), *Mutual
    Trespasses* (Ion, 1988), *Acquainted with the Night: Anth*
    (Rizzoli, 1997), *Partisan, Paris Rev, Massachusetts Rev,
    BPJ, Maryland Poetry Rev, Cream City Rev, Chelsea, Tin
    House*

Sanford Friedman   W
37 W 12 St, #10F
New York, NY 10011
    Pubs: *Rip Van Winkle* (Atheneum, 1980), *Still Life, A
    Haunted Woman, Totempole* (Dutton, 1975, 1968, 1965)

B. H. Friedman 🎤 ✈   W
439 E 51st St, 9E
New York, NY 10022, 212-755-5723
    Pubs: *Between the Flags* (Fiction Collective, 1990), *The
    Polygamist* (Atlantic, 1981), *Epoch*

Dorothy Friedman   P
582 E 2 St
Brooklyn, NY 11218, 718-633-1503
    Pubs: *Family Album, The Liberty Years* (Rio Edtns, 1989,
    1987), *Partisan Rev, California Qtly, Kayak, Ms.*

Nancy Bengis Friedman 🎤 ✈   P
551 4th St #2
Brooklyn, NY 11215, 718-499-8383
    Pubs: *Fine China: Anth* (Springhouse Edtns, 1993), *The Tie
    that Binds: Anth* (Papier-Mache Pr, 1992), *Natl Poetry Mag
    of the Lower East Side, Lips, New Pr, Eleven*

Norman Friedman 🎤   P
33-54 164 St
Flushing, NY 11358-1442, 718-353-3631
Internet: nfriedman18@aol.com
    Pubs: *The Magic Badge: Poems 1953-1984* (Slough Pr,
    1984), *Intl Poetry Rev, Centennial Rev, BPJ, New Mexico
    Qtly, New Voices, Georgia Rev, Nation, Texas Qtly*

Celestine Frost 🎤 ✈   P
PO Box 6877, Yorkville Sta, New York, NY 10128,
212-722-0446
    Pubs: *A Yelp in the Ideal* (Codhill Pr, 2002), *I Gathered My
    Ear from the Green Field* (Logodaedalus, 1998), *An
    Imagined Experience Over the Entrance* (Dusty Dog, 1993),
    Talisman, Juxta, Camellia, Epoch

Lewis Burke Frumkes   W
c/o The Writing Center, Marymount Manhattan College,
221 E 71 St, New York, NY 10021, 212-734-3073
    Pubs: *The Logophile's Orgy* (Delacorte, 1995),
    Metapunctuation (Dell, 1993), *How to Raise Your IQ By
    Eating Gifted Children* (McGraw-Hill, 1983), *Harper's,
    Punch, Reader's Digest*

Daniel Gabriel 🎤   P
211 Sixth Ave, #3A
Brooklyn, NY 11215-1220, 718-857-5669
    Pubs: *Columbus* (Gnosis Pr, 1993), *Sacco & Vanzetti* (Gull
    Bks, 1983),

Roger Gaess   P
47 Jane St, #16
New York, NY 10014, 212-691-8352
    Pubs: *Leaving the Bough* (International, 1982)

Jonathan Galassi 🎤 ✈   P
Farrar, Straus & Giroux, 19 Union Sq W, New York, NY 10003,
212-741-6900
    Pubs: *North Street* (HC, 2000), *Morning Run* (Paris Rev
    Edtns, 1988)

Tess Gallagher   P&W
c/o Amanda Urban, ICM, 40 W 57 St, New York, NY 10019
    Pubs: *At the Owl Woman Saloon* (Scribner, 1997), *Portable
    Kisses, My Black Horse* (Bloodaxe Pr, 1996, 1995), *Portable
    Kisses Expanded* (Capra Pr, 1994), *Zyzzyva, Glimmer Train,
    Sycamore Rev, Ploughshares, Indiana Rev, Atlantic, APR,
    Michigan Qtly Rev*

Mavis Gallant   W
Georges Borchardt Inc., 136 E 57 St, New York, NY 10022

James Gallant   W
c/o Noah Lukeman, AMG/Renaissance, 140 W 57 St, New
York, NY 10019, 212-956-2600
Internet: jtgallant@cs.com
    Pubs: *Press, Exquisite Corpse, Raritan, Rhino, Georgia Rev,
    Epoch, Kansas Qtly, Mississippi Rev, NAR, Massachusetts
    Rev, Story Qtly*

Kenneth Gangemi 🎤 ✈   P&W
211 E 5 St
New York, NY 10003, 212-777-4795
    Pubs: *The Volcanoes from Puebla, Olt, The Interceptor Pilot*
    (Marion Boyars, 1989, 1984, 1982)

Suzanne Gardinier   P&W
110 W 96 St, #8C
New York, NY 10025-6474
    Pubs: *A World That Will Hold All the People* (U Michigan Pr,
    1996), *The New World* (U Pitt Pr, 1993)

Nancy Bruff Gardner   P&W
200 E 66 St, #D803
New York, NY 10021, 212-752-8774
    Pubs: *Lively Scandals in Old Brooklyn Heights, Laughing
    Lady of Old Cape Cod* (iUniverse, 2001, 2001), *The Mist
    Maiden* (Dell, 1975), *My Talon in Your Heart* (Dutton, 1946)

Johanna Garfield   W
200 E 94 St, #1517
New York, NY 10128, 212-996-2568
Internet: jogarfield@aol.com
    Pubs: *Cousins* (Donald I Fine, 1990), *The Life of a Real Girl*
(St. Martin's Pr, 1986), *Ms., Reader's Digest, McCall's, Art &
Antiques, Paris Rev, American Art*

Peggy Garrison 🎤 ✈   P&W
74 E 7 St
New York, NY 10003-8417, 212-533-1996
    Pubs: *Ding the Bell* (Poetry NY, 1999), *Charing Cross
Bridge* (P&Q Pr, 1998), *Beloit Fiction, South Dakota Rev,
Poetry Now, The Smith, Ball State U Forum, Images,
Literary Rev, Slant, Global City Rev, Mudfish*

Ellen Gruber Garvey 🎤 ✈   P&W
202 St Marks Ave, #3
Brooklyn, NY 11238
Internet: egarvey@njcu.edu
    Pubs: *Tales of Magic Realism by Women: Anth, Speaking
for Ourselves: Anth* (Crossing Pr, 1990, 1990), *If I Had a
Hammer: Anth* (Papier-Mache, 1990), *The Tribe of Dina:
Anth* (Beacon Pr, 1989), *Minnesota Rev, Feminist Studies,
Paragraph, Bridges*

Serge Gavronsky 🎤 ✈   P
525 W End Ave, #12H
New York, NY 10024, 212-787-7068
Internet: sgavronsky@barnard.edu
    Pubs: *Temps mort* (Virgile, 2002), *Une toute autre histoire*
(Al Dante, 2002), *Sixty-Six for Starters* (Jensen/Daniels,
2002), *Ou l'ecume* (Collections Memiores, 2002), *Etait-ce le
vide* (Bradley Hutchenson, 2001), *Talisman, Lingo, Bitter
Oleander, Interstice*

Barrie Gellis   P
43-06 159 St, #D-2
Flushing, NY 11358, 718-961-3521
    Pubs: *We Speak for Peace: Anth* (KIT Inc, 1993), *Forum,
Pandemonium, Athena, Long Shot, Yellow Silk, Inside-
Outside, Poets on Photography, Genesis*

Kathleen E. George 🎤 ✈   W
c/o Anne Rittenberg, Literary Agency, 1201 Broadway, Ste
708, New York, NY 10001
    Pubs: *Taken* (Delacorte, 2001), *The Man in the Buick* (BkMk
Pr, 1999), *Rhythm in Drama* (U Pitt Pr, 1980), *Cimarron Rev,
Alaska Qtly Rev, Great Stream Rev, NAR, American Fiction,
Vignette*

Sally George   W
715 Carroll St
Brooklyn, NY 11215
    Pubs: *Frog Salad* (Scribner, 1981), *Ms., Redbook, NAR,
Conditions, Heresies, Massachusetts Rev*

Corinne Gerson   W
101 W 12 St, #2N
New York, NY 10011
    Pubs: *Cyberdog* (Royal Fireworks Pr, 1998), *Rendez-Vous
Au Zoo* (Rageout-Editeur, 1992), *My Grandfather the Spy*
(Walker, 1990)

Peter Gethers 🎤 ✈   W
c/o Random House Inc, 299 Park Ave, New York, NY 10171
    Pubs: *The Cat Who'll Live Forever, A Cat Abroad, The Cat
Who Went to Paris, Getting Blue, The Dandy* (Crown, 2001,
1994, 1991, 1987, 1978)

Andrew Gettler   P
2663 Heath Ave #6D
Bronx, NY 10463-7520, 718-884-1316
    Pubs: *A Condition, Not an Event* (New Spirit Pr, 1992),
Footsteps of a Ghost (Iniquity Pr, 1991), *Boston Lit Rev,
Excursus, Confrontation, Santa Clara Rev*

P. J. Gibson   PP
400 W 43 St, #14L
New York, NY 10036

Dagoberto Gilb 🎤 ✈   W
Grove Press, 841 Broadway, New York, NY 10003
    Pubs: *Gritos, The Woodcuts of Women, The Last Known
Residence of Mickey Acuna, The Magic of Blood* (Grove Pr,
2003, 2001, 1994, 1993), *Harper's, Threepenny Rev, New
Yorker, DoubleTake, Ploughshares, Texas Observer*

Ilsa Gilbert 🎤 ✈   P
203 Bleecker St, #9
New York, NY 10012-1456, 212-254-5289
    Pubs: *Zoo International, The Poet of Bleecker Street III, The
Poet of Bleecker Street II* (Downtown Music Prods, 2001,
2000, 1994), *Survivors & Other New York Poems* (Bard Pr,
1991), *And Then, Poet Lore, Quartet, Waterways,
Landscapes, St. Clements Qtly*

Saul B. Gilson   P
7 Sigma Pl
Bronx, NY 10421, 718-601-3105
    Pubs: *Basilisic* (Cross Cultural Lit Edtns, 1996), *New Re-
naissance, Annals of Internal Medicine*

Estelle Gilson   W
7 Sigma Pl
Bronx, NY 10471, 718-549-3979
    Pubs: *Dirty Goat, Present Tense, Midstream, Moment,
Columbia, New Renaissance, Other Voices, Congress
Monthly*

John Giorno 🎤 ✈   PP&P
222 Bowery
New York, NY 10012-4216, 212-925-6372
Internet: giornopoetry@attglobal.net
    Pubs: *You Got to Burn to Shine* (High Risk, 1994), *Grasping at Emptiness, Balling Buddha* (Kulchur Fdn, 1985, 1970), *Shit, Piss, Blood, Pus & Brains* (Painted Bride, 1978)

Daniela Gioseffi 🎤 ✈   PP&P&W
Poet USA, 57 Montague St #8G, Brooklyn, NY 11201-3356, 718-624-2165
Internet: daniela@garden.net
    Pubs: *Symbiosis: Poems* (Rattapallax Pr, 2002), *Going On: Poems, Word Wounds & Water Flowers* (Via/Purdue U, 2000, 1996), *In Bed with the Exotic Enemy: stories & novella* (Avisson, 1997), *Paris Rev, Nation, Ms., Prairie Schooner, Poetry East*

Nikki Giovanni   P
William Morrow & Co, 105 Madison Ave, New York, NY 10016

Todd Gitlin 🎤 ✈   P
New York Univ, Dept of Culture & Communication, 239 Greene St, Rm 735, New York, NY 10003
Internet: todd.gitlin@nyu.edu
    Pubs: *Sacrifice* (Metropolitan/Holt, 1999), *The Murder of Albert Einstein* (Bantam, 1994), *Nation, Civilization, Dissent*

Julia Glass   W
137 W 12 St
New York, NY 10011
    Pubs: *Amer Short Fiction, Bellingham Rev, Chicago Tribune*

Eleanor Glaze   W
Ellen Levine Literary Agency, 15 E 26 St, Ste 1801, New York, NY 10010, 212-889-0620
    Pubs: *Jaiyavara* (Peachtree, 1988), *Homeworks* (U Tennessee Pr, 1986), *Atlantic, New Yorker, Redbook, The Sun*

Judith Gleason   W
26 E 91 St #6B
New York, NY 10128, 212-534-2019
    Pubs: *Oya: In Praise of the Goddess* (Shambhala, 1987), *Leaf & Bone* (Viking, 1980)

Adele Glimm 🎤 ✈   W
120 E 81 St #16E
New York, NY 10028-1423
    Pubs: *Epoch, Redbook, Cosmopolitan, McCall's, Southern Humanities Rev, Good Housekeeping, Ellery Queen's Mystery Mag*

Tony Gloeggler 🎤 ✈   P
83-45 116 St, #2B
Richmond Hill, NY 11418, 718-441-8195
    Pubs: *One on One* (Pearl Edtns, 1999), *Full Court: A Literary Anth of Basketball* (Breakaway Bks, 1996), *Puerto del Sol, Mangrove, West Branch, Rattle, The Ledge, Graffiti Rag, NYQ, Chiron Rev, Rhino, Black Bear Rev, Mudfish, Yellow Silk*

Tereze Gluck   W
333 E 69 St #4J
New York, NY 10021, 212-535-5417
    Pubs: *Chelsea, Antioch Rev, Malahat Rev, Ascent, Epoch, Fiction, Alaska Qtly, Threepenny Rev, Story, Columbia*

John Godfrey   P
437 E 12 St, #32
New York, NY 10009, 212-475-6532
    Pubs: *Dabble: Poems 1966-1980* (Full Court Pr, 1982), *From the Other Side of the Century: Anth* (Sun & Moon Pr, 1994), *Lingo, Poetry NY, World, o.blek*

Ivan Gold   W
Mary Yost Associates, 59 E 54 St, New York, NY 10022, 212-980-4988
    Pubs: *Sams in a Dry Season, Nickel Miseries, Sick Friends* (Washington Square Pr, 1992, 1992, 1992)

Gerald Jay Goldberg   W
Georges Borchardt Inc, 136 E 57 St, New York, NY 10022
    Pubs: *Heart Payments* (Viking, 1982), *The Lynching of Orin Newfield* (Dial, 1970)

Myra Goldberg   W
Sarah Lawrence College, Writing Program, Bronxville, NY 10708, 914-337-0700
    Pubs: *Whistling & Other Stories* (Zoland Bks, 1993), *Representations of Motherhood: Anth* (Yale U Pr, 1994), *Ploughshares, NER, Tikkun, Feminist Studies*

Isaac Goldemberg   P&W
4555 Henry Hudson Pkwy, #703
Bronx, NY 10471-3844
    Pubs: *La Vida al Contado* (Ediciones Del Norte, 1992), *Play By Play* (Persea Bks, 1985)

Mike Golden   P&W
Black Market Press, 400 W 43 St, Ste 37K, New York, NY 10036
    Pubs: The Buddhist 3rd Class Junk Mail Oracle (Seven Stories Pr, 1999), Help Yourself: Anth, Crimes of the Beats: Anth, Unbearables: Anth (Autonomedia, 2002, 1998, 1995) The Outlaw Bible of American Poetry: Anth (Thunder's Mouth Pr, 1999)

Michael Goldman   P
425 Riverside Dr
New York, NY 10025

William Goldman   W
c/o Urban del Rey, Ballantine Books, 201 E 50 St, New York,
NY 10022
   Pubs: *Control, Tinsel* (Delacorte, 1982, 1979), *The Princess
   Bride* (Ballantine, 1977)

Lloyd Goldman   P
448 2nd St
Brooklyn, NY 11215-2503

Gloria Goldreich 🎤 ✈   W
356 Marbledale Rd
Tuckahoe, NY 10707-1716
   Pubs: *That Year of Our War, Years of Dreams, Mothers*
   (Little, Brown, 1994, 1992, 1989), *Commentary, Midstream,
   Redbook, McCall's, Moment*

Barbara Goldsmith   W
c/o Lynn Nesbit, Janklow & Nesbit Associates, 1021 Park Ave,
New York, NY 10028, 212-534-3637
   Pubs: *The Straw Man* (FSG, 1975), *Vanity Fair, New Yorker*

Jeanette Erlbaum Goldsmith 🎤 ✈   W
1483 E 34 St
Brooklyn, NY 11234, 718-253-3484
   Pubs: *Confrontation* (Long Island U, 1987), *Each in Her Own
   Way* (Queen of Swords Pr, 1994), *Whetstone, Hawaii Rev,
   Antioch Rev, Commentary, Malahat Rev, Mid-American Rev*

Howard Goldsmith   W
41-07 Bowne St, #6B
Flushing, NY 11355-5629, 718-886-5819
   Pubs: *Slap! Dash! Mark Twain at Work, Thomas Edison to
   the Rescue* (Simon & Schuster, 2003), *Science Through
   Stories* (McGraw-Hill, 1999), *Scholastic Storyworks, Short
   Story Intl, London Mystery, Disney Adventures*

Jewelle Gomez   P&W
Michele Karlsberg Publicity, 47 Dongan Hills Ave, Staten
Island, NY 10306, 718-980-4262
   Pubs: *Don't Explain, Oral Tradition, The Gilda Stories*
   (Firebrand Bks, 1998, 1996, 1991), *Essence, Ms., Black
   Scholar, Advocate, Qtly Black Rev, Zyzzyva, Curve*

Brad Gooch   P
Joy Harris Literary Agency, 156 Fith Ave, Ste 617, New York,
NY 10010, 212-924-6269
   Pubs: *Scary Kisses* (Putnam, 1988), *Jailbait & Other Stories*
   (Sea Horse Pr, 1984), *Paris Rev, Partisan Rev, Bomb,
   Between C&D, Shiny, Christopher Street*

Melinda Goodman   P
45 E 1 St, #4
New York, NY 10003
   Pubs: *Middle Sister* (MSG Pr, 1988), *My Lover Is a Woman:
   Anth* (Ballantine Bks, 1996), *The Arch of Love: Lesbian Love
   Poems: Anth* (Scribner, 1996), *Sinister Wisdom, Conditions,
   Heresies*

Mary Gordon   W
c/o Peter Matson, Sterling Lord Literistic, 65 Bleecker St, New
York, NY 10012, 212-780-6050
   Pubs: *The Rest of Life, The Other Side* (Viking Penguin,
   1993, 1989), *Spending* (Scribner, 1998), *Temporary Shelter,
   Men & Angels, The Company of Women, Final Payments*
   (Random Hse, 1987, 1985, 1981, 1978)

Coco Gordon 🎤 ✈   P
138 Duane St, #5SW
New York, NY 10013-3854, 212-285-1609
Internet: cocogord@mindspring.com
   Pubs: Knee (Ginocchio) (Porto Dei Santi Pr, 2000), Tikysk:
   Permaculture Getting to Know You (Foot Square Space,
   1997), Superskywoman (Leonardi V-Idea, 1995), Oreste 2:
   Anth (Venice Biennale, 2000), Pig Iron, New Observations,
   Aquaterra, Eternal Network

Fred Gordon   W
35 Carriage Rd
Great Neck, NY 11024
   Pubs: *Benjamin Grabbed His Glicken & Ran* (H&R, 1971)

hattie gossett   P&W
775 Riverside Dr, #6J
New York, NY 10032
   Pubs: *presenting . . . sister noblues* (Firebrand Bks, 1988),
   Seeing Jazz: Anth (Smithsonian/Chronicle Bks, 1998),
   *Conditions, Heresies, Sinister Wisdom, Essence,
   Womanews, Between Ourselves, Playbill*

Darcy Gottlieb 🎤   P
67 Orchard Beach Blvd
Port Washington, NY 11050-1427
   Pubs: *Matters of Contention* (Aesopus, 1979), *No Witness
   But Ourselves* (U Missouri Pr, 1973), *And What Great Beast:
   Poems at the End of the Century: Anth* (Ashland Poetry Pr,
   1999), *Beyond Lament: Anth* (Northwestern U Pr, 1998)

Amy Gottlieb   W
2575 Palisade Ave
Riverdale, NY 10463
Internet: rapubs@jtsa.edu
   Pubs: *Midstream, Other Voices, Puerto del Sol*

Lois Gould 🎤 ✈   W
Charlotte Sheedy Literary Agency, 65 Bleecker St, New York,
NY 10012, 212-780-9800
   Pubs: *No Brakes* (H Holt, 1997), *Medusa's Gift* (Knopf,
   1992), *Subject to Change* (FSG, 1988), *La Presidenta, A
   Sea-Change* (S&S, 1981, 1976)

Roberta Gould 🎤 ✈   P
315 E 18 St, #4R
New York, NY 10003, 212-982-6818
Internet: nobertag@ulster.net
    Pubs: *In Houses with Ladders, Not by Blood Alone* (Editores
    Lince, 2001, 1990), *Three Windows* (Reservoir Pr, 1997),
    Only Rock (Folder Edtns, 1985), *Rio On Line, Bridges, Stet,
    Home Planet, Confrontation, Green Mountains Rev*

Pascale Gousseland 🎤   P
117A E 71 St
New York, NY 10012, 212-472-6881
    Pubs: *Second Glance, Medicinal Purposes, Poems That
    Thump in the Dark, Nomad's Choir, Albatross, Thirteen,
    New Press*

Ignatius Graffeo   P
82-34 138 St, #6F
Kew Gardens, NY 11435, 718-847-1482
Internet: newspirit@gnn.com
    Pubs: *She Came with the Magazine, Xanthus* (New Spirit Pr,
    1995, 1993), *We Speak for Peace: Anth* (Kit Pubs, 1994),
    Poetry Digest, Maryland Poetry Rev

James Graham   P
PO Box 605, Cooper Sq Sta, New York, NY 10276
Internet: jasgraham@juno.com
    Pubs: *Search Engine: Difficult Path, One Skin* (Machete,
    1998, 1994), *Small Hours of the Night* (Curbstone Pr, 1996),
    Found Body (Soncino Bks, 1993), *Hungry Mind Rev, Rev:
    Latin America, Nexus, Cover, Machete, The Sun, Nexus,
    Harper's*

Shirley Ann Grau 🎤 ✈   W
JCA, 27 W 20 St, New York, NY 10011, 212-807-0888
    Pubs: *The Black Prince, The Roadwalkers, Keepers of the
    House* (Knopf, 1996, 1994, 1965)

Elizabeth Graver 🎤 ✈   W
Richard Parks Agency, 138 E 16 St, New York, NY 10003,
212-228-1786
Internet: graver@bc.edu
    Pubs: *The Honey Thief, Unravelling* (Hyperion, 1999, 1997),
    Have You Seen Me? (Ecco Pr, 1993), *O. Henry Prize
    Stories: Anths* (Anchor, 2001, 1996, 1994), *Pushcart Prize
    Stories: Anth* (Pushcart Pr, 2001), *Best American Short
    Stories: Anths* (HM, 2001, 1991)

Francine du Plessix Gray 🎤 ✈   W
Georges Borchardt Inc, 136 E 57 St, New York, NY 10022
    Pubs: *Adam & Eve & the City, October Blood* (S&S, 1987,
    1985), *New Yorker, Yale Rev, Harper's*

Dorothy Randall Gray   P&W
328 Flatbush Ave, Ste 148
Brooklyn, NY 11238, 718-638-6415
http://www.heartland.drg
    Pubs: *Soul Between the Lines* (Avon Bks, 1998), *Woman, A
    Taste of Tamarindo, The Passion Collective, Muse Blues*
    (Polaris Pr, 1996, 1994, 1991, 1990), *Frontiers, Binnewater
    Tides*

Richard Grayson   W
Linda Konner Literary Agency, 10 W 15 St, Ste 1918, New
York, NY 10011-6829
Internet: graysonric@aol.com
    Pubs: *I Survived Caracas Traffic* (Avisson Pr, 1996), *I Brake
    for Delmore Schwartz* (Zephyr, 1983)

Stephen Greco   P
134 Henry St
Brooklyn, NY 11201, 718-855-8759
    Pubs: *Penguin Book of Gay Short Stories: Anth* (Viking
    Penguin, 1994), *Flesh & the Word: Anth* (Dutton, 1992),
    Interview, 7 Days

Jessica Greenbaum 🎤 ✈   P
404 Vanderbilt Ave
Brooklyn, NY 11238-1505
Internet: greenbaum@marcusattorneys.com
    Pubs: *Inventing Difficulty* (Silverfish Rev Pr, 2000)

Joanne Greenberg   W
Wallace Literary Agency, 177 E 70 St, New York, NY 10021,
212-570-9090
    Pubs: *Where the Road Goes, No Reck'ning Made, In This
    Sign* (H Holt, 1998, 1993, 1970), *Literature: Anth* (Prentice
    Hall, 1998), *High Fantastic: Anth* (Ocean View Bks, 1995),
    Hadassah, Hudson Rev, Redbook, Denver Qtly

Harry Greenberg   P
321 W 94 St, #6-NE
New York, NY 10025, 212-866-3242
    Pubs: *Handbook of Poetic Forms: Anth, The Point: Anth*
    (Teachers & Writers, 1987, 1983), *Agni*

Henry L. Greene   P
58-27 212 St
Bayside, NY 11364
    Pubs: *Modern Images, Spoon River Qtly*

Ted Greenwald   P
206 E 17 St, #4-D
New York, NY 10003
    Pubs: *Word of Mouth* (Sun & Moon Pr, 1986), *Exit the Face*
    (w/R Bosman; MOMA, 1982)

Arthur Gregor P
c/o Sheep Meadow Pr, PO Box 1345, Riverdale-on-Hudson,
NY 10471, 718-548-5542
    Pubs: *The River Serpent, Secret Citizen* (Sheep Meadow Pr,
    1995, 1989), *Boulevard, Ploughshares, Nation, Hudson Rev*

Kathleen C. Griffin 🎤 ✈ P
6425 Broadway
Riverdale, NY 10471, 718-549-8405
Internet: kathleengriffin@gobi.com
    Pubs: *Newsletter, Waterways, Home Planet News*

Tom Grimes 🎤 ✈ W
Dunow-Carlson Literary Agency, 27 W 20 St, Suite 1003, New
York, NY 10011
Internet: tg02@swt.edu
    Pubs: *A Stone of the Heart* (Southern Methodist U Pr,
    1997), *City of God* (Picador, 1996), *Season's End* (Bison
    Bks, 1996)

Gwendolen Gross P&W
Elaine Koster Literary Agency, 55 Central Pk W, Ste 6, New
York, NY 10023
Internet: ggross@compuserve.com
    Pubs: *Amelia, Cold Mountain Rev, Fresh Ground, Global
    City Rev, Hubbub, Laurel Rev, MacGuffin, Madison Rev,
    Prism Intl, Red Cedar Rev, Salt Hill Jrnl, Santa Barbara Rev,
    Seattle Rev, Southern Humanities Rev, Wind Mag*

Ronald Gross P
17 Myrtle Dr
Great Neck, NY 11021, 516-487-0235
    Pubs:

Doris Grumbach W
c/o Timothy Seldes, Russell & Volkening Inc, 50 W 29 St, New
York, NY 10001, 212-684-6050
    Pubs: *The Pleasure of Their Company, The Presence of
    Absence, Life in a Day, Fifty Days of Solitude* (Beacon,
    2000, 1998, 1996, 1994), *Extra Innings, Coming into the
    End Zone* (Norton, 1993, 1991)

Barbara Guest P
49 W 16 St
New York, NY 10011
    Pubs: *Defensive Rapture, Fair Realism* (Sun & Moon Pr,
    1993, 1989), *Conjunctions, Sulfur, NAW*

Amy Guggenheim 🎤 ✈ PP
Pratt Institute, 200 Willoughby Ave, Brooklyn, NY 11215,
718-963-1977
Internet: agenheim@cs.com
    Pubs: *Sensitive Skin Festival, Havana Intl Theater Festival,
    Here, Pratt Institute, Home Theatre for Contemporary Art &
    Performance, La Mama Etc, Casa del Lago, Cleveland Per-
    formance Open, Performance Mix/DIA Art Fdn, American
    Letters & Commentary*

Joanna Gunderson 🎤 ✈ P
1148 5th Ave, #12B
New York, NY 10128, 212-348-4388
Internet: reddustjg@aol.com
    Pubs: *Kaleidoscape 1969* (Spuyten Duyvil, 2000), *The Field,
    Sights* (Red Dust, 1999, 1963), *Midland Rev, Rampike,
    How*(ever), *Frank, Northeast Jrnl*

Allan Gurganus W
c/o Amanda Urban, ICM, 40 W 57 St, New York, NY 10019,
212-556-5600
    Pubs: *The Practical Heart, Plays Well with Others, White
    People, Oldest Living Confederate Widow Tells All* (Knopf,
    2000, 1997, 1992, 1989), *New Yorker, Antaeus, Harper's,
    Granta, Atlantic, Yale Rev, Paris Rev*

C. W. Gusewelle W
Harvey Klinger, Inc, 301 W 53 St, New York, NY 10019
    Pubs: *The Rufus Chronicle: Another Autumn* (Ballantine
    Bks, 1998), *A Paris Notebook* (Lowell Pr, 1995), *Far from
    Any Coast: Pieces of America's Heartland* (U Missouri Pr,
    1989), *American Heritage, Antioch Rev, Virginia Qtly Rev,
    Audience, Harper's*

Rosa Guy W
Ellen Levine Literary Agency, 15 E 26 St, Ste 1801, New York,
NY 10010, 212-889-0620
    Pubs: The Sun, The Sea, A Touch of the Wind (Dutton,
    1995) The Ups & Downs of Carl Davis III, Paris, Pee Wee &
    Big Dog (Delacorte, 1989, 1984), My Love, My Love, or the
    Peasant Girl (H Holt, 1985)

Charles Hackenberry W
M Evans & Co Inc, 216 E 49 St, New York, NY 10017

Marilyn Hacker 🎤 ✈ P
230 W 105 St #136
New York, NY 10025, 212-678-1074
Internet: 110165.74@compuserve.com
    Pubs: *Desperanto, Squares & Courtyards, Winter Numbers,
    Selected Poems* (Norton, 2003, 2000, 1994, 1994), *Going
    Back to the River* (Random Hse, 1990), *Nation, Poetry, Paris
    Rev, TriQtly, Prairie Schooner*

Rachel Hadas 🎤 P
838 W End Ave, #3A
New York, NY 10025, 212-666-4482
Internet: rhadas@andromeda.rutgers.edu
    Pubs: *Indelible, Halfway Down the Hall, The Empty Bed
    (Wesleyan U Pr, 2001, 1998, 1995), Merrill, Cavafy, Poems
    & Dreams* (Michigan, 2000), *The Double Legacy* (Faber &
    Faber, 1995), *New Yorker, Threepenny Rev, Paris Rev, Yale
    Rev, New Republic*

Jessica Hagedorn   PP&W
Harold Schmidt Literary Agency, 343 W 12 St, #1B, New York,
NY 10014, 212-727-7473
    Pubs: *Danger and Beauty* (City Lights Pr, 2002), *The
    Gangster of Love, Dogeaters, Charlie Chan Is Dead: Anth*
    (Penguin, 1996, 1991, 1993)

Hannelore Hahn   P
PO Box 810, Gracie Sta, New York, NY 10028, 212-737-7536
Internet: dirhahn@aol.com
    Pubs: *Places, On the Way to Feed the Swans* (Tenth Hse
    Enterprises, 1990, 1982), *To Jump Or Not Jump: Anth*
    (Traveler's Tales Guides, 1998), *Network*

Kimiko Hahn   P
421 3rd St #1
Brooklyn, NY 11215
    Pubs: *The Unbearable Heart* (Kaya Pr, 1995), *Earshot, Air
    Pocket* (Hanging Loose, 1992, 1990), *Bomb, Manoa,
    American Voice, Ikon, River Styx, Mudfish, Tyuonyi*

Isidore Haiblum   W
160 W 77 St
New York, NY 10024
    Pubs: *Crystalworld, Specterworld* (Avon, 1992, 1991), *Bad
    Neighbors* (St. Martin's, 1990), *Out of Sync* (Del Ray, 1990)

Jana Haimsohn   PP
530 Canal St, #3-E
New York, NY 10013, 212-925-4071
    Pubs: *Collective Consciousness: Art Performances in the
    '70s Anth* (Performing Arts Journal Pubs, 1981)

Victoria Hallerman   P
65 Fort Hill Cir
Staten Island, NY 10301
Internet: vicki@omibusiness.com
    Pubs: *The Night Market, The Woman in the Magic Show*
    (Firm Ground Pr, 1998, 1995), *Poetry, Nation, SPR, Indiana
    Rev, Global City Rev, Pivot*

Nancy Hallinan 🎤 ✈   W
276 Riverside Dr, #2D
New York, NY 10025, 212-222-6936
    Pubs: *Sasakawa: Global Philanthropist* (Pergamon Pr,
    1981), *Night Swimmers, Rough Winds of May* (H&R, 1976,
    1955), *Voice from the Wings* (Knopf, 1965), *O. Henry Prize
    Stories Anth, Harper's, Cosmopolitan, Pulpsmith, American
    Vanguard, Cornhill, Touchstone*

Joan Halperin   P
23 Hastings Landing
Hastings-On-Hudson, NY 10706
    Pubs: *Connecticut River Rev, Poet Lore, Modern Images,
    Pudding, Goblets, Confrontation, NYQ, Echoes, Southern
    Poetry Jrnl, Tar River Poetry, Cimarron Rev*

Mary Stewart Hammond 🎤 ✈   P
1095 Park Ave, #4A
New York, NY 10128, 212-289-6264
    Pubs: *Out of Canaan, The Book of Elegies: Anth* (Norton,
    1991, 2001), *The KGB Bar Book of Poems: Anth* (HC,
    2000), *Where Books Fall Open: Anth* (Godine, 2001),
    *Boulevard, Field, Gettysburg Rev, NER, Atlantic, APR, New
    Yorker, New Criterion, Paris Rev*

Edward Hannibal   W
601 E 20 St, #11D
New York, NY 10010
    Pubs: *A Trace of Red* (Dial Pr, 1982), *Chocolate Days
    Popsicle Weeks* (HM, 1970)

Barbara Hantman 🎤   P
15-17 Utopia Pkwy
Whitestone, NY 11357, 718-352-2098
Internet: bh7254@aol.com
    Pubs: *Midstream, Pegasus Rev, Sunday Suitor Poetry Rev,
    Troubadour*

Rob Hardin   P&W
PO Box 2214, Stuyvesant Sta, New York, NY 10009,
212-477-1066
    Pubs: *Distorture* (BIB/FC2, 1997), *Forbidden Acts: Anth*
    (Avon, 1995), *Avant Pop: Anth* (Black Ice Bks, 1993),
    Michigan Rev, Sensitive Skin

Nancy Harding   W
Meredith Bernstein Literary Agency, 2112 Broadway, Ste
503A, New York, NY 10023
    Pubs: *Wind Child, The Silver Land* (Pocket Bks, 1990, 1989)

Jean Harfenist 🎤 ✈   W
c/o Sam Stoloff, The Frances Goldin Agency, 57 E. 11th St.,
Ste 5B, New York, NY 10003
Internet: harf@west.net
    Pubs: *A Brief History of the Flood* (Knopf, 2002), *Qtly West,
    Sycamore Rev, The Missouri Rev, Prism Intl, Crazyhorse,
    Cream City Rev, Nimrod Intl Jrnl, Hayden's Ferry Rev,
    Sonora Rev, Wisconsin Rev,*

Enid Harlow 🎤   W
175 Riverside Dr, #12L
New York, NY 10024
Internet: enidh3030@aol.com
    Pubs: *A Better Man* (Van Neste Bks, 2000), *Love's Shadow*
    (Crossing Pr, 1993), *American Fiction 4: Anth* (Birchlane Pr,
    1993), *Mediphors, TriQtly*

Curtis Harnack   W
205 W 57 St
New York, NY 10019, 212-757-9235
    Pubs: *The Attic, We Have All Gone Away* (Iowa State U Pr,
    1993, 1987), *American Short Fiction, Confrontation, Nation*

Joseph Harris   P&W
Ann Elmo Literary Agency, 60 E 42 St, New York, NY 10165,
212-661-2880
   Pubs: *Seriously Meeting Karl Shapiro, Life on the Line*
(Negative Capability Pr, 1993, 1992), *Georgia Rev, Prairie
Schooner*

Stephanie Hart   W
Fashion Institute of Technology, 227 W 27 St, New York, NY
10011, 212-760-7994
   Pubs: *Is There Any Way Out of Sixth Grade?* (Coward,
McCann & Geoghegan, 1978), *Mondo James Dean: Anth*
(St. Martin's, 1996), *Caprice*

Yukihide Maeshima Hartman   P
200 W 83 St, #2N
New York, NY 10024, 212-595-3092
   Pubs: *A Coloring Book* (Hanging Loose Pr, 1996), *New
Poems* (Empyreal Pr, 1991), *New Directions, Hanging
Loose, Telephone, Zymerzy, The World*

Steven Hartman   P
1610 Ave P, #6B
Brooklyn, NY 11229
   Pubs: *Pinched Nerves* (CCC, 1992), *Coffeehouse Poetry
Anth* (Bottom Dog Pr, 1996)

George Egon Hatvary   W
61 Jane St, #3B
New York, NY 10014
   Pubs: *The Murder of Edgar Allan Poe* (Carroll & Graf, 1997),
The Suitor (Avon, 1981), *Hawaii Rev, Hawaii Pacific Rev,
Hudson Rev, U Kansas City Rev, Short Story Intl*

Helen Haukeness   W
100 Bank St
New York, NY 10014
Internet: haukeness@aol.com
   Pubs: *Novel Writing: Anth* (Writer's Digest Bks, 1992), *Los
Angeles Times, CSM, NAR*

Marianne Hauser   W
Curtis Brown Ltd, 10 Astor Pl, New York, NY 10003-6935
   Pubs: *Me & My Mom, Prince Ishmael* (Sun & Moon Pr,
1993, 1989), *Fiction Intl, Parnassus*

Michael Hawley   W
642 E 14 St, #11
New York, NY 10009-3384, 212-673-4549
Internet: mhawl@aol.com
   Pubs: *New Yorker, Boston Rev, Sun Dog*

Annette Hayn 🎤   P
225-23 88 Ave
Queens Village, NY 11427, 718-465-8214
   Pubs: *Chamber Music, Enemy on the Way to School* (Poet's
Pr, 2001, 1994), *Caprice, Wind, Antenna, Telephone,
Painted Bride Qtly*

Shirley Hazzard   W
200 E 66 St, #C-1705
New York, NY 10021
   Pubs: *Countenance of Truth, The Transit of Venus* (Viking
Penguin, 1990, 1980), *New Yorker*

Carol Hebald 🎤 ✈   P&W
463 West St, #H660
New York, NY 10014-2036
Internet: chebald@aol.com
   Pubs: *Three Blind Mice & Clara Kleinschmidt* (Unicorn,
1989), *New Letters, Humanist, Antioch Rev, Caprice,
Confrontation, PEN Intl, Massachusetts Rev, Intl Poetry Rev*

Jennifer Michael Hecht 🎤 ✈   P
144 First Ave, #2
New York, NY 10009, 212-674-7526
www.jennifermichaelhecht.com
   Pubs: *The Next Ancient World* (Tupelo Pr, 2001), *Poems to
Live By In Uncertain Times: Anth* (Beacon Pr, 2001), *Best
American Poetry 1999: Anth* (Scribner, 1999), *Denver Qtly,
Antioch Rev, Prairie Schooner, River City, Salmagundi,
Poetry*

Ursula Hegi   W
Brandt & Hochman Literary Agents, 1501 Broadway, New York,
NY 10036
   Pubs: *Trudi and Pia* (Atheneum, 2003), *Hotel of the Saints,
The Vision of Emma Blau, Tearing the Silence: On Being
German in America, Salt Dancers, Stones from the River,
Floating in My Mother's Palm* (S&S, 2001, 2000, 1997,
1995, 1994, 1990)

Larry Heinemann 🎤 ✈   W
Ellen Levine Literary Agency, 15 E 26 St, New York, NY 10010,
212-889-0620
Internet: lheinema@depaul.edu
   Pubs: *Cooler by the Lake, Paco's Story* (FSG, 1992, 1986),
Harper's, Penthouse, Playboy, TriQtly, Van Nghe, Atlantic

George Held 🎤 ✈   P&W
285 W 4 St
New York, NY 10014-2222, 212-989-2591
Internet: geoheld7@aol.com
   Pubs: *Beyond Renewal* (Cedar Hill, 2001), *Open & Shut,
Salamander Love & Others* (Talent Hse Pr, 1999, 1998),
And What Rough Beast: Anth (Ashland Poetry Pr, 1999),
Blue Unicorn, Connecticut Rev, Chariton Rev

Richard Hell   P&W
437 E 12 St, #25
New York, NY 10009
   Pubs: *Artifact* (Hanuman, 1990), *Penguin Book of Rock &
Roll Writing: Anth* (Viking, 1992), *The World, Cuz, Verbal
Abuse, Portable Lower East Side*

Michael Heller 🎤 ✈   P&W
PO Box 1289, Stuyvesant Sta
New York, NY 10009-8953, 212-533-1928
Internet: mh7@nyu.edu
   Pubs: *Wordflow* (Talisman, 1997), *In the Builded Place*
   (Coffee Hse Pr, 1989), *Paris Rev, Conjunctions, Tel Aviv*
   Rev, Ohio Rev, Parnassus

J. V. Hellew 🎤 ✈   P
318 W 100 St, #7-A
New York, NY 10025-5372
Internet: joylyn@msn.com
   Pubs: *NYQ, Diarist's Jrnl, Little Mag, Hollins Critic, Portland*
   Rev, Voices Intl, Avenue

Bob Heman 🎤 ✈   P
PO Box 2165, Church St Sta
New York, NY 10008-2165
   Pubs: *Some Footnotes for the Future* (Luna Bisonte, 1986),
   15 Structures (Incurve Pr, 1986), *Yefief, First Intensity,*
   Caliban, Prose Poem, Artful Dodge, Ant-E-Nym, Juxta, Key
   Satch(el)

David Henderson   P
PO Box 1158, Cooper Sta
New York, NY 10276, 212-978-3901
   Pubs: *The Low East* (North Atlantic Bks, 1981), *Rap & Hip*
   Hop Voices (Pantheon, 1992)

Geoffrey Hendricks   PP
486 Greenwich St
New York, NY 10013
   Pubs: *Sky Anatomy* (Rainer Verlag, 1985), *White Walls*

Donna Henes 🎤 ✈   PP&P
PO Box 380403
Brooklyn, NY 11238-0403, 718-857-2247
Internet: cityshaman@aol.com
   Pubs: *Reverence to Her, Pt I* (CD; Io Prods, 1998),
   Celestially Auspicious Occasions (Perigee, 1996), *Dressing*
   Our Wounds on Warm Clothes (Astro Artz, 1982), *Isis*
   Rising: Anth (Isium Pr, 2000), *Free Spirit, New Visions,*
   Catalyst, Changes

Eileen Hennessy 🎤 ✈   P
PO Box 1470
New York, NY 10185-1470, 212-661-7445
   Pubs: *The Best of Writers at Work: Anth* (Pecan Grove Pr,
   1995), *The Next Parish Over: A Collection of Irish-American*
   Writing: Anth (New Rivers Pr, 1993), *Artful Dodge, Prairie*
   Schooner, Cream City Rev, Nimrod, Confluence, Lullwater
   Rev, SPR, Cimarron Rev

Barbara Henning   P
English Dept, Long Island Univ, University Plaza, Brooklyn, NY
11201, 718-488-1050
Internet: bhenning@phoenix.liu.edu
   Pubs: *Love Makes Thinking Dark, Smoking in the Twilight*
   Bar (United Artists, 1995, 1988), *Lingo, Poet Intl, Paris Rev,*
   Poetry NY, Talisman, Chain, Trois, The World, Fiction Intl,
   Lacanian Ink

Gerrit Henry   P
70 Seventh Ave, #5A
New York, NY 10011-6606
   Pubs: *The Mirrored Clubs of Hell* (Little, Brown, 1991), *The*
   Lecturer's Aria (Groundwater Pr, 1989), *Ecstatic*
   Occasions, Expedient Forms: Anth (Collier Bks, 1987), *Art*
   News, Art in America, Arts, Poetry, Paris Rev, Chelsea,
   Brooklyn Rev, NAW

James Leo Herlihy   W
c/o Jay Garon, 415 Central Pk W, New York, NY 10025

Grace Herman   P
370 1st Ave #9C
New York, NY 10010, 212-982-7197
   Pubs: *Set Against Darkness* (Natl Council of Jewish
   Women, 1992), *Blood & Bone: Poems by Physicians: Anth*
   (U Iowa Pr, 1998), *Anthology #19* (Bay Area Poets Coalition,
   1997), *Lilith Anth* (Jewish Women's Research Ctr, 1994),
   Poetalk, Comstock Rev

Joanna Herman 🎤 ✈   P&W
370 Riverside Dr, #10C
New York, NY 10025, 212-866-8817
Internet: jclapps@worldnet.att.net
   Pubs: *Massachusetts Rev, Kalliope, Crescent Rev, The*
   Critic, Paterson Lit Rev, VIA, Italian Americana, Earth's
   Daughters, Woman's Day

Calvin Hernton   P&W
Marie Brown Assoc Inc, 625 Broadway, New York, NY 10012
   Pubs: *The Sexual Mountain & Black Women Writers*
   (Doubleday/Anchor, 1987)

Ruth Herschberger   P
463 West St
New York, NY 10014-2010, 212-645-6050
www.poets.org/poets/
   Pubs: *Adam's Rib* (H&R, 1970), *Nature & Love Poems*
   (Eakins Pr, 1969), *A Way of Happening* (Pellegrini &
   Cudahy, 1948) *Botteghe Oscure, Kenyon Rev, Poetry*

Stella K. Hershan   W
2 Fifth Ave
New York, NY 10011, 212-533-9759
   Pubs: *The Naked Angel* (Pinnacle Bks, 1977), *Talent,*
   Pirquet Mag

Robert Hershon 🎤 ✈ P
231 Wyckoff St
Brooklyn, NY 11217-2208, 718-643-9559
Internet: print225@aol.com
 Pubs: *The German Lunatic, Into a Punchline: Poems 1984-1994* (Hanging Loose Pr, 2000, 1994), *How to Ride on the Woodlawn Express* (Sun, 1986), *The World, Poetry NW*

Frank Hertle P
401 E 74 St
New York, NY 10021, 212-861-7446
 Pubs: *The Resurrection Stone* (Writers Club Pr, 2001), *Cicada, Blue Unicorn, Gravida, Lake Superior Rev, Voices Intl*

Carol Hill 🎤 ✈ W
2 Fifth Ave, #19-U
New York, NY 10011
Internet: fonzcat@aol.com
 Pubs: *Henry James' Midnight Song* (Poseidon Pr, 1993), *The Eleven Million Mile High Dancer* (H Holt, 1985), *Let's Fall in Love, Jeremiah 8:20* (Random Hse, 1981, 1970)

Donna Hill 🎤 W
530 E 23 St, #6, New York, NY 10010-5029
 Pubs: *Shipwreck Season* (Clarion Bks, 1998), *Eerie Animals: Seven Stories* (Newfield, 1997), *More Stories to Dream On: Anth* (HM, 1993), *Murder Uptown* (Carroll & Graf, 1992), *First Your Penny* (Atheneum, 1985), *Alfred Hitchcock's Mystery Mag, Wreck & Rescue*

Kathleen Hill 🎤 ✈ W
106 Morningside Dr
New York, NY 10027, 212-662-0055
 Pubs: *Still Waters in Niger* (TriQtly Bks, 2002), *Best American Short Stories: Anth* (HM 2000), *DoubleTake, Yale Rev, Hudson Rev, Kenyon Rev, Prairie Schooner*

Daryl Hine 🎤 ✈ P&W
Alfred A Knopf Inc, 201 E 50 St, New York, NY 10022
 Pubs: *Ovid's Heroines* (Yale U Pr, 1991), *Postscripts* (Knopf, 1991)

Edward Hirsch 🎤 ✈ P
John Simon Guggenheim Memorial Fdn, 90 Park Ave, New York, NY 10016, 713-743-2956
 Pubs: *Lay Back The Darkness, On Love, Earthly Measures, The Night Parade, Wild Gratitude* (Knopf, 2003, 1998, 1994, 1989, 1986), *New Yorker, Paris Rev, APR, DoubleTake*

Douglas Hobbie 🎤 ✈ W
Donadio & Olson Inc, 121 W 27 St, Ste 704, New York, NY 10011, 212-691-8077
 Pubs: *This Time Last Year, Being Brett, The Day, Boomfell* (H Holt, 1998, 1996, 1993, 1991)

Rolaine Hochstein 🎤 ✈ W
c/o Emilie Jacobson, Curtis Brown Ltd, 10 Astor Pl, New York, NY 10003-6935
 Pubs: *Table 47* (Doubleday, 1983), *Stepping Out* (Norton, 1977), *O. Henry Prize Stories, Atlantic, NAR, Massachusetts Rev, Antioch Rev, Confrontation, Kalliope, Karamu*

William Hoffman W
Curtis Brown Ltd, 10 Astor Pl, New York, NY 10003-6935
 Pubs: *Tidewater Blood* (Algonquin, 1998), *Follow Me Home, Furors Die* (LSU Pr, 1994, 1990), *O. Henry Prize Stories: Anth* (Doubleday, 1996), *Sewanee Rev, Virginia Qtly Rev, Shenandoah*

William M. Hoffman P
c/o Mitch Douglas, ICM, 40 W 57 St, New York, NY 10019, 212-556-5600
 Pubs: *As Is* (Vintage/Random Hse, 1985), *Gay Plays* (Avon, 1979)

Jill Hoffman P&W
184 Franklin St, Ground Fl
New York, NY 10013, 212-219-9278
 Pubs: *Jilted* (S&S, 1993), *Mink Coat* (HRW, 1973), *New Yorker, New Republic, Mudfish, NW Rev, Now This, Helicon Nine*

Cliff Hogan 🎤 ✈ PP
89-32 88 St
Woodhaven, NY 11421-2529, 718-849-5576
 Pubs: *Waterfalls* (Muse Federation Ink Poets, 1987)

Kam Holifield P
2086 2nd Ave, #20A
New York, NY 10029
 Pubs: *Workshop Poems* (Big Apple Pub, 1989), *Haiku Anth* (Norton, 1999), *Pink Bulldozer: Anth* (Spring Street Haiku Group, 1999), *Timepieces: Anth* (Cloverleaf Bks, 1995), *Haiku Headlines, Frogpond, Vitis Vine, New Press Lit Qtly*

Maureen Holm P
115 W 104 St, #53
New York, NY 10025, 212-864-2823
Internet: MaureenholmNYC@aol.com
 Pubs: *Distance From the Tree: Anth* (Headwaters, 2002), *Drunken Boat, Rattapallax, Southern California Anth, Medicinal Purposes Lit Jrnl, Salonika*

Amy Holman 🎤 ✈ P&W
233 Smith St, #1
Brooklyn, NY 11231
Internet: Aocean63@aol.com
 Pubs: *Vanishing Twin* (Mitki/Mitki Pr, 2002), *Poems for a Beach House: Anth* (Salt Marsh Pottery Pr, 2003), *We the Creatures: Anth* (Dream Horse, 2003), *Best American Poetry 1999: Anth* (Scribner, 1999), *Rattapallax, Del Sol Rev, XConnect, Van Gogh's Ear*

Bob Holman 🎤 ✈   P
c/o Bowery Poetry Club, 308 Bowery, New York, NY 10012,
212-614-0505
Internet: holman@bard.edu
   Pubs: *Beach Simplifies Horizon* (Grenfell Pr, 1999), *In with
the Out Crowd* (Mouth Almighty/Mercury, 1998), *Bob
Holman's Collect Call of the Wild* (H Holt, 1995), *KGB Bar
Book of Poems: Anth* (Perennial, 2000), *Chrysanthemum,
Exquisite Corpse, Bomb, Talisman*

Doloris Holmes 🎤   PP&P
Director, White Mask Theatre/Press, 22 W 30 St, New York, NY
10001, 212-683-9332
Internet: janaiseast@aol.com
   Pubs: *Soul Poems, Upbeat Triangles of Pastime, Poems on
the Brain & Red Feet Too, Lady of the Grape Arbor* (White
Mask Pr, 1999, 1997, 1996, 1991), *Upfront Muse Intl Jrnl*

Darryl Holmes   P
Afrikan Poetry Theatre, 176-03 Jamaica Ave, Jamaica, NY
11432, 718-528-3392
   Pubs: *Wings Will Not Be Broken* (Third World Pr, 1990),
Catalyst Mag

Spencer Holst 🎤 ✈   P&W
55 Bethune St, #313-C
New York, NY 10014, 212-929-5770
   Pubs: *Brilliant Silence: A Book of Paragraphs & Sentences
& 13 Very, Very Short Stories, The Zebra Storyteller:
Collected Stories, Something to Read to Someone* (Station
Hill Pr, 2000, 1993, 1980)

A. M. Homes   W
Wylie Agency, 250 W 57 St, #2106, New York, NY 10107,
212-246-0069
   Pubs: *Things You Should Know, Music for Torching* (HC,
2002, 1999), *The End of Alice* (Scribner, 1996), *In a
Country of Mothers* (Knopf, 1993), *The Safety of Objects*
(Norton, 1990), *Jack* (Vintage, 1990), *New Yorker*

Peter Hood   P
15 Greenway Terr
Forest Hills, NY 11375, 718-263-9640

William Hooker   PP
444 W 52 St, #E
New York, NY 10019
   Pubs: *New Observations*

Susan Hoover 🎤 ✈   P
211 W 10 St, #6D
New York, NY 10014, 212-924-3765
Internet: misterborges@yahoo.com
   Pubs: *The Magnet & the Target* (New School Chapbook
Series, 1995), *Taxi Dancer* (Exotic Beauties Pr, 1977),
*Home Planet News, U Colorado Lit Mag, Granite, Cold
Mountain Rev, Isinglass Rev, Cover/Arts New York*

Doug Hornig   W
Jane Dystel Literary Management, 1 Union Sq W, New York,
NY 10003, 212-627-9100
Internet: jane@ocsny.com
   Pubs: *Stinger, Virus* (NAL, 1990, 1989), *Deep Dive,
Waterman* (Mysterious Pr, 1988, 1987)

Israel Horovitz   P&W
c/o Biff Liff, William Morris Agency, 1325 Ave of the Americas,
New York, NY 10019, 212-586-5100
   Pubs: *Horovitz: Collected Works* (Smith & Kraus, 1994),
Three Gloucester Plays (Doubleday/Fireside, 1993),
L'Avant-Scene

Richard Howard   P
23 Waverly Pl
New York, NY 10003, 212-228-6689
   Pubs: *Like Most Revelations* (Pantheon, 1994), *Trappings*
(Counterpoint, 1998), *No Traveller, Lining Up* (Atheneum
1987, 1983), *Paris Rev, Yale Rev*

Thomas J. Hubschman 🎤   W
473 17 St, #6
Brooklyn, NY 11215-6226
Internet: tjhubsc@dorsai.org
   Pubs: *Space Ark* (Saga SF, 2002), *Billy Boy* (Savvy Pr,
2001), *Space Ark* (Tower, 1981), *Alpha-II* (Manor, 1980),
*BBC World Service, Blue Penny Qtly, New York Pr, In Vivo,
Morpo Rev, Kudzu, Blue Moon Rev*

Vicki Hudspith   P
77 Bleecker St
New York, NY 10012
Internet: turbeville@earthlink.net
   Pubs: *White & Nervous* (Bench Pr, 1982), *Transfer, Mudfish,
Caprice, Pequod, Telephone, The World*

Sophie Hughes   P
49 W 12 St #2H
New York, NY 10011, 212-255-8144
   Pubs: *We Speak for Peace: Anth* (KIT, 1993), *Hollins Critic,
Interim, Potato Eyes, Poet's Edge, NeoVictorian/Cochlea,
Poem, Confrontation, Panhandler, Sidewalks, Echoes,
Writers' Forum, ProCreation*

Ingrid Hughes 🎤   P&W
311 E 9 St, #6
New York, NY 10003-7742, 212-254-0635
   Pubs: *All the Trees in the Ocean* (Pink Granite Pr, 2000),
Women in the Midrash: Anth (Jason Aronson, 1996),
*Birmingham Rev, Negative Capability, Blue Light Rev, West
Branch, Mudfish, Bad Henry, MPR, Massachusetts Rev*

Josephine Humphreys   W
Harriet Wasserman Literary Agency, 137 E 36 St, New York,
NY 10016
   Pubs: *The Fireman's Fair, Rich in Love, Dreams of Sleep*
(Viking, 1991, 1987, 1984)

Evan Hunter W
c/o Jane Gelfman, Gelfman Schneider Literary Agents, Inc.,
250 W 57 St, New York, NY 10107, 212-245-1993
   Pubs: *Fat Ollie's Book, The Moment She was Gone, Money,
Money, Money, Candyland, The Blackboard Jungle* (S&S,
2002, 2002, 2001, 2001, 1954)

Christian X. Hunter P&W
166 Suffolk St #C
New York, NY 10002, 212-228-7864
Internet: cxhunter@onepine.com
   Pubs: *Crimes of the Beats: Anth* (Autonomedia, 1998),
Verses That Hurt: Anth (St. Martin's Pr, 1997), *Ikon, Red
Tape, The World, Portable Lower East Side, Sensitive Skin,
New York Pr*

Jerrie W. Hurd ♦ ✈ W
Jane Chelius Literary Agency, 548 2 St, Brooklyn, NY 11215,
718-499-0236
Internet: jerriehurd@aol.com
   Pubs: *RavenEyed, HoopSnaked, Lady Pinkerton Gets Her
Man, Kate Bourke Shoots the Old West, Miss Ellie's Purple
Sage Saloon* (Pocket Bks, 2002, 2001, 1998, 1997, 1995),
Kansas Qtly, Antioch Rev

Johanna Hurwitz ♦ ✈ W
10 Spruce Pl
Great Neck, NY 11021, 516-829-6205
Internet: imhur@yahoo.com
   Pubs: *Peewee & Plush, Peewee's Tale* (North South, 2002,
2000), *Dear Emma, One Small Dog* (HC, 2002, 2000),
Faraway Summer (Morrow Junior Bks, 1998)

Eleanor Hyde W
343 E 74 St, #12L
New York, NY 10021, 212-861-2116
   Pubs: *Animal Instincts, In Murder We Trust* (Fawcett Bks,
1996, 1995), *Arizona Qtly, Cosmopolitan, Satire*

Colette Inez ♦ ✈ P
5 W 86 St
New York, NY 10024, 212-874-2009
   Pubs: *Clemency* (Carnegie Mellon U Pr, 1998), *Getting
Underway: New & Selected Poetry, Family Life* (Story Line
Pr, 1993, 1992), *Paris Rev, Barrow Street, Poetry NW,
Tamene, Kenyon Rev, Hudson Rev, Partisan Rev, Iowa Rev,
Ploughshares, Prairie Schooner*

Elizabeth Inness-Brown ♦ ✈ W
Carlisle & Co., 24 E 64 St, New York, NY 10021, 212-813-1881
Internet: mvc@carlisleco.com
   Pubs: *Burning Marguerite* (Knopf, 2002), *Here* (LSU, 1994),
Satin Palms (Fiction Intl Pr, 1981), *New Yorker, Glimmer
Train, Boulevard, NAR, Cream City Rev, Mississippi Rev,
Sycamore Rev*

Carole Ione ♦ ✈ P
Melanie Jackson Agency, 250 W 57 St, New York, NY 10107,
212-582-8585
www.deeplistening.org/ione
   Pubs: *This Is a Dream* (M.O.H. Pr, 2000), *Piramida Negra,
Selected Poems* (Live Letters Pr, 1991), *Pride of Family*
(Summit Bks, 1991), *The Night Train to Aswan: Anth* (Neterv
Edtns, 1998), *Spirits of the Passage: Anth* (S&S, 1997)

Susan Isaacs W
c/o Owen Laster, William Morris Agency, 1325 Ave of the
Americas, New York, NY 10019
   Pubs: *Shining Through, Almost Paradise* (H&R, 1988, 1984)

Rashidah Ismaili ♦ ✈ P
1851 Adam Clayton Powell Blvd
New York, NY 10026, 212-222-8631
   Pubs: *Missing in Action & Presumed Dead* (Africa World Pr,
1992), *Oniybo* (Shamal, 1986), *African Women: Anth*
(Heineman, 1995), *Soul Looks Back In Wonder: Anth* (Dial
Books, 1993), *Black Renaissance*

Peter Israel W
Georges Borchardt Inc, 136 E 57 St, New York, NY 10022,
212-753-5785

Philip Israel W
257 Beach 130 St
Belle Harbor, NY 11694, 718-945-0680
   Pubs: *Me & Brenda* (Norton, 1990), *Carlton Miscellany,
Transatlantic Rev*

Beverly Jablons ♦ W
63 E 9 St, #9K
New York, NY 10003-6334
   Pubs: *Dance Time* (Berkley, 1981), *Midstream, NAR*

Sheila Cathryn Jackson PP&P
PO Box 7554, FDR Sta
New York, NY 10150
   Pubs: *WomanStuff* (La Mama La Galleria, 1993), *Letters
from Texas* (New Works Project, 1993), *Manhattan Class Co
Theatre, Playwrights' Ctr*

Gale P. Jackson ♦ ✈ P&W
180 Prospect Park W
Brooklyn, NY 11215
Internet: stormimpri@aol.com
   Pubs: *Khoisan Tale of Beginnings & Ends, Bridge Suite:
Narrative Poems* (Storm Imprints, 1998, 1998), *Poets at
Work: Anth* (Just Buffalo Lit Ctr, 1996), *American Voice,
Ploughshares, Ikon, Callaloo, Black American Lit, Kenyon
Rev*

Mae Jackson   P
165 Clinton Ave, #2G
Brooklyn, NY 11205, 718-237-0762
    Pubs: *Can I Poet with You* (Broadside Pr, 1970), *Black
    Scholar, Essence, Encore, Nimrod*

Louise Jaffe 🎤 ✈   P
2411 E 3 St, #3E
Brooklyn, NY 11223, 718-998-0038
    Pubs: *Wisdom Revisited* (Adams Pr, 1987), *Which Lilith:
    Anth* (Jason Aronson, 1998), *Jewish Women's Literary
    Annual, Mid-Amer Poetry Rev, Buckle &, Iambs and
    Trochees, Medicinal Purposes, American Poets & Poetry,
    Sunday Suitor, New Press Lit Qtly*

John Jakes   W
Rembar & Curtis Attorneys, 19 W 44 St, New York, NY 10036
Internet: jjfiction@aol.com
    Pubs: *Charleston, On Secret Service, American Dreams*
    (Dutton, 2002, 2000, 1998), *Homeland* (Doubleday, 1993),
    In the Big Country: The Best Western Stories of John Jakes
    (Bantam, 1993), *Parade Mag*

Kelvin Christopher James 🎤 ✈   W
1295 5th Ave, #32F
New York, NY 10029
    Pubs: *A Fling with a Demon Lover* (HC, 1996), *Secrets,
    Jumping Ship & Other Stories* (Villard Bks, 1993, 1992),
    Leave to Stay: Anth (Virago, 1996), *Children of the Night:
    Anth* (Little, Brown, 1995), *Low Rent: Anth* (Grove Pr, 1994)

Elizabeth Janeway   W
350 E 79 St #8D
New York, NY 10021-9204

Ronald Wiley Janoff 🎤 ✈   P
1 Washington Sq Village, #15A
New York, NY 10012-1610, 212-995-8791
Internet: rwj1@nyu.edu
    Pubs: *Choice, Modern Poetry Studies, Abraxas, Hanging
    Loose, First Issue, Purchase Poetry Rev*

Tama Janowitz 🎤 ✈   W
c/o Betsy Lerner, The Gernet Co, 136 E 57 St, New York, NY
10022, 212-838-6467
    Pubs: *Area Code 212* (Bloomsbury U.K., 2002), *A Certain
    Age* (Doubleday/Anchor, 1998), *By the Shores of Gitchi
    Gumee, The Male Cross-Dresser Support Group* (Crown,
    1996, 1992), *New Yorker*

Lisa Jarnot   P
PO Box 185, Stuyvesant Sta, New York, NY 10009,
718-802-9575
    Pubs: *screens & tasted parallels, Black Bread, o.blek*

Gish Jen   W
Maxine Groffsky Literary Agency, 853 Broadway Ste 708, New
York, NY 10003
Internet: mgroffsley@aol.com
    Pubs: *Who's Irish* (Knopf 1999), *Mona in the Promised Land*
    (Knopf 1996), *Typical American* (HM 1991)

Ruth Prawer Jhabvala   W
400 E 52 St #7G
New York, NY 10022
    Pubs: *East Into Upper East* (Counterpoint, 1998), *Shards of
    Memory* (Doubleday, 1995), *Three Continents, Out of India,
    In Search of Love & Beauty* (Morrow, 1987, 1986, 1983),
    Counterpoint

Vita Marie Jimenez   P
567 81 St
Brooklyn, NY 11209, 718-630-5440
    Pubs: *To Grow Grapes, The Courtship of Mickey & Minnie* (A
    Little Pr, 1998, 1990), *Crunchy, Munchy Cookies* (Newbridge
    Comm, 1993), *The World, Poetry Project Newsletter,
    Hanging Loose*

Jacqueline Joan Johnson   P
Marie Brown Assoc Inc, 625 Broadway, New York, NY 10012,
718-574-4475
    Pubs: *A Gathering of Mother Tongues* (White Pine Pr,
    1998), *Beyond the Frontier* (Black Classical Pr, 1998), *Drum
    Voices* (U St. Louis Pr, 1994), *Streetlights: Illuminating Tales
    of the Urban Black Experience: Anth* (Viking Penguin, 1996),
    River Styx

Fenton Johnson   W
Malaga Baldi Literary Agency, 204 W 84th St, Suite 3C, New
York, NY 10024
Internet: johnfenton@aol.com
    Pubs: *Geography of the Heart* (Scribner, 1996), *Scissors,
    Paper, Rock* (Washington Square Pr, 1996), *Virginia Qtly
    Rev, Mother Jones, Sewanee Rev*

Halvard Johnson 🎤 ✈   P
55 Bethune St, #610C
New York, NY 10014, 212-691-2764
Internet: halvard@earthlink.net
    Pubs: *American Dispora: Anth* (Univ of Iowa Pr, 2001),
    Mixed Voices, This Sporting Life (Milkweed Edtns, 1991,
    1987), *Poethia, Sugar Mule, Valparaiso Rev, Florida Rev,
    Can We Have Our Ball Back, Tattoo Highway, Blue Moon
    Rev, CrossConnect, Poetry NY*

Judith E. Johnson   PP&P&W
890 W End Ave, #1A
New York, NY 10025, 212-866-2639
    Pubs: *The Ice Lizard* (Sheep Meadow Pr, 1992), *The Waste
    Trilogy* (Countryman Pr, 1979), *Partisan Rev, New Yorker,
    Little Mag, Hudson Rev, Caprice, Frontiers*

Tom Johnson P
Two-Eighteen Press, PO Box 218, Village Sta, New York, NY
10014-0218
Pubs: *The Voice of New Music* (Het Apollohuis, 1989),
Imaginary Music: Anth (Two-Eighteen Pr, 1976), *Unmuzzled
Ox, Black Box*

Kate K. Johnson 🎤 P
Sarah Lawrence College, Bronxville, NY 10708, 914-395-2316
Pubs: *Wind Somewhere, & Shade, This Perfect Life* (Miami
U Pr, 2001, 1993), *When Orchids Were Flowers* (Dragon
Gate, 1986), *Ploughshares, The Sun, Salt Jrnl, Luna,
Bloomsbury Rev, Decade, Poetry, One Meadway*

J. Chester Johnson 🎤 ✈ P
315 E 86 St, #16GE
New York, NY 10028-4780, 212-831-5063
Internet: jchester.gfa@prodigy.net
Pubs: *Curate's Chorus, Lazarus* (Juliet Pr, 1998, 1993), *Intl
Poetry Rev, Pegasus, The Iconoclast, Potpourri, Choice, NY
Times, SPR, Parnassus*

Nicholas Johnson 🎤 ✈ P
141 Huntington St
Brooklyn, NY 11231, 718-624-7305
Pubs: *Second Word Thursdays Anth* (Bright Hill Pr, 1999),
Anth of Magazine Verse & Yearbook of American Poetry
(Monitor Bk Co, 1997), *Men of Our Time: Anth* (U Georgia
Pr, 1992), *APR, Rattle, Rattapallax, The Jrnl, Pivot, Poetry
Wales, Troubadour, AL&C*

Gary Johnston 🎤 ✈ P
Blind Beggar Press, PO Box 437, Williamsbridge Sta, Bronx,
NY 10467
Pubs: *Crossings, Two* (Blind Beggar Pr, 1995, 1994), *Bum
Rush the Page: Anth* (Three Rivers Pr, 2001), *New Rain,
African Voices, Black Nation*

Gerald Jonas P
70 W 95 St, #5H
New York, NY 10025, 212-864-3949
Internet: GJonas1004@aol.com
Pubs: *Dancing* (Harry Abrams, 1992), *Poetry*

Hettie Jones 🎤 ✈ W
27 Cooper Sq
New York, NY 10003, 212-473-5193
Pubs: *Drive* (Hanging Loose Pr, 1998), *How I Became
Hettie Jones* (Grove Pr, 1996), *Big Star Fallin' Mama* (Viking,
1995), *Hanging Loose, Ploughshares, Global City Rev*

Kaylie Jones 🎤 ✈ W
Lantz-Harris Literary Agency, 156 5th Ave, Ste 617, New York,
NY 10010, 212-924-6269
Internet: kayliej@mindspring.com
Pubs: *Celeste Ascending, A Soldier's Daughter Never Cries*
(HC, 2000, 1998), *Quite the Other Way* (Doubleday, 1989)

Patricia Spears Jones 🎤 ✈ P
426 Sterling Pl, #1C
Brooklyn, NY 11238, 718-399-2356
Pubs: *Blood & Tears* (Painted Leaf Pr, 1999), *Poetry After
9/11: An Anthology of New York Poets* (Melville House,
2002), *Bum Rush the Page: A Def Poetry Jam: Anth* (Three
Rivers Pr, 2001), *Barrow St, Ploughshares, Crazy Horse*

JEM Jones McNeil 🎤 P&W
The Picture Poet, PO Box 23144, Hollis, NY 11423
Pubs: *Veiled Truths, Travelin on Faith/Travelin on Credit*
(Jones, 1992, 1982), *The Nubian Gallery: A Poetry Anth*
(Blacfax, 2002), *Poetry in Motion, Soldiers of the Light,
Blacfax Mag*

Erica Mann Jong P&W
c/o K D Burrows, 425 Park Ave, New York, NY 10022-5739,
212-980-6922
Pubs: *Fear of Fifty, Becoming Light* (HC, 1994, 1991)

Joanne Joseph 🎤 ✈ P
770 Amsterdam Ave, #4N
New York, NY 10025, 212-840-1234
Internet: joannejoseph@juno.com
Pubs: *Polaris Studio North, NYQ, Dirty Goat*

Stephen M. Joseph W
270 1st Ave, #8E
New York, NY 10009, 212-254-5078
Pubs: *Children in Fear* (HR&W, 1974), *The Me Nobody
Knows* (Avon, 1969)

Lawrence Joseph 🎤 ✈ P
St. John's Univ Law School, Jamaica, NY 11439,
718-990-6014
Pubs: *Lawyerland, Before Our Eyes* (FSG, 1997, 1993),
Curriculum Vitae, Shouting at No One (U Pitt Pr, 1988, 1983)

Ellen Kahaner W
79-10 34 Ave #4Y
Jackson Heights, NY 11372
Pubs: *Fourth Grade Loser* (Troll Inc, 1992), *Motorcycles*
(Capstone Pr, 1991), *Growing Up Female* (Rosen Pubs,
1991)

Anna Kainen P
689 Columbus Ave, #14B
New York, NY 10025
Pubs: *Whispers* (New York Poetry Fdn, 1986), *I Am Woman*
(Anna Kainen, 1983), *Plowman, The Qtly*

Layding Kaliba P
60 E 135 St, Apt 7C
New York, NY 10037, 212-690-2472
Pubs: *The Moon Is My Witness, Up on the Down Side*
(Single Action Prods, 1988, 1982)

Robert Kalich   W
240 Central Pk S
New York, NY 10019-1413
   Pubs: *A Twin Life* (Kudansha, 2002), *The Handicapper*
(Crown, 1981)

Laura Kalpakian 🎤 ✈   W
c/o Gelfman/Schneider, 250 W 57th St, New York, NY 10107,
212-245-1993
   Pubs: *Educating Waverly* (Morrow, 2002), *Steps and Exes*
(Avon, 2000), *Delinquent Variations* (Graywolf, 1999),
Caveat (J F Blair, 1998)

Marc Kaminsky   P
291 11th St
Brooklyn, NY 11215, 718-788-0250
   Pubs: *Target Populations* (Central Park Edtns, 1991), *The
Road from Hiroshima* (S&S, 1984), *Sun*

Linda Kampley   P
407 W 50 St, #3
New York, NY 10019
   Pubs: *Widener Rev, Soundings East, Connecticut River Rev,
Panhandler, Voices Intl, Cream City Rev*

Alan Kapelner   W
40 King St, #1A
New York, NY 10014, 212-242-7496
   Pubs: *All the Naked Heroes* (Braziller, 1965), *Lonely Boy
Blues* (Scribner, 1950), *New Voices*

Johanna Kaplan 🎤   W
411 W End Ave, #11E
New York, NY 10024-5722
   Pubs: *O My America!* (Syracuse U Pr, 1995), *Other People's
Lives* (Knopf, 1975), *Commentary*

Robert Kaplan   P&W
300 W 23 St, #14D
New York, NY 10011, 212-242-8687
Internet: rkaplan1@email.gc.cuny.edu
   Pubs: *A Loving Testimonial: Remembering Loved Ones Lost
to AIDS: Anth* (Crossing Pr, 1995), *Beyond Definition: Anth*
(Manic D Pr, 1994), *Evergreen Chronicles, Modern Words,
Anemone, Amethyst, RFD: A Country Jrnl for Gay Men
Everywhere, New Leaves Rev*

Allan Kaplan   P
45 Christopher St, #16G
New York, NY 10014
Internet: akaplan@worldnet.att.net
   Pubs: *Paper Airplane* (H&R, 1972), *Slant, Chiron Rev,
Washington Square Rev, GW Rev, Folio, Fine Madness,
Green Hills Lit Lantern, Wind, Hubbub, Gulf Stream,
Panhandler, Half Tones to Jubilee*

Arno Karlen   P&W
350 Bleecker St, #1P
New York, NY 10014
   Pubs: *New Letters, Antioch Rev*

Mollyne Karnofsky 🎤 ✈   PP
515 E 88 St, #1D
New York, NY 10128-7743, 212-517-8607
Internet: mkarnart@aol.com
   Pubs: *Places and Spaces* (Performance; Gallery X, 2002),
Collide: A Scope (Performance; Chuck Levitan Art Gallery,
1998), *Elemental Sounds/Equinox Life Line* (Performance;
Anth Film Archives, 1996)

Vickie Karp 🎤 ✈   P
Thirteen/WNET, 450 W 33 St, New York, NY 10001,
212-560-3123
Internet: karp@thirteen.org
   Pubs: *A Taxi to the Flame* (U South Carolina, 1999), *KGB
Bar Reader: Anth* (HC, 2000), *Best American Poetry: Anths*
(Macmillan, 1991, 1989), *New Yorker, New Republic, New
York Rev, Yale Rev, Paris Rev*

Jean Karsavina   W
c/o Knox Burger, 425 Madison Ave, New York, NY
10017-1110, 212-289-2368
   Pubs: *White Eagle, Dark Skies* (Scribner, 1975), *Tree by the
Water* (Young World Bks, 1949)

Samuel Kashner 🎤 ✈   P
c/o Sobel Weber Assoc.
146 E 19 St, New York, NY 10003
   Pubs: *Sinatraland* (Overlook Pr, 2000), *Don Quixote in
America, Hanging Loose 20 Year Anth* (Hanging Loose Pr,
1997, 1988), *Harvard Mag, riverrun, Verse, Salamander,
Mudfish, William & Mary Rev*

Ben Katchor   W
PO Box 2024, Cathedral Sta, New York, NY 10025,
212-665-8913
Internet: bkatchor@spacelab.net
   Pubs: *The Jew of New York* (Pantheon, 1999), *Julius Knipl,
Real Estate Photographer* (Little, Brown, 1996), *Cheap
Novelties* (Penguin, 1991), *D.C. City Paper, Forward, San
Francisco Weekly, Chicago New City, Metropolis Mag, River
Front Times*

Eliot Katz 🎤 ✈   P
Old Chelsea Sta, PO Box 1621, New York, NY 10113
Internet: unlcokingexits@earthlink.net
   Pubs: *Unlocking the Exits* (Coffee Hse Pr, 1999), *Space &
Other Poems for Love, Laughs, & Social Transformation*
(Northern Lights, 1990), *Poems for the Nation: Anth* (Seven
Stories Pr, 2000)

Leandro Katz PP
25 E 4 St
New York, NY 10003, 212-260-4254
    Pubs: *Death Trip* (Turt, 1990), *27 Windmills* (Viper's
Tongue, 1986)

Vincent Katz 🎤 ✈ P
211 W 19 St, 5 Fl
New York, NY 10011-4001
Internet: vincent@el.net
    Pubs: *Pearl* (PowerHouse Bks, 1998), *Boulevard
Transportation* (Tibor de Nagy Edtns, 1997), *Cabal of
Zealots* (Hanuman, 1988), *Carnegie Intl 1999/2000 Artists'
Reader, Bomb, Exquisite Corpse, New Censorship, Little
More, The World, The Fred, Ars Electronica*

Andrew Kaufman 🎤 ✈ P
585 Isham St #4E
New York, NY 10034, 212-304-8657
    Pubs: *Cinnamon Bay Sonnets* (Ctr for Book Arts, 1996),
*Atlanta Rev, Skid Row, Penthouse, Riversedge, Anth of Mag
Verse & Yearbook of American Poetry, Massachusetts Rev,
College English, Spoon River Poetry Rev, Crazyhorse*

Bel Kaufman W
1020 Park Ave, #20-A
New York, NY 10028, 212-288-8783
    Pubs: *Up the Down Staircase* (HC, 1991), *Love, Etc.*
(Prentice Hall, 1981), *Esquire, McCall's, Commonweal, New
Choices, Ladies' Home Jrnl, Saturday Rev of Lit, Today's
Education*

Rebecca Kavaler 🎤 ✈ W
425 Riverside Dr
New York, NY 10025, 212-865-4632
    Pubs: *A Little More Than Kin* (Hamilton Stone Edtns, 2002),
Tigers in the Wood (U Illinois Pr, 1986), *Doubting Castle*
(Schocken, 1984), *The Further Adventures of Brunhild* (U
Missouri Pr, 1978), *Carolina Qtly*

Marvin Kaye W
c/o Donald C Maass, Donald Maass Literary Agency, 157 W
57 St, Ste 1003, New York, NY 10019
    Pubs: *Fantastique* (St. Martin's Pr, 1993), *Ghosts of Night &
Morning, A Cold Blue Light* (Berkley, 1987, 1983)

Melanie Kaye/Kantrowitz P&W
922 8th Ave #3B
Brooklyn, NY 11215, 718-788-5333
Internet: mkk@netstep.net
    Pubs: *My Jewish Face & Other Stories* (Aunt Lute, 1990),
*Sinister Wisdom, Calyx, Bridges, Tikkun, Sojourner,
Women's Rev of Bks, Gay Community News*

Meg Kearney 🎤 P
National Book Fdn, 260 5th Ave Rm 904, New York, NY
10001, 212-685-0261
Internet: raven6364@aol.com
    Pubs: *An Unkindness of Ravens* (BOA Edtns, 2001), *Urban
Nature: Anth* (Milkweed, 2000), *Gettysburg Rev,
Ploughshares, DoubleTake, Agni, Black Warrior Rev, Third
Coast, Washington Square, Sycamore Rev, Florida Rev,
Pivto, Free Lunch, Passages North*

Celine Keating W
697 W End Ave, #5D
New York, NY 10025-6823,
212-666-9174
    Pubs: *North Stone Rev, Emry's Jrnl, Appearances, Echoes,
Prairie Schooner, Santa Clara Rev*

John Keeble 🎤 ✈ W
c/o Denise Shannon, ICM, 40 W 57 St, New York, NY 10019,
212-556-6727
Internet: jkeeble@mail.ewu.edu
    Pubs: *Out of the Channel* (HC, 1991), *Broken Ground* (H&R,
1987), *Outside*

Edmund Keeley 🎤 ✈ P&W
Georges Borchardt Inc, 136 E 57 St, New York, NY 10022,
212-753-5785
Internet: keeley@princeton.edu
    Pubs: *Some Wine for Remembrance* (White Pine Pr, 2001),
School for Pagan Lovers (Rutgers U Pr, 1993),
*Ploughshares, Antaeus, Harvard Rev, Mediterraneans, Intl
Qtly, TriQtly, Ontario Rev, Seattle Rev*

Joyce Keener W
Sarah Lazin Books, 126 5th Ave, Ste 300, New York, NY
10011, 212-989-5757
    Pubs: *Limits of Eden, Borderline* (Ace Bks, 1981, 1979),
Womanblood: Anth (Continuing Saga, 1981)

Tsipi Edith Keller P&W
235 E 40th St, #30-D
New York, NY 10016, 212-983-6104
Internet: tsipik@juno.com
    Pubs: *Leverage, The Prophet of Tenth Street* (Israel; Sifriat
Poalim, 1997, 1995), *Vintage Bk of Contemporary Poetry:
Anth* (Vintage Bks, 1996), *Partisan Rev, Seneca Rev, Prairie
Schooner, Between C&D, Minetta Rev, MPR, Mildred,
Present Tense, Cream City Rev*

William Melvin Kelley W
c/o The Wisdom Shop, PO Box 2658, New York, NY 10027
    Pubs: *A Different Drummer* (Doubleday, 1973)

William Kennedy W
Darhansoff & Verrill Agency, 1220 Park Ave, New York, NY
10128, 212-534-2479
    Pubs: *Very Old Bones, Quinn's Book, Ironweed* (Viking,
1992, 1988, 1983)

Raymond Kennedy   W
English Dept/Lewisohn Hall 615, Columbia Univ, New York, NY 10027
   Pubs: *The Bittersweet Age, Ride a Cockhorse* (Ticknor & Fields, 1994, 1991), *Lulu Incognito* (Vintage, 1988), *The Flower of the Republic* (Knopf, 1983)

Eileen Kennedy   P&W
631 E 23 St
Brooklyn, NY 11210
Internet: tcd543@aol.com
   Pubs: *Poetic License, Hodgepodge, Creative Juices, Northern Stars*

Bliem Kern   P
230 Riverside Dr, #15CC
New York, NY 10025-6172
   Pubs: *Temple of Sound, Hail Jupiter* (La Maison de la Bleame, 1995, 1995), *Spiritual Unity of Nations, Ingress, Ararita*

Katharine Kidde 🎤 ✈   P
335 E 51 St, #1G
New York, NY 10022, 212-755-9461
   Pubs: *Early Sky* (Writers Ink, 2002), *Sounding for Light* (Linear Arts, 1998), *Home Light: Along the Shore* (North Atlantic Rev, 1994), *NAR, Pegasus, Context South, Long Island Qtly, Maryland Poetry Rev, Whelks Walk Rev, Whole Notes*

Jamaica Kincaid   W
Farrar, Straus & Giroux, 19 Union Sq W, New York, NY 10003
   Pubs: *My Brother, A Small Place, At the Bottom of the River* (FSG, 1997, 1988, 1983), *Lucy, Annie John* (NAL, 1991, 1986)

Basil King 🎤 ✈   P&W
326-A 4 St
Brooklyn, NY 11215, 718-788-7927
   Pubs: *Identity, Ward Spasm* (Spuyten Duyvil, 2000, 2000), *The Complete Miniatures, Devotions* (Stop Pr, 1997), *Split Peas* (Zealot Pr, 1986), *Poetry NY, Synaesthetic, First Intensity, Box Kite*

Martha King 🎤 ✈   P
326-A 4 St
Brooklyn, NY 11215, 718-788-7927
Internet: gpwitd@aol.com
   Pubs: *Little Tales of Family & War* (Spuyten Duyvil, 2000), *Seventeen Walking Sticks* (Stop Pr, 1998), *The Taking of Hands: Anth* (New Rivers Pr, 1999), *House Organ, Poetry Project Newsletter, NAW, Bomb, Salt Lick, Carbuncle*

Gloria Devidas Kirchheimer 🎤 ✈   W
210 W 101 St, #15G
New York, NY 10025
   Pubs: *Goodbye, Evil Eye* (Holmes & Meier, 2000), *We Were So Beloved: Autobiography of a German Jewish Community* (U Pitt, 1997), *With Signs and Wonders: Anth* (Invisible Cities Pr, 2001)

Karl Kirchwey 🎤 ✈   P
54 Morningside Dr, #43
New York, NY 10025-1760, 212-316-0130
   Pubs: *At the Palace of Jove* (Putnam, 2002), *The Engrafted Word* (Holt, 1998), *Those I Guard* (HB, 1993), *A Wandering Island* (Princeton U Pr, 1990), *Best of the Best American Poetry 1988-1997: Anth* (Scribner, 1998), *Parnassus, New Yorker, New Republic, Nation*

Binnie Kirshenbaum 🎤 ✈   W
84 Charles St, #18
New York, NY 10014
Internet: binniex@aol.com
   Pubs: *Hester Among the Ruins* (Norton, 2002), *Pure Poetry* (S&S, 2000), *A Disturbance in One Place, On Mermaid Avenue* (Fromm Intl, 1994, 1993), *NER, BLQ, Mid-American Rev, Indiana Rev*

William Kistler   P
101 W 79 St, #22C
New York, NY 10024, 212-874-6150
   Pubs: *Notes Drawn from the River of Ecstasy, America February, The Elizabeth Sequence* (Council Oak Bks, 1996, 1991, 1989), *Poems of the Known World* (Arcade Pubs, 1995), *APR, Antaeus, Poetry Flash, Poetry Intl, New Criterion, New Directions Annual, Harper's*

Myra Klahr 🎤 ✈   P
40 E 9 St, #12L
New York, NY 10003, 212-505-2606
Internet: lingosmart@earthlink.net
   Pubs: *The Waiting Room* (Fiddlehead Pr, 1972), *Caprice, Sesheta, Unicorn, Hanging Loose, Squeezebox*

Sheila Solomon Klass 🎤 ✈   W
Elaine Markson Literary Agency, 44 Greenwhich Ave, New York, NY 10011
   Pubs: *Little Women Next Door, The Uncivil War, A Shooting Star* (Holiday Hse, 2000, 1997, 1996), *In a Cold Open Field* (Black Heron Pr, 1997), *Next Stop Nowhere, Rhino, Kool Ada* (Scholastic, 1995, 1993, 1991)

Irena Klepfisz   P
155 Atlantic Ave
Brooklyn, NY 11201, 718-855-2905
Internet: irkegoles@aol.com
   Pubs: *A Few Words in the Mother Tongue: Poems Selected & New* (Eighth Mountain Pr, 1990), *The Tribe of Dina: A Jewish Women's Anth* (Beacon, 1989), *Bridges, Ms.*

Nancy Kline 🎤 ✈ W
540 Prospect Ave
Brooklyn, NY 11215
    Pubs: *The Faithful* (Morrow, 1968), *Chelsea, Massachusetts Rev, Ascent, Playgirl, Boston Globe Sunday Mag, Nantucket Rev, Colorado Qtly, Weber Studies*

Jay Klokker P
311 E 9 St
New York, NY 10003
    Pubs: *Devil's Millhopper, BPJ, Bellingham Rev, Hanging Loose, State Street Rev*

Alison Knowles PP&P
122 Spring St
New York, NY 10012, 212-226-5703
    Pubs: *Event Scores* (Left Hand Bks, 1992), *A Bean Concordance* (Printed Edtns, 1983), *Aperture, New Wilderness*

John Knowles W
Curtis Brown Ltd, 10 Astor Pl, New York, NY 10003-6935, 212-473-5400
    Pubs: *A Stolen Past* (HRW, 1983), *Spreading Fires* (Random Hse, 1974), *A Separate Peace* (Macmillan, 1960), *Playboy, Esquire*

Stephen Koch 🎤 ✈ W
Carlisle & Co, 24 E 64 St, New York, NY 10021, 212-813-1881
Internet: stephenkoch41@msn.com
    Pubs: *The Bachelor's Bride* (Marion Boyars, 1986)

Ronald Koertge 🎤 ✈ P
c/o William Reiss, John Hawkins & Assoc, 71 W 23 St, Ste 1600, New York, NY 10010, 212-807-7040
Internet: ronkoe@earthlink.net
    Pubs: *Stoner & Spaz, The Brimstone Journals* (Candlewick Bks, 2002, 2001), *Geography of the Forehead, Making Love to Roget's Wife* (U Arkansas Pr, 2000, 1997)

Wayne Koestenbaum 🎤 ✈ P
c/o Faith Hamlin, Sanford J Greenburger Assoc, 55 Fifth Ave, New York, NY 10003
Internet: wkoestenbaum@aol.com
    Pubs: *The Milk of Inquiry, Rhapsodies of a Repeat Offender, Ode to Anna Moffo & Other Poems* (Persea, 2000, 1994, 1990), *New Yorker, Paris Rev, APR, Yale Rev*

Sheila Kohler 🎤 ✈ W
150 Columbus Ave. # 26A
New York, NY 10023, 212-362-6281
Internet: sheilakohler@hotmail.com
    Pubs: *The Children of Pithiviers* (Zoland, 2001), *One Girl* (Helicon Nine Edtns, 1999), *The House on R Street, The Perfect Place* (Knopf, 1994, 1989), *Miracles in America* (Vintage UK, 1990), *Best American Fiction: Anth* (HM, 1999)

Sybil Kollar 🎤 ✈ P&W
10 Clinton St, #11L
Brooklyn, NY 11201-2708, 718-858-4749
Internet: sybkollar@aol.com
    Pubs: *In Rooms We Come & Go* (Somers Rocks Pr, 1998), *Party Train: Anth* (New Rivers Pr, 1996), *Rattapallax, 5AM, Confrontation, Columbia, American Voice, Pivot, Lit Rev*

Edith Konecky 🎤 ✈ W
511 E 20 St, #9G
New York, NY 10010, 212-228-2253
    Pubs: *Allegra Maud Goldman* (Feminist Pr, 2001), *Past Sorrows and Coming Attractions, A Place at the Table* (Hamilton Stone Eds, 2001, 2000)

Hans Koning P&W
Frances Goldin Agency, 57 E 11th St, #5B, New York, NY 10003
    Pubs: *DeWitt's War: Bk,* (Pantheon, 1983), *America Made Me: Bk,* (Thunder's Mouth Pr, 1983), *Pursuit of a Woman: Bk,* (Brookline Bks, 1998), *The New Yorker, Partisan Rev*

Jean Hanff Korelitz 🎤 ✈ P&W
c/o Suzanne Gluck, William Morris Agency, 1325 Ave of the Americas, New York, NY 10019, 212-903-1169
    Pubs: *The Sabbathday River* (FSG, 1999), *A Jury of Her Peers* (Crown, 1996), *The Properties of Breath* (Bloodaxe/Dufour, 1988)

Richard Kostelanetz PP&P&W
PO Box 444, Prince St Sta, New York, NY 10012-0008
    Pubs: *Wordworks: Poems Selected & New* (BOA Edtns, 1993), *The New Poetries & Some Old* (Southern Illinois, 1991)

Dean Kostos 🎤 ✈ P&W
211 W 21 St, #5-W
New York, NY 10011-3144, 212-255-6860
Internet: Mayos2000@aol.com
    Pubs: *The Sentence that Ends with a Comma, Blood & Tears: Anth* (Painted Leaf, 1999, 1999), *Celestial Rust* (Red Dust, 1994), *Rattapallax, Anthropophagy.com, SW Rev, Boulevard, James White Rev, Poetry NY, Barrow Street, Chiron Rev*

Robert Kotlowitz 🎤 ✈ W
54 Riverside Dr
New York, NY 10024-6509, 212-787-0239
    Pubs: *Before Their Time, His Master's Voice, Boardwalk* (Knopf, 1997, 1992, 1976), *Sea Changes* (North Point Pr, 1986), *Somewhere Else* (Charterhouse, 1972)

Elaine Kraf W
72-26 Manse St
Forest Hills, NY 11375-6728, 718-544-3614
    Pubs: *The Princess of 72nd Street* (Dalkey Archives, 2000), *Find Him!* (Fiction Collective, 1977)

Daniel Krakauer   P
346 E 10 St #6
New York, NY 10009, 212-533-8537
    Pubs: *Poems for the Whole Family* (United Artists, 1994),
Out of This World: Anth (Crown, 1991), *Transfer, Tamarind,
Mag City, Downtown, The World, Cover*

Cynthia Kraman 🎤 ✈   P
16 Charles St
New York, NY 10014, 212-675-7435
    Pubs: *The Mexican Murals* (E.G. Pr, 1986), *Taking on the
Local Color* (Wesleyan U Pr, 1977), *Antaeus, Paris Rev,
Poetry Flash, Southern Rev*

Robert Kramer 🎤 ✈   P
Manhattan College, Language Dept, Riverdale, NY 10471,
718-862-7401
    Pubs: *From Action to Dynamic Silence* (Charles Schlacks,
1991), *Rattapallax, Home Planet News, Pivot, Poets, Night
Sun, Quarry West, Apocalypse*

David Kranes   W
Harold Matson Co Inc, 276 Fifth Ave, New York, NY 10001,
212-679-4490

Christine Kraus   P
151 2nd Ave, #2A
New York, NY 10003, 212-982-5603

Rochelle Kraut   P
334 E 11 St, #16
New York, NY 10003
    Pubs: *Art in America* (Little Light Bks, 1984), *Little Light, The
World, Mag City, Rocky Ledge*

Steven M. Krauzer   W
c/o Ginger Barber, William Morris Agency, 1325 Ave of the
Americas, New York, NY 10019, 212-255-6515
    Pubs: *Frame Work* (Bantam, 1989)

Nancy Kricorian 🎤 ✈   P
Witherspoon Assoc, 235 E 31 St, New York, NY 10016
    Pubs: *Dreams of Bread and Fire, Zabelle: A Novel* (Atlantic
Monthly Pr, 2002, 1998), *River Styx, Ararat, Literary Rev,
Mississippi Rev, Witness, Graham Hse Rev, Ikon, Caliban,
Heresies, Parnassus*

Leonard Kriegel   W
355 8th Ave, #19F
New York, NY 10001-4838, 212-243-7832
    Pubs: *Flying Solo* (Beacon, 1998), *Falling into Life* (North
Point Pr, 1991), *Quitting Time* (Pantheon, 1982)

Stanley Kunitz   P
37 W 12 St, #2J
New York, NY 10011-8503, 212-924-9155
    Pubs: *The Collected Poems, Passing Through: The Later
Poems* (Norton, 2000, 1995), *Next to Last Things* (Atlantic,
1985)

Tuli Kupferberg 🎤 ✈   W
160 6th Ave
New York, NY 10013, 212-925-3823
Internet: tuli@escape.com
    Pubs: *Teach Yourself Fucking* (Autonomedia, 2000), *Don't
Make Trouble* (Strolling Dog Pr, 1991), *Portable Beat
Reader: Anth* (Viking Penguin, 1992), *Home Planet News,
NY Press, Revolting News, MNN, Fugs, Against the Current,
Shadow*

Bill Kushner 🎤 ✈   P
319 W 22 St, #2A
New York, NY 10011-2675, 212-691-7276
    Pubs: *He Dreams of Waters* (Rattapallax Pr, 2000), *That
April* (United Artists Bks, 2000), *Best American Poetry
2002: Anth* (Scribner, 2002), *In Our Time: Anth* (St. Martin's
Pr, 1989)

Paul Kuttner   W
Dawnwood Press, 387 Park Ave S, 5th Fl, New York, NY
10016-8810
    Pubs: *The Iron Virgin, Absolute Proof, Condemned*
(Dawnwood Pr, 1987, 1984, 1983), *The Man Who Lost
Everything* (Sterling Pub, 1976)

Mary La Chapelle   W
275 Bronxville Rd
Bronxville, NY 10708-2801
    Pubs: *House of Heroes* (Vintage, 1990), *Sing Heavenly
Muse!, Warm Jrnl, Northern Lit Qtly*

Tom LaBar   W
436 W Broadway
New York, NY 10012

Martha J. LaBare 🎤 ✈   P
1 Old Fulton St
Brooklyn, NY 11201, 718-855-2896
Internet: martha_labare@bloomfield.edu
    Pubs: *Shooting Star & Other Poems* (Swollen Magpie Pr,
1982), *Footwork, Roof, Telephone, World, Poet & Critic*

Oliver Lake P
163 Adelphi St
Brooklyn, NY 11205

Wally Lamb 🎤 ✈ W
Linda Chester Literary Agency, 630 5th Ave, Ste 2662, New
York, NY 10111, 212-218-3350
Internet: wlamb@downcity.net
  Pubs: *I Know This Much Is True* (Regan Bks/HC, 1998),
  She's Come Undone (Pocket Bks/S&S, 1992), *Best of the
  Missouri Review: Fiction 1978-1990: Anth* (U Missouri Pr,
  1991), *Pushcart Prize XV Anth 1990*

Annette Henkin Landau 🎤 ✈ W
301 E 66 St, #16K
New York, NY 10021-6219, 212-861-7425
Internet: jwrcncjw@aol.com
  Pubs: *Best of Moment Mag: Anth* (Jason Aronson, 1987),
  *Confrontation, Commentary, Tikkun, Other Voices, Moment,
  Vignette, Jewish Women's Lit Annual*

Louise Landes Levi 🎤 ✈ P
c/o 508 E. 5th St., #10, New York, NY 10009, 917-435-1208
Internet: llevi32@hotmail.com
  Pubs: *Michaux's Michaux* (Corona Munch, 2002), *Makar/A
  Kar'Ma* (Woodbrue Pr, 2002), *Chorma* (Porto Dei Santi,
  2000), *Guru Punk* (Cool Grove Pr, 2000), *Extinction* (Left
  Hand Bks, 1990), *Lungfull, UR Voy, Fish Drum, Chain,
  Bigbridge, Friction, Milk*

Sandy Landsman W
43-57 Union St, #6C
Flushing, NY 11355, 516-921-0808
  Pubs: *Castaways on Chimp Island, The Gadget Factor*
  (Atheneum, 1986, 1984)

Marcia Lane PP
462 Amsterdam Ave
New York, NY 10024, 212-799-1196
Internet: storylane@aol.com
  Pubs: *Christoph Wants a Party* (Kane-Miller Bks, 1995),
  Picturing the Rose (H W Wilson, 1993), *National Storytelling
  Lit Jrnl, Creative Classroom*

George Lanning W
c/o Tony Outhwaite, JCR Inc, 27 W 20 St, Ste 1103, New York,
NY 10011

Alyssa A. Lappen 🎤 ✈ P
75 Livingston St 14C
Brooklyn, NY 11201, 718-852-0722
http://hometown.aol.com/alyssaalappen/myhomepage/index.
html
  Pubs: *Kota Press, The Pedastal Mag, New Works Rev,
  International Poetry Rev, Sow's Ear Poetry Rev, Switched-
  on Gutenberg, Midstream, Poetry Motel, Ruah,
  ForPoerty.com, Blueline*

Joan Larkin 🎤 ✈ P
331 21st Street
Brooklyn, NY 11215
Internet: larkin7@aol.com
  Pubs: *Sor Juana's Love Poems, Cold River* (Painted Leaf Pr,
  1997, 1997), *A Long Sound* (Granite Pr, 1986), *Gay &
  Lesbian Poetry in Our Time: Anth* (St. Martin's Pr, 1988),
  *APR, Global City Rev, Hanging Loose, Out Mag, Sing
  Heavenly Muse*

Wendy Wilder Larsen 🎤 ✈ P
439 E 51 St
New York, NY 10022-6473
  Pubs: *Braided Lives* (Minnesota Humanities Commission,
  1991), *Shallow Graves: Two Women and Vietnam* (Random
  Hse, 1986), *The KGB Bar Book of Poems: Anth* (HC,
  2000), *Outsiders: Anth, Night Out: Anth* (Milkweed Edtns,
  1999, 1997)

Pam Laskin 🎤 ✈ P&W
414 5th St
Brooklyn, NY 11215
  Pubs: *Trick or Treat, Till Death Do Us Part* (Wordrunner,
  2001), *Dear Hades* (New Spirit Pr, 1994), *In a Glass Ball*
  (Green Meadow Pr, 1992), *The Buried Treasure, Heroic
  Horses* (McGraw-Hill, 1998, 1998), *A Wish Upon a Star*
  (Magination, 1991), *Sassy, Sidewalk*

Michael Lassell P&W
114 Horatio St, #512
New York, NY 10014-1579, 212-206-7339
Internet: mjlassell@aol.com
  Pubs: *A Flame for the Touch That Matters* (Painted Leaf Pr,
  1998), *The Hard Way* (Kasak Bks, 1995), *Decade Dance*
  (Alyson, 1990), *City Lights Rev, Portable Lower East Side,
  Excursus, Central Park, Zyzzyva, Global City Rev, Hanging
  Loose*

Charles Keeling Lassiter P
1382 1st Ave, #19
New York, NY 10021-9526, 212-535-6075
  Pubs: *C.K. Lassiter: Drawings & Writing, 1957-1990*
  (Switzerland; Sylvia Acatos, 1990)

Kristin Lattany 🎤 W
c/o Jane Dystel Literary Management, 1 Union Sq W, New
York, NY 10003, 212-627-9100
Internet: klattany@comcast.net
  Pubs: *The Lakestown Rebellion* (Coffee Hse Pr, 2003),
  Buffaloed, Do Unto Others, Kinfolks (Ballantine, 2003, 2000,
  1996), *The Soul Brothers and Sister Lou* (The Women's Pr,
  1988), *God Bless the Child* (Howard U Pr, 1986), *Essence,
  Callaloo, Nation*

Lynne Lawner   P
Georges Borchardt Inc, 136 E 57 St, New York, NY 10022,
212-737-5619
Internet: lynlawner@aol.com
    Pubs: *Lives of the Courtesans* (Rizzoli, 1987), *Paris Rev,*
    Radcliffe Qtly, Confrontation, Chelsea, Georgia Rev, The
    Bridge

Kathleen Rockwell Lawrence 🎤 ✈   W
510 E 23 St, #13-B
New York, NY 10010, 212-533-7563
Internet: krlawrence2000@yahoo.com
    Pubs: *The Boys I Didn't Kiss* (British-American, 1990), *The*
    Last Room in Manhattan, Maud Gone (Atheneum, 1989,
    1986)

Jane Lazarre   W
Wendy Weil Agency Inc, 232 Madison Ave, Ste 1300, New
York, NY 10016, 212-685-0300
    Pubs: *Worlds Beyond My Control* (Dutton/NAL, 1991), *The*
    Powers of Charlotte (Crossing Pr, 1988), *The Mother Knot*
    (Beacon Pr, 1985)

Cynthia LeClaire   P&W
Philosophy Dept, St. Francis College, 180 Remsen St,
Brooklyn, NY 11201, 718-522-2300
    Pubs: *The Rape of Persephone* (New Spirit Pr, 1993),
    Homage to the Light (Black Swan Pr, 1985)

Roland Legiardi-Laura   P
295 E 8 St
New York, NY 10009, 212-529-9327
    Pubs: *Bomb, Appearances, The World, Telephone,*
    Lumen/Avenue A, Main Trend, Sunbury

David Lehman 🎤 ✈   P&W
104 MacDougal St, #1
New York, NY 10012
Internet: bestampoetry@aol.com
    Pubs: *The Evening Sun, The Daily Mirror, Valentine Place*
    (Scribner, 2002, 2000, 1996), *Operation Memory*
    (Princeton, 1990)

Eric Gabriel Lehman 🎤 ✈   W
Malaga Baldi Literary Agency, 204 W 84 St, Ste 3C, New York,
NY 10024, 212-579-5075
Internet: eglehman@accesshub.net
    Pubs: *Summer's House* (St. Martin's Pr, 2000), *Quaspeck,*
    Waterboys (Mercury Hse, 1993, 1989), *Best American Gay*
    Fiction 3: Anth (Back Bay Bks, 1998), *Confrontation, GSU*
    Review, James White Rev, New Letters, Modern Words

Christine Lehner   W
271 S Broadway
Hastings-on-Hudson, NY 10706-2906
    Pubs: *Expecting* (New Directions, 1982), *Agni, NAR,*
    Chelsea

Alan Lelchuk   W
Georges Borchardt Inc, 136 E 57 St, New York, NY 10022,
212-573-5785
    Pubs: *Ziff: A Life?* (Carrol & Graf, 2003), *Playing the Game*
    (Baskerville Pubs, 1995), *Brooklyn Boy* (McGraw-Hill, 1990),
    Miriam in Her Forties (HM, 1985), *American Mischief,*
    Miriam at Thirty-Four (FSG, 1974, 1974), *Atlantic, New*
    Republic

Gabrielle LeMay 🎤   P
250 W 99 St, #7A
New York, NY 10025
Internet: LeMayNYC@aol.com
    Pubs: *Ravishing DisUnities: Real Ghazals in English: Anth*
    (Wesleyan, 2000), *Heliotrope: A Jrnl of Poetry, The Ledge,*
    Rattapallax, Blue Mesa Rev, Paterson Lit Rev,
    Confrontation, River Oak Rev, Mudfish

John Leonard   W
Curtis Brown Ltd, 10 Astor Pl, New York, NY 10003-6935,
212-473-5400
    Pubs:

Estelle Leontief   P
37 Washington Sq W, #16B
New York, NY 10011-9123
    Pubs: *Sellie & Dee: A Friendship* (Chicory Blue Pr, 1993),
    Genia & Wassily: A Russian American Memoir (Zephyr Pr,
    1987), *Whatever Happens, Razerol* (Janus Pr, 1975, 1973),
    Sojourner, Florida Rev

Eleanor Lerman   P
10460 Queens Blvd, #20H
Flushing, NY 11375-7325
    Pubs: *Come the Sweet By & By* (U Massachusetts Pr,
    1975), *Armed Love* (Wesleyan U Pr, 1973)

Linda Lerner 🎤 ✈   P
PO Box 020292
Brooklyn, NY 11202-0007, 718-596-4583
Internet: llerner@mindspring.com
    Pubs: *Greatest Hits: 1989-2002* (Pudding Hse Pubs, 2002),
    No Earthly Sense Gets It Right (Lummox Pr, 2001),
    Anytimeblues (Ye Olde Font Shoppe Pr, 1999), *Ragged*
    Lion: Anth (Vagabond/Smith, 1999), *Blue Collar Rev,*
    Louisiana Rev, Rattle, Home Planet Rev

Rika Lesser 🎤 ✈   P
133 Henry St, #5
Brooklyn, NY 11201-2550, 718-852-1163
Internet: rika.lesser.mc.74@aya.yale.edu
    Pubs: *Growing Back* (U South Carolina Pr, 1997), *All We*
    Need of Hell (U North Texas Pr, 1995), *Etruscan Things*
    (Braziller, 1983), *New Republic, Threepenny Rev, Paris Rev,*
    New Yorker, Partisan, Poetry, Nation

Jan Heller Levi 🎤 ✈ P&W
244 Waverly Pl, #2B
New York, NY 10014-2246, 212-929-1951
Internet: janhellerlevi@cs.com
    Pubs: *Once I Gazed at You in Wonder* (LSU Pr, 1999), *TriQtly, Graham Hse Rev, Poetry East, Ploughshares, Pequod, Antioch Rev, River Styx, BPJ*

Toni Mergentime Levi 🎤 ✈ P
105 W 73 St, #4D
New York, NY 10023, 212-362-5481
Internet: tonimerg@cs.com
    Pubs: *For a Dancing Bear* (Three Mile Harbor, 1995), *Prairie Schooner, California Qtly, Manhattan Poetry Rev, Negative Capability, Crosscurrents, Texas Rev, Kansas Qtly, Confrontation*

Phillis Levin 🎤 ✈ P
535 W 110 St, #3-G
New York, NY 10025-2067, 212-865-9245
Internet: phillislevin@earthlink.net
    Pubs: *Mercury, The Penguin Book of the Sonnet: Anth* (Penguin Bks, 2001, 2001), *The Afterimage* (Copper Beech Pr, 1995), *Temples & Fields* (U Georgia Pr, 1988), *Atlantic, New Yorker, Paris Rev, New Republic, Poetry, Partisan Rev, Nation*

Anne-Marie Levine 🎤 ✈ P
156 E 89 St
New York, NY 10128
Internet: stinpilot@aol.com
    Pubs: *Bus Ride to a Blue Movie* (Pearl Edtns, 2003), *With Sophie* (Peapod Pr, 1999), *Euphorbia* (Provincetown Arts Pr, 1994), *Poetry After 9/11: An Anthology of New York Poets* (Melville Hse Pub, 2002), *Crossconnect, Parnassus, Ploughshares*

Howard Levy 🎤 ✈ P
70 E 96 St, #12B
New York, NY 10128
    Pubs: *A Day This Lit* (Cavankerry Pr, 2000), *Poetry, Paris Rev, Threepenny Rev, Gettysburg Rev, APR, Georgia Rev, Massachusetts Rev, Columbia*

Owen Levy W
217 Central Pk N
New York, NY 10026
    Pubs: *A Brother's Touch* (Pinnacle Bks, 1982)

Robert J. Levy P
595 W End Ave #4A
New York, NY 10024-1727, 212-799-6836
Internet: rjlevy@unitedmedia.com
    Pubs: *Chefs at Twilight* (Bacchae Pr, 1996), *The Perfection of Standing Aside* (South Coast Pr, 1993), *Paris Rev, Poetry, Georgia Rev, Southern Rev*

Richard Lewis 🎤 ✈ P
141 E 88 St, #3E
New York, NY 10128, 212-831-7717
Internet: rlewis212@aol.com
    Pubs: *In the Space of the Sky* (Harcourt, 2002), *The Bird of Imagining, Each Sky Has Its Words* (Touchstone Ctr Pub, 2002, 2000), *Living By Wonder* (Parabola Bks, 1998), *Poets at Work* (Just Buffalo Lit Ctr, 1995), *When Thought Is Young* (New Rivers Pr, 1992)

Owen Lewis PP
24 E 82 St
New York, NY 10028
    Pubs: *New Pictures at an Exhibition* (Alexander Browde, 1977), *Princeton Spectrum*

Harry Lewis 🎤 ✈ P
125 Barrow St
New York, NY 10014, 212-243-1393
    Pubs: *Two for One, Silly 1-14* (Little Rootie Tootie/Ikon Pr, 1994, 1992), *Global Rev, Coffee House Rev, Local Knowledge, Ikon, Sun, Number, Mulch, Transfer*

Marilyn Jaye Lewis 🎤 ✈ W
777 W End Ave
New York, NY 10025
Internet: mjaye@akula.com
    Pubs: *I Like Boys, Neptune & Surf* (MasQuerade Bks, 1999, 1998), *Frighten the Horses, Bad Attitude, Masquerade Erotic Jrnl*

Leslie Li 🎤 ✈ PP&W
235 East 31st St
New York, NY 10016
www.sover.net/~leslieli
    Pubs: *Bittersweet* (Audio; Tuttle Pub, 1994), *American Identities: Contemporary Multicultural Voices, 6th Bread Loaf Anth* (Univ Pr New England, 1994)

Herbert Lieberman W
Georges Borchardt Inc, 136 E 57 St, New York, NY 10022, 212-753-5785
    Pubs: *Widdershims, The Concierge* (Le Spoil, 2002, 1998), *The Girl with the Botticelli Eyes, Sandman Sleep* (St. Martin's Pr, 1996, 1992), *Shadow Dancers* (Little, Brown, 1989), *Nightbloom* (Putnam, 1984)

Herbert Liebman W
College of Staten Island, 2800 Victory Blvd, Staten Island, NY 10314, 212-242-1909
    Pubs: *Confrontation, Chelsea, PEN Syndicated Fiction, Paris Transcontinental, Midstream*

Kate Light   P
736 W End Ave
New York, NY 10025-6245, 212-222-9620
   Pubs: *The Laws of Falling Bodies* (Story Line Pr, 1997),
   *Paris Rev, Sparrow, Western Humanities Rev, Feminist
   Studies, Wisconsin Rev, Janus*

Frank Lima   P
147-20 35 Ave, #11-B
Flushing, NY 11354-3706, 718-961-0301
   Pubs: *Angel* (Liveright, 1976), *Underground with the Oriole*
   (Dutton, 1971)

Nancy Linde   P
20 Cliff St, #8E
Staten Island, NY 10305, 718-876-9293
   Pubs: *The Orange Cat Bistro* (Kensington, 1996), *Buckle,
   Symposium, Sojourner, 13th Moon, Promethean, Endymion*

Don Linder   P&W
243 Riverside Dr, #604
New York, NY 10025, 212-866-9001
Internet: dlinder@shiva.hunter.cuny.edu
   Pubs: *West Side Spirit, Other Voices, Mss., Beacon Rev,
   Stardancer, Inprint*

Elinor Lipman   W
William Morris Agency, 101 5th Ave, New York, NY 10003
   Pubs: *The Inn at Lake Devine* (Random Hse, 1998), *Isabel's
   Bed* (Pocket Bks, 1995), *The Way Men Act, Then She
   Found Me* (Washington Square Pr, 1993, 1991)

Marcia Lipson 🎤 ✈   P
900 W End Ave 16D
New York, NY 10025
Internet: mar.li@att.net
   Pubs: *Stories from Where We Live: Anth* (Milkweed Edtns,
   2001), *bite to eat place: Anth* (Redwood Coast Pr, 1995),
   *Appalachia, Cream City Rev, Barrow Street, Bridge,
   Gargoyle, Jewish Women's Lit Annual, Kerem, Paterson Lit
   Rev, Plum Rev, Yankee*

Gordon Lish   W
Four Walls Eight Windows, 39 W 14 St, New York, NY 10011,
212-206-4769
   Pubs: *Peru, The Mourner at the Door, Epigraph, Dear Mr.
   Capote, What I Know So Far* (Four Walls Eight Windows,
   1997, 1997, 1996, 1996, 1996)

Olga Litowinsky 🎤 ✈   W
Curtis Brown Ltd, 10 Astor Pl, New York, NY 10003-6935
Internet: olgalit@islanderis.net
   Pubs: *Boats for Bedtime* (Clarion, 2000), *The Pawloined
   Paper* (Big Red Chair Bks, 1998), *Oliver's High Flying
   Adventure* (as M. McBrier; Troll, 1986), *The High Voyage*
   (Viking, 1977)

Iris Litt 🎤 ✈   P&W
252 W 11 St
New York, NY 10014, 212-691-5420
Internet: irislitt@aol.com
   Pubs: *Word Love* (Cosmic Trend, 1996), *Confrontation,
   Caprice, Icarus, Travellers' Tales, Pacific Coast Jrnl,
   Onthebus, Lactuca, Earth's Daughters, Poetry Now, Central
   Park, Pearl*

Larry Litt 🎤 ✈   PP&W
3515 84th St, #3D
Jackson Heights, NY 11372, 718-478-2929
Internet: humornet@aol.com
   Pubs: *Aesop's America* (Oralit Pr, 1995), *eine DATA base*
   (Germany; Edition Cantz, 1993), *Art 20/21 The Turn of the
   Century* (S. Korea; Taejon Pr, 1993), *Downtown, Street
   News, The Fugue*

Susan Litwack   P
752 W End Ave, #6F
New York, NY 10025, 212-663-1379
   Pubs: *Mudfish, SPR, Outerbridge, Puerto del Sol, Cincinnati
   Poetry Rev, Zone*

Tsaurah Litzky 🎤 ✈   P
1 Old Fulton St
Brooklyn, NY 11201-6908, 718-875-1107
Internet: tsaurah@mindspring.com
   Pubs: *Kamikaze Lover* (Appearances, 1999), *Blessing
   Poems* (Synaethesia Pr, 1996), *Blue Bird Buddha of No
   Regrets* (Apathy Pr, 1994), *Best American Erotica: Anths*
   (S&S, 2001, 1999, 1997, 1995), *Unmade Bed: Anth*
   (Borders, 1999), *Long Shot, Rant, Pink Pages*

Jay Liveson 🎤 ✈   P
3671 Hudson Manor Terr
Riverdale, NY 10463, 718-796-3750
Internet: jlivesonmd@pol.net
   Pubs: *What Counts* (Fithian Pr, 2000), *Atlanta Rev,
   Mediphors, Judaism, New England Jrnl of Medicine, Modern
   Haiku, JAMA, Riverrun, Western Jrnl of Medicine, Einstein
   Qtly, Hollins Critic, Plainsongs*

Zelda Lockhart 🎤 ✈   P&W
Sally Wofford-Girand, 44 Greenwich Ave, New York, NY 10011,
212-243-8480
Internet: zl23@cornell.edu
   Pubs: *Sojourner, Wordwrights, Sinister Wisdom, Calyx*

Katinka Loeser   W
Watkins Loomis Agency Inc, 133 E 35 St, Ste 1, New York,
NY 10016
   Pubs: *The Archers at Home, Tomorrow Will Be Monday*
   (Atheneum, 1968, 1964), *New Yorker, McCall's*

Andrea Freud Loewenstein   P&W
462 5th St, #2
Brooklyn, NY 11215-3402
Internet: ziporah@earthlink.net
    Pubs: *The Worry Girl* (Firebrand Bks, 1992), *This Place*
    (Pandora Pr, 1984), *Conditions, Bad Attitude*

Eloise Loftin   P
77 Eastern Pkwy, #5B
Brooklyn, NY 11238, 718-783-7062

Robert Emmet Long   W
c/o Ruth Nathan, 80 Fifth Ave, #705, New York, NY 10011

Sabra Loomis   P
136 Waverly Pl, Apt 6E
New York, NY 10014
    Pubs: *Travelling on Blue* (Firm Ground Pr, 1998), *Rosetree*
    (Alice James Bks, 1989), *APR, American Voice, Poetry
    Ireland Rev, Cyphers, Salt Hill Jrnl, Salamander, Cincinnati
    Poetry Rev, Negative Capability*

Phillip Lopate 🎤 ✈   P&W
402 Sackett St
Brooklyn, NY 11231
Internet: plopate@aol.com
    Pubs: *Portrait of My Body* (Anchor, 1996), *Against Joie de
    Vivre* (Poseidon, 1989), *The Rug Merchant* (Viking, 1987),
    *Paris Rev, Harper's, Threepenny Rev, SW Rev, Parnassus,
    Boulevard*

Judy Lopatin   W
925 Union St, #6C
Brooklyn, NY 11215, 718-399-7903
    Pubs: *Modern Romances* (Fiction Collective, 1986), *AM Lit:
    Anth* (Edtns Druckhaus, 1992), *Lone Star Lit Qtly, VLS,
    Between C&D, Witness, Europe*

Barry Lopez   W
c/o Peter Matson, Sterling Lord Literistic, 65 Bleecker St, New
York, NY 10012, 212-780-6050
    Pubs: *Light Action in the Caribbean, Field Notes* (Knopf,
    2000, 1994), *Crow & Weasel* (North Point Pr, 1990), *Winter
    Count* (Scribner, 1981), *Georgia Rev, Paris Rev, Story,
    Esquire, American Short Fiction, Manoa*

Eileen Lottman   W
Karpfinger Agency, 357 W 20 St, New York, NY 10011-3379,
212-691-2690
    Pubs: *She & I* (Morrow, 1991), *After the Wind* (Dell, 1979)

Esther Louise 🎤 ✈   P
568-3 Louisiana Ave
Brooklyn, NY 11239, 718-942-3001
Internet: elm@con2.com
    Pubs: *Confirmations Anth* (Quill, 1983), *Essence, City,
    Obsidian, American Rag, Bopp, Freshtones*

Cortnie A. Lowe   PP&P
172 St Marks Ave
Brooklyn, NY 11238
    Pubs: *Hexagram* (Poets Union Pr, 1977), *Partisan Rev*

Marilyn Lowen   P
286 South St, #16A
New York, NY 10002, 212-227-5364
    Pubs: *Vague* (Fire Sign Pr, 1983), *Reflections: Anth* (Diana
    Pr, 1971), *City, New Women*

Bruce Lowery   W
Georges Borchardt Inc, 136 E 57 St, New York, NY 10022,
212-753-5785

Carmen D. Lucca 🎤 ✈   PP
3131 Grand Concourse
Bronx, NY 10468, 718-367-0780
    Pubs: *Bum Rush the Page: Anth* (Three Rivers Pr, 2001),
    The Spirit in the Woods: Anth (Daimler Chrysler, 2000),
    Maboiti, Carver of Birds, Bilingual Edtn (Poets' Refuge,
    2000), *Latino Mothers: Anth* (Lee & Low Bks, 2000)

Thomas Luhrmann   P
468 Riverside Dr, #82A
New York, NY 10027, 212-663-3372
    Pubs: *The Objects in the Garden* (Wesleyan U Pr, 1982)

K. Curtis Lyle   P
132-11 Foch Blvd
South Ozone Park, NY 11420, 718-659-4776
    Pubs: *Fifteen Predestination Weather Reports* (Beyond
    Baroque, 1976)

Charles H. Lynch 🎤 ✈   P
263 Eastern Pkwy, #5B
Brooklyn, NY 11238-6335, 718-638-3047
    Pubs: *Saint Ann's Rev, The Ledge, Rattapallax, Black Amer
    Lit Forum, World Order, Chelsea, Crab Orchard Rev*

Ellen Windy Aug Lytle   P&W
80 N Moore St, #9B
New York, NY 10013, 212-571-6774
    Pubs: *Factory Fish: Selected Short Fiction, MSS* (Linear
    Arts Pr, 1998, 1998), *Lettuce After Moon* (Ikon Pr, 1993),
    Down Under Manhattan Bridge: Anth (Dan Freeman, 1996),
    *Global City Rev, And Then, Crossroads, Downtown, Lowell
    Rev, Mind the Gap*

Jackson Mac Low 🎤 ✈   PP&P
42 N Moore St, #6
New York, NY 10013-2468, 212-226-3346
Internet: tarmac@pipeline.com
    Pubs: *20 Forties* (Zasterle, 1999), *Barnesbook* (Sun &
    Moon Pr, 1996), *42 Merzgedichte in Memoriam Kurt
    Schwitters* (Station Hill, 1994), *Sulfur, Talisman,
    Conjunctions, Crayon, Chain*

Norman MacAfee 🎤 ✈   P
55 W 11 St #8D
New York, NY 10011-8692, 212-924-8247
    Pubs: *A New Requiem* (Cheap Rev Pr, 1988), *Hanging Loose, The World, Rouge*

James MacGuire   P&W
412 E 55 St, Apt 3H
New York, NY 10022, 212-838-0651
Internet: jmacg52@aol.com
    Pubs: *Dusk on Lake Tanganyika* (Fermanagh Pr, 1999), *Ironwood, Southern Rev, America, Kansas Qtly*

Ginny MacKenzie   P&W
66 Grand St
New York, NY 10013, 212-966-5643
    Pubs: *By Morning* (Coyote Pr, 1984), *Boulevard, Iowa Rev, Agni, New Letters, Pequod, Ploughshares*

Elizabeth Macklin   P
207 W 14 St, #5F
New York, NY 10011
Internet: emacklin@earthlink.net
    Pubs: *You've Just Been Told, A Woman Kneeling in the Big City* (Norton, 2000, 1992), *The KGB Bar Book of Poems: Anth* (HC, 2000), *Best American Poetry: Anths* (Scribner, 1993, 1991), *New Republic, Paris Rev, Nation, Threepenny Rev, SW Rev, New Yorker, Lyra*

Phillip Mahony   P
PO Box 947
New York, NY 10021
    Pubs: *Supreme, Catching Bodies* (North Atlantic Bks, 1989, 1986)

Norman Mailer   W
ICM, 40 W 57 St, New York, NY 10019, 212-556-5600

Gerard Malanga 🎤 ✈   P
221 Mott St, #8
New York, NY 10012
www.gerardmalanga.com
    Pubs: *No Respect: New & Selected Poems 1964-2000* (Black Sparrow Pr, 2001), *Southwest Rev, Raritan, Massachusetts Rev, Agni*

Michael Malinowitz   P
55 Liberty St
New York, NY 10005-1003, 212-766-1941
    Pubs: *Michael's Ear* (Groundwater Pr, 1993), *Best American Poetry: Anth* (Scribner, 1988), *Private, Poetry Motel, Bad Henry Rev, Brooklyn Rev*

George Malko 🎤 ✈   W
36 W 84 St
New York, NY 10024
Internet: geemal@peoplepc.com
    Pubs: *Luna* (Pan Bks Ltd, 1980), *Take What You Will* (Pyramid Bks, 1975), *Inkwell, Red Rock Rev, North Dakota Qtly, Riversedge, Licking River Rev, Distillery, Pleiades*

Michael Malone 🎤 ✈   W
c/o Peter Matson, Sterling Lord Literistic, 65 Bleecker St., New York, NY 10012, 212-780-1690
    Pubs: *Dingley Falls, First Lady, Red Clay Blue Cadillac, The Last Noel* (Washington Square Bks, 2002, 2002, 2002, 2002), *Playboy, Nation, Partisan Rev*

Carolina Mancuso 🎤 ✈   W
c/o PSC, 123 7th Ave, Brooklyn, NY 11215
Internet: caro50@aol.com
    Pubs: *Word of Mouth, Vols II, I: Anth, Love, Struggle & Change: Anth* (Crossing Pr, 1991, 1990, 1988), *Amelia, Ikon*

Norman Manea   W
201 W 70 St, #10-I
New York, NY 10023
    Pubs: *The Black Envelope* (FSG, 1996), *On Clowns: The Dictator & the Artist* (Grove Pr, 1992), *TriQtly, Partisan, New Republic, Paris Rev, Salmagundi*

Peggy Mann   W
46 W 94 St
New York, NY 10025
    Pubs: *Reader's Digest, McCall's, Good Housekeeping*

D. Keith Mano   W
392 Central Pk W, #6P
New York, NY 10025
    Pubs: *The Fergus Dialogues* (Intl Scholars Pubs, 1998), *Take Five* (Dalkey Archive Pr, 1998), *Topless* (Random Hse, 1991), *Playboy, National Rev*

Jaime Manrique 🎤 ✈   P&W
33 Bank St, #5
New York, NY 10014, 212-929-4960
Internet: jmardila@aol.com
    Pubs: *Eminent Maricones: Arenas, Lorca, Puig, & Me* (U Wisconsin Pr, 1999), *Colombian Gold* (Painted Leaf Pr, 1998), *Twilight at the Equator* (Faber & Faber, 1997), *My Night with Federico Garcia Lorca* (Groundwater Pr, 1995)

Jan Marino   W
c/o Dorothy Markinko, McIntosh & Otis, 310 Madison Ave, New York, NY 10017
    Pubs: *Searching for Atticus* (S&S, 1997), *The Day That Elvis Came to Town* (Little, Brown, 1991)

George Maritime P
44 Cherwing Rd
Yonkers, NY 10701, 914-963-4971
    Pubs: *Noble Deeds, The Rap* (The New Pr, 1991, 1986),
Rose Colored Glasses: Anth (ABC No Rio, 1985)

Wendy Mark P
2 W 67 St #9D
New York, NY 10023
    Pubs: *Prairie Schooner, Literary Cupboard, Res Gestae*

Wallace Markfield W
15 Vista Way
Port Washington, NY 11050

David Markson W
215 W 10 St, #3E
New York, NY 10014-2913, 212-243-8688
    Pubs: *This is Not a Novel* (Counterpoint, 2001), *Reader's
Block, Wittgenstein's Mistress* (Dalkey Archive Pr, 1996,
1988)

Julia Markus W
Harriet Wasserman Agency, 137 E 36 St, New York, NY 10016
    Pubs: *A Change of Luck* (Viking Penguin, 1991), *American
Rose, Friends Along the Way, Uncle* (Dell, 1990, 1986, 1986)

Regina Marler W
Maia Gregory Assoc, 311 E 72 St, New York, NY 10021,
212-288-0310
    Pubs: *Carolina Qtly, Chattahoochee Rev, NAR, NW Rev*

Elizabeth Marraffino P
75 Bank St, #6H
New York, NY 10014, 212-691-9806
    Pubs: *Blue Moon for Ruby Tuesday* (Contact II Pub, 1981),
Choice, Sun, The Dream Book, Nation

Paule Marshall W
Faith Childs Literary Agency, 275 W 96 St, New York, NY
10025, 212-662-1232
    Pubs: *Brown Girl, Brownstones* (Feminist Pr, 1996), *The
Chosen Place, The Timeless People* (Vintage Pr, 1992),
Daughters (Atheneum, 1991), *Praisesong for the Widow*
(Putnam, 1983)

Charles Martin P
116 Pinehurst Ave, Hudson View Gardens #A-64
New York, NY 10033-1755, 212-781-3500
    Pubs: *What the Darkness Proposes, Steal the Bacon* (Johns
Hopkins U Pr, 1996, 1987), *Boulevard, Hellas, Formalist,
Threepenny Rev, Tennessee Qtly*

Paula Martinac 🎤 W
237 E 26 St, #2-E
New York, NY 10010-1952
Internet: pmartinac@aol.com
    Pubs: *Chicken* (Alyson Pub, 1997), *Home Movies, Out of
Time, Voyages Out* (Seal Pr, 1993, 1990, 1989), *Art &
Understanding, Queer City, Conditions, Sinister Wisdom,
Blithe Hse Qtly*

Andrew Marum W
3640 Johnson Ave, Apt 7F
Bronx, NY 10463, 212-601-3748
    Pubs: *Follies & Foibles* (Facts On File, 1984)

Donna Masini P&W
PO Box 5, Prince St Sta, New York, NY 10012, 212-260-0496
Internet: dlmasini@aol.com
    Pubs: *About Yvonne* (Norton, 1997), *The Kind of Danger*
(Beacon Pr, 1994), *Georgia Rev, Paris Rev, Parnassus,
Boulevard, VLS*

Carole Maso W
Georges Borchardt Inc, 136 E 57 St, New York, NY 10022,
212-753-5785
    Pubs: *Defiance* (Dutton, 1998), *The American Woman in the
Chinese Hat* (Plume, 1995), *Ghost Dance* (Ecco Pr, 1995),
*APR, Common Knowledge, Rev of Contemporary Fiction,
Bomb, Nerve, Conjunctions*

Bobbie Ann Mason 🎤 ✈ W
c/o Amanda Urban, ICM, 40 W 57 St, New York, NY 10019,
212-556-5764
    Pubs: *Zigzagging Down a Wild Trail, Clear Springs* (Random
Hse, 2001, 1999), *Midnight Magic* (Ecco Press, 1998),
Feather Crowns, Shiloh (HC, 1993, 1982), *Love Life,
Spence & Lila, In Country* (H&R, 1989, 1988, 1985),
Southern Rev, DoubleTake, Harper's, Story

Greg Masters 🎤 ✈ P&W
437 E 12 St, #26
New York, NY 10009-4042, 212-777-2714
www2.thorn.net/~gmasters
    Pubs: *My Women & Men, Part 2* (Crony Bks, 1980),
Nuyorican Poetry Anth (H Holt, 1994)

Harry Mathews 🎤 ✈ P&W
Maxine Groffsky Literary Agency, 2 Fifth Ave, New York, NY
10011, 212-473-0004
    Pubs: *The Human Country: Collected Stories, The
Journalist, Singular Pleasures* (Dalkey Archive Pr, 2002,
1997, 1993), *Oulipo Compendium* (Atlas Pr, 1998), *Out of
Bounds* (Burning Deck Pr, 1989), *The Orchard* (Bamberge
Bks, 1988), *Yale Rev*

Mindy Matijasevic 🎤 ✈ P&W
2877 Grand Concourse, #2J
Bronx, NY 10468, 718-933-9209
Internet: leunamzemog@aol.com
Pubs: *AllSpice Mag, Lynx Eye, Anna's House, Howling Dog, Portable Wall, Free Focus, Kana, Impetus, Rebirth of Artemis, A Taste of Summer, Amazon*

Peter Matthiessen W
Donadio & Olson, Inc., 121 W 27 St, Ste 704, New York, NY 10001, 212-691-8077

Sharon Mattlin P
60 E 4 St, #21
New York, NY 10003, 212-475-7110
Pubs: *The Big House: A Collection of Poets' Prose: Anth* (Ailanthus Pr, 1978), *Telephone, Dragonfly*

Susan Maurer 🎤 ✈ P
210 E 15 St, #9P
New York, NY 10003
Pubs: *By the Blue Light of the Morning Glory* (Linear Arts, 1997), *Help Yourself!: Anth* (Autonomedia, 2001), *Cafe Nico Anth* (Venom Pr, 1996), *Literary Imagination, Poetry, Salzburg Rev, Skidrow Penthouse, Gare du Nord, Virginia Qtly Rev, Crazyhorse*

Bernadette Mayer P&W
172 E 4 St, #9B
New York, NY 10009, 212-254-5308
Pubs: *The Formal Field of Kissing* (Catchword Papers, 1990), *Sonnets* (Tender Buttons, 1990)

Frances Mayes P&W
c/o Broadway Books, 1540 Broadway, New York, NY 10036, 212-782-8941
Pubs: *Swan, In Tuscany, Bella Tuscany, Under the Tuscan Sun* (Broadway Bks, 2002, 2000, 1998, 1997), *Ex Voto, Hours* (Lost Roads, 1995, 1984), *Atlantic, Virginia Qtly, Southern Rev, Iowa Rev, Gettysburg Rev*

Jane Mayhall P&W
15 W 67 St, #6MW
New York, NY 10023-6226
Pubs: *Treasury of American Short Stories: Anth* (Dell, 1994), *Best of Wind Literary Mag: Anth* (Wind Pubs, 1994), *Confrontation, Partisan Rev, New Renaissance, Hudson Rev, New Yorker, New Letters, Shenandoah*

Norma Fox Mazer W
Elaine Markson Literary Agency, 44 Greenwich Ave, New York, NY 10011, 212-243-8480
Pubs: *When She Was Good* (Arthur Levine/Scholastic, 1997), *Missing Pieces, Silver, After the Rain* (Morrow, 1995, 1988, 1987), *Heartbeat* (Bantam, 1989), *English Jrnl*

Jerome Mazzaro 🎤 ✈ P
392 Central Park W, Apt11J
New York, NY 10025-5819, 212-662-2605
Internet: jerrymazzaro@aol.com
Pubs: *War Games* (Xlibris, 2001), *Rubbings* (Quiet Hills, 1985), *The Caves of Love* (Jazz Pr, 1985), *From the Margin: Anth* (Purdue U Pr, 1990), *Accent, SW Rev, Colorado Rev, New Republic, Nation, Hudson Rev, Poetry, Sewanee Rev, Salmagundi*

Charles McCarry W
c/o Owen Laster, William Morris Agency, 1325 Ave of the Americas, New York, NY 10019, 212-586-5100
Pubs: *The Better Angels, The Secret Lovers* (Dutton, 1979, 1977)

Robbie McCauley PP
223 E 4 St, #3
New York, NY 10009, 212-473-1801
Internet: robbiamcc@msn.com

Rebecca McClanahan 🎤 ✈ P&W
331 W 57th St #211
New York, NY 10019, 212-245-3619
Internet: mcclanmuse@aol.com
Pubs: *Naked As Eve, The Intersection of X & Y* (Copper Beech Pr, 2000, 1996), *One Word Deep* (Ashland Poetry Pr, 1993), *Best American Poetry: Anth* (Scribner, 1998), *Southern Rev, Shenandoah, Kenyon Rev, Gettysburg Rev*

Suzanne McConnell 🎤 ✈ W
133 W 24 St, 5th Fl
New York, NY 10011-1936, 212-620-4196
Internet: smcconnell2@mindspring.com
Pubs: *Personal Fiction Writing: Anth* (Teachers & Writers, 1984), *Kalliope, Earth's Daughters, Fiddlehead, Green Mountains Rev, Calyx, Little Mag, Olive Tree Rev, Dreamworks, Appearances*

Mary Joneve McCormick P
427 W 51 St, #4E
New York, NY 10019
http://www.quicklink.com/~joneve
Pubs: *Small Bird Bones: Anth* (New Pr, 1993), *Single Flower, Japanophile, Soul to Soul, New Pr, Golden Isis, Smoke Signals, Nomad's Choir, Standard, Sisyphus*

James McCourt W
c/o Vincent Virga, 145 E 22 St, New York, NY 10003
Pubs: *Kaye Wayfaring in "Avenged"* (Knopf, 1984), *Mawrdew Czgowchwz* (FSG, 1975), *New Yorker*

Alice McDermott W
Harriet Wasserman Literary Agency, 137 E 36 St, New York, NY 10016
Pubs: *Charming Billy, At Weddings & Wakes, That Night* (FSG, 1998, 1992, 1987), *A Bigamist's Daughter* (Random Hse, 1982), *Ms., Mademoiselle*

Joyce McDonald 🎤 ✈ W
McIntosh and Otis Inc, 353 Lexington Ave, New York, NY 10016
Internet: jmcdonald@nac.net
 Pubs: *Shades of Simon Gray, Shadow People, Swallowing Stones, Comfort Creek* (Delacorte, 2001, 2000, 1997, 1996), *Homebody, Mail-Order Kid* (Putnam 1991, 1988)

Joseph McElroy W
Melanie Jackson Agency, 250 W 57 St, #1119, New York, NY 10107
 Pubs: *The Letter Left to Me* (Knopf, 1988), *Fathers & Sons: Anth* (Grove Pr, 1992)

Gardner McFall 🎤 ✈ P
924 W End Ave, #101
New York, NY 10025-3544, 212-678-1595
Internet: cathgm@aol.com
 Pubs: *The Pilot's Daughter* (Time Being Bks, 1996), *Naming the Animals* (Viking, 1994), *Contemporary Poetry of New England: Anth* (Middlebury College Pr, 2002), *Atlantic Monthly, Tin House, New Criterion, Nation, Ploughshares, Paris Rev, New Yorker*

Thomas McGuane W
Farrar, Straus & Giroux, 19 Union Sq W, New York, NY 10003, 212-741-6900

Brian McInerney P
200 W 81 St, #56
New York, NY 10024, 212-496-9084
 Pubs: *All My Life* (James L Weil, 1985), *The Photographs Are Still Here* (Smoot Pr, 1984), *Origin*

Taylor Mead PP&P&W
163 Ludlow St
New York, NY 10002
 Pubs: *Excerpts from Son of Andy Warhol* (Hanuman Bks, 1990), *Living with the Animals: Anth* (Faber & Faber, 1995), *Outlook, Boss*

Rosemari Mealy P
WBAI Radio, 505 8th Ave, New York, NY 10018, 212-279-0707
 Pubs: *Confirmations* (Morrow/Quill, 1983), *Mickle Street Rev, Shooting Star, Sunbury*

James Mechem 🎤 W
420 E 54 St #3E
New York, NY 10022-5180, 212-888-1392
 Pubs: *Welcome to Bangkok* (Fell Swoop, 1997), *Della* (Fault Pr, 1976), *Women Without Qualities* (Cafe Solo, 1973), *A Diary of Women* (Winter Hse Pr, 1970), *Joyful Noise: Anth* (Kings Estate, 1996)

Pablo Medina P&W
Elaine Markson Literary Agency, 44 Greenwich Avenue, New York, NY 10011
Internet: pfmedina@aol.com
 Pubs: *The Marks of Birth* (FSG, 1994), *Arching Into the Afterlife* (Bilingual Pr, 1991), *APR, Antioch Rev, Poetry, Pivot*

Tony Medina P
PO Box 335
New York, NY 10026, 212-982-3158
Internet: tonymedina@erols.com
 Pubs: *No Noose Is Good Noose* (Harlem River Pr, 1996), *Identity Lessons: Anth* (Viking Penguin, 1998), *Catch the Fire: Anth* (Riverhead Bks, 1998), *Long Shot, Vibe, African Voices, Paterson Lit Rev, Catalyst, Third World Viewpoints*

Susie Mee P
349 W 22 St
New York, NY 10011, 212-989-0405

Joshua Mehigan P
11 Sterling Place, #2C
Brooklyn, NY 11217
Internet: joshm@interport.net
 Pubs: *Confusing Weather* (Black Cat Pr, 1998), *Ploughshares, Verse, Poetry, Sewanee Rev, Pequod*

Ved Parkash Mehta W
Borchardt Agency, 136 E 57th St, 14th Floor, New York, NY 10022
 Pubs: *Three Stories of the Raj* (Scolar Pr, 1986), *Delinquent Chacha* (H&R, 1967), *Observer, Harper's, Statesman, New Yorker, Atlantic, Spectator*

Richard Meier P
16 Tompkins Pl
Brooklyn, NY 11231, 718-855-3683
 Pubs: *New Voices, 1984-1988: Anth* (Acad of American Poets, 1989), *APR, Chelsea, Mudfish, Phoebe, Graham Hse Rev, o.blek, Prairie Schooner*

Jesus Papoleto Melendez 🎤 ✈ P
PO Box 268
New York, NY 10029-0260, 212-828-5814
Internet: papoleto.poet@verizon.net
 Pubs: *Concertos on Market Street* (Kemetic Images, 1993), *Street Poetry* (Barlenmir Hse, 1972), *Bum Rush the Page: Anth* (Three Rivers Pr, 2001), *In Defense of Mumia: Anth* (Writers & Readers, 1996), *Centro*

D. H. Melhem 🎤 ✈ P&W
250 W 94 St, #2H
New York, NY 10025-6954, 212-865-9216
Internet: dhmelhem@worldnet.att.net
 Pubs: *Country: An Organic Poem* (CCC, 1998), *Rest in Love* (Confrontation Mag Pr, 1995), *Blight* (Riverrun Pr, 1995), *Confrontation, Ararat, Home Planet News, New Pr, Paintbrush, Medicinal Purposes, Graffiti Rag*

Daniel Meltzer   W
251 W 74 St, #3D
New York, NY 10023, 212-362-4116
Internet: dm22@nyu.edu
    Pubs: *The Square Root of Love* (Samuel French, 1979),
Pushcart Prize Anth (Pushcart Pr, 1997), *A Contemporary
Reader for Creative Writing: Anth* (HB, 1994), *Prize Stories
1992: The O. Henry Awards: Anth* (Doubleday, 1992),
Techno Tales, Story Qtly, Vignette

Samuel Menashe   P
75 Thompson St #15
New York, NY 10012, 212-925-4105
    Pubs: *Collected Poems* (National Poetry Fdn, 1986),
Penguin Modern Poets, Vol. 7: Anth (Penguin U.K., 1996),
An Introduction to Poetry: Anth (HC, 1994), *Partisan Rev,
New Yorker, Sunday Times London, Tundra*

Douglas A. Mendini   P&W
403 W 54 St, #1D
New York, NY 10019, 212-541-6328
    Pubs: *Country Living, MacGuffin, Modernsense, Real
Fiction, No, Clock Radio, Lactuca, Pudding, Details*

Claudia Menza   🎤   ✈   P
Claudia Menza Literary Agency, 1170 Broadway, New York,
NY 10001, 212-889-6850
    Pubs: *The Lunatics Ball, Cage of Wild Cries* (Mosaic Pr,
1994, 1990), *The Dream Book: Anth* (Schocken Pr, 1985),
L.A. Times, Ploughshares

Louise Meriwether   🎤   ✈   W
Ellen Levine Literary Agency, 15 E 26 St, Ste 801, New York,
NY 10010, 212-725-4501
Internet: lmeriwe123@aol.com
    Pubs: *Shadow Dancing* (Ballantine, 2000), *Fragments of
the Ark* (Pocket Bks, 1994), *Daddy Was a Number Runner*
(Feminist Pr, 1984), *Essence, Icarus, Black Scholar,
Harbor Rev*

Daphne Merkin   W
c/o Owen Laster, William Morris Agency, 1325 Ave of the
Americas, New York, NY 10019, 212-586-5100
    Pubs: *Enchantment* (HBJ, 1986), *Out of the Garden:
Women Writing on the Bible: Anth* (Ballantine, 1994), *New
Yorker, Partisan Rev, Esquire*

W. S. Merwin   P&W
Alfred A Knopf Inc, 299 Park Ave, New York, NY 10171,
212-572-2153
    Pubs: *The Pupil, The River Sound, Travels: Poems, The Lost
Upland, The Rain in the Trees* (Knopf, 2001, 2000, 1993,
1992, 1988), *New Yorker*

Shelley Messing   P&W
582 2nd St, #4C
Brooklyn, NY 11215, 718-768-2453
    Pubs: *Making Contact* (Voyage Out, 1978), *Women: A
Journal of Liberation, Moving Out, Sojourner*

Mike Metz   P
150 E 56 St, PHA
New York, NY 10022, 212-421-5443
    Pubs: *Street Fighting at Wall & Broad* (Macmillan, 1982)

Claire Michaels   P
35-50 82 St #6E
Jackson Heights, NY 11372, 718-672-7889
    Pubs: *Making Contact* (Willow Bee, 1989), *We Speak for
Peace: Anth* (KIT, 1993), *Poetpourri, Aurora, Pudding,
Parnassus, Wyoming: Hub of the Wheel*

Frank Michel   🎤   W
333 E 80 St, #3-I
New York, NY 10021-0664, 212-861-8258
Internet: fearstone@cs.com
    Pubs: *Witness, Bilingual Rev, American Writing, Gettysburg
Rev, Indiana Rev, Glimmer Train, Crescent Rev, Alaska Qtly
Rev, Qtly West*

Betty Miles   🎤   ✈   W
c/o Library Marketing, Random House, 225 Park Ave S, New
York, NY 10003, 212-254-1600
Internet: bmiles94@aol.com
    Pubs: *The Sky Is Falling, The Tortoise & the Hare* (S&S,
1998, 1998), *Hey! I'm Reading, Save the Earth, Sink or
Swim, I Would If I Could, Maudie & Me* (Knopf, 1995, 1991,
1986, 1982, 1980)

Ellen Miller   W
c/o Jennifer Rodolph Walsh, William Morris, 101 5th Ave, 11th
Floor, New York, NY 10003, 212-255-6515
    Pubs: *Like Being Killed* (Dutton, 1998)

Shelley Miller   🎤   P
299 W 12 St, #17H
New York, NY 10014
    Pubs: *World, Natl Poetry Mag of the Lower East Side, Tone,
Cover, SoHo Arts Weekly, Inner Harvest, Arts New York*

Walter James Miller   🎤   ✈   P
100 Bleecker St, #17-E
New York, NY 10012-2205, 212-674-1466
Internet: wjm2@nyu.edu
    Pubs: *Love's Mainland: New and Selected Poems* (Lintel,
2001), *Making An Angel* (Pylon, 1977), *Croton Rev, Lit Rev,
NYQ, Artemis, Poet Lore*

Stephen Paul Miller   P
60 E 8 St, #6P
New York, NY 10003, 212-677-6739
Internet: spmma@aol.com
    Pubs: *Art Is Boring for the Same Reason We Stayed in Viet
Nam* (Domestic Pr, 1992), *Best American Poetry: Anth*
(S&S, 1994), *Talisman*

Arthur Miller W
c/o Bridget Ashenberg, ICM, 40 W 57 St, New York, NY 10019, 212-556-5600
    Pubs: *The Creation of the World & Other Business, The Crucible, Death of a Salesman* (Viking Penguin, 1973, 1953, 1949)

Joyce Milton P
60 Plaza St, #6B
Brooklyn, NY 11238, 718-636-4471
    Pubs: *Save the Loonies* (Four Winds Pr, 1983), *The Rosenberg File* (HR&W, 1983)

Mark Mirsky W
English Dept, CCNY, Convent Ave & 138 St, New York, NY 10031, 212-650-5408
    Pubs: *The Red Adam* (Sun & Moon, 1990), *The Secret Table* (Macmillan, 1977), *The Qtly, Fiction, TriQtly, Mississippi Rev, Ways of Knowing, Partisan Rev, Massachusetts Rev*

Julia Mishkin P
408 W 57 St, Apt 8H
New York, NY 10019
Internet: juliamishkin@yahoo.com
    Pubs: *Cruel Duet* (QRL Poetry Series, 1986), *Poetry, Georgia Rev, Paris Rev, Nation, Iowa Rev*

Tom Mitchelson PP&W
524 W 143 St, #3
New York, NY 10032, 212-690-5040
    Pubs: *Untold Lies As Love Tales* (WBAI, 1994), *Street Lights: Illuminating Tales of the Urban Black Experience: Anth* (Viking Penguin, 1995)

Charles Molesworth P
109-23 71 Rd
Forest Hills, NY 11375, 718-268-8024
    Pubs: *Words to That Effect* (Seven Woods, 1981), *Salmagundi*

Ursule Molinaro W
65 E 2 St
New York, NY 10003, 212-982-2204
    Pubs: *Power Dreamers* (McPherson, 1994), *Fat Skeletons* (Serif London, 1993), *Obsession: Anth* (Serpent's Tail, 1995), *Caprice, Manoa*

Merle Molofsky 🎤 W
26 W Ninth St Suite 2B
New York, NY 10011
Internet: mmpsya@mindspring.com
    Pubs: *Notes for a Journey* (Limbo Bar & Grill Pr, 1985), *Hexagram* (Poets Union, 1978), *Junction*

Richard Monaco W
Adele Leone Agency, Cathedral Station, PO Box 2080, New York, NY 10025
    Pubs: *Unto the Beast* (Bantam/Spectra, 1987), *Runes* (Ace, 1984), *The Final Quest* (Berkley, 1982)

Timothy Monaghan 🎤 P
78-44 80 St
Glendale, NY 11385-7659
    Pubs: *5 A.M., Slipstream, Long Shot, NYQ, Negative Capability, Mudfish, Chiron Rev, Sulphur River, The Ledge, Poet Lore, Rattle, Birmingham Poetry Rev*

Susan Montez P
875 W 181 St, #1E
New York, NY 10033, 212-781-5433
    Pubs: *Radio Free Queens* (Braziller, 1994), *NYQ, 13th Moon, Artful Dodge, Cream City Rev, Hampden-Sydney Poetry Rev, Long Shot, Puerto del Sol, Asylum*

Honor Moore 🎤 ✈ P
276 Riverside Dr, #8A
New York, NY 10025, 212-663-3546
Internet: HonorM@aol.com
    Pubs: *Darling* (Grove, 2001), *The White Blackbird* (Penguin, 1997), *Memoir* (Chicory Blue, 1988), *Conjunctions, New Yorker, Seneca Rev, Paris Rev, APR*

Lorrie Moore W
Melanie Jackson Agency, 250 W 57 St, Ste 1119, New York, NY 10107
    Pubs: *Birds of America, Who Will Run the Frog Hospital?, Like Life, Anagrams* (Knopf, 1998, 1994, 1990, 1986), *Forgotten Helper* (Kipling, 1987), *New Yorker, Paris Rev*

Susanna Moore W
c/o Andrew Wylie, The Wylie Agency, 250 W 57 St, New York, NY 10107, 212-246-0069
    Pubs: *In the Cut, Sleeping Beauties* (Knopf, 1995, 1993), *The Whiteness of Bones* (Doubleday, 1989), *My Old Sweetheart* (HM, 1983)

Speer Morgan W
c/o Esther Newberg, ICM, 40 W 57 St, New York, NY 10019, 573-882-4460
Internet: morganr@missouri.edu
    Pubs: *The Freshour Cylinders* (MacMurray & Beck, 1998), *The Whipping Boy* (HM, 1994), *The Assemblers* (Dutton, 1986), *Brother Enemy* (Little, Brown, 1981), *Belle Starr* (Atlantic, 1979), *Harper's, Atlantic, Prairie Schooner, Iowa Rev*

Kyoko Mori P&W
Ann Rittenberg Agency, 14 Montgomery Pl, Brooklyn, NY 11215, 212-886-9317
    Pubs: *Polite Lies, The Dream of Water, Shizuko's Daughter* (H Holt, 1998, 1996, 1993), *Prairie Schooner, Missouri Rev, Kenyon Rev, American Scholar, Crosscurrents, Denver Qtly, Paterson Rev*

James Cliftonne Morris　　　　　　P&W
Rivercross Publishing, 127 E 59 St, New York, NY 10022,
800-451-4522
　　Pubs: *Potpourri from a Black Pen* (Rivercross Pr, 1995),
　　Poem of Love in the Long Run (Professional Pr, 1994),
　　Phylon, Freedomways

Mary Morris　🎤　✈　　　　　　P&W
Ellen Levine Literary Agency, 15 E 26 St, New York, NY 10010,
212-889-0620
Internet: mmorris@mail.slc.edu
　　Pubs: *Acts of God* (Picador, 2000), *House Arrest, A
　　Mother's Love, The Waiting Room* (Doubleday, 1996, 1993,
　　1989), *Ontario Rev, Paris Rev, Boulevard, Epoch,
　　Crosscurrents*

Toni Morrison　　　　　　　　　W
1 CM, 40 W. 57th St.
New York, NY 10019
　　Pubs: *Paradise, Jazz, Tar Baby, Song of Solomon, Sula*
　　(Knopf, 1998, 1992, 1981, 1977, 1974), *Beloved* (Random
　　Hse, 1987)

Julia Morrison　✈　　　　　　　P
Seagate Music, 595 Columbus Ave, #9P, New York, NY
10024-1930
　　Pubs: *Smile Right to the Bone* (Seagate, 1989), *New World
　　Writing, Accent, Poetry, Prism Intl*

Lillian Morrison　🎤　　　　　　P
116 Pinehurst Ave, #F42
New York, NY 10033, 212-928-2662
　　Pubs: *Way to Go! Sports Poems, Whistling the Morning In*
　　(Boyds Mills Pr, 2001, 1992), *Confrontation, American
　　Writing, Light, Aethlon*

Charlie Morrow　　　　　　　　PP&P
365 W End Ave
New York, NY 10024, 212-799-0636
　　Pubs: *Exiled in the Word: Anth* (Copper Canyon Pr, 1989),
　　Ear Collective, Raven, Unmuzzled Ox

Bradford Morrow　　　　　　　W
21 E 10 St, Apt 3E
New York, NY 10003
　　Pubs: *Trinity Fields* (Viking Penguin, 1995), *The New Gothic*
　　(Random Hse/Vintage, 1993), *The Almanac Branch* (Linden
　　Pr/S&S, 1991), *Conjunctions, VLS*

Carl Morse　🎤　✈　　　　　　P
460 W 24 St, #17B
New York, NY 10011
　　Pubs: *Columbia Anth of Gay Literature* (Columbia U Pr,
　　1998), *Queer Dog: Anth* (Cleis Pr, 1997), *The Badboy Book
　　of Erotic Poetry: Anth* (Masquerade Bks, 1995), *Gay &
　　Lesbian Poetry in Our Time: Anth* (St. Martin's Pr, 1988),
　　Poetry London

Jo-Ann Mort　　　　　　　　　P
40 Prospect Pk W, Apt 3C
Brooklyn, NY 11215, 718-499-6261
　　Pubs: *Without a Single Answer: Poems on Contemporary
　　Israel: Anth* (Magnes Museum, 1990), *Social Text, Stand,
　　Jewish Qtly, Pequod, Midstream*

Bette Ann Moskowitz　　　　　　W
Jonathan Dolger Agency, 49 E 96 St, New York, NY 10028,
212-427-1853
　　Pubs: *Leaving Barney* (H Holt, 1988), *Appearances*

Stanley Moss　　　　　　　　　P
Sheep Meadow Press, PO Box 1345, Riverdale-on-Hudson,
NY 10471
　　Pubs: *The Intelligence of Clouds* (HBJ, 1989), *Skull of Adam*
　　(Horizon Pr, 1979), *Poetry*

Isaac Elchanan Mozeson　　　　　P
24 5th Ave, #1223
New York, NY 10011, 212-260-4314
Internet: mozeson@yahoo.com
　　Pubs: *The Watcher & Other Poems* (Decalogue Bks, 1990),
　　Jewish Frontier

Marnie Mueller　🎤　✈　　　　　P&W
119 W 77 St #5
New York, NY 10024
　　Pubs: *My Mother's Island, The Climate of the Country,
　　Green Fires* (Curbstone Pr, 2002, 1999, 1999), *VLS, River
　　Styx, Qtly West, Laurel Rev, Clinton Street, Five Fingers Rev*

Maureen Mulhern　🎤　✈　　　　P
440 E 88 St
New York, NY 10128, 212-369-8791
Internet: maureenmulhern@yahoo.com
　　Pubs: *Parallax* (Wesleyan, 1986), *Poetry, Crazyhorse,
　　Phoebe, Prairie Schooner, Indiana Rev, Denver Qtly*

Jerrold Mundis　　　　　　　　W
c/o Merrilee Heifetz, The Writers House, 21 W 26 St, New
York, NY 10010, 212-685-2605
　　Pubs: *The Dogs* (Berkley, 1988), *The Retreat* (Warner, 1985)

Hester Mundis　　　　　　　　W
Harold Ober Assoc, 425 Madison Ave, New York, NY 10017,
212-759-8600
Internet: rfvw@ulster.net
　　Pubs: *Just Humor Me* (Random Hse, 1996), *101 Ways to
　　Avoid Reincarnation* (Workman Pub, 1989)

Carole Murray　　　　　　　　P
214 Riverside Dr, #207
New York, NY 10025, 212-666-5967
　　Pubs: *NAR, Driftwood East, Milkweed, Amelia, Cedar Rock,
　　Womanchild*

Eileen Myles   P
86 E 3 St, #3C
New York, NY 10003, 212-982-4703
Internet: easte8@aol.com
    Pubs: *Maxfield Parrish: Early & New Poems, Chelsea Girls*
    (Black Sparrow Pr, 1995, 1994), *APR, Denver Qtly,*
    Valentine, Jejeune, XXXFruit, Zing

Marie Myung-Ok Lee 🎤 ✈   W
Charlotte Sheedy, Charlotte Sheedy Literary Agency, 65
Bleecker St., New York, NY 10017
Internet: marie_g_lee@yahoo.com
    Pubs: *Finding My Voice, Necessary Roughness* (HC, 2001,
    1996), *Kenyon Rev, Amer Voice, Asian Pacific Amer Jrnl*

Zakee Nadir   P
159 Ashford St
Brooklyn, NY 11207, 718-277-3916
    Pubs: *Don't Run, Listen* (Poet Tential Unltd, 1979)

Robert Nathan   W
350 Central Pk W
New York, NY 10025
    Pubs: *The White Tiger* (S&S, 1987), *Rising Higher* (Dial,
    1981), *Harper's, New Republic, New York*

Elinor Nauen 🎤 ✈   P
27 1st Ave, #9
New York, NY 10003-9447, 212-677-3792
Internet: enauen@aol.com
    Pubs: *American Guys* (Hanging Loose Pr, 1997), *Ladies,*
    Start Your Engines: Anth, Diamonds Are a Girl's Best
    Friend: Anth (Faber & Faber, 1997, 1994), *The World,*
    Exquisite Corpse, Long Shot, Fiction, Gas, Koff, NAW

Gloria Naylor 🎤 ✈   W
Sterling Lord Literistic, 65 Bleecker St, New York, NY 10012,
212-780-6050
    Pubs: *The Men of Brewster Place* (Hyperion, 1998), *Bailey's*
    Cafe (HBJ, 1992), *Children of the Night: The Best Short*
    Stories By Black Writers: Anth (Little, Brown, 1996)

Peter Neill 🎤 ✈   W
165 John St
New York, NY 10038, 212-825-3600
Internet: pneill@compuserve.com
    Pubs: *On a Painted Ocean* (NYU Pr, 1999), *Maritime*
    America (Balsam Pr, 1996), *Acoma* (Leete's Island Bks,
    1978), *Mock Turtle Soup* (Viking/Grossman, 1972), *A Time*
    Piece (Grossman, 1970), *American Sea Writing: Anth*
    (Library of America, 2001)

Stanley Nelson   P
454 37 St
Brooklyn, NY 11232, 718-788-6088
    Pubs: *Immigrant: Books III, II, I* (Birch Brook Pr, 1995, 1993,
    1990), *Long Shot, The Smith, Pinched Nerve, Kansas Qtly,*
    Confrontation, For Now

Vernita Nemec   PP
361 Canal St
New York, NY 10013, 212-925-4419

Cindy Nemser   W
41 Montgomery Pl
Brooklyn, NY 11215, 718-857-9456
    Pubs: *Eve's Delight* (Pinnacle, 1982), *Feminist Art Jrnl,*
    Women: A Jrnl of Liberation, Free Press

Amos Neufeld   P
65 W 90 St, #9E
New York, NY 10024, 212-496-0683
    Pubs: *Blood to Remember: American Poets on the*
    Holocaust: Anth (Texas Tech U Pr, 1991), *Ghosts of the*
    Holocaust: Anth (Wayne State U Pr, 1989), *Response*

Joachim Neugroschel   P
447 Beach 136 St
Belle Harbor, NY 11694, 718-318-2147
    Pubs: *Extensions, Just Before Sailing*

Wade Newman 🎤 ✈   P
505 E 14 St, #9C
New York, NY 10009, 212-598-9483
Internet: wnewman@earthlink.net
    Pubs: *Testaments* (Somers Rocks Pr, 1996), *Edge City Rev,*
    Pivot, Amer Arts Qtly, Kenyon Rev, Croton Rev, Cumberland
    Poetry Rev, Crosscurrents, Nebo, Nimrod, Confrontation

Leslie Newman   W
Georges Borchardt Inc, 136 E 57 St, New York, NY 10022,
212-753-5785

Fae Myenne Ng   W
Donadio & Olson Inc, 121 W 27 St, Ste 704, New York,
NY 10001
    Pubs: *Bone* (Hyperion, 1993), *Charlie Chan Is Dead: Anth*
    (Penguin, 1994), *Harper's, Pushcart Prize XII*

Nina daVinci Nichols 🎤 ✈   W
305 W 13 St, #5H
New York, NY 10014, 212-924-1423
    Pubs: *Pirandello & Film* (U Nebraska Pr, 1996), *Ariadne's*
    Lives (Fairleigh Dickinson U Pr, 1995), *Child of the Night*
    (Bantam, 1985), *Behind the Veil: Anth* (Eden Pr, 1982),
    Stages, American Bk Rev, Shakespeare Bulletin

M. M. Nichols   P
311 E 50 St, #5H
New York, NY 10022-7941, 212-759-8733
    Pubs: *Haiku World: Anth* (Kodansha Intl, 1996), *Timepieces:*
    Anth (Cloverleaf Bks 1993), *Wind in the Long Grass: Anth*
    (S&S, 1991), *The Formalist, Salamander, Waterways,*
    Modern Haiku, Frogpond

Richard Nickson P
205 W 19 St
New York, NY 10011, 212-989-7833
    Pubs: *Stones: A Book of Epigrams* (Lithic Pr, 1998), *Cause at Heart* (w/Junius Scales; U Georgia Pr, 1987), *Staves* (Moretus Pr, 1977)

Hugh Nissenson W
411 W End Ave
New York, NY 10024, 212-873-5193

Kathryn Nocerino 🎤 P
139 W 19 St, #2B
New York, NY 10011
    Pubs: *Death of the Plankton Bar & Grill, Wax Lips* (New Rivers Pr, 1987, 1980), *Candles in the Daytime* (Warthog Pr, 1986), *City Secrets: New York: Anth* (The Little Bookroom, 2002), *Growing Up Ethnic in America: Anth* (Penguin Bks, 1999)

Suzanne Noguere 🎤 ✈ P
27 W 96 St #12B
New York, NY 10025, 212-865-1045
Internet: snoguere@eclipse.net
    Pubs: *Whirling Round the Sun* (Midmarch Arts Pr, 1996), *Second Word Thursdays: Anth* (Bright Hill Pr, 1999), *A Formal Feeling Comes: Anth* (Story Line Pr, 1994), *Rattapallax, Heliotrope, Poetry, Nation, Lit Rev, Sparrow*

James Nordlund P
318 Third Ave, Apt 553
New York, NY 10010
    Pubs: *Serendipity, Jones Av., Pink Cadillac, Poets Fantasy*

Constance Norgren P
303A 16 St
Brooklyn, NY 11215-5504
    Pubs: *Yankee, Northland Qtly, Minnesota Rev, Tendril, Louisville Rev, Poetry Rev, Confrontation*

Lissette Norman 🎤 ✈ P
4 Chester Pl, #5B
Staten Island, NY 10304
Internet: LaPoetaDR@cs.com
    Pubs: *Role Call: A Generational Anth of Social and Political Black Lit & Art: Anth* (Third World Pr, 2002), *Bum Rush the Page: A Def Poetry Jam: Anth* (Three Rivers Pr, 2001), *Moving Beyond Boundaries: Anth* (New York U Pr, 1995), *African Voices, DIALOGUE*

Charles North P
c/o English Dept., Pace Univ, 1 Pace Plaza, New York, NY 10038
    Pubs: *The Nearness of the Way You Look Tonight* (Adventures in Poetry Pr, 2001), *New & Selected Poems* (Sun & Moon Pr, 1999), *The Year of the Olive Oil* (Hanging Loose Pr, 1989)

Sudie Nostrand 🎤 P
11 Waverly Pl E
New York, NY 10003
    Pubs: *Bless the Day: Anth* (Kodansha America, 1998), *California Qtly, Illya's Honey, Poetry Motel, Cumberland Poetry Rev, Kansas Qtly, Louisville Rev, Birmingham Poetry Rev, Greensboro Rev*

Craig Nova 🎤 ✈ W
Peter Matson, Sterling Lord Literistic, 65 Bleecker St, New York, NY 10012, 212-780-6050
Internet: nova@sover.net
    Pubs: *Wetware* (Crown, 2002), *Universal Donor, Book of Dreams* (HM, 1998, 1994), *Trombone* (Grove, 1992), *The Good Son* (Bantam Doubleday Dell, 1982), *Esquire, Paris Rev*

Barbara Novack 🎤 ✈ P
134-18 228 St
Laurelton, NY 11413-2441, 718-527-3674
    Pubs: *On a Sea of Sighs, A Rainbow in the Sand, Still Life* (Michael Gaily Bks, 1999, 1999, 1999), *CQ, Long Island Qtly, South Coast Poetry Jrnl, Cape Rock, Alms House Sampler, Verve, Nassau Rev*

Minda Novek PP
226 W 47 St, 2nd Fl
New York, NY 10036-1413, 212-921-9040
    Pubs: *Daily News Sunday Supplement, Adamant Jrnl, Seaport Mag*

D. Nurkse 🎤 ✈ P
598 17 St, #1
Brooklyn, NY 11218, 718-788-0024
    Pubs: *Leaving Xaia, Voices Over Water* (Four Way Bks, 2000, 1996), *Staggered Lights* (Owl Creek Pr, 1990), *Shadow Wars* (Hanging Loose, 1988), *APR, Poetry, Kenyon Rev, Hudson Rev, New Yorker, Hanging Loose*

Michael O'Brien P
400 W 23 St, #6L
New York, NY 10011
Internet: michaelobrien@mindspring.com
    Pubs: *Sills: Selected Poems of Michael O'Brien* (Zoland Bks, 2000), *The Floor & the Breath, Veil, Hard Rain* (Cairn Edtns, 1994, 1986), *Blue Springs* (Sun, 1976)

Francis V. O'Connor 🎤 ✈ P
250 E 73 St, #11C
New York, NY 10021-4310, 212-988-8927
Internet: fvoc@aol.com
    Pubs: *Twelve Sonnets for the Abstract Expressionists* (Art Jrnl, 1988), *And What Rough Beast: Anth* (Ashland Poetry Pr, 1999), *Creative Insight, Whelks Walk Rev*

Stephen O'Connor   P&W
Witherspoon Assoc, 235 E 31 St, New York, NY 10016,
212-889-8626
  Pubs: *Rescue* (Harmony Bks, 1989), *Columbia,
  Massachusetts Rev, The Qtly, Fiction Intl, Partisan Rev,
  Hubbub*

Ned O'Gorman   P
2 Lincoln Sq
New York, NY 10023, 212-799-0806

Jennifer O'Grady 🎤   P
250 W 94 St, #6D
New York, NY 10025-6954
Internet: jogrady1@aol.com
  Pubs: *White* (Mid-List Pr, 1999), *American Poetry: Anth*
  (Carnegie Mellon, 2000), *Yale Rev, Kalliope, Colorado Rev,
  Antioch Rev, Georgia Rev, Poetry, Poetry East, Seneca Rev,
  Southern Rev, Harper's, 13th Moon, Western Humanities
  Rev, SW Rev, Kenyon Rev*

Sidney Offit 🎤   W
23 E 69 St
New York, NY 10021
  Pubs: *He Had It Made* (Beckham Classic Reprint, 1999),
  The Bookie's Son, A Memoir (St. Martin's Pr, 1995), *What
  Kind of Guy Do You Think I Am?* (Lippincott, 1970)

Valery Oisteanu 🎤 ✈   P
170 2nd Ave, #2A
New York, NY 10003, 212-777-3597
  Pubs: *The King of Penguins, Zen-Dada Meditations for the
  3rd Millennium* (Linear Arts Pr, 2001, 1998), *Temporary
  Immortality, Passport to Eternal Life, Moons of Venus* (Pass
  Pr, 1996, 1992, 1990), *New Observations, Long Shot*

Adrian Oktenberg 🎤 ✈   P
c/o Ellen Yaroshevsky, CLC, 55 5th Ave, Rm 1116, New York,
NY 10003-4301, 212-790-0410
  Pubs: *The Bosnia Elegies* (Paris Pr, 1997), *Drawing in the
  Dirt* (Malachite & Agate, 1997), *Luna, Qtly West, Prairie
  Schooner, Provincetown Arts, Salamander, WRB,
  American Voice*

Sharon Olds   P
Alfred A Knopf Inc, 201 E 50 St, New York, NY 10022
  Pubs: *The Gold Cell, The Dead & the Living* (Knopf, 1987,
  1984), *Satan Says* (U Pitt Pr, 1980)

Sondra Spatt Olsen   W
201 W 16 St, #10A
New York, NY 10011
  Pubs: *Traps* (U Iowa Pr, 1991), *Yale Rev, Ontario Rev, New
  Yorker, Iowa Rev, Boulevard, Redbook, Mississippi Rev,
  Confrontation, Qtly West*

Gregory Orfalea   P&W
Tom Wallace, The Wallace Agency, 177 E 70 St, New York, NY
10021, 212-570-9090
  Pubs: *Messengers of the Lost Battalion* (The Free Pr, 1995),
  Before the Flames (U Texas Pr, 1988), *Antioch Rev, TriQtly,
  CSM, Epoch*

Miguel A. Ortiz   P
516 Seventh St
Brooklyn, NY 11215

Susan Osterman 🎤 ✈   P
610 W 115 St #94
New York, NY 10025, 212-678-1115
  Pubs: *A Head of Her Time* (Theo, 1996), *Strip Mining*
  (Cambric Pr, 1987), *Clark Street Rev, Village Voice, Cover*

Suzanne Ostro 🎤   P&W
321 W 94 St, #2W
New York, NY 10025
Internet: pombooks@aol.com
  Pubs: *Dream of the Whale* (Toothpaste Pr, 1982), *Demoli-
  tion Zone, The Talking of Hands: Anth* (New Rivers Pr, 1975,
  1998), *Bearing Life: Anth* (Feminist Pr, 2001), *River Styx,
  Exquisite Corpse, Paris Rev, Partisan Rev, Open Places,
  Yardbird*

Iris Owens   W
c/o Arlene Donovan, ICM, 40 W 57 St, New York, NY 10019,
212-556-5600

Kent Jorgensen Ozarow   P
4 Edgewood Pl
Great Neck, NY 11024, 516-466-0976
  Pubs: *Poetry Now, Confrontation, Croton Rev, Xanadu,
  Paris Rev, West Hills Rev, Alura, Yankee*

Cynthia Ozick   W
c/o Theron Raines, Raines & Raines, 71 Park Ave, New York,
NY 10016
  Pubs: *Quarrel & Quandary, Fame & Folly* (Knopf, 2000,
  1996), *The Puttermesser Papers* (Vintage, 1998), *A Cynthia
  Ozick Reader* (Indiana U Pr, 1996)

Richard Pa   P
210 E 15 St, #14K
New York, NY 10003, 212-420-1854
  Pubs: *Landscape of Skin & Single Rooms* (Monday Morning
  Pr, 1973), *Chester H. Jones Anth* (Chester H. Jones Fdn,
  1997), *Prairie Schooner, Paris Rev, Windless Orchard*

William Packard   P&W
232 W 14 St, #2A
New York, NY 10011, 212-255-8531
  Pubs: *Art of Poetry Writing* (St. Martin's Pr, 1990), *The
  Poet's Dictionary* (H&R, 1989)

Eve Packer 🎤 ✈   PP&P
78 Bank St, #17
New York, NY 10014-2102, 212-243-3496
Internet: evebpacker@aol.com
　　Pubs: *window: 911, west frm 42nd* (CDs; Altsax Records,
　　2001, 1998), *that look* (CD; Boxholder, 2000), *Showworld*
　　(Kango Pub, 1996), *skulls head samba* (fly-by-night pr,
　　1994), *Tribes, Poetry in Performance, Sculpture, Knitting
　　Factory, Bowery Poetry Club*

Ron Padgett   P&W
342 E 13 St, #6
New York, NY 10003-5811, 212-477-4472
　　Pubs: *You Never Know, Great Balls of Fire* (Coffee Hse Pr,
　　2002, 1990), *New & Selected Poems* (Godine, 1995)

Maggie Paley 🎤   W
c/o Jane Gelfman, Gelfman Schneider Literary Agents. Inc.,
250 W 57 St, #2515, New York, NY 10107
　　Pubs: *Elephant* (Groundwater Pr, 1990), *Bad Manners*
　　(Clarkson Potter, 1986), *Mudfish, New Observations*

Marion Palm 🎤 ✈   P
705 41 St, #17
Brooklyn, NY 11232
　　Pubs: *Islands of the Blest* (Print Ctr, 1993), *Nightingale Day
　　Songs* (Wingate Pr, 1984), *Working Mother, Big Apple,
　　Minneapolis Star & Tribune*

Bruce Palmer   W
180 Riverside Dr
New York, NY 10024, 212-595-6651
　　Pubs: *The Karma Charmer* (Harmony Bks, 1994)

Anne Paolucci   P&W
166-25 Powells Cove Blvd
Beechhurst, NY 11357, 718-767-8380
　　Pubs: *Terminal Degrees* (Novella, 1997), *Queensboro
　　Bridge & Other Poems* (Potpourri Pubs, 1995), *Three Short
　　Plays* (Griffon Hse Pubs, 1995), *The World & I, Pirandello
　　Society Annual, Choice, Kenyon Rev, Prism, Poetry*

Jim Papa 🎤 ✈   P&W
Dept of English, York College (CUNY), Jamaica, NY 11451,
718-262-3720
Internet: papa@york.cuny.edu
　　Pubs: *In Autumn: Anth* (Birnham Wood, 1994), *Snowy Egret,
　　Petroglyph, Isle, Fire Island Tide, NAR, Long Island Qtly,
　　College English, Wordsmith, Plainsong, Panhandler,
　　Madison Rev*

Helen Papell 🎤   P
720 W End Ave
New York, NY 10025-6299, 212-316-5821
　　Pubs: *Talking with Eve Leah Hagar Miriam* (Jewish Women's
　　Resource Ctr, 1996), *Lilith: Anth* (Jason Aronson, 1999),
　　Sarah's Daughters Sing: Anth (KTAV, 1990), *Verve, Metis,
　　Mildred, Negative Capability, Prairie Schooner, Jewish
　　Women's Lit*

Matthew Paris   P&W
645 E 14 St, Apt 9E
New York, NY 10009, 212-995-0299
　　Pubs: *The Holy City* (Carpenter Pr, 1979), *Mystery* (Avon
　　Bks, 1973), *Home Planet News, Generalist Papers, The
　　Phoenix, Downtown, New Worlds, Brooklyn Lit Rev, Bright
　　Hill*

Gwendolyn M. Parker   W
Marie Brown Assoc Inc, 625 Broadway, New York, NY 10012,
212-533-5534
Internet: gmcdparker@juno.com
　　Pubs: *Trespassing: My Sojourn in the Halls of Privilege,
　　These Same Long Bones* (HM, 1997, 1994)

Vincent Passaro   W
Georges Borchardt Inc, 136 E 57 St, New York, NY 10022,
212-753-5785
　　Pubs: *Lust, Violence, Sin, Magic: Esquire Anth* (Atlantic
　　Monthly Pr, 1993), *Best of the West: Anth* (Norton, 1992),
　　Harper's, Story, Willow Springs, NAW

Beth Passaro   W
514 W 110 St, #21
New York, NY 10025, 212-662-6224
Internet: oddsyntax@aol.com
　　Pubs: *Columbia, NW Rev*

Ben Passikoff   P
73-07 164 St
Flushing, NY 11366
Internet: benpas969@aol.com
　　Pubs: *Atlanta Rev, Harvard Rev, Texas Rev, Rattle, Qtly Rev
　　of Lit, Poetry Intl, Sarah Lawrence Rev, Small Pond Mag,
　　Verve, Connecticut River Rev, Madison Rev, Painted Bride
　　Qtly, Interim, Literal Latte*

Ned Pastor 🎤 ✈   P
1200 Midland Ave
Bronxville, NY 10708-6412, 914-337-4214
Internet: n_pastor@dellnet.com
　　Pubs: *Lighten Up: Anth* (Meadowbrook Pr, 1999, 1998),
　　Golf: Anth (Meadowbrook Pr, 1996), *Treasury of Light Verse:
　　Anth* (Random Hse, 1995), *Sometime the Cow Kick Your
　　Head: Anth* (Bits Pr, 1988), *Pennsylvania Poetry Society
　　Prize Poems, Amelia, Light*

Ann Patchett   W
c/o Lisa Bankoff, ICM, 40 W 57 St, New York, NY 10019,
212-556-5600
　　Pubs: *Taft, The Patron Saint of Liars* (HM, 1994, 1992)

Kathryn Paulsen 🎤 ✈   W
341 W 24th St, #17H
New York, NY 10011
Internet: gauchette@yahoo.com
　　Pubs: *New Letters, West Branch, Sundog, Cottonwood Rev,
　　New Constellations*

Molly Peacock 🎤 ✈   P&W
505 E 14 St, #3-G
New York, NY 10009, 212-677-3535
Internet: peacockmol@aol.com
    Pubs: *Cornucopia: New & Selected Poems, Original Love*
(Norton, 2002, 1995), *Take Heart, Raw Heaven* (Random
Hse, 1989, 1984), *And Live Apart* (U Missouri Pr, 1980)

Pamela Manche Pearce   P&W
PO Box 1848
New York, NY 10021, 212-879-7935
    Pubs: *Mondo Greco, Ararat, Straight Ahead Intl, Samba,
Brooklyn Rev, Hellenic Times*

Gerry Gomez Pearlberg 🎤 ✈   P&W
418 Bergen St
Brooklyn, NY 11217, 718-638-1233
Internet: ggpwrite@aol.com
    Pubs: *Mr. Bluebird* (Painted Leaf, 2001), *Marianne Faithfull's
Cigarette, Queer Dog: Homo/Pup/Poetry: Anth* (Cleis Pr,
1998, 1997), *The Best American Erotica: Anth* (Macmillan,
1994), *Women on Women 2: Anth* (Plume, 1993), *Gulf
Coast, Pleiades, Chelsea, Beloit*

Fredda S. Pearlson 🎤 ✈   P
350 Bleecker St
New York, NY 10014-2602
    Pubs: *The Dolphin's Arc: Anth* (SCOP, 1989), *Wisconsin
Rev, Helicon Nine, Stone Country, Chrysalis, Little Mag,
Centennial Rev, California Qtly*

Robert Pease   W
500 E 77 St, #1017
New York, NY 10021
    Pubs: *The Associate Professor* (S&S, 1967)

Richard Peck   P&W
c/o Delacorte Press, 245 E 47 St, New York, NY 10017
    Pubs: *Remembering the Good Times, This Family of
Women* (Delacorte, 1985, 1983)

Sylvia Peck   W
136 W 75 St, #3C
New York, NY 10023
Internet: rossdhu@compuserve.com
    Pubs: *Kelsey's Raven, Seal Child* (Morrow Junior, 1992,
1989)

Anca Pedvis   P
625 Main St #1233
New York, NY 10044, 212-319-5339
Internet: sbfam14@mindspring.com
    Pubs: *Romanian Writers in New York: Anth* (Vestala Press,
1998), *Cartea Romaneasca, Romania Literara, Pen &
Brush Club*

Ted Pejovich 🎤 ✈   W
233 W 99 St, #6E
New York, NY 10025-5017, 212-663-7621
    Pubs: *The State of California* (Knopf, 1989), *The Qtly,
Kenyon Rev, Story Qtly*

Derek Pell   P&W
Donadio & Olson Inc, 121 W 27 St, Ste 704, New York, NY
10001
    Pubs: *Morbid Curiosities* (Jonathan Cape, 1983),
Expurgations (Hyena, 1981), *Playboy, Benzene*

Michael M. Pendragon   P&W
Radio City Station, POB 719, New York, NY 10101-0719
    Pubs: *Poetry Motel, Afterthoughts, Portal, Maverick Pr,
Clinton Chronicles, Grim Commander Fright Library,
Barefoot Grass Jrnl, Terror Tales, Blue Lady, Pluto's
Orchard, Visionary Tongue, Nasty Piece of Work*

Edmund Pennant   P
2902 210 St
Bayside, NY 11360, 718-229-6104
Internet: penbard@aol.com
    Pubs: *Askance & Strangely: New & Selected Poems, The
Wildebeest of Carmine Street* (Orchises Pr, 1993, 1990),
*Confrontation, Shenandoah, American Scholar, Pivot, NER,
Madison Rev*

Willie Perdomo 🎤 ✈   PP&P
PO Box 1363
New York, NY 10113
Internet: papo421@aol.com
    Pubs: *Visiting Langston* (Holt/Byr, 2002), *Postcards of El
Barrio* (Isla Negra Pr, 2002), *Where a Nickel Costs a Dime*
(Norton, 1996), *Wachale!: Anth* (Cricket Bks, 2002), *Listen
Up!: Anth* (One World, 1999), *Aaron Davis Hall, Lincoln
Center*

Victor Perera   W
Watkins Loomis Agency, Inc, 133 E 35 St, Ste 1, New York, NY
10016, 212-532-0080
    Pubs: *Rites: A Guatemalan Boyhood* (HBJ, 1986), *Atlantic,
New Yorker, Harper's, Nation*

Deborah Perlberg   W
305 E 6 St #7
New York, NY 10003
    Pubs: *Cliff House* (M Evans, 1990), *Heartaches High
School, Heartaches* (Fawcett/Ballantine, 1987, 1983)

Rick Pernod 🎤 ✈   P
4414 Cayuga Ave
Bronx, NY 10471
Internet: exoterica@aol.com
    Pubs: *New Rain: Poetry By Men: Anth* (Blind Beggar Pr,
1999), *Alaska Qtly Rev, Medicinal Purposes, Minding the
Gap, Paterson Lit Rev, Rattapallax*

John Perreault   P
54 E 7 St
New York, NY 10003, 212-677-3504
  Pubs: *Hotel Death & Other Tales* (Sun & Moon Pr, 1989),
  Harry (Coach Hse, 1974)

Kathrin Perutz   W
16 Avalon Rd
Great Neck, NY 11021, 516-482-0804
  Pubs: *Writing for Love & Money* (U Arkansas Pr, 1991),
  Faces (Pseudonym: Joanna Kingsley; Bantam, 1987)

Keith Peterson   W
Deborah Schneider, Agent, 250 W 57 St, #1007, New York, NY
10107, 212-941-8050
  Pubs: *The Scarred Man* (Doubleday, 1990), *Rough Justice*
  (Bantam, 1989), *Ellery Queen*

Ann Petry   P&W
Russell & Volkening Inc, 50 W 29 St, New York, NY 10001
  Pubs: *Miss Muriel, The Narrows, The Street* (HM, 1971,
  1953, 1946), *New Yorker*

Simon Pettet ♪ ✈   P
437 E 12 St #6
New York, NY 10009
  Pubs: *Abundant Treasures* (w/Duncan Hannah; Granary
  Bks, 2001), *Selected Poems* (Talisman Hse, 1996), *Talking
  Pictures* (w/Rudy Burckhardt; Zoland, 1994), *Twenty One
  Love* (Microbrigade, 1990)

D. F. Petteys   P
90 Bank St
New York, NY 10014, 212-989-4528
  Pubs: *Against Infinity* (Primary Pr, 1979), *Lying Awake*
  (Lillian Pr, 1977)

Richard Pevear   P
313 W 107 St
New York, NY 10025, 212-662-7190
  Pubs: *Exchanges* (Spuyten Duyvil, 1982), *Night Talk*
  (Princeton U Pr, 1977), *Hudson Rev, Occident*

Robert Phillips ♪ ✈   P&W
Wieser & Wieser Inc, 25 E 21 St, 6th Fl, New York, NY 10010,
212-260-0860
  Pubs: *Spinach Days, Breakdown Lane* (Johns Hopkins U Pr,
  2000, 1994), *Public Landing Revisited* (Story Line Pr, 1992),
  Personal Accounts (Ontario Rev Pr, 1986), *Paris Rev,
  Hudson Rev, New Yorker, Poetry, Nation*

Louis Phillips ♪ ✈   P&W
375 Riverside Dr, #14-C
New York, NY 10025, 212-866-9643
  Pubs: *Bus to the Moon* (Fort Schuyler Pr, 2000), *A Dream of
  Countries Where No One Dare Live* (SMU Pr, 1993), *Hot
  Corner: Baseball Writings* (Livingston U Pr, 1996), *Georgia
  Rev, Massachusetts Rev, Epoch*

Wanda Phipps ♪ ✈   P
470 State St
Brooklyn, NY 11217, 718-852-1722
Internet: wanda@interport.net
  Pubs: *Zither Mood* (CD-Rom; Faux Pr, 2002), *Your Last
  Illusion or Break Up Sonnets* (Situations, 2001), *The
  Portable Boog Reader: Anth* (Boog Lit, 2000), *Verses That
  Hurt: Pleasure & Pain from the Poemfone Poets* (St. Martin's
  Pr, 1997)

Bruce Piasecki   P
c/o Lettie Lee, Ann Elmo Literary Agency, 60 E 42 St, New
York, NY 10017, 212-661-2880
  Pubs: *In Search of Environmental Excellence* (S&S, 1990),
  America's Future (Greenwood, 1988)

Felice Picano   P&W
The Malaga Baldi Agency, 208 W 84th St, Suite 3C, New York,
NY 10024
Internet: felicepic@aol.com
  Pubs: *The Lure, Onyx, The Book of Lies, The New York
  Years* (Alyson Pubs, 2002, 2001, 2000, 2000), *A House on
  the Ocean, A House on the Bay* (Faber & Faber, 1997), *Like
  People in History* (Viking, 1995), *Window Elegies* (Close
  Grip Pr, 1985)

Pedro Juan Pietri   P
400 W 43 St, #38E
New York, NY 10036, 212-244-4270
  Pubs: *An Alternate* (Hayden Bk Co, 1980), *The Blue & the
  Gray* (Cherry Valley Edtns, 1975)

Kevin Pilkington   P
520 E 72 St #LP
New York, NY 10021, 212-535-0533
  Pubs: *Ready to Eat the Sky* (River City Pubs, 2003),
  Birthday Poems, A Celebration: Anth (Thunder's Mouth Pr,
  2002), *Contemporary Poems of New England: Anth*
  (Middlebury, 2002), *Spare Change* (La Jolla Poets Pr, 1997),
  Getting By (The Ledge, 1996), *Poetry*

Thomas Pinnock   PP
265 Bainbridge St
Brooklyn, NY 11233, 718-467-0563
  Pubs: *Essence, Everybody's*

Beverly Pion   P
58-19 251 St
Little Neck, NY 11362, 718-225-3019
  Pubs: *Sunlight on the Moon: Anth* (Carpenter Gothic, 2000),
  Long Island Qtly: Anth (Birnam Wood, 1997), *Eve's Legacy,
  Crone's Nest: Wisdom of the Elderwoman, Taproot, Lit Rev*

Hilary Plattner 🎤 ✈ P&W
501 17 St
Brooklyn, NY 11215, 718-369-0068
Internet: hplattner@brooklynwriters.org
    Pubs: *Fence, The Ledge, Cider Press Rev, Gulf Coast, Mudfish, Brownstone Rev, Bellowing Ark, GSU Rev, Poetry Motel*

Susan Pliner 🎤 ✈ P
2501 Palisade Ave, #E-1
Bronx, NY 10463-6104, 718-796-2885
    Pubs: *Paris Rev, Pivot, APR, Greenfield Rev, Kenyon Rev*

Tamra Plotnick 🎤 ✈ P&W
397 16 St #1
Brooklyn, NY 11215, 718-499-5774
Internet: tplotnick@pace.edu
    Pubs: *Global City Rev, Poetry Project Newsletter, Caprice, Curare, A Gathering of the Tribes*

Carol Polcovar P
145 E 27 St 1A
New York, NY 10016, 718-499-0497
Internet: carolpolcovar@cs.com
    Pubs: *Riddle* (Tiresis I, 1983), *Partisan Rev, Bitterroot, Helen Rev*

Ellin Ronee Pollachek W
525 E 83 St, Apt 2W
New York, NY 10028
Internet: EllinsPlace@aol.com
    Pubs: *Total Immersion-Amikveh Anthology: Anth,* (Jason Aronson Inc.), *Seasons: Bk,* (Zebra Books, 1980 & 1988), *The Bridge, Wisconsin Rev, Focus Mag*

Eileen Pollack 🎤 ✈ W
c/o Maria Massie, Witherspoon Assoc, 235 E 31 St, New York, NY 10016, 212-889-8626
Internet: epollack@umich.edu
    Pubs: *Paradise, New York* (Temple U Pr, 1998), *The Rabbi in the Attic & Other Stories* (Delphinium, 1991), *Pushcart Prize XX, XVI: Anths* (Pushcart Pr, 1996, 1992), *NER, Ploughshares, Prairie Schooner, Michigan Qtly Rev, Agni, Literary Rev*

Shirley B. Pollan-Cohen 🎤 PP&P
2939 Grand Concourse, #4C
Bronx, NY 10468-1708, 718-289-5679
    Pubs: *Connections, Grub Street, Bronx Roots, Garland, Jewish Currents, Hieroglyphics Pr*

Elizabeth Pollet W
463 West St, #D-817
New York, NY 10014
    Pubs: *A Family Romance* (NAL, 1951)

Katha Pollitt P
317 W 93 St
New York, NY 10025
    Pubs: *Antarctic Traveller* (Knopf, 1982), *The Best American Poetry: Anth* (Scribner, 1991), *New Yorker, Antaeus, Atlantic, Nation, Poetry*

Edward Pomerantz 🎤 ✈ W
351 W 24 St, #10F
New York, NY 10011-1517, 212-255-6277
Internet: ejp20@columbia.edu
    Pubs: *Into It* (iuniverse.com, 2000), *Brisburial Play* (Magic Circle Pr, 1981), *Tyuonyi*

Marie Ponsot P
340 E 93 St, #2J
New York, NY 10128
    Pubs: *The Bird Catcher, The Green Dark, Admit Impediment* (Knopf, 1998, 1988, 1981), *Commonweal, The Jrnl, New Yorker, Paris Rev, Ploughshares, Gulf Coast, Kenyon Rev*

Melinda Camber Porter P
c/o Faith Hamlin, Sanford J Greenburger Assoc., 55 5th Ave, New York, NY 10003, 212-206-5600
Internet: flicekjr@pipeline.com
    Pubs: *Badlands, The Art of Love* (Writers & Readers, 1996, 1993)

Cally Pourakis P
11 Nortema Ct
New Hyde Park, NY 11040-2031, 516-437-9511
    Pubs: *Thirteen Poetry Mag, Haiku Zasshi Zo, Salome, Bitterroot, Calli's Tales, Hoosier Challenger*

David Poyer 🎤 ✈ W
Sloan Harris, ICM, 40 W 57th St, New York, NY 10019
    Pubs: *Black Storm, Tomahawk, The Passage* (St. Martin's Pr, 2002, 1998, 1995), *Fire on the Waters* (S&S, 2001)

Penelope Prentice W
Garland Publishing Inc, 717 Fifth Ave, New York, NY 10022-8101, 212-308-9399
    Pubs: *The Pinter Aesthetic: The Erotic Aesthetic* (Garland Pub, 1994), *Boundary II, 20th Century Literary Tales, Wisconsin Rev, Spree, Cithara, Paper Curtain*

Richard Price W
Janklow & Nesbit Associates, 598 Madison Ave, New York, NY 10022-1614
    Pubs: *Freedomland* (Broadway Bks, 1998), *Clockers, Ladies Man, Bloodbrothers* (HM, 1992, 1978, 1976), *The Breaks* (S&S, 1984)

Ron Price ♦ ⊀   P
Liberal Arts, The Juilliard School, 60 Lincoln Center Plaza,
New York, NY 10023-6588, 212799500 x346
Internet: ronprice@juilliard.edu
  Pubs: *A Small Song Called Ash from the Fire* (Rattapallax
  Pr, 2001), *A Crucible for the Left Hand* (Wubbie Productions
  for Exoterica, 1998), *Leviathan Qtly, One Trick Pony, Poetry,
  Zone 3,*

William Price ♦   W
292 Clermont Ave
Brooklyn, NY 11205
  Pubs: *The Potlatch Run* (Dutton, 1971), *Evergreen Rev,
  Saturday Evening Post*

Robert Prochaska ♦ ⊀   P
3972 52 St
Woodside, NY 11377-3257, 718-457-3432
  Pubs: *Fourfront* (Bearstone, 1982), *Pipe Dream, Exquisite
  Corpse, Louisville Rev, Slipstream, Woodrose, Rhode
  Island Rev, Moody Street Irregulars*

James Purdy   P&W
236 Henry St
Brooklyn, NY 11201, 718-858-0015
  Pubs: *Out with the Stars* (Peter Owen Ltd, 1992), *63:
  Dream Palace, Collected Stories 1956-1986* (Black Sparrow
  Pr, 1991)

Thomas Pynchon   W
c/o Ray Roberts, Henry Holt & Co Inc, 115 W 18 St, New York,
NY 10011
  Pubs: *Mason & Dixon* (H Holt, 1997), *Vineland* (Little, Brown,
  1990), *Gravity's Rainbow* (Penguin, 1987), *V.* (H&R, 1986)

David Quintavalle ♦ ⊀   P
36 Commerce St
New York, NY 10014-3755
  Pubs: *The Carl Chronicles, Inky Star* (P&Q Pr, 1999, 1998),
  *Frogpond, Modern Words, Green Hills Lit Lantern, Global
  City Rev, Gulfstream Mag, Mudfish 11, Slant*

Margo Rabb ♦ ⊀   W
1498 3rd Ave, #5
New York, NY 10028
Internet: margorabb@aol.com
  Pubs: *New Stories from the South: Anth* (Algonquin Bks,
  2000), *Best New American Voices: Anth* (HB, 2000),
  Atlantic, Zoetrope, Seventeen, Glimmer Train, The Sun

Anna Rabinowitz ♦ ⊀   P
850 Park Ave
New York, NY 10021-1845, 212-734-2233
Internet: rabanna@aol.com
  Pubs: *Darkling* (Tupelo Pr, 2001), *At the Site of Inside Out*
  (U Massachusetts Pr, 1997), *KGB Bar Book of Poems: Anth*
  (Harper, 2000), *Best American Poetry: Anth* (Scribner,
  1989), *Lit, Verse, Volt, Atlantic, SW Rev, Paris Rev, NAW,
  Sonora Rev, Colorado Rev*

Nahid Rachlin   W
300 E 93 St, Apt 43-D
New York, NY 10128, 212-996-3478
  Pubs: *Heart's Desire, Married to a Stranger, Veils* (City
  Lights, 1995, 1994, 1993), *Foreigner* (Norton, 1979), *Fiction,
  Shenandoah, Ararat, Redbook, Literary Rev, Columbia,
  Confrontation, Natural History*

Dotson Rader   W
Janklow & Nesbit Associates, 445 Park Ave, New York,
NY 10022
  Pubs: *Tennessee: Cry of the Heart* (Doubleday, 1985), *Beau
  Monde* (Random Hse, 1980), *Esquire, Paris Rev*

Keith Rahmmings   P&W
PO Box 371
Brooklyn, NY 11230
  Pubs: *Lost & Found Times, Qwertyuiop, Glassworks, So &
  So, NRG, Star-Web-Paper, Assembling*

Heidi Rain   P
73 Kermit Place
Brooklyn, NY 11218, 718-437-1431
Internet: heidirain@aol.com
  Pubs: *Mirrors of the Soul* (Modern Poetry Society, 1995),
  Seasons: Anth (Poets Under Glass, 1994), *Rag Shock,
  Saturn Series, Copulation: Erotic Lit, Salonika, Medicinal
  Purposes, New Press Lit Qtly, Nomad's Choir, Wings*

Diane Raintree   P
360 W 21 St
New York, NY 10011-3305, 212-242-2387
  Pubs: *The Wind in Our Sails* (Midnight Sun, 1982), *Global
  City Rev, Slow Motion Mag, Tamarind, Helen Rev, NYQ*

Alice Ramirez   W
Donald MacCampbell Inc, PO Box 20191, New York, NY
10025-1518
  Pubs: *Bright Glows the Dawn* (Pseudonym: Santa Arroyo;
  Leisure Historical Romance, 1984)

Victor Rangel-Ribeiro ♦ ⊀   W
172-28 83 Ave
Jamaica, NY 11432-2104, 718-658-7064
Internet: vrangelrib@aol.com
  Pubs: *Loving Ayesha* (India; HC, 2002), *Tivolem* (Milkweed
  Edtns, 1998), *Ferry Crossings: Anth* (India; Penguin, 1999),
  Iowa Rev, NAR, Literary Rev

Claudia Rankine   P
c/o Grove/Atlantic, 841 Broadway, New York, NY 10003
Internet: jlcr@earthlink.net
  Pubs: *The End of the Alphabet* (Grove Pr, 1998), *Nothing in
  Nature Is Private* (Cleveland Poetry Pr, 1994)

Phyllis Raphael 🎤 ✈   W
Writing Program, Columbia Univ, 612 Lewisohn Hall, New
York, NY 10027, 212-595-5286
Internet: pr4@columbia.edu
 Pubs: *They Got What They Wanted* (Norton, 1972),
 Seasons of Women: Anth (Norton/BOMC, 1995), *Boulevard,*
 PEN Syndicated Fiction

Carolyn Raphael 🎤 ✈   P
Queensborough Community College, English Dept, Springfield
Blvd, Bayside, NY 11364, 718-631-6303
 Pubs: *Diagrams of Bittersweet* (Somers Rocks Pr, 1997),
 The Formalist, Cumberland Poetry Rev, Pivot, The Lyric,
 Edge City Rev, Orbis

Rebecca Rass   W
54 W 16 St, #14C
New York, NY 10011, 212-627-9122
Internet: rebecarass@aol.com
 Pubs: *From A-Z* (Proza, 1985), *The Mountain, The Fairy Tales*
 of My Mind (Lintel, 1982, 1978), *Solo: Women on Woman*
 Alone (Dell, 1977), *Moznaim, Zero Mag, Seven Days*

Carter Ratcliff 🎤   P
26 Beaver St
New York, NY 10004-2311, 212-825-9012
 Pubs: *Give Me Tomorrow* (Vehicle, 1983), *Fever Coast*
 (Kulchur Pr, 1973), *KGB Bar Book of Poems: Anth* (Harper,
 2000), *Out of this World: Anth* (Crown, 1991), *The World*
 Anth (Bobbs-Merrill, 1969)

Rochelle Ratner 🎤 ✈   P&W
609 Columbus Ave, #16F
New York, NY 10024-1433, 212-769-0498
Internet: rochelleratner@mindspring.com
 Pubs: *House & Home* (Marsh Hawk Pr, 2004), *Zodiac Arrest*
 (Ridgeway Pr, 1995), *Lion's Share* (Coffee Hse Pr, 1992),
 Someday Songs: Poems Toward a Personal History (BkMk
 Pr, 1992), *Bearing Life: Anth* (Feminist Pr, 2000), *Antaeus,*
 Nation, Hanging Loose

John Rechy   W
Georges Borchardt Inc, 136 E 57 St, New York, NY 10022,
212-753-5785
 Pubs: *Our Lady of Babylon, The Miraculous Day of Amalia*
 Gomez (Arcade, 1996, 1991), *Marilyn's Daughter, Bodies &*
 Soul (Carroll & Graf, 1988, 1983)

Liam Rector 🎤 ✈   P
300 E 34 St #3-J
New York, NY 10016, 212-779-7549
Internet: liamrector@aol.com
 Pubs: *American Prodigal* (Story Line, 1994), *The Sorrow of*
 Architecture (Dragon Gate, 1984), *Ploughshares, Slate,*
 Paris Rev, New Republic, APR, Agni

Victoria Redel 🎤 ✈   P&W
90 Riverside Dr #12A
New York, NY 10024-5318, 212-873-2502
Internet: vredel@aol.com
 Pubs: *Loverboy* (Harcourt, 2002), *Where the Road Bottoms*
 Out (Knopf, 1995), *Already the World* (Kent State U Pr,
 1995), *Nothing Makes You Free: Anth* (Norton, 2002), *Poets*
 of the New Century: Anth (Godine, 2001), *Antioch Rev,*
 Missouri Rev, The Qtly, Epoch

Gomer Rees   P
325 Riverside Dr, #3
New York, NY 10025, 212-865-7035
 Pubs: *Loves, Etc, Choice, NYQ, Chelsea, Purchase Poetry*
 Rev, Studies in Contemporary Satire

Gail Regier   W
c/o Matthew Bialer, William Morris Agency, 1325 Ave of the
Americas, New York, NY 10019
 Pubs: *Laurel Rev, New Virginia Rev, Greensboro Rev, Zone*
 3, Emrys Jrnl, Yarrow, Atlantic

Regina Reibstein   P
26 Oxford Blvd
Great Neck, NY 11023
516-487-6839
 Pubs: *Midstream, SWRev, California Qtly, Poem, Skylark*
 Qtly, Judaism, Pale Fire Rev

Edward V. Reiff   P
18 Baker Hill Rd
Great Neck, NY 11023
 Pubs: *Visions Harbor Mag*

Barbara Eve Reiss   P
1290 Madison Ave, #2N
New York, NY 10128, 212-369-8663
 Pubs: *Family Mirrors* (HM, 1991), *Tangled Vines: Anth* (HBJ,
 1992), *Antaeus, Agni, Nation, Virginia Qtly Rev*

Gertrude Reiss 🎤   P&W
74 Beaumont St
Brooklyn, NY 11235-4104, 718-615-0327
 Pubs: *The Perceptive I* (NTC Pub Group, 1997), *Legacies*
 (HC, 1993), *Menorah, New Press, Jewish Currents, Outloud,*
 Oxalis, Riverrun, Pumpkin Stories

Rose Reitter   P
25 Forest Ave
Hastings-on-Hudson, NY 10706, 914-478-3077
 Pubs: *The Pomegranate Series, Voices Intl, Attention*
 Please

Sally Renfro   P
401 E 64 St, #2D
New York, NY 10021-7590
 Pubs: *13th Moon, Atlantic, Texas Qtly*

Vittoria Repetto 🎤 ✈   P
24 Mulberry St, #4R
New York, NY 10013-4360, 212-267-1434
   Pubs: *Head for the Van Wyck* (Monkey Cat Pr, 1994),
   Unsettling America: Anth (Penguin, 1994), *Paterson Lit Rev,*
   Voices in Italian Americana, Mudfish, Lips

Naomi Replansky 🎤   P
711 Amsterdam Ave, #8E
New York, NY 10025-6916, 212-666-1233
   Pubs: *The Dangerous World: New & Selected Poems*
   (Another Chicago Pr, 1994), *Ring Song* (Scribner, 1952),
   Ploughshares, Feminist Studies, NYQ

A. Wanjiku H Reynolds   P
Ngoma's Gourd, Inc, PO Box 24, W Farms Sq Sta, Bronx,
NY 10460
   Pubs: *Cognac & Collard Greens* (Single Action Productions,
   1986), *A Gathering of Hands: Anth* (Ngoma's Gourd, 1991)

Richard Rhodes 🎤 ✈   W
Janklow & Nesbit Associates, 455 Park Ave, New York, NY
10022-2606, 212-421-1700
Internet: rhodesr@pantheon.yale.edu
   Pubs: *Masters of Death, Why They Kill* (Knopf, 2002, 2000),
   The Making of the Atomic Bomb (S&S, 1986)

Martha Rhodes   P
80 N Moore St, #33J
New York, NY 10013, 212-571-4683
   Pubs: *At the Gate* (Provincetown Arts Pr, 1995), *Agni,*
   Boston Rev, Harvard Rev, Ploughshares, Virginia Rev

M. Z. Ribalow 🎤 ✈   P
431 E 20 St, #4C
New York, NY 10010-7507, 212-777-3538
   Pubs: *Fishdrum, NYQ, Paris Rev, Literary Rev*

Adrienne Rich   P
W W Norton, 500 5 Ave, New York, NY 10110, 212-354-5500
   Pubs: *Midnight Salvage, What Is Found There, An Atlas of*
   the Difficult World (Norton, 1999, 1993, 1991), *Kenyon Rev,*
   APR, Sulfur

Arthur Rifkin   P
7 Fourth Rd
Great Neck, NY 11021
   Pubs: *Lake Superior Rev, Bitterroot, Encore, Poet Lore,*
   Dodeca

Mindy Rinkewich   P&W
290 9th Ave #5F
New York, NY 10001, 212-242-4445
   Pubs: *The White Beyond the Forest* (CCC, 1992), *Lips,*
   Schmate, Bitterroot, Poet Lore

Louis Reyes Rivera 🎤 ✈   P
Shamal Books Inc, GPO Box 16, New York, NY 10116-0016,
718-622-4426
   Pubs: *Scattered Scripture, This One for You, Who Pays the*
   Cost (Shamal Bks, 1997, 1984, 1977), *Blind Beggar,*
   Sunbury

Edward Rivera   W
321 W 100 St, #6
New York, NY 10025
   Pubs: *Family Installments* (Morrow, 1982), *New American*
   Rev, Bilingual Rev, New York Mag

Agnes Robertson   P
3100 Brighton 2nd St, #6J
Brooklyn, NY 11235, 718-934-3018
   Pubs: *The Me Inside of Me, The Chestnut Tree* (Gull Bks,
   1987, 1987)

Natalie Robins 🎤 ✈   P
c/o Lynn Nesbit, Janklow & Nesbit Associates, 445 Park Ave,
New York, NY 10022, 212-421-1700
Internet: nrobins@escape.com
   Pubs: *Eclipse* (Swallow Pr, 1981)

Corinne Robins 🎤 ✈   W
83 Wooster St
New York, NY 10012-4376, 212-925-3714
   Pubs: *Marble Goddesses with Technicolor Skins* (Segue,
   2000), *Facing It* (Pratt, 1996), *The Pluralist Era* (H&R,
   1984), *American Book Rev, ACM, NAW, Caprice, Poetry NY,*
   Confrontation, Situation

Jill Robinson   W
c/o Lynn Nesbit, Janklow & Nesbit Associates, 445 Park Ave,
New York, NY 10022, 212-421-1700
   Pubs: *Perdido* (Knopf, 1978), *Bed/Time/Story* (Random
   Hse, 1974)

John Robinson 🎤 ✈   W
William Moris Agency, 1325 Ave of the Americas, New York,
NY 10019
Internet: jrobi28@aol.com
   Pubs: *Legends of the Lost* (Northland, 1989), *January's*
   Dream (Green Street Pr, 1985), *Ploughshares*

Jeremy Robinson   P
275 Central Pk W, #12E
New York, NY 10024, 212-362-0574
   Pubs:

Ruthann Robson 🎤 ✈   P&W
CUNY School of Law, 65-21 Main St, Flushing, NY 11367,
718-340-4447
Internet: robson@mail.law.cuny.edu
   Pubs: *The Struggle For Happiness, A/K/S, Another Mother*
   (St. Martin's Pr, 2000, 1997, 1995), *Masks* (Leapfrog Pr,
   1999)

Michael Rogers   W
c/o Gail Hochman, Brandt & Hochman Literary Agents, 1501
Broadway, New York, NY 10036, 212-840-5760
Internet: rogersm@washpost.com
  Pubs: *Forbidden Sequence* (Bantam, 1988), *Silicon Valley*
  (S&S, 1982), *Esquire, Playboy, West, Manhattan Inc*

Gilbert Rogin   W
Sports Illustrated, Time-Life Building, New York, NY 10020,
212-556-3123

Rose Romano   P
c/o Malefemmina Press, 4211 Fort Hamilton Pkwy, Brooklyn,
NY 11219
  Pubs: *Vendetta* (malafemmina pr, 1990), *Slipstream,
  Waterways, Common Lives, Footwork, Women's Studies
  Qtly, Italian Americana*

Marcus Rome ♦ ⊀   P
2727 Palisade Ave
Riverdale, NY 10463-1018, 718-548-7330
  Pubs: *Out of Darkness* (St. Bede's Pubs, 2000),
  Repercussions, Abreactions (Birch Brook Pr, 2000, 1989),
  Visual Eyes (Ziggurat Pr, 1997), *Red Owl, Wordsmith, The
  Bridge, Vincent Brothers Rev, Pacific Coast Jrnl*

Cheryl Romney-Brown   P
c/o Philippa Brophy, Sterling Lord Literistic, 65 Bleecker St,
New York, NY 10012, 212-780-6050
  Pubs: *Circling Home* (Scripta Humanistica, 1989), *American
  Beauties: Anth* (Abrams, 1993)

William Pitt Root ♦ ⊀   P
English Dept, Hunter College, 695 Park Ave, New York, NY
10021, 520-791-2816
Internet: wprpoet@ATTGLOBAL.NET
  Pubs: Stories from Where We Live: The California Coast
  (Milkweed, 2002), Stories from Where We Live: The Gulf
  Coast (Milkweed, 2002), *Orpheus & Co* (New England Pr,
  2000), *And What Rough Beast: Anth* (Ashland Pr, 1999),

Rose Rosberg   P
880 W 181 St, #4-I
New York, NY 10033, 212-928-7089
  Pubs: *Chrysalis* (Swedenborg Fdn, 1995), *The Country of
  Connections* (University Edtns, 1993), *Breathe In, Breathe
  Out* (Singular Speech Pr, 1992), *Pacific Coast Jrnl, Poetry
  Digest, Skylark, American Poets & Poetry, Lyric,
  Neovictorian, Comstock Rev*

Joel Rose   W
104 Charlton St, #4E
New York, NY 10014, 212-633-2996
Internet: joeyrose@nyc.rr.com
  Pubs: *New York Sawed in Half* (Bloomsbury, 2001), *Kill Kill
  Faster Faster* (Crown, 1997), *Kill the Poor* (Atlantic Monthly
  Pr, 1988), *Love Is Strange: Anth* (Norton, 1993), *Between
  C&D: Anth* (Penguin, 1988)

Norma Rosen ♦   W
Gloria Loomis, Watkins Loomis Agency, Inc, 133 E 35 St, New
York, NY 10016, 212-532-0080
  Pubs: *Biblical Women Unbound,* (JPS, 1997), *John & Anzia,
  At the Center* (Syracuse U Pr, 1997, 1996), *Accidents of
  Influence* (SUNY Pr, 1992), *Tikkun, Lilith*

Judith Rosenberg ♦ ⊀   P
1010 5th Ave, #11D
New York, NY 10028, 212-288-4773
Internet: jrosenberg7@nyc.rr.com
  Pubs: *Paterson Lit Rev, Antigonish Rev, Atlanta Rev,
  Louisville Rev, Women's Rev of Bks, Worcester Rev*

Alice Rosenblitt ♦ ⊀   P
47-25 43 St, #1F
Woodside, NY 11377-6229, 718-937-2891
Internet: arosenblitt@lagcc.cuny.edu
  Pubs: *Celebrating Women: 20 Years of Co-Education: Anth*
  (Yale Women's Ctr, 1990), *Long Shot, Natl Poetry Mag of
  the Lower East Side, La Mia Ink, Pome*

Linda Rosenkrantz   W
Howard Morhaim Agency, 841 Broadway, Ste 604, New York,
NY 10003, 212-529-4433
  Pubs: *SoHo, Gone Hollywood* (Co-author; Doubleday,
  1981, 1979)

Carole Rosenthal   W
37 1/2 St Marks Pl, #B2
New York, NY 10003, 212-228-4289
  Pubs: *Best of the Underground: Anth* (Rhinoceros Mass
  Market Edtns, 1998), *Powers of Desire: Anth* (Monthly Rev
  Pr, 1983), *Dreamworks, Confrontation, Minnesota Rev,
  Mother Jones, Ellery Queen's Mystery Mag, Other Voices,
  Cream City Rev*

Barbara Rosenthal ♦ ⊀   PP&P&W
The Media Loft, 463 West St, #A-628, New York,
NY 10014-2035, 212-924-4893
  Pubs: *Soul & Psyche, Homo Futurus, Sensations, Clues to
  Myself* (Visual Studies Wkshp, 1998, 1986, 1986, 1980),
  Cradle & All: Anth (Faber & Faber, 1990), *Parting Gifts,
  Kopy Kultur, Spit, Feelings, Afterimage, Umbrella,
  MacGuffin, Bohemian Chronicle*

Bob Rosenthal   P
367 E 10 St #14
New York, NY 10009, 212-477-2487
Internet: rosevalley@allenginsbergtrust.com
  Pubs: *Rude Awakenings* (Yellow Pr, 1982), *Lies About the
  Flesh* (Frontward Bks, 1977), *Mag City*

Martha Rosler   W
143 McGuinness Blvd
Brooklyn, NY 11222, 718-383-2277
  Pubs: *3 Works* (Nova Scotia, 1981), *Service* (Printed Matter,
  1978), *Heresies*

Elizabeth Rosner 🎤 ✈   P&W
Joelle Delbourgo, 450 7th Ave, Ste 3004, New York, NY
10123, 212-279-9027
Internet: erosner900@aol.com
    Pubs: *The Solitaire Bird* (Ballantine, 2001), *Gravity* (Small
    Poetry Pr, 1998), *SPR, Faultline, Blue Mesa Rev, Poetry
    East, ACM, Cream City Rev*

Terrence Ross   W
8 Spring St, #4RW
New York, NY 10012
    Pubs: *Bitter Graces* (Avon, 1980)

Judith Rossner   W
Wendy Weil Agency Inc, 232 Madison Ave, Ste 1300, New
York, NY 10016, 212-685-0030
    Pubs: *Perfidia* (Talese/Doubleday, 1997), *Olivia* (Crown,
    1994), *His Little Women* (Summit, 1990), *August* (HM,
    1983), *Emmeline, Attachments, Looking for Mr. Goodbar*
    (S&S, 1980, 1977, 1975), *Any Minute I Can Split* (McGraw
    Hill, 1972)

Philip Roth   W
Farrar, Straus & Giroux, 19 Union Sq W, New York, NY 10003

Joyce Andrea Rothenberg 🎤 ✈   PP&P
PO Box 6041, FDR Sta, New York, NY 10150-6041
Internet: joyan_us@yahoo.com
    Pubs: *The Symphony Is Barely Audible* (Symphony Pr,
    1991), *Phatitude*

Earl Rovit   W
309 W 109 St, #6G
New York, NY 10025
    Pubs: *Crossings, A Far Cry, The Player King* (HBJ, 1973,
    1967, 1965)

Ann Rower   W
60-82 60 Dr
Maspeth, NY 11378-3536, 212-966-6737
    Pubs: *If You're a Girl* (Semiotext(e), *1990)*

Peter Rubie   W
Peter Rubie Literary Agency, 240 W 35 St. Ste100, New York,
NY 10001
    Pubs: *Werewolf* (Longmeadow Pr, 1992), *Mindbender* (Lynx
    Bks, 1989)

Kathryn Ruby   P
180 Cabrini Blvd, #71
New York, NY 10033, 212-781-3833
    Pubs: *Twentieth Century Views* (Prentice-Hall, 1979), *We
    Become New* (Bantam, 1975), *Rio*

Mark Rudman   P
817 W End Ave, #4A
New York, NY 10025, 212-666-3648
    Pubs: *Rider* (Wesleyan U Pr, 1994), *Diverse Voices* (Story
    Line Pr, 1993), *The Nowhere Steps* (Sheep Meadow Pr,
    1990), *APR, Harper's, Paris Rev, New Yorker*

Raphael Rudnik   P
511 Warren St
Brooklyn, NY 11217-2723
    Pubs: *Frank 207* (Ohio U Pr, 1982), *Pequod, Kentucky Rev*

Frazier Russell   P&W
405 Westminster Road, #LB3
Brooklyn, NY 11216, 718-826-8427
    Pubs: *How We Are Spared, Four Way Books Reader: Anth*
    (Four Way Bks, 2000, 1996), *Fweivel: The Day Will Come*
    (Ridgeway Pr, 1996), *Ploughshares, Global City Rev,
    American Voice, Marlboro Rev, Phoebe*

Suzanne Ruta   W
55 Bethune St, Apt B647
New York, NY 10014-2010, 212-675-5170
    Pubs: *Stalin in the Bronx & Other Stories* (Grove Pr, 1987),
    Wigwag, VLS, Grand Street

Thaddeus Rutkowski 🎤 ✈   W
249 Eldridge St, #7
New York, NY 10002-1336, 212-387-0056
Internet: thadrand@earthlink.net
    Pubs: *Roughhouse* (Kaya, 1999), *The Naughty Bits: Anth*
    (Three Rivers/Crown, 2001), *Help Yourself!: Anth*
    (Autonomedia, 2001), *Outlaw Bible of Amer Poetry: Anth*
    (Thunder's Mouth Pr, 1999), *Fiction Mag, American Letters
    & Commentary, Long Shot, Phatasmagoria*

Lester Rutsky   P
2930 W 5 St
Brooklyn, NY 11224

Margaret Ryan 🎤 ✈   P
250 W 104 St #63
New York, NY 10025-4282, 212-666-2591
    Pubs: *Black Raspberries* (Parsonage Pr, 1986), *Filling Out a
    Life* (Front Street, 1981), *The American Scholar,
    Rattapallax, Nation, Poetry, Confrontation, Kansas Qtly*

Elizabeth-Ann Sachs   W
c/o Anne Borchardt, Georges Borchardt Inc, 136 E 57 St, New
York, NY 10022, 212-753-5785
    Pubs: *Mountain Bike Madness, The Boy Who Ate Dog
    Biscuits* (Random Hse, 1994, 1989), *Just Like Always*
    (Aladdin Bks, 1991)

Howard Sage 🎤 ✈   P
720 Greenwich St, #4H
New York, NY 10014-2574, 212-627-8959
Internet: hs15@is.nyu.edu
   Pubs: *Fictional Flights: Anth* (Heinle & Heinle, 1993), *Folio,
   New Voices*

Raymond Saint-Pierre 🎤 ✈   P
Street/Editions, 25 Cumming at Seaman, Ste 3B, New York,
NY 10034, 212-304-2265
Internet: streeteditions@juno.com
   Pubs: *Orgasms of Light* (Gay Sunshine Pr, 1976), *Hell's
   Kitchen: Anth* (Public Pr, 1999), *One Teacher in Ten: Anth*
   (Alyson Pub, 1994), *Long Island Qtly, Fox Cry Rev, Haight
   Ashbury Lit Jrnl, Edgz, Latino Stuff Rev, Bay Windows,
   Prophetic Voices, Amherst Rev*

Jerome Sala   P
298 Mulberry St, #3L
New York, NY 10012, 212-941-8724
Internet: jsala@cm.timeinc.com
   Pubs: *Raw Deal: New & Selected Poems* (Another Chicago
   Pr, 1994), *The Trip* (Highlander Pr, 1987), *Aerial, Exquisite
   Corpse, NAW, Onthebus, Ploughshares*

Joseph S. Salemi 🎤 ✈   P
3222 61 St
Woodside, NY 11377-2030, 718-932-5351
   Pubs: *Masquerade, Nonsense Couplets, Formal Complaints*
   (Somers Rocks Pr, 2000, 1999, 1997), *Pivot, Crisis, Iambs
   & Trochees, Connecticut River Rev, Light, Carolina Qtly,
   Hellas, Cumberland Poetry Rev, Blue Unicorn, Formalist,
   Satire, Sparrow, Edge City Rev*

J. D. Salinger   W
Harold Ober Assoc, 425 Madison Ave, New York, NY 10017,
212-759-8600

James Salter   W
c/o Peter Matson, Sterling Lord Literistic, 65 Bleecker St, New
York, NY 10012, 212-780-6050
   Pubs: *Cassada* (Counterpoint, 2000), *The Hunters* (Vintage,
   1999), *Solo Faces, Dusk & Other Stories, Light Years, A
   Sport & a Pastime* (North Point Pr, 1998, 1988, 1982, 1980),
   Esquire

Thomas Sanchez   W
c/o Esther Newberg, ICM, 40 W 57 St, New York, NY 10019
   Pubs: *King Bongo, Day of the Bees* (Knopf-Vintage, 2003,
   2001)

Ronni Sandroff   W
Elaine Markson Literary Agency, 44 Greenwich Ave, New York,
NY 10011
   Pubs: *Fighting Back* (Jove, 1979), *Party, Party/Girlfriends*
   (Knopf, 1975)

Myro Sandunes   W
The Dramatists Guild, 1501 Broadway, Ste 101, New York, NY
10036, 212-398-9366
   Pubs: *The Go-Between, Placebo* (Albatross Pub, 1983, 1983)

Reuben Sandwich   PP
688 Tompkins Ave
Staten Island, NY 10305
   Pubs: *The Shredder*

Rosemarie Santini 🎤 ✈   W
296 W 11 St
New York, NY 10014-2495
Internet: rosantini@earthlink.net
   Pubs: *Blood Sisters, Private Lives* (Pocket Bks, 1990, 1989),
   The Disenchanted Diva, A Swell Style of Murder (St.
   Martin's, 1988, 1986), *Music Lesson, Movie Murder, Sins of
   the Father, New Mystery Mag*

Sapphire 🎤 ✈   W
521 41 St #D-4
Brooklyn, NY 11232
Internet: sapphire1100@aol.com
   Pubs: *Black Wings & Blind Angels, Push* (Knopf, 1999,
   1996), *American Dreams* (High Risk Bks, 1994), *Wann bitte
   findet das Leben statt?: Anth* (Germany; Rowohlt, 1998),
   Black Scholar, New Yorker, Bomb

Helen Saslow   P
3626 Kings Hwy #5L
Brooklyn, NY 11234-2751
   Pubs: *Arctic Summer* (Barlenmir Hse, 1974), *The Villanelle:
   The Evolution of a Poetic Form: Anth* (U Idaho Pr, 1987),
   *NYQ, Glassworks, Confrontation, Hellcoal Annual, Hanging
   Loose, Small Pond*

Steven Sater   P
c/o Mike Lubin, William Morris Agency, 1325 Ave of the
Americas, New York, NY 10019, 212-586-5100
   Pubs: *Take Ten: Anth* (Vintage, 1997), *Portland Rev, Poems
   & Plays, Confrontation, Rockford Rev, Hawaii Rev,
   MacGuffin*

Tom Savage 🎤 ✈   P
622 E 11 St, #14
New York, NY 10009-4140, 212-533-3893
   Pubs: *Help Yourself!: Anth, Unbearables: Anth*
   (Autonomedia, 2002, 1995), *Downtown Poets: Anth*
   (Montclair Takilma Pub, 1999), *Out of This World: Anth*
   (Crown, 1991), *New York Times, Cyberpoems*

Sally Savic   P&W
Melanie Jackson Agency, 250 W 57 St, #1119, New York, NY
10107
   Pubs: *Elysian Fields* (Scribner, 1988), *Cosmopolitan, Intro*

Lynwood Sawyer ♀ ✈ W
85 State St, #5
Brooklyn, NY 11201-5534, 718-237-2296
Internet: uncertain@altavista.com
  Pubs: *Uncertain Currency* (Avocet Pr, 2000), *Hawaii Pacific Rev, Art Access, Pembroke Rev, Just Pulp, St. Andrews Rev, Ellery Queen's Mystery Mag*

Ann Scaglione P
244-23 73 Ave
Douglaston, NY 11362, 718-523-8839
  Pubs: *Vega, Arulo, Modern Images*

Hindy Lauer Schachter ♀ W
420 E 64 St
New York, NY 10021-7853
  Pubs: *Intl Poetry Rev, Response, Jewish Frontier*

Sandy Rochelle Schachter ♀ ✈ PP
438 W 23 St, #A
New York, NY 10011-2165, 212-929-6245
Internet: chelsea438@aol.com
  Pubs: *Poems from the Heart* (The Plowman, 1992), *The Players' Club, Barnes and Noble, Lincoln Center Outdoors, Medicine Show Ensemble Theatre, Connecticut River Rev, Visions Intl*

Robert Schirmer W
24 1st St
Brooklyn, NY 11231-5002
  Pubs: *Living with Strangers* (NYU Pr, 1991), *NER, Indiana Rev, Greensboro Rev, New Letters*

Murray Schisgal W
275 Central Pk W
New York, NY 10024-3015
  Pubs: *Days & Nights of a French Horn Player* (Little, Brown, 1980), *Luv & Other Plays* (Dodd, Mead, 1983)

Peter Schjeldahl P
53 St Marks Pl
New York, NY 10003, 212-674-5889
  Pubs: *Since 1964: New & Selected Poems* (Sun Pr, 1978)

Tobias Schneebaum W
463 West St, #410A
New York, NY 10014, 212-691-0022
  Pubs: *Embodied Spirits* (Peabody Museum of Salem, 1990), *Where the Spirits Dwell, Keep the River on Your Right* (Grove, 1988, 1969)

Carolee Schneemann ♀ ✈ PP&P
114 W 29 St
New York, NY 10001
Internet: caroleel2@aol.com
  Pubs: *Imaging Her Erotics* (MIT Pr, 2000), *A Book of the Book, Vulva's Morphia* (Granary Bks, 2000, 1997), *More Than Meat Joy* (McPherson & Co, 1996), *Deep Down* (Faber & Faber, 1988), *Parts of a Body House Book* (U.K.; Beau Geste Pr, 1972), *White Walls Jrnl*

Bart Schneider ♀ ✈ P
c/o Gloria Loomis, Watkins Loomis Agency Inc, 133 E 35 St, New York, NY 10016, 212-532-0080
  Pubs: *Secret Love, Blue Bossa* (Viking, 2001, 1998), *Race* (Crown, 1997), *Seasons of the Game* (Elysian Fields, 1992), *Water for a Stranger* (Blue Teal Pr, 1979), *Teachers & Writers Mag*

Elizabeth Lynn Schneider P
480 2nd St
Brooklyn, NY 11215, 718-768-6296
  Pubs:

L. J. Schneiderman W
c/o Marcia Amsterdam Agency, 41 W 82 St, New York, NY 10024-5613, 212-873-4945
Internet: ljs@ucsd.edu
  Pubs: *The Appointment* (S&S, 1991), *Sea Nymphs by the Hour* (Bobbs-Merrill, 1972), *Confrontation, Ascent, Kansas Qtly, Chouteau Rev, Black Warrior Rev*

Lynda Schor ♀ ✈ W
463 West St, #610C
New York, NY 10014, 212-691-6337
Internet: lyndaschor@msn.com
  Pubs: *Appetities* (Hamilton Stone Edtns, 2001), *True Love & Real Romance* (Coward, McCann, 1979), *The Mother Reader: Anth* (Seven Stories Pr, 2001), *Bearing Life: Anth* (Feminist Pr, 2000), *Witness, Cream City Rev, Quarter After Eight, Playboy, Confrontation*

Roni Schotter ♀ ✈ W
c/o Susan Cohen, The Writers House, 21 W 26 St, New York, NY 10010, 914-478-3231
  Pubs: *Purim Play, Passover Magic, A Fruit & Vegetable Man* (Little, Brown, 1998, 1995, 1993), *Nothing Ever Happens on 90th Street, Dreamland* (Orchard Bks, 1997, 1996), *When Crocodiles Clean Up* (Macmillan, 1993)

Peninnah Schram ♀ ✈ PP&P&W
525 W End Ave, #8C
New York, NY 10024, 212-787-0626
  Pubs: *A Chanukah Blessing* (UAHC Pr, 2000), *Tales of Elijah the Prophet, Jewish Stories One Generation Tells Another, Stories Within Stories: From the Jewish Oral Tradition: Anth* (Jason Aronson, 1991, 1987, 2000)

Susan Schreibman P
372 5th Ave, #4N
New York, NY 10018, 212-695-2947
   Pubs: *Poetry Ireland, Footwork, Atlanta Rev, Poet Lore, Dreamworks, Wind, Crazyquilt, Amelia*

Grace Schulman 🎤 ✈ P
1 University Pl, #14-F
New York, NY 10003-4519, 212-533-0235
   Pubs: *Days of Wonder: New and Selected Poems, The Paintings of Our Lives* (HM, 2002, 2001), *For That Day Only, Hemispheres* (Sheep Meadow Pr, 1994, 1984), *New Yorker, Paris Rev, Boulevard, Pequod, Kenyon Rev, Poetry*

Sarah Schulman 🎤 ✈ W
406 E 9 St, #20
New York, NY 10009-4972, 212-982-1033
   Pubs: *Shimmer* (Avon, 1998), *Rat Bohemia* (E.P. Dutton, 1995), *Empathy* (Plume, 1993)

Helen Schulman W
252 W 85 St, #8A
New York, NY 10024
   Pubs: *Out of Time* (Atheneum, 1991), *Not a Free Show* (Knopf, 1988), *Antioch Rev, NAR, Story Qtly, The Qtly, Arete*

Philip Schultz 🎤 ✈ P&W
c/o Georges Borchardt, Inc, 136 E 57 St, New York, NY 10022, 212-753-5785
Internet: gusandbenya@earthlink.net
   Pubs: *The Holy Worm of Praise* (Harcourt, 2002), *Deep Within the Ravine, Like Wings* (Viking, 1984, 1978), *New American Poets of the '90s: Anth* (Godine, 1991), *New Yorker, Poetry Chicago, Nation*

David Schultz 🎤 ✈ P&W
162-31 9th Ave #4A
Whitestone, NY 11357-2010, 718-767-7455
Internet: davidtrans@aol.com
   Pubs: *Liquid Pony Ink, Somniloquy, Poesie USA, Footwork, Horizontes, Transition, Ambrosia, The Haven, Tin Wreath, Italian-Americana*

Elaine Schwager 🎤 ✈ P
228 W 22 St
New York, NY 10011-2701, 212-807-1225
Internet: esschwager@aol.com
   Pubs: *I Want Your Chair* (Rattapallax Pr, 2000), *It Is the Poem Singing in Your Eyes: Anth* (Harper, 1971), *City in all Directions: Anth* (Macmillan, 1969), *Rattapallax, Literal Latte, Writ, Armadillo*

Lynne Sharon Schwartz 🎤 ✈ W
50 Morningside Dr, #31
New York, NY 10025
   Pubs: *Face to Face, Ruined by Reading* (Beacon, 2000, 1996), *In the Family Way* (Morrow, 1999), *Leaving Brooklyn* (HM, 1989)

Marian Schwartz W
c/o Emilie Jacobson, Curtis Brown Ltd, 10 Astor Pl, New York, NY 10003-6935
   Pubs: *Realities* (St. Martin's Pr, 1981)

Leonard Schwartz 🎤 ✈ P
120 Cabrini Blvd, #96
New York, NY 10033
   Pubs: *The Tower of Diverse Shores, New & Selected Poems: Words Before the Articulate* (Talisman Hse, 2003, 1997), *Gnostic Blessing* (Goats & Compasses Pr, 1992), *First Intensity, Five Fingers Rev, Talisman, Poetry NY, Pequod*

Sheila Schwartz W
15 W 72nd St
New York, NY 10023, 212-877-3192
Internet: sheilarsch@aol.com
   Pubs: *The Little Terrorist* (Xlibris, 2001), *The Most Popular Girl, Bigger Is Better* (Crosswinds, 1987, 1987), *Sorority* (Warner, 1987)

Doris Schwerin W
317 W 83 St, #4W
New York, NY 10024
   Pubs: *The Tree That Cried* (Caedmon Bks, 1986), *Cat & I* (H&R, 1990), *Leanna, Diary of a Pigeon Watcher* (Morrow, 1978, 1976), *Rainbow Walkers* (Villard/Random Hse, 1986), *The Tomorrow Book* (Pantheon, 1984)

Armand Schwerner PP&P
20 Bay St Landing, #B-3C
Staten Island, NY 10301, 718-442-3784
Internet: schwerner@cuny.campus.mci.net
   Pubs: *The Tablets I-XXVI* (National Poetry Fdn, 1998), *Poems for the Millennium: Anth* (U California Pr, 1996), *Conjunctions, Sulfur, Tyuonyi, Talisman*

Ilka Scobie P
39 Great Jones St
New York, NY 10012
Internet: zeblw@aol.com
   Pubs: *Any Island* (Soncino Pr, 1997), *There for the Taking* (For Zoas Pr, 1979), *Long Shot, Poetry in Performance, Phatitude, New Observations*

Virginia Scott P
255 Fieldston Terr, #3A
Bronx, NY 10471
   Pubs: *Toward Appomattox, The Witness Box* (Motherroot Pubs, 1985), *Prairie Schooner, Antigonish Rev, American Voice*

Peter Seaton 🎤 ✈ P
229 E 25 St, #3A
New York, NY 10010, 212-683-1449
   Pubs: *Crisis Intervention* (Tuumba Pr, 1983), *The Son Master* (Roof Bks, 1982), *Agreement* (Asylum's Pr, 1978)

Lore Segal 🎤 ✈   W
280 Riverside Dr, #12K
New York, NY 10025-9031
Internet: lsegal70@aol.com
    Pubs: *Morris the Artist* (Farrar, Straus, 2003), *Other People's Houses, Her First American* (New Pr, 1994, 1994), *The Story of King Saul & King David* (Schocken, 1991), *Eliza's Kitchen: Anth* (Blue Cathedral, 2000), *Best American Short Stories: Anth* (HM, 1990)

Edith Segal   P
60 Plaza St, #3A
Brooklyn, NY 11238
    Pubs: *Tributes & Trumpets, A Time to Thunder* (Philmark Pr, 1986, 1982)

Frederick Seidel   P
Farrar, Straus & Giroux, 19 Union Sq W, New York, NY 10003, 212-741-6900
    Pubs: *Going Fast, My Tokyo* (FSG, 1998, 1991), *Poems 1959-1979, These Days* (Knopf, 1989, 1989), *Sunrise* (Viking Penguin, 1980)

Hugh Seidman 🎤 ✈   P
463 West St, #H822
New York, NY 10014-2038, 212-255-5847
    Pubs: *Selected Poems: 1965-1995, People Live, They Have Lives* (Miami U Pr, 1995, 1992)

Robert J. Seidman 🎤 ✈   W
Gelfman Schneider, 250 W 57 St, New York, NY 10107
Internet: seidman@ix.netcom.com
    Pubs: *Bucks County Idyll* (S&S, 1980), *One Smart Indian* (Overlook Pr, 1979)

Bernice Selden   W
808 W End Ave, #507
New York, NY 10025, 212-222-5819
    Pubs: *The Mill Girls* (Atheneum, 1983), *Music in My Heart* (Dutton, 1982)

Robyn Selman   P
62 W 11 St, #3F
New York, NY 10011
    Pubs: *Directions to My House* (U Pittsburgh Pr, 1995), *Best American Poetry: Anths* (Macmillan, 1995, 1991), *Paris Rev, Prairie Schooner, American Voice, Puerto del Sol, Ploughshares, Kenyon Rev, APR*

Vijay Seshadri   P
Sarah Lawrence College, 1 Mead Way, Bronxville, NY 10708, 914-395-2280
Internet: seshadri@mail.slc.edu
    Pubs: *Wild Kingdom* (Graywolf Pr, 1996), *New Yorker*

Vikram Seth   P&W
c/o Irene Skolnick, Curtis Brown Ltd, 10 Astor Pl, New York, NY 10003-6935, 212-473-5400
    Pubs: *All You Who Sleep Tonight* (Knopf, 1990), *The Golden Gate* (Random Hse, 1986)

Elaine Sexton 🎤 ✈   P
7 Carmine St, #9
New York, NY 10014, 212-727-0306
Internet: esexton@harris-pub.com
    Pubs: *Sleuth* (New Issues Pr, 2003), *APR, CSM, Prairie Schooner, 5 AM, New Letters, Rattapallax, Women's Review of Books, Larcom Rev, Hubbub*

Bob Shacochis 🎤 ✈   W
c/o Gail Hochman, Brandt & Hochman Literary Agents, 1501 Broadway, New York, NY 10036, 212-840-5760
    Pubs: *The Women Who Lost Her Soul* (Grove Atlantic, 2003), *Swimming in the Volcano* (Scribner, 1993), *The Next New World, Easy in the Islands* (Crown, 1989, 1985), *Paris Rev, Harper's, Esquire, Outside*

R. L. Shafner   W
100 W 92 St, #8A
New York, NY 10025, 212-496-0979
    Pubs: *Stop Me if You've Heard This* (Signet, 1986), *Formations, TriQtly, Shankpainter*

Myra Shapiro 🎤 ✈   P
111 4th Ave, #12I
New York, NY 10003-5243, 212-995-0659
    Pubs: *I'll See You Thursday* (Blue Sofa Pr, 1996), *Bronx Accent: Anth* (Rutgers Univ Pr, 2000), *Best Amer Poetry: Anth* (Scribner, 1999), *Harvard Rev, Ploughshares, Ohio Rev*

Dee Shapiro   P&W
28 Clover Dr
Great Neck, NY 11021-1819
Internet: betiren1@aol.com
    Pubs: *Blueline, Small Pond Mag of Lit, Black Bear Rev, Chiron Rev, New Press Lit Qtly*

David Shapiro   P
3001 Henry Hudson Pkwy #3B
Riverdale, NY 10463, 718-601-3425
    Pubs: *After a Lost Original, House Blown Apart, To an Idea* (Overlook, 1994, 1988, 1984), *Lingo, NAW, Boulevard, New Yorker, Paris Rev*

Harvey Shapiro 🎤 ✈   P
43 Pierrepont St
Brooklyn, NY 11201-3362, 718-858-3765
    Pubs: *How Charlie Shavers Died and Other Poems, Selected Poems* (Wesleyan, 2001, 1997)

Peter Sharpe 🎤 ✈   P
Wagner College, 1 Campus Rd, Staten Island, NY 10301,
718-390-3370
Internet: psharpe@wagner.edu
    Pubs: *Lost Goods & Stray Beasts* (Rowan Tree Pr, 1983),
    *Massachusetts Rev, Tendril, Harbor Rev, Southern Rev,
    Davidson Miscellany, Poet Lore*

Brenda Shaughnessy   P
Farrar, Straus & Giroux, 19 Union Sq W, New York, NY 10003,
212-741-6900
    Pubs: *Interview with Sudden Joy* (FSG, 1999), *Paris Rev,
    Yale Rev, Chelsea*

Don Shea   W
102 E 22 St, #5G
New York, NY 10010
Internet: dshea11741@aol.com
    Pubs: *New York Sex: Anth* (Painted Leaf Pr, 1998), *Fast
    Fiction: Anth* (Story Pr, 1997), *Flash Fiction: Anth* (Norton,
    1992), *NAR, Gettysburg Rev, The Lit Rev, The Qtly,
    Confrontation, High Plains Lit Rev, Crescent Rev, Onthebus,
    Descant*

Laurie Sheck   P
303 Mercer St, Apt A-502
New York, NY 10003
Internet: jlpeck1098@aol.com
    Pubs: *Io at Night, The Willow Grove: Anth* (Knopf, 1990,
    1996), *Amaranth* (U Georgia Pr, 1981), *Best American
    Poetry: Anths* (MacMillan, 2000, 1991), *New Yorker, Poetry,
    Iowa Rev*

Jackie Sheeler 🎤 ✈   P
PO Box 1401
New York, NY 10026
Internet: jackie@poetz.com
    Pubs: *The Memory Factory* (Buttonwood Pr, 2002), *Bum
    Rush the Page: A Def Poetry Jam: Anth* (Three Rivers Pr,
    2001), *Sleeping with Dionysus* (Crossing Pr, 1994), *Long
    Shot, Rattapallax, Medicinal Purposes, Visions, Slant*

Evelyn Shefner   W
230 E 15 St, #5N
New York, NY 10003-3943, 212-242-5810
    Pubs: *Common Body, Royal Bones* (Coffee Hse Pr, 1987),
    O. Henry Prize Stories: Anth (Doubleday, 1979), *Southern
    Rev, Negative Capability, The Bridge*

Susan Sherman 🎤 ✈   P
305 E 6 St, #3
New York, NY 10003
Internet: shermansu@aol.com
    Pubs: *Casualties of War* (Venom Pr, 1998), *The Color of the
    Heart* (Curbstone Pr, 1990), *We Stand Our Ground* (Co-
    author; Ikon Bks, 1988), *A Gathering of the Tribes, Long
    Shot, Heresies, Poetry, APR*

James Sherry   P&W
300 Bowery
New York, NY 10012, 212-353-0555
    Pubs: *Our Nuclear Heritage* (Sun & Moon Pr, 1991), *The
    Word I Like White Paint Considered* (Awede, 1986), *Popular
    Fiction* (Roof Bks, 1985)

David Shetzline   W
ICM, 40 W 57 St, New York, NY 10019, 212-556-5600

Ann Allen Shockley 🎤 ✈   W
Carole Abel Literary Agent, 160 W 87 St, #7D, New York, NY
10024, 212-724-1168
    Pubs: *Loving Her* (Northeastern U Pr, 1997), *Homeworks:
    Anth* (U Tenn Pr, 1996), *Women in the Trees: Anth* (Beacon
    Pr, 1996), *Revolutionary Tales: Anth* (Dell, 1995), *Centers of
    the Self: Anth* (Hill & Wang, 1994), *Calling the Wind: Anth*
    (Harper, 1993)

Enid Shomer 🎤 ✈   P&W
173 Riverside Dr, #2Y
New York, NY 10024-1615, 212-580-4207
Internet: enidshomer@aol.com
    Pubs: *Stars at Noon, Black Drum, This Close to the Earth* (U
    Arkansas Pr, 2001, 1997, 1992), *Imaginary Men* (U Iowa Pr,
    1993), *New Yorker, Atlantic, Paris Rev, Poetry, New
    Criterion, Georgia Rev, Modern Maturity*

Susan Richards Shreve   W
Russell & Volkening Inc, 50 W 29 St, New York, NY 10001,
212-684-6050
Internet: SRSHREVE@aol.com
    Pubs: *Plum & Jaggers* (FSG, 2000), *The Visiting Physician,
    The Train Home, Daughters of the New World* (Doubleday,
    1996, 1993, 1992), *A Country of Strangers* (S&S, 1989)

Kenneth Siegelman 🎤   P
2225 W 5 St
Brooklyn, NY 11223
Internet: pkorolenko@aol.com
    Pubs: *Critical Thinking Through Poetry* (Gifted Education Pr,
    1997), *Urbania, American Imprints, Through Global
    Currents* (Modern Images Pr, 1996, 1994, 1993),
    Parnassus, Poet

Alan Siegler 🎤 ✈   W
c/o Carolyn Trager, 171 W 79 St, New York, NY 10024
Internet: alansiegler@highplanet.com
    Pubs: *Icarus, Midstream*

Eleni Sikelianos 🎤 ✈   P
106 Ridge St, #2D
New York, NY 10002
Internet: sikelianos@aol.com
    Pubs: *Of Sun, Of History, Of Seeing* (Coffee Hse, 2001),
    Book of Tendons (Post-Apollo Pr, 1997), *To Speak While
    Dreaming* (Selva Edtns, 1993), *New American Poets: Anth*
    (Talisman, 1999), *The World, Grand Street, Verse, Sulfur,
    Skanky Possum*

Joan Silber 🎤 ✈   W
43 Bond St
New York, NY 10012-2463, 212-228-9728
Internet: jksilber@earthlink.net
    Pubs: *Lucky Us* (Algonquin, 2001), *In My Other Life*
    (Sarabande, 2000), *In the City, Household Words* (Viking,
    1987, 1980), *Pushcart Prize XXV: Anth* (Pushcart Pr, 2000),
    Ploughshares, VLS, New Yorker, Paris Rev

Layle Silbert 🎤   P&W
Seven Stories Press, 140 Watts St, New York, NY 10013,
212-226-8760
    Pubs: *The Free Thinkers* (Seven Stories Pr, 2000), *New
    York, New York* (St. Andrews Pr, 1996), *Burkah & Other
    Stories* (Host Pubs, 1992), *Imaginary People & Other
    Strangers* (Exile Pr, 1985), *Denver Qtly, Salmagundi,
    Michigan Qtly Rev, Confrontation*

Lari Field Siler   W
361 E 50 St
New York, NY 10022, 212-759-7364
    Pubs: *Adrienne's House* (HR&W, 1979), *Epicure, True Love,
    Teens Today*

Christopher Silver   W
300 Central Pk W
New York, NY 10024, 413-238-7769

Ruth M. Silver   P
374 Eastern Pkwy
Brooklyn, NY 11225
    Pubs: *Brooklyn Book Fair: Anth* (Somrie Pr, 1984), *Brooklyn
    College Lit Rev*

Shirley J. Simmons   P
JAF Box 7496, GPO, New York, NY 10116
    Pubs: *Song of Circe* (Art & Oxygen, 1988), *Liberation*
    (Platen Pub, 1986), *Up Against the Wall*

Laura Simms   PP&P
814 Broadway, #3
New York, NY 10003, 212-674-3479
    Pubs: *Moon & Otter & Frog* (Hyperion, 1995), *Chosen Tales:
    Anth* (Rosen, 1995), *Revisioning the Myth of Demeter &
    Persephone: Anth* (Shambala, 1994)

Ana Maria Simo   W
New Dramatists, 424 W 44 St, New York, NY 10036

Jane Simon 🎤   P
145 Central Pk W
New York, NY 10023, 212-877-3566
Internet: js145@msn.com
    Pubs: *Incisions* (Croton Rev Pr, 1989), *On Wings of Spirit:
    Anth* (American Physicians' Poetry Assoc, 2000), *UCLA
    Poet Physician Anth* (UCLA Pr, 1990), *Poet, Black Buzzard
    Rev, New Voices*

Mona Simpson   P&W
c/o Amanda Urban, ICM, 40 W 57 St, New York, NY 10019,
212-556-5600
    Pubs: *Anywhere But Here* (Knopf, 1987)

Abiola Sinclair   PP&P
Black History Magazine, 2565 Broadway MBE 262, New York,
NY 10025, 212-662-2942
Internet: blackhistorymag@pipeline.com
    Pubs: *Black History Mag, Charleston Chronicle, New York
    Beacon, Daily Challenge, Black Mask, Big Red,
    Amsterdam News*

Davida Singer   P
223 W 105 St, #3FW
New York, NY 10025-3968, 212-663-3937
    Pubs: *Khupe* (CD; Recording, 1997), *Shelter Island Poems*
    (Canio's Edtns, 1995), *Ignite, Response, Little Mag,
    Passager, Caprice, Sinister Wisdom*

Frieda Singer 🎤   P
161-08 Jewel Ave, #1-C
Flushing, NY 11365, 718-591-2288
    Pubs: *Voices of the Holocaust: Anth* (Perfection Learning,
    2000), *Which Lilith: Anth* (Jason Aronson, 1999), *Blood to
    Remember: Anth* (Texas Tech U Pr, 1992), *Poetpourri, The
    Formalist, South Florida Poetry Rev, Negative Capability*

Ravi Singh   P
225 E 5 St, #4D
New York, NY 10003, 212-475-0212
    Pubs: *Long Song to the One I Love* (White Lion, 1986),
    Another World: Anth (Crown, 1992), *Grand Union, Exquisite
    Corpse, Cover*

Harriet Sirof 🎤   W
792 E 21 St
Brooklyn, NY 11210-1042, 718-859-3296
Internet: hsirof@aol.com
    Pubs: *Bring Back Yesterday, Because She's My Friend*
    (Atheneum, 1996, 1993)

Hal Sirowitz 🎤 ✈   P
144-45 Sanford Ave, #2C
Flushing, NY 11355, 718-461-7892
    Pubs: *My Therapist Said, Mother Said* (Crown, 1998,
    1996), *Word of Mouth: Poems Featured on NPR's All
    Things Considered: Anth* (Vintage, 2003), *Good Poems:
    Anth: CD* (Penguin Audiobks, 2002), *Ploughshares,
    Chelsea, The Ledge*

Denis Sivack 🎤 ✈   P
1165 E 54 St, #4-F
Brooklyn, NY 11234-2426
    Pubs: *Gargoyle, Weber Studies, Esprit*

Arnold Skemer   W
58-09 205 St
Bayside, NY 11364-1712, 718-428-9368
  Pubs: *Investigations of the Cyberneticist, The Ruins of the
  City, Momus, B* (Phrygian Pr, 1999, 1998, 1997, 1996),
  *Paradoxism, Lost & Found Times, Transmoog, Drop Forge,
  Meat Epoch, Generator, New Surrealism*

Morty Sklar 🎤 ✈   P
35-50 85 St, Apt 8E
Jackson Heights, NY 11372-5540, 718-426-8788
Internet: msklar@mindspring.com
  Pubs: *To the White Lady* (The Spirit That Moves Us Pr,
  1999), *The First Poem* (Snapper Pr, 1987), *The Night We
  Stood Up For Our Rights* (Toothpaste Pr, 1977), *From A to
  Z: Anth* (Swallow Pr, 1980), *New Letters, NYQ, World Letter,
  Smiling Dog, Pearl*

Bob Slaymaker 🎤 ✈   P&W
415 W 24 St, #4F
New York, NY 10011, 212-558-3601
Internet: bob@bobslaymaker.com
  Pubs: *Blue Mesa, NAR, Pif, Texas Observer, Exquisite
  Corpse, Poetry Ireland Rev, US Latino Rev, Callaloo, CSM,
  Essence, Gargoyle, Natl Catholic Reporter, NYQ, Orbis,
  Press, River Styx, Weber Studies, Writers' Forum, Zuzu's
  Petals Qtly*

Henry Slesar   W
125 E 72 St, #12-A
New York, NY 10021, 212-628-1741
  Pubs: *Death on Television* (U Illinois Pr, 1989), *Murders
  Most Macabre* (Avon Bks, 1986), *Ellery Queen's Mystery
  Mag, Alfred Hitchcock's Mystery*

John C. Smedley   W
14 Oakdale Dr
Hastings-on-Hudson, NY 10706
  Pubs: *The Villager, St. Andrews Rev, Phantasm*

Barbara Smith 🎤 ✈   P&W
Charlotte Sheedy Literary Agency, 65 Bleecker St, 12th Fl,
New York, NY 10012
  Pubs: *Yours in Struggle* (Firebrand Bks, 1984), *Home Girls:
  Black Feminist Anth* (Kitchen Table, 1983), *Ms., The
  Guardian, American Voice, Black Scholar, Village Voice*

Robert L. Smith   P
271 E 78 St
New York, NY 10021, 212-734-3474
  Pubs: *Refractions* (Dragon's Teeth, 1979), *Galley Sail Rev,
  Roanoke Rev, Orbis, Long Pond Rev*

Charlie Smith 🎤 ✈   P&W
Maria Carvainis Literary Agency, 235 W End Ave, New York,
NY 10023, 212-580-1559
  Pubs: *Heroin, Before & After* (Norton, 2000, 1995), *Shine
  Hawk* (U Georgia Pr, 1998), *Cheap Ticket to Heaven* (H
  Holt, 1996), *New Yorker, Paris Rev, Fence, Open City,
  Poetry, APR, New Republic*

C. W. Smith   W
Elaine Markson Literary Agency, 44 Greenwich Ave, New York,
NY 10011, 212-243-8480
  Pubs: *Thin Men of Haddam* (Texas Christian U Pr, 1990),
  Uncle Dad (Berkley Bks, 1989), *Buffalo Nickel* (Poseidon,
  1989), *Esquire, Quartet*

Patti Smith   P
c/o Ina Lea Meibach, Meibach Epstein Reiss & Regis,
680 Fifth Ave, Ste 500, New York, NY 10019
  Pubs:

Dinitia Smith   W
210 W 101 St, #3J
New York, NY 10025, 212-864-3866
  Pubs: *Remember This* (H Holt, 1989), *The Hard Rain* (Dial
  Pr, 1980), *Hudson Rev, Pequod*

Phil Demise Smith 🎤 ✈   P
421 Hudson St, #220
New York, NY 10014-3647, 212-989-7845
Internet: philsmith@waresforart.com
  Pubs: Constant Variations, The Lost Supper/The Last
  Generation (w/Gunter Temech) (Gegenshein, 1993, 1990)

Harry Smith 🎤 ✈   P
69 Joralemon St
Brooklyn, NY 11201-4003, 718-834-1212
Internet: thesmith@aol.com
  Pubs: *The Sexy Sixties, Two Friends II* (w/Menke Katz),
  Ballads for the Possessed (Birch Brook Pr, 2002, 1988, 1987)

Leora Skolkin Smith   W
61 Lexington Ave, #4G
New York, NY 10010
  Pubs: *Hystera* (Persea Bks, 1979), *Sarah Lawrence Rev*

John J. Soldo 🎤 ✈   P
1627 81 St
Brooklyn, NY 11214-2107, 718-259-8016
  Pubs: *Sonnets for Our Risorgimento, In the Indies*
  (Brunswick Pub, 1993, 1991), *High Plains Scenarios*
  (Earthwise Pub, 1992), *Encore, Parnassus, Omnific*

Stacey Sollfrey   P
1117 E 86 St, Downstairs
Brooklyn, NY 11236, 718-209-9840
  Pubs: *Feeling the Roof of a Mouth That Hangs Open*
  (w/Sheila Murphy; Luna Bisonte Prod, 1991), *Lost & Found
  Times, Impetus, Fine Madness*

Barbara Probst Solomon 🎤   W
c/o Jennifer Lyons, The Writers House, 21 W 26 St, New York,
NY 10010, 212-961-0636
    Pubs: *Arriving Where We Started, The Beat of Life* (Great
    Marsh Pr, 1999, 1999), *Smart Hearts in the City* (HB, 1992),
    Horse Trading & Ecstasy (Northpoint, 1989), *Short Flights*
    (Viking Pr, 1983)

Susan Sontag   W
Wylie Agency, 250 W 57 St, New York, NY 10107
    Pubs: *Where the Stess Falls, In America, The Volcano
    Lover, A Susan Sontag Reader, Under the Sign of Saturn, I,
    Etcetera* (FSG, 2001, 1999, 1992, 1982, 1981, 1978)

Gilbert Sorrentino   W
c/o Mel Berger, William Morris Agency, 1325 Ave of the
Americas, New York, NY 10019
    Pubs: *Little Casino* (Coffee Hse, 2002), *Gold Fools* (Green
    Integer, 2001), *Pack of Lies, Under the Shadow, Misterioso,
    Rose Theatre* (Dalkey Archive, 1997, 1991, 1989, 1987),
    Red the Fiend (Fromm Intl, 1995), *Odd Number* (North
    Point, 1985)

Peter Sourian   W
30 E 70 St
New York, NY 10021
    Pubs: *At the French Embassy in Sofia* (Ashod Pr, 1992),
    Drawing, Annandale, Ararat, Nation

Ellease Southerland   P&W
Marie Brown Associates Inc, 625 Broadway, New York, NY
10012, 917-863-6528
Internet: eoseye@aol.com
    Pubs: *A Feast of Fools* (Africana Legacy Pr, 1998), *Let the
    Lion Eat Straw* (Scribner, 1979), *Calling the Wind: Anth*
    (Harper Perennial, 1993), *Breaking Ice: Anth* (Penguin,
    1990), *Massachusetts Rev, Poet Lore*

Tom Spanbauer   W
Donadio & Olson Inc, 121 W 27 St, Ste 704, New York, NY
10001, 212-691-8077
    Pubs: *Les Chiens de L'Enfer* (Gallimard, 1989), *Faraway
    Places* (Putnam, 1988), *Mississippi Mud*

Al Spector   P
69-31 222 St
Bayside, NY 11364, 718-224-8950
    Pubs: *Whispers of Spring* (The Plowman, 1994), *Bogg,
    Midwest Poetry Rev, Wind, Orphic Lute, Chicago Street*

Scott Spencer   W
c/o HarperCollins, 10 E 53rd St, New York, NY 10022
    Pubs: *A Ship Made of Paper* (HC, 2003), *The Rich Man's
    Table, Men in Black, Secret Anniversaries* (Knopf, 1998,
    1995, 1990)

Katia Spiegelman   W
392 Sackett St, 2nd Fl
Brooklyn, NY 11231, 718-858-1404
    Pubs: *Peculiar Politics, Soul Catcher* (Marion Boyars Pub,
    1993, 1990)

Peter Spielberg 🎤 ✈   W
321 W 24 S, Apt 13F
New York, NY 10011, 212-989-4298
    Pubs: *The Noctambulists, Hearsay* (Fiction Collective Two,
    2001, 1992), *Crash-Landing* (Fiction Collective, 1985),
    Fiction Intl, Europe, Mississippi Rev

Norman Spinrad   W
c/o Jane Rotrosen, 318 E 51 St, New York, NY 10022,
212-752-1038

Nancy Springer   W
Jean V. Naggar Literary Agency, 216 E 75 St, Ste 1E, New
York, NY 10021
    Pubs: *I Am Mordred* (Philomel, 1998), *Fair Peril, Larque on
    the Wing* (Avon, 1996, 1994), *Alfred Hitchcock's Mystery,
    Mag of Fantasy & Sci-Fi, Cricket, Boys Life, Pirate Writings*

Stephen Stark   W
c/o Lisa Ross, Spieler Agency, 154 W 57 St, New York, NY
10019, 212-757-4439
    Pubs: *Second Son* (H Holt, 1992), *The Outskirts* (Algonquin
    Bks, 1988), *New Yorker, The Jrnl*

Robert Steiner   W
Georges Borchardt Inc, 136 E 57 St, New York, NY 10022
    Pubs: *Toward a Grammar of Abstraction* (Pennsylvania
    State Pr, 1993), *Broadway Melody of 1999, Matinee* (Fiction
    Collective Two, 1993, 1991)

Stephen Stepanchev 🎤 ✈   P
140-60 Beech Ave, #3C
Flushing, NY 11355-2830, 718-539-4463
    Pubs: *Seven Horizons* (Orchises Pr, 1997), *Descent* (Stone
    Hse Pr, 1988), *Poetry, New Yorker, New Criterion,
    Commonweal, Interim, NYQ*

Jack Stephens   P&W
51 7th Ave S, #5C
New York, NY 10014-6705
    Pubs: *Vector Love* (Haw River Bks, 1990), *Triangulation*
    (Crown, 1990), *Prairie Schooner, APR*

Michael Stephens   P&W
520 W 110 St, #5C
New York, NY 10025
    Pubs: *The Brooklyn Book of the Dead* (Dalkey Archive,
    1994), *Green Dreams* (U Georgia Pr, 1994), *Fiction, Ontario
    Rev, Pequod*

Phyllis Stern 🎤 ✈ P
167 W 71 St, Apt 9
New York, NY 10023-3833, 212-799-4365
Internet: s6mkjphyllis@netscape.com
Pubs: *Making Contact: Anth* (Voyage Out Pr, 1978), *Lilith,
Womanews, Home Planet News*

Daniel Stern W
Georges Borchardt Inc, 136 E 57 St, New York, NY 10022
Pubs: *In the Country of the Young, One Day's Perfect
Weather* (SMU Pr, 2000, 1999), *Twice Upon a Time* (Norton,
1992), *Twice-Told Tales* (Paris Rev Edtns, 1989), *An Urban
Affair* (S&S, 1980), *Paris Rev, Raritan, Columbia*

Margaret Stetler 🎤 ✈ P
189-49 45th Dr
Flushing, NY 11358-3412, 718-353-2185
Internet: mastetler@aol.com
Pubs: *The Naming of the Soul* (Four Zoas, 1980), *West
Wind Rev, Womanchild, Small Pond Rev, Kosmos, Pegasus
Dreaming, Telephone*

Nikki Stiller P&W
622 W 114th St
New York, NY 10025-7973, 212224326
Internet: nso40247@aol.com
Pubs: *On Both Frontiers: Poems of Youth and Age, Notes of
a Jewish Nun* (CCC, 1999, 1992), *Poetry NY, Shaking Eve's
Tree, Response, Primavera, Midstream, Jewish Currents*

William R. Stimson W
333 W 21 St, Apt 2FW
New York, NY 10011, 212-675-1213
Internet: stimson_bill@bah.com
Pubs: *Parting Gifts, Snowy Egret, New Thought Jrnl*

B. E. Stock 🎤 ✈ P
c/o Dolan, 28 Vesey St, PMB 2143, New York, NY 10007-2906
Pubs: *We Speak for Peace: Anth* (KIT Pr, 1993), *Flash!Point,
Sonnet Scroll, Orbis, Blue Unicorn, Lyric, New Pr, Spring,
Array, Karamu, Skylark, Poems That Jump in the Dark,
Piedmont Lit Rev, Edge City Rev*

Norman Stock 🎤 ✈ P
77-11 35 Ave #2P
Jackson Heights, NY 11372-4633, 718-898-1762
Internet: stockn@mail.montclair.edu
Pubs: *Buying Breakfast for My Kamikaze Pilot* (Gibbs Smith,
1994), *Barrow Street, Verse, New Republic, College English,
NYQ, Denver Qtly, NER, Asylum*

Carolyn Stoloff P
32 Union Sq E, Rm 911
New York, NY 10003, 212-473-0256
Pubs: *Reaching for Honey* (Red Hen Pr, 2003), *You Came
to Meet Someone Else* (Asylum Arts Pr, 1993), *Bomb, New
Yorker, Partisan Rev, Southern Rev*

Alma Stone W
523 W 112 St
New York, NY 10025

Laurie Stone 🎤 ✈ W
808 W End Ave
New York, NY 10025-5369, 212-663-7011
Internet: lstonehere@aol.com
Pubs: *Close to the Bone* (Grove, 1997), *Laughing in the
Dark* (Ecco, 1997), *Starting with Serge* (Doubleday, 1990),
TriQtly, New Letters, VLS, Nation, New Yorker

Alison J. Stone 🎤 ✈ P
230 E 15 St, #7F
New York, NY 10003-3944
Internet: nygoddess@aol.com
Pubs: *Sweet Nothings: Rock & Roll in American Poetry:
Anth* (Indiana U Pr, 1994), *Catholic Girls: Anth* (Plume,
1992), *Paris Rev, Poetry, Ploughshares, NYQ, Artful Dodge,
Witness, Many Mountains Moving*

James Story 🎤 ✈ P
500 9th St, #3F
Brooklyn, NY 11215-4112, 718-768-6919
Pubs: *Paper Boat, Berkeley Poetry Rev, Home Planet News,
Karamu, Now, Poets*

Mark Strand P&W
c/o Harry Ford, Alfred A Knopf Inc, 201 E 50 St, New York,
NY 10022
Pubs: *Dark Harbor* (Knopf, 1993), *Hopper: Anth* (Ecco Pr,
1994)

Dennis Straus PP&P&W
PO Box 176
Rockaway Park, NY 11694-0176, 718-474-6547
www.ascher/straus.com
Pubs: *ABC Street* (Green Integer, 2002), *The Menaced
Assassin, The Other Planet, Red Moon/Red Lake*
(McPherson, 1989, 1988, 1988), *NAW, Central Park,
Confrontation, Exile*

John Strausbaugh P&W
New York Press
333 7th Ave, NYC 10001, 212-244-2282
Internet: john@nypress.com
Pubs: *Rock Til You Drop* (Verso, 2001), *Reflections on the
Birth of the Elvis Faith, Alone with the President* (Blast Bks,
1995, 1994), *Red Zone, Flying Fish* (Dolphin-Moon, 1988,
1986), *High Performance, Bartleby*

Brad Strickland 🎤 ✈ W
Richard Curtis Assoc, 171 E 74 St, New York, NY 10021,
212-772-7393
Pubs: *Pirate Hunter: Mutiny* (S&S, 2002), *The Tower at the
End of the World, When Mack Came Back, Ghost in the
Mirror* (w/J. Bellairs) (Dial, 2002, 2001, 2000, 1993), *Stow-
aways* (Pocket, 1994), *Dragon's Plunder* (Atheneum, 1992)

Stephanie Strickland 🎤 ✈ P
1175 York Ave, 16B
New York, NY 10021-7175, 212-759-5175
Internet: strickla@mail.slc.edu
Pubs: *V* (Penguin, 2002), *True North Hypertext* (Eastgate Systems, 1998), *True North* (U Notre Dame Pr, 1997), *The Red Virgin: A Poem of Simone Weil* (U Wisconsin Pr, 1993), *Paris Rev, Grand Street, Fence*

Vicki Stringer 🎤 P
5614 Netherland Ave, #1G
Riverdale, NY 10471
Internet: vicrvdl@msn.com
Pubs: *Still Waters: Anth* (Poetry Today, 1997), *Troubadour, Amelia, American Poets & Poetry, Light, Lucidity, Nostalgia*

Chris Stroffolino P
331 13 St, Apt 4L
Brooklyn, NY 11215-5022, 201-459-9245
Pubs: *Oops* (Pavement Saw Pr, 1994), *APR, Lift, First Intensity, o.blek, Lingo, Painted Bride Qtly, Talisman, Caliban, Sulfur*

Victoria Sullivan 🎤 ✈ P
620 W 116 St, #21
New York, NY 10027-7044, 212-749-7685
Pubs: *The Divided Bed* (Hatch-Billops, 1982), *When a Lifemate Dies: Anth* (Fairview Pr, 1997), *Medicinal Purposes, NE Corridor, Chadakoin Rev, Pivot, Manhattan Poetry Rev, 13th Moon, Cape Rock, Artist & Influence, Poetry in Performance*

Mark Sullivan P
630 Ft Washington Ave, Apt 2J
New York, NY 10040, 212-740-0013
Internet: Mpsullivan@aol.com
Pubs: *Willow Springs, Orion, Bomb*

David Surface W
81 St James Pl
Brooklyn, NY 11238
Pubs: *Four Minute Fictions: Anth* (Word Beat Pr, 1987), *DoubleTake, Artful Dodge, Fiction, Crazyhorse, Willow Springs*

Linda Svendsen 🎤 ✈ W
Robin Straus Agency, 229 E 79 St, New York, NY 10021, 212-472-3282
Pubs: *Marine Life* (FSG, 1992), *Oxford Book of Stories by Canadian Women: Anth* (Oxford, 1999), *Penguin Bk of Stories by Canadian Women: Anth* (Penguin, 1998)

Terese Svoboda 🎤 ✈ P
56 Ludlow St
New York, NY 10002
Internet: teresesvo@aol.com
Pubs: *Treason* (Zoo Pr, 2002), *Trailer Girl, A Drink Called Paradise* (Conterpoint Pr, 2001, 2000), *Mere Mortals, All Aberration* (U Georgia Pr, 1995, 1985), *Cannibal* (NYU Pr, 1994), *Laughing Africa* (U Iowa Pr, 1990)

Brian Swann P
Faculty of Humanities, The Cooper Union, 41 Cooper Sq, New York, NY 10003, 212-353-4279
Internet: swann@cooper.edu
Pubs: *Wearing the Morning Star* (Random Hse, 1996), *Song of the Sky* (U Massachusetts Pr, 1993), *The Plot of the Mice* (Capra Pr, 1986)

Roberta M. Swann 🎤 ✈ P&W
19 Stuyvesant Oval, #8B
New York, NY 10009-2027, 212-533-8705
Internet: swann@cooper.edu
Pubs: *Yellow Silk* (Crown, 1990), *Everything Happens Suddenly, The Model Life* (Ancient Mariner Pr, 1989, 1988), *Indiana Rev, Kenyon Rev, Queen's Qtly, American Voice, New Letters, NAR, Ploughshares*

Lois Swann W
22 Sagamore Rd, #5D
Bronxville, NY 10708, 914-961-8104
Pubs: *Torn Covenants, The Mists of Manittoo* (Scribner, 1981, 1976)

Burton Swartz 🎤 ✈ PP
235 W 107 St, #234
New York, NY 10025-3020, 212-866-0118
Pubs: *Grasshoppers* (Amer Theatre of Actors, NYC, 1999), *Eastside Roulette* (Homegrown Theatre, NYC, 1999), *The Hidden, Once Upon a Deal* (Riant Theatre, 1998, 1996), *Downbeat, Columbia Spectator, College Times, Show Business, National Star Chronicle*

Karen Swenson 🎤 ✈ P
25 W 54 St, #12E
New York, NY 10019-5404, 212-586-8507
Internet: karswen@aol.com
Pubs: *A Daughter's Latitude, The Landlady in Bangkok* (Copper Canyon, 1999, 1994), *A Sense of Direction* (The Smith, 1990), *Attic of Ideals* (Doubleday, 1974), *New Yorker, Saturday Rev*

Janet Sylvester P
W W Norton, 500 5th Ave, New York, NY 10110, 212-354-5500
Pubs: *The Mark of Flesh* (Norton, 1997), *That Mulberry Wine* (Wesleyan, 1985), *Best American Poetry: Anth* (Scribner, 1994), *Boulevard, TriQtly, Shenandoah*

Ryder Syvertsen 🎤 W
612 Castleton Ave
Staten Island, NY 10301, 718-981-9973
Internet: rydersyv@yahoo.com
    Pubs: *C.A.D.S. #1-8* (Pinnacle Bks, 1990, 1985), *Mystic
    Rebel, Doomsday Warrior* (Zebra Bks, 1989, 1986), *Psychic
    Spawn* (Popular Library, 1987)

Sherri Szeman 🎤 ✈ P&W
c/o Jennifer Hengen, Sterling Lord Literistic, 65 Bleecker St,
New York, NY 10012, 212-780-6050
    Pubs: *Only with the Heart, Kommandant's Mistress* (Arcade,
    2000), *Writer, Chicago Rev, Kenyon Rev, Centennial Rev*

Marilynn Talal 🎤 ✈ P
308 E 79 St, #4E
New York, NY 10021-0906
    Pubs: *Our Own Clues: Poets of the Lake 2: Anth* (Our Lady
    of the Lake U Pr, 1993), *Blood to Remember: Anth* (Texas
    Tech U Pr, 1991), *Western Humanities Rev, Poetry, New
    Republic, The Qtly*

Amy Tan W
G P Putnam's Sons, 375 Hudson St, New York, NY 10014
    Pubs: *The Bonesetter's Daughter, The Kitchen God's Wife,
    The Joy Luck Club* (Putnam, 2001, 1991, 1989), *The
    Hundred Secret Senses* (Ivy Bks, 1996), *Atlantic, SF Focus,
    Seventeen*

Anne Tardos 🎤 ✈ P
42 N Moore St
New York, NY 10013
Internet: annetardos@att.net
    Pubs: *The Dik-dik's Solitude, New and Selected Works*
    (Granary Bks, 2002, 2002), *UXUDO* (Tuumba Pr/O Bks,
    1999), *Mayg-shem Fish* (Potes & Poets, 1995), *Cat Licked
    the Garlic* (Tsunami Edtns, 1992), *Conjunctions, Chain, The
    Germ, Crayon, Pom2*

Meredith Tax 🎤 ✈ W
c/o Women's World, 208 W 30 St, #901, New York, NY 10001
Internet: wworld@igc.org
    Pubs: *Families* (Feminist Pr, 1996), *Union Square, Rivington
    Street* (Morrow, 1988, 1982), *The Rising of Women* (Monthly
    Rev, 1980), *Nation*

Theodore Taylor W
c/o Gloria Loomis, Watkins Loomis Agency Inc, 133 E 35 St,
Ste 1, New York, NY 10016
    Pubs: *Rogue Wave, The Bomb, To Kill the Leopard, Timothy
    of the Cay* (HB, 1996, 1995, 1993, 1993)

Conciere Taylor P
67-08 Parsons Blvd, #6B
Flushing, NY 11365-2955
    Pubs: *In Concert: Anth, Shock Treatment: Anth* (Peak
    Output, 1989, 1988), *Rapunzel, Rapunzel: Anth* (Kathryn
    Machan Aal, 1979), *Earth's Daughters, Scapes, Whetstone,
    Slugfest, Calliope*

Richard Tayson 🎤 ✈ P
86-75 Midland Parkway, # 4N
Jamaica, NY 11432, 718-523-0370
Internet: rtayson@earthlink.net
    Pubs: *Best of Prairie Schooner: Anth* (U NE, 2001), *Word of
    Mouth: A Gay Poetry Anth* (Talisman Hse, 2000), *American
    Poetry, Next Generation: Anth* (Carnegie Mellon, 2000), *The
    World in Us, Lesbian & Gay Poetry of the Next Wave: Anth*
    (St Martin's Pr, 2000)

Fiona Templeton 🎤 ✈ PP&P
100 St Marks Pl, #7
New York, NY 10009-5822
    Pubs: *Delirium of Interpretations* (Green Integer, 2002),
    oops the join (rempress, 1997), *Hi Cowboy* (Mainstream,
    1997), *Cells of Release, You The City* (Roof Bks, 1997,
    1990), *London* (Sun & Moon Pr, 1984)

Megan Terry 🎤 ✈ PP&P
Marton Agency, 1 Union Sq W, Rm 612, New York, NY
10003-3303, 212-255-1908
Internet: jschmidm@aol.com
    Pubs: *Star Path Moon Stop* (Seoul, Korea, 1996), *Right
    Brain Vacation Photos* (Omaha Magic Theatre Pr, 1991),
    College Money: Anth (Meriwether Pr, 2003), *Fireworks: Anth*
    (Smith & Kraus, 1995)

Nadja Tesich W
855 W End Ave, #7A
New York, NY 10025
Internet: savage@qcvaxa.acc.qc.edu
    Pubs: *Shadow Partisan, American Fiction: Anth* (New Rivers
    Pr, 1989, 1995), *Mademoiselle, Kenyon Rev, Confrontation,
    ACM, City Lights Rev, Nation, 13th Moon*

Catherine Texier W
255 E 7 St
New York, NY 10009, 212-677-4748
    Pubs: *Panic Blood, Love Me Tender* (Viking, 1990, 1987),
    New Observations, Bomb, Heresies

Marcelle Thiebaux W
305 W 86 St, #11A
New York, NY 10024, 212-362-9906
    Pubs: *Literal Latte, Cream City Rev, Karamu, Twisted, El
    Gato Tuerto/The One-Eyed Cat*

James Alexander Thom 🎤 ✈ W
c/o Mitch Douglas, ICM, 40 W 57 St, New York, NY 10019
    Pubs: *Spectator Sport* (Universe, 2001), *Sign-Talker, The
    Red Heart, Panther in the Sky, Staying Out of Hell, The
    Children of First Man, From Sea to Shining Sea, Follow the
    River, Long Knife* (Ballantine, 2000, 1998, 1989, 1985, 1984,
    1984, 1981, 1979)

Abigail Thomas 🎤 ✈   P&W
395 Riverside Dr
New York, NY 10025-1859, 212-864-6867
   Pubs: *Herb's Pajamas, An Actual Life, Getting Over Tom*
   (Algonquin, 1998, 1996, 1994), *DoubleTake, Missouri Rev,*
   Paris Rev, Nation

Charles Columbus Thomas   P
1245 Park Ave, #11K
New York, NY 10028, 212-876-9464

Joyce Carol Thomas   P
c/o Mitch Douglas, ICM, 40 W 57 St, New York, NY 10019
   Pubs: *Journey, The Golden Pasture* (Scholastic, 1988,
   1986), *Watergirl* (Avon, 1986)

Barbara Thompson   W
205 W 57 St
New York, NY 10019, 212-581-5448
   Pubs: *The Pushcart Prize Anthology, Shenandoah, McCall's,*
   Paris Rev

Sharon Thompson   W
PO Box 20739, Tompkins Sq Sta, New York, NY 10009
   Pubs: *Powers of Desire* (Monthly Rev Pr, 1983), *Village*
   Voice, Heresies, Feminist Studies

John A. Thompson   P&W
418 Central Pk W
New York, NY 10025, 212-749-1256
   Pubs: *The Founding of English Metre* (Columbia U Pr, 1988)

Newton Thornburg   W
Don Congdon Assoc Inc, 156 5th Ave, Ste 625, New York, NY
10010-7002, 212-645-1229
   Pubs: *Beautiful Kate, Valhalla, Black Angus* (Little, Brown,
   1982, 1980, 1978)

Judith Thurman   P
445 E 86 St, #15D
New York, NY 10028
   Pubs: *Magic Lantern, Flashlight & Other Poems* (Atheneum,
   1978, 1976)

Irene Tiersten   W
JET Literary Assoc, 124 E 84 St, New York, NY 10028,
212-879-2578
Internet: tiersten@ix.netcom.com
   Pubs: *One Big Happy Family* (The Reader Project, 1990),
   Among Friends (St. Martin's, 1982), *Mediphors, First for*
   Women, New Directions

Carl Tiktin   W
87 Alta Ave
Yonkers, NY 10705, 914-968-3655
   Pubs: *Ron, The Hourglass Man* (Arbor Hse, 1979, 1978)

Gioia Timpanelli   PP
c/o Ira Silverberg, Donadio & Olson, Inc., 121 W 27 St, Ste
704, New York, NY 10001, 212-691-8077
   Pubs: *Sometimes the Soul* (Vintage Pr, 2000), *The Milk of*
   Almonds: Italian American Women Writers on Food and
   Culture: Anth (The Feminist Pr, 2002), *American Letters &*
   Commentary

Arthur Tobias   P
229 W 97 St, Apt 4J
New York, NY 10025-5611, 212-665-2962
   Pubs: *The View from Cold Mountain* (White Pine, 1982),
   Choice, Epoch, Ironwood, White Pine Jrnl

James Tolan 🎤 ✈   P
110 Bement Ave
Staten Island, NY 10310-1500, 718-273-9447
Internet: jimtolan@mindspring.com
   Pubs: *Coffeehouse Poetry Anth* (Bottom Dog Pr, 1996),
   What Have You Lost: Anth (Greenwillow, 1999), *American*
   Lit Rev, Atlanta Rev, The Baffler, Indiana Rev, Intl Qtly, Luna,
   The Qtly, Salt Hill Jrnl, Wisconsin Rev

Vincent J. Tomeo 🎤 ✈   P
PO Box 52-7203
Flushing, NY 11352-7203, 718-961-6208
Internet: Mmin2@aol.com
   Pubs: *EDGZ: Anth* (Blaine R. Hammond, 2002),
   Grandmother Earth (Life Pr, 2002), *Mausoleum/Mortis Es*
   Veritus (Crow Ravenscar, 2002), *Subway: Anth* (P&Q Pr,
   2002), *The Neovictorian/Cochlea*

Lydia Tomkiw   P
85 E 3 St, #A3
New York, NY 10003-9040, 212-982-7256
Internet: ltnyc@aol.com
   Pubs: *Unbearables: Anth* (Autonomedia, 1995), *Walk on the*
   Wild Side: Anth (Macmillan, 1994), *Aerial, B-City, Joe*
   Soap's Canoe, Brooklyn Rev

Yasunao Tone   PP
307 W Broadway, 3rd Fl
New York, NY 10013, 212-966-0945
   Pubs: *Solo for Wounded* (CD; Tzadik, 1997), *Musica*
   Iconologos, Trio for a Flute Player & Lyrictron in Upper Air
   Observation (CDs; Lovely Music, 1994, 1991),
   Conjunctions, Music

Mike Topp 🎤 ✈   P
8 Stuyvesant Oval, #8H
New York, NY 10009, 212-673-2766
Internet: mike_topp@hotmail.com
   Pubs: *I Used to be Ashamed of My Striped Face* (Elimae
   Bks, 2002), *Bad Luck, Basho's Milk Dud, Six Short Stories &*
   Seven Short Poems (Low-Tech Press, 2001, 1999, 1997),
   The Outlaw Bible of American Poetry: Anth. (Thunder's
   Mouth, 1999)

Juanita Torrence-Thompson 🎤 ✈   P&W
PO Box 751205
Forest Hills, NY 11375
Internet: jtth@aol.com
    Pubs: *Pedestal, Curbside Rev, Paterson Lit Rev, Montserrat Rev, Snail's Pace Rev, San Fernando Poetry Jrnl, Chaminade Lit Rev, CQ, Green Hills Lit Lantern, Yefief, AIM, Caprice, Tucumcari, Appearances, Array Mag, Women's Work*

Edwin Torres 🎤 ✈   PP&P
87 E 2nd St, #5D
New York, NY 10003
Internet: brainlingo@earthlink.net
    Pubs: *The All-Union Day of the Shock Worker* (Roof Bks, 2001), *Onomalingua: Noise Songs and Poetry* (e-book), *Short Fuse: Anth* (Rattapallax Pr, 2000, 2002), *Fractured Humorous* (Subpress, 1999), *Role Call: Anth* (Third World Pr, 2002), *World, Chain, Pom Pom*

Tony Towle   P
75 Hudson St, #2
New York, NY 10013, 212-619-4524
Internet: ttowlepoet@aol.com
    Pubs: *The History of the Invitation, Some Musical Episodes, Broadway 2: Anth* (Hanging Loose Pr, 2001, 1992, 1989), *New & Selected Poems 1963-1983* (Kulchur, 1983), *Postmodern American Poetry: Anth* (Norton, 1994), *Arshile, Otis Run, Hanging Loose, The World*

Peter Trachtenberg   W
c/o Gloria Loomis, Watkins Loomis Agency Inc, 133 E 35 St, Ste 1, New York, NY 10016
    Pubs: *The Casanova Complex* (S&S, 1988), *Mademoiselle, Der Stern, Chicago*

Patricia Traxler 🎤 ✈   P&W
Brandt & Hochman Literary Agents, 1501 Broadway, New York, NY 10036
    Pubs: *Blood* (St. Martin's Pr, 2001), *Forbidden Words* (U Missouri Pr, 1994), *Best American Poetry: Anth* (Scribner, 1994), *Kenyon Rev, Ploughshares, Nation, Glimmer Train, Ms., Agni*

Calvin Trillin   W
12 Grove St
New York, NY 10014, 212-243-3455

David Trinidad 🎤 ✈   P
401 W Broadway, #1
New York, NY 10012, 212-274-9529
Internet: david_trinidad@hotmail.com
    Pubs: *Plasticville* (Turtle Point Pr, 2000), *Answer Song* (High Risk/Serpent's Tail, 1994), *Hand Over Heart: Poems 1981-1988* (Amethyst Pr, 1991)

Frederic Tuten 🎤 ✈   W
Watkins Loomis Agency Inc, 133 E 35 St, Ste 1, New York, NY 10016, 212-532-0080
    Pubs: *The Green Hour* (Norton, 2002), *Van Gogh's Bad Cafe, Tintin in the New World* (Morrow, 1997, 1993), *Tallien* (FSG, 1988), *TriQtly, Fiction, Global City Rev*

David Unger 🎤 ✈   P
157 Waverly, #3A
Brooklyn, NY 11205
    Pubs: *Life in the Damn Tropics* (Syracuse U Pr, 2002), *Tropical Synagogues: Latin American Jewish Writing Anth* (Holmes & Meiers, 1994), *Neither Caterpillar Nor Butterfly* (Es Que Somos Muy Pobres Pr, 1986)

John Updike   P&W
Alfred A Knopf Inc, 201 E 50 St, New York, NY 10022, 212-751-2600
    Pubs: *Trust Me, Roger's Version, The Witches of Eastwick* (Knopf, 1987, 1987, 1984), *New Yorker*

Robert Upton   W
419 W 22 St
New York, NY 10011, 212-989-5349
    Pubs: *The Big Tour* (Berkely, 2002), *A Killing in Real Estate, The Faberge Egg* (Dutton, 1990, 1988), *Dead on the Stick* (Viking, 1986)

Jean Valentine 🎤 ✈   P
527 W 110 St, #81
New York, NY 10025-2082, 212-866-9740
    Pubs: *Cradle of Real Life* (Wesleyan U Pr, 2000), *Growing Darkness, Growing Light* (Carnegie Mellon, 1997), *The River at Wolf, Home Deep Blue* (Alice James Bks, 1992, 1989), *Field, New Yorker, APR*

Anthony Valerio 🎤   W
106 Charles St, #14
New York, NY 10014-2695, 212-675-4685
    Pubs: *Lefty and the Button Men, The Mediterranean Runs Through Brooklyn* (Xlibris, 2000, 2000), *Paris Rev, Paris Transcontinental*

Nicholas Valinotti   P
448 Bergen St, #4C
Brooklyn, NY 11217
    Pubs: *Brooklyn Rev, Cathartic, Galley Sail Rev, Home Planet News, Cottonwood, The Archer, Ailanthus, Cover, Mudfish*

Carmen Valle   P&W
71 E 4 St, #6A
New York, NY 10003, 212-673-7824
    Pubs: *Entre la Vigilia y el Sueno de las Fieras, Desde Marruecos Te Escribo* (Instituto de Cultura Puertorriqena, 1994, 1992), *Trasimagen, Balcon*

Henry Van Dyke   W
40 Waterside Plaza, #16-L
New York, NY 10010, 212-683-5587
    Pubs: *Lunacy & Caprice* (Ballantine, 1987), *Dead Piano,
    Blood of Strawberries, Ladies of the Rachmaninoff Eyes*
    (FSG, 1971, 1968, 1965), *Afro-American Short Story Anth*
    (HC, 1993), *Antioch Rev, Story Qtly*

Ronald Vance   W
10 W 18 St
New York, NY 10011
    Pubs: *Interstate, O.ars, Benzene, Clown War, Sun & Moon*

Herminio Vargas   P
Brooklyn College, Bedford Ave & Ave H, Brooklyn, NY 11210

Susan Varon 🎤 ✈   P
136 E 76th St, #3D
New York, NY 10021-2830, 212-744-1564
Internet: pearlhunter1@juno.com
    Pubs: *Midwest Qtly, Mangrove, Slant, Spillway, Outerbridge,
    South Coast Poetry Jrnl, Snail's Pace Rev, Passager,
    Defined Providence, Passages North, Third Coast, Green
    Mountains Rev, Rattle*

Ed Vega   W
S Bergholz Literary Services, 17 W 10 St, #5, New York, NY
10011, 212-387-0545
    Pubs: *Casualty Report, Mendoza's Dreams, The Comeback*
    (Arte Publico Pr, 1991, 1987, 1985), *Portable Lower East
    Side, MBM*

Richard Vetere 🎤 ✈   P&W
53-40 62 St
Maspeth, NY 11378-1208, 718-939-9398
Internet: vetrich88@aol.com
    Pubs: *The Third Miracle* (S&S, 1998), *A Dream of Angels*
    (Northwoods Pr, 1984), *Memories of Human Hands*
    (Manyland Bks, 1976), *Poets On, Dreamworks, Cobweb,
    Orbis, Hybrid, Abraxas*

Gore Vidal   W
William Morris Agency, 1325 Ave of the Americas, New York,
NY 10019

Joseph Viertel   W
c/o Owen Laster, William Morris Agency, 1325 Ave of the
Americas, New York, NY 10019, 212-586-5100
    Pubs: *Lifelines, Monkey on a String* (S&S, 1982, 1968), *To
    Love & Corrupt* (Random Hse, 1962)

David Vigoda   W
Ann Elmo Literary Agency, 60 E 42 St, New York, NY 10017
    Pubs: *Nucleus* (Baronet Publishing, 1980)

Michael Villanueva   P
437 E 12 St, #17
New York, NY 10009, 212-673-1671
    Pubs: *Nice to See You: Homage to Ted Berrigan: Anth*
    (Coffee Hse, 1988), *Transfer, Cover, Gandhabba*

Vincent Virga 🎤 ✈   W
Elaine Markson Literary Agency, 44 Greenwich Ave, New York,
NY 10011, 212-243-8480
    Pubs: *Vadriel Vail, Gaywyck* (Alyson, 2001, 2000), *A
    Comfortable Corner* (Avon, 1982)

Tricia Vita   W
42 Perry St
New York, NY 10014-7307
    Pubs: *Yankee, Boston Rev, Provincetown Arts, Ms., Games
    Mag, Shocked & Amazed!*

Susan Volchok 🎤 ✈   W
303 W 66 St
New York, NY 10023-6305, 212-787-4262
Internet: suzev@aol.com
    Pubs: *The Best American Erotica: Anth* (Touchstone, 2003),
    *Virginia Qtly Rev, New Novel Rev, 13th Moon, Paris
    Transcontinental, Kenyon Rev, Asylum Annual,
    Confrontation, Hayden's Ferry Rev*

Lenore Von Stein 🎤 ✈   PP
29 Charles St
New York, NY 10014
Internet: vonstein687@earthlink.net
    Pubs: *I Haven't Been Able to Lie and Tell the Truth,
    Tolerating Ambition, Blind Love = Porno?, Love Is Dead*
    (CDs: 1687, Inc, 2002, 1999, 1996, 1993)

Dina von Zweck   P&W
80 Beekman St
New York, NY 10038-1879, 212-732-1020
    Pubs: *Halloween & Other Poems, Sam Shepard's Dog*
    (White Deer Bks, 1985, 1984), *Helicon 9, Modularist Rev,
    Berkshire Rev, New Letters*

Kurt Vonnegut   W
c/o Donald C Farber, Hartman & Craven LLP, 460 Park Ave, 11
Fl, New York, NY 10022-1906
    Pubs: *God Bless You, Dr. Kevorkian* (Seven Stories Pr,
    2000), *Timequake, Hocus Pocus, Bluebeard* (Putnam, 1997,
    1990, 1987)

Susan Vreeland 🎤 ✈   W
Barbara Braun Assoc, 115 W 18 St, 5th Fl, New York, NY
10011, 212-604-9023
Internet: susan@svreeland.com
    Pubs: *The Passion of Artemisia, Girl in Hyacinth Blue*
    (Penguin, 2003, 2000), *What Love Sees* (Thorndike/S&S,
    1996), *NER, New Millennium, Dominion Rev, Missouri Rev,
    Confrontation, Manoa, Alaska Qtly Rev*

Chuck Wachtel P&W
337 E 5 St, #5FW
New York, NY 10003, 212-673-1511
  Pubs: *Because We Are Here: Stories & Novellas, The Gates* (Viking Penguin, 1996, 1993), *Joe the Engineer* (Morrow, 1983), *The World, Sun, Hanging Loose, Nation, Village Voice, Witness, Pequod*

Derek Walcott P
Farrar, Straus & Giroux, 19 Union Sq W, New York, NY 10003
  Pubs: *The Star-Apple Kingdom* (FSG, 1979)

William Walden P
30 E 9 St, #4K
New York, NY 10003
  Pubs: *New Yorker, Atlantic, Georgia Rev, Massachusetts Rev, Light, Punch*

Mel Waldman P&W
1660 E 13 St, #D2
Brooklyn, NY 11229, 718-375-1474
  Pubs: *Festina Lente* (Somrie Pr, 1982), *The Saint, Espionage Mag, Pulpsmith, Prelude to Fantasy*

Wendy Walker 🎤 ✈ W
855 W End Ave, #6A
New York, NY 10025-4995, 212-865-2932
  Pubs: *Stories Out of Omarie, The Secret Service* (Sun & Moon Pr, 1995, 1992), *Facture, Chain, Conjunctions, Fiction Intl, Parnassus*

Alice Walker P&W
Wendy Weil Agency Inc, 232 Madison Ave, Ste 1300, New York, NY 10016, 212-685-0030
  Pubs: *Absolute Trust in the Goodness of the Earth, The Way Forward is with a Broken Heart, By the Light of My Fathers Smile, Anything We Love Can Be Saved* (Random Hse, 2002, 2000, 1998, 1997)

Pamela Walker W
239 W 256 St
Bronx, NY 10471
  Pubs: *World in Our Words* (Blair Pr/Prentice-Hall, 1997), *Twyla* (Prentice-Hall/Berkley, 1976), *The Whole Story: Anth* (Bench Pr, 1995), *Hawaii Rev, Iowa Woman*

Barry Wallenstein 🎤 ✈ P
340 Riverside Dr, #7B
New York, NY 10025-3436, 212-222-2556
  Pubs: *A Measure of Conduct, The Short Life of the Five Minute Dancer* (Ridgeway Pr, 1999, 1993), *Love & Crush* (Persea, 1991), *Poetry Wales, Pequod, Ploughshares, Laurel Rev*

Rhoda Waller 🎤 ✈ P
370 W 11 St, #4
New York, NY 10014-6246
  Pubs: *Sea Sky Light* (Private, 1999), *Love is Ageless: Anth* (Lompico Creek Pr, 2002), *Between Worlds, Plumed Horn, Black Maria, Cummington Rev, Ikon*

Irene Wanner 🎤 ✈ W
Donadio & Olson Inc, 121 W 27 St, Ste 704, New York, NY 10001, 212-691-8077
Internet: iwanner@u.washington.edu
  Pubs: *Sailing to Corinth* (Owl Creek Pr, 1988), *Circle of Women: Anth* (Penguin, 1994), *Antaeus, Antioch Rev, Ploughshares, NW Rev, Blue Mesa Rev, New Orphic Rev*

Constance Warloe W
Linda Chester Literary Agency, 630 5th Ave, Rockefeller Ctr, New York, NY 10111, 212-439-0881
Internet: cwdenim@aol.com
  Pubs: *The Legend of Olivia Cosmos Montevideo* (Atlantic Monthly Pr, 1994)

Larkin Warren P
315 W 23 St, #11-B
New York, NY 10011
  Pubs: *Old Sheets* (Alice James Bks, 1979), *Qtly West, Ohio Rev, River Reporter, Good Housekeeping, Small Pond, Yankee, Mississippi Rev, Tendril, Mid-American Rev, Akros*

Lewis Warsh P
112 Milton St
Brooklyn, NY 11222-2502, 718-857-5974
  Pubs: *Money Under the Table* (Trip Street Pr, 1997), *Avenue of Escape* (Long News, 1995), *A Free Man* (Sun & Moon, 1991)

Burton D. Wasserman 🎤 P
191 Winding Brook Rd
New Rochelle, NY 10804-1920, 914-235-2256
  Pubs: *Between the Totems of Labor and Love* (Fithian Pr, 2001), *The XY Files: Anth* (Sherman Asher Pub, 1997), *Images of the Holocaust: Anth* (NTC Pub Group, 1996), *Blood to Remember: Anth* (Texas Tech U Pr, 1991), *Atlanta Rev, California Qtly, Black River Rev*

Chocolate Waters PP&P&W
415 W 44 St, #7
New York, NY 10036, 212-581-6820
Internet: c-w@chocolatewaters.com
  Pubs: *Stand Up Poetry: Anth* (U IA Pr, 2002), *Chocolate Waters Uncensored* (CD), *Ladies & Gentlemen: The Hudson Pier Poets: Anth* (Eggplant Pr, 2001, 2001) *Mom: Candid Memories* (Alyson Pubs, 1998), *Pedestal Mag, Stirring, Libido, Mudfish, Westerly*

Gordon R. Watkins　　　　　　　　P
675 Water St, #19D
New York, NY 10002

Vivienne Wechter 🎤 ✈　　　　　　P
Artist in Residence, Fordham Univ, FMH 230, Bronx, NY
10458, 718-817-4898
　　Pubs: *A View from the Ark* (Barlenmir Hse, 1975), *Arts
　　Interaction, Other Voices*

James L. Weil　　　　　　　　　P
103 Van Etten Blvd
New Rochelle, NY 10804-2319, 914-636-7569
　　Pubs: *Gregory's Last Stand and Other Lasts* (Kelly-
　　Winterton Pr, 2001), *Founding Fathers* (Origin Pr, 1997),
　　*Hummingbird, Harvard Mag, Potlatch, Notre Dame Rev,
　　Shearsman, Tel-Let*

Bibi Wein 🎤 ✈　　　　　　　　W
210 W 101 St, #9-A
New York, NY 10025-5035
　　Pubs: *Yes* (HBJ, 1969), *Ariadne's Thread: Anth* (H&R, 1982),
　　*Kalliope, Mademoiselle, Iris, Permafrost, Other Voices,
　　American Letters & Commentary*

Estha Weiner 🎤 ✈　　　　　　　P
214 W 30th St, 9th Fl
New York, NY 10001, 212-279-2657
Internet: esthalynne@hotmail.com
　　Pubs: *The Poets Grim: Anth* (Story Line Pr, 2003), *New
　　Republic, Barrow Street, Brilliant Corners, Rattapallax, Lit,
　　Global City Rev*

Jeff Weinstein　　　　　　　　W
54 E 7 St
New York, NY 10003, 212-677-3504
　　Pubs: *Life in San Diego* (Sun & Moon, 1982), *Pushcart
　　Prize IV Anth, Crawl Out Your Window*

Marjorie Welish 🎤 ✈　　　　　　P
225 W 10 St, #2C
New York, NY 10014-2974
　　Pubs: *The Annotated "Here"* (Coffee Hse Pr, 2000),
　　Begetting Textile (Equipage, 2000), *Else, in Substance*
　　(Paradigm Pr, 1999), *Casting Sequences* (U Georgia Pr,
　　1993), *Moving Borders: Anth* (Talisman Hse, 1998)

Sheila Weller　　　　　　　　W
39 Jane St, #5A
New York, NY 10014
　　Pubs: *Hansel & Gretel in Beverly Hills* (Morrow, 1978), *Ms.,
　　Redbook*

Mac Wellman 🎤 ✈　　　　　　　P
c/o Buddy Thomas, ICM, 40 W 57 St, New York, NY 10019,
212-556-5720
Internet: mwellman@brooklyn.cuny.edu
　　Pubs: *Miniature* (Roof Bks, 2002), *Annie Salem, The Land
　　Beyond the Forest, The Fortuneteller, A Shelf in Woop's
　　Clothing* (Sun & Moon Pr, 1996, 1995, 1991, 1990)

Rebecca Wells　　　　　　　　W
Jonathan Dolger Agency, 49 E 96 St, #9B, New York, NY
10128, 212-427-1853
　　Pubs: *Divine Secrets of the Ya-Ya Sisterhood, Little Altars
　　Everywhere* (HC, 1996), *Mississippi Rev*

Kate Wenner　　　　　　　　W
Elaine Markson Literary Agency, 44 Greenwich Ave, New York,
NY 10011
　　Pubs: *Shamba Letu* (HM 1970)

Eliot Werbner　　　　　　　　P
1150 E 22 St
Brooklyn, NY 11210-3620
　　Pubs: *Prelude* (The Four Seas, 1930), *Blue Unicorn, The
　　Lyric, Western Poetry, The Archer*

Judith Werner 🎤 ✈　　　　　　　P
24 Joralemon St, #E125
Brooklyn, NY 11201, 718-643-2262
　　Pubs: *Sixteen Voices: Anth* (Mariposa Pub, 1994), *Calyx,
　　Mid-America Poetry Rev, Sulphur River Rev, Asheville
　　Poetry Rev, Rattle, Comstock Rev, Medicinal Purposes,
　　South Dakota Rev, Bridges, The Lyric, ELF, Yankee, Slant,
　　Sow's Ear*

Evelyn Wexler 🎤　　　　　　　P
5550 Fieldston Rd, #7D
Bronx, NY 10471-2522, 718-549-4636
Internet: evwex@aol.com
　　Pubs: *Dark and Light: New and Selected Poems* (Xlibris,
　　2002), *Occupied Territory, The Geisha House* (Mayapple Pr,
　　1994, 1992), *Beyond Lament: Anth* (Northwestern U Pr,
　　1998), *ACM, Nimrod, Negative Capability, Classical Outlook*

Susan Wheeler 🎤 ✈　　　　　　P
37 Washington Sq W, #10A
New York, NY 10011-9100, 212-254-3984
Internet: susanwheeler@earthlink.net
　　Pubs: *Source Codes* (SALT, 2000), *Smokes* (Four Way
　　Bks, 1998), *Bag o' Diamonds* (U Georgia Pr, 1993), *Best
　　American Poetry: Anth* (Macmillan, 1996), *New Yorker,
　　Paris Rev*

Kate Wheeler　　　　　　　　W
Witherspoon & Chernoff, 157 W 57 St, Ste 700, New York,
NY 10019
　　Pubs: *Not Where I Started From* (HM, 1993), *O. Henry
　　Awards: Anth* (Doubleday, 1992), *Threepenny Rev, Black
　　Warrior Rev, Gettysburg Rev*

Edgar White P&W
New Dramatists, 424 W 44 St, New York, NY 10036,
212-757-6960
    Pubs: *The Rising* (Marion Boyars Pub, 1990)

Edmund White W
313 W 22 St, #2D
New York, NY 10011, 212-989-7084
    Pubs: *The Married Man* (Knopf, 2000), *A Boy's Own Story,
States of Desire* (Dutton, 1982, 1980)

Wendy White-Ring 🎤 ✈ W
Trident Media Group, 152 West 57th Street, 16th Floor, New
York, NY 10019, 212-262-4810
Internet: whitering@qwest.net
    Pubs: *Micro Fiction: Anth* (Norton, 1996), *Breaking Up Is
Hard to Do: Anth* (Crossing Pr, 1994), *NAR, American Lit
Rev, Sun Dog, Great Stream Rev, Crescent Rev*

Anne Whitehouse 🎤 ✈ P&W
340 Riverside Dr
New York, NY 10024-3423, 212-749-5377
    Pubs: *Fall Love* (Xlibris Pubs, 2002), *The Surveyor's Hand*
(Compton Pr, 1981), *Boulevard, American Voice, Buffalo
Spree*

Nathan Whiting 🎤 ✈ P
105 Buckingham Rd, #6D
Brooklyn, NY 11226-4330, 718-856-6248
    Pubs: *Contemplations* (MAF Pr, 1987), *Light Talks a Lot*
(Agni, 1983)

George Whitmore P
10 Downing St, #5T
New York, NY 10014
    Pubs: *The Confessions of Danny Slocum* (St. Martin's,
1980), *On the Line: Anth* (Crossing Pr, 1981)

Frances Whyatt P
61 Jane St, #9G
New York, NY 10014, 212-255-7378
    Pubs: *A Real Man & Other Stories* (British American/Paris
Rev Edtns, 1990), *McCall's*

Brooke Wiese P
230 E 97 St, Apt 4W
New York, NY 10029
    Pubs: *At the Edge of the World* (Ledge Pr, 2000), *My Lover
Is a Woman: Anth* (Ballantine Bks, 1996), *American Tanka,
Atlanta Rev, Brooklyn Rev, Confluence, Flyway, Hawai'i Rev,
Laurel Rev, Ledge, Plainsongs, Pleiades, Poetry Motel,
Tucumcari Lit Rev*

Roslyn Willett 🎤 ✈ W
441 W End Ave, #15A
New York, NY 10024, 212-787-6060
    Pubs: *Hawaii Pacific Rev, Phantasmagoria, Feminist
Studies, Prairie Star, Papyrus, Short Stories Bimonthly, Art
& Understanding, Timber Creek Rev, Words of Wisdom*

Gary Williams P
36 E 4 St, Apt 2
New York, NY 10003, 212-982-7602
    Pubs: *Waterways, Pan Arts Mag, Jane, Manhattan Poetry
Rev, Home Planet News*

Edward F. Williams 🎤 ✈ PP
1633 Sterling Pl, #4H
Brooklyn, NY 11233-4970, 718-735-6153
    Pubs: *E. F. Williams, Urban Poet* (CD; Libra Productions,
1999)

C. K. Williams 🎤 ✈ P
c/o Jonathan Galassi, Farrar, Straus & Giroux, 19 Union Sq W,
New York, NY 10003
Internet: ckwilliams@compuserve.com
    Pubs: *Misgivings, Repair, The Vigil, Selected Poems, A
Dream of Mind, Flesh & Blood* (FSG, 2000, 1999, 1997,
1994, 1992, 1987), *Tar* (Random Hse, 1983), *New Yorker,
APR*

Regina E. Williams P
132-11 Foch Blvd
South Ozone Park, NY 11420, 718-322-9550
    Pubs: *Our Work & God's World* (Presbyterian Pub Hse,
1988), *New Rain: Anth* (Blind Beggar, 1988)

Paul Hastings Wilson W
314 E 84 St
New York, NY 10028
    Pubs: *Turning Islands* (Avon, 1977), *Center*

Martha Wilson PP&W
Founding Director, Franklin Furnace Archive, Inc, 45 John St,
#611, New York, NY 10038-3706, 212-766-2606
www.franklinfurnace.org

William S. Wilson W
458 W 25 St
New York, NY 10001-6502, 212-989-2229
Internet: parllw@aol.com
    Pubs: *Birthplace* (North Point Pr, 1982), *Why I Don't Write
Like Franz Kafka* (Ecco/Norton, 1977)

Leigh Allison Wilson W
c/o Elizabeth McKee, Harold Matson Co Inc, 276 5th Ave, New
York, NY 10001
    Pubs: *Wind: Stories* (Morrow, 1989), *From the Bottom Up*
(Penguin, 1984), *Harper's, Grand Street*

Fran Winant   P
PO Box 398, Stuyvesant Sta, New York, NY 10009
  Pubs: *Goddess of Lesbian Dreams, Dyke Jacket, Looking at Women* (Violet Pr, 1980, 1976, 1971)

Ronna Wineberg (Blaser) 🎤 ✈   W
7-13 Washington Sq North, #46B
New York, NY 10003
Internet: ronnagroup@aol.com
  Pubs: *A Tennessee Landscape, People & Places: Anth* (Cool Springs Pr, 1996), *So to Speak, Writers Forum, Berkeley Fiction Rev, Sou'wester, South Dakota Rev, American Way, Midstream, Colorado Rev*

David Winn   W
English Dept, Hunter College, 695 Park Ave, New York, NY 10021
Internet: dwinn@hejira.hunter.cuny.edu
  Pubs: *Gangland* (Knopf, 1982)

Mary Winters 🎤 ✈   P
434 E 52 St, #4E
New York, NY 10022-6402, 212-753-3320
  Pubs: *A Pocket History of the World* (Nightshade Pr, 1996), *Anth of Mag Verse & Yearbook of American Poetry: Anth* (Monitor Bk Co, 1997), *Qtly West, Commonweal, Press, Poetry East, Poet Lore, Gulf Coast*

Elizabeth Winthrop 🎤 ✈   W
250 W 90 St, #6A
New York, NY 10024-1123
Internet: winthrop50@aol.com
  Pubs: *Halloween Hats, Dumpy La Rue* (HH, 2002, 2001), *Dear Mr. President* (Winslow Pr, 2001), *Promises* (Clarion, 2000), *Island Justice* (Morrow, 1998), *The Battle for the Castle* (Holiday Hse, 1993), *Best American Short Stories: Anth* (HM, 1992)

William Wiser   W
c/o Emilie Jacobson, Curtis Brown Ltd, 10 Astor Pl, New York, NY 10003-6935

Ellen Wisoff   P
1782 E 19 St
Brooklyn, NY 11229, 718-375-2355
  Pubs: *Partisan Rev, Denver Qtly, Sun & Moon, NY Arts Jrnl, Zone, City*

Francine Witte   P
PO Box 101
New York, NY 10024
Internet: franigirl@aol.com
  Pubs: *Calliope, Poet & Critic, Connecticut River Rev, Florida Rev, Bellingham Rev, Tar River Poetry, Outerbridge*

Larry Woiwode 🎤 ✈   P&W
Donadio & Olson Inc, 121 W 27 St, New York, NY 10001, 212-691-8077
Internet: woiwode@ctctel.com
  Pubs: *Beyond the Bedroom Wall* (Graywolf, 1997), *Silent Passengers* (Atheneum, 1993), *Acts* (Harper SF, 1993), *Even Tide* (FSG, 1977), *New Yorker, Paris Rev, Image, Atlantic, Harper's*

Linda Wolfe   W
c/o Lynn Nesbit, Janklow & Nesbit Assoc, 598 Madison Ave, New York, NY 10022-1614
  Pubs: *Love Me to Death* (Pocket Bks, 1998), *Professor & the Prostitute* (HM, 1986), *Private Practices* (S&S, 1980), *Cosmopolitan, Woman, Ladies' Home Jrnl*

Eunice Wolfgram   P
c/o Raymond Ross, 47 E Houston St, #3, New York, NY 10012, 212-966-0897
  Pubs: *Three Hundred Chinese & Other Events* (Home Planet Pub, 1975)

Meg Wolitzer   W
c/o Peter Matson, Sterling Lord Literistic, 65 Bleecker St, New York, NY 10012, 212-780-6050
  Pubs: *This Is Your Life* (Crown, 1988), *Hidden Pictures* (HM, 1986)

Hilma Wolitzer 🎤 ✈   W
500 E 85 St, #18H
New York, NY 10028-7456, 212-861-8062
Internet: hilma@att.net
  Pubs: *The Company of Writers* (Penguin, 2001), *Tunnel of Love* (HC, 1994), *Silver, In the Palomar Arms, Hearts* (FSG, 1988, 1983, 1980), *In the Flesh* (Morrow, 1977)

Diane Wolkstein   PP&P
10 Patchin Pl, 1 Fl
New York, NY 10011
  Pubs: *DreamSongs, Abulafia, Part of My Heart* (Cloudstone Pr, 1992), *The First Love Stories* (H&R, 1991), *Oom Razoom* (Morrow, 1991)

Janet S. Wong 🎤 ✈   P
c/o Margaret McElderry, Simon & Schuster, 1230 Ave of the Americas, New York, NY 10020-1586
www.janetwong.com
  Pubs: *Night Garden, The Rainbow Hand, Behind the Wheel, A Suitcase of Seaweed & Other Poems* (S&S, 2000, 1999, 1999, 1996), *Good Luck Gold & Other Poems* (Macmillan, 1994)

Jacqueline Woodson   W
Charlotte Sheedy Literary Agency, 65 Bleecker St, New York, NY 10012, 212-780-9800
  Pubs: *Autobiography of a Family Photo* (Dutton, 1995), *I Hadn't Meant to Tell You This* (Delacorte, 1994), *Kenyon Rev, American Voice*

Dale Worsley   W
150 Lafayette Ave, #1
Brooklyn, NY 11238, 718-789-3640
   Pubs: *The Focus Changes of August Previco* (Vanguard,
   1980), *Hoy* (NPR Broadcast, 1992)

Charles S. Wright   W
Farrar, Straus & Giroux, 19 Union Sq W, New York, NY 10003,
212-741-6900
   Pubs: *The Wig, The Messenger* (FSG, 1966, 1963)

K. C. Wright   W
c/o D Kossow, Becker & London, 400 E 56 St #10B, New York,
NY 10022
   Pubs: *Everyman's Dream* (Carlyle Pr, 1978)

Sarah Elizabeth Wright   P&W
780 W End Ave, #1D
New York, NY 10025
   Pubs: *A Philip Randolph* (S&S/Silver Burdett, 1990), *This
   Child's Gonna Live* (Feminist Pr, 1986), *Black Scholar*

Stephen Wright   W
PO Box 1341, FDR Sta, New York, NY 10150, 212-213-4382
   Pubs: *The Adventures of Sandy West, Private Eye* (Mystery
   Notebook Edtns, 1986)

Jeffrey Cyphers Wright   P
632 E 14 St, #18
New York, NY 10009, 212-673-1152
   Pubs: *Out Loud: Nuyorican Poets Cafe Anth* (H Holt, 1995),
   Out of this World: Anth (Crown, 1991), *Up Late: Anth* (Four
   Walls, Eight Windows, 1987), *Exquisite Corpse*

Robert Wrigley   🎤   ✈   P
c/o Penguin Putnam
375 Hudson St
New York, NY 10014
   Pubs: *Reign of Snakes, In the Bank of Beautiful Sins*
   (Penguin, 1999, 1995), *What My Father Believed, Moon in a
   Mason Jar* (U Illinois Pr, 1991, 1986)

Karen Wunsch   🎤   W
325 Central Park W, #7W
New York, NY 10025, 212-663-7575
Internet: wunschkaren@hotmail.com
   Pubs: *Living & Learning* (Avon, 1972), *Press, North Dakota
   Qtly, Confrontation, Epoch*

Emanuel Xavier   🎤   ✈   PP&P&W
c/o Shifty Entertainment, 336 W 17th St, Ste 2C, New York, NY
10011, 212-741-2062
Internet: emanuelxavier9@aol.com
   Pubs: *Americano, Of The Flesh: Anth* (Suspect Thoughts Pr,
   2002, 2002), *Christ-Like, Besame Mucho* (Painted Leaf Pr,
   1999, 1999), *Virgins, Guerrillas & Locas: Anth Best Gay
   Erotica 1997: Anth* (Cleis Pr, 1999, 1997), *Men on Men:
   Anth* (Plume, 1999), *Long Shot*

Susan Yankowitz   🎤   ✈   W
Phyllis Wender, Rosenstone/Wender, 38 E 29 St #10, New
York, NY 10016, 212-725-9445
Internet: syankowitz@aol.com
   Pubs: *Night Sky* (Samuel French, 1996), *Silent Witness*
   (Knopf, 1976), *Excavators: Anth* (Gnosis Pr, 1993), *Taking
   The Fall: Anth* (Parnassus, 1986), *Samuel French, QRL,
   Parnassus, Gnosis, Solo, Heresies, Performing Arts Jrnl,
   Yale Theatre, Poetry in Rev*

Camille D. Yarbrough   PP&P
80 St Nicholas Ave Apt 4G
New York, NY 10026-2922, 212-491-9503
   Pubs: *Tamika & the Wisdom Rings* (Random Hse, 1994),
   The Shimmershine Queens (Putnam-Paperstar, 1989), *The
   Little Tree Growin in the Shade, Cornrows* (Coward,
   McCann, 1985, 1979), *Black Collegian*

Jose Yaryura-Tobias   P&W
935 Northern Blvd, #102
Great Neck, NY 11021
   Pubs: *El Ser Humano Integral* (Mexico; Diana, 1992), *The
   Integral Being* (H Holt, 1987), *Circular* (Botella al Mar, 1983)

John Yau   P
PO Box 1910, Canal St Sta, New York, NY 10013
   Pubs: *Radiant Silhouette: New & Selected Works* (Black
   Sparrow Pr, 1989), *APR, Sulfur, Sun*

Rafael Yglesias   W
18 E 12 St, #9B
New York, NY 10003
   Pubs: *Dr. Neruda's Cure for Evil, Fearless* (Warner Bks,
   1996, 1993), *The Murderer Next Door* (Crown, 1990), *Only
   Children* (Ballantine, 1989)

Helen Yglesias   W
1261 5th Ave, Rm 1303
New York, NY 10029, 212-427-2892
   Pubs: *The Girls* (Ballantine, 2000), *How She Died, The
   Saviors* (HM, 1992, 1987), *Sweetsir* (S&S, 1981), *Family
   Feeling* (Dial, 1975)

Jane Breskin Zalben   🎤   ✈   P&W
70 South Rd
Port Washington, NY 11050-2601, 516-944-8590
Internet: janezalben@hotmail.com
   Pubs: *Let There Be Light: Poems for Repairing the World*
   (Dutton, 2002), *Pearl's Passover, To Every Season,
   Unfinished Dreams* (S&S, 2002, 1999, 1996), *Beni's Family
   Treasury, Beni's Family Cookbook* (H Holt, 1999, 1996),
   New York Times, Newsday

Bill Zavatsky 🎤 ✈ P
100 W 92 St, #9D
New York, NY 10025-7503, 212-496-2956
Internet: bzav@earthlink.net
Pubs: *For Steve Royal & Other Poems* (COPE, 1985),
Theories of Rain & Other Poems (Sun, 1975), *Out of This
World: Anth* (Crown, 1991)

George Zebrowski 🎤 ✈ W
Richard Curtis Assoc Inc, 171 E 74 St, New York, NY 10021,
518-439-1994
Internet: sarzeb@compuserve.com
Pubs: *Cave of Stars* (Harper, 2000), *Brute Orbits* (Harper
Prism, 1998), *The Sunspacers Trilogy* (White Wolf, 1996),
The Killing Star (Avon/Morrow, 1995), *Stranger Suns*
(Bantam, 1991), *The Monadic Universe* (Ace, 1985)

Kip Zegers P
English Dept, Hunter College High School, 71 E 94 St, New
York, NY 10128, 212-884-3011
Pubs: *The American Floor* (Mayapple Pr, 1996), *The
Promise Is* (Humana Pr, 1985)

Lisa Zeidner P&W
Denise Shannon, ICM, 40 W 57 St, New York, NY 10019, 212-
556-6727
Pubs: *Layover* (Random Hse, 1999), *Limited Partnerships*
(North Point Pr, 1989), *Pocket Sundial* (U Wisconsin Pr, 1988)

David Zeiger 🎤 ✈ P
9 Fourth Rd
Great Neck, NY 11021-1505, 516-466-2977
Pubs: *Life on My Breath* (Sarna Pr, 1995), *Through a Child's
Eyes: Anth* (Plain View Pr, 2001), *Mixed Voices: Anth*
(Milkweed Edtns, 1991), *Free Lunch, Wordsmith, Minnesota
Rev, Midstream, Slant*

Lila Zeiger 🎤 ✈ P
PO Box 4518
Great Neck, NY 11023, 516-466-2977
Pubs: *The Way to Castle Garden* (State Street Pr, 1982),
Fiction Intl, Paris Rev, Georgia Rev, New Republic

Roger Zelazny W
c/o Kirby McCauley, Pimlico Agency, 155 E 77th St, Ste 1A,
New York, NY 10021, 212-628-9729
Pubs: *Knight of Shadows, Frost & Fire* (Morrow, 1989,
1989), *A Dark Traveling* (Avon, 1989)

Joel Zeltzer P
407 W 50 St, #3
New York, NY 10019
Pubs: *Shadows in Light* (Poets Pr, 1985), *Daring Poetry
Qtly, Green Feather Mag, MacGuffin*

Patricia Zelver W
Wallace Literary Agency, 177 E 70 St, New York, NY 10021,
212-772-9090
Pubs: *The Wonderful Towers of Watts* (Morrow, 1995), *The
Wedding of Don Otavio* (Tambourine Bks, 1993), *A Man of
Middle Age* (H Holt, 1974), *Ascent, Ohio Rev, Shenandoah,
Atlantic, Virginia Qtly, Esquire, Redbook, Cosmopolitan*

Elizabeth Zelvin 🎤 ✈ P
115 W 86th St
New York, NY 10024-3410, 212-724-0494
Internet: lizzelvin@aol.com
Pubs: *Gifts & Secrets: Poems of the Therapeutic
Relationship, I Am the Daughter* (New Rivers, 1999, 1981),
Sarah's Daughters Sing: Anth (KTAV Pub Hse, 1990),
Caprice, Home Planet News, Jewish Women's Lit Annual

Alan Ziegler P&W
45 Sutton Pl S
New York, NY 10022, 212-751-6244
Internet: az8@columbia.edu
Pubs: *The Green Grass of Flatbush* (Word Beat Pr, 1986),
So Much to Do (Release Pr, 1981), *New Yorker, Paris Rev*

Bette Ziegler W
45 Sutton Place South, #8J
New York, NY 10022, 212-751-6244
Pubs: *Older Women/Younger Men* (Doubleday, 1979), *An
Affair for Tomorrow* (HBJ, 1978)

Edra Ziesk 🎤 ✈ W
444 E 85 St, #4B
New York, NY 10028
Pubs: *A Cold Spring* (Algonquin, 2002), *Acceptable Losses*
(SMU Pr, 1996), *Alaska Qtly Rev, Arkansas Rev, Folio,
Other Voices, Playgirl, Salmon*

Thomas Zigal 🎤 ✈ W
c/o Esther Newberg, ICM, 40 W 57th St, New York, NY 10019
Internet: tzigal@mail.utexas.edu
Pubs: *Pariah, Hardrock Stiff, Into Thin Air* (Dell Paperback,
2000, 1997, 1996), *Playland* (Thorp Springs, 1982),
Western Edge (Calliope Pr, 1982), *New Letters, Texas Qtly*

Evan Zimroth 🎤 ✈ P
Lydia Wills Artists Agency, 230 W 55 St, New York, NY 10019
Pubs: *Gangsters* (Crown, 1996), *Giselle Considers Her
Future* (Carnegie Mellon U Pr, 1996), *Dead, Dinner, or
Naked* (TriQtly, 1993)

Harriet Zinnes 🎤 ✈ P&W
25 W 54 St, #6A
New York, NY 10019-5404, 212-582-8315
Internet: hzinnes@aol.com
Pubs: *Drawing on the Wall* (Marsh Hawk Pr, 2002),
Listening to the Rain (Wild Honey Pr, 2002), *The Radiant
Absurdity of Desire* (Avisson Pr, 1998), *My, Haven't the
Flowers Been?* (Magic Circle Pr, 1995), *Ravishing
Disunities: Anth* (Wesleyan, 2000), *APR*

Nonyaniso Zinza   P
c/o DuEwa, 630108 Spuyten Duyvil St, Bronx, NY 10463,
212-796-3070
   Pubs: *Affirmations, Declarations & Blues* (DuEwa, Inc., 1988)

Larry Zirlin 🎤 ✈   P
411 Clinton St, #5
Brooklyn, NY 11231-3544, 718-858-6229
Internet: larryz@worldnet.att.net
   Pubs: *Under the Tongue* (Hanging Loose Pr, 1992), *Awake
   for No Reason* (Cross Country Pr, 1979), *The World, Paris
   Rev, Hanging Loose, Transfer*

Edward Zuckrow   P
303 Marcy Ave
Brooklyn, NY 11211, 718-782-3616
   Pubs: *Slowly, Out of Stones* (The Horizon, 1980), *The Death
   of Horn & Hardart* (Smith, 1971)

Ellen Zweig   P
93 E 3 St
Brooklyn, NY 11218, 718-972-7290
   Pubs: *Impressions of Africa* (e.g. Pr, 1986), *Women & Performance, De Zaak, Unsound, Moving Letters, Assembling*

NORTH CAROLINA

Beth Adamour   W
1804 W Friendly Ave
Greensboro, NC 27403
   Pubs: *Kansas Qtly, West Branch, Nimrod, Mid-American
   Rev, Crescent Rev*

Betty Adcock 🎤 ✈   P
817 Runnymede Rd
Raleigh, NC 27607, 919-787-2407
   Pubs: *Intervale: New & Selected Poems, The Difficult Wheel,
   Beholdings* (LSU Pr, 2000, 1995, 1988), *Inventions of
   Farewell: Anth* (Norton, 2001), *Georgia Rev, Southern Rev,
   TriQtly, Gettysburg Rev*

Maya Angelou   P
3240 Valley Rd
Winston-Salem, NC 27106

James Applewhite   P
606 November Dr
Durham, NC 27712, 919-383-7734
   Pubs: *Daytime & Starlight, A History of the River* (LSU Pr,
   1997, 1993), *River Writing: An Eno Journal* (Princeton U Pr,
   1988), *Antaeus, APR, Atlantic, Poetry, Southern Rev,
   Esquire*

Jacqueline Ariail   W
1018 Monmouth Ave
Durham, NC 27701, 919-682-7809
Internet: ariail@unity.ncsu.edu
   Pubs: *Fever: Erotic Writing By Women: Anth* (HC, 1994),
   Redbook

Daphne Athas   P&W
English Dept, 435 Greenlaw Hall, Univ North Carolina, Chapel
Hill, NC 27514, 919-962-5481
Internet: dathas@email.unc.edu
   Pubs: *Entering Ephesus* (Second Chance, 1991), *Crumbs
   for the Bogeyman* (St. Andrews Pr, 1991), *Cora* (Viking,
   1978), *Southern Rev, Black Warrior Rev, Spectator, Carolina
   Qtly, Solo, Shenandoah*

Ellyn Bache 🎤 ✈   W
2314 Waverly Dr
Wilmington, NC 28403
   Pubs: *Holiday Miracles: A Christmas/Hanukkah Story*
   (Banks Channel Bks, 2001), *The Activist's Daughter*
   (Spinsters Ink, 1997), *Safe Passage* (Bantam, 1994), *The
   Value of Kindness* (Helicon Nine Edtns, 1993), *Festival in
   Fire Season* (August Hse, 1992)

John Balaban 🎤 ✈   P&W
Dept of English, North Carolina State Univ, Campus Box 8105,
Raleigh, NC 27695, 919-515-1836
Internet: tbalaban@msn.com
   Pubs: *Locusts at the Edge of Summer, Words for My
   Daughter* (Copper Canyon Pr, 1997, 1991), *Coming Down
   Again* (S&S, 1989), *Blue Mountain* (Unicorn, 1982),
   Harper's, TriQtly, Ploughshares

Gerald Barrax 🎤 ✈   P
808 Cooper Road
Raleigh, NC 27610, 919-255-6140
Internet: gbarrax@nc.rr.com
   Pubs: *From a Person Sitting in Darkness: New & Selected
   Poems* (LSU Pr, 1998), *Leaning Against the Sun* (U
   Arkansas Pr, 1992), *The Deaths of Animals & Lesser Gods*
   (U Kentucky, 1984), *APR, Gettysburg Rev, Prairie Schooner,
   Callaloo, Georgia Rev*

Coyla Barry   P
7020 Knotty Pine Dr
Chapel Hill, NC 27517
Internet: coyla@mindspring.com
   Pubs: *Creature and Creature* (North Carolina Writers
   Network, 2001), *The Denny Poems: Anth* (Billee Murray
   Denny Fdn, 1988), *An Anth of Haiku by People of the US
   and Canada* (Japan Airlines, 1988), *SunDog, Nimrod,
   Greensboro Rev, Tar River Poetry*

Ronald H. Bayes 🎤 ✈   P
St. Andrews Presbyterian College, Dogwood Mile, Laurinburg,
NC 28352, 919-277-5000
www.sapc.edu
  Pubs: *Chainsong for the Muse* (Northern Lights, 1993),
  Prescott Street Reader: Anth (Prescott Street Pr, 1995),
  *Solo, Oysterboy Rev, Pembroke Mag, Prairie Schooner, NW
  Rev, TriQtly, Prism Intl*

Jeffrey Beam 🎤 ✈   P
Golgonooza at Frog Level, PO Box 83, Chapel Hill, NC 27514,
919-967-2470
Internet: jeffbeam@email.unc.edu
  Pubs: *What We Have Lost: New & Selected Poems* (Green
  Finch, 2002), *An Elizabethan Bestiary: Retold* (Horse &
  Buggy, 1999), *Visions of Dame Kind* (The Jargon Society,
  1995), *The Fountain* (North Carolina Wesleyan, 1992),
  Carolina Qtly, North Carolina Lit Rev

Doris Betts   W
Alumni Distinguished Prof, English Dept, UNC-Chapel Hill,
230 Greenlaw Hall, CB#3520, Chapel Hill, NC 27599-3520,
919-962-4006
Internet: dbetts@cphl.mindspring.com
  Pubs: *Beasts of the Southern Wild* (Scribner, 1998), *The
  Sharp Teeth of Love, Souls Raised From the Dead, Heading
  West* (Knopf, 1997, 1994, 1982)

Robert Bixby 🎤 ✈   P&W
3413 Wilshire
Greensboro, NC 27408
Internet: rbixby@aol.com
  Pubs: *Carolina Qtly, Omni, Sow's Ear, Passages North,
  Celery, Lactuca, Gypsy, Greensboro Rev, Oxalis*

Patrick Bizzaro 🎤 ✈   P
East Carolina Univ, Dept of English, Greenville, NC 27858,
919-328-6751
Internet: bizzarop@mail.ecu.edu
  Pubs: *Fear of the Coming Drought* (Mount Olive College Pr,
  2000), *Undressing the Mannequin* (Third Lung Pr, 1989),
  Violence (Tamarack Edtns, 1978), *NYQ, Poetry Now, Tar
  River Poetry, River City, Asheville Poetry Rev, SPR*

James Breeden 🎤 ✈   P&W
610 Wendy Way
Durham, NC 27712-9246, 919-471-7000
  Pubs: *Main Street Rag, Iodine, Urban Hiker, Xavier Rev,
  Wind Lit Jrnl, Modern Haiku, Wellspring, Piedmont Lit Rev,
  Arts Line*

Sue Ellen Bridgers   W
PO Box 248
Sylva, NC 28779-0248, 704-586-6271
  Pubs: *All We Know of Heaven* (Banks Channel Bks, 1996),
  Keeping Christina (HC, 1993)

Bill Brittain   W
17 Wisteria Dr
Asheville, NC 28804, 704-252-7104
  Pubs: *Shape-Changer, The Ghost From Beneath the Sea,
  Wings, Professor Popkin's Prodigious Polish* (HC, 1994,
  1992, 1991, 1990)

Sally Buckner 🎤 ✈   P
3231 Birnamwood Rd
Raleigh, NC 27607, 919-782-3636
  Pubs: *Strawberry Harvest* (St. Andrews Pr, 1986), *Pembroke
  Mag, Crab Creek Rev, Christian Century*

Kathryn Stripling Byer 🎤 ✈   P
PO Box 489
Cullowhee, NC 28723, 828-293-5695
Internet: jbyer@wpoff.wcu.edu
  Pubs: *Catching Light, Black Shawl, Wildwood Flower* (LSU
  Pr, 2002, 1998, 1992), *The Girl in the Midst of the Harvest*
  (Texas Tech Pr, 1986), *Arts & Letters, Callaloo, Crab
  Orchard Rev, Southern Rev, Georgia Rev, Greensboro Rev,
  SPR, Shenandoah, Carolina Qtly*

Mary Belle Campbell   P
53 Pine Lake Dr
Whispering Pines, NC 28327-9388, 910-949-3993
  Pubs: *Anima, Intl Poetry Rev, Pembroke, St. Andrews Rev,
  Stone Country*

Joan L. Cannon 🎤   P&W
207 B Ridgeside Terr
Morganton, NC 28655-2656, 828-439-8339
Internet: joancannon@hci.net
  Pubs: *Elf, Expressions, Grit, Odessa Poetry Rev, Pulpsmith,
  Seacoast Life, Modern Woodman, Thema, Cappers*

Fred Chappell 🎤 ✈   P&W
305 Kensington Rd
Greensboro, NC 27403, 336-275-8851
  Pubs: *Family Gathering* (LSU Pr, 2002), *Look Back All the
  Green Valley, Farewell, I'm Bound to Leave You* (Picador,
  1999, 1996), *The Fred Chappell Reader* (St Martin's, 1991),
  Saturday Evening Post, Harper's, Georgia Rev, Poetry

Richard Chess 🎤 ✈   P
Univ of North Carolina Asheville, Dept of Literature &
Language CPO#2130, Asheville, NC 28804
Internet: rchess@bulldog.unca.edu
  Pubs: *Tekiah* (Georgia Pr, 1994), *Telling & Remembering:
  Anth* (Beacon Pr, 1997), *Ascent, Tampa Rev*

Avery Grenfell Church   P
2749 Park Oak Dr
Clemmons, NC 27012, 336-766-7737
  Pubs: *Rainbows of the Mind* (Modern Images, 1982),
  Dakota: Plains & Fancy: Anth (Vermilion Lit Project/South
  Dakota, 1989), *San Fernando Poetry Jrnl, Bardic Echoes,
  Orphic Lute, Poets' Paper, Amer Bard, Parnassus Lit Jrnl*

Jim Clark 🎤 ✈   P&W
4706 Quaker Rd
Wilson, NC 27893, 252-243-9736
Internet: jclark14@nc.rr.com
  Pubs: *Handiwork* (St. Andrews Pr, 1998), *Dancing on
  Canaan's Ruins* (Eternal Delight Pub, 1997), *Witnessing
  Earth: Anth* (Catamount Pr, 1994), *Cross Roads, Denver
  Qtly, SPR, Georgia Rev, Prairie Schooner, Greensboro Rev,
  Appalachian Heritage*

Kent Cooper   W
1124 Woodburn Rd
Durham, NC 27705-5738
  Pubs: *Fame & Fortune* (Playboy Bks, 1981), *Below Houston
  Street, The Minnesota Strip* (Manor Bks, 1978, 1978),
  Paterson Lit Rev, Living Blues

Helen M. Copeland   W
1850 Maryland Ave
Charlotte, NC 28209, 704-375-3022
  Pubs: *Endangered Specimen & Other Poems From a Lay
  Naturalist* (St. Andrews, 1988)

Robert Cumming 🎤   P&W
PO Box 1047
Davidson, NC 28036-1047, 704-896-3479
Internet: rdgcumming@mindspring.com
  Pubs: *45/96: Anth* (Ninety-Six Pr, 1994), *Chattahoochee
  Rev, SPR*

Christopher Davis   P
English Dept, Univ North Carolina, Charlotte, NC 28223,
704-547-2296
  Pubs: *The Tyrant of the Past & the Slave of the Future*
  (Texas Tech U Pr, 1989), *Sonora Rev, Black Warrior Rev,
  Ploughshares, Denver Qtly, Amer Voice*

Thadious M. Davis   P
English Dept, Univ North Carolina, Chapel Hill, NC 27514,
919-967-3778
  Pubs: *Black Scholar, Obsidian, South & West, Black Amer
  Lit Forum*

Angela Davis-Gardner 🎤 ✈   W
English Dept, Box 8105, North Carolina State Univ, Raleigh,
NC 27695-8105, 919-515-4173
Internet: agardner@unity.ncsu.edu
  Pubs: *Forms of Shelter* (Ticknor & Fields, 1991), *Felice*
  (Random Hse, 1982), *Close to Home: Anth* (John F Blair,
  1998), *A Few Thousand Words About Love: Anth* (St.
  Martin's, 1998), *Between Friends: Anth* (HM, 1994),
  Shenandoah, Crescent Rev, Greensboro Rev

Irene Dayton   P
209 S Hillandale Dr
East Flat Rock, NC 28726-2609, 828-693-4014
Internet: bendayton@isa.com
  Pubs: *Sobs of the Violins* (White Maine Pub, 2000), *In
  Oxbow of Time's River, Seven Times the Wind* (Windy Row,
  1978, 1977), *North Stone Rev, Women Artist News, Lit Rev*

Ann Deagon 🎤 ✈   P&W
802 Woodbrook Dr
Greensboro, NC 27410-3278, 336-292-5273
Internet: anndeagon@worldnet.att.net
  Pubs: *The Polo Poems* (U Nebraska-Omaha, 1990), *The
  Diver's Tomb* (St. Martin's/Marek, 1985)

Stuart Dischell 🎤 ✈   P
1614 W End Pl
Greensboro, NC 27403-1758, 336-334-4695
Internet: dischell@uncg.edu
  Pubs: *Evenings & Avenues* (Penguin, 1996), *Good Hope
  Road* (Viking/Penguin, 1993)

Julia Nunnally Duncan   P
379 Paxton Creek Rd
Marion, NC 28752
Internet: jnundun@hotmail.com

Pam Durban   W
Greenlaw Hall, UNC, Dept of Eng CB#3520, Chapill Hill, NC
27516
  Pubs: *So Far Back* (Picador USA, 2000), *The Laughing
  Place* (Scribner, 1993), *All Set About With Fever Trees*
  (Godine, 1985), *Best American Short Stories of the
  Century: Anth* (Houghton-Mifflin, 1999), *Southern Rev,
  Georgia Rev, TriQtly*

Charles Edward Eaton   P&W
808 Greenwood Rd
Chapel Hill, NC 27514-3908, 919-942-4775
  Pubs: *The Jogger by the Sea, The Scout in Summer, The
  Country of the Blue, New & Selected Stories 1959-1989*
  (Cornwall, 2000, 1998, 1994, 1989), *Sewanee Rev,
  Salmagundi, New Letters, Antioch Rev, Hollins Critic,
  Centennial Rev*

Julie Fay 🎤 ✈   P
158 Kingfisher Dr
Blounts Creek, NC 27814-9802, 252-975-6709
Internet: fayj@mail.ecu.edu
  Pubs: *The Woman Behind You* (U Pitt Pr, 1999), *Portraits of
  Women* (Ahsahta, 1991), *Images of Women in Literature*
  (HM, 1990), *In Every Mirror* (Owl Creek, 1985), *New
  American Poets: Anth* (Hardscrabble, 2000), *Ploughshares,
  Prairie Schooner, Alaska Qtly*

Thomas Feeny　　　　　　　　　　　　　　　　　　P
306 Chamberlain St
Raleigh, NC 27607-7312, 919-515-9281
Internet: feeny@social.chass.ncsu.edu
　　Pubs: *The Paternal Orientation of Ramon Perez de Ayala*
　　(Spain; Albatros-Hispanofila, 1985), *Puerto del Sol, Poets*
　　On, Hiram Poetry Rev, Cape Rock, Verve, Comstock Rev,
　　Sulphur, Timber Creek Rev, Mankato Poetry Rev, GW Rev,
　　RE:AL

Candace Flynt　♀　✈　　　　　　　　　　　　　W
2005 Madison Ave
Greensboro, NC 27403-1511, 336-373-1025
　　Pubs: *Mother Love* (FSG, 1987), *Sins of Omission* (Random
　　Hse, 1984), *Chasing Dad* (Dial, 1980)

Marita Garin　　　　　　　　　　　　　　　　　P
PO Box 503
Black Mountain, NC 28711-0503, 828-669-7819
　　Pubs: *Verse, Tar River Poetry, Oxford Mag, Kansas Qtly,*
　　Cumberland Poetry Rev, Kenyon Rev

Philip Gerard　♀　✈　　　　　　　　　　　　W
6231 Tortoise Ln
Wilmington, NC 28409
Internet: PhilipGerard@worldnet.att.net
　　Pubs: *Desert Kill* (Morrow, 1994), *Cape Fear Rising,*
　　Hatteras Light (John F Blair, 1994, 1987), *Carolina Style,*
　　NER, Puerto del Sol, Hawaii Rev

Grace Evelyn Loving Gibson　　　　　　　　　P
709 McLean St
Laurinburg, NC 28352, 919-276-1769
Internet: gibsongl@+artan.sapc.edu
　　Pubs: *Frayed Edges, Drake's Branch, Home in Time* (St.
　　Andrews Pr, 1995, 1982, 1977)

Marie Gilbert　♀　✈　　　　　　　　　　　　P
2 St Simons Sq
Greensboro, NC 27408-3833, 336-288-3051
Internet: Ragmrg@worldnet.att.net
　　Pubs: *Brookgreen Oaks* (Downhome Pr, 1999), *Word &*
　　Witness: 100 Years of NC Poetry: Anth (Carolina Academic
　　Pr, 1999), *Connexions, Myrtle Beach Back When* (St.
　　Andrews, 1994, 1990)

Marianne Gingher　♀　✈　　　　　　　　　　W
Univ North Carolina, Dept of English, CB#3520, Chapel Hill,
NC 27599, 919-962-0468
Internet: mbging@email.unc.edu
　　Pubs: *How to Have a Happy Childhood* (John F Blair, 2000),
　　Teen Angel, Bobby Rex's Greatest Hit (Atheneum, 1988,
　　1986), *New Virginia Rev, NAR, Redbook, Southern Rev*

Judy Goldman　♀　✈　　　　　　　　　　　　P
1121 Scotland Ave
Charlotte, NC 28207-2572, 704-334-6868
Internet: judygoldman@earthlink.net
　　Pubs: *The Slow Way Back* (Morrow, 1999), *Wanting to*
　　Know the End (Silverfish Rev Pr, 1993), *Holding Back*
　　Winter (St. Andrews Pr, 1987), *Ohio Rev, Kenyon Rev,*
　　Southern Rev, Crazyhorse, Shenandoah, Prairie Schooner,
　　Gettysburg Rev

Robert Waters Grey　♀　✈　　　　　　　　　P
2577 Essex Dr
Concord, NC 28025, 704-795-0920
　　Pubs: *Saving the Dead* (Briarpatch Pr, 1992), *Poet & Critic,*
　　Black Warrior Rev, Sycamore Rev, Kansas Qtly, Hollins
　　Critic, Willow Springs

Frank Borden Hanes　　　　　　　　　　　　　W
1057 W Kent Rd
Winston-Salem, NC 27104
　　Pubs: *The Seeds of Ares* (Briarpatch Pr, 1977), *The Fleet*
　　Rabble (Popular Library, 1967), *Jackknife John* (Naylor,
　　1964), *The Bat Brothers, Abel Anders* (Farrar Straus &
　　Young, 1953, 1951)

Suzan Shown Harjo　　　　　　　　　　　　　P
99 Pressley Rd
Asheville, NC 28805-1345

William Harmon　♀　✈　　　　　　　　　　　P
Univ North Carolina, English Dept, CB #3520, Chapel Hill, NC
27599-3520
Internet: wharmon03@mindspring.com
　　Pubs: *Mutatis Mutandis* (Wesleyan U Pr, 1985), *One Long*
　　Poem (LSU Pr, 1982), *Carolina Qtly, Agni, Sewanee Rev,*
　　Poetry, Partisan Rev, Free Lunch

Rabiul Hasan　　　　　　　　　　　　　　　　P
2609 MacGregor Downs Rd, #17
Greenville, NC 27834, 252-752-5556
　　Pubs: *Mississippi Writers: Reflections of Childhood & Youth*
　　Anth (Jackson & London/U Pr Mississippi, 1988), *New Earth*
　　Rev, Aura Literary/Arts Rev, Piddiddle

Ardis Messick Hatch　　　　　　　　　　　　P
414 Oakridge Rd
Cary, NC 27511-4544
　　Pubs: *The Illusion of Water* (St. Andrews Pr, 1980), *To*
　　Defend a Form (Teachers & Writers, 1978)

Tom Hawkins　　　　　　　　　　　　　　　P&W
5020 Oak Park Rd
Raleigh, NC 27612-3025, 919-782-3009
　　Pubs: *Paper Crown* (BkMk Pr, 1989), *Flash Fiction: Anth*
　　(Norton, 1992), *Greensboro Rev, Kansas Qtly, Sequoia Rev,*
　　Carolina Qtly, South Carolina Rev, Ploughshares

Carol Bessent Hayman P
618 Ann St
Beaufort, NC 28516-2204, 252-728-7088
Pubs: *A Garden of Virtues* (Abingdon Pr, 1996), *Images & Echoes of Beaufort-By-The-Sea* (Mt. Olive College Pr, 1993), *Ideals, Listen, Marriage & Family Living, Mature Living, Our State, Down Home in North Carolina, Carolina Country*

Robert R. Hentz P&W
415 Chunns Cove Rd, 900A
Asheville, NC 28805, 704-252-9064
Pubs: *Cape Rock, Hellas, Riverrun, Silhouette, Poem, Cold Mountain Rev, Sonoma Mandala, The Panhandler*

M. L. Hester 🎤 ✈ P
Avisson Press, PO Box 38816, Greensboro, NC 27438, 336-288-6989
Pubs: *Another Jackie Robinson, With Crockett at the Alamo* (Tudor Pubs, 1996, 1995), *Poetry Now, Amer Scholar, Minnesota Rev*

Lonnie Hodge 🎤 ✈ P
179 Hoover Ave
Concord, NC 28025, 704-782-7423
Pubs: *Unrisen Son* (Sandstone Pr, 2000), *Fishing for the Moon* (Sandstone Pr, 1994), *Shadow of the Peaks* (Crossroads, 1985), *America, Bridge, Passages North, Fujimi, Kansas Qtly, Alabama Lit Rev, Colorado North Qtly, Appalachia, Sulphur River Rev*

Judy Hogan 🎤 ✈ P
PO Box 253
Moncure, NC 27559-0253, 919-545-9932
Internet: judyhogan@mindspring.com
Pubs: *Acheron and the Swans* (Thorp Springs Pr, 2003), *Beaver Soul* (Kostroma Writers Org, 1997), *Light Food* (Latitudes Pr, 1989), *Caprice, News and Observer, Wellspring, Chapel Hill Herald, Small Press, Arts Jrnl, Pembroke, Crucible, Lit Kostroma*

David Brendan Hopes 🎤 ✈ P&W
Literature Dept, Univ North Carolina, 1 University Heights, Asheville, NC 28804-3251, 828-254-6057
Internet: davehopes@aol.com
Pubs: *Bird Songs of the Mesozoic, A Sense of the Morning* (Milkweed Edtns, 2000, 1999), *A Childhood in the Milky Way* (U Akron Pr, 1998), *Blood Rose* (Urthona Pr, 1996), *The Sacred Place* (U Utah Pr, 1996), *Atlanta Rev, Cafe Bellas Artes, Salmon*

Maria Ingram P
111 Stratford Rd
Winston-Salem, NC 27104, 919-722-7271
Pubs: *Thirtieth Year to Heaven* (Jackpine Pr, 1980), *Maria* (Red Clay Bks, 1976)

Robert Inman 🎤 ✈ W
PO Box 470788
Charlotte, NC 28247-0788, 704-542-6156
www.robert-inman.com
Pubs: *Dairy Queen Days, Old Dogs and Children, Home Fires Burning* (Little, Brown & Co, 1997, 1991, 1987)

Susan S. Kelly W
522 Woodland Dr
Greensboro, NC 27408, 336-275-5499
Internet: sskelly@nr.infi.net
Pubs: *How Close We Come* (Warner Bks, 1999), *Iowa Woman, Crescent Rev*

Carol Klein W
1-103 Carolina Meadows
Chapel Hill, NC 27517
Internet: czklein@aol.com
Pubs: *Permafrost, The Iconoclast, Green Mountains Rev, Kinesis, Rockhurst Rev, Patomac, North Atlantic Rev, Widener Rev*

Stephen Knauth P
805 E Worthington Ave
Charlotte, NC 28203
Internet: rwss@mindspring.com
Pubs: *The River I Know You By, Twenty Shadows* (Four Way Bks, 1998, 1995), *The Pine Figures* (Dooryard Pr, 1986), *Virginia Qlty Rev, Prairie Schooner, Pacific Rev, Puerto del Sol, Alaska Qtly Rev, Ironwood, Kansas Qtly, MPR, NAR*

Carrie Knowles 🎤 ✈ P&W
315 S Boylan Ave
Raleigh, NC 27603-1907, 919-833-6022
Internet: cwriter@bellsouth.net
Pubs: *Cardinal: Anth* (Jacan Pr, 1986), *The Sun, TasteFull, Mothers Today, Beyond Baroque, Carolina Qtly, Glimmer Train*

Howard D. Koenig P
3306 Middle Sound Rd
Wilmington, NC 28405
Pubs: *Profiles in Leadership* (Quest, 1981), *Lyrical Iowa, Amer Poet*

Mary Kratt 🎤 ✈ P
7001 Sardis Rd
Charlotte, NC 28270-6057, 704-366-0297
Pubs: *Valley* (Sow's Ear Pr, 2000), *Small Potatoes* (St. Andrews Pr, 1999), *On the Steep Side* (Briarpatch Pr, 1993), *The Only Thing I Fear Is a Cow & a Drunken Man* (Carolina Wren Pr, 1991), *SPR, Yankee, Tar River, Spoon River Qtly, Texas Rev, Shenandoah*

Richard Krawiec ♀ ⊀   P&W
319 Wilmot Dr
Raleigh, NC 27602, 919-859-9297
Internet: rkrawiec@mindspring.com
   Pubs: *And Fools of God, Faith in What?, Voices from Home:
   The North Carolina Anth* (Avisson Pr, 2000, 1997, 1998),
   Time Sharing (Viking Penguin, 1987), *Shenandoah,
   Witness, Cream City Rev, The Qtly, Many Mountains
   Moving, The Other Side*

Sandra Lake Lassen   P
1499 Lakeside Dr
West Jefferson, NC 28694-7291
   Pubs: *Womanwrit* (Miller, 1982), *Amaranth Rev, Wordart,
   Touchstone, Amer Scholar, Chiron Rev*

Brenda Kay Ledford ♀ ⊀   P
450 Swaims Rd
Hayesville, NC 28904
   Pubs: *Writers Cramp, Roswell Lit Rev, Aurorean, Lyricist,
   River's Edge, Pembroke Mag, New Thought Jrnl, Mobius,
   Asheville Poetry Rev, Appalachian Heritage*

Lou Lipsitz ♀   P
168 Lake Ellen Dr
Chapel Hill, NC 27514-1937, 919-942-9574
Internet: loulipsitz@earthlink.net
   Pubs: *Seeking the Hook* (Signal Bks, 1998), *American
   Democracy* (St. Martin's Pr, 1993), *Reflections on Samson*
   (Kayak, 1977), *NW Rev, New Letters, New Republic, The
   Sun, Witness, Southern Rev*

Don Mager   P
Johnson C Smith Univ, English Dept, Charlotte, NC 28216,
704-378-1295
   Pubs: *Good Turns, That Which Is Owed to Death* (Main
   Street Rag Pr, 2001, 1998), *Borderings* (Union County
   Writers', 1998), *Glosses* (St Andrews Pr, 1992), *To Track the
   Wounded One* (Ridgeway, 1988), *River Styx, Lyricist, St.
   Andrews Rev, Sun Dog*

E. T. Malone, Jr.   P
PO Box 18124
Raleigh, NC 27619
Internet: diocese_of_nc.parti@ecunet.org
   Pubs: *The View from Wrightsville Beach* (Lit Lantern Pr,
   1988), *Pembroke, St. Andrews Rev, Communicant*

Allen Mandelbaum   P
William Kenan Jr., Prof of Humanities, Wake Forest Univ, PO
Drawer 7228, Winston-Salem, NC 27109, 336-758-5135
   Pubs: *The Savantasse of Montparnasse* (Sheep Meadow
   Pr, 1988), *A Lied of Letter Press* (Pennyroyal, 1980),
   Chelmaxioms (Godine, 1978), *Leaves of Absence* (Living
   Hand, 1976), *Journeyman* (Schocken Bks, 1967), *Denver
   Qtly, Poetry*

Harry A. Maxson   P
North Carolina Wesleyan Univ, 3400 N Wesleyan Blvd, Rocky
Mount, NC 27804
Internet: max34@ix.netcom.com
   Pubs: *The Curley Poems* (Frank Cat Pr, 1994), *Walker in the
   Storm* (K M Gentile Pub, 1981), *Turning the Wood* (Cedar
   Creek Pr, 1976), *Kansas Qtly, Cimarron Rev, New Rev, The
   Ledge, Nation*

Barbara J. Mayer ♀ ⊀   P&W
805 Heatherly Rd
Mooresville, NC 28115-2778, 704-663-7593
Internet: dmayer5@juno.com
   Pubs: *Peacock* (Mount Olive Pr, 2005), *Earth and Soul: Anth*
   (North Carolina Poetry Project, 2001), *I Am Becoming the
   Woman I've Wanted: Anth* (Papier-Mache Pr, 1994), *Filtered
   Images: Anth* (Vintage '45 Pr, 1992), *Atlanta Rev*

Jean McCamy   P
145 W Sycamore Ave
Wake Forest, NC 27587, 919-556-5342
   Pubs: *Uwharrie Rev, Davidson Miscellany, SPR, St.
   Andrews Rev*

Michael McFee ♀ ⊀   P
English Dept, UNC-Chapel Hill, Greenlaw Hall CB# 3520,
Chapel Hill, NC 27599-3520, 919-962-3461
Internet: mcfee@email.unc.edu
   Pubs: *Earthly* (Carnegie Mellon U Pr, 2001), *The Language
   They Speak Is Things to Eat: Anth* (UNC Pr, 1994), *Poetry,
   Hudson Rev, Southern Rev*

Jane Mead ♀ ⊀   P
PO Box 7896, Reynolda Station, Winston-Salem, NC 27109,
336-758-5382
Internet: meadjw@wfu.edu
   Pubs: *House of Poured-Out Waters* (U Illinois Pr, 2001), *The
   Lord & the General Din of the World* (Sarabande Bks, 1996)

Thomas Meyer ♀ ⊀   P
PO Box 10
Highlands, NC 28741-0010, 828-526-4461
Internet: meyer@jargonbooks.com
   Pubs: *At Dusk Iridescent* (Jargon Society, 2000), *Monotypes
   & Tracings* (Enitharmon Pr, 1994), *Conjunctions, First
   Intensity, Oyster Boy Rev*

Shirley Moody   P
4300 Windsor Pl
Raleigh, NC 27609-5968, 919-469-1314
   Pubs: *Charmers, Four North Carolina Women Poets: Anth*
   (St. Andrews Pr, 1990, 1982), *SPR, Crucible*

Lenard D. Moore 🎤 ✈ P
North Carolina State Univ, English Dept, Tompkins Hall,
Raleigh, NC 27695, 919-515-4127
Internet: ldmoore@social.chass.ncsu.edu
Pubs: *Forever Home* (St. Andrews Pr, 1996), *The Garden
Thrives* (HC, 1996), *Soulfires* (Penguin, 1996), *African Amer
Rev, Callaloo, North Carolina Lit Rev, Black Scholar,
Colorado Rev, North Dakota Qtly, Crab Orchard Rev*

Ruth Moose 🎤 ✈ P&W
14 Matchwood
Pittsboro, NC 27312, 919-929-0376
Internet: rumoo@email.unc.edu
Pubs: *Smith Grove* (Sow's Ear Pr, 1997), *Dreams in Color*
(August Hse, 1989), *The Wreath Ribbon & Other Stories* (St.
Andrews, 1986), *12 Christmas Stories by North Carolina
Writers: Anth* (Down Home Pr, 1997), *Atlantic, Redbook*

Jack Nestor P&W
119 Leslie Dr
Chapel Hill, NC 27516
Pubs: *Love Is Ageless* (Serala Pr, 1987), *Stone Country,
Slow Motion Mag, Laurel Rev, Open Mag, Wittenberg Rev,
Ascent, Columbia, Jrnl of New Jersey Poets*

P. B. Newman P
Queens College, Charlotte, NC 28274
Pubs: *The George Washington Poems* (Briarpatch Pr,
1986), *Tar River Poetry, River City, Kennebec, Apalachee
Qtly, Carolina Qtly, SPR, Sun*

Suzanne Newton W
829-A Barringer Dr
Raleigh, NC 27606, 919-851-4710
Pubs: *Where Are You When I Need You?, A Place Between,
An End to Perfect* (Viking, 1991, 1986, 1984)

Claudio Oswald Niedworok PP
Mt Pisgah Church Rd
Broadway, NC 27505-0718, 919-499-2565
Internet: knightt@foto.infi.net
Pubs: *Seafarers* (Vision Era Concepts, 1996)

Valerie Nieman P&W
1313 Hawthorne Ave
Reidsville, NC 27320-5904
Internet: vneiman@nr.infi.net
Pubs: *How We Live* (State Street Pr, 1996), *Slipping Out of
Old Eve* (Sing Heavenly Muse, 1988), *Modern Arthurian Lit:
Anth* (Garland Pub, 1992), *Poetry, New Letters, West
Branch, Kenyon Rev, Antietam Rev*

Sallie Nixon 🎤 P
Covenant Village, 1351 Robinwood Rd, #A-8, Gastonia, NC
28054-1671
Pubs: *Spiraling* (Persephone Pr, 1990), *Second Grace*
(Moore Pub Co, 1977), *Pembroke Mag, Crucible, Sandhills
Rev*

Linda Orr P
Romance Languages Dept, Duke Univ, Durham, NC 27706,
919-684-3706
Pubs: *A Certain X* (L'Epervier Pr, 1980), *Antioch Rev, Paris
Rev, Pequod, Agni*

Tom Page 🎤 ✈ P
PO Box 747
Spruce Pine, NC 28777, 828-766-7633
Internet: madux@yahoo.com
Pubs: *Going Places With the Kids, The Fort Scott Poems*
(Free Soil Pr, 1997, 1994), *The Name of the Place* (John
Brown Pr, 1989), *Minnesota Rev, Phoenix, Caprice, Viet
Nam Generation, Blue Light, Pemmican, Galley Sail*

Sallie Page W
PO Box 64
Lynn, NC 28750
Pubs: *Grab-a-nickel, Potato Eyes, Lonzie's, Pine Mtn Sand
& Gravel, Art/Life, St. Andrews Rev, Spindrift, Aura,
Mountain Rev*

Leslie Parker 🎤 ✈ P
5004 Hiddenbrook Ct
McLeansville, NC 27301-9775, 336-621-7316
Pubs: *A Turn in Time: Anth* (TransVerse Pr, 1999), *Cold Mtn
Rev, Half Tones to Jubilee, Bay Leaves, Hawaii Rev, Black
Buzzard Rev, Infinity Ltd, Byline, Elk River Rev, Panhandler,
Poetpourri, Cape Rock*

Peggy Payne W
512 St Mary's St
Raleigh, NC 27605, 919-833-8021
Pubs: *Revelation* (S&S, 1988), *New Stories From the South:
Anth* (Algonquin, 1987), *Cosmopolitan, Ms., McCall's,
Family Circle, Travel & Leisure*

Gail J. Peck P
250 King Owen Ct
Charlotte, NC 28211, 704-364-1944
Internet: 74601,1420@compuserve.com
Pubs: *Drop Zone* (Texas Rev, 1995), *New River* (Harper,
1993), *Uncommonplace: Anth* (LSU Pr, 1998), *Southern
Rev, Cimarron Rev, Carolina Qtly, High Plains Lit Rev,
Southern Poetry, Malahat, Mangrove, Greensboro Rev,
Cape Rock*

Henry Petroski P
2528 Wrightwood Ave
Durham, NC 27705-5830, 919-489-9416
Pubs: *Paperboy, The Book on the Bookshelf, Remaking the
World, Engineers of Dreams* (Knopf, 2002, 1999, 1997,
1995), *Invention by Design* (Harvard U Pr, 1996), *Design
Paradigms* (Cambridge U Pr, 1994), *Virginia Qtly Rev, Amer
Scientist*

Catherine Petroski W
2528 Wrightwood Ave
Durham, NC 27705-5830, 919-489-9416
Internet: petroski@mindspring.com
  Pubs: *A Bride's Passage* (Northeastern U Pr, 1997), *The Summer That Lasted Forever* (HM, 1984), *I Know Some Things: Anth* (Faber & Faber, 1993), *Virginia Qtly Rev, NAR*

Diana Pinckney 🎤 ✈ P
2215 Malvern Rd
Charlotte, NC 28207-2625, 704-377-6159
Internet: pinckpat@aol.com
  Pubs: *White Linen* (Nightshade Pr, 1998), *Fishing With Tall Women* (Persephone Pr, 1996), *Word & Witness: Anth* (Carolina Academic Pr, 1999), *SPR, Tar River, Sandhills Rev, Chattahoochee Rev, Pembroke, Cream City Rev*

Deborah Pope 🎤 ✈ P
Dept of English, Duke Univ, Durham, NC 27708, 919-684-2741
  Pubs: *Falling Out of the Sky, Mortal World, Fanatic Heart* (LSU Pr, 1999, 1995, 1992), *Poetry, Georgia Rev, Southern Rev, Shenandoah, Poetry NW, Threepenny Rev*

Joe Ashby Porter 🎤 ✈ W
2411 W Club Blvd
Durham, NC 27705, 919-286-7075
Internet: japorter@duke.edu
  Pubs: *Touch Wood* (Turtle Point, 2002), *Resident Aliens* (New Amsterdam, 2000), *Lithuania: Short Stories, The Kentucky Stories* (Johns Hopkins U, 1990, 1983), *Kenyon Rev, Yale Rev, Harper's, TriQtly, Fiction, Raritan, Antaeus, Iowa Rev*

Dannye Romine Powell 🎤 ✈ P
700 E Park Ave
Charlotte, NC 28203-5146, 704-334-0902
Internet: dannye700@aol.com
  Pubs: *The Ecstasy of Regret, At Every Wedding Someone Stays Home* (U Arkansas Pr, 2002, 1994), *America's Foremost Writers on Libraries: Anth* (Doubleday, 1989), *Ploughshares, Field, River Styx, New Republic, Georgia Rev, Gettysburg Rev, Prairie Schooner*

Charles F. Powers 🎤 ✈ W
1412 Rock Creek Ln
Cary, NC 27511, 919-467-2629
Internet: moyesmax@aol.com
  Pubs: *A Matter of Honor* (First East Coast Theatre & Publishing Co, 1982)

Reynolds Price P&W
PO Box 99014
Durham, NC 27708-9014
  Pubs: *Private Contentment, Vital Provisions, The Source of Light* (Atheneum, 1984, 1982, 1981)

Glenis Redmond 🎤 ✈ PP&P
PO Box 4142
Asheville, NC 28805, 800-476-6240
Internet: poetica11@aol.com
  Pubs: *Backbone* (Underground Epics, 2000), *360∞: A Revolution of Black Poets: Anth* (Black Words, 1998), *Catch the Fire: Anth* (Riverhead Bks 1998), *Out of the Rough: Anth* (Novello Festival Pr, 2001), *Bum Rush the Page: Anth* (Three Rivers Pr, 2001)

Tony Reevy P&W
2222 W Club Blvd
Durham, NC 27704-4225, 919-515-3339
Internet: tony_reevy@ncsu.edu
  Pubs: *Now & Then, Charlotte Poetry Rev, Piedmont Pedlar, Asheville Poetry Rev, Bath Avenue Newsletter*

Jonathan K. Rice 🎤 ✈ P
PO Box 18548
Charlotte, NC 28218-0548, 704-595-9526
Internet: iodineopencut@aol.com
  Pubs: *Slipstream, Bogg, Parting Gifts, Red Owl Mag, Blue Collar Rev, Main Street Rag, Wellspring, Cold Mountain Rev, Comstock Rev*

David Rigsbee P
315 Oakwood Ave
Raleigh, NC 27601, 919-821-9851
Internet: drigsbee@earthlink.net
  Pubs: *A Skeptic's Notebook: Longer Poems* (St. Andrews Pr, 1997), *Your Heart Will Fly Away* (The Smith, 1992), *Stamping Ground* (Ardis, 1976), *APR, New Yorker, Iowa Rev, Ironwood, Southern Rev, Georgia Rev, Ohio Rev, Willow Springs*

E. M. Schorb 🎤 ✈ P&W
PO Box 1461
Mooresville, NC 28115-1461, 704-660-5453
Internet: paschorb@aol.com
  Pubs: *Paradise Square, Scenario for Scorsese* (Denlinger's Pub, 2000, 2000), *Murderer's Day* (Purdue U Pr, 1998)

James Seay P
530 Bowden Rd
Chapel Hill, NC 27516-5505, 919-929-9094
  Pubs: *Open Field, Understory: New & Selected Poems* (LSU Pr, 1997), *The Light As They Found It* (Morrow, 1990)

Mabelle M. Segrest P
811 Onslow St
Durham, NC 27705-4244
  Pubs: *My Mama's Dead Squirrel* (Firebrand Bks, 1985), *Southern Exposure, Feminary, Conditions*

Rudy P. Shackelford 🎤 ✈ P
4156 Lattice Rd
Wilson, NC 27893
  Pubs: *Dreamers Wine, Poems, A Visual Diary & Poems, Gathering Voices, Bamboo Harp, Rosewood, Ascend the Hill*

Alan Shapiro P
Univ North Carolina, Chapel Hill, NC 27599, 919-962-1994
Internet: 1shapiro@email.unc.edu
Pubs: *The Dead Alive & Busy, Mixed Company, Covenant* (U Chicago Pr, 2000, 1997, 1996), *In Praise of the Impure* (Northwestern U Pr, 1992), *Happy Hour, The Courtesy* (U Chicago, 1987, 1983), *After the Digging* (Elpenor Bks, 1981)

Janet Beeler Shaw P&W
46 Newcross N
Asheville, NC 28805-9213, 704-298-8999
Pubs: *Taking Leave* (Viking, 1987), *Dowry* (U Missouri Pr, 1978), *Atlantic, Redbook, TriQtly, Shenandoah, SW Rev, Esquire*

Bynum Shaw W
2700 Speas Rd
Winston-Salem, NC 27106, 336-924-1644
Pubs: *Oh, Promised Land!* (Stratford Bks, 1992), *Days of Power, Nights of Fear* (St. Martin's, 1980), *The Nazi Hunter* (Norton, 1969)

Nancy Simpson P
472 Old Cherry Mtn Trail
Hayesville, NC 28904, 828-389-6497
Internet: nance@webworkz.com
Pubs: *Night Student, Across Water* (State Street Pr, 1985, 1983), *Poets for Peace: Anth* (Chapel Hill Pr, 2002), *Word & Witness: Anth* (Carolina Academic Pr, 1999), *Georgia Rev, Prairie Schooner, Indiana Rev, Florida Rev, New Virginia Rev, SPR, Confrontation*

Lee Smith W
219 N Churton St
Hillsborough, NC 27278
Pubs: *Fair & Tender Ladies, Oral History* (Putnam, 1988, 1981), *Atlantic, Southern Exposure, New York Times*

John Thom Spach W
PO Box 11408
Winston-Salem, NC 27116-1408, 336-724-6774
Pubs: *Time Out From Texas* (John F Blair, 1970), *Great Commanders in Action: Anth* (Cowles Enthusiast Media, 1996), *Augusta Spectator, The State, Military History, Cowboy, American Civil War, Retired Officer, Saturday Evening Post, Grit, Reader's Digest*

Elizabeth Spencer W
402 Longleaf Dr
Chapel Hill, NC 27517, 919-929-2115
Pubs: *The Southern Woman* (Modern Library, 2001), *Landscapes of the Heart* (Random Hse, 1998), *The Light in the Piazza, The Snare* (U Pr Mississippi, 1996, 1993), *The Voice at the Back Door* (LSU Pr, 1994), *Boulevard, Southern Rev, Story, New Yorker, Atlantic*

Max Steele W
English Dept, Univ North Carolina, Chapel Hill, NC 27514, 919-962-5481
Pubs: *The Hat of My Mother* (Algonquin Bks, 1988), *Story, Paris Rev*

Shelby Stephenson 🎤 ✈ P
UNC Pembroke, Pembroke Magazine, Box 1510, Pembroke, NC 28372-1510, 919-521-4214
Internet: shelbystephenson@mindspring.com
Pubs: *Greatest Hits* (Pudding Hse, 2002), *The Persimmon Tree Carol* (Juniper Pr, 2002), *Fiddledeedee* (The Bunny & The Crocodile Pr, 2001), *Poor People* (Nightshade Pr, 1998), *Plankhouse* (North Carolina Wesleyan College Pr, 1993), *Poetry NW, Hudson Rev, Bits*

John Stokes P
124 Windemere Rd
Wilmington, NC 28405
Pubs: *Texas Qtly, Voices Intl, The Poet, Pembroke Mag, Crucible*

Lori Storie-Pahlitzsch P&W
864 Red Fox Rd
Columbus, NC 28722, 828-894-8741
Pubs: *45/96: South Carolina Poetry Anth* (96 Pr, 1994), *Looking for Home: Anth* (Milkweed Edtns, 1990), *Poetry NW, Pleiades, Blue Unicorn, Crescent Rev, Poet Lore, Laurel Rev*

Julie Suk 🎤 ✈ P
845 Greentree Dr
Charlotte, NC 28211-2731, 704-366-8956
Pubs: *The Angel of Obsession* (U Arkansas Pr, 1992), *Heartwood* (Briarpatch Pr, 1991), *The Chariton Rev, Chelsea, Tar River Poetry, Poetry, Shenandoah*

Chuck Sullivan P
1100 E 34 St
Charlotte, NC 28205, 704-334-3496
Pubs: *Alphabet of Grace: New & Selected Poems* (Sandstone Pr, 1995), *Longing for the Harmonies* (St Andrews Pr, 1992), *The Juggler on the Radio* (Briarpatch Pr, 1987), *The Catechism of Hearts* (Red Clay Bks, 1979)

Charleen Whisnant Swansea P
404 Deming Dr
Chapel Hill, NC 27514
Internet: mindwok@aol.com
Pubs: *The Red Clay Reader Reader* (Tryon Pr, 2002), *Mindworks* (South Carolina Educational TV, 1990), *Word Magic* (Doubleday, 1976), *SPR*

Nancy McFadden Tilly 🎤 ✈ W
628 Kensington Dr
Chapel Hill, NC 27514-6731, 919-929-8880
Pubs: *Golden Girl* (FSG, 1985), *Potato Eyes, Writer to Writer, Pembroke Mag, Raleigh News & Observer, Carolina Qtly, Cotton Boll, Writer's Choice, Albany Rev*

Stephanie S. Tolan 🎤 ✈   P&W
4511 Eagle Lake Dr N
Charlotte, NC 28217-3001
Internet: steft@carolina.rr.com
　　Pubs: *Surviving the Applewhites, Flight of the Raven* (HC,
　　2002, 2001), *Ordinary Miracles, The Face in the Mirror,*
　　Welcome to the Ark, Who's There?, Save Halloween!
　　(Morrow, 1999, 1998, 1996, 1994, 1993)

Kermit Turner   W
Lenoir-Rhyne College, Box 418, Hickory, NC 28601,
704-328-1741
　　Pubs: *These Rebel Powers* (Frederick Warne & Co, 1979),
　　Greensboro Rev, Roanoke Rev, Phylon

Pamela Uschuk   P
Center for Women Writers, PO Box 10548 Salem College,
Winston-Salem, NC 27108, 336-722-3221
Internet: marchu@attglobal.net
　　Pubs: *One-Legged Dancer, Finding Peaches in the Desert*
　　(Wings Pr, 2002, 2000), *Without Birds, Without Flowers,*
　　Without Trees (Flume, 1991), *Light From Dead Stars* (Full
　　Count, 1981), *Amer Voice, Parnassus Rev, Agni, Poetry,*
　　Nimrod, Parabola

Linda Wagner-Martin   P&W
English Department, Univ of North Carolina, Chapel Hill,
Chapel Hill, NC 27599-3520, 919-962-8765
Internet: wagnerl@prodigy.net
　　Pubs: *Sylvia Plath: A Biography* (S&S, 1987), *Sylvia Plath:*
　　Essays (GK Hall, 1984)

Thomas N. Walters   P
5211 Melbourne Rd
Raleigh, NC 27606, 919-851-4899
　　Pubs: *Always Next August, Seeing in the Dark* (Moore Pub
　　Co, 1976, 1972)

Robert Watson 🎤   P&W
9-D Fountain Manor Dr
Greensboro, NC 27405-8032, 336-274-9962
　　Pubs: *The Pendulum: New & Selected Poems* (LSU Pr,
　　1995), *Night Blooming Cactus* (Atheneum, 1980), *Poetry,*
　　Harper's, New Yorker, Georgia Rev, Shenandoah

Susan C. Weinberg   W
English Dept, Appalachian State Univ, Boone, NC 28608,
704-262-2871
Internet: weinbergsc@appstate.edu
　　Pubs: *Voices From Home: North Carolina Prose Anth*
　　(Avisson Pr, 1997), *Gettysburg Rev, Other Voices, Gargoyle,*
　　Indiana Rev, MacGuffin, Third Coast, Washington Rev,
　　Mississippi Rev

John Foster West   P&W
157 West Ln
Boone, NC 28607-8605, 828-295-7704
　　Pubs: *Lift Up Your Head, Tom Dooley* (Down Home Pr,
　　1993), *The Summer People* (Appalachian Consortium Pr,
　　1988), *Wry Wine* (John F Blair Pub, 1977), *Time Was*
　　(Random Hse, 1965), *Southern Rev, Atlantic, SW Rev, Cold*
　　Mountain Rev, Crucible

Nina A. Wicker   P
2356 Minter School Rd
Sanford, NC 27332-2494
　　Pubs: *October Rain on My Window* (Honeybrook Pr, 1984),
　　Heiwa: Anth (U Hawaii Pr, 1996), *Haiku Moment: Anth*
　　(Charles E Tuttle, 1993), *The Haiku Hundred: Anth* (Iron Pr,
　　1992), *Modern Haiku, Woodnotes*

Carol Lynn Wilkinson   P
PO Box 19312
Raleigh, NC 27609
　　Pubs: *Taste of Remembered Wine* (North Carolina Rev Pr,
　　1975), *Wind, Miscellany*

Jonathan Williams 🎤 ✈   P
PO Box 10
Highlands, NC 28741-0010, 828-526-4461
Internet: jwms@jargonbooks.com
　　Pubs: *Blackbird Dust* (Turtle Pt Pr, 2000), *A Palpable Elysium*
　　(Godine, 2000), *Quote, Unquote* (Ten Speed Pr, 1989)

Dede Wilson 🎤 ✈   P
2409 Knollwood Rd
Charlotte, NC 28211-2707, 704-365-6846
　　Pubs: *Sea of Small Tears* (Main St Rag, 2001), *Glass* (Scots
　　Plaid Pr, 1998), *Spoon River Poetry Rev, New Orleans*
　　Poetry Rev, SPR, Iowa Woman, Cream City Rev, Painted
　　Bride Qtly, Flyway, Carolina Qtly, Tar River Poetry Rev

Emily Herring Wilson 🎤 ✈   P
3381 Timberlake Ln
Winston-Salem, NC 27106, 910-759-2309
　　Pubs: *To Fly Without Hurry* (St. Andrews Pr, 2001), *Hope &*
　　Dignity (Temple U Pr, 1983)

Lee Zacharias 🎤 ✈   W
UNCG PO Box 26170, English Dept, Greensboro,
NC 27402-6170
Internet: zachpeny@aol.com
　　Pubs: *Lessons* (HM, 1981), *Helping Muriel Make It Through*
　　the Night (LSU Pr, 1976), *Southern Rev, Southern Qtly, New*
　　Virginia Rev, Southern California Anth, New Territory,
　　Redbook, Kansas Qtly

NORTH DAKOTA

Madelyn Camrud P
815 40 Ave, Apt 121F
Grand Forks, ND 58201, 701-772-2828
 Pubs: *Prairie Volcano* (Dacotah Territory & St. Ives, 1995),
This House Is Filled With Cracks (New Rivers Pr, 1994),
North Dakota Qtly, Kalliope, Nebraska Rev

Rita Johnson P
PO Box 877
Stanley, ND 58784
 Pubs: *Plainswoman, Georgia Rev, Great River Rev, DeKalb
Lit Arts Jrnl, Oxygen*

David Martinson P
English Dept, North Dakota State Univ, Minard 322 F,
University Sta, Fargo, ND 58105
Internet: davimart@badlands.nodak.edu
 Pubs: *A Little Primer of Tom McGrath* (Shining Times, 1998),
Hinges (Aluminum Canoe, 1996), *Nation, Dacotah Territory,
Pemmican, Minnesota Monthly, Floating Island, ACM*

Jay Meek 🎤 ✈ P
English Dept, Univ North Dakota, Box 7209, University Stn,
Grand Forks, ND 58203, 701-777-3321
 Pubs: *Memphis Letters, Headlands, Windows* (Carnegie
Mellon U Pr, 2001, 1997, 1994), *BPJ, Crazyhorse, Great
River Rev, Ohio Rev, Prose Poem*

Martha George Meek P
English Dept, Univ North Dakota, Box 8237, University Sta,
Grand Forks, ND 58202, 701-777-6391
 Pubs: *Rude Noises* (Dacotah Territory Pr, 1995), *Preludes:
Anth* (Mount Holyoke College, 1973)

Rodney Nelson P&W
510-4th Ave N #305
Fargo, ND 58102-4848, 701-293-1777
 Pubs: *Villy Sadness* (New Rivers Pr, 1987), *Thor's Home*
(Holmganger's Pr, 1984), *American Letters & Comments*

OHIO

Steve Abbott 🎤 ✈ P
91 E Duncan St
Columbus, OH 43202, 614-268-5006
Internet: sabbott@cscc.edu
 Pubs: *A Short History of the Word* (Pudding Hse, 1996),
Coffeehouse Poetry Anth (Bottom Dog Pr, 1996), *Pavement
Saw, Wind, Birmingham Poetry Rev, Heartlands Today*

Lee K. Abbott 🎤 ✈ W
4536 Carriage Hill Ln
Upper Arlington, OH 43220, 614-459-0197
Internet: abbott.4@osu.edu
 Pubs: *Wet Places at Noon* (U Iowa Pr, 1997), *Living After
Midnight, Dreams of Distant Lives* (Putnam, 1991, 1989),
Atlantic, Harper's, Georgia Rev, Kenyon Rev

Laura Albrecht P
6217 Carmin Ave
Dayton, OH 45427-2058
 Pubs: *Skid* (WSU Prods, 1994), *Poetry Gumball* (Voicebox
Pubs, 1993), *CQ, Coe Rev, Maverick Pr, Ohio Poetry Rev,
Steam Ticket, Work*

Pamela Alexander P
Creative Writing Program, Rice Hall, Oberlin College, Oberlin,
OH 44074, 440-775-6567
Internet: pamela.alexander@oberlin.edu
 Pubs: *Inland* (Iowa U Pr, 1997), *Commonwealth of Wings*
(Wesleyan, 1991), *Navigable Waterways* (Yale U Pr, 1985),
*Atlantic, New Yorker, Orion, Shankpainter, Denver Qtly,
TriQtly, Marlboro Rev, Agni*

Maggie Anderson 🎤 ✈ P
124 Forest Dr
Kent, OH 44240-2270, 330-672-2067
 Pubs: *Windfall, A Space Filled with Moving, Cold Comfort* (U
Pitt Pr, 2000, 1992, 1986), *Years That Answer* (H&R, 1980),
*Alaska Qtly, Marlboro Rev, The Journal, Poetry East, APR,
Ohio Rev, Third Coast*

Julian Anderson 🎤 W
159 Riverview Park
Columbus, OH 43214
 Pubs: *Empire Under Glass* (Faber & Faber, 1996), *Pushcart
Prize XXIV: Anth* (Pushcart Pr, 1999), *Kenyon Rev,
Southern Rev, Cleveland Plain Dealer, la fontana, The Jrnl*

Nuala Archer P
English Dept, Cleveland State Univ, Cleveland, OH 44115
 Pubs: *Two Women, Two Shores* (w/Medbh McGuckian; New
Poets Series, 1989), *Epoch, Poetry Australia*

Rane Arroyo 🎤 ✈ P
3925 Watson Av
Toledo, OH 43612, 419-476-1578
Internet: rarroyo@utoledo.edu
 Pubs: *Home Movies of Narcissus* (U Arizona Pr, 2002), *Pale
Ramon* (Zoland Bks, 1998), *The Singing Shark* (Bilingual Pr,
1996), *Death Cab for Cutie* (New Sins Pr, 1991), *Nimrod,
Kenyon Rev, Spoon River Qtly, Americas Rev,
Ploughshares, Many Mountains Moving*

Russell Atkins   P
6005 Grand Ave
Cleveland, OH 44104, 216-431-7116
  Pubs: *The Garden Thrives: Anth* (HC, 1996), *Voices of
  Cleveland: Anth* (Cleveland State U, 1996), *Beyond the
  Reef: Anth* (Houghton, 1991), *Letters to America: Anth*
  (Wayne State U Pr, 1995), *Scarecrow Poetry: Anth* (Ashland
  Poetry Pr, 1994), *Crayon, Splitcity*

David Baker ♦ ✈   P
135 Granview Rd
Granville, OH 43023, 740-587-1269
Internet: baker@denison.edu
  Pubs: *Changeable Thunder, Truth About Small Towns, After
  the Reunion, Sweet Home, Saturday Night* (U of Arkansas
  Pr, 2001, 1998, 1994, 1991), *Haunts* (Cleveland State U Pr,
  1985), *Atlantic, New Yorker, Poetry, Nation, Yale Rev,
  Kenyon Rev*

David Baratier ♦ ✈   P
PO Box 6291
Columbus, OH 43206, 614-445-0534
Internet: baratier@megsinet.net
  Pubs: *In It What's In It* (Spuyten Duyvil, 2002), *The Fall of
  Because* (Pudding Hse, 1999), *American Poetry: Anth*
  (Carnegie Mellon, 2000), *Clockpunchers: Anth* (Partisan Pr,
  2000), *Salt Hill, Heartlands Today, Southeast Rev, Denver
  Qtly, Fourteen Hills*

Panos D. Bardis   P&W
2533 Orkney Dr
Toledo, OH 43606
  Pubs: *A Cosmic Whirl of Melodies* (Literary Endeavor,
  1985), *Ivan & Artemis* (Pageant Pr, 1957), *Abira Digest,
  Poetry Project Four, Hellenic Times*

Steven Bauer ♦ ✈   P&W
Miami Univ, English Dept, Oxford, OH 45056, 765-732-3768
Internet: bauersa@muohio.edu
  Pubs: *Cat of a Different Color* (Delacorte, 2000), *Strange &
  Wonderful Tale of RBT McDoodle* (S&S, 1999), *Daylight
  Savings* (Peregrine Smith, 1989), *Dog People: Anth*
  (Artisan/Workman, 1995), *Hopewell Rev, Missouri Rev,
  Indiana Rev, High Plains Lit Rev*

Gail Bellamy ♦ ✈   P
3422 E Scarborough Rd
Cleveland Heights, OH 44118-3412
Internet: sgbellamy@mac.com
  Pubs: *Victual Reality* (Pudding House, 2000), *Food Poems:
  Anth* (Bottom Dog Pr, 1998), *Detours: Anth* (Lonesome
  Traveler Pub, 1997), *Earth's Daughters, Cosmopolitan,
  Rolling Stone*

John M. Bennett ♦ ✈   P
Luna Bisonte Prods, 137 Leland Ave, Columbus, OH 43214,
614-846-4126
Internet: bennet.23@osu.edu
  Pubs: *rOlling COMBers* (Potes & Poets Pr, 2000), *Mailer
  Leaves Ham* (Pantograph Pr, 1999), *Know Other* (Luna
  Bisonte Prods, 1998), *Seasons* (Spectacular Diseases,
  1997), *Door Door* (Juxta/3300 Pr, 1997), *Prime Sway*
  (Texture Pr, 1996), *Caliban, DOC(K)S, Texture*

Paul Bennett ♦   P&W
Poet in Residence, Denison Univ, Granville, OH 43023,
614-587-6688
  Pubs: *Max: The Tale of a Waggish Dog* (Mayhaven Pub,
  1998), *Appalachian Mettle* (Savage Pr, 1997), *Follow the
  River* (Orchard Bks, 1987), *Building a House* (Limekiln Pr,
  1986), *Agni, CSM, Delmar*

Maureen Bloomfield ♦ ✈   P
1555 Donaldson Pl
Cincinnati, OH 45223-1713, 513-681-0037
  Pubs: *Error & Angels* (U South Carolina Pr, 1997),
  *Ploughshares, Southern Rev, Cincinnati Poetry Rev, New
  Republic, Poetry, Shenandoah*

Don Bogen ♦ ✈   P
362 Terrace Ave
Cincinnati, OH 45220, 513-221-2699
Internet: donald.bogen@uc.edu
  Pubs: *The Known World, After the Splendid Display*
  (Wesleyan, 1997, 1986), *Nation, New Republic, Yale Rev,
  Paris Rev, Poetry, Partisan Rev*

Phil Boiarski   P
839 Lakefield Dr
Galloway, OH 43119, 614-870-6623
Internet: pboiarsk@freenet.columbus.oh.us
  Pubs: *Cornered* (Logan Elm Pr, 1990), *Coal & Ice* (Yellow
  Pages Pr, 1980), *Paris Rev, California Qtly, Rocky Mtn Rev,
  Green House, Ohio Jrnl, Handbook*

Jennifer Bosveld ♦ ✈   P
Pudding House Writers Innovation Center, 60 N Main St,
Johnstown, OH 43031, 740-967-6060
Internet: pudding@johnstown.net
  Pubs: *The Magic Fish, Prayers to Protest: Poems That
  Center & Bless: Anth, Unitarian Universalist Poets: Anth*
  (Pudding Hse Pub, 2002, 1998, 1996), *Coffeehouse Poetry
  Anth* (Bottom Dog Pr, 1996), *Bottomfish, Heaven Bone,
  Chiron Rev, Negative Capability*

Daniel Bourne ♦ ✈   P
College of Wooster, English Dept, Wooster, OH 44691,
216-263-2577
Internet: dbourne@wooster.edu
  Pubs: *The Household Gods* (Cleveland State U Pr, 1995),
  *APR, Shenandoah, Prairie Schooner, Field, Poetry NW,
  Salmagundi*

Philip Brady   P
Youngstown State Univ, English Dept, Youngstown,
OH 44555-3415, 216-742-1952
Internet: psbrady@cc.ysu.edu
    Pubs: *Forged Correspondences* (New Myths, 1996), *Plague
    Country* (Mbira Pr, 1990), *College English, Poetry NW,
    Massachusetts Rev, Honest Ulsterman, Centennial Rev*

David Breithaupt ♪ ✈   P&W
22900 Caves Rd
Gambier, OH 43022, 740-427-4170
Internet: David_Breithaupt@hotmail.com
    Pubs: *Thus Spake the Corpse, Vol. 2: Anth* (Black Sparrow
    Pr, 2000), *Exquisite Corpse, Kumquat Merinque, Beet, The
    Krellullin, Rant*

Denise Brennan Watson ♪ ✈   P&W
PO Box 68081
Cincinnati, OH 45206-0081
Internet: brennan7@earthlink.net
    Pubs: *Food and Other Enemies* (Essex Pr, 2000), *The
    Undertow of Hunger* (Finishing Line Pr, 1999), *Revelations
    II: Anth* (U Cincinnati Pr, 1999), *Lucid Stone*

Robert L. Brimm ♪ ✈   P
1120 Carlisle Ave
Dayton, OH 45420-1917, 937-254-5165
Internet: rbrimm@aol.com
    Pubs: *Rockford Rev, Cape Rock, Palo Alto Rev, Poetry
    Motel, Poem, Potpourri, Midwest Poetry Rev, Riverrun,
    Sisters Today, American Scholar*

Ira Beryl Brukner   P
203 West South College St
Yellow Springs, OH 45387, 937-767-1937
    Pubs: *Questions, Short Poems, Water & Air* (Junction Pr,
    1998)

Michael J. Bugeja   P&W
Special Assistant to the President, Ohio Univ, Cutler Hall 110,
Athens, OH 45701, 740-593-2329
    Pubs: *Millennium's End* (Archer Pr, 1999), *Talk* (Arkansas
    Pr, 1998), *Flight from Valhalla* (Livingston U Pr, 1993),
    Platonic Love (Orchises Pr, 1991), *Poetry, Harper's, TriQtly,
    Georgia Rev, Kenyon Rev*

Grace Butcher ♪ ✈   P
PO Box 274
Chardon, OH 44024, 440-286-3840
Internet: grace_butcher@msn.com
    Pubs: *Child, House, World* (Hiram Poetry Rev, 1991),
    Rumors of Ecstasy (Barnwood, 1981), *Before I Go Out on
    the Road* (Cleveland State U Pr, 1979)

Catherine A. Callaghan ♪ ✈   PP&P
Ohio State Univ, 222 Oxley Hall, 1712 Neil Ave, Columbus, OH
43210-1298, 614-292-5880
    Pubs: *Other Worlds: Poems on Prints by M.C. Escher*
    (Pudding Hse, 1999), *Haiku Poems: Anth* (Bottom Dog Pr,
    1999), *The Poet's Job: To Go Too Far: Anth, I Name Myself
    Daughter & It Is Good: Anth* (Sophia Bks, 1985, 1981),
    Pudding Mag, Dragonfly, Timber Creek

Neil Carpathios ♪ ✈   P
376 49th St NW
Canton, OH 44709, 330-499-7768
Internet: CantonCarp@aol.com
    Pubs: *Greatest Hits* (Pudding House Pubs, 2002), *The
    Weight of the Heart* (Blue Light Pr, 2000), *Intimate Kisses:
    Anth* (New World Library, 2001), *Our Mothers, Our Selves:
    Anth* (Bergin & Garvey, 1996), *I The Father* (Millennium Pr,
    1993)

Ellin Carter ♪ ✈   P
414 Arcadia Ave
Columbus, OH 43202-2406, 614-267-8798
Internet: carter.3@osu.edu
    Pubs: *What This Is & Why* (Richmond Waters Pr, 1992),
    Kalliope, GW Rev, Earth's Daughters, Caprice, Prose Poem

David Citino ♪ ✈   P
English Dept, Denney Hall, Ohio State Univ, 164 W 17 Ave,
Columbus, OH 43210, 614-292-4856
Internet: citino.1@osu.edu
    Pubs: *The News and Other Poems* (U Notre Dame Pr,
    2002), *The Book of Appassionata: Collected Poems, The
    Discipline: New & Selected Poems, 1980-1992* (Ohio State
    U Pr, 1998, 1992), *Antioch Rev, Poetry, Kenyon Rev, Yale
    Rev, Salmagundi, NER, Georgia Rev*

Marian Clover   P&W
611 Yaronia Dr S
Columbus, OH 43214, 614-267-9201
    Pubs: *NAR, Kansas Qtly, Essence, Review 76, Review 74*

Lawrence Coates   W
514 N Prospect St
Bowling, OH 43402, 419-352-2722
Internet: coatesl@bgnet.bgsu.edu
    Pubs: *The Master of Monterey, The Blossom Festival* (U
    Nevada Pr, 2003, 1999), *Connecticut Rev, Blue Mesa Rev,
    Contemporary Satire, Writers' Forum, Long Story, Toyon,
    Santa Clara Rev, Missouri Rev*

E. R. Cole   P
274 E 214 St
Cleveland, OH 44123
    Pubs: *songpoems/poemsongs* (Weyburne, 1988), *Uneasy
    Camber* (Greystone Pr, 1986), *Northland Qtly*

Joan C. Connor 🎤 ✈   W
Ohio Univ, 327 Ellis Hall, English Dept, Athens, OH 45701,
740-593-2754
Internet: connor@ohiou.edu
    Pubs: *Matter of the Heart* (13th Moon, 2000), *We Who Live
Apart, Here on Old Rte. 7* (U Missouri Pr, 2000, 1997),
*Kenyon Rev, TriQtly, Gettysburg Rev, Shenandoah,
Southern Rev, NAR, Manoa, Arts & Letters*

David Craig 🎤 ✈   P&W
690 Overlook Dr N
Wintersville, OH 43953, 740-282-6950
Internet: dcraig@franuniv.edu
    Pubs: *Mercy's Face: New & Selected Poems, 1980-2000,
The Roof of Heaven* (Franciscan U Pr, 2001, 1998), *Place
of Passage* (Story Line Pr, 2000), *Our Lady of the Outfield,
The Cheese Stands Alone* (CMJ Pub, 1999, 1997),
Heartlands Today, Hiram Poetry Rev

James Cummins 🎤 ✈   P
ML-#0033, Univ Cincinnati, Elliston Poetry Collection,
Cincinnati, OH 45221-0033, 513-556-1570
Internet: james.cummins@uc.edu
    Pubs: *Portrait in a Spoon* (U South Carolina Pr, 1997), *The
Whole Truth* (North Point, 1986), *Paris Rev, Ploughshares,
Shenandoah, New Republic*

Kiki DeLancey 🎤 ✈   W
617 N 7th St
Cambridge, OH 43725
Internet: kiki@cambridgeoh.com
    Pubs: *Coal Miner's Holiday* (Sarabande Bks, 2002), *The
Styles, Rain Crow, Brilliant Corners, Oxford Mag, Carve,
Mississippi Rev, Quarter After Eight, Boston Rev, Primavera,
Bridge, Arden, Epiphany, Karamu*

Kent H. Dixon   W
Wittenberg Univ, PO Box 720, Springfield, OH 45501,
937-327-7069
www.wittenberg.edu
    Pubs: *Kansas Qtly, Arkansas Rev, Grand Tour, Gettysburg
Rev, Georgia Rev, TriQtly, Shenandoah, Iowa Rev, American
Prospect, Libido*

Wayne Dodd 🎤 ✈   P
11292 Peach Ridge Rd
Athens, OH 45701, 740-592-3409
    Pubs: *The Blue Salvages, Of Desire & Disorder* (Carnegie
Mellon Pr, 1998, 1994), *Toward the End of the Century* (U
Iowa, 1992), *Gettysburg Rev, Iowa Rev, Antioch, Georgia
Rev*

John Drury 🎤 ✈   P
2824 Werk Rd
Cincinnati, OH 45211, 513-389-0303
Internet: druryjp@email.uc.edu
    Pubs: *The Disappearing Town* (Miami U Pr, 2000), *The
Stray Ghost* (State Street, 1987), *APR, Lit Rev, New
Republic, Paris Rev, Poetry NW, Southern Rev, Verse,
Western Humanities Rev*

Leatrice Joy W. Emeruwa 🎤 ✈   P
PO Box 21755
Cleveland, OH 44121, 216-381-3027
Internet: lemeruwa@aol.com
    Pubs: *A Jazzzzzzz Poem* (Burning Pr, 1997), *Voices of
Cleveland: Anth* (Cleveland State U Pr, 1996)

John Engle 🎤 ✈   P
1127 Neeld Dr
Xenia, OH 45385
    Pubs: *Tree People, Laugh Lightly II* (Engle's Angle, 1990,
1989), *Writer's Digest, Lake Effect, Poetpourri, Byline,
Science of Mind, Unity*

Cathryn Essinger 🎤 ✈   P
225 Crestwood Dr
Troy, OH 45373, 937-335-1724
Internet: maybe@erinet.com
    Pubs: *A Desk in the Elephant House* (TX Tech Univ Pr,
1998), *Grrrrr:Anth* (CB Follett, 2000), *Qtly West, Mid-Amer
Rev, Talking River, Grand Lakes Rev, Poetry, Poetry
Northwest, Yankee, The Ledge*

Angie Estes 🎤 ✈   P
242 N Liberty St
Delaware, OH 43015-1647, 614-292-0270
Internet: aestes@calpoly.edu
    Pubs: *Voice-Over* (Oberlin College Pr, 2002), *The
Extraordinary Tide: Anth* (Columbia Univ Pr, 2001), *The
Uses of Passion* (Peregrine Smith Bks, 1995), *Geography of
Home: Anth* (Heyday Bks, 1999), *Queer Dog: Anth* (Cleis Pr,
1997), *Paris Rev, Ploughshares*

Kathy Fagan 🎤 ✈   P
English Dept, Ohio State Univ, 164 W 17 Ave, Columbus, OH
43210, 614-292-0270
Internet: fagan.3@osu.edu
    Pubs: *Moving & St. Rage* (UNT, 1999), *The Raft* (Dutton,
1985), *Paris Rev, Missouri Rev, Ploughshares, Shenandoah,
New Republic, Kenyon Rev*

Laurence S. Fallis   P&W
4457 Woodglen St, Apt D
Kent, OH 44240-6954, 216-296-3765
    Pubs: *Arizona Qtly, Woodrider, Texas Qtly, Blue Cloud Qtly,
Orion, Middle Way, Invisible City*

Ross Feld   P&W
6934 Miami Ave Room 23
Cincinnati, OH 45243, 513-271-3405
Internet: rfrites@sprintmail.com
  Pubs: *Shapes Mistaken, Only Shorter* (North Point, 1989,
  1982), *Harper's, Parnassus*

B. Felton   P&W
17102 Ridgeton Dr
Cleveland, OH 44128, 216-991-9245
  Pubs: *Conclusions* (B Felton, 1971)

Barbara Fialkowski   P
Creative Writing Program, Bowling Green State Univ, Hannah
Hall, Bowling Green, OH 43403, 419-372-8370
  Pubs: *Framing* (Croissant Pr, 1978), *New Virginia Rev, NAR,
  Abraxas, Poetry Now*

Annie Finch 🎤 ✈   P
376 Howell Ave
Cincinnati, OH 45220-2015, 513-961-4982
Internet: finchar@muohio.edu
  Pubs: *Calenders* (Tupelo Pr, 2002), *Eve, The Poet's Grimm:
  Anth* (Story Line Pr, 1997, 2002), *Visiting Emily: Anth* (Iowa
  Univ Pr, 2001), *Book of the Sonnet: Anth* (Penguin, 2000),
  Ravishing DisUnities: Anth (Wesleyan, 2000), *Yale Rev,
  Poetry, Partisan Rev*

Norman M. Finkelstein 🎤 ✈   P
Xavier Univ, English Dept, 3800 Victory Pkwy, Cincinnati, OH
45207-4446, 513-745-2041
Internet: finkelst@xavier.xu.edu
  Pubs: *Columns: Track Vol II, Track* (Spuyten Duyvil, 2002,
  1999), *The Ritual of New Creation* (SUNY Pr, 1992),
  Restless Messengers (U Georgia Pr, 1992), *Denver Qtly,
  Salmagundi, Pequod, Hambone, Talisman, Notre Dame Rev,
  Colorado Rev*

Robert Flanagan 🎤 ✈   P&W
181 N Liberty St
Delaware, OH 43015-1642, 740-369-4820
Internet: rjflanag@cc.owu.edu
  Pubs: *Getting By, In Buckeye Country, Loving Power*
  (Bottom Dog, 1996, 1994, 1990), *Norton Bk of American
  Short Stories: Anth* (Norton, 1988), *Civic Arts Rev, Illinois
  Qtly, Chicago, Fiction, Kansas Qtly, NW Rev, Ohio Rev*

Deborah Fleming   P
2525 CR 775
Perrysville, OH 44864, 419-938-7305
Internet: dfleming@ashland.edu
  Pubs: *Learning the Trade* (Locust Hill, 1992), *Hiram Poetry
  Rev, Pennsylvania Rev, Green River Rev, The Jrnl,
  Crosscurrents, Sucarnochee Rev, Organization &
  Environment, Pike Creek Rev, Ibis*

Robert R. Fox 🎤 ✈   P&W
Ohio Arts Council, 727 E Main St, Columbus, OH 43205-1796,
614-466-2613
Internet: bfox@oac.state.oh.us
  Pubs: *Columbia Companion to the 20th Century Short
  Story: Anth* (Columbia U Pr, 2000), *Jrnl of Appalachian
  Studies, Pine Mountain Sand & Gravel, 5 a.m.*

Christopher Franke   P
c/o Deciduous, 1456 W 54 St, Cleveland, OH 44102,
216-651-7725
Internet: frankepoet@hotmail.com
  Pubs: *Paren's Thesis* (Burning Pr, 1997),
  frankeana/miscellangy (deciduous/worded print, 1996), *=5*
  (Wm. Busta Gallery, 1994), *Artcrimes, SplitCity, Listening
  Eye, Coffeehouse Poetry Anth*

Stuart Friebert   P
172 Elm
Oberlin, OH 44074
  Pubs: *Funeral Pie* (Four Way Bks, 1996), *The Darmstadt
  Orchids* (BkMk Pr, 1993), *Paris Rev, The Qtly, Iowa Rev,
  Paterson Rev*

Diane Furtney 🎤 ✈   P
297 E Deshler
Columbus, OH 43206-2710, 614-444-1812
  Pubs: *Murder in the New Age* (as D.J.H. Jones; U New
  Mexico Pr, 2000), *Murder at the MLA* (as D.J.H. Jones; U
  Georgia Pr, 1993), *Destination Rooms* (Riverstone Pr,
  1980), *Chicago Rev, Kenyon Rev, Iowa Rev*

Zona Gale   P
3877 Indian Rd
Toledo, OH 43606
  Pubs: *Her Soul Beneath the Bone* (U Illinois Pr, 1988),
  Spirits & Seasons (Heatherdown Pr, 1982)

David C. D. Gansz 🎤 ✈   P
221 Pyle Road
Clarksville, OH 45113, 937-289-3708
Internet: david_gansz@wilmington.edu
  Pubs: *Millennial Scriptions* (OtherWind Pr, 2000), *Ashen
  Meal*

David Lee Garrison 🎤 ✈   P
Dept of Modern Languages, Wright State Univ, Dayton, OH
45435, 937-775-2641
Internet: dgarrison@desire.wright.edu
  Pubs: *Inside the Sound of Rain* (Vincent Brothers Co, 1997),
  Blue Oboe (Wyndham Hall Pr, 1984), *Wind, Whiskey Island
  Mag, Comstock Rev, Denver Qtly, Laurel Rev, Vincent
  Brothers Rev, The Listening Eye, Poem, The Classical
  Outlook, Classical and Modern Lit*

Bill Garten ♪ ⊀   P
7673 Yennicook Way
Hudson, OH 44236, 330-808-4013
Internet: redlol2@aol.com
    Pubs: *Wild Sweet Notes: Anth* (Publisher's Place Inc, 2000),
*Rattle, Chaminade Lit Rev, Asheville Poetry Rev, Hawaii
Rev, Interim, Fish Stories, Boderlands, Blueline, Antietam
Rev, Portland Rev*

John Gerlach   P
140 Meadowhill Ln
Moreland Hills, OH 44022
    Pubs: *NAR, Ohio Rev, Prairie Schooner*

Elton Glaser ♪ ⊀   P
Univ of Akron Press, Akron, OH 44325-1703, 330-836-3388
Internet: eglaser@uakron.edu
    Pubs: *Pelican Tracks, Winter Amnesties* (Southern Illinois U
Pr, 2003, 2000), *Color Photographs of the Ruins* (U Pitt Pr,
1992), *Tropical Depressions* (U Iowa Pr, 1988), *Georgia
Rev, Parnassus, Poetry NW, Poetry*

William Greenway ♪ ⊀   P
English Dept, Youngstown State Univ, Youngstown, OH 44555,
330-742-3418
Internet: WillGreenway@aol.com
    Pubs: *Ascending Order, Simmer Dim, How the Dead Bury
the Dead* (U Akron, 2003, 1999, 1994), *Where We've Been*
(Breitenbush Bks, 1987), *Poetry, APR, Southern Rev, Poetry
NW, Prairie Schooner, Shenandoah*

Gordon Grigsby   P
625 Edgecliff Dr
Columbus, OH 43235, 614-847-1780
    Pubs: *Mid-Ohio Elegies* (Logan Elm Pr, 1985), *West Coast
Rev, SPR, Mickle Street Rev*

Jeff Gundy ♪ ⊀   P
Bluffton College, English Dept, Bluffton, OH 45817-1196,
419-358-3283
Internet: gundyj@bluffton.edu
    Pubs: *Rhapsody with Dark Matter* (Bottom Dog, 2000),
Flatlands (Cleveland State U Pr, 1995), *The Sun, NAR,
Georgia Rev, Exquisite Corpse, Laurel Rev*

Mark Halliday ♪ ⊀   P
English Dept, Ohio Univ, Athens, OH 45705, 740-593-2758
Internet: hallidam@ohio.edu
    Pubs: *Selfwolf* (U Chicago Pr, 1999), *Tasker Street* (U
Massachusetts Pr, 1992), *Little Star* (Morrow, 1987)

Yvonne Moore Hardenbrook   P
1757 Willow Way Cir N
Columbus, OH 43220, 614-459-4339
    Pubs: *Out of Season: Anth* (Amagansett Pr, 1993), *A
Gathering of Poets: Anth* (Kent State U Pr, 1992), *Amelia,
Brussels Sprout, Frogpond, Modern Haiku*

Donald M. Hassler ♪ ⊀   P
1226 Woodhill Dr
Kent, OH 44240, 330-672-2676
Internet: extrap@kent.edu
    Pubs: *A Gathering of Poets: Anth* (Kent State U Pr, 1992),
*The Finnish American, Extrapolation, Hellas, Tar River
Poetry, Onionhead, Above the Bridge, Hiram Poetry Rev,
Descant*

Laurie Henry   P
2824 Werk Rd
Cincinnati, OH 45211, 513-389-0303
Internet: henrylj@email.uc.edu
    Pubs: *Restoring the Chateau of the Marquis de Sade*
(Silverfish Rev Pr, 1985), *APR, Poetry NW*

Michelle Herman   W
Director, MFA Prog in Creative Writing, Ohio State Univ, 164 W
17 Ave, Columbus, OH 43210, 614-292-5767
Internet: herman.2@osu.edu
    Pubs: *A New & Glorious Life* (Carnegie Mellon U Pr, 1998),
Missing (Ohio State U, 1990), *Twenty Under Thirty: Anth*
(Scribner, 1986)

Terry Hermsen   P
25 Weber Rd
Columbus, OH 43202
    Pubs: *Child Aloft in Ohio Theatre, 36 Spokes: The Bicycle
Poems* (Bottom Dog Pr, 1995, 1985), *Images, Kansas Qtly,
The Plough, The Jrnl, Nimrod, Antigonish, Confluence,
Outerbridge, Hiram Poetry Rev, South Dakota Rev, Descant*

Garrison L. Hilliard   P&W
PO Box 25102
Cincinnati, OH 45225, 513-251-3747
www.efn.org/~garrison
    Pubs: *This Is a Romance (?)* (QCB Pr, 1994), *Minotaur, Aim,
Leatherneck, Small Pond, Innisfree*

Andrew Hudgins ♪ ⊀   P
Dept of English, Ohio State Univ, 421 Denny Hall, 164 W 17th
Ave, Columbus, OH 43210, 614-292-6065
    Pubs: *Babylon in a Jar* (Mariner Bks, 2001), *The Glass
Hammer: A Southern Childhood, The Never-Ending* (HM,
1994, 1991)

Robert Hudzik ♪ ⊀   P
403 Miami Ave
Terrace Park, OH 45174-1146, 513-248-2965
    Pubs: *From the Tree* (Alms Hse Pr, 1995), *Poetry, Poet Lore,
Cincinnati Poetry Rev, Slow Loris Reader, Hiram Poetry
Rev, Poetry NW*

Lynne Hugo 🎤 ✈ P&W
PO Box 454
Oxford, OH 45056, 513-523-4774
Internet: lynnephugo@aol.com
   Pubs: *Baby's Breath* (Synergistic Pr, 2000), *Swimming Lessons* (w/A.T. Villegas; Morrow, 1998), *A Progress of Miracles* (San Diego Poets Pr, 1993), *The Time Change* (Ampersand Pr, 1992), *The Qtly, Prairie Schooner, Cincinnati Poetry Rev, Mid-American Rev*

Bonnie Jacobson 🎤 ✈ P
24395 Shaker Blvd
Cleveland, OH 44122-2346, 216-831-1916
   Pubs: *In Joanna's House* (Cleveland State U Poetry Center, 1998), *Stopping for Time* (GreenTower Pr, 1989), *I Have My Own Song for It: Anth* (U of Akron, 2002), *Potpourri, Gettysburg Rev, Iowa Rev, Tar River Poetry*

Steven James Joyce P&W
60 Stewart Ave
Mansfield, OH 44906, 419-525-2780
Internet: joyce.3@osu.edu
   Pubs: *Intl Qtly, Minimus, Kimera*

Jack R. Justice P
9023 Shadetree Dr
Cincinnati, OH 45242, 513-793-1969
   Pubs: *Blue Unicorn, Sou'wester, Hampden-Sydney, Kentucky Poetry Rev, Stone Country, Wind, Samisdat*

Bella Briansky Kalter W
5 Lenox Ln
Cincinnati, OH 45229
   Pubs: *Lilian and Athena* (Xlibris, 2001), *Ohio's Heritage, American Israelite, U Kansas City Rev, St. Anthony Messenger, Backbone*

Daniel Kaminsky P
7116 Deveny Ave
Cleveland, OH 44105, 216-883-3683
   Pubs: *Snout to Snout, Voices of Cleveland: Anth* (Cleveland State U Pr, 1974, 1996), *Pig Iron*

J. Patrick Kelly 🎤 P
7336 Blue Boar Ct
Cincinnati, OH 45230-2181, 513-232-8962
   Pubs: *Touchstone, Son of Fat Tuesday, Ellipsis, Sierra Nevada Rev, Voices Intl, Bellowing Ark, Licking River Rev, Ascent, Mississippi Valley Rev, Louisville Rev*

Diane Kendig 🎤 ✈ P
235 Lexington Ave
Findlay, OH 45840-3709, 419-424-5965
Internet: kendig@mail.findlay.edu
   Pubs: *Tunnel of Flute Song* (Cleveland State U Pr, 1980), *Grrrr: Anth* (Arctos, 2000), *U.S. 1 Worksheets, Minnesota Rev, Cincinnati Poetry Rev, Kalliope*

Laura Ballard Kennelly 🎤 ✈ P
PO Box 626
Berea, OH 44017-0626, 216-243-4842
Internet: lkennelly@aol.com
   Pubs: *A Certain Attitude, A Measured Response* (Pecan Grove Pr, 1995, 1993), *Passage of Mrs. Jung* (Norton Coker Pr, 1990), *Redneck Rev, New Texas '92, La Carta De Oliver, San Jose Studies, Faultline, Ohio Writer*

Harley King P
875 Maple St
Perrysburg, OH 43551
Internet: hgking@aol.com
   Pubs: *Like a Hammer* (Mariposa Pr, 2002), *Mother Don't Lock Me in that Closet* (Keller U Pr, 1989), *Empty Playground* (K&K Communications, 1980)

Robert Kinsley 🎤 ✈ P
6 Old Peach Ridge Rd
Athens, OH 45701-1342, 740-597-2760
Internet: kinsley@ohio.edu
   Pubs: *Field Stones, Endangered Species* (Orchises Pr, 1997, 1989), *Yankee Mag, Tar River Poetry*

Christina Kiplinger Robinson P&W
PO Box 2729
Canton, OH 44720
Internet: christinarobinson@yahoo.com
   Pubs: *Aliens & Lovers* (Unique Graphics, 1985), *Undinal Songs, Footsteps*

Leonard Kress P
834 Louisiana Ave
Perrysburg, OH 43551, 419-872-0398
Internet: lkress@owens.cc.oh.us
   Pubs: *Sappho's Apples* (HarrowGate Pr, 2000), *Centralia Mine Fire* (Flume Pr, 1987), *From the Life & Death of Chopin* (Lalka, 1976), *APR, Missouri Rev, New Letters, Massachusetts Rev*

Lolette Beth Kuby P
English Dept, Cleveland State Univ, E 22 & Euclid Ave, Cleveland, OH 44115, 216-932-4842
   Pubs: *The Mama Stories* (Bottom Dog Pr, 1995), *In Enormous Water* (Cleveland State U Pr, 1981), *Midwest Qtly, American Scholar, Proteus, Caesura, Nightsun, The Long Story*

Wayne Kvam 🎤 ✈ P
Kent State Univ, English Dept, Kent, OH 44242, 216-672-2676
   Pubs: *Denver Qtly, Intl Poetry Rev, Centennial Rev, Exile: A Literary Qtly*

Denise Reynolds Laubacher P
422 East St
Minerva, OH 44657, 216-868-3808
   Pubs: *Collective Works 1983-1987, Incognito* (Adams, 1987, 1985), *Whiskey Island, Touchstone*

Edward Lense P
400 Piedmont Rd
Columbus, OH 43214
Internet: elense@att.net
    Pubs: *Buried Voices* (Logan Elm Pr, 1982), *The Spirit That Moves Us, Greenfield Rev, Antioch Rev, Cimarron Rev, AWP Chronicle*

Kenneth Leonhardt P&W
4644 Rumpke Rd
Cincinnati, OH 45245-1122
Internet: mteacher@skycorp.net
    Pubs: *Goners* (University Edtns, 1996), *Sex Scells* (Fithian Pr, 1994), *Light, Bogg, Iconoclast, Abbey, Lilliput Rev, Higginsville Reader*

Robert Lietz P
8780 Dostego Pike
Custar, OH 43511
Internet: r-lietz@onu.edu
    Pubs: *Running in Place, At Park & East Division* (L'Epervier, 1979, 1979)

Joel A. Lipman P
English Dept, Univ Toledo, Toledo, OH 43606-3390, 419-841-3733
    Pubs: *The Real Ideal* (Luna Bisonte, 1996), *Machete Chemistry/Panades Physics* (Cubola New Art, 1994), *Fiction Intl, Generator, Exquisite Corpse*

Ernest Lockridge W
143 W South St
Worthington, OH 43085, 614-885-8964
    Pubs: *Flying Elbows, Prince Elmo's Fire* (Stein & Day, 1975, 1974), *New Jrnl, Ohio Jrnl*

Sandra Love 🎤 ✈ W
898 E Hyde Rd
Yellow Springs, OH 45387, 937-767-2700
    Pubs: *Dive for the Sun* (HM, 1982), *Life on the Line: Anth* (Negative Capability Pr, 1992), *Iowa Woman, South Dakota Rev, Kansas Qtly*

R. Nikolas Macioci 🎤 ✈ P
1506 Frebis Ave
Columbus, OH 43206-3721
    Pubs: *Greatest Hits: 1986-2000* (Pudding House Pubs, 2001), *Why Dance?* (Singular Speech Pr, 1997), *Cafes of Childhood* (Event Horizon Pr, 1992), *Raintown Rev, Mad Poets Rev, Owen Wister Rev, Zone 3, Tampa Rev, Appalachee Qtly, Crazyquilt*

James Magner, Jr. P
John Carroll Univ, English Dept, Cleveland, OH 44118, 216-397-4221
    Pubs: *Rose of My Flowering Night, Till No Light Leaps* (Golden Quill Pr, 1985, 1981), *America*

Doug Martin P
English Dept, Bowling Green State Univ, Bowling Green, OH 43403, 419-352-2822
    Pubs: *RE:AL, James White Rev, Riverrun, B City, Wormwood, Soundings: A Jrnl of the Living Arts, Malcontent, Eidos*

Herbert Woodward Martin P
5193 Chapin St
Dayton, OH 45429-1905, 937-434-0969
Internet: herbert.martin@notes.udayton.edu
    Pubs: *In His Own Voice* (Ohio U Pr, 2002), *A Rock Against the Wind* (Berkley Pub Group, 1996), *Grand Street, Ploughshares, Chaminade Rev, Poetry, Crone's Nest*

Lee Martin 🎤 ✈ W
English Dept, Ohio State Univ, 164 West 17th Ave, Columbus, OH 43210-1370, 614-292-0648
Internet: martin.1199@osu.edu
    Pubs: *Quakertown, From Our House* (Dutton, 2001, 2000), *The Least You Need to Know* (Sarabande Bks, 1996), *Harper's, Georgia Rev, Story, DoubleTake, Glimmer Train*

Jack Matthews W
Ohio Univ, English Dept, Athens, OH 45701, 614-593-2757
    Pubs: *Ghostly Populations, Booking in the Heartland* (Johns Hopkins U Pr, 1986, 1986), *Kenyon Rev*

Wendell Mayo 🎤 ✈ W
English Dept, Bowling Green State Univ, Bowling Green, OH 43403, 419-372-7399
Internet: wmayo@bgnet.bgsu.edu
    Pubs: *B. Horror & Other Stories* (Livingston, 1999), *In Lithuanian Wood* (White Pine 1999), *Centaur of the North* (Arte Publico Pr, 1996), *City Wilds: Anth* (U Georgia Pr, 2002), *Harvard Rev, Threepenny Rev, Lit Rev, Missouri Rev, New Letters, Yale Rev, NAR*

Janet McAdams P&W
Kenyon College, English Dept, Gambier, OH 43022, 740-427-5206
Internet: McAdamsj@kenyon.edu
    Pubs: *The Island of Lost Luggage* (U Arizona Pr, 2000), *Crab Orchard Rev, Ascent Fall, Women's Rev of Books, Lullwater Rev*

Howard McCord 🎤 ✈ P&W
15431 Sand Ridge Rd
Bowling Green, OH 43402, 419-352-5549
Internet: texian555@aol.com
    Pubs: *McCord: The Poems* (Bloody Twin Pr, 2002), *Bone/Hueso* (Russell McKnight, 2000), *The Man Who Walked to the Moon* (McPherson & Co, 1997), *The Wisdom of Silenus* (St. Andrews Pr, 1996), *Thus Spake the Corpse, Vol. 2: Anth* (Black Sparrow Pr, 2000)

Robert E. McDonough 🎤 ✈ P
10581 State Rte 82
Windham, OH 44288
Internet: remcd@config.com
    Pubs: *No Other World* (Cleveland State U Pr, 1988),
*Minnesota Rev, Mississippi Valley Rev, Windless Orchard,
Cornfield Rev, West Branch*

Robert McGovern 🎤 ✈ P
935 CR 1754
Ashland, OH 44805, 419-289-0499
Internet: rgovern@ashland.edu
    Pubs: *Selected Poems, Scarecrow Poetry, A Feast of Flesh
& Other Occasions* (Ashland Poetry Pr, 2000, 1994, 1971),
*Nation, Kansas Qtly, Hiram Poetry Rev, New Laurel Rev,
Hollins Critic, Christian Century, Blue Unicorn*

Erin McGraw 🎤 ✈ W
English Dept, ML 69, Univ Cincinnati, Cincinnati,
OH 45221-0069, 513-556-0923
    Pubs: *Lies of the Saints* (Chronicle Bks, 1996), *Bodies at
Sea* (U Illinois Pr, 1989), *Georgia Rev, Southern Rev,
Ascent, Kenyon Rev, Atlantic*

William McLaughlin P
20865 Chagrin Blvd, #1
Cleveland, OH 44122, 216-752-8330
    Pubs: *At Rest in the Midwest* (Cleveland State U Pr, 1982),
*Amherst Rev, Black Fly Rev, Cape Rock, Oxford Mag, Inlet,
Nebo, Kansas Qtly*

Joseph McLaughlin 🎤 ✈ P&W
186 Pegasus Dr, NW
Dover, OH 44622-8609, 330-343-1602
Internet: JosephMcL@aol.com
    Pubs: *Greatest Hits: 1970-2000* (Pudding House, 2001),
Memory, In Your Country (Pale Horse Pr, 1995), *Ilya's
Honey, Poetry Midwest, Facets, Urban Spaghetti, The
Listening Eye, The Formalist, SPR, Hiram Poetry Rev*

William McMillen P
824 Oak Knoll Dr
Perrysburg, OH 43551, 419-874-1596
    Pubs: *NAR, Prairie Schooner, Black Warrior Rev, Ohio Jrnl*

Roberta Mendel 🎤 P
23511 Chagrin Blvd #519
Beachwood, OH 44122-5539, 216-378-2253
    Pubs: *Ritter's Writers are Blossoming: Anth* (Ritter Public
Library, 2000), *Indicting God: Anth* (Academic & Arts Pr,
1999), *Travels Through Time: Anth* (Creative With Words
Pub, 1998), *Mushroom Dreams, Writer's Ink, Mandrake,
Etcetera*

Larry Michaels 🎤 ✈ P
548 Robindale Ave
Toledo, OH 43616, 419-697-5550
Internet: michaelsOH@aol.com
    Pubs: *Parnassus, The Writer, Poetry Today, Prophetic
Voices, Piedmont Lit Rev, Wind, Orphic Lute, Lyric*

John N. Miller 🎤 ✈ P
428 W College St
Granville, OH 43023, 740-587-4432
    Pubs: *In the Western World* (Spoon River Poetry, 1979),
Articles of War: Anth (U Arkansas Pr, 1990), *Small Pond,
NAR, Bellowing Ark, Atlanta Rev, Passages North, Hawaii
Rev, Tar River Poetry, Chariton Rev*

Lloyd L. Mills P
English Dept, Kent State Univ, Kent, OH 44242, 330-673-6826
Internet: lmills@kent.edu
    Pubs: *Unreconciled Passions, Dry with a Twist: Anth* (Poets
League of Greater Cleveland, 1993, 1997), *Laughter & Dry
Mockery* (Commercial Pr, 1988), *Sics, New Laurel Rev,
Louisiana Rev, Blue Unicorn*

Robert Miltner 🎤 ✈ P&W
English Dept, Kent State Univ Stark Campus, 6000 Frank Rd
NW, Canton, OH 44720, 330-499-9600
Internet: rmiltner@stark.kent.edu
    Pubs: *Ghost of a Chance* (Zygote Pr, 2002), *Four Crows on
a Phone Line* (Spare Change Pr, 2002), *A Box of Light*
(Pudding Hse Pubs, 2002), *On the Off-Ramp* (Implosion Pr,
1996), *I Have My Own Song for It: Anth* (Akron U Pr, 2002),
Pleiades, EnterText, Diagram

Richard Morgan P
Ohio Dominican College, English Dept, 1216 Sunbury Rd,
Columbus, OH 43219, 614-846-0917
    Pubs: *Love & Anger* (ARN, 1982), *Tiger in the Air* (Blue Dog,
1979), *West Coast Rev, Rocky Mountain Rev*

Scott H. Mulrane P
1708 Bruck St
Columbus, OH 43207-1972
    Pubs: *Cincinnati Poetry Rev, Oxford Mag, Cream City Rev,
Sequoia, Galley Sail, Mudfish*

George Myers, Jr. W
The Columbus Dispatch, 34 S 3rd St, Columbus, OH 43215,
614-461-5265
    Pubs: *Jump Hope* (Cumberland, 1992), *Worlds Without End*
(Another Chicago Pr, 1990), *The Literary Rev, Seattle Rev,
Ploughshares, The Qtly, Gargoyle, NAW*

Alan Napier   P
3799 Olmsby Dr
Brimfield, OH 44240, 330-678-1686
Internet: sherlockarts@icgroup.net
    Pubs: *Atomic Ghost* (Coffee Hse Pr, 1995), *Fathers: A*
    Collection of Poems: Anth (St. Martin's Pr, 1997), *Hiram*
    Poetry Rev, SPR, Negative Capability, Colorado Rev, Key
    West Rev, Chelsea

James R. Nichols   W
Muskingum College, English Dept, New Concord, OH 43762,
614-826-8265
    Pubs: *Afterwords* (Intl U Pr, 1987), *Children of the Sea*
    (Blair, 1977), *Phoebe, Bitterroot, Encore*

Mwatabu Okantah 🎤 ✈   P
PO Box 13613
Akron, OH 44334, 330-672-0161
Internet: mokantah@kent.edu
    Pubs: *Cheikh Anta Diop: Poem for the Living* (Black History
    Museum/Umum Loh Pubs, 1997), *Collage* (Lotus Pr, 1984),
    Afreeka Brass (Cleveland State U, 1983)

Bea Opengart   P
1511 Chase Ave, Apt A
Cincinnati, OH 45223, 513-681-0729
    Pubs: *Erotica* (Owl Creek Pr, 1995), *American Voice, Iowa*
    Rev, Apalachee Qtly, The Jrnl, Shenandoah, Southern
    Humanities Rev

Gary Bernard Pacernick 🎤 ✈   P
English Dept, Wright State Univ, Dayton, OH 45409-2345,
513-873-3136
    Pubs: *The Jewish Poems* (Wright State U Pr, 1985),
    Wanderers (Prasada Pr, 1985), *Poetry East, APR, Ohio Rev,*
    Tikkun, NAR, Poetry Now

Janis L. Pallister 🎤   P
1249 Brownwood Dr
Bowling Green, OH 43402-3535, 419-353-9513
Internet: jpallis@dacor.net
    Pubs: *Shadows of Madness, At the Eighth Station, Sursum*
    Corda (Geryon, 1991, 1983, 1982), *Practices of the Wind:*
    Anth (Nicolas Kogon, 1997)

James Parlett   P
6878 Solon Blvd
Solon, OH 44139
    Pubs: *News of the Assassin* (Raincrow, 1978), *Atlantic,*
    Poetry NW, Cape Rock, En Passant

Nancy Pelletier   W
c/o Pansing, 624 5th St, Marietta, OH 45750-1910
    Pubs: *Happy Families* (Collins, 1986), *The Rearrangement*
    (Paperback-Paperbooks, 1986), *Twigs*

Jane Piirto 🎤 ✈   P&W
233 W Walnut St
Ashland, OH 44805-3148, 419-281-6516
Internet: jpiirto@ashland.edu
    Pubs: *A Location in the Upper Peninsula* (Sampo Pub,
    1994), *The Three-Week Trance Diet* (Carpenter Pr, 1986),
    South Dakota Rev, Denver Qtly

Frank Polite   P
2537 Ohio Ave
Youngstown, OH 44504, 216-746-3955
    Pubs: *Flamingo* (Pangborn Bks, 1990), *Letters of Transit*
    (City Miner, 1979), *Harper's, Nation, Free Lunch, New*
    Yorker, Exquisite Corpse, Ohio Rev

Lynn Powell 🎤 ✈   P
171 E College St
Oberlin, OH 44074-1770, 440-775-2276
Internet: lynn.powell@oberlin.edu
    Pubs: *Old & New Testaments* (U Wisconsin Pr, 1995),
    Southern Rev, Image, Seneca Rev, Poetry, Gettysburg Rev,
    Paris Rev

Robert Pringle 🎤 ✈   P
11210 Gorsuch Rd
Galena, OH 43021, 614-965-4158
    Pubs: *Cold Front* (Pudding Hse Pr, 1998), *Here's to*
    Humanity: Anth (The People's Pr, 2000), *Afterthoughts,*
    Orbis, Psychopoetica, Pudding Mag, Onionhead, Dream
    Intl Qtly, Poetry Motel, Envoi, Green's Mag, Paris/Atlantic,
    Vol. No.

Rose Mary Prosen   P
2300 Overlook Rd, #506
Cleveland Heights, OH 44106, 216-791-6145
    Pubs: *Ethnic Literature & Culture in the U.S.A.: Anth* (Peter
    Lang, 1996), *Voices of Cleveland: Anth* (Cleveland State U,
    1996), *Whiskey Island, Dry with a Twist, Writing Our Lives*

Nicholas Ranson 🎤 ✈   P
Univ Akron, English Dept, Akron, OH 44325-0001,
330-972-7606
Internet: nickranson@uakron.edu
    Pubs: *Track Made Good* (Bits Pr, 1977), *Mississippi Rev,*
    Lake Superior Rev, Wind

James Reiss 🎤 ✈   P
English Dept, Miami Univ, Bachelor Hall, Oxford,
OH 45056-3414, 513-529-5110
Internet: reissja@muohio.edu
    Pubs: *Ten Thousand Good Mornings, The Parable of Fire*
    (Carnegie Mellon, 2002, 1996), *The Breathers* (Ecco Pr,
    1974), *Atlantic, New Yorker, Poetry, Nation, New Republic,*
    Paris Rev

Peter Roberts 🎤 ✈ P
1205 Laurelwood Rd
Mansfield, OH 44907-2328, 419-756-1460
Internet: peterroberts@compuserve.com
    Pubs: *Skylark, Nebo, William & Mary Rev, Small Pond, Star*Line, NYQ, Confrontation, Beyond Baroque, Abbey, Frisson*

Linda Goodman Robiner 🎤 ✈ P&W
2648 S Belvoir Blvd
Cleveland, OH 44118-4661, 216-397-9473
Internet: lgrobiner@aol.com
    Pubs: *Reverse Fairy Tale* (Pudding Hse Pub, 1997), *Mothers & Daughters: Anth* (Harmony Bks, 2002), *We Used to Be Wives: Anth* (Fithian Pr, 2002), *Maryland Rev, North Atlantic Rev, Graham House Rev, Black River Rev, William & Mary Rev, CQ, Neovictorian*

Marge Rogers 🎤 ✈ P
5340 Silverdome Dr
Dayton, OH 45414-3648, 937-233-4822
Internet: Doma513@aol.com
    Pubs: *Memories of the Heart* (GWR Pr, 2002), *Lucidity, Hodge Podge, Common Threads, Poets at Work, Our Journey, Poetry in Motion, Byline Mag, Writers Block*

Bill Roorbach 🎤 ✈ P
English Dept, Ohio State Univ, 164 W 17 Ave, Columbus, OH
43215-1326, 614-292-0648
Internet: roorbach.1@osu.edu
    Pubs: *Harper's, Granta, Iowa Rev, Witness*

Lynne Carol Rose 🎤 ✈ P
3911 Tamara Dr
Grove City, OH 43123-2832, 614-871-5840
    Pubs: *Child of the Washed World* (American Studies Pr, 1984), *Kingdom of Three* (Green River, 1980)

J. Allyn Rosser 🎤 ✈ P
12750 Rich Ln
Athens, OH 45701-9011
Internet: rosserj@oak.cats.ohiou.edu
    Pubs: *Bright Moves* (Northeastern U Pr, 1990), *Ploughshares, Alaska Qtly Rev, Poetry, Paris Rev, Hudson Rev, Georgia Rev, Denver Qtly, Ontario Rev, Crazyhorse, Gettysburg Rev*

Joel Rudinger P
208 Ohio St
Huron, OH 44839-1514, 419-433-8151
    Pubs: *Lovers & Celebrations* (Dearborn Pr, 1984), *First Edition: 40 Poems* (Gull Pr, 1975)

Timothy Russell 🎤 ✈ W
202 Daniels St
Toronto, OH 43964-1340
Internet: timothyrussell@earthlink.net
    Pubs: *Adversaria* (TriQtly Bks/Northwestern U Pr, 1993), *Artful Dodge, Cincinnati Poetry Rev, Hiram Poetry Rev, Kestrel, Poetry, West Branch*

David Schloss 🎤 ✈ P
358 Bryant Ave, #1
Cincinnati, OH 45220-1628, 513-281-3551
Internet: schlosd@muohio.edu
    Pubs: *Sex Lives of the Poor & Obscure* (Carnegie Mellon Pr, 2002), *Legends* (Windmill Pr, 1976), *The Beloved* (Ashland Poetry Pr, 1973), *Poetry, Paris Rev, Western Humanities Rev, Iowa Rev, Antaeus*

Amy Jo Schoonover 🎤 ✈ P
3520 State Rte 56
Mechanicsburg, OH 43044-9714, 937-834-2666
    Pubs: *Amy Jo Schoonover's Greatest Hits* (Pudding House, 2001), *New & Used Poems* (Lake Shore Pub, 1988), *Kansas Qtly, Hiram Poetry Rev, Cape Rock, Negative Capability, Western Ohio Jrnl, Lyric, Limestone Circle*

Pearl Bloch Segall 🎤 P
425 Hunters Hollow SE
Warren, OH 44484-2367, 330-856-5565
    Pubs: *Amelia, Poetpourri, Pinehurst Jrnl*

Marilyn Weymouth Seguin 🎤 ✈ W
1830 Highbridge Rd
Cuyahoga Falls, OH 44223-1827, 330-928-6907
Internet: mseguin@kent.edu
    Pubs: *Where Duty Calls, Dogs of War, Silver Ribbon Skinny, The Bell Keeper, Song of Courage, Song of Freedom* (Branden Bks, 1999, 1997, 1996, 1995, 1993)

Christopher Seid P
3909 Criswell Dr
Columbus, OH 43220-4935
Internet: christopher_seid@excite.com
    Pubs: *Prayers to the Other Life* (Helicon Nine Edtns, 1997)

Joseph Semenovich P
6100 Laurent Dr
Cleveland, OH 44129-5973, 440-884-5887
    Pubs: *The Peter Poems* (Trout Creek Pr, 1984), *Prothalamion* (Textile Bridge Pr, 1982), *Webster Rev, Dog River Rev, Slipstream, Rain City Rev*

Tim Shay W
7227 Scottwood Ave
Cincinnati, OH 45237-3128
    Pubs: *Green's Mag, Short Stuff Mag, Prolific Writer, Fiction, Valley Views, Live Writers, Fiction Cincinnati*

Glenn Sheldon 🎤 ✈   P
3925 Watson Av
Toledo, OH 43612, 419-476-1578
Internet: gsheldon@utnet.utoledo.edu
Pubs: *Eagle or Beak* (Seffron Pub, 1995), *Wolves in Brown Wedding Gowns* (New Sins Pr, 1991), *Janus Head, CafÈ Rev, Puerto del Sol, Rio Grande Rev, Mudfish, Marquee, Spoon River Qtly, Limestone*

David Shevin 🎤 ✈   P
1453 N Broad St #6
Fairborn, OH 45324, 937-878-9320
Internet: shevin@compuserve.com
Pubs: *Three Miles from Luckey, Needles & Needs, Dunbar: Suns & Dominions: Anth* (Bottom Dog, 2002, 1994, 1999), *Growl & Other Poems: Anth* (Carpenter Pr, 1990), *Confluence, The Crisis, Exquisite Corpse, Tikkun, Descant, The Jrnl*

Kay Sloan   P&W
English Dept, Miami Univ, Oxford, OH 45056, 513-529-2227
Pubs: *Worry Beads* (Louisiana State U Pr, 1991), *Southern Exposure, Oxford Mag, Southern Rev, Pudding*

Monica E. Smith 🎤 ✈   P
8990 SR 287
West Liberty, OH 43357
Internet: monica@expressocafe.org
Pubs: *Steel Point Qtly, Skyline Pubs, Poesy, Jrnl of Modern Writing, Story House Pr, Lucid Moon, Ibbetson Street Pr*

Larry Smith   P&W
Firelands College of BGSU, English Dept, Huron, OH 44839, 419-433-5560x20663
Internet: lsmithdog@aol.com
Pubs: *Thoreau's Lost Journal* (Westron, 2001), *Beyond Rust* (Bottom Dog Pr, 1995), *Steel Valley: Postcards & Letters* (Pig Iron Pr, 1993), *Utne Reader, Shambhala Sun, Parabola, Heartlands Today, Humanist*

Francis J. Smith   P
John Carroll Univ, 20700 N Park Blvd, Rodman Hall, University Heights, OH 44118, 216-397-4546
Pubs: *All Is a Prize* (Pterodactyl Pr, 1989), *First Prelude* (Loyola U Pr, 1981), *America, Light, College English, Aethlon*

Tricia Springstubb   W
1816 Wilton Rd
Cleveland Heights, OH 44118
Pubs: *Two Plus One Goes Ape, Two Plus One Makes Trouble* (Scholastic, 1995, 1991)

John Stickney   P
4545 W 214
Cleveland, OH 44126
Pubs: *Rampike, Caliban, Generator, Mississippi Rev, NYQ, Semiotext(e), Exquisite Corpse, Atticus Rev*

Gloria Still   P
1439 Alameda Ave
Lakewood, OH 44107-4920
Pubs: *Free Songs* (Writers' Center Pr, 1992), *Indiana Rev, Hopewell Rev, Woman Poet, Arts Indiana Literary Supplement, Passages in Nonviolence*

Terry Stokes 🎤 ✈   P&W
PO Box 19359
Cincinnati, OH 45219, 513-556-0939
Pubs: *Sportin' News* (Raccoon Bks, 1985), *Intimate Apparel* (Release Pr, 1980), *Issuing of Scars* (Bartholomew's Cobble, 1981), *Paris Rev, Gettysburg Rev, Hanging Loose*

Myrna Stone 🎤 ✈   P
6526 Jaysville-St Johns Rd
Greenville, OH 45331
Internet: myrnastone@woh.rr.com
Pubs: *I Have My Own Song for It: Modern Poems of Ohio: Anth* (U of Akron Pr, 2002), *Flora Poetica: The Chatto Book of Botanical Verse: Anth* (Chatto & Windus, 2001), *The Art of Loss* (MI U Pr, 2001), *Nimrod, River Styx, Poetry, Ploughshares, Green Mtns Rev*

Lorraine J. Sutton   P
914 Franklin Ave
Columbus, OH 43205
Pubs: *Saycred Laydy* (Sunbury Pr, 1975), *Ms., Latin New York, Conditions, West End*

Charles A. Taormina   P&W
860 Chalker St
Akron, OH 44310-2116, 330-434-5106
Pubs: *Moments* (1st Bks, 1998), *Rain Folio* (Renaissance Workshop, 1998), *Blue Ridge Rev, Gargoyle, William & Mary Rev, Samisdat, Fool's Jrnl*

Robert L. Tener 🎤   P
PO Box 182
Rootstown, OH 44272-0182
Pubs: *A Dialogue of Marriage* (Plowman, 1989), *Laughter & Dry Mockery* (Kent, 1988), *Blue Unicorn, Green's Mag, Studies in Contemporary Satire*

James Thomas 🎤 ✈   W
802 Green St
Yellow Springs, OH 45387-1409, 937-767-9445
Internet: green802@aol.com
Pubs: *Pictures, Moving* (Dragon Gate, 1986), *Flash Fiction: Anth, Sudden Fiction: Anth* (Norton, 1996, 1994), *Carolina Qtly, Esquire, Cimarron, Epoch, Mississippi Rev, Crazyhorse*

Sharon Thomson ♀ ✈ PP&P
932 O'Bannonville Rd.
Loveland, OH 45140, 513-683-2340
Internet: sharonthomson@juno.com
  Pubs: *Sharon Thomson Greatest Hits 1973-2000, Home Again* (Pudding Hse, 2001, 2000), *Many Lights in Many Windows: Anth, Writer's Community: Anth* (Milkweed Edtns, 1997, 1997), *Grailville Poets: Anth* (Grailville, 1995), *Aspect, Poetry, Pequod, Anthenaeum*

John Thorndike ♀ ✈ W
13034 McDougal Rd
Athens, OH 45701-9731
Internet: johnthorndike@compuserve.com
  Pubs: *Another Way Home* (Crown, 1996), *The Potato Baron* (Villard, 1989), *Anna Delaney's Child* (Macmillan, 1986)

Caroline Totten W
140 Santa Clara NW
Canton, OH 44709, 330-493-0913
Internet: caltotn@aol.com
  Pubs: *Venture: Ohio Voices: Anth* (Creative Works Pubs, 2002), *Montage* (Media Turf, 1997), *Best of 1995 Ohio Poetry: Anth* (Ohio Poetry Day Assn, 1995), *Insight, Remington Rev*

Ann Townsend ♀ ✈ P
Denison Univ, English Dept, Granville, OH 43023, 740-587-6331
Internet: townsend@denison.edu
  Pubs: *Dime Store Erotics* (Silverfish Rev Pr, 1998), *New American Poets: Anth* (U Pr New England, 2000), *New Young American Poets: Anth* (Southern Illinois U Pr, 2000), *Poetry, The Nation, Georgia Rev, Southern Rev*

Leonard Trawick ♀ ✈ P
Cleveland State Univ, English Dept, Cleveland, OH 44115
Internet: l.trawick@csuohio.edu
  Pubs: *Greatest Hits: 1965-2000* (Pudding House Pubs, 2001), *Beastmorfs* (Cleveland State U Poetry Ctr, 1994), *Sometime the Cow Kick Your Head: Anth* (Bits Pr, 1988), *Laurel Rev, Poetry, BPJ, Phase & Cycle*

Alberta T. Turner P
482 Caskey Ct
Oberlin, OH 44074, 440-775-7844
  Pubs: *Beginning with And: New & Selected Poems* (Bottom Dog Pr, 1994), *Responses to Poetry* (Longman, 1990), *Stand, The Jrnl, South Carolina Rev, American Lit Rev*

Jim Villani P&W
Pig Iron Press, PO Box 237, Youngstown, OH 44501, 216-783-1269
  Pubs: *Moment in Bronze, Stars on Lake* (Fantome Pr, 1990, 1989), *Cincinnati Poetry Rev, Salome*

Diane Vreuls W
131 Sycamore
Oberlin, OH 44074, 216-774-1737
  Pubs: *Let Us Know* (Viking, 1986), *Are We There Yet?* (Avon, 1976), *New Yorker, Paris Rev, Massachusetts Rev*

F. Keith Wahle P
3357 Citrus Ln
Cincinnati, OH 45239, 513-923-3136
  Pubs: *A Choice of Killers* (Morgan Pr, 1998), *Almost Happy* (Rumba Train, 1980), *The Qtly, Yellow Silk, Cincinnati Poetry Rev*

Mary E. Weems P
10602 Lamountier Ave
Cleveland, OH 44104-4848
  Pubs: *White* (Wick Chapbook Kent State U Pr, 1997), *Fembles* (The Heartlands Today, 1996), *Blackeyed* (Burning Pr, 1994), *A Hole in the Ghetto: Anth* (CSU Poetry Ctr, 1995), *Pearl, Listening Eye*

Etta Ruth Weigl P
56 Kendal Dr
Oberlin, OH 44074, 216-774-6101
  Pubs: *Seventh Age, Meltwater* (Stereopticon Pr, 1988, 1982), *Poetry Now, And, Williwaw*

William Wells ♀ ✈ P
4240 Campus Dr
Lima, OH 45804-3576, 419-995-8213
Internet: wellswalt@tec.oh.us
  Pubs: *Conversing with the Light* (Anhinga Pr, 1988), *Prairie Schooner, Hudson Rev, Denver Qtly, Ohio Rev, Boulevard, Poetry NW, SPR, Poetry East, Stand, Cimarron Rev, Yale Rev, Poetry Durham*

Dallas Wiebe ♀ ✈ W
582 McAlpin Ave
Cincinnati, OH 45220-1534, 513-281-4767
  Pubs: *Our Asian Journey* (Canada; MLR Edtns, 1997), *Going to the Mountain, The Transparent Eye-Ball & Other Stories* (Burning Deck, 1988, 1982), *Paris Rev, NAR, First Intensity*

Austin Wright ♀ ✈ W
601 Maple Trace
Cincinnati, OH 45246, 513-782-6413
Internet: austin.wright@uc.edu
  Pubs: *Disciples, Telling Time, After Gregory, Tony & Susan* (Baskerville, 1997, 1995, 1994, 1993), *Recalcitrance, Faulkner & the Professors* (U Iowa Pr, 1990)

Laura Yeager ♀ ✈ W
3788 Kay Dr
Stow, OH 44224, 330-686-0760
Internet: lauried710@att.net
  Pubs: *NAR, Ohio Short Fiction, Kaleidoscope, Paris Rev, Missouri Rev*

David Young 🎤 ✈   P
English Dept, Oberlin College, Oberlin, OH 44074,
216-775-8576
Internet: david.young@oberlin.net
   Pubs: *At the White Window, Seasoning, Night Thoughts &
   Henry Vaughn* (Ohio State U Pr, 2000, 1999, 1994)

Thomas Young 🎤 ✈   P
2658 N 4 St
Columbus, OH 43202-2404, 614-267-1682
Internet: tygertom2@cs.com
   Pubs: *Binary Alliances: A Novel of the Information Age*
   (Xlibris, 2000), *Ohio Jrnl, Waves, Graffiti, You Gotta Suit Up
   for 'Em All, The Smudge*

Nancy Zafris   W
71 E Lincoln St
Columbus, OH 43215, 614-228-7251
Internet: nancy_zafris@msn.com
   Pubs: *Into the Silence* (Green Street Pr, 1998), *Did My
   Mama Like to Dance?* (Avon Bks, 1994), *The People I Know*
   (U Georgia Pr, 1990), *Kenyon Rev, Witness, Missouri Rev*

Nancy Zafris   W
71 East Lincoln Street
Columbus, OH 43215
Internet: nancy_zafris@msn.com
   Pubs: *The People I Know* (U of GA, 1990), *Wind, Story Qtly,
   Black Warrior Rev, Alaska Qtly Rev*

Zena Zipporah   P
3544 Fairmount Blvd
Shaker Heights, OH 44118-4354, 216-932-1547
   Pubs: *In the Sacred Manner of the Buffalo, Lost Tribes,
   Victoriana-In Love with Words* (Zipporah, 1989, 1988, 1987),
   Akros Rev

OKLAHOMA

Ivy Bloch   P
2109 E 25 Pl
Tulsa, OK 74114-2917, 918-742-8293
   Pubs: *Midwest Qtly, Plainsong, Nimrod, Chariton Rev, SPR,
   Mississippi Valley Rev*

William J. Bly   P
2701 S Juniper Ave, #101
Broken Arrow, OK 74012-7731
   Pubs: *Memories of Second Street, Land of the Living* (Pine
   Woods Pr, 1986, 1985), *Poetry Now*

Alfred Corn   P&W
Oklahoma State University, Dept of English, 205 Morrill Hall,
Stillwater, OK 74078-4069, 405-744-9473
Internet: Verb3k@aol.com
   Pubs: *Part of his Story* (Mid-List Pr, 1997), *Present*
   (Counterpoint, 1997), *Autobiographies, The West Door*
   (Viking Penguin, 1992, 1988), *Notes from a Child of
   Paradise* (Viking, 1984), *A Call in the Midst of a Crowd*
   (Viking, 1978)

Mark Cox   P
Oklahoma State Univ, English Dept, 205 Morrill, Stillwater, OK
74078, 405-744-9474
Internet: markcox@okstate.edu
   Pubs: *Thirty-Seven Years from the Stone* (U Pitt Pr, 1998),
   Smoulder (Godine, 1989), *Poetry, APR, NER, NAR, Poetry
   East, Poetry NW*

J. Madison Davis   W
1112 Lincoln Green
Norman, OK 73072-7521, 405-447-3756
   Pubs: *Red Knight, Bloody Marko, White Rook* (Walker & Co,
   1992, 1991, 1990), *Conversations with Robertson Davies* (U
   Mississippi Pr, 1989)

George Economou 🎤 ✈   P
1401 Magnolia St
Norman, OK 73072-6827, 405-364-5797
   Pubs: *Century Dead Center & Other Poems* (Left Hand Bks,
   1997), *Harmonies & Fits* (Point Riders, 1987), *Backwoods
   Broadsides, Cover, Grand Street, Poetry NY, Sulfur, Texture,
   ACM, APR*

Toni Graham 🎤 ✈   W
118 Payne St
Stillwater, OK 74074, 405-624-2864
   Pubs: *The Daiquiri Girls* (U Massachusetts Pr, 1998),
   *Meridian, Beloit Fiction Jrnl, Other Voices, Chiron Rev,
   Mississippi Rev, American Fiction, Ascent, Clockwatch Rev,
   Worcester Rev, Green Mountains Rev, Writers' Forum,
   Mississippi Mud, The Bridge*

Arn Henderson   P
1208 Barkley Ave
Norman, OK 73071, 405-364-6770
   Pubs: *Document for an Anonymous Indian, The Point Riders
   Great Plains Poetry Anth* (Point Riders Pr, 1974, 1982)

Geary Hobson 🎤 ✈   P&W
English Dept, Univ Oklahoma, Norman, OK 73019-0240,
405-325-6231
Internet: geary.hobson-1@ou.edu
   Pubs: *The Last of the OFos* (U Arizona Pr, 2000),
   Aniyunwiya (Greenfield Rev Pr, 1995), *Deer Hunting &
   Other Poems* (Point Riders Pr, 1990), *The Remembered
   Earth* (U New Mexico Pr, 1981), *Rampike, Crisp Blue
   Edges, Quilt, Nimrod*

Sherry Lachance   P
4765 SE 23
Del City, OK 73115

Mary McAnally 🎤 ✈   P
76 N Yorktown
Tulsa, OK 74110-5214, 918-583-3651
    Pubs: *Stations* (Pemmican, 1995), *Fat Poems* (Cardinal Pr,
    1990), *Coming of Age in Oklahoma* (Point Riders Pr, 1985),
    The Absence of the Father & the Dance of the Zygotes
    (Shadow Pr, 1981), *Poems from the Animal Heart* (Full
    Court Pr, 1979)

Susan Smith Nash   P&W
3760 Cedar Ridge Dr
Norman, OK 73072-4621, 405-366-7730
    Pubs: *Liquid Babylon* (Potes & Poets, 1994), *The Airport Is
    My Etude* (Paradigm Pr, 1993), *Pornography* (Generator Pr,
    1992), *o.blek, Washington Rev, ACM, Aerial*

Perry Oldham   P
2940 Huntleigh Dr
Oklahoma City, OK 73120
    Pubs: *Higher Ground* (Mercury Pr, 1987), *Vinh Long*
    (Northwoods, 1977)

Rochelle Owens 🎤 ✈   P
1401 Magnolia
Norman, OK 73072-6827, 405-364-5797
    Pubs: *Luca: Discourse on Life & Death, New & Selected
    Poems 1961-1996* (Junction Pr, 2000, 1997), *Poems for the
    New Millennium Vol. 2: Anth* (U California Pr, 1998), *Sulfur,
    Abacus, Talisman, Temblor, ACM, Texture*

G. Palmer, Jr.   P
Rte 3
Carnegie, OK 73015, 405-654-2353
    Pubs: *American Indian Literature Anth* (U Oklahoma Pr,
    1979)

Alice Lindsay Price 🎤 ✈   P
3113 S Florence Ave
Tulsa, OK 74105-2407, 918-748-4411
    Pubs: *Cranes* (La Alameda Pr, 2001), *Swans of the World*
    (Council Oak Bks, 1994), *Our Dismembered Shadow* (Ena
    Pr, 1980), *Nimrod, Rhino, Commonweal, Phoenix*

S. David Price   P
2542 NW 12
Oklahoma City, OK 73107-5418
    Pubs: *Summer Snow* (Daybreak, 1977), *Joyful Noise, Texas
    Rev, Writer, Encore, Driftwood East, Counsel*

Francine Ringold 🎤 ✈   P
3215 S Yorktown
Tulsa, OK 74105, 918-745-9234
Internet: RINGOLDFI@CS.COM
    Pubs: *Every Other One* (Coman & Assoc, 2000), *The
    Trouble with Voices: Selected Poetry, Making Your Own
    Mark: A Guide to Creative Writing and Drawing for Senior
    Citizens* (Council Oak Bks, 1995, 1989), *Nimrod, Phoenix,
    Borderlands, Puerto del Sol, SW Rev*

Paul B. Solyn   P
525 49th St
Oklahoma City, OK 73118
    Pubs: *Mistress Quickly's Garden* (Raintree Pr, 1978), *New
    Letters, Minnesota Rev, Northeast*

Tim Tharp   W
800 N Mission Rd, #4
Okmulgee, OK 74447
    Pubs: *Falling Dark* (Milkweed Edtns, 1999)

Gordon Weaver   P&W
Cimarron Review, English Dept, Oklahoma State Univ,
Stillwater, OK 74078, 405-744-6140
    Pubs: *Men Who Would Be Good* (TriQtly Bks, 1991), *Manoa,
    TriQtly*

Carolyne Wright 🎤 ✈   P&W
University of Oklahoma, English Dept., Norman,
OK 73019-0240, 405-329-8259
Internet: carolyne.eulene@juno.com
    Pubs: *Under the Sign of Cancer* (Invisible Cities, 2003),
    Seasons of Mangos & Brainfire (Lynx Hse Pr, 2000), *Poets
    of the New Century: Anth* (Godine, 2001), *Like Thunder:
    Anth* (U Iowa Pr, 2002), *Michigan Qtly Rev, New England
    Rev, NAR, New Yorker, Iowa Rev*

OREGON

Howard Aaron   P
2428 NE 20
Portland, OR 97212, 503-282-4904
    Pubs: *Retina* (Confluence Pr, 1979), *What the Worms
    Ignore . . .* (Jawbone Pr, 1979), *Porch*

Diana Abu-Jaber 🎤 ✈   W
Dept. of English, Portland State Univ, Portland, OR 97207
    Pubs: *Crescent* (Norton, 2003), *Arabian Jazz* (HB, 1993)

Duane Ackerson 🎤 ✈   P&W
1850 Corina Dr SE
Salem, OR 97302-1624, 503-581-9075
Internet: ackerson@navicom.com
    Pubs: *The Bird at the End of the Universe* (TM Pr, 1997),
    The Eggplant (Confluence Pr, 1977), *Yankee, NW Rev,
    Chelsea, Prairie Schooner, CSM*

Cathy Ackerson 🎤 ✈   P
1850 Corina Dr SE
Salem, OR 97302-1624, 503-581-9075
Internet: ackerson@navicom.com
    Pubs: *Poets West: Anth* (Perivale Pr, 1976), *But Is It
Poetry?: Anth* (Dragonfly Pr, 1972), *Dragonfly, Caprice,
Outpost, Out of Sight, NW Rev*

Henry Melton Alley 🎤 ✈   W
Honors College, 1293 Univ Oregon, Eugene, OR 97403,
541-346-2513
Internet: halley@oregon.uoregon.edu
    Pubs: *Umbrella of Glass* (Breitenbush Bks, 1988), *The
Lattice* (Ariadne Pr, 1986), *Clackamas Lit Rev, Virginia Qtly
Rev, Seattle Rev*

Erland Anderson 🎤 ✈   P
565 Fairview
Ashland, OR 97520, 541-482-4029
Internet: eand1@aol.com
    Pubs: *Searchings for Modesto* (Talent Hse Pr, 1993),
Moorpark Rev, American Scholar, Calapooya Collage

Dori Appel   P&W
PO Box 1364
Ashland, OR 97520, 541-482-2735
Internet: applcart@mind.net
    Pubs: *Girl Talk* (w/Myers; Samuel French, 1992), *At Our
Core: Anth, Grow Old Along with Me: Anth* (Papier-Mache
Pr, 1998, 1996), *Prairie Schooner, Yankee, Ascent, Calyx,
Southern Humanities, Kalliope*

Lois Baker 🎤 ✈   P&W
6819 SW 32 Ave
Portland, OR 97219-1826, 503-244-1826
Internet: lbaker@imagina.com
    Pubs: *Tracers* (Howlett Pr, 1992), *Partial Clearing* (Press-22,
1976), *Playing With a Full Deck: Anth* (26 Bks, 1999),
*Poetry, Poetry NW, Prism Intl, Calyx, Penthouse, Colorado
State Qtly*

Tim Barnes   P
Portland Community College, PO Box 19000, Portland, OR
97280-0990, 503-977-4638
Internet: tbarnes@zeus.cc.pcc.edu
    Pubs: *Falling Through Leaves* (Marino Pr, 1995), *Star Hill
Farm & the Grain of What Is Gone* (Skookum's Tongue Pr,
1994), *Fine Madness, Puerto del Sol*

Judith Barrington 🎤 ✈   P
622 SE 29 Ave
Portland, OR 97214-3026, 503-236-9862
Internet: soapston@teleport.com
    Pubs: *History & Geography, Trying to Be an Honest
Woman* (8th Mtn Pr, 1989, 1985), *Poetry London, GSU
Rev, Stand, Chattahoochee Rev, Americas Rev, Rialto,
Kenyon, Sonora, American Voice, Ploughshares, Women's
Rev of Bks, 13th Moon*

Elizabeth Bartlett   P
5550 Bethel Heights Rd NW
Salem, OR 97304-9730
    Pubs: *Around the Clock* (St. Andrews, 1989), *Candles*
(Autograph Edtns, 1988), *Harper's, Virginia Qtly, Denver
Qtly, Ellery Queen's Qtly, NAR, Literary Rev, National Forum*

M. F. Beal 🎤 ✈   W
PO Box 161
Seal Rock, OR 97376-0161
    Pubs: *Angel Dance* (Crossing Pr, 1990), *End of Days* (H&R,
1982), *West Coast Fiction: Anth* (Bantam, 1979), *Atlantic,
Paris Rev, Calyx, Caprice*

David Biespiel 🎤 ✈   P
The Attic, 4423 SE Hawthorne, Portland, OR 97215-3164,
503-963-8783
    Pubs: *Shattering Air* (BOA Edtns, 1996)

Kathleen M. Bogan   P
3523 SW Jerald Ct
Portland, OR 97201, 503-228-5663
    Pubs: *Prairie Hearts: Women's Writings on the Midwest:
Anth* (Feminist Writers Guild, 1996), *Convolvulus,
Confrontation, Writers' Forum, Alaska Qtly Rev, Encodings*

Karen Braucher 🎤 ✈   P
3326 SW 64 Pl
Portland, OR 97221, 503-291-1431
Internet: braucher@portlandia.com
    Pubs: *Sending Messages Over Inconceivable Distances,
Heaven's Net* (Bacchae Pr, 2000, 1997), *Spoon River
Poetry Rev, Nimrod*

Robert Brown   P
The Bacchae Press, 10 6th St, Ste 215, Astoria, OR 97103
Internet: rbrown@oregonreview.com
    Pubs: *Sleepwalking with Mayakovsky* (Kent State U Pr,
1994), *Poem, ELF, Poetry NW, New Virginia Rev, Kansas
Qtly*

Julie Brown   W
1434 6 St
Astoria, OR 97103-5315
    Pubs: *Indiana Rev, Southern Rev, Madison Rev, Hayden's
Ferry Rev, Cream City Rev, Michigan Rev*

Douglas G. Campbell 🎤   P
9310 SW 18 Pl
Portland, OR 97219-6456, 503-246-3286
Internet: dcampbell@georgefox.edu
    Pubs: *When the Wind Stops* (Counterpoint Pub, 1992), *In
Our Own Voices: Anth* (Oregon Writers Colony, 1986), *River
Sedge, Rockhurst Rev, The Dakota, This, Voices in the
Wilderness, Gravida, A New Song*

Henry Carlile 🎤 ✈   P&W
7349 SE 30 Ave
Portland, OR 97202-8836, 503-774-0944
Internet: hcarlile@spiritone.com
 Pubs: *Rain* (Carnegie Mellon, 1994), *Running Lights*
 (Dragon Gate, 1981), *Southern Rev, Poetry, Crazyhorse,*
 Shenandoah, Ohio Rev, APR

Deb Casey   P
Academic Learning Services, Univ Oregon, Eugene, OR
97403, 503-346-3226
Internet: wkcasey@oregon.uoregon.edu
 Pubs: *Daredevil Research* (Peter Lang Pub, 1997), *For a*
 Living: Anth (U Illinois Pr, 1995), *Zyzzyva, Kenyon Rev,*
 River Styx, Ploughshares, Massachusetts Rev, Prairie
 Schooner, Graham Hse Rev, Calyx

Kent Clair Chamberlain 🎤 ✈   P&W
625 Holly St
Ashland, OR 97520-2927
 Pubs: *Phaer Wind* (Pauper Pr, 1992), *Rarely Published*
 (Blue Willow Pr, 1977), *Voodoo Souls Qtly, Promise/Purple*
 Rose Pubs, Lyriklife, Current Accounts/Bank Street Writers,
 Object Lesson, Atrocity, Danger, GSC, Ozark Muse, Muse
 Letter, Carpe Laureate Diem

Leonard Cirino 🎤 ✈   P
685 9th St
Springfield, OR 97477, 541-345-9635
Internet: ljcpfp@msn.com
 Pubs: *War Horses, The Sane Man Speaks* (Anabasis, 2000,
 2000), *American Minotaur, 96 Sonnets Facing Conviction,*
 The Terrible Wilderness of Self (Cedar Hill Pub, 2000, 1999,
 1998), *Henry's Will* (Mandrake Pr, 1995), *Amherst Rev,*
 Grasslimb, Lungfish

Walt Curtis 🎤 ✈   P&W
306 NE Holman
Portland, OR 97211, 503-285-8279
Internet: waltcurtis@hotmail.com
 Pubs: *Salmon Song* (26 Bks, 1995), *Journey Across*
 America, The Roses of Portland (Out of the Ashes Pr, 1979,
 1975), *Rhymes for Alice Blue Light* (Lynx Hse, 1984),
 Mississippi Mud, Mr Cogito, Gay Sunshine, Atlantic

Annie Dawid 🎤 ✈   P&W
0615 SW Palatine Hill Rd, #58
Portland, OR 97219-7879, 503-768-7405
Internet: david@lclark.edu
 Pubs: *Lily in the Desert* (Carnegie Mellon, 2001), *York Ferry*
 (Cane Hill Pr, 1993), *American Fiction: Anth* (New Rivers Pr,
 1999), *Beyond Lament: Anth* (Northwestern U Pr, 1998),
 Arts & Letters, Phoebe, Art & Academe, Toyon

Steven Dimeo 🎤   W
800 NE 3 Ave
Hillsboro, OR 97124-2321, 503-640-1375
 Pubs: *Great Midwestern Qtly, Indigenous Fiction,*
 Uncommon Reader, Wildfire, Seattle Times, Michigan Qtly
 Rev, Amazing Stories, Descant, Crosscurrents

Thomas Doulis   W
2236 NE Regents Dr
Portland, OR 97212, 503-287-3484
Internet: hhtd@odin.ccpdx.edu
 Pubs: *Landmarks of Our Past* (Holy Trinity, 1983), *Toward*
 the Authentic Church: Anth (Light & Life, 1996)

Barbara Drake 🎤 ✈   P&W
6104 NW Lilac Hill Rd
Yamhill, OR 97148-8328, 503-662-3373
Internet: bdrake@linfield.edu
 Pubs: *Peace at Heart* (Oregon State U Pr, 1998), *Space*
 Before A (26 Bks, 1996), *Bees in Wet Weather* (Canoe Pr,
 1992), *What We Say to Strangers* (Breitenbush, 1986),
 Portland Lights: Anth (Nine Lights, 1999), *Sumac Reader:*
 Anth (MSU Pr, 1997)

Albert Drake   P&W
9727 SE Reedway St
Portland, OR 97266-3738, 503-771-6779
 Pubs: *Fifties Flashback* (Fisher Bks, 1999), *Flat Out,*
 Herding Goats (Flat Out, 1994, 1989), *Epoch, Best*
 American Short Stories

David Elsey 🎤 ✈   P
2139 W Burnside, #202
Portland, OR 97210-5543, 503-241-5404
 Pubs: *Gray Light* (Smellfeast, 1995), *Off the Beaten Track:*
 Anth (Quiet Lion Pr, 1992), *Poetry Now, Hubbub, Small*
 Pond Rev, Gryphon, Rhino

Pat Enders   P
Clackamas Press, 21730 SE Hwy 224, Clackamas, OR 97015
 Pubs: *Pioneer Woman, Poetry Oregon, St. Andrews Rev*

Elizabeth Engstrom 🎤 ✈   W
598 Brookside Drive
Eugene, OR 97405, 541-484-1682
Internet: liz@elizabethengstrom.com
 Pubs: *Suspicions* (Triple Tree, 2002), *Lizard Wine* (Dell,
 1995), *Nightmare Flower* (TOR, 1992), *Fantasy & Sci Fi*
 Mag, Cemetery Dance, Bone

Tess Enroth   P&W
8222 SW Capitol Hwy
Portland, OR 97219-3625, 503-977-2539
Internet: tessmce@aol.com
 Pubs: *Her Soul Beneath the Bone: Anth* (U Illinois Pr, 1988),
 Cottonwood, Lake Effect, Wide Open Mag

Garrett Epps   W
Univ Oregon School of Law, Eugene, OR 97403
    Pubs: *The Floating Island* (HM, 1985), *The Shad Treatment*
(Putnam, 1977)

Esther Erford   P
1313 Lincoln St, #1002
Eugene, OR 97401-3965
    Pubs: *South Coast Poetry Jrnl, Connecticut River Rev,*
Galley Sail Rev, Slant, Voices Intl

Alice Evans   P&W
4635 Larkwood St
Eugene, OR 97405-3987
    Pubs: *Solo: Women Going It Alone in the Wilderness: Anth,*
Another Wilderness: New Outdoor Writing By Women: Anth
(Seal Pr, 1996, 1994), *Clinton Street Qtly*

Sandra Foushee 🎤 ✈   P
PO Box 541
Manzanita, OR 97130-0541, 503-717-0112
    Pubs: *The Light That Stops Us* (Night Sky, 1990), *Back to*
Essentials (Bristlecone Pr, 1984), *Seattle Rev,*
Ploughshares, Poetry & Prose, Westwind Rev, Prairie
Schooner

Vi Gale   P&W
Prescott Street Press, PO Box 40312, Portland,
OR 97240-0312, 503-254-2922
    Pubs: *Odd Flowers & Short Eared Owls, Prescott Street*
Reader: Anth (Prescott Street Pr, 1984, 1995), *Clearwater*
(Swallow, 1974)

Ken Gerner   P
PO Box 10881
Portland, OR 97210
    Pubs: *Throwing Shadows* (Copper Canyon Pr, 1985),
CutBank, Willow Springs

Martha Gies 🎤 ✈   W
2109 NE Rodney Ave
Portland, OR 97212-3739, 503-287-4394
    Pubs: *A Celestial Omnibus: Anth* (Beacon Pr, 1997),
Storming Heaven's Gate: Anth (Plume/Penguin, 1997), *The*
World Begins Here: Anth (Oregon State U Pr, 1993), *The*
Time of Our Lives: Anth (Crossing Pr, 1993), *Orion, Left*
Bank, Zyzzyva, Cream City Rev

Jane Glazer 🎤 ✈   P
Adrienne Lee Press, PO Box 309, Monmouth, OR 97361,
503-838-1220
Internet: xelamuse@aol.com
    Pubs: *Go Where the Landshed Takes You* (Daniel & Daniel,
2003), *Some Trick of Light* (Adrienne Lee Pr, 1993), *Fresh*
Water: Anth (Pudding Hse Pub, 2000), *Claiming the Spirit*
Within; Anth (Beacon Pr, 1996), *Berkeley Poetry Rev*

Jim Grabill 🎤 ✈   P
9835 SW 53 Ave
Portland, OR 97219-5827, 503-977-0331
    Pubs: *An Indigo Scent after the Rain* (MSU Pr/Lynx Hse,
2002), *Lame Duck Eternity* (26 Bks, 2000), *Listening to the*
Leaves Form, Poem Rising Out of the Earth & Standing Up
in Someone (Lynx Hse Pr, 1997, 1994), *Through the Green*
Fire (Holy Cow! Pr, 1995)

Cecelia Hagen 🎤 ✈   P&W
2972 Madison St
Eugene, OR 97405, 541-345-7386
Internet: cecelia_hagen@ous.edu
    Pubs: *Fringe Living* (26 Books Pr, 1999), *Caffeine Destiny,*
Web del Sol, Portlandia, Poet & Critic, Exquisite Corpse,
Prairie Schooner, Willow Springs, Seattle Rev, Puerto del Sol

John Haislip 🎤 ✈   P
925 Park Ave
Eugene, OR 97404-6502
    Pubs: *Seal Rock* (Barnwood Pr, 1987), *American Poets in*
1976: Anth (Bobbs-Merrill, 1976)

James Byron Hall   P&W
1413 Oak Street
Lake Oswego, OR 97034-4743
    Pubs: *I Like It Better Now* (U Arkansas Pr, 1992),
Bereavements (Story Line Pr, 1991), *New Directions, New*
Letters, Esquire

Miriam Halliday-Borkowski   P
955 SE Richland Ave
Corvallis, OR 97333, 541-754-3704
Internet: miriamborkowski@hotmail.com
    Pubs: *For the Beloved* (Handbuilt Bks/San Raphael, 1996),
Travelling Poet, Columbia, Beatitude, Kansas Qtly, Spirit
That Moves Us

Robert D. Hoeft   P
1374 SW 37th St
Pendleton, OR 97801, 503-276-1989
Internet: rhoeft@uci.net
    Pubs: *Greatest Hits: 1960-2000* (Pudding Hse, 2001), *What*
Are You Doing? (Trout Creek Pr, 1986), *Out of Work*
(Winewood Pub, 1983), *Exhibits at a Retirement Home*
(Wings Pr, 1982), *Tools* (Mosaic Pr, 1982), *Green's Mag*

Michael Holstein   P
228 West St
Ashland, OR 97520, 503-488-1099
  Pubs: *Alura Qtly, Phoebus Mag, Poets On, BPJ,
Crosscurrents*

Garrett Kaoru Hongo   P
Univ Oregon, Program in Creative Writing, Eugene, OR
97405, 503-346-0545
  Pubs: *The River of Heaven* (Knopf, 1988), *The Open Boat:
Anth* (Anchor Bks, 1993), *Ploughshares, Zyzzyva, Field,
Antaeus, Bamboo Ridge, Agni*

Lawson Fusao Inada   P&W
Southern Oregon State College, English Dept, Ashland, OR
97520, 541-552-6639
  Pubs: *Legends from Camp* (Coffee Hse Pr, 1993)

Stephen R. Jones 🎤 ✈   P
24407 Decker Rd
Corvallis, OR 97333, 541-929-5505
Internet: jonesa@onid.orst.edu
  Pubs: *Willamette Jrnl of Liberal Arts, Manzanita Qtly,
Calapooya Collage, Eloquent Umbrella, NW Rev, Oregon
English Jrnl, Greenfield Rev, Fireweed*

Susan Kenyon   P
2060 Willamette St
Eugene, OR 97405
  Pubs: *Western Humanities Rev
Accent, NWRev, Atlantic, California Rev*

Ken Kesey 🎤 ✈   W
85829 Ridgeway Rd
Pleasant Hill, OR 97455-9627, 541-746-1572
Internet: kenk@efn.org
  Pubs: *Last Go Round, Sailor Song, Sometimes a Great
Nation, One Flew Over the Cuckoo's Nest* (Viking, 1994,
1992, 1964, 1962)

David Kherdian 🎤 ✈   P
600 W. 12 th St
McMinnville, OR 97128, 503-434-9558
Internet: tavit@earthlink.net
  Pubs: *Seeds of Light: Poems from a Gurdjieff Community*
(Stopinder Bks, 2002), *The Neighborhood Years* (Bottom
Dog Pr, 2000), *I Called It Home* (Blue Crane Bks, 1997), *My
Racine* (Forkroads Pr, 1997, 1994)

Lee Crawley Kirk 🎤 ✈   P
PO Box 5432
Eugene, OR 97405-0432, 541-683-7033
Internet: leekirk@continet.com
  Pubs: *From Here We Speak: Anth* (Oregon State U Pr,
1993), *Stafford's Road* (Adrienne Lee Pr, 1991), *Portlander,
Daughters of Nyx, Wormwood Rev, Fireweed, Calapooya
Collage*

Elio Emiliano Ligi   P
c/o Eric Blair, Uncommon Sense, PO Box 430, Banks, OR
97106-0430
Internet: garyligi@mac.com
  Pubs: *The Diversabomber* (Dehumanities, 1995), *How I
Shot Down KAL007* (Sodoms Insane Pub, 1994), *CSM*

Robert Hill Long   P&W
1910 Charnelton St
Eugene, OR 97405-2818, 541-686-6223
webdelsol.com/long/
  Pubs: *The Effigies* (Plinth Bks, 1998), *The Work of the Bow*
(Cleveland State U Poetry Center, 1997), *Poetry, Zyzzyva,
Shenandoah, DoubleTake, Manoa, Prose Poem*

Jack E. Lorts 🎤 ✈   P
PO Box 474
Fossil, OR 97830-0474, 541-763-3060
Internet: jclorts@centurytel.net
  Pubs: *The Great Oregon Serial Poem* (Talent House Pr,
2001), *Poetry Motel, Quantum Tao, Arizona Qtly, Kansas
Qtly, English Jrnl, Oregon English Jrnl, Abbey, Fireweed,
Fishtrap, Anth #10*

Manna Lowenfels   P
20950 SW Rock Creek Rd
Sheridan, OR 97378, 503-843-2465
Internet: manna@delphian.org
  Pubs: *The New Woman Speaks & Other Poems* (Buffalo
Bks, 1979), *Sunbury, Connections*

David Lunde 🎤 ✈   P&W
2218 McPherson St
North Bend, OR 97459, 541-751-1646
Internet: davelunde@earthlink.net
  Pubs: *Nightfishing in Great Sky River, 2001: Anth*
(Anamnesis Pr, 1999, 2001), *Blues for Port City,
Uncommonplaces: Anth* (Mayapple Pr, 1995, 2000),
Asimov's Sci Fi Mag, Renditions, Literary Rev, Poetry

Joan Maiers 🎤 ✈   P
PO Box 33
Marylhurst, OR 97036-0033, 503-636-8955
  Pubs: *Tcha Teemanwi* (Knot Hse, 2001), *Blooming in the
Shade: Anth* (Media Weavers, 1997), *Out of Season: Anth*
(Amagansett Pr, 1993), *If I Had a Hammer: Anth* (Papier-
Mache Pr, 1990), *Jrnl of Pastoral Care, The Other Side,
New Press Literary Qtly, Hubbub*

Katherine Marsh   P&W
PO Box 613
Salem, OR 97308-0613
Internet: stone_ally@hotmail.com
  Pubs: *Voices from the White Noise* (Gaff Pr, 2000), *Painting
Daisies Yellow: Anth, Little Verse, Big Thoughts: Anth*
(Golden Apple Pr, 1995, 1995), *Canadian Writers Jrnl, Hard
Row to Hoe, Writers Gazette, PDX, Stop, Palo Alto Rev,
Fighting Chance Mag*

Robert McDowell P
Story Line Press, Three Oaks Farm, PO Box 1240, Ashland,
OR 97525-0055, 541-512-8792
    Pubs: *The Diviners* (Peterloo Poets, 1995), *Quiet Money* (H
    Holt, 1987), *At the House of the Tin Man* (Chowder Pr,
    1983), *Hudson Rev, Kenyon Rev, Sewanee Rev, New
    Criterion, Harvard Rev, Poetry*

David Memmott P&W
PO Box 3235
La Grande, OR 97850, 541-963-0723
Internet: wordcraft@oregontrail.net
    Pubs: *Within the Walls of Jericho* (26 Bks, 1998), *The
    Larger Earth* (Permeable Pr, 1996), *Once Upon a Midnight*
    (Unnameable Pr, 1995), *Nebula 27* (HB, 1993), *Oregon
    East, Co-Lingua, Airfish, Point No Point, The Temple, Mag
    of Speculative Poetry*

Rob Hollis Miller P
PO Box 865
Union, OR 97883, 503-562-5091
    Pubs: *The Boy Whose Shoesocks Ran Away* (Primavera,
    1982), *Shanghai Creek Fire* (St. Andrews, 1979)

Gary Miranda P
1172 SE 55 St
Portland, OR 97215, 503-239-9174
    Pubs: *Grace Period* (Princeton, 1983)

Rodger Moody ♀ ⤢ P
3020 Charnelton St
Eugene, OR 97405-3379, 541-344-5060
Internet: myst8385@aol.com
    Pubs: *Unbending Intent* (26 Bks Pr, 1997), *From Here We
    Speak: Anth* (Oregon State U Pr, 1993), *Pleiades, South
    Dakota Rev, Zyzzyva, Caliban*

F. A. Nettelbeck P
PO Box 336
Beatty, OR 97621, 503-533-2486
    Pubs: *Ecosystems Collapsing* (Inkblot Pubs, 1992),
    Americruiser (Illuminati, 1983), *Gas, Bombay Gin, Painted
    Bride Qtly, Rain City Rev*

Michael Niflis P
6920 Whiskey Creek Rd
Tillamook, OR 97141-8316, 503-842-6755
    Pubs: *From Here We Speak: Anth* (Oregon State U Pr,
    1993), *Poetry, Esquire, Partisan Rev, American Scholar,
    Commonweal, CSM, Harper's, New Republic, Virginia Qtly*

Verlena Orr ♀ P
1907 NW Hoyt
Portland, OR 97209-1224, 503-224-1849
    Pubs: *Woman Who Hears Voices* (Future Tense Pr, 1998),
    Graining the Mare: The Poetry of Ranch Women: Anth
    (Gibbs Smith, 1994), *From Here We Speak: Anth* (Oregon
    State U Pr, 1993), *Poet & Critic, Colorado Rev*

Robyn Parnell ♀ ⤢ W
343 NE 15 Ct
Hillsboro, OR 97124-3459, 503-681-9818
Internet: robyn@wagnell.com
    Pubs: *This Here & Now* (Scrivenery Pr, 2000), *Children's
    Storybook: Anth* (Cherubic Pr, 1997), *Strictly Fiction: Anth*
    (Potpourri, 1995), *Feminist Parenting: Anth* (Crossing Pr,
    1994), *Satire, Oasis, Lynx Eye, Mobius, Bellowing Ark,
    Belletrist Rev, ProCreation*

A. B. Paulson W
c/o English Dept, Portland State Univ, PO Box 751, Portland,
OR 97207, 503-725-3521
Internet: ab@nh1.nh.pdx.edu
    Pubs: *Watchman Tell Us of the Night* (Viking Penguin,
    1987), *Georgia Rev*

Paulann Petersen ♀ ⤢ P
8403 SE 11th Ave
Portland, OR 97202, 503-236-5229
Internet: ppetersen@jps.net
    Pubs: *Blood-Silk* (Quiet Lion Pr, 2002), *The Wild Awake,
    Under the Sign of a Neon Wolf* (Confluence Press, 2002,
    1989), *Fabrication* (26 Books, 1996), *The Animal Bride*
    (Trask Hse Bks, 1994), *Poetry, New Republic, Prairie
    Schooner, Poetry NW, Yellow Silk*

Jarold Ramsey ♀ ⤢ P
5884 NW Highway #26
Madras, OR 97741
Internet: JWR1937@madras.net
    Pubs: *Hand-Shadows* (QRL, 1989), *Dermographia*
    (Cornstalk Pr, 1982), *Atlantic, NW Rev, QRL, Poetry NW,
    Nation, Chelsea, American Scholar*

Dan Raphael ♀ ⤢ P
6735 SE 78 St
Portland, OR 97206-7116, 503-777-0406
Internet: raphael@aracnet.com
    Pubs: *Showing Light a Good Time, Clear to Where,
    Molecular Jam* (Jazz Police, 2001, 2000, 1996), *Dan
    Raphael: Greatest Hits* (Pudding Hse Pub, 2001), *Isn't How
    We Got Here* (Unnum, 1999), *Trees Through the Road* (Nine
    Muses, 1997), *Heaven Bone, The Temple*

Carlos Reyes ♀ ⤢ P
3222 NE Schuyler
Portland, OR 97212-5131, 503-287-9806
Internet: isacar@aol.com
    Pubs: *A Suitcase Full of Crows* (Bluestem, 1995),
    Nightmarks (Lynx Hse, 1990), *Men of Our Time: Anth* (U
    Georgia, 1992), *West Coast Rev*

Howard W. Robertson ♀ ⤢ P
PO Box 50204
Eugene, OR 97405, 541-344-6206
Internet: robertsons2@earthlink.net
    Pubs: *Nest, Literal Latte, Nimrod, Fireweed, Ergo*

Bruce Holland Rogers 🎤 ✈ P&W
1485 E Briarcliff Lane
Eugene, OR 97404-3268, 541-689-6735
Internet: bruce@sff.net
  Pubs: *Flaming Arrows* (IFD Publishing, 2001), *Wind Over Heaven* (Wildside Pr, 2000), *The Pushcart Prize: Anth* (Pushcart Pr, 2000), *Year's Best Mystery & Suspense Stories: Anth* (Walker & Co, 1994), *Flash Fiction: Anth* (Norton, 1992), *N Amer Rev*

Elaine Romaine 🎤 P
5017 SE 40 Ave
Portland, OR 97206-4221, 503-788-9034
  Pubs: *Breaking Up: Anth* (Crossing Pr, 1994), *Passion: Anth* (Peconic Gallery, 1994), *The Dream Book: Anth* (Schocken Bks, 1985), *Interim, Bellowing Ark, City Primeval, New Letters, NAR, Oyez*

Helen Ronan P
344 E 14 Ave
Eugene, OR 97401, 503-687-0419
  Pubs: *Petrified Thunder, Cloud Shadows* (Oregon State Pr, 1989, 1989), *Brussels Sprout, Dragonfly, Modern Haiku, Frogpond, Haiku Canada, New Cicada*

Lex Runciman 🎤 ✈ P
Linfield College, English Dept, McMinnville, OR 97128, 503-434-2583
Internet: lruncim@linfield.edu
  Pubs: *Continuo* (Salmon Pub, 2002), *The Admirations* (Lynx Hse Pr, 1989), *Luck* (Owl Creek Pr, 1981), *Who Are the Rich & Where Do They Live?: Anth* (Poetry East Pr, 2000), *ISLE, Meridian, Verse, Fireweed, NER, Missouri Rev, Willow Springs*

Biff Russ P
9448 SW Wood Parkway
Portland, OR 97219
  Pubs: *Black Method* (Helicon Nine Edtns, 1991), *Fathers: Anth* (St. Martin's Pr, 1997), *Prairie Schooner, Cream City Rev, Poetry East, Indiana Rev, Berkeley Poetry Rev, Passages North, Boulevard*

Vern Rutsala P
2404 NE 24 Ave
Portland, OR 97212-4828, 503-281-5872
  Pubs: *Little-Known Sports* (U Massachusetts Pr, 1994), *Selected Poems* (Story Line, 1991), *Ruined Cities* (Carnegie Mellon, 1987)

Harley L. Sachs 🎤 ✈ P&W
2545 SW Terwilliger Blvd #222
Portland, OR 97201
Internet: hlsachs@mtu.edu
  Pubs: *Ben Zakkai's Coffin* (Zumaya Pubs, 2002), *The Mystery Club Solves a Murder* (Idevlo, 2002), *Threads of the Covenant* (Isaac Nathan Pubs, 1995), *Irma Quarterdeck Reports* (Wescott Cove Pub, 1991)

Ralph Salisbury P&W
2377 Charnelton
Eugene, OR 97405-2859, 541-343-5101
Internet: salwendt@oregon.uoregon.edu
  Pubs: *Rainbows of Stone* (U Arizona Pr, 2000), *The Last Rattlesnake Throw & Other Stories* (U Oklahoma Pr, 1998), *One Indian & Two Chiefs* (Navaho Comm College Pr, 1993), *Earth Song Sky Spirit* (Doubleday, 1993), *Chariton Rev, Poetry Chicago, New Yorker*

Maxine Scates 🎤 ✈ P
1500 Skyline Park Loop
Eugene, OR 97405-4466, 541-687-2758
Internet: mscates@teleport.com
  Pubs: *Toluca Street* (U Pittsburgh Pr, 1989), *Zyzzyva, Crab Orchard Rev, Women's Rev of Bks, Massachusetts Rev, Prairie Schooner, Poetry East, APR, Agni, Crazyhorse, Ironwood*

Willa Schneberg P
2524 SW Sheffield
Portland, OR 97201, 503-248-4136
  Pubs: *In the Margins of the World* (Plain View Pr, 2001), *Bearing Witness, Teaching the Holocaust: Anth* (Heineman, 2001), *Claiming the Spirit Within: Anth* (Beacon, 2000), *APR, Salmagundi, Virginia Qtly Rev, Americas Rev, Hawaii Pacific Rev, Exquisite Corpse*

Penelope Scambly Schott 🎤 ✈ P
507 NW Skyline Crest Rd
Portland, OR 97229, 503-291-0159
Internet: penelopeschott@compuserve.com
  Pubs: *Penelope: The Story of the Half-Scalped Woman* (U Pr Florida, 1999), *The Perfect Mother* (Snake Nation Pr, 1994), *These Are My Same Hands* (State Street Pr, 1989), *A Little Ignorance* (Potter, 1986), *Amer Poetry Rev, Nimrod, Amer Voice, Georgia Rev*

Sandra Scofield 🎤 ✈ W
PO Box 3329
Ashland, OR 97520, 541-488-0324
  Pubs: *Plain Seeing, A Chance to See Egypt* (HC, 1997, 1996), *Opal on Dry Ground* (Villard, 1994), *More Than Allies, Walking Dunes, Beyond Deserving, Gringa* (Permanent Press, 1993, 1992, 1990, 1989)

Peter Sears P
2845 NW Royal Oakes Dr
Corvallis, OR 97330
  Pubs: *Saturday Rev, SPR, Field, Poetry NW, BPJ*

Chris Semansky 🎤 ✈   P
5536 NE 25th
Portland, OR 97211
Internet: cks18@attbi.com
    Pubs: *Death, But at a Good Price* (Story Line Pr, 1991),
    Blindsided (26 Bks, 1998), *Folio, College English, Exquisite
    Corpse, ND Qtly, MN Rev, Mississippi Rev, Genre,
    American Letters & Commentary, New Orleans Rev, Poetry
    New York*

Dale Shank   W
2375 Madrona Lane
Canby, OR 97013
Internet: dshank@teleport.com
    Pubs: *Powder, Joint Endeavor, Akros Rev, Before the Sun,
    Croton Rev, U Portland Rev, Exquisite Corpse*

Brenda Shaw   P&W
3475 Harris St
Eugene, OR 97405
    Pubs: *The Dark Well* (Audenreed Pr, 1997), *Dog Music:
    Anth* (St. Martin's Pr, 1996), *Each in Her Own Way: Anth*
    (Queen of Swords Pr, 1994), *Scottish Stories 1985: Anth*
    (Collins, 1985), *Fireweed, Pacifica, Mediphors, Northlight,
    Inscape, Word, Envoi, Spectrum*

Steven Sher 🎤 ✈   P&W
3930 NW Witham Hill Dr, #197
Corvallis, OR 97330, 541-752-5949
Internet: shlomosher@hotmail.com
    Pubs: *At the Willamette* (Solo Pr, 2003), *Thirty-Six* (Creative
    Arts Bk Co, 2002), *Flying Through Glass* (Outloudbks,
    2001), *Traveler's Advisory* (Trout Creek Pr, 1994), *Man with
    a Thousand Eyes & Other Stories* (Gull Bks, 1989)

Jim Shugrue 🎤 ✈   P
5344 SE 38 Ave
Portland, OR 97202-4208, 503-775-0370
Internet: jim.shugrue@reed.edu
    Pubs: *Icewater* (Trask Hse Bks, 1998), *Small Things
    Screaming* (26 Bks, 1995), *American Diaspora: Anth* (U
    Iowa Pr, 2001), *Connecticut River Rev, Qtly West, Intl Qtly,
    Poetry East, ACM*

Floyd Skloot 🎤 ✈   P&W
5680 Karla's Ln
Amity, OR 97101-2316, 503-835-2230
Internet: fskloot@vicklink.com
    Pubs: *The Fiddler's Trance* (Bucknell, 2001), *The Evening
    Light, The Open Door, The Night-Side* (Story Line Pr, 2000,
    1997, 1996), *Music Appreciation* (U Pr Florida, 1994),
    *Atlantic, Harper's, Poetry, American Scholar, New Criterion,
    Virginia Qtly Rev*

Peter Spiro   W
C/O Sharon Laughlin, Box 105, Wasco, OR 97065
Internet: peterspiro@aol.com
    Pubs: *The United States of Poetry: Anth* (Abrams, 1996),
    Aloud: Voices from the Nuyorican Poets Cafe: Anth (H Holt,
    1994), *Poetry NY, Outerbridge, Flex, Maryland Rev*

Primus St. John 🎤 ✈   P
Portland State Univ, PO Box 751, Portland, OR 97207-0751,
503-725-3578
Internet: stjohnp@pdx.edu
    Pubs: *Communion, Skins on the Earth* (Copper Canyon Pr,
    1999, 1976), *Dreamer, Love Is Not a Consolation It Is a
    Light* (Carnegie Mellon U Pr, 1990, 1982), *APR*

Kim R. Stafford   P
Northwest Writing Institute, Lewis & Clark College, Campus
Box 100, Portland, OR 97219, 503-768-7745
    Pubs: *Having Everything Right* (Sasquatch Bks, 1996),
    Lochsa Road: A Pilgrim in the West (Confluence Pr, 1991),
    Atlantic, Virginia Qtly Rev, The Sun

Lisa Malinowski Steinman 🎤 ✈   P
Reed College, English Dept, Portland, OR 97202-4208,
503-775-0370
Internet: lisa.steinman@reed.edu
    Pubs: *Ordinary Songs* (26 Bks, 1996), *A Book of Other
    Days, All That Comes to Light* (Arrowood Bks, 1993, 1989),
    *Notre Dame Rev, Prairie Schooner, Chariton Rev, Michigan
    Qtly, Poetry East, Threepenny Rev*

Sandra Stone   P&W
2650 SW 106 Ave
Portland, OR 77225-4313, 503-292-3296
    Pubs: *Cocktails with Brueghel at the Museum Cafe*
    (Cleveland State U Poetry Ctr, 1997), *The Qtly, Ms., Poetry
    NW, New Republic*

Thomas Strand   P
PO Box 83706
Portland, OR 97283
    Pubs: *Oregon East* (Eastern Oregon State College, 1985),
    The Best of Poetic Space: Anth 1987-91 (Poetic Space,
    1991), *Desperado, Incoming, Poetic Space*

Gloria Sykee   W
11057 SW Summerfield Dr, #10
Tigard, OR 97224, 503-684-1434
    Pubs: *Carolina Qtly, Prairie Schooner, Kansas Qtly*

Mark Thalman 🎤 ✈   P
3310 Hillside Way
Forest Grove, OR 97116, 503-357-4042
Internet: oregonpoet@aol.com
    Pubs: *Chariton Rev, Poetry, Fireweed, Pearl, From Here We
    Speak, Whetstone*

George Venn 🎤 ✈   P
706 B Ave
La Grande, OR 97850-1133, 541-962-0380
Internet: venng@eou.edu
  Pubs: *West of Paradise* (Ice River Pr, 1999), *Marking the Magic Circle, From Here We Speak: Anth* (Oregon State U Pr, 1987, 1994), *Portland Lights: Anth* (Nine Lights, 1999), *Prescott Street Reader: Anth* (Prescott Street Pr, 1995), Oregon English

Doyle Wesley Walls 🎤 ✈   P
English Dept, Pacific Univ, Forest Grove, OR 97116, 503-359-2992
Internet: wallsdw@pacificu.edu
  Pubs: *Sweet Nothings: Anth* (Indiana U Pr, 1994), *From Here We Speak: Anth* (Oregon State U Pr, 1993), *NYQ, Poet & Critic, Cimarron Rev, Minnesota Rev, BPJ*

Patricia J. Ware   P
4733 NE 17 Ave
Portland, OR 97211-5705, 503-232-9756
  Pubs: *CutBank, Slackwater Rev, Calyx, Portland Rev, Fedora, Poetry Seattle, Willamette Week*

Roger Weaver 🎤 ✈   P
712 NW 13
Corvallis, OR 97330-5953, 541-753-9955
Internet: weaverr@onid.orst.edu
  Pubs: *Standing on Earth, Throwing These Sequins at the Stars, Traveling on the Great Wheel* (Gardyloo Pr, 1992), *Twenty-One Waking Dreams* (Trout Creek Pr, 1986), *The Orange & Other Poems* (Press-22, 1978), *NAR, Massachusetts Rev, NW Rev*

Ingrid Wendt 🎤 ✈   W
2377 Charnelton
Eugene, OR 97405-2859, 541-343-5101
Internet: IngridWendt@compuserve.com
  Pubs: *Blow the Candle Out* (Pecan Grove Pr, 2002), *Singing the Mozart Requiem* (Breitenbush Bks, 1987), *Moving the House* (BOA Edtns, 1980), *No More Masks: Anth* (HC, 1993), *Prairie Schooner, Nimrod, Poetry, Ms., Calyx, Massachusetts Rev*

Leslie What 🎤 ✈   W
PO Box 5412
Eugene, OR 97405
Internet: what@radarangels.com
  Pubs: *Sweet & Sour Tongue* (Wildside Pr, 2001), *2001 Nebula Awards Showcase: Anth* (Harcourt, 2001), *Bending the Landscape: Anth* (Overlook Pr, 2001), *Beyond Lament: Poets Bearing Witness: Anth* (Northwestern U Pr, 1998)

Elizabeth Whitbeck   P&W
32200 SW French Prairie, A-106
Wilsonville, OR 97070, 503-694-5475
  Pubs: *Take This Woman* (Macmillan, 1947), *NE Corridor, Creativity Unlimited, Time of Singing, The Writing Self, Zantia, Pegasus Rev*

Hannah Wilson 🎤 ✈   P&W
2660 Emerald St
Eugene, OR 97403
Internet: hana@mindspring.com
  Pubs: *Line Drives: 100 Contemporary Baseball Poems: Anth* (Southern Illinois U Pr, 2002), *The Wedding Cake in the Middle of the Road: Anth* (Norton, 1992), *Prairie Schooner, Calyx, Earth's Daughters, Other Voices, Turnstile*

John Witte 🎤 ✈   P
1170 Barber Dr
Eugene, OR 97405-4413, 541-346-3957
  Pubs: *Loving the Days* (Wesleyan, 1978), *Kenyon Rev, Ohio Rev, NER, New Yorker, Paris Rev, APR, Iowa Rev, Antaeus*

PENNSYLVANIA

Nathalie F. Anderson 🎤 ✈   P
3 Rutledge Ave
Morton, PA 19070, 610-690-1213
Internet: nanders1@swarthmore.edu
  Pubs: *Following Fred Astaire* (Word Works Pr, 1999), *My Hand, My Only Map* (House of Keys, 1978), *Paris Rev, SPR, Madison Rev, Spazio Humano, Prairie Schooner, Cimarron Rev*

Teresa Anderson 🎤   P
PO Box 65
Starucca, PA 18462
  Pubs: *Speaking in Sign* (West End Pr, 1978), *This Same Sky: Anth* (S&S, 1996), *Pemmican, Manoa, Paterson Lit Rev, New Poets: Women, Best Friends, Anima, Sunsprout*

Ron Androla   P
1624 W Grandview Blvd, Apt 1
Erie, PA 16509
http://members.xoom.com/androla/
  Pubs: *Splattered in Erie* (Smiling Dog Pr, 1996), *It's a Pretty World* (Non Compos Mentis Pr, 1996), *Poetry Motel, Atom Mind, Chiron Rev, Wooden Head Rev*

Bim Angst 🎤 ✈   P&W
PO Box 157
Hegins, PA 17938, 570-682-4366
Internet: bimangst@epix.net
  Pubs: *An Intricate Weave: Anth* (Iris Edtns, 1997), *Coal Seam: Anth* (U Scranton Pr, 1994), *West Branch, Spoon River, BPJ, Poetry Now*

Kenneth L. Arnold   P
6363 Germantown Ave
Philadelphia, PA 19144, 215-844-1892

J. T. Barbarese 🎤 ✈   P
7128 Cresheim Rd
Philadelphia, PA 19119-2429, 215-247-9575
Internet: barbares@camden.rutgers.edu
    Pubs: *New Science, Under the Blue Moon* (U Georgia,
    1989, 1985), *Georgia Rev, Chelsea, Story Qtly, Sewanee
    Rev, Denver Qtly, Southern Rev, Atlantic, NAR, Boulevard*

Marilyn Bates 🎤 ✈   P&W
126 Swallow Hill Ct
Pittsburgh, PA 15220
Internet: bbatest+@pitt.edu
    Pubs: *It Could Drive You Crazy* (Small Poetry Pr, 2002), *And
    What Rough Beast: Anth* (Ashland Poetry Pr, 1999),
    *MacGuffin, Comstock Rev, Potomac Rev, Santa Clara Rev,
    Paterson Lit Rev*

Jean Baur 🎤 ✈   P
29 Green Ridge Rd
Yardley, PA 19067, 215-493-4257
Internet: jbaur@eudoramail.com
    Pubs: *Bucks County Writer, The Helen Rev, Confrontation,
    Green River Rev*

Robin Becker 🎤 ✈   P
215 Academy St
Boalsburg, PA 16827-1438, 814-466-3326
Internet: rxb20@psu.edu
    Pubs: *The Horse Fair, All-American Girl, Giacometti's Dog*
    (U Pitt Pr, 2000, 1995, 1990), *Backtalk* (Alice James Bks,
    1982), *Prairie Schooner, New Virginia Rev, APR, Kenyon
    Rev, Ploughshares, Amicus Jrnl*

Stephen Berg   P
2005 Mt Vernon St
Philadelphia, PA 19130

Jane Bernstein 🎤 ✈   W
English Dept, Carnegie Mellon Univ, Pittsburgh,
PA 15213-3890, 412-268-6445
Internet: janebern+@andrew.cmu.edu
    Pubs: *Loving Rachel* (Little, Brown, 1988), *Seven Minutes in
    Heaven* (Fawcett, 1986), *Ms., The Sun, Prairie Schooner*

Becky Birtha   P&W
32 Scottsdale Rd
Philadelphia, PA 19050
    Pubs: *The Forbidden Poems* (Seal, 1991), *Breaking Ice:
    Anth of Contemporary African-American Fiction* (Penguin
    1990), *We Are the Stories We Tell: Anth* (Pantheon, 1990)

Lili Bita 🎤 ✈   P
326 Bryn Mawr Ave
Bala Cynwyd, PA 19004, 610-667-2224
Internet: lilibita@hotmail.com
    Pubs: *Lethe, The Scorpion* (Pella, 2001, 1998), *Striking the
    Sky* (European Arts Center, 1997), *Excavations, Firewalkers*
    (Lyra Pr, 1985, 1984), *Agenda, APR, Caprice, Intl Poetry
    Rev, Nea Hesperia, Mad Poets Rev*

Karen Blomain 🎤 ✈   P
English Dept, Kutztown Univ, Kutztown, PA 19530,
610-683-4335
Internet: lefloog@aol.com
    Pubs: *A Trick of Light* (Toby Pr, 2001), *Normal Ave.,
    Borrowed Light* (Nightshade Pr, 1998, 1993), *Coalseam:
    Poems* (U Scranton, 1993), *Pittsburgh Qtly, Passages North,
    Painted Bride Qtly, MacGuffin, Sun, Negative Capability,
    One Trick Pony*

Louise A. Blum   W
English Dept, Mansfield Univ, Mansfield, PA 16933,
717-662-4597
Internet: lblum@mnsfld.edu
    Pubs: *Amnesty* (Alyson Pubs, 1995), *Love's Shadow: Anth*
    (Crossing Pr, 1992), *West, Cream City Rev, Poetic Space,
    Columbia, Sonora Rev*

Deborah Bogen   P
1112 N Highland Ave
Pittsburgh, PA 15206, 412-362-8446
Internet: Dbbogen@aol.com
    Pubs: *The Spirit of Pregnancy: Anth* (Contemporary Bks,
    2000), *Proposing on the Brooklyn Bridge: Anth* (Grayson
    Bks, 2003), *Field, Mudfish, Poetry Intl, JAMA, Bucket, Lyric,
    Pittsburgh Qtly, Poet Lore, Santa Monica Rev, Sandhills Rev*

William O. Boggs 🎤 ✈   P
English Dept, Slippery Rock Univ, Slippery Rock, PA 16057,
412-738-2348
Internet: william.boggs@sru.edu
    Pubs: *Eddy Johnson's American Dream* (Hiram Poetry Rev,
    1990), *Swimming in Clear Water* (Dacotah Territory Pr,
    1989), *Hiram Poetry Rev, Poetrytonight.com, Pennsylvania
    English*

Roger Bower   P
Cameron Star Rte
Waynesburg, PA 15370, 412-852-1448
    Pubs: *Editor's Choice II Anth, Space & Time, Abraxas, Pig
    Iron, Pudding, Colorado State Rev*

Greg Bowers   P
1010 Prospect Rd
Red Lion, PA 17356
    Pubs: *The Reunion* (Trunk Pr, 1977)

James Brasfield 🎤 ✈ P
Pennsylvania State Univ, 117 Burrowes, English Dept,
University Park, PA 16802-6200, 814-865-9795
Internet: jeb16@psu.edu
    Pubs: *Agni, American Scholar, Colorado Rev, Crazyhorse,
    Prairie Schooner*

Beth Phillips Brown 🎤 ✈ P
P.O. Box 1046
Media, PA 19063, 610-566-2810
Internet: philipsbrown@earthlink.net
    Pubs: *A Celtic Daybook & Compendium of Lore, Invisible
    Threads* (White Pine Pr, 1987, 1983), *Painted Bride Qtly,
    U.S. 1 Worksheets, Full Moon, White Pine Jrnl*

Deborah Burnham P
327 N 34
Philadelphia, PA 19104
    Pubs: *Anna & the Steel Mill* (Texas Tech, 1995), *Virginia Qtly
    Rev, West Branch, Literary Rev, Kansas Qtly*

Christopher Bursk 🎤 ✈ P
704 Hulmeville Ave
Langhorne Manor, PA 19047, 215-752-5101
    Pubs: *Cell Count* (Texas Tech, 1997), *The One True Religion*
    (Qtly Rev, 1997), *The Way Water Rubs Stone* (Word Works,
    1989), *Places of Comfort, Places of Justice* (San Jose,
    1987), *Making Wings* (State Street Pr, 1983), *APR*

Anthony Butts 🎤 ✈ P
Dept of English, Carnegie-Mellon University, 5000 Forbes Ave,
Pittsburgh, PA 15213-3890, 412-268-9156
Internet: ab2s@andrew.cmu.edu
    Pubs: *Little Low Heaven, Fifth Season* (New Issues, 2003,
    1997), *Evolution* (Sutton Hoo Pr, 1998), *Giant Steps: Anth*
    (Morrow, 2000), *American Poetry, The Next Generation*
    (CMU Pr, 2000)

Shulamith Wechter Caine 🎤 ✈ P
122 Grasmere Rd
Bala Cynwyd, PA 19004, 215-667-5990
    Pubs: *Love Fugue* (Silverfish Pr, 1998), *World & Local News*
    (Alms Hse Pr, 1988), *APR, American Scholar, Negative
    Capability, SPR, Kalliope*

Rosemary Cappello P
1919 Chestnut St, #1721
Philadelphia, PA 19103, 215-568-1145
    Pubs: *Sig* (Peter Chaloner, 1988), *Pearl 22: Anth* (Pearl,
    1995), *Voices in Italian Americana: Anth* (Bordighera, Inc.,
    1994), *Schuylkill Valley Jrnl*

Robert L. Carothers P
English Dept, Edinboro State College, Edinboro, PA 16444,
814-732-2736

Jody Carr 🎤 ✈ W
2210 Lehigh Pkwy N
Allentown, PA 18103, 610-820-5710
Internet: wrichick@aol.com
    Pubs: *Monday's Child* (HC, 1999), *My Beautiful, Fat Friend*
    (Crosswinds, 1988), *No Regrets* (Dial Bks, 1982)

Diana Cavallo 🎤 ✈ W
1919 Chestnut St, #1015
Philadelphia, PA 19103-3415, 215-665-0698
    Pubs: *A Bridge of Leaves, The Voices We Carry: Anth*
    (Guernica Edtns, 1997, 1994), *From the Margin to the
    Center: Anth* (Purdue U Pr, 1990), *Confrontation*

Joel Chace 🎤 ✈ P
300 E Seminary St
Mercersburg, PA 17236, 717-328-3824
Internet: joel_chace@mercersburg.edu
    Pubs: *O-d-e* (Runaway Spoon Pr, 2000), *Greatest Hits*
    (Pudding Hse, 2000), *Uncertain Relations, The Melancholy
    of Yorick* (Birch Brook, 2000, 1998), *Twentieth Century
    Deaths* (Singular Speech, 1997), *Veer, 6ix, Xtream, Lost &
    Found Times, Aught*

Diana Chang 🎤 ✈ P&W
1400 Waverly Rd, Apt B126
Gladwyne, PA 19035-1263
Internet: dherr15171@aol.com
    Pubs: *The Mind's Amazement* (Live Poets Society, 1998),
    Intersecting Circles: Anth (Bamboo Ridge Pr, 1999), *Yellow
    Light: Anth* (Temple U Pr, 1999), *Sea Change, Blue Sand
    Mag, Montserrat Rev*

A. V. Christie P
474 Conestoga Rd
Malvern, PA 19355, 610-725-1989
Internet: johnfattibene@juno.com
    Pubs: *Nine Skies* (U Illinois Pr, 1997), *Black & Blues*
    (Itinerant Pr, 1985), *The Bread Loaf Anth of New American
    Poets* (U Pr of New England, 2000), *Orpheus & Company:
    Anth* (U Pr of New England, 1999), *APR, Ploughshares,
    Excerpt, The Jrnl*

Michael Clark W
Humanities Dept, Widener Univ, 1 University Pl, Chester, PA
19013, 610-499-4354
Internet: clark@widener.edu
    Pubs: *Our Roots Grow Deeper Than We Know: Anth* (U
    Pittsburgh Pr, 1985), *Arizona Qtly, Outerbridge*

John Clarke P
RD 1, Stone Jug Rd
Biglerville, PA 17307, 717-677-7438
    Pubs: *Inland Tide* (Snowy Road Pr, 1981), *Texas Rev,
    Kansas Qtly, New Yorker, Atlantic, Colorado Qtly*

Lance Clewett 🎤 ✈   P
8 Cave Hill Dr
Carlisle, PA 17013-1203, 717-249-6912
Internet: bluemoon51@juno.com
   Pubs: *One Fast Trout* (Paco Bks, 1997), *Diesel Flowers*
(Warm Spring Pr, 1992)

Marion Deutsche Cohen   P
2203 Spruce St
Philadelphia, PA 19103, 215-732-7723
   Pubs: *Dirty Details* (Temple U Pr, 1996), *Epsilon Country*
(Ctr for Thanatology Research, 1995), *The Sitting-Down
Hug* (Liberal Pr, 1989), *Plain Brown Wrapper, Palo Alto Rev,
Ikon, Abraxas*

James H. Comey 🎤   W
105 Treaty Rd
Drexel Hill, PA 19026
Internet: drjimcomey@aol.com
   Pubs: *The Magnificent Red Button, Three Moons Till
Tomorrow, The Eagle's Claw, The Dragon Singer, The
Monster in the Woods* (Stages of Imagination, 2000, 1999,
1998, 1997, 1996)

Marjorie Lenore Comfort 🎤   P
41 W Corydon St
Bradford, PA 16701-2233, 814-368-5742
Internet: marcom6@juno.com
   Pubs: *Comstock Rev, Poet's Page, Poetic Celebration,
Cer*ber*us, Lucid Moon, Alpha Beat Soup, Tiotis,
Parnassus, Arachne*

Julie Cooper-Fratrik   P
5553 Rte 412
Riegelsville, PA 18077
Internet: juliec@ot.com
   Pubs: *The Leap Years* (Beacon Pr, 2000), *APR, Rhino, The
Styles, Quarter After Eight*

Anita R. Cornwell   W
3220 Powelton Ave
Philadelphia, PA 19104
   Pubs: *The Girls of Summer* (New Seed Pr, 1989), *Black
Lesbian in White America* (Naiad Pr, 1983), *Revolutionary
Tales: Anth* (Dell, 1995), *Romantic Naiad: Anth* (Naiad, 1993)

Gerald Costanzo 🎤 ✈   P
366 Parker Dr
Pittsburgh, PA 15216-1324, 412-268-2861
   Pubs: *Great Disguise* (Aan, 2000), *Nobody Lives on Arthur
Godfrey Boulevard* (BOA Edtns, 1993), *Amer Poetry: The
Next Generation: Anth* (Carnegie Mellon, 2000), *Devins
Award: Anth* (U Missouri Pr, 1998), *Nation, APR,
Ploughshares, NAR, Ohio Rev, Georgia Rev*

Barbara Crooker 🎤 ✈   P
7928 Woodsbluff Rd
Fogelsville, PA 18051, 610-395-5845
Internet: bcrooker@ix.netcom.com
   Pubs: *Ordinary Life* (Byline Pr, 2001), *The White Poems*
(Barnwood Pubs, 2001), *In the Late Summer Garden* (H&H
Pr, 1998), *Obbligato* (Linwood Pub, 1992), *Boomer Girls:
Anth* (U Iowa Pr, 1999), *Reading & Writing from Literature:
Anth* (Houghton Mifflin, 2000)

David C. Cruse   P
5220 W Master St
Philadelphia, PA 19139

Craig Czury   P
914 Leiszs Bridge
Reading, PA 19605-2322, 610-921-0216
Internet: czury@aol.com
   Pubs: *Unreconciled Faces* (Foot Hills Pub, 1999),
Shadow/Orphan Shadow, Obit Hotel (Pine Pr, 1996, 1993),
Fine Line that Screams: Anth (Endless Mountains Rev,
1993), *Five Finger Rev, Parnassus*

Susan Daily   P
523 Magee Ave
Philadelphia, PA 19111, 215-725-5831
   Pubs: *Newsart, Hot Water Rev, Painted Bride Qtly, Palm of
Your Hand, Ampersand Mag*

Jim (Ray) Daniels 🎤 ✈   P
Carnegie Mellon Univ, English Dept, Pittsburgh, PA 15213,
412-268-2842
Internet: jd6s@andrew.cmu.edu
   Pubs: *Detroit Tales* (Michigan State U Pr, 2002), *Night with
Drive-By Shooting Stars* (New Issues Pr, 2002), *Digger's
Blues* (Adastra Pr, 2002), *Blue Jesus* (Carnegie Mellon U
Pr, 2000), *No Pets* (Bottom Dog Pr, 1999)

Edmund Dantes 🎤 ✈   P
501 Franklin St
East Pittsburgh, PA 15112-1109, 412-241-0671
Internet: edantes@netscape.net

Almitra David 🎤 ✈   P
986 N Randolph St
Philadelphia, PA 19123, 215-922-4563
   Pubs: *Between the Sea & Home* (Eighth Mtn Pr, 1993),
Impulse to Fly (Perugia Pr, 1998), *Annie Crow
Road/Chesapeake* (Potter Pr, 1988), *Building the Cathedral*
(Slash & Burn, 1986)

George Deaux   W
English Dept, Temple Univ, Philadelphia, PA 19122,
215-787-7560
   Pubs: *Superworm* (S&S, 1968)

R. DeBacco P
Westmoreland Community College, College Sta, Youngwood,
PA 15697, 724-925-4033
    Pubs: *New Voices, Whiskey Island Mag, Atavist, MacGuffin,
South Coast Poetry Jrnl, Tightrope, Loyalhanna Rev,
Ecphorizer, Ko, Archer, Modern Haiku, Amelia*

Toi Derricotte ♪ ✈ P
6700 Edgerton Ave
Pittsburgh, PA 15208, 412-624-6527
Internet: toiderri@mindspring.com
    Pubs: *Natural Birth* (Firebrand, 2000), *Tender, Captivity* (U
Pitt Pr, 1997, 1995), *Empress of the Death House* (Lotus Pr,
1988), *Callaloo, Paris Rev, Iowa Rev*

John Dewitt ♪ ✈ P
221 Buttonwood Way
Glenside, PA 19038
    Pubs: *Finger Food* (Synapse, 1982), *A New Geography of
Poets: Anth* (U Arkansas Pr, 1992), *New American Rev, #,
Spectrum, Painted Bride Qtly, Lace Rev, Hydrant*

Gregory Djanikian ♪ ✈ P
English Dept, Univ Pennsylvania, 119 Bennett Hall,
Philadelphia, PA 19104, 215-898-7341
Internet: djanikia@english.upenn.edu
    Pubs: *Years Later, About Distance, Falling Deeply Into
America* (Carnegie Mellon U Pr, 2000, 1995, 1989), *Best
American Poems 2000: Anth* (Scribner, 2000), *Poetry,
American Scholar, Georgia Rev, Poetry NW, Iowa Rev*

Patricia Dobler ♪ ✈ P
English Dept, Carlow College, 3333 5th Ave, Pittsburgh, PA
15213, 412-578-6032
Internet: pdobler@carlow.edu
    Pubs: *UXB* (Mill Hunk Bks, 1991), *Talking to Strangers*
(U Wisconsin Pr, 1986), *Ohio Rev, Ploughshares, SPR,
Mid-American Rev, 5 A.M.*

John Dolis ♪ ✈ P
711 Summit Pointe
Scranton, PA 18508-1049, 570-961-9787
Internet: jjd3@psu.edu
    Pubs: Time Flies: Butterflies, Bl( )nk Space (Runaway
Spoon Pr, 1999, 1993), *Antennae, Logo, Daedalus, New
Orleans Rev*

George Dowden P
c/o Corinne Thomas, 27 Ward St, Ridley Park, PA 19078,
215-532-6784
    Pubs: *A Message to Isis* (Moving I, 1977), *Renew
Jerusalem* (Symra Pr, 1969), *Evergreen Rev*

Robert C. S. Downs ♪ ✈ W
764 W Hamilton Ave
State College, PA 16801, 814-234-0747
Internet: rcd4@psu.edu
    Pubs: *The Fifth Season* (Counterpoint, 2000), *Living
Together* (St. Martin's, 1983), *Cimarron Rev, Sundog*

Rachel Blau DuPlessis ♪ ✈ P
211 Rutgers Ave
Swarthmore, PA 19081-1715, 610-328-4116
Internet: rdupless@temple.edu
    Pubs: *Drafts 1-38, Toll* (Wesleyan U Pr, 2001), *Drafts 15-
XXX, The Fold; Drafts 3-14* (Potes & Poets, 1997, 1991),
The Pink Guitar (Routledge, 1990), *How 2, Sulfur,
Conjunctions, Hambone, Chain, Chelsea, Iowa Rev*

Howard Linn Edsall W
105 Innis Way
Malvern, PA 19355-2135, 201-744-8434
    Pubs: *Successful Farming, Harper's, Saturday Evening
Post, The American, London Graphic, Holland's*

W. D. Ehrhart ♪ ✈ P
6845 Anderson St
Philadelphia, PA 19119-1423, 215-848-2068
Internet: wdehrhart@worldnet.att.net
    Pubs: *Beautiful Wreckage* (Adastra Pr, 1999), *NAR,
Cimmaron Rev, APR, Virginia Qtly Rev*

Karen Elias P
RD2, Box 279-C
Lock Haven, PA 17745, 717-748-1632
    Pubs: *Sinister Wisdom, 13th Moon, Second Wave, Feminist
Studies, Women/Poems IV, Anima*

Edith Muesing Ellwood ♪ ✈ P&W
RR1 PML 178
Bushkill, PA 18324, 570-588-3111
Internet: edithmellwood@earthlink.net
    Pubs: *Doctor's Waiting Room* (Potpourri Pub Co, 2001), *Old
Man Snoring* (Modern Haiku, 2001), *Expressions Mag,
Parent to Parent, Black Bough, Haiku Headlines, Brussels
Sprout, Inkstone, Dragonfly, Summer Rain, After the
Shouting*

Lynn Emanuel ♪ ✈ P
Univ of Pittsburgh, Dept of English, Pittsburgh, PA 15260,
412-624-4036
Internet: emanuel@pitt.edu
    Pubs: *Then, Suddenly* (U Pittsburgh Pr, 1999), *The Dig &
Hotel Fiesta* (U Illinois Pr, 1995), *Best American Poetry:
Anths* (Scribner, 1998-2001), *Parnassus, Hudson Rev,
Ploughshares, APR*

Aisha Eshe P
Community College Philadelphia, 17 & Spring Garden,
Philadelphia, PA 19130
    Pubs: *Grain* (Saskatchewan Writers Guild, 1994), *Life on the
Line* (Negative Capability Pr, 1992), *Catalyst, Dream
Network, Women's Recovery Network, Athena*

Joann Marie Everett P
2224 Ogden Ave
Bensalem, PA 19020, 215-244-0525
  Pubs: *Angel Wisdom & a Woman's Song, Seasons in Thunder Valley, Whispered Beginnings* (Jasmine Pr, 1996, 1986, 1984), *Calliope*

Samuel Exler 🎤 ✈ P
307 E Roumfort Rd
Philadelphia, PA 19119-1031
  Pubs: *River Poems* (Slapering Hol Pr, 1992), *Ambition, Fertility, Loneliness* (Lintel, 1982), *Beyond Lament: Anth* (Northwestern U Pr, 1998), *Poetry East, Plainsong, NYQ, Literary Rev, And Rev*

Sascha Feinstein 🎤 ✈ P
Lycoming College, English Dept, Williamsport, PA 17701, 570-321-4279
Internet: feinstei@lycoming.edu
  Pubs: *Misterioso* (Copper Canyon, 2000), *The Second Set: Anth* (Indiana U Pr, 1996), *The Jazz Poetry Anth* (Indiana U Pr, 1991), *APR, Ploughshares, NER, Missouri Rev, NAR, Denver Qtly, Hayden's Ferry Rev*

Al Ferber 🎤 ✈ P
1110 Sheffield Ct
Bensalem, PA 19020-4824, 215-638-2791
Internet: catfer87@aol.com
  Pubs: *Gus* (Cutting Edge Pub, 1994), *Badlands* (Johnston Green Pub, 1986), *Echos, Blue Buildings, Berkeley Poets Co-op, Painted Bride Qtly*

Charles Fergus W
RD2, 340 Mountain Rd
Port Matilda, PA 16870, 814-692-5097
  Pubs: *Shadow Catcher* (Soho Pr, 1991)

Rina Ferrarelli P
224 Adeline Ave
Pittsburgh, PA 15228, 412-341-8009
Internet: rferrarelli@mail.earthlink.net
  Pubs: *A Whole Other Ball Game* (Noonday Pr, 1997), *Home Is A Foreign Country* (Eadmer Pr, 1996), *Dreamsearch* (malafemmina, 1992), *The Art of Life: Anth* (South-Western Educational Pub, 1998), *The Runner's Literary Companion: Anth* (Breakaway Pr, 1994)

Ken Fifer 🎤 ✈ P
5525 Spring Dr
Center Valley, PA 18034-9312
  Pubs: *Falling Man* (Ithaca Hse, 1979), *Partisan Rev, Ploughshares, New Letters, Poetry Now*

Gary Fincke P&W
3 Melody Ln
Selinsgrove, PA 17870, 717-372-4164
Internet: gfincke@susqu.edu
  Pubs: *The Almanac for Desire* (BkMk Pr, 2000), *The Technology of Paradise* (Avisson Pr, 1998), *Emergency Calls* (U Missouri Pr, 1996), *Inventing Angels* (Zoland Bks, 1994), *Paris Rev, Harper's, Kenyon Rev, Poetry, Georgia Rev, Gettysburg Rev*

Sandra Gould Ford W
7123 Race St
Pittsburgh, PA 15208, 412-731-7039
  Pubs: *ELF, Obsidian II, Confluence, James River Rev, Shooting Star Rev*

Robert Freedman P
30 E Market St, #3
Bethlehem, PA 18018, 610-868-5137
Internet: rlfreed@pipeline.com
  Pubs: *Creeping Bent, Yarrow, Endless Mountains Rev, West Branch, Onthebus, Calapooya Collage, Four Quarters, NYQ, Poet Lore*

Catherine Gammon W
Univ Pittsburgh, English Dept, Pittsburgh, PA 15260-0001
Internet: cathg+@pitt.edu
  Pubs: *Isabel Out of the Rain* (Mercury Hse, 1991), *Cape Discovery: Anth* (Sheep Meadow, 1994), *Manoa, Ploughshares, Kenyon, Central Park, Iowa Rev*

Tom Gatten 🎤 ✈ P&W
105 E Curtin St, #15
Bellefonte, PA 16823-1737, 814-353-0532
Internet: tomgatten123@hotmail.com
  Pubs: *The Kojo Hand* (1st Bks Library, 2001), *Mapper of Mists* (Hre Lo Wambli Pr, 1974), *The Workshop: Anth* (Hyperion, 1999), *The Sumac Reader: Anth* (Michigan State U Pr, 1996), *Fiction Midwest, Shenandoah*

Greg Geleta 🎤 ✈ P
1017 S 48 St
Philadelphia, PA 19143-3508, 215-704-6969
  Pubs: *The Year I Learned to Drive, Jazz Elegies* (Axe Factory Pr, 1988, 1985), *Snail's Pace Rev, Artful Dodge, New Stone Circle, Onion River Rev, Axe Factory*

Julia Geleta P&W
427 Carpenter Ln
Philadelphia, PA 19119, 215-844-7678
Internet: jblum@ga.k12.par.us
  Pubs: *Meeting Tessie* (Singing Horse Pr, 1994), *Artificial Memory* (Leave Bks, 1994), *Parallelism* (Abacus/Potes & Poets Pr, 1989), *Topography* (Center, 1983), *Aerial, Paper Air, 6IX, The World, Chain, Brief, Central Park*

Robert Gibb 🎤 ✈ P
5036 Revenue St
Homestead, PA 15120-1227, 412-243-5332
 Pubs: *Origins of Evening* (Norton, 1997), *Fugue for a Late
 Snow, The Winter House* (U Missouri Pr, 1993, 1984),
 Momentary Days (Walt Whitman Ctr, 1988)

C. S. Giscombe P
Pennsylvania State Univ, English Dept, Burrowes Bldg,
University Park, PA 16802, 814-865-6381
 Pubs: *Giscome Road, Here* (Dalkey Archive Pr, 1998, 1994),
 *o.blek, River Styx, Obsidian II, Situation, NAW, ACM,
 Callaloo, Hambone*

Ann K. Glasner W
Kennedy House 2209, 1901 J F Kennedy Blvd, Philadelphia,
PA 19103, 215-561-5874
 Pubs: *Summer Awakening* (Lancer Bks, 1971)

Patricia J. Goodrich 🎤 ✈ P
PO Box 473
Richlandtown, PA 18955-0473
Internet: pgoodric@cbsd.org
 Pubs: *Sidelights* (Kali Moma Pr, 1995), *Intricate Lacing*
 (Nightshade Pr, 1992), *Zone 3, Yarrow, Mediphors, Folio,
 Footwork, New Jersey Jrnl*

Carol Granato P
2506 S 18 St
Philadelphia, PA 19145, 215-334-5412
 Pubs: *The Universe & Beyond* (Garnet Pub, 1999),
 *Epiphany, Snake Nation, Seems, American Goat, The
 Formalist, Prophetic Voices, Midwest Qtly, Poem, Rockford
 Rev, Troubadour, Neovictorian, riverrun, The Lyric*

Ray Greenblatt P
Box 2000, Church Farm School
Paoli, PA 19301, 610-363-7500
 Pubs: *Strange Forest of Words* (Plowman Pubs, 2002),
 *America, Drexel Online Jrnl, English Jrnl, International
 Poetry Rev, Midwest Qtly*

Sam Gridley 🎤 ✈ W
Box 13267
Philadelphia, PA 19101
 Pubs: *Cream City Rev, The Long Story, Other Voices,
 Calapooya Collage, Epoch, Cottonwood, South Dakota Rev,
 Cimarron Rev, American Short Fiction*

Alexandra Grilikhes 🎤 ✈ P&W
4343 Manayunk Ave
Philadelphia, PA 19128-4930, 215-483-7051
 Pubs: *Yin Fire* (Haworth Pr, 2001), *Shaman Body* (Branch
 Redd Bks, 1996), *The Reveries* (Insight to Riot Pr, 1994),
 The Blue Scar (Folder Edtns, 1988), *On Women Artists*
 (Cleis, 1981), *Fishdrum, Pleiades, Seattle Rev, TDR*

Emily Grosholz 🎤 ✈ P
Pennsylvania State Univ, 240 Sparks Bldg, Philosophy,
University Park, PA 16802, 814-865-6397
Internet: erg2@psu.edu
 Pubs: *The Abacus of Years* (David R. Godine Pub Inc,
 2002), *Eden* (Johns Hopkins U Pr, 1992), *Shores &
 Headlands* (Princeton U Pr, 1988), *Michigan Qtly Rev, Tar
 River Poetry, Sewanee Rev, Hudson Rev, Poetry*

Lee Gutkind 🎤 ✈ W
5501 Walnut St, #202
Pittsburgh, PA 15232-1811, 412-688-0304
Internet: info@creativenonfiction.org
 Pubs: *Connecting: Anth* (Putnam, 1998)

H.T. 🎤 ✈ P&W
Kutztown Univ, English Dept, Kutztown, PA 19530,
610-683-4337
Internet: ht6ix@aol.com
 Pubs: *Resurrection Papers* (Chax Pr, 2002), *Practicing
 Amnesia* (Singing Horse Pr, 2000), *The Fray* (Kutztown Pub,
 2000), *Circus Freex* (Standing Stones Pr/Pine Pr, 1995),
 Voiceunders (Texture Pr, 1993), *Five Fingers Rev, Chain,
 Key Satch*(el), *13th Moon*

John Haag P&W
379 Moose Run Rd
Bellefonte, PA 16823, 814-355-7578
 Pubs: *Stones Don't Float* (Ohio State U Pr, 1996), *Atlantis at
 $5 a Day* (NAR, 1991), *The Brine Breather* (Kayak Bks,
 1971), *The Mirrored Man* (Reading U Pr, 1961), *Poetry,
 Talking River Rev, Fugue*

Sy Hakim 🎤 ✈ P&W
3726 Manayunk Ave
Philadelphia, PA 19128-3705, 215-482-0853
Internet: syhakim23@msn.com
 Pubs: *Michaelangelo's Call, Eleanor, Goodbye* (Poet
 Gallery/Century Pr, 1998, 1988), *Dan River Anth* (Dan River
 Pr, 2000), *California Qtly, American Writing*

Ruth Hammond 🎤 ✈ W
2321 Eldridge St
Pittsburgh, PA 15217-2305
Internet: ruthhammondpa@cs.com
 Pubs: *Lake Street Rev, Northeast Mag, Newsday, Portland
 Oregonian, Minneapolis Tribune, Kansas Qtly*

William J. Harris P
103 Cherry Ridge
State College, PA 16803, 814-867-1381
 Pubs: *The Garden Thrives: Anth* (HC, 1996), *In Search of
 Color Everywhere: Anth* (Stewart, Tabori & Chang, 1994)

Dev Hathaway W
314 N Morris St
Shippensburg, PA 17257, 717-530-5943
 Pubs: *The Widow's Boy* (Lynx Hse, 1992), *Black Warrior
 Rev, Carolina Qtly, Missouri Rev, Greensboro Rev*

G. W. Hawkes   W
Lycoming College, English Dept, Williamsport, PA 17701,
570-321-4336
Internet: hawkes@lycoming.edu
   Pubs: *Gambler's Rose, Surveyor, Semaphore* (MacMurray &
   Beck, 2000, 1998, 1998), *Playing Out of the Deep Woods,
   Spies in the Blue Smoke: Stories* (U Missouri Pr, 1995,
   1992), *Atlantic, GQ, Ploughshares, Missouri Rev*

Samuel Hazo 🎤 ✈   P&W
International Poetry Forum, 4415 Fifth Ave, Webster Hall,
Pittsburgh, PA 15213
   Pubs: *The Autobiographers of Everybody* (Intl Poetry Forum,
   2000), *As They Sail, The Holy Surprise of Right Now, The
   Past Won't Stay Behind You* (U Arkansas Pr, 1999, 1996,
   1993), *Spying for God* (Byblos Pr, 1999), *The Pages of Day
   & Night* (Marlboro, 1994)

Sonya Hess   P
Virginia Kidd Agency, 538 E Harford St, Box 278, Milford, PA
18337, 717-296-6205
   Pubs: *Kingdom of Lost Waters* (Ahsata Pr, 1993),
   Constellations of the Inner Eye (Puckerbrush Pr, 1991),
   Grand Street, Iowa Woman, Hiram Poetry Rev

Alan Hines   W
PO Box 262
Solebury, PA 18963-0262, 215-862-3898
   Pubs: *Square Dance* (H&R, 1984), *St. Andrews Rev, Texas
   Qtly, Junction*

Tony Hoagland   P
6637 Dalzell Pl
Pgh International Airport, PA 14217-1141, 412-624-7765
Internet: thglnd@aol.com
   Pubs: *Donkey Gospel, Sweet Ruin* (Graywolf, 1998, 1992),
   History of Desire (Moon Pony Pr, 1990), *Talking to Stay
   Warm* (Coffee Cup Pr, 1986), *A Change in Plans* (San
   Pedro, 1985)

Allen Hoey   P
804 Bismark Way
King of Prussia, PA 19406-3214, 215-992-1088
   Pubs: *What Persists* (Liberty Street Bks, 1992), *A Fire in the
   Cold House of Being* (Walt Whitman Ctr, 1987), *Georgia
   Rev, Hudson Rev, Poetry, Southern Rev*

Daniel Hoffman 🎤 ✈   P
502 Cedar Ln
Swarthmore, PA 19081-1105, 610-544-4438
   Pubs: *Darkening Water, Middens of the Tribe* (LSU, 2002,
   1996), *Words to Create a World* (U Michigan Pr, 1992),
   Hudson Rev, Sewanee Rev, Boulevard, Gettysburg Rev

Cynthia Hogue 🎤 ✈   P
Bucknell Univ, Stadler Center For Poetry, Lewisburg, PA
17837, 570-577-1944
Internet: hogue@bucknell.edu
   Pubs: *Flux* (New Issues Pr, 2002), *The Never Wife*
   (Mammoth Pr, 1999), *The Woman in Red* (Ahsahta Pr,
   1990), *Where the Parallels Cross* (White Knights Pr, 1984),
   *Southern Rev, APR, NAR, Ploughshares, Spoon River
   Poetry Rev, Puerto del Sol, West Branch*

Margaret Holley   P
1184A MacPherson Dr
West Chester, PA 19380, 610-344-4992
Internet: mholley@brynmawr.edu
   Pubs: *Kore in Bloom, Morning Star* (Copper Beech Pr, 1998,
   1992), *The Smoke Tree* (Bluestem Pr, 1991), *Prairie
   Schooner, Boulevard, Poetry, Southern Rev, Gettysburg
   Rev, Nation, Shenandoah*

Charlotte Holmes 🎤 ✈   W
Pennsylvania State Univ, English Dept, University Park,
PA 16802, 814-865-9126
Internet: cxh18@psu.edu
   Pubs: *Gifts & Other Stories* (Confluence Pr, 1994), *The
   Family Track: Anth* (U Illinois Pr, 1998), *New Stories from the
   South: Anth* (Algonquin Bks, 1988), *Grand Street, Carolina
   Qtly, Epoch, Story, New Yorker, Antioch Rev, New Letters,
   Columbia*

C. J. Houghtaling 🎤 ✈   P
RD2, Box 241
Middlebury Center, PA 16935, 570-376-2821
Internet: cjhoughtaling@usa.net
   Pubs: *Filtered Images: Anth* (Vintage 45 Pr, 1992),
   Meanderings: Anth (Foothills, 1992), *Wild West, Literary Jrnl,
   Wolf Head Qtly, Fox Cry, Open Bone, Byline Mag, Endless
   Mountain Rev, Dogwood Tales, South Coast Poetry Jrnl*

Carolyn Fairweather Hughes   P
548 Greenhurst Dr
Pittsburgh, PA 15243, 412-344-6850
   Pubs: *For She Is the Tree of Life: Anth* (Conari Pr, 1995), *We
   Speak for Peace: Anth* (KIT Pubs, 1993), *Pittsburgh Qtly,
   Slant, Wind, Poets On, Lactuca*

Bruce Hunsberger   W
3616 Willingham Ave
Reading, PA 19605-1156, 610-929-2017
   Pubs: *Railroad Street* (Lyle Stuart, 1970), *Alfred Hitchcock's
   Mystery, Nantucket Rev, Seattle Rev, John O'Hara Jrnl,
   Redbook*

Mary Jean Irion 🎤 ✈   P
Chautauqua Writers' Center, 149 Kready Ave, Millersville, PA
17551, 717-872-8337
Internet: mjirion@aol.com
   Pubs: *Holding On* (Heatherstone Pr, 1984), *Poetry, Prairie
   Schooner, NER, Western Humanities Rev, Southern
   Humanities Rev, Poet Lore*

Haywood Jackson P
9A Carothers Dr
Turtle Creek, PA 15145, 412-824-6814
Pubs: *Fellow Travelers* (Samisdat, 1981), *APR, Poetry Now, NYQ, The Little Mag*

Annette Williams Jaffee W
PO Box 26, River Rd
Lumberville, PA 18733
Pubs: *The Dangerous Age* (Leapfrog Pr, 1999), *Recent History* (Putnam, 1988), *Adult Education* (Ontario Review Pr, 1981), *Ploughshares*

Martin James W
Peekner Literary Agency Inc, 3121 Portage Rd, Bethlehem, PA 18017, 215-974-9158
Pubs: *Zombie House, Night Glow* (Pinnacle Bks, 1990, 1989), *5 A.M., Mystery Scene, Cemetery Dance*

Lou Janac P
PO Box 342
Mechanicsburg, PA 17055, 717-774-0253

Suzan Jivan PP
818 N Taney St
Philadelphia, PA 19130-1817
Pubs: *Long Pond Rev*

Julia Kasdorf 🎤 ✈ P
Penn State English Dept, Burrowes Building, University Park, PA 16802-6200, 717-737-4996
Internet: jkasdorf@mcis.messiah.edu
Pubs: *Eve's Striptease, Sleeping Preacher* (U Pitt Pr, 1998, 1992)

Susan Rea Katz P
535 Valley Park Rd
Phoenixville, PA 19460, 610-933-3496
Internet: katz@netaxs.com
Pubs: *Mrs. Brown on Exhibit and Other Museum Poems, Snowdrops for Cousin Ruth* (S&S, 2002, 1998), *Sutured Words* (Aviva Pr, 1987), *Passages North Anth* (Milkweed Edtns, 1990), *American Scholar, Louisville Rev, Maryland Poetry Rev, Alaska Qtly Rev*

Candace E. Kaucher 🎤 ✈ P
1126 Robeson St, 1st Floor
Reading, PA 19604, 610-396-1126
Internet: candyman1654@msn.com
Pubs: *An Anth of New (American) Poets* (Talisman House Pubs, 1998), *NYQ, Painted Bride Qtly, 6ix, Synergism, W'ORCs Aloud Allowed*

Linda Keegan P
141 Friar Ln
McMurray, PA 15317, 724-941-1279
Internet: keegan@nb.net
Pubs: *Heeding the Wind* (Still Waters Pr, 1995), *Greedy for Sunlight* (M. Wurster, 1992), *Poet Lore, New Virginia Rev, Zone 3, Cape Rock, Pittsburgh Qtly, The Herb Companion*

Joseph J. Kelly P
Pennsylvania Humanities Council, 325 Chestnut St, Ste 715, Philadelphia, PA 19106-2607, 215-925-1005
Internet: jkelly@pahumanities.org
Pubs: *Only Morning in Her Shoes: Anth* (Utah State U Pr, 1990), *Chariton Rev, Visions, Plains Poetry Jrnl, Kansas Qtly, Poet Lore, Hiram Poetry Rev*

Miriam Kessler 🎤 ✈ P
2008 Highland Cir
Camp Hill, PA 17011-5920, 717-761-4830
Pubs: *Beyond Lament* (Northwestern Univ Press, 1998), *I Feel a Little Jumpy Around You* (S&S, 1996), *Someone to Pour the Wine* (Ragged Edge Pr, 1996), *Blood to Remember: Anth* (Texas Tech U Pr, 1991), *Cries of the Spirit: Anth* (Beacon Pr, 1990), *Kalliope*

John A. Kessler P
18 Birdie Ln
Reading, PA 19607
Internet: jandmkess@aol.com
Pubs: *Library of Congress Bicentennial: Anth* (Library of Congress, 1999), *Hidden Oak, Poetic License, Reading Eagle, Bookends, Smile, Neovictorian, Riverrun*

Kerry Shawn Keys P
14 Joseph Dr
Boiling Springs, PA 17007, 717-241-6033
Internet: kkeys@paonline.com
Pubs: *Ch'antscapes* (Pine Pr, 1998), *Krajina Supu Vultures' Country* (Votobia, 1996), *Decoy's Desire* (Pennywhistle Pr, 1993), *The Hearing* (Paco Bks, 1992), *Nation, Ploughshares, Iowa Rev, Kayak, Wilderness, 100 Words, Blue Guitar, Michigan Qtly Rev*

Maurice Kilwien Guevara 🎤 ✈ P&W
English Dept, Indiana Univ of Pennsylvania, Indiana, PA 15705-1094, 724-357-2261
Internet: mauricio@iup.edu
Pubs: *Autobiography of So-and-So* (New Issues Pr, 2001), *New Poems of the River Spirits* (U Pitt Pr, 1996), *Postmortem* (U Georgia Pr, 1994), *Learning By Heart: Anth* (U Iowa Pr, 1999), *The Best of Cream City Rev: Anth* (U Wisconsin-Milwaukee, 1997), *Parnassus*

Yong Ik Kim W
1030 Macon Ave
Pittsburgh, PA 15218, 412-243-9495
Pubs: *Blue in the Seed & Other Stories* (Shi-Sa Yong Wo Sa, 1989), *The Diving Gourd* (Knopf, 1963), *Hudson Rev, New Yorker, Atlantic, TriQtly, Sewanee Rev*

Dorothy E. King   PP
PenOwl Productions, PO Box 3872, Harrisburg,
PA 17105-3872, 717-234-3886
     Pubs: *Love in Time* (PenOwl Pr, 1983), *Essence, Chicago
Sheet, Mobius*

Claude F. Koch   W
128 W Highland Ave
Philadelphia, PA 19118, 215-247-4270
     Pubs: *Light in Silence* (Dodd Mead, 1958), *O. Henry Prize
Stories: Anth* (Doubleday, 1985), *Sewanee Rev, Antioch
Rev, Southern Rev, Four Quarters, Spirit*

Sandra Kohler   ⚲   ✈   P
225 S Market St
Selinsgrove, PA 17870-1813, 570-374-8497
Internet: hagendaz@ptd.net
     Pubs: *The Country of Women* (Calyx Bks, 1995), *Colorado
Rev, Black Warrior Rev, Pleiades, Gettysburg Rev, New
Republic, Southern Rev, APR, Calyx, Prairie Schooner*

William Krasner   ⚲   ✈   W
538 Berwyn Ave
Berwyn, PA 19312, 610-647-1527
     Pubs: *The Gambler* (Harper Perennial, 1987), *Resort to
Murder* (Scribner Classic, 1985), *Harper's, Trans-Action,
Society*

Peter Krok   ⚲   ✈   P
240 Golf Hills Rd
Haverton, PA 19083-1026, 610-789-4692
Internet: macpoet1@aol.com
     Pubs: *Midwest Qtly, Poem, Blue Unicorn, Connecticut Rev,
One Trick Pony, Mid-Amer Poetry Rev, New Zoo Rev,
Schuylkill Valley Jrnl*

Will Lane   P
1420 Russel Tavern Rd
Gettysburg, PA 17325
Internet: wlane@gettysburg.edu
     Pubs: *In the Barn of the God, Elegy for Virginia Redding*
(Mad River Pr, 1999, 1989), *Moonlight Standing in as
Cordelia, Hang Together: Anth* (Hanging Loose Pr, 1981,
1985), *Windless Orchard, Lit Rev, Minnesota Rev*

Ursula K. Le Guin   ⚲   ✈   P&W
Virginia Kidd Agency, Box 278, Milford, PA 18337
     Pubs: *The Birthday of the World* (HC, 2002), *The Other
Wind, Tales From Earthsea, The Telling* (Harcourt, 2001,
2001, 2000), *Sixty Odd* (Shambhala, 1999)

Harper Lee   W
c/o J. B. Lippincott Company, E Washington Sq, Philadelphia,
PA 19105, 215-238-4200

Lynn Levin   ⚲   ✈   P
1850 Dover Rd
Southampton, PA 18966-4550, 215-364-2423
     Pubs: *A Few Questions About Paradise* (Loonfeather Pr,
2000), *Poetry NY, Kerem, NAR, New Laurel Rev,
Loonfeather, Poetry Miscellany, Nebraska Rev, Green Hills
Literary Lantern, Yellow Silk II, Hanging Loose, Cedar Hill
Rev, Drexel Online Jrnl*

Bahman Levin   P&W
c/o Concourse Press, PO Box 8265, Philadelphia, PA 19101,
215-262-0497
     Pubs: *Dead Reckoning, Rooted in Volcanic Ashes, The
Night's Journey* (Concourse Pr, 1992, 1987, 1984),
Confrontation Anth (Long Island U, 1992)

Harriet Levin   P
Drexel University, Humanities Dept, McAlister Hall, 32nd &
Chestnut Sts, 5th Fl, Philadelphia, PA 19104, 215-895-2441
Internet: millanhl@dunx1.ocs.drexel.edu
     Pubs: *The Christmas Show* (Beacon Pr, 1996), *West
Branch, Partisan Rev, New Letters, Nimrod, Iowa Rev,
American Voice*

Robert Lima   ⚲   ✈   P
Pennsylvania State Univ, N 352 Burrowes Bldg, University
Park, PA 16802, 814-865-4252
Internet: RXL2@psu.edu
     Pubs: *Sardinia/Sardegna* (Bordighera Intl, 2000), *Mayaland*
(Editorial Betania, 1992), *The Olde Ground* (Society of Inter-
Celtic Arts & Culture, 1985), *2001: A Science Fiction Poetry
Anth* (Anamnesis, 2001), *Uncommonplaces: Anth* (Mayapple
Pr, 2000)

Jack Lindeman   ⚲   ✈   P
133 S Franklin St
Fleetwood, PA 19522-1810, 610-944-9554
Internet: jklnfltwpt@enter.net
     Pubs: *From Both Sides Now* (Scribner, 1998), *Twenty-One
Poems* (Atlantis Edtns, 1963), *Illya's Honey, Kerf, Itnl Poetry
Rev, Phantasmagoria, Forum, Images, Chiron Rev, Poetry
Motel, Calapooya, Rhino, Bellowing Ark, Eureka Lit Mag,
Blue Unicorn, Poet's Page*

George Looney   ⚲   ✈   P
Penn State Erie/The Behrend College, School of Humanities
and Social Sciences, Station Rd, Erie, PA 16563-1501,
814-898-6281
Internet: gol1@psu.edu
     Pubs: *Greatest Hits: 1990-2000* (Pudding Hse, 2001),
Attendant Ghosts (Cleveland State U Pr, 2000), *Animals
Housed in the Pleasure of Flesh* (Bluestem Pr, 1995), *West
Branch, Witness, Kenyon Rev, Ascent, Willow Springs,
Southern Rev*

Roger A. Lopata 🎤 ✈   W
1300 Medford Rd
Wynnewood, PA 19096-2419
Internet: ralopata@earthlink.net
  Pubs: *Other Voices, Painted Bride Qtly, Sou'wester, Hawaii Pacific Rev, Turnstile, Worcester Rev, Panhandler, Midland Rev, Pointed Circle, Hudson Valley Echoes*

Marjorie Maddox   P&W
Lock Haven University, Lock Haven, PA 17745, 570-893-2044
Internet: mmaddoxh@suscom.net

Jeanne Mahon 🎤 ✈   P
84 Yankee Ridge Rd
Mercer, PA 16137-2644, 412-346-6466
  Pubs: *The Wolf in the Wood* (Pangborn Bks, 1996), *English Jrnl, Cimarron Rev, Creeping Bent, Cutbank, Pig Iron, West Branch*

Jody Mahorsky   P&W
281 Nazareth Pike
Bethlehem, PA 18020, 610-759-8341
Internet: jessebers@yahoo.com
  Pubs: *Impressions* (Quill Bks, 1986), *PARA*phrase, Cottage Cheese, Poetalk, Night Roses, AKA: Writer, See of Tranquility, The Creative Spirit, Spirit of the Muse, First Time, Golden Isis, Prophetic Voices, Cosmic Trend, Poetry Peddler, Me 2*

Charles Edward Mann 🎤 ✈   P
PO Box 752
Langhorne, PA 19047, 215-943-3398
Internet: agincour@comcast.net
  Pubs: *After the Pledge of Allegiance* (Pudding Hse, 2000), *American Poetry Rev, Threepenny Rev, Cream City Rev, Southern Humanities Rev, Greensboro Rev, NYQ*

Joanne M. Marinelli   P&W
158 N 23 St, Apt 514
Philadelphia, PA 19103
Internet: the-palsied-poet@worldnet.att.net
  Pubs: *Like Fire* (Crawlspace Pr, 1988), *Onionhead Lit Qtly, G.W. Rev, South Carolina Rev, Poetpourri, Pendragon, Parnassus Lit Jrnl*

Gigi Marino   P
1657 Leisure Acres Rd
Allenwood, PA 17810, 570-547-6628
Internet: gmarino@bucknell.edu
  Pubs: *Catholic Boys & Girls: Anth, Catholic Girls: Anth* (Penguin/NAL, 1994, 1992), *Willow Springs, Graham Hse Rev, South Florida Poetry Rev*

Paul Raymond Martin 🎤 ✈   P&W
18304 Porky St
Saegertown, PA 16433-3356, 814-763-1549
  Pubs: *ByLine, Lynx Eye, Stoneflower, Happy, New Thought Jrnl, Oceana, Eclipse, Nuthouse, Show & Tell, Superior Poetry News, Roswell Lit Rev, Second Tuesday Anthology, Fiction Primer, Virago, Poetry in Motion, 247 artzine*

Hilary Masters 🎤 ✈   W
Carnegie Mellon Univ, Dept of English, Pittsburgh, PA 15213, 412-268-6443
Internet: hm05@andrew.cmu.edu
  Pubs: *In Montaigne's Tower* (U Missouri Pr, 2000), *Home Is the Exile* (Permanent Pr, 1996), *Best Amer Essays: Anth* (HM, 1999), *Best Essays of 1998: Anth* (Doubleday, 1998), *Success: New & Selected Stories* (St. Martin's, 1992), *Kenyon Rev, West Branch*

Dawna M. Maydak   P
Hickory on the Green, 7074 Clubview Dr, South Fayette, PA 15017-1097
  Pubs: *Ten: Poems* (R&R Pr, 1988), *Because the Death of a Rose* (Earthwise Pub, 1983), *Eleven*

Jane McCafferty   W
5927 Bryant Ct
Pittsburgh, PA 15206, 412-665-0561
Internet: danjanemclowe@msn.com
  Pubs: *Autumn and Manuel, Thank You For The Music, One Heart* (Harper Collins 2003, 2003, 2000), *Director of the World* (U Pitt Pr, 1992), *Story, Seattle Rev, West Branch, Alaska Qtly Rev*

Dorothy McCartney   P&W
PO Box 29
Westtown, PA 19395
  Pubs: *Lemmus Lemmus & Other Poems* (Branden Pr, 1973), *Poet Lore, Modern Haiku, Storytime*

Leslie Anne McIlroy 🎤 ✈   P
333 Pitt St, #2
Pittsburgh, PA 15221-3332, 412-241-2049
Internet: lesanne@ix.netcom.com
  Pubs: *Gravel* (Slipstream, 1997), *American Poetry: Anth* (Carnegie Mellon U Pr, 2000), *E: Emily Dickinson Award Anth* (Universities West Pr, 1999), *MacGuffin, Main Street Rag, ACM, Ledge*

Louis McKee 🎤 ✈   P
PO Box 11186
Philadelphia, PA 19136-6186, 215-331-7389
Internet: lmckee4148@aol.com
  Pubs: *Greatest Hits* (Pudding Hse, 2002), *Loose Change* (Marsh River Edtns, 2001), *Right As Rain* (Nova Hse, 2000), *River Architecture* (Cynic Pr, 1999), *The True Speed of Things* (Nightshade Pr, 1990), *The New Geography of Poets: Anth* (U Arkansas, 1992), *APR*

Frank McQuilkin   P
1708 S 16 St
Philadelphia, PA 19145
    Pubs: *Southern Humanities Rev, San Jose Studies,*
    America, Painted Bride Qtly, Sparrow

Robert Randolph Medcalf, Jr.   P&W
185 N Main St
Apt 6, PO Box 746
Biglerville, PA 17307, 717-677-7437
Internet: robmedcalfjr@earthlink.net
    Pubs: *The Unique Anthology #1: Anth* (Promartian Pr,
    2002), *Star*Line, Strange Horizons, Dreams and*
    Nightmares

Diane Hamill Metzger   P&W
c/o Caldwells, 240 W Ridley Ave, Norwood, PA 19074
    Pubs: *Coralline Ornaments* (Weed Patch Pr, 1980), *Pearl,*
    South Coast Poetry Jrnl, Collages & Bricolages, Anima,
    Philadelphia Poets, Hob-Nob, Long Islander

Ann E. Michael 🎤 ✈   P
2380 Brunner Rd
Emmaus, PA 18049
Internet: juanitafb@aol.com
    Pubs: *I Have My Own Song for It: Anth* (U Akron Pr, 2002),
    Inside Grief: Anth (Wise Pr, 2001), *Essential Love: Anth*
    (Grayson Bks/Poetworks, 2000), *Bitter Oleander, Comstock*
    Rev, Coe Rev, Runes, California Qtly, Natural Bridge, Buckle
    &, Cottonwood, Thema

Thomas Milligan   P
561 College Ave, B203
Lancaster, PA 17603
Internet: tmilligan5640@hotmail.com
    Pubs: *Virginia Qtly Rev, New Mexico Humanities Rev,*
    Georgia Rev, Jeopardy, West Branch

David Milton   W
3210 Garbett St
McKeesport, PA 15132

John Paul Minarik   P&W
1600 Walters Mill Rd
Somerset, PA 15510-0005, 724-847-9575
Internet: minarikj@asme.org
    Pubs: *Past the Unknown, Remembered Gate* (Greenfield
    Rev, 1981), *Pittsburgh & Tri-State Area Poets: Anth* (Squirrel
    Hill Poetry Wkshp, 1992), *Confrontation*

Carol Artman Montgomery   P
3115 Perrysville Ave
Pittsburgh, PA 15214, 412-231-1591
    Pubs: *Starting Something* (Los Hombres Pr, 1992), *Outlines*
    (Swamp Pr, 1990)

Dinty W. Moore 🎤 ✈   W
916 26th Ave
Altoona, PA 16601, 814-949-5154
Internet: dinty@psu.edu
    Pubs: *Toothpick Men* (Mammoth, 1999), *The Accidental*
    Buddhist, The Emperor's Virtual Clothes (Algonquin, 1997,
    1995), *Catholic Girls: Anth* (Plume/Penguin, 1992), *Utne*
    Reader, Fourth Genre, Arts & Letters, Georgia Rev, Iowa Rev

Edwin Moses   W
1625 Almond St
Williamsport, PA 17701, 717-323-6496
    Pubs: *Nine Sisters Dancing* (Fithian Pr, 1996), *Astonishment*
    of Heart, One Smart Kid (MacMillan, 1984, 1982)

P. D. Murphy   P
English Dept, Univ Pennsylvania, Indiana, PA 15705
    Pubs: *CQ, Pinchpenny, Kindling, Gold Dust, Poetry Rev,*
    Taurus, Asylum, Sonoma Mandala

Manini Nayar   W
512 Brittany Dr
State College, PA 16803
    Pubs: *London Mag, Signals, Stand Mag, Malahat Rev,*
    Parnassus

Kirk Nesset 🎤 ✈   P&W
Allegheny College, Dept of English, Meadville, PA 16335,
814-332-4331
Internet: knesset@alleg.edu
    Pubs: *Antioch Rev, Chelsea, Cimarron Rev, Fiction, Folio,*
    Green Mountains Rev, Hawaii Rev, Mudfish, NER, Nimrod,
    Paris Rev, Ploughshares, Poet Lore, Prairie Schooner,
    Seattle Rev, Spoon River Poetry Rev, Witness

Joseph Nicholson   P&W
RR3, Box 396E
Mill Hall, PA 17751-9519
Internet: jnicholson@eagle.lhup.edu
    Pubs: *The Dam Builder* (Fault Pr, 1977), *Missouri Rev, West*
    Branch, New Letters, Mississippi Rev, Poetry Now,
    Wormwood Rev

Richard R. O'Keefe   P
PO Box 10506
State College, PA 16805
    Pubs: *Rumors of Autumn* (Hierophant Bks, 1984), *Uccello's*
    Horse (Three Rivers Pr, 1972)

Ed Ochester 🎤 ✈   P
RD1, Box 174
Shelocta, PA 15774-9511, 724-354-4753
Internet: edochester@yourinter.net
    Pubs: *Land of Cockaigne* (Story Line Pr, 2001), *Snow White*
    Horses (Autumn Hse Pr, 2000), *Nation, Virginia Qtly Rev,*
    Third Coast, Tin House, Ploughshares, Prairie Schooner,
    Poetry, Pearl

Toby Olson 🎤 ✈   P&W
275 S 19 St, Ste 7
Philadelphia, PA 19103-5710, 215-732-8296
    Pubs: *Human Nature* (New Directions, 2000), *Write Letter to
    Billy, Unfinished Building* (Coffee Hse, 2000, 1993), *At Sea*
    (S&S, 1993), *Seaview* (New Directions, 1982),
    Conjunctions, Gettysburg Rev

Peter Oresick   P
6342 Jackson St
Pittsburgh, PA 15206-2232, 412-741-6860
Internet: POresick@aol.com
    Pubs: *For a Living: Anth* (U Illinois Pr, 1995), *Pittsburgh Book
    of Contemporary American Poetry: Anth* (U Pitt Pr, 1993)

Gil Ott 🎤 ✈   P
Singing Horse Press, PO Box 40034, Philadelphia,
PA 19106-0034, 215-844-7678
Internet: singinghorse@erols.com
    Pubs: *Pact* (Singing Horse, 2002), *Traffic, Wheel* (Chax,
    2000, 1992), *The Whole Note* (Zasterle, 1997), *Public
    Domain* (Potes & Poets, 1989)

Karl Patten 🎤 ✈   P
232 S 3 St
Lewisburg, PA 17837-1912, 717-522-0070
    Pubs: *Touch* (Bucknell U Pr, 1998), *The Impossible Reaches*
    (Dorcas Pr, 1992), *Controlled Burn, The Progressive, The
    New Renaissance, Yarrow, Amer Literary Rev, 5 A.M.,
    Graham Hse Rev, Pikeville Rev, Connecticut Rev,
    Mississippi Valley Rev, Greensboro Rev*

Jean Pearson   P
PO Box 417
Bethlehem, PA 18016, 215-867-6447
    Pubs: *On Speaking Terms with Earth* (Great Elm Pr, 1988),
    Earth Prayers Anth, APR

James A. Perkins   P&W
Westminster College, Box 62, New Wilmington, PA 16172,
412-946-7347
Internet: jperkins@westminster.edu
    Pubs: *Snakes, Butterbeans, & the Discovery of Electricity*
    (Dawn Valley Pr, 1990), *Southern Rev, Footwork, U.S. 1
    Worksheets, Mississippi Rev*

Pamela M. Perkins-Frederick   P
PO Box F-3
Feasterville, PA 19053-0003, 215-757-7229
Internet: herbnpam@voicenet.com
    Pubs: *A Leaf Gnawed to Lace* (Petoskey Stone Pr, 1992),
    Medical Heritage, Other Poetry, BPJ, Images, The Sun

Walt Peterson   P
5837 Beacon St
Pittsburgh, PA 15217, 412-422-8129
    Pubs: *Image Song* (Seton Hill College, 1994), *Rebuilding
    the Porch* (Nightshade Pr, 1990), *Potato Eyes, Pittsburgh
    Qtly, Language Bridges, Samisdat*

Natalie L. M. Petesch   W
6320 Crombie St
Pittsburgh, PA 15217-2511, 412-521-2802
    Pubs: *The Immigrant Train & Other Stories, Justina of
    Andalusia & Other Stories* (Swallow Pr/Ohio U Pr, 1996,
    1990), *The Bridge, Artful Dodge, Kansas Qtly, Chariton Rev,
    Confrontation*

Anthony Petrosky   P
1109 DeVictor Pl
Pittsburgh, PA 15206, 412-361-5783
    Pubs: *Red & Yellow Boat* (LSU, 1994), *Georgia Rev, Bastard
    Rev, Prairie Schooner, College English*

Sanford Pinsker 🎤 ✈   P
Franklin and Marshall College, English Dept, Lancaster, PA
17603, 717-393-1483
    Pubs: *Sketches of Spain, Local News* (Plowman Pr, 1992,
    1989), *Whales at Play* (Northwoods Pr, 1986), *Georgia Rev,
    Salmagundi, Centennial Rev*

Kenneth Pobo 🎤 ✈   P
123 Folsom Ave
Folsom, PA 19033
Internet: kenneth.g.pobo@widener.edu
    Pubs: *Ordering: A Season in My Garden* (Higganum Hills
    Bks, 2001), *A Barbaric Yawp on the Rocks Please* (Alpha
    Beat Pr, 1996), *Ravens & Bad Bananas* (Osric Pubs, 1995),
    Atlanta Rev, James White Rev

Jad Reilly 🎤 ✈   P
2842 E Devereaux Ave
Philadelphia, PA 19149-3013, 215-289-3659
    Pubs: *Mozart Park* (Nightlight Pr, 1984), *Poets Theater: Anth*
    (H&H Pr, 2000), *Visions Intl, CPU Rev, Aloha, Impetus*

Barbara Reisner   P
3026 Congress St
Allentown, PA 18104, 610-439-1610
    Pubs: *Poems* (Creeping Bent Pr, 1993), *MPR, Laurel Rev,
    Blue Buildings, Shirim, Graham Hse Rev, Yarrow, Wind,
    Bellingham Rev, River Styx*

John Repp 🎤 ✈   P
408 Colorado Dr
Erie, PA 16505, 814-456-5169
Internet: jrepp@edinboro.edu
    Pubs: *The Old West (and other tales)* (March Street Pr,
    2002) *Things Work Out* (Palanquin Pr, 1998), *Thirst Like
    This* (U Missouri Pr, 1990), *Puerto del Sol, Iowa Rev,
    Greensboro Rev, Many Mountains Moving*

Michael D. Riley 🎤 ✈   P
1705 Lititz Pike
Lancaster, PA 17601-6509, 717-569-6377
Internet: mdr1@psu.edu
    Pubs: *Circling the Stones* (Creighton U Pr, 2002),
    Scrimshaw: Citizens of Bone (Lightning Tree Pr, 1988),
    *Talking River Rev, S Dakota Rev, The Ledge, Iron Horse Lit
    Rev, Poetry, Poetry Ireland Rev*

Len Roberts 🎤 ✈   P
2443 Wassergass Rd
Hellertown, PA 18055, 610-838-6716
    Pubs: *The Silent Singer: New & Selected Poems, The
    Trouble-Making Finch, Counting the Black Angels* (U Illinois
    Pr, 2001, 1998, 1994), *Partisan Rev, APR, Paris Rev,
    Poetry, Hudson Rev, Georgia Rev*

Judith R. Robinson 🎤 ✈   P&W
4712 Bayard St
Pittsburgh, PA 15213, 412-681-3018
    Pubs: *The Beautiful Wife and Other Stories* (Aegina Pr,
    1996), *Poems for All: Anth* (24th Street Irregulars Pr, 2002),
    Crossing Limits: Anth (Crossing Limits Pr, 1996), *Taproot,
    Pittsburgh Qtly, Poet's Pen, Byline, Midstream*

Margaret A. Robinson   P
Widener Univ, Chester, PA 19013
    Pubs: *A Woman of Her Tribe* (Fawcett, 1992), *Courting
    Emma Howe* (Ballantine, 1989)

Rosaly DeMaios Roffman 🎤 ✈   P
2580 Evergreen Dr
Indiana, PA 15701, 724-349-2296
Internet: rroffman@iup.edu
    Pubs: *Going to Bed Whole* (University Pr IV, 1993), *I Am
    Becoming the Woman I've Wanted: Anth* (Papier-Mache Pr,
    1997), *Life on the Line: Anth* (Negative Capability Pr, 1992),
    A Gathering of Poets: Anth (Kent State U, 1992), *MacGuffin*

Judith Root   P
Carnegie Mellon Univ Press, PO Box 21, Pittsburgh, PA
15213, 412-268-2861
    Pubs: *Weaving the Sheets* (Carnegie Mellon U Pr, 1988),
    The Paris Rev Anth (Norton, 1990), *Nation, Commonweal,
    William & Mary Rev, Tar River Poetry, Poetry, APR, New
    Republic*

Judith Rose 🎤 ✈   P&W
Allegheny College, Meadville, PA 16335
Internet: jrose@alleg.edu
    Pubs: *Women's Studies Qtrly, Prairie Schooner, Indiana
    Rev, Iowa Rev, Virginia Qtly Rev, Equinox, Carbuncle*

Savina Roxas 🎤 ✈   P
265 Sleepy Hollow
Pittsburgh, PA 15216, 412-561-3557
Internet: roxi50@aol.com
    Pubs: *Sacrificial Mix* (P. Gaglia Inc, 1992), *The Art of Life:
    Anth* (South Western Educational Pub, 1998), *Footwork:
    Paterson Lit Rev Anth* (Passaic Comm College, 1995), *For
    She Is the Tree of Life: Grandmothers Anth* (Conari Pr,
    1994), *Taproot, Passager*

Gibbons Ruark 🎤 ✈   P
45 Morgan Hollow Way
Landenberg, PA 19350-1048, 610-255-3454
Internet: gruark@udel.edu
    Pubs: *Passing Through Customs, Rescue the Perishing*
    (LSU Pr, 1999, 1991), *Keeping Company* (Johns Hopkins,
    1983), *New Republic, Shenandoah*

Sonia Sanchez   P
Temple Univ, English Dept, Philadelphia, PA 19122,
215-787-1796
    Pubs: *Under a Soprano Sky* (Africa World, 1987), *Homegirls
    & Handgrenades* (Thunder's Mouth, 1984)

Walter Sanders   W
266 Burley Ridge Rd
Mansfield, PA 16933
    Pubs: *Four-Minute Fictions: Anth* (WordBeat Pr, 1988),
    NAR, West Branch, North Dakota Qtly

Sally Love Saunders 🎤 ✈   P
609 Rose Hill Rd
Broomall, PA 19008, 610-356-0849
    Pubs: *Manna, New York Times, Times Intl, London Times*

Judy Schaefer 🎤 ✈   P
PO Box 90153
Harrisburg, PA 17109-0153, 717-651-0519
Internet: jschaefer@mindspring.com
    Pubs: *Harvesting the Dew* (Vista, 1997), *Between the
    Heartbeats* (U Iowa Pr, 1995), *Academic Medicine, Amer
    Jrnl of Nursing, Pediatric Nursing, The Lancet*

Peter Schneeman   W
English Dept, Pennsylvania State Univ, 104 Burrowes Bldg,
University Park, PA 16802, 814-865-6381
    Pubs: *Through the Finger Goggles: Stories* (U Missouri Pr,
    1982), *Americas Rev, Salmagundi*

Mike Schneider 🎤 ✈   P
119 Gordon St
Pittsburgh, PA 15218-1605, 412-371-4523
Internet: schneider@psc.edu
    Pubs: *Poetry, Main Street Rag, Mudfish, Poet Lore,
    Sycamore Rev, Yawp, Antietam Rev, Notre Dame Rev,
    Atlanta Rev, Heart Qtly*

Rhoda Josephson Schwartz　　　P&W
1901 JFK Blvd, #2321
Philadelphia, PA 19103-1520, 215-563-3768
　　Pubs: *Worlds of Literature: Anth* (Norton, 1994, 1989), *Chicago Rev, Nation, Kansas Qtly, APR*

Joel L. Schwartz　　　W
1245 Highland Ave, Ste 202
Abington, PA 19001-3714
　　Pubs: *Upchuck Summer's Revenge* (Delacorte, 1990), *The Great Spaghetti Showdown* (Dell, 1988)

Kathleen M. Sewalk　　　P
3589 Menoher Blvd
Johnston, PA 15905-5505
　　Pubs: *Along the Way, Singing of Fruit, Generations of Excellence, On Holiday, Past the Conemaugh Yards* (Tunnel Pr Ltd, 1996, 1996, 1993, 1992, 1987)

Dr. M. P. A. Sheaffer 🎤 ✈　　　P
Millersville Univ, Humanities Division, Millersville, PA 17551
　　Pubs: *Moonrocks & Metaphysical Turnips* (MAF Pr, 2001), *Paths* (Community of Poets Series, 2000), *Requiem Suite, Still a Miracle* (Millersville U Pr, 1992, 1987), *Lacquer Birds & Leaves of Brass* (Four Seasons Pr, 1986)

Ron Silliman　　　P
262 Orchard Rd
Paoli, PA 19301-1116, 610-251-2214
Internet: rsillima@ix.netcom.com
　　Pubs: *Xing* (Meow, 1996), *N/O* (Roof, 1994), *Toner* (Potes & Poets, 1993), *Jones* (Generator Pr, 1993), *Paris Rev, Poetry, Sulfur, Iowa Rev, Zyzzyva, Conjunctions, Object, Mirage, Grist On-Line, Object Permanence*

Randall Silvis　　　W
PO Box 297
St Petersburg, PA 16054, 724-659-2922
Internet: rrbns@juno.com
　　Pubs: *Dead Man Falling* (Carroll & Graf, 1996), *An Occasional Hell* (Permanent Pr, 1993), *Manoa, Destination Discovery, Pittsburgh Mag, CSM, Prism Intl*

Michael Simms 🎤 ✈　　　P
219 Bigham St
Pittsburgh, PA 15211-1431
　　Pubs: *The Fire-Eater* (Del Rogers, 1987), *Migration* (Breitenbush, 1985), *CafÈ Rev, Mid-American Rev, West Branch, SW Rev, Black Warrior Rev, 5 A.M., Pittsburgh Qtly*

Deloris Slesiensky　　　P&W
74 Dug Rd
Wyoming, PA 18644-9374
　　Pubs: *Wild Onions, Plaza, Mobius, Psychopoetica, Moments in Time, Pittston Thursday Dispatch*

David Small 🎤 ✈　　　W
532 Grandview Ave
Camp Hill, PA 17011-1812, 717-763-0374
Internet: dsmall1007@aol.com
　　Pubs: *Alone, The River in Winter, Almost Famous* (Norton, 1991, 1987, 1982)

Ronald F. Smits　　　P
Box 466
Ford City, PA 16226, 412-763-7024
　　Pubs: *Mourning Dove* (Ball State U Pr, 1979), *Tar River Poetry, Wilderness, Puerto del Sol, Free Lunch, Connecticut River Rev, The Bridge*

Judith Sornberger　　　P
141 S Main St
Mansfield, PA 16933, 717-662-7735
　　Pubs: *BiFocals Barbie: A Midlife Pantheon, Judith Beheading Holofernes* (Talent Hse Pr, 1996, 1993), *Open Heart* (Calyx Bks, 1993), *Prairie Schooner, Puerto del Sol, West Branch, American Voice, Calyx, Hawaii Pacific Rev*

Eileen Spinelli　　　P
Ray Lincoln, 7900 Old York Rd, 107B, Elkins Park, PA 19027
　　Pubs: *Somebody Loves You, Mr. Hatch* (Bradbury, 1990), *A Room of One's Own, Muse, Footwork*

Will Stanton　　　W
925 Wilhelm Rd
Harrisburg, PA 17111, 717-564-1881
　　Pubs: *The Old Familiar Booby Traps of Home* (Doubleday, 1977), *New Yorker, Atlantic, Redbook*

Sharon Sheehe Stark　　　P&W
23 Blue Rocks Rd
Lenhartsville, PA 19534, 610-756-6048
　　Pubs: *Wrestling Season, The Dealer's Yard & Other Stories* (Morrow, 1987, 1985), *Atlantic*

Irving Stettner　　　P
RR2, Box 280
Harveys Lake, PA 18618
　　Pubs: *Beggars in Paradise* (Writers Unlimited, 1991), *Self-Portrait* (Sun Dog, 1991), *Anais, World Letter*

Alex Stiber　　　P
1133 Sunrise Dr
Pittsburgh, PA 15243-1945
　　Pubs: *American Voice, Stone Country, Long Pond Rev, Fiddlehead, Event, Louisville Rev*

Adrienne Su 🎤 ✈   P
English Dept, Dickinson College, PO Box 1773, Carlisle, PA
17013-2896, 717-245-1347
Internet: sua@dickinson.edu
Pubs: *Middle Kingdom* (Alice James Bks, 1997), *New
American Poets: Anth* (U Pr New England, 2000), *Best
American Poetry: Anth* (Scribner, 2000), *Electronic Poetry
Rev, 88, Indiana Rev, New Letters, Prairie Schooner*

John Taggart   P
295 E Creek Rd
Newburg, PA 17240, 717-423-5565
Pubs: *Poems for the New Millennium: Anth* (U California Pr,
1998), *Crosses* (Sun & Moon, 1998), *Conjunctions, Five
Fingers Rev, Hambone, Sulfur, Talisman, To, Chicago Rev*

Myron Taube   W
English Dept, Univ Pittsburgh, Pittsburgh, PA 15260,
412-624-6532
Pubs: *Kansas Qtly, Texas Qtly, Wind, Cimarron Rev*

John Alfred Taylor   P
395 N Wade Ave
Washington, PA 15301, 724-228-0968
Pubs: *Castle Fantastic, Year's Best Horror Stories: Anth*
(Daw, 1996, 1983), *West Branch, Asimov's Science Fiction,
New Letters, Twilight Zone Mag*

Robert Love Taylor, Jr. 🎤 ✈   W
English Dept, Bucknell Univ, Lewisburg, PA 17837,
570-577-1440
Internet: rtaylor@bucknell.edu
Pubs: *Lady of Spain, The Lost Sister* (Algonquin Bks,
1992, 1989), *Southern Rev, Hudson Rev, Shenandoah,
Georgia Rev*

Philip Terman 🎤 ✈   P
4606 Scrubgrass Rd
Grove City, PA 16127-8716, 814-786-7270
Internet: terman@clarion.edu
Pubs: *The House of Sages* (Mammoth Pr, 1998), *What
Survives* (Sow's Ear Pr, 1993), *Poetry, Kenyon Rev, NER,
NAR, Poetry NW, SPR*

Elaine Terranova 🎤 ✈   P
1912 Panama St
Philadelphia, PA 19103
Internet: eterranova@ccp.cc.pa.us
Pubs: *The Dog's Heart* (Orchises Pr, 2002), *Damages, A
Gift of Tongues: Anth* (Copper Canyon Pr, 1996, 1996), *The
Cult of the Right Hand* (Doubleday, 1991), *Sixty Years of
Amer Poetry: Anth* (Harry Abrams, 1997), *Prairie Schooner,
Poet Lore, New Yorker, 88*

John A. Thompson, Sr. 🎤 ✈   P
137 Pointview Rd
Pittsburgh, PA 15227-3131, 412-885-3798
Internet: nitewriterarts@aol.com
Pubs: *Medicinal Purposes, Droplet Jrnl, Poetic Soul, Broken
Streets, Writer's Info, Green Feather, Wind Mag, Parnassus
Lit Jrnl, Haiku Zasshi Zo, Prophetic Voices*

J. C. Todd 🎤 ✈   P
339 S 4 St
Philadelphia, PA 19106-4219, 215-625-2449
Internet: jctodd66@aol.com
Pubs: *Nightshade, Entering Pisces* (Pine Pr, 1995, 1984),
*APR, Drunken Boat, Crab Orchard Rev, Paris Rev, Virginia
Qtly Rev, Prairie Schooner, BPJ*

Ronald Tranquilla 🎤 ✈   P&W
Saint Vincent College, 300 Fraser Purchase Rd, Latrobe, PA
15650-2690, 724-539-9761
Internet: ron.tranquilla@email.stvincent.edu
Pubs: *Loyalhanna Rev, New Rev, West Branch, Great
Stream Rev, Violent Milk, Marginal Rev, Hollins Critic,
Rocky Mtn Rev, Small Pond Mag, Monmouth Rev, Haiku
Highlights, New American & Canadian Poetry*

Tommy Trantino   W
Writers Unlimited, Inc, Box 280, Rte 2, Harveys Lake, PA
18618, 717-675-3447
Pubs: *Lock the Lock* (Bantam, 1975), *Village Voice, People
Mag, Stroker Mag*

Lee Upton 🎤 ✈   P
English Dept, Lafayette College, Easton, PA 18042,
610-330-5250
Internet: uptonlee@lafayette.edu
Pubs: *Civilian Histories* (U Georgia, 2000), *Approximate
Darling* (U Georgia, 1996), *No Mercy* (Atlantic Monthly,
1989), *APR, Field, Yale Rev, Poetry*

William F. Vanwert   P&W
7200 Cresheim Rd, #C-1
Philadelphia, PA 19119, 215-248-4715
Pubs: *Missing in Action* (York Pr, 1991), *The Discovery of
Chocolate* (Word Beat Pr, 1987), *TriQtly, NAR, Western
Humanities Rev, Chelsea, Boulevard, Georgia Rev*

Jack Veasey 🎤 ✈   P
37-A W 2nd St
Hummelstown, PA 17036, 717-566-9237
Pubs: *The Moon in the Nest* (Crosstown Bks, 2002), *Tennis
with Baseball Bats* (Warm Spring Pr, 1995), *Sweet Jesus:
Anth* (Anthology Pr, 2003), *A Loving Testimony: Anth*
(Crossing Pr, 1995), *Experimental Forest, Christopher
Street, Pittsburgh Qtly, Oxalis*

Jon Volkmer   P&W
English Dept, Ursinus College, Collegeville, PA 19426,
610-489-4111
Internet: jvolkmer@acad.ursinus.edu
    Pubs: *Painted Bride Qtly, Texas Rev, Folio, Dancing Shadow Pr, South Dakota Rev, Crosscurrents, Carolina Qtly, Hellas, Cimarron Rev, Prairie Schooner, Seattle Rev*

Jeanne Murray Walker 🎤 ✈   P
742 S Latches Ln
Merion, PA 19066-1614
Internet: jwalker@udel.edu
    Pubs: *Gaining Time* (Copper Beech, 1998), *Stranger Than Fiction* (QRL, 1993), *Coming Into History, Nailing Up the Home Sweet Home* (Cleveland State U Pr, 1990, 1980), *APR, Poetry, Nation, Partisan Rev, Georgia Rev*

T. H. S. Wallace 🎤 ✈   P
3032 Logan St
Camp Hill, PA 17011-2947, 717-737-6489
Internet: thswallace@aol.com
    Pubs: *When the World's Foundation Shifts, Raw on the Bars of Longing* (Rabbit Pr, 1998, 1994), *None Were So Clear* (New Foundation Pub, 1996), *Voices from the Peace Tree: Anth* (Rabbit Pr, 2000), *Midwest Qtly, Cumberland Poetry Rev*

Mark Thomas Wangberg   P
593 Hansell Rd
Wynnewood, PA 19096, 215-649-6007
    Pubs: *The Third Coast: Anth* (Wayne State U Pr, 1976), *U.S. 1, Poets, Bellingham Rev, 5 A.M., South Dakota Rev*

Robert G. Weaver   W
Box 194, RD 1, Petersburg, PA 16669, 814-667-3530
    Pubs: *Just Pulp, Manhunt*

Bruce Weigl   P
English Dept, Burrowes Bldg, Pennsylvania State Univ,
University Park, PA 16802, 814-865-7105
    Pubs: *Sweet Lorrain, What Saves Us* (TriQtly Bks, 1996, 1992), *Song of Napalm* (Atlantic Monthly Pr, 1988), *The Monkey Wars* (U Georgia Pr, 1985), *TriQtly*

Sanford Weiss   P
542 Headquarters Rd
Ottsville, PA 18942, 610-847-2238
Internet: sweiss@epix.net
    Pubs: *Poetry, Kayak, Poetry Now, Yankee, BPJ*

William Welsh 🎤 ✈   P&W
501 Franklin St
East Pittsburgh, PA 15112-1109, 412-824-0679
Internet: grapie@stargate.net
    Pubs: *Being Pretty Doesn't Help at All* (Ancient Mariner Pr, 1989), *You Can't Get There from Here* (Neumenon Pr, 1986), *Maple Leaf Rag: Anth* (Portals Pr, 1995), *New Orleans Rev, Interstate, Maple Leaf Rag, Slow Loris Reader, Pittsburgh Qtly, Gravida*

Richard Wertime 🎤 ✈   W
Beaver College, English Dept, Glenside, PA 19038-3295,
215-572-2963
Internet: wertime@beaver.edu
    Pubs: *The Ploughshares Reader: Anth* (Pushcart, 1985), *NE Corridor, Centerstage, Hudson Rev, Ploughshares*

Maureen Williams   P&W
RD3, Box 3292
Uniondale, PA 18470, 717-679-2745
    Pubs: *A Loving Voice: Anth* (Charles Pr, 1992), *Women of the 14th Moon: Anth* (Crossing Pr, 1991), *Keltic Fringe, Black Mountain Rev, Endless Mountain Rev, Broomstick*

Kimmika L. H. Williams 🎤 ✈   PP
Temple Univ, Anthropology Dept, Philadelphia, PA 19122,
215-204-8417
Internet: kwilli01@temple.edu
    Pubs: *Signs of the Time: Culture Pop, Epic Memory: Places & Spaces I've Been, Envisioning a Sea of Dry Bones, Mine Eyes Have Seen Into the Millennium: Anth* (Three Goat Pr, 1999, 1995, 1994, 2000), *Di-Verse City 2000: Anth* (AIPF, 2000), *Hip Mama, Sisters*

Craig Williamson   W
English Dept, Swarthmore College, Swarthmore, PA 19081,
215-328-8152
    Pubs: *Feast of Creatures* (U Penn Pr, 1982), *Senghor's Poems* (England; Rex Collings Ltd, 1976)

Eleanor Wilner 🎤 ✈   P
324 S 12 St
Philadelphia, PA 19107-5947, 215-546-4237
Internet: pophys@aol.com
    Pubs: *Reversing the Spell* (Copper Canyon, 1998), *Otherwise, Sarah's Choice, Shekhinah* (U Chicago Pr, 1993, 1989, 1984)

Jet Wimp   P
Math & Computers Dept, Drexel Univ, Philadelphia, PA 19104,
215-895-2658
    Pubs: *Against Infinity* (Primary Pr, 1978), *The Drowning Place* (Moore College of Art, 1974)

Marion Winik   P
Rr 4
Glen Rock, PA 17327-9804
    Pubs: *Boy Crazy* (Slough Press, 1986), *Nonstop* (Cedar Rock, 1981)

Michael Wurster 🎤 ✈   P
PO Box 4279
Pittsburgh, PA 15203-0279, 412-481-7636
    Pubs: *The Snake Charmer's Daughter* (Elemenope, 2000), *The Cruelty of the Desert* (Cottage Wordsmiths, 1989), *Janus Head, Unwound, The Antigonish Rev, 5AM, Old Red Kimono, Bogg, Pleiades, Poet Lore*

Yvonne P
c/o Chameleon Productions, Inc, Greene Street Artists Corp,
5225 Greene St, Loft #16, Philadelphia, PA 19144
Internet: iwilla@earthlink.net
    Pubs: *Iwilla/Rise, Iwilla/Scourge* (Chameleon Prod, 1999,
1987), *An Ear to the Ground: Anth* (U Georgia, 1989)

Robert Zaller 🎤 ✈ P
326 Bryn Mawr Ave
Bala Cynwyd, PA 19004-2822, 610-667-2224
Internet: rzaller@msn.com
    Pubs: *For Empedocles* (European Arts Center, 1996),
Invisible Music (Mavridis Pr, 1988), *Lives of the Poet*
(Barlenmir Hse, 1974), *Meridian Bound: Anth* (Meridian
Writers Collective, 2000), *APR, Sea Change, Mad Poets
Rev, Schuylkill Valley Rev, Agenda*

Anne Yusavage Zellars W
RD2, Box 403
Valencia, PA 16059, 412-898-3019
    Pubs: *Oxford Mag, South Carolina Rev, Room of One's
Own, West Branch, Women's Qtly Rev, Bloodroot*

PUERTO RICO

David Dayton 🎤 ✈ P
580 Cruz Maria/Bellas Lomas
Mayaguez, PR 00682-7571, 787-833-9242
Internet: ddayton@caribe.net
    Pubs: *The Lost Body of Childhood* (Copper Beech, 1979)

Jose Emilio Gonzalez P
Univ Puerto Rico, Box 2-3056, Rio Piedras, PR 00931,
809-751-8266

E. W. Northnagel P&W
PO Box 6155
San Juan, PR 00914-6155
    Pubs: *Twenty-Five for Tony* (Cibola Studio, 1968), *Phase &
Cycle, Pegasus Rev, CQ, Poetry Motel*

Carmen Puigdollers P&W
Condominio Francia #5E, 1551 Rosario St, Santurce, PR
00911, 809-721-8379
    Pubs: *Homenaje Poetico A Josemilio Gonzalez: Anth* (U
Puerto Rico, 1993), *Interamericana, A Proposito Revista
Literaria*

Magaly Quinones 🎤 P
PO Box 22269, University Stn, San Juan, PR 00931-2269,
787-764-0000
Internet: mquinone@rrpac.upr.clu.edu
    Pubs: *Suenos de Papel* (Editorial Universidad de Puerto
Rico, 1996), *Razon de Lucha, Razon de Amor, Nombrar*
(Editorial Mairena, 1989, 1985)

Etnairis Rivera 🎤 ✈ P
Arrigoitia 515
San Juan, PR 00918-2648, 787-627-5273
Internet: etnairisrivera@yahoo.com
    Pubs: *Intervenidos, Entre Ciudades Y Casi Paraisos, Canto
De La Pachamama* (Instituto De Cultura Puertorriquena,
2002, 1995, 1976), *El Viaje De Los Besos* (Ed.De La
Universidad De Puerto Rico, 2000)

RHODE ISLAND

Tom Ahern 🎤 ✈ P
16 High St, #4
Westerly, RI 02891, 401-596-8480

William Allen P
118 Gibbs Ave
Newport, RI 02840, 401-842-0832
    Pubs: *Sevastopol: On Photos of War* (Xenos, 1997), *The
Man on the Moon* (NYU/Persea Pr, 1987), *Iowa Rev,
Newport Rev, Spazio Humano, Denver Qtly, Prairie
Schooner, American Voice*

Mark Anderson P
English Dept, Rhode Island College, 600 Mt Pleasant Ave,
Providence, RI 02908, 401-456-8804
    Pubs: *Serious Joy* (Orchises Pr, 1990), *The Broken Boat*
(Ithaca Hse, 1978), *Poetry, Hudson Rev*

Randy Blasing 🎤 ✈ P
528 Great Rd
Lincoln, RI 02865, 401-722-1551
    Pubs: *Second Home* (Copper Beach Pr, 2001), *Graphic
Scenes, The Double House of Life* (Persea Bks, 1994, 1989)

Cathleen Calbert P
English Dept, Rhode Island College, 600 Mt Pleasant Ave,
Providence, RI 02908, 401-456-8678
Internet: ccalbert@ric.edu
    Pubs: *Bad Judgment* (Sarabande Bks, 1999), *Lessons in
Space* (U Pr Florida, 1997), *My Summer As a Bride*
(Riverstone Pr, 1995), *Best American Poetry: Anth* (S&S,
1995), *Paris Rev, Nation, New Republic, Hudson Rev,
Ploughshares*

David Cashman P
23 Burlington St
Providence, RI 02906
    Pubs: *Modern Haiku, Brussels Sprout*

Tom Chandler 🎤 ✈ P
44 Summit Ave
Providence, RI 02906
Internet: tchandle@bryant.edu
    Pubs: *Wingbones* (Signal Bks, 1997), *One Tree Forest, The
Sound the Moon Makes As It Watches* (The Poet's Pr, 1992,
1988), *Poetry, Ontario Rev, Boulevard, Literary Rev, NYQ*

Martha Christina 🎙 ✈   P
17 Union St
Bristol, RI 02809
    Pubs: *What Have You Lost?* (Greenwillow, 1999), *Staying Found* (Fleur de Lis, 1997), *Crab Orchard Rev, Connecticut Rev, Louisville Rev, Prairie Schooner, Tar River Poetry*

Dave Church 🎙 ✈   PP&P
30 Forest St
Providence, RI 02906, 401-521-4728
    Pubs: *Hack Job* (Green Bean Pr, 2002), *Bebop Rebop: CD* (Aftermath Bks, 2002), *A Good Life It Is These Days* (Microbe Pr, 2001), *Paris/Atlantic, Rattle, Nerve Cowboy, Maelstrom, Angelfish, Nedge*

Geoffrey D. Clark 🎙   W
PO Box 43
Bristol, RI 02809-0043, 401-245-4369
Internet: WAYPAMGEOF@aol.com
    Pubs: *Rabbit Fever, All the Way Home* (Avisson Pr, 2000, 1997), *Jackdog Summer* (Hi Jinx Pr, 1996), *Schooling the Spirit* (Asylum Arts, 1993), *Ruffian on the Stairs* (Story Pr, 1988), *Witness, NE Corridor, Ploughshares, Mississippi Rev, Pittsburgh Qtly*

Thomas Cobb   P
Rhode Island College, English Dept, Providence, RI 02908, 401-456-8115
    Pubs: *Crazy Heart* (H&R, 1987), *We Shall Curse the Dead* (Desert First Works, 1976)

Leonard Cochran   P
Providence College, Providence, RI 02918-0001, 401-865-2358
    Pubs: *Formalist, Tennessee Qtly, Atlantic, Harvard Mag, America, Spirit, Yankee, Christian Century*

Patricia Cumming 🎙 ✈   P
Box 251
Adamsville, RI 02801, 508-636-2403
    Pubs: *Mother to Daughter, Daughter to Mother: Anth* (Feminist Pr, 1984), *Letter from an Outlying Province, Afterwards* (Alice James Bks, 1976, 1974), *ACM, Riverrun, Home Planet News, Crone's Nest, Timber Creek Rev*

Tina Marie Egnoski 🎙 ✈   P&W
124 Rogers Ave
Barrington, RI 02806, 401-437-2210
    Pubs: *Life on the Line: Anth* (Negative Capability Pr, 1992), *Cimarron Rev, Dark Horse Lit Rev, Hawaii Paific Rev, Louisville Rev, Clackamas Lit Rev, Fish Stories, Rhode Islander Mag, Cream City Rev, Laurel Rev, Rockford Rev, Mississippi Valley Rev*

Caroline Finkelstein   P
170 Westminster St
Providence, RI 02903
    Pubs: *Germany* (Carnegie Mellon U Pr, 1995), *Windows Facing East* (Dragon Gate, 1986), *APR, Poetry, Antioch, TriQtly, Virginia Qtly Rev, Willow Springs*

Forrest Gander 🎙 ✈   P
351 Nayatt Rd
Barrington, RI 02806-4336
    Pubs: *Torn Awake, Science & Steepleflower* (New Directions, 2001, 1998), *Deeds of Utmost Kindness* (Wesleyan, 1994), *Lynchburg* (U Pitt Pr, 1993)

Lora Jean Gardiner   P
25 Glenwood Dr
North Kingstown, RI 02852
    Pubs: *In Native Woods* (Rhode Island State Poetry Society, 1985), *Chrysalis, Green's Mag, Lyric*

Christopher Gilbert 🎙 ✈   P
56 Ardoene St
Providence, RI 02907-3409, 401-461-5707
Internet: cgilbert@bristol.mass.edu
    Pubs: *Across the Mutual Landscape* (Graywolf, 1984), *Massachusetts Rev, African-American Lit Rev, Urbanus, Crab Apple Rev, Graham Hse Rev, Ploughshares, Indiana Rev, William & Mary Rev, Callaloo*

Michael S. Harper   P
Brown Univ, Box 1852, Providence, RI 02912, 401-863-2393
    Pubs: *Honorable Amendments* (U Illinois Pr, 1994), *Every Shut Eye Ain't Asleep: Anth* (Little, Brown, 1994), *New Yorker, Obsidian*

Edwin Honig 🎙 ✈   P
229 Medway St
Providence, RI 02906, 401-831-1027
    Pubs: *Time and Again* (Xlibris, 2001), *The Imminence of Love* (Texas Ctr for Writers Pr, 1993), *Always Astonished* (City Lights, 1986), *Mentor Book of Major American Poets: Anth* (Penguin, 1983), *Alea, City Lights Rev, Agni*

Peter Johnson 🎙 ✈   P&W
Providence College, English Dept, Providence, RI 02918
Internet: pjohnson@providence.edu
    Pubs: *Miracles and Mortifications* (White Pine Pr, 2001), *I'm a Man* (Raincrow Pr, 1998), *Pretty Happy!* (White Pine Pr, 1997)

Caroline Knox 🎙 ✈   P
Adamsville, RI 02801-0245, 508-636-4138
Internet: cbjknox@aol.com
    Pubs: *A Beaker: New and Selected Poems* (Verse Pr, 2002), *Sleepers Wake* (Timken Pubs, 1994), *To Newfoundland* (U Georgia Pr, 1989), *Poetry, American Scholar, New Republic, Harvard, Verse, Paris Rev*

Kathryn Kulpa 🎤 ✈ W
49 Shangri-la Ln
Middletown, RI 02842
Internet: kathrynka@yahoo.com
    Pubs: *Hayden's Ferry Rev, Bellevue Lit Rev, Margin, Carve, Indigenous Fiction, Florida Rev, Asimov's, Parting Gifts, Madison Rev, Minimus, Seventeen, Larcom Rev, Quality Women's Fiction*

Betsy Lincoln 🎤 ✈ P
247 Fishing Cove Rd
Wickford, RI 02852, 401-295-5547
Internet: blincolnl@netsense.net
    Pubs: *News of the Living* (Premier Poets Chapbook Series, 1999), *Further Along* (Arbor Pr, 1990), *Momentary Stays* (Weaver Pubs, 1976), *Sojourner, NE Jrnl, Newport Rev, Crone's Nest*

Peter Mandel P
239 Transit St
Providence, RI 02906, 401-831-5227
    Pubs: *If One Lived on the Equator* (Nightshade Pr, 1993), *Harper's, Yankee, Poetry NW, Laurel Rev, Pulpsmith, Dusty Dog*

Susan Onthank Mates W
52 Bluff Rd
Barrington, RI 02806
    Pubs: *The Good Doctor* (U Iowa Pr, 1994), *Pushcart Prize XIX Anth* (Pushcart Pr, 1994), *TriQtly, NW Rev, Sou'wester, Arkansas Rev*

F. X. Mathews W
497 Old North Rd
Kingston, RI 02881, 401-789-7338
    Pubs: *The Frog in the Bottom of the Well, The Concrete Judasbird* (HM, 1971, 1968)

Edward McCrorie 🎤 ✈ P
English Dept, Providence College, Providence, RI 02918
    Pubs: *Needle Man* (Chestnut Hills Pr, 1999), *After a Cremation* (Thorpe Springs Pr, 1974), *Ariel, Confluence, Tennessee Qtly, NE Corridor, New Press Literary Qtly, BPJ, Little Mag, Spirit*

Robert McRoberts P
8 Emery Rd
Warren, RI 02885, 401-245-5321

Richard O'Connell P
3 West View Dr
West Kingston, RI 02892, 401-539-5044
    Pubs: *The Bright Tower, Voyages, Retro Worlds: Selected Poems* (U Salzburg, 1997, 1995, 1993), *Dawn Crossing, Fractals, American Obits, The Caliban Poems* (Atlantis Edtns, 2002, 2002, 2002, 1992), *New Yorker, Paris Rev, Atlantic*

Lawrence T. O'Neill P
PO Box 9
Carolina, RI 02812-0009
    Pubs: *Chrysalis, Daguerreotypes, With Fire & Smoke* (Shadow Pr, 2002, 1991, 1976)

Tom Ockerse P
37 Woodbury St
Providence, RI 02906
    Pubs: *T.O.P.* (Tom Ockerse Edtns, 1970), *The A-Z Book* (Colorcraft-Brussel Pub, 1969)

Jane Lunin Perel P
135 Canonchet Ave
Warwick, RI 02888, 401-865-2490
Internet: jlperel@providence.edu
    Pubs: *The Sea Is Not Full* (Le'Dory Pub Hse, 1990), *Blowing Kisses to the Sharks* (Copper Beech Pr, 1978), *Alembic, 13th Moon, Poetry Northwest, Carolina Qtly, The Voice, West Coast Writer's Conspiracy, Choice, Massachusetts Rev*

Paul Petrie P
200 Dendron Rd
Peace Dale, RI 02879, 401-783-8644
    Pubs: *The Runners* (Slow Loris Pr, 1988), *Strange Gravity* (Tidal Pr, 1984), *Atlantic, Poetry*

Nancy Potter W
298 Hillsdale Rd
West Kingston, RI 02892, 401-539-2156
    Pubs: *Legacies* (U Illinois Pr, 1987), *Indiana Rev, Kansas Qtly, Cotton Boll, Paragraph, Alaska Qtly*

Laurence J. Sasso, Jr. 🎤 ✈ P
145 Mann School Rd
Esmond, RI 02917, 401-231-1402
    Pubs: *The Olney Street Group Anth* (Olney Street Pr, 1989), *Italian-Americana, Texas Rev, Yankee, Santa Fe Literary Rev*

Carl Senna P
365 Angell St, #3
Providence, RI 02906
    Pubs: *Parachute Shop Blues: Poetry of New Orleans* (Xavier U Pr, 1972)

John Shaw W
28 Oaklawn St, #302
Cranston, RI 02920-9375, 401-944-5633
    Pubs: *Libido, New Renaissance, Turnstile, Brown Rev, NAR, Onion Head, New Oregon Rev, Phantasm, Moosehead Rev, Spectrum, Back Bay View*

Meredith Steinbach   W
English Dept, Brown Univ, Box 1852, Providence, RI 02912,
401-863-3526
Internet: meredith_steinbach@brown.edu
  Pubs: *The Birth of the World As We Know It; or Teiresias*
  (Northwestern U Pr, 1996), *Zara* (TriQtly Bks, 1996), *Here
  Lies the Water* (Another Chicago Pr, 1990), *Prize Stories,
  1990: The O. Henry Awards* (Anchor, 1990), *Southwest Rev,
  Antioch Rev*

Nancy Sullivan   P
Hillsdale Rd
West Kingston, RI 02892, 401-539-2156
  Pubs: *Telling It* (Godine, 1976), *Treasury of English Short
  Stories: Anth* (Doubleday, 1985), *Iowa Rev*

John Tagliabue 🎤 ✈   P
Wayland Manor Apt 412, 500 Angell St, Providence, RI 02906,
401-272-1766
  Pubs: *New & Selected Poems: 1942-1997* (National Poetry
  Fdn, 1998), *The Great Day* (Alembic Pr, 1984), *The
  Doorless Door* (Grossman, 1970), *Contemporary Poetry of
  New England: Anth* (U Pr of New England, 2002),
  Puckerbrush Rev, VIA

Rosmarie Waldrop 🎤 ✈   P
71 Elmgrove Ave
Providence, RI 02906-4132, 401-351-0015
  Pubs: *The Hanky of Pippin's Daughter + A Form/of Taking/It
  All* (Northwestern Univ Pr, 2001), *Reluctant Gravities, A Key
  Into the Language of America* (New Directions, 1999, 1994),
  Split Infinities (Singing Horse, 1998), *Another Language*
  (Talisman Hse, 1997)

Keith Waldrop   P
71 Elmgrove Ave
Providence, RI 02906
  Pubs: *The Locality Principle* (Avec, 1995), *Light While There
  Is Light* (Sun & Moon, 1993), *The Opposite of Letting the
  Mind Wander* (Lost Roads, 1990)

Craig Watson 🎤 ✈   P
211 Conanicus Ave
Jamestown, RI 02835-1520, 401-423-2390
Internet: csw1@idt.net
  Pubs: *Free Will* (Roof, 2000), *Reason* (Zasterle, 1998),
  Picture of the Picture of the Image in the Glass (O Pr, 1992),
  Unsuspended Animation (Paradigm Pr, 1990), *After
  Calculus* (Burning Deck, 1988)

Ed Weyhing   W
20 Murphy Cir
Middletown, RI 02842-6234, 401-846-1981
Internet: edweyhing@worldnet.att.net
  Pubs: *Generation to Generation: Anth* (Papier-Mache Pr,
  1998), *How the Weather Was: Anth* (Ampersand Pr, 1990),
  *Nimrod, Short Story, Cimarron Rev, Witness, Glimmer Train,
  Crescent Rev, Nexus*

Ruth Whitman   P
40 Tuckerman Ave
Middletown, RI 02842, 401-846-3737
  Pubs: *Hatshepsut, Speak to Me, Laughing Gas: New &
  Selected Poems* (Wayne State U Pr, 1992, 1991), *New
  Republic, American Voice*

Thomas Wilson   W
6 Bush St
Newport, RI 02840
  Pubs: *American Fiction, Ellery Queen, Paris Rev, Antaeus*

C. D. Wright 🎤 ✈   P
351 Nayatt Rd
Barrington, RI 02806-4336, 401-245-8069
Internet: wrightcd@aol.com
  Pubs: *Deepstep Come Shining* (Copper Canyon, 1998),
  Tremble (Ecco Pr, 1996), *Just Whistle* (Kelsey Street Pr,
  1993), *String Light* (U Georgia Pr, 1991), *Conjunctions,
  Sulfur, Arshile*

SOUTH CAROLINA

Gilbert Allen 🎤 ✈   P&W
English Dept, Furman Univ, Greenville, SC 29613,
864-294-3152
Internet: gil.allen@furman.edu
  Pubs: *Driving to Distraction, Commandments at Eleven,
  Second Chances* (Orchises, 2003, 1994, 1991), *American
  Scholar, Georgia Rev, Shenandoah, Southern Rev, Tampa
  Rev*

Paul Allen 🎤 ✈   P
English Dept, College of Charleston, Charleston, SC 29424,
843-953-5659
Internet: allenp@cofc.edu
  Pubs: *American Crawl* (U North Texas Pr, 1997), *Four
  Passes* (Glebe Street Pr, 1994), *Iowa Rev, Laurel Rev, Viet
  Nam Generation, Madison Rev, Ontario Rev*

Syed Amanuddin   P
790 McKay St
Sumter, SC 29150
  Pubs: *Poems* (Apt Bks, 1984), *World Poetry in English*
  (Humanities Pr, 1982)

Franklin Ashley   W
College of Applied Sciences, Univ South Carolina, Columbia,
SC 29208, 803-777-2560

Claire Bateman   P
Fine Arts Center, 1613 W Washington St, Greenville, SC
29601, 864-241-3327
Internet: bateman7@juno.com
    Pubs: *At the Funeral of the Ether* (Ninety-Six Pr, 1998),
    Friction (Eighth Mountain Pr, 1998), *The Bicycle Slow Race,
    The Wesleyan Tradition: Anth* (Wesleyan, 1993, 1991), *The
    Kenyon Poets: Anth* (Kenyon Rev, 1989), *Georgia Rev, NER,
    Paris Rev*

William C. Burns   P
126 Forestdale Drive
Taylors, SC 29687-3728
Internet: sunhawk@infi.net
    Pubs: *Crack Pressures Recalled* (Ali Baba Pr, 1984), *Texas
    Rev, Yankee, Kenyon Rev, Sewanee Rev*

Alice Cabaniss   P
1405 Sarsfield Ave
Camden, SC 29020-2941, 803-713-0662
    Pubs: The Dark Bus (Saltcatcher Pr, 1975), 45/96: Anth
    (Ninety-Six Pr, 1996) *Portfolio, Circus Maximus, A Shout in
    the Street, Appalachian Heritage, The Devil's Millhopper,
    Points*

J. Clontz   P
PO Box 30302
Charleston, SC 29407-0302, 803-571-4683
    Pubs: *Haiku Headlines, Night Roses, Frogpond, Lamp-Post,
    Candelabrum*

Phebe Davidson 🎙 ✈   P
11 Inverness W
Aiken, SC 29803-5962, 803-642-3992
Internet: phebed@aiken.sc.edu
    Pubs: *Dreameater* (Delaware Valley, 1998), *Conversations
    with the World* (Trilogy Bks, 1998), *Two Seasons, Milk &
    Brittle Bone* (Muse-Pie Pr, 1993, 1991), *Kenyon Rev,
    Literary Rev, Poetry East, Calliope, SPR*

Kwame Dawes 🎙 ✈   P
4 Doral Ct
Columbia, SC 29229, 803-777-2096
Internet: dawesk@gwm.sc.edu
    Pubs: *Mapmaker* (Smith Doorstop, 2001), *One Love*
    (Metheun, 2001), *Midland* (Ohio U Pr, 2001), *Resisting the
    Anomie* (Goose Lane Edtn,1995), *Shook Foil, Requiem,
    Jacko Jacobus, Prophets* (Peepal Tree Bks, 1997, 1996,
    1996, 1995), *Callaloo, Black Renaissance*

Fred Dings 🎙 ✈   P
Univ of South Carolina, Dept of English, Columbia, SC 29208,
803-777-2012
Internet: dings@gwm.sc.edu
    Pubs: *Eulogy for a Private Man* (TriQtly Bks, 1999), *After the
    Solstice* (Orchises Pr, 1993), *TriQtly, Poetry, Paris Rev, New
    Republic, New Yorker, Western Humanities Rev*

Scott Ely   W
Winthrop College, English Dept, Rock Hill, SC 29730,
803-323-2131
    Pubs: *Overgrown with Love* (U Arkansas Pr, 1993), *Pit Bull,
    Starlight* (Weidenfeld & Nicolson, 1988, 1987)

Marta Fenyves   P
937 Bowman Rd, #125
Mount Pleasant, SC 29464
    Pubs: *From a Distance* (Warthog Pr, 1981), *Celebrating
    Gaia: Anth* (Sweet Annie Pr, 2000), *Exile: Anth* (Milkweed,
    1990), *Messages from the Heart, Home Planet News,
    Relativity, NYQ, Helen Rev*

Stephen Gardner 🎙 ✈   P
English Dept, Univ South Carolina Aiken, 471 University Pkwy,
Aiken, SC 29801, 803-641-3239
Internet: steveg@usca.edu
    Pubs: *This Book Belongs to Eva* (Palanquin Pr, 1996),
    *Louisiana Literature, Texas Rev, Southern Rev, California
    Qtly, Kansas Qtly, Poetry NW, Connecticut Rev, Nebraska
    Rev, Widener Rev, New Delta Rev, SPR, Mississippi Rev*

Vertamae Grosvenor   P&W
c/o Penn Center, PO Box 126, Frogmore, SC 29920

Dan Huntley   P
1089 Cedar Spring Rd
York, SC 29745
    Pubs: *SPR, Kudzu, Graffiti, Hob-Nob*

Vera Kistler   W
123 Edwards Ave
Darlington, SC 29532, 843-393-3191
    Pubs: *Birds of a Feather, Deaf Violets* (Melantrich, 1986,
    1982), *Too Much Heaven* (C.S. Spisovatel, 1985),
    *Sandlapper, State, Zapad, Metamorphosis, Choice,
    Spektrum*

J. Calvin Koonts   P
Professor Emeritus, Erskine College, Washington St, Due
West, SC 29639, 813-379-2360
    Pubs: *Lines: Opus 8* (Jacobs Pr, 1994), *Under the Umbrella*
    (Sandlapper Pr, 1971)

Margaret Lally 🎙 ✈   P
PO Box 30494
Charleston, SC 29417-0494, 843-953-7908
Internet: lallym@citadel.edu
    Pubs: *Juliana's Room* (Bits Pr, 1988), *Ohio Rev, Literary
    Rev, Kenyon Rev, Hudson Rev*

John Lane P
Wofford College, Box 101, Spartanburg, SC 29303,
864-597-4518
Internet: laneje@wofford.edu
  Pubs: *Against Information & Other Poems* (New Nature Pr,
  1996), *In Short: Short Creative Nonfiction: Anth* (Norton,
  1996), *Virginia Qtly Rev, Nimrod*

Bryan Eugene Lindsay P
109 Greenbriar Rd
Spartanburg, SC 29302, 803-573-7277
  Pubs: *New Orleans Rev, SPR, Epos, Human Voice Qtly,
  Foxfire, Prickly Pear*

Bret Lott W
English Dept, College of Charleston, Charleston, SC 29424,
843-953-5650
  Pubs: *The Hunt Club* (Villard, 1998), *Fathers, Sons, &
  Brothers* (HB, 1997), *Reed's Beach, Jewel* (Pocket Bks,
  1993, 1991), *Antioch Rev, Story, Prairie Schooner, Witness,
  New Letters, Iowa Rev, Gettysburg Rev, Southern Rev,
  Ascent, Notre Dame Rev*

Susan Ludvigson P
330 Marion St
Rock Hill, SC 29730, 803-328-9207
  Pubs: *To Find the Gold, The Beautiful Noon of No Shadow,
  The Swimmer* (LSU Pr, 1990, 1986, 1984)

Nelljean McConeghey P
c/o Rice, 203 Sherwood Dr, Conway, SC 29526
  Pubs: *BPJ, Calyx, Cold Mountain Rev, New Mexico
  Humanities Rev*

Susan Meyers ♀ ✈ P
PO Box 188
Summerville, SC 29484, 843-821-9238
Internet: BardOwl2@aol.com
  Pubs: *Lessons in Leaving* (Persephone Pr, 1998), *Word &
  Witness: Anth* (Carolina Academic Pr, 1999), *Christian
  Century, NC Lit Rev, Crazyhorse, Tar River Poetry, Asheville
  Poetry Rev, Greensboro Rev*

Horace Mungin ♀ ✈ P&W
152 McArn Rd
Ridgeville, SC 29472, 843-875-3886
Internet: horacemungin@msn.com
  Pubs: *Sleepy Willie Sings the Blues* (Xlibris, 2002), *Sleepy
  Willie Talks About Life* (R&M Pub, 1991), *The Ninety-Six
  Sampler of South Carolina Poetry: Anth* (Ninety-Six Pr,
  1994), *Essence*

Eugene Platt ♀ ✈ P&W
734 Gilmore Ct
Charleston, SC 29412-9043, 843-795-9442
  Pubs: *Summer Days with Daughter* (Hawkes Pub, 1999),
  Bubba, Missy & Me (Tradd Street Pr, 1992), *South Carolina
  State Line* (Huguley Co, 1980), *Charleston Mag, Tar River
  Poetry, Crazyhorse, South Carolina Rev, Poet Lore, Poem,
  Christianity & the Arts*

Robert S. Poole W
2913 Kennedy St
Columbia, SC 29205, 803-799-3964
Internet: robtpoole@hotmail.com
  Pubs: *Inheritance: Anth* (Hub City, 2001), *Cardinal Anth*
  (Jaccar Pr, 1986), *Greensboro Rev, Fiction*

Ron Rash P&W
320 Princess Grace Ave
Clemson, SC 29631-1216, 864-653-8791
  Pubs: *Eureka Mill, The Night the New Jesus Fell to Earth*
  (Bench Pr, 1998, 1994)

Fran B. Reed W
PO Box 23481
Hilton Head Island, SC 29926, 212-592-3510
Internet: ML 888888@aol.com
  Pubs: *Black Mexican Necklace* (Dominie, 1990), *A Dream
  with Storms* (New Readers Pr, 1990), *Female Patient*

Ennis Rees P
2921 Pruitt Dr
Columbia, SC 29204
  Pubs: *Selected Poems* (U South Carolina Pr, 1973),
  Southern Rev, New Republic

Rosa Shand ♀ ✈ W
189 Clifton Ave
Spartanburg, SC 29302-1435, 864-582-2302
Internet: rosashand@mindspring.com
  Pubs: *The Gravity of Sunlight* (Soho Pr, 2000), *New
  Southern Harmonies: 4 Emerging Fiction Writers: Anth*
  (Holocene Pr, 1998), *Massachusetts Rev, Southern Rev,
  Virginia Qtly Rev, Shenandoah*

Bennie Lee Sinclair P&W
PO Box 345
Cleveland, SC 29635, 864-836-8489
  Pubs: *The Endangered* (Ninety-Six Pr, 1993), *The Lynching*
  (Walker & Sons, 1992), *New Rev, NAR, Ellery Queen,
  Foxfire, South Carolina Rev, Asheville Poetry Rev*

Warren Slesinger 🎤 ✈   P
2507 Brighton Ln
Beaufort, SC 29902, 843-322-0532
Internet: slesin@iscc.net
    Pubs: *Warren Slesinger Greatest Hits* (Pudding Hse Pr,
2003), *With Some Justification* (Windhover Pr, 1984),
Poems for a Beach House: Anth (Salt Marsh Pr, 2003),
*Antioch Rev, Iowa Rev, The Prose Poem, APR, Georgia
Rev, NAR, NW Rev, The Rivers Poetry Jrnl*

Laura Stamps   P&W
PO Box 212534
Columbia, SC 29221-2534, 803-749-8579
Internet: laurastamps@mindspring.com
    Pubs: *Poetry Motel, Maelstrom, Concrete Wolf, Ancient
Paths, Erete's Bloom, Alive Now, American Writing*

Mark Steadman   W
450 Pin du Lac Dr
Central, SC 29630, 864-639-6673
Internet: mcafee@clemson.edu
    Pubs: *Bang-Up Season* (Longstreet Pr, 1990), *Angel Child,
An American Christmas: Anth* (Peachtree, 1987, 1986), *A
Lion's Share, McAfee County* (Holt, Rinehart & Winston
1976, 1971), *South Carolina Rev, Southern Rev, Nova*

Dennis Ward Stiles 🎤 ✈   P
656 Harbor Creek Dr
Charleston, SC 29412-3203, 843-762-2957
    Pubs: *Saigon Tea* (Palanquin Pr, 2000), *Asheville Poetry
Rev, Florida Rev, Hanging Loose, Laurel Rev, New Delta
Rev, Poetry NW, Puerto del Sol, SPR*

David Tillinghast 🎤 ✈   P&W
Clemson Univ, English Dept, Clemson, SC 29631-1366,
864-656-5412
    Pubs: *Women Hoping for Rain & Other Poems* (State Sreet
Pr, 1987), *Texas Rev, Southern Rev, Georgia Rev, Virginia
Qtly Rev, Ploughshares*

Deno Trakas 🎤 ✈   P
Wofford College, 429 N Church St, Spartanburg, SC 29303
Internet: trakasdp@wofford.edu
    Pubs: *Human & Puny, New Southern Harmonies, The
Shuffle of Wings* (Holocene Pr, 1999, 1998, 1990), *45/96:
South Carolina Poetry Anth* (96 Pr, 1994), *From the Green
Horseshoe: Anth* (U South Carolina Pr, 1987)

Laura Puccia Valtorta   W
2009 Lincoln St
Columbia, SC 29201, 803-765-0508
    Pubs: *Family Meal, A Living Culture in Durham* (Carolina
Wren Pr, 1993, 1987)

SOUTH DAKOTA

David Allan Evans 🎤 ✈   P&W
1432 2nd St
Brookings, SD 57006, 605-692-5214
Internet: evans@brookings.net
    Pubs: *Double Happiness: Two Lives in China* (USD Pr,
1995), *Hanging Out with the Crows* (BkMk Pr, 1991),
Perfect in Their Art: Anth (S Illinois U Pr, 2002), *Motion: Anth*
(U Iowa Pr, 2001), *NAR, Southern Rev, Aethlon, Chariton
Rev, Poetry Northwest*

Tom Hansen   P
1803 N Kline
Aberdeen, SD 57401, 605-225-0272
    Pubs: *Northern Centinel, Midwest Qtly, Kansas Qtly, Great
River Rev, Literary Rev, Iowa Rev, Anima, Prairie Schooner,
Willow Springs, Changing Men*

Donald Harington   W
Art Dept, Solberg Hall, South Dakota State Univ, Brookings,
SD 57007
    Pubs: *The Architecture of the Arkansas Ozarks* (Little,
Brown, 1975), *Esquire*

Linda M. Hasselstrom 🎤 ✈   P&W
Windbreak House Writing Retreat, PO Box 169, Hermosa, SD
57744, 605-255-4064
Internet: info@windbreakhouse.com
    Pubs: *Bitter Creek Junction* (High Plains Pr, 2001), *Dakota
Bones: Collected Poems* (Spoon River Poetry, 1993), *Land
Circle* (Fulcrum, 1991)

Adrian C. Louis   P
PO Box 1990
Pine Ridge, SD 57770-1990
Internet: louisa@southwest.msus.edu
    Pubs: *Wild Indians & Other Creatures* (U Nevada Pr, 1996),
Skins (Crown, 1995), *Ploughshares, New Letters, Kenyon
Rev, TriQtly, Exquisite Corpse, Chicago Rev*

Janice H. Mikesell 🎤 ✈   PP&P&W
PO Box 87945
Sioux Falls, SD 57105
    Pubs: *For Better and Worse* (Hen's Teeth, 2002), *Charity:
Anth* (Red Rock Pr, 2002), *Mid-America Poetry Rev, BB:
Capers*

John R. Milton   P&W
630 Thomas
Vermillion, SD 57069

Kathleen Norris 🎤 ✈   P&W
PO Box 570
Lemmon, SD 57638
    Pubs: *Journey: New & Selected Poems* (Pittsburgh, 2002),
The Virgin of Bennington, The Cloister Walk (Riverhead,
2002, 1996), *Dakota* (Ticknor & Fields, 1993)

Geraldine Sanford 🎤 P&W
306 W 36 St, #22
Sioux Falls, SD 57105, 605-332-6090
Pubs: *Unverified Sightings* (Dakota East, 1996), *As Far As I Can See* (Windflower Pr, 1989), *Women's Encounters With the Mental Health Establishment: Anth* (Haworth Pr, 2002), *South Dakota Rev, South Dakota Mag*

Sandra Abena Songbird Naylor 🎤 ✈ P&W
863 1/2 St James St
Rapid City, SD 57701
Internet: abenasongbird@hotmail.com
Pubs: *Bitterroot* (Freedom Voices Pr, 2000), *The Spirit in the Words: Anth: Anths* (DaimlerChrysler, 2000, 1999), *Di-Verse-City 2000: Anth* (Austin Poets Intl, 2000), *My Home As I Remember: Anth* (Natural Heritage/Natural History Inc, 2000), *Vermillion*

TENNESSEE

Deborah Adams P&W
Jin Publicists, 504 Cedar Forest Ct, Nashville, TN 37221, 615-356-3086
http://members.aol.com/dkadams
Pubs: *All the Blood Relations, All the Deadly Beloved, All the Hungry Mothers* (Ballantine, 1997, 1996, 1994), *Murderous Intent, Funny Bones, Murder They Wrote 2, Deadly Women, Canine Capers, Malice Domestic 3*

Tina Barr 🎤 ✈ P
English Dept, Rhodes College, 2000 N Pkwy, Memphis, TN 38112-1690, 901-843-3979
Internet: tinabarr@rhodes.edu
Pubs: *Red Land, Black Land* (Longleaf Pr, 2002), *The Fugitive Eye* (Painted Bride Qtly, 1997), *At Dusk on Naskeag Point* (Flume Pr, 1984), *Southern Rev, SW Rev, APR, Louisiana Lit, Harvard Rev, Chelsea, Boulevard*

Scott Bates P
Box 1263, 735 University Ave, Sewanee, TN 37375-1000, 615-598-5843
Pubs: *Merry Green Peace, Lupo's Fables* (Jump-Off Mountain, 1990, 1983), *Delos*

John Bensko 🎤 ✈ P
PO Box 40042
Memphis, TN 38174-0042, 901-726-9187
Pubs: *The Iron City* (U Illinois Pr, 2000), *The Waterman's Children* (U Mass Pr, 1994), *Green Soldiers* (Yale U Pr, 1981), *Poetry, Poetry NW, New Letters, NER, Iowa Rev, Georgia Rev*

Diann Blakely 🎤 ✈ P
3037 Woodlawn Dr
Nashville, TN 37215-1140, 615-297-6026
Internet: dblakely@aol.com
Pubs: *Farewell My Lovelies* (Story Line Pr, 2000), *Hurricane Walk* (BOA Edtns, 1992)

Gaylord Brewer P
7165 Primrose LN
Lascassas, TN 37085-4709, 615-898-2712
Internet: glorewer@mtsu.edu
Pubs: *Presently a Beast* (Coreopsis Bks, 1996), *Qtly West, NYQ, Lullwater Rev, RE:AL, U of Windsor Rev, Puerto del Sol, Ellipsis, Chelsea, Conneticut Rev, Crab Orchard Rev, Poet Lore*

James Brooks 🎤 ✈ P&W
114 Malone Hollow Rd
Jonesborough, TN 37659, 615-753-7831
Internet: comeback@usit.net
Pubs: *Comeback of the Bears* (Scruffy City, 2000), *South Carolina Rev, Davidson Miscellany, Cold Mountain Rev, Wisconsin Rev*

Melissa Cannon P
141 Neese Dr, #E18
Nashville, TN 37211-2750, 615-832-1813
Pubs: *A Formal Feeling Comes, Sleeping with Dionysus* (Crossing Pr, 1994, 1994), *Bogg, Kenyon Rev, Lyric, Ploughshares, Shockbox, Tight*

Jill Carpenter 🎤 ✈ P&W
PO Box 3271
Sewanee, TN 37375, 931-598-0795
Internet: jill@infoave.net
Pubs: *Fingerlings* (Catamount Pr, 1995), *Anth of Frogs & Toads: Anth* (Ione Pr, 1998), *Amelia, Birmingham Poetry Rev, Exquisite Corpse, New Mexico Humanities Rev, Utah Wilderness Assoc Rev, Passager*

Blair Carr W
PO Box 2138
Memphis, TN 38088-2138
Pubs: *Flashbacks, A Case of Black or White* (Kudzu Pub, 1998, 1996)

Kevin Christianson 🎤 ✈ P
English Dept, Tennessee Tech Univ, Box 5053, Cookeville, TN 38505, 931-372-3351
Internet: kchristianson@tntech.edu
Pubs: *Seven Deadly Witnesses* (Broom Street Theatre Pr, 1971), *Libido, Rockford Rev, The Formalist, Z Misc, Turnstile, Connecticut River Rev, Protea, Black Bear Rev, Lynx Eye, Minnesota Rev, New Letters*

Suzanne Underwood Clark 🎤 ✈ P
721 Pennsylvania Ave
Bristol, TN 37620
Internet: capriole10@yahoo.com
Pubs: *What a Light Thing, This Stone, Weather of the House* (Sow's Ear Pr, 1999, 1994), *Sketches of Home* (Canon Pr, 1998), *Quilt Anthology* (Quilt Digest Pr, 1994), *Lullwater Rev, Shenandoah, SPR, Image, Appalachian Jrnl, Sow's Ear Poetry Rev*

Jay Clayton   W
English Dept, Vanderbilt Univ, Nashville, TN 37235,
615-322-2541
    Pubs: *Denver Qtly, SW Rev, Kansas Qtly, Southern Rev*

Robert Cowser 🎤 ✈   P
120 Virginia St
Martin, TN 38237, 731-587-2729
    Pubs: *Sulphur River Rev, RE:AL, Context South, New
    Ground, Jackson Purchase Jrnl, Sulphur River*

Margaret Danner   P
Poet-In-Residence, Lemoyne Owen College, Memphis, TN
38126

Harry Norman Dean   P
920 Haywood Dr NW
Cleveland, TN 37312-3929, 423-476-6950
    Pubs: *A Sheltered Life* (Rowan Mountain Pr, 1991),
    Appalachia Inside Out: Anth (U Tennessee Pr, 1995), *Poetry
    Miscellany, Cumberland Poetry Rev, Appalachian Heritage,
    Samisdat, Number One, Mountain Ways*

Victor M. Depta   P
Professor of English, Univ of Tennessee at Martin, Martin, TN
38237, 901-587-7300
Internet: sales@blairmtp.com
    Pubs: *Gate of Paradise, Silence of Blackberries* (Blair Mtn
    Pr, 2000, 1999), *A Doorkeeper in the House* (Ion Bks,
    1993), *Idol & Sanctuary* (University Edtns, 1993), *Aura,
    Sonoma Mandala, Centennial Rev, Negative Capability*

Ora Wilbert Eads   P
812 W Hemlock St
LaFollette, TN 37766
    Pubs: *Tranquility, Heavenly Light* (Banner Bks, 1994, 1993),
    Crystal Rainbow, Omnific

Neal Ellis   P
3561 Hanna Dr
Memphis, TN 38128, 901-386-2684
    Pubs: *Gayoso Street Rev, Voices Intl, Memphis Tennessee
    Anth*

Steve Eng   P&W
PO Box 111864
Nashville, TN 37222-1864
    Pubs: *All Aboard, SPWAO: Anth, Poets of Fantastic: Anth*
    (SPWAO, 1992, 1992), *Worlds of Fantasy & Horror,
    Beatlicks' Nashville Poetry Newsletter, Fantasy
    Commentator, Nashville Banner, Night Songs, Amanita
    Brandy, Nightmare Express*

David Flynn   P&W
303 Crestmeade Dr
Nashville, TN 37221, 615-354-1063
Internet: davidflynn@mindspring.com
    Pubs: *Stand, The Qtly, Intl Qtly, Panurge, Story Qtly,
    Confrontation, Paris Transcontinental*

Dorothy Foltz-Gray   P
5900 Wade Ln
Knoxville, TN 37912
    Pubs: *Homewords: Anth of Tennessee Writers* (U Tennessee
    Pr, 1986), *Mississippi Rev, Poet Lore, College English*

Shelby Foote   W
542 E Parkway S
Memphis, TN 38104-4362
    Pubs: *September, September* (Random Hse, 1977), *Jordan
    County, Shiloh, Love in a Dry Season, Follow Me Down,
    Tournament* (Dial Pr, 1954, 1952, 1951, 1950, 1949)

Charlotte Gafford   P
7325 Walker Rd
Fairview, TN 37062-8142, 615-799-2546
Internet: gkxk32c@prodigy.com
    Pubs: *The Pond Woman* (Kudzu Pr, 1989), *SPR, Iowa Rev,
    NER*

Isabel Joshlin Glaser 🎤   PP&P&W
5383 Mason Rd
Memphis, TN 38120-1707, 901-685-5597
Internet: isajglaser@yahoo.com
    Pubs: *American History Through Poetry: Anth* (Boyds Mills
    Pr/Wordsong, 2003), *Dreams of Glory: Anth* (Atheneum,
    1995), *Cicada, Prairie Schooner, Greensboro Rev, Cricket,
    School Mag, Instructor, Mississippi Rev*

Malcolm Glass   P
PO Box 137
Clarksville, TN 37041-0137, 615-648-7882
Internet: glassm@apsu01.apsu.edu
    Pubs: *The Dinky Line, Wiggins Poems* (Bucksnort, 1991,
    1984), *In the Shadow of the Gourd* (New Rivers Pr, 1990),
    Sewanee Rev

George Grace 🎤 ✈   P&W
1030 Leatherwood Rd
White Bluff, TN 37187
Internet: gdgart@aol.com
    Pubs: *Buffalo Pr Anth, Pure Light, Textile Bridge Pr, Moody
    Street Irregulars: Jack Kerouac Newsletter*

Roy Neil Graves 🎤 ✈   P
Univ Tennessee, English Dept, Martin, TN 38238,
901-587-7301
Internet: ngraves@utm.edu
    Pubs: *Somewhere on the Interstate* (Ion Bks, 1987), *Always
    at Home Here: 6 Tennessee Poets: Anth* (McGraw-Hill,
    1998), *Homeworks: Anth* (U Tennessee Pr, 1996), *New
    Ground, Bean Switch, Manana, Distillery, Runner's World*

Larry D. Griffin 🎤 ✈ P&W
Dyersburg State Community College, 1510 Lake Rd,
Dyersburg, TN 38024, 901-286-3371
Internet: lgriffin@dscclan.dscc.cc.tn.us
 Pubs: *Larry D Griffin Gold* (Pudding Hse, 2000), *Airspace*
(Slough, 1990), *A Gathering of Samphire* (Poetry Around,
1990), *Oyster Boy, 2 River Rev, Cimarron Rev, RiverSedge,
Poetry Ireland Rev, Blue Unicorn, Dock*(s)

Martha Whitmore Hickman 🎤 ✈ W
2034 Castleman Dr
Nashville, TN 37215, 615-292-9529
Internet: mjwhickman@aol.com
 Pubs: *Such Good People* (Warner Bks, 1996), *Fullness of
Time: Short Stories of Women & Aging: Anth* (Abingdon Pr,
1997), *Weavings, Christian Century, Highlights, Image*

Cary Holladay 🎤 ✈ W
23 S Evergreen St
Memphis, TN 38104-3918, 901-278-7510
 Pubs: *The Palace of Wasted Footsteps* (U Missouri Pr,
1998), *The People Down South* (U Illinois Pr, 1989), *The O.
Henry Awards: Anth* (Anchor Bks, 1999), *Kenyon Rev,
Alaska Qtly Rev, Chelsea, Literary Rev, Oxford American,
Chattahoochee Rev, Epoch, NW Rev*

Richard Jackson 🎤 ✈ P
3413 Alta Vista Dr
Chattanooga, TN 37411, 423-624-7279
Internet: svobodni@aol.com
 Pubs: *Half-Lives* (Invisible Cities Pr, 2002), *Heartwall* (U
Mass Pr, 2000), *Heart's Bridge* (Aureole Pr, 1999), *Alive All
Day* (Cleveland State U Pr, 1992), *Worlds Apart,
Dismantling Time* (U Alabama Pr, 1989, 1987), *Gettysburg
Rev, Crazyhorse, NER, NAR*

Mark Jarman 🎤 ✈ P
English Dept, Vanderbilt Univ, Nashville, TN 37235,
615-322-2618
Internet: mark.jarman@vanderbilt.edu
 Pubs: *Unholy Sonnets, Questions for Ecclesiastes, Iris*
(Story Line Pr, 2000, 1997, 1992), *APR, Hudson Rev, New
Yorker, Southern Rev, New Criterion, Threepenny Rev,
Atlantic, Kenyon Rev, Sewanee Rev*

Marilyn Kallet 🎤 ✈ P
Director, Creative Writing, Univ Tennessee, Knoxville, TN
37996, 865-974-6947
Internet: mkallet@utk.edu
 Pubs: *Sleeping with One Eye Open: Women Writers & the
Art of Survival: Anth* (U Georgia Pr, 1999), *How to Get Heat
Without Fire* (New Messenger/New Millennium, 1996),
Worlds in Our Words: Anth (Blair Pr/Prentice Hall, 1996),
New Letters, Prairie Schooner

Richard Kelly P
Univ Tennessee, McClung Tower, English Dept, Knoxville, TN
37919
 Pubs: *Lewis Carroll, Daphne du Maurier* (G.K. Hall, 1990,
1987), *V.S. Naipaul* (Continuum, 1989)

Tamara Beryl Latham 🎤 P
5816 Brentwood Trace
Brentwood, TN 37027
Internet: T_Latham@msn.com
 Pubs: *Raintown Rev, Tucumcari Literary Rev, High Tide,
Songs of Innocence, Starburst, Candlelight Memories,
Painting Daisies Yellow, Penny Dreadful*

Shara McCallum 🎤 ✈ P
Univ of Memphis, Dept of English, Memphis, TN 38152,
901-678-4771
Internet: sssmm@earthlink.net
 Pubs: *Song of Thieves, Water Between Us* (U Pitt Pr, 2003,
1999), *Beyond the Frontier: Anth* (Black Classics Pr, 2002),
New American Poets: Anth (U Pr New England, 2000),
*Ploughshares, Callaloo, Prairie Schooner, Iowa Rev, Antioch
Rev, Caribbean Writer*

Ellis K. Meacham W
414 S Crest Rd
Chattanooga, TN 37404, 615-624-1887
 Pubs: *For King & Company, On the Company's Service*
(Little, Brown, 1976, 1968)

Corey J. Mesler 🎤 P&W
1954 Young Ave
Memphis, TN 38104-5643, 901-274-4718
Internet: resolemcrey@yahoo.com
 Pubs: *Talk* (Livingston Pr, 2002), *New Stories from the
South: Anth* (Algonguin Books, 2002), *Full Court: Anth*
(Breakaway Bks, 1996), *Pindeldyboz, Yellow Silk, Poet Lore,
Rhino, Visions Intl, Southern Voices, Slant*

Ben Norwood P&W
6219 Les Waggoner Rd
Franklin, TN 37067-8115, 615-395-7563
 Pubs: *Travois: An Anth of Texas Poetry* (Thorp Springs Pr,
1976), *Sulphur River, Negative Capability, Unity, Stone Drum*

Gordon Osing P
1056 Blythe St
Memphis, TN 38104
 Pubs: *A Town Down River* (St. Luke's Pr, 1984), *From the
Boundary Waters* (Memphis State U, 1982)

William Page 🎤 ✈ P
5551 Derron Ave
Memphis, TN 38115-2323, 901-363-2216
Internet: wpagemem@aol.com
 Pubs: *William Page Greatest Hits: 1970-2000* (Pudding
House Pubs, 2001), *Bodies Not Our Own* (Memphis State
U Pr, 1986), *American Literary Rev, NAR, Literary Rev,
SW Rev*

Barbara Shirk Parish 🎤   P&W
4293 Beechcliff Ln
Memphis, TN 38128-3423, 901-388-4384
    Pubs: *Maverick Western Verse: Anth* (Gibbs Smith, 1994),
    The Kentucky Book: Anth (Courier Journal, 1979), *Pegasus,*
    Small Pond, Green's Mag, Dry Crik Rev, Little Balkins Rev

Wyatt Prunty   P
Sewanee Writers' Conference, Univ of the South, 310 St
Luke's Hall, Sewanee, TN 37383-1000, 615-598-1159
Internet: wprunty@sewanee.edu
    Pubs: *Unarmed and Dangerous: New and Selected Poems,*
    Since the Noon Mail Stopped, The Run of the House (Johns
    Hopkins U Pr, 2000, 1997, 1993), *New Criterion, New*
    Republic, New Yorker, Oxford American, Sewanee Review,
    Southern Rev, Yale Rev

N. Scott Reynolds   P
301 28th Ave N, Apt 1206
Nashville, TN 37203
Internet: natscott@msn.com
    Pubs: *First Songs from the Midden* (Nephtys Inc.),
    Something We Can't Name: Anth (Octus Orbus), *Kameleon,*
    Tea Party Electronic Mag, Wired Art for Wired Hearts,
    Crumpled Papers, Beatlicks Nashville Poetry Newsletter,
    Flying Dog, CafÈ Daze, Radio Beds

J. C. Robison   W
Brentwood Academy, 219 Granny White Pike, Brentwood, TN
37027
    Pubs: *Peter Taylor: A Study of the Short Fiction* (Twayne,
    1988), *Texas Rev, Chariton Rev, Cimarron*

Bobby Caudle Rogers 🎤 ✈   P
UU Box 3136, 1050 Union Univ Dr., Jackson, TN 38107,
731-661-5107
Internet: brogers@uu.edu
    Pubs: *Georgia Rev, Greensboro Rev, Southern Rev,*
    Shenandoah, Puerto del Sol, Meridian

Abby Jane Rosenthal   P
650 S Greer
Memphis, TN 38111
    Pubs: *Ardor's Hut* (Alembic Pr, 1985), *Alaska Qtly Rev,*
    Kalliope, CutBank, Bloomsbury Rev

Frank Russell   P
501 Park Ctr
Nashville, TN 37205, 615-386-9731
    Pubs: *Dinner with Dr. Rocksteady* (Ion Bks, 1987), *Poetry,*
    Chariton Rev, Poetry NW

George Addison Scarbrough 🎤   P
100 Darwin Ln
Oak Ridge, TN 37830-4021, 866-482-2793
    Pubs: *Tellico Blue* (Iris Pr, 1999), *Southern Lit: Anth*
    (Prentice Hall, 2000), *Poetry, Southern Rev, Iron Mountain*
    Rev, Emory Valley Rev, Now & Then, Appalachian Rev, New
    Orleans Rev, Atlantic, Harper's, Saturday Rev, New
    Republic

Joan Silva   P
118 W Outer Dr
Oak Ridge, TN 37830-8611
    Pubs: *Attila* (Black Scarab Pr, 1976), *Slipstream, Tandava,*
    Pteranadon, Contact II, Exquisite Corpse, Gryphon, Prickly
    Pear

Ken Smith   P
1129 Clermont Dr
Chattanooga, TN 37415-3601
Internet: kenneth-smith@utc.edu

Arthur Smith   P
Univ Tennessee, 301 McClung Tower/English Dept, Knoxville,
TN 37996, 865-974-5401
Internet: artsmith@utk.edu
    Pubs: *The Late World, Orders of Affection* (Carnegie Mellon
    U Pr, 2002, 1996), *Elegy on Independence Day* (U Pitt Pr,
    1985), *Nation, Crazyhorse, NAR*

Rosemary Stephens   P&W
64 N Yates Rd
Memphis, TN 38120
    Pubs: *Eve's Navel* (South & West, 1976), *Seventeen,*
    Mississippi Rev, SPR

Arthur J. Stewart 🎤 ✈   P
2061 Crooked Oak Dr
Lenoir City, TN 37771-7898, 423-986-5935
Internet: astewart@utk.edu
    Pubs: *Songs from Unsung Worlds: Anth* (Birkhauser, 1985),
    Southern Voices in Every Direction: Anth (Bell Buckle/Iris Pr,
    1997), *Lullwater Rev, Quantum Tao, Sow's Ear Poetry Rev,*
    ELF, Now & Then: The Appalachian Mag, New Millennium
    Writings

James Summerville   W
2911 Woodlawn Dr
Nashville, TN 37215, 615-298-5830
Internet: mapheus@prodigy.net
    Pubs: *With Kennedy and Other Stories* (Xlibris, 1998),
    Homewords: Anth (U Tennessee, 1986), *Lake Superior Rev,*
    Green River Rev, Old Hickory Rev

Heather Tosteson 🎤 ✈   P&W
PO Box 282
Chattanooga, TN 37401
Internet: toteson@bellsouth.net
    Pubs: *Nimrod, Nation, Pequod, Calyx, SPR, New Virginia*
    Rev, Cottonwood Rev, Southern Rev, NW Rev

Frederick O. Waage 🎤   W
East Tennessee State Univ, Box 23081, Johnson City, TN
37614, 615-929-7466
Internet: waage@xtn.net
   Pubs: *Greatest Hits* (Pudding Hse, 2000), *Minestrone*
   (Pudding, 1983), *The End of the World* (Gallimaufry, 1977),
   SPR, California Qtly, Antigonish Rev

Minnie Warburton   W
Pink Flamingo Studios, 201 Kentucky Ave, Sewanee,
TN 37375
   Pubs: *Mykonos* (Coward, McCann, Geoghegan, 1979), *Jove
   Romances, Bantam Romance*

Jon Manchip White   P&W
5620 Pinellas Dr
Knoxville, TN 37919-4118, 423-558-8578
   Pubs: *Whistling Past the Churchyard, Journeying Boy*
   (Atlantic Monthly Pr, 1992, 1991)

Lola White   P
5040 Villa Crest Dr
Nashville, TN 37220
   Pubs: *Thunder: Silence* (Red Girl Pr, 1992), *Potato Eyes,
   New River Free Pr, Tendril, Aspect, Zeugma, Cat's Eye,
   Pluma True, CSM, Dark Horse*

Allen Wier 🎤 ✈   W
English Dept, Univ Tennessee, 301 McClung Tower, Knoxville,
TN 37996-0430, 865-974-5401
Internet: awier@utk.edu
   Pubs: *Tehano* (Overlook Pr, 2001), *A Place for Outlaws*
   (H&R, 1989), *Departing As Air* (S&S, 1983), *Southern Rev,
   Texas Rev, Mid-American Rev*

Don Williams 🎤 ✈   W
PO Box 2463
Knoxville, TN 37901, 865-428-0389
Internet: DonWilliams7@att.net
   Pubs: *Christmas Blues: Anth* (Amador Pr, 1996), *A
   Tennessee Landscape: Anth* (Cool Springs Pr, 1996),
   Homeworks: Anth (U Tennessee Pr, 1996), *Voices from the
   Valley: Anth* (Knoxville Writers Guild, 1994), *New Millennium
   Writings*

Charles Wyatt   P&W
3810 Central Ave
Nashville, TN 37205, 615-385-2456
   Pubs: *The Spirit Autobiography of S. M. Jones* (Texas Rev
   Pr, 2002), *Listening to Mozart* (U Iowa Pr, 1995), *Kenyon
   Rev, Sewanee Rev, NER, TriQtly, Hanging Loose, BPJ*

TEXAS

Virginia T. Abercrombie 🎤   P
2 Smithdale Ct
Houston, TX 77024
Internet: vtaber@usa.net
   Pubs: *Greatest Hits* (Pudding Hse Pr, 2001), *Suddenly*
   (Martin Hse, 1998), *Songs for the Century, Houston Party
   File, Leaf Raker* (Brown Rabbit Pr, 1998, 1986, 1983), *Back
   to Your Roots: Anth* (Houston Poetry Fest, 1991), *Visions
   Intl, Illyas, Honey, Pleiades*

Neal Abramson 🎤 ✈   P
1000 W Spring Valley Rd, #229
Richardson, TX 75080, 972-231-3732
   Pubs: *Sojourn, Lactuca, Amoeba, Unmuzzled Ox, City West
   End, Confrontation*

Alan P. Akmakjian   P&W
2200 Waterview Pkwy, #2134
Richardson, TX 75080-2268
   Pubs: *And What Rough Beast: Poems at the End of the
   Century* (Ashland U Pr, 1999), *California Picnic & Other
   Poems* (Northwoods Pr, 1998), *Let the Sun Go* (MAF Pr,
   1993), *Ararat, Atom Mind, Black Bear Rev, New Thought
   Jrnl, Onthebus, Wormwood Rev*

Silvia Berta Alaniz   P
821 Carver St
Alice, TX 78332
   Pubs: *Perceptions, Writing for Our Lives, Dream Intl Qtly,
   Poetic Eloquence, Expressions, Tight, Moving Out, Stone
   Drum, Up Against the Wall, Notebook, Aura, Avocet, Pacific
   Coast Jrnl, Reflect, Mind in Motion*

Max Apple   W
Rice Univ, PO Box 1892, Houston, TX 77251, 713-527-8101
   Pubs: *Roommates, Zip* (Warner Bks, 1994, 1986), *The
   Propheteers, Free Agents* (H&R, 1987, 1984), *Ploughshares*

Terry Lee Armstrong 🎤 ✈   P
4219 Flint Hill St
San Antonio, TX 78230-1619
   Pubs: *When the Soul Speaks, Call it Love* (Armstrong Pub,
   1990, 1989), *Lone Stars Mag, Omnific Mag*

Carolyn Banks 🎤 ✈   W
223 Riverwood
Bastrop, TX 78602-7616, 512-303-1531
Internet: studio@onr.com
   Pubs: *Mr. Right* (Permanent Pr, 1999), *A Horse to Die For,
   Death on the Diagonal, Murder Well Bred, Groomed for
   Death, Death By Dressage* (Fawcett, 1996, 1996, 1995,
   1994, 1993), *Tart Tales: Elegant Erotic Stories* (Carroll &
   Graf, 1993)

Wendy Barker 🎤 ✈ P
Univ of Texas, 6900 North Loop 1604 West, San Antonio, TX
78249-0643, 210-492-8152
Internet: wbarker@utsa.edu
Pubs: *Way of Whiteness* (Wings Pr, 2000), *Eve Remembers*
(Aark Arts Pr, 1996), *Let the Ice Speak* (Ithaca Hse Bks,
1991), *Winter Chickens & Other Poems* (Corona Pub, 1990),
*Partisan Rev, Michigan Qtly Rev, Poetry, NAR, American
Scholar, Prairie Schooner*

Charles Behlen 🎤 ✈ P
501 W Industrial Dr, Apt 503- B
Sulphur Springs, TX 75482, 505-438-9384
Internet: cwbehlen@yahoo.com
Pubs: *Texas Weather* (Trilobite Pr, 1999), *Texas in Poetry:
Anth* (Texas Christian U Pr, 2002), *Borderlands*

Michael Berryhill P
Fort Worth Star-Telegram, 400 W 7 St, Fort Worth, TX 76102

Michael C. Blumenthal P
3311 Merrie Lynn Ave
Austin, TX 78722, 512-457-8856
Internet: mcblume@attglobal.net
Pubs: *Dusty Angel* (BOA Edts, 1999), *The Wages of
Goodness* (U Missouri Pr, 1992), *Against Romance* (Viking
Penguin, 1987), *Marriage: Anth* (Poseidon, 1991), *Poetry,
Nation, Agni, American Scholar, Paris Rev, Ploughshares*

Bruce Bond P
1505 Laurelwood
Denton, TX 76201, 940-565-0849
Internet: bond@unt.edu
Pubs: *The Throats of Narcissus* (U of Arkansas, 2001),
Radiography (BOA, 1997), *The Afternoon of Paradise* (QRL,
1991), *Independence Days* (Woodley Pr, 1990), *The
Possible* (Silverfish Rev Pr, 1995)

Eugene G. E. Botelho P
PO Box 925
Eagle Pass, TX 78853-0925, 830-773-8790
Pubs: *For Better, for Worse* (All American Pr, 1981),
I Wonder As I Wander (Northwoods, 1978)

Michael Bracken 🎤 ✈ W
1120 N 45th St
Waco, TX 76710, 254-752-0839
Internet: Michael@CrimeFictionWriter.com
Pubs: *Canvas Bleeding, All White Girls, Tequila Sunrise, Bad
Girls* (Wildside Press, 2002, 2001, 2000, 2000), *In the Town
of Dreams Unborn and Memories Dying* (Barley Bks, 2000)

David Breeden 🎤 ✈ P&W
1424 Fifth St.
Kerrville, TX 78028, 830-792-7274
Internet: dbreeden@schreiner.edu
Pubs: *Artistas* (Superior Bks, 2001), *Another Number* (Silver
Phoenix Pr, 2000), *Guiltless Traveller, Building a Boat*
(March Street Pr, 1996, 1995), *Double-Headed End Wrench*
(Cloverdale Pr, 1992)

Van K. Brock 🎤 ✈ P
317 Lexington Ave, #227
San Antonio, TX 78215, 210-226-8952
Internet: vbrock@mailer.fsu.edu
Pubs: *Unspeakable Strangers* (Anhinga Pr, 1995), *The
Window* (Chase Ave Pr, 1981), *The Made Thing: Anth* (U
Arkansas Pr, 1999), *Holocaust Poetry: Anth* (St. Martin's Pr,
1995), *Ploughshares, NER, New Yorker, Sewanee Rev,
Southern Rev*

J. W. Brown P
3500 Rankin St
Dallas, TX 75205, 214-739-6566
Pubs: *Pawn Rev, DeKalb Literary Arts Jrnl, SW Rev, Texas
Qtly*

William S. Burford P
4201 Stonegate Blvd, #217
Fort Worth, TX 76109, 817-926-1480
Pubs: *A Beginning* (Norton, 1968), *A World* (U Texas Pr,
1962), *The Poetry Anth: Sixty-Five Years of America's
Distinguished Verse Mag* (HM, 1978), *Nation*

Robert Grant Burns P
PO Box 763
Jacksonville, TX 75766
Pubs: *Selected Poems* (Waltonhof, 1993)

Harry Burrus P
1266 Fountain View
Houston, TX 77057-2204, 713-784-2802
Internet: Gama1266@aol.com
Pubs: *Cartouche, The Jaguar Portfolio, Without Feathers*
(Black Tie Press, 1995, 1991, 1990)

Bobby Byrd P
2709 Louisville
El Paso, TX 79930, 915-566-9072
Pubs: *On the Transmigration of Souls in El Paso* (Cinco
Puntos Pr, 1993), *Get Some Fuses for the House* (North
Atlantic Bks, 1987)

Jean Calkins 🎤 P
14281 Shoredale Ln
Farmers Branch, TX 75234-2045
Internet: nystxn@fastlane.net
  Pubs: *Passages, Win Place Show, Seasons of the Mind* (JC
  Pr, 2000, 1999, 1999), *Against All Odds, Portrait of
  Insomnia* (Inky Pr, 1995, 1995), *Black Creek Rev,
  Parnassus, Smile, Apropos, Potpourri, Haiku Headlines,
  Humoresque, Vantage Point, Pegasus*

Ewing Campbell W
Texas A&M Univ, English Dept, College Station, TX
77843-4227, 409-845-8342
Internet: rec025b@venus.tamu.edu
  Pubs: *Madonna, Maleva* (York Pr, 1995), *The Tex-Mex
  Express* (Spectrum Pr, 1993), *London Mag, NER, Kenyon
  Rev, Chicago Rev, Cimarron Rev*

Vincent Canizarro, Jr. P
8285 Collier Rd
Beaumont, TX 77706, 713-866-3612
  Pubs: *The Poet*

Wendy Taylor Carlisle 🎤 ✈ P
19 Dogwood Lake Dr
Texarkana, TX 75503
Internet: carlisle@vidnet.net
  Pubs: *Reading Berryman to the Dog* (Jacaranda Pr, 2000),
  *Monserrat Rev, Cider Press Rev, Texas Observer,
  Borderlands*

Warren Carrier 🎤 ✈ P
69 Colony Park Cir
Galveston, TX 77551-1737, 409-744-5511
  Pubs: *Risking the Wind* (Birch Brook, 2000), *Justice at
  Christmas, Death of a Poet* (Denlinger, 2000, 1999),
  *Harvard Mag, Formalist, Ohio Rev, Visions Intl, Pembroke
  Mag, Wallace Stevens Jrnl*

Jane Chance 🎤 ✈ P
English Dept, MS30, Rice Univ, PO Box 1892, Houston, TX
77251-1892, 713-348-2625
Internet: jchance@rice.edu
  Pubs: *Christine de Pizan's Letter of Othea to Hector* (Boydell
  & Brewer, 1997), *Literary Rev, Southern Humanities Rev,
  Primavera, Ariel, New America*

Charlotte Cheatham P
Galveston Arts Ctr On Strand, 202 Kempner, Galveston, TX
77550, 713-765-6309
  Pubs: *Gjelsness, Joy Drake*

Paul Christensen 🎤 ✈ P
Texas A&M Univ, English Dept, College Sta, TX 77843-4227,
979-845-8330
Internet: p-christensen@neo.tamu.edu
  Pubs: *I Have My Own Song for It* (U Akron Pr, 2002), *Blue
  Alleys: Prose Poems* (Stone River Pr, 2001), *Like Thunder:
  American Poets Respond to Violence: Anth* (U Iowa Pr,
  2002), *Water Stone, Sou'wester, Quarter After Eight,
  Antioch Rev, SW Rev*

LaVerne Harrell Clark 🎤 ✈ W
604 Main St
Smithville, TX 78957, 512-237-2796
Internet: ldlhclark@aol.com
  Pubs: *Keepers of the Earth* (Cinco Puntos Pr, 1997), *A New
  Dimension of an Old Affinity* (Writers on the Plains Pr,
  1996), *21 Texas Women Writers: Anth* (Texas A&M U Pr,
  2003), *Pembroke, St. Andrews Rev, Vanderbilt Street Rev,
  Southwestern Amer Lit*

L. D. Clark W
604 Main St
Smithville, TX 78957, 512-237-2756
  Pubs: *A Bright Tragic Thing* (Cinco Puntos Pr, 1992), *A
  Charge of Angels* (Confluence Pr, 1987), *The Fifth Wind*
  (Blue Moon Pr, 1981)

Richard Cole P
5125 McDade Dr
Austin, TX 78735, 512-891-9276
  Pubs: *Success Stories* (Limestone Bks, 1998), *The Glass
  Children* (U Georgia Pr, 1986), *Chicago Rev, New Yorker,
  Hudson Rev, Denver Qtly, The Sun*

Paul David Colgin P
2308 Neeley Ave
Midland, TX 79705, 915-682-6609
Internet: paulcolgin@apex2000.net
  Pubs: *Yankee, Sulphur, Pearl, Nexus, Black Fly Rev,
  Kinesis, Pittsburgh Qtly, Sou'wester, Oxford Mag, Iconoclast,
  Tomorrow Mag, Xanadu*

Joe Coomer W
1951 NW Parkway
Azle, TX 76020
  Pubs: *Apologizing to Dogs* (Scribner, 1999), *Sailing in a
  Spoonful of Water* (Picador, 1997), *Beachcombing for a
  Shipwrecked God* (Greywolf, 1995), *The Loop, Dream
  House* (Faber & Faber, 1992, 1992), *A Flatland Fable* (Texas
  Monthly Pr, 1986)

Carol Cullar P&W
Rte 2, Box 4915
Eagle Pass, TX 78852-9605, 210-773-1836
Internet: mavpress@admin.hilconet.com
  Pubs: *Inexplicable Burnings* (Pr of the Guadalupe, 1992),
  Wind Eyes: A Woman's Reader & Writing Source: Anth (Plain
  View Pr, 1997), *Texas Short Fiction: Anth, Texas In Poetry:
  Anth* (Ctr for Texas Studies, 1996, 1994), *NYQ, RE:AL*

Chip Dameron 🎤 ✈ P
4853 Lakeway Dr
Brownsville, TX 78520, 956-350-0031
Internet: dameron@utb.edu
    Pubs: *Greatest Hits* (Pudding Hse Pub, 2001), *Hook and Bloodline* (Wings Pr, 2000), *Night Spiders, Morning Milk, Definition of Hours* (Hawk Pr, 1990), *In the Magnetic Arena* (Latitudes, 1987), *New Texas 95, Sulphur*

William Virgil Davis 🎤 ✈ P
2633 Lake Oaks Rd
Waco, TX 76710-1616, 254-772-3198
Internet: william_davis@baylor.edu
    Pubs: *One Way to Reconstruct the Scene* (Yale U Pr, 1980), *Poetry, New Criterion, Gettysburg Rev, Hudson Rev, Atlantic*

Angela de Hoyos P
M&A Editions, 10120 State Hwy 16 S, San Antonio, TX 78224
Internet: elmohe@earthlink.net
    Pubs: *Woman, Woman* (Arte Publico Pr, 1985), *Selected Poems/Selecciones* (Dezkalzo Pr, 1979)

Nephtali Deleon P&W
1411 Betty Dr
San Antonio, TX 78224

Jeffrey DeLotto P
Texas Wesleyan Univ, 1201 Wesleyan, Fort Worth, TX 76105, 817-531-4909
    Pubs: *Anthology of New England Writers: Voices at the Door* (Maverick Pr, 1995), *New Texas 91: Anth* (U North Texas Pr, 1991), *Aura Literary/Arts Rev, College English, Preying Mantis, Horny Toad*

Cara Diaconoff 🎤 ✈ P&W
TCU English Dept, TCU Box 297270, Fort Worth, TX 76129
Internet: c.diaconoff@tcu.edu
    Pubs: *Other Voices, Indiana Rev, South Dakota Rev, Descant, Hurakan*

Jerry Ellison ✈ P
Rte 3 Box 377
Gilmer, TX 75644-9537, 903-725-6283
Internet: peacewds@etex.net
    Pubs: *Never Again Summer* (College Poetry Rev, 1969), *Death Chant: Anth* (Silver Spur, 1962), *Sulphur, Borderlands, Avocet, Bellowing Ark*

Robert A. Fink 🎤 ✈ P
Hardin-Simmons Univ, Box 15114, Abilene, TX 79698, 915-670-1214
    Pubs: *Beyond Where the West Begins* (Friends of the Abilene Public Library, 1999), *The Tongues of Men & of Angels* (Texas Tech U Pr, 1995), *The Ghostly Hitchhiker* (Corona Pub, 1989), *Azimuth Points* (Sam Houston State U, 1981), *Poetry NW, Poetry*

Robert Flynn W
Trinity Univ, 715 Stadium Dr, San Antonio, TX 78212, 210-736-7575
Internet: rflynn@trinity.edu
    Pubs: *Living with the Hyenas* (TCU Pr, 1995), *The Last Klick* (Baskerville Pub, 1994), *A Personal War in Viet Nam* (Texas A&M U, 1989), *Image*

Peter Fogo 🎤 ✈ P&W
PO Box 7743
Pasadena, TX 77508-7743, 713-941-5227
Internet: bear2000@ev1.net
    Pubs: *Bitterroot* (Dead End Street Pr, 2001), *A Language That Keeps Company with the Moon* (Mackinations Pr, 1992), *Single Again* (Raspberry Pr, 1980), *And What Rough Beast: Anth* (Ashland U Pr, 1999), *Midwest Qtly, Black Bear Rev, Prairie Winds, Ellipsis*

Larry L. Fontenot 🎤 P
2543 The Highlands Drive
Sugar Land, TX 77478
Internet: poboy@hotmail.com
    Pubs: *Choices & Consequences* (Maverick Pr, 1997), *Sulphur River Lit Rev, Chachalaca Poetry Rev, Snow Monkey, Melic Rev, River Sedge, Minimus, El Locofoco, Maverick Pr, i.e. mag*

Ken Fontenot 🎤 ✈ P
1221 Algarita, #162
Austin, TX 78704-4413
Internet: poetry12748@prodigy.net
    Pubs: *All My Animals & Stars* (Slough Pr, 1989), *After the Days of Miami* (Longmeasure Pr, 1980), *APR, Kenyon Rev, Southern Rev, NAR*

Margot Fraser W
Southern Methodist Univ Press, Box 415, Dallas, TX 75275, 214-768-1432
    Pubs: *Careless Weeds, The Laying Out of Gussie Hoot* (SMU Pr, 1993, 1990), *Negative Capability*

Laura Furman 🎤 ✈ W
English Dept, Univ Texas, Austin, TX 78712-1164, 512-471-8385
Internet: ljfurman@mail.utexas.edu
    Pubs: *Drinking With the Cook, Watch Time Fly, The Glass House, The Shadow Line, Tuxedo Park, Ordinary Paradise* (Winedale Pub, 2001, 2001, 2001, 2000, 2000, 1998), *Threepenny Rev, Yale Rev, Preservation Mag, New Yorker, Ploughshares, SW Rev*

G. N. Gabbard P&W
PO Box 602
New Boston, TX 75570-2206, 903-628-2788
    Pubs: *A Mask for Beowulf, Knights Errand, Daily Nous, Dragon Raid* (Flea King Bks, 1992, 1992, 1991, 1985)

Roberto A. Galvan   P
Southwest Texas State Univ, LBJ Dr, San Marcos, TX 78666,
512-245-2360
    Pubs: *Poemas En Espanol Por Un Mexiamericano* (Mexican
American Cultural Center Pr, 1977)

Greg Garrett   W
Baylor Univ, English Dept, Waco, TX 76798, 254-710-6879
Internet: greg_garrett@baylor.edu
    Pubs: *Texas Short Fiction: Anth* (ALE Pub, 1995), *Writers'
Forum, High Plains Lit Rev, Grain, South Dakota Rev,
Laurel Rev, Negative Capability*

Daniel Garza   P
5 Briarwood Cir
Richardson, TX 75080

Zulfikar Ghose   P&W
Univ Texas, English Dept, Austin, TX 78712-1164
    Pubs: *The Triple Mirror of the Self* (Bloomsbury, 1992),
Selected Poems (Oxford U Pr, 1991)

Miguel Gonzalez-Gerth   P
Harry Ransom Humanities Center, Univ Texas, Austin, TX
78712, 512-471-8157
    Pubs: *Palabras Inutilez* (Spain; Taller Fernandez Ciudad,
1988)

Jennifer Grotz 🎤 ✈   P
823 1/2 Tulane
Houston, TX 77007, 713-869-7154
Internet: jennifer.grotz@prodigy.net
    Pubs: *Cusp* (Houghton Mifflin, 2003), *Not Body* (Urban
Editions, 2001), *TriQtly, NER, Black Warrior Rev,
Ploughshares*

Juan G. Guevara   P
PO Box 446
Benavides, TX 78341, 512-256-3308

James Haining   P
Salt Lick Press/LHB, PO Box 15471, Austin, TX 78761-5471,
512-450-0952
    Pubs: *A Child's Garden* (Salt Lick Pr, 1987), *Beowulf to
Beatles & Beyond* (Macmillan, 1981)

Devin Harrison   P
601 Petersburg St
Castroville, TX 78009-4538
    Pubs: *Lactuca, Riverrun, Passages North, Windless
Orchard, Poem, Panhandler, South Dakota Rev*

Don Hendrie, Jr.   W
714 Tuxedo Ave
San Antonio, TX 78209
    Pubs: *A Criminal Journey, Blount's Anvil* (Lynx Hse Pr,
1990, 1980)

Louise Horton   P&W
Brighton Gardens, 4401 Spicewood Springs Rd, #232, Austin,
TX 78759-8589
    Pubs: *Southern Humanities Rev*

Timothy Houghton   P
English Dept, Univ Houston, Creative Writing Program,
Houston, TX 77204-3012, 713-743-2390
    Pubs: *Below Two Skies* (Orchises Pr, 1993), *High Bridges*
(Stride Pr, 1989), *Denver Qtly, Stand Mag, College English*

Diane Hueter 🎤 ✈   P
5210 15th
Lubbock, TX 79416, 806-795-2391
Internet: lildw@lib.ttu.edu
    Pubs: *Times of Sorrow/Times of Grace: Anth* (Backwaters
Pr, 2002), *In the Middle: Midwestern Women Poets: Anth*
(BKMK Pr, 1985), *Iris, Iowa Woman, Borderlands: Texas
Poetry Rev, Clackamas Lit Rev, Texas Rev*

Albert Huffstickler   P
312 E 43 St, #103
Austin, TX 78751, 512-459-3472
    Pubs: *Quinlen, City of the Rain* (Press of Circumstance,
1998, 1993), *Working on My Death Chant* (Back Yard Pr,
1992), *Poetry East, Poetry Motel, Heeltap, First Class,
Rattle, Galley Sail*

Guida Jackson 🎤   W
PO Box 130233
Spring, TX 77393-0233
Internet: panthercreek3@hotmail.com
    Pubs: *Red Boots & Attitude: Anth* (Eakin Pr, 2002), *Virginia
Diaspora* (Heritage Bks, 1992), *Women Who Ruled* (ABC-
CLIO, 1990), *Heart to Hearth* (Prism, 1989), *Passing
Through* (S&S, 1989), *New Texas: Anth* (U Mary Hardin
Baylor Pr, 2001)

Dan Kaderli   P&W
English Division, Univ Texas, 6900 Loop 1604 W, San Antonio,
TX 78249-0691, 512-691-4165
    Pubs: *The Lyric, Tucumcari Rev, Reflect, Bogg, SPSM&H,
Iota, Negative Capability, Star Poets 2, Plains Poetry Jrnl,
Howling Mantra, Pegasus, Spitball*

Cynthia King 🎤   W
5306 Institute Ln
Houston, TX 77005-1820, 713-526-0232
Internet: tonibking@aol.com
    Pubs: *Sailing Home* (Putnam, 1982), *Beggars & Choosers*
(Viking, 1980), *Good Housekeeping*

Judith Kroll   P
3003 Gilbert St
Austin, TX 78703, 512-320-0546
Internet: xerxes2001@aol.com
    Pubs: *Our Elephant & That Child* (Qtly Rev Poetry Series,
1991), *In the Temperate Zone* (Scribner, 1974), *Poetry,
Kenyon Rev, Southern Rev*

Patricia Clare Lamb   P
3614 Montrose Blvd, Ste 405
Houston, TX 77006-4651
Internet: harbottle@aol.com
    Pubs: *The Long Love, All Men By Nature* (Harbottle Pr,
    1998, 1993), *Branch Redd Rev, Plains Poetry Jrnl, Midwest
    Qtly Rev, Commonweal*

James Langdon   P&W
1202 Seagler Rd, #60
Houston, TX 77042, 713-266-1229
    Pubs: *Chicago Rev, Contempora, Descant, Maple Leaf Rag,
    New Orleans Rev, Rapport*

Barbara D. Langham ♦ ✈   W
B.D. Langham Public Relations, 800 Bering Dr, Suite 310,
Houston, TX 77057, 713-961-4235
    Pubs: *NAR, Bellingham Rev, Descant, Fiction Texas,
    Crosscurrents, Pig Iron*

William Laufer   W
PO Box 8308
The Woodlands, TX 77387-3295
    Pubs: *Sudenly IV, Suddenly III, Suddenly 2000, Suddenly II:
    Anths* (Martin Hse, 2002, 2001, 2000, 1999), *P, Four Sea
    Interludes, Surrogates Fiction & Art* (Third Coast
    Letterpress, 1998, 1996, 1995), *The Indochina Suite*
    (Touchstone Pr, 1994)

Anne Leaton   W
3209 College Ave
Forth Worth, TX 76110, 817-923-7308
    Pubs: *Blackbird, Bye Bye* (Virago Pr, 1989), *Pearl* (Knopf,
    1989), *Esquire, Transatlantic Rev, Storia, Cosmopolitan*

J. R. LeMaster ♦ ✈   P
201 Harrington Ave
Waco, TX 76706-1519, 254-754-4358
    Internet: J_R_LeMaster@Baylor.edu
    Pubs: *Purple Bamboo, First Person, Second* (Tagore Inst of
    Creative Writing, 1988, 1983)

Jim Linebarger ♦ ✈   P
210 Solar Way
Denton, TX 76207, 940-243-9020
    Internet: jline@metronet.com
    Pubs: *Anecdotal Evidence* (Point Riders Pr, 1993), *The
    Worcester Poems* (Trilobite Pr, 1991), *SW Rev, Wormwood
    Rev, SE Rev, Southern Humanities Rev*

Marianne McNeil Logan ♦ ✈   P
7003 Amarillo Blvd E, #16
Amarillo, TX 79107, 806-374-4354
    Pubs: *Designed by Heritage* (PR Pub, 1998), *Girls Write
    Cowboy Poetry Too* (Nostalgic Nook Pr, 1990), *Pudgy
    Parodies* (Tanglewood, 1988), *NLAPW Mag, Stand, Poets
    Forum Mag*

Patricia Looker ♦ ✈   P&W
PO Box 1551
Bellaire, TX 77401-1551, 713-432-7873
    Internet: lookerpsyc@aol.com
    Pubs: *Straight Ahead, Wellspring, Apalachee Qtly, Forum,
    Quartet, Whetstone, Blonde on Blonde*

Marianne Loyd   P
3704 Tompkins
Baytown, TX 77521
    Pubs: *Stone Country, Uroboros, Tamarack, New Letters*

Grant Lyons ♦   W
2923 Woodcrest
San Antonio, TX 78209-3047, 210-822-5409
    Internet: gmlyons@swbell.net
    Pubs: *4.4.4.* (U Missouri Pr, 1977), *Negative Capability,
    Seattle Rev, Confrontation, Cimarron Rev, NW Rev,
    Redbook*

Cynthia Macdonald   P
1400 Hermann Dr, #8E
Houston, TX 77004, 713-520-6598
    Internet: cmacdo@compassnet.com
    Pubs: *Living Wills: New & Selected Poems, Alternate Means
    of Transport* (Knopf, 1991, 1985)

Kenard Marlowe ♦ ✈   P
3401 Cartagena Dr
Corpus Christi, TX 78418-3922, 361-937-5215
    Pubs: *Thinking Allowed* (IN Pub, 1994)

Janet McCann ♦ ✈   P
Texas A&M Univ, English Dept, College Station,
TX 77843-4227, 409-845-8316
    Internet: jmccann1@tamu.edu
    Pubs: *Looking for Buddha in the Barbed Wire Garden*
    (Avisson Pr, 1996), *Afterword* (Franciscan U Pr, 1990),
    Borderlands, Christian Century

Cormac McCarthy   W
1510 N Brown
El Paso, TX 79902

Walt McDonald ♦ ✈   P&W
English Dept, Texas Tech Univ, Lubbock, TX 79409,
806-742-2501
    Internet: walt.mmcdonald@ttu.edu
    Pubs: *All Occasions* (U Notre Dame Pr, 2000), *Blessings
    the Body Gave* (Ohio State U Pr, 1998), *Counting Survivors*
    (U Pitt Pr, 1995), *Night Landings* (H&R, 1989), *American
    Scholar, Atlantic, Poetry, Sewanee Rev, Southern Rev, APR*

Neill Megaw   P
2805 Bowman Ave
Austin, TX 78703, 512-472-5522
    Pubs: *The Spectator, Negative Capability, Sequoia, Hellas,
    The Lyric, South Coast Poetry Jrnl, The Formalist*

Christopher Middleton 🎤 ✈ P
Univ Texas, Dept Germanic Languages, Austin, TX 78712,
512-471-4123
   Pubs: *The Word Pavilion and Selected Poems, Intimate
Chronicles, The Balcony Tree* (Sheep Meadow Pr, 2001,
1996, 1992), *Twenty Tropes for Doctor Dark* (Enitharmon Pr,
2000), *In the Mirror of the Eighth King* (Sun & Moon Pr, 1999)

Bryce Milligan 🎤 ✈ P&W
627 E Guenther
San Antonio, TX 78210-1134, 210-271-7805
Internet: milligan@wingspress.com
   Pubs: *Brigid's Cloak* (Eerdmans Pub, 2003), *Alms for
Oblivion* (Aark/London, 2002), *Prince of Ireland* (Holiday
Hse, 2001), *Comanche Captive, Battle of the Alamo* (Eakin
Pr, 2000, 1999), *Lawmen* (Disney Pr, 1994), *Working the
Stone* (Wings Pr, 1993)

A. G. Mojtabai 🎤 ✈ P&W
2329 Woodside
Amarillo, TX 79124-1036, 806-433-5851
   Pubs: *Soon* (Zoland Bks, 1998), *Blessed Assurance*
(Syracuse U Pr, 1997), *Ordinary Time, Called Out*
(Doubleday, 1994, 1989)

Jane P. Moreland P&W
503 Shadywood
Houston, TX 77057, 713-975-6711
Internet: jpmore@prodigy.net
   Pubs: *Iowa Rev, Mademoiselle, Poetry, Poetry NW,
Georgia Rev*

E'Lane Carlisle Murray P&W
433 Haroldson Pl
Corpus Christi, TX 78412, 512-991-5294
   Pubs: *The Lace of Tough Mesquite: A Texas Heritage* (Eakin
Pr, 1993), *Southern Living, Texas Highways*

Jack Myers P
Southern Methodist Univ, English Dept, Dallas, TX 75275,
214-768-4369
   Pubs: *Blindsided, New American Poets of the '90s: Anth*
(Godine, 1992, 1992), *Poetry, Esquire, APR*

Isabel Nathaniel 🎤 ✈ P
18040 Midway Rd, Villa #215
Dallas, TX 75287, 972-380-6128
Internet: isabeln@aol.com
   Pubs: *Poetry in Motion from Coast to Coast: Anth* (Norton,
2002), *The Dominion of Lights* (Copper Beech Pr, 1996),
Ravishing DisUnities: Anth (Wesleyan U Pr, 2000), *Poetry,
Nation, Field, Ploughshares, Prairie Schooner, The Jrnl*

Kim L. Neidigh P&W
231 Radiance Ave
San Antonio, TX 78218
   Pubs: *Poetry Forum Jrnl, Wicked Mystic, Realm of the
Vampire, Ripples, Deathrealm, Bloodrake, Pursuit*

Sheryl L. Nelms 🎤 ✈ P
PO Box 674
Azle, TX 76098-0674, 817-444-1149
Internet: slnelms@aol.com
   Pubs: *The Secrets of the Wind* (Kitty Litter Pr, 2002), *Aunt
Emma Collected Teeth* (Sweet Annie Pr, 1999), *Friday Night
Desperate* (IM Pr, 1997), *Land of the Blue Paloverde*
(Shooting Star Pr, 1995), *Their Combs Turn Red in the
Spring* (Northwoods Pr, 1984)

Warren Norwood P&W
500 Green Tree
Weatherford, TX 76087-8909, 817-596-5201
Internet: gigi-warren-norwood@worldnet.att.net
   Pubs: *True Jaguar* (Bantam, 1988), *Space Opera: Anth* (Del
Rey, 1996), *Twilight Zone, Lookout, Green Fuse*

David Offutt 🎤 ✈ P
759 Redwood #3
Rockport, TX 78382-5961, 888-522-6464
Internet: doffutt@academicplanet.com
   Pubs: *Now That It's Quiet, The Byzantine Virgin, A
Perishable Good* (Inflammable Pr, 2002, 2001, 1997), *Ship
of Fools, Raintown Rev, Chachalaca, Free Lunch, Maverick
Pr, Tucumcari*

Dave Oliphant 🎤 ✈ P&W
Univ Texas, Main 201, Austin, TX 78712, 512-331-1557
Internet: doliphant@mail.utexas.edu
   Pubs: *Memories of Texas Towns & Cities* (Host, 2000), *New
Texas, New Letters, Colorado Qtly, College English, South
Dakota Rev*

Joe Olvera P&W
12400 Rojas Dr, #49
El Paso, TX 79927, 915-592-9870
Internet: olvera@freewwweb.com
   Pubs: *Drugs: Frankly Speaking* (SW Pub, 1980), *Voces de
la Gente* (Mictla Pub, 1972)

Carolyn Osborn 🎤 ✈ W
3612 Windsor Rd
Austin, TX 78703-1538, 512-472-4533
   Pubs: *Warriors & Maidens* (Texas Christian U Pr, 1991), *The
O. Henry Awards: Anth* (Doubleday, 1991), *Witness, SW
Rev, Antioch Rev*

Keddy Ann Outlaw 🎤 ✈ P&W
3003 Linkwood Dr
Houston, TX 77025-3813, 713-668-8273
Internet: koutlaw@usa.net
   Pubs: *At Our Core: Anth, I Am Becoming the Woman I've
Wanted: Anth* (Papier-Mache, 1998, 1994), *Texas Short
Stories: Anth* (Browder Springs, 1999, 1997), *Texas Short
Fiction III: Anth* (ALE Pub, 1996)

Leslie Palmer 🎤 ✈   P
Univ North Texas, English Dept, Denton, TX 76203,
817-387-5460
    Pubs: *Disgraceland* (Pine Tree Pr, 2000), *Swollen Foot, The
    Devil Sells Ice Cream* (Windy-Dawn, 1999, 1994), *Ode to a
    Frozen Dog* (Laughing Bear, 1992), *Poetry & Audience,
    Green's Mag, Blue Jacket, Cape Rock, Southern
    Humanities Rev, Linq*

Dave Parsons 🎤 ✈   P
414 Oak Hill
Conroe, TX 77304-1906, 409-539-2466
Internet: dmparsons@txucom.net
    Pubs: *Editing Sky* (Texas Rev Pr, 1999), *Texas Rev, Gulf
    Coast, Southwestern American Lit, Anth of Magazine Verse
    & Yearbook of Poetry, Louisiana Lit, Touchstone,
    Standpoints*

Tom Person   P
PO Box 613322
Dallas, TX 75261-3322, 817-283-6303
Internet: tom@laughingbear.com
    Pubs: *Small Pr, NYQ, Nexus, Interstate, Iron, Coffeehouse
    Poets Qtly*

Estela Portillo   P&W
131 Clairemont
El Paso, TX 79912, 915-584-8841

Ron Querry   W
2415 E Musser
Laredo, TX 78043-2434, 011-524-1523542
Internet: ronquerry@mpsnet.com.mx
    Pubs: *Bad Medicine, The Death of Bernadette Lefthand*
    (Bantam Bks, 1998, 1995), *I See By My Get-Up*
    (U Oklahoma Pr, 1994)

S. Ramnath   P&W
PO Box 371823
El Paso, TX 79937-1823, 915-592-3701
Internet: an193@rgfn.epcc.edu
    Pubs: *Eye of the Beast* (Vergin Pr, 1986), *Rings in a Tree
    Trunk* (India; Writers Workshop, 1976), *Bedside Prayers:
    Anth* (Harper SF, 1997), *Willow Springs, Weber Studies,
    Press, Litspeak, Kerf, Arkansas Qtly, Quixote Qtly,
    Maverick Pr*

Pedro Revuelta   P
c/o Gutierrez Revuelta, Univ Houston, Spanish Dept, Houston,
TX 77204-3784, 713-749-3064
    Pubs: *Accidentes Y Otros Recursos* (Spain; Ediciones
    Libertarias, 1990), *Complejas Perspectivas* (Spain; Editorial
    Origenes, 1988), *Maize, el ultimo vuelo*

Diane Reynolds 🎤 ✈   P
600 Barwood Pk, #1716
Austin, TX 78753-6454, 512-415-7389
Internet: dianereynolds@swbell.net
    Pubs: *Travois: An Anth of Texas Writers* (Wings Pr, 1977),
    *Southern Poetry Rev, Cortland Rev, Adirondack Rev, Red
    River Rev, Liberty Hill Poetry Rev, Poesy, Lit Rev,*

Clay Reynolds 🎤 ✈   W
909 Hilton Pl
Denton, TX 76201-8605, 940-566-2512
Internet: rclayr@aol.com
    Pubs: *Monuments* (Texas Tech U Pr, 2000), *Players* (Carroll
    & Graf, 1998), *Rage, Franklin's Crossing* (NAL/Signet, 1994,
    1993), *Descant, Writers' Forum, Texas Rev, i.e. Mag,
    Cimarron Rev, Concho River Rev*

Brian Paul Robertson   P
516 Tamarack
McAllen, TX 78501

Amber Rollins 🎤 ✈   W
6618 Laura Ann Ct
Fort Worth, TX 76118-6278, 817-284-4322
Internet: amberrollins@hotmail.com
    Pubs: *Living Buddhism, Not My Small Diary, World Tribune,
    EOTU, Paper Bag, Fiction Forum, The Torch, DC, After
    Hours, Being, Bahlasti Papers, Starsong, Outrage*

Rolando Romo 🎤 ✈   W
6951 Heron
Houston, TX 77087, 713-643-5612
Internet: rmr_2000@yahoo.com

Paul Ruffin 🎤 ✈   P&W
2014 Avenue N 1/2
Huntsville, TX 77340, 936-295-5645
Internet: eng_pdr@shsu.edu
    Pubs: *Pompeii Man* (Louisiana Lit Pr, 2002), *Islands,
    Women, and God, Circling, Circling* (Browder Springs Pr,
    2001, 1997), *The Man Who Would Be God* (SMU Pr, 1993),
    *Southern Rev, Michigan Qtly Rev, Georgia Rev, ALR,
    Alaska Qtly Rev, Poetry*

Annette Sanford   W
Box 596
Ganado, TX 77962, 512-771-3654
    Pubs: *Lasting Attachments, Common Bonds: Stories By &
    About Texas Women: Anth* (SMU Pr, 1989, 1990), *Story,
    American Short Fiction*

Rainer Schulte   P
Center for Translation Studies, Univ Texas-Dallas, Box 830688,
Richardson, TX 75083-0688, 972-883-2092
    Pubs: *The Other Side of the Word* (Texas Writers, 1978),
    Suicide at the Piano (Sono Nis, 1970)

Daryl Scroggins 🎤 ✈   W
6200 Bryan Pkwy
Dallas, TX 75214-4302, 214-821-9317
Internet: darylscrog@yahoo.com
  Pubs: *Winter Investments* (Trilobite Pr, 2002), *The Game of
  Kings* (Rancho Loco Pr, 2001), *Quarter After Eight,
  webdelsol, Pearl, NW Rev, Carolina Qtly*

Jan Epton Seale 🎤 ✈   P
400 Sycamore
McAllen, TX 78501-2227, 956-686-4033
  Pubs: *Red Boots & Attitude* (Eakin Pr, 2002), *The Yin of It*
  (Pecan Grove Pr, 2000), *Airlift* (TCU Pr, 1992), *MacGuffin,
  Midwest Poetry Rev, Visions, Yale Rev, Texas Monthly,
  Passages North, Blue Mesa, COE Rev*

Wendell P. Sexton   P
4302 Rosebud Dr
Houston, TX 77053, 713-435-0867
  Pubs: *Poets Corner* (Office Duplication Classes, 1975)

John E. Smelcer 🎤 ✈   P
7202 Eastphal Circle
Corpus Christi, TX 78413
Internet: jpsmelcer@aol.com
  Pubs: *Riversongs* (CPR, 2001), *Songs from an Outcast*
  (UCLA, 2000), *Kesugi Ridge* (Aureole Pr, 1995), *Here First:
  Anth* (RH, 2000), *Poetry Comes Up: Anth* (Utah U Pr, 2000),
  *Atlantic Rev, Prairie Schooner, Ploughshares, Iowa Rev,
  Yale Rev, Antioch Rev*

Samuel B. Southwell   W
1217 W Main
Houston, TX 77006
  Pubs: *Kenneth Burke & Martin Heidegger: With a Note
  Against Deconstructionism* (U Florida, 1988), *If All the
  Rebels Die* (Doubleday, 1966)

L. Sprague de Camp   W
3453 Hearst Castle Way
Plano, TX 75025
  Pubs: *Rivers of Time, The Enchanter Reborn* (w/C. Stasheff)
  (Baen Bks, 1993, 1992), *Analog, Asimov's Sci Fi,
  Command, Nature, Expanse*

Kristi Sprinkle   P&W
8105 Coyote Ridge
Austin, TX 78737
Internet: kristi@bga.com
  Pubs: *Freelight, Paramour, Austin Chronicle*

Cathy Stern 🎤 ✈   P
12427 Old Oaks Dr
Houston, TX 77024-4911, 713-465-8017
  Pubs: *Suddenly V: Anth* (Martin Hse Pr, 2003), *Echoes for a
  New Room: Anth* (Brown Rabbit Press, 1998), *A Wider
  Giving: Anth* (Chicory Blue Pr, 1988), *Paris Rev, New
  Republic, Shenandoah*

Alex Stevens   P
801 Rutland
Houston, TX 77007
  Pubs: *New Yorker, Poetry, Georgia Rev, New Republic*

Gail Donohue Storey 🎤 ✈   P&W
3907 Swarthmore
Houston, TX 77005-3611, 713-669-9318
  Pubs: *God's Country Club, The Lord's Motel* (Persea Bks,
  1996, 1992), *Fiction, NAR, Chicago Rev, Gulf Coast,
  Ellipses, Mississippi Valley Rev*

James L. Stowe   W
709 Baltimore
El Paso, TX 79902
  Pubs: *Winter Stalk* (S&S, 1978)

Semon Strobos   W
2281 Bretzke Ln
New Braunfels, TX 78132, 210-609-0527
Internet: strobat@compuserve.net
  Pubs: *NAR, Epoch, Chariton Rev, Antioch Rev, Descant,
  Alabama Literary Rev*

Belinda Subraman   P
PO Box 370322
El Paso, TX 79937-0322, 915-566-1858
Internet: subraman1@msn.com
  Pubs: *Notes of a Human Warehouse Engineer* (Nerve
  Cowboy, 1998), *Finding Reality in Myth* (Chiron Rev Pr,
  1996), *Between the Cracks: Anth* (Daedalus, 1996), *Mondo
  Barbie: Anth* (St. Martin's Pr, 1993), *Arkansas Rev, India
  Currents, Best Texas Writing*

Thea Temple   P&W
3109 Caribou Ct
Mesquite, TX 75181, 972-222-3973
Internet: jmyers@post.cis.smu.edu
  Pubs: *River Styx, Sycamore Rev, Yellow Silk, Chiron Rev,
  Beloit Fiction Jrnl, The New Press, Alabama Literary Rev,
  Japanophile*

Heriberto Teran   P
2314 Baltimore St
Laredo, TX 78040, 512-722-7435

Larry D. Thomas 🎤 ✈   P
2006 Commonwealth
Houston, TX 77006-1804, 713-523-8147
  Pubs: *Lighthouse Keeper* (Timberline, 2000), *Midwest Qtly,
  Louisiana Lit, Cottonwood, JAMA, Whole Notes, Plainsongs,
  Intl Poetry Rev, Southwestern Amer Lit, Green Hills Lit
  Lantern, Amer Indian Culture/Research Jrnl, Blue Violin,
  Modern Haiku*

Lorenzo Thomas 🎤 ✈   P
Box 14645
Houston, TX 77221, 713-221-8475
Internet: thomasl@zeus.dt.uh.edu
    Pubs: *The Bathers* (Reed & Cannon, 1981), *Chances Are
    Few* (Blue Wind Pr, 1979), *Postmodern American Poetry:
    Anth* (Norton, 1994), *Ploughshares, Long News*

Ruby C. Tolliver   W
1806 Pin Oak Ln
Conroe, TX 77302, 409-756-4659
    Pubs: *Boomer's Kids, Blind Bess, Buddy & M* (Hendrick-Long
    Pub, 1992, 1990), *Have Gun, Need Bullets* (TCU Pr, 1991)

Frederick Turner   P&W
School of Arts & Humanities, Univ Texas-Dallas, Richardson,
TX 75083, 214-690-2777
    Pubs: *April Wind, Beauty* (U Pr Virginia, 1992, 1992),
    Tempest, Flute & Oz (Persea Bks, 1991), *Harper's, Poetry*

Leslie Ullman 🎤 ✈   P
Creative Writing Program, Univ Texas, English Dept, El Paso,
TX 79968, 505-874-3068
Internet: lullman@utep.edu
    Pubs: *Slow Work Through Sand* (U Iowa Pr, 1998), *Dreams
    By No One's Daughter* (U Pitt Pr, 1987), *Natural Histories*
    (Yale U Pr, 1979), *Poetry, Kenyon Rev, Bloomsbury Rev*

Leo Vroman   P
1600 Texas St
Fort Worth, TX 76102, 817-870-1172
Internet: lvroman@elash.net
    Pubs: *Psalmen en Andere Gedichten* (Amsterdam; Querido,
    1997), *Flight 800/Vlucht 800, Love, Greatly Enlarged* (CCC,
    1997, 1992)

Brian Walker   P
PO Box 5143
Lubbock, TX 79417
    Pubs: *Fiddlehead, Poetry Ireland Rev, Poetry Wales,
    Transnational Perspectives, Bitterroot*

William Wenthe 🎤 ✈   P
Dept of English, Box 43091, Texas Tech Univ, Lubbock, TX
79410, 806-742-2501
Internet: wwenthe@ttacs.ttu.edu
    Pubs: *Not Till We Are Lost* (LSU Pr, 2003), *Birds of Hoboken*
    (Orchises Pr, 1995), *Pushcart Prize: Anths* (Pushcart Pr,
    2002, 2000), *Best Texas Writing I: Anth* (Rancho Loco Pr,
    1998), *Image, Laurel Rev, Orion, Southern Rev, Meridian,
    Press, Georgia Rev*

Kenneth Wheatcroft-Pardue 🎤 ✈   P
1805 Robinwood Dr
Forth Worth, TX 76111-6110, 817-834-3341
Internet: kwheatcroftpardue@yahoo.com
    Pubs: *Sleepy Tree I: Anth* (Sleepy Tree Pr, 1980), *Pitchfork,
    Blind Man's Rainbow, California Qtly, Poetry Motel, Concho
    River Rev*

Thomas Whitbread   P
English Dept, Univ Texas, Austin, TX 78712, 512-471-4991
    Pubs: *Whomp & Moonshiver* (BOA Edtns, 1982), *Four
    Infinitives* (H&R, 1964)

Brenda Black White   P
2508 Washington
Commerce, TX 75428, 903-886-3822
    Pubs: *Callahan County* (Plainview Pr, 1988), *New Texas '95:
    Anth, Texas in Poetry: Anth* (Ctr for Texas Studies, 1995,
    1994), *RE:AL, Ms., Confrontation*

J. Whitebird   W
13815 Bay Gardens Dr
Sugar Land, TX 77478-1723, 281-494-1380
    Pubs: *Heat & Other Stories* (Arbiter Pr, 1990), *The North
    Beach Papers* (Suck Egg Mule Pr, 1985), *Crosscurrents,
    Plainswoman, Poemail*

Scott Wiggerman 🎤 ✈   P
1310 Crestwood Rd
Austin, TX 78722, 512-467-0678
Internet: swiggerman@austin.rr.com
    Pubs: *Vegetables and Other Relationships* (Plain View Pr,
    2000), *New Dudes: Gents, Bad Boys & Barbarians: Anth*
    (Windstorm Creative, 2002), *Portals: Anth* (PoetWorks Pr,
    2002), *Cancer Poetry Project: Anth* (Fairview Press, 2001),
    Midwest Poetry Rev, Gertrude

Chris Willerton   P
English Dept, Abilene Christian Univ, ACU Box 29142,
Abilene, TX 79699, 915-674-2259
Internet: willerto@nicanor.acu.edu
    Pubs: *Texas in Poetry: Anth* (Browder Springs Pr, 2002),
    Londale Hotel (Eastgate Systems, 2002)

Lex Williford 🎤   W
Eng Mail Code 00526, UTEP HUD 113, 500 W Univ Ave, El
Paso, TX 79968-0526, 915-443-1931
Internet: lex@utep.edu
    Pubs: *Macauley's Thumb* (U Iowa Pr, 1994), *Scribner's Anth
    of Contemporary Short Fiction* (S&S, 1999), *Glimmer Train,
    Sou'wester, Fiction, Qtly West, New Texas, Laurel Rev,
    Virginia Qtly Rev, Story Qtly, Southern Rev, Shenandoah*

Miles Wilson   P&W
906 Clyde St
San Marcos, TX 78666, 512-392-9643
    Pubs: *Line of Fall* (U Iowa Pr, 1989), *Gettysburg Rev,
    Georgia Rev, Poetry, SW Rev, NAR, Iowa Rev*

Steve Wilson 🎤 ✈   P
English Dept, Southwest Texas State Univ, San Marcos, TX
78666, 512-245-2163
Internet: sw13@swt.edu
    Pubs: *The Singapore Express, Allegory Dance* (Black Tie Pr,
    1994, 1991), *American Poetry: Anth* (Carnegie Mellon U Pr,
    2000), *What Have You Lost?: Anth* (Greenwillow Bks, 1999),
    Yankee Mag, Commonweal, America, CSM, New Letters

Bryan Woolley   W
18040 Midway Rd, Villa 215
Dallas, TX 75287, 214-380-6128
    Pubs: *The Bride Wore Crimson, The Edge of the West*
    (Texas Western, 1993, 1990), *Time & Place* (TCU, 1985)

John Works   W
1600 Forest Trail
Austin, TX 78703
    Pubs: *Thank You Queen Isabella* (Texas A&M U, 1986),
    Humanities Rev, Cottonwood Rev

Robert Wynne 🎤 ✈   P
7936 Clear Brook Circle
Fort Worth, TX 76123
Internet: RobertWynne@Bigfoot.com
    Pubs: *Uno* (Comrades/Xlibris, 2002), *Smaller than God*
    (Black Moss Pr, 2001), *Henry's Creature: Poems and*
    Stories on the Automobile: Anth (Black Moss Pr, 2000), *Call*
    the Sun Down (VCP Pr, 1999), *Driving* (Inevitable Pr, 1997)

UTAH

Christopher Arigo 🎤 ✈   P
1014 E 100 South, #2
Salt Lake City, UT 84102, 801-322-3105
Internet: chrisarigo@yahoo.com
    Pubs: *Lit Interim* (Pavement Saw Pr, 2002), *Fine Madness,*
    Phoebe, Fourteen Hills, Whiskey Island Mag

Margaret Pabst Battin   W
Philosophy Dept, Univ of Utah, Salt Lake City, UT 84112,
801-581-6608
    Pubs: *The Least Worst Death* (Oxford U Pr, 1994)

Kenneth W. Brewer 🎤 ✈   P
651 Canyon Rd
Logan, UT 84321-4240, 435-752-5494
Internet: kbrewer@english.usu.edu
    Pubs: *The Place in Between* (Limberlost Pr, 1998), *To*
    Remember What Is Lost (Utah State U Pr, 1989), *Great &*
    Peculiar Beauty, A Utah Reader: Anth (Gibbs Smith, 1995),
    Poetry NW, Kansas Qtly

Alissandru (Alex) Caldiero 🎤 ✈   PP&P
1978 N 100 E
Orem, UT 84057, 801-224-8642
Internet: wordshaker@usa.net
    Pubs: *Various Atmospheres* (Signature Bks, 1998), *Text-*
    Sounds Texts (Morrow, 1980), *A Dictionary of the Avant-*
    Gardes: Anth (Routledge, 2001), *Clown War, Handbook,*
    Screens & Tasted Parallels, Canyon Echo

Joan Gilgun   W
1700 S 800 E
Lewiston, UT 84320
    Pubs: *The Uncle* (Cadmus Edtns, 1982), *Dialogue, New*
    Voices, Innisfree, Western Humanities Rev

Edward L. Hart   P
1401 Cherry Ln
Provo, UT 84604, 801-375-0871
    Pubs: *To Utah* (Brigham Young U Pr, 1979), *BPJ, Western*
    Humanities Rev

Robin Hemley   W
Dept of English, Univ of Utah, 255 South Central Campus Dr,
Rm 3500, Salt Lake City, UT 84109, 801-581-3022
Internet: rhemley@msn.com
    Pubs: *The Big Ear* (Blair, 1995), *The Last Studebaker*
    (Graywolf, 1992), *All You Can Eat* (Atlantic Monthly Pr,
    1988), *NAR, Prairie Schooner, Ploughshares, Story,*
    Boulevard, Manoa

Robert L. Jones   P
Univ Utah, English Dept, 341 0SH, Salt Lake City, UT 84112
    Pubs: *Wild Onion* (Graywolf Pr, 1985), *The Space I Occupy*
    (Skywriting, 1977), *Kansas Qtly*

Lance Larsen 🎤 ✈   P
Poetry Editor: Literature and Belief, 3077 JKHB, Brigham
Young U, Provo, UT 84602, 801-378-8104
Internet: Lance_Larsen@byu.edu
    Pubs: *Erasable Walls* (New Issues Pr, 1998), *American*
    Poetry: Anth (Carnegie Mellon U Pr, 2000), *Times Lit*
    Supplement, Southern Rev, Paris Rev, Kenyon Rev, New
    Republic, Field, Southern Rev, Threepenny Rev,
    Salmagundi, New England Rev

David Lee 🎤 ✈   P
Dept of Language & Literature, Southern Utah State College,
Cedar City, UT 84720, 801-586-7835
Internet: lee_d@suu.edu
    Pubs: *Incident at Thompson Slough* (Wood Works Pr, 2004),
    A Legacy of Shadows, News from Down to the CafÈ, Day's
    Work (Copper Canyon Pr, 1999, 1999, 1990), *Paragonah*
    Canyon, Autumn (Brooding Heron Pr, 1988)

Harris Lenowitz   P
Middle East Center, Univ Utah, Salt Lake City, UT 84112, 801-
581-6181
    Pubs: *Transparencies: Jewish Pages* (Finch Lane, 1985),
    The Sayings of Yakov Frank (Tree, 1978)

Lynne Butler Oaks   W
3945 S Wasatch Blvd, #260
Salt Lake City, UT 84124, 801-321-1808
    Pubs: *Missouri Rev, Fiction Intl, Story Qtly, The Qtly, Utah*
    Holiday

Jacqueline Osherow   P
Univ Utah, English Dept, 3500 LNCO, Salt Lake City, UT 84112
Internet: jacqueline.osherow@m.cc.utah.edu
    Pubs: *With a Moon in Transit* (Grove Poetry, 1996),
    Conversations with Survivors, Looking for Angels in New
    York (U Georgia Pr, 1994, 1988), *Paris Rev, New Republic,*
    TriQtly, Partisan Rev, SW Rev, Boulevard

Donald Revell 🎤 ✈   P
English Dept, Univ Utah, Salt Lake City, UT 84112,
801-581-6168
Internet: Donald.Revell@m.cc.utah.edu
 Pubs: *Arcady, There Are Three, Beautiful Shirt, Erasures,
 New Dark Ages* (Wesleyan, 2002, 1998, 1994, 1992, 1990),
 *Antaeus, APR, Grand Street, Conjunctions, Partisan Rev,
 Kenyon Rev*

Stephen Ruffus   P
c/o Utah Arts Council, 617 E South Temple, Salt Lake City, UT
84102, 801-533-5895
 Pubs: *Qtly West, Westigan Rev, Western Humanities Rev*

Natasha Saje   P
Westminster College, 1840 1300 East, Salt Lake City, UT
84105, 801-488-1692
Internet: n-saje@wcslc.edu
 Pubs: *Red Under the Skin* (U Pittsburgh Pr, 1994), *Poetry,
 Shenandoah, American Voice, Denver Qtly, Ploughshares*

Richard Schramm   P
Univ Utah, English Dept, Salt Lake City, UT 84112
 Pubs: *Rooted in Silence* (Bobbs-Merrill, 1972), *New Yorker,
 Antaeus, APR*

Emma Lou Thayne   P&W
1965 St Mary's Dr
Salt Lake City, UT 84108, 801-581-1260
 Pubs: *All God's Critters Got a Place in the Choir* (w/L.T.
 Ulrich; Aspen, 1995), *Things Happen: Poems of Survival*
 (Signature Bks, 1991), *Network*

Melanie Rae Thon 🎤 ✈   W
Dept of English, Univ of Utah, 255 S Central Campus Dr, Rm
3500, Salt Lake City, UT 84112-0494
 Pubs: *Sweet Hearts* (HM, 2001), *First, Body* (H Holt, 1998),
 Iona Moon (Plume, 1994), *Girls in the Grass, Meteors in
 August* (Random Hse, 1991, 1990), *Five Points, Image: A
 Jrnl, Granta, Paris Rev, Ontario Rev, Antaeus, Hudson Rev,
 Ploughshares*

David Widup   P
1930 E Sunridge Cir
Sandy, UT 84093
Internet: david_widup@bdhq.bd.com
 Pubs: *In Country* (w/Michael Andrews), *Over to You*
 (w/Stellasue Lee Bombshelter Pr, 1994, 1991), *ACM, Icarus
 Rev, Spillway, Onthebus, Rattle*

VERMONT

Thomas Absher   P
Vermont College, Montpelier, VT 05679, 802-828-8820
 Pubs: *The Calling* (Alice James Bks, 1987), *Forms of Praise*
 (Ohio State U Pr, 1981), *Ploughshares, Poetry, Nation*

Laurie Alberts 🎤 ✈   W
PO Box 258
Westminster, VT 05158
Internet: lalberts@sover.net
 Pubs: *Lost Daughters, The Price of Land in Shelby* (U Pr
 New England, 1999, 1996), *Goodnight Silky Sullivan* (U
 Missouri Pr, 1995), *Tempting Fate* (HM, 1987)

Joan Aleshire 🎤 ✈   P
223 Mitchell Rd
Cuttingsville, VT 05738, 802-492-3550
 Pubs: *The Yellow Transparents* (Four Way Bks, 1997), *This
 Far* (QRL, 1987), *Cloud Train* (Texas Tech, 1982), *Outsiders:
 Anth* (Milkweed, 1999), *Staring Back: Anth* (Dutton, 1997),
 Marlboro Rev, Barrow Street, QRL, Nation, Seneca Rev

Frank Anthony 🎤 ✈   P
151 Main St, PO Box 483
Windsor, VT 05089, 802-674-2315
Internet: newvtpoet@aol.com
 Pubs: *First Family, Down Gullah, The Conch Chronicle, The
 Brussels Book, The Amsterdam Papers, The Magic Bench*
 (New Vision Pubs, 2003, 2000, 1999, 1998, 1997, 1996),
 Evening Vespers (Rosecroft Pr, 2002), *Curious Rooms,
 Artisan, Parnassus, Poetry Mag*

Bob Arnold   P
1604 River Rd
Guilford, VT 05301, 802-254-4242
Internet: poetry@sover.net
 Pubs: *Dream Come True* (Tel-Let, 2001), *Honeymoon*
 (Granite Pr, 2000), *Once in Vermont* (Gnomon Pr, 1999),
 Good Poems: Anth (Viking/Penguin, 2002), *Clothes Line:
 Anth* (Abrams, 2001), *Home: Anth* (Abrams, 1999),
 Outsiders: Anth (Milkweed Edtns, 1999)

E. RL. Barna 🎤 ✈   P
80 Park St
Brandon, VT 05733, 802-247-3146
Internet: gotobarn@sover.net
 Pubs: *Atlanta Rev, Agni, Firehouse, Worcester Rev, Long-
 house, Afterthought, Mothering, Softball, Gob*

Ben Belitt   P
PO Box 88
North Bennington, VT 05257-0088, 802-442-5956
 Pubs: *Graffiti & Other Poems* (Erewhon, 1990), *Possessions*
 (Godine, 1986), *Nowhere But Light* (U Chicago Pr, 1970),
 Salmagundi, Yale Rev, Southern Rev

T. Alan Broughton 🎤 ✈   P&W
124 Spruce St
Burlington, VT 05401-4522, 802-864-4250
Internet: tbrought@zoo.uvm.edu
 Pubs: *Suicidal Tendencies* (Cntr for Lit Publishing, Colorado
 State Univ, 2003), *The Origin of Green, In the Country of
 Elegies, Preparing to Be Happy* (Carnegie Mellon U Pr,
 2001, 1995, 1988)

David Budbill 🎤 ✈ P
4592 E Hill Rd
Wolcott, VT 05680-4149, 802-888-3729
Internet: budbill@sover.net
    Pubs: *Moment to Moment* (Copper Canyon Pr, 1999),
    Judevine: The Complete Poems (Chelsea Green, 1991),
    Why I Came to Judevine (White Pine, 1987), *Green
    Mountains Rev, Harper's, New Virginia Rev, The Sun, Cedar
    Hill Rev, Graffiti Rag, Maine Times, Ohio Rev*

Rhoda Carroll P
RR5, Box 1030, 2047 Elm St
Montpelier, VT 05602, 802-229-0037
Internet: rhoda@norwich.edu
    Pubs: *Slant, Nebraska Rev, Green Mountains Rev, Poet
    Lore, Visions Intl, Lake Effect, Laurel Rev, Texas Rev,
    Northern Rev, Tar River Poetry, Louisville Rev*

George R. Clay W
Wild Farm
Arlington, VT 05250, 802-362-1656

Greg Delanty 🎤 ✈ P
3 Berry St
Burlington, VT 05401
Internet: ninenine@together.net
    Pubs: *Leper's Walk* (Carcanet Pr, 2001), *The Fifth Province*
    (Traffic Street Pr, 2000), *The Hellbox* (Oxford U Pr, 1998),
    American Wake (Dufour Edtns, 1995), *Southward* (Louisiana
    U Pr, 1992), *Cast in the Fire* (Dolmen Pr, 1986)

Chard deNiord P
137 Birch Lane
Putney, VT 05346, 802-387-5309
    Pubs: *Asleep in the Fire* (U Alabama Pr, 1990), *Poems for a
    Small Planet: A Bread Loaf Anth* (U Pr New England, 1993),
    Harvard Mag, Denver Qtly, NAR, NER, Iowa Rev

Rickey Gard Diamond 🎤 ✈ W
56 Browns Mill Rd
Montpelier, VT 05602, 802-223-7911
Internet: rdiamond@norwich.edu
    Pubs: *Second Sight* (HC, 1999), *Other Voices, Writers' Bar-
    B-Q, Plainswoman, Kalliope, Sewanee Rev, Louisville Rev*

Susan M. Dodd W
Bennington College, Bennington, VT 05201
    Pubs: *Hell-Bent Men & Their Cities, Mamaw, No Earthly
    Notion* (Viking, 1990, 1988, 1986), *New Yorker*

Ellen Dudley 🎤 ✈ P
The Marlboro Rev, PO Box 243, Marlboro, VT 05344,
802-254-4938
Internet: dudley@sover.net
    Pubs: *Slow Burn* (Provincetown Arts Pr 1997), *Outsiders:
    Anth* (Milkweed Edtns 1999), *TriQtly, Agni, Massachusetts
    Rev*

Margaret Edwards P&W
Univ of Vermont, English Dept, 400 Old Mill, Burlington, VT
05405, 802-862-4468
    Pubs: *Best American Short Stories: Anth* (HM, 1986),
    Virginia Qtly Rev, Vermont History

Kenward Elmslie P&W
c/o Poets Corner
Calais, VT 05648, 802-456-8123
    Pubs: *Routine Disruptions* (Coffee Hse Pr, 1998), *Pay Dirt*
    (Bamberger Bks, 1992), *Sung Sex* (Kulchur Fdn, 1989), *26
    Bars* (Z Pr, 1987), *NAW, o.blek, Conjunctions*

John Engels P
221 Shelburne St
Burlington, VT 05401, 802-865-2543
    Pubs: *Walking to Cootehill* (U Pr New England, 1993),
    Cardinals in the Ice Age (Graywolf Pr, 1987), *Weather-Fear*
    (U Georgia Pr, 1982)

James Facos 🎤 ✈ P&W
333 Elm St
Montpelier, VT 05602-2213
    Pubs: *The Silver Lady* (Thorndike Pr, 1995), *Morning's
    Come Singing* (American Poetry Pr, 1981), *Bk of Light
    Verse: Anth* (Norton, 1986), *New Press Lit Qtly, Negative
    Capability, Stories, The Leading Edge*

Terry Farish 🎤 ✈ W
Steerforth Press, PO Box 70, South Royalton, VT 05068, 802-
763-2808
Internet: farish@nh.ultranet.com
    Pubs: *House in Earnest, If the Tiger* (Steerforth Pr, 2000,
    1995), *Talking in Animal, Shelter for a Seabird, Why I'm
    Already Blue* (Greenwillow, 1996, 1990, 1989), *Flower
    Shadows* (Morrow, 1992)

Alvin Feinman P
PO Box 655
North Bennington, VT 05257

Daniel Mark Fogel 🎤 ✈ P
112 S Williams St, Englesby House
Burlington, VT 05401-3406, 802-656-8998
Internet: danile.fogel@uvm.edu
    Pubs: *A Trick of Resilience* (Ithaca, 1975), *Southern Rev,
    National Forum, Western Humanities*

Ellen Frye W
7 Third Ave
White River Jct, VT 05001
Internet: ellen.frye@dartmouth.edu
    Pubs: *Amazon Story Bones* (Spinsters Ink, 1994), *The
    Other Sappho* (Firebrand Bks, 1989), *Calyx, Short Fiction
    By Women*

Lyle Glazier   P&W
RD 3, Niles Rd
Bennington, VT 05201-4959, 802-442-9459
    Pubs: *Prefatory Lyrics* (Coffee Hse Pr, 1991), *Azubah Nye* (White Pine Pr, 1988), *Origin, Longhouse, Shadow/Play, Tel-Let, New Yorker, Story*

Florence Grossman   P
PO Box 352
Bondville, VT 05340-0352
    Pubs: *Listening to the Bells* (Heinemann Boynton/Cook, 1991), *Nation, Poetry, New Criterion*

Robert Hahn   P
155 College Hill
Johnson, VT 05656-9134, 802-635-1246
Internet: hahnr@badger.jsc.vsc.edu
    Pubs: *No Messages* (U Notre Dame Pr, 2001), *All Clear* (U South Carolina Pr, 1996), *Ontario Rev, Paris Rev, SW Rev, Yale Rev, Partisan Rev*

H. Douglas Hall   P
RD
Cuttingsville, VT 05738, 802-492-3517
    Pubs: *Road Apple Rev, Loon, The Sun, Poetry Now, Northern New England Rev*

Pamela Harrison 🎤 ✈   P
PO Box 1106
Norwich, VT 05055-1106, 802-649-2946
    Pubs: *Greatest Hits: 1981-2000* (Pudding Hse, 2001), *Noah's Daughter, The Panhandler* (U West Florida Pr, 1988), *College Handbook of Creative Writing: Anth* (HBJ, 1991), *BPJ, Yankee, Poetry, Cimarron Rev, Laurel Rev, Green Mountains Rev, Sow's Ear*

Shelby Hearon   W
246 S Union
Burlington, VT 05401, 802-660-4349
    Pubs: *Ella in Bloom, Footprints, Life Estates, Hug Dancing* (Knopf, 2000, 1996, 1994, 1991), *Redbook, Cosmopolitan, Southwest Rev, Southern Rev*

Bruce Hesselbach 🎤 ✈   P&W
43 Bruce Brook Rd
Newfane, VT 05345
Internet: hessel@sover.net
    Pubs: *The Lyric, Piedmont Lit Rev, Reflect, Waterways*

Geof Hewitt 🎤 ✈   P
PO Box 51
Calais, VT 05648-0051, 802-828-3111
    Pubs: *Only What's Imagined* (Kumquat Pr, 2000), *Just Worlds* (Ithaca Hse, 1989)

Edward Hoagland   W
RR1, Box 2977
Bennington, VT 05201-9735, 802-442-2088
    Pubs: *Compass Points* (Pantheon, 2001), *Balancing Acts, Heart's Desire* (S&S, 1992, 1988)

David Huddle 🎤 ✈   P&W
34 N Willams St
Burlington, VT 05401-3304, 802-864-6111
Internet: dhuddle@zoo.uvm.edu
    Pubs: *Grayscale, Summer Lake* (LSU Pr, 2003, 1999), *La Tour Dreams of the Wolf Girl, Story of a Million Years* (HM, 2002, 1999), *Not: A Trio* (U Notre Dame Pr, 2000), *Story, APR, Kenyon Rev, Antioch, Epoch, Field, Poetry*

John Irving   W
The Turnbull Agency, PO Box 757, Dorset, VT 05251
    Pubs: *The Fourth Hand, A Widow for One Year, A Son of the Circus* (Random Hse, 2001, 1998, 1994), *The Cider House Rules* (Morrow, 1985)

Galway Kinnell   P&W
Sheffield, VT 05966
    Pubs: *When One Has Lived a Long Time Alone* (Knopf, 1990), *The Past, Selected Poems* (HM, 1985, 1982)

Sydney Lea 🎤 ✈   P&W
PO Box 9
Newbury, VT 05051-0009, 802-866-5458
Internet: leabaron@aol.com
    Pubs: *Pursuit of a Wound: New Poems, To the Bone: New & Selected Poems* (U Illinois Pr, 2000, 1996), *Hunting the Whole Way Home* (U Pr New England, 1995), *New Yorker, Atlantic, Georgia Rev*

Gary Lenhart 🎤 ✈   P
166 Beaver Meadow Rd
Norwich, VT 05055
    Pubs: *Father & Son Night, Light Heart* (Hanging Loose, 1999, 1991), *One at a Time* (United Artists, 1983), *APR, The World, Hanging Loose, Poetry Flash*

Daniel Lusk   P&W
PO Box 369
Jonesville, VT 05466, 802-434-5688
Internet: dlusk@pop.uvm.edu
    Pubs: *Kissing the Ground: New & Selected Poems* (Onion River 1999), *The Cow Wars* (Nightshade 1995), *Painted Bride Qtly, Green Mountains Rev, APR, St. Andrews Rev, New Letters, New American Rev*

Gary Margolis 🎤 ✈ P
Middlebury College, Carr Hall, Middlebury, VT 05753,
802-493-5141
Internet: margolis@middlebury.edu
   Pubs: *Falling Awake, The Day We Still Stand Here* (U
Georgia Pr, 1986, 1983), *Poetry, TriQtly*

Lynn Martin 🎤 ✈ P
50 Westgate Dr
Brattleboro, VT 05301-8935, 802-257-7748
Internet: poetlynn@sover.net
   Pubs: *A Song About a Walk* (Sweet Annie Pr, 2000), *A Red
Hat* (Bloodstone, 1999), *Heartbeat of New England: Anth*
(Tiger Moon, 2000), *My Lover Is a Woman: Anth*
(Ballantine, 1996)

Jean R. Matthew W
Box 147
Marshfield, VT 05658
Internet: jmatthew@plainfield.bypass.com
   Pubs: *Testimony: Stories* (U Missouri Pr, 1987), *Missouri
Rev, Black Warrior Rev, Crescent Rev, Southern
Humanities Rev*

Don Mitchell W
RD #2 Box 2680
Vergennes, VT 05491, 802-545-2278
   Pubs: *The Souls of Lambs* (HM, 1979), *Thumb Tripping*
(Little, Brown, 1970), *Boston Mag, Yankee, Country Jrnl,
Harper's, Atlantic, Esquire*

Peter Money 🎤 ✈ P
PO Box 487, 214 Old Barn Ln
Brownsville, VT 05037, 802-484-8939
Internet: ruralwanab@aol.com
   Pubs: *Finding It* (Mille Grazie, 2000), *Between Ourselves*
(Backwoods, 1997), *These Are My Shoes* (Boz, 1991), *The
Sun, Solo, Provincetown Arts, APR, North Dakota Qtly,
Writer's Almanac, House Organ, Art/Life*

Patty Mucha P
RD 3
St Johnsbury, VT 05819
   Pubs: *See Vermont* (Poets Mimeo Co-op, 1979), *Telephone,
New Wilderness Audiographics*

Patrick O'Connor P
PO Box 296
Killington, VT 05751-0296, 802-422-9399
Internet: mapplucia@aol.com
   Pubs: *No Poem for Fritz* (Colorado Qtly, 1978), *The Prayers
of Man: Anth* (Ivan Oblensky, 1960), *Dance Mag, Voices
Israel*

Dzvinia Orlowsky 🎤 ✈ P
669 Forest St
Marshfield, VT 02050
   Pubs: *Except for One Obscene Brushstroke, Edge of
House, A Handful of Bees* (Carnegie Mellon U Pr, 2002,
1999, 1994)

Robert Pack P
Sperry Rd
Middlebury, VT 05753

Grace Paley 🎤 ✈ P&W
PO Box 620
Thetford Hill, VT 05074
   Pubs: *Begin Again, Just As I Thought, The Collected Stories*
(FSG, 2000, 1998, 1994), *New & Collected Poems* (Tilbury
Pr, 1992), *Long Walks & Intimate Talks* (Feminist Pr, 1991)

Verbena Pastor P&W
Graduate Program, Vermont College of Norwich Univ,
Montpelier, VT 05602, 802-828-8831
Internet: vpastor@norwich.edu
   Pubs: *Kiria Andreov* (Rain Crow Publishing, 1997), *Penny
Dreadful, Green's Mag, The European, 100 Words, Alfred
Hitchcock's Mystery, Ellery Queen's Mystery, Yellow Silk,
Bostonia, Stories*

Angela Patten 🎤 ✈ P
Carraig Binn, PO Box 369, Jonesville, VT 05466,
802-434-5688
Internet: angelapatten@hotmail.com
   Pubs: *Still Listening, The White Page: An Bhileog Bhan Anth*
(Ireland: Salmon Pub, 1999, 1999), *Onion River: Six
Vermont Poets: Anth* (RNM Inc, 1997), *Poetry Ireland Rev,
Literary Rev, Prairie Schooner, Voices Int'l, Waterford Rev*

Linda Peavy 🎤 ✈ P&W
169 Garron Rd
Middletown Springs, VT 05757-4222, 802-235-2844
Internet: crazywoman@vermontel.com
   Pubs: *Frontier House* (w/S. Shaw and U. Smith), *Frontier
Children, Pioneer Women* (Atria, 2002, 1999, 1997),
Women in Waiting in the Westward Movement (w/U. Smith;
U Oklahoma Pr, 1994), *Hard Love: Anth* (Queen of Swords
Pr, 1997), *Kalliope, Poets On*

John Pember 🎤 ✈ P
PO Box 185
Dorset, VT 05251-0185, 802-362-8189
Internet: poemz2@sover.net
   Pubs: *Rope to the Barn* (White Eagle Coffee Store Pr,
1993), *Under a Gull's Wing: Anth* (Down the Shore Pub,
1996), *Footwork, Fresh Ground, Sunrust, Jrnl of New
Jersey Poets, Calypso, Poetpourri, Without Halos, Northern
New England Rev*

Verandah Porche 🎤 ✈   P
45 Old County Rd
Guilford, VT 09301, 802-254-2442
Internet: verandah@sover.net
    Pubs: *Glancing Off* (See-Through Pr, 1987), *The Body's
Symmetry* (H&R, 1975), *CSM, Chrysalis Reader, Ms., New
Boston Rev*

Burt Porter 🎤 ✈   P
1101 Heights Rd
Glover, VT 05839, 802-525-3037
    Pubs: *Rhymes of the Magical World* (Other Media Pr, 1995),
Crows & Angels (Bread & Puppet Pr, 1993), *Hellas, The
Lyric, Poet, Classical Outlook, The Formalist*

Martha Ramsey 🎤 ✈   P
PO Box 1001
Putney, VT 05346, 802-387-2884
    Pubs: *Blood Stories* (Cleveland State U Poetry Ctr, 1996),
*Boulevard, Passages North, New Letters, American Voice,
Soundings East, Sojourner*

Julia Randall 🎤   P
23 Church St
North Bennington, VT 05257-9534
    Pubs: *The Path to Fairview: New & Selected, Moving in
Memory* (LSU, 1992, 1987), *Southern Rev, Ploughshares,
Kenyon Rev*

F. D. Reeve 🎤 ✈   P&W
PO Box 14
Wilmington, VT 05363-0014
Internet: lcsfdr@sover.net
    Pubs: *The Blue Boat on the St. Anne* (Story Line, 2003),
*The Urban Stampede and Other Poems, The Moon and
Other Failures* (Michigan State, 2002, 1999), *Concrete
Music* (Pyncheon Hse, 1992), *Agni, Connecticut, Margie,
Sewanee, Poetry, APR, Hudson*

Kate Riley   W
RD2, Box 455A
Johnson, VT 05656, 802-635-7021
Internet: rileyk@vscacs.vsc.edu
    Pubs: *Other Voices, Green Mountains Rev, Kalliope*

Stephen Sandy 🎤 ✈   P
PO Box 276
Shaftsbury, VT 05262, 802-442-8496
Internet: sandys@bennington.edu
    Pubs: *Surface Impressions, Black Box, The Thread* (LSU Pr,
2002, 1999, 1998), *Thanksgiving Over the Water, Man in
the Open Air* (Knopf, 1992, 1988), *Partisan Rev, Paris Rev,
Ploughshares, New Yorker, Southern Rev, Atlantic, APR,
Kenyon Rev, Southwest Rev*

Jim Schley 🎤 ✈   P
Blue Moon Cooperative, 24 Blue Moon Rd, South Strafford, VT
05070-7703
Internet: jschley@sover.net
    Pubs: *One Another* (Chapiteau, 1999), *Best American
Spiritual Writing: Anth* (HC, 2000), *Articulations: Anth* (U
Iowa Pr, 1994), *Orion, Northern Woodlands, Ironwood,
Crazyhorse, Garrison Keillor's Writer's Almanac*

Roger W. Shattuck   P
231 Forge Hill Rd
Lincoln, VT 05443-9184
    Pubs: *Half Tame* (U Texas, 1964), *Harper's, New Republic,
New Yorker, Poetry, Virginia Qtly Rev*

Neil Shepard 🎤 ✈   P
Writing & Literature Dept, Johnson State College, Johnson,
VT 05656
Internet: shepardn@badger.jsc.vsc.edu
    Pubs: *I'm Here Because I Lost My Way, Scavenging the
Country for a Heartbeat* (Mid-List Pr, 1998, 1993), *TriQtly,
Chelsea, Western Humanities Rev, Poetry East, Denver
Qtly, Southern Rev, Antioch Rev, Paris Rev, Ploughshares,
New England Rev, Ontario Rev*

Allen Shepherd   W
487 S Willard St
Burlington, VT 05401, 802-863-5672
    Pubs: *Kansas Qtly, Colorado Qtly, New Yorker, New Arts
Rev, Cimarron Rev*

Joe Sherman   W
Box 22
Montgomery, VT 05470
    Pubs: *Fast Lane on a Dirt Road* (Countryman Pr, 1991), *A
Thousand Voices* (Rutledge Hill, 1987), *The House at
Shelburne Farms* (Paul Eriksen, 1986)

Jane Shore 🎤 ✈   P
459 Peck Hill Road
East Calais, VT 05650
    Pubs: *Happy Family, Music Minus One* (Picador USA, 1999,
1996), *The Minute Hand, Eye Level* (U Mass Pr, 1987,
1977) *Salmagundi, Pequod, TriQtly*

Frank Short   P
12 Burnell Terr
St Albans, VT 05478-1803, 802-524-3749
    Pubs: *Bits, Bitterroot, Blue Unicorn, Chowder Rev, High-
Coo, Poet Lore, Poetry Now, Snakeroot*

Tom Smith 🎤 ✈   P
PO Box 223
Castleton, VT 05735-0223, 802-468-2277
    Pubs: *Trash* (Red Moon, 2000), *Waiting on Pentecost*
(Birch Brook, 1999), *Cow'sleap* (Fithian, 1999), *Iowa Rev,
Crazyhorse*

Erin St. Mawr 🎤 ✈   P
Box 91
Dorset, VT 05251
Internet: wrdwrt@sover.net
   Pubs: *1969-1998* (WordWright of Princeton, 2000),
Micronesia: The Sound of an Image (Cider Barrel Pr, 1979),
*Urthkin, Interstate, Aieee, New York Culture Rev, Stile,
Attention Please, Star West, Washout Rev, Veins*

Wendy Stevens   P&W
PO Box 189
Waterbury Center, VT 05677
   Pubs: *True Life Adventure Stories: Anth* (Crossing Pr, 1983),
Fight Back: Anth (Cleis Pr, 1981), *Nimrod*

Ruth Stone   P
788 Hathaway Rd
Goshen, VT 05733
   Pubs: *In the Next Galaxy* (Copper Canyon Pr, 2002), *Mother
Stone's Nursery Rhymes* (MBIRA, 1992), *Who Is the
Widow's Muse, Second Hand Coat* (Yellow Moon Pr, 1991,
1991), *Iowa Rev, Boulevard, American Voice, APR*

Floyd C. Stuart 🎤 ✈   P
6 North St
Northfield, VT 05663
   Pubs: *The Spirit That Moves Us: Anth* (The Spirit That
Moves Us Pr, 1982), *Travelling America with Today's Poets:
Anth* (Macmillan, 1976), *BPJ*

Susan Thomas   P&W
1010 Ennis Hill Rd
Marshfield, VT 05658
Internet: duh@together.net
   Pubs: *Kalliope, Midstream, Nimrod, Feminist Studies,
Southern Humanities Rev, Spoon River Poetry Rev, Atlanta
Rev*

Joyce A. Thomas 🎤 ✈   P
PO Box 24
Castleton, VT 05735-0024, 802-468-5104
   Pubs: *Skins* (Fithian Pr, 2001), *Orpheus & Company:
Contemporary Poems on Greek Mythology: Anth* (U Pr of
New England, 1999), *Of Frogs & Toads: Anth* (Ione Pr,
1998), *JAMA, Florida Rev, blueLINE*

Lynn Manning Valente 🎤 ✈   P&W
PO Box 9
Marlboro, VT 05344-0009, 802-254-2876
Internet: lynnvalente@hotmail.com
   Pubs: *Live and Learn: Anth, Dynamics of Choice: Anth*
(Chrysalis Bks, 2001, 1999), *Anth of New England Writers,
Longhouse, Northeast, Visions, Poetry Now, Jam ToDay, Pig
Iron, Poetry Motel*

Ellen Bryant Voigt 🎤 ✈   P
Box 128
Marshfield, VT 05658-0128, 802-563-2707
   Pubs: *Shadow of Heaven, Kyrie, Two Trees, The Lotus
Flowers, The Forces of Plenty* (Norton, 2002, 1995, 1992,
1987, 1983), *The Flexible Lyric* (U Georgia Pr, 1999), *Five
Points, New Yorker, Atlantic*

Roger Weingarten 🎤 ✈   P
MFA in Writing, Vermont College, Montpelier, VT 05602,
802-828-8638
   Pubs: *Ghost Wrestling, Infant Bonds of Joy, Shadow
Shadow, Poets of the New Century: Anth* (Godine, 1997,
1990, 1986, 2001), *88, Barrow St, Prairie Schooner,
Poetry East, NAR, APR, Paris Rev, Poetry, New Yorker,
Prague Revue*

Mame Willey 🎤 ✈   P&W
PO Box 147
So. Strafford, VT 05070, 802-765-4432
Internet: jhenkel@juno.com
   Pubs: *Anthology of New England Writers* (New England
Writers, 1998), *Cumberland Poetry Rev, Poetry Motel,
California Qtly, New Press Lit Qtly, Albany Rev, Hudson Rev,
Colorado Qtly, Mississippi Rev, Hanging Loose, Blueline,
U.S. 1 Worksheets*

Norman Williams   W
381 S Union St
Burlington, VT 05401
   Pubs: *The Unlovely Child* (Knopf, 1985), *New Yorker, Verse*

Nancy Means Wright 🎤 ✈   W
1777 Ridge Rd
Cornwall, VT 05753, 802-462-2719
Internet: nancyden@shoreham.net
   Pubs: *Fire & Ice* (Worldwide Library, 2002), *Stolen Honey,
Poison Apples, Harvest of Bones, Mad Season* (St. Martin's
Pr, 2002, 2000, 1998, 1996), *Walking Up Into the Volcano*
(Pudding Hse, 2000), *Down the Strings* (Dutton, 1982),
American Lit Rev

VIRGINIA

B. Chelsea Adams 🎤 ✈   P&W
5510 Piney Woods Rd
Riner, VA 24149-1647, 540-382-1778
Internet: bmadams@radford.edu
   Pubs: *Looking for a Landing* (Sow's Ear Pr, 2000), *Sampler:
Anth* (Alms Hse Pr, 1993), *Lucid Stone, Potato Eyes, Thin
Air, CQ, Poet Lore, Southwestern Rev, Union Street Rev,
Albany Rev, Virginia English Bulletin*

Jennifer Atkinson   P
George Mason Univ, English Dept, MSN3E4, 4400 University
Dr, Fairfax, VA 22030, 703-993-1177
Internet: jatkins2@gmu.edu
   Pubs: *The Dogwood Tree* (U of Alabama Pr, 1990), *The
Drowned City* (Northeastern U Pr, 2000)

Judy Light Ayyildiz 🎤 ✈ P
4930 Hunting Hills Cir
Roanoke, VA 24014-4961, 703-774-8440
Internet: jayyildiz@aol.com
    Pubs: *Mud River* (Lintel Pr, 1988), *Smuggled Seeds* (Gusto Pr, 1981), *Hawaii Pacific Rev, Artemis, MacGuffin, New Renaissance, Pig Iron Pr, Blackwater Rev, Sow's Ear, Potato Eyes, NYQ*

Mary Balazs P
English Dept, Virginia Military Institute, 411 Scott Shipp Hall, Lexington, VA 24450, 703-464-7240
    Pubs: *Out of Darkness* (Phase & Cycle Pr, 1993), *Pierced by a Ray of Sun: Anth, Peeling the Onion: Anth* (HC, 1995, 1993), *Pivot, Shenandoah, Kalliope, Roanoke Rev, Christianity & Literature, Arts & Letters*

D. N. Baldwin W
PO Box 82
Basye, VA 22810
Internet: dbaldwin@shentel.net
    Pubs: *Blue Mesa Rev, Florida Rev, American Short Fiction, Washington Rev, Hawaii Rev, Chiron Rev*

Jill Bart P&W
3012 Spotswood Cay
Williamsburg, VA 23185, 757-220-2101
    Pubs: *Heart's Eye, First Light* (Paumanok Pr, 2002, 1988), *Beyond Lament: Anth* (Northwestern U Pr, 1998), *Of Frogs and Toads* (Ione Pr, 1998), *Out of Season* (Amaganset Pr, 1997), *The Naked & the Nude* (Birnham Wood, 1993), *Baltimore Rev, West Wind Rev, LIQ*

Steven Barza 🎤 ✈ P&W
2123 Floyd Ave
Richmond, VA 23220
Internet: sbarza@richmond.edu
    Pubs: *Man Overboard* (Finishing Line Pr, 2002), *Wisconsin Rev, New Letters, Kit-Cat Rev, Tennessee Qtly, Black Warrior Rev, Writers' Forum*

Dorothy Ussery Bass P
Riverview Farm, Rte 1, Box 64, Rice, VA 23966, 804-392-4974
    Pubs: *NYQ, Gyre, Lyric, Hoosier Challenge, Archer, Mountainside Qtly, Appalachian Heritage*

Jefferson D. Bates 🎤 P
11939 Escalante Ct
Reston, VA 20191-1843, 703-758-0258
Internet: jefbates@netscape.net
    Pubs: *The Poets of Tallwood: Anth* (Learning In Retirement Institute, 1998), *Jazzbo Brown from Reston Town, Poems for Old Geezers & Young Whippersnappers* (Pogment Pr, 1993, 1990), *Qtly of Light Verse, Reston Rev*

Richard Bausch W
George Mason Univ, English Dept, 4400 Univ Dr, Fairfax, VA 22030, 703-349-0609
    Pubs: *Rare & Endangered Species, Rebel Powers* (Seymour Lawrence/HM, 1994, 1993), *The Fireman's Wife & Other Stories* (S&S, 1990), *New Yorker, Esquire*

Mel Belin 🎤 ✈ P
1600 N Oak St #1633
Arlington, VA 22209
    Pubs: *Flesh That Was Chrysalis* (Word Works, 1999), *Midstream, Connecticut River Rev, Phoebe, Cape Rock, Cumberland Poetry Rev, Poet Lore, Potomac Rev, Blue Unicorn, Wind Mag, Jewish Spectator, The Lyric, South Coast Poetry Jrnl*

Joe David Bellamy 🎤 ✈ P&W
1145 Lawson Cove Cir
Virginia Beach, VA 23455-6824
Internet: litlux@aol.com
    Pubs: *Atomic Love: A Novella & Eight Stories* (U Arkansas Pr, 1993), *Suzi Sinzinnati* (Penguin, 1991), *Story, Ploughshares, NAR, Paris Rev*

Patsy Anne Bickerstaff 🎤 ✈ P
PO Box 156
Weyers Cave, VA 24486-0156
    Pubs: *City Rain* (Librado Pr, 1989), *The Lyric, Flash!Point, Raintown Rev, Cumberland Poetry Rev, Piedmont Literary Rev, Ariel, Bellingham Rev, Caprice, Edge City Rev*

Peter Blair P&W
Georgetown U, 118 Univ Gardens, Apt 1, Charlottesville, VA 22903, 804-977-7916
    Pubs: *Last Heat* (Word Works Pr, 2000), *Furnace Greens* (Defined Providence Pr, 1998), *A Round, Fair Distance from the Furnace* (White Eagle Coffee Store Pr, 1993), *And Rev, Poetry East, Crazyhorse, River City*

Dean Blehert 🎤 P
11919 Moss Point Ln
Reston, VA 20194, 703-471-7907
Internet: dean@blehert.com
    Pubs: *Kill the Children* (Argonne House Pr, 2001), *Please, Lord, Make Me a Famous Poet or at Least Less Fat, I Swear He Was Laughing* (Words & Pictures Pr, 1999, 1996), *Poems for Adults and Other Children* (Pogment Pr, 1988)

Adrian Blevins P
3328 Forest Hill Ave NW
Roanoke, VA 24102
Internet: justycel@worldnet.att.net
    Pubs: *The Man Who Went Out for Cigarettes* (Bright Hill Pr, 1997), *Lucid Stone, Massachusetts Rev, Southern Rev, Sow's Ear Poetry Rev*

Edward Brash   P
1906 Windmill Ln
Alexandria, VA 22307, 703-765-1760
   Pubs: *Poetry, Atlantic, American Scholar, Partisan Rev, Mademoiselle*

David Bristol 🎤 ✈   P&W
1206 N Stuart St
Arlington, VA 22201, 703-841-1914
   Pubs: *Toad and Other Poems* (The Bunny and the Crocodile
   Pr, 2002), *Paradise & Cash* (Washington Writer's Pub Hse,
   1980), *Arlington Arts, Minimus, Beltway, Hayotzer, Kansas
   Qtly, Aerial, Washington Rev, New Laurel Rev*

Skylar Hamilton Burris 🎤   P
PO Box 7505
Fairfax Station, VA 22039
http://ancientpaths.literatureclassics.com
   Pubs: *AIM, The Lyric, Bible Advocate, Tucumari Lit Rev, The
   Green Tricycle*

Mary Patricia Carroll   P&W
528 Ocean Trace Arch, #H
Virginia Beach, VA 23451-5412
   Pubs: *The Creative Woman, Skylight, Black Bear Rev*

Travis Charbeneau   W
3421 Hanover Ave
Richmond, VA 23221-2735, 804-358-0417
Internet: travchar@mindspring.com
   Pubs: *The Sun, Utne Reader, Esquire, Dallas Life Mag,
   Atlanta Constitution, World Monitor, In These Times*

Elaine Raco Chase 🎤 ✈   W
4333 Majestic Ln
Fairfax, VA 22033, 703-378-9580
Internet: elainerc@juno.com
   Pubs: *Double Occupancy, Dare the Devil, Video Vixen,
   Calculated Risk* (Thorndike, 2002, 2001, 2000, 1999), *The
   Amateur Detective* (Writer's Digest Bks, 1996), *Partners in
   Crime: Anth* (Signet Paperback, 1995)

Emily Blair Chewning 🎤 ✈   P
6088 Leeds Manor Rd
Hume, VA 22639, 202-944-9644
Internet: twob1@aol.com
   Pubs: *Anatomy Illustrated* (S&S, 1980), *The Illustrated
   Flower* (Crown, 1979), *Family Life, Art & Antiques*

John I. Church   P
7216 Evans Mill Rd
McLean, VA 22101, 703-790-0428
   Pubs: *Hoosier College Poet* (The Friendly Pr, 1984),
   Windless Orchard, Patterns, Compass, Rhino

Rita Ciresi   W
Hollins College, PO Box 9642, Roanoke, VA 24020,
540-362-6318
Internet: ciresir@minnie.hollins.edu
   Pubs: *Mother Rocket* (U Georgia Pr, 1993), *Blue Italian:
   Anth* (Ecco Pr, 1996), *Prairie Schooner, South Carolina Rev,
   Oregon Rev, Alaska Qtly Rev, New Delta Rev, Italian
   Americana*

Mark Craver   P
Orchises Press, PO Box 20602, Alexandria, VA 22320-1602
Internet: mwcraver@aol.com
   Pubs: *They Came for What You Love, Seven Crowns for the
   White Lady of the Other World & Blood Poems* (Orchises,
   1998, 1992), *The Problem of Grace* (Lost Roads, 1986)

William Davey   P&W
Michelle Mordant, Literary Agent, PO Box 129, Keene, VA
22946, 434-977-0404
   Pubs: *Bitter Rainbow* (Edtns Carrefour, 2000), *Lost
   Adulteries, Trial of Pythagoras* (Alyscamps Pr, 1997, 1996),
   Angry Dust (Beijing, 1993), *Dawn Breaks the Heart* (Howell,
   Soskin, 1941), *Arms, Angels, Epitaphs* (Rydal Pr, 1935),
   Thalia, Massacre, Lyric

Tom De Haven   W
14106 Huntgate Woods Rd
Midlothian, VA 23112-4355, 804-744-6288
   Pubs: *Walker of Worlds* (Bantam/Doubleday, 1990),
   Sunburn Lake, Freaks' Amour, Funny Papers (Penguin,
   1989, 1986, 1986)

R. H. W. Dillard 🎤 ✈   P&W
Hollins Univ, Box 9671, Roanoke, VA 24020-1671,
540-362-6316
Internet: rdillard@hollins.edu
   Pubs: *Omniphobia, Just Here, Just Now* (LSU Pr, 1995,
   1994)

Gregory Donovan 🎤 ✈   P&W
Virginia Commonwealth Univ, English Dept, PO Box 842005,
Richmond, VA 23284-2005, 804-828-4507
Internet: gdonovan@vcu.edu
   Pubs: *Calling His Children Home* (U Missouri Pr, 1993),
   *Mss., Hayden's Ferry Rev, Southern Rev, NER, CutBank,
   South Coast Poetry Jrnl, Alaskan Qtly Rev*

Rita Dove 🎤 ✈   P
PO Box 400121, Univ Virginia, English Dept, 219 Bryan Hall,
Charlottesville, VA 22904-4121, 804-924-6618
Internet: rfd4b@virginia.edu
   Pubs: *On the Bus with Rosa Parks, Mother Love, Grace
   Notes* (Norton, 2000, 1995, 1989), *The Darker Face of the
   Earth* (Oberon, 1999), *Selected Poems* (Pantheon, 1993),
   Thomas & Beulah, Museum, Yellow House on the Corner
   (Carnegie Mellon, 1986, 1983, 1980)

John Elsberg 🎤 ✈   P
422 N Cleveland St
Arlington, VA 22201, 703-243-6019
    Pubs: *Sailor* (New Hope Intl, 2002), *Small Exchange*
    (Lilliput, 1999), *A Week in the Lake District* (Soffietto
    Eds/Red Moon Pr, 1998), *Offsets* (Kings Estate Pr, 1998),
    Broken Poems for Evita (Runaway Spoon Pr, 1997),
    Randomness of E (Semiquasi Pr, 1995)

Anthony Esler   W
416 Harriet Tubman Dr
Williamsburg, VA 23187
    Pubs: *The Western World* (S&S, 1997), *Bastion*
    (MacDonald, 1982), *Babylon* (Morrow, 1980)

Edward Falco   P&W
English Dept, Virginia Tech, Blacksburg, VA 24061-0112,
540-951-4112
Internet: efalco@vt.edu
    Pubs: *A Dream with Demons* (Eastgate Systems, 1997),
    Acid (U Notre Dame, 1996), *Pushcart Prize: Anth* (Pushcart
    Pr, 1999), *Atlantic, Ploughshares, TriQtly, Best American
    Short Stories 1995, Playboy*

Mark Farrington   W
13 E Windsor Ave
Alexandria, VA 22301
Internet: mfarring@gmu.edu
    Pubs: *Mountain Pr, Berkshire Writers Inc, Union Street Rev,
    Phoebe, Bennington Booklet, Louisville Rev*

Stanley Field   P&W
6315 Nicholson St
Falls Church, VA 22044
    Pubs: *The Freelancer* (Poetica Pr, 1984), *West Wind Rev,
    Women's Household, Minnesota Ink, Green's Mag, A Loving
    Voice, Animal Tales, Albatross, Cats*

Carolyn Forche   P
English Dept MS3E4, George Mason Univ, 4400 University Dr,
Fairfax, VA 22030, 301-320-2934
Internet: cforchem@osf1.gmu.edu
    Pubs: *The Angel of History, The Country Between Us* (HC,
    1994, 1982)

Kathleen Ford   W
630 Ivy Farm Dr
Charlottesville, VA 22901-8848
    Pubs: *Jeffrey County* (St. Martin's Pr, 1986), *Ladies' Home
    Jrnl, Southern Rev, Redbook, Yankee*

Jay Bradford Fowler   P
3710 Lee Hwy, #220
Arlington, VA 22207-3721, 703-538-5892
    Pubs: *The Soul* (Shangri La Pubs, 1996), *Writing Down the
    Light* (Orchises Pr, 1988), *Poet Lore, Yankee, Shenandoah,
    Phoebe, APR, Cosmic Trend*

Anne Hobson Freeman   P&W
314 Oyster Shell Ln
Callao, VA 22435
    Pubs: *The Style of a Law Firm, Eight Gentlemen from
    Virginia* (Algonquin, 1989, 1989), *Virginia Qtly Rev, McCall's,
    Mademoiselle, Cosmopolitan*

Serena Fusek 🎤 ✈   P
PO Box 3095
Newport News, VA 23603-0095, 757-887-9253
Internet: sfusek@skiffscreek.com
    Pubs: *The Night Screams with Jaguar's Voice, Miles Melt
    Like Winter* (Skiff's Creek Pr, 1998, 1997), *The Color of
    Poison* (Slipstream Pr, 1991), *Bitter Oleander, Nerve
    Cowboy, Slipstream, Thin Coyote, Virginia Adversaria,
    Frisson*

Louis Gallo   P&W
Radford Univ, English Dept, Radford, VA 24142, 703-831-5264
Internet: lgallo@runet.edu
    Pubs: *Missouri Rev, Berkeley Fiction Rev, MacGuffin,
    Baltimore Rev, Green Hills Rev, Rhino, Evansville Rev,
    Mangrove, New Orleans Rev, Brownstone Rev, Maple Leaf
    Rag, Greensboro Rev, Habersham Rev, GAIA, Louisiana Lit,
    American Lit Rev, Glimmer Train*

Patricia Garfinkel 🎤 ✈   P
900 N Stuart St, #1001
Arlington, VA 22203, 703-620-2945
Internet: pgarfink@nsf.gov
    Pubs: *Making the Skeleton Dance* (George Braziller Pub,
    2000), *From the Red Eye of Jupiter* (Washington Writer's
    Pub Hse, 1990), *Ram's Horn* (Window Pr, 1980), *Seattle
    Rev, Hollins Critic, Pittsburgh Qtly, Visions Intl, Negative
    Capability, California Qtly*

George Garrett 🎤 ✈   P&W
1845 Wayside Pl
Charlottesville, VA 22903-1630, 434-979-5366
    Pubs: *Days of Our Lives Lie in Fragments* (LSU Pr, 1998),
    *The King of Babylon Shall Not Come Against You, Whistling
    in the Dark* (HB, 1998, 1992)

Joseph Garrison   P
265 Thornrose Ave
Staunton, VA 24401, 540-885-7475
    Pubs: *Landscape & Distance: Poets from Virginia* (U Pr
    Virginia, 1975), *Hampden-Sydney Poetry Review: Anth*
    (Hampden-Sydney, 1990), *Carolina Qtly, South Carolina
    Rev, Poetry NW, SW Rev, SPR, Theology Today*

Beth George   P
13456 Muir Kirk Ln
Herndon, VA 22071, 703-435-3112
    Pubs: *Poet Lore, Wisconsin Rev, West Branch, Sou'wester,
    South Dakota Rev, Artemis, Kentucky Poetry Rev, Lip
    Service*

Bernadette K. Geyer 🎤 ✈   P
1020 N Stafford St #400
Arlington, VA 22201
     Pubs: *What Remains* (Argonne Hse Pr, 2001), *Gargoyle,*
     Minimus, Roanoke Rev, Le Petite Zine, Mid-America
     Poetry Rev

Wesley Gibson   W
342 S Laurel St, Apt B
Richmond, VA 23220
     Pubs: *Shelter* (Harmony Bks, 1992), *New Virginia Rev*

Robert L. Giron 🎤 ✈   P&W
5200 N 1 St
Arlington, VA 22203-1252, 703-351-0079
Internet: writerrobertgiron@yahoo.com
     Pubs: *Texas: Anth* (Sam Houston Sate U Pr, 1979),
     Amphora Rev, Art Form Mag, The Great Lawn

Guy LeCharles Gonzalez 🎤 ✈   PP&P
PO Box 8801
Norfolk, VA 23503
Internet: glecharles@aol.com
     Pubs: *Burning Down the House* (w/R. Bonair-Agard, et al:
     Soft Skull, 2000), *di-verse-city 2000: Anth* (AIPF, 2000), *Will*
     Work for Peace: Anth (zeropanik pr, 1999), *Austin Intl Poetry*
     Festival (2000, 1999), *National Poetry Slam* (1999, 1998),
     SoUPFest (1999)

Courtenay Graham-Gazaway   P
PO Box 754
Earlysville, VA 22936-0754
     Pubs: *17 Syllables, Iona* (GramWel Studios & Stills Pr, 1985,
     1985), *Harvard Advocate*

Bernice Grohskopf   W
116 Turtle Creek Rd, #11
Charlottesville, VA 22901-6760, 804-296-8044
Internet: bergrow@aol.com
     Pubs: *End of Summer* (Avon, 1982), *Tell Me Your Dream*
     (Scholastic, 1981), *PEN Anth* (Ballantine, 1985), *Harvard*
     Library Bulletin, Virginia Qtly Rev

Cathryn Hankla 🎤 ✈   P&W
Hollins Univ, English Dept, Box 9677, Roanoke, VA 24020,
540-362-6278
Internet: chankla@hollins.edu
     Pubs: *Texas School Book Depository, Negative History,*
     Afterimages, Yellow Shoe Poets: Anth (LSU Pr, 2000, 1997,
     1991, 2000), *A Blue Moon in Poorwater* (U Virginia Pr,
     1998), *Buck & Wing: Anth* (Shenandoah, 2000), *Virginia*
     Qtly Rev, Prairie Schooner

Charles L. Hayes 🎤 ✈   W
PO Box 6995
Radford, VA 24142-6995, 703-831-5231
     Pubs: *Sou'wester, St. Andrews Rev, Phoebe, Yellow Silk*

Ellen Herbert 🎤 ✈   W
2929 Rosemary Ln
Falls Church, VA 22042-1857, 703-532-4544
Internet: jhh1@msn.com
     Pubs: *Life on the Line: Anth* (Negative Capability Pr, 1992),
     Negative Capability, Demos, Dexter Rev, Sonora Rev,
     Crescent Rev, First for Women, Pennsylvania English

Susan Heroy   P
3133 Windsorview Dr
Richmond, VA 23225, 804-272-7111
     Pubs: *Prairie Schooner, SPR, Three Rivers Poetry Jrnl, New*
     Virginia Rev, Artemis

Neva Herrington 🎤 ✈   P&W
6712 W Wakefield Dr, #B-2
Alexandria, VA 22307-6746, 703-765-0388
     Pubs: *Blue Stone* (Still Point Pr, 1986), *Worcester Rev,*
     Connecticut Rev, Chariton Rev, Southern Rev, SW Rev,
     Wind, New Letters, Confrontation, Union Street Rev

Lynn Dean Hunter 🎤 ✈   P&W
PO Box 4053
Virginia Beach, VA 23454, 804-496-8289
Internet: ldhunter@aol.com
     Pubs: *Excuses* (Watermark Literary Pr, 1996), *Powhatan*
     Rev, Poet's Domain, Blackwater Rev, Crone's Nest, Ghent
     Mag, Virginian-Pilot, Crescent Rev, Thema

Lucky Jacobs   P
203 Santa Clara Dr
Richmond, VA 23229
     Pubs: *The Book of Love* (East Coast Edtns, 1993), *Our*
     Eyes, Like Walls (Konglomerati, 1981), *Poetry Now, Intro 7,*
     Artemis, Hollins Critic, SPR

Kate Jennings   P
12816 Cross Creek Ln
Herndon, VA 22071, 703-476-5814
     Pubs: *Malice* (Devil's Millhopper Pr, 1988), *Birth Stories:*
     Anth (Crossing, 1984), *Hudson Rev*

Edward P. Jones 🎤 ✈   W
4300 Old Dominion Dr, #914
Arlington, VA 22207-3227, 703-522-6720
     Pubs: *Lost in the City* (Morrow, 1992)

William Keens   P
The Keens Company, 200 N Little Falls St, #303, Falls Church,
VA 22046
     Pubs: *Dear Anyone* (Penumbra Pr, 1977), *APR, Poetry,*
     Seneca Rev, Ohio Rev

Helene Barker Kiser ♀ ✦   P
2470 Rivermont Ave
Lynchburg, VA 24503-1411, 434-846-1921
Internet: inkbiz@earthlink.net
    Pubs: *Topography* (Linear Arts Bks, 1998), *Salonika Qtly,
    Hawai'i Rev, Chachalaca Poetry Rev, Indiana Rev,
    Sycamore Rev, Borderlands Texas Poetry Rev, Poet Lore*

Peter Klappert ♀ ✦   P
MS 3E4 Eng Dept, George Mason Univ, Fairfax, VA 22030,
202-483-3822
Internet: petermail@earthlink.net
    Pubs: *Chokecherries: New & Selected Poems, 1966-1996*
    (Orchises, 2000), *The Idiot Princess of the Last Dynasty*
    (Knopf, 1984), *Lugging Vegetables to Nantucket* (Yale,
    1971), *Atlantic, Harper's, Antaeus, Ploughshares*

Carolyn Kreiter-Foronda ♀ ✦   P
5966 Annaberg Pl
Burke, VA 22015, 703-503-9743
Internet: foronda@erols.com
    Pubs: *Death Comes Riding, Gathering Light* (SCOP Pubs,
    1999, 1993), *Contrary Visions* (Scripta Humanistica, 1988),
    *Prairie Schooner, Antioch Rev, Mid-American Rev, Poet
    Lore, Hispanic Culture Rev, Antietam Rev*

Elisabeth Kuhn ♀ ✦   P
VA Commonwealth Univ, English Dept, Box 842005,
Richmond, VA 23284-2005, 804-285-2535
Internet: kuhnelisa@aol.com
    Pubs: *Unbearable Uncertainty: Anth* (Pioneer Valley Breast
    Cancer Network, 2000), *Intl Poetry Rev, Windsor Rev,
    Troubador, Formalist, Paterson Lit Rev, LiNQ, 96 Inc, Ledge,
    Urban Spaghetti, Sow's Ear Poetry Rev, Stitches, Chiron
    Rev, Herb Network*

Jeanne Larsen ♀ ✦   P&W
Hollins Univ, Box 9542, Roanoke, VA 24020-1542,
540-362-6276
Internet: jlarsen@hollins.edu
    Pubs: *Manchu Palaces* (H Holt, 1997), *Silk Road* (H
    Holt/BOMC, 1989), *NER, Georgia Rev, New Virginia Rev,
    Yarrow, Greensboro Rev, 5 A.M.*

Monty S. Leitch ♀ ✦   W
113 Huffville Rd
Pilot, VA 24138-1679, 540-651-4502
Internet: mleitch@swva.net
    Pubs: *Grandmother Histories: Anth* (Syracuse U, 1998),
    *Writer's Yearbook '95, Hollins Mag, Artemis, Radford U Mag,
    Virginia Country, Mountain Rev, Roanoker, Window,
    Shenandoah, Union Street Rev*

Janet Lembke ♀ ✦   P
210 N Madison St
Staunton, VA 24401-3359, 540-886-4180
Internet: janetlembke@yahoo.com
    Pubs: *Euripides' Hecuba* (Oxford U Pr, 1991), *Looking for
    Eagles* (Lyons & Burford, 1990), *Audubon, NAR, Sierra*

Judy Longley   P
1001 Wildmere Pl
Charlottesville, VA 22901, 804-973-0780
    Pubs: *My Journey Toward You* (Helicon Nine Edtns, 1993),
    Rowing Past Eden (Nightshade Pr, 1993), *Parallel Lives*
    (Owl Creek Pr, 1990), *Poetry, Southern Rev*

Katie Letcher Lyle   P&W
110 W McDowell St
Lexington, VA 24450, 540-463-5439
Internet: krlyle@cfw.com
    Pubs: *The Foraging Gourmet* (Lyons & Burford, 1997), *The
    Men Who Wanted Seven Wives, Scalded to Death by the
    Steam* (Algonquin, 1986, 1983), *Virginia Qtly Rev,
    Shenandoah, Sierra Mag, Country Jrnl, Blue Ridge Country*

Edward C. Lynskey   P
9124 Bramble Place
Annandale, VA 22003-4014
Internet: lynskey@erols.com
    Pubs: *The Tree Surgeon's Gift* (Scripta, 1990), *Teeth of the
    Hydra* (Crop Dust Pr, 1986), *Atlantic, APR, Chicago Rev,
    Southwest, America, Commonweal*

Mike Maggio ♀ ✦   P&W
1549 Coomber Court
Herndon, VA 20170, 703-437-7740
Internet: mikemaggio@aol.com
    Pubs: *Sifting Through the Madness* (Xlibris, 2001),
    Oranges from Palestine (Mardi Gras Pr, 1996), *Your Secret
    Is Safe with Me* (Cassette; Black Bear Pub, 1988), *Blue
    Cathedral: Anth* (Red Hen Pr, 2000), *Bedside Prayers:
    Anth* (Harper, 1997)

Anita Mathias ♀ ✦   P
104 Richard's Patent
Williamsburg, VA 23185-5118, 757-564-0355
Internet: mathias@widomaker.com
    Pubs: *The Best Spiritual Writing: Anths* (HarperSF, 2000,
    1999), *Tanzania on Tuesday: Anth* (New Rivers Pr, 1997),
    The Best of Writers at Work: Anth (Northwest Pub, 1994),
    *Virginia Qtly Rev, Commonweal, New Letters, London Mag,
    America, Notre Dame Mag*

Deirdra McAfee ♀ ✦   W
1503 Willingham Rd
Richmond, VA 23233-4727, 804-750-1338
Internet: dhmca@aol.com
    Pubs: *Turnstile, Willow Springs, Ambergris, Confrontation*

David McAleavey ♀ ✦   P
3305 N George Mason Dr
Arlington, VA 22207-1859, 703-532-8546
Internet: dmca@gwu.edu
    Pubs: *Greatest Hits: 1971-2000* (Pudding Hse, 2001),
    Holding Obsidian (WWPH, 1985), *Poetry, Nedge,
    Ploughshares, Situation*

Jane McIlvaine McClary   W
Box 326
Middleburg, VA 22117
    Pubs: *Maggie Royal, A Portion for Foxes* (S&S, 1982, 1972),
Middleburg Life, Virginia Country

Sharyn McCrumb 🎤 ✈   W
c/o Laree Hinshelwood, PO Box 495, Shawsville, VA 24162,
540-268-2807
www.sharynmccrumb.com
    Pubs: *The Songcatcher, The Ballad of Frankie Silver, The
Rosewood Casket* (Dutton, 2001, 1998, 1996), *She Walks
These Hills, Hangman's Beautiful Daughter, If Ever I Return,
Pretty Peggy-O* (Scribner, 1994, 1992, 1990), *Appalachian
Heritage, Writer's Digest*

Heather Ross Miller 🎤 ✈   P&W
402 Morningside Dr
Lexington, VA 24450, 540-464-6534
Internet: hmiller2@carolina.rt.com
    Pubs: *Days of Love & Murder* (Green Tower Pr, 2000),
Champeen (S Methodist U Pr, 1999), *In the Funny Papers,
Friends & Assassins* (U Missouri Pr, 1995, 1993), *Georgia
Rev, Louisiana Lit, Witness, Sandhills Rev, Crab Orchard
Rev, Potato Eyes, Southern Rev*

Miles David Moore 🎤 ✈   P
5913 Mayflower Ct, #102
Alexandria, VA 22312, 703-256-9275
Internet: miles3855@aol.com
    Pubs: *Buddha Isn't Laughing* (Argonne Hotel Pr, 1999),
*Winners: A Retrospective of the Washington Prize, Bears of
Paris* (Word Works, 1999, 1995), *Pivot, Word Wrights, NYQ,
Poet Lore, Sulphur, Bogg, Minimus, Writer's Jrnl*

Elaine Moore   W
420 Ole Dirt Rd
Great Falls, VA 22066-1103, 703-444-3499
Internet: elaine@elainemoore.com
    Pubs: *Phoebe, Virginia Country, Modern Short Stories*

Elizabeth Seydel Morgan   P
504 Honaker Ave
Richmond, VA 23226, 804-285-2153
    Pubs: *The Governor of Desire, Parties* (LSU Pr, 1993,
1988), *Southern Rev, Poetry, Prairie Schooner, Georgia
Rev, Virginia Qtly, Iowa Rev*

Michael Mott 🎤 ✈   P&W
122 The Colony
Williamsburg, VA 23185-3157, 757-220-1042
    Pubs: *Woman & the Sea: Selected Poems, Counting the
Grasses* (Anhinga, 1999, 1980), *Corday* (Black Buzzard Pr,
1995), *Georgia Rev, Sewanee Rev, Stand, American
Scholar, Verse, Tar River Poetry, Kenyon Rev*

Elisabeth Murawski 🎤 ✈   P
6804 Kenyon Dr
Alexandria, VA 22307-1535, 703-768-4504
Internet: emurawski@juno.com
    Pubs: *Troubled by an Angel* (Cleveland State U Pr, 1997),
Moon & Mercury, Hungry As We Are: Anth (Washington
Writers Pub Hse, 1990, 1995), *Yale Rev, Field, Qtly West,
Crazy Horse, Virginia Qtly Rev, Literary Rev, American
Voice, Grand Street, Ohio Rev, APR*

Mary Hayne North   P
6020 Piney Woods Rd
Riner, VA 24149
    Pubs: *From Mt. San Angelo: Anth* (AAUP, 1987)

Tom O'Grady 🎤 ✈   P
PO Box 126
Hampden-Sydney, VA 23943
Internet: togrady@hsc.edu
    Pubs: *The Same Earth, The Same Sky, Sun, Moon & Stars*
(Tryon Pub, 2002, 1996), *In the Room of the Just Born*
(Dolphin-Moon, 1989), *Poet Lore, Connecticut Rev, North
Atlantic Rev, Maryland Poetry Rev, Chrysalis, New Letters*

Renee Ellen Olander 🎤 ✈   P
College of Arts & Letters, Old Dominion Univ, Interdisciplinary
Teacher Prep, Norfolk, VA 23529, 757-683-4044
Internet: rolander@odu.edu
    Pubs: *Verse & Universe: Anth* (Milkweed Edtns, 1998), *13th
Moon, Snake Nation Rev, Sistersong: Women Across
Cultures, Artword Qtly, Amelia*

Bill Oliver 🎤 ✈   W
Dept of English and Fine Arts, Virginia Military Institute,
Lexington, VA 24450, 540-464-7045
    Pubs: *Women & Children First* (Mid-List Pr 1998), *Laurel
Rev, Virginia Qtly Rev, Florida Rev, Descant, Indiana Rev,
Kansas Qtly, Carolina Qtly, Cimarron Rev, New Letters*

Gregory Orr 🎤 ✈   P
2006 Hessian Rd
Charlottesville, VA 22903-1219, 804-293-4831
Internet: gso@virginia.edu
    Pubs: *The Caged Owl, Orpheus & Eurydice* (Copper
Canyon Pr, 2003, 2000), *City of Salt* (U Pitt Pr, 1995)

Mary Overton 🎤 ✈   W
5122 Dahlgreen Pl
Burke, VA 22015-1500
Internet: maoverton@hotmail.com
    Pubs: *The Wine of Astonishment* (La Questa Pr, 1997),
*Glimmer Train, Potomac Rev, Wordwrights, Belletrist Rev,
Spelunker Flophouse, Southern Anth*

Cheryl Pallant 🎤 ✈ P&W
108 S Colonial Ave
Richmond, VA 23221-3518, 804-355-7524
Internet: cpallant@mail1.vcu.edu
    Pubs: *Into Stillness, Uncommon Grammer Cloth* (Station
Hill Pr, 2003, 2001), *Spontaneities* (Belladonna Bks, 2001),
*Confrontation, NYQ, Wormwood Rev, Crescent Rev,
Oxford Mag*

Eric Pankey 🎤 ✈ P
4213 Lenox Dr
Fairfax, VA 22032
Internet: epankey@gmu.edu
    Pubs: *Cenotaph, Apocrypha, The Late Romances* (Knopf,
2000, 1998, 1997), *Heartwood, For the New Year,*
(Atheneum, 1988, 1984)

Richard Peabody 🎤 ✈ P&W
3819 N 13 St
Arlington, VA 22201, 703-525-9296
Internet: hedgehog2@erols.com
    Pubs: *Sugar Mountain, Mood Vertigo* (Argonne Hotel, 2000,
1999), *Buoyancy* (Gut Punch, 1995), *Paraffin Days*
(Cumberland, 1995), *Short Fuse: Anth* (Rattapallax, 2002),
*Iodine, Main St Rag, Red Booth Rev, Frantic Egg,
Barcelona Rev, Word Wrights, Hollins Critic*

Jim Peterson 🎤 ✈ P
555 Elmwood Ave
Lynchburg, VA 24503-4411, 804-845-2735
Internet: jepete1@aol.com
    Pubs: *The Owning Stone* (Red Hen Pr, 2000), *Jim
Peterson's Greatest Hits* (Pudding Hse Pr, 2000), *An
Afternoon with K, Carvings on a Prayer Tree* (Holocene Pr,
1996, 1994), *The Man Who Grew Silent* (Bench Pr, 1989),
Poetry NW, Shenandoah, Georgia Rev

Leslie Pietrzyk 🎤 ✈ W
3201 Elmwood Dr
Alexandria, VA 22303
Internet: lpietr@aol.com
    Pubs: *Pears on a Willow Tree* (Avon/Bard, 1998), *The Sun,
Columbia, TriQtly, Gettysburg Rev, Iowa Rev, NER,
Shenandoah*

Richard Plant 🎤 ✈ W
English Dept, Mary Baldwin College, Staunton, VA 24401,
540-887-7284
Internet: rplant@cit.mbc.edu
    Pubs: *Three Novellas: Anth* (Texas Rev Pr, 1997), *Sudden
Fiction: Anth* (Norton, 1996), *The O. Henry Awards: Anth*
(Doubleday, 1989), *Best Stories from New Writers: Anth*
(Writer's Digest Bks, 1989), *South Dakota Rev, Cimarron Rev*

Simone Poirier-Bures 🎤 ✈ W
7547 Cedar Grove Ln
Radford, VA 24141, 540-731-1814
Internet: poirier@vt.edu
    Pubs: *Nicole* (Pottersfield Pr, 2001), *That Shining Place,
Candyman* (Oberon Pr, 1995, 1994), *Virginia Qtly Rev,
Dalhousie Rev, Connecticut Rev, Pennsylvania Rev, Crazy-
horse, Florida Rev*

Barbara Ann Porte 🎤 ✈ W
PO Box 16627
Arlington, VA 22215
    Pubs: *Beauty and the Serpent: Thirteen Tales of Unnatural
Animals* (S&S, 2001), *If You Ever Get Lost* (HC, 2000),
He's Sorry, She's Sorry, They're Sorry, Too (Hanging Loose
Pr, 1998)

Ken Poyner 🎤 ✈ P
PO Box 14452
Norfolk, VA 23518
Internet: kpoyner@prodigy.net
    Pubs: *Sciences, Social* (Palaquin Bks, 1995), *Cordwood* (22
Pr, 1985), *Iowa Rev, West Branch, Poet Lore, Western
Humanities Rev, Yarrow, Black Fly Rev*

Philip Raisor P
PO Box 61623
Virginia Beach, VA 23466-1623, 804-489-3345
    Pubs: *Kansas Qtly, Arete, Poetry NW, Literary Rev,
Southern Rev, Tar River Poetry*

Paula Rankin P
89 Gum Grove Dr
Newport News, VA 23601-2705, 804-591-8350
    Pubs: *Your Rightful Childhood, Divorce: A Romance, To the
House Ghost* (Carnegie Mellon U Pr, 1996, 1990, 1985)

Kristen Staby Rembold 🎤 ✈ P&W
102 Bennington Rd
Charlottesville, VA 22901, 804-296-3086
    Pubs: *Felicity* (Mid-List Pr, 1994), *Coming Into This World*
(Hot Pepper Pr, 1992), *SPR, Green Mountains Rev,
Passages North, Artemis, Nimrod, South Dakota Rev, Iowa
Woman, Appalachia, CQ*

Lisa Ress P
1414 5 St SW
Roanoke, VA 24016-4508
    Pubs: *Flight Patterns* (U Pr Virginia, 1985), *Kalliope,
Farmer's Market, Spoon River Qtly, Sycamore Rev, Denver
Rev, Yarrow*

Kurt Rheinheimer W
1862 Arlington Rd SW
Roanoke, VA 24015-2859, 540-981-1307
    Pubs: *New Stories from the South: Anths* (Algonquin Bks,
1999, 1989, 1986), *Michigan Qtly Rev, Southern, Playgirl,
Shenandoah, Carolina Qtly, Redbook, Story Qtly,
Greensboro Rev*

Evelyn Ritchie   P
817 St Christopher's Rd
Richmond, VA 23226, 804-262-0664
    Pubs: *New Virginia Rev, Richmond Qtly, Forms, Lyric,*
Midwest Poetry Rev

Kim Roberts 🎤 ✈   P
Cultural Affairs Division, 3700 S Four Mile Run, Arlington, VA
22206, 703-228-1839
Internet: ellipse@erols.com
    Pubs: *The Wishbone Galaxy* (Washington Writers Pub Hse,
1994), *American Poetry: The Next Generation: Anth*
(Carnegie Mellon, 2000), *Southwest Rev, Barrow St, Ohio*
Rev, Sonora Rev, High Plains Literary Rev, Confrontation,
New Letters, Crosscurrents

Renee Roper-Jackson   P
380 E Washington St
Suffolk, VA 23434
    Pubs: *Changes: Anth* (White Swan Pr, 1987), *Truly Fine,*
Abbey Mag, Columbia

John B. Rosenman   P
Norfolk State Univ, 2401 Corprew Ave, English Dept, Norfolk,
VA 23504
    Pubs: *The Best Laugh Last* (McPherson & Co., 1983),
Yankee, Croton Rev, Xanadu, Phoebe

Irene Rouse 🎤 ✈   P
Box 310
Atlantic, VA 23303-0310, 757-824-4090
Internet: irbooks@dmv.com
    Pubs: *Private Mythologies* (Argonne Hotel Pr, 1999), *Mary-*
land Millennial Anth (St. Mary's College, 2000), *Poetry*
Baltimore: Anth (Wordhouse, 1997), *Wordwrights!, Potato*
Eyes

John D. Ruemmler   W
815 W Main St
Charlottesville, VA 22901, 804-295-8393
    Pubs: *Smoke on the Water* (Shoe Tree Pr, 1992), *Brothers in*
Arms (Lynx Pr, 1988), *Albemarle, Stranger*

Viette Sandbank   P
4800 Fillmore Ave, #419
Alexandria, VA 22311
    Pubs: *Alive & Gazing at You* (Northwoods, 1984), *Coming*
Through the Wry (Praying Mantis, 1982), *The Poet's*
Domain: Anth (Road Pub, 1991), *The Lyric*

Ben Satterfield 🎤 ✈   P&W
403 Upham Pl NW
Vienna, VA 22180
    Pubs: *Apocalypse Now: Anth* (Red Hen Press, 2000), *2000:*
Here's to Humanity: Anth (People's Pr, 2000), *Light,*
Baltimore Rev, Rambunctious Rev, Art Times, American
Dissident

Roger Sauls   P
2235 Monument Ave
Richmond, VA 23220-2746, 804-358-2958
    Pubs: *Hard Weather* (Bench Pr, 1987), *Light* (Loom Pr,
1975), *Ohio Rev, Ploughshares, Shenandoah*

Nancy Schoenberger 🎤 ✈   P
College of William & Mary, PO Box 8795 English Dept,
Williamsburg, VA 23187-8795, 757-221-2439
Internet: njscho@facstaff.wm.edu
    Pubs: *Long Like a River* (NYU Pr, 1998), *Girl on a White*
Porch (U Missouri Pr, 1987), *The Taxidermist's Daughter*
(Calliopea Pr, 1979), *Southern Rev, Poetry, NER, New*
Yorker, Ploughshares

Nancy Scott   P
PO Box 179
Sperryville, VA 22740-0179
    Pubs: *Rhino, Eleven, Windchimes, Phoebus, Womansong,*
Ten Years & Then Some, NYQ, Poetry Now, Modern Haiku,
New Virginia Rev, Phoebe, Shades of Gray

Tim Seibles 🎤 ✈   P
Old Dominion Univ, English Dept, Norfolk, VA 23529,
757-625-3843
Internet: tseibles@odu.edu
    Pubs: *Hammerlock, Hurdy-Gurdy* (Cleveland State U Pr,
1999, 1992), *Ten Miles an Hour* (Mille Grazie Pr, 1998),
Kerosene (Ampersand Pr, 1995), *Body Moves* (Corona Pr,
1988), *Outsiders: Anth, Verse & Universe: Anth* (Milkweed
Edtns, 1999, 1997), *Harper's Ferry*

Richard Shaw   P
1503 Scandia Cir
Reston, VA 20190
    Pubs: *Sleeping Beauty/Kabuki* (U Minnesota Pr, 1975)

Ellen Harvey Showell   W
1200 N Cleveland St
Arlington, VA 22201, 703-525-8872
Internet: eshowell@erols.com
    Pubs: *Cecelia & the Blue Mountain Boy* (Lothrop, Lee &
Shepard, 1983), *The Ghost of Tillie Jean Cassaway* (Four
Winds Pr, 1978)

Ron Smith   P
616 Maple Ave
Richmond, VA 23226
Internet: smithjron@aol.com
    Pubs: *Running Again in Hollywood Cemetery* (U Florida,
1988), *Southern Rev, Virginia Qtly Rev, Kenyon Rev,*
Georgia Rev, Nation, NER

R. T. Smith 🎤 ✈   P
Washington & Lee Univ, Troubadour Theater, 2nd Fl,
Lexington, VA 24450, 540-463-8908
Internet: rodsmith@wlu.edu
    Pubs: *Brightwood, Messenger, Trespasser* (LSU Pr, 2003,
2001, 1996), *Sewanee Rev, Missouri Rev, Atlantic, Poetry,
Georgia Rev, Gettysburg Rev, Southern Rev*

Lisa Solod 🎤 ✈   W
310 Enfield Rd
Lexington, VA 24450-1756, 540-463-7637
Internet: lisa@rockbridge.net
    Pubs: *Summer's Love, Winter's Discontent: Anth*
(Lonesome Traveller Pr, 1999), *The Inn Near Kyoto: Anth*
(New Rivers Pr, 1998), *Lonzie's Fried Chicken, American
Voice, Housewife-Writer's Forum, Tales of the Heart,
Parting Gifts*

Margo Solod 🎤 ✈   P
PO Box 113
Lexington, VA 24450-0113, 540-464-6242
Internet: 70664.2126@compuserve.com
    Pubs: *Photo Cries Real Tears* (Talent Hse Pr, 1999), *Still
Life with Trucks* (Tortilla Pr, 1996), *Outside the Kremlin*
(Nightshade Pr, 1996), *Voices of East Tennessee: Anth*
(Knoxville Writers Guild, 2000), *What Have We Lost: Anth*
(Green Willow, 1998)

Katherine Soniat 🎤 ✈   P
Virginia Polytechnic Inst & SU, English Dept, Blacksburg, VA
24061-0112, 540-231-7728
Internet: ksoniat@vt.edu
    Pubs: *Alluvial* (Bucknell U Pr, 2001), *A Shared Life* (U Iowa
Pr, 1993), *Cracking Eggs* (U Pr Florida, 1990), *NAR, Poetry,
Nation, New Republic, Southern Rev, Iowa Rev*

Lisa Russ Spaar   P
English Dept, Univ Virginia, 219 Bryan Hall, Charlottesville, VA
22903, 804-924-6675
Internet: lrs9e@virginia.edu
    Pubs: *Blind Boy on Skates* (Trilobite Pr, 1987), *Cellar*
(Alderman, 1983), *Poetry, Shenandoah, Poetry East, Crazy-
horse, Virginia Qtly Rev, Tendril*

Sofia M. Starnes 🎤 ✈   P
4951 Burnley Dr.
Williamsburg, VA 23188
Internet: whsstarnes@widomaker.com
    Pubs: *A Commerce of Moments* (Pavement Saw Pr, 2002),
Turnings: Writing on Women's Transformations: Anth (Old
Diminion U), *The Poet's Domain: Anth* (Road Pub, 1995),
*Southern Poetry Rev, Laurel Rev, Hayden's Ferry Rev,
Marlboro Rev, Hawaii Pacific Rev*

Bradley R. Strahan 🎤 ✈   P
1007 Ficklen Rd
Fredricksburg, VA 22405-2101
    Pubs: *Conjurer's Gallery* (CCC, 2002), *Crocodile Man* (The
Smith, 1990), *First Things, Crosscurrents, Onthebus, Hollins
Critic, Seattle Rev, Confrontation, Christian Century,
Sources, America, Soundings East*

Dabney Stuart 🎤 ✈   P
30 Edmondson Ave
Lexington, VA 24450-1904, 540-463-5663
Internet: stuartd@wlu.edu
    Pubs: *The Man Who Loved Cezanne, Settlers, Long Gone,
Light Years, Sweet Lucy Wine, Narcissus Dreaming* (LSU,
2003, 1999, 1996, 1994, 1992, 1990), *No Visible Means of
Support, The Way to Cobbs Creek, Second Sight*
(U Missouri Pr, 2001, 1997, 1996)

Jitu Tambuzi   P
Tambuzi Pub, 208 E Grace St, Richmond, VA 23219-1916,
804-649-3149
    Pubs: *A Voice Within* (King Pub, 1979), *New Renaissance,
Universal Black Writer*

Eleanor Ross Taylor   P&W
1841 Wayside Pl
Charlottesville, VA 22903
    Pubs: *Days Going/Days Coming Back* (U Utah, 1992), *New
& Selected Poems* (Stuart Wright, 1984), *Parnassus,
Seneca Rev, Ploughshares, Shenandoah, Virginia Qtly Rev*

William Tester   W
8 Partridge Hill Rd
Richmond, VA 23233-6219
Internet: wteste@vcu.edu
    Pubs: *Darling* (Knopf, 1992), *Grand Street, Prairie
Schooner, Esquire, The Qtly, Fiction, TriQtly, NAR, Black
Warrior, Witness*

Hilary Tham 🎤 ✈   P&W
2600 N Upshur St
Arlington, VA 22207-4026, 703-527-4568
Internet: hilarytham@aol.com
    Pubs: *Reality Check* (Kings Estate Pr, 2001), *Counting*
(Word Works, 2000), *Lane with No Name: Memoirs &
Poems* (Lynne Rienner Pub, 1997), *Men & Other Strange
Myths: Poems* (Three Continents Pr, 1994), *Mondo Barbie:
Anth* (St. Martin's, 1993), *Antietam Rev*

Carla Theodore 🎤   P
60 Ecology Ln
Woodville, VA 22749-1715, 540-987-8813
    Pubs: *Somebody's Brother, Rural Water, Peter & the Guru*
(Samisdat, 1983, 1980, 1979), *Jewish Currents, Kansas
Qtly, Jump River Rev, Dark Horse, San Fernando Poetry
Jrnl, Princeton Spectrum*

Jack Trammell ♦ ✈   P
241 Willow Brook Rd
Bumpass, VA 23024-3001, 804-556-4394
Internet: jacktrammell@yahoo.com
 Pubs: *Sarah's Last Secret, The Saints Departed, Retrun to
 Treasure Island* (Hard Shell, 2002, 2002, 2000), *Beyond the
 County Line, Appalachian Dreams* (Escape, 2000, 1998)

John R. Tucker ♦ ✈   P
4627 Buckhorn Ridge
Fairfax, VA 22030-6171
 Pubs: *Poetry Church Collection Vol. 4 & 3* (Feather Bks,
 2002, 2001), *AIM, Poetry Church Collection: Anth, Vol 3 & 4,
 Feather Books, Poetry Church Mag, Dream Intl Qtly, Seed-
 house, Literally Horses, Mobius, Bread of Life Mag,
 Plowman*

Charles Vandersee ♦ ✈   P
Dept of English, Univ Virginia, 219 Bryan Hall, PO Box
400121, Charlottesville, VA 22904-4121, 804-924-8877
Internet: cav7w@virginia.edu
 Pubs: *Indiana Rev, Ohio Rev, Georgia Rev, Sewanee Rev,
 Poetry East, Poetry, Ironwood, Iris, Timbuktu*

Angela Vogel   P
PO Box 36760
Richmond, VA 23235
http://members.aol.com/newzoopoet
 Pubs: *CQ, Evansville Rev, Cream City Rev, Cape Rock,
 Black Dirt*

Edward G. Williams   W
3837 Betsy Crescent, PH
Virginia Beach, VA 23456-1610, 804-471-2781
 Pubs: *Not Like Niggers* (St. Martin's Pr, 1970), *A Galaxy of
 Black Writing: Anth* (Moore Pub Co., 1971), *The Alumnus*

Charles Wright ♦ ✈   P
940 Locust Ave
Charlottesville, VA 22901-4030, 804-979-2373
 Pubs: *Negative Blue, Black Zodiac, Chickamauga, The
 World of the 10,000 Things,* (FSG, 2000, 1997, 1995, 1990),
 Halflife (U Michigan Pr, 1988)

VIRGIN ISLANDS

Marty Campbell   W
5016 Estate Boetzberg
Christiansted, VI 00820-4516, 340-692-9935
Internet: ad144@virgin.usvi.net
 Pubs: *Companion to Senya* (MarCrafts, 1989), *Saint Sea*
 (Blondo, 1986), *Caribbean Writer, Hammers, Road Map of
 My Soul, Collage, Magical Blend, Lilliput Rev*

David Gershator ♦ ✈   P
PO Box 303353
St Thomas, VI 00803-3353
Internet: gershator@islands.vi
 Pubs: *Palampam Day* (Cavendish, 1997), *Elijah's Child*
 (CCC, 1992), *Play Mas* (Downtown Poets, 1981), *Frogpond,
 Home Planet News, Caribbean Writer*

Phillis Gershator ♦ ✈   P&W
PO Box 303353
St Thomas, VI 00803-3353
Internet: gershator@islands.vi
 Pubs: *The Babysitter Sings, When It Starts to Snow* (HHolt,
 2003, 1998), *Only One Cowry, ZZZNG-ZZZNG-ZZZNG*
 (Orchard, 2000, 1998), *Caribbean Writer, Home Planet
 News, Cricket, Spider, Ladybug*

Oyoko Loving   P
Box 24742 Christiansted
St Croix, VI 00824, 809-778-7480
 Pubs: *Remember When* (Jet Publishing, 1974)

WASHINGTON

Catherine Austin Alexander ♦ ✈   W
9506 Ravenna Ave NE, #105
Seattle, WA 98115-2402, 206-616-7550
Internet: catalexander@yahoo.com
 Pubs: *I Thought My Father Was God: Anth* (HH, 2001),
 *Snow Monkey, Intersections, Higginsville Reader, Mosaic,
 Synapse, Children Churches & Daddies, Sidewalks,
 Mediphors, Spindrift, Amer Jones Building & Maintenance,
 North Atlantic Rev*

Jody Aliesan ♦ ✈   P
5032 22 Ave NE, Apt E
Seattle, WA 98105, 206-524-8365
Internet: aliesanj@earthlink.net
 Pubs: *Loving in Time of War* (Blue Begonia Pr, 1999),
 Desperate for a Clearing (Grey Spider Pr, 1998), *Grief
 Sweat* (Broken Moon Pr, 1991), *Deadsnake Apotheosis,
 Natural Bridge, nycBigCityLit, Many Mountains Moving, L.A.
 Times, Contemporary Qtly*

Judith Anne Azrael ♦ ✈   P&W
PO Box 165
Lummi Island, WA 98262, 360-758-2042
 Pubs: *Twelve Black Horses* (Salmon Run Pr, 1998), *Apple
 Tree Poems, Antelope Are Running* (Confluence, 1983,
 1978), *Shenandoah, The Sun, Rosebud, Minnesota Rev,
 Nation, Yale Rev, CSM, Western Humanities Rev, SPR*

Deborah Bacharach P
137 N 78th St
Seattle, WA 98103
Internet: Bacharah@aol.com
Pubs: *Many Mountains Moving, Kalliope, Bellowing Ark, College English, Atom Mind, Stuff, Slipstream, South Coast Poetry Jrnl, Wellspring, Bridges, Soundings East, Paramour, Poet Lore*

June Frankland Baker 🎤 P
614 Lynnwood Ct
Richland, WA 99352-1860, 509-375-0842
Pubs: *Blueline Anthology: Anth* (Syracuse U Pr, 2003), *Woven on Wind: Anth* (HM, 2001), *Potpourri, Artful Doge, CSM, Flyway, SPR, Poetry NW, Commonweal, Poet Lore*

Sharon Baker W
1125 SW Normandy Terr
Seattle, WA 98166, 206-243-9004
Pubs: *Burning Tears of Sassurum, Journey to Membliar* (Avon, 1988, 1987)

Christianne Balk 🎤 ✈ P
PO Box 15633
Seattle, WA 98115-0633, 206-523-6543
Pubs: *Desiring Flight* (Purdue U Pr, 1995), *Bindweed* (Macmillan, 1986), *New Yorker, Michigan Rev, Seattle Rev, Heartland, Pequod, Crazy Horse*

Carol Jane Bangs 🎤 ✈ P&W
PO Box 92
Nordland, WA 98358, 360-379-0268
Internet: cbangs@olympus.net
Pubs: *The Bones of the Earth* (New Directions, 1983), *Verse & Universe: Anth* (Milkweed Edtns, 1999), *Intro to Poetry: Anth* (Norton, 1995), *Willow Springs, Colorado Rev, Indiana Rev, Ploughshares*

Mary Barnard P&W
5565 E Evergreen Blvd, #3406
Vancouver, WA 98661-6672
Pubs: *Nantucket Genesis, Time & the White Tigress* (Breitenbush Bks, 1988, 1986), *American Poetry, The 20th Century, Vol 2: Anth* (LOA, 2000), *Paldeuma*

W. D. Barnes P
7611-15th NE
Seattle, WA 98115, 206-523-8946
Pubs: *Fragments, Vagabond, Phantasm, Harvest, Minnesota Poetry Jrnl*

Bruce Beasley 🎤 ✈ P
2225 Victor St
Bellingham, WA 98225
Internet: bruce@cc.wwu.edu
Pubs: *Signs & Abominations* (Wesleyan U Pr, 2000), *Summer Mystagogia* (U Colorado Pr, 1996), *The Creation* (Ohio State U Pr, 1994), *Spirituals* (Wesleyan U Pr, 1988)

John Bennett 🎤 ✈ W
605 E 5 Ave
Ellensburg, WA 98926, 509-962-8471
www.eburg.com/~vagabond
Pubs: *The Moth Eaters* (Angelfish Pr, 1998), *Domestic Violence* (Foursep Pr, 1998), *Bodo* (Mata Pubs, 1997), *Outlaw Bible of American Poetry: Anth* (Thunder's Mouth Pr, 1999), *Rattle, Arkansas Rev, NW Rev, Pudding, Columbia, Pangolin Papers*

Beth Bentley P
8762 25 Pl NE
Seattle, WA 98115, 206-525-3508
Pubs: *Little Fires* (Cune Pr, 1998), *The Purely Visible* (Sea Pen Pr, 1980), *Country of Resemblances* (Ohio U Pr, 1976), *Best American Poetry: Anth* (Macmillan, 1989), *Gettysburg Rev, Fine Madness, Poetry NW*

James Bertolino P
PO Box 1157
Anacortes, WA 98221, 206-293-6274
Pubs: *The Writer's Journal* (Dell Pub, 1997), *Snail River, First Credo* (QRL, 1994, 1986), *Amicus Jrnl, Wilderness, Onthebus, Raven Chronicles, Seattle Rev, Caliban, Ploughshares, Montserrat Rev, Gargoyle, The Temple*

Linda Bierds 🎤 ✈ P
4326 NE Rhodes End
Bainbridge Island, WA 98110, 206-780-2015
Internet: lbierds@u.washington.edu
Pubs: *The Seconds* (Putnum, 2001), *The Profile Makers, The Ghost Trio, Heart & Perimeter, The Stillness The Dancing* (H Holt, 1997, 1994, 1991, 1988), *Flights of the Harvest-Mare* (Ahsahta, 1985)

Laurie Blauner 🎤 P&W
7549 27 Ave NW
Seattle, WA 98117
Pubs: *Somebody* (Black Heron Pr, 2002), *Facing the Facts* (Orchises Pr, 2002), *Children of Gravity* (Owl Creek Pr, 1989, 1996)

Alice Bloch 🎤 ✈ W
4055 SW Henderson St
Seattle, WA 98136-2541
Internet: AliceBloch@attbi.com
Pubs: *The Law of Return, Lifetime Guarantee* (Alyson Pub, 1983, 1981), *Hers 2: Brilliant New Fiction by Lesbian Writers: Anth* (Faber & Faber, 1997)

Marian Blue 🎤 ✈ P&W
PO Box 145
Clinton, WA 98236, 360-341-1630
Internet: blueyude@whidbey.com
Pubs: *Tiller & the Pen* (Eighth Moon Pr, 1994), *Snowy Egret, Eureka Lit Mag, Cold Mountain Rev, Exhibition, Mankato Poetry Rev, Dominion Rev*

Marcia Blumenthal   P&W
1134 Hendricks
Port Townsend, WA 98368-2309, 360-385-4560
Internet: mlewton@olympus.net
    Pubs: *In the Heart of Town, Still Digging* (Barnwood Pr,
1985), *Flying Island, Thema, Iowa Woman, Ms., Indiana
Rev, Whiskey Island*

Malcolm J. Bosse   W
1407 E Madison, #30
Seattle, WA 98122
    Pubs: *The Vast Memory of Love, Mister Touch* (HM, 1992,
1991), *Stranger at the Gate, Fire in Heaven* (S&S, 1988,
1986)

David Bosworth   W
Univ Washington, English Dept, GN-30, Seattle, WA 98115,
206-543-2682
    Pubs: *From My Father, Singing* (Pushcart Pr, 1986), *The
Death of Descartes* (Pittsburgh Pr, 1981)

Randall Brock   🎤   P
PO Box 1673
Spokane, WA 99210
    Pubs: *Weave* (Found Street Pr, 1994), *Poetalk: Anth* (Bay
Area Poets Coalition, 2002), *Deep Down Things: Anth*
(Washington State U Pr, 1990), *American Muse, Cairn,
Pegasus, Kimera, Moon Reader, Echoes, Blind Man's
Rainbow, Poetic Realm*

John Brummet   P
8531 NW 24th
Seattle, WA 98117, 206-784-8393
    Pubs: *Negative Capability, Electrum, Common Ground,
Concerning Poetry*

Thomas Brush   P
17217 SE 42 Pl
Issaquah, WA 98027, 206-746-9189
    Pubs: *Even Money* (Seapen Pr, 1988), *Opening Night* (Owl
Creek Pr, 1981), *Poetry, Poetry NW, Indiana Rev, Tar River
Rev, Fine Madness, Qtly West*

Sharon Bryan   P
125 Jackson St
Port Townsend, WA 98368, 360555767
Internet: sharonbrya@aol.com
    Pubs: *Flying Blind* (Sarabande Bks, 1996), *Where We
Stand: Anth* (Norton, 1994), *Paris Rev, Atlantic, Tar River
Poetry, Nation, APR, Seattle Rev*

Gregory Burnham   W
PO Box 13129
Burton, WA 98013-0129, 206-463-4006
    Pubs: *Flash Fiction: Anth* (Norton, 1992), *Vital Lines: Anth*
(St. Martin's Pr, 1991), *Harper's, Indiana Rev, Turnstile,
Puerto del Sol, Black Ice*

E. G. Burrows   P
20319 92nd Ave W
Edmonds, WA 98020-2991, 425-775-5383
    Pubs: *Sailing As Before* (TDM Pr, 2001), *The Birds Under
the Earth* (Owl Creek Pr, 1996), *Wildsong: Anth* (U Georgia
Pr, 1998), *Poet Lore, Emrys, Baybury Rev, North Dakota
Rev, Abraxas, Wisconsin Rev, Comstock Rev, Santa
Barbara Rev, Montserrat Rev, Iowa Rev*

Jack Cady   🎤   ✈   W
PO Box 872
Port Townsend, WA 98368-0872, 360-385-1670
Internet: erewhon@olympus.net
    Pubs: *Ghostland* (Scorpius Pub, 2001), *The Hauntings of
Hood Canal, The Off Season, Street* (St. Martin's, 2001,
1996, 1994), *The Night We Buried Road Dog* (Dreamhaven,
1998), *Inagehi, The Sons of Noah* (Broken Moon Pr, 1994,
1992), Glimmer Train, Portland Rev*

Janet Cannon   🎤   ✈   P
PO Box 17263
Seattle, WA 98107
Internet: j.c@islewrite.com
    Pubs: *The Last Night in New York* (Homeward, 1984),
*Poetry CafÈ, NYQ, Helicon Nine, Berkeley Poetry Rev,
Slant, George Washington Rev, New Mexico Humanities
Rev, Beatitude 33*

Kris Christensen   🎤   ✈   P
2119 S Monroe St
Spokane, WA 99203, 509-363-1826
    Pubs: *Pontoon: An Anth of WA State Poets* (Floating Bridge
Pr, 2001), *Many Mountains Moving, Iowa Rev, Kalliope, Iris,
Puerto del Sol, Hayden's Ferry Rev, Hawaii Pacific Rev,
Hubbub, Passages North*

Chrystos   🎤   ✈   P
3900 Pleasant Beach Dr NE
Bainbridge Island, WA 98110-3215, 206-842-7207
    Pubs: *Fire Power* (Press Gang, 1995), *Fugitive Colors*
(Cleveland State U Poetry Ctr, 1994), *Reinventing the
Enemy's Language: Anth* (Norton, 1996)

Thomas Churchill   🎤   ✈   W
PO Box 232
Langley, WA 98260-0232, 360-730-4634
Internet: pearlisl@whidbey.com
    Pubs: *Triumph Over Marcos* (Open Hand, 1995), *Centralia
Dead March* (Curbstone, 1980), *Island Independent, Rev of
Contemporary Fiction*

Linda J. Clifton   🎤   P&W
Clifton Consulting, 4462 Whitman Ave N, Seattle,
WA 98103-7347
Internet: lclifton1@mindspring.com
    Pubs: *Shadowmarks* (Blue Begonia Pr, 1994), *Crab Creek
Rev: Anth* (Crab Creek Rev, 1994), *Calyx, Gold Dust,
Tinderbox*

Jim Cody P
1055 NW 96 St
Shoreline, WA 98177
Internet: ngjmc@ttacs.ttu.edu
  Pubs: *My Body Is a Flute* (A Place of Herons Pr, 1994), *A Book of Wonders* (Cedarshouse Pr, 1988), *Prayer to Fish* (Slough Pr, 1984), *Lynx, Exquisite Corpse*

Phyllis Collier 🎤 ✈ P
905 E Tacoma Av
Ellensburg, WA 98926
Internet: pkcollier@elltel.net
  Pubs: *Willow Springs, Cape Rock, West Wind Rev, South Dakota Rev, Cumberland Poetry Rev, Mississippi Valley Rev, Puerto del Sol, Green Mountains Rev, Poet Lore, College English, Poetry NW, Nimrod*

Sharon Cumberland 🎤 ✈ P
Dept of English, Seattle Univ, 900 Broadway, Seattle, WA 98122-4460, 206-296-5423
Internet: slc@seattleu.edu
  Pubs: *Sharon Cumberland: Greatest Hits 1985-2000* (Pudding House Pubs, 2002), *The Arithmetic of Mourning* (Green Rock Pr, 1998), *Nelson Mandelamandela: Anth* (Three Continents Pr, 1989), *Ploughshares, Kalliope, BPJ, Iowa Rev, Mickle Street Rev, Contact II*

Madeline DeFrees 🎤 ✈ P
7548 11 Ave NW
Seattle, WA 98117-4143, 206-789-9109
  Pubs: *Blue Dusk* (Copper Canyon Pr, 2001), *Double Dutch* (Red Wing Pr, 1999), *Possible Sibyls* (Lynx Hse Pr, 1991), *Imaginary Ancestors* (Broken Moon Pr, 1990), *A Millennium Reflection: Anth* (Seattle Arts Commission, 1999), *Yale Rev, Paris Rev, Ploughshares*

Anita Endrezze 🎤 ✈ P
5010 Fowler Ave
Everett, WA 98203
Internet: aendrezze@worldnet.att.net
  Pubs: *throwing fire at the Sun, water at the Moon* (U of Arizona, 2000), *Lost Rivers* (Making Waves Pr, 1997), *at the helm of twilight* (Broken Moon Pr, 1992), *Harper & Row's 20th Century of Native American Poetry: Anth* (H&R, 1988)

Anita N. Feng 🎤 ✈ P
300 SW Forest Dr
Issaquah, WA 98027, 425-557-8764
Internet: anita@anitasocarinas.com
  Pubs: *Internal Strategies* (U Akron Pr, 1996), *NW Rev, Ploughshares, Primavera, Prairie Schooner, Black Warrior Rev, Nimrod*

Lorraine Ferra 🎤 ✈ P
PO Box 93
Port Townsend, WA 98368-0093, 360-385-7568
Internet: lferra@cablespeed.com
  Pubs: *Eating Bread* (Kuhn Spit Pr, 1994), *This Should Be Enough: Anth* (Skagit River Poetry Fest, 2002), *Poet & Critic, Qtly West, Florida Rev, Country Jrnl, Seattle Rev, Iris, Bellowing Ark*

Hollis Giammatteo 🎤 ✈ P&W
2911 1 Ave, #103
Seattle, WA 98121-1086
Internet: hoax@w-link.net
  Pubs: *Secrets* (Blue Heron Pub, 1996), *Left Bank, APR, Prairie Schooner, Nimrod, Calyx, Feminist Studies, NAR, Ms., Salmagundi*

Carole L. Glickfeld 🎤 ✈ W
731 Broadway E
Seattle, WA 98102-4674, 206-322-7953
Internet: clg238@earthlink.net
  Pubs: *Swimming Toward the Ocean* (Knopf, 2001), *Useful Gifts, Flannery O'Connor Award Selected Stories: Anth* (U Georgia Pr, 1989), *Her Face in the Mirror: Anth* (Beacon Pr, 1994, 1992), *Ohio Rev, Confrontation*

Samuel Green 🎤 ✈ P
101 Bookmonger Rd
Waldron Island, WA 98297
Internet: bhpress@pocketmail.com
  Pubs: *Vertebrae* (Eastern Washington U Pr, 1994), *Working in the Dark, Communion* (Grey Spider Pr, 1998, 1993), *Poetry, Poetry NW, Prairie Schooner, SPR, Yellow Silk*

Joseph Green 🎤 ✈ P
930 Cascade Dr
Longview, WA 98632, 360-577-1724
Internet: josgreen@teleport.com
  Pubs: *The End of Forgiveness* (Floating Bridge Pr, 2001), *Greatest Hits: 1975 - 2000* (Pudding House Pr, 2001), *Deluxe Motel, His Inadequate Vocabulary* (Knute Skinner, 1991, 1987), *Line Drives: Anth* (So. Illinois U Pr, 2002)

Michael Gregory P
1132 NW 56 St
Seattle, WA 98107
Internet: eebmpg@aa.net
  Pubs: *The World Abandoned by Numbers* (Owl Creek Pr, 1992), *Denver Qtly, Western Humanities Rev, SPR, Cape Rock, Phoebe, Telescope, Amelia, Nimrod, Crazyhorse, New Delta Rev, ACM, Passages North, Crab Creek Rev*

Ben Groff 🎤 ✈ W
17832 66 Pl, W
Lynnwood, WA 98037-7115, 425-745-8855
Internet: bengroff@aol.com
  Pubs: *Pushcart Prize XVI: Anth* (Pushcart Pr, 1992), *Alaska Qtly Rev, Crab Creek Rev, Permafrost, Iowa Rev, NW Rev*

Carol Guess 🎤 ✈ P&W
Western Washington Univ, Dept of English, MS 9055,
Bellingham, WA 98225, 206-782-1868
Internet: guessc@cc.wwu.edu
Pubs: *Love Is a Map I Must Not Set on Fire* (Odd Girls Pr,
2003), *Switch* (Calyx Bks, 1998), *Seeing Dell* (Cleis Pr, 1996)

Theodore Hall 🎤 ✈ P
PO Box 317
Rainier, WA 98576-0317
Internet: drtedhall@aol.com
Pubs: *Intro I* (Bantam, 1968), *NYQ, Maps, Greenfield Rev,
NE Jrnl, Shenandoah, Stony Hills, Poet*

Mark W. Halperin 🎤 ✈ P
Central Washington Univ, English Dept, Ellensburg, WA
98926-7558, 509-963-3511
Internet: halperin@cwu.edu
Pubs: *Time as Distance* (New Issues/Western Michigan U
Pr, 2001), *A Measure of Islands* (Wesleyan, 1990), *A Place
Made Fast* (Copper Canyon Pr, 1982), *Iowa Rev, Seneca,
Shenandoah, Seattle Rev, NW Rev*

Sam Hamill 🎤 ✈ P
Copper Canyon Press, PO Box 271, Port Townsend, WA
98368, 206-385-4925
Internet: sam@coppercanyonpress.org
Pubs: *Dumb Luck, Gratitude* (BOA Edtns, 2002, 1998),
Destination Zero: Poems 1970-1995 (White Pine Pr, 1995),
Tricycle, APR, Poetry East, Ploughshares

Blaine Hammond 🎤 ✈ P
PO Box 543
Ocean Park, WA 98640-0543, 360-665-4248
Internet: padredoc@willapabay.org
Pubs: *Sand Script: Anth* (North Coast Writers, 1998), *Bogg,
Plainsongs, LSR, Chachalaca Rev, Byline, Minnesota Rev,
Acorn, Pemmican, Prairie Jrnl, Crossroads, Psychopoetica,
Kimera, Seattle Rev, South Dakota Rev, Antiskios,
Bouillabaisse, Free Lunch*

Nixeon Civille Handy P
262 Woodland Dr
Lacey, WA 98503, 206-438-5328
Pubs: *River as Metaphor* (Gorham, 1992), *A Little Leaven*
(Kings Pr, 1987), *NYQ, NER/BLQ, Oregon East, Chariton
Rev, Skylark, Connecticut Rev, Bellowing Ark*

Edward Harkness 🎤 ✈ P
14903 Linden Ave N
Shoreline, WA 98133-6516, 206-367-6574
Internet: eharkness@ctc.edu
Pubs: *Saying the Necessary* (Pleasure Boat Studio, 2000),
Water Color Portrait of a Bamboo Rake (Brooding Heron Pr,
1994), *Fiddle Wrapped in a Gunnysack* (Dooryard, 1984),
Seattle Rev, Portland Rev

George W. Harper W
1208 S 27 St, #C-2
Tacoma, WA 98409, 206-272-1034
Pubs: *Gypsy Earth* (Doubleday, 1983)

Jana Harris 🎤 ✈ P&W
32814 120th St SE
Sultan, WA 98294-9605, 360-793-1848
Internet: jnh@u.washington.edu
Pubs: *Pearl of Ruby City* (St. Martin's Pr, 1998), *Dust of
Everyday Life* (Sasquatch Pr, 1997), *Oh How Can I Keep
on Singing?, Sourlands, Untitled Poetry* (Ontario Rev Pr,
1993, 1989, 1989), *Manhattan As a Second Language*
(H&R, 1980)

Barbara Hiesiger PP
202 NW 43 St
Seattle, WA 98107-4328

Alicia Hokanson P
Box 10657
Bainbridge Island, WA 98110
Pubs: *Mapping the Distance* (Breitenbush, 1989),
Phosphorous (Brooding Heron, 1984), *Poetry USA,
Exhibition, Literary Center Qtly*

Emily Newman Holt P
1704 1st Ave N
Seattle, WA 98109, 206-283-3455
Pubs: *Encore, Up Against the Wall Mother, Blue Unicorn*

A. J. Hovde P
1400 Chuckanut Dr
Bellingham, WA 98226, 206-673-8073
Pubs: *A.J. Hovde: Selected Poems* (Fairhaven College Pr,
1981), *New Laurel Rev, Kansas Qtly*

Joan Howell P
Colorado College, 1975 Wynoochee Valley Rd, Montesano,
WA 98563, 360-249-2005
Internet: wynooche@techline.com
Pubs: *A Letter to Myself to Water* (Jonesalley Pr, 1995), *Our
Lady of the Harbor* (Seapen Pr, 1985), *Yale Rev, SPR,
Poetry NW*

Christopher Howell 🎤 ✈ P
420 W 24th
Spokane, WA 99203-1922, 509-624-4894
Internet: cnhowell@ewu.edu
Pubs: *Memory & Heaven* (Eastern Washington U Pr, 1997),
Sweet Afton (True Directions, 1991), *Pushcart Prize: Anth*
(Pushcart Pr, 1999), *Harper's, Gettysburg Rev, NAR, NW
Rev, Iowa Rev, Poetry NW, Hudson Rev, Ironwood*

Barbara Hull   P
18027 10th Place NE
Poulsbo, WA 98370, 360-779-5075
Internet: bhull36@altbi.com
   Pubs: *This House She Dreams In* (Kuhn Spit Pr, 1990),
   *Quarry West, California Qtly, Seattle Rev, Interim, Poet Lore,
   Poetry Seattle, Footwork*

Paul Hunter 🎤 ✈   P
4131 Greenwood N
Seattle, WA 98103-7017, 206-633-5647
www.woodworkspress.com
   Pubs: *Clown Car, Lay of the Land* (Wood Works, 2000,
   1997), *It Loves Me It Loves Me Not* (Now Its Up To You Pr,
   1992), *Mockingbird* (Jawbone Pr, 1981), *Alaska Fisherman's
   Jrnl, Fine Madness, NAR, Poetry, Poetry NW, Point No
   Point, Beloit*

Richard Ives 🎤 ✈   P
2693 S Camano Dr
Camano Island, WA 98282
Internet: ivesrich@yahoo.com
   Pubs: *Evidence of Fire* (Owl Creek Pr, 1989), *Notes from
   the Water Journals* (Confluence Pr, 1980), *Iowa Rev, Poetry
   NW, NW Rev, Mississippi Rev, Virginia Qtly Rev*

Sibyl James 🎤 ✈   P&W
1712 22nd Ave, S
Seattle, WA 98144-4514, 206-323-7516
   Pubs: *The Bakery of the Three Whores* (Ink Poet Pr, 1994),
   The Adventures of Stout Mama (Papier-Mache Pr, 1993), *In
   China with Harpo & Karl, The White Junk of Love, Again*
   (Calyx Bks, 1990, 1986)

Charles Johnson   W
English Dept, GN-30, Univ Washington, Seattle, WA 98195,
206-543-2690
   Pubs: *Middle Passage, Sorcerer's Apprentice* (Atheneum,
   1990, 1986), *Dialogue, American Visions*

Thom Jones   P&W
2438 31st Ave NW
Olympia, WA 98502, 360-866-8039
   Pubs: *Cold Snap, The Pugilist at Rest* (Little, Brown, 1995,
   1993), *Madmen & Bassoons, Footbridge to India* (India;
   Writers Workshop, 1992, 1990), *New Yorker, Esquire,
   Harper's, Playboy, Buzz*

R. P. Jones   P
7102 Interlaaken Dr SW
Tacoma, WA 98499-1805, 206-531-7422
   Pubs: *The Rest Is Silence* (Broken Moon Pr, 1984), *Waiting
   for Spring* (Circinatum Pr, 1978)

Sy M. Kahn   P
1212 Holcomb St
Port Townsend, WA 98368, 360-385-9499
Internet: kahnandbaker@olympus.net
   Pubs: *Between Tedium & Terror: A Soldier's Diary, 1943-45*
   (U Illinois Pr, 1993), *Facing Mirrors* (Two Windows, 1980),
   Another Time (Sydon, Inc, 1968), *Jrnl of Modern Literature,
   Midwest Qtly, College English, South Carolina Rev*

Lonny Kaneko 🎤   P
Highline College, PO Box 98000, Des Moines,
WA 98198-9800, 206-878-3710
Internet: lkaneko@highline.edu
   Pubs: *Coming Home from Camp* (Brooding Heron Pr, 1986),
   Asian Amer Lit: Anth (HC, 1995), *The Big Aiiieeee!: Anth*
   (NAL, 1991), *An Ear to the Ground: Anth* (U of Georgia Pr,
   1989), *Crossing the River: Anth* (The Permanent Pr, 1987),
   Seattle Rev, Amer Jrnl

Linda M. Kay   P
8110 175th Ave KPS
Longbranch, WA 98351
Internet: lkcoquille@aol.com
   Pubs: *Only Morning in Her Shoes: Anth* (Utah State U Pr,
   1990), *Nebo, Poem, Sierra Nevada College Rev, ByLine,
   Cold Mountain Rev, Jacaranda, Prairie Schooner,
   Primavera, Slant, Voices Intl*

John E. Keegan 🎤 ✈   W
7722 22nd Ave NE
Seattle, WA 98115-4512
Internet: johnkeegan@dwt.com
   Pubs: *Piper* (Permanent Pr, 2001), *Clearwater Summer*
   (Carroll & Graf, 1994), *New Orleans Rev*

R.J. Keeler 🎤 ✈   P
2649 NW 63rd St., Ste A
Seattle, WA 98107, 206-781-0344
Internet: Robert.J.Keeler@IEEE.ORG
   Pubs: *Friends Bulletin, tight, Ploughshares, The New Times*

Richard L. Kenney   P
Univ Washington, English Dept, 354330, Seattle,
WA 98195, 206-543-2690
   Pubs: *The Invention of the Zero* (Knopf, 1993), *Orrery*
   (Atheneum, 1985), *The Evolution of the Flightless Bird*
   (Yale U Pr, 1983)

Alex Kuo 🎤 ✈   P
PO Box 2237
Pullman, WA 99165, 509-335-4901
Internet: alexkuo@wsu.edu
   Pubs: Lipstick and Other Stories, Chinese Opera (Asia
   2000, 2000),This Fierce Geography (Limberlost, 1999),
   Changing the River (Reed & Cannon, 1986), New Letters
   from Hiroshima (Greenfield, 1974), The Window Tree (Windy
   Row, 1971), Chicago Rev, Caliban

Susan Landgraf   P
4828 51st Ave, S
Seattle, WA 98118, 206-721-0208
    Pubs: *Spoon River Qtly, South Florida Poetry Rev, Calyx,
    Ploughshares, Nimrod, Cincinnati Poetry Rev*

R. A. Larson   P
9600 Occidental
Yakima, WA 98903, 509-965-4547
    Pubs: *Of Wind, A Hawk, & Kiona* (Confluence Pr, 1978),
    Silverfish Rev, Brix, Kingfisher

Alan Chong Lau 🎤 ✈   P
5005 Phinney Ave N, #302
Seattle, WA 98103-6047
    Pubs: *Blues & Greens* (U Hawaii Pr, 2000), *What Book!?:
    Anth* (Parallax Pr, 1998), *Highway 99: Anth* (Heyday Bks,
    1996), *The Open Boat Poems from Asian America: Anth*
    (Anchor Bks, 1993), *American Dragons: Anth* (HC, 1993)

Ellen Levine   P
838 NE 83 St
Seattle, WA 98115
    Pubs: *Poetry NW, Georgia Rev, SPR, Poetry Now, Calyx,
    Kansas Qtly*

Evelyn Livingston   W
71 Windship Dr
Port Townsend, WA 98368-9545, 360-385-2063
    Pubs: *Digging for Roots: Dalmo'ma 5 Anth* (Empty Bowl Pr,
    1985), *Confrontation, Pennsylvania Rev, Indiana Rev,
    Georgia Rev, Crosscurrents, New Letters, Interim*

Jeanne Lohmann 🎤 ✈   P
2501 Washington SE
Olympia, WA 98501-2962, 360-705-3735
Internet: jlohmann@olywa.net
    Pubs: *Flying Horses, Granite Under Water* (Fithian Pr, 2000,
    1996), *Prayers to Protest* (Pudding Hse, 1998), *Between
    Silence & Answer* (Pendle Hill, 1994), *Wild Song: Anth* (U
    Georgia Pr, 1998), *Cries of the Spirit: Anth* (Beacon Pr,
    1991), *Bitter Oleander*

Kenneth MacLean   P
522 Decatur St SW
Olympia, WA 98502, 360-753-1175
Internet: kenver@oly.net
    Pubs: *Blue Heron's Sky* (Latitudes Pr, 1990), *The Long Way
    Home* (Inchbird Pr, 1982), *Prism Intl, Poetry Seattle,
    Calapooya Collage, Concerning Poetry*

Stephen Manes 🎤 ✈   W
1122 E Pike St, #588
Seattle, WA 98122-3916, 206-722-2525
Internet: steve@cranky.com
    Pubs: *An Almost Perfect Game, Comedy High* (Scholastic,
    1995, 1992), *Make Four Million Dollars by Next Thursday*
    (Bantam, 1990), *Be a Perfect Person in Just Three Days!*
    (HM,1982)

Laureen D. Mar   P&W
3811 S Horton St
Seattle, WA 98144-7027, 206-722-3482
    Pubs: *Charlie Chan Is Dead: Anth* (Penguin, 1993),
    Breaking Silence: Anth (Greenfield Rev Pr, 1983), *Contact
    II, Greenfield Rev, Seattle Rev*

Carlos M. Martinez 🎤 ✈   P
9116 1st Ave
Seattle, WA 98115-2705, 206-528-0543
Internet: carlmart1@yahoo.com
    Pubs: *Pontoon #5: Anth* (Floating Bridge Pr, 2002), *Yawp,
    4th St, Firefly, Pitt Qtly, Black Bear Rev, Crab Creek Rev*

John Constantine Mastor 🎤   P
505 NE 70 St # 308
Seattle, WA 98115-5403, 206-525-1081
    Pubs: *Studio Portrait, Glorious Morning, Bountiful Light* (The
    Plowman, 1999, 1996, 1995), *The Musing Place, Time of
    Singing, My Legacy, Broken Streets, Purpose, Rio Grande
    Pr, Bellowing Ark, Uprising, Aim Qtly, Poetic Realm*

William H. Matchett   P
1017 Minor Ave, #702
Seattle, WA 98104-1303, 206-682-6730
    Pubs: *Fireweed* (Tidal Pr, 1980), *Water Ouzel* (HM, 1955),
    *New Yorker, Harper's, Harvard, New Republic,
    Ploughshares, SPR*

Rita Z. Mazur 🎤 ✈   P
2332 Ferndale
Richland, WA 99352-1975, 509-375-4210
    Pubs: *The Great Blue Heron & Other Poems* (Adrienne Lee
    Pr, 1996), *Tanka Splendor* (AHA Bks, 1995), *Rain: Anth* (NW
    Region HSA, 1997), *Frogpond, American Tanka, Cherry
    Blossom, Black Bough, Modern Haiku, Passager*

James J. McAuley   P
1011 W 25 St
Spokane, WA 99203, 509-747-0896
    Pubs: *Coming & Going, New & Selected Work* (U Arkansas
    Pr, 1989), *Recital* (Dolmen/Colin Smythe, 1982), *Irish Times,
    Shenandoah, Cimarron Rev, Poetry NW*

Joanne McCarthy   P
1322 N Cascade
Tacoma, WA 98406-1113, 253-752-3462
    Pubs: *Shadowlight* (Broken Moon Pr, 1989), *Times of
    Sorrow, Times of Grace: Anth* (Backwater Pr, 2002), *At Our
    Core: Anth* (Papier-Mache Pr, 1998), *Claiming the Spirit
    Within: Anth* (Beacon Pr, 1996), *Runes, Calyx, Green Fuse,
    Kalliope, Writers' Forum*

Michael McClure 🎤 ✈ P&W
c/o Denise Enck, Empty Mirror Books Agency, PO Box 972,
Mukilteo, WA 98275
Internet: denise@emptymirrorbooks.com
    Pubs: *Plum Stones* (O Bks, 2002), *Here's a Word: CD* (Rare
Angel, 2001), *Third Mind: Video* (Empty Mirror Bks, 2000),
Touching the Edge (Shambhala, 1999), *Huge Dreams,
Three Poems* (Penguin, 1999, 1995), *Rain Mirror* (New
Directions, 1999)

Colleen J. McElroy 🎤 ✈ P&W
c/o Elizabeth Wales, Wales Literary Agency, PO Box 9428,
Seattle, WA 98109, 206-284-7114
    Pubs: *Over the Lip of the World* (U Washington Pr, 1999),
Travelling Music (Story Line Pr, 1998), *A Long Way from St.
Louie* (Coffee Hse Pr, 1997), *What Madness Brought Me
Here* (Wesleyan U, 1990), *Best American Poetry: Anth*
(Scribner, 2001), *Seneca Rev*

John McFarland 🎤 ✈ W
2320 10th Ave E, #5
Seattle, WA 98102-4076, 206-323-7053
Internet: jbmcfar@yahoo.com
    Pubs: *The Exploding Frog & Other Fables* (Little, Brown,
1981), *Contra/Diction: Anth* (Arsenal Pulp Pr, 1998), *The
Next Parish Over: Anth* (New Rivers Pr, 1993), *Stringtown,
Mediphors, Ararat, Caliban, Cricket*

Heather McHugh P
English Dept, Box 354330, Univ Washington, Seattle, WA
98195-4330, 206-543-2483
http://spondee.com
    Pubs: *Broken English: Poetry & Partiality, The Father of the
Predicaments, Hinge & Sign: Poems 1968-1993* (Wesleyan,
1999, 1999, 1994)

Robert McNamara 🎤 ✈ P
Univ Washington, English Dept, Box 354330, Seattle, WA
98195-4330, 206-543-7131
Internet: rmcnamar@u.washington.edu
    Pubs: *Second Messengers* (Wesleyan U Pr, 1990), *Ohio
Rev, Agni, Missouri Rev, Field, Gettysburg Rev, Antioch Rev,
NW Rev*

Melinda Mueller 🎤 ✈ P
7704 16th Ave NW
Seattle, WA 98117-5419, 206-323-6600
    Pubs: *What the Ice Gets* (Van West Co, 2000), *Apocrypha*
(Grey Spider Pr, 1998), *Asleep in Another Country*
(Jawbone Pr, 1979), *Best American Poetry: Anth*
(MacMillan, 1990)

Duane Niatum 🎤 ✈ P&W
c/o D. Kopta, 4408 Phinney Ave N, Seattle, WA 98103,
206-633-0702
    Pubs: *The Crooked Beak of Love* (West End Pr, 2000),
Drawings of the Song Animals: New & Selected Poems
(Holy Cow! Pr, 1991), *North Dakota Qtly, Prairie Schooner,
Puerto del Sol, Canadian Literature, Archae Mag, Seattle
Rev, Michigan Qtly Rev, Chariton Rev*

Carol Orlock 🎤 ✈ W
920 2nd Ave W
Seattle, WA 98119, 206-283-0680
    Pubs: *The Hedge, The Ribbon* (Broken Moon Pr, 1993), *The
Goddess Letters* (St. Martin's Pr, 1987), *Century, Willow
Springs, Calyx, Crab Creek Rev*

Hans Ostrom 🎤 ✈ P&W
English Dept, Univ of Puget Sound, 1500 N Warner, Tacoma,
WA 98416, 206-756-3434
Internet: ostrom@ups.edu
    Pubs: *Subjects Apprehended: Poems* (Pudding Hse Pr,
2000), *Metro* (Longman, 2000), *Water's Night* (Mariposite
Pr, 1993), *Three to Get Ready* (Cliffhanger Pr, 1991),
*Ploughshares, Poetry NW, Redbook, California Qtly, South
Carolina Rev*

Lori Jo Oswald P&W
12401 SE 320 St, #HS
Auburn, WA 98092-3622
    Pubs: *Poetry North Rev, Day Tonight/Night Today, Alura,
Negative Capability, Nettles & Nutmeg*

Eileen Owen P
2709 128th St SE
Everett, WA 98208, 206-337-1231
    Pubs: *Facing the Weather Side* (Basilisk Pr, 1985), *Calyx,
Cincinnati Rev, South Dakota Rev*

Dixie Lee Partridge P
1817 Marshall Ct
Richland, WA 99351-2483, 509-943-4007
    Pubs: *Watermark* (Saturday Pr, 1991), *Deer in the
Haystacks* (Ahsahta Pr, 1984), *Poetry, Commonweal, SPR,
Ploughshares, Passages North, Georgia Rev, Northern
Lights*

Lucia Perillo 🎤 ✈ P
James Rudy, 513 S Quince St, Olympia, WA 98501
    Pubs: *The Oldest Map with the Name America* (Random
Hse, 1999), *The Body Mutinies* (Purdue U Pr, 1996),
Dangerous Life (Northeastern U Pr, 1989), *New Yorker,
Ploughshares, Atlantic, Kenyon Rev, Poetry East*

Terry Lee Persun 🎤 ✈   P&W
836 Calhoun St
Port Townsend, WA 98368, 360-379-3375
Internet: tpersun@waypt.com
> Pubs: *Barn Tarote, The Witness Tress, In the Story* (Implosive Pr, 1999, 1998, 1996), *Three Lives* (ph Pub,1996), *Plant-Animal-I* (March St Pr, 1994), *Hollow Goodbyes* (Mulberry Pr, 1991), *Dandelion Soul* (Nightshade Pr, 1990)

Anne Pitkin   P
6809 Dayton Ave N
Seattle, WA 98103, 206-789-4623
> Pubs: *Yellow* (Arrowood Bks, 1989), *Poetry, Prairie Schooner, Ironwood, Malahat, Seattle Rev*

Randall Platt 🎤 ✈   W
1126 Pt Fosdick Dr NW
Gig Harbor, WA 98335-8810
Internet: royal@harbornet.com
> Pubs: *The Likes of Me* (Random Hse, 2000), *The 1898 Baseball Fe-As-Ko, The Cornerstone, The Royalscope Fe-As-Ko, The Four Arrows Fe-As-Ko* (Catbird Pr, 2000, 1998, 1997, 1991), *Honor Bright* (Doubleday, 1998), *Out of the Forest Clearing* (John Daniel, 1991)

Darryl Ponicsan   W
PO Box 10036
Bainbridge Island, WA 98110
> Pubs: *The Ringmaster, Tom Mix Died for Your Sins* (Delacorte/Dell, 1978, 1975)

Charles Potts 🎤 ✈   P
PO Box 100
Walla Walla, WA 99362-0033, 509-529-0813
Internet: tsunami@innw.net
> Pubs: *Across the North Pacific* (Slough Pr, 2002), *Slash and Burn, Lost River Mountain* (Blue Begonia, 2001, 1999), *Nature Lovers* (Pleasure Boat Studio, 2000), *Little Lord Shiva* (Glass Eye Bks, 1999), *Fascist Haikus* (Acid Pr, 1999)

Joseph Powell 🎤 ✈   P
221 Cross Creek Dr
Ellensburg, WA 98926, 509-925-5312
Internet: powellj@cluster.cwu.edu
> Pubs: *Getting Here, Quarterly Rev of Literature 50th Anniversary Anth* (QRL, 1997, 1993), *Counting the Change, Winter Insomnia* (Arrowhead, 1993, 1993), *Poetry, Seattle Rev, Tar River Poetry, Nebraska Rev*

Marjorie Power 🎤 ✈   P
508 O'Farrell Ave
Olympia, WA 98501-3470, 360-352-7025
Internet: birdbrane@attbi.com
> Pubs: *The Complete Tishku, Cave Poems, Tishku After She Created Men* (Lone Willow Pr, 2003, 1998, 1996), *Living with It* (Wampeter Pr, 1983), *Zone 3, Atlanta Rev, Poet Lore, Blue Unicorn, Malahat Rev*

Belle Randall 🎤 ✈   P
1202 N. 42 St.
Seattle, WA 98103, 206-633-2744
Internet: bellerandall@prosody.org
> Pubs: *Say Uncle, Drop Dead Beautiful* (Wood Works Pr, 2002, 1998), *The Gift of Tongues: Anth* (Copper Canyon Pr, 1996), *Wallace Stegner Anth* (Stanford U Pr, 1989), *Threepenny Rev, Common Knowledge*

Bill W.M. Ransom 🎤 ✈   P&W
1505 Division St SW
Olympia, WA 98502, 360-705-2521
www.sfwa.org/members/ransom
> Pubs: *Sleight of Hand* (Far Cry Pr, 2000), *Jaguar* (Wildside Pr, 2000), *Learning the Ropes* (Utah State U Pr, 1995), *Burn* (Putnam-Berkley Pub, 1995), *In Praise of Pedagogy: Anth* (Calendar Pr, 2000), *Thirteen Ways of Looking for a Poem: Anth* (Longman, 1999)

Susan Rich 🎤 ✈   P
3417 60th Ave SW
Seattle, WA 98116-2819, 206-878-3710x3253
Internet: srich@highline.edu
> Pubs: *The Cartographer's Tongue* (White Pine Pr, 2000), *Alaska Qtly Rev, Bridges, DoubleTake, Glimmer Train, Harvard Mag, Massachusetts Rev, Many Mountains Moving, Poet Lore, SPR, Santa Barbara Rev, Sojourner*

Sherry A. Rind 🎤 ✈   P
321 NE 115 St
Seattle, WA 98125, 206-364-0804
Internet: airebird@hotmail.com
> Pubs: *A Fall Out the Door* (Confluence Pr, 1994), *The Hawk in the Backyard* (Anhinga Pr, 1985), *Poetry NW, SPR*

Judith Roche 🎤 ✈   P
178 Lake Dell Ave
Seattle, WA 98122-6309, 206-329-4687
Internet: judith@onereel.org
> Pubs: *Myrrh, My Life as a Screamer* (Black Heron Pr, 1994), *Ghosts* (Empty Bowl Pr, 1984), *Raven Chronicles, Willow Springs, Duckabush Jrnl, Yellow Silk*

Mary Elizabeth Ryan 🎤 ✈   W
WordCrafters Northwest, 4137 University Way NE, Ste 202, Seattle, WA 98105-6263, 206-632-2593
Internet: mary.e.ryan@gte.net
> Pubs: *Alias, The Trouble with Perfect, Me, My Sister, & I, My Sister Is Driving Me Crazy* (S&S, 1997, 1995, 1992, 1991), *I'd Rather Be Dancing* (Delacorte Pr, 1989), *Tails of Terror: Anth* (Lyric, 1999)

Sal Salasin ✈   P
840 W Nickerson St, #11
Seattle, WA 98119-1448
> Pubs: *Optima Suavidad* (Greenbean Pr, 1999), *Casa de Caca* (Apathy Poets Pr, 1990), *Stepping Off the Plane* (Another Chicago Pr, 1988), *Exquisite Corpse, ACM, NAW, Sensitive Skin, Real Poetik*

Eric Schmidt PP
1517 12th Ave, #Mezz
Seattle, WA 98122-3932
   Pubs: *The Freezing No to All Questions Prison of Bent Things: Verse Play*

Julianne Seeman 🎤 ✈ P
English Dept, Bellevue Community College, Arts & Humanities
Div, #A255M, Bellevue, WA 98004, 206-526-0698
Internet: jseeman2@msn.com
   Pubs: *Enough Light to See* (Anhinga Pr, 1989)

Janet Seery P
2505 42 Ave W
Seattle, WA 98119-3606
   Pubs: *Washout Rev, Greenfield Rev, Kudzu, Wisconsin Rev, Nantucket Rev, Buckle, Bloodroot*

David Shields W
Dept of English, Univ of Washington, Box 354330, Seattle, WA
98195-4330, 205-543-2247
Internet: dshields@u.washington.edu
   Pubs: *Remote, Dead Languages* (Knopf, 1996, 1989),
Harper's, Village Voice, Utne Reader

Sondra Shulman W
934 E Allison St
Seattle, WA 98102, 206-329-6493
   Pubs: *Moon People* (Baskerville Pub, 1994), *Scrittori Ebrei Americani* (Tascabili Bom Pi Ant, 1989), *Ascent, Massachusetts Rev, Antioch Rev, Kansas Qtly, Bumbershoot*

Red Shuttleworth 🎤 ✈ P
10482 Rd 16 NE
Moses Lake, WA 98837-9356, 509-766-9104
   Pubs: *Western Settings* (U Nevada Pr, 2000), *All These Bullets* (Logan Hse Pr, 1997), *Western Movie* (Signpost Pr, 1990), *Coyotes with Wings* (Gorse Pr, 1990), *Neon, Alaska Qtly Rev, New Mexico Humanities Rev, West Branch*

Sarah Singer 🎤 P
2360 43 Ave E, #415
Seattle, WA 98112-2703, 206-726-8103
   Pubs: *The Gathering, Of Love & Shoes* (William L. Bauhan, 1992, 1987), *Palomar Showcase: Anths* (Palomar Branch Pr, 1999, 1998, 1997), *Glimpses: Anth* (King Cty Public Art Prgm, 1997), *Shakespeare Newsletter, Voices Intl, Lyric, Judaism, Poets West, Penwoman*

Judith Skillman 🎤 ✈ P
14206 SE 45 Pl
Bellevue, WA 98006-2308, 206-644-4026
   Pubs: *Red Town* (Silverfish Rev Pr, 2001), *Sweetbrier, Storm, Beethoven & the Birds* (Blue Begonia Pr, 2001, 1998, 1996), *JAMA, Southern Rev, NW Rev, Iowa Rev, Prairie Schooner, Poetry*

James M. Snydal 🎤 ✈ P
11034 Old Creosote Hill Rd
Bainbridge Island, WA 98110-2154, 206-842-1273
Internet: snydal5@hotmail.com
   Pubs: *Do Not Surrender, Near the Cathedral* (Dry Bones Pr, 2001, 1995), *Blueberry Pie* (Wood Works, 1998), *Living in America* (New Thought Jrnl Pr, 1997), *To Range Widely Over Possibilities* (Full Moon Pub, 1996), *Poetry Wales, Onthebus, Chiron, Bloomsbury*

Maya Sonenberg 🎤 ✈ W
English Dept, Univ Washington, Box 354330, Seattle, WA
98195-4330, 206-543-9865
Internet: mayas@u.washington.edu
   Pubs: *Cartographies* (U Pitt Pr, 1989), *American Fiction X: Anth* (New Rivers Pr, 1999), *Alaska Qtly Rev, American Short Fiction, Cream City Rev, Grand Street, Chelsea, Santa Monica Rev*

Sandi Sonnenfeld 🎤 ✈ W
125 N 105 St
Seattle, WA 98133-8701
Internet: SanWar1@earthlink.net
   Pubs: *Sex & the City: Anth* (Serpent's Tail, 1989), *Hayden's Ferry Rev, ACM, Margin: Exploring Magic Realism, Raven Chronicles, Onion River Rev, Voices West, This Mag, Salmon Mag, CPU Rev, Emrys Jrnl, Ion, Sojourner, Written Arts*

Michael Spence 🎤 ✈ P
5810 S 144 St
Tukwila, WA 98168-4550, 206-431-6874
   Pubs: *Adam Chooses* (Rose Alley Pr, 1998), *The Spine* (Purdue U Pr, 1987), *Poetry Comes Up Where It Can: Anth* (U Utah Pr, 2000), *N Amer Rev, Chariton Rev, Hollins Critic, Poetry NW, Seattle Rev, S Humanities Rev, Tar River Poetry*

Stephen Sundin 🎤 ✈ P
21 Alpine Way
Longview, WA 98632
Internet: stateofsss@aol.com
   Pubs: *Playing with a Full Deck: Anth* (26 Bks, 1999), *ACM, Artful Dodge, Denver Qtly, Key Satch(el), Luna, Mudfish, NYQ, Paragraph, Poet Lore, Prose Poem, Pivot, Quarter After Eight, Thin Air, Wolf Head Qtly*

Joan Swift 🎤 ✈ P
18520 Sound View Pl
Edmonds, WA 98020-2355, 425-776-2391
Internet: jayswift@msn.com
   Pubs: *The Tiger Iris* (BOA Edtns, 1999), *Intricate Moves* (Chicory Blue Pr, 1997), *The Dark Path of Our Names* (Dragon Gate, 1985), *Parts of Speech* (Confluence Pr, 1978), *The Yale Rev, Poetry, DoubleTake, Ploughshares*

Gordon Taylor   W
3920 SW 109 St
Seattle, WA 98146-1652

Velande P. Taylor, PhD 🎤   P&W
910 Marion St, #1008
Seattle, WA 98104-1273, 206-621-1376
    Pubs: *Zodiac Affair, Between the Lines, Copper Flowers,
    Tales from the Archetypal World* (WordCraft Bks, 2000, 1999,
    1999, 1998), *Pacific Mag, Verses Mag, Extended Hands*

Gary Thompson 🎤 ✈   P
875 Puget Dr SE
Port Orchard, WA 98366-8504
Internet: gary.thompson3@worldnet.att.net
    Pubs: *On John Muir's Trail* (Bear Star Pr, 1999), *As for
    Living* (Red Wing Pr, 1995), *Hold Fast* (Confluence Pr,
    1984), *Colorado Rev, Laurel Rev, Nebraska Rev, Writers'
    Forum, Hayden's Ferry Rev, Chariton Rev*

Gail Tremblay   P
The Evergreen State College, Olympia, WA 98505,
206-866-6000
    Pubs: *Indian Singing in 20th Century America* (Calyx,
    1990), *Harper's Anth of 20th Century Native American
    Poetry* (Harper SF, 1986), *Wooster Rev, Calyx, Denver Qtly,
    NW Rev*

Wayne Ude   W
PO Box 145
Clinton, WA 98236, 206-341-1630
    Pubs: *Maybe I Will Do Something* (HM, 1993), *Buffalo &
    Other Stories* (Lynx Hse Pr, 1991), *Three Coyote Tales*
    (Lone Oak Pr, 1989), *Ploughshares, NAR*

Michael Upchurch   W
9725 Sand Point Way NE
Seattle, WA 98115-2650
Internet: michaelupchurch@msn.com
    Pubs: *Passive Intruder* (Norton, 1995), *The Flame Forest*
    (Available Pr/Ballantine, 1989), *Carolina Qtly, American
    Scholar, Glimmer Train*

Craig Van Riper 🎤 ✈   P
1630 E Lynn St
Seattle, WA 98112-2130, 206-329-5972
Internet: craigvanriper@earthlink.net
    Pubs: *Convenient Danger* (Pecan Grove Pr, 2000), *Making
    the Path While You Walk* (Sagittarius Pr, 1993), *Seattle
    Poets & Photographers: Anth* (U Washington Pr, 1999),
    *Spoon River Qtly, Passages North, SPR, Onthebus, Five
    Fingers Rev, Score, Coe Rev*

Nance Van Winckel 🎤 ✈   P&W
12506 S Gardener
Cheney, WA 99004-9513, 509-448-6155
Internet: nancev@sisna.com
    Pubs: *Beside Ourselves* (Miami U Pr, 2002), *Curtain Creek
    Farm* (Persea, 2000), *After a Spell, The Dirt* (Miami U Pr,
    1998, 1994), *Limited Lifetime Warranty* (U Missouri Pr,
    1994), *DoubleTake, Gettysburg Rev, Poetry, New Letters,
    APR, Nation, NAR, Poetry NW*

David Wagoner   P&W
4820-168 St #2
Lynnwood, WA 98037, 425-745-5400
    Pubs: *The House of Song, Traveling Light: Collected and
    New Poems, Walt Whitman Bathing* (U Illinois Pr, 2002,
    1999, 1996), *Through the Forest* (Atlantic Monthly Pr, 1987)

Edith M. Walden   P
PO Box 9493
Seattle, WA 98109
    Pubs: *Iowa Rev, Luna Tack, Calyx, Slackwater Rev,
    Rapunzel Rapunzel, Nethula Jrnl, Pig Iron*

Robert R. Ward 🎤 ✈   P
PO Box 45637
Seattle, WA 98145, 206-440-0791
    Pubs: *Notes on an Urban Ecology* (Primeval Pr, 1998),
    *Kansas Qtly, Arkansas Rev, Midday Moon, Tar River Poetry,
    Sulphur River, Seattle Rev, Outposts Poetry Rev, Imago,
    MacGuffin, Permafrost, Santa Clara Rev, Cafe Solo,
    Farmer's Market, Snowy Egret*

Michael Frank Warlum   P
4412 50 Ave SW
Seattle, WA 98116, 206-935-8615
    Pubs: *The Keating Dynasty* (NAL/Signet, 1986), *A Bullet for
    Bradford* (Carousel, 1981)

Emily Warn   P
1723 27th Ave
Seattle, WA 98122, 206-322-8750
Internet: dogwood@msn.com
    Pubs: *The Novice Insomniac, The Leaf Path* (Copper
    Canyon Pr, 1996, 1982), *Kenyon Rev, Cream City Rev,
    SPR, CutBank, Mississippi Mud*

Irving Warner   W
312 Gehrke Rd
Port Angeles, WA 98362
Internet: irvingwarner@olympus.net
    Pubs: *From Timberline to Tidepool: Anth* (Copper Canyon,
    1984), *Montana Rev, Cimarron Rev, Colorado Rev*

Jan Widgery   W
8605 NE 12 St
Medina, WA 98039-3904, 425-454-9358
Internet: jwidgery@msn.com
    Pubs: *Trumpet at the Gates, The Adversary* (Doubleday,
    1970, 1966), *Good Housekeeping*

Barbara Wilson   W
523 N 84 St
Seattle, WA 98103-4309, 206-781-9612
www.witescn.org
  Pubs: *Blue Windows* (Picador USA, 1997), *If You Had a
  Family* (Seal Pr, 1996)

Shawn H. Wong   P&W
Univ Washington, Asian American Studies, GN-80, Seattle,
WA 98195
  Pubs: *The Big Aiiieeee!: Anth* (NAL, 1991), *Before
  Columbus Fiction Anth, Before Columbus Poetry Anth*
  (Norton, 1992, 1992)

Sara Jorgenson Woodbury   P
PO Box 676
Spokane, WA 99210-4059, 509-458-0454
  Pubs: *A Field, A Mountain, Ways of Silence, Edge of Night*
  (Writer's Works, 2001, 2000, 1999), *Dreams, Shadows of
  the Moon* (Papermill, 1996, 1991)

WEST VIRGINIA

Jean Anaporte-Easton ♦ ⊀   P
110 Town Ct
Charleston, WV 25312-1130, 304-744-9776
  Pubs: *Free Songs* (Writers' Center Pr, 1992), *With a Fly's
  Eye, Whale's Wit, & Woman's Heart* (Cleis Pr, 1989), *13th
  Moon, Mid-American Rev, Mildred, One Trick Pony, Kestrel,
  Callaloo*

Grace Cavalieri ♦ ⊀   P
PO Box 416
Hedgesville, WV 25427-0416, 304-754-8847
Internet: grace7623@aol.com
  Pubs: *Cuffed Frays, Sit Down Says Love* (Argonne House
  Pr, 2001, 2000), *Heart on a Leash* (Red Dragon Pr, 1999),
  Pinecrest Rest Haven (WordWorks, 1998), *Migrations,
  Poems* (Vision Library Pubs, 1995, 1994), *Pembroke Mag*

Lloyd Davis   P
West Virginia Univ, Morgantown, WV 26506, 304-293-3107
  Pubs: *The Way All Rivers Run* (Une Pr, 1982), *Fishing the
  Lower Jackson* (Best Cellar, 1974)

Mark DeFoe ♦ ⊀   P&W
28 Central Ave
Buckhannon, WV 26201, 304-472-0667
Internet: defoe@wvwc.edu
  Pubs: *Aviary, Palmate* (Pringle Tree Pr, 2001, 1988), *Air*
  (GreenTower Pr, 1998), *Bringing Home Breakfast* (Black
  Willow, 1982), *Poetry, Kenyon Rev, Paris Rev, Yale Rev,
  Michigan Qtly Rev, Poetry Intl, CSM, Denver Qtly, S
  Humanities Rev, Black Warrior Rev*

Marc Harshman ♦ ⊀   P
PO Box 2111
Wheeling, WV 26003, 304-243-9711
  Pubs: *Rose of Sharon* (Mad River, 1999), *Turning Out the
  Stones* (State Street Pr, 1983), *Learning By Heart: Anth*
  (U Iowa Pr, 1999), *Wild Song: Anth* (U Georgia Pr, 1998),
  Theology Today, Christianity and Lit, 5 AM, Shenandoah,
  Wilderness, Sycamore Rev

Robert G. Head   P
c/o Bookstore, 104 S Jefferson, Lewisburg, WV 24901
  Pubs: *Refuges of Value, Selected Poems* (Book & Mineral
  Investment Corp, 1993, 1988), *Jrnl of Sister Moon,
  Malcontent*

Eugene L. Jeffers ♦ ⊀   W
891 Bayer Rd
Hedgesville, WV 25427, 304-229-0305
  Pubs: *Beyond Darkness* (Eagle & Palm Pub, 2000), *A
  Rumor of Distant Tribes* (Ariadne Pr, 1994), *Pulpsmith,
  Crosscurrents, Orbis, Virginia Country*

Sandra Marshburn ♦ ⊀   P
201 Viking Rd
Charleston, WV 25302, 304-342-4450
Internet: marshbsh@mail.wvsc.edu
  Pubs: *Undertow* (March Street Pr, 1992), *Controlled Flight*
  (Alms Hse Pr, 1990), *Now & Then, Antietam Rev, Wind,
  Flyway, Yankee, Cincinnati Poetry Rev, Devil's Millhopper,
  MacGuffin, Midwest Qtly, Tar River Poetry*

Llewellyn T. McKernan ♦ ⊀   P
Rte 10, Box 4639B
Barboursville, WV 25504, 304-733-5054
  Pubs: *Short & Simple Annals* (West Virginia Humanities
  Council, 1983), *Bloodroot: Essays on Place by Appalachian
  Women Writers: Anth* (U Kentucky Pr, 1998), *Kenyon Rev,
  SPR, Antietam Rev, Kalliope, Nimrod, Appalachian Jrnl*

John McKernan ♦ ⊀   P
Marshall Univ, English Dept, Huntington, WV 25701,
304-696-6499
Internet: mckernan@marshall.edu
  Pubs: *Postcard from Dublin* (Dead Metaphor Pr, 1999),
  Walking Along the Missouri River (Lost Roads, 1977), *Paris
  Rev, Field, Harvard, Ohio Rev, Prairie Schooner, Virginia
  Qtly Rev*

Irene McKinney ♦ ⊀   P
Rte 1, Box 118C
Belington, WV 26250, 304-823-3041
Internet: McKinney_i@wvwc.edu
  Pubs: *Six O'Clock Mine Report* (U of Pittsburgh Pr, 1989),
  Kenyon Rev, Poetry, Salmagundi, NW Rev, MA Rev

John S. Morris   P
English Dept, Davis & Elkins College, Elkins, WV 26241,
304-636-1900
    Pubs: *Bean Street* (Lost Roads, 1977), *America, Central
Appalachian Rev, Shenandoah, Laurel Rev*

John O'Brien 🎤 ✈   P&W
PO Box 148
Franklin, WV 26807
    Pubs: *At Home in the Heart of Appalachia* (Knopf, 2001),
*Country Jrnl, Massachusetts Rev, Gray's Sporting Journal,
Hudson Rev, Iowa Rev, Madrona*

Barbara Smith 🎤 ✈   P&W
16 Willis Ln
Philippi, WV 26416, 304-457-3038
Internet: smith_b@ab.edu
    Pubs: *The Circumstance of Death, Six Miles Out* (Mountain
State Pr, 2001, 1981), *Wild Sweet Notes: Anth* (Publishers
Place, 2000), *Appalachian Inside Out: Anth* (U Tennessee Pr,
1995), *Potomac Rev, Women's Words, Pine Mountain, Sand
and Gravel*

Richard Thorman   W
325 Silver Rd
Berkeley Springs, WV 25411
    Pubs: *Hardly Working* (LSU Pr, 1990), *Bachman's Law*
(Norton, 1981), *Sewanee Rev, The Long Story*

Ed Zahniser 🎤 ✈   P&W
PO Box 955
Shepherdstown, WV 25443-0955, 304-876-2442
    Pubs: *A Calendar of Worship & Other Poems* (Plane Bucket
Pr, 1995), *Shepherdstown Historic Firsts* (Four Seasons Bks,
1992), *Antietam Rev, December, Kestrel, The Other Side*

WISCONSIN

Robert Alexander 🎤 ✈   P
3440 Lake Mendota Dr
Madison, WI 53705-1471, 608-238-5076
Internet: alex@mailbag.com
    Pubs: *Five Forks: Waterloo of the Confederacy* (Michigan
State U Pr, 2003), *White Pine Sucker River, The Party
Train: Anth* (New Rivers Pr, 1993, 1996), *Luna, Flyway,
Prose Poem*

Antler 🎤 ✈   P
c/o Inland Ocean, PO Box 11502, Milwaukee, WI 53211
    Pubs: *Selected Poems* (Soft Skull, 2000), *September 11,
2001: American Writers Respond: Anth* (Etruscan, 2002),
Poems of the Natural World: Anth (U Georgia, 1998),
American Poets Say Goodbye to the 20th Century: Anth (4
Walls 8 Windows, 1996)

Norbert Blei   W
PO Box 33
Ellison Bay, WI 54210, 414-854-2413
Internet: nblei@mail.doorcounty-wi.com
    Pubs: *Chi Town, Neighborhood, The Ghost of Sandburg's
Phizzog, The Door* (Ellis Pr, 1990, 1987, 1986, 1985), *New
Yorker, TriQtly, Chicago Mag*

Thomas Bontly   W
Creative Writing, English Dept, Univ Wisconsin-Milwaukee, PO
Box 413, Milwaukee, WI 53201-0413, 414-229-4530
Internet: bontly@uwm.edu
    Pubs: *The Giant's Shadow* (Random Hse, 1989), *Celestial
Chess* (Ballantine, 1980), *Sewanee Rev, Denver Qtly,
Cream City Rev, Redbook, McCall's, Esquire*

Harriet Brown 🎤 ✈   P
2515 Chamberlain Ave
Madison, WI 53705-3828, 608-233-6191
Internet: hnbrown@gdinet.com
    Pubs: *The Good-Bye Window* (U Wisconsin Pr, 1998),
*Atlanta Rev, Prairie Schooner, Wisconsin Poets Calendar,
Ms.*

Gary C. Busha   P&W
3123 S Kennedy Dr
Sturtevant, WI 53177
    Pubs: *Lines on Lake Winnebago* (Marsh River Edtns, 2002),
The Skeptics's Dream, Willowdown (Wolfsong Pub, 1996,
1995), *Root River Poets Anth, Abraxas, Wisconsin Poet's
Calendar, Page 5*

Alden R. Carter 🎤 ✈   W
1113 W Onstad Dr
Marshfield, WI 54449, 715-389-1108
Internet: acarterwriter@tznet.com
    Pubs: *Crescent Moon* (Holiday Hse, 1999), *Bull Catcher,
Between a Rock & a Hard Place, Dogwolf* (Scholastic, 1997,
1995, 1994), *RoboDad, Up Country, Sheila's Dying*
(Putnam, 1990, 1989, 1987)

DeWitt Clinton 🎤 ✈   P
3567 N Murray
Shorewood, WI 53211-2525, 414-332-4582
Internet: clintond@mail.uww.edu
    Pubs: *Divine Inspiration* (Oxford U Pr, 1998), *And What
Rough Beast: Anth* (Ashland Poetry Pr, 1999), *Louisiana
Literature, Voices Israel, Southern California Jrnl, Southern
Anth, Image*

Keith Cohen 🎤 ✈   W
149 Dayton Row
Madison, WI 53703-4604
Internet: lkcohen@wisc.edu
    Pubs: *Writing in a Film Age* (U Pr Colorado, 1991), *L'Esprit
Createur*

Mark Dintenfass   W
Lawrence Univ, Appleton, WI 54911
Internet: mldin@aol.com
     Pubs: *A Loving Place, Old World, New World* (Morrow, 1986, 1982)

Karl Elder 🎤 ✈   P
Lakeland College, Box 359, Sheboygan, WI 53082-0359, 920-565-3871
Internet: kelder@excel.net
     Pubs: *A Man in Pieces* (Prickly Pear Pr, 1994), *The Pushcart Prize: Anth* (Pushcart Pr, 2001), *Best American Poetry: Anth* (Scribner, 2000), *Chicago Rev, BPJ*

Roberta Fabiani   P
PO Box 716
Burlington, WI 53105
Internet: berta@execpc.com
     Pubs: *Artery: Anth* (No Pr Pubs, 2001), *Wisconsin Academy Science, Arts and Letters: Anth* (Arria, 1999), *Free Verse, Burlington Area Arts Council Newsletter, Writer's Block, Wisconsin Fellowship of Poets Museletter*

Jean Feraca   P
1418 Winslow Ln
Madison, WI 53711, 608-273-0402
     Pubs: *Crossing the Great Divide* (Wisconsin Academy of Sciences, Arts & Letters, 1992), *The Dream Book: Anth* (Schocken Bks, 1985), *APR, Southern Rev, Nation*

Susan Firer 🎤 ✈   P
4816 N Bartlett Ave
Milwaukee, WI 53217, 414-332-7534
Internet: sfirer@uwm.edu
     Pubs: *The Laugh We Make When We Fall* (Backwaters Pr, 2002), *The Lives of the Saints & Everything* (Cleveland State U Pr, 1993), *The Underground Communion Rail* (West End Pr, 1992)

Doug Flaherty   P
1011 Babcock St
Neenah, WI 54956-5114, 414-722-5826
     Pubs: *Last Hunt: Anth* (Wolfsong Pub, 1998), *Good Thief Come Home: Selected Poems* (Prickly Pear Pr, 1990), *New Yorker, Nation, NAR, QRL, Poetry NW, Carolina Qtly*

Steven D. Fortney 🎤 ✈   P
501 W South St
Stoughton, WI 53589, 608-873-3917
Internet: sfortney@wisc.edu
     Pubs: *Greatest Hits* (Pudding Hse, 2003), *The Gazebo* (Waubesa Pr, 2001), *The Thomas Jesus: A Novella, Heg: A Novella* (Badger Bks, 2000, 1998), *This Sporting Life: Anth* (Milkweed Edtns, 1996), *East West: A Poetry Annual: Anth* (Cape Cod Writers, 1992)

Abby Frucht 🎤 ✈   W
Legion Place
Oshkosh, WI 54901
     Pubs: *Polly's Ghost, Life Before Death* (Scribner, 2000, 1997), *Are You Mine?* (Grove Pr, 1993), *Licorice* (Graywolf, 1990), *Fruit of the Month* (U Iowa Pr, 1987)

Frederick Gaines   P
621 N Badger Ave
Appleton, WI 54914, 414-731-0786

Brent Goodman 🎤 ✈   P
771 S Dickinson St
Madison, WI 53703, 608-256-5047
Internet: brentg@tos.net
     Pubs: *Wrong Horoscope* (Thorngate Rd, 1999), *Trees & the Slowest River* (Sarasota Poetry Theater Pr 1999), *American Poetry at the End of the Millennium: Anth* (Green Mountains Rev, 1997), *A First Light: Anth* (Calypso Pub, 1997), *Tampa Rev, Poetry, Zone 3*

George Gott   P
804 N 19 St
Superior, WI 54880-2902, 715-394-7512
     Pubs: *Here & There* (Linwood Pub, 1989), *Birds & Horses* (Poetry North Rev, 1984)

John Goulet 🎤 ✈   W
3489 N Frederick Ave
Milwaukee, WI 53211-2902, 414-332-5141
Internet: goulet@csd.uwm.edu
     Pubs: *Yvette in America* (Colorado U Pr, 2000), *Oh's Profit* (Morrow, 1975), *Brooklyn Rev, Alaska Qtly Rev, Denver Qtly, Crescent Rev, Folio, Sonoro Rev, Intro*

David M. Graham 🎤 ✈   P
215 Elm St
Ripon, WI 54971-1441, 920-748-5806
Internet: grahamd@mail.ripon.edu
     Pubs: *Greatest Hits 1975-2000* (Pudding House 2001), *Stutter Monk, A Mind of Winter* (Flume Pr, 2000, 2000), *Doggedness* (Devil's Millhopper Pr, 1991), *Second Wind* (Texas Tech U Pr, 1990), *Magic Shows* (Cleveland State U Poetry Ctr, 1986)

R. Chris Halla 🎤 ✈   P&W
1724 N Whitney Dr
Appleton, WI 54914, 920-731-2257
Internet: shagbark@vbe.com
     Pubs: *Water* (Wolfsong, 1994), *Northeast, Seems, Poetry Now*

C. J. Hribal 🎤 ✈   W
2831 W McKinley Blvd
Milwaukee, WI 53208-2928, 414-933-3555
Internet: cjhribal@marquette.edu
     Pubs: *The Clouds in Memphis* (U Mass Pr, 2000), *American Beauty* (S&S, 1987), *Matty's Heart, The Boundaries of Twilight: Anth* (New Rivers Pr, 1984, 1991)

Ellen Hunnicutt   W
PO Box 62
Big Bend, WI 53103-0062, 262-662-2740
Internet: wh@execpc.com
   Pubs: *Suite for Calliope* (Walker & Co, 1987), *In the Music Library* (U Pitt Pr, 1987), *The Whole Story: Anth* (Bench Pr, 2000), *Flash Fiction: Anth* (Norton, 1992), *Story, Prairie Schooner, Cimarron Rev, Indiana Rev*

John Judson   P
1310 Shorewood Dr
La Crosse, WI 54601
   Pubs: *The Years Before the Braves Left Boston* (Shagbark Pr, 2000), *The Inardo Poems, Muse(sic)* (Juniper Pr, 1996, 1993), *The Baseball Poems, My Father's Brown Sweater: Anth* (Page Five, 1992, 1996), *The Long Story, Poem, Elysian Fields, NAR, Ohio Rev*

Reinhold Johannes Kaebitzsch   P
PO Box 3495
Madison, WI 53704-0495, 608-241-3949
   Pubs: *Red Snow, Quiscunsin, Papagaio* (Red Mountain, 1992, 1986, 1983), *Piankeshaw on Blue Horses* (White Anvil, 1983)

John Koethe 🎤 ✈   P
2666 N Hackett Ave
Milwaukee, WI 53211, 414-964-5107
   Pubs: *North Point North: New and Selected Poems, The Constructor, Falling Water* (HC, 2002, 1999, 1997), *The Late Wisconsin Spring* (Princeton U Pr, 1984)

David Kubach   P
404 N Walbridge Ave, #6
Madison, WI 53714, 608-244-2538
   Pubs: *First Things* (Holmgangers Pr, 1980), *Wisconsin Poetry: Anth* (Wisconsin Academy of Sciences, Arts, & Letters, 1991), *Painted Bride Qtly, Slant*

Donald D. Kummings   P
Univ Wisconsin-Parkside, English Dept, Kenosha, WI 53141, 262-595-2525
   Pubs: *The Open Road Trip* (Geryon Pr, 1989), *The Dolphin's Arc: Anth* (SCOP Productions, 1989)

D. J. Lachance 🎤 ✈   W
1722 N 58 St
Milwaukee, WI 53208-1618, 414-453-4678
Internet: djlachance@usa.net
   Pubs: *Inside Grief: Anth* (Wise Pr, 2001), *Poetry Motel, Book Lovers, Art Forum, Poettalk, Collages & Bricolages, The Plaza, Pleiades, Philae*

Peg Carlson Lauber 🎤 ✈   P
1105 Bradley Ave
Eau Claire, WI 54701-6520, 715-835-0363
Internet: laubermc@uwec.edu
   Pubs: *Locked in the Wayne County Courthouse, A Change in Weather* (Rhiannon Pr, 1980, 1978), *Kalliope, Wind, Synaesthetic, Poetry Motel, Georgetown Rev, River Oak Rev, Windhover, Pike Creek Rev, Snail's Pace, Lucid Stone, Hodgepodge*

John Lehman 🎤 ✈   P&W
315 E Water St
Cambridge, WI 53523, 608-235-2377
Internet: santerra@aol.com
   Pubs: *Greatest Unknown Poet* (Zelda Wilde Pubs, 2002), *Dogs Dream of Running* (Salmon Run Pr, 2001), *Shrine of the Tooth Fairy* (Cambridge Bk Rev Pr, 1998), *Wisconsin Academy Rev, Free Verse, Cup of Poems, Cambridge Book Rev, Rosebud*

Carl Lindner   P
Univ Wisconsin-Parkside, Box 2000, Kenosha, WI 53141, 414-595-2392
Internet: lindnerc@it.uwp.edu
   Pubs: *Shooting Baskets in a Dark Gymnasium* (Linwood, 1984), *Vampire* (Spoon River Poetry Pr, 1977), *Poetry, Slant, Literary Rev, Iowa Rev, Greensboro Rev*

Karen Loeb 🎤 ✈   P&W
Univ Wisconsin-Eau Claire, English Dept, Eau Claire, WI 54702, 715-836-3140
Internet: loebk@uwec.edu
   Pubs: *Jump Rope Queen & Other Stories* (New Rivers Pr, 1993), *100 Percent Pure Florida Fiction Anth* (U Pr Florida, 2000), *If I Had a Hammer: Anth* (Papier-Mache Pr, 1990), *Crania OnLine, Widener Rev, Lullwater Rev, South Dakota Rev, Footworks*

Arthur Madson   P
419 Pleasant
Whitewater, WI 53190, 414-473-4791
   Pubs: *Blue-Eyed Boy* (Lake Shore Pub, 1993), *Coming Up Sequined* (Fireweed Pr, 1990), *Midwest Poetry Rev, Samisdat, Anemone, South Carolina Rev, Wisconsin Academy Rev*

David Martin 🎤 ✈   P
7123 Cedar St
Wauwatosa, WI 53213
Internet: damartin64@aol.com
   Pubs: *Seattle Rev, Red Cedar Rev, Oyez Rev, Qtly West, Cream City Rev, Wisconsin Rev, College English, Slant, Poetry Motel*

Tom McKeown 🎙 ✈   P
1220 N Gammon Rd
Middleton, WI 53562-3806, 608-836-1612
    Pubs: *Three Hundred Tigers* (Zephyr Pub, 1994), *Invitation of the Mirrors* (Wisconsin Rev Pr, 1985), *New Yorker, Nation, Yale Rev, Atlantic, Harper's, Commonweal*

Lee Merrill 🎙 ✈   P
217 E 3 St
Washburn, WI 54891, 715-373-2300
Internet: lmerrill@cheqwet.net
    Pubs: *Seven Lake Superior Poets: Anth* (Bear Cult Pr, 1979), *Plainsong, Great Lakes Rev, Northeast*

Stephen M. Miller   P
Univ Wisconsin Press, 2537 Daniels St, Madison, WI 53718-6772, 608-224-3882
    Pubs: *Backwaters* (Peridot Pr, 1983), *The Last Camp in America* (Midwestern Writers Pub Hse, 1982), *Midatlantic Rev, Stardancer, Rolling Stone*

Oscar Mireles 🎙 ✈   P
1301 Wheeler Rd
Madison, WI 53704
danenet.wicip.org/latino
    Pubs: *Black & Brown begin with the letter "B", I Didn't Know There Were Latinos in Wisconsin: 30 Hispanic Writers: Anth, Weehcohnson Latino Writers: Anth, Second Generation: Anth* (Focus Communications Inc, 2000, 1999, 1998, 1985), *U.S. Latino Rev*

Mary Moran   P&W
PO Box 3012
Madison, WI 53704
    Pubs: *In Celebration of the Muse* (M Pr, 1987), *Fireworks!* (Women's Pr, 1987), *Sinister Wisdom*

Sandra Sylvia Nelson 🎙 ✈   P&W
4519 S Pine Ave
Milwaukee, WI 53207-5210, 414-294-0280
    Pubs: *Exploring Poetry: Anth, Exploring Literature: Anth* (Longman, 2002, 2001), *Hard Choices: Anth* (Iowa Rev Pr, 1996), *Yankee, Iowa Rev, Ms., Mid-American Rev, NAR, Virginia Qtly Rev, BPJ*

Mary F. O'Sullivan   W
N 1079 Lauterbach Rd
La Crosse, WI 54601
    Pubs: *Webs Inviolate, Common Lives/Lesbian Lives, Earth's Daughters, Touchstone*

Franco Pagnucci 🎙 ✈   P
8717 Mockingbird Road
Platteville, WI 53818-9763, 608-348-8662
Internet: fpagnucci@yahoo.com
    Pubs: *Ancient Moves, I Never Had a Pet* (Bur Oak Pr, 1998, 1992), *Out Harmsen's Way* (Fireweed Pr, 1991), *Best American Poetry: Anth* (Scribner, 1999), *American Voices: Anth* (Mayfield, 1996), *College English*

Susan Peterson   P
Box 81
Ephraim, WI 54211
    Pubs: *Preparing the Fields* (Spoon River Poetry Pr, 1985), *Cincinnati Poetry Rev, Calliope*

Sara Rath 🎙 ✈   P&W
1605 Legion Dr
Elm Grove, WI 53122-1706, 262-789-8618
Internet: sararath@aol.com
    Pubs: *Dancing with a Cowboy* (Wisconsin Academy of Sciences, Arts & Letters, 1991), *Remembering the Wilderness* (Northword Pr, 1983), *Boston Rev, Green Mountains, Arkham Collector, Contemporary Rev, Great River Rev, Wisconsin Academy Rev*

Jocelyn Riley 🎙 ✈   W
PO Box 5264
Madison, WI 53705, 608-271-7083
Internet: herownword@aol.com
    Pubs: *Crazy Quilt, Only My Mouth Is Smiling* (Bantam, 1986, 1986), *Wisconsin Woman, Wisconsin Trails, Wisconsin Academy Rev, Buffalo Spree, Spokane Woman, Crossing Press Anth*

Sheila Roberts   P&W
Univ Wisconsin, English Dept, PO Box 413, Milwaukee, WI 53201-0413, 414-229-4530
    Pubs: *Purple Yams* (Penguin, 2001), *Daughters & Other Dutiful Women: Poems, Coming In* (Justified Pr, 1995, 1993), *New Contrast, Printed Matter*

Tobin F. Rockey   P
PO Box 795
Green Bay, WI 54305, 414-437-6608
    Pubs: *Bitterroot, Above the Bridge, Wisconsin Poets, Peninsula Rev, Around the Bay, Baybury Rev*

William Robert Rodriguez   P
1802 Redwood Ln
Madison, WI 53711-3332, 608-274-2096
    Pubs: *the shoe shine parlor poems* (Ghost Pony Pr, 1984), *A Multicultural Reader II: Anth* (Perfection Learning Co, 2000), *Welcome to Your Life: Anth* (Milkweed, 1998), *The Party Train: Anth* (New Rivers Pr, 1996)

Andrew J. Roffers   W
14022 W Tiffany Pl
New Berlin, WI 53151, 262-784-3729
    Pubs: *Short Story Forum, My Legacy, Penny-A-Liner, Expressions Jrnl*

Martin Jack Rosenblum 🎤 ✈ P
2521 E Stratford Court
Shorewood, WI 53211-2635, 414-332-7474
  Pubs: *Spirit Fugitive* (Holy Ranger Texts, 2002), *Places to Go, No Freedom, Honey, Down on the Spirit Farm* (Wheel to Reel Pub, 2001, 2000, 1993), *The Holy Ranger: Harley-Davidson Poems* (Ranger Intl, 1989), *Conjunction* (Lion Pub, 1987)

Lisa M. Ruffolo W
2125 Chamberlain Ave
Madison, WI 53705-3977
  Pubs: *Tanzania on Tuesday, Holidays* (New Rivers Pr, 1997, 1987), *Voices That We Carry* (Guernica, 1993), *From the Margin: Anth* (Purdue U Pr, 1991), *Mademoiselle, Cosmopolitan*

R.M. Ryan 🎤 ✈ P&W
332 E Acacia Rd
Milwaukee, WI 53217-4234, 414-352-2902
  Pubs: *The Golden Rules* (Hi Jinx Pr, 1998), *Goldilocks in Later Life, Yellow Shoe Poets: Anth* (LSU, 1980, 1999), *Dreams & Secrets: Anth* (Woodland Pattern Bk Ctr, 1993), *Faultline, Light, New Republic, ACM, Exquisite Corpse, Wisconsin Academy Rev*

Ted Schaefer 🎤 ✈ P&W
403 Center St
Lake Geneva, WI 53147-1905, 262-248-7729
Internet: trish@genevaonline.com
  Pubs: *The Summer People* (Singing Wind Pr, 1978), *After Drought* (Raindust Pr, 1976), *From A to Z: Anth* (Swallow, 1981), *Village Voice, Story Qtly, New Letters, Kansas Qtly, Wisconsin Rev, ACM, Chariton Rev, Webster Rev, NW Rev, Cottonwood Rev*

Willa Schmidt P&W
2020 University Ave, #317
Madison, WI 53705-3965
  Pubs: *Crimson Online, Ambergris, Iowa Woman, St. Anthony Messenger*

Robert Schuler 🎤 ✈ P
E 4549 479th Ave
Menomonie, WI 54751, 715-235-6525
Internet: schulerr@uwstout.edu
  Pubs: *Red Cedar Suite* (Friends of the Red Cedar Trail, 1999), *Grace: A Book of Days* (Wolfsong Pr, 1995), *Blueline: Anth* (Syracuse U Pr, 2003), *Imagining Home, Inheriting the Earth: Anths* (U Minnesota Pr, 1995, 1993), *Hummingbird, Caliban, Northeast*

John Kingsley Shannon P&W
200 S Vincennes Cir
Racine, WI 53402
  Pubs: *Loom, The Shrine of the White Owl, Randy, Hosea Jackson* (Caledonia Pr, 1992, 1991, 1983, 1980)

Lynn Shoemaker P
172 N Esterly Ave
Whitewater, WI 53190
  Pubs: *Hands* (Lynx Hse Pr, 1982), *Dreams & Secrets: Anth* (Woodland Pattern Book Center, 1993), *Poet Lore, Salthouse, Oxford Mag, Groundswell*

Alan Shucard P
Univ Wisconsin-Parkside, Box 2000, Kenosha, WI 53141-2000, 414-595-2392
  Pubs: *Modern American Poetry: 1865-1950, American Poetry: The Puritans Through Walt Whitman* (Twayne, 1989, 1988)

Mary Shumway P
PO Box 815
Plover, WI 54467-0815
  Pubs: *Legends & Other Voices: Selected & New Poems, Practicing Vivaldi* (Juniper Pr, 1992, 1981)

Shoshauna Shy 🎤 ✈ P
878 Woodrow St
Madison, WI 53711-1959, 608-238-7937
Internet: shaunshy@netscape.net
  Pubs: *Poetry NW, Comstock Rev, West Wind Rev, Samsara Qtly*

Robert Siegel P&W
Univ Wisconsin, PO Box 413, English Dept, Milwaukee, WI 53201, 414-229-4511
  Pubs: *White Whale, Whalesong* (Harper SF, 1991, 1991), *In a Pig's Eye* (Florida, 1985), *Cream City Rev, Sewanee Rev, Atlantic*

Carol Sklenicka 🎤 ✈ W
332 E Acacia Rd
Milwaukee, WI 53217
Internet: sklen@mixcom.com
  Pubs: *Dreams & Secrets: Anth* (Woodland Pattern, 1993), *Clackamas Lit Rev, Iowa Woman, Sou'wester, Confrontation, Cream City Rev, Military Lifestyle, Transactions*

Thomas R. Smith 🎤 ✈ P
523 State St
River Falls, WI 54022-2237, 715-425-2137
Internet: thosmith@spacestar.net
  Pubs: *The Dark Indigo Current, Horse of Earth* (Holy Cow! Pr, 2000, 1994), *Best American Poetry: Anth* (Scribner, 1999), *Witness, The Thousands, Bitter Oleander, Agni, Bloomsbury Rev*

Angela Sorby P
Marquette Univ, PO Box 1881, Milkwaukee, WI 53201-1881, 414-288-7263
Internet: sorby@marquette.edu
  Pubs: *Distance Learning* (New Issues Pr, 1998)

Robert Spiess P
Modern Haiku, PO Box, Madison, WI 53701-1752,
608-233-2738
Pubs: *Modern Haiku*

David Steingass P
1510 Drake St
Madison, WI 53711
Pubs: *New Roads Old Towns: Anth* (U Wisconsin Platteville
Pr, 1988), *Poetry, Mid-American Rev, Northeast*

Porter Stewart P
Milwaukee Inner City Council, 642 W North Ave, Milwaukee,
WI 53212
Pubs: *Passing By* (U Connecticut Lutheran Church, 1970),
Ethiop, The Flame

Ingrid Swanberg ♀ ✈ P
PO Box 260113
Madison, WI 53726-0113, 608-238-0175
Internet: ghostponypress@hotmail.com
Pubs: *Eight Poems* (Light & Dust, 2001), *Letter to
Persephone & Other Poems* (Rhiannon Pr, 1984),
*Northeast, Lips, Wisconsin Academy Rev, Orisis, Le
Geupard*

Bruce Taylor P
Univ Wisconsin, English Dept, Eau Claire, WI 54702,
715-836-2639
Internet: taylorb@uwec.edu
Pubs: *Why That Man Talks That* (Upriver Pr, 1994), *This Day*
(Juniper Pr, 1993), *Poetry, Nation, Chicago Rev, NW Rev,
Gulf Coast, NYQ*

Marilyn L. Taylor ♀ ✈ P
2825 E Newport Ave
Milwaukee, WI 53211-2922, 414-332-3455
Internet: mlt@csd.uwm.edu
Pubs: *Greatest Hits* (Pudding Hse Pubs, 2001), *Exit Only*
(Anamnesis Pr, 2001), *Shadows Like These* (Wm. Caxton,
1994), *New Voices: Anth* (Academy of Amer Poets, 2001),
Smaller Than God: Anth (Black Moss, 2001), *Claiming the
Spirit: Anth* (Beacon, 1996)

Alison Townsend ♀ ✈ P
1409 Lake Kegonsa Rd
Stoughton, WI 53589, 608-873-8304
Internet: townsena@mail.uww.edu
Pubs: *The Blue Dress* (White Pine Pr, 2003), *What the Body
Knows* (Parallel Pr, 2002), *Fruitflesh: Anth* (Harper San
Francisco, 2002), *Boomer Girls: Anth* (Univ of Iowa, 1999),
Claiming the Spirit Within: Anth (Beacon Pr, 1996),
Southern Rev, NAR, Nimrod

Dennis Trudell ♀ ✈ P
309 N Brearly St
Madison, WI 53703-1601
Pubs: *Fragments in Us: Recent & Earlier Poems* (U
Wisconsin Pr, 1996), *Full Court: Basketball Literary Anth*
(Breakaway Bks, 1996), *O. Henry Prize Stories: Anth*
(Northwoods Pr, 1994)

Barbara Vroman ♀ ✈ W
N4721 9th Dr
Hancock, WI 54943-7617, 715-249-5407
Pubs: *Linger Not at Chebar: A Novel of Burma* (Angel Pr
Wisconsin, 1992), *Sons of Thunder, Tomorrow Is a River*
(Phunn Pub, 1981, 1977)

Ronald Wallace ♀ ✈ P
Univ Wisconsin, English Dept, 600 N Park, Madison, WI
53706, 608-263-3705
Internet: rwallace@facstaff.wisc.edu
Pubs: *Quick Bright Things* (Mid-List, 2000), *Long for this
World: New & Selected Poems, The Uses of Adversity,
Time's Fancy* (U Pitt Pr, 2003, 1998, 1994), *Paris Rev,
Ploughshares, Southern Rev, Poetry, Poetry NW*

Larry Watson P&W
English Dept, Univ Wisconsin, Stevens Point, WI 54481,
715-346-4757
Internet: lwatson@uwspmail.uwsp.edu
Pubs: *Justice, Montana 1948* (Milkweed Edtns, 1995, 1993),
Leaving Dakota (Song Pr, 1983), *NER, Black Warrior Rev,
Cimarron Rev, Gettysburg Rev, Kansas Qtly*

Marvin Weaver P
Wisconsin Arts Board, 131 W Wilson St, #301, Madison, WI
53702, 608-266-0190
Pubs: *Hearts & Gizzards* (Curveship Pr, 1977),
Contemporary North Carolina Poetry: Anth (Blair, 1977)

J. D. Whitney P
829 E Thomas St
Wausau, WI 54403-6448, 715-843-5533
Internet: jdwhitne@uwcmail.uwc.edu
Pubs: *What Grandmother Says* (March Street Pr, 1994), *sd*
(Spoon River Poetry Pr, 1988), *Word of Mouth* (Juniper,
1986)

Doris T. Wight P
122 8th Ave
Baraboo, WI 53913-2109, 608-356-6997
Internet: dorisight@charter.net
Pubs: *Seeking Promethean Woman in the New Poetry*
(Peter Lang, 1988), *Christian Science Monitor, Mississippi
Valley Rev, Yale Jrnl of Law & Feminism, Language & Style,
Wisconsin Rev, Dekalb Literary Arts Jrnl*

Jeffrey Winke 🎤 ✈   P
1705 N 68 St
Wauwatosa, WI 53213-2307, 414-453-3244
Internet: win9@earthlink.net
 Pubs: *Row of Pine* (Distant Thunder Pr, 1994), *Against
 Natural Impulse* (Boog Lit, 1992)

Karl Young   P
7112 27th Ave
Kenosha, WI 53143-5218
Internet: lndb@concentric.net
 Pubs: *Milestones Set 1* (Landlocked Pr, 1987), *To Dream
 Kalapuya* (Truck Pr, 1977), *Poems for the Millennium, Vol 2:
 Anth* (U California Pr, 1998)

Christina Zawadiwsky 🎤 ✈   P
1641 N Humboldt
Milwaukee, WI 53202-2111, 414-272-4592
Internet: xristia@evrosport.com
 Pubs: *Desperation, Isolation, What Will Be, I Began to
 Dream* (Where the Waters Meet, 1999, 1998, 1997, 1996),
 The Hand on the Head of Lazarus (Ion Bks, 1986)

Paul Zimmer   P
Box 1068, Rt 1, Soldiers Grove, WI 54655, 608-624-5742
 Pubs: *Crossing to Sunlight: Selected Poems* (U Georgia Pr,
 1996), *Big Blue Train* (U Arkansas Pr, 1994), *Georgia Rev,
 Southern Rev, Gettysburg Rev, Poetry NW, NER, Prairie
 Schooner, Harper's*

WYOMING

Martha Clark Cummings   W
111 E Arapahoe #1
Thermopolis, WY 82443, 307-864-2235
Internet: mcumngs@trib.com
 Pubs: *Mono Lake* (Rowbarge Pr, 1995), *Love's Shadow*
 (Crossing Pr, 1993), *Common Lives/Lesbian Lives, Pearl,
 NAR, Kalliope, Hurricane Alice, Sojourner*

Richard F. Fleck   P&W
English Dept, Univ Wyoming, Laramie, WY 82071,
307-766-2650
 Pubs: *Deep Woods* (Peregrine Smith, 1990), *Earthen
 Wayfarer* (Writers Hse, 1988), *Trumpeter*

Dainis Hazners   P&W
PO Box 442
Story, WY 82842-0442
 Pubs: *Plains Poetry Rev, South Carolina Rev, South Florida
 Poetry Rev, North Dakota Qtly, Alaska Qtly Rev, SPR,
 Connecticut River Rev, Apocalypse*

Charles Levendosky 🎤 ✈   P
714 E 22 St
Casper, WY 82601, 307-237-0884
Internet: levendos@trib.com
 Pubs: *Circle of Light* (High Plains Pr, 1995), *Hands & Other
 Poems* (Point Riders Pr, 1986), *Dacotah Territory, Poetry
 Now, Poetry On, Poetry Rev, APR, Northern Lights*

Vicki Lindner   W
Univ Wyoming, Box 3353, Laramie, WY 82071, 307-766-2384
 Pubs: *Outlaw Games* (Dial Pr, 1982), *Ploughshares, Kenyon
 Rev, Northern Lights, Terrain, Gastronomica, New York
 Stories*

W. Dale Nelson 🎤 ✈   P&W
1719 Downey St
Laramie, WY 82072-1918, 307-742-0737
 Pubs: *Interim, Imago, Small Pond, Western Humanities Rev,
 New Yorker, Antietam Rev, NW Rev, Poetry NW, Yankee,
 Blue Unicorn*

C. L. Rawlins   P&W
PO Box 51
Boulder, WY 82923, 307-537-5298
 Pubs: *In Gravity National Park* (U Nevada Pr, 1998), *Broken
 Country, Sky's Witness* (H Holt, 1996, 1993), *A Ceremony
 on Bare Ground* (Utah State Pr, 1985), *Ploughshares,
 Poetry Ireland, Poetry Wales, NAR*

Tom Rea 🎤 ✈   P
1756 S Chestnut St
Casper, WY 82601-4531, 307-235-9021
Internet: trea@trib.com
 Pubs: *Smith & Other Poems* (Dooryard Pr, 1985), *Man in a
 Rowboat* (Copper Canyon Pr, 1977), *What Have You Lost?:
 Anth* (Greenwillow Bks, 1999)

David Romtvedt 🎤 ✈   P&W
457 N Main
Buffalo, WY 82834-1732, 307-684-2194
Internet: romtvedt@wyoming.com
 Pubs: *Certainty* (White Pine Pr, 1996), *A Flower Whose
 Name I Do Not Know* (Copper Canyon Pr, 1992)

Tim Sandlin   W
Box 1974
Jackson, WY 83001, 307-733-1212
Internet: 71430.2262@compuserve.com
 Pubs: *Social Blunders, Sorrow Floats, Skipped Parts*
 (H Holt, 1995, 1992, 1991)

Stephen J. Thorpe   W
117 1/2 W Wentworth St
Newcastle, WY 82701
 Pubs: *Walking Wounded* (Bantam, 1984), *Encounter,
 California Qtly, Smackwarm*

AFRICA

Don Meredith   W
Lamu Island, PO Box 173, Kenya, Africa
Internet: lamupoly@africaonline.co.ke
  Pubs: *Where the Tigers Were* (U South Carolina Pr, 2001),
  Wing Walking & Other Stories (Texas Rev Pr, 2001), *Home
  Movies, Morning Line* (Avon, 1982, 1980), *Folio, Kingfisher,
  Greensboro Rev, Texas Rev, Slipstream, Short Story Rev*

ARABIAN GULF

Dione A. Tongal 🎤 ✈   P&W
c/o Dod M. Tongal, c/o NODCO, PO Box 50033, Boha, Qatar,
Arabian Gulf
Internet: cuddlycuttie13@hotmail.com
  Pubs: *That Morning Star Girl* (Upstream Productions 1999)

AUSTRALIA

Jeri Kroll 🎤 ✈   P
29 Methuen St
Fitzroy, Adelaide 5082, South Australia
Internet: jeri.kroll@flinders.edu.au
  Pubs: *Riding the Blues* (Lothian, 2001), *Fit for a Prince*
  (Omnibus, 2001), *Beyond Blue, Better than Blue* (Longman,
  1998, 1997), *Bruise, Goliath* (Longman, 1998), *Storie, the
  write side/Pomeriggio/Afternoon/ten to six: Anth* (Leconte,
  2001), *Salt, Southern Rev*

Joan Nestle 🎤 ✈   P&W
c/o D. Olto, Carlton 3053, 17/261 Nicholson St,
Australia 03-9348-1491
Internet: joannenestle@aol.com
  Pubs: *Gender Queer: Voices from Beyond the Binary*
  (Alyson Pubs, 2002), *A Fragile Union* (Cleis Pr, 1998), *A
  Restricted Country* (Pandora, 1996), *Vintage Bk of Intl
  Lesbian Fiction* (Vintage, 1999), *Women on Women 3: Anth*
  (Plume, 1996)

Laura Jan Shore   P&W
Lot 1 Johnsons Rd, Huonbrook 2482 NSW, Australia
  Pubs: *The Sacred Moon Tree* (Bradbury Pr, 1986), *Croton
  Rev, Blue Unicorn, WomanSource*

AUSTRIA

Herbert Kuhner 🎤 ✈   P&W
Gentzgasse 14/4/11
A-1180 Vienna, Austria, 014792469
Internet: harry.k@vienna.at
  Pubs: *Love of Austria* (Vienna; Apple Pub, 1998), *Minki the
  Nazi Cat & the Human Side* (Verlag der Theodor Kramer
  Gesellschaft, 1998), *Will the Stars Fall* (Austrian Lit Forum,
  1995)

BELGIUM

David Henson   P
Avenue Jacques Pastur 18, B-1180 Uccle, Belgium
  Pubs: *Wedging Oaks Into Acorns* (Uzza No Pr, 1979),
  Pikestaff Forum, Laurel Rev, Poetry Now

Phillip Sterling   P&W
Rue Garde Dieu, 33, 4031 Angleur, Belgium
  Pubs: *Passages North, Seneca Rev, South Florida Poetry
  Rev, Slant, MacGuffin, Hayden's Ferry Rev, Sucarnochee
  Rev*

BOLIVIA

Richard Hughes 🎤 ✈   W
Casilla 6572, Torres Sofer, Cochabamba, Bolivia
  Pubs: *Isla Grande* (Silver Mountain Pr, 1994)

BOTSWANA

Keorapetse William Kgositsile   P
Univ Botswana, Private Bag 0022, Gabarone, Botswana

CANADA

Robert Allen   P
Box 169, Ayer's Cliff, Quebec J0B 1C0, Canada, 819-838-5921
  Pubs: *The Hawryliw Process: Vol II, Vol I* (Porcupine's Quill
  Pr, 1981, 1980)

Bert Almon 🎤 ✈   P
Univ of Alberta, English Dept, Edmonton, Alberta T6G 2E5,
Canada, 403-492-7809
Internet: Bert.Almon@ualberta.ca
  Pubs: *Hesitation Before Birth* (Beach Holme, 2002), *Mind
  the Gap* (Ekstasis, 1998), *Earth Prime* (Brick, 1995), *Calling
  Texas* (Thistledown Pr, 1990), *TLS, Southern Rev, Malahat
  Rev, Poetry East, Chicago Rev, Poetry Durham, Orbis*

George Amabile   P
Univ Manitoba, English Dept, Winnipeg, Manitoba R3R 2N2,
Canada, 204-453-3107
  Pubs: *The Presence of Fire* (McClelland & Stewart, 1982),
  Ideas of Shelter (Turnstone, 1981), *Saturday Night,
  Canadian Lit, Canadian Fiction Mag*

Margaret Atwood 🎤 ✈   P&W
c/o Jennifer Osti, Asst to M Atwood, McClelland & Stewart,
481 University Ave, Ste 800, Toronto, Ontario, Canada
  Pubs: *Blind Ambition, Alias Grace* (Nan A Talese Bks, 2002,
  1996), *Morning in the Burned House* (HM, 1995), *The
  Handmaid's Tale* (HM, 1986)

Peter Aroniawenrate Blue Cloud P&W
Box 86, Kahnawake, Quebec J0L 1B0, Canada
  Pubs: *Clans of Many Nations, The Other Side of Nowhere, Elderberry Flute Song* (White Pine Pr, 1995, 1990, 1988)

Richard Emil Braun 🎤 P
PO Box 178, Errington, BC V0R 1V0, Canada
Internet: krbraun@bcsupernet.com
  Pubs: *The Snow Man Is No One* (Corriedale Pr, 2001), *Last Man In* (Jargon Society, 1990)

Robert Clayton Casto P
67 Forman Ave, Toronto, Ontario M4S 2R4, Canada
  Pubs: *The Arrivals* (The Studio Pr, 1980), *Midatlantic Rev, Waves, NYQ, New Orleans Rev*

Ann Copeland W
Carol Bonnett, MGA, 10 Saint Mary St, Ste 510
Toronto, Ontario M4Y 1P9, Canada, 416-964-3302
  Pubs: *The Back Room* (HC, 1991), *The Golden Thread* (Viking Penguin, 1989)

James Deahl P
237 Prospect St S
Hamilton, Ontario L8M 2Z6, Canada, 905-312-1779
  Pubs: *Even This Land Was Born of Light* (Moonstone Pr, 1993), *Heartland, Opening the Stone Heart* (Envoi Poets Pubs, 1993, 1992)

John Ditsky P
English Dept, Univ Windsor
Windsor, Ontario N9B 3P4, Canada, 313-963-6112
  Pubs: *Friend & Lover* (Ontario Rev, 1981), *New Letters, Ontario Rev, Fiddlehead, NAR*

Magie Dominic 🎤 ✈ P
c/o League of Canadian Poets, Toronto, ON M5T 1A5, 54
Wolsely St, Canada, 4164868525
Internet: magiedominic@hotmail.com
  Pubs: *Countering the Myths: Anth, Outrage: Anth* (Women's Pr, 1996, 1993), *The Village Voice, Toronto Globe & Mail, New York Times, Pottersfield Portfolio, Prairie Jrnl, ARC*

Real Faucher P
82 Main St N, Windsor
Quebec J1S 2C6, Canada, 819-845-4446
  Pubs: *Touching the Emptiness* (Ansuda Pr, 1983), *Fires & Crucifixions* (Samisdat Pr, 1980), *Wind*

John Bart Gerald W
206 St Patrick's St
Ottawa, Ontario K1N 5K3, Canada, 613-241-1312
  Pubs: *Internal Exile, New Englanders, Geometry* (Gerald & Maas, 1992, 1992, 1989)

Joanna McClelland Glass
400 Walmer Road, Apt 2308, Toronto, M5P 2X7, Canada
Internet: kate1129105@cs.com
  Pubs: *Woman Wanted* (St. Martin's Pr, 1985), *Reflections on a Mountain Summer* (Knopf, 1974)

Carole Glasser-Langille 🎤 ✈ P
Lunenburg County, PO Box 1531, Nova Scotia B0J 2C0, Canada, 9026343187
Internet: carole.langille@ns.sympatico.ca
  Pubs: *Late in a Slow Time* (Mansfield Pr, 2003), *In Cannon Cave* (Brick Bks, 1997), *All That Glitters in Water* (New Poetry Series, 1990), *Words Out There: Anth* (Roseway Pr, 2000)

Roger Greenwald 🎤 ✈ P
Innis College, 2 Sussex Ave, Univ Toronto, Toronto, Ontario M5S 1J5, Canada, 4169782662
Internet: roger@chass.utoronto.ca
  Pubs: *Connecting Flight* (Williams-Wallace, 1993), *Pequod, Saturday Night, Prism Intl, Great River Rev, Texas Observer, Leviathan Qtly*

Jane Eaton Hamilton 🎤 ✈ P&W
Vancouver BC, Hillcrest Park POB 74056, Vancouver, BC V5V 5C8, Canada, 604 4379492
Internet: jane@janeeatonhamilton.com
  Pubs: *Hunger* (Oberon Pr, 2002), *Going Santa Fe* (League of Canadian Poets, 1997), *Steam-Cleaning Love, Body Rain* (Brick Bks, 1993, 1991), *July Nights and Other Stories* (Douglas and McIntyre, 1992)

Mark Holmgren P
11119 72 Ave, Edmonton, Alberta T6G 0B3, Canada
  Pubs: *Poetry Now, Syncline, Paper Bag Poems, Nit Wit, Small Pond, Dark Horse*

Lewis Horne W
1213 Elliott St,
Saskatoon, SK S7N 0V5, Canada, 3062444145
  Pubs: *What Do Ducks Do in Winter* (Signature Bks, 1993), *The Seventh Day* (Thistledown, 1982), *Barrow Street, Other Voices, Fiddlehead, Colorado Rev, South Dakota Rev, Canadian Fiction Mag, Greensboro Rev, Southern Rev*

Mary Stewart Kean P&W
14981 Beachview Ave
White Rock, BC V4B 1P2, Canada
  Pubs: *Critical Minutes* (Rocky Ledge Cottage Edtns, 1985), *Bombay Gin, Windhorse, Camera*

W. P. Kinsella 🎤 ✈ W
9442 Nowell
Chilliwack, BC V2P 4X7, Canada, 6047939716
Internet: buzzard2_99@yahoo.com
  Pubs: *Shoeless Joe* (Mariner Bks, 1999), *The Secret of the Northern Lights* (Thistledown Pr, 1998), *If Wishes Were Horses, The Winter Helen Dropped By, The Dixon Cornbelt League, Brother Frank's Gospel Hour, Box Socials* (HC, 1997, 1995, 1994, 1992, 1991)

William Kuhns   W
RR1, Alcove, Quebec J0X 1A0, Canada, 819-459-2523

Peter Levitt 🎤 ✈   P
121 Central Ave
Salt Spring Island BC V8K 2P4, Canada, 2505379795
Internet: levgram@saltspring.com
    Pubs: *One Hundred Butterflies; Bright Root, Dark Root*
(Broken Moon Pr, 1992, 1991), *A Book of Light* (Amargi Pr,
1982), *Poetry/L.A.*

Judith McCombs   P
67 Sullivan St
Toronto, Ontario M5T 1C2, Canada
    Pubs: *Against Nature: Wilderness Poems* (Dustbooks, 1981)

Eugene McNamara 🎤 ✈   P&W
English Dept, Univ Windsor, Windsor, Ontario N9B 2T3,
Canada
    Pubs: *Waterfalls* (Coteau Bks, 2000), *Forcing the Field: New
& Selected Poems* (Mosaic Pr, 1998), *The Moving Light*
(Wolsak & Wynn, 1986), *Best Canadian Stories 90: Anth*
(Oberon Pr, 1990), *Ontario Rev, Witness*

Albert F. Moritz 🎤 ✈   P
14 Alpha Ave
Toronto, Ontario M4X 1J3, Canada
    Pubs: *Early Poems* (Insomniac, 2002), *Conflicting Desire*
(Ekstasis, 2000), *Best Amer Poetry: Anth* (Scribner, 1998),
Paris Rev, Partisan Rev, APR

Simon J. Ortiz   P&W
276 George St, Apt 204
Toronto Canada M5R2P6, 416-946-3451
    Pubs: *A Good Journey* (Sun Tracks/U Arizona Pr, 1984),
Fightin' (Thunder's Mouth Pr, 1983)

Pamela Porter 🎤 ✈   P
11347 Peregrine Pl
Sidney, BC V8L 5S3, Canada, 250-655-5204
Internet: paige1@shaw.ca
    Pubs: *Poems for the Luminous World* (Frog Hollow Pr,
2002), *Atlanta Rev, Clackamas Rev, Descant, 13th Moon,
Iowa Woman, Borderlands, Theology Today, Seattle Rev,
Phoebe, Equinox, The Other Side, Sojourner, Commonweal*

Leon Rooke   W
49 Oak St, Winnipeg, MB R3M 3P6, Canada, 2044880315
Internet: leonrooke@cs.com
    Pubs: *Who Do You Love?* (Canada; McClelland & Stewart,
1992), *A Good Baby* (Vintage, 1990), *How I Saved the
Province* (Oolichan, 1989)

Aaron Schneider 🎤 ✈   P
RR4, Baddeck
Nova Scotia B0E 1B0, Canada, 902-929-2063
Internet: rschneid@uccb.ns.ca
    Pubs: *Wild Honey* (Breton Bks, 1998), *Landmarks: Anth*
(Acorn Pr, 2001)

Robin Skelton   P
1255 Victoria Ave
Victoria, BC, V8S 4P3, Canada, 604-592-7032

Lynn Strongin 🎤   P
1370 Beach Dr, Victoria, BC V8S 2N6, Canada
Internet: yosunt@home.com
    Pubs: *Bones & Kim* (Spinsters Ink, 1980),
Countrywoman/Surgeon (L'Epervier, 1979), *Visiting Emily:
Anth* (U Iowa Pr, 2000), *Shenandoah, Southern Humanities
Rev, Prism Intl*

Audrey Thomas
RR 2, Galiano, British Columbia V0N 1P0, Canada

W. D. Valgardson 🎤 ✈   W
Creative Writing Dept/Box 1700, Univ Victoria, Victoria, BC
V8W 2Y2, Canada, 2507217306
Internet: wvalgard@uvic.ca
    Pubs: *Frances, The Divorced Kids' Club, Garbage Creek &
Other Stories, Thor* (Groundwood, 2000, 1999, 1998, 1996,
1995)

Ian Young 🎤 ✈   P
2483 Gerrard St E
Scarborough, Ontario, M1N 1W7, Canada, 416-691-9838
    Pubs: *A Day for a Lay* (Barricade, 1999), *The Mammoth
Book of Gay Short Stories* (Robinson, 1997), *Between the
Cracks* (Daedalus, 1996), *The AIDS Dissidents* (Scarecrow
Pr, 1992), *Sex Magick* (Stubblejumper Pr, 1986)

CAYMAN ISLANDS

David V. Hughey 🎤   P
International College, Newlands Campus, 595 Hirst Rd,
P0136SAU, Cayman Islands, 3459471100
Internet: dvhughley@mailcity.com
    Pubs: *Driftwood East, Orphic Lute, Piedmont Lit Rev*

DENMARK

Thomas E. Kennedy   P&W
Fragariavej 12, DK-2900 Hellerup, Denmark, 45-31-622269
    Pubs: *American Fiction: Anth* (Birch Lane, 1990), *New
Letters, Virginia Qtly Rev, New Delta Rev, Chariton Rev,
Missouri Rev, Cimarron Rev*

EGYPT

David Graham Dubois   W
76 Nile St, Apt 24, Cairo, Giza, Egypt

ENGLAND

Dannie Abse 🎤 ✈   P
85 Hodford Rd, London NW11 8NH, England, 4471458196
   Pubs: *Be Seated, Thou* (Sheep Meadow Pr, 2000),
Remembrance of Crimes Past, White Coat, Purple Coat
(Persea Bks, 1992, 1990)

Joan Alexander   W
Coachman's Cottage/33 Grove Rd, Barnes, London SW13
OHH, England, 081-876-5338
Internet: joan.cornwath@zoom.com.uk
   Pubs: *The Life of Mabel Strickland* (Progress Press, 1996),
Voices & Echoes: Tales of Colonial Women: Anth (Quartet,
1983)

Alba Ambert 🎤 ✈   P&W
Orchard House, Queens Rd, Richmond Univ, Richmond,
Surrey TW10 6JP, England, 44 208332 0526
Internet: amberta@richmond.ac.uk
   Pubs: *The Eighth Continent & Other Stories, A Perfect
Silence* (Arte Publico Pr, 1997, 1995), *The Mirror Is Always
There, The Fifth Sun* (Cactus Pub, 1992, 1989), *Americas
Rev, Mango Season, Southern California Anth*

Joan Montgomery Byles   P
The Coach House, Hinton NN135NF, England
   Pubs: *Wind, Blueline, Tickleace, The PEN*

Mary Carter   W
Amer Inst for Foreign Study, Dilke House, Malet St, London
WC1E 7JA, England
   Pubs: *Tell Me My Name* (Morrow, 1975), *A Member of the
Family* (Doubleday, 1974), *Mid-Amer Rev*

Judith Chernaik 🎤 ✈   W
Poems on the Underground, 124 Mansfield Rd, London NW3,
England, 02074851930
   Pubs: *Love's Children* (Knopf, 1992), *Leah* (Macmillan,
1987), *The Daughter* (Harper, 1981), *Double Fault* (Putnam,
1975), *TLS*

John T. Daniel   P
71 Alma Rd, Plymouth, Devon, England

Florence Elon   P
26 Whittlesex St, London SE1 8TA, England
   Pubs: *Self-Made* (Secker & Warburg, 1984), *Paris Rev,
Poetry, Sewanee Rev, New Yorker*

Ruth Fainlight 🎤 ✈   P
14 Ladbroke Terr, London W11 3PG, England
Internet: ruthfainlight@writersartists.net
   Pubs: *Selected Poems* (Sinclair-Stevenson, 1995), *Burning
Wire, Sugar-Paper Blue* (Dufour Editions, 2003, 1998), *New
Yorker, Threepenny Rev*

Martha Gelhorn   W
72 Cadogan Sq, London SW1, England

Penelope Gilliatt   W
c/o A. P. Watt, 20 John St, London C1N 2DL, England
   Pubs: *New Yorker, Hic Haec Hoc, Fat Chance*

John Lahr   W
11A Chalcott Gdns, England's Lane
Hampstead, London NW3, England

Anne Lambton   W
15 Bellevue Rd
Wandsworth Common, London SW17 7EB, England
   Pubs: *Thoroughbred Style* (Salam Hse, 1987), *Lady* (Jove
Pr, 1981), *The Daughter* (Berkley, 1978)

George Lamming   W
14A Highbury Pl, London N5, England, 212-534-2019
   Pubs: *Santeria, Bronx* (Atheneum, 1975)

Doris Lessing   W
c/o Jonathan Clowes Ltd., 10 Iron Bridge House, Bridge
Approach/London NW1 8BD, England
   Pubs: *The Real Thing: Stories & Sketches, African Laughter*
(HC, 1992, 1992), *The Fifth Child, The Good Terrorist*
(Knopf, 1988, 1987)

Liliane Lijn   P&W
99 Camden Mews, London NW1 9BU, England, 071-485-8524
Internet: lijn@lineone.net
   Pubs: *Crossing Map* (Thames & Hudson, 1983), *Six Throws
of the Oracular Keys* (Edtns Nepe, 1983)

Tom Lowenstein   P
c/o Deborah Rogers, 20 Powis Mews, Westbourn Pk Rd,
London, W11 1JN, England, 071-221-3717
   Pubs: *Filibustering in Samsara* (London; Many Pr, 1987),
Eskimo Poems From Canada & Greenland: Anth (U Pitt Pr,
1974)

Mairi MacInnes 🎤 ✈   P
31 Huntington Rd., York, Y031 8RL, England, 1904633362
Internet: mairimccormick@dial.pipex.com
   Pubs: *The Pebble* (U Illinois Pr, 2000), *The Ghostwriter,
Elsewhere & Back* (Bloodaxe, 1999, 1993), *The Quondam
Wives* (Louisiana State U Pr, 1993), *The House on the
Ridge Road* (Rowan Tree, 1988), *Herring, Oatmeal* (QRL,
1981), *Hudson Rev, New Yorker, Stand*

Joan Michelson 🎤 ✈   P&W
8 Greig Close
London, N8 8PB, England, 011442083400008
  Pubs: *Coming Late to Motherhood: Anth* (Thorsons Pub, 1984), *Calyx, Alaska Qtly Rev, Bete Noire, Panurge*

David Plante   W
c/o Deborah Rogers, 20 Powis Mews, Westbourn Pk Rd, London W11 1JN, England
  Pubs: *The Accident* (Ticknor & Fields, 1991), *The Native, Difficult Women, The Woods, The Country* (Atheneum, 1987, 1983, 1982, 1981)

Frederic Michael Raphael   W
The Wick, Langham, Colchester, Essex, England

Mary Jo Salter   P
64 Muswell Rd, London N10 2BE, England
  Pubs: *Henry Purcell in Japan* (Knopf, 1986), *New Yorker, Southwestern Rev, Atlantic*

Clancy Sigal   W
Elaine Greene Ltd
31 Newington Green, London N16, England
  Pubs: *Zone of the Interior* (Crowell, 1975), *Going Away* (HM, 1961)

Agnes Stein   P&W
1 Carlingford Rd, London NW3 1RY, England, 071-435-4858
Internet: steinage81@aol.com
  Pubs: *Color Composition, Windy Times* (Red Dust, 1985, 1984), *Cumberland Poetry. Rev, River City, Ambit, Rialto, Kansas Qtly*

Anne Stevenson 🎤 ✈   P
38 Western Hill
Durham DH1 4RJ, England, 01913862115
Internet: anne.steveson@dial.pipex.com
  Pubs: *Hearing With My Fingers* (Thumbscrew Pr, 2002), *The Collected Poems, Granny Scarecrow* (Bloodaxe Bks, 2000, 2000), *Hudson Rev, Michigan Qtly Rev, PN Rev, Partisan Rev, TLS, Stand, NER, Poetry Rev*

Ted Walker   P&W
David Higham Associates, Ltd, 115-8 Lower John St, Golden Sq, London WIR 4HA, England
  Pubs: *In Spain, Hands at a Live Fire* (Secker & Warburg, 1987, 1987)

John J. Wieners   P
Jonathan Cape, Ltd, 30 Bedford Sq, London NW3, England
  Pubs: *O! Khan Collar with Tong Tie, Selected Poems* (Black Sparrow Pr, 1988, 1986), *San Francisco Sentinel, Ten Zone*

FRANCE

Grace Andreacchi   P&W
c/o E. Hadas, BP 11, 61320 Carrouges, France
  Pubs: *Give My Heart Ease* (Permanent Pr, 1989), *Calapooya Collage*

Samuel Astrachan   W
La Juverde, 84220 Gordes, France, 90-72-00-66
  Pubs: *Malaparte in Jassy* (Wayne State U, 1989), *Katz-Cohen* (Macmillan, 1978), *Rejoice* (Dial, 1970)

Ian Ayres 🎤 ✈   P&W
1 Place du General Leclerc, 94160 Saint-Mande, France, 01133143280807
Internet: ianayres@noos.fr
  Pubs: *Private Parts* (French Connection Pr, 2002), *Fantasies Made Flesh: Anth* (Starbooks, 2002), *The HarpWeaver, Global Tapestry Jrnl, RFD, Defiance, Rattle, EIDOS, The Church-Wellesley Rev, Libido, Verandah, Cover Mag*

Nina Bogin   P
5 Rue Du Chantoiseau, Vescemont 90200 Giromagny, France, 84-29-51-80
  Pubs: *In the North* (Graywolf, 1989), *Ironwood, Agenda, Kenyon Rev, APR, Iowa Rev, Stand, CQ*

Anthony Burgess   W
44 Rue Grimaldi, Monte Carlo, Principality of Monaco, France

Roger Dickinson-Brown   P
93, Rue De L'Eglise, Bethisy-St-Martin
60320 Bethisy-St-Pierre, France, 03 44 39 51 12
Internet: clownsong2000@yahoo.com
  Pubs: *Southern Rev, Canto, Agenda, Synthesis, Song, Intermuse*

Michel R. Doret, Ph.D. 🎤 ✈   P
Editions Amon Ra, 1364 Rue de Gex, Ornex/Maconnex 01210, France, 50-41-44-87
Internet: mdor26@aol.com
  Pubs: *Les Mamelles de Lutece* (La Nouvelle Proue, 1995), *Divagations* (La Nouvelle Proue, 1994), *Hier et demain* (La Nouvelle Proue, 1990), *Volutes* (La Nouvelle Proue, 1988), *Situation Poesie 83* (Editions Saint-Germain-Des Pres, 1984) *Portique*

James A. Emanuel 🎤 ✈   P
Boîte Postale 339
75266 Paris Cedex 06, France, 1-45-49-3266
  Pubs: The Force and the Reckoning, Whole Grain (Lotus, 2001, 1991) Jazz from the Haiku King (Broadside Pr, 1999), De la Rage au Coeur (France; Amiot-Lenganey, 1992)

Susan Fox 🎤 ✈   P
La Bordelière, Segrie Fontaine 61100, France
Internet: bordeliere@wanadoo.fr
  Pubs: *Poetry, Paris Rev, Boulevard, Minnesota Rev, Chicago Rev, Women's Studies*

Jeffrey Greene 🎤 ✈   P
42 rue du Cherche-Midi, 75006 Paris, France,
01133145492643
Internet: jeffrey.Greene@wanadoo.fr
  Pubs: *American Spirituals* (Northeastern U Pr, 1998), *To the Left of the Worshiper* (Alice James Bks, 1991), *Glimpses of the Invisible World in New Haven* (Coreopsis Bks, 1995), *Parnassus, New Yorker, Ploughshares, Boulevard, Poetry*

Yuri Mamleyev   W
142 rue Legendre, 75017 Paris, France, 42-63-51-61
  Pubs: *The Eternal House* (Fiction Lit, 1992), *The Voice From Nothingness* (Worker of Moscow, 1991), *Drown My Head* (Union Bks Ctr, 1990), *Lettre Intl*

Alice Notley 🎤 ✈   P
21 Rue de Messageries, Paris, 75010, France, 0145230848
Internet: notleya@aol.com
  Pubs: *Disobedience, Mysteries of Small Houses, The Descent of Alette* (Penguin, 2001, 1998, 1996)

Albert Russo 🎤 ✈   W
BP 640, 75826 Paris cedex 17, France, 33147664459
www.albertrusso.com
  Pubs: *Eclipse Over Lake Tanganyika, Mixed Blood* (Domhan Bks, 2000, 2000), *Zapinette à New York* (France; Edtns Hors Commerce, 2000), *L'amant de mon pere* (France; Le Nouvel Athanor, 2000), *Volcano Rev, Short Story Intl, Amelia, Edinburgh Rev*

GERMANY

Jay Dougherty   P
Essener Str 73, 4320 Hattingen 16, Germany, 49-2324-42721
  Pubs: *The Process Poet Writes Back* (Parkville/Howling Dog, 1987), *Chiron Rev, Sonoma Mandala*

Eva Curlee Doyle 🎤 ✈   W
HQ Useucom, Cmr 480, Box 638, APO, AE 09128
Internet: ecd916@yahoo.com
  Pubs: *Lower Than the Angels: Anth* (Lite Circle Books, 1999), *America's Intercultural Mag, About Such Things, George's Last Gift: Pupose, 1997*

Gabriele Glang 🎤 ✈   P
Bonwiedenweg 21, 73312 Geislingen-Tükheim, Germany, 01149733143695
Internet: gabiglang@compuserve.com
  Pubs: *Stark Naked on a Cold Irish Morning, In a Certain Place: Anth* (SCOP Pub, 1990, 2000), *Wenn ich einen Vorschlag machen düfte: Anth* (Germany; Eislinger Edtns, 1996), *Eislinger Zeitung, Stuttgarrter Zeitung, NWZ Geislingen, NWZ Göpingen, Quarry*

Tom Whalen   W
Hasenbergstr. 15, 70178 Stuttgart, GERMANY, 497116741894
Internet: WhalenTom@aol.com
  Pubs: *Winter Coat, Elongated Figures* (Red Dust, 1998, 1991), *Newcomer's Guide to the Afterlife* (w/Daniel Quinn; Bantam Bks, 1997), *Roithamer's Universe* (Portals Pr, 1996), *Ploughshares, Seattle Rev, Georgia Rev, Iowa Rev, NW Rev, Fiction Intl, The Qtly, NAR*

GREECE

Yannis A. Phillis   P
Aghiou Markou St, Technical Univ of Crete, Chania 73132 Greece, Greece, 01130821064437
  Pubs: *Mother Earth Intl, Kaleidoscope, Philia*

Ann Rivers 🎤 ✈   P
Hydra 180 40, Greece
Internet: annrivers2002@yahoo.com
  Pubs: *Pilgrimage and Early Poems* (Hydra Pr, 2000), *A World of Difference* (Persephone Pr, 1995), *Samos Wine* (Mammon Pr, 1987), *Pembroke Mag, St. Andrews Rev*

Jessie Schell   W
Anatolia College, Thessaloniki, Greece
  Pubs: *Sudina* (Avon, 1977), *O. Henry Awards: Prize Stories Anth* (Doubleday, 1978), *McCall's*

Vassilis Zambaras   P
21 K Fotopoulou, Meligalas, Messenias, 24002, Greece, 0724-22313
  Pubs: *How the Net Is Gripped: Anth* (Stride Pubs, 1992), *Aural* (Singing Horse, 1985), *Sentences* (Querencia, 1976), *Poetry Salzburg Rev, Salt River Rev, Chiron Rev, Maverick Mag, Poetry NW, Shearsman, Text, Sthrn Poetry Rev, Wisconson Rev, W Coast Rev*

INDIA

Terry Kennedy 🎤 ✈   P&W
3/677 Coconut Grove, Prasanthi Nilayam AP 515134, South India
  Pubs: *Open Letter to My Priest Perpetrator* (Tiger Moon Pubs, 1994), *Sexual Harassment: Anth* (Crossing Pr, 1993), *Heart, Organ, Part of the Body* (Second Coming Pr, 1981), *Ludlow Fugue* (Wampeter Pr, 1980), *Durango* (The Smith, 1979), *Splitshift, Vol. No.*

INDONESIA

James Penha 🎤 ✈   P
Jakarta International School, PO Box 1078 JKS, Jakarta 12010, Indonesia
Internet: jpenha@yahoo.com
   Pubs: *Greatest Hits* (Pudding Hse Pubs, 2000), *Back of the Dragon* (Omega Cat Pr, 1992), *Storie, Waterways, Columbia Rev, Wired Art From Wired Hearts, Thema*

IRELAND

Chris Agee 🎤 ✈   P
102 N Parade, Belfast BT7 2GJ, Ireland, 00442890641644
Internet: cagee2@visteon.com
   Pubs: *First Light, In the New Hampshire Woods* (Dedalus, 2003, 1992), *Bk of Irish-American Poetry: Anth* (Notre Dame U Pr, 2003), *TLS, APR, Orion, New Statesman, Irish Times*

Theodore Deppe   P
Gortahork, Meenala
County Donegal, IRELAND, 3537480958
Internet: deppe@eircom.net
   Pubs: *Cape Clear: New and Selected Poems* (Salmon Bks, 2002), *The Wanderer King, Children of the Air* (Alice James Bks, 1996, 1990), *Kenyon, Harper's, Poetry, Boulevard, Poetry NW, Crazyhorse*

Thomas Kinsella   P
Laragh, Killalane, County Wicklow, Ireland
   Pubs: *Songs of the Psyche, Her Vertical Smile* (Ireland; Pepper Cannister, 1985, 1985)

Knute Skinner 🎤 ✈   P
Killaspuglonane
Lahinch, County Clare, Ireland, 011353657072064
Internet: kielskin@eircom.net
   Pubs: *Stretches* (Ireland; Salmon Pub, 2002), *An Afternoon Quiet* (Pudding Hse Pubs, 1998)

David S. Van Buren   P
24 Brompton Ct
Castleknock, Dublin 15, Ireland, 35318210080
Internet: vanburen@indigo.ie
   Pubs: *Maryland Poetry Rev, Hiram Poetry Rev, Cutbank, Mid-Atlantic Rev, Spectrum, Wind*

ISRAEL

Karen Alkalay-Gut 🎤 ✈   P
Tel Aviv Univ, English Dept, Ramat Aviv 69978, Israel
Internet: gut22@post.tau.ac.il
   Pubs: *So Far So Good, In My Skin, The Love of Clothes & Nakedness* (Israel; Sivan, 2002, 2000, 1999), *Avra Cadivra* (ZeBook Pr, 2002), *High Maintenance* (Canada: Neamh, 2001), *Harmonies/Disharmonies* (Israel; Etc. Edtns, 1994), *Ignorant Armies* (CCC, 1994)

Robert Friend   P
PO Box 4634
Jerusalem, Israel, 634998
   Pubs: *Dancing With a Tiger* (Beth-Shalom Pr, 1990), *5 A.M., Jerusalem Post, Atlantic, West Hills Rev, Jewish Frontier, Midstream, Bay Windows, Ariel*

Hadassah Haskale   P
PO Box 9358
9190 Jerusalem, Israel, 01197226411951
Internet: haskale@netvision.net.il
   Pubs: *Inscape* (Laughing Moon Pubs, 1992; Cassette: Marcos Allen, 1992), *Between Me & Thee* (Illuminations, 1982), *Inkslinger's Rev, Cochlea, Seven Gates, Puerto del Sol, Beyond Baroque, Illuminations, Hoopoe*

Lisa Katz 🎤 ✈   P
PO Box 8588
Jerusalem, 91084, Israel, 01197225662627
Internet: lisakatz@netvision.net.il
   Pubs: *Leviathan Qtly, Bridges, Reading Rm, Kerem, Mississippi Rev, Nimrod, Judaism 193*

Shirley Kaufman 🎤 ✈   P
7 Rashba St, 92264
Jerusalem, Israel, 97225618869
   Pubs: *Threshold, Roots in the Air* (Copper Canyon Pr, 2003, 1996), *APR, Paris Rev, Field, Iowa Rev*

Sharon Kessler 🎤 ✈   P
49 Hashmonaim St
37000 Pardes Hanna, Israel, 972466373351
Internet: sharkess@netvision.net.il
   Pubs: *Ghosts of the Holocaust* (Wayne State U Pr, 1989), *The Jewish Woman's Book of Wisdom: Anth* (Birch Lane Pr, 1998), *Without a Single Answer: Anth* (J. Magnes Museum, 1990), *Crab Creek Rev, Phatitude, Exit 13, Hawaii Rev, Tel Aviv Rev, Ariel, Tikkun*

Ruth Finer Mintz   P
Neve Granot, Block 3, Ent 5, Rehov Avraham Granot, Jerusalem 93706, Israel, 792-724
   Pubs: *Endor* (Massada, 1985), *Auguries Charm Amulets, Poems* (Jonathan David Pub, 1983)

Reva Sharon   P
13 Balfour St
Jerusalem 92102, Israel, 02-630608
   Pubs: *Pool of the Morning Wind* (Shemesh, 1989), *Under Open Sky* (Fordham U, 1986), *Ariel, Arc*

Lois Michal Unger 🎤 ✈   P
9 Bialik St
Tel Aviv 63324, Israel, 97235255497
Internet: lois_michal_u@yahoo.com
   Pubs: *The Glass Lies Shattered All Around 9* (Sivan, 2000), *Tomorrow We Play Beersheva* (Lamed Bks, 1992), *White Rain in Jerusalem: Anth* (Yaran Golan Pub Hse, 1997)

Linda Stern Zisquit 🎤 ✈ P
PO Box 8448
Jerusalem 91084, Israel, 97225639567
Internet: mslz@pluto.mscc.huji.ac.il
  Pubs: *Unopened Letters* (Sheep Meadow Pr, 1996), *Ritual Bath* (Broken Moon Pr, 1993), *Paris Rev, Ploughshares, Boston Rev, Harvard Rev, Tikkun*

ITALY

Salvatore Galioto P
Via Bruno Buozzi, 15, Montecatini Terme, 51016, Italy
  Pubs: *Is Anybody Listening* (Allicorn Pr, 1990), *Snow Summits: Anth* (Cerulean Pr, 1988), *San Fernando Poetry Jrnl, Imago*

Gerald Barttett Parks 🎤 ✈ P
CP 1879
Trieste, 34125, Italy, 0405582346
Internet: parks@sslmit.univ.trieste.it
  Pubs: *Lumen* (Italy; Corbo e Fiore, 1992), *Epodi ed Epigrammi* (Italy; Art Gallery Club, 1987), *Phatitude, World Order, Mickle Street Rev*

Edmund Quincy P
Via Grande Albergo, 6, San Remo, Imperia 18038, Italy, 9184-79881
  Pubs: *Lyrical Ways, Random Weirdness, Moana-Pacific Qtly, Chock, Lyric, Country Poet*

Nat Scammacca P&W
Co-op Ed Antigruppo Siciliano, Via Argenteria, Km 4, Trapani, Sicily 91100, Italy, 001-0923538681
  Pubs: *Ericepeo III, II, I* (Co-op Ed Antigruppo Siciliano/CCC, 1990, 1990, 1990), *Sikano l'Americano!, Bye Bye America* (CCC, 1989, 1986)

JAPAN

Price Caldwell W
Meisei University, Tokyo, JAPAN, 0425893615
Internet: price@mail.hinocatv.ne.jp
  Pubs: *Mississippi Writers: Reflections of Childhood & Youth: Anth* (U Mississippi Pr, 1985), *Best American Short Stories 1977: Anth* (HM, 1978), *Carleton Miscellany, Georgia Rev, Image, Mississippi Rev, New Orleans Rev*

William I. Elliott P
4834 Mutsuura, Kanazawa-ku, Kanto Gakuin Univ, Kamariya-cho, Yokohama 236, Japan, 45-786-7202
  Pubs: *62 Sonnets & Definitions* (Katydid Pr, 1992), *Doers of the Word, Floating the River in Melancholy* (Prescott Street Pr, 1991, 1989)

Morgan Gibson P&W
3-17-604 Sakashita-cho
Isogo-ku, Yokohama 235-003, Japan
  Pubs: *Among Buddhas in Japan, Tantric Poetry of Kukai* (White Pine Pr, 1988), *The Great Brook Book* (Four Zoas, 1981), *Dark Summer, Stones Glow Like Lovers' Eyes* (Morgan Pr, 1977, 1970), *Mayors of Marble* (Great Lakes Bks, 1966), *Farmer's Market, Cold-drill*

Jesse Glass 🎤 ✈ P
Meikai Univ/8 Akemi, Urayasu-shi, Chiba-Ken, Foreign Language Dept, 279-8550 Japan, Japan
Internet: ahadada@gol.com
  Pubs: *Dear Walt: Poems Inspired by the Life and Work of Walt Whitman: Anth* (U Iowa Pr, 2003), *The Book of Doll, Against the Agony of Matter, Song for Arepo* (Revanche-Hoya, 1999, 1999, 1999), *The Life & Death of Peter Stubbe* (Birch Brook Pr, 1995)

John Gribble P
1-7-66-406 Fuji-Machi, Nishi-Tokyo, Tokyo 202-0014, JAPAN
Internet: gribblej@gol.com
  Pubs: *Ravishing Disunities: Anth* (Wesleyan U Pr, 2000), *Poesie Yaponesia: Anth* (Printed Matter Pr, 2000), *Wind Five Folded: Anth* (AHA Bks, 1994), *The Ledge, Pearl, Peregrine, Heliotrope, Maryland Poetry Rev, Tundra, Yomimono, Verve, Birmingham Poetry Rev*

Thomas Heffernan 🎤 ✈ P
1-52-1 Shimo-Ishiki-Cho, Kagoshima Kenritsu Tanki-Daigaku, Kagoshima-Shi 890-0005, Japan, 81992587502
Internet: thomasheffernan@yahoo.com
  Pubs: *Gathering in Ireland* (New Hse Bks, 1996), *City Renewing Itself* (Peloria Pr, 1983), *The Liam Poems* (Dragon's Teeth, 1981), *At the Year's Turning: Anth* (Dedalus Pr, 1998), *Wherever Home Begins: Anth* (Orchard Bks, 1995), *Mainichi, Frog Pond*

Suzanne Kamata 🎤 ✈ W
Hiroshima, Matsushige-Cho, Itano-Gun, Tokushima-Ken 771-0220, 113-6 Ninokoshi, Kitakawamukai, Aza,, Japan, 81886997574
Internet: suekamata@msn.com
  Pubs: *Beacon Best of 1999: Anth* (Beacon Pr, 1999), *New York Stories, Calyx, Kyoto Jrnl, Wingspan*

Drew McCord Stroud P
Temple Univ, 1-16-7 Kamiochiai, Shinjuku-ku, Tokyo 161, Japan
    Pubs: *The Hospitality of Circumstance, Poamorio, Lines Drawn Towards* (Saru, 1988, 1984, 1980)

MEXICO

Diana Anhalt P
Sierra Chalchihui 215-9a, Lomas Chapultepec, Mexico D.F., MX, 11000, Mexico
Internet: dianalt@mail.internet.com
    Pubs: *Buckle &, Daybreak, Lucid Stone*

Jennifer Clement ✸ P&W
Tulipan 359 (esq. Azucena), Col El Toro, Del Magdalena Contreras, Mexico DF, 10610, Mexico
Internet: 74751.513@compuserve.com
    Pubs: *Lady of the Broom* (Aldus 2002), *A True Story Based on Lies, Widow Basquiat* (Canongate Bks, 2001, 2000), *Newton's Sailor, The Next Stranger* (Ediciones El Tucan de Virginia, 1997, 1993)

Kent Gardien P&W
Colonia Ranchos Cortes, Calle Nardo 137, 62120 Cuernavaca, Morelos, Mexico, 73-13-2269
    Pubs: *The Way We Write Now: Anth* (Citadel Pr, 1995), *Antioch Rev, Qtly West, Glimmer Train, Writers' Forum, Paris Rev*

Michael Hogan ✸ ✈ P&W
English Dept, Colegio Americano, Colomos 2100/APDO 6-280, Guadalajara, Jalisco, Mexico, 011523336420061
Internet: mhogan@infosel.net.mx
    Pubs: *Imperfect Geographies* (Q-Trips, 1999), *Making Our Own Rules* (Greenfield Rev, 1989)

Robert O. Nystedt P
Apdo 377 Cuautitlan-Izcalli, Edo el Mexico 54701, Mexico
    Pubs: *Stone Country, Taurus, Negative Capability, Nexus, Touchstone, Brushfire, Garcia Lorca Rev*

Robert Joe Stout ✸ ✈ P&W
Caja Postal 220, La Paz, BCS, CP 23000
Internet: bobstout@journalist.com
    Pubs: *They Still Play Baseball the Old Way* (White Eagle Coffee Store Pr, 1994), *City Lights* (Stout, 1992), *Interim, South Dakota Rev, Beloit Poetry Jrnl, Mid-America Poetry Rev, Georgetown Rev, Notre Dame Mag, Penthouse, Christian Century*

MOROCCO

Victor Hernandez Cruz ✸ ✈ P
Secteur 8 #1027, Hay Salam Sale, Ouivvan, Morocco, 787-732-8458
    Pubs: *Maraca: New & Selected Poems, Panoramas, Red Beans* (Coffee Hse Pr, 1998, 1991, 2001), *Paper Dance: Anth* (Persea Bks, 1995), *A Gathering of the Tribes, See, River Styx, Massachusetts Rev*

NETHERLANDS

Izzy Abrahami ✸ ✈ W
Koninginneweg 89, 1075 CJ Amsterdam, The Netherlands, 31 20 6710616
Internet: antv@com-all.nl
    Pubs: *The Game* (Scribner, 1973), *Omni Mag, Media & Methods*

Rachel Pollack P&W
Balthasar Floriszstratt 30-III, 1071 VD Amsterdam, Netherlands, 763924
    Pubs: *The New Tarot* (Aquarian, 1989), *Unquenchable Fire* (Century, 1988), *Interzone, Semiotext*(e)

NORWAY

Rasma Haidri ✸ ✈ P
Norway
Internet: razma@online.no
    Pubs: *Essential Love: Anth* (Grayson Bks, 2000), *The Pocket Poetry Parenting Guide: Anth* (Pudding Hse Pr, 1999), *Nimrod, Earth's Daughters, Fine Madness, Fish Stories, Lullwater Rev, Passages North, Prairie Schooner*

PAKISTAN

Alamgir Hashmi ✸ ✈ P
House 40, Street 25, G-10/2, Islamabad, Pakistan, 92512298951
Internet: alamgirhashmi@hotmail.com
    Pubs: *A Choice of Hashmi's Verse* (England: Oxford U Pr, 1997), *Poetry Rev, New Letters, Chelsea, Washington Rev, Postmodern Culture*

SOUTH AFRICA

Mireya Robles P
Dept of Europe Studies, Univ Natal, King George Ave
Durban 4001, South Africa
  Pubs: *Profecia Y Luz En La Poesia de Maya Islas* (M&A
  Edtns, 1987)

SOUTH KOREA

Tom Crawford P
Chonnam National University, 406 Kyosu #300, Yong-Bong
Dong, Kwangju 500-757, South Korea, 062-520-6099
Internet: yd@chonnam.chonnam.ac.kr
  Pubs: *China Dancing, Lauds* (Cedar Hse Bks, 1996, 1993),
  If It Weren't for These Trees (Lynx Hse Pr, 1986), *I Want to
  Say Listen* (Ironwood Pr, 1980), *Malahat*

TRINIDAD

Lennox Raphael P
Home Theatre, Ten Pelham St, Belmont, Port-Of-Spain,
Trinidad

UNITED ARAB EMIRATES

Gerald Timothy Gordon P
Dept. of English Language & Literature, The Univ of Sharjah,
P.O. Box 27272, Sharjah, U.A.E
Internet: gtimothy@simon.pu.edu.tw
  Pubs: *Out of Season: Anth* (Amagansett Pr, 1992), *Mixed
  Voices: Anth* (Milkweed Edtns, 1991), *Art Times, Spitball,
  Pacific Coast Jrnl, American Literary Rev*

Alphabetical Index
of All Writers

Index of
Performance Poets

Index of
Languages

Index of
Identity

Irish-Catholic

Israeli

Israeli American

Italian-American

Jamaican American

Japanese-American

Jewish

Index of
Community Groups

Miller, E. Ethelbert 97
Miller, Carolyn 51
Miller, A. McA 105
Milligan, Bryce 438
Miltner, Robert 390
Miner, Valerie 204
Mish, Jo 268
Mnookin, Wendy 178
Moldaw, Carol 240
Money, Peter 446
Monsour, Leslie 52
Moore, Dinty W. 415
Moore, Richard 179
Moran, Daniel
  Thomas 269
Morgan, Robert 269
Morin, Edward 195
Morressy, John 221
Morro, Henry J. 53
Morse, Carl 339
Morton, Bridget
  Balthrop 106
Moskowitz, Faye 97
Mueller, Marnie 339
Mungin, Horace 426
Murawski, Elisabeth 454
Murphy, Patricia 8
Murphy, Sheila Ellen 8
Murphy, Jr., George
  E. 106
Myung-Ok Lee, Marie 340
Naiden, James 204
Najarian, Peter 53
Nelms, Sheryl L. 438
Nelson, Crawdad 54
Nelson, Howard 269
Nelson, Ray Faraday 54
Nelson, Sandra
  Sylvia 473
Nelson-Humphries, Dr.
  Tessa 240
Nemec, David 54
Newman, Wade 340
Niatum, Duane 465
Nobles, Edward 151
Nocerino, Kathryn 341
Nordhaus, Jean 97
Noto, John 55
Novack, Barbara 341
O'Grady, Tom 454
Ochester, Ed 415

Oden, Gloria 158
Offit, Sidney 342
Ogden, Hugh 91
Okantah, Mwatabu 391
Oles, Carole Simmons 56
Olivas, Daniel A. 56
Olson, Toby 416
Orlowsky, Dzvinia 446
Osborn, John Jay 56
Osborn, William P. 195
Osterman, Susan 342
Owen, Maureen A. 91
Packer, Eve 343
Pagnucci, Franco 473
Pallant, Cheryl 455
Palm, Marion 343
Palmer, Leslie 439
Palmer, David 196
Parish, Barbara Shirk 431
Paschen, Elise 125
Pastan, Linda 158
Pastrone, Nicolas 8
Patten, Angela 446
Paulsen, Michelle 211
Pawlak, Mark 180
Peabody, Richard 455
Pearlman, Bill 241
Peattie, Noel 58
Peavy, Linda 446
Pejovich, Ted 344
Pelton, Theodore 271
Penn, William S. 196
Perchik, Simon 271
Perdomo, Willie 344
Pesetsky, Bette 271
Petersen, Paulann 401
Peterson, Jim 455
Pfingston, Roger 133
Phelan, Tom 271
Piercy, Marge 181
Pietrzyk, Leslie 455
Pirolli, John Paul 181
Platt, Donald 133
Pliner, Susan 346
Pobo, Kenneth 416
Pollack, Eileen 346
Pomerantz, Edward 346
Poole, Francis 94
Porte, Barbara Ann 455
Porter, Joe Ashby 379
Posner, Richard 272

Potts, Charles 466
Powell, Dannye
  Romine 379
Pray, Ralph E. 59
Pringle, Robert 391
Raab, Lawrence 182
Rachel, Naomi 83
Radavich, David 126
Radke, Charles 59
Ragan, James 60
Ramsey, Jarold 401
Randlev Smith, Karen 60
Random, Jack 60
Rangel-Ribeiro, Victor 347
Ransom, Bill W.M. 466
Raphael, Dan 401
Raphael, Carolyn 348
Ratzlaff, Keith 136
Ray, David 9
Ray, Judy 9
Rector, Liam 348
Reeve, F. D. 447
Rendleman, Danny 196
Reno, Dawn E. 107
Revard, Carter 212
Rhodes, Jewell Parker 9
Rivera, Etnairis 421
Robbins, Richard 205
Roberts, Dave 107
Roberts, Len 417
Roberts, Peter 392
Robertson, Howard
  W. 401
Robiner, Linda
  Goodman 392
Robinson, John 349
Roche, Judith 466
Rodia, Becky 92
Rodning, Charles
  Bernard 2
Roeske, Paulette 133
Rogers, Marge 392
Rogers, Bruce Holland 402
Rogers, Del Marie 241
Rogoff, Jay 274
Rogow, Zack 61
Romero, Leo 241
Romo, Rolando 439
Rosenblitt, Alice 350
Rosenblum, Martin
  Jack 474

Ross, Gary Earl 274
Rossiter, Charles 126
Rothenberg, Jerome 62
Roxas, Savina 417
Rubin, Larry 113
Rudy, Dorothy 233
Rutkowski, Thaddeus 351
Ryan, R.M. 474
Sagan, Miriam 241
Sage, Howard 352
Saint-Pierre,
  Raymond 352
Salas, Floyd 62
Saleh, Dennis 62
Sanfield, Steve 63
Sanfilip, Thomas 126
Sasso, Jr., Laurence
  J. 423
Saunders, Sally Love 417
Savage, Tom 352
Sax, Boria 275
Scarbrough, George
  Addison 431
Scates, Maxine 402
Schaefer, Ted 474
Schefflein, Susan 275
Schelling, Andrew 83
Schevill, James 63
Schneider, Mike 417
Schoenberger, Nancy 456
Schoenl, William 196
Schram, Peninnah 353
Schreiber, Jan 184
Schroeder, Gary 84
Schuler, Robert 474
Schultz, Philip 354
Schwalberg, Carol 63
Schwartz, Howard 212
Schwartz, Leonard 354
Scofield, Sandra 402
Scollins-Mantha,
  Brandi 233
Scrimgeour, James R. 92
Script, Dee Rossi 276
See, Carolyn 64
Seiler, Barry 276
Serrano, Nina 64
Sethi, Robbie Clipper 233
Shaffer, Eric Paul 116
Shaik, Fatima 233
Shand, Rosa 426

Women of Color

Women's Groups

Women's Support Groups

Workshops on Nature Writing

Writing Groups

Youth

Index of Literary Agents

Carol Abel Literary Agent

Shockley, Ann Allen   356

AMG/Renaissance

Gallant, James   309

The Anderson Literary Agency

Corrigan, John   299

Malaga Baldi Literary Agency

Lehman, Eric Gabriel   329

Steven Barclay Agency

Nye, Naomi Shihab   55

Susan Bergholtz

Alvarez, Julia   286
Cisneros, Sandra   297

Georges Borchardt, Inc.

Allen, Roberta   286
Ashbery, John   287
Begley, Louis   289
Boyle, T. Coraghessan   292
Coover, Robert   299
Flam, Jack   307
Goldberg, Gerald Jay   311
Israel, Peter   320
Keeley, Edmund   324
Lawner, Lynn   329
Lelchuk, Alan   329
Lieberman, Herbert   330
Lowery, Bruce   332
Maso, Carole   334
Mehta, Ved Parkash   336
Newman, Leslie   340
Passaro, Vincent   343
Rechy, John   348
Sachs, Elizabeth-Ann   351
Steiner, Robert   359
Stern, Daniel   360

Brandt & Hochman Literary

Berry, Eliot   290
Dunn, Robert   304

Hegi, Ursula   316
Rogers, Michael   350
Shacochis, Bob   355
Traxler, Patricia   364

Barbara Braun Assoc.

Vreeland, Susan   365

Marie Brown Associates

Southerland, Ellease   359

Burns & Clegg

Doty, Mark   303

Carlisle & Co.

Casey, John   296
Inness-Brown, Elizabeth   320
Koch, Stephen   326

Maria Carvainis Literary Agency

Smith, Charlie   358

Chelsea Forum

Cofer, Judith Ortiz   298

Linda Chester Literary Agency

Lamb, Wally   328

Molly Malone Cook Agency

Oliver, Mary   180

Curtis Brown Ltd

Hauser, Marianne   316
Hochstein, Rolaine   318
Hoffman, William   318
Knowles, John   326
Leonard, John   329
Litowinsky, Olga   331
Schwartz, Marian   354
Seth, Vikram   355
Wiser, William   369

Joelle Delbourgo Assoc

Rosner, Elizabeth   351

Donadio & Olson, Inc.

Agee, Joel   285
Bernstein, Burton   290
Calisher, Hortense   295
Ehle, John   304
Hobbie, Douglas   318
Matthiessen, Peter   335
Ng, Fay Myenne   340
Pell, Derek   344
Spanbauer, Tom   359
Timpanelli, Gioia   363
Wanner, Irene   366
Woiwode, Larry   369

Dunow & Carlson Agency

Dark, Alice Elliott   300
Davenport, Kiana   301
Grimes, Tom   314

Donald Gastwirth & Associates

Kuhlken, Ken   90

Gelfman Schneider Literary Agency

Hunter, Evan   320
Kalpakian, Laura   323
Paley, Maggie   343
Seidman, Robert J.   355

The Gernet Co.

Janowitz, Tama   321

Susan Gleason Literary Agency

Bauer, Tricia   289

Goodman Assoc

Cassill, Kay   296

Sanford Greenburger Associates

Allen, Paula Gunn   286

Maxine Groffsky Literary Agency

Canin, Ethan   295
Jen, Gish   321
Mathews, Harry   334

Hamilburg Agency

Burkholz, Herbert   21

Joy Harris Literary Agency

Gooch, Brad   312

Hartman & Craven, LLP

Vonnegut, Kurt   365

Frederick Hill Assoc

Cohan, Tony   24

ICM

Bird, Sarah   290
Black, David   18
Carey, Peter   295
Cooper, Bernard   299
Cravens, Gwyneth   299
Davis, Lydia   301
Doctorow, E.L.   303
Dolan, J. D.   303
Ford, Richard   308
Gallagher, Tess   309
Gurganus, Allan   314
Hoffman, William M.   318
Keeble, John   324
Mailer, Norman   333
Mason, Bobbie Ann   334
Miller, Arthur   338
Morgan, Speer   338
Owens, Iris   342
Patchett, Ann   343
Sanchez, Thomas   352
Shetzline, David   356
Simpson, Mona   357
Thomas, Joyce Carol   363
Wellman, Mac   367
Zeidner, Lisa   371

Melanie Jackson Agency

Ione, Carole   320
McElroy, Joseph   336
Moore, Lorrie   338
Savic, Sally   352

Janklow & Nesbit Associates

Beattie, Ann   289
Bryan, C.D.B.   294